GROLIER

ENCYCLOPEDIA
OF KNOWLEDGE

Grolier Incorporated
Danbury, Connecticut

1993 Printing

ISBN 0-7172-5300-7 (complete set)
ISBN 0-7172-5319-8 (volume 19)

Printed and manufactured in the United States of America.

This publication is an abridged version of the *Academic American Encyclopedia*.

3 4 5 6 7 8 9 10

UNICEF see UNITED NATIONS CHILDREN'S FUND

unicorn In both Western and Eastern mythology, the unicorn is a fabulous animal resembling a horse but with a single long horn growing out of its forehead. Those who drank out of its horn were protected from poisoning, stomach trouble, and epilepsy. According to medieval European folklore and art, the unicorn could be captured only by a virgin, thus symbolizing the power of spiritual love over fierceness. The medieval Christian church elaborated this story into an allegory of the incarnation and death of Christ. In Chinese mythology the unicorn presides over literature.

One of the six panels from the Lady with the Unicorn *tapestry (c.1490–1500) portrays a maiden with a docile unicorn, a legendary creature variously represented throughout history as a fantastic animal resembling a horse with a single horn projecting from its forehead. (Musée de Cluny, Paris.)*

unidentified flying object An unidentified flying object (UFO) is an unusual aerial or potentially airborne object that cannot be readily identified. Approximately 90% of raw UFO reports are interpreted as misperceptions of conventional objects, hoaxes, or hallucinations. The remaining 10% constitute the UFO enigma.

The date of the earliest UFO sighting is unknown. Some UFO researchers believe that there were UFO sightings in ancient times. The evidence for such sightings, however, is scanty and therefore purely speculative. Most UFO researchers date the beginning of the UFO phenomenon with the sighting of dirigiblelike "mystery airships" over the United States during 1896–97. The next significant group of reports came during World War II from Allied and Axis pilots who reported seeing strange metallike objects, which they called "foo fighters," in controlled flight around their planes. In 1946 people in Europe, particularly Scandinavia, reported large-scale sightings of silent "ghost rockets." None of these phenomena has been satisfactorily explained.

The UFO phenomenon entered public consciousness on June 24, 1947, when private pilot Kenneth Arnold reported sighting nine circular objects flying across his airplane's path in the skies over the state of Washington. He described their movements as being like "saucers skipping over water" and the term *flying saucer* was born.

Since 1947 there have been UFO sightings in nearly every country. Occasionally the number of sightings rapidly increases and a UFO wave ensues. For instance, UFO waves occurred in France and Italy in 1954, in New Guinea in 1958, and in the USSR in 1967. In the United States, waves occurred in 1947, 1952, 1957, 1965–67, and 1973. UFO researchers have been unable to predict or explain UFO waves. Attempts to link them to media publicity about UFOs, hysterical contagion, or societal stress" have proved unsuccessful. Although intensive publicity has prompted people to report sightings they had previously made, such publicity is not considered responsible for new reports.

Witnesses report a great variety of sizes and shapes of UFOs, including amorphous and changing-shape objects. The classic "two bowls joined at the rim" shape is reported often, but reports of objects shaped like cigars, squares, balls, triangles, rings, and hats are also common.

The U.S. Air Force attempted to study the UFO phenomenon from 1948 to 1969 through its Project Blue Book. After collecting reports for 21 years, it concluded that UFOs did not represent a threat to the national security, and it could find no evidence that UFOs were of extraterrestrial origin. In 1953, however, the Central Intelligence Agency suggested that the USSR might be able to use "flying-saucer hysteria" as a psychological warfare weapon against the United States. Therefore, from 1953 to 1969, the U.S. Air Force was concerned mainly with the incidence of UFO reports and never seriously considered the idea that UFOs per se might represent anomalous or unique phenomena.

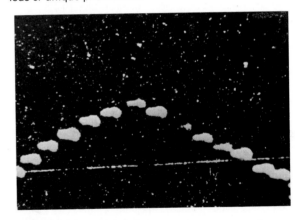

This photo of the "Lubbock Lights"—seen over Lubbock, Tex., on at least 14 occasions during late 1951—is one of several analyzed by the U.S. Air Force, which concluded that the photos were not a hoax. Reanalysis indicated that the lights were reflections from birds.

unified field theory In the early years of the 20th century classical attempts were made, principally by Albert Einstein, to unify two of the fundamental forces of nature, gravitation and electromagnetism. After presenting his theory of gravitation (the general theory of RELATIVITY), Einstein set out to reconcile his results with the description of electromagnetism given by Maxwell's equations. Einstein's failure to form a successful unified field theory must be judged in light of the fact that two of the fundamental forces, the weak and strong nuclear forces, had not been discovered.

More-recent attempts at unification have been made from the quite different point of view of merging the quantum field theories that describe (or are supposed to describe) the four fundamental interactions of gravity, electromagnetism, and the weak and the strong nuclear interactions. The most successful unification so far has been given by Steven Weinberg, Abdus Salam, and Sheldon Glashow, joining electromagnetism and the weak interactions (see ELECTROWEAK THEORY). In the simplest version of this type of unified gauge theory, forces are transmitted by the exchange of four different types of particles called bosons, which are assumed to be massless. By means of a "broken symmetry" an effective generation of masses occurs, with three bosons, W^+, W^-, and Z^0 particles, having masses on the order of 50 to 100 times the mass of the proton, and a 4th boson, the photon, remaining massless. The W and Z bosons were detected by high-energy experiments at the CERN laboratories in 1983. Weinberg, Salam, and Glashow shared the 1979 Nobel Prize for physics for their model.

Many other unified theories, involving the strong interaction (GRAND UNIFICATION THEORIES) and even gravitation (supersymmetry theories) have recently been proposed. Such schemes to date have unavoidable and questionable consequences, such as the removal of the separate conservation of baryon and lepton number; they predict that a proton could decay into a lepton plus pions—an improbable event that is being searched for at the present.

---

uniformitarianism   The concept that "the present is the key to the past," developed (1788) by the Scottish geologist James HUTTON, embodies the principle that in the past, geological processes operated according to the same natural laws that apply today. The name *uniformitarianism* was applied (1830) to the concept by Sir Charles LYELL.

At the end of the 18th century, geology was in its infancy. CATASTROPHISM—the concept that the Earth was shaped by unique, violent events—was rampant, and some philosophical underpinning was needed to curb the wild fantasies of unbridled speculation. Because geology is primarily an observational science, it lacks some of the rigor of chemistry and physics, where simple, repeatable laboratory experiments may often settle disputed theories. In Hutton's day, therefore, geology needed a standard for testing theories. Hutton asserted that "the past history of our globe must be explained by what can be seen to be happening now." Past geologic events were to be explained by processes that could be tested by observation somewhere in the modern world. This approach had the effect of stimulating investigation into contemporary geologic processes, and it simplified investigations of Earth history by eliminating from immediate consideration the more extreme catastrophist explanations.

Lyell's subsequent writings, particularly the many editions of his *Principles of Geology* (3 vols., 1830–33), popularized the uniformitarian idea among English-speaking geologists. His work extended the concept to include the assertion that past geologic processes have operated at a more or less constant rate equivalent to the rates seen today, which tend to be quite slow.

One of the most important influences of uniformitarianism was on the development of the theory of evolution. Charles Darwin read Lyell's *Principles,* and the two became close friends and correspondents. Although Lyell was slow to accept the transmutation of species, he strongly urged his colleague to publish his ideas and eventually become a convert. In Darwin's *On the Origin of Species* (1859) the emphasis is on slow, gradual processes operating over eons of time, which is the hallmark of Lyellian uniformitarianism. The vast period of time available for evolution is now indisputably documented by radioisotope dating of rocks billions of years old; whether evolution is an essentially uniform and gradual process or one punctuated by rapid bursts of change is a subject of current debate.

union, labor   see LABOR UNION

Union College   Established in 1795, Union College was made part of Union University in 1873, along with Albany Medical College (1839), Albany Law School (1951), Dudley Observatory (1852), and Albany College of Pharmacy (1881). A private coeducational liberal arts school in Schenectady, N.Y., Union College was the first liberal arts college to have an engineering program.

Union Islands   see TOKELAU ISLANDS

Union Jack   The Union Jack is the flag of the United Kingdom of Great Britain and Northern Ireland. It combines the crosses of Saint George of England, Saint Andrew of Scotland, and Saint Patrick of Ireland. Its origin is nautical; a jack is a small identifying flag usually flown on the bow of a ship. The flag in its present form has been in use since 1801, when Ireland joined the Union. Its colors are red, white, and blue, and variations of it are incorporated into the official flags of many former British dependencies.

Union Leagues   The Union Leagues were formed during the U.S. Civil War to foster allegiance to the U.S. government. The first units appeared throughout the North in 1862, and in May 1863 a Washington-based national council was created. The Union Leagues distributed patriotic literature, promoted interracial recruiting for the Union armies, and raised funds for soldier relief.

After the Civil War the Union Leagues survived primarily as social clubs in the North. In the South, however, they served for a time to establish Republican party organizations. At first, some antisecessionist Southern whites joined, but most of them resigned when the clubs, controlled by radical Republicans, began admitting African Americans in 1867.

Union Pacific Railroad   see TRANSCONTINENTAL RAIL-ROAD

Union party   The Union party was organized in the United States in 1936 by right-wing critics of President Franklin D. Roosevelt. Its major founders were Father Charles E. COUGHLIN, popular anti-Semitic radio priest; Fascist sympathizer Gerald L. K. Smith, head of the late Huey Long's Share the Wealth Movement; and Dr. Francis E. TOWNSEND, old-age pension advocate. It nominated U.S. representative William Lemke, Republican of North Dakota, for president and Thomas C. O'Brien for vice-president. Because of poor campaign strategy, indifferent press coverage, and gross miscalculation of popular support, the party polled only 892,378 votes and soon disintegrated.

The name *Union party* was also briefly adopted by the Republicans in 1864, when they renominated Abraham Lincoln for president and adopted War Democrat Andrew Johnson as his running mate. The name was soon dropped.

---

union shop   A place of employment where all workers must belong to a union is called a union shop. Anyone may be employed but within a stated time must join the union. This specified time period varies within each industry and according to the contractual agreement between management and labor. The union shop differs from the CLOSED SHOP, where all persons hired must already be union members, and from the OPEN SHOP, where employees need not join a union. Union shops are banned in states where RIGHT-TO-WORK LAWS prescribe an open-shop arrangement.

Union of Soviet Socialist Republics   The former Union of Soviet Socialist Republics (USSR), also known as the Soviet Union, was the largest country in the world, encompassing one-sixth of the Earth's land surface. Its 22,228,000 km² (8,582,280 mi²) made up the eastern half of Europe and the northern third of Asia. As it existed from 1922 to 1991, the Soviet Union was a tightly controlled Communist state comprising 15 union republics, the largest of which was RUSSIA. In 1991, after several years of turmoil, the already weakened Soviet Communist party was removed from power. Most of the republics then declared their independence, and at the end of the year 11 of them formed a new non-Communist Commonwealth of Independent States (CIS).

The USSR was formed on Dec. 30, 1922, and originally consisted of 4 member republics. Through subdivision and annexation, the number of full, or "union," republics increased to 15 by the end of World War II. Within most Soviet republics smaller ethnic groups received territorial representation. The massive political upheaval

---

AT A GLANCE

UNION OF SOVIET SOCIALIST REPUBLICS

Land: Area: 22,403,200 km² (8,649,800 mi²). Capital and largest city: Moscow (1991 est. pop., 8,801,500).

People: Population (1991 est.): 284,000,000. Density: 13 persons per km² (34 per mi²). Distribution (1990): 66% urban, 34% rural. Official language: Russian. Major religions: Eastern Orthodoxy and other Christian churches, Islam, Judaism.

Government: Type: federal republic. Legislature: Supreme Soviet. Political subdivisions: 15 union republics.

Economy: GNP (1989): $2,420 billion; $8,375 per capita. Labor distribution (1989): agriculture—18%; mining and manufacturing—28%; construction—10%; transportation and communications—8%; trade—8%; services—19%; other—9%. Foreign trade (1989): imports—$118.8 billion; exports—$113 billion. Currency: 1 ruble = 100 kopeks.

Education and Health: Literacy (1990): 99% of adult population. Universities (1989): 69. Hospital beds (1989): 3,762,600. Physicians (1989): 1,119,400. Life expectancy (1990): women—74; men—65. Infant mortality (1990): 24 per 1,000 live births.

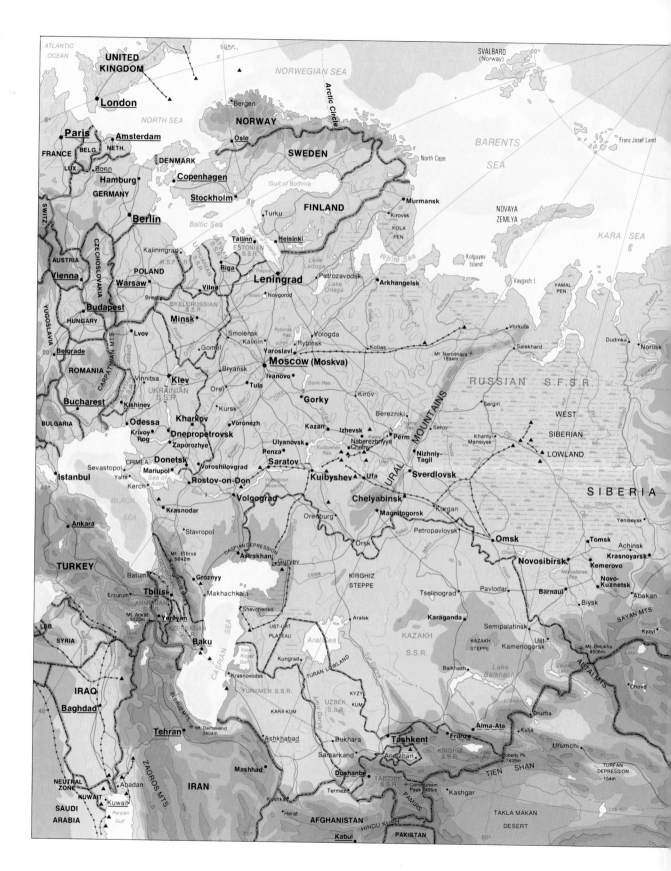

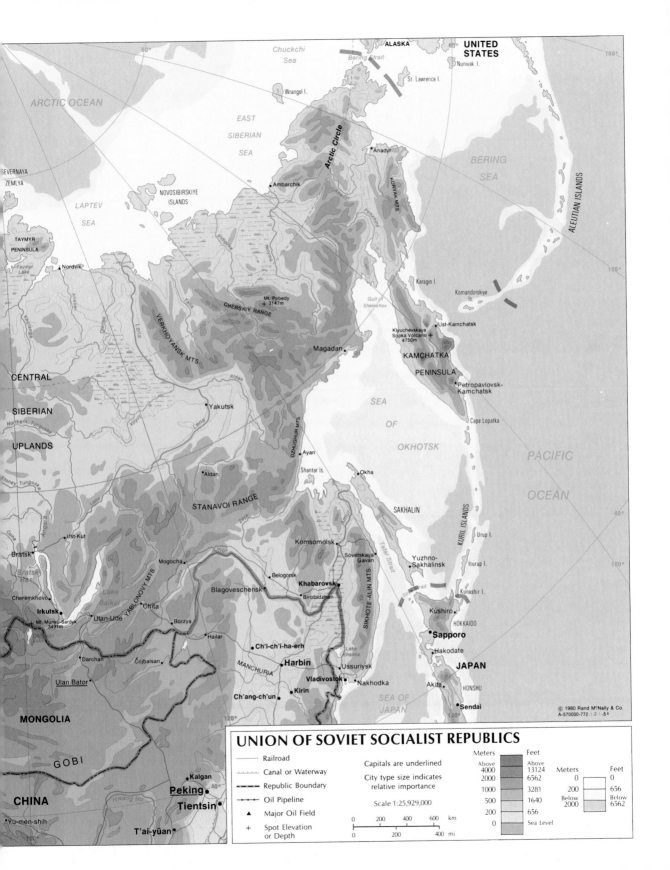

ARCTIC OCEAN

Chuckchi
Sea

ALASKA

UNITED
STATES

Bering Strait

Nunivak I.

St. Lawrence I.

Wrangel I.

EAST
SIBERIAN
SEA

BERING
SEA

SEVERNAYA
ZEMLYA

LAPTEV
SEA

NOVOSIBIRSKIYE
ISLANDS

Ambarchik

Anadyr

KORYAK MTS.

ALEUTIAN ISLANDS

TAYMYR
PENINSULA

Taymyr
Lake

Nordvik

Karagin I.

Komandorskiye
Is.

Mt. Pobedy
3147m

CHERSKIY RANGE

VERKHOYANSK MTS.

Gulf of
Shelekhov

Klyuchevskaya
Sopka Volcano
4750m

Ust-Kamchatsk

CENTRAL

Magadan

KAMCHATKA
PENINSULA

Petropavlovsk-
Kamchatsk

SIBERIAN

Yakutsk

SEA

UPLANDS

OF

Northern Tunguska

DZHUGDHUR MTS.

Ayan

OKHOTSK

PACIFIC

Cape Lopatka

Stoney Tunguska

Aldan

Shantar Is.

Okha

OCEAN

STANAVOI RANGE

Ust-Kut

SAKHALIN

KURIL ISLANDS

Bratsk

Komsomolsk

Urup I.

Bratsk
Res.

Mogocha

Sovetskaya
Gavan

Yuzhno-
Sakhalinsk

Iturup I.

Cheremkhovo

Belogorsk

Lake
Baikal

YABLONOVY MTS.

Blagoveschensk

Khabarovsk

Kunashir I.

Irkutsk

Mt. Munku-Sardyk
3491m

Chita

Birobidzhan

SIKHOTE-ALIN MTS.

Kushiro

Ulan-Ude

Borzya

HOKKAIDO

Darchan

Hailar

Sapporo

Čojbalsan

Ch'i-ch'i-ha-erh

Lake
Khanka

Hakodate

Ulan Bator

MANCHURIA

Harbin

Ussuriysk

JAPAN

Vladivostok

Nakhodka

Akita

MONGOLIA

Ch'ang-ch'un

Kirin

HONSHU

GOBI

SEA OF
JAPAN

Sendai

Kalgan

CHINA

Peking

40°

Tientsin

Yu-men-shih

Hwang Ho

T'ai-yüan

© 1980 Rand McNally & Co.
A-570000-772- -2- -5⁸

UNION OF SOVIET SOCIALIST REPUBLICS

———	Railroad
+++++	Canal or Waterway
—·—·—	Republic Boundary
—•—•—	Oil Pipeline
▲	Major Oil Field
+	Spot Elevation or Depth

Capitals are underlined

City type size indicates
relative importance

Scale 1:25,929,000

0   200   400   600 km

0   200   400 mi

Meters	Feet		
Above 4000	Above 13124	Meters	Feet
2000	6562	0	0
1000	3281	200	656
500	1640	Below 2000	Below 6562
200	656		
0	Sea Level		

Overlooking the Moscow River is the Kremlin, the city's old fortress, and today the seat of the Russian government. Seen here are the Water Tower (left), part of the Kremlin wall; the Great Palace of the Kremlin (center); and the domes of the Kremlin cathedrals (right).

ushered in by Mikhail GORBACHEV in 1985 led to an outpouring of long-suppressed nationalism. In several places ethnic conflicts erupted in violence. Together with a disintegrating economy, this finally led to the USSR's collapse.

From the October Revolution of 1917 until the late 1980s, the whole Soviet system was dominated by the Communist party, whose leading role was enshrined in the constitution. In March 1990 the Communist party formally renounced its monopoly on power, and in August 1991 its 74-year rule was effectively terminated.

The USSR contained an abundance of raw material, fuel, and power resources, which began to be extensively exploited during the industrialization drive of the 1930s. From the very beginning, heavy industry was stressed at the expense of consumer goods and services. In agriculture the USSR was the world's largest producer of several crops, but because of widespread inefficiency the country could not feed its population and had to import wheat. Despite advances in such fields as military and aerospace technology, the USSR lagged years behind the West in the development and application of newer, computer-based technology.

The Soviet Union was more or less coextensive with the Russian Empire, which was overthrown by the RUSSIAN REVOLUTIONS OF 1917. A civil war followed in which the Bolsheviks (see BOLSHEVIKS AND MENSHEVIKS), later the Communist party, led by V. I. LENIN, prevailed. After Lenin's death (1924), Joseph STALIN seized power, defeating in turn the Left Opposition under Leon TROTSKY and the Right Oppositionists, including Nikolai BUKHARIN.

Stalin collectivized agriculture and provided the country with a modern industrial base, but at the cost of massive social dislocation, violence, and loss of life. No less traumatic was the GREAT PURGE of 1936–38, a reign of terror in which millions perished.

The death of Stalin in 1953 was followed by a "thaw" in cultural policy and a period of economic and political reform under Nikita S. KHRUSHCHEV. In October 1964, however, Khrushchev was forced to resign. His successor, Leonid I. BREZHNEV, presided over a period of political stability and economic prosperity and also improved relations with the West, through a policy that became known as détente.

In Brezhnev's last years, however, economic stagnation and social malaise set in, and after the Soviet intervention in Afghanistan in 1979, East-West tensions increased. Brezhnev's two short-lived successors, Yuri ANDROPOV (1982–84) and Konstantin CHERNENKO (1984–85), were followed by Mikhail Gorbachev, who inaugurated a period of unprecedented reform and innovation.

Under the watchwords of GLASNOST ("openness") and PERESTROIKA ("restructuring"), Gorbachev encouraged free discussion of issues, reorganized the government on a more democratic basis, and relaxed the system of strict censorship and political repression. In the new atmosphere of freedom, nationalism reemerged within the constituent republics, accompanied in some cases by outbreaks of ethnic violence. In Eastern Europe the removal of the threat of Soviet intervention contributed to the fall of Communist-dominated governments.

As old governing structures gradually fell away, a worsening of economic conditions led to widespread strikes and protests and mass defections from the Communist party. In August 1991 party hard-liners attempted a last-gasp coup against President Gorbachev but were thwarted by massive popular opposition. In the aftermath, Gorbachev resigned as party chief, Communist rule was effectively ended, and the Soviet Union formally ceased to exist on Dec. 25, 1991.

Land and Resources

The broad Russian (or East European) plain extends from the Baltic Sea to the URAL MOUNTAINS. The plain is bordered in the extreme northwest by the uplands of KARELIA and the mountains of the Kola Peninsula; in the southwest and south by the moderately high CARPATHIAN and Crimean mountain ranges; in the southeast by the much higher CAUCASUS MOUNTAINS; and in the east by the less formidable Ural Mountains, which constitute the traditional boundary between Europe and Asia.

To the east of the Urals lies SIBERIA, which consists of a largely swampy West Siberian Plain; the Central Siberian Plateau, bounded by the YENISEI RIVER on the west and the LENA RIVER on the east; and a series of mountain ranges between the Lena and the Pacific Ocean. Jutting out from eastern Siberia is the KAMCHATKA PENINSULA, which along with the KURIL ISLANDS lying to its south forms part of the East Asian volcanic arc.

The highest mountain ranges of the former USSR lie along its southern border. In addition to the Caucasus, which rise to a maximum height of 5,642 m (18,510 ft) at Mount ELBRUS, they include the PAMIRS on the border with Afghanistan, the TIAN SHAN on the Chinese frontier, and the ALTAI MOUNTAINS on the border of Mongolia. The highest mountain of the USSR was COMMUNISM PEAK (7,495 m/24,590 ft), in the Pamirs in TADZHIKISTAN.

Soviet territory included many large islands and island groups. In the Pacific, these include the Kuril Islands, SAKHALIN, and the easternmost extension of the Aleutian chain. Arctic islands include FRANZ JOSEF LAND, NOVAYA ZEMLYA, the Novosibirskye Islands, Severnaya Zemlya, and WRANGEL ISLAND. All these islands are now part of the Russian Federation.

Soils. Along the Arctic coast is a band of infertile tundra soil that is more or less permanently frozen. South of the tundra lies the gray brown belt of taiga soils roughly corresponding to the coniferous forest zone and constituting a third of the country.

Farther still to the south stretches the black-earth (chernozem) zone, occupying about 9% of the country and nearly half the world's area of this soil type. Rich in humus, it is the most fertile soil belt. Beyond the Caspian Sea to the south, the soil contains less moisture and humus. The semidesert and desert areas of Central Asia have gray-earth soils (serozems), which are high in salt content. Red-earth soils are present in parts of the Caucasus and the foothills of the Central Asian ranges.

Climate. With the exception of the southern Far Eastern coast, which has a foggy monsoonal climate and the Baltic and Black Sea littorals, the climate almost everywhere in the former Soviet Union is markedly continental. Four latitudinal climatic belts can be discerned. The far north displays an Arctic climate. Mean temperatures in summer hover around the freezing point and in January reach –50° C (–58°F) at Verkhoyansk in eastern Siberia, where the world's lowest temperature outside of Antarctica has been recorded. Northern European Russia and Siberia above 60° north latitude are in a subarctic belt; the remainder of European Russia and Siberia as well as most of Central Asia are in the temperate belt; and parts of Transcaucasia and the southernmost areas of Central Asia are subtropical.

In winter a cold continental air mass situated over eastern Siberia spreads cold, dry air throughout much of the rest of the country. Mean temperatures for January are in most places below freezing. Precipitation is greatest in the west, where 200 to 300 mm (8 to 12 in) are recorded between October and March, and least in Central Asia and eastern Siberia, where only 50 to 100 mm (2 to 4 in) fall.

In summer a system of low pressure covers the former Soviet territory, except the southern Russian plain. Westerly winds bring moisture-laden air from the Atlantic; precipitation averages 500 mm (20 in) in the west but only 150–200 mm (6–8 in) in eastern Siberia. The heaviest rainfall, up to 1,200 mm (47 in), is in the western Caucasus.

Drainage. About half of all rivers in the former USSR drain into the Arctic Ocean. The largest of these are the Northern DVINA and Pechora in European Russia and the OB, Yenisei, Lena, and Kolyma of Siberia. The largest Far Eastern river, which drains into the Pacific, is the AMUR. The Atlantic Ocean ultimately receives the waters of rivers that empty into the Black Sea (the Danube, DNEPR, and DNESTR), the Sea of Azov (DON and Kuban) and the Baltic Sea (the NEVA and Western DVINA). The internal Caspian-Aral drainage basin covers the eastern Caucasus, the southeastern part of the Russian plain, the Turan plain, and the Pamir and Tian Shan ranges. The VOLGA River, the longest in Europe, and the Ural flow into the CASPIAN SEA; the AMU DARYA and SYR DARYA drain into the ARAL SEA.

The Caucasus, one of the principal mountain ranges of the former USSR, lies between the Black Sea and the Caspian Sea, forming a natural boundary between Europe and Asia. Its maximum elevation, Mount Elbrus, is the highest mountain in Europe.

The USSR contained approximately 270,000 lakes, including five of the world's largest: the Caspian and Aral seas, Lake BAIKAL, Lake Balkhash, and Lake LADOGA. Marshlands cover nearly 10% of former Soviet territory.

Vegetation and Animal Life. Vegetation in the tundra, in the far north, is restricted to mosses, lichens, and scrub; animal life includes the Arctic fox, reindeer, lemmings, and in summer, migratory geese, ducks, and swans. The largest vegetational zone is the TAIGA, in which coniferous forests of fir, pine, and larch harbor elks, deer, brown bears, lynx, sables, squirrels, and foxes. Toward the south, broad-leaved trees such as birch, oak, maple, lime, and ash are interspersed with the conifers and in this area are found deer, wild pig, and mink. Farther south, the mixed-grass and grassy steppe is now almost entirely under the plow. The most common animals are burrowing rodents (marmot, jerboa, hamster) and such birds as the kestrel, lark, and eagle. Finally, the southernmost zone consists of semidesert and desert vegetation such as dry grasses, wormwood, and saltwort that support jackals, lizards, spiders, ravens, and bustards.

Natural Resources. The Soviet Union had a wide variety of mineral resources. Coal reserves are widely scattered. Oil is found mainly in the Volga-Urals area, the North Caucasus, western Siberia, and at Baku in Azerbaijan. Natural gas is extracted principally from the Volga-Urals, Ukraine, and western Siberia. Soviet iron-ore reserves accounted for approximately 40% of the world's total. Manganese, copper, chromium, magnesium, nickel, and tungsten are also produced in large quantities. Gold production is thought to rank second in the world.

Arable land constitutes only 10% of former Soviet territory, while another 17% consists of meadows and pastures. About 40% of the country is forested. Water resources are abundant but unevenly distributed.

People

More than 100 distinct ethnic or nationality groups existed in the USSR. Of the 15 former republics, the largest and most populous was RUSSIA, in which Great Russians predominate. Two other Slavic peoples are concentrated in UKRAINE and Belarus (see BELORUSSIA). MOLDOVA is inhabited mainly by people ethnically and linguistically identical with Romanians. Lithuanians, Latvians, and Estonians comprise the core nationality groups within each of the three Baltic republics—LITHUANIA, LATVIA and ESTONIA—though Russians constitute a sizable minority, particularly in the latter two. The three Transcaucasian republics—ARMENIA, GEORGIA, and AZERBAIJAN—are based on the largest nationality groups in that region. The remaining five republics, constituting Soviet Central Asia, are KAZAKHSTAN, UZBEKISTAN, Tajikistan (see TADZHIKISTAN), TURKMENISTAN, and Kyrgyzstan (see KIRGHIZIA). The Uzbeks are the most numerous of the Central Asian peoples. Other larger ethnic groups include the Tatars, Bashkirs, and Poles. In recent years heavy emigration has depleted the ranks of Jews and Germans. Indigenous Siberian peoples are widely scattered.

Language. Russian was the official language of the USSR. Ukrainian and Belorussian are closely related to

Russian and together with it make up the main SLAVIC LANGUAGES spoken within the country. Other Indo-European languages are the two BALTIC LANGUAGES, Latvian and Lithuanian; Romanian, the Romance language of the Moldavians; Armenian; and the Iranian language of the Tadzhiks and Ossetes. Four subfamilies of URAL-ALTAIC LANGUAGES existed in the Soviet Union: Turkic, Finno-Ugric, Kalmyk and Buryat, and Tungusic. Ethnic groups used their indigenous language as a second official language within their particular national territory.

Religion. Before the revolution, Russian orthodoxy was closely integrated into the structure of the tsarist state, but after 1918 church and state were officially separated, and atheism became the main pillar of the new Communist ideology. Until Gorbachev's rule, harassment of believers was a standard feature of the Soviet system.

It has been estimated that 40% of the population are religious believers. The Russian Orthodox church, which

Orthodox Christianity and Islam are the two principal religions of the former USSR. (Right) A Russian Orthodox priest stands in front of a church built in the traditional Russian style. Many churches and monasteries closed during the period of repressive Communist rule have now been reopened. (Below) Muslim men worship in a mosque in Dushanbe, capital city of Tajikistan.

celebrated 1,000 years of Christianity in 1988, commands the membership of the dominant Slavic groups (except for sizable numbers of Ukrainians who are affiliated with a branch of Catholicism) as well as Moldavians and some Finno-Ugric peoples. Western Christianity is represented by Catholicism (primarily among the Lithuanians), Lutheranism (among Latvians and Estonians), and other Protestant groups. Both the Armenians and Georgians have their national Christian churches.

The Turkic-speaking peoples of the former USSR are mainly Muslims, making Islam the second most important religious faith in the country. Buddhism, the predominant religion among the Mongolic-language groups, and Judaism have smaller, though still significant, numbers of believers.

Demography. Soviet history was marked by several demographic catastrophes. The civil war that followed World War I was accompanied by widespread epidemics and a process of deurbanization. Then a severe famine struck in 1921–22 and again in 1932–33, as a result of Stalin's collectivization campaign, particularly in Ukraine and the North Caucasus. The greatest catastrophe of all was World War II, which cost the USSR about 28 million lives, and when indirect losses (fewer births and increased mortality resulting from lower standards of living) are taken into account, perhaps as many as 50 million people.

Roughly two-thirds of the Soviet population lived in urban areas. The 22 cities with populations in excess of one million are: Moscow, Leningrad, Gorky, Kuibyshev, and Kazan in European Russia; Sverdlovsk, Chelyabinsk, Perm, and Ufa in the Urals; Novosibirsk and Omsk in Siberia; Kiev, Kharkov, Dnepropetrovsk, Odessa, and Donetsk in Ukraine; Minsk in Belarus; Baku, Tbilisi, and Yerevan in Transcaucasia; and Tashkent and Alma-Ata in Central Asia.

Education. Before 1917 only about 20% of the adult population was literate. When the Communists came to power, they created a nationwide system of secular schools and by the 1960s had virtually elimated illiteracy. Until recently, the primary aim at all levels of Soviet education was to produce politically upright citizens trained in specific skills needed for building the Soviet economy. Formal teaching methods stressed repetition and memorization rather than problem-solving skills. The curriculum was uniform throughout the country.

Schooling begins at age six or seven and is compulsory for ten years. About 40% of students continue their education in vocational schools. There is an extensive system of universities and other institutes of higher learning, some of which, particularly in the sciences, have produced world-renowned scholars.

The political changes of recent years have greatly affected such disciplines as literature, history, and social studies. Old textbooks, permeated by the Communist ideology, are being discarded, but the writing of new textbooks is far from complete.

Health. The medical and dental professions are socialized, but private practice is now being permitted. About two-thirds of all doctors are women. Doctors' salaries are below manual workers' wages. Medical care is free, but the quality—especially in small towns and rural areas—is low. The lack of medicines, modern instruments, prosthetic devices, and wheelchairs has been more pronounced in recent years. For decades alcoholism has been a major public-health problem.

Science. State support for scientific research has been extensive. Research is conducted in thousands of institutes, mostly under the authority of the Academy of Sciences and its affiliates. The fate of science has varied considerably under successive Soviet administrations. In the 1920s the natural sciences were relatively unaffected by the political struggles. In the Stalin era, however, scientists were forced to conform to official scientific doctrines laid down by the party, and scientific progress suffered as a result. In more recent decades, Soviet science has made great strides in certain fields but has lagged behind the West in terms of the application of theoretical work. The computer revolution is only beginning to penetrate the post-Soviet society.

The Arts. From the classical refinement of the ballet and impassioned poetry readings to the slapstick humor of the circus, the arts occupied an especially important place in Soviet life and often provided the only refuge from life's daily frustrations. During the 1920s the arts were swept by several competing movements, which sought to translate the revolutionary dynamism in politics into a new vision of culture. Prominent poets included Anna Akhmatova, Osip Mandelstam, Boris Pasternak, Vladimir Mayakovsky, and Sergei Yesenin. Prose writers, such as Isaak Babel, Mikhail Bulgakov, and Mikhail Zoshchenko, vividly and often humorously captured the contradictions of the times in their short stories. Also noteworthy were the films of Sergei Eisenstein and Dziga Vertov and the graphics of El Lissitsky.

All this came to an end in the early 1930s, when writers and other artists came under heavy pressure from the Communist party to portray the "passion for construction." Construction novels, such as Valentin Katayev's

Dancers of Moscow's Bolshoi Ballet rehearse Giselle. *The Bolshoi is today acknowledged as the premier dance company of Russia and one of the finest in the world.*

Time Forward! (1932; Eng. trans., 1933), served as prototypes for the officially prescribed doctrine of SOCIALIST REALISM. Fine arts, music, and architecture felt the impact of socialist realism as well.

Even in the context of such limitations, some Soviet writers and artists managed to enrich Soviet and world culture. Mikhail SHOLOKHOV was awarded (1965) a Nobel prize, largely on the strength of his novel *And Quiet Flows the Don* (4 vols., 1928–40; Eng. trans. in 2 vols., 1934–40); Sergei PROKOFIEV, Dmitry SHOSTAKOVICH, and Aram KHATCHATURIAN each composed a large body of music that has entered the classical repertoire; Soviet ballet also maintained its high standards.

On the death of Stalin, literary controls were relaxed. A new generation of poets emerged, among whom Yevgeny YEVTUSHENKO and Andrei VOZNESENSKY were most prominent. Still, restrictions on what could be published persisted. Pasternak's novel *Doctor Zhivago* (1958) had to be published abroad, setting a precedent that was followed by other authors, including Aleksandr SOLZHENITSYN. In addition to *tamizdat* (works published abroad), many authors resorted to circulating their works in the form of *samizdat* ("self-publishing").

By the 1980s, censorship had become increasingly arbitrary and ineffective. Novelists such as Yuri Trifonov, Fedor Abramov, Valerii Rasputin, Sergei Zalygin, Anatoli Rybakov, Fazil Iskander, and Chinghiz Aitmatov explored a wide range of themes, many of them critical of the Soviet way of life. Under the policy of *glasnost*, the works of previously forbidden authors were published in enormous editions, and the range of cultural discourse expanded to unprecedented proportions.

Economic Activity

The chief characteristic of the Soviet economic system was the direct administration of all industry, transportation, construction, trade, and a substantial part of agricultural production by central state institutions. The only exceptions were the collective farms, the family plots belonging to collective farmers, and the collective-farm-market sector of retail trade.

The USSR enjoyed considerable economic growth in the 1950s and '60s, but the failure of the party to effectively administer more complex economic processes kept growth rates low in the 1970s and early 1980s. After 1985 the Soviet government tried to dismantle the "administrative-command system of economic management," but the various partial reforms (including the reintroduction of limited private enterprise and decentralization of economic decision making) led to a virtual economic collapse. Widespread shortages, rationing of basic goods, labor unrest, and the disintegration of political and economic authority worsened in 1990 and 1991. A new prescription for a radical overhaul of the Soviet economy, with massive help from the West, began to emerge in 1991, but was derailed by the USSR's collapse late that year.

Manufacturing. The USSR was the world's leading producer of a number of important industrial goods, including pig iron, cement, steel, and chemicals. Industrial plants are

(Above) *The Karaganda steel mill in Kazakhstan symbolizes the state-run Soviet heavy industry created during the Stalin era as prescribed by Marxist-Leninist doctrine.* (Below) *As the former Soviet republics move toward a market economy, more industrial enterprises will be in the hands of private individuals such as this manager of a nonferrous-metals plant.*

typically large but far behind the West in automation. The greatest concentration of manufacturing is in Ukraine, near traditional sources of fuel, and in the Central Industrial Region, extending from Moscow east to Gorky.

Mining. The Soviet Union was essentially self-sufficient in raw materials and fuels. The Krivoi Rog area in eastern Ukraine has long been a center of iron-ore mining. Coal is produced in widely scattered areas, from the Donets Basin in Ukraine and the Pechora River region in northern Russia, to the KUZNETSK BASIN of western Siberia and the Karaganda Basin in Kazakhstan. The Urals are the source for most nonferrous minerals, except for gold, which is mined in the Lena River basin and in the Tian Shan mountains of Central Asia.

The Baku oil fields, once the major petroleum-producing area in the country, are all but depleted. Newer areas, particularly in the Volga-Urals region, the Tyumen district of western Siberia, and the Tenghiz oil fields of Kazakhstan, are being developed. The USSR was also a major supplier of natural gas to Western Europe.

Energy. The essential problem for Soviet planners was how to tap the nearly unlimited reserves to the east of the Urals. One strategy consisted of developing means of transportation that would convey large quantities of energy from the east to the more populated and industrialized areas of the country in the west. The other was to locate new industry in Siberia and encourage migration there.

The use of coal declined considerably. Petroleum, gas, hydroelectric, and nuclear power were all developed rapidly after 1960. Nuclear power was generated, especially in the European part of the country, but the program suffered a major setback in April 1986, when several explosions occurred at the CHERNOBYL plant north of Kiev, in the worst accident in the history of nuclear-power generation. Fossil-fuel production, particularly in western Siberia, also has resulted in devastating environmental damage and a major public-health crisis.

Agriculture. Soviet agriculture traditionally consisted of three distinct institutional arrangements: state farms, which operate more or less as industrial enterprises; collective farms, cooperative units that sell a fixed quota of their output to the state at predetermined prices and remunerate their members on the basis of a complex system of labor inputs; and small private plots. Reforms of the late 1980s made possible extended leaseholding, outright purchase and consolidation of farms, and other arrangements.

Flax and dairy farming are prominent in the far north. South of this zone, potatoes, rye, and hemp are cultivated, and livestock production is carried out extensively. Further to the south, in the broad steppe region, wheat, barley, corn, and sunflowers are the principal crops, though in western Ukraine sugar beets are the main crop. The drier, eastern part of the steppe supports sheep grazing and cotton production. Fruits and vegetables are abundant in the small subtropical areas of the Crimea, the southern Caucasus, and Central Asia.

The Achilles' heel of the Soviet economy, agriculture suffered from lack of motivation among farm workers, out-migration of talented youth to the cities, mismanagement, inefficient utilization of machinery, and the inadequacy of infrastructures, such as paved roads and storage facilities. It has been estimated that up to one-third of produce rotted in transit. Unfortunately, none of these problems is amenable to improvement in the near future.

Forestry. The USSR ranked as the world's leading producer of timber. The locus of the industry shifted from the depleted forests of central European Russia northward and, more recently, eastward into Siberia. The processing of the timber into pulp, paper, particle board, and plywood benefited in recent decades from the expansion of the electricity grid and the chemicals industry but has been a major source of water pollution, particularly in Lake Baikal.

Fishing. The USSR, along with Japan, had one of the world's largest fishing industries. Dried and salted fish have long been a feature of the Russian diet, and the USSR was the leading producer of caviar—the processed salted roe of sturgeon—culled mainly from the Caspian Sea.

Transportation. The need for transporting large quantities of bulk items over long distances and the predominant flatness of the terrain made railroads the principal mode of transport.

The TRANS-SIBERIAN RAILROAD, completed in 1916, opened up Siberia and the Russian Far East to settlement. During the 1920s the Turksib line linked the Central Asian cities of Tashkent and Alma-Ata to the rest of the nation's rail network. The Baikal-Amur Mainline (BAM) was built in the 1970s and early 1980s. Electrical systems—tram and trolley bus services—played a crucial role in urban and suburban passenger conveyance. Subways served all the largest Soviet cities.

Road transport was limited mainly to short-haul movements, connecting farms with railheads. Inland water transport made up only a small proportion of overall freight movement. The Volga system was the main artery,

Combines harvest wheat on a state farm in Ukraine. The Soviet collectivized agricultural system, imposed by Stalin in the 1930s at a cost of millions of human lives, failed to perform effectively, forcing the USSR to rely on imported grain for its food supply.

linking Moscow with the Caspian Sea and the Urals and, via the Volga-Don canal, the Ukrainian republic and the Black Sea ports. The Soviet merchant marine was one of the world's largest.

Air transport was used mostly for passenger travel. Serving more than 3,500 localities within the USSR and linking it to countries in Europe, Africa, Asia, and North America, Soviet air transport accounted for approximately one-quarter of the world total by volume of traffic.

Trade. Goods were distributed in five different ways in the USSR. First in terms of total sales were state outlets that sold items at a uniform price throughout the country. Until the late 1980s, the prices remained stable for several decades. Second, there were consumer cooperatives that primarily served rural regions. Prices were generally higher than in state stores, but the quality and variety of produce were better. The third type consisted of collective farm markets where prices were determined by supply and demand. This principle also governed the sale of goods by cooperative stores that were established as part of Gorbachev's economic reforms. Finally, retail sales occurred informally, either by barter arrangement or through the sale of used or contraband goods.

Foreign trade played a relatively minor role in Soviet economic activity, partly because of the country's rich and diverse economic base and partly because self-sufficiency was long a cardinal principle of economic policy. After World War II the other Communist countries, grouped in the COUNCIL FOR MUTUAL ECONOMIC ASSISTANCE (Comecon), became the main trading partners of the USSR.

The composition of Soviet exports and imports reflected the intermediate level of the country's development. Earnings from the export of raw materials such as oil, timber, coal, and natural gas were used to purchase capital equipment and some consumer goods. The Soviet Union's need for advanced technology from the industrialized West had exceeded its ability to find markets there for its own goods.

Communications. The Soviet mass media were developed as organs of the party intended to encourage identification with and participation in officially approved activities. In the era of *glasnost*, all this changed.

The major national newspapers—at least until August 1991—were PRAVDA, the Communist party daily, and IZVESTIA, the more liberal government paper. The weeklies *Ogonek* and *Argumenty i fakty* were in the forefront of the new free journalism. Moscow continued to be the center of the broadcast media. By use of communications satellites, its programs were transmitted to all parts of the USSR and could be picked up in foreign lands as well. "Vremia," the main television news program, was said to have a nightly audience of 200 million people.

The chief impact of *glasnost* was to enliven the Soviet media, enabling it to express a wide range of viewpoints in a variety of formats. Investigative reporting, vivid accounts of political unrest, crime and accidents occurring within the Soviet Union, revelations about the past, particularly about the crimes of the Stalin era, and debates about current issues began to appear regularly.

Government

The USSR was officially a federation of 15 union republics.

The Communist Party. Policy-making, personnel selection, and supervision of public activities were the main functions of the party. The party itself developed as a highly centralized body, with its nucleus consisting of the Moscow-based Central Committee, Politburo, and Secretariat.

At the 1990 May Day parade in Moscow, antigovernment protesters wait behind police lines to join the march. This was the first time that "unofficial" groups were allowed to participate in the parade.

Muscovites gather to read political posters before elections for the Congress of People's Deputies in March 1989. On the left is a photograph of the radical democratic reformer Boris Yeltsin.

The Central Committee consisted of several hundred members, elected by the all-union congress. The much smaller Politburo was composed of full and candidate members, chosen from the Central Committee. The general secretary of the party traditionally presided over its meetings and spoke in the name of the Politburo. The Secretariat implemented party policies.

Until the reforms associated with Gorbachev's leadership, all important positions in the party and government were filled by party members who previously had been cleared by higher party bodies. Through this power of *nomenklatura*, the party apparatus ensured itself of direct access to and control over all state institutions, production enterprises, and public organizations.

Among the reforms engineered by Gorbachev were limited tenure for all party officials, multiple candidates, secret-ballot elections, and the encouragement of free-wheeling debate. Under his leadership, the party became a motley and highly unstable body. Communist parties in individual republics declared themselves independent of Moscow control, and many members, impatient with the pace of change, resigned.

The failed coup by party hard-liners in August 1991 marked the demise of Communist authority. Denouncing the Central Committee, Politburo, and Secretariat for not opposing the coup, Gorbachev resigned as general secretary and ordered the party leadership to step down. Individual republics shut down party offices, and the Soviet Parliament voted to suspend all party activity.

Other Political Groups. Even before August 1991 the Communist party had ceased to be the only political force. Many new groups had been formed since 1985; they included the right-wing anti-Semitic Pamyat, the ultraconservative Soyuz, various anarchist and monarchist groups, and Democratic Russia, a coalition of opposition parties.

National and Local Governments. Soviet government traditionally represented a vast pyramidal structure, with local village, city, and country SOVIETS (councils) at the base and the Supreme Soviet at the apex. One of the pri-

mary goals of Gorbachev's political reforms was the transfer of power from the Communist party to freely elected representative bodies. The degree of autonomy or sovereignty exercised by local soviets was not clearly determined in the last years of the USSR, and the overall erosion of political authority hastened the disintegration of the country. Members of the Supreme Soviet are chosen by a Congress of People's Deputies.

In March 1990 the Congress of People's Deputies created a new executive office, the presidency of the USSR, and elected Mikhail Gorbachev as the first president. In the months that followed, Gorbachev gradually enhanced the authority of this new position, shifting the decision-making power from the Communist party apparatus and concentrating it in the presidency. His control over the USSR was challenged, however, by the growing power of the presidents of the 15 republics, especially Boris YELTSIN of the Russian republic. The end of Communist power in August 1991 and the rush to secession by individual republics culminated in the formal disbanding of the union and its replacement by the Commonwealth of Independent States (CIS), a much looser alliance of 11 former Soviet republics. The three Baltic states and Georgia did not join the CIS.

Law and the Judiciary. The Supreme Court of the USSR, whose members were appointed by the Supreme Soviet, was the highest judicial body in the land. Most cases were handled by People's Courts, in which a professional judge was assisted by two lay assessors. The judge, nominated by the party, was formally elected by the district's constituents. Assessors, the Soviet equivalent of a jury, usually concurred with the judge's decision.

Armed Forces. The USSR's immense size and limited access to oceans favored the development of a large land army supported by a tactical air force. Acquisition of nuclear weapons and long-range and medium-range missiles

Relaxation of government repression under the Gorbachev regime led to the emergence of separatist movements in many Soviet republics. In January 1990, members of the Azerbaijan People's Front destroy barbed-wire barriers along the Soviet-Iranian border, demanding union with fellow Azerbaijanis on the other side.

greatly enhanced the army's strategic capabilities. The Soviet navy had a significant presence in the Atlantic, northern Pacific, and Indian oceans as well as in the Mediterranean Sea. For decades the armed forces were the only efficiently functioning sector of the Soviet system.

The Soviet armed forces consisted of five major service branches: the army, the navy, the strategic rocket forces, the air force, and the air-defense forces. There was also a sizable paramilitary force consisting of border guards and security troops under the direction of the KGB. The Communist party traditionally maintained close control of the armed forces, but that authority disintegrated during the August 1991 coup attempt as the military backed down and sided with prodemocracy demonstrators.

The armed forces were affected by recent upheavals in other ways as well. Hundreds of thousands of troops stationed in Eastern Europe were being gradually withdrawn, the Warsaw Pact was abolished in early 1991, and conscripts in a number of insurgent republics began resisting the military service. On the other hand, army units had been used in a number of violent nationalist conflicts.

See also: COMMUNISM; RUSSIA/UNION OF SOVIET SOCIALIST REPUBLICS, HISTORY OF; RUSSIAN ART AND ARCHITECTURE; RUSSIAN LITERATURE; RUSSIAN MUSIC.

Unitarian Universalist Association

The Unitarian Universalist Association was formed in 1961 by consolidation of the American Unitarian Association (1825) and the Universalist Church of America (1793). At its headquarters in Boston, the association carries on common activities, such as church extension, ministerial settlement, and preparation of educational materials, but it does not exercise hierarchical control. Its philosophy is one of religious liberalism, stressing the value of human freedom and rejecting dogmatic formulations. Humanitarian concerns are entrusted to a related organization, the Unitarian Universalist Service Committee. The denomination is connected with similar groups abroad through the International Association for Religious Freedom.

Unitarianism

Unitarianism is a form of Christianity that asserts that God is one person, the Father, rather than three persons in one, as the doctrine of the Trinity holds. A number of religious groups in Transylvania, Poland, Great Britain, and North America have been designated as unitarian because of this belief. As significant, however, has been the confidence of these groups in the reasoning and moral abilities of people—in contrast to traditions that emphasize original sin and human depravity—and their avoidance of dogma.

Modern Unitarianism dates to the period of the Protestant Reformation. A Unitarian movement has existed in Transylvania since the 1560s, when the leader was Francis David (1510–79). In Poland, Unitarianism flourished for a hundred years as the Minor Reformed Church until persecution forced (1660) its adherents into exile. The key figure in the Polish movement was Faustus Socinus (1539–1604; see SOCINIANISM). Isolated individual unitarians lived in England in the 1600s, most notably John BIDDLE, but Unitarianism developed as a formal movement in the 1700s, partly within the Church of England but mainly in dissenting circles.

In America the religious liberalism that came to be known as Unitarianism appeared within the congregational churches in Massachusetts as a reaction against the revivalism of the GREAT AWAKENING (1740–43). The election (1805) of Henry Ware as Hollis Professor of Divinity at Harvard University touched off a controversy, as a result of which the liberals became a separate denomination. William Ellery CHANNING's sermon entitled "Unitarian Christianity" (1819) was an influential statement of their beliefs.

In 1838, Ralph Waldo EMERSON's divinity school address declared that religious truth should be based on the authority of inner consciousness, not on external historical proofs. More conservative Unitarians were critical of Emerson and his followers, known as transcendentalists. Since the controversy over TRANSCENDENTALISM, some within the denomination have always felt it important to maintain continuity with the Christian tradition, whereas others have found Christianity to be intellectually limited and emotionally restrictive.

In 1961 the Unitarians merged with the Universalists in the Unitarian Universalist Association.

Unitas, Johnny

[yoo-ny'-tuhs]   John Unitas, b. Pittsburgh, Pa., May 7, 1933, an American professional football player, was considered by many to be the greatest quarterback of his era. After a college career at the University of Louisville, he was drafted by the Pittsburgh Steelers of the National Football League (NFL) but did not qualify for the team in the 1955 season. Unitas earned a living that year playing semiprofessional football for $6 per game. The next year he joined the Baltimore Colts, and in 17 seasons as their quarterback he led them to 4 NFL championships. During his career Unitas threw touchdown passes in 47 consecutive games, and in 23 games he passed for more than 300 yd, marks that are both NFL records. He completed 2,830 passes (out of 5,186 attempts) for 40,239 yd and 290 touchdowns—all NFL career records when he retired. Unitas was the Player of the Year in 1959, 1964, and 1967, and he made 10 Pro Bowl appearances. Traded to the San Diego Chargers in 1973, he played there for 1 year before retiring. In 1979 he was elected to the Pro Football Hall of Fame.

United Arab Emirates

The United Arab Emirates (UAE)—composed of the sheikhdoms of Abu Dhabi, Dubai, Sharjah, Ras al-Khaimah, Umm al-Qaiwain, Ajman, and Fujairah—is located on a flat coastal plain of the Arabian Peninsula, along the Persian Gulf. The borders with Qatar on the northwest, Saudi Arabia on the south and west, and Oman on the east are undefined, as are the borders between the individual sheikhdoms. Two neutral zones are shared by several sheikhdoms.

AT A GLANCE

UNITED ARAB EMIRATES

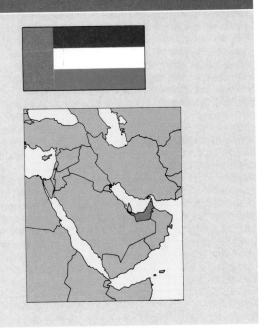

Land: Area: 83,600 km² (32,278 mi²). Capital and largest city: Abu Dhabi (1981 pop., 243,000).

People: Population (1990 est.): 2,253,624. Density: 27 persons per km² (70 per mi²). Distribution (1987 est): 81% urban, 19% rural. Official language: Arabic. Major religion: Islam.

Government: Type: federation of emirates. Legislature: Federal National Council. Political subdivisions: 7 emirates.

Economy: GNP (1989): $28.45 billion; $18,430 per capita. Labor distribution (1986): public administration and services—36%; construction—25%; trade—14%; manufacturing—6%; agriculture—5%; mining—2%. Foreign trade (1988 est.): imports—$8.5 billion; exports—$10.6 billion. Currency: 1 UAE dirham = 100 fils.

Education and Health: Literacy (1986): 73% of adult population. Universities (1987): 1. Hospital beds (1985): 5,817. Physicians (1985): 2,361. Life expectancy (1990): women—73; men—69. Infant mortality (1990): 24 per 1,000 live births.

Land, People, and Economy

About 80% of the UAE's area is in Abu Dhabi. The climate is hot and dry, with mean January temperatures of 18° C (65° F) and mean July temperatures of 33° C (92° F). Rainfall averages 152 mm (6 in) annually. The major resource is petroleum.

Only 42% of the inhabitants are Arabs because the petroleum boom has brought in a flood of foreign workers. About 50% of the population are South Asian. The native population is overwhelmingly Muslim (95%). ABU DHABI, the capital, and DUBAI are the chief cities. Six years of primary education are free and compulsory. Health services are good because of extensive social services provided by petroleum wealth.

Petroleum, first exported in 1962, dominates the economy of the UAE. By 1985 this once-underdeveloped region had the world's highest per capita income—$19,120—even though its petroleum revenues declined in the 1980s because of a world oil glut. The new wealth has been invested in capital improvements and social services in all the emirates, although petroleum production is concentrated in Abu Dhabi and Dubai. Industrial development is primarily petroleum related and is hampered by a lack of trained personnel and other raw materials. Limited irrigated agriculture, fishing, poultry raising, and sheep herding provide domestic food sources.

History and Government

At one time this area was known as the "Pirate Coast," reflecting the major occupation of the inhabitants. To protect its ships, Great Britain, beginning in 1820, made several treaties with the Arab leaders outlawing sea battles. Britain handled foreign relations for the area, then known as Trucial Oman or the Trucial States. The United

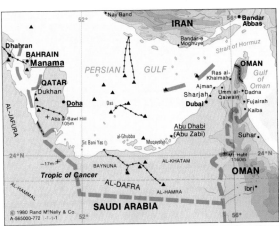

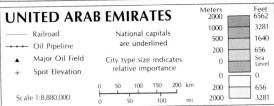

UNITED ARAB EMIRATES

		Meters	Feet
—— Railroad	National capitals	2000	6562
·+·+· Oil Pipeline	are underlined	1000	3281
▲ Major Oil Field	City type size indicates	500	1640
+ Spot Elevation	relative importance	200	656
		0	Sea Level

Scale 1:8,880,000

Arab Emirates gained full independence on Dec. 2, 1971, although Ras al-Khaimah did not join until 1972. There are no elections or legal political parties; authority rests with the seven hereditary sheikhs, who control their own domains and choose a president from among their number. Zaid bin Sultan al-Nahayan, of Abu Dhabi, has been president since 1971. Like other members of the Gulf Cooperation Council (formed 1981), the UAE provided troops and financial and logistical support for the allied war effort in the 1991 GULF WAR.

___

United Arab Republic The United Arab Republic (UAR) was a short-lived federation of Egypt and Syria formed in February 1958 with President Gamal Abdel Nasser of Egypt as head of state. The founders hoped that the federation might lead to the ultimate unification of all Arab peoples. Syria, however, became disenchanted by Egypt's domination of the federation and left the union in September 1961. Yemen (Sana), which had joined the UAR in a trade pact known as the United Arab States, left the association shortly thereafter. Egypt retained United Arab Republic as its official name until 1971.

___

United Auto Workers The International Union, United Automobile, Aerospace and Agricultural Implement Workers of America (UAW) is an industrial union for workers, engineers, and technicians involved in the manufacturing of automobiles, aircraft, and farm equipment. The UAW was formed in 1935 as an American Federation of Labor affiliate but left the AFL the following year to join the newly formed Congress of Industrial Organizations (CIO). After a hard-fought struggle that included a nationwide sit-down strike in General Motors plants in 1937, the UAW won recognition by the automobile industry. In 1969, under the leadership of Walter P. REUTHER, the union withdrew from the AFL-CIO and became independent; it reaffiliated in 1981. In March 1985 the Canadian council of the UAW, with about 10 percent of the total UAW membership, voted to form a separate union.

___

United Church of Christ The United Church of Christ was established in 1957 as a union of the Congregational Christian Churches and the Evangelical and Reformed Church. Its roots lie in the teachings of such 16th-century reformers as Martin Luther and Ulrich Zwingli and in CONGREGATIONALISM.

The basic unit of the United Church is the local church, which is guaranteed autonomy, or freedom, in the decisions it makes. That freedom is the "freedom of the gospel," however, and every corporate body within the church—whether a local church, a conference, or the General Synod—is supposed to make its decisions in the light of the gospel and out of a sense of responsibility to the whole fellowship.

The General Synod of the United Church of Christ,

which meets biennially, is the representative, deliberative body composed of 675–725 delegates elected by the conferences. The officers of the church and the General Synod are the president, secretary, and director of finance and treasurer. The national program agencies include the United Church Board for World Ministries, United Church Board for Homeland Ministries, Office for Church in Society, Office of Communication, Stewardship Council, United Church Foundation Pension Boards, and Commission for Racial Justice. The United Church of Christ is a member of the National Council of Churches, the World Council of Churches, and the World Alliance of Reformed Churches.

United Empire Loyalists see LOYALISTS

United Farm Workers of America see CHAVEZ, CESAR

___

United Irishmen, Society of The Society of United Irishmen, inspired by the French Revolution, was founded in 1791 to seek parliamentary reform and legal equality for all Irish. Its leaders included Belfast Presbyterian merchants and such Dublin intellectuals as Wolfe TONE. They found support among rural Presbyterians in Ulster and among Roman Catholic peasants. After war broke out (1793) between Great Britain and France the society began advocating violent revolution and was harshly suppressed by the British. Spurred by promises of French support, the movement planned a rebellion in 1798, resulting only in three isolated local revolts that were quickly put down.

___

United Kingdom The United Kingdom of Great Britain and Northern Ireland lies at the northwestern edge of Europe, separated from the European mainland by the ENGLISH CHANNEL and the NORTH SEA. It consists of the formerly separate kingdoms of ENGLAND and SCOTLAND, the principality of WALES—which are collectively referred to as GREAT BRITAIN—and the six counties of NORTHERN IRELAND. Other integral parts of the United Kingdom are the outlying HEBRIDES, ORKNEY ISLANDS, and SHETLAND ISLANDS, off the coast of Scotland; Anglesey (see GWYNEDD), off the coast of Wales; and the ISLE OF WIGHT and the SCILLY ISLANDS, off the southern and southwestern coasts of England, respectively. Separate from the kingdom but administered by the crown are the ISLE OF MAN, located in the Irish Sea; and the CHANNEL ISLANDS, located off the northwest coast of France.

England is the largest and most populous unit in the kingdom, with an area of 130,439 km^2 (50,363 mi^2) and a population (1988 est.) of 47,536,300. Wales, located to the west, has an area of 20,768 km^2 (8,018 mi^2) and 2,857,000 (1988 est.) inhabitants; it became part of the English kingdom in 1282. Scotland—with an area of 78,783 km^2 (30,418 mi^2) and 5,094,000 (1988 est.) inhabitants—lies to the north. Scotland and England

AT A GLANCE

UNITED KINGDOM OF GREAT BRITAIN AND NORTHERN IRELAND

Land: Area: 244,110 km^2 (94,251 mi^2). Capital and largest city: London (1988 est. pop., 6,735,400).

People: Population (1990 est.): 57,384,000. Density: 235 persons per km^2 (609 per mi^2). Distribution (1989): 90% urban, 10% rural. Official language: English. Major religions: Anglicanism (Church of England), Roman Catholicism, Presbyterianism (Church of Scotland).

Government: Type: constitutional monarchy. Legislature: Parliament. Political subdivisions: England (45 counties and Greater London); Scotland (9 regions and 3 "island districts"); Wales (8 counties); Northern Ireland (6 counties or 26 districts).

Economy: GNP (1989): $834.2 billion; $14,570 per capita. Labor distribution (1988): manufacturing and construction—22%; services—17%; trade—16%; government—9%; agriculture—1%; finance—9%; other—26%. Foreign trade (1989): imports—$189 billion; exports—$151 billion. Currency: 1 pound sterling = 100 new pence.

Education and Health: Literacy (1990): 99% of adult population. Universities (1989): 45. Hospital beds (1987): 388,700. Physicians (1986): 87,900. Life expectancy (1990): women—79; men—73. Infant mortality (1990): 7 per 1,000 live births.

were ruled by the same monarchs after 1603 and were united in 1707 to form the kingdom of Great Britain. Ireland was made an integral part of the kingdom in 1801, changing the official name to the United Kingdom of Great Britain and Ireland. The present name was adopted after the partition of Ireland in 1921. Northern Ireland has an area of 14,120 km^2 (5,452 mi^2) and a population of 1,578,100 (1988 est.).

Commonly described as "in Europe but not of it," Great Britain and Ireland remained relatively isolated from world events until the 15th century, when the Age of Discovery placed them on the world's newly charted sea lanes and trading routes. Increasingly, the island nation looked across the seas and established overseas colonies, forming the enormous BRITISH EMPIRE. Many of these colonies chose to retain trade and other ties to Britain when granted independence and are today part of the COMMONWEALTH OF NATIONS; because of these ties, however, the United Kingdom's entry into the EUROPEAN COMMUNITY (EC) in 1973 was preceded by lengthy negotiations and dispute.

The INDUSTRIAL REVOLUTION began in the United Kingdom, but in the 20th century competition from more recently industrialized countries as well as the loss of its colonies brought an economic decline. In the 1960s and '70s severe labor disputes, unprecedented inflation, and declining exports contributed to a series of economic crises; but in the 1980s the country enjoyed a long period of prosperity.

The United Kingdom is heavily urbanized. To protect the remaining countryside, the government has established ten national parks in the most scenic areas—DARTMOOR, the LAKE DISTRICT, the Pennines, the Snowdonia, the Pembrokeshire coast, North York Moors, Yorkshire Dales, Northumbria, Exmoor, and the Brecon Beacons.

Land and Resources

Lowland England. The largest area of flat plain occurs in The Fens, located on the east coast around The Wash. Before they were drained to produce a rich agricultural landscape, The Fens were marshland. Smaller flat areas are found along the HUMBER RIVER estuary farther north on the east coast; along the Thames below London; and in Romney Marsh, in the southeastern county of Kent. Elsewhere, lowland England in the south and east is rolling country with a variety of landforms. Especially prominent are the low hills and scarps developed on chalk rocks of Cretaceous age, which occur in the North and South downs to the south of London and in Salisbury Plain. Northwestward from Salisbury Plain, the chalk hills form the prominent Chiltern Hills to the northwest of London;

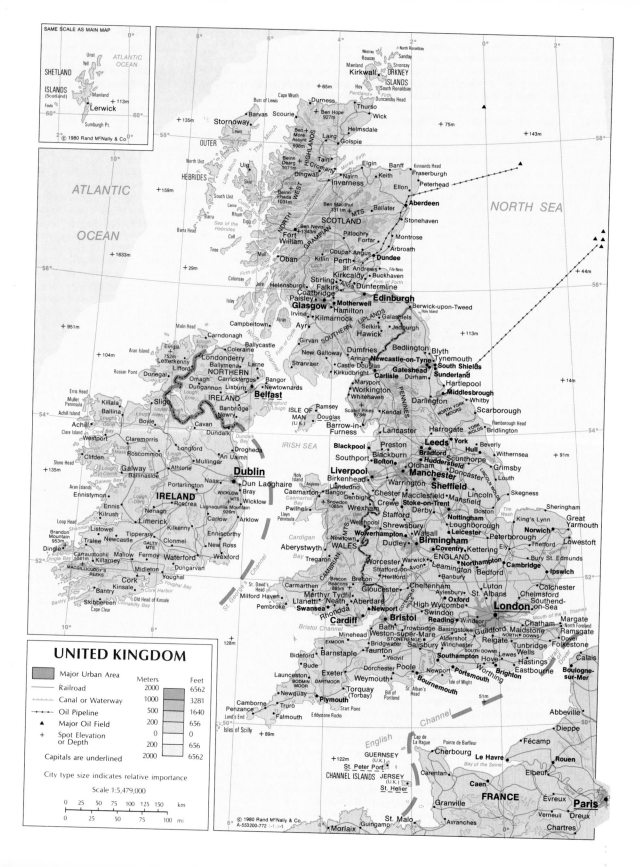

UNITED KINGDOM

| Major Urban Area |
| Railroad |
| Canal or Waterway |
| Oil Pipeline |
| Major Oil Field |
| Spot Elevation or Depth |
| Capitals are underlined |

Meters	Feet
2000	6562
1000	3281
500	1640
200	656
0	0
200	656
2000	6562

City type size indicates relative importance

Scale 1:5,479,000

0 25 50 75 100 125 150 km

0 25 50 75 100 mi

© 1980 Rand McNally & Co.
A-553200-772 -1-1-1

fall to lower elevations in the hills of East Anglia (Norfolk and Suffolk counties); and farther north form the Lincoln and York wolds on each side of the Humber estuary.

To the west rise a northeast-trending series of uplands developed on limestones of Jurassic age. They extend from the southern county of Dorset to the North York moors on England's northeast coast, and include the Cotswolds.

Also prominent in lowland England are the Mendip Hills in the southwest near Bristol; Exmoor in Dunkery Beacon farther west; Dartmoor, a granite-formed upland in High Willhays in the southwestern peninsula; and the Malvern Hills between GLOUCESTER and WORCESTER. Glacial deposits greatly modify topography and landforms north of an irregular line joining the River Thames and the Bristol Channel.

Upland England. Uplands predominate in northern and western England. The most extensive uplands are the PENNINES, which rise to 893 m (2,930 ft) in Cross Fell. The Pennines are bordered on both sides by discontinuous coalfields, and the open moorlands of the Pennines contrast starkly with the sprawling industrial cities near the coal deposits. Numerous broad river valleys, known locally as dales, drain eastward across the mountains into the Vale of York. West of the Pennines are the Lancashire and Cheshire plains and farther north is England's scenic

One of Britain's historic landmarks is the Tower of London, a medieval fortress dating back to the time of William the Conqueror (late 11th century). Once famous as a prison and place of execution, the Tower is now a museum and the repository of the crown jewels.

Dedicated in 1984, the Thames Flood Barrier at Woolwich protects London from being flooded by high tides from the North Sea. The visible portion consists of a line of concrete piers with rounded steel tops. Attached to the piers are gates on the riverbed that can be raised to form a barrier against a rising tide.

Lake District, which rises to 978 m (3,210 ft) in Scafell Pike, England's highest peak.

Wales and Scotland. The topography of Wales and Scotland is dominated by mountains and uplands. The highest mountain in Wales is Snowdon, which rises to 1,085 m (3,560 ft). In South Wales the Brecon Beacons rise to 886 m (2,907 ft). The principal lowlands in Wales are on the island of Anglesey and along the western coasts of Caernarvon and Cardigan bays.

Southern Scotland is dominated by low ranges of the Southern Uplands. To the north are the geologically complex, down-faulted Scottish Central Lowlands that extend northeastward across the country from the Firth of Clyde on the west coast to the firths (estuaries) of Tay and Forth on the east coast. North and west of the Central Lowlands are the HIGHLANDS, a large upland region divided by the Glen More (Great Glen), a deep depression that extends from Fort William to Inverness and is occupied in part by Loch (lake) NESS. Narrow lowlands border the Highlands in the east. The rugged western Highlands include BEN NEVIS, the highest point in the United Kingdom (1,343m/ 4,406 ft). The Cairngorm Mountains are the most extensive area of mountainous terrain in the Highlands. On the western island of SKYE, the scenic Cuillin Hills rise to more than 900 m (3,000 ft).

Northern Ireland. The structural depression forming the Scottish Central Lowlands extends southwestward across the Irish Sea to form the area of lowlands surrounding Lough (lake) NEAGH, which is situated to the west of Belfast in Northern Ireland. Scenic mountains of low elevation border the lowlands area on all sides. To the northeast rise the Antrim Mountains, which reach the sea on the north coast in the famous steps of the GIANT'S CAUSEWAY. The Sperrin Mountains form the northwestern edge of the depression. On the southern edge of the depression are the Mourne Mountains, south of Belfast, which rise to 852 m (2,796 ft) in Slieve Donard, the highest point in Northern Ireland.

The ruins of the 14th-century fortress Dunluce Castle overlook basaltic cliffs in County Antrim, the northeasternmost portion of Northern Ireland. Ramore Head, where the castle is located, extends into the North Channel, which separates Northern Ireland from Scotland.

Soils. The richest soils include the reclaimed alluvial deposits in The Fens, alluvial soils along the Mersey River and west coast, and brick earths and other deep soils in the London basin. Elsewhere, modern methods of fertilization make natural fertility less important than such other conditions as soil texture, drainage, climate, and slope. In general terms, soils in the drier east and south are used mainly for crops, and soils in the more humid west and north and in some clay areas are used mainly for dairying.

Climate. The United Kingdom has a highly variable temperate marine west-coast type of climate. Relatively few periods of continuously dry weather occur. Much more common is the variable weather that occurs as cyclonic depressions sweep in from the Atlantic Ocean, bringing high winds and abundant rainfall to the west in winter and lower amounts of rainfall in summer. Mountainous west-coast areas generally receive more than 2,540 mm (100 in) of rain a year, but rainfall amounts diminish rapidly eastward. The driest areas surround the Thames estuary in southeastern England, where less than 500 mm (20 in) of rain falls each year. In the wetter western areas, 2 out of 3 days are usually rainy; in the drier east, rain falls on almost one out of every two days. No permanent snows exist, but snow may lie on the ground for 2 months or more in the Highlands; it covers the ground for about 18 days in Aberdeen and an average of 6 days in London. In summer, a more normal decrease in temperature from south to north occurs; average July temperatures range from about 17° C (63° F) on the southern coast and in London, to 12° C (54° F) in the north of Scotland.

Drainage. The SEVERN and THAMES are the longest rivers. Other major rivers are the AVON, CLYDE, FORTH, MERSEY, TAY, TRENT, TWEED, Ouse, Tees, and Tyne. These and other rivers are all used for shipping, water supplies, or hydroelectric power; their flow is, accordingly, highly regulated. An intricate canal system, now largely abandoned, dates from the early Industrial Revolution.

Vegetation and Animal Life. Although forests cover only 7% of the land area, the British landscape presents a characteristically wooded appearance. This impression stems mainly from the presence of many trees in hedgerows and pastures, coverts planted for game birds, shelter belts planted beside farmhouses and exposed fields, and ornamental plantings on great estates. The largest forests in England occur in the Breckland to the northeast of Cambridge; in Kielder Forest in Northumberland; and as the remnants of the historic Forest of Dean (in Gloucestershire) and Sherwood Forest (in Nottinghamshire); and the New Forest (in Hampshire), a former royal hunting preserve. Expanses of treeless moorland cover much of the Pennines, Highlands, and other exposed upland areas; on the drier moors heather predominates, and on the wetter moors various grasses and mosses are prevalent. Alpine flora occur at high elevations in the Cairngorms and other parts of the Highlands. Game birds include grouse, on the moors, and pheasants; deer and foxes are hunted in many areas.

Resources. The United Kingdom has long been rich in energy resources but deficient in food and industrial raw materials. Extensive coal deposits occur around the eastern and western edges of the Pennines, in South Wales, in the western MIDLANDS (Birmingham area), and in the Scottish Central Lowland. Easily accessible coal seams are, however, largely exhausted. Large deposits of petroleum and natural gas under the North Sea came into commercial production in 1975, and by the end of the 1980s the United Kingdom was largely self-sufficient in petroleum.

Other mineral deposits are of small importance. They include tin, low-grade iron ores, kaolinite (china clay), and sands and gravels. Of the total land area about 30% is used for crops and 50% for pasture.

People

About 83% of the total population live in England, 9% in Scotland, 5% in Wales, and 3% in Northern Ireland.

More than 2% are non-Caucasian immigrants who arrived in recent decades from the British West Indies, Pakistan, India, and other Commonwealth or former Commonwealth countries.

The nonimmigrant population is primarily descended from a mixture of Europeans that have at different times invaded and occupied the islands. Traces of early settlement go back to the Paleolithic era, but the first main occupation was by CELTS, who came by direct migration from continental Europe and also as travelers along the western sea routes linking Brittany to Cornwall, Ireland, Scotland, and the Orkney and Shetland islands. The Roman occupation began in AD 43. Most of the English Lowland was eventually romanized. ANGLO-SAXONS came after the decline of Roman Britain and colonized most of the English lowland after the 5th century; they failed, like the Romans, to colonize the north and west, and the division between an Anglo-Saxon south and east and a predominantly Celtic north and west has persisted to this day. Danes settled alongside the English in the 9th century and briefly controlled northeastern and central parts of the English lowland as the DANELAW. The Danish invasions were part of large-scale VIKING movements from the 9th to 11th centuries. NORMANS conquered England in 1066. Anglo-Normans had conquered Wales by 1284 but did not anglicize the population much beyond the towns and castles they established along the lowland fringes of North and South Wales; they were also unable to subdue the Scots. Added to this early ethnic mixture were later refugees from continental Europe, such as the French HUGUENOTS; many Irish migrants in the 18th and 19th centuries; Poles and other displaced persons during and after World War II; and since the 1960s more than 1.3 million Asian, West Indian, and other nonwhite immigrants.

Language. The official language is English. Other languages include the CELTIC LANGUAGES: Welsh, the national language of Wales, and Scottish Gaelic, so named to distinguish it from Irish Gaelic, the national language of Ireland. Most Welsh speakers are concentrated in the rural northern and western counties of Wales, where they constitute about 75% of the total population; all but a few are also recorded as English speaking. Since 1967, Welsh has enjoyed parity with English in governmental and legal matters throughout Wales. Scottish Gaelic is used primarily in the western Highlands and on the islands.

Religion. The Anglican Church of England (see ENGLAND, CHURCH OF) and the Presbyterian Church of Scotland (see SCOTLAND, CHURCH OF) are established churches, but neither is subsidized by the state. Wales has no established church, nor has Northern Ireland, which is approximately two-thirds Protestant and one-third Roman Catholic. The Church of England has the nominal support of about 60% of the English; about 40% of all Scots support the Church of Scotland. Roman Catholicism is heavily represented in large industrial cities with Irish and continental European immigrant workers. Methodist, Baptist, and United Reform (Presbyterian and Congregational) churches are found almost everywhere in England and Wales; in Scotland the Episcopal (Anglican) church has small numbers of adherents in most towns. About 450,000 Jews live in the United Kingdom, mainly

(Left) *This workers' community is located near textile factories in Lancashire, in the moorlands of northwestern England, where textile manufacture is most concentrated.* (Below) *The town of Worsley, in northwestern England, is noted for its historic houses and landmarks. The Bridgewater Canal, constructed during the 18th century, helped change the character of Worsley from an agricultural community to a coal-mining and textile center.*

in the London area. In addition, recent immigrants have established Islamic mosques and Hindu and Sikh temples in some cities.

Demography. The United Kingdom is one of the most densely populated nations in Europe. The most densely populated part of the United Kingdom is England, with 364 persons per km^2 (944 per mi^2) in 1988; Scotland has a density of 65 per km^2 (167 per mi^2); Wales, 138 per km^2 (356 per mi^2); and Northern Ireland, 112 per km^2 (289 per mi^2). About 35% of the total population is concentrated in the Greater London area and seven other conurbations (continuously built-up urban areas)—Central Clydeside (based on GLASGOW), Tyne and Wear (based on the central cities of NEWCASTLE UPON TYNE and Sunderland), Merseyside (LIVERPOOL and environs), Greater MANCHESTER, West Yorkshire (based on LEEDS and BRADFORD), South Yorkshire (based on SHEFFIELD), and the West Midlands (BIRMINGHAM and the Black Country). The most sparsely populated areas are the Highlands of Scotland, upland areas of Wales, and the Pennines.

Areas of most rapid population growth are in outer London, where several of the post-1945 NEW TOWNS (designed to relieve urban congestion) are located, in the western Midlands; and in the eastern Midlands around DERBY and NOTTINGHAM. By contrast, the old textile and other industrial towns of the Pennines are declining, and stagnation is also seen in the industrialized northeast of England and in most of Scotland. The greatest losses of population are occurring in the mining valleys of South Wales and in inner-city areas of Liverpool, Manchester, and Glasgow.

Education and Health. Education is free and compulsory for children between the ages of 5 and 16. Nursery schools are also provided for children under 5, but the number of such schools does not meet the demand. In most cases children in the BRITISH EDUCATION system move from a junior to a senior school at age 11. Current educational policy is for comprehensive schools to educate all children up to age 16.

The old grammar schools are now almost completely merged into the comprehensive system of education, although some have chosen to become independent. As independent schools, they, like such prestigious "public" (private) schools as ETON COLLEGE, RUGBY SCHOOL, and Winchester College, no longer receive state aid but are required to maintain the same standards of staffing and equipment as the state schools. Higher education is provided at 36 universities in England and Wales, including the prestigious universities of CAMBRIDGE, LONDON, and OXFORD; at 8 in Scotland; and at 2 in Northern Ireland. In addition, 7 university colleges and medical and technological institutions are allied with the University of Wales.

Medical care is provided free or for a small charge to most of the population through the National Health Service. In addition, a small minority financially able to do so choose to remain outside the system and be private, fee-paying patients of hospitals, physicians, and dentists. Normally, no costs are incurred by the patient for routine medical care, including visits to the doctor's office, house calls, or hospitalization as a patient or outpatient.

The Arts. More than 35,000 books are published annually in the United Kingdom, including paperback editions. For the nation's vast literary heritage see separate articles on ENGLISH LITERATURE, SCOTTISH LITERATURE, and WELSH LITERATURE. Foremost painters include William HOGARTH, Thomas GAINSBOROUGH, Joseph Mallord William TURNER, John CONSTABLE, and William BLAKE (see ENGLISH ART AND ARCHITECTURE). The works of these and other painters are maintained at the NATIONAL GALLERY, the TATE GALLERY, and other galleries in London and in some larger cities outside London. Leading composers of ENGLISH MUSIC include Henry PURCELL, Edward ELGAR, Ralph VAUGHAN WILLIAMS, and Benjamin BRITTEN. The Albert Hall and Royal Festival Hall are important concert centers in London, and first-class orchestras are maintained in London, Liverpool, Manchester, and Birmingham and by the BBC (British Broadcasting Corporation). The GLYNDEBOURNE OPERA FESTIVAL, ROYAL BALLET, Royal Opera, and English National Opera (formerly Sadler's Wells Opera) are all internationally famous. In Wales *eisteddfods*, festivals of music (especially choral music) and art, are held throughout the year, the most famous being the Royal National Eisteddfod. In Scotland the major event in the arts is the three-week annual Edinburgh International Festival of Music, Drama, and Art at the end of the summer.

Economic Activity

In the 14th and 15th centuries, England developed a flourishing wool trade with the Continent and a cottage-based textile industry in sheep-raising areas of the Cotswolds, the Pennines, East Anglia (Norwich area), and the southwest. In the 18th century the invention of power-driven textile machinery revolutionized this earlier industry, and spinning and weaving operations moved out of the home and into factories. Steam engines, fueled by coal, replaced waterpower after the 1780s, and the coalfields developed as major industrial centers. Lancashire (west Pennines) developed as a cotton textile center; Yorkshire (east Pennines), as the center of woolen manufactures; Birmingham and the Black Country (West Midlands), as a center for the manufacture of machinery and precision equipment; and the Glasgow area, as a shipbuilding and metallurgical center. By 1851 the United Kingdom was the world's leading industrial nation. It lost this industrial preeminence after the 1920s as other nations began to industrialize. It experimented with the nationalization of steel and other key industries in the 1940s and, despite widespread opposition, joined the EC in 1973. After two decades of economic crises, the 1980s saw a continuous economic growth. During this period, Prime Minister Margaret THATCHER also initiated a major reprivatization of nationalized industries.

Manufacturing. About 30% of the 5.2 million workers in manufacturing are engaged in the metallurgical and engineering industries. Increasing efficiency of production and elimination of uneconomic plants continue to reduce the numbers working in manufacturing. The main centers of industry are in the coalfields of northern England and Scotland, in the western Midlands, and around the major ports, including London.

During Glasgow's growth as a major port, extensive ship- yards and dock installations were constructed along both banks of the Clyde River. By the early 1800s, Glas- gow—Scotland's largest city—had established itself as a shipbuilding and industrial center.

Mining. Petroleum is the principal mineral produced, and production approached the self-sufficiency level of 2 million barrels a day in the 1980s. Natural gas is produced in association with petroleum. Coal is also mined, but employment in the coal industry has dropped significantly because of loss of export markets, increasing use of petroleum and other fuels, and exhaustion of easily worked coal seams in the coalfields. Sands and gravels are of considerable economic significance; iron ores, tin, and kaolinite (china clay) are of lesser importance.

Energy. In 1988 the United Kingdom ranked second in Europe, after West Germany, in electricity production, with an output of 308 billion kW h. Hydroelectricity is produced mainly in the Scottish Highlands and in south-western Scotland. In 1989, 39 nuclear reactors provided almost 22% of all electricity.

Agriculture. Approximately three-fourths of all the land area of England and Wales is used for farming, excluding moorlands used for grazing; in Scotland less than one-fourth of the total area is farmed. The main crops are wheat, barley, oats, peas, beans, vegetables, sugar beets, and green fodder crops. Livestock farming, mainly for beef and dairy products, is also important; and sheep farming predominates on higher ground. Truck farming (called market gardening in the United Kingdom) is important near London and other large cities and on the south coast. Flowers and early potatoes are a specialty in mild and sheltered areas of Cornwall and the Scilly Islands.

Forestry and Fishing. Forestry is of minor national importance. In some areas the state-owned forests have become economically important as tourist attractions; in other areas, including the Lake District, reforestation is opposed for fear that it would spoil open mountain views and thereby damage a thriving tourist industry. Fishing has long been a major activity, and large fishing ports include Lerwick (in the Shetland Islands), Aberdeen, Grimsby, Hull, Lowestoft, North Shields, and Yarmouth on the east coast, and Fleetwood and Milford Haven on the west coast.

Transportation. More than 2,400 km (1,490 mi) of high-speed motorways supplement the United Kingdom's older and slower highway system based on 13,161 km (8,178 mi) of trunk roads radiating out from London. Railroads were nationalized in 1947, and service was reduced and modernized by British Railways (BR). Except for the Manchester Ship Canal, canals and canalized rivers carry little freight today. The busiest ports—some brought to recent prominence by North Sea oil—are London, Milford Haven, Hartlepool, Forth, Grimsby, Southampton, Shetland (Sullom Voe), Orkney (Flotta), Liverpool, and Manchester.

Trade. Imports generally exceed exports by value, but the difference is usually balanced by income from worldwide financial, insurance, and transport services and from an increasingly successful tourist industry. More than half of all exports consist of electrical equipment, aircraft and aircraft engines, road vehicles and tractors, scientific instruments, and other metallurgical and engineering products. Other leading exports are chemical products and textiles. The four main groups of imports are semimanufactured goods; manufactured articles; raw materials; and food, drink, and tobacco.

Government

The United Kingdom is a constitutional monarchy with a

parliamentary form of government. The ruling sovereign (since 1952) is Queen ELIZABETH II; the heir apparent is Prince CHARLES. As head of state the sovereign ceremonially opens each new session of Parliament and entrusts executive authority to the prime minister (since 1990, John MAJOR) and the cabinet. Legislative authority rests with a bicameral Parliament, but effective power lies more with the directly elected 650-member House of Commons (lower house) than with the House of Lords (upper house), consisting of hereditary and life peers. The prime minister is appointed by the sovereign as the leader of the majority party or coalition of parties in the House of Commons. The maximum term of Parliament is 5 years.

The principal political parties are the CONSERVATIVE PARTY, led by John Major, and the LABOUR PARTY, led by Neil KINNOCK. Other parties include the Social and Liberal Democrats, formed in 1988 by a merger of the LIBERAL PARTY and the Social Democratic party; the Communist party; and the locally important Ulster Unionist party, the Scottish National party, and the Plaid Cymru (Welsh Nationalist party).

Plans to provide devolution (home rule) to Scotland and Wales ended in 1979, when voters in Wales rejected a plan to establish a Welsh assembly in Cardiff, and voters in Scotland approved, but with less than the necessary majority, establishment of a separate assembly for Scotland in Edinburgh. Home rule in Northern Ireland was ended in 1972 because of continuing Protestant-Catholic hostilities. Government of Northern Ireland now rests with the secretary of state for Northern Ireland.

Local government in England underwent major reorganization in 1974. Local administration is now managed through 6 metropolitan counties; 39 nonmetropolitan counties; and Greater London. The 6 metropolitan counties are the conurbations of Tyne and Wear, Merseyside,

Among Liverpool's Pier Head group of office buildings is the Royal Liver Building (1908–10). Located on the Mersey River in northwestern England, Liverpool has been a major port since the 18th century.

Greater Manchester, West Yorkshire, South Yorkshire, and the West Midlands.

British dependencies overseas include Gibraltar, Bermuda, the British Virgin Islands, the Falkland Islands, the Turks and Caicos Islands, the Cayman Islands, Montserrat, Hong Kong, the British Indian Ocean Territory, Saint Helena, Ascension, Tristan da Cunha, and the Pitcairn Islands.

See also: GREAT BRITAIN, HISTORY OF; separate articles on counties and major cities and land features in the United Kingdom.

Queen Elizabeth II, on horseback, reviews a parade of Guards at the entrance to Buckingham Palace in London. The palace, designed (1825) by John Nash, is the principal residence of the British monarch.

United Methodist Church   see METHODISM

United Mine Workers of America   The United Mine Workers of America (UMW) is an independent labor union, organized on an industrial basis, comprising workers in the coal industry. It was founded in 1890 through the merger of several earlier organizations.

Always militant, it almost disintegrated several times from economic depression, employer hostility, and periodic unemployment. In 1897 it initiated a successful organization drive; in 1898 it achieved an 8-hour work day in the important areas of western Pennsylvania, Indiana, Ohio, and Illinois. John L. LEWIS headed the union from 1920 to 1960. During that period the UMW was at the center of the militant labor movement. When the National Industrial Recovery Act (NIRA) of 1933 guaranteed a union's right to bargain and to organize, Lewis fought to organize other industrial unions, but the American Federation of Labor (AFL) refused to support him. He then created the Committee for Industrial Organization, which became (1938) the Congress of Industrial Organizations (CIO), for which the UMW provided support until it withdrew in 1942. Following World War II the UMW's agreement to automation in mining cost many miners their jobs but brought greater benefits to those remaining. The union rejoined the AFL in 1946 but again became independent in 1947.

Lewis was succeeded (1960) as president by Thomas Kennedy, after whose death (1963) W. A. "Tony" Boyle assumed leadership. Boyle's opponent Joseph Yablonski was murdered in 1969; Boyle was subsequently forced out (1972) of the presidency and convicted (1974) of the murder. Arnold Miller then became president. He was succeeded by Samuel Church in 1979, who was defeated in 1982 UMW elections by Richard Trumka. In the mid-1980s the UMW had more than 210,000 active or retired members.

United Nations   The United Nations (UN) is a general international organization established at the end of World War II to promote international peace and security. It is the second such organization, having replaced the LEAGUE OF NATIONS, which was founded in the aftermath of World War I. UN headquarters is in New York City.

Origins

The United Nations officially came into existence on Oct. 24, 1945, when 51 original members ratified its charter. The main purposes of the organization were to "save succeeding generations from the scourge of war"; develop friendly relations among states; cooperate in solving international economic, social, cultural, and humanitarian problems; and promote respect for human rights and fundamental freedoms.

To enable it to work toward its goals the UN was equipped with six major organs: the Security Council, General Assembly, Economic and Social Council, Trusteeship Council, INTERNATIONAL COURT OF JUSTICE, and the Secretariat. In addition, a number of specialized agencies were attached to the UN system to deal with specific international problems.

Structure and Powers

The Security Council. The organ with the primary responsibility for maintaining peace and security is the Security Council. Originally the Security Council had 11 members, but now it has 15. Five of these—China, France, the USSR, Great Britain, and the United States—are permanent members. The other ten members are elected by the General Assembly for 2-year terms. Each member of the council has one vote. Decisions on matters of procedure must carry by an affirmative vote of at least 9 of the 15 members. Decisions on substantive matters also require nine votes, with no negative vote from any of the five permanent members. This is the so-called Great Power unanimity rule, often referred to as the "veto." All five permanent members have exercised the veto right at one time or another. If a permanent member does not support a decision but has no desire to block it through a veto, it may abstain; an abstention is not regarded as a veto.

Under the charter, all members of the UN agree to accept and carry out the decisions of the council. While other organs of the UN make recommendations to governments, the council alone has the power to make decisions which member states are obligated under the charter to carry out. When a dispute leads to open warfare, the council may decide on cease-fire directives, enforcement measures, or collective military action. Sometimes it sends UN observers or peacekeeping forces to help reduce tensions in troubled areas.

A state that is not a member of the UN or is a member of the UN but not of the Security Council may participate, without vote, in its discussions when the council considers that the country's interests are specially affected.

The General Assembly. The General Assembly, composed of all member states of the UN, is the main deliberative organ of the UN. It has no power to compel action by any government, but its recommendations carry moral weight as an expression of world opinion. As new problems arise, the General Assembly initiates activities to deal with them. The General Assembly, consequently, has encouraged humanitarian relief efforts, development programs, campaigns against colonialism and racism, and the negotiation of treaties and other agreements on matters of global concern, such as the Law of the Sea.

The General Assembly expanded its role during the Korean War. Under the Uniting for Peace resolution, adopted by the General Assembly in November 1950, the assembly gave itself the power to take action if the Security Council, because of the lack of unanimity of its permanent members, fails to act in a case where there appears to be a threat to the peace, a breach of the peace, or an act of aggression.

Each member of the General Assembly has one vote. Decisions on important questions—such as recommendations on peace and security; admission, suspension, and expulsion of members; and budgetary matters—need a two-thirds majority. Decisions on other questions are by simple majority. The regular session begins each year on the third Tuesday in September and continues usually until mid-December.

The Economic and Social Council. The Economic and Social Council, under the authority of the General Assembly, coordinates the economic and social work of the UN and the specialized agencies and institutions. The council makes recommendations and initiates activities relating to development, world trade, natural resources, human rights, population, social welfare, science and technology, and many other economic and social questions.

The council has 54 members. One-third of its members are elected each year by the General Assembly for a 3-year term of office. Voting in the Economic and Social Council is by simple majority; each member has one vote.

Trusteeship Council. The Trusteeship Council was established to deal with nonindependent territories previously held under League of Nations mandate, territories taken from the defeated World War II powers, and such other territories as might be handed over to it by their possessors. It operates under the authority of the General Assembly.

The Trusteeship Council consists of representatives of those states which administer trust territories, representatives of permanent members of the Security Council that do not administer trust territories, and enough others to assure that membership is divided equally between administering and nonadministering states. The principal activities of the Trusteeship Council have included receiving annual reports from the administering states and periodically visiting the territories. Since its establishment the Trusteeship Council has seen the 11 trust territories originally under its control transformed into other entities.

International Court of Justice. The International Court of Justice receives cases from states and international organizations. The court is also empowered to give advisory opinions when requested to do so by organs of the UN and specialized agencies. Generally, states have preferred to resolve their disputes outside of the jurisdiction of the court.

Secretariat. The first secretary-general of the United Nations was Trygve LIE of Norway, who served until 1953. Dag HAMMARSKJÖLD, of Sweden, served from 1953 until his death in a plane crash in Africa in 1961, when he was succeeded by U THANT of Burma. Kurt WALDHEIM of Austria served two consecutive terms from January 1972 to December 1981. In January 1982, Javier PÉREZ DE CUÉLLAR of Peru began a five-year term, which was extended, in October 1986, through 1991.

The Secretariat, an international staff working at UN headquarters and in the field, carries out the day-to-day work of the UN. Each staff member takes an oath not to seek or receive instructions from any outside authority; under the UN Charter, each member state undertakes not to seek to influence the Secretariat in the discharge of its duties. In practice, however, this provision has been violated.

The work of the secretary-general and the staff is varied and includes providing mediation in resolving international disputes; administering peacekeeping operations; preparing surveys of world economic trends and problems; studying human rights and natural resources; organizing international conferences; compiling statistics; and interpreting speeches, translating documents, and servicing the communications media of the world with information about the UN.

Specialized Agencies. The specialized agencies attached to the United Nations system can be divided roughly into two groups. The first group, the major purpose of which is to broaden and facilitate communications among nations, includes the Universal Postal Union (UPU; see POSTAL UNION, UNIVERSAL), the INTERNATIONAL CIVIL AVIATION ORGANIZATION (ICAO), the WORLD METEOROLOGICAL ORGANIZATION (WMO), the International Telecommunication Union (ITU), and the Inter-Governmental Maritime Consultative Organization (IMCO). The second group may be called the "welfare" agencies, in the sense

The United Nations Security Council, comprising five permanent and ten temporary members, was conceived as the principal peacekeeping body of the UN. Unlike other organs of the UN, the Security Council is able to make decisions binding on all members of the organization.

that each is intended to improve world economic, social, and cultural conditions and thus build defenses for peace. The oldest of these is the INTERNATIONAL LABOR ORGANIZATION (ILO). Other agencies in this group include the FOOD AND AGRICULTURE ORGANIZATION (FAO), the WORLD HEALTH ORGANIZATION (WHO), the UNITED NATIONS EDUCATIONAL, SCIENTIFIC, AND CULTURAL ORGANIZATION (UNESCO), the WORLD BANK, the INTERNATIONAL DEVELOPMENT ASSOCIATION (IDA), the INTERNATIONAL FINANCE CORPORATION (IFC), the INTERNATIONAL MONETARY FUND (IMF), the INTERNATIONAL ATOMIC ENERGY AGENCY (IAEA), the GENERAL AGREEMENT ON TARIFFS AND TRADE (GATT), the Office of the United Nations High Commissioner for Refugees (UNHCR; see REFUGEES, OFFICE OF THE UNITED NATIONS HIGH COMMISSIONER FOR), and the United Nations Relief and Works Agency for Palestine Refugees (UNRWA).

Developments since 1945

The UN has experienced many changes since 1945 when the United States was the most dominant of the 51 states in the organization. Today, as a result of the attainment of independence by most colonies, the organization has about three times (159 in 1991) as many member states. Switzerland, North Korea, and South Korea are among the few independent nations that are not members of the UN. Today, too, the representatives from Africa, Asia, and Latin America play major roles in its affairs, and the USSR is much more influential in the UN today than it was in 1945.

The cold war between the United States and the USSR had a serious impact on the UN, as did the rise of the colonial world to self-government and the increased interdependence among nations. One effect of the cold war was the opposition from 1949 until 1971 by the United States to the admission of the People's Republic of China to the UN. When Communist China was finally admitted in 1971, the Republic of China (Taiwan) lost its seat.

Militarily, the UN reflected the rising international tensions both between the USSR and the United States and also among emerging nations. When Soviet-supported North Korea invaded American-supported South Korea in June 1950, the Security Council—with the USSR absent—called upon all members to "repel the armed attack." Because almost 90 percent of the non-Korean forces fighting under the UN flag were U.S. forces, the UN unified command was primarily a U.S. operation.

The United Nations has since engaged in other military activities, but these have not been on the scale of the Korean War, nor were the military forces of the United States directly involved. The UN established several major peacekeeping forces in the Middle East, Africa, and Cyprus.

The UN military action in the Middle East was considerably less dramatic than the Korean campaign. The first United Nations Emergency Force (UNEF) that was dispatched to the troubled area in 1956 never exceeded 6,000 troops. UNEF was not meant to be a fighting army; its purpose was to serve as a symbol of the UN's involvement, which, it was hoped, would succeed in bringing about the neutralization of the disputed areas. It constituted for the first time a genuine international police force not dominated by any single power. In fact, all the great powers were specifically excluded from it.

The second United Nations Emergency Force (UNEF II) was established immediately after the conclusion of the war between Israel and its Arab neighbors in late October 1973. The force was deployed by the Security Council along the disengagement line that had been negotiated between Israel and Egypt by U.S. secretary of state Henry Kissinger. In May 1974, in the wake of the disengagement arrangement that had been worked out by Secretary Kissinger between Israel and Syria, the Security Council established a small (1,250-person) UN Disengagement Observer Force drawn from UNEF. They were transferred for patrol duty to the Golan Heights. In an attempt to separate Israelis and Palestinian guerrillas, the UN Interim Forces in Lebanon (UNIFIL) was established in 1978. By mid-1982, 7,000 troops had been deployed to southern Lebanon, they were brushed aside when Israel occupied west Beirut in September 1982, but they stayed on.

Perhaps the most complex military challenge to confront the United Nations was the one that occurred in the Congo between 1960 and 1964. The UN force of 20,000 mostly African troops had to attempt to keep brutal tribal warfare to a minimum, assume some governmental functions, and forestall great power intervention.

In March 1964 yet another peacekeeping experiment was launched, this time in Cyprus. When the Greek and Turkish communities on that island found themselves unable to resolve their differences and civil war became an increasingly ominous threat, the Security Council met in emergency session and authorized a peace force. Three thousand British troops already on the island were deputized as UN policemen, and in addition Canada, Sweden, Ireland, and Finland contributed troops, bringing the total to 7,000.

Along with its peacekeeping operations, the UN has also been responsible for a number of important treaties in the area of arms control. Most significant among these are the treaties demilitarizing outer space (1967), prohibiting the spread of nuclear weapons (1968), prohibiting the emplacement of nuclear weapons on the ocean floors (1971), imposing a ban on biochemical warfare (1975), and establishing a ban on environmental warfare (1976).

The 1970s witnessed an integrated approach by the United Nations to deal with some of the world's most critical nonmilitary problems. A series of global conferences was organized under UN auspices to address the main challenges facing the world. The first of these was a World Conference on the Human Environment held in Stockholm in 1972. The year 1974 saw a number of global conferences concerned with such matters as raw materials and development, the law of the sea, world population, and world food. All these conferences emphasized the need to respond to global challenges with global initiatives. This "planetary management" movement continued to gather momentum during the 1970s and 1980s with more international conferences dealing with such subjects as the status of women, human rights, urban growth, the spread of deserts, and, once more, population and the law of the sea.

Until recently the United Nations was the object of considerable criticism from many quarters due to its seeming inability to deal with political crises, particularly those involving conflicting interests of the United States and the Soviet Union. This criticism overlooked the fact that many disputes were brought to the UN only when the participants had already failed to resolve the crisis and it had become acute, even violent. The voting rules of the General Assembly, which give each member one vote, regardless of its size, were also criticized.

The United Nations peacekeeping forces were awarded the Nobel Peace Prize in 1988, and by 1990 the easing of East-West tensions had led to a dramatic increase in the UN's effectiveness. The most conspicuous evidence of change was the UN's cohesive response to the 1990 Iraqi invasion of Kuwait. The UN also played a central, mediating role in the 1988 cease-fire in the IRAN-IRAQ WAR, the 1989 withdrawal of Soviet forces from Afghanistan, and independence for Namibia (1990), and UN peacekeeping forces supervised peace accords in such countries as Angola, Cambodia, and El Salvador. The UN continued efforts to peacefully resolve conflicts in Cyprus, Somalia, the Balkans, and elsewhere.

UN membership increased in the 1990s with the breakup of the USSR and Yugoslavia and the admission of North and South Korea, the Marshall Islands, and the Federated States of Micronesia. In 1992, Yugoslavia became the first nation ever to be expelled from the organization.

United Nations Children's Fund The United Nations Children's Fund (UNICEF) was established as the United Nations International Children's Emergency Fund in 1946 at the General Assembly's first session. Originally it was responsible for assisting child welfare programs in countries devastated by World War II, but after 1950 its scope expanded to developing nations. UNICEF helps governments develop nutrition programs and child health and welfare services and gives direct aid (food and medical supplies) to children in emergency situations.

UNICEF was awarded the Nobel Peace Prize (1965). It is governed by a 41-nation executive board elected by the UN Economic and Social Council and administered by an executive director headquartered in New York City. UNICEF is financed totally by voluntary contributions and activities such as the sale of greeting cards.

United Nations Educational, Scientific, and Cultural Organization The United Nations Educational, Scientific, and Cultural Organization, or UNESCO, was established at a London conference in November 1945. In 1946 it became a specialized agency of the United Nations. Its purpose was to further the cause of peace through education and research. The organization is a successor to the League of Nations International Committee on Intellectual Cooperation.

UNESCO's activities fall into the following general categories: expanding and directing education so as to enable the people of every country to further their own development; helping to establish the scientific and technological foundations through which every country can make better use of its resources; encouraging national cultural values and the preservation of cultural heritage; developing communication for the balanced flow of information and information systems for the universal pooling of knowledge; and promoting the social sciences as instruments for the realization of human rights, justice, and peace.

Like other specialized organizations of the UN, UNESCO has its own budget, constitution, and separate organization. UNESCO is guided by the General Conference composed of one representative from each member country. It meets biennially to approve a program and budget. An Executive Board consisting of 45 members elected by the General Conference meets two or three times a year and is responsible for executing the program of the General Conference. The Secretariat carries out the program. It consists of a director-general and an international staff, headquartered in Paris. In 1990, UNESCO had 156 members.

In December 1984 the United States withdrew from UNESCO because of the agency's inefficient administration and increased politicization, including attacks against Western press freedom. The United Kingdom and Singapore withdrew at the end of 1985.

United Negro College Fund The United Negro College Fund, founded in 1944, is an association of fully accredited private colleges, universities, and professional schools primarily for African-American students. Its chief purpose is fund raising; it also advises its member schools and coordinates research on higher education for blacks.

United Presbyterian Church see PRESBYTERIANISM

United Press International see PRESS AGENCIES AND SYNDICATES

United Service Organizations The United Service Organizations (USO) were founded in 1941 to provide United States military personnel with clubs and centers that serve social, educational, and religious needs. A civilian federation, the USO is staffed largely by unpaid volunteers and funded by private contributions. The organizations operate service facilities and outreach programs in hundreds of U.S. and overseas locations.

United States The United States of America is located in the middle of the North American continent. The 48 states of the conterminous United States stretch from the Atlantic Ocean in the east, where the country has a

---

AT A GLANCE

UNITED STATES OF AMERICA

Land: Area: 9,809,390 km^2 (3,787,425 mi^2). Capital: Washington, D.C. (1990 pop., 609,909). Largest city: New York (1990 pop., 7,322,564).

People: Population (1990): 249,632,692. Density: 27.15 persons per km^2 (70.3 per mi^2). Distribution (1990): 74% urban, 26% rural. Official language: English. Major religions: Protestantism, Roman Catholicism, Judaism.

Government: Type: federal republic. Legislature: Congress. Political subdivisions: 50 states, 1 federal district.

Economy: GNP (1990): $5.5 trillion; $21,800 per capita. Labor distribution (1990): agriculture—2.8%; manufacturing—17.8%; mining—0.6%; services—16.2%; public administration and defense—15.9%; construction—6.7%; public utilities, transportation, and communication—6.7%; trade—20.4%; finance—11.0%; other—1.9%. Foreign trade (1991): imports—$509.3 billion; exports—$421.8 billion. Currency: 1 dollar = 100 cents.

Education and Health: Literacy (1991): 98% of adult population. Universities and colleges (1988): 3,690. Hospital beds (1988): 1,241,000. Physicians (1988): 612,000. Life expectancy (1991): women—79; men—72. Infant mortality (1991): 10 per 1,000 live births.

6,000-km-long (3,700-mi) coastline—including the Gulf of Mexico—to the Pacific, where the coast stretches for 2,100 km (1,300 mi). The United States shares borders with only two other countries. In the north the border extends across the width of both Canada and the United States and between Alaska (the 49th state) and Canada for 8,900 km (5,500 mi); in the south the shorter border with Mexico is 3,111 km (1,933 mi) long. Hawaii (the 50th state) is composed of a group of Pacific islands about 3,400 km (2,100 mi) southwest of San Francisco; Alaska occupies the northwestern extremity of North America, with a 10,700-km (6,700-mi) coastline on the Pacific and Arctic oceans.

The United States is the world's fourth largest country (after Russia, Canada, and China) and the third most populous (after China and India). The 50 states are blessed with a variety of mineral, agricultural, water, and other land resources that provide the basis for a highly productive economy—in fact, the United States is the world's wealthiest nation. For most of the 20th century the country has enjoyed economic preeminence throughout the world, particularly during the post–World War II era. Yet within the United States, the population, per capita wealth, and general welfare are unevenly distributed, with areas of affluence often contiguous with areas of poverty. Beginning in the early 1970s the United States faced economic difficulties brought on by a high foreign-trade deficit, the declining value of the dollar abroad, high governmental spending, and inflation. During the 1980s, inflation was brought under control and tax-cut-

ting stimulated economic expansion in some sectors, although there was stagnation in others. The trade deficit remained, however, and the national debt burgeoned as never before. In 1990–92 the nation experienced a persistent recession and a concomitant rise in the unemployment rate.

The United States plays a prominent role in world affairs and is an influential member of such multinational organizations as the United Nations (headquartered in New York City) and the World Bank (headquartered in Washington, D.C.). The United States, a capitalist nation, has frequently found itself in opposition to the USSR, the most powerful Communist country, although by 1990 there was greater cooperation between the two countries.

The United States came into existence as a result of the AMERICAN REVOLUTION (1775–83), during which the original 13 states declared and won their independence from Great Britain. During the 19th century, while the European powers built worldwide empires, the young United States focused on expansion across the North American continent and on internal development. Nevertheless, the country gradually acquired some overseas territories, collectively known as the UNITED STATES OUTLYING TERRITORIES, that it continues to administer. These include GUAM and PUERTO RICO (both acquired in 1899); AMERICAN SAMOA (acquired in 1900); the PANAMA CANAL ZONE (acquired in 1903 but scheduled for return to Panama by the year 2000); and the U.S. VIRGIN ISLANDS (acquired in 1917). The Trust Territory of the Pacific Islands (see PACIFIC ISLANDS, TRUST TERRITORY OF THE) was established in

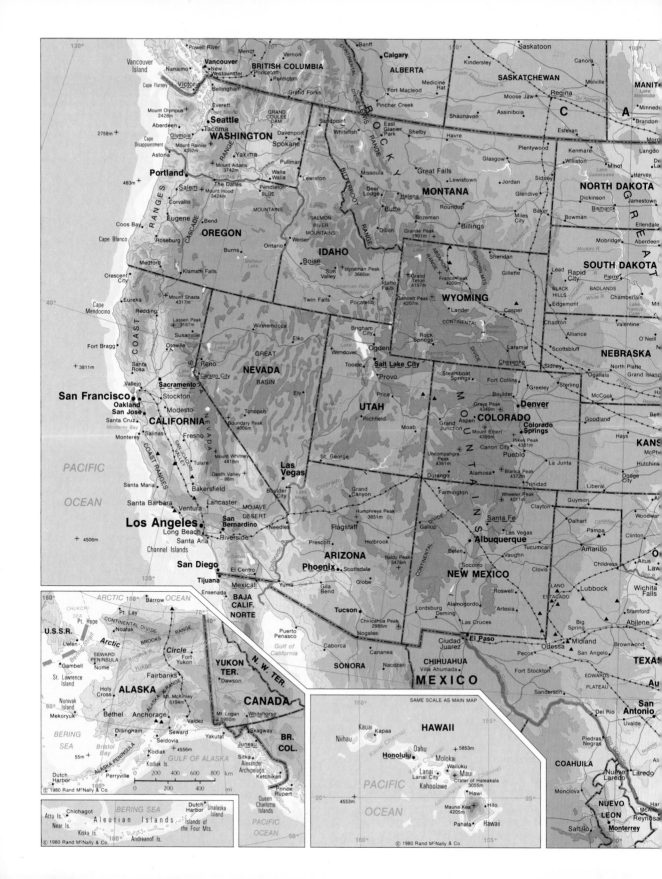

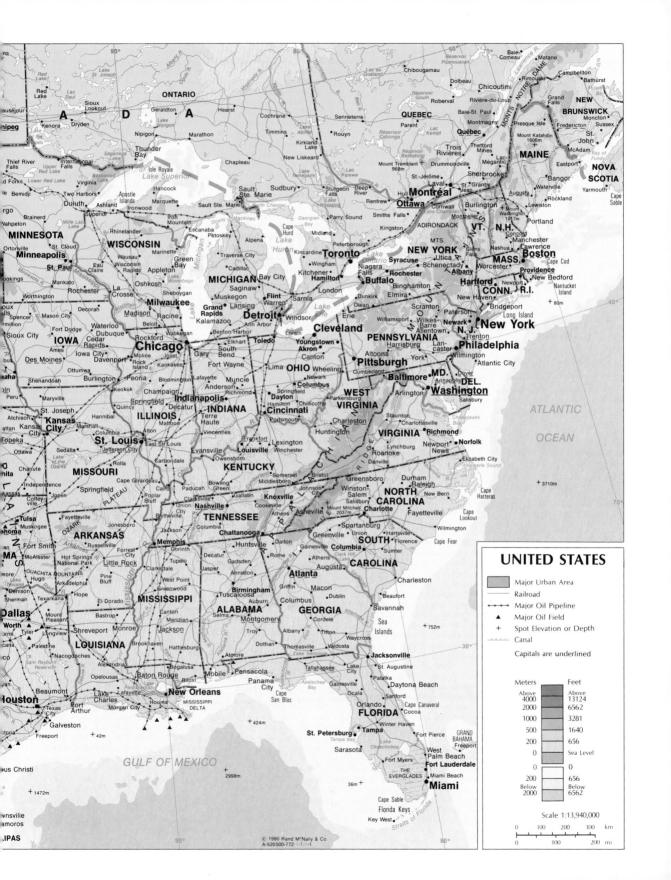

1947 to govern the CAROLINE ISLANDS, MARIANA ISLANDS, and MARSHALL ISLANDS.

Land and Resources

The United States covers 9,372,575 km² (3,618,770 mi²), which divide into several large natural regions, each with unique topography, geology, and resources.

Eastern United States. Along the coasts of the Gulf of Mexico and the Atlantic Ocean northward to Long Island is a coastal plain, almost all of it below 100 m (300 ft) in altitude and with an average width of 160–320 km (100–200 mi). Except for the muddy delta of the Mississippi River, the shores of the plain are sandy, most of them with barrier beaches surmounted by dunes and backed by shallow, muddy estuaries of brackish or salt water. These include marshlands, so-called wetlands, that are biologically important because they breed quantities of the primitive plants and animals that provide the basic food supply for all higher organisms living there.

The coastal plain extends under the Gulf of Mexico and Atlantic Ocean, more than 320 km (200 mi) in places, where it forms the continental shelf. LONG ISLAND, MARTHA'S VINEYARD, NANTUCKET ISLAND, and Block Island are actually tops of coastal-plain hills.

Inland from the coastal plain, and almost parallel to the Atlantic coast, is the APPALACHIAN MOUNTAIN system, which extends from Alabama and Georgia north to Canada; in New England the old rocks of the highlands extend to the coast and form rocky shores. The Appalachian Mountains divide into natural regions. To the east, bordering the Atlantic coastal plain, is a transitional zone, the PIEDMONT PLATEAU, which has elevations ranging from approximately 100 to 300 m (300 to 1,000 ft) above sea level. The boundary between the Piedmont and the coastal plain is an escarpment across which the rivers tumble in falls to the lower coastal plain. This Fall Line marks the head of navigation, and cities of the urban corridor—such as Trenton, N.J., Philadelphia, Wilmington, Del., Baltimore, Md., Washington, D.C., and Richmond, Va.—are located on the Fall Line. In NEW ENGLAND

The restored mansions and historic town houses of Charleston, S.C., preserve the era of the seaport's prosperity during America's colonial period.

are found the GREEN MOUNTAINS, the WHITE MOUNTAINS, and the BERKSHIRE HILLS. Farther south the mountain ridges of the BLUE RIDGE reach 2,037 m (6,687 ft) at Mount MITCHELL in North Carolina, the highest point east of the Mississippi River. West of the Blue Ridge is a hilly region called the Ridge and Valley Province, about 40–120 km (25–75 mi) wide. Farther west are the coal-rich and mountainous Appalachian Plateaus; the easternmost portion, ALLEGHENY MOUNTAINS (or Plateau), mostly between 300 and 1,000 m (1,000 and 3,300 ft) in altitude, rise up abruptly from the Ridge and Valley Province. Throughout the Appalachian Plateaus as a whole local relief commonly exceeds 500 m (1,600 ft). To the west of the GREAT SMOKY MOUNTAINS, the Ridge and Valley Province separates them from the CUMBERLAND PLATEAU.

The Nubble Lighthouse, built in 1879, is one of the many warning beacons posted along the perilously rocky coast of Maine. The nearby community of York, now restored as a colonial village, was the first English settlement in America to receive (1641) a city charter.

Denver, the capital of Colorado, is situated on a plateau at the base of the Front Range of the Rocky Mountains in the north central portion of the state. The dome of the capitol is gilded with gold from Colorado's mines.

Midwest. The Appalachians give way to a central lowland and the GREAT PLAINS that extend 1,600 km (1,000 mi) west to the Rocky Mountains and reach from Canada south to the Gulf coastal plain. Some highland areas in the Midwest are the OZARK Mountains in Arkansas and Missouri, the Ouachita Mountains in Arkansas and Oklahoma, the MESABI RANGE in Minnesota, and the BLACK HILLS in South Dakota. The lowest part of the region is along the Mississippi River, at about 300 m (1,000 ft). West of the river the plains rise westward to the 1.6-km-high (1-mi) base of the Rocky Mountains.

Rockies and Great Basin. The ROCKY MOUNTAINS, extending northward from New Mexico into Canada, have many summit ridges higher than 3,000 m (10,000 ft), and many peaks reach above 4,250 m (14,000 ft). The highest point in the U.S. portion of the Rockies, Mount EL-BERT, reaches 4,399 m (14,432 ft) in Colorado. The

Rockies form a bold, east-facing mountain front—including the dramatic Front Range in Colorado.

Beyond the Rockies are elevated plateaus. In the south is the COLORADO PLATEAU, averaging about 1,500 m (5,000 ft) above sea level. The plateau is cut by spectacular canyons, including the GRAND CANYON of the Colorado River.

West of the Colorado Plateau is the GREAT BASIN, part of the BASIN AND RANGE PROVINCE. It consists of scores of closed desert basins separated by equally numerous mountainous ridges. Most of the basins range between 1,200 and 1,500 m (4,000 and 5,000 ft) in altitude. The mountain ranges separating the basins are mostly 500 to 2,000 m (1,500 to 6,000 ft) higher. South of the Great Basin is a lower area also without exterior drainage and including DEATH VALLEY and the SALTON SEA, both below sea level. East of the Colorado River,

The world's largest dormant volcanic crater, produced over eons by the eruptions of Haleakala, covers 49 km2 (19 mi2) of the Hawaiian island of Maui. The crater and surrounding area became part of a national park in 1916.

more desert basins and ranges extend east to the Great Plains. The RIO GRANDE, rising in southwestern Colorado and flowing south through New Mexico, connects several of these basins.

West Coast. Much larger basins and ranges form the Pacific Mountains. In California is the SIERRA NEVADA, about 725 km (450 mi) long and 125 km (75 mi) wide. The highest peak, Mount WHITNEY, reaches 4,418 m (14,494 ft). In northernmost California and in Oregon and Washington the Sierra gives way to the volcanic CASCADE RANGE. Mount RAINIER reaches 4,392 m (14,410 ft). West of these mountains are broad, long basins—the Great Valley in central California and the valley of the WILLAMETTE RIVER and Puget Trough in Oregon and Washington. West of the basins are the COAST RANGES, which extend from California to Alaska. Almost no continental shelf borders the Pacific coast.

Alaska and Hawaii. Alaska consists of mountain ranges curving concentrically around the Gulf of Alaska and extending west in an arc forming the ALEUTIAN ISLANDS. North America's highest point, Mount MCKINLEY (6,194 m/20,320 ft), is in the Alaska Range. North of these mountains is a broad plateau bisected by the Yukon River. Farther to the north is the BROOKS RANGE, the northern base of which slopes to the Arctic Ocean, including the oil-rich PRUDHOE BAY area.

Hawaii, the 50th state, located near the center of the Pacific Ocean, consists of volcanic islands aligned in a northwesterly direction. Active volcanoes, KILAUEA and MAUNA LOA, are located on Hawaii, the southeasternmost island.

Juneau, the capital of Alaska, occupies a narrow coastal strip in the southeastern portion of the state. Like many Alaskan cities, Juneau was founded by prospectors seeking gold during the late 19th century.

Geologic Structure. Like other continents, North America has a central nucleus called a shield. The CANADIAN SHIELD, as it is termed, is mostly in Canada but extends southward into the United States at Lake Superior. Shield rocks are more than 1 billion years old, and some are 4 billion years old. In the central lowland and Appalachian region, surrounding the exposed shield, is a stable platform, underlain by shield rocks but overlain by younger sedimentary rocks, averaging about 1,700 to 3,000 m (5,600 to 10,000 ft) thick. These sedimentary rocks are 1 billion to 225 million years old (late Precambrian and Paleozoic). Overlying these in the western part of the stable platform are younger sedimentary formations 60 to 150 million years old (Mesozoic). All these sedimentary rocks are generally almost horizontal; mountains are few—the Black Hills, the southern Rockies, and mountains in Oklahoma and Arkansas are exceptions.

The eastern and western edges of the stable platform were downwarped to form linear troughs thousands of kilometers long and hundreds of kilometers wide. These troughs (or geosynclines) were then flooded by seas. The trough along the eastern edge of the platform, the present-day site of the Appalachians, accumulated sediments approximately 12,000 m (40,000 ft) thick. West of the platform, at the site of the Great Basin, the sediments accumulated to thicknesses exceeding 30,500 m (100,000 ft). After formation of the troughs, the sides were squeezed together, and the sedimentary formations were folded, faulted, uplifted, and subsequently sculptured by erosion to form the mountains along the east and west sides of the continent.

During the last 65 million years (the Cenozoic Era), the Atlantic and Gulf coastal plains were submerged and the western United States was uplifted in a broad arch extending from the Mississippi River to the Pacific. The basins and ranges developed largely by faulting of the previously folded and arched rocks.

Surface Deposits and Soils. In the southeastern United States the ground is clayey and thick. Iron was disseminated through the clay, staining it red. Similar soil formed along the very wet northwest coast of the United States. In less humid parts of the country the ground contains little clay. In humid regions, such as the Appalachians, 95% of the mountainsides are covered with colluvium—loose, weathered rock debris. Even in the Rocky Mountains more than 80% of the ground is covered with colluvium.

Other extensive surface deposits include those of the Pleistocene glaciers that covered Canada and extended into the northern United States. They reached as far south as Long Island, northern Pennsylvania, the Ohio and Missouri rivers, and Puget Sound lowland. In hilly New England, the deposits are stony; on the plains, less so.

In the central United States the glacial deposits and much of the country to the south are covered by wind-laid silt (loess). These deposits form some of the best agricultural land in the United States.

Lake deposits are numerous in glaciated areas, but they are most extensive in the desert depressions of the

Great Basin. Even Death Valley, where annual precipitation averages only about 38 mm (1.5 in), had a lake approximately 180 m (600 ft) deep. The east part of the Great Basin contained Pleistocene Lake Bonneville, which covered 52,000 km² (20,000 mi²) and had a maximum depth of 300 m (1,000 ft). GREAT SALT LAKE is a salt-brine remainder from that Pleistocene lake, as are the BONNEVILLE SALT FLATS. Death Valley is now without a lake but has a salt pan.

Despite conservation efforts, the United States continues to deplete its soil resources by erosion and loss of organic matter.

Climate. Most of the United States has a continental climate, characterized by considerable annual variability. Coastal regions, moderated by the oceans, have less variable climates; Hawaii has slight variability, with most of the variation due to elevation. Alaska is partly cold-wet and partly cold-dry. Much of the northern half of the state is permanently frozen.

The eastern United States is humid, with annual precipitation averaging more than 500 mm (20 in). The western part of the country—beginning approximately at 100° west longitude—except for the mountains and the maritime Pacific coast, is mostly semiarid with annual precipitation averaging between 250 mm (10 in) and 500 mm, but parts are arid with annual precipitation averaging less than 250 mm. The western mountains receive about 500 mm of precipitation yearly. The northwestern coast receives more than 2,500 mm (100 in) of precipitation each year.

The country's temperatures are heavily influenced by latitude and by proximity to the oceans. In the northeastern part of the country the average annual temperature in New York is 13° C (55° F). Farther south is a subtropical

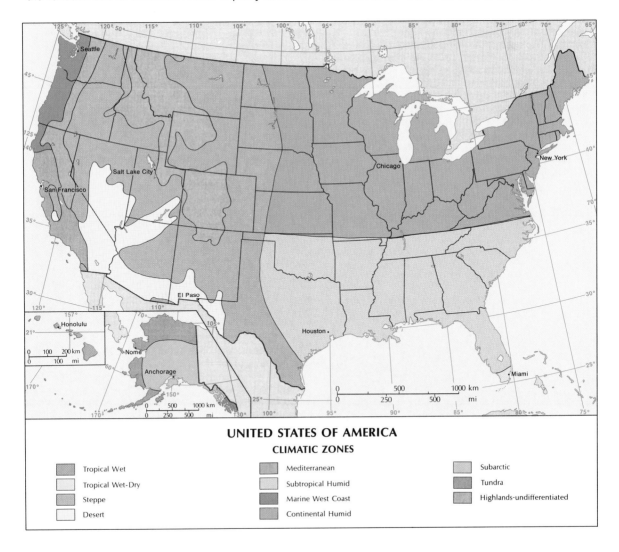

UNITED STATES OF AMERICA

CLIMATIC ZONES

Tropical Wet
Tropical Wet-Dry
Steppe
Desert
Mediterranean
Subtropical Humid
Marine West Coast
Continental Humid
Subarctic
Tundra
Highlands-undifferentiated

zone: Charleston, S.C., has an average annual temperature of 19° C (66° F). The only tropical zone of the United States occurs in southern Florida, and Miami experiences an average temperature of 24° C (75° F). In the central United States seasonal differences are more extreme. In Minneapolis, Minn., the average temperature is 7° C (45° F), whereas in Tulsa, Okla., only about 2° farther west but 1,030 km (640 mi) south, the temperature averages 16° C (61° F). Along the west coast, temperatures, moderated by the ocean, are mild. Portland, Oreg., has an average annual temperature of 12° C (54° F); Los Angeles, in the Mediterranean climate zone, experiences a temperature of 17° C (63° F).

Climate hazards in the United States include hurricanes along the Gulf and Atlantic coasts, tornadoes in the southeast and central states, hail on the western plains, dry electric storms that cause forest fires on western mountains, floods in the central and eastern states and along the Pacific coast in winter, and droughts in most of the western states.

Rivers and Lakes. Inland water covers about 200,000 km² (78,500 mi²), or almost 2% of the total area of the United States. The MISSISSIPPI RIVER, flowing south across the eastern half of the conterminous United States, is major both in length (3,779 km/2,348 mi) and in annual discharge (18,200 m³ per sec/650,000 ft³ per sec). By contrast, the COLORADO RIVER (Colorado) is about one-third as long as the Mississippi River system, but its average annual discharge is only 2% as great. An area along the Atlantic seaboard, only slightly larger than the Colorado River basin, has 20 rivers—including the CONNECTICUT RIVER, DELAWARE RIVER, HUDSON RIVER, and SUSQUEHANNA RIVER—each only one-third as long as the Colorado but together discharging 20 times as much as it does.

(Right) *Olympic National Park is famous for its coniferous rain forest, which lies along the windward (western) slopes of the Olympic Mountains of northwestern Washington, the area receiving the greatest annual rainfall in the continental United States.*

(Below) *The Mississippi River, the longest inland waterway in the United States, flows 3,779 km (2,348 mi) from its source, at Lake Itasca in north central Minnesota, to its mouth, on the Gulf of Mexico.*

The rocks of Bryce Canyon National Park, in southwest Utah, have been sculpted by wind and rain into a myriad of colorful shapes. The canyons of the park are about 300 m (1,000 ft) deep in places.

In terms of discharge, the major rivers, in addition to the Mississippi, are the ST. LAWRENCE RIVER, OHIO RIVER, MISSOURI RIVER, COLUMBIA RIVER, and SNAKE RIVER. The YUKON RIVER is Alaska's principal river.

Lakes and peat bogs are numerous in the glaciated parts of the United States, especially in northern Minnesota. The lakes are small and used primarily for recreation, but the GREAT LAKES are important arteries of transportation. Florida has lakes and bogs at limestone sinks, including Lake OKEECHOBEE. The troughs of the Great Basin have mostly ephemeral lakes. The Salton Sea and Great Salt Lake are saline. Many of the lakes, especially in the west, have been created by dams; Lake MEAD has the greatest capacity.

Vegetation. The vegetation of the United States is varied. In Florida the subtropical vegetation includes man-

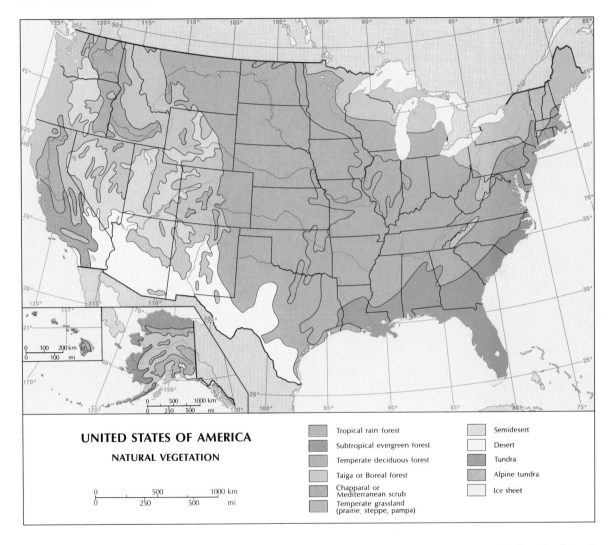

UNITED STATES OF AMERICA

NATURAL VEGETATION

Tropical rain forest	Semidesert
Subtropical evergreen forest	Desert
Temperate deciduous forest	Tundra
Taiga or Boreal forest	Alpine tundra
Chapparal or Mediterranean scrub	Ice sheet
Temperate grassland (prairie, steppe, pampa)	

grove and palmetto. Farther north in the southeastern states, forests of loblolly and slash pines grade north near the Tennessee River to hardwood forest with oak and hickory. In the Great Lakes region white pine appears, and north of this are fir and spruce. In Alaska, north of the spruce zone, is tundra.

Striking differences also occur between the humid east and the arid west. Hardwood forest extends westward beyond the Mississippi River, giving way to grassland on the plains. Rocky Mountain forests are chiefly coniferous, with pine and Douglas fir near the base and spruce and true fir extending upward to the timberline (3,500 m/ 11,500 ft in the Southern Rockies). Above that the growing season is too short for trees.

West of the Rockies desert shrubs occur, with patches of woodland or forest on the isolated mountain ranges. Forests rather like those in the Rockies grow on the eastern slopes of the Sierra Nevada and the Cascades; the

western slopes have evergreen oaks with Douglas fir and, on the Sierra Nevada, sequoia. The central Coast Ranges have redwood, grading north to Douglas fir and spruce, and grading south to a scrubby growth known as chapparal.

Resources. Agriculturally, the United States is richly productive. Most of the eastern two-thirds of the conterminous United States is arable; the land of the western United States is used mostly for grazing but has considerable irrigated lands for crops. The principal U.S. crops are: fruit, truck-farming products, and special crops (including rice and sugarcane) along the Gulf coast, in irrigated areas of the west, and near urban areas in the east; cotton in the southeastern states and on some irrigated lands in the west; tobacco, peanuts, fruit, and general farm products on the Atlantic coastal plain and in the eastern Appalachians; dairy products and hay in the northern states; and corn, wheat, and soybeans on the plains.

Livestock on farms habitually totals over 100 million

cattle and additional millions of hogs and sheep and hundreds of millions of chickens and turkeys.

Commercial forests cover more than 2,000,000 km^2 (800,000 mi^2), especially in the northwestern, northern midwestern, and the southeastern states. They produce—in addition to lumber—paper pulp, resins, and syrup.

Changing interests in water resources are reflected in the history of water management. First, the need for transportation led to the building of canals, such as the ERIE CANAL, in the eastern states in the early 19th century. Second came the great period of flood control, especially along the Mississippi River. Third came a period of large-scale development of irrigation systems in the west, beginning around the turn of the century. Fourth came a

period of developing hydroelectricity, beginning during the 1930s. Today's principal concern is pollution control. In the future will come a stage when controls will be needed to prevent groundwater withdrawals from exceeding recharge.

Mineral production, although less than 2% of the gross national product (GNP), is vitally important. Although the United States has more than its share of minerals, domestic production of many minerals is less than demand, necessitating imports. Fossil-fuel shortages combined with high demand threatens the United States with severe economic problems. Alternate sources of energy such as solar, geothermal, and wind energy are in the early stages of development.

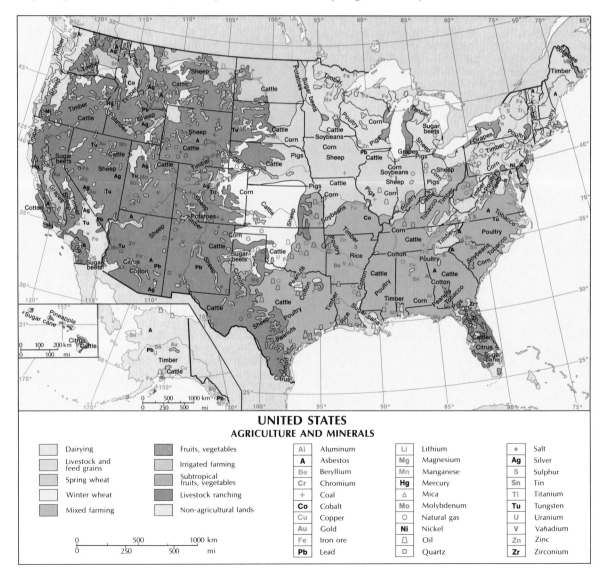

UNITED STATES
AGRICULTURE AND MINERALS

Dairying	Fruits, vegetables	Al	Aluminum	Li	Lithium	• Salt
Livestock and feed grains	Irrigated farming	A	Asbestos	Mg	Magnesium	Ag Silver
Spring wheat	Subtropical fruits, vegetables	Be	Beryllium	Mn	Manganese	S Sulphur
Winter wheat	Livestock ranching	Cr	Chromium	Hg	Mercury	Sn Tin
Mixed farming	Non-agricultural lands	+	Coal	△	Mica	Ti Titanium
		Co	Cobalt	Mo	Molybdenum	Tu Tungsten
		Cu	Copper	○	Natural gas	U Uranium
		Au	Gold	Ni	Nickel	V Vanadium
		Fe	Iron ore	△	Oil	Zn Zinc
		Pb	Lead	□	Quartz	Zr Zirconium

Vast fields of wheat, such as these in Washington State, cover 23,002,000 ha (56,839,000 acres) of the nation's land surface. Wheat is the fourth most valuable crop cultivated in the United States, ranking behind corn, soybeans, and hay.

People

Prior to the discovery (1492) of the New World by Christopher Columbus the area of the United States had an Indian population averaging only about 1 person per 13 to 26 km² (roughly 1 person per 5 to 10 mi²). When George Washington was president in 1790 the population had grown to almost 4,000,000; only 5 cities had populations exceeding 10,000. During the next 100 years the population doubled 4 times—to about 8 million in 1815, to 16 million in 1840, to 32 million in 1861–62, and to 64 million in 1890. The population was more than 120 million by 1930 and about 250 million in 1990.

Ethnic Composition. In 1990 the native American population (see INDIANS, AMERICAN; ESKIMO; and ALEUT) totaled more than 1.9 million. Of the Indians, who constitute the overwhelming majority, approximately half live on some 275 reservations. Most reservation land is located in Arizona, New Mexico, Utah, South Dakota, Washington, and Montana. The half of the Indian population off reservations live mostly in cities, especially in the north, central, and western states and in Alaska.

About 12.1% of the total population—29,986,060 persons (1990)—are black, almost all descendants of slaves (see AFRICAN AMERICANS). The vast majority of Americans, however, are descended from Europeans. During the colonial period most settlers came from the British Isles and settled along the eastern seaboard; the French settled the St. Lawrence River valley. The first great IMMIGRATION wave—from 1820 to 1860—saw the arrival of more than 5 million new Americans. Of these, 90% were from England, Ireland, and Germany. By the middle of the 19th century the culture and customs of western Europe dominated the United States.

After the Civil War, immigration increased dramatically; between 1860 and 1920, about 29 million persons arrived. The composition of the immigrant population had shifted, and most came from eastern and southern Europe—Russia, Poland, the Balkans, and Italy. During the same period increasing numbers of Asians, especially Chinese and Japanese, migrated to the Pacific coast and to Hawaii (see ASIAN AMERICANS). White immigrants mixed to a considerable degree with the earlier western European stocks, beginning the so-called American melting pot. In the southern part of the country, where most blacks lived, however, the races were segregated until the middle of the 20th century, and although diminishing, de facto segregation remains a national problem.

The total population of Spanish origin in the United States is probably about 30 million. Of that number, some 22.4 million are legal Hispanic residents, and the others are illegal aliens. In southern Texas, New Mexico, Arizona, and southern California, a considerable percentage of the population is of Mexican-American origin (see CHICANO). Each year thousands more enter the United

Taos, N.Mex., is the site of a community of Pueblo Indians. The two communal structures there, one four stories and the other five stories high, are the home of about 1,800 people.

The skyline of Chicago features several of the world's tallest buildings. From the observation deck of the twin-spired John Hancock Center visitors can see portions of four states—Illinois, Indiana, Michigan, and Wisconsin. Lake Michigan appears in the background.

States, most illegally, because of overpopulation in Mexico and greater opportunities in the United States. The eastern states have also experienced an influx of Spanish-speaking immigrants from Central America and the Caribbean, especially Puerto Rico and Cuba. Most live in the cities, especially New York and Miami. (See also HISPANIC AMERICANS.)

Religion. More than half of all Americans are practicing Protestants, with Baptists outnumbering members of other individual denominations, including those of the Methodists, Lutherans, Presbyterians, Episcopalians, Latter-day Saints, Pentacostalists, Churches of Christ, and United Church of Christ. Nearly 22% of the U.S. population are Roman Catholic. About 1.6% belong to Eastern Orthodox churches, and another 2.4% are Jewish. Other major world religions—Buddhism, Hinduism, Islam, and the many tribal religions, notably from Africa—are lightly represented in the United States.

Demography. The annual rate of population increase in the United States is 1.02% (1980–90). In 1990, 77.5% of the total population lived in metropolitan areas. There were 39 metropolitan areas within more than 1 million inhabitants, and 24 cities had more than 500,000 residents in the city center: BALTIMORE, BOSTON, CHICAGO, CLEVELAND, COLUMBUS (Ohio), DALLAS, DETROIT, EL PASO, HOUSTON, INDIANAPOLIS, JACKSONVILLE, LOS ANGELES, MEMPHIS, MILWAUKEE, NASHVILLE-Davidson, NEW YORK, PHILADELPHIA, PHOENIX, SAN ANTONIO, SAN DIEGO, SAN FRANCISCO, SAN JOSE, SEATTLE, and WASHINGTON, D.C.

Urban problems have developed in many U.S. cities because large numbers of the more affluent whites have moved out of the city centers to the suburbs. Much light industry and other businesses have followed them. Thus many large cities are faced with decaying downtown and residential areas—often primarily the home of blacks and Hispanics. As a consequence the tax base of many cities has been eroded, and almost every major city faces financial difficulties.

In 1990 the country's overall population density was 26.6 persons per km^2 (69.0 per mi^2), but great regional variations exist. Through the 1970s and 1980s some areas, mostly the northeastern and the north central states, experienced a decline in population, whereas other states, such as Arizona, Florida, Nevada, and Texas—in the Sunbelt—experienced higher-than-average increases due to in-migration. The birthrate in the United States is 16 per 1,000 inhabitants (1987), and the death rate, 9 per 1,000.

Health and Education. In 1987 the United States had almost 7,000 hospitals, and an average of 5.3 hospital beds for every 1,000 inhabitants. About 612,000 physicians were practicing. In 1990 female residents of the United States had a life expectancy of about 80 years at birth, whereas for males it was 73 years. The average life expectancy at birth for all whites in 1988 was 75.5 years; for blacks, however, it was 69.5 years, although that figure increased from 45 years in 1920. The nation's infant mortality rate was 10 per 1,000 live births in 1990, one of the world's lowest rates.

Illiteracy has been almost eliminated in the United States. The median school years completed by U.S. citizens 25 years and older in 1988 was 12.7 years.

Education is required between the ages of 5 and 16. In 1990, 40.8 million pupils attended public schools; an estimated 5.3 million students attended private schools. Of the nation's 3,587 institutions of higher education (1987), 2,135 are 4-year institutions, and the remainder are 2-year schools. In 1990 an estimated 10.3 million students attended public colleges and universities, and 2.9 million studied at private institutions. For a more detailed description of the country's educational system, see UNITED STATES, EDUCATION IN THE.

Communications. In 1988 there were 1,642 daily newspapers published in the United States, more than

50 of them in languages other than English. The English-language papers had a total circulation of 62,700,000. Among the best-known of the dailies with circulations exceeding 500,000 are the *Chicago Tribune*, NEW YORK TIMES, WASHINGTON POST, and the *Los Angeles Times*; the *St. Louis Post-Dispatch*, *Atlanta Constitution*, *Miami Herald*, and *Toledo Blade* are also important. The *Christian Science Monitor*, WALL STREET JOURNAL, and *USA Today* are the principal nationally circulated dailies.

The country is served by 4,932 AM and 4,155 FM radio stations (1988). There are 176 million television sets in the United States and more than 1,000 commercial stations. In addition, cable television and public television are now popular alternatives to commercial television, which had been dominated by 3 networks; in 1988, 324 public stations and 8,500 cable systems operated.

Economic Activity

In 1989 the gross national product (GNP) of the United States reached $5.2 trillion, the highest in the world. The per-capita income of $21,082 is also among the world's highest.

Agriculture, fishing, and forestry together contribute about 2.5% of the GNP. The leading crops, in order of value, are corn, soybeans, hay, wheat, cotton, tobacco, sorghum, rice, and potatoes. The United States is the world's leading producer of meat, soybeans, and corn, and the second largest producer of wheat, tobacco, hogs, and cattle.

Forests cover about 3,000,000 km^2 (1,200,000 mi^2), but of that total only about one-third is commercial timberland. Forests yield an annual income of several hundred million dollars. Income from the U.S. fishing industry was $3.5 billion in 1988. The Pacific states—especially Alaska and California—lead the nation in the

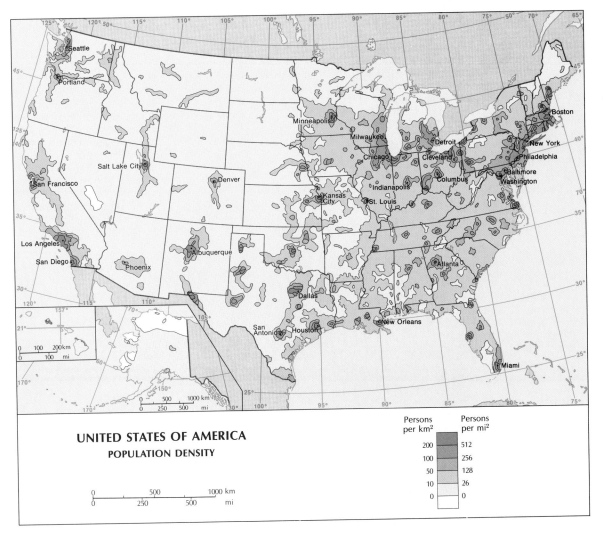

UNITED STATES OF AMERICA
POPULATION DENSITY

Persons per km^2	Persons per mi^2
200	512
100	256
50	128
10	26
0	0

A flock of sheep graze in a farm pasture in an Appalachian valley of West Virginia. The Appalachian Mountains are the most extensive mountain system in the eastern portion of the United States.

value of their catch; Louisiana, on the Gulf coast, is also a leading producer.

Industry contributes almost one-fifth of the GNP. In 1987 the value added by manufacturing was $1.2 trillion. The leading industries, in order of value, are transportation equipment, processed foods, chemicals, industrial machinery and equipment, printing and publishing, fabricated metal products, instruments and related products, electrical and electronic equipment, paper and allied products, and primary metals. The country is a world leader in production and export in heavy industry, especially primary metals (steel, aluminum, copper); in transportation equipment, such as automobiles; and in printing and publishing.

In 1988 the United States produced 2.7 trillion kW h of electricity, the highest in the world. Of that total, approximately 57% was derived from coal, 5.5% from petroleum, 9.5% from natural gas, 19.5% from nuclear power, and 8.5% from hydroelectricity. Of the petroleum used for energy production, about one-third or more is imported. The country's total installed capacity is 723.9 million kW (1988).

Mining accounts for less than 2% of the GNP but produced $85.4 billion in 1987, 92% of which was derived from mineral fuels—coal, natural gas, and petroleum. The principal minerals, in order of value, are petroleum, natural gas, coal, portland cement, stone, copper, iron ore, sand and gravel, phosphates, lime, clay, salt, uranium, molybdenum, zinc, sulfur, lead, silver, and gold.

As in the other highly developed countries—the so-called postindustrial nations—the service sector, widely defined, in the United States accounts for the largest percentage of the GNP (almost 72% in 1987). The service sector produced $3.5 trillion in 1987.

Tourism is also an important industry. In 1990, 39 million foreign tourists visited the country, spending more than $51 billion.

As recently as 1975, U.S. exports were 10% greater than imports. In the 1980s, however, the U.S. trade balance reversed, sparked by large increases in the cost of petroleum imports. In 1989 the U.S. trade deficit was $123.8 billion.

In addition to petroleum, principal imports are automobiles, nonelectrical machinery, electrical equipment, and chemicals. The principal industrial exports are machinery, transportation equipment, and chemicals; soybeans and corn are the leading agricultural exports.

In 1987 the United States had 6,234,652 km (3,874,026 mi) of highways. Rail tracks totaled 240,000 km (150,000 mi) in 1988. Of all passenger traffic in 1988, 81% was by private automobile, 8% by air, and less than 2% by rail and bus. During the same year, how-

The Statue of Liberty, the famous landmark in New York Harbor, was presented as a gift from France to the United States in 1886. The massive sculpture, the island on which it rests, and nearby Ellis Island—formerly a major immigration port—are maintained as a national monument.

This massive oil refining complex is situated near Perth Amboy, in northeastern New Jersey. This portion of the state has been one of the nation's centers of oil refining since the 1870s, when Bayonne became the terminus of an oil pipeline operated by John D. Rockefeller.

ever, 37% of freight was carried by rail and 25% by motor vehicles. Leading U.S. seaports include New York, New Orleans, Houston, and Baton Rouge, La. St. Louis is the nation's leading inland port.

Government

The United States has a democratic government, meaning that it is "elected by the people and for the people." Every adult (aged 18 and over) can vote. Voters usually choose between the two political parties that dominate U.S. politics—the DEMOCRATIC PARTY and the REPUBLICAN PARTY.

The country has a federal system of government in which power is divided between the national, or federal, government and the governments of the 50 states. A third level of government is provided at the local level by municipal and county authorities. Theoretically the responsibilities of the different levels are delineated in the federal (see CONSTITUTION OF THE UNITED STATES) and state constitutions, although actually the responsibilities overlap.

The federal government and each of the 50 state governments are divided into three branches—executive, legislative, and judicial. Municipal and county governments are more varied but to a considerable degree are patterned after the federal and state models. The executive branch of the federal government is headed by the president (see PRESIDENT OF THE UNITED STATES) and vice-president, elected every 4 years. The administrative duties of the executive branch are divided among 14 departments: State, Treasury, Defense, Justice, Interior, Agriculture, Commerce, Labor, Health and Human Services, Housing and Urban Development, Transportation, Energy, Education, and Veterans Affairs. Numerous fed-

Trading on the New York Stock Exchange is now accomplished largely through computers. This has facilitated the development of a global market in financial securities. When the New York Market crashed on Oct. 19, 1987, the panic spread instantly to other financial centers. The severity of the plunge—a record 22.6% in New York—was attributed by some observers to massive computerized selling.

eral agencies, including those for regulation of the private sector (see GOVERNMENT REGULATION), supplement the activities of these departments. The secretary of each department sits on the cabinet, the president's principal advisory body.

The legislative branch of the federal government—the CONGRESS OF THE UNITED STATES—consists of a 100-member SENATE, with 2 senators elected from each state, and a HOUSE OF REPRESENTATIVES, with 435 elected members, one for approximately every 570,000 persons. Senators serve 6-year terms and representatives serve for 2 years. Similarly, most states have 2 legislative bodies, although Nebraska has a unicameral body of 49 members. The chief executive of each state is the GOVERNOR.

The federal judicial branch consists of the SUPREME COURT OF THE UNITED STATES—the nation's highest judicial body—with a chief justice and eight other members appointed by the president with the advice and consent of the Senate; and 90 district courts, at least one in each state. They consider violations of federal law and certain civil cases involving persons in different states. Decisions may be appealed to the 12 U.S. appellate courts. Each state has a system of courts paralleling the federal system.

State and local governments have responsibility for such local services as water supply, waste disposal, police and fire protection, hospitals and health, parks and recreation, schools, and libraries, but to a considerable degree each of these activities is shared by all levels of government including the federal government. The federal government alone has responsibility for national defense, but even this responsibility is shared with the individual states to the degree that each state has its own national guard or militia.

See also: AMERICAN ART AND ARCHITECTURE; AMERICAN LITERATURE; AMERICAN MUSIC; NORTH AMERICA; and separate articles on each U.S. state, important cities, and major land features.

United States, education in the   Public education in the United States takes place in more than 85,000 elementary and secondary schools and in more than 3,200 private and public colleges, COMMUNITY AND JUNIOR COLLEGES, and UNIVERSITIES. In addition, PRIVATE SCHOOLS, PRESCHOOL EDUCATION programs, ADULT EDUCATION programs, federal INDIAN SCHOOLS, and schools on federal installations abroad are components of the U.S. educational system. Almost 88% of the regular day-school students and almost 73% of the students in higher education are enrolled in public institutions.

Although enrollments were low early in the 20th century, by the 1980s almost all 5- to 13-year-olds and more than 90% of 5- to 17-year-olds were enrolled in school. The proportion of 17-year-olds with high school diplomas has increased from 7% in 1901 to almost 74% today; another 10% earn diplomas by the time they are 29 years of age. Seventy percent of all persons over 25 years of age complete four years of high school education or higher.

Significant changes in school enrollments result from both nationwide changes in the birthrate and regional differences in population growth. The areas of major growth are the southern and western states; the areas of decline or stable growth include urbanized northeastern and central states. Urban systems remain large and unwieldy. More than one-third of the elementary and secondary students in Arizona are in Phoenix, and the New York City school system, with almost a million students, is larger than that of any state west of the Mississippi except California and Texas. Population shifts from these urban schools are resulting in an increasing proportion of low-income racial and ethnic minority students.

In the early 1980s, 9% of public-school costs were paid by federal sources, 48% by state sources, and 43% by local sources. Until the 1970s more than 50% came from local sources. Expenditures per pupil vary greatly among the 50 states, and there is also dramatic variation among school districts within a state, reflecting relative local wealth.

Local Authority

American public education began in the late 18th century as a local endeavor, with citizens taking the initiative to clear land, build schools, hire teachers, raise funds, and determine who would supervise the operation. This early tradition explains the long-standing American conviction that public schools are primarily the responsibility of the communities they serve. During the late 19th century the emphasis of schools at the postprimary level shifted from a common basic learning for all students to a differentiated curriculum to prepare young people for varied social roles. From about the 1860s on, professionally trained teachers and administrators were common. At this time, schools became increasingly secular. Compulsory-attendance laws became widespread early in the 20th century. By the 1920s the responsibility for supervision had largely been assumed by professional staff, and the size of school boards was reduced. Now school-board powers include hiring and reviewing the performance of the superintendent, setting policy guidelines, and approving administrative actions and recommendations. Some districts have the power to levy taxes within state-imposed limits. In these instances school boards tend to be involved in budget making and district finances. The extent of board involvement in school policy-making and hiring varies with the interests of the members.

State Authority

Formal control of American public schools is in the hands of the individual states. The powers of local school boards are, in all states, delegated by state governments. In general, states reserve the power to legislate and to enforce policy guidelines, academic standards, and accreditation review procedures. State legislation determines the system of school finance, criteria for licensing school personnel, and the ages of compulsory attendance. State agencies are responsible for curriculum review, quality control, and general supervision of the educational institutions. States cannot bar private education but can exercise indirect control over private institutions through

CURRICULUM requirements, ACCREDITATION standards, and criteria for the licensing of professional staff.

State influence on education was encouraged by the common-school movement (from about 1830 to 1860), which was particularly strong in the northern and midwestern states. Advocates of common schools sought to establish more schools and to organize systems of comparable schools within the states. The effort focused on elementary education, but growing support for public high schools was also generated. By 1861 most Union states had active state school offices, and by 1900 about half of the states had them. At first they merely collected data, recommended improvements, and inspected and compared schools. The wider powers that characterize them today developed in the 20th century.

Federal Intervention

Until after the Civil War both houses of Congress refused to establish standing committees on education on the grounds that the subject fell within state prerogatives. Nevertheless, new states were required to reserve land for the support of schools, and in the late 1830s surplus federal funds were returned to states to be used for a number of purposes, including education. It was at this time that the common-school movement developed. Education programs for Indian tribes began before 1820. When the Department of Agriculture was established (1862), educational services constituted one of its major assignments. The FREEDMEN'S BUREAU, instituted in 1865, also offered educational services. A U.S. Department of Education was approved in 1867 but later was reorganized as a bureau in the Department of the Interior, where it played only a minor role for almost a century.

The major federal educational legislation of the 19th century was the Morrill Act (1862). It offered land grants to the states for endowing and maintaining at least one college that would promote scientific, agricultural, industrial, and military studies. A second act (1890) provided continuing federal support for LAND-GRANT COLLEGES. These annual appropriations were to be withheld from states practicing segregation unless separate agricultural and mechanical BLACK COLLEGES were provided. The law led to the creation of 17 land-grant institutions for blacks. Among the land-grant colleges are such distinguished institutions as Cornell and Rutgers universities, Michigan State University, the University of Illinois, and Texas Agricultural and Mechanical University. In the first half of the 20th century, Congress approved aid for VOCATIONAL EDUCATION, for education-related public works during the Depression, for veterans education through the G.I. BILL OF RIGHTS, and for school districts affected by the school-age children of federal employees.

Recent Developments. The National Defense Education Act (NDEA) of 1958 approved the use of federal funds to support science and mathematics education and modern foreign-language instruction. Funds from the NDEA were employed to strengthen secondary-school and college programs and to underwrite low-interest loans to students in higher education. The ELEMENTARY AND SECONDARY EDUCATION ACT OF 1965 (ESEA) represented the most direct federal intervention in education in U.S. history. In making funds available to local and state education agencies offering programs for economically and educationally disadvantaged children, ESEA committed the federal government to enhancing equal educational opportunity. Major infusions of federal funds to support education followed throughout the 1960s. The Education Consolidation and Improvement Act of 1981 altered the mode of distributing a large portion of federal education funds by consolidating 42 programs into 7 programs fundable through block grants to the states.

Federal intervention has neither augmented local and state operating budgets nor exercised direct control over education. Rather, it has been problem focused, targeted at particular populations, and limited in duration. The principal agency is the U.S. Department of Education.

Supreme Court Decisions. In its decision in BROWN v. BOARD OF EDUCATION OF TOPEKA, KANSAS (1954), the U.S. Supreme Court barred the de jure segregation of students by race, ruling that separate schools were inherently unequal. It was the first of a series of decisions directly promoting school desegregation. UNIVERSITY OF CALIFORNIA v. BAKKE (1978) approved admissions policies that seek to promote the inclusion of certain groups but barred the use of group quotas.

Other U.S. Supreme Court decisions of recent decades have established major precedents in the areas of student rights, school finance, and access to education. *Tinker* v. *Des Moines Independent Community School District* (1969) upheld the constitutional rights to freedom of speech and expression of public-school students and teachers, a ruling that has been applied to decisions involving underground newspapers, demonstrations, and refusal to participate in patriotic exercises. *Goss* v. *Lopez* (1975) guaranteed due process to students in cases involving suspension and expulsion. *San Antonio Independent School District* v. *Rodriguez* (1973) held that school finance reform is a matter to be resolved by state lawmakers and not a constitutional issue. *Mueller et al.* v. *Allen et al.* (1983) upheld a Minnesota law allowing tax deductions for the costs of public and private education.

Current Issues

Two issues facing American education are the declining enrollments—which will require program curtailments, the abandonment of facilities, and staff reductions—and the question of whether there should be BILINGUAL EDUCATION. Both issues will be intensified by changes in the nation's demography. The school-age population represents a decreasing proportion of the total population. Fewer taxpayers directly concerned as parents with the quality of schools may result in further reductions in educational spending. Absolute and proportional increases in the Spanish-speaking population affect the controversy over the language of instruction.

Recent studies have indicated significant declines in student achievement in reading, mathematics, science, and social studies. Students in inner-city schools, especially those from low-income and minority-group families, generally test lower than their suburban, middle-class counterparts. In 1983 several critical reports recommended sweeping curriculum and policy changes to raise student achievement, including a longer school day and academic year, additional high school graduation requirements in the sciences and mathematics, competency testing in basic areas of study, and higher admissions requirements for colleges and universities. Studies later in the decade confirmed the poor performance of U.S. students compared with those of students from other developed nations, and reiterated the recommendations for reform.

The lack of qualified teachers, especially in science and mathematics, continues. The problem results from a combination of factors. Women, historically the major source of school personnel, are moving into different professions. Relative to others with similar levels of education, teachers are underpaid. Recent studies indicate strong dissatisfaction among teachers with their working conditions. As a consequence, both the number and the quality of teacher candidates have fallen. Merit pay for teachers and creation of new career paths for outstanding teachers have been proposed as ways to attract a greater number of able people into the profession. The proposals offer long-term career incentives, but teacher organizations fear that such proposals may supplant efforts to correct the salary inequities of teachers generally.

See also: GRADUATE EDUCATION; MIDDLE SCHOOLS AND JUNIOR HIGH SCHOOLS; PRIMARY EDUCATION; SECONDARY EDUCATION.

United States, history of the Many peoples have contributed to the development of the United States of America, a vast nation that arose from a scattering of British colonial outposts in the New World. The first humans to inhabit the North American continent were migrants from northeast Asia who established settlements in North America as early as 8000 BC and possibly much earlier (see NORTH AMERICAN ARCHAEOLOGY). By about AD 1500 the native peoples of the areas north of the Rio Grande had developed a variety of different cultures (see INDIANS, AMERICAN). The vast region stretching eastward from the Rocky Mountains to the Atlantic Ocean was relatively sparsely populated by tribes whose economies were generally based on hunting and gathering, fishing, and farming.

VIKINGS explored the North American mainland in the 10th and 11th centuries and settled there briefly (see VINLAND). Of more lasting importance, however, was the first voyage (1492–93) of Christopher COLUMBUS, which inaugurated an age of great European EXPLORATION of the Western Hemisphere. Various European states (including Spain, France, England, the Netherlands, and Portugal) and their trading companies sent out expeditions to explore the New World during the century and a half that followed.

The Spanish claimed Florida, Mexico, and the region west of the Mississippi River, although they concentrated their settlement south of the Rio Grande. The French explored much of what became Canada and established several settlements there. Of most significance, howev-

Christopher Columbus, portrayed (1519) by the Italian painter Sebastiano del Piombo, initiated the exploration and colonization of the New World when he discovered the lands of the Western Hemisphere. (Metropolitan Museum of Art, New York City.)

er, for the subsequent development of the United States, was the English colonization of the region along the Atlantic coast.

British Colonies in North America

In England internal stability under Elizabeth I (r. 1558–1603) and an expanding economy combined with a bold intellectual ferment to produce a soaring self-confidence. Ireland experienced the first impact: by the beginning of the 17th century it had been wholly subjugated by the English. Scottish and English Protestants were dispatched to "colonize" where the savage Irish, as they were called, had been expelled, especially in the northern provinces. Then, entrepreneurs began to look to North America, claimed by England on the basis of John CABOT's voyages of discovery (1497–99).

The Chesapeake Colonies. The English had failed in their attempts in the 1580s to found a colony at ROANOKE on the Virginia coast. In 1606, however, the LONDON

New Amsterdam, renamed New York when the English claimed (1664) the area from the Dutch, became the second largest port in the colonies by the late 1700s. (New York Public Library.)

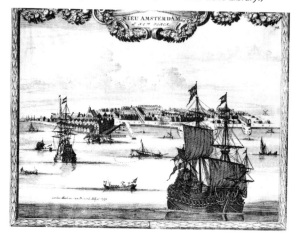

COMPANY, established to exploit North American resources, sent settlers to what in 1607 became JAMESTOWN, the first permanent English colony in the New World. The colonists suffered extreme hardships, and by 1622, of the more than 10,000 who had immigrated, only 2,000 remained alive. In 1624 control of the failing company passed to the crown, making Virginia a royal colony. Soon the tobacco trade was flourishing, and with a legislature (the House of Burgesses, established in 1619) and an abundance of land, the colony entered a period of prosperity. Individual farms, available at low cost, were worked primarily by white indentured servants (laborers who were bound to work for a number of years to pay for their passage before receiving full freedom). The Chesapeake Bay area became a land of opportunity for poor English people.

In 1632, Maryland was granted to the CALVERT family as a personal possession, to serve as a refuge for Roman Catholics. Protestants also flooded into the colony, and in 1649 the Toleration Act was issued, guaranteeing freedom of worship in Maryland to all Trinitarian Christians.

The New England Colonies. In 1620, Puritan Separatists, later called PILGRIMS, sailed on the MAYFLOWER to New England, establishing PLYMOUTH COLONY, the first permanent settlement there. They were followed in 1629 by other Puritans (see PURITANISM), under the auspices of the MASSACHUSETTS BAY COMPANY, who settled the area around Boston. During the Great Puritan Migration that followed (1629–42), about 16,000 settlers arrived in the Massachusetts Bay Colony. The strictly Calvinist Puritans set out to build a "city on a hill" intended to provide a model of godly living for the world. Dissidents of a Baptist orientation founded Rhode Island (chartered 1644). In 1639, Puritans on what was then the frontier established the Fundamental Orders of Connecticut, the first written constitution in North America; the colony was chartered

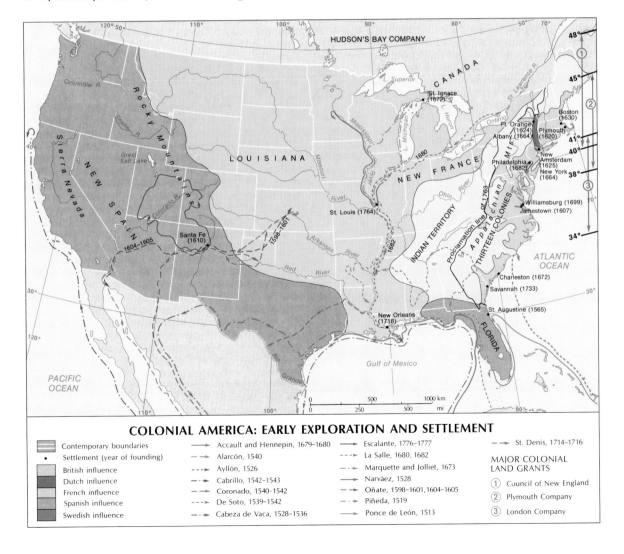

COLONIAL AMERICA: EARLY EXPLORATION AND SETTLEMENT

- Contemporary boundaries
- • Settlement (year of founding)
- British influence
- Dutch influence
- French influence
- Spanish influence
- Swedish influence

→ Accault and Hennepin, 1679–1680
–→ Alarcón, 1540
---→ Ayllón, 1526
–·→ Cabrillo, 1542–1543
→ Coronado, 1540–1542
---→ De Soto, 1539–1542
–·–→ Cabeza de Vaca, 1528–1536

→ Escalante, 1776–1777
---→ La Salle, 1680, 1682
–·–→ Marquette and Jolliet, 1673
→ Narváez, 1528
–·–→ Oñate, 1598–1601, 1604–1605
–·→ Piñeda, 1519
→ Ponce de León, 1513

– –→ St. Denis, 1714–1716

MAJOR COLONIAL LAND GRANTS
① Council of New England
② Plymouth Company
③ London Company

in 1662. The settlements in New Hampshire that sprang up in the 1620s were finally proclaimed a separate royal colony in 1679. Plymouth later became (1691) part of the royal colony of Massachusetts.

The Restoration Colonies. A long era (1642–60) of turmoil in England ended with the restoration of the Stuarts in the person of Charles II. An amazing period ensued, during which colonies were founded and other acquisitions were made. In 1663, Carolina was chartered; settlement began in 1670, and from the start the colony flourished. The territory later came under royal control as South Carolina (1721) and North Carolina (1729).

In 1664 an English fleet arrived to claim by right of prior discovery the land along the Hudson and Delaware rivers that had been settled and occupied by the Dutch since 1624. Most of NEW NETHERLAND now became New York colony, and its principal settlement, New Amsterdam, became the city of New York. New York colony, already multiethnic and strongly commercial in spirit, came under control of the crown in 1685. New Jersey, sparsely settled by the Dutch, Swedes, and others, was also part of this English claim. Its proprietors divided it into East and West Jersey in 1676, but the colony was reunited as a royal province in 1702. In 1681, Pennsylvania, and in 1682, what eventually became (1776) Delaware, were granted to William PENN, who founded a great Quaker settlement in and around Philadelphia.

Indian Wars. In 1675 disease-ridden and poverty-stricken Indians in New England set off KING PHILIP'S WAR against the whites. Almost every Massachusetts town experienced the horror of Indian warfare; thousands on both sides were slaughtered before King Philip, the Wampanoag chief, was killed in 1676 and the war ended. Virginians, appalled at this event, in 1676 began attacking the

William Penn's treaty (c.1682) with the Delaware Indians is dramatized in this painting. Penn's liberal policies, including payment for Indian lands, made Pennsylvania one of the most prosperous colonies. (Abby Aldrich Rockefeller Folk Art Collection, Williamsburg, Va.)

Occaneechee despite the disapproval of the royal governor, Sir William BERKELEY. Then, under Nathaniel Bacon, dissatisfied and angry colonists expelled Berkeley from Jamestown and proclaimed Bacon's Laws, which gave the right to vote to all freedmen. Royal troops soon arrived to put down BACON'S REBELLION.

Along the Mohawk River in New York, the Five Nations of the IROQUOIS LEAGUE maintained their powerful confederacy with its sophisticated governing structure and strong religious faith. Allies of the English against the French along the St. Lawrence River, they dominated a vast region westward to Lake Superior with their powerful and well-organized armies. The FRENCH AND INDIAN WARS, a series of great wars between the two European powers and their Indian allies, ended in 1763 when French rule was eradicated from North America and Canada was placed under the British crown.

18th-Century Social and Economic Developments. In the 1700s the British colonies grew rapidly in population and wealth. Trade and cities flourished. The 250,000 settlers who had lived in the mainland colonies to the south of Canada in 1700 became 2,250,000 by 1775 and grew to 5,300,000 by 1800.

Several non-English ethnic groups migrated to the British colonies in large numbers during the 18th century. By 1775, Germans, who settled primarily in the Middle Colonies but also in the back-country South, numbered about 250,000. They were members of the Lutheran and German Reformed (Calvinist) churches or of pietist sects (Moravians, Mennonites, Amish, and the like); the pietists, in particular, tended to live separately, avoiding English-speaking peoples. From the 1730s waves of Scots-Irish immigrants, numbering perhaps 250,000 by the time of the Revolution, swelled the ranks of the non-English group. Forming dense settlements in Pennsylvania, as well as in New York's Hudson Valley and in the back-country South, they brought with them the Presbyterian church. The colony of Georgia was granted in 1732 to reformers, led by James OGLETHORPE, who envisioned it as an asylum for English debtors, as well as a buffer against Spanish Florida. Georgia, too, was colonized by many non-English people.

The Growth of Slavery. Slaves from Africa were used in small numbers in the colonies from about 1619 (see AFRICAN AMERICANS; SLAVERY). After British merchants joined the Dutch in the slave trade later in the 17th century, prices tumbled and increasing numbers of African Americans were transported into the Southern colonies to be used for plantation labor. Slaves were also used in the Northern colonies, but in far fewer numbers.

The expansion of slavery was the most fateful event of the pre-Revolutionary years. Virginia had only about 16,000 slaves in 1700; by 1770 it held more than 187,000, or almost half the population of the colony. In low country South Carolina, with its rice and indigo plantations, only 25,000 out of a total population of 100,000 were white in 1775. Fearful whites mounted slave patrols and exacted savage penalties on transgression in order to maintain black passivity.

Meanwhile, on the basis of abundant slave labor, great

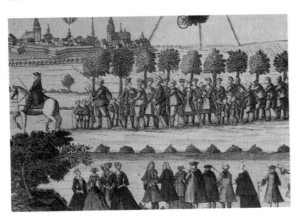

A German engraving (1732) portrays Lutherans from Salzburg, Austria, departing for the New World. During the 18th century many German Protestants emigrated to North America to escape religious persecution.

plantations emerged, creating sharp distinctions in wealth among whites. Southern society was dominated by the aristocracy; however, whites of all classes were united in their fear of blacks. Miscegenation was common, especially where slaves were most numerous, and mulattoes were regarded as black, not white. An almost total absence of government in this sparsely settled, rural Southern environment resulted in complete license on the part of owners in the treatment of their slaves. Paradoxically, the ideal of liberty—of freedom from all restraints—was powerful in the Southern white mind.

Religious Trends. As transatlantic trade increased, communication between the colonies and England became closer, and English customs and institutions exerted a stronger influence on the Americans. The Church of England, the established church in the Southern colonies and in the four counties in and around New York City, grew in status and influence. At the same time, in both Britain and America, an increasingly rationalistic and scientific outlook, born in the science of Sir Isaac NEWTON and the philosophy of John LOCKE, made religious observance more logical and of this world. Deism and so-called natural religion scoffed at Christianity and the Bible as a collection of ancient superstitions.

Then from England came an upsurge of evangelical Protestantism, led by John Wesley (the eventual founder of the Methodist church; see WESLEY family) and George WHITEFIELD. It sought to combat the new rationalism and foster a revival of enthusiasm in Christian faith and worship. Beginning in 1738, with Whitefield's arrival in the colonies, a movement known as the GREAT AWAKENING swept the colonials, gaining strength from an earlier outbreak of revivalism in Massachusetts (1734–35) led by Jonathan EDWARDS. Intensely democratic in spirit, the Great Awakening was the first intercolonial cultural movement. It vastly reenergized a Puritanism that, since the mid-1600s, had lost its vigor. All churches were electrified by its power—either in support or in opposition.

The American Revolution

By the middle of the 18th century the wave of American expansion was beginning to top the Appalachian rise and move into the valley of the Ohio. Colonial land companies looked covetously to that frontier. The French, foreseeing a serious threat to their fur trade with the Indians, acted decisively. In 1749 they sent an expedition to reinforce their claim to the Ohio Valley and subsequently established a string of forts there. The British and the colonists were forced to respond to the move or suffer the loss of the vast interior, long claimed by both British and French. The French and Indian War (1754–63) that resulted became a worldwide conflict, called the SEVEN YEARS' WAR in Europe. At its end, the British had taken over most of France's colonial empire as well as Spanish Florida and had become dominant in North America, except for Spain's possessions west of the Mississippi River.

Rising Tensions. The tremendous cost of the war itself and the huge responsibility accompanying the new possessions left Britain with an immense war debt and heavy administrative costs. At the same time the elimination of French rule in North America lifted the burden of fear of that power from the colonists, inducing them to be more independent-minded.

London authorities attempted to meet the costs of imperial administration by levying a tax on the colonials; the STAMP ACT of 1765 required a tax on all public documents, newspapers, notes and bonds, and almost every other printed paper. A raging controversy that brought business practically to a standstill erupted in the colonies. A Stamp Act Congress, a gathering of representatives from nine colonies, met in New York in October 1765 to issue a solemn protest. It held that the colonials possessed the same rights and liberties as did the British at home, among which was the principle that "no taxes be imposed on them but with their own consent, given personally or by their representatives." In March 1766, Parliament repealed the Stamp Act; it passed the Declaratory

An American cartoon portrays a procession of British dignitaries mourning the demise of the Stamp Act of 1765. This tax legislation was repealed (1766) when the colonists boycotted British goods.

Act, asserting its complete sovereignty over the colonies.

Thereafter the transatlantic controversy was rarely quiet. The colonists regarded the standing army of about 6,000 troops maintained by London in the colonies after 1763 with great suspicion—such a peacetime force had never been present before. British authorities defended the force as necessary to preserve peace on the frontier, especially after PONTIAC'S REBELLION (1763–65), which had been launched by the brilliant Indian leader Pontiac to expel the British from the interior and restore French rule. In another attempt to quell Indian unrest, London established the Proclamation Line of 1763. Set along the crest of the Appalachians, the line represented a limit imposed on colonial movement west until a more effective Indian program could be developed.

In the cultural politics of the British Empire, American colonists were an out-group; they bitterly resented the disdain and derision shown them by the metropolitan English. Furthermore, most free colonists belonged to subgroups: Dissenters (the Congregationalists in New England and the Presbyterians and Baptists in New York and the South, non-English peoples with ancient reasons for hating the English (the Scots-Irish), outsiders in a British-dominated society (Germans and Dutch), or slave-owners sharply conscious of the distaste with which they were regarded by the British at home.

The current ideology among many colonists was that of republicanism. The radicalism of the 18th century, it called for grounding government in the people, giving them the vote, holding frequent elections, abolishing established churches, and separating the powers of government to guard against tyranny. Republicans also advocated that most offices be elective and that government be kept simple, limited, and respectful of the rights of citizens.

Deterioration of Imperial Ties. In this prickly atmosphere London's heavy-handedness caused angry reactions on the part of Americans. The Quartering Act of 1765 ordered colonial assemblies to house the standing army. In 1767 the TOWNSHEND ACTS levied tariffs on many articles imported into the colonies. These imports were designed to raise funds to pay wages to the army as well as to the royal governors and judges, who had formerly been dependent on colonial assemblies for their salaries. Nonimportation associations immediately sprang up in the colonies to boycott British goods. When mob attacks prevented commissioners from enforcing the revenue laws, part of the army was placed (1768) in Boston to protect the commissioners. This action confirmed the colonists' suspicion that the troops were maintained in the colonies to deprive them of their liberty. In March 1770 a group of soldiers fired into a crowd that was harassing them, killing five persons; news of the BOSTON MASSACRE spread through the colonies.

London now repealed all the Townshend duties except for that on tea. The economic centralization long reflected in the NAVIGATION ACTS—which compelled much of the colonial trade to pass through Britain on its way to the European continent—nonetheless served to remind colonials of the heavy price exacted from them for membership in the empire. The Sugar Act of 1764, latest in a

The Boston Massacre (Mar. 5, 1770), in which British troops fired on a rioting crowd and killed five men, is depicted in an engraving by the Boston silversmith Paul Revere. (New York Public Library.)

long line of such restrictive measures, produced by its taxes a huge revenue for the crown. By 1776 it drained from the colonies about £600,000, an enormous sum. The colonial balance of trade with England was always unfavorable for the Americans, who found it difficult to retain enough cash to purchase necessary goods.

In 1772 the crown, having earlier declared its right to dismiss colonial judges at its pleasure, said it would pay directly the salaries of governors and judges in Massachusetts. Samuel ADAMS, a passionate republican, immediately created the intercolonial Committee of Correspondence. Revolutionary sentiment mounted. In December 1773 swarms of colonials disguised as Mohawks boarded recently arrived tea ships in Boston harbor, flinging their cargo into the water. The furious royal government responded to this BOSTON TEA PARTY by the so-called INTOLERABLE ACTS of 1774, practically eliminating self-government in Massachusetts and closing Boston's port.

Virginia moved to support Massachusetts by convening the First CONTINENTAL CONGRESS in Philadelphia in the fall of 1774. It drew up declarations of rights and grievances and called for nonimportation of British goods. Colonial militia began drilling in the Massachusetts countryside.

The War for Independence. In April 1775, Gen. Thomas GAGE in Boston was instructed to take the offensive against the Massachusetts troublemakers, now declared traitors to the crown. Charged with ending the training of militia and gathering all arms and ammunition in colonial hands, on April 19, Gage sent 800 soldiers to Concord to commandeer arms. On that day, the Battles of LEXINGTON AND CONCORD took place, royal troops fled back to Boston, and American campfires began burning around the city. The war of the AMERICAN REVOLUTION had begun.

It soon became a world war, with England's European enemies gladly joining in opposing England in order to gain revenge for past humiliations. British forces were engaged in battle from the Caribbean and the American colonies to the coasts of India. Furthermore, the rebelling 13 colonies were widely scattered in a huge wilderness and were occupied by a people most of whom were in arms. The dispersion of the American population meant that the small (by modern standards) cities of New York, Boston, and Philadelphia could be taken and held for long periods without affecting the outcome.

Within a brief period after the Battle of Concord, practically all royal authority disappeared from the 13 colonies. Rebel governments were established in each colony, and the Continental Congress in Philadelphia provided a rudimentary national government. The task now before the British was to fight their way back onto the continent, reestablish royal governments in each colony, and defeat the colonial army. By March 1776 the British evacuated Boston, moving to take and hold New York City. Within days of the British arrival in New York, however, the Congress in Philadelphia issued (July 4) the DECLARATION OF INDEPENDENCE. In December 1776, Gen. George WASHINGTON reversed the early trend of American defeats by a stunning victory at Trenton, N.J. (see TRENTON, BATTLE OF). Thereafter, as the fighting wore on and the cause survived, Washington became in America and abroad a symbol of strength and great bravery.

In February 1778 the French joined the conflict by signing an alliance with the Continental Congress. With the aid of the French fleet the British army in the north was reduced to a bridgehead at New York City. Shifting its efforts to the south, the royal army campaigned through Georgia and the Carolinas between 1778 and 1780, marching to the James Peninsula, in Virginia, in 1781. There, in the YORKTOWN CAMPAIGN, by the combined efforts of Washington's troops and the French army and navy, Lord CORNWALLIS was forced to surrender on Oct. 19, 1781. The fighting, effectively, was over. In September 1783 the Treaty of Paris secured American independence on generous terms. The new nation was given an immense domain that ran westward to the Mississippi River (except for Britain's Canadian colonies and East and West Florida, which reverted to Spanish rule).

A New Nation

The first federal constitution of the new American republic was the ARTICLES OF CONFEDERATION. With ratification of that document in 1781, the nation had adopted its formal name, the United States of America.

Government under the Articles of Confederation. Under the Articles the only national institution was the Confederation Congress, with limited powers not unlike those of the United Nations. The states retained their sovereignty, with each state government selecting representatives to sit in the Congress. No national executive or judiciary had been established. Each state delegation received an equal vote on all issues. Congress was charged with carrying on the foreign relations of the United States, but because it had no taxing powers (it could only request funds from the states), it had no strength to back up its diplomacy. In addition, it had no jurisdiction over interstate commerce; each state could erect tariffs against its neighbors.

The Confederation Congress, however, achieved one great victory: it succeeded in bringing all 13 of the states to agree on a plan for organizing and governing the western territories (the "public lands") beyond the Appalachians. Three ordinances dealing with the Northwest (1784, 1785, and 1787) provided that new states established in the western regions would be equal in status to the older ones. After a territorial stage of quasi self-gov-

(Left) *As the British fleet sailed out of New York Harbor on Nov. 25, 1783, an American sailor, David Van Arsdale, succeeded in climbing the flagpole greased by the British, to unfurl the flag of the new American nation.* (Below) *John Trumbull's* The Death of General Mercer at the Battle of Princeton *portrays the thick of the action in this engagement, which helped change the failing fortunes of the American Revolution.*

ernment, they would pass to full statehood. The land in the NORTHWEST TERRITORY (the Old Northwest, that is, the area north of the Ohio River) would be surveyed in square parcels, 6 mi (9.7 km) on a side, divided into 36 sections, and sold to settlers at low cost; one plot would be reserved for the support of public schools. Furthermore, slavery was declared illegal in the Northwest Territory. (The Southwest Territory, below the Ohio, was organized by the later federal Congress in 1790 as slave country.)

The Confederation Congress, however, did not survive. Because of its lack of taxing power, its currency was of little value; widespread social turbulence in the separate states led many Americans to despair of the new nation. Indeed, so did other nations. The new United States was so weak that it was regarded contemptuously all over the world, and its diplomats were ignored.

The Constitutional Convention of 1787. In 1787 the CONSTITUTIONAL CONVENTION met in Philadelphia. Deciding to start afresh and fashion a new national government independent of, and superior to, the states, the delegates made a crucial decision: the nation's source of sovereignty was to lie in the people directly, not in the existing states. Using the British Parliament as a model, they provided for a CONGRESS OF THE UNITED STATES that would have two houses to check and balance each other. One house would be elected directly by the people of each state, with representation proportionate to population; the other would provide for two senators for each state, to be chosen by the state legislatures.

The powers of the national government included regulation of interstate and foreign commerce, foreign affairs and defense, and Indian affairs; control of the national domain; and promotion of "the general Welfare." Most important, the Congress was empowered to levy "taxes, duties, imposts, and excises." The states were prohibited from carrying on foreign relations, coining money, passing ex post facto laws, impairing the obligations of contracts, and establishing tariffs. Furthermore, if social turbulence within a state became serious, the federal government, following invitation by the legislature or the executive of that state, could bring in troops to insure "a republican form of government."

An engraving shows President George Washington (left) with members of his first cabinet—(from left) Gen. Henry Knox, secretary of war; Alexander Hamilton, secretary of the treasury; Thomas Jefferson, secretary of state; and Edmund Randolph, the first attorney general.

The elective office of PRESIDENT OF THE UNITED STATES was created. Chosen by a special body (an ELECTORAL COLLEGE), the president would be an independent and powerful national leader, effectively in command of the government. The Constitutional Convention also created a fully independent SUPREME COURT OF THE UNITED STATES, members of which could be removed only if they committed a crime. Then, most important, the document that was drawn up at Philadelphia stated that the Constitution, as well as laws and treaties made under the authority of the U.S. government, "shall be the supreme Law of the Land."

Ratification of the proposed constitution was completed (1788) and the CONSTITUTION OF THE UNITED STATES became operative. The Bill of Rights, preserving individual liberties, was then drafted by the first Congress and became the first ten amendments to the Constitution.

The Constitution of the United States was drawn up in Philadelphia in 1787 and ratified by the required nine states by June 21, 1788. It superseded the Articles of Confederation and laid the foundations of the federal system of government.

Diverging Visions of the American Republic. George Washington was unanimously elected chief executive, the only president so honored. He was inaugurated in the temporary capital, New York City, on Apr. 30, 1789. The unanimity expressed in Washington's election, however, would prove short-lived.

Under the leadership of Secretary of the Treasury Alexander HAMILTON, Congress pledged (1790) the revenues of the federal government to pay off all the outstanding debt of the old Articles of Confederation government as well as the state debts. At one stroke, the financial credit of the new government was assured. Southerners, however, mistrusted the plan, claiming that it served only to enrich Northern speculators because the southern states had largely paid off their debts. Many Southerners feared, too, that the new nation would be dominated by New Englanders, whose criticism of Southern slavery and living styles offended them. Before assenting to the funding proposal, the Southerners had obtained agreement that the national capital (after 10 years in Philadelphia) would be placed in the South, on the Potomac River.

In 1791, Hamilton persuaded Congress to charter the BANK OF THE UNITED STATES, modeled after the Bank of England. Primarily private (some of its trustees would be federally appointed), it would receive and hold the government's revenues, issue currency and regulate that of state-chartered banks, and be free to invest as it saw fit the federal tax moneys in its vaults. Because it would control the largest pool of capital in the country, it could shape the growth of the national economy. Hamilton also proposed (with limited success) that protective tariffs be established to exclude foreign goods and thus stimulate the development of U.S. factories. In short, he laid out the economic philosophy of what became the FEDERALIST PARTY: that the government should actively encourage economic growth by providing aid to capitalists. Flourishing cities and a vigorous industrial order: this was the American future he envisioned. His position gained the support of the elites in New York City and Philadelphia as well as broad-based support among the Yankees of New England.

On the other hand, Southerners, a rural and widely dispersed people, feared the cities and the power of remote bankers. With Thomas JEFFERSON they worked to counteract the Federalists' vision of the United States. Southerners rejected the concept of an active government, preferring one committed to laissez-faire (that is, allowing people to act without government interference) in all areas—economic and cultural. Jefferson declared that close ties between government and capitalists would inevitably lead to corruption and exploitation. In his view, schemers would use graft to secure special advantages (tariffs, bounties, and the like) that would allow them to profiteer at the community's expense.

The Middle Atlantic states at first supported the Federalists, who won a second term for Washington in 1792 and elected John ADAMS to the presidency in 1796. However, many of the Scots-Irish, Germans, and Dutch in these states disliked Yankees and distrusted financiers and business proprietors. The growing working class in Philadelphia and New York City turned against the Federalists' elitism. By 1800 the ethnic minorities of the Middle Atlantic states helped swing that region behind Jefferson, a Virginian, and his Democratic-Republican party, giving the presidency to Jefferson. Thereafter, until 1860, with few intermissions, the South and the Middle Atlantic states together dominated the federal government. Although the U.S. Constitution had made no mention of POLITICAL PARTIES, it had taken only a decade for the development of a party system that roughly reflected two diverging visions for the new republic. Political parties would remain an integral part of the American system of government.

The Democratic Republic. As president, Jefferson attempted to implement the Democratic-Republican vision of America; he cut back the central government's activities, reducing the size of the court system, letting excise taxes lapse, and contracting the military forces. Paradoxically, in what was perhaps Jefferson's greatest achievement as president, he vastly increased the scope of U.S. power: the securing of the LOUISIANA PURCHASE (1803) from France practically doubled American territory, placing the western boundary of the United States along the base of the Rocky Mountains.

In 1811, under Jefferson's successor, James MADISON, the 20-year charter of the Bank of the United States was allowed to lapse, further eroding the Federalists' program. Renewed warfare between Britain and France, during which American foreign trade was progressively throttled down almost to nothing, led eventually to the WAR OF 1812. The British insisted on the right freely to commandeer U.S. cargoes as contraband and to impress American sailors into their navy. To many Americans the republic seemed in grave peril.

With reluctance and against unanimous Federalist opposition, Congress made the decision to go to war against Britain. Except for some initial naval victories, the war went badly for the Americans. Western Indians, under the gifted TECUMSEH, fought on the British side. In 1814, however, an invading army from Canada was repelled. Then, just as a peace treaty was being concluded in Ghent (Belgium), Andrew JACKSON crushed another invading British army as it sought to take New Orleans. The war thus ended on a triumphant note, and the republic was confirmed. The Federalists, who in the HARTFORD CONVENTION (in Connecticut, 1814) had capped their opposition to the war with demands for major changes in the Constitution, now were regarded as disloyal, and by the 1820s their party dissolved. Robbed of their enemy, Jeffersonian Democratic-Republicans broke into factions, effectively disappearing as a national party.

An Age of Boundlessness: 1815–50

The volatile and expansive years from 1815 to 1850 were, in many ways, an age of boundlessness when limits that had previously curbed human aspirations seemed to disappear.

Economic and Cultural Ferment. After 1815 the American economy began to expand rapidly. The cotton boom in the South spread settlement swiftly across the Gulf Plains: the Deep South was born. Farmers also moved

Thousands of Americans crossed the plains in covered wagons during the westward migration of 1815–50. Quicksand along river crossings in Nebraska's Platte valley was one of many obstacles they encountered.

into the Lake Plains north of the Ohio River, their migration greatly accelerating after the completion of the ERIE CANAL in 1825. Practically all Indians east of the Mississippi were placed on small reservations or forced to move to the Great Plains beyond the Missouri River. Canals and railroads opened the interior to swift expansion of both settlement and trade. In the Midwest many new cities, such as Chicago, appeared, as enormous empires of wheat and livestock farms came into being. From 1815 to 1850 a new western state entered the Union, on the average, every 2½ years.

The westward movement of the FRONTIER was matched in the Northeast by rapid economic development. National productivity surged during the 1820s; prices spurted to a peak during the 1830s and dropped for a time during the 1840s; both prices and productivity soared upward

Miners sought gold in riverbeds during the California gold rush (1848–49), which stimulated rapid economic, agricultural, and industrial growth in the Far West. (Museum of Fine Arts, Boston.)

again during the 1850s, reaching new heights. A business cycle had appeared, producing periods of boom and bust, and the factory system became well developed. After the GOLD RUSH that began in California in 1848–49, industrial development was further stimulated during the 1850s by the arrival of $500 million in gold and silver from the Sierra Nevada and other western regions. Land values rose, and hundreds of new communities appeared in the western states.

Meanwhile, white manhood suffrage became the rule, and most offices were made elective. A communications revolution centering in the inexpensive newspaper and in a national fascination with mass education (except in the South) sent literacy rates soaring. The Second Great Awakening (1787–1825), a new religious revival that originated in New England, spread an evangelical excitement across the country. In its wake a ferment of social reform swept the Northern states. The slave system of the South spread westward as rapidly as the free labor system of the North, and during the 1830s ABOLITIONISTS mounted a crusade against slavery.

Expansion of the American Domain. The years 1815–50 brought further expansion of the national domain. During the 1840s a sense of MANIFEST DESTINY seized the American mind, and continent-wide expansion seemed inevitable. Texas, which had declared its independence from Mexico in 1835–36 (see TEXAS REVOLUTION), was annexed in 1845. Then a dispute with Mexico concerning the Rio Grande as the border of Texas led to the MEXICAN WAR (1846–48). While U.S. armies invaded the heartland of Mexico to gain victory, other forces sliced off the northern half of that country—the provinces of New Mexico and Alta California. In the Treaty of GUADALUPE HIDALGO (1848), $15 million was paid for the Mexican cession of those provinces, more than 3 million km² (roughly 1 million m²).

In 1846, Britain and the United States settled the OREGON QUESTION, concluding a treaty that divided the Oregon Country at the 49th parallel and bringing the Pacific

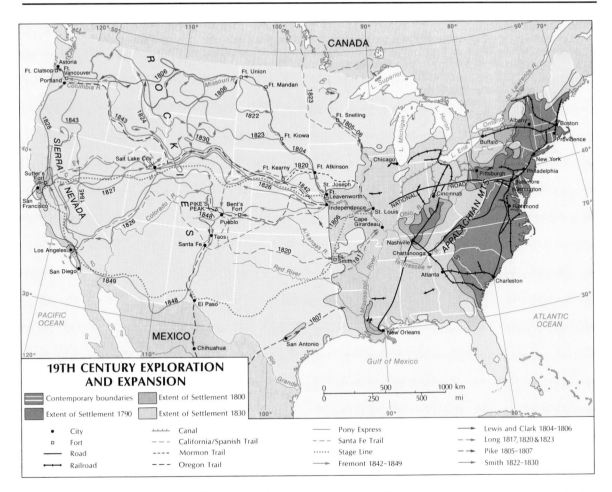

19TH CENTURY EXPLORATION AND EXPANSION

▤ Contemporary boundaries	▨ Extent of Settlement 1800
▨ Extent of Settlement 1790	░ Extent of Settlement 1830

• City	┴┴┴ Canal	—— Pony Express	——→ Lewis and Clark 1804–1806
▫ Fort	- - - California/Spanish Trail	- - - Santa Fe Trail	—•→ Long 1817, 1820 & 1823
—— Road	- - - - Mormon Trail	······ Stage Line	—••→ Pike 1805–1807
↦ Railroad	- - - Oregon Trail	——→ Fremont 1842–1849	——→ Smith 1822–1830

Acquisition of the Louisiana Territory in 1803 spurred exploration across the continent by government-sponsored expeditions and independent parties, particularly fur trappers and traders. They blazed westward routes later used by the wagon trains of emigrants.

Northwest into the American nation. In addition, by the GADSDEN PURCHASE of 1853 the United States acquired (for $10 million) the southern portions of the present states of New Mexico and Arizona. By 1860 the Union comprised 33 states. Fed by a high birthrate and by the heavy immigration from Ireland and Germany that surged dramatically during the 1840s, the nation's population was leaping upward: from 9.6 million in 1820 to 23 million in 1850 and 31.5 million in 1860.

Domestic Politics: 1815–46. In a nationalist frame of mind at the end of the War of 1812, Congress chartered the Second Bank of the United States in 1816, erected the first protective tariff (see TARIFF ACTS), and supported internal improvements (roads and bridges) to open the interior. President James MONROE presided (1817–25) over the so-called Era of Good Feelings, followed by John Quincy ADAMS (1825–29).

Chief Justice John MARSHALL led the Supreme Court in

a crucial series of decisions, beginning in 1819. He declared that within its powers the federal government could not be interfered with by the states (MCCULLOCH V. MARYLAND) and that regulation of interstate and international commerce was solely a federal preserve (GIBBONS V. OGDEN). In 1820, in the MISSOURI COMPROMISE, Congress took charge of the question of slavery in the territories by declaring it illegal above 36°30' in the huge region acquired by the Louisiana Purchase. Witnessing the Latin American revolutions against Spanish rule, the American government in 1823 asserted its paramountcy in the Western Hemisphere by issuing the MONROE DOCTRINE. In diplomatic but clear language it stated that the United States would fight to exclude further European extensions of sovereignty into its hemisphere.

During Andrew JACKSON's presidency (1829–37) a sharp bipolarization occurred again in the nation's politics. Of Scots-Irish descent, Jackson hated the English,

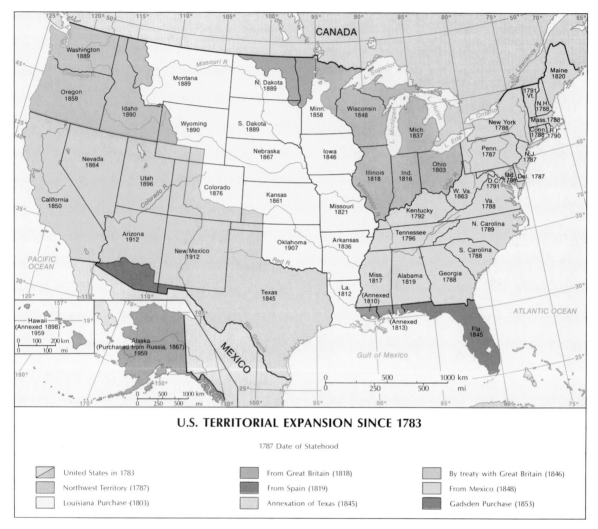

U.S. TERRITORIAL EXPANSION SINCE 1783

1787 Date of Statehood

United States in 1783	From Great Britain (1818)	By treaty with Great Britain (1846)
Northwest Territory (1787)	From Spain (1819)	From Mexico (1848)
Louisiana Purchase (1803)	Annexation of Texas (1845)	Gadsden Purchase (1853)

Between 1783, when the western boundary of the United States was set at the Mississippi River, and 1853, the year of the Gadsden Purchase, the country expanded threefold to its present continental limits.

and he was, in turn, as thoroughly disliked by New Englanders, who thought him violent and barbaric. He made enemies in the South, as well, when in 1832 South Carolina, asserting superior STATE RIGHTS, attempted to declare null and void within its borders the tariff of 1828 (see NULLIFICATION). In his Nullification Proclamation (1832), Jackson declared that the federal government was supreme according to the Constitution. He skillfully outmaneuvered the South Carolinians, forcing them to relent. In 1832 he vetoed the rechartering of the Second Bank of the United States on the grounds that it caused the booms and busts that so alarmed the country and that it served the wealthy while exploiting the farmers and working people. To oppose him, the old Federalist coalition

was reborn in the form of the American WHIG PARTY. With a DEMOCRATIC PARTY emerging behind Jackson and embodying the old Jeffersonian Democratic-Republican coalition, two-party rivalries appeared in every state. By the 1840s modern mass political parties, organized down into every ward and precinct, had appeared.

Led by Henry CLAY and Daniel WEBSTER, the Whigs called for protective tariffs, a national bank, and internal improvements to stimulate the economy. Yankees, who by now had migrated in great numbers into the Midwest, leaned strongly toward the Whigs. Many Southerners tended to vote for Whig candidates too.

Democrats continued to condemn banks and tariffs as sources of corruption and exploitation, and in Jefferson's tradition insisted on cultural laissez-faire, the freedom of people to live as they desired. The minority out-groups—Irish Catholics and Germans—concurred, voting strongly Democratic. During Martin VAN BUREN's presidency (1837–41) Democrats succeeded in entirely separating banking and government in the INDEPENDENT TREASURY SYSTEM, by which the government stored and controlled its own funds. A brief Whig interlude under William Henry HARRISON (1841) and John TYLER (1841–45) was followed by the presidency of the Democrat James K. POLK (1845–49).

Growing Sectional Conflicts. President Polk's war with Mexico ripped open the slavery question again. Was it to be allowed in the new territories? The WILMOT PROVISO (1846), which would have excluded slavery, became a rallying point for both sides, being voted on again and again in Congress and successfully held off by Southerners. Abolitionism, led by William Lloyd GARRISON and others and now strong in many Northern circles, called for the immediate emancipation of slaves with no compensation to slaveowners. Most Northern whites disliked blacks and did not support abolition; they did want to disallow slavery in the territories so they could be preserved for white settlement based on Northern ideals: free labor, dignity of work, and economic progress.

In 1848, Northerners impatient with both of the existing parties formed the FREE-SOIL PARTY. By polling 300,000 votes for their candidate, Martin Van Buren, they denied victory to the Democrats and put the Whig Zachary TAYLOR in the White House (1849–50; on his death Millard FILLMORE became president, 1850–53). The COMPROMISE OF 1850 seemed to settle the slavery expansion issue by the principle of POPULAR SOVEREIGNTY, allowing the people who lived in the Mexican cession to decide for themselves. A strong FUGITIVE SLAVE LAW was also passed in 1850, giving new powers to slaveowners to reach into Northern states to recapture escaped slaves.

The Civil War Era

As the 1850s began, it seemed for a time that the issue of slavery and other sectional differences between North and South might eventually be reconciled. But with the westward thrust of the American nation, all attempts at compromise were thwarted, and diverging economic, political, and philosophical interests became more apparent. The resulting civil war fundamentally transformed the American nation.

Political Fragmentation. In 1854 the KANSAS-NEBRASKA ACT threw open the huge unorganized lands of the Louisiana Purchase to popular sovereignty, repealing the Missouri Compromise line of 1820. The North exploded in rage. Thousands defected from the Whig party to establish a new and much more antisouthern body (and one wholly limited to the Northern states), the REPUBLICAN PARTY. The Republicans were aided by an enormous anti-Catholic outburst underway at the same time, aimed at the large wave of Irish Catholic immigration. Anti-Catholicism was already draining away Whigs to a new organization, the American party, soon known as the KNOW-NOTHING

PARTY. When in 1856 disagreements over slavery sundered the party, the anti-Catholics joined the Republicans.

In Kansas civil war broke out between proslavery and antislavery advocates, as settlers attempted to formalize their position on the institution prior to the territory's admission as a state. The Democratic presidents Franklin PIERCE (1853–57) and James BUCHANAN (1857–61) appeared to favor the proslavery group in Kansas despite its use of fraud and violence. In 1857 the Supreme Court, Southern dominated, intensified Northern alarm in its decision in the case of DRED SCOTT V. SANDFORD. The Court ruled that Congress had no authority to exclude slavery from the territories and thus, that the Missouri Compromise line had been unconstitutional all along. Thousands of Northerners now became convinced that the national government intended to make slavery a nationwide institution.

In 1860 the political system became completely fragmented. The Democrats split into Northern and Southern wings, presenting two different candidates for the presidency; the small CONSTITUTIONAL UNION PARTY attempted to rally the former Whigs behind a third. The Republicans, however, were able to secure the election of Abraham LINCOLN.

Southerners had viewed the rise of the Yankee-dominated Republican party with great alarm. They were convinced that the party was secretly controlled by abolitionists (although most Northerners detested the abolitionists) and that Yankees believed in using government to enforce their moralistic crusades. In 1859, John BROWN led a raid on the federal arsenal at Harpers Ferry, Va., hoping to incite a slave insurrection. His action—and his subsequent deification by some Northerners—helped persuade Southerners that emancipation of the slaves, if northerners obtained control of the country, was sooner or later inevitable.

Secession. Southern leaders had threatened to leave the Union if Lincoln won the election of 1860. Many South Carolinians, in particular, were convinced that Republican-sponsored emancipation would lead to bloody massacres as blacks sought vengeance against whites. In order to prevent this horror, South Carolina seceded in December 1860, soon after Lincoln's victory. Before Lincoln's inauguration (March 1861) six more states followed (Mississippi, Florida, Alabama, Georgia, Louisiana, and Texas). In February their representatives gathered in Montgomery, Ala., to form the CONFEDERATE STATES OF AMERICA. On Apr. 12, 1861, when President Lincoln moved to reprovision the federal troops at FORT SUMTER, in Charleston Harbor, Confederate shore batteries launched a 34-hour battering of the installation, forcing its surrender. The U.S. CIVIL WAR had begun.

The War between the States. Lincoln moved swiftly. On April 15 he called the remaining states to provide 75,000 troops to put down the Confederacy; Virginia, Arkansas, North Carolina, and Tennessee reluctantly seceded. The capital of the Confederacy moved to Richmond. On July 21, 1861, the first major battle between Union and Confederate forces occurred—at Bull Run (see BULL RUN, BATTLES OF), south of Washington, D.C.—resulting in a

(Above) *At the first Battle of Bull Run, on July 21, 1861, Gen. Thomas J. Jackson earned his nickname, Stonewall, in holding the Confederate line against a Union advance. The South's victory shattered Northern complacency.* (Right) *Even early in the Civil War the Union foot soldier* (right) *was more formally equipped than his Confederate counterpart. As the war disrupted the already limited industrial capacity of the South, Confederate supplies became so scarce that some men marched barefoot.*

dramatic Southern victory. Thereafter, both sides settled down to a long conflict.

It became an immense struggle. With a total U.S. population of fewer than 32 million, the number of dead reached 620,000 (360,000 Northerners out of an army of about 1.5 million and 260,000 Southerners in an army of about 1 million). In 1861 about 22 million people lived in the North, compared with about 9 million people in the South, of whom 3.5 million were black. Al-

Gen. William T. Sherman, Gen. Ulysses S. Grant, and Rear Adm. David D. Porter advise President Abraham Lincoln on the conduct of the Civil War in this painting by G.P.A. Healy. (1894; White House Collection.)

though the North possessed a vigorous system of industry and a well-developed railroad network, it had to invade and defeat the opposition in order to win; the South had only to defend its borders. The conflict was not so uneven as it seemed.

Lincoln launched an all-out effort: he declared a naval blockade of the Confederacy; worked hard to maintain the loyalty of the slaveholding border states (Delaware, Maryland, Kentucky, and Missouri); invaded Tennessee to gain a base of power in the heart of the Confederacy; issued the EMANCIPATION PROCLAMATION, declaring slavery dead wherever rebellion existed; cut the South in two by taking the Mississippi River; and looked for a general who could win. In 1864, Lincoln brought Gen. Ulysses S. GRANT to Washington to face the brilliant Confederate commander, Robert E. LEE.

By mid-1863 the South was in desperate straits, lacking both food and supplies. A great northward thrust was turned back at Gettysburg, Pa., in July of that year (see GETTYSBURG, BATTLE OF). Thereafter, Grant mounted a relentless campaign that hammered down toward Richmond, at hideous cost in casualties. Union general William T. SHERMAN, meanwhile, was slashing through Georgia to the sea, leaving a wide swath of total destruction, and then turning northward through the Carolinas. By April 1865, Grant had finally rounded Lee's flank, and on the 9th of that month, Lee surrendered at APPOMATTOX COURT HOUSE. The Civil War was over.

Reconstruction. A week after Appomattox, Lincoln was assassinated. Andrew JOHNSON assumed office and moved quickly to establish a plan for RECONSTRUCTION. He asked Southern whites only to repudiate debts owed by the

Confederacy, declare secession null and void, and ratify the 13th Amendment (which declared slavery illegal). When Congress convened in December 1865, newly elected Southerners were already on the scene waiting to be admitted to their seats. Many of them had been elected on the basis of BLACK CODES, established in the Southern states in 1865–66 to restore a form of quasi slavery. To the shocked and angered North, it seemed that the sufferings endured in the war had been in vain: politics as before the war—only now with a powerful Southern Democratic bloc in Congress—would resume.

The Republican majority in Congress refused to admit southern legislators to their seats until a congressional committee reexamined the entire question of Reconstruction. Soon, Radical Republicans (those who wished to use the victory as an opportunity to remake the South in the Yankee image) were in open conflict with Johnson, led by Sen. Charles SUMNER of Massachusetts and Rep. Thaddeus STEVENS (New England-born) of Pennsylvania. Johnson attempted to terminate the FREEDMEN'S BUREAU (an agency established in 1865 to aid refugees) and to veto legislation aimed at protecting the civil rights of former slaves (see CIVIL RIGHTS ACTS).

The 14TH AMENDMENT made all persons born or naturalized in the country U.S. citizens and forbade any state to interfere with their fundamental civil rights. In March 1867 all state governments in the South were terminated and military occupation established. Federal commanders were charged with reconstructing Southern governments through constitutional conventions, to which delegates were to be elected by universal male suffrage. After a new state government was in operation and had ratified the 14th Amendment, its representatives would be admitted to Congress. In February 1868 an impeachment effort sought unsuccessfully to remove President Johnson from office.

The Republican majority in Congress made no signifi-

Locomotives of the Union Pacific and Central Pacific railways meet at Promontory Point, Utah, marking the completion of the first transcontinental railroad. The event occurred on May 10, 1869.

cant effort to create social equality for African Americans. It merely gave them the vote and ensured them equal protection under the law (trial by jury, freedom of movement, the right to hold office and any employment, and the like). In 1870 the 15th Amendment, which made it illegal to deny the vote on the grounds of race, was ratified.

In 1868, Republican Ulysses S. Grant was elected president with electoral votes gained in occupied Southern states. Democrats alleged that Radical Reconstruction was not genuinely concerned with aiding African Americans but with using their votes in the South to keep the Republicans in power in Congress and to retain protective tariffs and other aids to industrialists. When evidence of corruption surfaced during the Grant administration, Democrats declared that it proved that the outcome of Republican friendliness to capitalists was graft and plunder.

By 1870 the anti-Southern mood that had supported Radical Reconstruction had faded, as had the surge of concern for African Americans in the South. New domestic problems were emerging. A resurgence of white voting in the South, together with the use of violence to intimidate African Americans and their white sympathizers, brought Southern states back into Democratic hands. Northerners, awakened to economic questions by the depression that began in 1873 and lasted for 5 years, tacitly agreed to return the race issue to the control of Southern whites.

After the disputed election of 1876, amid evidence of electoral corruption, the Republican presidential candidate promised to withdraw the last federal occupation troops from the South. The election was decided by a congressional electoral commission, and Rutherford B. HAYES became president. He withdrew (1877) the troops; Reconstruction was over.

The Gilded Age

The era known as the GILDED AGE (1870s to 1890s) was a time of vigorous, exploitative individualism. Despite widespread suffering by industrial workers, southern sharecroppers, displaced American Indians, and other groups, a mood of optimism possessed the United States.

Industrialization and Large-Scale Exploitation of Natural Resources. During the Gilded Age ambitious and imaginative capitalists ranged the continent looking for new opportunities. Business lurched erratically from upswings to slumps, while the country's industrial base grew rapidly. Factories and mines labored heavily through these years to provide the raw materials and finished products needed for expansion of the railroad system. In 1865 (as construction of the first TRANSCONTINENTAL RAILROAD was underway; completed 1869) approximately 56,000 km (35,000 mi) of track stretched across the United States; by 1910 the total reached about 386,000 km (240,000 mi) of interconnected uniform-gauge track.

After new gold and silver discoveries in the late 1850s, until about 1875, individual prospectors explored the western country and desert basins in search of mineral riches. Then mining corporations took over, using hired laborers and eastern-trained engineers. Indians were either brutally exterminated or placed on small reservations. Warfare with the Great Plains Indians broke out in 1864; these INDIAN WARS did not entirely subside until after the slaughtering of the buffalo herds, the basis of Indian life, which had occurred by the mid-1880s. Through the DAWES ACT of 1887, which forced most Indians to choose 160-acre (65-ha) allotments within their reservations, reformers hoped to break down tribal bonds and induce Indians to take up sedentary agriculture.

Cattle ranching was the first large-scale enterprise to invade the Great Plains beginning in the late 1860s. By the 1880s, however, the open range began to give way to fenced pastureland and to agriculture, made possible by the newly invented barbed-wire fence and by "dry farming," a technique of preserving soil moisture by frequent plowing. Millions of farmers moved into the high plains west of the 100th meridian. So huge was their grain output that slumping world prices beginning in the mid-1880s put them into severe financial straits. Meanwhile, the vast continental sweep between Kansas and California became filled with new states.

By the early 1900s the nation's economy, tied together by the railroads into a single market, was dominated by a small number of large firms. With great size, however, came large and complex problems. In 1887, Congress created the INTERSTATE COMMERCE COMMISSION to curb cutthroat competition among the railroads and to ensure that railroad rates were "reasonable and just." In 1890, on the other hand, Congress attempted to restore competition through passage of the SHERMAN ANTI-TRUST ACT, which declared illegal trusts and other combinations that restrained trade. The U.S. Supreme Court favored laissez-faire and consistently blocked both federal and state efforts to regulate private business.

New Social Groupings: Immigrants, Urbanites, and Union Members. In 1890 the American people numbered 63 million, double the 1860 population. During these years the nation's cities underwent tremendous growth. Many new urbanites came from the American countryside, but many others came from abroad. From 1860 to 1890 more than 10 million immigrants arrived in the United States; from 1890 to 1920, 15 million more arrived (see IMMIGRATION). Most were concentrated in northern cities: by 1910, 75 percent of immigrants lived in urban areas, while fewer than 50 percent of native-born Americans did so. In the 1880s the so-called new immigration began: in addition to the Germans, Scandinavians, Irish, and others of the older immigrant groups, came the Italians, Poles, Hungarians, Bohemians, Greeks, and Jews (from central and eastern Europe, especially Russia). Roman Catholics grew in number from 1.6 million in 1850 to 12 million in 1900, producing a renewed outburst of bitter anti-Catholic nativism in the 1880s. The large cities, with their saloons, theaters, dance halls, and immigrant slums, were feared by many native American Protestants, who lived primarily in small cities and the rural countryside.

The outbreak of labor protests from the 1870s on, often characterized by immigrant workers opposing native-born employers, intensified the hostility. In 1878 the KNIGHTS OF LABOR formed, opening its ranks to all working people, skilled or unskilled. Internal stresses soon broke it apart, however, and the American Federation of Labor, under Samuel GOMPERS, formed to take its place. Concentrating on skilled craftworkers and tight organization, the new union endured.

Domestic Politics. Gilded Age politics became a contest between evenly balanced Republicans and Democrats. Winning elections by small margins, they alternated in their control of Congress and the White House. Five Republicans served as presidents: Hayes; James A. GARFIELD (1881); Chester A. ARTHUR (1881–85), who succeeded Garfield on his assassination; Benjamin HARRISON (1889–93); and William McKINLEY (1897–1901). Democrat Grover CLEVELAND served two terms as U.S. president (1885–89; 1893–97).

In the Great Plains and the South, grain and cotton farmers, suffering from falling crop prices, demanded currency inflation to raise prices. By 1892 a POPULIST PARTY had appeared, to call for free coinage of silver to achieve this goal. Cleveland resisted, stating that such a monetary policy would destroy confidence, prolong the depression that began in 1893, and injure city consumers. In 1896 the Democrats, taken over by southern and western inflationists, ran William Jennings BRYAN on a FREE SILVER platform. Ethnic voters surged into the Republican ranks—for the depression was a disastrous one, and the Republican party had always urged active government intervention to stimulate the economy. In addition, as city dwellers they feared inflation. William McKinley's election began a long period of one-party (Republican) domination in the Northern states and in Washington.

The Progressive Era

During the period known as the Progressive Era (1890s to about 1920) the U.S. government became increasingly activist in both domestic and foreign policy. Progressive, that is, reform-minded, political leaders sought to extend their vision of a just and rational order to all areas of society and some, indeed, to all reaches of the globe.

Immigrants crowd the decks of a ship bound for New York in 1893. More than 25 million Europeans immigrated to the United States between 1860 and 1920. Many flocked to urban centers along the eastern seaboard.

America Looks Outward. During the 1890s, U.S. foreign policy became aggressively activist. As American industrial productivity grew, many reformers urged the need for foreign markets. Others held that the United States had a mission to carry Anglo-Saxon culture to all of humankind, to spread law and order and American civilization. In 1895 the United States intervened bluntly in the VENEZUELA BOUNDARY DISPUTE between Venezuela and imperial Britain, warning that, under the Monroe Doctrine, American force might be used if Venezuela were not treated equitably. A Cuban revolution against Spain, begun in 1895, finally led to the SPANISH-AMERICAN WAR (1898), undertaken to free Cuba. From that war the United States emerged with a protectorate over Cuba and an island empire consisting of the Philippines, Puerto Rico, and Guam. The United States also annexed the Hawaiian Islands in 1898, completing a bridge to the markets of the Far East. In 1900 the American government announced the OPEN DOOR POLICY, pledging to support continued Chinese independence as well as equal access for all nations to China's markets.

William McKinley's assassination brought Theodore ROOSEVELT to the presidency in 1901. A proud patriot, he sought to make the United States a great power in the world. In 1903 he aided Panama in becoming independent of Colombia, then secured from Panama the right for the United States to build and control a canal through the isthmus. In 1904, in the Roosevelt Corollary to the Monroe Doctrine, he asserted the right of the United States to intervene in the internal affairs of Western Hemisphere nations to prevent "chronic wrongdoing." The following year his good offices helped end the Russo-Japanese War. Having much strengthened the navy, Roosevelt sent (1907) the Great White Fleet on a spectacular round-the-world cruise to display American power.

Progressivism at Home. Meanwhile, the Progressive Era was also underway in domestic politics. City governments were transformed, becoming relatively honest and efficient; social workers labored to improve slum housing, health, and education; and in many states reform movements democratized, purified, and humanized government. Under Roosevelt the national government strengthened or created regulatory agencies that exerted increasing influence over business enterprise, promoted conservation, and attempted to protect consumers from fraudulent labeling and adulteration of products. Beginning in 1902, Roosevelt also used the Justice Department and lawsuits (or the threat of them) to mount a revived assault on monopoly under the Sherman Anti-Trust Law. William Howard TAFT, his successor as president (1909–13), drew back in his policies, continuing only the antitrust campaign. He approved passage of the 16th Amendment (the income tax amendment, 1913), however; in time it would transform the federal government by giving it access to enormous revenues.

Republicans were split in the election of 1912. The regular nomination went to Taft, and a short-lived PROGRESSIVE PARTY was formed to run Theodore Roosevelt. Democrat Woodrow WILSON (1913–21) was therefore able to win the presidency. Attacking corporate power, he won a drastic lowering of the tariff (1913) and establishment of a Tariff Commission (1916); creation of the FEDERAL RESERVE SYSTEM (1913) to supervise banking and currency; a broadened antimonopoly program under the Clayton Anti-Trust Act (1914); control over the hours of labor on the railroads (Adamson Act, 1916); and creation of a body to ensure fair and open competition in business (Fair Trade Commission, 1914).

During the Progressive Era, Southern governments imposed a wide range of JIM CROW LAWS on African Americans, using the rationale that such legalization of segregation resulted in a more orderly, systematic electoral system and society. Many of the steps that had been taken toward racial equality during the Reconstruction period were thus reversed. The federal government upheld the principle of racial segregation in the U.S. Supreme Court case PLESSY V. FERGUSON (1896), as long as African Americans were provided with "separate but equal" facilities. In the face of the rigidly segregated society that confronted them, African Americans themselves were divided concerning the appropriate course of action. Since 1895, Booker T. WASHINGTON had urged that African Americans should not actively agitate for equality but should acquire craft skills, work industriously, and convince whites of their abilities. W. E. B. DU BOIS insisted instead that African Americans ceaselessly protest Jim Crow laws, demand education in the highest professions as well as in crafts, and work for complete social integration. In 1910 the NATIONAL ASSOCIATION FOR THE ADVANCEMENT OF COLORED PEOPLE (NAACP) was founded to advance these ideals.

Intervention and World War. President Taft continued to stress the economic aspects of Roosevelt's interventionist spirit. Under Taft's foreign policy (called dollar diplomacy) U.S. firms were encouraged to increase investments in countries bordering the Caribbean in the hope that the American economic presence would ensure political stability there. President Wilson went a step further, seeking not simply to maintain order but to advance democracy and self-rule. He sent troops into Haiti and into the Dominican Republic to put an end to the chaos of revolution, making both virtual protectorates of the United States. With Nicaragua he achieved the same end by diplomacy. In hope of tumbling the Mexican dictator Victoriano Huerta, Wilson sent troops to occupy the Mexican port city of Veracruz and keep from Huerta its import revenues. The Mexicans were deeply offended, and Wilson withdrew American forces. The bloody civil war that racked Mexico until 1920 sent the first large migration of Mexicans, perhaps a million people, into the United States (see CHICANO).

After the outbreak of World War I in August 1914, Wilson sought vainly to bring peace. In early 1917, however, Germany's unrestricted use of submarine attacks against neutral as well as Allied shipping inflamed American opinion for war (see LUSITANIA). Wilson decided that if the United States was to have any hope of influencing world affairs, it was imperative that it enter the war and fight to protect democracy against what he called German autocracy.

America's entry (April 1917) into the war was the cli-

Army recruits march out of an armory en route to training camp during World War I. The United States entered the war on Apr. 6, 1917, with an army of 200,000 men. By the end of the conflict this number had expanded to 4 million.

Members of the Equal Suffrage League of St. Louis, Mo., demonstrate for their cause. Although the suffrage movement began decades earlier, nationwide suffrage for women did not become a reality until 1920, when the 19th Amendment was ratified.

max of the Progressive Era: Wilson's aim was the extension of democracy and the creation of a just world order. In January 1918 he issued his FOURTEEN POINTS as a proposed basis for peace. The addition of more than a million American troops to the Allied armies turned the balance against the Germans in 1918, and an armistice on November 11 ended the war. At the PARIS PEACE CONFERENCE, however, Wilson failed in much of his program, for the other Allies were not interested in a "peace without victory." He had even less success at home. The Senate refused to accept the peace treaty he brought them or to allow the United States to join the LEAGUE OF NATIONS he had sought to establish.

The United States Turns Inward: The 1920s and 1930s

After its participation in the conflagration then known as the Great War, the American nation was ready to turn inward and concentrate on domestic affairs.

The 1920s: Decade of Optimism. By the 1920s innovative forces thrusting into American life were creating a new way of living. The automobile produced mobility and a blurring of the traditional rural-urban split. The radio and motion pictures inaugurated a national culture, one built on new, urban values. In 1920 the U.S. census showed, for the first time, that a majority of Americans lived in cities of 2,500 people or more. The 19th Amendment (1920) gave women the vote in national politics and symbolized their persistence in efforts to break out of old patterns of domesticity.

Traditional WASP (white, Anglo-Saxon Protestant) America fought the new ways. The adoption of PROHIBITION in 1919 (with ratification of the 18th Amendment) had been a victory of Yankee moral values over those of immigrants, but now many of the great cities practically ignored the measure. The Russian Revolution of 1917 sent a "Red Scare" shivering through the country in 1919–20; suspicion centered on labor unions as alleged instru-

ments of Moscow. The KU KLUX KLAN, stronger in the Northern Republican countryside than in the South, attacked the so-called New Negro, who returned from the fighting in France with a new sense of personal dignity (the HARLEM RENAISSANCE expressed this spirit through the arts), and the millions of Roman Catholics and Jews who had been flooding into the country since the 1890s. The Immigration Law of 1924 established a quota system that discriminated against all groups except northern and western Europeans.

Three Republican presidents occupied the White House during the 1920s. Warren G. HARDING, a conservative, was swept into office by a landslide victory in 1920. He proved an inept president, and his administration was racked by scandals, including that of TEAPOT DOME. Calvin COOLIDGE, who succeeded to the office on Harding's death (1923), worshiped business as much as he detested government. Herbert HOOVER, an engineer,

During a rustic outing Thomas Edison (left) poses with three other notable Americans, naturalist John Burroughs and Henry Ford, the automobile manufacturer (seated on water wheel), and Harvey Firestone (right), founder of the world's largest rubber company.

brought to the presidency (1929–33) a deep faith in the essential soundness of capitalism, which to him represented the fullest expression of individualism.

The 1930s: Decade of Depression. The stock-market crash of October 1929 initiated a long economic decline that accelerated into a world catastrophe, the DEPRESSION OF THE 1930s. By 1933, 14 million Americans were unemployed, industrial production was down to one-third of its 1929 level, and national income had dropped by more than half. In the presence of deep national despair, Democratic challenger Franklin D. ROOSEVELT easily defeated Hoover in the 1932 presidential election. After his inauguration, the NEW DEAL exploded in a whirlwind of legislation.

A new era commenced in American history. The federal government under Roosevelt experienced a vast expansion in its authority, especially over the economy. Roosevelt had a strong sense of community; he distrusted unchecked individualism and sympathized with suffering people. He nourished, however, no brooding rancor against the U.S. system. He sought to save capitalism, not supplant it.

Recovery was Roosevelt's first task. In the First New Deal (1933–35) he attempted to muster a spirit of emergency and rally all interests behind a common effort in which something was provided for everyone. Excessive competition and production were blamed for the collapse. Therefore, business proprietors and farmers were allowed to cooperate in establishing prices that would provide them with a profitable return and induce an upward turn (under the NATIONAL RECOVERY ADMINISTRATION and the AGRICULTURAL ADJUSTMENT ADMINISTRATION). By 1935, however, 10 million were still unemployed, and the U.S. Supreme Court was ruling such agencies unconstitutional.

The Second New Deal (1935–38) was more antibusiness and proconsumer. Roosevelt turned to vastly increased relief spending (under the WORKS PROGRESS ADMINISTRATION) to pump up consumer buying power. In 1933 he had decided to take the nation off the GOLD STANDARD. This monetary policy and the spending to aid the unemployed succeeded in moving the economy toward recovery before 1940, when the impact of war-induced

Margaret Bourke-White captured some of the irony of American life during the late 1930s in her photograph of black flood victims in a breadline beneath a patriotically idyllic billboard.

buying from Europe accelerated such movement.

The impact of the New Deal was perhaps strongest and most lasting in its basic reform measures. Farm prices were supported and farm plantings centrally planned; the money supply became a federal, not private, responsibility under a strengthened Federal Reserve Board; and stock exchanges were put under regulation of the SECURITIES AND EXCHANGE COMMISSION. The FEDERAL DEPOSIT INSURANCE CORPORATION insured bank deposits, and banking practices were closely supervised under the Banking Act of 1933; the NATIONAL LABOR RELATIONS ACT made relations between employers and employees a matter of public concern and control; and under the direction of agencies such as the TENNESSEE VALLEY AUTHORITY government facilities supplied electrical power to entire regions, providing a standard for private utilities.

For the majority of the population, New Deal legislation defined minimum standards of living: the Fair Labor Standards Act set MINIMUM WAGE and maximum-hour limitations and included a prohibition on child labor in interstate commerce; the Social Security Act (see SOCIAL SECURITY) made provisions for old-age and disability pensions, unemployment insurance, monthly payments to mothers living alone with dependent children, and direct assistance to the blind and crippled. In addition, the New Deal helped make it possible for organized unions to gain higher wages; in 1938 the Congress of Industrial Organizations (CIO) was formed; members were organized by industry rather than by craft.

Meanwhile, totalitarian movements abroad were inducing world crisis. Congress, mirroring public opinion, had grown disenchanted with the U.S. entry into World War I. This spirit of isolationism led to the passage (1935–37) of a series of neutrality acts that Congress hoped would prevent involvements like those of 1914–17.

A World Power

The spirit of isolationism eroded steadily as Americans

A painting (c.1934) by Ben Shahn lampoons the actions of bootleggers who defied the 18th Amendment, which prohibited the sale of alcoholic beverages in the United States. (Museum of the City of New York.)

Oily fumes from burning battleships fill the air after Japan's attack (Dec. 7, 1941) on the U.S. naval base at Pearl Harbor, Hawaii. The raid, which crippled the U.S. Pacific fleet, precipitated U.S. entry into World War II.

U.S. troops wade ashore in a dramatic photograph taken during the Allied landings on the Normandy beaches on June 6, 1944. This invasion of German-held France constituted the largest amphibious operation in history.

watched the aggressive moves of Adolf Hitler and his allies. President Roosevelt and the American people finally concluded that the United States could not survive as a nation, nor could Western civilization endure, if Hitler and fascism gained dominance over Europe. During the world war that followed, the United States became a major world power.

Total War: 1941–45. In September 1940, Congress established the first peacetime draft in American history, and 6 months later it authorized Roosevelt to transfer munitions to Great Britain, now standing practically alone against Hitler, by a procedure called LEND-LEASE. On Dec. 7, 1941, the Japanese reacted to stiffening American diplomacy against its expansion into Southeast Asia by attacking the U.S. fleet at PEARL HARBOR in the Hawaiian Islands. In this one stroke Japan ended American isolationist sentiment, forced the United States into World War II, and unified the American people as never before in total war.

The first American military decision was to concentrate on defeating Hitler while fighting a holding action in the Pacific. The next was to form an alliance with Great Britain so close that even military commands were jointly staffed. The year 1942 was devoted to halting, after many defeats, the outward spread of Japanese power and to keeping Hitler's forces from overwhelming America's British and Soviet allies. By May 1943, American and British forces had defeated the German armies in North Africa.

In 2 months the Allies were fighting the Germans in Sicily and Italy; at the same time U.S. forces in the Pacific were pushing in toward the Japanese home islands by means of an island-hopping offensive. On the long Russian front, German armies were being defeated and pushed back toward their borders. In June 1944 a huge Allied force landed on the French coast, an invasion preceded by 2 years of intense day-and-night bombing of Germany by British and American aircraft. By August 1944, Paris was recaptured. On Apr. 30, 1945, Hitler committed suicide. Peace in Europe followed shortly.

The Pacific war continued, the Japanese home islands being rendered practically defenseless by July 1945. American aerial attacks burned out city after city. In April, Harry S. TRUMAN had succeeded to the presidency on Roosevelt's death. Advised that the alternative would be an invasion in which multitudes would perish, including many thousands of young Americans, he authorized use of the recently tested atomic bomb. On August 6 the city of Hiroshima was obliterated; on August 9 the same fate came to Nagasaki. Within a week, a cease-fire was achieved.

The political shape of the postwar world was set at the YALTA CONFERENCE (February 1945) among Roosevelt, Joseph Stalin, and Winston Churchill. Soviet occupation of

Allied leaders (seated, left to right) *Churchill, Roosevelt, and Stalin pose for a portrait during their consultations at Yalta (February 1945). The decisions reached at the Yalta Conference largely shaped the geopolitics of the postwar era.*

Eastern European countries overrun by the Red Army was accepted, in return for a pledge to allow democratic governments to rise within them. Soviet and Allied occupation zones in Germany were established, with Berlin, deep in the Soviet zone, to be jointly administered. In return for Soviet assistance in the invasion of Japan (which was eventually not needed), it was agreed that certain possessions in the Far East and rights in Manchuria, lost to the Japanese long before, would be restored to the USSR. Soon it was clear that the kind of democratic government envisioned by the Americans was not going to be allowed in the Eastern European countries under Soviet control, nor, as the Soviets pointed out, was the United States ready to admit the Soviets to any role in the occupation and government of Japan, whose occupation was under the command of Gen. Douglas MACARTHUR.

Cold-War Years. The breach widened steadily. Americans became convinced that the Soviets were seeking to communize not only the Soviet-occupied countries, but also Turkey, Greece, and Western Europe. In February 1946, Stalin declared in Moscow that there could never be a lasting peace with capitalism. Shortly thereafter, Churchill warned of the "iron curtain" that had descended across the middle of Europe. The COLD WAR had begun.

In March 1947, Truman asked Congress for funds to shore up Turkey and Greece, both under Soviet pressure, and announced the Truman Doctrine: that "it must be the policy of the United States to support free peoples who are resisting attempted subjugation by armed minorities or by outside pressures." Then the MARSHALL PLAN (named for George C. MARSHALL, U.S. chief of staff during the war and at this time secretary of state), approved by Congress in April 1948, sent $12 billion to the devastated countries of Europe to help them rebuild and fend off communism.

True to its Democratic tradition, the Truman administration stressed multilateral diplomacy; that is, the building of an international order based on joint decision making. Nationalism, it was believed, must be tamed. The United Nations received strong American support. Meanwhile, the United States continued the drive toward a lowering of world tariffs (begun in the 1930s). In 1947 in the GENERAL AGREEMENT ON TARIFFS AND TRADE, 23 nations participated in an extensive mutual lowering of trade barriers. In 1948, at American initiative, the ORGANIZATION OF AMERICAN STATES was established to provide a regional multilateral consultative body in the Western Hemisphere. Within Europe, the Common Market emerged.

Toward the USSR, the basic American policy was that known as containment: building "situations of strength" around its vast perimeter to prevent the outward spread of communism. A series of East-West crises, most dramatically the Berlin Blockade of 1948–49, led to the creation (April 1949) of the NORTH ATLANTIC TREATY ORGANIZATION. The NATO alliance sought to link the United States militarily to Western Europe (including Greece and Turkey) by making an attack against one member an attack against all. As Europe recovered its prosperity, the focus of East-West confrontation shifted to Asia, where the British, French, and Dutch empires were collapsing and the Communist revolution in China was moving toward its victory (October 1949). In June 1950 the North Korean army invaded South Korea. The United Nations Security Council (which the Soviets were then boycotting) called on UN members jointly to repel this attack. Shortly afterward, a multinational force under Gen. Douglas MacArthur was battling to turn back North Korean forces in the KOREAN WAR. As the UN army swept northward to the Manchurian border, Chinese forces flooded southward to resist them, and a long, bloody seesaw war ensued. An armistice was not signed until July 1953, following 150,000 American casualties and millions of deaths among the Koreans and Chinese.

Domestic Developments during the Truman Years. In 1945, President Truman called on Congress to launch another program of domestic reform, but the nation was indifferent. It was riding a wave of affluence such as it had never dreamed of in the past. Tens of millions of people found themselves moving upward into a middle-class way of life. What fascinated Americans was the so-called baby boom—a huge increase in the birthrate (the population was at 150 million by 1950 and 179 million by 1960)—and the need to house new families and teach their children.

In the presence of rapidly rising inflation, labor unions called thousands of strikes, leading in 1948 to passage of the Taft-Hartley Act (see LABOR-MANAGEMENT RELATIONS ACT), which somewhat limited the powers of unions. In 1955 merger negotiations were completed for the formation of the AMERICAN FEDERATION OF LABOR AND CONGRESS OF INDUSTRIAL ORGANIZATIONS (AFL-CIO); more than 85 percent of all union members were now in one organization.

Fears that Russian communism was taking over the entire world grew pervasive. Soviet spy rings were discovered in the United States, Canada, and Great Britain. In 1948–50 a trial for perjury led to the conviction of a former State Department official, Alger HISS, accused of passing secrets to the Soviets. In 1950 a Soviet spy ring was uncovered in the Los Alamos atomic installation. These events, together with the explosion (1949) of a Soviet atomic bomb and the victory (1949) of the Communists in China, prompted a widespread conviction that subversive conspiracies within the American government were leading toward Soviet triumph.

In February 1950, Republican Senator Joseph R. McCARTHY of Wisconsin began a 4-year national crisis, during which he insisted repeatedly that he had direct evidence of such conspiracies in the federal government, even in the army. The entire country seemed swept up in a hysteria in which anyone left of center was attacked as a subversive. A program to root out alleged security risks in the national government destroyed the State Department's corps of experts on Far Eastern and Soviet affairs. The Truman administration's practice of foreign policy was brought practically to a halt. In 1952, Dwight D. EISENHOWER, nationally revered supreme commander in Europe during World War II, was elected president (1953–61) on the Republican ticket, but soon McCarthy was attacking him as well for running a "weak, immoral, and cowardly" foreign policy. In 1954 a long and dramatic series of

Sen. Joseph R. McCarthy, who vaulted into prominence through his crusade against alleged Communists in government, appears during the Army-McCarthy hearings in 1954.

uals for their beliefs or associations.

No decision of the Warren Court was more historic than that in Brown v. Board of Education of Topeka, Kansas (1954), which ruled unanimously that racial segregation in the public schools was unconstitutional. Other decisions struck down segregation in all public facilities and in elections and marriage laws. The separate-but-equal principle was cast aside, and the Second Reconstruction could get under way. Now African Americans could charge that the statutory discrimination that tied them down and kept them in a secondary caste was illegal, a fact that added enormous moral weight to their fight against segregation.

Eisenhower's foreign policy, under Secretary of State John Foster Dulles, was more nationalist and unilateral than Truman's. American-dominated alliances ringed the Soviet and Chinese perimeters. Persistent recessions in the American economy hobbled the national growth rate while the Soviet and Western European economies surged dramatically. An aggressive Nikita Khrushchev, Soviet premier, trumpeted that communism would bury capitalism and boasted of Moscow's powerful intercontinental missiles while encouraging so-called wars of liberation in Southeast Asia and elsewhere.

congressional hearings, the first to be nationally televised, destroyed McCarthy's credibility. He was censured by the Senate, and a measure of national stability returned.

The Eisenhower Years. Eisenhower declared himself uninterested in repealing the New Deal, but he was socially and economically conservative, and his presidency saw the enactment of few reforms. His appointment of Earl Warren as chief justice of the Supreme Court, however, led to a Court that suddenly seized so bold and active a role in national life that many called it revolutionary. During Warren's long tenure (1953–69), the Court swept away the legal basis for racial discrimination; ruled that every person must be represented equally in state legislatures and in the U.S. House of Representatives; changed criminal-justice procedures by ensuring crucial rights to the accused; broadened the artist's right to publish works shocking to the general public; and in major ways limited the government's ability to penalize individ-

The United States since 1960: New Challenges to the American System

In the years following 1960, the cold war wound down, and attention focused on social and cultural rebellions at home. Involvement in a long war in Asia and scandals that reached into the White House severely shook the nation.

The Kennedy Years. The Democratic senator John F. Kennedy won the presidency in a narrow victory over Vice-President Richard M. Nixon in 1960. The charismatic Kennedy stimulated a startling burst of national enthusiasm and aroused high hopes among the young and the disadvantaged. Within 3 years his Peace Corps (see ACTION) sent about 10,000 Americans (mostly young people) abroad to work in 46 countries. He also proposed massive tariff cuts between the increasingly protectionist

Four men who served as presidents of the United States (left to right) John F. Kennedy, Lyndon B. Johnson, Dwight D. Eisenhower and Harry S. Truman, occupied the front pew during the funeral services for former Speaker of the House Sam Rayburn (November 1961), who served in that position longer than any other person in the nation's history.

Standing to attention as well as his suit permits, astronaut Edwin "Buzz" Aldrin salutes the U.S. flag as it waves over the lunar surface. Aldrin, copilot of the lunar lander on the epochal Apollo 11 mission (July 1969), became the second man to set foot on the Moon.

European Common Market and the world at large. (The so-called Kennedy Round of tariff negotiations concluded in 1967 with the largest and widest tariff cuts in modern history.) In June 1961, Kennedy gave the nation a common goal: to place an American on the Moon. On July 20, 1969, the APOLLO PROGRAM succeeded in landing astronauts on the Moon.

Kennedy blundered into a major defeat within 3 months of entering the White House. He kept in motion a plan sponsored by the CENTRAL INTELLIGENCE AGENCY (CIA) and begun by the Eisenhower administration to land an invasion force in Cuba, which under Fidel Castro had become a Communist state and a Soviet state. The BAY OF PIGS INVASION failed in April 1961, utterly and completely. In October 1962, Kennedy discovered that the Soviets were rapidly building missile emplacements in Cuba. Surrounding the island with a naval blockade, he induced the Soviets to desist and dismantle the sites. The relieved world discovered that, when pushed to the crisis point, the two major powers could stop short of nuclear war. This CUBAN MISSILE CRISIS effectively ended the cold war.

The atomic bomb now seemed defused, and Moscow seemed ready to negotiate on crucial issues. A new and more relaxed relationship developed slowly into the U.S.-Soviet détente that emerged in the late 1960s and persisted through the 1970s. A test-ban treaty, the Moscow Agreement (see ARMS CONTROL), signed in October 1963 symbolized the opening of the new relationship.

In this new environment of security, American culture broke loose into multiplying swift changes. The media were filled with discussions of the rapidly changing styles of dress and behavior among the young; of the "new woman" (or the "liberated woman," as she became known); of new sexual practices and attitudes and new life-styles.

On Nov. 22, 1963, the Kennedy presidency came to an end with his assassination. Vice-President Lyndon B. JOHNSON was sworn in as his successor.

The Struggle for Civil Rights. Since the 1950s, the Reverend Martin Luther KING Jr., and others had been leading the fight against segregationist practices. In 1957, Congress enacted the first civil rights law since 1875, prohibiting interference with African-Americans' right to vote. In 1962, President Kenndy asked Congress to enact a law to guarantee equal access to all public accommodations, forbid discrimination in any state program receiving federal aid, and outlaw discrimination in employment and voting. After Kennedy's death, President Johnson prodded Congress into enacting (August 1965) a voting-rights bill that eliminated all qualifying tests for registration that had as their objective limiting the right to vote to whites.

The civil rights phase of the black revolution had reached its legislative and judicial summit. Then, from 1964 to 1968, more than a hundred U.S. cities were swept by RACE RIOTS. In 1968 the nation swung rightward in its politics and chose as president Richard M. Nixon, who was not in favor of using federal power to aid the disadvantaged. Individual advancement, he believed, had to come by individual effort.

Fundamental changes continued nonetheless in relations between whites and blacks. Entrance requirements for schools and colleges were changed; hundreds of communities sought to work out equitable arrangements to end de facto segregation in the schools; graduate programs searched for African-American applicants; and integration in jobs and in the professions expanded. African Americans moved into the mainstream of the party system, and the daily impact of television helped make them, seen in shows and commercial advertisements, seem an integral part of a pluralistic nation.

Mexican Americans and Puerto Ricans were also becoming more prominent in American life. Reaching the level of 9 million by the 1960s, Hispanic Americans had become the second largest ethnic minority and were as-

Martin Luther King, Jr. (front row, second from right) leads his supporters on the "freedom march" from Selma to Montgomery, Ala., in 1965. The march was part of a drive to register black voters throughout the South.

serting their right to equitable treatment in politics, in culture, and in economic affairs.

Kennedy-Johnson Legislative Accomplishments. In his first 3 months of office, Kennedy sent 39 messages and letters to Congress asking for reform legislation—messages dealing with health care, education, housing and community development, civil rights, transportation, and many other areas. His narrow margin of victory in 1960, however, had not seemed a mandate for change, and an entrenched coalition of Republicans and conservative Southern Democrats in Congress had prevented the achievement of many of Kennedy's legislative goals by the time of his death. Johnson, who in 1964 won an enormous victory over the Republican presidential candidate, Barry GOLDWATER, and carried on his coattails a large Democratic congressional majority, proceeded with consummate political skill to enact this broad program.

Johnson launched his WAR ON POVERTY, which focused on children and young people, providing them with better education and remedial training, and Congress created a domestic peace corps, Volunteers in Service to America (VISTA). Huge sums went to the states for education. MEDICARE was enacted in 1965, providing millions of elderly Americans with a kind of security from the costs of illness that they had never known before. The Economic Development Administration moved into depressed areas, such as Appalachia. Billions were appropriated for urban redevelopment and public housing.

At War in Vietnam. The VIETNAM WAR, however, destroyed the Johnson presidency. The United States had been the protector of South Vietnam since 1954, when the Geneva Conference had divided Vietnam into a Communist North and a pro-Western South. By 1961 an internal revolution had brought the South Vietnamese regime to the point of toppling. President Kennedy sent in 15,000 military advisors and large supplies of munitions. By 1964 it

A U.S. soldier looks on as a Vietnamese mother cradles her child after learning of her husband's death. The Vietnam War, which took the lives of about 1.7 million people, including 50,000 Americans, and devastated Vietnam, deeply divided the people of the United States.

was clear that a collapse was again impending. In April 1965, Johnson began sending U.S. ground troops to Vietnam, the total reaching nearly 550,000 in early 1969. Still victory eluded the United States. Responding to mass public protests that put the nation in a state of near-insurrection—and in recognition of fruitless American casualties, which in 1967 passed 100,000—Johnson decided in March 1968 to begin deescalation. At the same time, he announced that he would not run for reelection.

Foreign Policy under Nixon. When Richard M. Nixon became president in 1969, he profoundly changed U.S. foreign policy. He announced his "Vietnamization" policy, which meant a slow withdrawal of U.S. forces and a heavy building up of the South Vietnamese army. In the 3 years 1969–71, 15,000 more Americans nonetheless died fighting in Vietnam. In April 1970, Nixon launched a huge invasion of Cambodia in a vain attempt to clear out Communist "sanctuaries."

Then, most dramatically, he deflected world attention by ending the long American quarantine of Communist China, visiting Beijing in February 1972 for general discussions on all matters of mutual concern—a move that led to the establishment (1979) of diplomatic relations.

In May 1972, Nixon became the first U.S. president to consult with Soviet leaders in Moscow, leaving with major agreements relating to trade, cooperation in space programs and other fields of technology, cultural exchanges, and many other areas. In November he won a landslide victory over the Democratic nominee, Sen. George McGovern. The following January, Nixon announced a successful end to the Vietnamese negotiations: a cease-fire was established and an exchange of prisoners provided for. It would be another 2 years, however, before all Americans were evacuated from Vietnam, with a final American death toll of 58,000.

Watergate. Before the year 1973 was out, Nixon's administration had fallen into the gravest scandal in U.S. history. By March 1974 the stunning events of the WATERGATE crisis and associated villainies had led to the resignation of more than a dozen high officials—including the vice-president, Spiro T. AGNEW (for the acceptance of graft)—and the indictment or conviction of many others. Their criminal acts included burglary, forgery, illegal wiretapping and electronic surveillance, perjury, obstruction of justice, bribery, and many other offenses.

The crisis began on June 17, 1972, when five members of Nixon's Special Investigations Unit (created without congressional authorization) were arrested while burglarizing the national Democratic party offices in the Watergate office-and-apartment complex in Washington, D.C. A frantic effort then began, urged on by the president, to cover up links between the Watergate burglars and the executive branch. Congressional investigations, however, uncovered evidence of millions of dollars jammed into White House office safes and sluiced about from hand to hand to finance shady dealings, of elaborate procedures for covering tracks and destroying papers, and of tapes recording the president's conversations with his aides.

On July 24, 1974, the Supreme Court ordered Nixon to deliver his Oval Office tapes to Congress. This order, in

On Apr. 29, 1974, President Nixon announced his release to the House Judiciary Committee of edited transcripts of his taped conversations relating to the Watergate scandal. Three months later he was forced to surrender the tapes themselves, and on Aug. 9, 1974, he resigned.

turn, led to the revelation that he had directly approved the cover-up. Informed by Republican congressional leaders of his certain conviction in forthcoming impeachment proceedings, Richard Nixon resigned the presidency on Aug. 9, 1974. Gerald R. FORD, who had been appointed vice-president after Agnew's resignation, became president.

The Third Century Begins. As the nation approached its bicentennial anniversary, its cities found themselves in grave difficulties: its nonwhite peoples still lagged far behind the whites in income and opportunity; unemployment seemed fixed at a level of more than 6 percent, which, for minorities and the young, translated into much higher figures; and inflation threatened to erode the buying power of everyone in the country.

Most of these problems continued to plague the American nation during the presidency (1977–81) of Jimmy CARTER, Democrat of Georgia, who defeated Ford in the 1976 election. Carter brought to the presidency an informality and sense of piety. He arranged negotiations for an Egyptian-Israeli peace treaty (signed in 1979) and guided the Panama Canal treaty through narrow Senate approval (1978). Carter also had to deal with shortages of petroleum that threatened to bring the energy-hungry U.S. economy to a standstill, with soaring inflation rates, with the taking (1979) of U.S. hostages by Iranian militants (see IRANIAN HOSTAGE CRISIS), and with an international crisis precipitated by Soviet intervention (1979) in Afghanistan. His popularity waned as problems remained unsolved, and in 1980 the voters turned overwhelmingly to the conservative Republican candidate, Ronald REAGAN.

The Reagan Era. The release of the U.S. hostages in Iran on the same day as Reagan's inauguration launched the new administration on a wave of euphoria. Reagan persuaded the Congress to cut government spending for welfare, increase outlays for defense, reduce taxes, and deregulate private enterprise. His "supply side" economic policy (dubbed "Reaganomics" by the media) anticipated that lower taxes and a freer market would stimulate investment and that a prosperous, expanding economy would increase employment, reduce inflation, and provide enough government revenue to eliminate future budget deficits.

The "Reagan Revolution" helped cut inflation, but unemployment rose dramatically, and the United States experienced its worst recession since the 1930s. The annual federal deficit soared to $117 billion, almost twice as high as it had ever been. Beginning in 1983, however, the economy rebounded sharply, and 11 million new jobs were created. The Reagan recovery did little for rural America or for the declining industrial regions of the Midwest. Nearly 33 million Americans—one out of every seven—were reported as living below the poverty line.

A staunch anti-communist, Reagan set out to fight communism in Central America and the Caribbean. To quash a Communist revolt in El Salvador, Reagan committed military advisors and financial aid to the Salvadoran government. Determined to oust Nicaragua's pro-Communist Sandinista government, he gave covert aid to antigovernment rebels—known as the contras—in defiance of a congressional ban on such aid. In 1983 he used military force to topple a pro-Cuban regime on the Caribbean island of Grenada.

Reagan and his running mate, George Bush, easily defeated their Democratic opponents, Walter MONDALE and Geraldine FERRARO, in 1984, but the Democrats maintained control of Congress. Repeated failure by the president and Congress to agree on budget reductions kept the deficit at record levels. Disputes over the control of trade policy also worsened the imbalance of imports over exports, which rose to $161 billion in 1987.

At the end of Reagan's tenure the Republican party could boast that Reagan's administration had helped create 16.5 million new jobs, bring down the unemployment

An inactive steel mill in Youngstown, Ohio, exemplifies the decline of the smokestack industries. The United States has made the transition to a "postindustrial" economy, one based increasingly on the service sectors.

The Iran-contra affair, involving secret arms sales to Iran and the diversion of profits to Nicaraguan "contra" rebels, led to joint televised hearings by U.S. House and Senate committees during the summer of 1987. A chief witness was Lt. Col. Oliver North (left).

rate to a 17-year low, cut double-digit inflation to about 4%, and raise the gross national product by one-third. Democrats, on the other hand, could criticize "Reaganomics" for promoting prosperity at the expense of the poor and the nation's future well-being. The number of people below the poverty line rose by 8 million. By borrowing rather than taxing to rearm, Reagan mortgaged the financial future. Moreover, persistent trade and budget deficits made the United States a debtor nation for the first time since 1914.

A major scandal of Reagan's second term was the IRAN-CONTRA AFFAIR, in which national security advisor John M. Poindexter, marine lieutenant colonel Oliver North, and

President Ronald Reagan (left) greets Soviet leader Mikhail Gorbachev at the White House in December 1987. The two leaders signed a historic arms-control measure that eliminated an entire class of nuclear weapons, intermediate-range missiles.

other administration officials were involved in a secret scheme to sell arms to Iran, diverting some of the proceeds to the contra rebels in Nicaragua. Investigation of this affair by Congress in 1987 damaged the administration's image.

Ironically, developments in foreign affairs during Ronald Reagan's second term led this most anti-Communist of presidents into a new, harmonious relationship with the Soviet Union and to sign the first superpower treaty that actually reduced nuclear armaments. He and Soviet leader Mikhail Gorbachev held four summit meetings.

The Bush Administration. The remarkable reduction in cold-war tensions, combined with the promise of continued prosperity with no increase in taxes, carried Republicans George BUSH and Dan QUAYLE to victory over Democratic candidates Michael DUKAKIS and Lloyd BENTSEN in 1988. Lacking his predecessor's strong personal following and facing a Democratic-controlled Congress, Bush sought to govern in a more moderate, middle-of-the-road way than Reagan. The rapid demise of communism in Eastern Europe in 1989–90 and upheaval in the USSR in 1991 provided him an opportunity to ease international tensions and to reclaim U.S. primacy in world affairs. Bush intervened militarily in Panama in 1989 to overthrow its president, Manuel Noriega. In mid-1990, responding to Iraq's invasion and annexation of Kuwait, he ordered more than 400,000 U.S. troops to the Persian Gulf region to defend Saudi Arabia. When Iraqi troops refused to withdraw from Kuwait in January 1991, he authorized a massive bombing attack, and then ground assault, on Iraq and its forces in Kuwait, and won a swift victory. (See GULF WAR.)

Decisive in acting abroad, Bush failed at home to adequately address a persistent recession starting in 1990. That year, despite the recession, he and congressional leaders agreed to a deficit-reduction package that raised federal taxes, thereby breaking his "no new taxes" campaign pledge of 1988. A conservative revolt led by political columnist Pat Buchanan moved Bush to the right, and with the economy still stagnant, many moderates deserted him in his 1992 reelection bid. Democrat Bill CLINTON, apparently unhurt by the independent candidacy of H. Ross PEROT, campaigned on a theme of change and won a solid victory.

See also: AMERICAN ART AND ARCHITECTURE; AMERICAN LITERATURE; AMERICAN MUSIC; UNITED STATES.

United States Air Force Academy The United States Air Force Academy, founded in 1954 near Colorado Springs, Colo., educates and trains men and women for service in the U.S. Air Force. Admission is by congressional appointment. Graduates receive the bachelor of science degree and commissions as second lieutenants in the U.S. Air Force. The government pays for tuition and room and board and also pays students a basic salary.

United States Coast Guard Academy The United States Coast Guard Academy educates and trains men and women for duty in the U.S. Coast Guard, a service within the Department of Transportation and, in wartime, a highly specialized part of the U.S. Navy. The academy, founded in 1876, is in New London, Conn. Admission to the academy is by competition and not by congressional appointment. Graduates receive the bachelor of science degree and appointments as ensigns in the U.S. Coast Guard. They must serve at least 5 years in the Coast Guard, whose functions include port safety, marine environmental protection, icebreaking, and enforcement of maritime laws.

United States Geological Survey

The United States Geological Survey is a federal agency charged with the classification of public lands, the preparation of geologic and topographic maps, and the investigation of mineral resources in the United States. The Geological Survey is within the Department of the Interior and is primarily a research and fact-finding agency.

Early in the 19th century geology was incidental to federal expeditions because federally sponsored science, a form of public works, raised constitutional questions. Congress eventually followed foreign and state examples, however, and authorized (beginning in 1867) four western surveys with geology as their main purpose. The federal surveys, supervised by the War and Interior departments, were Clarence King's Geological Exploration of the 40th Parallel, Ferdinand Hayden's Geological and Geographical Survey of the Territories, John Wesley POWELL's Geographical and Geological Survey of the Rocky Mountain Region, and George M. Wheeler's Geographical Survey West of the 100th Meridian.

After rivalry developed among the civilian directors of the western surveys, Congress accepted the recommendation of the National Academy of Sciences that the functions of the several surveys be consolidated into one permanent agency. President Rutherford B. Hayes signed the bill establishing (1879) the Geological Survey. A legal interpretation of the enabling act restricted the agency to the West until 1882, when Congress extended the scope of its work to the eastern states. In recent years, the Geological Survey has tended to concentrate on natural resources and environmental problems.

United States Merchant Marine Academy

The United States Merchant Marine Academy, at Kings Point, N.Y., trains men and women to serve in the U.S. Merchant Marine industry and for inactive duty as ensigns in the U.S. Naval Reserve. The academy, founded in 1943 and operated by the Maritime Administration, requires students (midshipmen) to be nominated for admittance. The government provides tuition, room and board, and a basic salary to students, who spend some time at sea. Graduates earn the bachelor of science degree and the Merchant Marine license as a third mate or a third assistant engineer and must serve in the naval reserve for 6 years.

United States Military Academy

The United States Military Academy, at West Point, N.Y., trains and educates the future officers of the regular U.S. Army. Since 1976, women have been admitted to the academy, and the first women cadets graduated in 1980. Admission to the academy, known as West Point, is by nomination by specified official sources (the vice-president, senators, and U.S. representatives), who are entitled to nominate more candidates than will ultimately be accepted. Students from the U.S. dependencies and the District of Columbia may be nominated. Children of deceased or disabled veterans and of career military personnel of any of the armed forces are also eligible for appointment to West Point. Limited numbers of cadets may be from the other American republics and the Philippines. They may not, however, receive a commission in the U.S. Army upon graduation.

The 4-year program of study leads to the bachelor of science degree. Graduates, who receive commissions as second lieutenants, must serve in the U.S. Army for 5 years. The government provides tuition, room, and board. Cadets also receive one-half of a second lieutenant's basic pay.

The academy was established in 1802 in a Hudson River fortress dating from the American Revolution. The entire post is now a national monument. The school was founded to free American soldiers from wartime reliance on foreign military engineers, artillerymen, and drillmasters. Colonel Sylvanus Thayer, superintendent from 1817 to 1833, established West Point's tradition of academic excellence by insisting on regular study habits and a well-qualified faculty and by requiring every cadet to pass every course or make up his failure. During the first half of the 19th century, West Point emphasized civil engineering, and for its first few decades it was the best civil engineering school in the country.

Since 1900 and especially since the end of World War

Cadets at the U.S. Military Academy practice drill techniques on the parade grounds. The academy is located at West Point, a military post on the Hudson River in New York State that dates back to 1778.

II, more emphasis has been placed on a balanced curriculum that includes the social sciences, the humanities, and ethics, and on military leadership and management. Although the corps of cadets was almost doubled in 1964, the U.S. Military Academy is still considered to be a small school with small classes and with an intensive academic, physical, and military training curriculum.

United States Naval Academy The United States Naval Academy, at Annapolis, Md., educates and trains men and women for service in the U.S. Navy or Marine Corps. Admission to the academy, known as Annapolis, is by nomination by the president, vice-president, senators, U.S. representatives, and the secretary of the navy. Students from the U.S. dependencies and the District of Columbia may be nominated. Children of deceased or disabled veterans, of military personnel missing in action, and of prisoners of war are eligible for nomination to Annapolis. Qualified children of Medal of Honor recipients are admitted. Up to 40 cadets from foreign countries may be designated by the U.S. secretary of defense. The list of eligible countries changes annually. These cadets may not receive a commission in the U.S. Navy or Marine Corps.

The 4-year program of study leads to the bachelor of science degree. Graduates, who receive commissions as second lieutenants in the marine corps or as ensigns in the navy, must serve for 5 years. The government provides tuition and room and board. Cadets also receive a basic pay out of which other needs are paid. The academy, a U.S. National Historic Site, was founded as the Naval School in 1845 at Fort Severn in Annapolis to replace

Assembled midshipmen (students) stand at parade rest during an awards ceremony at the U.S. Naval Academy in Annapolis, Md.

training by naval schoolmasters and other officers on warships on active service. Its founder was Secretary of the Navy George BANCROFT, a noted historian. The course sandwiched 3 years of sea duty between an entering and a final year on shore. Since 1850, when the school was reorganized and given its present name, it has had a 4-year curriculum similar to that of the U.S. Military Academy, with two summer cruises for intensive practical training. The curriculum includes practical engineering, science, and leadership courses of particular concern to the U.S. Navy and required and elective courses in the sciences and liberal arts. Unlike the military and air force academies, Annapolis has both a tenured civilian and a military faculty.

United States Naval Observatory The United States Naval Observatory, established in 1842 at Washington, D.C., as an outgrowth of the Navy Department's Depot of Charts and Instruments, has responsibilities in the broad areas of navigation, time, and fundamental celestial reference systems. Because of these duties it is one of the few institutions in the world to undertake astrometry—the determination, through continual observations, of the positions and motions of the Sun, the Moon, the planets, and principal stars. The data collected form the basis of the Nautical Almanac and ephemeris time.

At the Washington site, 6-in (15-cm) and 7-in (18-cm) transit circles, specially designed telescopes that make observations only as an object crosses the meridian, are used to measure accurate positions of celestial bodies. Two photographic zenith tubes determine mean solar time, and many ATOMIC CLOCKS determine atomic time. The observatory's master clock establishes standard time for the United States. A 61-in (155-cm) astrometric reflector in Flagstaff, Ariz., measures distances of faint nearby stars, and a 40-in (102-cm) Ritchey Chretien reflector, also at Flagstaff, observes comets and minor planets. The 26-in (66-cm) refractor, still in operation in Washington, was the instrument Asaph Hall used to discover the two moons of Mars in 1877.

United States outlying territories The United States exercises sovereignty over 12 outlying territories. Since 1959, when Alaska and Hawaii achieved statehood, the United States has had no incorporated territories—those in which the U.S. Constitution applies. Unincorporated territories, or possessions, can be either organized or unorganized. Organized territories are governed by congressional legislation functioning much as a state constitution. Unorganized territories have no such bodies of legislation. GUAM and the U.S. VIRGIN ISLANDS are organized territories. Unorganized territories are AMERICAN SAMOA; MIDWAY; WAKE ISLAND; Howland, Baker, and Jarvis islands; Johnston Atoll; Kingman Reef; Navassa Island; and Palmyra Island.

U.S. commonwealth status offers more local autonomy than that afforded a possession. The government functions under a constitution adopted by local residents following

U.S. congressional enabling legislation. PUERTO RICO and the Northern MARIANA ISLANDS are U.S. commonwealths.

The United States also administered the Trust Territory of the PACIFIC ISLANDS under trusteeship granted by the United Nations (see TRUST TERRITORY). These islands were formerly under the mandate system of the League of Nations. In 1986 the Northern Mariana Islands became a U.S. commonwealth, and the MARSHALL ISLANDS and the Federated States of MICRONESIA (YAP, Kosrae, Ponape, and Truk islands) gained limited independence in free association with the United States, which provides economic assistance and remains responsible for their defense. The UN Trusteeship Council approved a similar compact of free association for PALAU in 1988, despite a continuing dispute between Palau and the United States over the compact's interpretation.

Of the U.S. territories, Baker and Howland islands, Johnston Atoll, and Navassa Island were claimed under the Guano Islands Act of 1856. The act enables the United States to assume possession of an unoccupied, unclaimed area to extract GUANO deposits for fertilizer. American Samoa was acquired through agreements with the islands' residents. Uninhabited Kingman Reef was annexed, as were Midway and Wake islands. Palmyra Island was annexed with Hawaii; Puerto Rico was ceded to the United States by Spain; and the U.S. Virgin Islands were purchased from Denmark.

United States Student Association

The United States Student Association, formed in 1978 by the merger of the U.S. National Student Association (1947) and the National Student Lobby (1971), is a confederation of 425 American college student governments. It is a lobbying organization for students, giving them a voice in the Department of Education, and acts as a clearinghouse for information on student concerns. Its headquarters is in Washington, D.C.

United States Trust Territory of the Pacific Islands   see PACIFIC ISLANDS, TRUST TERRITORY OF THE

United States Weather Bureau   see NATIONAL WEATHER SERVICE

United Steelworkers of America

The United Steelworkers of America (USWA) is a labor union made up of workers in the steel, aluminum, and other metal-refining industries. Its affiliation with the American Federation of Labor and Congress of Industrial Organizations (AFL-CIO) dates back to its origin as the Steel Workers Organizing Committee (SWOC) of the Committee for Industrial Organization. Organized in 1936 as an industrial union, the SWOC was aided by the growth in the demand for steel before and during World War II. In 1942 the constitution was rewritten giving the union its present name. Under President Philip Murray the USWA absorbed unionized aluminum workers and later, under I. W. Abel, workers in other metal, smelting, mining, and technical industries.

United Way of America   see FUND-RAISING

units, physical

Measurement systems have been developed as needed to describe and quantitate physical systems or experimental situations. Human civilizations early developed systems of measurement for areas of land, for amounts of water, food, and other materials, and for duration of time. In each case, the quantity to be measured is specified by giving its size in terms of a numerical relationship to another similar quantity. A reference quantity becomes a unit for this measurement when it is chosen to have a numerical value of unity, such as 1 year or 1 bushel.

Measurement systems, such as the metric system and the English system, can be based on a convenient and arbitrary selection of a limited number of independent units, chosen by convention. All other units can be related algebraically to this set of units. For example, there need not be a separate unit for speed; it can be expressed as distance divided by time. The International System of Units, or the SI (from the original *Système International d'Unités*; see METRIC SYSTEM), is based on seven fundamental units. It now forms the basis for both international commerce and communication in science and technology and is replacing the local system of measurement that had evolved within each country.

Base Units. All measurable physical quantities can be described in terms of a limited number of units, called base units. The metric system specifies seven quantities

PRESENT DEFINITION OF THE BASE UNITS OF THE SI

Unit of Length (meter):   The meter is the length of the path traveled by light in a vacuum during a time interval of 1/299,792,458 of a second.

Unit of Mass (kilogram):   The kilogram is equal to the mass of the international prototype of the kilogram.

Unit of Time (second):   The second is the duration of 9,192,631,770 periods of the radiation corresponding to the transition between the two hyperfine levels of the ground state of the cesium-133 atom.

Unit of Electric Current (ampere):   The ampere is that constant current which, if maintained in two straight parallel conductors of infinite lengths and of negligible circular cross section, placed 1 meter apart in vacuum, would produce between these conductors a force equal to 2×10^{-7} newton per meter of length.

Unit of Thermodynamic Temperature (kelvin):   The kelvin is the fraction 1/273.16 of the thermodynamic temperature of the triple point of water.

Unit of Amount of substance (mole):   The mole is the amount of substance of a system that contains as many elementary entities as there are atoms in 0.012 kilogram of carbon-12.

Unit of Luminous Intensity (candela):   The candela is the luminous intensity, in the perpendicular direction, of a surface of 1/600,000 square meter of a blackbody at the temperature of freezing platinum under a pressure of 101,325 newtons per square meter.

whose units of measurement are units of length, mass, time, electric current, thermodynamic temperature, amount of substance, and luminous intensity. Other units of measurement are called derived units and, in principle, can be formed by combining the base units. Certain of these derived units have been given names of their own. For example, the metric unit of force is the newton, derived from mass times acceleration (which itself is derived from distance divided by time squared).

Standards. To assure that measurements of identical objects would be the same wherever they are made, a set of physical standards is required. The unit of length, the meter, was defined in 1791 by the French National Assembly to be one ten-millionth of the length of the quadrant of the Earth's meridian, and its physical realization was the length of a sintered platinum-iridium bar maintained under standard atmospheric conditions in the Archives of the Republic in Paris. The meter has since been redefined in terms of the speed of light in vacuum. The unit of mass, the kilogram, is the mass of a cubic decimeter (0.001 cubic meter) of water at 4° C (39° F), the temperature of maximum density. It, too, is represented by a platinum-iridium body.

Customary Units. The system of units built around the common English units of pound, foot, and degree Fahrenheit for the units of mass, length, and temperature evolved in Europe through practical use over many centuries. In the United States, the modern system of English units is commonly called the customary units. Similar systems developed in different countries.

CGS Units. The CGS (centimeter-gram-second) system of units is the oldest of several extended versions of the metric system. It developed as an attempt to define a system that could be derived from a limited set of base units: the unit of length was the centimeter (cm), 1/100 of the length of the meter bar maintained in Paris; the unit of mass was the gram (g), 1/1000 of the kilogram; and the unit of time, the second (s), was determined from astronomical observations. The units for most other quantities were derived by using the systems of equations

TABLE 1: EXAMPLES OF SI DERIVED UNITS EXPRESSED IN TERMS OF BASE UNITS

Quantity	SI Unit	
	Name	Symbol
Area	Square meter	m^2
Volume	Cubic meter	m^3
Speed (velocity)	Meter per second	m/s
Acceleration	Meter per second squared	m/s^2
Wave number	Waves per meter	m^{-1}
Mass density	Kilogram per cubic meter	kg/m^3
Current density	Ampere per square meter	A/m^2
Magnetic field strength	Ampere per meter	A/m
Concentration (of amount of substance)	Mole per cubic meter	mol/m^3
Specific volume	Cubic meter per kilogram	m^3/kg
Luminance	Candela per square meter	cd/m^2

TABLE 2: SI DERIVED UNITS WITH SPECIAL NAMES

Quantity	SI Unit			
	Name	Symbol	Expression in Terms of Other Units	Expression in Terms of SI Base Units
Frequency	Hertz	Hz		s^{-1}
Force	Newton	N		$m \cdot kg \cdot s^{-2}$
Pressure	Pascal	Pa	N/m^2	$m^{-1} \cdot kg \cdot s^{-2}$
Energy, work, quantity of heat	Joule	J	N·m	$m^2 \cdot kg \cdot s^{-2}$
Power, radiant flux	Watt	W	J/s	$m^2 \cdot kg \cdot s^{-3}$
Quantity of electricity, electric charge	Coulomb	C	A·s	$s \cdot A$
Electric potential, potential difference, electromotive force	Volt	V	W/A	$m^2 \cdot kg \cdot s^{-3} \cdot A^{-1}$
Capacitance	Farad	F	C/V	$m^{-2} \cdot kg^{-1} \cdot s^4 \cdot A^2$
Electric resistance	Ohm	Ω	V/A	$m^2 \cdot kg \cdot s^{-3} \cdot A^{-2}$
Conductance	Siemens	s	a/v	$M^{-2} \cdot kg^{-1} \cdot s^3 \cdot A^2$
Magnetic flux	Weber	Wb	V·s	$m^2 \cdot kg \cdot s^{-2} \cdot A^{-1}$
Magnetic flux density	Tesla	T	Wb/m^2	$kg \cdot s^{-2} \cdot A^{-1}$
Inductance	Henry	H	Wb/A	$m^2 \cdot kg \cdot s^{-2} \cdot A^{-2}$
Luminous flux	Lumen	lm		cd·sr*
Illuminance	Lux	lx		$m^{-2} \cdot cd \cdot sr*$
Celsius temperature	Degree Celsius	°C		K

*In this expression the steradian (sr) is treated as a base unit.

relating different quantities, but new definitions were needed for other units, particularly in the relatively new fields of electricity and magnetism.

MKS Units. The size of the CGS units made it difficult to accept them as practical units, especially in the growing electrical industry. To get around this difficulty, a new fundamental unit of current was defined, based on the coulomb, the unit of charge, which was set at 1 coulomb = 0.10 abcoulomb. The MKS system was thus determined by four base units—the meter, the kilogram, the second, and the ampere (1 coulomb per second)—and is sometimes referred to as the MKSA system.

Gaussian Units. A hybrid CGS system of both electrostatic and electromagnetic units has been used in the solution of problems clearly either electrostatic or electromagnetic in nature. The system is called the gaussian system of units.

Gravitational Units. For certain engineering applications it was found convenient to use the unit of force as a base unit, instead of the unit of mass. In this system the unit of mass is defined as the unit of force divided by the unit of gravitational acceleration, hence the term gravitational unit.

SI (International System of Units). The General Conference on Weights and Measures, which was established by the Treaty of the Meter (1875) and which normally meets

TABLE 3: EXAMPLES OF SI DERIVED UNITS EXPRESSED BY MEANS OF SPECIAL NAMES

| Quantity Base Units | SI Unit | | |
	Name	Expression in Terms of SI Symbol	
Dynamic viscosity	Pascal second	Pa•s	$m^{-1}•kg•s^{-1}$
Moment of force	Meter newton	N•m	$m^2 kg•s^{-2}$
Surface tension	Newton per meter	N/m	$kg•s^{-2}$
Power density, heat flux density, irradiance	Watt per square meter	W/m^2	$kg•s^{-2}$
Heat capacity, entropy	Joule per kelvin	J/K	$m^2•kg•s^{-2}K^{-1}$
Specific heat capacity, specific entropy	Joule per kilogram kelvin	J/(kg•K)	$m^2•s^{-2}•K^{-1}$
Specific energy	Joule per kilogram	J/kg	$m^2•s^{-2}$
Thermal conductivity	Watt per meter kelvin	W/(m•K)	$m•kg•s^{-3}•K^{-1}$
Energy density	Joule per cubic meter	J/m^3	$m^{-1}•kg•s^{-2}$
Electric field strength	Volt per meter	V/m	$m•kg•s^{-3}•A^{-1}$
Electric charge density	Coulomb per cubic meter	C/m^3	$m^{-3}•s•A^{-1}$
Electric flux density	Coulomb per square meter	C/m^2	$m^{-2}•s•A$
Permittivity	Farad per meter	F/m	$m^{-3}•kg^{-1}•s^4•A^2$

every 6 years, has assumed the responsibility for establishing a rational system of units. To describe completely all independent physical measurements, three new base units were introduced. To the four base units of the MKS system (the meter, the kilogram, the second, and the ampere) were added the units for the quantities of temperature (the kelvin, K), amount of substance (the mole, mol), and luminous intensity (the candela, cd). In 1960 the General Conference laid down rules for prefixes and the derived and supplementary units.

See also: ATOMIC CONSTANTS; MEASUREMENT.

UNIVAC   UNIVAC (Universal Automatic Computer) is the trade name of a line of electronic digital COMPUTERS produced by the Remington-Rand Univac Division of the Sperry-Rand Corporation. The first of these, the UNIVAC I computer built by Remington-Rand and accepted by the U.S. Bureau of the Census in April 1951, is generally credited as being the first commercially available stored-program electronic digital computer. Its design was based on the EDVAC, a machine planned by John Presper Eckert and John W. MAUCHLY in association with John VON NEUMANN at the Moore School of Electrical Engineering of the University of Pennsylvania in 1946.

UNIVAC I employed for memory a unique system based on binary acoustic signals. It had twin arithmetic units run in parallel for error detection and converted binary information from memory into "words," each

consisting of 12 alphabetic or decimal quantities. Arithmetic was performed on these words at a rate of 2,000 additions or 450 multiplications per second. Internal memory capacity was 1,000 words. Provision was made for high rates of data exchange with an external magnetic tape memory of large capacity and with high-speed printers. UNIVAC I was intended for statistical usage. By 1958 nearly 50 of the computers had been produced, but all of them have subsequently been phased out of service. The current UNIVAC 1100 series of computer systems, which began in the early 1960s, comprises a number of medium to large general-purpose data-processing models.

universal language   SEE LANGUAGES, ARTIFICIAL

Universal Postal Union   SEE POSTAL UNION, UNIVERSAL

universal time   SEE TIME

universalism   Universalism is the theological doctrine that all souls will ultimately be saved and that there are no torments of hell. Universalism has been asserted at various times in different contexts throughout the history of the Christian church, as for example by Origen in the 3d century. As an organized religious movement, however, universalism dates from the late 1700s in America, where its early leaders were Hosea Ballou, John MURRAY, and Elhanan Winchester. As a form of religious liberalism, it has had close contacts with UNITARIANISM throughout its history. The Universalist Church of America and the American Unitarian Association merged in 1961 to form a single denomination, the UNITARIAN UNIVERSALIST ASSOCIATION.

universals   In philosophy, universals are general terms or abstract concepts, of which there may be particular individual instances. For example, *red* is a universal, of which the red square is an instance. Universals are considered essential to thought and language, but differing views exist as to their origin and nature of existence. A realist (see REALISM, philosophy), such as Plato, maintains that universals are eternal objects existing independently of the mind, although not in space and time. Conceptualists, such as Saint Thomas Aquinas and Saint Augustine, hold that universals are ideas in the mind of God or abstractions of the human intellect, as opposed to independent objects. Nominalists (see NOMINALISM), such as the medieval William of Occam and the contemporary Nelson Goodman, argue that universals are merely words, used to refer to the similarity among objects considered collectively.

universe   The term *universe*, in astronomy, refers to all known and inferred celestial materials, including the Earth, and to the space-time continuum in which they exist. The study of the universe as a whole is called COSMOLOGY.

Mythology and religion provide many CREATION AC-

COUNTS of the origin of the universe. Through the centuries people also learned increasingly more about its physical nature. By the late 20th century the most widely accepted scientific theory of the origin of the universe was the BIG BANG THEORY. In elaborations of this concept, the universe is described as having expanded extremely rapidly, some 14 to 20 billion years ago, from an initial singularity, or "point" of virtual nothingness (see INFLATIONARY THEORY). According to the conceptually difficult general RELATIVITY theory, the universe has neither boundary nor center but is self-contained within the curvature of space-time. The physical universe appears to consist of vast "bubbles" of seemingly empty space, the "surface" of these bubbles being a frothlike network of EXTRAGALACTIC SYSTEMS of stars such as our own Milky Way system (see GALAXY, THE).

Some versions of current inflationary theory suggest that an infinity of universes might be capable of forming as did the known universe. These universes, however, would forever lie beyond the possibility of contact with this one.

university　Universities and colleges are institutions that offer education beyond the secondary (preparatory or high school) level. This broad category includes colleges offering only undergraduate preparation; universities offering undergraduate and GRADUATE EDUCATION; freestanding professional schools offering degrees in law, divinity, medicine, engineering, and architecture; and two-year COMMUNITY AND JUNIOR COLLEGES offering technical, vocational, and liberal arts programs.

In general, a college offers degree programs (see DEGREE, ACADEMIC) for undergraduate students, but it may also have master's degree programs. The university is usually dedicated to three comprehensive activities: instruction leading to undergraduate, graduate, and professional degrees; research geared to expanding the frontiers of knowledge; and outreach or dissemination of learning beyond the boundaries of the institution through the printed word, scholarly associations, formal and informal instruction, and worldwide telecommunications and computer linkages.

National systems of higher education in general are geared to serving youth between the ages of 17 and 25. The percentage of students enrolled has been growing appreciably. Where once higher education was reserved for a small elite, today university education in many countries is a massive social enterprise.

History of the University

The general features of the university's present form, including prescribed curricula, formal examinations, and degrees, had their beginnings in medieval Europe in the 11th and 12th centuries. Among the several centers for learning that arose, two in particular, Bologna and Paris, served as models for the rest. Bologna developed primarily as a corporation of students, whereas Paris arose as an institution of masters. The medieval Latin term *universitas* meant a community or corporation of any kind, but

over time it came to mean a center for advanced learning with legal standing and various special privileges.

Most of the early students and masters were clerics or members of religious orders, but membership was not restrictive and soon included physicians, lawyers, and other learned men. Over time the universities won increasing autonomy to establish their own methods of self-governance, including the right to select their members and leaders and to determine the content and direction of their studies.

Often migrations of students and masters out of the older universities were the impetus for the founding of new centers. Out of one such migration from Paris, OXFORD UNIVERSITY was formed. Oxford adopted the master-dominated pattern of Paris and became an important center of scholarship in England. Another migration, from Oxford, led to the development of CAMBRIDGE UNIVERSITY in the early 13th century. During the same period such universities as Montpellier (1220), Padua (1222), Salamanca (c.1230), and Coimbra (1292) arose in France, Italy, and the Iberian peninsula. With the founding of Charles University (1348) in Prague and universities in Kraków (1364), Vienna (1365), Heidelberg (1386), and Uppsala (1477), universities spread throughout the Holy Roman Empire, central Europe, and Scandinavia.

Universities were crucial to the cultural and social vitality of the West. Throughout the Renaissance, Reformation, and Counter-Reformation, the universities were vital centers of intellectual stimulation and essential sources of leadership, both civil and ecclesiastical. During the great periods of exploration and settlement of North and South America, the university was part of the cultural legacy that was transplanted. By the early 17th century, centers of higher education had been founded in Peru, Mexico, New France (or Canada), and New England.

In the 19th century universities assumed their contemporary forms in most of the nations of Europe as well as in North and South America. Several forces converged to stimulate their expansion. As education became more secularized and more widespread, the churches, both Catholic and Protestant, increasingly lost control of institutions of learning to the nation-state, which everywhere assumed greater authority for supporting and controlling education at all levels. Nationalism increased throughout the century, carrying with it the belief that each nation needed an educational system specially geared to its particular values and goals. The rise of science and the accompanying belief in progress also contributed to the growth and importance of the university as a center of intellectual activity.

19th-Century Development in Europe. Germany developed the most successful and influential national system of higher education. The jewel in its crown was the University of Berlin, founded in 1810. Built on the principle of free inquiry for both teachers and students, the University of Berlin attracted scholars from around the world. The seminar, the scientific laboratory, and the monographic study were products of the new form of intellectual inquiry and were widely copied in other countries.

In France a national system of higher education was

established in 1806 during the Napoleonic era. Napoleon centralized education under the "University of France," which had responsibility for all education from primary to university levels. Standardized curricula, schedules, and examinations were the hallmarks. Subsequent demands among French university faculty and students in the 19th and 20th centuries centered on gaining greater autonomy and access. In England in the 19th century a number of new universities were created in response to the growth of industrial cities such as Manchester. Today Britain has more than 40 universities, the bulk of which were established following World War II.

In the 19th and early 20th centuries, India, Canada, and Australia, then parts of the British Empire, also established important centers of learning. Japan established the University of Tokyo in 1877, and toward the end of the century China permitted some international exchange that promoted growth and change in its universities.

20th-Century Developments. With the end of the colonial era following World War II, the number of universities worldwide increased dramatically as newly independent nations in Africa and Asia established their own institutions of higher learning. Another development, in response to the increasing demand for higher education, has been the tremendous growth in size of some universities. For instance, the National Autonomous University of Mexico now has more than 300,000 students. Exchange programs, which allow students to take part or all of their education in a foreign country, are still another development in contemporary higher education. Professors often teach abroad. Whereas once a college or university was confined to the narrow boundaries of its location, today's universities can be thought of as global enterprises linking scholars around the world.

Development of the U.S. University

The universities and colleges in the United States developed several distinct forms. The earliest, Harvard College (see HARVARD UNIVERSITY), was founded in 1636, not long after the first settlers arrived in New England, with the primary intention of training clergymen and other leaders. These aims guided the founding of eight other colonial colleges, including WILLIAM AND MARY (1693), YALE (1701), and COLUMBIA (1754), during the next 140 years. All of the colleges were begun and supported by religious groups; each was staffed and led mainly by clergy; and each had as a central purpose the education of church and civic leaders.

The curriculum of the early colleges included Latin, Greek, Hebrew, logic, rhetoric, ancient history, and mathematics. Scientific topics, modern languages, and literature were added slowly. Most learning was by rote; all courses were prescribed, and discipline was strictly observed. Teachers were typically young men preparing for the clergy or other professions. Only the college president served for a relatively long period, often combining his duties with preaching in a local church. Unlike the faculty-governed European universities, lay boards of trustees directed the policies and finances of the American college.

During the 19th century a number of different types of colleges and universities developed to serve the growing diversity of educational needs. In 1819, Thomas Jefferson founded the University of Virginia (see VIRGINIA, UNIVERSITY OF), one of the earliest state universities. Several other states began ventures in higher education, usually with a practical, nonsectarian intent. State schools in Maryland, Pennsylvania, and Michigan, offering agriculture, engineering, and applied-science curricula, were opened, whereas older colleges such as Harvard, Yale, and DARTMOUTH added scientific schools. Normal schools were instituted in response to a growing demand for elementary and secondary school teachers; many later expanded into comprehensive colleges, whereas others were incorporated in existing universities. Similarly, professional schools for law and medicine were begun or incorporated into other institutions.

The Land-Grant College Act, or Morrill Act, passed by Congress in 1862, offered federal lands to states that would establish colleges to prepare students in agriculture and the mechanical arts. Eventually, LAND-GRANT COLLEGES and universities developed in all 50 states, providing a broad range of applied, scientific courses; accessible, low-cost education; and a comprehensive curriculum including both undergraduate and graduate programs. A number of these public universities subsequently earned top academic reputations.

In 1876, The JOHNS HOPKINS UNIVERSITY was founded in Baltimore, Md., as the first U.S. institution to embody the German ideal of university education. From that time forward graduate education became an important aspect of many institutions. Older ones, such as Harvard and Yale, and new ones, such as Stanford and Chicago, adopted the aims of advanced learning conducted in a spirit of free inquiry. Faculty members henceforth were expected to hold Ph.D. degrees and to engage in research and publication along with teaching.

Specialized forms of education developed simultaneously to meet the needs of women, blacks, and certain religious groups. Higher education for women began with the seminary, which offered a form of education distinct from that provided for men. OBERLIN COLLEGE, opened in 1833, became the first coeducational, degree-granting institution. Eventually, all state colleges and universities became coeducational. Today women constitute about 54% of total enrollments, and COEDUCATION is the predominant form of higher education for both women and men (although a number of single-sex colleges continue to thrive).

Although a few blacks attended college before 1850, BLACK COLLEGES, such as HAMPTON and TUSKEGEE institutes, arose only after the Civil War. Not until the 1960s did blacks in practice win the right to be admitted on an equal basis with whites to state institutions throughout all sections of the country. Catholics and Jews, as well as the various Protestant denominations, also established their own colleges. Many of these institutions, such as GEORGETOWN UNIVERSITY and YESHIVA UNIVERSITY, having achieved academic distinction, attract students from other backgrounds as well. Indeed, the extensive access to higher education for people of many different social and economic backgrounds is a hallmark of the U.S. system of higher education.

During the 20th century there was a great expansion in the number of U.S. institutions of higher learning, the number of students enrolled, and the kinds of programs available. In 1940 there were 1,708 colleges and universities serving approximately 1,388,000 students. Fifty years later, more than 3,500 two-year and four-year institutions served nearly 13 million students. This expansion was due in part to greater federal and state support.

The G.I. BILL OF RIGHTS legislation of 1944 accounted for one enrollment surge by enabling World War II veterans to attend universities and colleges under government sponsorship. The "baby boom" that followed the war swelled enrollment in the 1960s and '70s. Returning adults now constitute a rapidly increasing college population group, many of them attending part-time. Among the institutions created during this period to address the needs of new population groups, community and technical colleges have grown tremendously. Today there are more than 1,450 public and private two-year colleges offering a wide range of college-transfer, technical, and practical programs. More than 40 percent of all students in U.S. higher education are enrolled in these colleges.

During World War II and afterward, scientific and technological advances encouraged by the government stimulated many changes in universities. Research rapidly supplanted teaching as a primary preoccupation of many faculty members, and outreach programs for credit and noncredit have extended education beyond the boundaries of many campuses. Many new fields of knowledge, such as biotechnology and nuclear medicine, have developed, and faculty specialists are frequently called upon by business and government to help solve problems.

Problems Facing Higher Education

The late 20th century has been called the Information Age. With the advent of computers and advanced telecommunications, the explosion of knowledge in many disciplines, and a rising sense of global community, universities find themselves in the middle rather than on the periphery of social change. Demand for university education has never been greater worldwide, but universities face many problems. Despite strong demand, many countries do not have the resources to build universities or to hire faculty. Older universities often lack resources to modernize their laboratories and classrooms. Faculty members are expensive to train and often find jobs in industry or government more attractive and lucrative. Industry has grown impatient with the slowness of the university response and has begun to train its own personnel.

Because the cost of education in recent years has grown faster than has family income, U.S. students have difficulty paying for higher education. As a result, wealthy students, who usually receive better preparatory schooling, gain admission, whereas students from poorer families, or who are members of minority groups, are shut out. Often these poorer students must settle for a less-expensive and lower-quality education—or none at all. Measures to mitigate this trend include OPEN ADMIS-

SION, affirmative action, various forms of government aid, and the expansion of public institutions.

As governments contribute a greater share of the revenues on which universities and colleges depend, the autonomy of institutions with regard to their policies and practices is often threatened. In more-centralized countries, human-resource allocations may override educational needs. The autonomy of the university is never permanent; it must be reestablished from time to time. This is never more obvious than in the frequent disputes over ACADEMIC FREEDOM. Universities traditionally reserve the right to teach and research freely, but those outside the university may object to what is taught or researched or may wish to direct it to their own ends.

In the United States, universities also face the prospect of declining enrollments, which could lead to some colleges either cutting back or closing altogether. With public colleges enrolling nearly 80 percent of all students, the vitality of the private sector is diminished and the burden on taxpayers is further exacerbated.

Dominance by universities in the higher-education system has been faulted for causing an erosion of the undergraduate curriculum by overspecialization and an overemphasis on research at the expense of teaching. The curriculum is also criticized for being insensitive to the contributions of non-Western and nonwhite people. Hence the university's traditional role as preserver and disseminator of a society's culture can conflict with changing definitions of what is important to know. Finally, there is a persistent struggle to maintain quality in the face of various demands to serve increasingly diverse constituencies, to respond to more and different social needs, and to preserve the ancient traditions and prerogatives of the university while simultaneously creating the means for change.

———

University of California v. Bakke   In the case of *University of California* v. *Bakke* (1978), the U.S. Supreme Court held that even though universities may consider race and ethnic origins as factors in evaluating candidates for admission, universities may not establish fixed racial quotas. The case arose when the medical school of the University of California at Davis twice rejected Allan Bakke's application while admitting members of racial minorities who had lower test scores. Bakke charged that the medical school's policy of setting aside 16 of 100 positions for racial minorities was a violation of the equal protection clause of the 14th Amendment.

In a complex 5–4 decision the Supreme Court ordered that Bakke be admitted. Four of the majority, including Chief Justice Warren Burger, ruled against the university on the ground that it had violated the Civil Rights Act of 1964, which provided that no person might be excluded from any federally funded institution because of race. The decision was viewed by some as a setback for U.S. blacks in their struggle for equality. Others saw it as a vindication of an individual's right to be judged on the basis of merit rather than race.

See also: EQUAL OPPORTUNITY.

unknown soldier The unknown soldier is an unidentified wartime casualty who has, since World War I, been memorialized by various countries as a representative of all those who died in their nation's service. In Paris, France, the tomb for the unknown soldier lies under the Arc de Triomphe (Arch of Triumph). In London, England, the unknown soldier's tomb is in Westminster Abbey. In the United States, four unknown servicemen—one from each world war, one from the Korean War, and one from the Vietnam War—are now buried in the Tomb of the Unknowns at Arlington National Cemetery in Virginia.

Unser (family) The Unsers are a family of American racing-car drivers. **Robert William Unser**, b. Albuquerque, N.Mex., Feb. 20, 1934, known as Bobby, won the Indianapolis 500-mi (804.7-km) race in 1968, 1975, and 1981. He started racing in 1949. Bobby Unser gained early fame in the Pike's Peak Hill Climb, which he won 12 times. In 1963 he entered his first Indianapolis race, and in 1968, the year of his first victory there, he gained the United States Auto Club (USAC) National Championship. He was National Champion again in 1974. During his career Bobby won more than 25 National Championship races.

His brother, **Al Unser**, b. Albuquerque, N.Mex., May 29, 1933, won the Indianapolis 500-mi race in 1970, 1971, 1978, and 1987; he was the second man to win the race four times. Al competed in numerous Pike's Peak Hill Climb races, finishing second in 1960 and 1962 and first in 1964 and 1965. In 1968, he finished third in the USAC National Championship rankings; in 1969, 1977, and 1978 he was ranked second, and he achieved first-place ranking in 1970. During his career Al won more than 35 National Championship races.

Jerry Unser, the father of Bobby and Al, competed in numerous Pike's Peak Hill Climb races.

Untouchables Untouchables, now called Harijans, have traditionally occupied the lowest place in the CASTE system of Hindu India; they were called untouchable because they were considered to be outside the confines of caste. Their impurity derived from their traditional occupations, which might involve the taking of life (fishermen), working with carcasses (leatherworkers), or touching bodily wastes (laundrymen, sweepers). Traditionally, they were banned from Hindu temples; in parts of South India even the sight of an Untouchable was sufficient to pollute a member of a higher caste. In 1949 the Indian government outlawed the use of the term *Untouchables*. The group has been reclassified as the "scheduled castes" and has been granted special educational and political privileges. Today it is illegal to discriminate against a Harijan, yet they remain generally at the bottom of the caste hierarchy, performing the most menial roles demanded by society. The scheduled castes numbered more than 100 million in the 1980s.

Upanishads [oo-pan'-i-shadz] The Upanishads are chronologically the latest portions of the VEDAS, the sacred texts of Hinduism. The earliest Upanishads, probably dating from 900 to 600 BC, represent the first development of philosophical reflections in Sanskrit literature; later works have also been accepted from time to time as Upanishads. The material the Upanishads comprise is part poetry, part prose. They contain didactic stories, allegories, and passages for meditation, a number of which are repeated in more than one Upanishad or elsewhere in the Vedic corpus. The fundamental concern of the Upanishads is the nature of reality. They teach the identity of the individual soul (atman) with the universal essence soul (Brahman). Because they are the final portions of the Vedas, they are also known as VEDANTA, "the end of the Vedas," and their thought, as interpreted in succeeding centuries, is likewise known as Vedanta.

upas tree [yoo'-puhs] Upas tree is the common name for *Antiaris toxicaria* in the family Moraceae. Native to the tropics of Africa and Asia, these trees may reach 76 m (250 ft) high. They bear oblong, deciduous leaves and small pear-shaped fruits (drupes). The latex of the upas is highly toxic and has been used for poisoning arrows. In some areas the tree was fabled to be so poisonous that humans or animals who came close to it died.

Updike, John [uhp'-dyk] Famous among contemporary writers for his rich, elegant prose and the craftsmanship of his short stories and his many novels, John Hoyer Updike, b. Shillington, Pa., Mar. 18, 1932, was trained as a graphic artist. As an English major at Harvard (1950–54), he contributed cartoons, verse, and parodies to the *Harvard Lampoon*. Following a Knox Fellowship at

Photo Jill Krementz © 1978

John Updike began his writing career in the mid-1950s with short stories in the New Yorker *and has since written novels, poems, and critical pieces noted for their brilliant use of the language. Although Updike often explores the conflict between mundane existence and the possibility of higher purpose, he is also capable of writing lighter fare, such as* The Witches of Eastwick *(1984).*

the Ruskin School of Drawing and Fine Arts at Oxford (1954–55), Updike became a staff writer for the *New Yorker*. In 1957 he moved to Massachusetts to devote himself to fiction.

Middle-class manners, Updike's favorite subject, are examined from almost every possible perspective. The novel *Rabbit Run* (1960) and the story collection *Pigeon Feathers* (1962) are representative works from Updike's early period. Like Rabbit, many of Updike's later characters confuse sexuality with spiritual ecstasy, notably in *Couples* (1968). Updike's fondness for writing books in series has produced four Rabbit novels (the third, *Rabbit is Rich*, 1981, won a Pulitzer Prize); two books about the misadventures of Henry Bech (*Bech: A Book*, 1970; *Bech Is Back*, 1982); and three novels that, in different ways, refer to *The Scarlet Letter* of Nathaniel Hawthorne: *A Month of Sundays* (1975), *Roger's Version* (1986), and *S* (1988), in which the main character is a contemporary Hester Prynne.

Updike has also achieved a reputation as a poet and a perceptive book reviewer in his pieces for the *New Yorker*. In 1989, two works of nonfiction, *Self-Consciousness*, a collection of memoirs, and *Just Looking*, essays on art, were published.

UPI   see PRESS AGENCIES AND SYNDICATES

Upjohn, Richard   The architect Richard Upjohn, b. England, Jan. 22, 1802, d. Feb. 17, 1878, came to the United States in 1829 and devoted most of his career to the design of churches. His Trinity Church in New York City (1839–46) became the paradigm of fastidiously composed and detailed GOTHIC REVIVAL churches in America; Upjohn himself produced many variations of it. Often more original and sympathetic were his small rural churches built of wood. These became so popular that he published a group of designs and instructions for building them in *Upjohn's Rural Architecture* (1852).

Upper Volta   see BURKINA FASO

Uppsala [uhp'-sah-lah]   The city of Uppsala, a major Swedish cultural center, lies about 70 km (45 mi) north of Stockholm and has a population of 164,754 (1990 est.). Manufactures include machinery, clothing, drugs, musical instruments, and food products. Printing and publishing are also important. The University of Uppsala (1477) is Sweden's oldest institution of higher learning.

Gamla Uppsala, now a suburb 5 km (3 mi) to the north of the modern city, was the religious and political capital of the Vikings. Uppsala became the seat of the archbishop of Sweden in 1164 and a royal residence in the next century. The philosopher Emanuel Swedenborg and the scientist Carolus Linnaeus are buried in the 15th-century cathedral.

---

upwelling, oceanic   Oceanic upwelling is the slow ascending motion of deep water toward the surface; up-welling is produced primarily by the action of surface winds. The water typically comes from depths of less than a few hundred meters, and it is usually lower in temperature and higher in nutrients than the surface water it replaces.

Upwelling along the coasts (usually western) of continents is associated with the north-south winds blowing along these coasts. These winds produce a movement of water within the uppermost layer of the sea (the Ekman layer; see OCEAN CURRENTS), to the right of the wind direction in the Northern Hemisphere and to the left in the Southern Hemisphere. When the movement in this layer (called Ekman transport) is directed offshore, deeper water will flow toward shore and will well up near the coast. This process tends to intensify in low latitudes. The significant open-ocean upwelling in equatorial regions of both the Atlantic and the Pacific oceans is associated with a divergence in the surface Ekman transport produced by easterly winds near the equator.

Upwelling regions are marked by a depression in surface water temperature. Cold upwelled water along the western coasts of continents generally lowers air temperature, which increases the relative humidity and frequently produces fog. Upwelled water is often deficient in oxygen and rich in dissolved nutrients (phosphates, nitrates, silicates). The supply of nutrients to the surface layers leads to increased photosynthesis by phytoplankton; as a result, regions of upwelling, such as along the Peruvian Coast, are among the ocean's most biologically productive areas. Upwelling around the Antarctic continent is responsible for huge blooms of phytoplankton, which form the basis of the marine food chain. Periodically, upwelling in the eastern Pacific is negated by a current called EL NIÑO, with devastating effects on Peru's anchovy fisheries.

Ur   The ruins of Ur (modern Muqayyar), the ancient Sumerian capital and religious center that the Bible identifies as the early home of Abraham, lie about 300 km (187 mi) southeast of Baghdad, Iraq, and about 15 km (9.4 mi) southwest of the Euphrates River, which once flowed past the city. Modern studies have produced evidence that prehistoric occupation of the site (5th millennium BC) was interrupted by a flood that was formerly believed to have been the one described in Genesis. The city flourished during the 3d millennium BC, briefly serving (c.2500 BC) as the capital of SUMER under kings of the 1st dynasty of Ur. An extensive cemetery of approximately this period yielded several so-called Royal Tombs. Important persons were buried in these tombs, not only with magnificent treasures of gold, silver, and semiprecious stones, but also with their retinues of servants, ceremonial carts and animals, furniture, and utensils.

Following a period of Akkadian rule (c.2371–2230 BC), the city became the center of a Mesopotamian empire under the 3d dynasty of Ur, founded (c.2100 BC) by Ur-Nammu. Many of the important buildings on the site date from this period. Sacked (c.2000 BC) by the Elamites, Ur remained an important religious center main-

The ziggurat at Ur, the religious and commercial center of Sumer from c.2120 to 2006 BC, was constructed during the reign of King Urnammu and rebuilt during the 6th century BC.

tained by successive kings of Babylonia, in particular by the Neo-Babylonian kings Nebuchadnezzar II (r. 605–562 BC) and Nabonidus (d. c.538 BC). After the Achaemenid period (c.550 to 330 BC), the city declined, and its abandonment (4th century BC) may have resulted from a breakdown in the irrigation system after a change in the river's course.

The city walls, rebuilt (c.2100) by Ur-Nammu, enclose an oval area of about 33 ha (82 acres). Three main building complexes have been excavated: the raised ZIGGURAT and temple precinct surrounded by Nebuchadnezzar's retaining wall; the palace and temple of Nabonidus in the northeast section; and a residential quarter in the southeast part of the city. The residential quarter contains private houses of the early 2d millennium BC, the time at which Abraham is said to have lived at Ur. Cuneiform tablets from this area give information about the city's involvement in foreign trading during the late 3d and early 2d millennia BC, when Mesopotamian exports were transported to DILMUN (modern Bahrain) in the Persian Gulf, and there exchanged for copper and ivory from the East.

The site of Ur was discovered in 1852, but not until the excavations carried out (1922–34) under the direction of Sir Leonard Woolley was detailed evidence of the city's history uncovered and present-day knowledge of early Mesopotamian culture substantially increased. Many objects from the Royal Tombs are now in the British Museum (London) and the Baghdad and University of Pennsylvania museums.

Ur-Nammu, King of Ur [ur-nah'-moo]   Ur-Nammu was the first king (r. c.2112–c.2095 BC) of the 3d dynasty of Sumerian kings at UR in southern MESOPOTAMIA. He was the author of the oldest known law code and built the lower part of the pyramidal temple (ziggurat) at Ur. His son Shulgi (r. c.2094–c.2047) succeeded him.

Ural-Altaic languages [yur'-ul-ahl-tay'-ik]   The many Ural-Altaic languages—constituting the Uralic and the Altaic languages—extend from Scandinavia, Hungary, and the Balkans in the West, to the easternmost reaches of the Amur and the island of Sakhalin, and from the Arctic Ocean to central Asia. According to some investigators, JAPANESE and KOREAN should also be considered Altaic languages. All of the Uralic languages have been shown to be related—the vocabulary and grammar of each member language can be examined in the light of productive-predictive correspondences—but Altaic is not a language family in the same sense, as similar correspondences have yet to be discovered for it.

Uralic Languages

The Uralic languages are traditionally divided into two major branches, Finno-Ugric and Samoyed. Finno-Ugric in turn contains two subgroups: Finnic and Ugric. The former is divided into the Baltic-Finnic, Volga-Finnic, and Permian languages; the latter comprises Hungarian and the Ob-Ugric languages.

Baltic-Finnic. Finnish and Estonian are the best known of the Baltic-Finnic languages. Others are Karelian, spoken in northwestern Russia and eastern Finland; Veps, spoken between the Dnepr and the Volga; Votian, spoken in the Udmurt Autonomous Republic of the USSR; and Livonian, spoken in the Livonia district of Latvia. Lapp is similar in structure to Finnish, but the various Lapp dialects—spoken in Norway, Sweden, Finland, and the Kola Peninsula of Russia—diverge greatly from each other.

Finnish has many cases, 12 of which are productive. Another pervasive feature of the language is consonant gradation, such as the t/d alternation found in the declination of the Finnish word for "hundred": nominative sata, genitive sadan, ablative sadalta, partitive sataa, and so on.

Volga-Finnic and Permian. Mordvinian, spoken along the middle Volga, and Cheremis, spoken in the district where the Kama joins the Volga, constitute the Volga-Finnic language group. Both are close to Finnish in grammar and vocabulary. Less like Finnish are the Permian languages—Zyrien and Votyak, spoken in northeastern European Russia.

Ugric. The Finnic languages are more or less geographically contiguous, but the Ugric languages lie at opposite ends of the Finno-Ugric area—Hungarian occupying the extreme west, and the Ob-Ugric languages, Vogul and Ostyak, the extreme east, in the Ob Valley beyond the Urals. One of the most striking Ugric linguistic features is the so-called objective conjugation. In Hungarian, for instance, adok means "I give," and adom means "I give it" or "I give them." Thus the object of the verb—"it" or "them"—is incorporated in the verb form.

Hungarian has more productive cases—upward of 20—than even Finnish has. Vogul and Ostyak, however, have only four to seven cases, depending on the dialect. The Ugric languages have no consonant gradation.

Samoyed. The Samoyed languages are the easternmost representatives of Uralic. Presumably they were the first to separate, as a group, from the original, proto-Uralic language. They are spoken in the northeastern corner of Europe, near Zyrian, and in north central Siberia. Yurak,

Tavgi, and Yenisei form a North Samoyed group, distinguished from the South Samoyed language, Selkup.

Loanwords and Early Records. In the course of their histories, the individual Uralic languages have come into contact with a great many languages from other families—Turkic, Germanic, Baltic (an earlier form of Latvian and Lithuanian), and Slavic. Finnish *kuningas*, "king," for instance, is an early loan from a Germanic language, hence its resemblance to English *king* and German *König*.

The oldest significant text written in a Uralic language is a funeral sermon in Hungarian from about 1195. Finnish and Estonian texts survive from the Protestant Reformation; the reformer of the Finns, Michael Agricola (1512–57), also translated the Bible into Finnish. Zyrien was recorded in the 15th century by Saint Stephen of Perm, apostle of the Zyriens, who fashioned its alphabet.

Altaic Languages

The Altaic languages are spread over an area even larger than that covered by the Uralic. Of the three branches of Altaic, Turkic ranges from Anatolia to the Volga basin and central Asia; Mongolian extends from China and Mongolia as far west as the lower Volga and Afghanistan; and Manchu-Tungus occupies the northern coast of northeastern Siberia, and runs as far south as the Amur and as far west as the Yenisei.

Turkic. Written evidence of the Turkic languages begins with the Orkhon inscriptions of the 8th century AD, found near the river Selenga in Mongolia, and continues wherever and whenever a Turkic population came into contact with one of the higher religions. Knowledge of one Turkic language usually enables an investigator to analyze words and simple sentences in any other Turkic language except Chuvash. To explain this, it is hypothesized that an original, proto-Turkic language split into two branches: West Turkic and East Turkic. West Turkic went its own way, both phonetically and in terms of contact with other languages, and eventually became Chuvash, spoken in the Volga Basin in the Chuvash Autonomous Republic of the USSR.

The speakers of East Turkic must have split up only comparatively recently into the many present-day languages, usually classed into five subdivisions: Oghuz, mainly represented by Turkish, the language of Turkey; Kipchak, with over a dozen languages, including Kazan Tatar, Kazakh, Kirghiz, and Bashkir; Sayan Turkic, represented by Tuvin, Altai, Shor, and several other languages; Turki, represented primarily by Uighur and Uzbek; and Yakut, comprising Yakut Proper, Khakas, and Dolgan.

Mongolian. Despite their considerable geographical dispersion, the present-day Mongolian languages or dialects are all closely related. The military conquests of Genghis Khan in the 13th century brought the Mongols well into Europe, and to this day traces of Mongolian may be discovered in a few provinces of Afghanistan and among the Kalmyk-Mongols in the Kalmyk Autonomous Republic of the USSR.

Khalkha is the language of the Mongols of the Mongolian People's Republic, with its capital at Ulan Bator.

Buriat is spoken in the Buriat Autonomous Republic of the USSR. Other Mongolian languages include Dagur, in northwestern Manchuria and the Chinese province of Xinjiang (Sinkiang); Monguor, in Qinghai (Tsinghai) province; Kalmyk; Oirat; Moghol; Santa; Paongan; and Yellow Uigur.

Manchu-Tungus. Just as the Turkic languages can be thought of as the western wing of Altaic, the Manchu-Tungus—also known simply as the Tungus—languages constitute the eastern wing. Most of these languages have been known only since the 19th century, but two of them, Manchu and Jurzhen, are preserved in historical records that go back much further. Manchu, now spoken by only a few thousand people, was the original language of the tribe of horsemen that became the Qing dynasty and occupied the Chinese throne from 1644 to 1912. Similarly, Jurzhen, now extinct, was the language of the tribes that became the Jin dynasty, ruling from 1115 to 1234.

The Manchu-Tungus languages fall into two groups. South Tungus includes Manchu, Goldi, Olcha, Orok, Udihe, and Orochon. The North Tungus languages are Eveneki, or Tungus Proper, and Even, also known as Lamut.

The Relation between Uralic and Altaic

The grammatical structures of Uralic and Altaic are similar, and about 70 words in each group appear to be cognates. The correspondences between the two groups of languages are unsystematic, however. They could be the result of borrowing or chance, or the parallels between Uralic and Altaic may be slight because the two groups split apart long ago.

In addition to the Ural-Altaic hypothesis (that Uralic and Altaic form a superfamily of languages), there is also an Indo-Uralic hypothesis, in which Uralic is linked with the INDO-EUROPEAN LANGUAGES; a Uralic-Yukagir hypothesis, linking Uralic and Yukagir, a Paleosiberian language; a Uralic-Luorawetlan (another Paleosiberian language or language family) hypothesis; a Uralic-Eskaleut (Eskimo and Aleut) hypothesis (see INDIAN LANGUAGES, AMERICAN); an Altaic-Korean hypothesis; an Altaic-Japanese hypothesis; and an Altaic-Ainu hypothesis—Ainu being the language of the prehistoric inhabitants of the northern islands of Japan.

Ural Mountains [yur'-ul]   The Ural Mountains in the USSR extend from near the coast of the Arctic Ocean southward for more than 2,000 km (1,250 mi). Traditionally they form the boundary between Europe and Asia, but they do not constitute a significant boundary within the USSR. The tallest peak, Mount Narodnaya, reaches 1,894 m (6,214 ft), but much of the range is below 1,000 m (3,280 ft). The mountains are drained by the Pechora, Ural, Kama, and Tobol rivers.

The Urals are built of parallel ridges trending north-south. They were formed in the course of the Hercynian Earth movements (about 250 million years ago). Toward the south the range broadens into a plateau, where Archaean rocks are to be found. Throughout its length the range has been intruded by granitic and other igneous rocks, which today give rise to the greatest relief. The

Urals were glaciated, and the effects of glacial erosion are especially evident in the north.

Toward the arctic, the mountains are covered with low-growing tundra, but elsewhere a sparse coniferous forest dominates. The central and southern Urals contain great mineral wealth, particularly iron ore, bauxite, copper, and zinc, as well as many rarer minerals. The southern Urals are flanked by coalfields and petroleum fields. These resources have given rise to smelting, metallurgical, and engineering industries, and to large industrial centers, including CHELYABINSK, MAGNITOGORSK, and SVERDLOVSK.

Exploration of the Urals began in the 11th century and continued into the 17th century. Industrialization of the region began in the 18th century with the exploitation of the area's vast mineral resources.

Ural River   The Ural River is a 2,535-km-long (1,575-mi) river in the Russian and Kazakh republics of the USSR, with a drainage area of 231,000 km^2 (89,190 mi^2). It rises in the Ural Mountains and flows south past the industrial city of Magnitogorsk, then west to Uralsk, where it turns south and continues through a semidesert area to its delta at Guryev on the northern shore of the Caspian Sea. The river is navigable to Uralsk during the ice-free season.

Uralic languages   see URAL-ALTAIC LANGUAGES

Uraniborg Observatory   see BRAHE, TYCHO

uranium   Uranium is a heavy, radioactive metal and a member of the ACTINIDE SERIES in the PERIODIC TABLE. Its atomic weight is 238.029, and its atomic number is 92. Its name and its chemical symbol, U, are derived from Uranus, because that planet was discovered a few years before the discovery of the element. A compound of uranium (uranium oxide) was discovered in the uranium ore pitchblende by the German chemist M. H. Klaproth in 1789. Klaproth believed that he had isolated the element, but this was not achieved until 1841, when the French chemist E. M. Péligot reduced uranium tetrachloride with potassium in a platinum crucible to obtain elementary uranium. It was in uranium-containing crystals that the French physicist A. H. Becquerel discovered RADIOACTIVITY in 1896.

Uranium is not as rare as was once believed. Widely distributed in the Earth's crust, uranium occurs to the extent of about 0.0004%, making the metal more plentiful than mercury, antimony, or silver. Before World War II, uranium was of interest as a source of RADIUM for medical use, and as a coloring agent in glass and ceramic glazes, in which it produces a yellow green color (vaseline glass). With the advent of the nuclear age, uranium now occupies a key position in nuclear weapons and NUCLEAR ENERGY.

Uranium has three naturally occurring isotopes: the most abundant is ^{238}U (99.276%), occurring with ^{235}U (0.7196%) and ^{234}U (0.0057%). There are 14 isotopes in all, each radioactive. Except for traces of neptunium and plutonium, uranium is the heaviest atom found in nature.

Physical Properties. Pure uranium is a dense, silvery white metal that melts at 1,132° C and boils at 3,818° C. Uranium has three different ALLOTROPES, or crystalline forms. The phase changes between these crystalline forms are important considerations in the design of metallic fuel rods for nuclear reactors. Uranium is a poor conductor of electricity, and it is soft, although it will harden when machined.

Chemical Properties. Uranium is a strongly electropositive element and is easily oxidized. When a massive sample of uranium is exposed to air, the surface is oxidized and protects the rest of the metal from oxidation near room temperature.

In its chemical compounds uranium exhibits four common oxidation states: +3, +4, +5, and +6. Uranium reacts readily with most nonmetals and dissolves slowly in dilute mineral acids. The metal dissolves rapidly in oxidizing acids, such as nitric acid, yielding (in nitric acid) uranyl nitrate, $UO_2(NO_3)_2$. Much of the aqueous chemistry of uranium is dominated by the uranyl ion, UO_2^{2+}, and its derivatives. The metal is inert to basic solutions.

An important compound of uranium is the hexafluoride, UF_6. Uranium hexafluoride is volatile and, in the absence of water, chemically stable. Fractional diffusion of large volumes of this compound was used to separate ^{235}U from ^{238}U for use in the ATOMIC BOMB.

Radioactivity. Each of the naturally occurring isotopes of uranium are radioactive and decay by the following nuclear transformations:

$$^{238}_{92}U \rightarrow\ ^{234}_{90}Th + ^4_2He \qquad t_{1/2} = 4.5 \times 10^9 \text{ years}$$
$$^{235}_{92}U \rightarrow\ ^{231}_{90}Th + ^4_2He \qquad t_{1/2} = 7.1 \times 10^8 \text{ years}$$
$$^{234}_{92}U \rightarrow\ ^{230}_{90}Th + ^4_2He \qquad t_{1/2} = 2.5 \times 10^5 \text{ years}$$

The half-life of each isotope is given by $t_{1/2}$. Each of the resulting thorium isotopes is also radioactive. The ^{238}U isotope decay begins a series of nuclear transformations, called the uranium series, that ends with the nonradioactive lead isotope, ^{206}Pb.

Mineralogy. Uranium is always found combined with other elements. In igneous rocks it exists in the +4 oxidation state. A large ion, it tends to be excluded from ferromagnesian minerals that crystallize early in the geochemical process, instead becoming concentrated in residual liquids during the final stages of crystallization. In intermediate and granitic rocks, uranium typically substitutes for calcium in apatite and for zirconium in zircon.

When exposed to more-oxidizing conditions near the Earth's surface, primary uranium minerals are readily oxidized to the highly soluble +6 oxidation state. Much of the oxidized uranium in solution ultimately reaches the oceans, where it may be selectively removed and incorporated into marine phosphorite deposits, adsorbed by clay minerals, or incorporated in the carbonate skeletons of organisms such as corals. Marine phosphorites constitute large uranium resources in Africa, the Soviet Union, Brazil, the Mediterranean region, and the United States. In

Florida these low-grade deposits are extensively mined for their phosphate, which makes recovery of the uranium feasible.

Several important primary uranium ores exist, including uraninite (essentially UO_2), pitchblende (a massive form of uraninite, including more-oxidized forms such as U_3O_8), and carnotite (a complex oxide that contains potassium and vanadium as well). The largest quantities of uranium ore are mined from the Blind River area in Ontario, Canada. More than 99% of the uranium now being mined in the United States comes from sedimentary deposits in New Mexico, Wyoming, Texas, Colorado, and Utah.

Production. No deposits of concentrated uranium ore have been discovered. As a result, uranium must be extracted from ores containing less than 0.1% uranium, so that substantial, complex processing of the ores is required. Usually it is necessary to preconcentrate the ore by grinding and by flotation or similar processes. The preconcentrated ore is then leached to bring the uranium compounds into solution. The resulting solution is filtered, absorbed onto an ion-exchange resin, eluted, precipitated, and purified to yield uranyl nitrate, which may be converted to other uranium compounds or reduced to yield the pure metal.

Nuclear Fission. In 1939 two German scientists, Otto HAHN and Fritz Strassman, reported that when ^{235}U absorbs slow neutrons, it forms ^{236}U, which then undergoes nuclear fission, splitting into two large fragments plus several neutrons. A typical fission reaction is

$$^{235}_{92}U + ^{1}_{0}n \rightarrow ^{236}_{92}U \rightarrow ^{90}_{36}Kr + ^{143}_{56}Ba + 3^{1}_{0}n$$

This reaction releases a tremendous amount of energy: the fission of a kilogram of ^{235}U produces about 2.5 million times as much energy as is produced by the burning of a kilogram of coal. The fission fragments include more neutrons that can cause fission of nearby ^{235}U atoms, thus setting up a nuclear CHAIN REACTION. This and similar chain reactions are the source of energy for many nuclear reactors.

Uranium Reprocessing. Uranium oxide enriched with ^{235}U is used as fuel in nuclear reactors. Eventually, the accumulation of products of nuclear fission will stop the chain reaction. Before this point is reached the fuel assembly is removed and the fuel must either be disposed of or reprocessed to remove the radioactive fission products. It is estimated that if the spent nuclear fuel were reprocessed, 30% less uranium ore would need to be mined for a given amount of power.

Uranium depleted of its fissionable isotope is used for a few nonnuclear purposes. Uranyl nitrate is used as a colored glaze for porcelain and glass and as an intensifier in photography. Uranyl acetate is used in dry copying inks and as a reagent in analytical chemistry. Because of its great density, the metal is used in inertial guidance systems, counterweights and ballast, and as a shielding material.

––

Uranus (astronomy) [yoo-ray'-nuhs]   Uranus is the seventh planet (see PLANETS AND PLANETARY SYSTEMS) from the Sun and was the first to be discovered since ancient times. Sir William HERSCHEL first observed the planet through a telescope on Mar. 13, 1781, seeing a featureless bluish green disk that he nevertheless recognized as a highly unusual object. Although Herschel wished to call the newly discovered planet Georgium Sidus (Georgian Star) for King George III of England, and although many French astronomers referred to it as Herschel, Johann Bode's proposal of the name Uranus—the mythological father of Saturn—was over the years accepted more and more widely and finally became universal in the mid-19th century.

The only spacecraft to encounter Uranus thus far, VOYAGER 2, collected data on the planet and its rings and satellites over a four-month period, between Nov. 4, 1985, and Feb. 25, 1986. Voyager 2 passed within 107,000 km (66,500 mi) of the center of Uranus—about 81,450 km (50,625 mi) above its cloud tops—on Jan. 24, 1986.

Appearance. Although it was discovered with a telescope, Uranus reaches a maximum brightness of magnitude 5.5 and can be seen by the naked eye as a faint point of light in a clear, moonless sky. In Voyager 2 photos, Uranus appears as a generally featureless disk, except for considerable darkening toward the edges. Faint banding is seen in contrast-enhanced images, as are transitory cloud plumes.

Orbit and Rotation. Uranus's average distance from the Sun is 2.875 billion km (1.786 billion mi), and the planet takes 84.013 years to make one complete revolution about the Sun. The orbit has an eccentricity of 0.0472 and an inclination of 0°46'. Its period of rotation was determined by Voyager 2 to be 17.24 hours (±0.01 hours). One startling aspect of Uranus is that its rotation axis is inclined 97°54' from its orbital plane. This means that the poles of Uranus lie nearly in the plane of its orbit around the Sun.

Physical Characteristics. Uranus has an equatorial diameter of 51,100 km (31,750 mi), almost precisely four times that of the Earth, and a mass 14.58 times that of the Earth. The dark absorption bands discovered in 1869 in the red part of the spectrum of Uranus were identified in 1932 as being caused by methane gas in Uranus's atmosphere. This red absorption is the major cause of the blue green color of the planet; the methane absorbs much of the red light from the impinging white sunlight, leaving a bluish green color in the reflected sunlight. Measurements by Voyager 2 verified that hydrogen is the main constituent of the visible atmosphere. Helium is the other major constituent, about 15% (±5%) in terms of molecular weight, which is a larger percentage than in the atmospheres of either Jupiter or Saturn. Together, hydrogen and helium make up more than 99% of Uranus's atmosphere, which extends to a depth of about 8,000 km (5,000 mi). A layer of methane ice clouds was detected by Voyager 2 near a pressure level of about one atmosphere. Deep within Uranus exists a superheated water ocean, perhaps 10,000 km (6,000 mi) deep, which contains large concentrations of ionized chemicals. It is in this ocean that Uranus's magnetic field may originate. Beneath this ionic ocean, an Earth-sized core of molten rocky materials is believed to exist. The magnetic field it-

SATELLITES AND RINGS OF URANUS

Name	Average Distance from Center of Uranus km	Average Distance from Center of Uranus mi	Period of Revolution (days)	Diameter or Ring Width km	Diameter or Ring Width mi	Orbital Inclination (degrees)	Orbital Eccentricity
1986U2R ring	38,000	24,000		2,500	1,500	0?	0?
6 ring	41,850	26,000		2	1	0.063	0.0010
5 ring	42,240	26,250		3	2	0.052	0.0019
4 ring	42,580	26,460		2	1	0.032	0.0011
Alpha ring	44,730	27,790		10	6	0.014	0.0008
Beta ring	45,670	28,380		9	6	0.005	0.0004
Eta ring	47,180	29,320		2	1	0.002	0.000
Gamma ring	47,630	29,600		3	2	0.011	0.000
Delta ring	48,310	30,020		6	4	0.004	0.000
Cordelia	49,700	30,900	0.33	40	25	0?	0?
1986U1R ring	50,040	31,090		2	1	0.001	0.0079
Epsilon ring	51,160	31,790		58	36	0?	0?
Ophelia	53,800	33,400	0.38	50	30	0?	0?
Bianca	59,200	36,800	0.43	50	30	0?	0?
Cressida	61,800	38,400	0.46	60	35	0?	0?
Desdemona	62,700	39,000	0.48	60	35	0?	0?
Juliet	64,600	40,100	0.49	80	50	0?	0?
Portia	66,100	41,100	0.51	80	50	0?	0?
Rosalind	69,900	43,400	0.56	60	35	0?	0?
Belinda	75,300	46,800	0.62	60	35	0?	0?
Puck	86,000	53,400	0.76	170	105	0?	0?
Miranda	129,900	80,700	1.41	484	301	4.2	0.0027
Ariel	190,900	118,600	2.52	1,160	720	0.3	0.0034
Umbriel	266,000	165,300	4.15	1,190	740	0.36	0.0050
Titania	436,300	271,100	8.70	1,610	1,000	0.14	0.0022
Oberon	583,400	362,500	13.46	1,550	960	0.10	0.0008

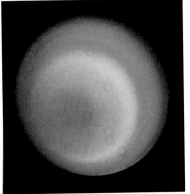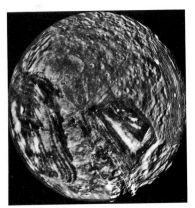

(Left) *Uranus, seen as it would appear to human eyes from the vantage point of* Voyager 2, *is a featureless disk.* (Center) *A false-color view, however, reveals some details about the hood of smog covering the south polar area. The small circles in these photos are actually image-processing defects.* (Right) *The innermost major moon, Miranda, has a chaotic surface in which old, heavily cratered terrain is interrupted by younger regions marked by scarps, ridges, and dark and bright bands.*

self is tilted 60° to the rotation axis and is offset from the center of the planet, by about one third of Uranus's radius, toward the north pole.

Infrared measurements from *Voyager 2* indicate that Uranus has an effective temperature of –214° C (–353° F). Unlike the other giant planets, there is no evidence of any significant internal heat source.

Rings. The discovery on Mar. 10, 1977, that Uranus has rings was one of the most unexpected and exciting events of modern planetary astronomy. Subsequent observations have indicated the presence of 10 narrow rings of dark particles and one broad, diffuse ring, in addition to 100 or more possibly transient ringlets of dust-sized particles seen only in *Voyager 2* images of the backlighted rings.

The outermost ring (called the epsilon ring), in marked contrast to the rings of Saturn, has almost no particles smaller than about 20 cm (8 in). The other rings also seem to be deficient in small particles.

Satellites. Uranus has five major satellites: MIRANDA, discovered by Gerard Kuiper in 1948; Ariel and Umbriel, discovered by William Lassell in 1851; and Titania and Oberon, discovered by William Herschel in 1787. Ten small satellites were also discovered in *Voyager 2* photographs, all of them orbiting Uranus well inside the orbit of Miranda. The five major satellites—and probably the ten smaller ones as well—appear to be in synchronous rotation; that is, they keep their same faces toward Uranus as they orbit the planet. Much like the ring particles, the smaller satellites appear to have surfaces as dark as coal. The major satellites have somewhat brighter surfaces, reflecting from 19% (Umbriel) to 40% (Ariel) of the sunlight that falls on them. In addition to being the darkest of the major satellites, Umbriel also has the fewest geological features. The other four satellites display increasingly complex geologies with decreasing distance from Uranus.

Oberon and Titania are remarkably similar in size, density color, and reflectivity. Titania, however, has a much larger fraction of small craters and more fractures across its surface, implying that Titania has a geologically younger surface. Oberon has one mountain that rises to an altitude of at least 20 km (12 mi) above the surrounding surface.

Although Umbriel and Ariel have similar diameters and densities, they differ dramatically in the appearance of their surfaces. Ariel's surface is literally covered with fractures and fault systems. Parallel fractures in several areas bound valleys that appear to have glacierlike flows along their floors. Water-ammonia ices become fluid at much lower temperatures than pure water ice and might form the observed glaciers.

Miranda is the innermost and smallest of the major moons. Its surface consists of an old, heavily cratered, rolling terrain with relatively uniform reflectivity, and a younger, complex terrain in three nearly rectangular regions characterized by parallel grooves, an abundance of vertical structures, and large brightness differences. The materials out of which Miranda was formed may not have melded together to form a uniform surface; its present bizarre appearance may be a frozen record of the late stages of the development of this satellite.

See also: SOLAR SYSTEM.

Uranus (mythology) In Greek mythology Uranus represented the sky or heaven. He was both the son and husband of GAEA, the earth, by whom he fathered first the hundred-handed giants and the CYCLOPES, whom he banished to Tartarus, and later the TITANS. Gaea, angry because her children were imprisoned, set the Titans against Uranus. CRONUS, their leader, castrated Uranus and succeeded him as ruler of the universe. According to Hesiod's *Theogony*, APHRODITE was born of the foam of Uranus's discarded genitals as they fell in the sea. Blood falling on the earth from the wound engendered the FURIES.

Urartu [oor-ahr'-too] The ancient kingdom of Urartu, centered in eastern Turkey, extended at the height of its prominence (8th century BC) into present-day northwestern Iran, Soviet Transcaucasia, and northern Syria. The Assyrians regarded Urartu as a threat by the 9th century BC, although references to Urartu already appear in Assyrian records dating from approximately 400 years earlier. Driven (late 8th century) from northern Syria, the Urartians subsequently were conquered by the Medes in the early 6th century BC, after years of hostilities with the Assyrians, Cimmerians, and Scythians.

Urban, Joseph [ur'-buhn] The architect and artist Joseph Urban, b. Vienna, May 26, 1872, d. July 10, 1933, distinguished himself by the wide range of his work. His architectural projects included the interior of Vienna's Municipal Building (1903), a castle (1900) for Count Esterhazy in Hungary, the Tsar Bridge (1903) over the Neva River in Russia, and Austrian exhibition buildings at Paris (1900) and St. Louis (1904). In the United States, Urban was best known as a scenic designer for the Metropolitan Opera Company (1918–33) and for the Ziegfeld Follies (beginning in 1914) in New York City. He also practiced architecture in New York: the Ziegfeld Theater (1927; demolished) and New School for Social Research (1930).

urban anthropology Urban anthropology is a relatively new but important subfield of cultural anthropology that focuses on the city as the locus of research. Traditionally, anthropologists have studied small, usually preliterate groups in remote areas. As complex industrial society penetrated into even isolated regions, however, many anthropologists began to redirect their field work toward the study of former hunter-gatherer groups and especially of farmers who migrated into the cities as laborers. Among the questions that currently interest urban anthropologists are the causes and perpetuation of urban poverty (the so-called culture of poverty controversy); adaptive strategies of kin and nonkin networks, such as voluntary associations; and the relationship between ethnicity and social stratification.

urban climate Urban climates are special cases of MICROCLIMATES, the study of which is of great importance in the conservation of energy and in air-pollution control. The most radical of the climatic changes caused by humans tend to be those from urbanization.

The city's microclimatic energy budget is different from that of rural areas in several ways. The large vertical surface areas of tall buildings expose a huge portion of the city to the Sun, allowing increased absorption of longwave and shortwave radiation. The surface materials are rocklike, with high conductivities, heat capacities, and reflectivities, and the surfaces are relatively impervious to moisture, which leads to rapid dispersal of rain and snow.

In addition, the city generates artificial heat and moisture because of its traffic, industries, and domestic heating and cooling. Last, the city is also a vast source of atmospheric contaminants that are by-products of its daily activities. As a result, urban environments, in contrast to rural ones, have undergone decreases in incident solar radiation, visibility, and horizontal wind speed but have shown increases in air pollution, air temperature, fog, cloudiness, rainfall, snowfall, and the number of thunderstorms.

The existence of urban heat islands (and coexisting cold islands because of the shading effect of tall buildings) has long been recognized. The complex and constantly changing mosaic of heat and cold islands influences urban ecology in a variety of ways. Heat islands raise minimum temperatures at night, and vertical temperature profiles over cities indicate multiple inversions that inhibit the escape of pollutants. As urbanization increases, escaping heat plumes may combine to form larger regional heat islands, producing a stronger convection cell and feeding local heat islands with already polluted air.

Urban League, National   A U.S. interracial organization, the National Urban League was founded in 1910 to provide community services and to secure equal opportunities for black citizens. Initially concerned with providing new jobs for blacks in industry and in aiding southern migrants who had moved into northern cities, after World War II the league became more directly involved in civil rights issues and in the improvement of employment and housing opportunities for American blacks.

urban planning   Urban planning can be defined variously as the formulation of alternative patterns of urban settlement, the rational use of resources to alleviate urban problems, and the provision of a city's physical and social infrastructure—transportation, utilities, housing, community facilities, and services. More simply, it is the art of building cities.

Contemporary urban planning draws upon many disciplines. The social sciences quantify the size and characteristics of the future population, its needs, and its occupational structure and income distribution. ARCHITECTURE, ENGINEERING, LANDSCAPE ARCHITECTURE, and urban design provide the three-dimensional solutions that are the expression of broad development policy decisions. The science of ecology permits an increasingly accurate measurement of the environmental consequences of development and the control of their adverse effects. Law and political science provide the principal legislative and bureaucratic mechanisms that are used to implement planning decisions. Although planning may anticipate the need for jobs, shelter, transportation, education, health, or recreation, its effectiveness is limited to putting restraints on private property rights and providing incentives to influence individual choices.

History of Urban Planning

The human desire to shape the urban environment goes back to the earliest known cities that developed in the Fertile Crescent and in India between 5000 and 3500 BC. Even though ancient cities were small by modern standards, their populations were frequently crowded within a defensive wall. Developmental pressures within a restricted area almost certainly resulted in legal restrictions regarding private property rights. The city's rulers built and maintained works of public utility—defensive walls and citadels, bridges and roads, temples and markets—while laws protected public ways and private property from encroachments.

Urban Planning in the Ancient World. Ancient civilizations occasionally planned new cities or major additions to existing settlements. The most widespread plan was a rectangular or grid street pattern that allowed considerable flexibility in the size of blocks while maintaining a clear visual order. Noteworthy examples of this type of city plan include Kahun (Egypt, *c.*1890 BC), whose workers' quarter is separated by an internal wall from the wealthier districts, and MILETUS (Anatolia, 479 BC), whose reconstruction was carried out in strict accord with the planning principles attributed to the Greek planner HIPPODAMUS OF MILETUS.

By the 4th century BC a theory of urban planning already existed, as evidenced in the writings of Hippocrates, Plato, and Aristotle. It addressed issues of site selection and orientation, as influenced by natural features and climate; city form, including the optimal location for major buildings; the size and composition of the population; and urban government and laws. These theories were later modified and amplified into a veritable textbook on urban planning, VITRUVIUS's *De architectura* (after 27 BC; trans. as *Ten Books on Architecture*, 1826 and 1914). This work standardized the city plans that the Roman engineers used in the innumerable fortified settlements and provincial cities that they built throughout the empire. The typical Roman plan consisted of two perpendicular main streets running north-south (*cardo*) and east-west (*decumanus*) with the city's main civic and mercantile square (*forum*) located at their intersection.

In 3d-century Rome building regulations prescribed construction standards, maximum allowable building heights on public ways, and minimum setbacks from other buildings. At various times the imperial government interfered directly in housing—for example, forcing owners to rebuild fire-damaged structures under penalty of confiscation (edict of Vespasian, AD *c.*70) or to repair dilapidated buildings (edict of Hadrian, AD *c.*129).

Medieval European Cities. Most of the Roman planning regulations fell into disuse during the protracted period of urban decadence that followed the dismembering (AD 476) of the empire, and they were not revived when European cities started flourishing again in the 10th and 11th centuries. They were replaced by a system of customary obligations that assigned to burgesses and guilds, or to work parties of residents, such traditional responsibilities of urban government as clearing refuse, maintaining highways, keeping the watch, and even repairing the city's walls.

Occasionally, when the establishment of a new settlement provided an opportunity to create a physical order, the simple geometry of the rectangular grid plan prevailed again, as in such late-medieval French *bastides* as Aigues-Mortes (1240) or Montpazier (1284), or the northern European trading cities of the Hanseatic League. Medieval theories of the city form were explicitly stated in Albrecht Dürer's idealized fortified capital of a kingdom in *Etliche Underricht zu Befestigung der Stett, Schlosz und Flecken* (1527; Guide to the Fortification of City, Castle, and Town), whose rigid spatial organization grouped classes by social status and segregated such noxious buildings as slaughterhouses, tanneries, and ironworks.

Renaissance Urban Planning. The shape of the city became more complicated as a result of improvements in the techniques of war and the reawakened interest in urban aesthetics in the Renaissance. The greater power of siege artillery required the replacement of vertical city walls with angular fortifications, whose sloping planes deflected the impact of iron cannonballs. Aesthetically, cities were embellished by widening streets and opening up squares. Straight avenues culminating in a monumental square ornamented with symmetrical buildings in the classical style became fashionable in the more prosperous European cities.

Starting in the middle of the 15th century, Italian theorists created a voluminous body of literature on the theory of urban planning. Largely inspired by Vitruvius, it treated aesthetics as well as such pragmatic questions as the design of fortifications, construction techniques, the location of specific facilities, and the supply of water. The theories of Leon Battista ALBERTI in *De re aedificatoria* (c.1450; trans. as *On Architecture*, 1726) and of Andrea PALLADIO in *I quattro libri d'architettura* (1570; trans. as *The Four Books of Architecture*, 1716), among many others, established an urban style whose influence was felt throughout the Western World. The aesthetic principles of the time were given their full rein in the layout of new towns, including Palmanova (Italy, 1593), Willemstad (The Netherlands, 1583), and Versailles (France, 1665).

The plan prepared for a fourfold extension of Amsterdam (The Netherlands, 1612) offers an exceptional example of a comprehensive effort to combine aesthetic and functional aspirations. Its three wide concentric canals, interconnected by smaller waterways radiating from the old town center, delineated a series of functional zones, with strict development controls governing the frontage of buildings on the canals, the use to which they could be put, their maximum height, and the general appearance of the building facade. These regulations were enforced through covenants between the Town Council, which had reclaimed the land and constructed canals and streets, and the purchaser of each lot.

The influence of Renaissance planning is also to be found in many of the new cities founded by Europeans in the Americas and in Asia. The Spanish colonial cities owed their rectangular plan and main square surrounded by the principal church and the government building to the Royal Ordinances of 1573 (*Leyes de las Indias*). William Penn's plan for Philadelphia (1682) and that for Montreal (1672) embodied the accepted planning principles of the time.

Origins of Contemporary Planning. Many of the problems that still plague our cities—slums, environmental pollution, social and economic segregation—came about during the Industrial Revolution. The incapacity of urban governments to enlarge their traditional responsibilities at a time when cities were developing rapidly led to the proliferation of substandard buildings, the intermingling of noisome industries and housing, and a density of development that overtaxed primitive water supplies and sewerage systems. At the end of the 19th century, almost 40 percent of the population of New York City, in large part newly arrived immigrants, lived in overcrowded tenements, many of whose rooms had no outside windows. Similar conditions prevailed in London, Berlin, Paris, Chicago, and other large cities. Infant mortality was high,

(Below, left to right) *Six typical housing patterns are illustrated by these maps, each representing 40 ha (100 acres). Three areas of single-family dwellings show both symmetrical construction on individual plots and houses clustered around cul-de-sacs in a wooded setting.*

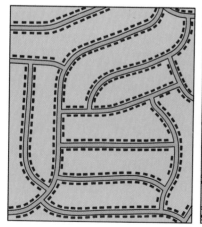 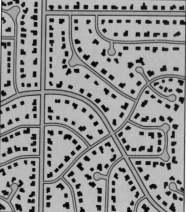 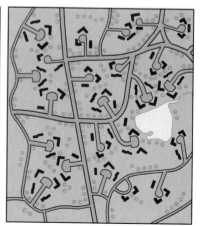

and cholera epidemics broke out frequently.

In England the Health of the Towns Act (1868) empowered municipalities to prescribe sanitary standards for housing and to issue a "closing order" when a dwelling was "unfit for human habitation," whereas the Public Health Act (1875) allowed towns to regulate new buildings and mandated the construction of water and sewer systems and the removal of refuse. Elsewhere in Europe new districts were planned on the urban fringe, replacing the now-obsolete fortifications, as in Vienna (1856) and Copenhagen (1865). Slums were cleared and broad avenues pierced through older districts, as in Paris, where Baron Georges Eugène HAUSSMANN launched (1848) an ambitious plan in the course of which more than 40 percent of the city's houses were torn down and replaced with new buildings, while new districts were laid out on the periphery and an extensive system of parks was created.

In the United States, Pierre Charles L'ENFANT had laid out (1791) the new capital of Washington, D.C., on an enormous scale, with a rectangular street grid laid over a plan of radial avenues, with squares and circles at major intersections. Urban improvements had been limited to parks in the 19th century, but the European approach was popularized by Chicago's World's Columbian Exposition of 1893, whose dazzling white plaster buildings lining landscaped avenues fired the imagination of visitors with a vision of a more aesthetic and efficient urban environment. Yet, despite improvements generated by the "City Beautiful" movement, city governments found imposing even minimal controls on private property politically difficult. The construction of unhealthy "old law" tenements was not outlawed in New York until 1901, and the new standards, prescribing an air shaft to ventilate inside rooms, were only marginally better. Only 22 cities had adopted height-restriction regulations by 1913; the first comprehensive zoning ordinance, specifying permitted uses as well as density of development, was not adopted in New York City until 1916.

Contemporary Urban Planning

Effective urban planning comprises clear development objectives as well as the means to carry them out. A city may choose to develop its unbuilt land, revitalize its downtown area, demolish its slums and replace them with new buildings, or any combination of these objectives. Its development objectives, usually combining social and physical aspects, are set forth in a comprehensive plan, which documents existing conditions, analyzes the causes of various shortcomings, and explores alternative solutions. By comparing the social, economic, and political costs and advantages of possible solutions, a preferred alternative can be selected and detailed.

The implementation of a plan occurs over many years; its progress is a function of the city's ability to finance it as well as of the plan's political viability. The means at the city's disposal may range from the use of its normal regulatory powers to legislate for the health, safety, and general welfare of the population to direct intervention in the private market through tax incentives, the purchase of land and buildings by eminent domain, or demolition of unsafe structures.

Zoning and Subdivision. Zoning and subdivision regulations are the powers most commonly used to regulate private development. Zoning separates land uses that are deemed incompatible by dividing the city into districts where only structures for specified uses, such as single-family homes, apartments, retail, or industry, can be built. Minimum lot sizes, maximum building heights, and setbacks from property lines are commonly part of zoning. Subdivision regulations prescribe the site-planning standards to be used in housing developments. They specify road widths and turning radii, sidewalk dimensions, utilities and drainage, street lighting, and landscaping. Together with building and health codes, zoning and subdivision regulations can effectively control the quality of new construction.

In cities, modern high-rise apartment blocks allow a greater density of population without creating the uniformity of 19th-century rowhouses. As shown in the illustration on the extreme right, all these patterns are sometimes mixed in the same area.

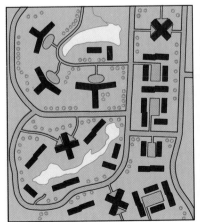

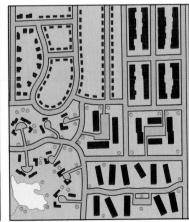

Urban Renewal in the United States. In the United States, direct government intervention was the keystone of urban renewal. Intended in part to eliminate substandard housing, which was estimated to account for 19 percent of dwellings in cities of 100,000 or more population, the urban-renewal legislation that was adopted as part of the 1949 Housing Act postulated a cooperative process between the public and private sectors. Local governments purchased land containing a specified percentage of substandard structures, prepared a reuse plan, undertook necessary demolition, provided new streets and utilities, and sold the improved parcels to private developers willing to build in accordance with the renewal plan. The difference between the public costs of the project and the resale value of the land was shared between the federal and local governments, the federal share amounting to two-thirds of the net cost. More than 2,000 projects with an average area of 29 ha (72 acres) were initiated under this controversial program; its major shortcomings were the displacement of low-income families and a failure to construct as many low- and moderate-income housing units as had been demolished.

In the United States the magnitude of necessary public intervention has prevented the establishment of NEW TOWNS from becoming official policy.

Urban Planning since 1960. In the United States and in most Western industrialized countries, urban planning is now commonly understood to include the delivery of social services, the development of employment opportunities for the economically disadvantaged, the search for housing solutions that avoid the stigma of public housing projects, and the protection of the environment. In the developing countries of the Third World, a lack of investment capital and rates of urbanization two to three times higher than in the West, resulting from rapid population growth and migration from rural areas, have created problems of unprecedented magnitude. Planning has tended to be a centralized government function whose major preoccupation has been the allocation of scarce resources to projects furthering national economic development objectives rather than the protection of the environment or the aesthetic appearance of cities.

urban renewal   see CITY

Urban II, Pope   Urban II, b. *c.*1042, d. July 24, 1099, was pope from 1088 until his death. He was a Frenchman named Odo. His great achievement was the continuance into the last years of the century—and in the face of opposition from Holy Roman Emperor HENRY IV— of the far-ranging ecclesiastical reform begun by Pope GREGORY VII.

Urban became prior of the great reforming monastery of Cluny. Going to Rome in 1078, he was created cardinal by Gregory VII. As pope, succeeding Victor III, Urban had to vindicate his own legitimacy against an antipope— Clement III—who was sponsored by Henry IV. He contrived nonetheless to vindicate the preeminence of the papacy in Latin Christendom, not only by leading the reform but also by launching the First CRUSADE in 1095. A cult developed around Urban soon after his death, and Leo XIII beatified him in 1881. Feast day: July 29.

Urban VI, Pope   Urban VI, b. *c.*1318, d. Oct. 15, 1389, pope from 1378 until his death, precipitated the Great SCHISM of the Western church. Originally named Bartolomeo Prignano, he was chosen to succeed Pope Gregory XI by a papal conclave strongly influenced by the Roman populace's demand for a Roman or Italian pope. Although known previously as an able administrator, as pope Urban acted in such a high-handed manner that he alienated the cardinals, and questions were raised about his sanity. Within a few months the powerful French cardinals returned to Avignon, declared Urban's election invalid, and elected Robert of Geneva (Clement VII) as "antipope." Thus the Great Schism began. Clement's supporters included Queen JOAN I of Naples. Urban secured her overthrow (1381) by Charles of Durazzo (CHARLES III of Naples) but later led an expedition against Charles during which Urban was captured (1383–84). On his release he had five cardinals executed for conspiracy against him.

Urban VIII, Pope   Urban VIII, b. Apr. 5, 1568, d. July 29, 1644, was pope from 1623 until his death. A Florentine aristocrat named Maffeo Barberini, he was named a cardinal in 1606 and bishop of Spoleto. As pope he encouraged the religious life by canonizing a number of saints and approving new orders. He revised the breviary, the missal, and the pontifical, and fostered missionary work by founding (1627) the Urban College of Propaganda. Urban also sponsored extensive building of military fortifications in the Papal States.

Urban's fear of Habsburg domination in Europe led him to favor France in the Thirty Years' War, although he tried to prevent Cardinal Richelieu's alliance with Sweden. Within Italy he was defeated in a war (1642–44) with the Farnese duke of Parma.

Urdu language   see INDO-IRANIAN LANGUAGES

urea [yur-ee'-uh]   The formation of urea and its excretion in the urine is the body's principal means of eliminating excess nitrogen derived from amino acids, which are the components of protein. Urea is a simple organic molecule, $CO(NH_2)_2$, in which almost half of the molecular weight is accounted for by nitrogen.

Urea is formed in the liver as the product of a set of biochemical reactions called the urea cycle. Although the urea cycle is complex, its net effect is the formation of urea molecules by combining nitrogen from the amino groups of amino acids with carbon and oxygen from carbon dioxide. Urea is carried from the liver by the bloodstream, and in the kidneys it is removed from the blood and concentrated for excretion. If the kidneys fail, blood-urea concentration may rise to high levels, a toxic condition known as uremia.

uremia [yur-ee'-mee-uh] *Uremia* is the term used to describe the wide variety of symptoms and physical abnormalities that result from the kidneys' failure to remove nitrogenous waste products normally excreted in the urine. The toxic effects of uremia affect virtually all human organs. The most common symptoms are high blood pressure, swelling (edema) of the ankles, nausea, vomiting, and weight loss. Anemia is almost always present because high blood levels of urea, one of the nitrogenous substances, shorten the life span of red blood cells. Other symptoms may include irritation of the heart sac (pericarditis), bleeding, muscle twitches, and itching (pruritus). In the later stages uremia causes agitation alternating with stupor, convulsions, coma, and ultimately death. Analysis of blood chemistries shows elevated levels of urea, creatinine, uric acid, phosphorus, and hydrogen ion. The levels of other minerals, hormones, and vitamins are abnormal as well. Removal of the toxins and improvement of the body's overload of fluids and acid are possible with the artificial kidney (hemodialysis), and patients are usually restored to a reasonably good state of health (see KIDNEY, ARTIFICIAL).

ureter see EXCRETORY SYSTEM

urethra see EXCRETORY SYSTEM

Urey, Harold Clayton [yur'-ee] Harold Clayton Urey, b. Walkerton, Ind., Apr. 29, 1893, d. Jan. 5, 1981, was awarded the 1934 Nobel Prize for chemistry for the discovery and isolation of deuterium (heavy hydrogen). Because of this recognition as a Nobel laureate and his experience in isotope separation, Urey was brought into the wartime Manhattan Project as head of the gaseous-diffusion project for uranium separation. Soon after the war, however, he began to speak out against the misuse of nuclear energy. His later research involved such diverse fields as geochemistry, astrophysics, and the origin of life.

uric acid [yur'-ik] Uric acid, the main end product of purine metabolism in humans and other primates, is derived from adenine and guanine, two purines that are important constituents of nucleic acids (DNA and RNA). In birds and reptiles, uric acid, a nitrogen-rich compound, performs the same function as UREA in mammals—ridding the body of excess nitrogen derived from amino acids. Birds and reptiles do not produce urea.

Uric acid is only slightly soluble, a property that accounts for the symptoms of GOUT, a disease in which levels of uric acid in the blood are elevated either from excess uric-acid formation or from impaired uric-acid excretion by the kidneys. The limited solubility of uric acid also causes the development of kidney stones; excess deposits of uric acid in the joints result in a condition called gouty arthritis, in which movement of a joint is accompanied by severe pain.

urine Urine is an aqueous solution, ranging from a liquid to a semisolid, formed by the EXCRETORY SYSTEM in animals and released from the body. It is composed of organic and inorganic substances, primarily metabolic waste products and water. Organisms have varying requirements for water, and this is reflected in their urine composition. Freshwater-drinking animals, for example, may need to rid their bodies of excess water. As a consequence, their urine will be dilute. Desert and marine mammals need to avoid water loss, and their urine can be very highly concentrated.

Birds and reptiles produce a urine that is white and composed of uric-acid crystals suspended in solution. It is mixed with fecal matter before expulsion. Land insects expel a nearly solid urine, and in some species it is stored as a body pigment rather than expelled. Amphibians and fish release a liquid solution of urea. In humans as well as other mammals, urine is formed in the kidneys. It is essentially a filtration of blood plasma, excluding most large molecules such as albumin. In the average person, about 120 ml (3.6 fl oz) of filtrate are derived from 650 ml (19.5 fl oz) of plasma each minute by both kidneys. About 99 percent of the sodium, chloride, and water of the filtrate is reabsorbed before the urine exits the kidneys, leaving only approximately 1 ml of urine per minute for excretion. In the average adult, about 1,200–2,000 ml (40–67 fl oz) of urine are formed each day.

Because the kidney is the only way to eliminate nonvolatile acids from the body, urine is usually acidic. In addition, the kidney is the primary route for excretion of metabolic end products, such as urea and uric acid from protein metabolism. Human urine also contains creatinine, inorganic salts, and the pigmented products of blood breakdown, such as urochrome, which gives urine its characteristic yellowish color. If kidney function decreases sufficiently, the body retains toxic substances, which leads to the development of UREMIA.

The various regulatory and excretory mechanisms of the kidneys allow the urine composition to vary, and thus they maintain the constancy and volume of the fluid compartments of the body while eliminating unwanted substances.

Because most kidney diseases and several systemic diseases cause abnormal findings during chemical and microscopic examination of the urine, urinalysis is an important laboratory test in clinical medicine.

Uris, Leon [yur'-is] An American novelist and screenwriter, Leon Uris, b. Baltimore, Md., Aug. 3, 1924, is famous for his massive, best-selling adventure novels in which a fictitious protagonist is placed in a semifactual historical context, such as the founding of the Israeli state (*Exodus*, 1959; film, 1961), the Berlin airlift (*Armageddon*, 1964), the Cuban missile crisis (*Topaz*, 1967; film, 1969), or the 1916 Easter Rising in Ireland (*Trinity*, 1976). Several of his novels have been adapted for film and television, and Uris has also written original screenplays, such as *Gunfight at the OK Corral* (1957).

Urmia, Lake [oor'-mee-uh]   Lake Urmia is a salt lake in north Iran, which has a maximum depth of 16 m (52 ft) and an area ranging from 3,885 to 5,955 km² (1,500 to 2,300 mi²), depending on the season. The largest lake in Iran, it forms an interior drainage basin that receives water from the mountains but has no outlet. Ferry service links Sharifkhaneh and Gelemkhaneh. Migrating flamingos and pelicans frequent the lake, and on the small volcanic islands, leopards are common.

Urochordata   see TUNICATE

urogenital diseases   Urogenital diseases include diseases of the urinary tract of the EXCRETORY SYSTEM—from the KIDNEY to the external opening of the urethra—and of the tract of the REPRODUCTIVE SYSTEM. These diseases are commonly grouped for convenience because in males the two tracts share the terminal end and in females the tracts, although separate, are contiguous. Thus in either sex a problem in one tract is likely to affect the other. The medical specialties most directly concerned with urogenital diseases are GYNECOLOGY and urology; both involve the urinary tract, but the former specializes in female and the latter in male genital-tract disorders. The illnesses studied include INFECTIOUS DISEASES, tumors, congenital (inborn) disorders, allergy and immunity problems, and diseases of other body systems or of general metabolism that also affect the urinary and genital tracts, such as cardiovascular diseases and diabetes.

Urinary-Tract Diseases. Among the more serious KIDNEY DISEASES are glomerulonephritis, nephrosis, and pyelonephritis. Of the many observed forms of glomerulonephritis, most show evidence of deposits of antibody-antigen complexes in the glomeruli, the kidney's filtering units; thus one common form of the disease occurs 2 to 3 weeks after an infection of the throat or skin with streptococci. Most cases are temporary, but a few become chronic, leading to kidney failure and UREMIA. Nephrosis, or nephrotic syndrome, is an outpouring of protein into the urine due to glomerular damage. This condition is not itself a disease but a symptom observed in the course of chronic glomerulonephritis, multiple myeloma, lupus erythematosus, or other serious diseases. Pyelonephritis is a serious infection of kidney tissue that can result in permanent damage if not treated promptly. It usually results from bacterial infections of the BLADDER (see also CYSTITIS) or of the ureter, the tube ascending from the bladder to the kidney.

Infections of the urethra are collectively known as urethritis. Such infections include CHLAMYDIA and GONORRHEA (see also VENEREAL DISEASES), among others.

Another urinary-tract affliction is the development of KIDNEY STONES and bladder stones; such stones also commonly arise in conjunction with infections. Stones are caused by the precipitation of insoluble materials from the URINE; some persons with GOUT form uric-acid stones, and some persons with tumors of the parathyroid glands form calcium stones. Small stones become trapped as

they descend into the ureter, and the waves of contraction to move them along produce the extremely painful condition known as ureteral COLIC.

Male Genital-Tract Diseases. One site along the male genital tract that is a frequent source of problems in middle and older age is the PROSTATE GLAND. The gland surrounds the urethra just below the bladder; because of this location, the prostate compresses the posterior urethra when it is enlarged by infections (prostatitis) or by benign tumors. The compression obstructs urinary flow and, if severe enough and continued over a long period of time, results in urinary-tract infection, severe renal damage, and uremia. Cancer of the prostate is uncommon in men under the age of 60, but its incidence increases steadily thereafter.

Female Genital-Tract Diseases. The vagina, uterus, and associated glands of the female genital tract are all common sites of venereal diseases and of a number of nonvenereal infections due to other bacteria and yeasts. Bacteria that move upward from the vagina during menstruation are also responsible for major problems of the fallopian tubes; such infections result in abscess of the tubes and in localized PERITONITIS. This serious and painful condition is known as pelvic inflammatory disease (PID). The condition can also lead to scarring of the fallopian tubes, which is a major cause of infertility.

A number of benign and malignant cysts and tumors can develop in the female genital tract, including endometriosis—a benign transplant of cells from the uterine lining (endometrium) cast off during menstruation. In the endometrium itself, malignancies occur with increasing frequency among the elderly; malignancies of the uterine muscle, called leiomyosarcomas, are seen more occasionally, but the benign tumors called leiomyomas are also fairly common.

The PAP test is routinely given in the United States to detect cancer of the neck of the uterus, or cervix. The vagina and associated glands are not common sites for tumors, except for the increased frequency of vaginal carcinomas seen in daughters of women who were treated with large doses of progestins (sex hormones) while pregnant.

Urquiza, Justo José de [oor-kee'-sah]   Justo José de Urquiza, b. Oct. 18, 1801, d. Apr. 11, 1870, an Argentine statesman and soldier, helped lead his country toward unity and constitutional government. For a time Urquiza served the dictator Juan Manuel de ROSAS as principal field commander. In 1841 he became governor of Entre Ríos, introducing educational, fiscal, and administrative reforms.

In 1852, Urquiza and other governors joined with liberals, exiles, and Brazilian forces to defeat Rosas at the Battle of Monte Caseros. Urquiza then became provisional dictator of the Argentine Confederation; he sanctioned a new constitution (1853) based on that of the United States. In 1854 he was inaugurated president, but his efforts to achieve unity were hindered by the secession of Buenos Aires. Urquiza lost decisive battles against Buenos Aires at Cepeda in 1859 and at Pavón in 1861. His position in Entre Ríos declined, and he and his sons were assassinated by a follower of a political rival.

Ursa Major   see Big Dipper

Ursa Minor   see Little Dipper

Ursúa, Pedro de [oor-soo'-ah]   Pedro de Ursúa, c.1510–1561, was a Spanish soldier and explorer of South America. He went to the New World in 1545 and then fought the Indians of New Granada. After serving (1546) as governor of Bogotá, in what is now Colombia, he founded (1549) Pamplona, which he governed from 1549 to 1550. In 1558, Ursúa went to Peru, and two years later he was joined by the adventurer Lope de Aguirre (c.1518–61) in a search for gold and for the headwaters of the Amazon River. It is believed that Aguirre murdered Ursúa on that journey.

Ursula, Saint [ur'-suh-luh]   The subject of popular legend during the Middle Ages, Saint Ursula was a 4th-century British princess and martyr. Returning from a pilgrimage to Rome, she and her 11,000 virgin companions were massacred at Cologne by the Huns. She is the patron saint of the Ursuline nuns (founded 1544). Feast day: Oct. 21 (suppressed in 1969).

Uruguay [yur'-uh-gway or oo-roo-gwy']   Uruguay, the second smallest country in South America, forms a wedge between Argentina on the west and Brazil on the north and east. On the south is the Atlantic and the Río de la Plata estuary. The Uruguay River follows the country's western border, suggesting the name during the colonial period—Banda Oriental (east bank). Almost half of Uruguay's inhabitants live in Montevideo, the capital and only large city.

Land and Resources

The countryside consists of rolling hills and prairies. An extension of the Brazilian Highlands lies in the northeast. The Cuchilla Grande (Grand Hills) runs from the northeast toward the south. Sandy beaches along the coast are the basis for a large tourist industry. Punta del Este, an internationally popular resort, is located there. The southern plains extend from the rich alluvial soil at the Río de la Plata estuary north along the Uruguay River to Salto.

Climate. Temperatures range from about 10° C (50° F) in July to 22° C (71° F) in February. Precipitation is adequate, with a mean annual rainfall of about 890 mm (35 in) increasing northward.

Drainage. The Cuchilla Grande acts as a drainage divide. Lakes and lagoons are numerous, some reaching 180 km² (70 mi²) in size. The largest lake in South America is the artificial Embalse del Río Negro, covering about 10,400 km² (4,000 mi²).

Vegetation and Animal Life. Most of Uruguay is covered with grassland. Wildlife has greatly diminished; jaguars and pumas have become rare, and capybaras, foxes, deer,

armadillos, and alligators are also declining in numbers. The American ostrich, or rhea, is now found infrequently, but many other bird species inhabit the country.

People

Of the 3 million Uruguayans, more than 85% are of European—predominantly Spanish and Italian—origin. A small number of mestizos and blacks have survived, whereas the original Charrúa Indian population has been totally absorbed. Spanish is the official language. Roman Catholicism is the religion of two-thirds of the population.

Education and Health. Illiteracy is among the lowest in Latin America, and a publicly financed program provides free education up to the university level. The University of the Republic (1849) is located in Montevideo. Inadequate classroom space presents a major problem, as does the surplus of graduates in professional fields forced to seek jobs abroad.

The health-care system provides adequate medical services for everyone. The government has traditionally paid much attention to preventative medicine.

The Arts. A major representation in Uruguayan literature, drama, and music is the cowboylike gaucho. Foremost among 20th-century writers have been essayist José Enrique Rodó, short-story writer Horacio Quiroga, poet Juana de Ibarbourou, and novelists Mario Benedetti and

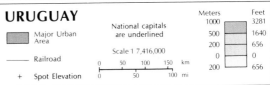

URUGUAY

Major Urban Area

National capitals are underlined

Railroad

Spot Elevation

Scale 1:7,416,000

Meters	Feet
1000	3281
500	1640
200	656
0	0
200	656

ORIENTAL REPUBLIC OF URUGUAY

Land: Area: 176,215 km^2 (68,037 mi^2). Capital and largest city: Montevideo (1985 pop., 1,311,976).

People: Population (1990 est.): 3,033,000. Density: 17 persons per km^2 (45 per mi^2). Distribution (1985): 86% urban, 14% rural. Official language: Spanish. Major religion: Roman Catholicism.

Government: Type: republic. Legislature: National Congress. Political subdivisions: 19 departments.

Economy: GNP (1989): $8 billion; $2,620 per capita. Labor distribution (1985): manufacturing—18%; government and services—31%; agriculture—15%; commerce—12%; utilities, construction, transport, and communication—12%; other—12%. Foreign trade (1989): imports—$1.1 billion; exports—$1.5 billion. Currency: 1 new Uruguayan peso = 100 centésimos.

Education and Health: Literacy (1990): 94% of adult population. Universities (1987) 1. Hospital beds (1983): 23,400. Physicians (1987): 6,679. Life expectancy (1990): women—76; men—70. Infant mortality (1990): 22 per 1,000 live births.

Juan Carlos Onetti. Cultural activities are centered in Montevideo, where art and architecture have imitated European schools.

Economic Activity

Increased urbanization has forced the development of intensive agriculture, but in the interior, sheep and cattle grazing occupy more than 80% of the land. Uruguay is largely self-sufficient in food production. It exploits its forest resources to a limited extent.

Public policy promotes industrialization in spite of the lack of minerals. The government established Uruguay's largest meat-packing operation, encouraged the formation of dairy cooperatives, and created a publicly owned petroleum refinery. The major industries continue to be agriculturally based. The development of the fishing industry was begun in the 1970s. The principal export items are wool, meat, and leather. Primary imports include petroleum, raw materials, chemicals, and machinery. In the late 1980s, the major economic problems included high inflation and frequent strikes.

Government and History

Democracy in Uruguay collapsed in 1973 with a takeover by the armed forces. Labor unions and political parties were outlawed, and the independent judiciary was abolished.

On Mar. 1, 1985, Uruguay returned to its democratic tradition, after 12 years of military rule, when a centrist, Julio María Sanguinetti, took office as president. He had won the November 1984 election as the Colorado party candidate. The bicameral congress, dissolved in 1973, was restored, and a National Constituent Assembly was formed in 1985 to draw up a series of constitutional reforms. Late in 1989, Luis Alberto Lacalle of the National (Blanco) party won the presidential elections.

Uruguay was the last colony settled by Spain in the Americas. Spain sent (1624) missionaries among the Charrúa Indians and founded (1726) Montevideo as a counter to Portuguese ambitions in the Río de la Plata estuary. In 1811 revolutionaries from the Banda Oriental, led by José Gervasio ARTIGAS, joined with the forces of Buenos Aires junta in expelling the Spanish. An attempted federal union with Argentina failed because the latter sought to impose a centralized government on the Banda Oriental. Artigas, however, was unable to maintain Uruguayan independence against Brazil, which annexed the Banda Oriental in 1821.

In 1825 the group called the Thirty-three Immortals, led by Juan Antonio LAVALLEJA, declared Uruguay's independence. War ensued, but both Argentina and Brazil recognized that independence in 1828.

A gaucho herds beef cattle in the rolling grasslands of central Uruguay. Livestock raising has long been a major economic activity in this South American nation. Today cattle and sheep continue to provide the meat, hides, and wool that are the nation's chief exports.

Civil strife soon developed in the new country between two parties: the Blancos, led by Manuel Oribe, and the Colorados, led by Fructuoso RIVERA. Oribe was supported by Juan Manuel de ROSAS of Argentina, and war continued until the overthrow (1852) of Rosas. Renewed conflict between the Colorados and Blancos and intervention by Paraguay helped precipitate the War of the TRIPLE ALLIANCE (1865–70).

Peace and prosperity were finally achieved after 1903 under the leadership of President José Batlle y Ordóñez. Few of his political and social reforms were actually adopted, but he laid the groundwork for later reforms. In 1919 a new constitution was adopted, providing for a *colegiado*, a plural executive modeled on the Swiss pattern. The system was abolished in 1933, and for the next ten years a mild dictatorship prevailed. A modified *colegiado* system was reintroduced in 1951.

After the mid-20th century, economic problems began to strain the political stability of the country. By the mid-1960s, strikes and riots had become prominent features of the sociopolitical scene. The 1967 return to presidential government did not alleviate the situation, and in the late 1960s, Marxist terrorist urban guerrillas called the Tupamaro National Liberation Front sought violent revolution. Between 1973 and 1976 the popularly elected government was eased out of office by the powerful armed forces, and by the late 1970s the regime held thousands of political prisoners. In 1984 the military permitted presidential elections. The victor, Julio Sanguinetti of the Colorado party, had pledged that there would be no purges for past military abuses and in 1986 signed an amnesty bill, upheld in a 1989 referendum.

Uruguay River   The Uruguay River, 1,610 km (1,000 mi) long, is a major South American river, draining approximately 307,000 km^2 (118,530 mi^2). Its two main headstreams, the Pelotas and Canoas, rise about 65 km (40 mi) west of the Atlantic coast in southeastern Brazil and join near Piratuba. The river flows west and then turns southwest, flowing first along the Argentina-Brazil border and farther south along the Argentina-Uruguay border. The Uruguay empties into the RÍO DE LA PLATA. It is navigable to Salto, 305 km (190 mi) upstream.

Uruk [oo'-ruk]   The ancient Sumerian city of Uruk (biblical Erech; modern Warka) lies 250 km (156 mi) southeast of Baghdad, Iraq. First settled (*c.*5000 BC) by the prehistoric inhabitants of Mesopotamia, the city developed (late 4th millennium BC) around the two sacred centers of Kullab and Eanna, which have yielded such evidence of early Sumerian civilization as monumental temples (at Eanna) decorated with cone mosaics, sophisticated sculpture, glyptic art, and some examples of the first writing, which was pictographic. In the early 3d millennium BC, a 9.5-km-long (6-mi) city wall was built (according to tradition, by semimythological King Gilgamesh) to enclose an area of about 8.75 km^2 (3.4 mi^2). Only intermittently independent, Uruk was subject to the Ur empire (*c.*2100–2000 BC) and to successive kings of Babylonia and Assyria, most of whom maintained its temples, as did the later Seleucids. Settlement declined during the Parthian period (247 BC–AD 226).

U.S. Information Agency   The U.S. Information Agency is an independent agency of the executive branch of the U.S. government founded in 1953. In 1977 it was merged with the Bureau of Educational and Cultural Affairs of the Department of State and was called for a few years the International Communications Agency. Its purpose is to spread information about the United States abroad, to inform the U.S. government about foreign opinion regarding the United States, and to arrange cultural and educational exchanges with foreign countries. The agency maintains libraries, reading rooms, and information centers in about 125 countries. Its largest component, the VOICE OF AMERICA, launched Radio Martí, to Cuba, in 1985.

U.S.A.   *U.S.A.* (1938), a novel by John Dos Passos, is an epic study from a radical-liberal point of view of the commercial vulgarization of American life from the beginning of the 20th century through the Depression of the 1930s. Divided into three books—*The 42nd Parallel* (1930), *1919* (1932), and *The Big Money* (1936)—*U.S.A.* is a collage of four kinds of materials: "Newsreels," recounting significant events through newspaper headlines, popular song lyrics, and other documentary sources; "Camera Eye," containing perceptions of such events through an anonymous stream-of-consciousness; poison-pen biographical sketches of the celebrities of the period; and long chapters from the linked histories of more than a dozen representative types of people.

Ushuaia [oo-swy'-ah]   Ushuaia (1980 pop., 10,998), Argentina, founded as a Protestant mission in 1870, is the southernmost city in the world and the capital of Tierra del Fuego National Territory. Its port faces the Beagle Channel. Industries include sheep raising, lumbering, fishing, trapping, and tourism.

Usman dan Fodio   Usman dan Fodio, 1754–1817, Islamic teacher and writer, led an Islamic reform movement that overthrew the Hausa city-state kingdoms of northern Nigeria and replaced them with a FULANI-dominated empire called the Sokoto caliphate. As head of a community advocating the purification of Islam, he directed the jihad (holy war) against the Hausa kingdoms that began in 1804. Within four years, his forces gained the upper hand. Usman acted as spiritual leader of the new Sokoto caliphate while others tended to its administration.

USO   see UNITED SERVICE ORGANIZATIONS

Ussher, James [uhsh'-ur]   The Irish scholar and Anglican archbishop James Ussher, b. Jan. 4, 1581, d. Mar. 21, 1656, is best remembered for his long-accepted system of biblical chronology, which set the date of creation at 4004 BC. Ordained in 1601, he was professor of divinity at Trinity College, Dublin, before becoming bishop of Meath (1621) and archbishop of Armagh (1625). Ussher's scholarship was wide ranging and profound, and he made use of original manuscript sources. His greatest achievement was identifying the seven authentic letters of Ignatius of Antioch. His library, including the magnificent Book of Kells, is preserved at Trinity College.

USSR   see UNION OF SOVIET SOCIALIST REPUBLICS; RUSSIA/UNION OF SOVIET SOCIALIST REPUBLICS, HISTORY OF

Ustinov, Peter [yoo'-sti-nawf]   The actor, director, producer, playwright, and author Peter Ustinov, b. London, Apr. 16, 1921, has appeared in scores of plays and films, winning Academy Awards for his performances in *Spartacus* (1960) and *Topkapi* (1964) and three Emmy Awards for his television work. A prolific author, he has written short stories (*Add a Dash of Pity*, 1959), novels (*The Loser*, 1960), an autobiography (*Dear Me*, 1977), *Ustinov in Russia* (1987), and screen and stage plays.

usury   Usury, the practice of charging an excessive rate of INTEREST on a loan, is regulated by many governments, and in the United States by state laws. The term originally meant any profit made from the loan of money. The Old Testament forbids the taking of interest. The medieval church also banned usury, although the prohibition eventually disappeared. Islamic law, however, still forbids the practice.

In the United States the need for borrowed money was especially acute as the Western frontier advanced. The populist movement of the latter 1800s was fueled in part by Western demands for regulated, low-interest loans, and many present state usury laws originated during this period. In recent years, most states have raised usury limits to conform with generally rising interest rates. A few states have eliminated usury laws entirely, counting on competition to keep interest rates from soaring.

Utah   Centrally located in the Rocky Mountain region, midway between Canada and Mexico, Utah is bordered by Wyoming on the northeast, Colorado on the east, Arizona on the south, Nevada on the west, and Idaho on the north. Utah is the 3d highest state in the United States, with an average elevation of 1,859 m (6,100 ft). Except for a projection of Wyoming into its northeastern corner, Utah would be rectangular in shape, measuring 440 km (275 mi) from east to west and 555 km (345 mi) from north to south. Settled by Mormon pioneers fleeing persecution in Illinois, Utah continues to have a large Mormon population. The state derives its name from the Ute Indians, who live in the Uinta Basin southeast of the capital, Salt Lake City.

Land and Resources

The spine of the ROCKY MOUNTAINS runs down the middle of Utah, with the COLORADO PLATEAU to the east and the GREAT BASIN to the west. The part of the Rockies keeping to the main north-south axis is called the WASATCH RANGE. The Uinta Mountains, extending more than 160 km (100 mi) just below the Utah–Wyoming border, represent the longest east-west-trending range in the United States; Utah's highest point, Kings Peak, at 4,123 m (13,528 ft), lies within this range. The Great Basin—the third largest region of interior drainage in the world—encompasses steep mountain ranges separated by broad desert flats.

Soils. Utah's soils range from the red and gray desert soils in the valleys to the alpine soils of the mountains. Most fertile are the alluvials and brown steppe—chestnut and chernozem loams formed along the bases of mountains.

AT A GLANCE

UTAH

Land: Area: 219,901 km² (84,904 mi²); rank: 13th. Capital and largest city: Salt Lake City (1990 pop., 159,936). Counties: 29. Elevations: highest—4,123 m (13,528 ft), at Kings Peak; lowest—610 m (2,000 ft), at Beaverdam Wash (Creek).

People: Population (1990): 1,727,784; rank: 35th; density: 8.1 persons per km² (21 per mi²). Distribution (1990): 87% urban, 13% rural. Average annual change (1980–90): +1.8%.

Government (1993): Governor: Mike Leavitt, Republican. U.S. Congress: Senate—2 Republicans; House—2 Democrats, 1 Republican. Electoral college votes: 5. State legislature: 29 senators, 75 representatives.

Economy: State personal income (1989): $22.3 billion; rank: 37th. Median family income (1989): $33,246; rank: 25th. Agriculture: income (1989)—$748 million. Lumber production (1991): not available. Mining (nonfuel): value (1988)—$1 billion. Manufacturing: value added (1987)—$4.9 billion. Services: value (1987)—$5.5 billion.

Miscellany: Statehood: Jan. 4, 1896; the 45th state. Nickname: Beehive State; tree: blue spruce; motto: Industry; song: "Utah, We Love Thee."

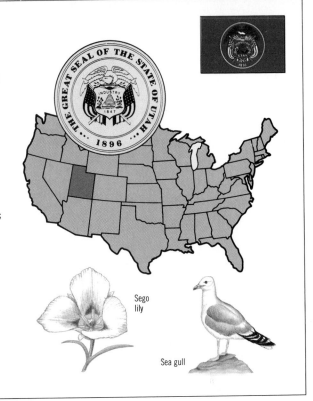

Sego lily

Sea gull

Rivers and Lakes. Eastern Utah drains into the COLORADO RIVER and its branches; major tributaries of the Colorado include the GREEN RIVER and the San Juan. Streams in the western part of the state—such as the Jordan, Bear, Provo, Sevier, and Weber—flow into the Great Basin. The Virgin River in southwestern Utah empties into Lake Mead. In the extreme northwestern corner of the state, the Raft River drains into the Snake River.

In prehistoric times, Lake Bonneville, an inland sea, covered a large part of western Utah. The GREAT SALT LAKE—the largest natural lake west of the Mississippi and the largest salt lake in the Western Hemisphere—is a remnant of Lake Bonneville, as are the BONNEVILLE SALT FLATS. Utah Lake, the state's largest natural freshwater lake, is dwarfed by the artificial Lake Powell—300 km (185 mi) from end to end.

Climate. Utah is the second driest state in the nation, with an average annual precipitation of 330 mm (13 in). Whereas the Great Salt Lake Desert receives only 127 mm (5 in) of precipitation per year, however, part of the Wasatch Range receives about 1,020 mm (40 in). During the summer, average temperatures range between 18° C (65° F) and 28° C (83° F). In winter, temperatures fall below freezing, except in the southeastern corner of the state.

Vegetation and Animal Life. The vegetation of Utah's low-lying deserts includes the Joshua tree, creosote bush, mesquite, and subtropical cacti. In the foothills piñon pine and gnarled juniper appear, and mountain flora include the blue spruce—the state tree—as well as the ponderosa pine, lodgepole pine, Douglas fir, Englemann spruce, and alpine fir. The nation's oldest trees, bristlecone pines, grow near the timberline, with some specimens dating back 3,000 years. The most common deciduous tree, the so-called quaking aspen, forms large stands at elevations well above 2,130 m (7,000 ft).

Although elk and a few moose inhabit the northern mountains, and pronghorn antelope and wild mustangs roam the western desert valleys, Utah's most prevalent big-game animal is the mule deer. Small buffalo herds can still be found in the Henry Mountains in the southeast and on Antelope Island in the Great Salt Lake, but desert bighorn sheep are limited to Zion and Canyonlands national parks. Cougars occupy the high mountain country. Smaller animals include the fur-bearing beaver, mink, marten, weasel, muskrat, badger, fox, and ringtail cat. The Great Basin rattlesnake is one of the most venomous creatures in North America.

The state's lakes and streams contain bass, catfish,

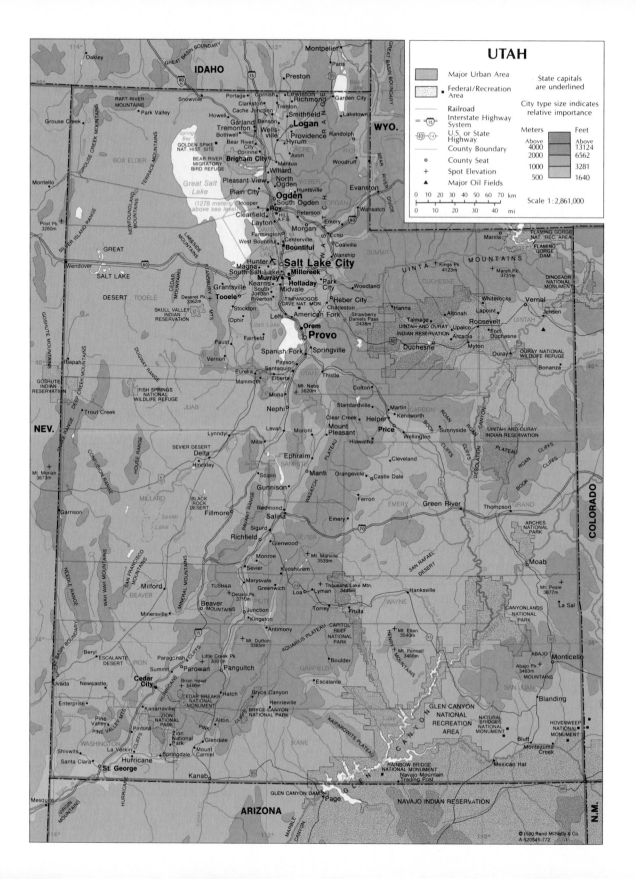

Utah sucker, carp, yellow perch, and rainbow, brook, and brown trout. A unique subspecies, the Utah cutthroat trout, is found only in the Deep Creek Mountains of western Utah. Utah hosts hundreds of species of migratory birds. Game birds include the Hungarian and chukar partridge, ring-necked pheasant, sage grouse, and wild turkey; birds of prey include the bald and golden eagle, vultures, and several varieties of hawks. The sea gull earned its status as the state bird when in 1848 flocks of them devoured the millions of crickets that threatened to destroy the Mormon pioneers' first crops.

Resources. More than 200 commercially usable minerals are present in Utah, including rich deposits of copper, gold, molybdenum, and silver. Coal, natural gas, and oil are found in the Colorado Plateau, and deposits of oil and gas are found in the northwestern area of the state. Almost 30% of Utah's total land area is forested; the forests are located in the state's mountainous areas.

People

During the 20th century, Utah's population has doubled almost every 40 years—from 276,749 in 1900, to 507,847 in 1930 and 1,059,273 in 1970. The population increased by almost 40% between 1970 and 1980 and by 18% between 1980 and 1990, making Utah one of the fastest-growing states in the country. The most densely populated area, the Wasatch Front, contains the state's three largest cities—SALT LAKE CITY, OGDEN (53 km/33 mi to the north), and PROVO (61 km/38 mi to the south). Their metropolitan populations account for much of Utah's population. Utah has by far the highest birthrate and one of the lowest death rates in the United States.

Hispanic Americans constitute the largest ethnic minority in Utah. Utah also has small African-American and American Indian populations. Most Indians belong to the UTE, NAVAJO, PAIUTE, and SHOSHONI tribes. About 70% of the state's inhabitants are members of the Church of Jesus Christ of Latter-day Saints (see MORMONISM).

Education. One of the first acts of the Mormon settlers was to establish the University of Deseret in the parlor of an adobe cabin in Salt Lake City in 1850. This, the first public university west of the Mississippi, changed its name to the University of Utah in 1892. Today the state system includes three other 4-year institutions of higher education. Utah's best-known private institution of higher learning, Mormon-supported BRIGHAM YOUNG UNIVERSITY, was established at Provo in 1875.

Culture. Salt Lake City's much-traveled Mormon Tabernacle Choir is world famous. Salt Lake City's Bicentennial Arts Complex houses the internationally recognized Utah Symphony; the Ballet West, considered one of the best classical ballet companies in the nation; the Utah Repertory Dance Theatre and the Ririe-Woodbury Company, both noted for modern dance; and the Salt Lake Art Center. The Museums of Fine Arts and of Natural History on the University of Utah campus house the state's principal collections.

Historical Sites and Recreational Areas. The Golden Spike National Historic Site at Promontory, Utah, commemorates the joining on May 10, 1869, of the Union Pacific Railroad from the east and the Central Pacific from the west to complete the nation's first transconti-

(Left) *Sandstone monoliths formed through eons of erosion rise nearly 100 m (330 ft) above the desert floor along the Utah-Arizona border. This portion of the Navajo Indian Reservation is maintained for tourists as the Monument Valley Navajo Tribal Park.* (Below) *The copper-plated dome of Utah's state capitol* (left), *in Salt Lake City, rises to a height of 87 m (285 ft). Salt Lake City, the state's largest city, was founded in 1847 by Mormons fleeing religious persecution.*

nental railroad. The restored Beehive House, built in 1855 in Salt Lake City, was the home of Brigham Young; and on the capital's Temple Square stand the Salt Lake City Tabernacle and the Mormon Temple.

Each year several million tourists visit Utah. They are attracted by Bryce Canyon National Park and Zion National Park as well as Arches, Canyonlands, and Capitol Reef national parks.

Communications. Of the state's daily newspapers, the two largest are in Salt Lake City—the *Tribune,* a morning paper, and the *Deseret News,* an evening daily. Other dailies include the *Ogden Standard-Examiner* and the *Provo Daily Herald*, both evening papers. Radio broadcasting is provided by a number of AM and FM stations.

Economic Activity

Service industries account for about 75% of Utah's gross state product, and government in particular wields an important economic influence in the state. About 70% of Utah's lands are under federal control, and many civilian workers are on federal payrolls. Others are employed by the military or defense industries.

Agriculture. Of every 40 ha (100 acres) of land in Utah, only about 1.6 ha (4 acres) are suitable for cultivation. Livestock provides about 75% of the state's agricultural income, with beef cattle ranking first in value, followed by dairy products, turkeys, and hay. The most important crops are hay, wheat, and cherries. Other crops include alfalfa seed, apples, barley, onions, potatoes, sugar beets, and greenhouse products. Many fruits and vegetables are grown in north central Utah.

Forestry. National forests cover significant areas of Utah, but most of the land is not available for commercial timber enterprises. Among the trees that are harvested are the ponderosa pine, white fir, Douglas fir, Englemann spruce, subalpine fir, lodgepole pine, and aspen. The Dixie National Forest has large ponderosa pine stands. Panguitch, a town in southern Utah, is a sawmilling center.

Mining. Fuels account for the majority of Utah's mineral output, and petroleum is the state's leading mineral. Utah's second most valuable mineral is coal. Utah also has reserves of natural gas.

The most valuable nonfuel mineral found in the state is copper, and Utah ranks among the leading U.S. states in copper production. Utah also has rich deposits of gold, molybdenum, silver, lead, and zinc, and its iron-mining operations are among the largest in the western United States. Utah is also a leading producer of beryllium and Gilsonite and has significant reserves of uranium. Phosphate and potash are used for fertilizer. Besides the sodium chloride obtained from evaporating beds along the southern and eastern shores of the Great Salt Lake, several minerals in solution are extracted from lake brines, including magnesium, chlorine, magnesium chloride, potassium sulfate, sodium sulfate, lithium, bromine, and boron.

Manufacturing. Utah's manufacturing is centered in the Salt Lake City area and in Cache, Utah, and Weber counties. Major state industries produce nonelectrical machinery, transportation equipment, and food products.

Other manufactures include electrical machinery and equipment; printing and publishing; petroleum and coal products; fabricated metals; chemical products; stone, clay, and glass products; and textiles.

Transportation. Utah is advantageously located on three interstate highways; I-15 crosses the state from north to south, and I-80 and I-70 are major east-west highways. Major railroads are the Union Pacific and the Denver and Rio Grande Western. Amtrak provides passenger service. Utah's busiest airport is the Salt Lake City International Airport.

Energy. Most of Utah's electrical power comes from coal-fired steam units, but hydroelectric units produce some electricity. Most electricity is supplied by the privately owned Utah Power and Light Company. Natural gas and oil are also energy sources in Utah.

Government and Politics

Utah's constitution of 1896 included the provision—unusual at that time—that women were allowed to vote. The state's governor serves a 4-year term and may be reelected indefinitely; the legislature consists of the senate, whose 29 members (one from each county) serve 4-year terms, and the house of representatives, whose 75 members serve 2-year terms. Utah's highest court is the supreme court; it has 5 justices who serve 10-year terms. Utah voters tend to be politically conservative and generally have voted Republican in presidential elections.

History

Prehistoric humans arrived in the Great Basin more than 10,000 years ago. The earliest ANASAZI, known as the Basket Makers, developed their culture on the Colorado Plateau over 2,000 years ago; they were followed by the PUEBLO Indian tribes. More recent arrivals were the Ute, Paiute, Goshiute, and Navajo Indians, who inhabited the state when the first white settlers arrived.

Early European Explorers. In 1776 two Franciscan missionaries, Silvestre Vélez de Escalante and Francisco Atanasio Domínguez, led an expedition into the "Northern Mystery" in order to establish a road from Santa Fe to the Spanish missions in California. By the mid-1820s, fur trappers and traders, including William Henry ASHLEY, James BRIDGER, and Jedediah Strong SMITH, had arrived; two other traders, Peter Skene Ogden and Etienne Provost, have given their names to Utah's second and third largest cities, Ogden and Provo.

In 1843–44, John C. FRÉMONT, of the U.S. Army Topographical Engineers, conducted the first scientific survey of the Great Basin. Also during the 1840s several parties of settlers traversed northern Utah on their way to California. In 1846 the ill-fated DONNER PARTY blazed the first trail through Emigration Canyon—the same route followed a year later by the Mormon pioneers.

The Mormons. The next chapter in Utah's history began at Carthage, Ill., on June 27, 1844, when Joseph SMITH, the founder of Mormonism, and his brother Hyrum were taken from jail and shot by a hostile mob. Persecution of Smith's followers—called Mormons—continued, and in the spring of 1847 most of them headed west, led by

Brigham YOUNG. The first pioneers entered the Great Salt Lake valley in July 1847.

When the Mormons came to Utah it still belonged to Mexico. A year later, at the conclusion of the Mexican War, it became part of the United States, and in 1849 the Mormons established the State of Deseret (a name from the *Book of Mormon* meaning "honeybee" and signifying industriousness) and requested admission to the Union. Congress, however, refused to recognize Deseret—which stretched from Oregon to Mexico and as far west as the Sierra Nevada—and instead created the Territory of Utah, covering a much smaller area, with Brigham Young as governor. Soon afterward conflicts broke out between the Indians, especially the Ute, and the new settlers. Intermittent fighting continued until 1867, when the Ute settled on a reservation.

Before long, antagonisms developed between Utah and the federal government, which opposed the Mormon practice of polygamy. During the Utah War (1857–58), President James Buchanan sent troops to Utah, along with a new governor. During this period of tension and resentment, a party of Mormons led by John Doyle LEE attacked a group of non-Mormons traveling through the territory in the so-called MOUNTAIN MEADOWS MASSACRE (September 1857). Congress finally granted Utah statehood in 1896, six years after the Mormons renounced their practice of polygamy.

Industrialization. The completion of the transcontinental railroad in 1869 brought new settlers—many of them non-Mormon—and a boom in both agriculture and industry. Silver, gold, lead, and zinc were discovered, and large-scale copper production began in 1907. Soon afterward several important new irrigation projects brought thousands of hectares of additional land under cultivation.

The two world wars stimulated mining and manufacturing, and by the early 1960s, Utah was no longer primarily an agricultural state. Hydroelectric projects such as those at Flaming Gorge and Glen Canyon dams (1964) have also encouraged industrial growth and urbanization.

Utamaro [oo-tah'-mah-roh] Regarded as one of the greatest masters of UKIYO-E, the Japanese artist Utamaro, 1753–1806, dominated the art of the print in Edo (Tokyo) during the 1790s with his elegantly styled portraits of beautiful women. Little is known of his life. His family name was Kitagawa, originally Toriyama, but he used other names as well. At its zenith in the early 1790s, Utamaro's art conveyed a sweetness and grace unmatched by his contemporaries. His intuitive grasp of feminine style enabled him to capture a certain erotic element in his half-length portraits, which were notable also for their clear, fresh color. Utamaro's work influenced not only his contemporaries but also Western artists, including Henri de Toulouse-Lautrec.

Ute [yoot] The Ute are a North American Indian tribe belonging to the Shoshonean division of the Uto-Aztecan linguistic stock. Their territory formerly extended from eastern Colorado into northern New Mexico, northeastern Arizona, and Utah. Before the introduction (c.1640) of the horse, the Ute lived in small groups. They harvested wild seeds and roots and organized rabbit and antelope drives.

By 1706 the Ute had turned to raiding the PUEBLO Indians and the Spanish in New Mexico for horses and livestock. Ute culture took on a Plains overlay with the introduction of the tepee, eagle warbonnets, and the scalp dance. Mormon settlement of Utah further disrupted the Ute way of life. During the 1870s and '80s mining interests forced the Northern Ute from treaty lands, and they were eventually consolidated on the Uintah and Ouray reservations in northeastern Utah; the Southern Ute were confined (1877) to a small strip of southwestern Colorado. In 1989 the Ute population was an estimated 5,298.

uterus see PREGNANCY AND BIRTH; REPRODUCTIVE SYSTEM, HUMAN

Utica [yoo'-ti-kuh] Utica, the seat of Oneida County, lies in central New York on the Mohawk River, 135 km (85 mi) west of Albany. It has a population of 68,637 (1990). Once a textile center, Utica is now dominated by the manufacture of electronic equipment, cutlery, paper and dairy products, and air conditioners. Settled in 1773 on the site of Fort Schuyler (1758), Utica was burned in an Indian and Loyalist attack in 1776 but was resettled after the American Revolution. The completion of the Erie Canal through Utica spurred the city's development.

utilitarianism Utilitarianism is a theory in moral philosophy by which actions are judged to be right or wrong according to their consequences. A dictum made famous by the utilitarian Jeremy BENTHAM is that an individual should seek "the greatest happiness of the greatest number." Utilitarians who equate happiness with pleasure are termed *hedonistic utilitarians*; those who regard happiness as incapable of reduction to any single notion such as pleasure are called *ideal* or *pluralistic utilitarians*.

Utilitarianism had its origins among the British philosophers of the 17th and 18th centuries. Its principal modern statements, however, come from Bentham, primarily in his *Introduction to the Principles of Morals and Legislation* (1789); from John Stuart MILL, chiefly in *Utilitarianism* (1863); and from Henry SIDGWICK, in *The Methods of Ethics* (1874).

Utilitarianism has an affinity with EMPIRICISM, the view that all knowledge arises from experience. By rejecting tradition, authority, or any supernatural basis for morality, utilitarianism makes human welfare the ultimate standard of right and wrong. It has thus often been associated with reform movements and causes.

Critics of utilitarianism usually argue that such actions as lying or cheating are wrong in themselves, apart from any ill consequences that might result. They point out that utilitarians must approve of lying and cheating if and when such actions promote positive consequences or the general welfare of society.

Some utilitarians believe that the principle of utility should be applied to the evaluation of each individual act. Such a view is termed *act utilitarianism*. Others believe that the principle should be applied only to moral rules or general categories of actions. This view is labeled *rule utilitarianism*.

utility, public   see PUBLIC UTILITY

—

utopias   Utopias are conceptions of ideal societies in which the social, political, and economic evils afflicting humankind have been eradicated and in which the state functions for the good and happiness of all. The use of the word *utopia* (which means "no place" in Greek) to designate a perfect society began with the publication in 1516 of Saint Thomas MORE's famous *Utopia*, depicting the way of life and social institutions on an imaginary island. More's *Utopia* gained a wide audience, and the term was subsequently applied to all such concepts advanced by social thinkers and visionaries.

Plato's REPUBLIC, written in the 4th century BC, is generally regarded as the earliest and greatest work in the genre of utopian literature, although the biblical Garden of Eden (see EDEN, GARDEN OF) might be described as a utopia. Other famous utopian works include Tommaso Campanella's *The City of the Sun* (1623; Eng. trans., 1937), Francis BACON's *New Atlantis* (1627), James Harrington's *Oceana* (1656), Samuel BUTLER's *Erewhon* (1872), Edward Bellamy's *Looking Backward* (1888), and William Morris's *News from Nowhere* (1891). Influential 20th-century examples of the genre include H. G. Wells's *Modern Utopia* (1905) and *Walden Two* (1948), by the behavioral psychologist B. F. Skinner.

During the 19th century numerous attempts were made actually to establish utopian communities. Most were experiments in utopian socialism, such as those advocated by the comte de SAINT-SIMON, Charles FOURIER, and Étienne CABET in France, Robert OWEN in Britain and the United States, and his son Robert Dale OWEN in the United States. Although they differed considerably in their specific views, these utopian thinkers concurred in the belief that ideal societies could be created without much difficulty, starting with the formation of small cooperative communities made up of their followers. Saint-Simon believed that future happiness was tied to industrial growth. Fourier, in contrast, favored agricultural communities in which people lived in small, self-sufficient "phalanxes" free from the restraints imposed by civilization. Experimental settlements based on the theories of the utopians were set up in Europe and the United States and included Robert Owen's famous cooperative communities in NEW HARMONY, Ind., and New Lanark, Scotland. Most did not long survive; one of the longest lasting was ONEIDA COMMUNITY, in New York State, which lasted from 1848 to 1881. By the middle of the 19th century the utopian socialists were beginning to be eclipsed by more militant radical movements.

Much recent writing has focused on scientific utopias in advanced technological societies. The publication of satiric antiutopias, sometimes called dystopias, has also continued. Prominent examples of this genre are Aldous Huxley's BRAVE NEW WORLD, George Orwell's NINETEEN EIGHTY-FOUR, and Kurt Vonnegut's *Player Piano* (1951).

—

Utrecht   [yoo'-trekt or oo'-trekt]   Utrecht, a city in the central Netherlands and capital of Utrecht province, is located about 30 km (20 mi) southeast of Amsterdam. The city's population is 230,634 (1989 est.). Crossed by canals, railroads, and branches of the Rhine River, Utrecht is a major transportation, trade, and financial center. Metal, wood, chemical, and food products are manufactured there. Historic landmarks include two sunken canals, the Gothic Dom tower (1321–83), and Utrecht Cathedral (1254–1517). Utrecht is the site of a state university (1636), seat of the Roman Catholic archbishop of the Netherlands, and a center for Old Catholics (Jansenists).

Utrecht grew around a Roman fortress (AD c.48). Saint Williborord, the city's first bishop (c.690), converted the northern Netherlands to Christianity. Medieval Utrecht was a cloth-weaving town ruled, along with the surrounding province, by its bishops. The Habsburgs took control in 1527, but in 1579 seven provinces of the north formed the Union of Utrecht to drive out the Spanish (see DUTCH REVOLT). The city then became a Calvinist stronghold. In 1713 the War of Spanish Succession was concluded by the Treaty of Utrecht. The city was occupied by the French in 1795 and served as the residence of Louis Bonaparte during his reign (1806–10) as king of Holland.

Utrecht, Peace of   see SPANISH SUCCESSION, WAR OF THE

—

Utrillo, Maurice   [oo-tree'-oh]   The French painter Maurice Utrillo, b. Dec. 26, 1883, d. Nov. 5, 1955, is known for his many uniquely personal interpretations of Parisian street scenes. A natural son of Suzanne VALADON, herself a painter and artists' model, he began to paint in about 1901, while convalescing from the first of many breakdowns due to alcoholism. The streets of Montmartre, sometimes copied from postcards, were often his theme, and he captured the tawdry, dismal atmosphere of this humble quarter with striking authenticity.

Utrillo began with a somber palette, but he soon came under the influence of impressionism, which, from 1905 onward, affected his brushwork and his use of color. The *Landscape at Pierrefitte* (1905; collection of Ailsa Mellon Bruce, New York City) is an example. His best pictures are those from the "white period" (1908–14), when he developed an interest in white buildings and his canvases began to show a rougher surface texture. His palette sugarcane are raised for cash. Important industrial products are sugar, textiles, and leather; the main handicrafts are silk weaving, metal enameling, and ceramic manufacturing. The TAJ MAHAL in AGRA is a world-famous landmark.

Buddha is said to have preached his first sermon at SARNATH near Varanasi, where Emperor Asoka later installed a stupa (shrine). Muslim rulers were in control for most of the period from 1194 to 1724. During the Indian Mutiny (1857–58), Uttar Pradesh was the center of anti-British resistance.

Uxmal [oosh-mahl'] Uxmal, in the rolling Puuc hills of northwestern Yucatán, Mexico, was a major regional capital of the Classic MAYA. The center of Puuc-style architecture, Uxmal had long, ranging buildings that were faced with thin stone veneers ("Puuc" stones) and adorned with ornate stone mosaics and sculptures attached with tenons. Although other, smaller cities of the region made buildings in this style, those of Uxmal have unusual engineering refinements, such as a slight outward lean that makes the structures appear elegant and light.

Many of the finest constructions at Uxmal were made during the reign of Lord Chac (d. c.907), a prominent 9th-century king and the last known ruler. The Great Pyramid and the final version of the Pyramid of the Magician were completed during his or his father's reign. The ball court, Nunnery Quadrangle, and House of the Governor are all testaments of Puuc lyricism at its height during Lord Chac's regime.

Uxmal was abandoned in the 10th century with the ascent of CHICHÉN ITZÁ to its east. At the time of the Spanish conquest, the powerful Xiu family claimed to have built Uxmal, but this is now thought to be unlikely.

Sacré-Coeur *(1924), by the 20th-century French artist Maurice Utrillo, is a colorful view of the famed Parisian basilica on the summit of Montmartre. (Mme. Jean Walther Collection, Paris.)*

changed also, the impressionist scale being replaced by silky grays, delicate pinks, and strong blues. During the final period, from 1914 on, Utrillo's colors again became brighter and his paintings less somber in mood.

Uttar Pradesh [u'-tahr prah'-dish] Uttar Pradesh is a state of northern India, bounded by Tibet and Nepal. It has an area of 294,411 km^2 (113,673 mi^2). Its population of 139,031,130 (1991) is the largest of any Indian state. The state capital is LUCKNOW. The greater portion of the state lies within the GANGES RIVER Plain. In the northwest are the HIMALAYAS. Nanda Devi is the tallest peak in Uttar Pradesh (7,817 m/25,645 ft). The population is predominantly Hindu. KANPUR is the state's largest city and an important industrial center. VARANASI, Hardwar, and Mathura are major Hindu pilgrim centers. Other cities include Aligarh (a university town), Allahabad, and Bareilly.

Agriculture is the basis of the economy; the state is India's largest wheat producer. Other food crops are rice, sorghum, millet, barley, and corn. Cotton, peanuts, and

Uzbekistan Uzbekistan was formerly one of the republics of the USSR, but it became independent in 1991. Located in Central Asia, it has an area of 447,400 km^2 (172,742 mi^2) and a population of 20,325,000 (1992 est.). The capital is TASHKENT (1991 est. pop., 2,113,300). Bordered by Kazakhstan on the north and west, Turkmenistan on the southwest, Afghanistan on the south, and Tajikistan and Kyrgyzstan on the east, the country extends from the TIAN SHAN mountain system to the ARAL SEA. The northwestern lowland portion of Uzbekistan is occupied by the KYZYL KUM desert, lying between the SYR DARYA and AMU DARYA rivers.

The population is concentrated in oases and irrigated valleys. The Uzbek, who make up 71% of the total, are Sunni Muslims, speak a Turkic language, and are traditionally cotton farmers. The Uzbek traditionally maintain bride-price, DOWRIES, and close kin LINEAGES. Russians, who represent 8% of the population, are mainly city dwellers. The Karakalpak, a Kipchak Turkic-speaking people, live in an autonomous area.

The province's most populous (1989) cities are, in addition to the capital, SAMARKAND (366,000), Namangan

(308,000), Andizhan (293,000), Bukhara (224,000), Fergana (200,000), and Kokand (182,000).

Economic activities are centered in Tashkent and in the Tian Shan's Fergana Valley. Important mineral industries process natural gas; coal (Angren); steel (Bekabad); copper, zinc, and molybdenum (Almalyk); gold (Zarafshan); and uranium (Yangiabad).

Uzbekistan was the USSR's largest cotton producer, accounting for more than 60% of Soviet output; the cotton area has been expanded through irrigation. Other important agricultural products are alfalfa, dried fruit, and karakul, or Persian lamb skins.

The Uzbek, who assumed a distinctive ethnic identity during the 16th century, were historically part of the khanates of Khiva, Bukhara, and Kokand. These khanates were conquered by Russia in the 1860s and '70s. The Uzbek were constituted as a Soviet republic in 1924. Under Mikhail Gorbachev, Uzbekistan began to claim greater autonomy and resist Moscow's Russification policies. Since becoming independent, the country has been ruled by former Communists who stress the need for Central Asian cooperation.

	GERMAN-GOTHIC	CLASSICAL LATIN	EARLY LATIN	ETRUSCAN	CLASSICAL GREEK	EARLY GREEK	EARLY ARAMAIC	EARLY HEBREW	PHOENICIAN

V   V/v is the twenty-second letter of the English alphabet. Both the letter and its position in the alphabet were derived from the Latin alphabet, which derived it from the Greek by way of the Etruscan. When the Greeks adapted a Semitic writing system, the Semitic sign *waw* was given two uses. One form of the sign was used as consonantal *w* and called *digamma*; although lost in the Greek alphabet, this sign eventually became the English letter *F/f*. A variant form of *waw* was used for vocalic *u*, called *upsilon*, and placed at the end of the alphabet after *tau*. This sign was adopted in the Etruscan alphabet and thence came into the Latin alphabet as *V/v*. The Latin alphabet used *V/v* for both consonantal *w* and vocalic *u*. In late Latin, however, the sound of *w* became *v*, and the sounds *u, v,* and *w* were generally not distinguished in writing. Eventually the letters *U/u* and *W/w* were derived from Latin *V/v* to differentiate the various sounds.

The sound of *V/v* is a voiced labiodental continuant—the voiced counterpart of *f*—made by expelling the voiced breath between the lower lip and the upper teeth as in *vice* or *love*.

V-1   The German V-1 flying bomb, or buzz bomb, known originally as the Fieseler Fi 103, was the first of the "weapons of vengeance," named in response to Allied air assaults on Germany during World War II. It emerged from proposals made in 1939, and the first flight test was made at Peenemünde in December 1941. The V-1 was used to attack London from sites near Calais, France, beginning in June 1944. More than 8,000 were launched against London alone.

The V-1 was actually a small, pilotless plane, having an overall length of 7.9 m (25.9 ft) and a wingspan of 5.3 m (17.3 ft). It weighed 2,180 kg (4,806 lb), including gasoline fuel and an 850-kg (1,874-lb) warhead. Powered by a pulse-jet engine and ramp-launched, the V-1 flew a preset distance. Then it was put into a dive, and its engine cut out, giving the population below only a few seconds in which to take cover.

V-2   The V-2, or Vengeance Weapon 2, was a liquid-propellant rocket developed at Peenemünde, Germany, between 1938 and 1942 under the technical direction of Wernher VON BRAUN. The rocket was part of a development series known as Aggregate, begun under the auspices of the German army at Kummersdorf in 1932. The V-2, fourth in the series, was also known as the A-4. Originally intended for battlefield use, it was eventually used to bomb Britain and other countries.

The V-2 stood over 14 m (46 ft) tall and at lift-off weighed 12,873 kg (28,380 lb), including a 998-kg (2,201-lb) warhead. It reached a maximum speed of about 5,705 km/h (3,545 mph) and had a range of about 320 km (200 mi).

Although the first successful V-2 test occurred on Oct. 3, 1942, it was not until July 27, 1943, that Adolf Hitler authorized full-scale development of the rocket. More than 4,300 were launched between Sept. 6, 1944, and Mar. 27, 1945, against London and southeastern England, Antwerp, and other targets. Much postwar rocket technology was based on the V-2 (see ROCKETS AND MISSILES).

V-E Day and V-J Day   V-E Day and V-J Day are the historic dates marking the end of WORLD WAR II (1939–

45), a conflict fought on two main fronts—the European and Pacific theaters. V-E (Victory in Europe) Day was celebrated on May 8, 1945, following the surrender of Germany to the Allied forces. V-J (Victory over Japan) Day designates Sept. 2, 1945, the day on which Japan formally surrendered. It had sued for peace on August 10, following the Allied dropping of atomic bombs on the Japanese cities of Hiroshima (August 6) and Nagasaki (August 9).

vaccination Vaccination is the inoculation of a person (or animal) in order to bring about IMMUNITY to an infectious (pathogenic) organism. The term (from the Latin *vacca*, "cow") originally meant immunization against SMALLPOX, because the procedure originated in 1796 when the English physician Edward JENNER discovered that milkmaids who had contracted the mild disease cowpox (vaccinia) were immune to smallpox. The development of a cowpox vaccine against smallpox has since led to the production of vaccines against a wide range of diseases.

Vaccination is based on the ability of a person's immune system to respond much more effectively and rapidly to a microorganism the second or third time that the elements of the immune system encounter the invading organism. It was in this way, for example, that the milkmaids' immune systems were "primed" by the cowpox virus to respond effectively to the closely related smallpox virus.

A vaccine may consist of living organisms that are weakened, or attenuated, in a laboratory so that they create immunity but do not cause disease. It may also consist of related organisms that cause a similar but milder disease, of killed organisms, or of extracts of the organisms that can induce the desired immune response and subsequent immunity but do not cause the disease. Periodic booster immunization is recommended with most vaccines, because the immunity caused by the initial inoculation may decrease with time. The time interval before booster shots are required varies greatly with the type of vaccine.

Vaccination has occasional complications. Thus patients with a poorly functioning immune system have particular problems with certain vaccines. Immunodeficient patients may develop acute poliomyelitis from the attenuated-virus vaccine, for example, although they do not develop the disease from killed polio virus. Transient problems with mild fevers, muscle aches, and tenderness at the inoculation site are also common to many vaccines. Control of serious disease by vaccination, however, is usually worth such risks.

Most of the exceptionally effective vaccines are viral vaccines (see VIRUS), such as those for measles, mumps, and rubella. Influenza vaccines are recommended for individuals at high risk for serious infections of the lungs. Because influenza strains are different almost every year, vaccination should be carried out yearly in the susceptible population. Vaccination for yellow fever and certain types of hepatitis are also of proven efficacy. Also available are vaccines for certain bacterial infections (see BACTERIA), such as typhoid fever, cholera, diphtheria, whooping cough, and tetanus. Among new vaccines being developed are vaccines against malaria, leprosy, and dengue fever. Researchers are also exploring the production of multipurpose vaccines through genetic engineering, using entities such as the vaccinia virus or the bacterium known as BCG to carry genes from several disease organisms.

See also: DISEASES, CHILDHOOD.

vaccinia Vaccinia, the COWPOX virus, is closely related to the variola, or SMALLPOX, virus. The term *vaccine* derives from vaccinia, because in the 18th century the English physician Edward JENNER used the vaccinia virus to develop the first successful preventive treatment for a communicable disease, smallpox; the treatment made possible the subsequent eradication of that disease. Vaccinia is currently of special interest in GENETIC ENGINEERING for several reasons. Adverse reactions to the virus are rare and well understood, so it is considered safe; it is more easily transportable than most viruses, because it can be freeze-dried and remain effective; its administration is simple; and it is a large virus, making possible the use of recombinant-DNA techniques to create new vaccines. That is, genes from another virus can be spliced into vaccinia, creating a hybrid vaccine effective against both viruses.

vacuum A vacuum may be defined most simply as a volume of space that contains no matter. On the Earth's surface this means, in practice, a volume from which as much matter has been removed as current technology makes possible, with the whole range of partial vacuums in between. In this sense, a perfect vacuum probably does not exist even in the depths of space, in the vast stretches between galaxies. Any given volume of space is likely to contain at least one or more particle of matter or one or more units of energy, which is the equivalent of matter (see RELATIVITY).

In physics the concept of a vacuum is more complex. According to QUANTUM MECHANICS and elementary particle theory (see FUNDAMENTAL PARTICLES), an ideal vacuum would be one that had a zero energy level besides lacking matter. Theory holds, however, that no such vacuum can exist. Even a vacuum with no measurable energy level is only a so-called "virtual" vacuum. Vacuum fluctuations are constantly producing "virtual" particles there that appear and disappear. The concept that a vacuum itself has structure is basic to modern physics and has been supported experimentally. It is also basic to current COSMOLOGY theories, according to which the entire universe arose from a virtual vacuum.

In the practical sense of a volume lacking as much matter as technology permits, a vacuum was first produced experimentally in the 17th century by the German physicist Otto von GUERICKE. Attempts to produce high vacuums were spurred in the later 19th century by the need to study such phenomena as electric discharges in gases. The electric light bulb, which had to be evacuated to prevent the filament from burning, emphasized the need for high-speed industrial vacuum pumps. Many such pumps were developed in the 20th century, including the rotary mercury pump, the molecular pump, and the cryogenic pump. Vacuums with PRESSURES as low as 10^{-15} mm of mercury have been attained (see BAROMETER). Besides their applications in science and advanced technology (see ELECTRON TUBE), vacuums are of use in practical ways. That is, the pressure differential between a vacuum and its surroundings is used to make vacuum cleaners, air and water pumps, and the carburetor, among other devices.

vacuum cleaner   The vacuum cleaner is an electrical appliance for removing dust and dirt from floors, walls, or furniture. An electric motor drives a high-speed fan, creating a vacuum that draws a current of air into a suction nozzle. Dirt is loosened by brushes or agitators attached to the nozzle and then drawn through a fabric or paper bag that allows air but not the dirt particles to escape. The bag must be emptied or discarded when full. The upright cleaner consists of a long-handled assembly containing motor, fan, brush, and agitator. Canister cleaners contain a motor and fan in a cylindrical or spherical housing to which a flexible hose with suction nozzle is connected.

Suction carpet sweepers with mechanically operated fans or bellows were invented in the 1850s, but the small electric motor had to be invented before the vacuum cleaner could be successfully produced. One of the first portable electric cleaners was developed by James Murray Spangler, who sold his rights to the machine to William Henry Hoover, the first manufacturer to mass-produce vacuum cleaners successfully.

vacuum tube   see ELECTRON TUBE

Vaduz [fah-doots']   Vaduz (1990 est. pop., 4,874) is the capital of the principality of Liechtenstein, located on the Swiss border 80 km (50 mi) southeast of Zurich, Switzerland. The ruling prince's residence, Vaduz castle, overlooks the town and the upper Rhine River valley. Vaduz dates from the 14th century and is a flourishing tourist center.

vagrancy   Vagrancy is a charge made against those who are perceived as drifters, loiterers, bums, prostitutes, gamblers, beggars, destitute persons unable to find or keep employment, or persons who simply refuse regular employment. Vagrants are sometimes arrested, although they may not have committed crimes. From a legal standpoint vagrancy has been a controversial matter. It invites community disapproval and arrest; in the United States, however, many vagrancy ordinances have been deemed too vague and in violation of due process. For example, it is increasingly recognized that many people in a state of HOMELESSNESS ought not to be categorized or treated as vagrants.

Vaiont Dam [vy-awnt']   The Vaiont Dam, the world's highest thin-arch DAM, located on the Vaiont River in the Italian Alps, was overtopped by a rock slide on Oct. 9, 1963, in the worst dam disaster since the Johnstown flood in 1889. Water and rocks thrown high above the crest of the dam destroyed everything in their path for several kilometers downstream, and about 3,000 lives were lost in the disaster. The slide was caused by adverse geological conditions in the dam area, a progressive weakening of the rock mass, and the effect of the impounded water on the stability of the steep rock slope.

Valadon, Suzanne [vah-lah-dohn']   Suzanne Valadon, b. Marie Clémentine Valadon, Sept. 23, 1865, d. Apr. 19, 1938, was a versatile French painter of the human figure, landscape, and still life. While modeling for Pierre Auguste Renoir and Henri de Toulouse-Lautrec, she became acquainted with Edgar Degas, who was impressed with her artistic ability. Her paintings are characterized by strong outlines and bright colors. Having achieved success with her own work, she also inspired her son, Maurice UTRILLO, to become a painter.

Valdez [val-deez']   Valdez (1990 pop., 4,068), a port city on Prince William Sound in south central Alaska, is the southern terminus of the petroleum pipeline from PRUDHOE Bay. The city is also a center for mining, hunting, and fishing. Founded in 1898, Valdez was devastated by an earthquake in 1964 and rebuilt on safer ground to the west. In 1989 the *Exxon Valdez* spilled 41.6 million l (11 million gal) of oil into the waters off Valdez, causing immense environmental damage and killing much wildlife.

Valdivia, Pedro de [vahl-dee'-vee-ah]   The Spanish conquistador and explorer Pedro de Valdivia, c.1500–1554, extended Spanish rule in Latin America south from Peru into Chile. He entered military service in Spain and participated in the conquest of Venezuela in 1535. In 1538, Valdivia joined Francisco PIZARRO in Peru, and two years later he left Cuzco with a small group of Spaniards and about 1,000 Indians, determined to establish a colony in Chile. After crossing the coastal desert, he founded (1541) the city of Santiago. Valdivia returned to Peru in 1547 and, as a reward for his support of the viceroy, Pedro de la Gasca, against the rebellion of Gonzalo Pizarro, was made governor of Chile in 1549. He founded Concepción the following year and extended his conquests farther south. In 1554, however, while trying to suppress an uprising of the Araucanian Indians, Valdivia was taken prisoner and tortured to death.

valence [vay'-luhns]   The valence of an atom or RADICAL represents the number of CHEMICAL BONDS that the atom or radical may form. The idea of valence was first introduced in 1868, even though the principles of bonding were not understood. Electrochemical studies showed that elements formed positive or negative ions. Hydrogen formed H^+ and was assigned the valence of +1, and the valence of chlorine, which formed Cl^-, became −1. Water (H_2O) consists of two atoms of hydrogen combined with one atom of oxygen, so the valence of oxygen was determined to be −2, because the sum of the total valences of all the atoms in a compound must equal zero. Some compounds contain a group of atoms, called a radical, that react as a unit. In nitric acid (HNO_3), for example, a valence of −1 was assigned to the entire nitrate (NO_3) unit.

In modern chemistry, the terms *oxidation state* and *oxidation number* have replaced *valence* except in describing the number of bonds of an atom or radical in a compound. The oxidation number of an atom is the number of electrons the atom has gained, lost, or shared when it bonds with another atom. In the case of sodium chloride (NaCl), the sodium atom transfers one electron to the chlorine atom, so sodium has an oxidation number of +1 (sodium is in the +1 oxidation state) and chlorine an oxidation number of −1 (the −1 oxidation state).

An element may have several oxidation states by being able to bond in different ways. Nitrogen, for example, forms five compounds with oxygen: N_2O, NO, N_2O_3, NO_2 (= N_2O_4), and N_2O_5, with oxidation numbers +1, +2, +3, +4, and +5, respectively.

Valencia (city in Spain) [vah-layn'-thee-ah]

Valencia, a city in eastern Spain and capital of Valencia autonomous region and Valencia province, is situated about 300 km (190 mi) southeast of Madrid. Its population is 732,491 (1987 est.). Valencia lies in a fertile plain, cut off from the rest of Spain by the mountainous rim of the Meseta. On the south bank of the Turia River, about 3 km (2 mi) from the Mediterranean coast, the city is served by its seaport at El Grao. Its people mainly speak Spanish, although Valencia lies within the traditional Catalan region.

Oranges, rice, vegetables, wine, and olive oil are exported through El Grao. Valencia's industries include food processing, distilling, shipbuilding, textile weaving, metallurgy, and tourism. Among the historic sites are two gates from the 14th-century city walls; the Gothic Cathedral of La Seo (13th–15th century); and the Gothic Lonja, or silk exchange (15th century). Valencia is the seat of an archdiocese and the site of a university (1500).

Valencia was settled by the Romans (138 BC) and called Valentia. It was captured by the Visigoths in AD 413 and by the Moors in 714. Valencia was the capital of the Moorish kingdom of Valencia (1021–1238), although the city was retaken and ruled by El Cid from 1094 to his death five years later. It was reconquered by James I of Aragon in 1238. Valencia prospered commercially and culturally under the medieval kings of Aragon. The city suffered damage in the Peninsular War and Spanish Civil War, when it served as the Loyalist capital in 1936–37 and again in 1939.

Valencia (city in Venezuela) [vah-layn'-see-ah]

Valencia (1990 est. pop., 955,005) is the third largest city in Venezuela and a leading industrial center. Located 120 km (75 mi) southwest of Caracas, in the agriculturally productive central highlands of northern Venezuela, it processes sugarcane, cotton, coffee, and tobacco and produces a wide variety of manufactured items, including feeds, fertilizers, pharmaceuticals, plastics, tires, automobiles, and clothing. It is the capital of Carabobo state and the site of the state university (1852). The 18th-century cathedral is a major feature. Valencia was founded by the Spanish in 1555 and served briefly as the capital of Venezuela in 1812 and 1830.

Valencia (region in Spain)

Valencia is a province located along the Mediterranean Sea in eastern Spain, covering an area of 10,763 km² (4,156 mi²). The population of 2,135,381 (1987 est.) is concentrated mainly in the coastal areas. The city of Valencia is the region's capital and principal urban center. Valencia's main agricultural products are citrus fruits, vegetables, dates, and rice. Olive oil is also an important product. Mineral deposits include marble and gypsum. Textile and chemical industries are well developed. The region is well known for its coastal resorts and for the ruins of many old Iberian towns.

Valencia was colonized by the Greeks and the Carthaginians. In the 8th century the Moors invaded the area. The emirate of Valencia was established in 1021 and El Cid ruled from 1094 to 1099. James I of Aragon conquered the region in 1238.

Valens, Roman Emperor in the East [vay'-luhnz]

Valens, b. c.328, d. Aug. 9, 378, ruled the eastern part of the Roman Empire after being appointed (364) coemperor by his brother, VALENTINIAN I, emperor in the West. An Arian Christian, Valens persecuted orthodox Christians. In 369 he defeated the Visigoths, but nine years later he was killed in the Visigoths' great victory over the Romans at Adrianople.

Valentine, Saint

The name Saint Valentine is given to two legendary Christian martyrs whose feasts were formerly observed on February 14. One, believed to be a Roman priest martyred c.269 during the persecution of Claudius the Goth, was buried on the Flaminian Way; the second was probably a bishop of Terni martyred in Rome. It is possible that these two legends were based on real people or, as some believe, one person. The association of Saint Valentine's Day with love and courtship may have arisen from the coincidence of the date with the Roman festival of LUPERCALIA. In 1969 the feast day was dropped from the Roman church calendar.

Valentinian I, Roman Emperor in the West

[val-uhn-tin'-ee-uhn] Valentinian I, b. 321, d. Nov. 17,

375, was Roman emperor in the West (364–75); his brother VALENS commanded (364–78) in the East. Valentinian served ably under Emperors Julian and Jovian, and his troops proclaimed him emperor at Nicaea upon Jovian's death. Valentinian fought the Alemanni successfully in Gaul and kept Roman power stable in Africa and Britain; he also built a system of frontier defenses in the north. Valentinian was notably tolerant of the Christians.

Valentinian II, Roman Emperor in the West

Valentinian II, b. c.371, d. May 15, 392, Roman emperor in the West (375–92), succeeded his father, Valentinian I. He ruled with his brother GRATIAN, controlling Italy, Africa, and Illyricum during a period of religious strife between the Arian and Nicene Christians. Gratian was murdered by the usurper Maximus, who forced Valentinian to flee Italy (387). Restored to power by THEODOSIUS I in 388, Valentinian was later murdered, possibly by Arbogast of the Franks.

Valentinian III, Roman Emperor in the West

Valentinian III, b. July 2, 419, d. Mar. 16, 455, was Roman emperor in the West (425–55), following the usurper John (r. 423–25). During Valentinian's minority, his mother, Galla Placidia, served as regent, followed in 433 by the powerful general AETIUS, who became the actual ruler of the West. Valentinian never took effective interest in affairs of state, although the empire was torn by barbarian invasions and religious discontinuity during his reign. In 444 he and Pope LEO I agreed that the bishop of Rome had authority over the provincial churches. In 454, Valentinian personally murdered Aetius and was in turn murdered by Aetius's followers.

Valentino, Rudolph

[val-uhn-tee'-noh] The greatest Latin lover of the American silent screen, Rudolph Val-

Rudolph Valentino, displaying the sultry charms and commanding presence that won him an international following, appears in Son of the Sheik *(1926), his last film.*

entino, b. Rodolfo d'Antonguolla, Italy, May 6, 1895, d. Aug. 23, 1926, was catapulted to stardom by *The Four Horsemen of the Apocalypse* (1921) and remained an irresistible attraction until his death. His hypnotic eyes, flashing smile, and slicked-back hair added up to magic in such films as *The Sheik* (1921), *Blood and Sand* (1922), *Monsieur Beaucaire* (1924), *The Eagle* (1925), and *Son of the Sheik* (1926).

Valentinus

[val-uhn-ty'-nuhs] Valentinus, fl. 2d century AD, was a leading exponent of GNOSTICISM in both Alexandria and Rome. An Egyptian by birth, he spent many years (c.136–c.160) in Rome, where he aspired to become pope. When unsuccessful in this effort, he turned against the Roman church. He was excommunicated in Rome for his teachings.

Valentinus was the most intellectual of the gnostic leaders and developed a gnosticism attractive enough to gain followers in both the East and West. Eastern Valentinianism was Docetist, claiming that Christ had a "pneumatic" body totally subject to the influence of the Spirit. Western (Italian) Valentinians taught a modified DOCETISM, attributing to Christ a "psychic" body, not fully "gnostic," but capable of salvation through perfect knowledge.

Valera, Eamon de   see DE VALERA, EAMON

Valéry, Paul

[vah-lay-ree'] Paul Ambroise Valéry, b. Sète, France, Oct. 30, 1871, d. July 20, 1945, was the greatest French poet of the 20th century. Evidence of his intellectual range is provided by the five volumes of essays entitled *Variety* (1924–44; Eng. trans., 1927, 1938) and the 29 volumes of *Cahiers* (Notebooks, 1957–61).

Valéry's early poetry was influenced by symbolist aesthetics in general and by the work of Stéphane MALLARMÉ in particular. It was collected in *Album de vers anciens, 1890–1900* (Album of Old Verses, 1920). His reputation during his first years in Paris also owed much to two prose works: *Introduction to the Method of Leonardo da Vinci* (1895; Eng. trans., 1929) showed his admiration for a fellow polymath, and *The Evening with Monsieur Teste* (1896; Eng. trans., 1925) examined a fictional monster with an entirely abstract intellect. In 1917, Valéry published one of his finest poems, *La Jeune Parque* (trans. as *The Young Fate*, 1970), a combination of enigmatic beauty and difficult, allusive SYMBOLISM. His poetic reputation was finally sealed by the publication of *Charmes* (1922; rev. 1926), which collected such celebrated longer poems as *The Graveyard by the Sea* (1920; Eng. trans., 1932) and *Fragments du Narcisse, La Pythie, and Ébauche d'un serpent* (Sketch of a Serpent, 1922). This poetry is austere, controlled, and intensely intellectual, yet suggestive and evocative in its use of imagery and sound.

Two much-admired prose works, *Eupalinos: or, The Architect* (Eng. trans., 1932) and *Dance and the Soul* (Eng. trans., 1951), were written in the form of Socratic dialogues and published together in 1923. The architect achieves dynamic repose; the dancer embodies controlled dynamism. Two later works in dialogue form are *Idée fixe* (1932; Eng. trans., 1965) and *Dialogue de l'arbre* (Dialogue of the Tree, 1943).

At the end of World War I, Valéry had written on the crisis of Western civilization. He continued to view the contemporary world with some asperity in *Reflections on the World Today* (1933; Eng. trans., 1948). These writings show his gift for aphorisms, also characteristic of *Rhumbs* (1926; Eng. trans., 1970). On his death he left an unfinished play, *My Faust* (Eng. trans., 1960), which was posthumously published in 1946.

Valhalla [val-hal'-uh]   In Norse mythology Valhalla was the most beautiful mansion in ASGARD, where the heroes slain in battle feasted each night with ODIN on the boar Schrimnir and mead from the goat Heldrun. The heroes rode out each morning and fought one another until they were cut to pieces; they recovered from their wounds each evening.

Valium [val'-ee-uhm]   Valium, a trade name for diazepam, is in the benzodiazepine group of drugs (as is Librium) and is the best-known and most widely prescribed minor TRANQUILIZER. Introduced in 1963, it effectively relieves tension and anxiety and may be useful in the treatment of the symptoms of acute alcohol withdrawal. Valium is often used, with other measures, to treat lower back pain, because it relieves skeletal-muscle spasms.

Excessive doses of Valium or doses in combination with alcohol or other nervous-system depressants may cause excessive sedation or decreased dexterity. Valium is frequently abused and may be habit-forming (see DRUG ABUSE).

Valkyries [val-keer'-eez]   In Norse mythology the Valkyries were nine semidivine virgins—priestesses of the mother goddess FREYA—who rode armed on horseback to battlefields and decided who would live and who would die. They carried half of the dead heroes to VALHALLA, Odin's palace in Asgard, and waited on them at their feasts. Their leader was BRUNHILD.

Valladolid [vahl-yah-doh-leed']   Valladolid, the capital of Valladolid province in north central Spain, is situated on the Pisuerga River, about 160 km (100 mi) northwest of Madrid. It has a population of 329,206 (1987 est.). Valladolid's economy is based on processing the province's cereals, vegetables, and sugarcane. Chemicals, textiles, metal products, wine, and leather are produced. Historic sites include the 13th-century Church of San Pablo, the unfinished cathedral (begun 1580s), the Colegio de San Gregorio, the Rivadavia palace, and a monument to Christopher Columbus. The city's university was founded in 1346.

A city of obscure origins, Valladolid was liberated from the Moors in the 10th century and became part of the kingdom of León-Castile. It was the seat of the Castilian and later Spanish royal courts in the 14th and 15th centuries and during the reign (1600–06) of Philip III. Valladolid was damaged in the Peninsular War and occupied by Nationalist forces in the Spanish Civil War (1936–39).

Vallandigham, Clement L. [vuh-lan'-dig-ham] The American politician Clement Laird Vallandigham, b. New Lisbon, Ohio, July 29, 1820, d. June 17, 1871, gained notoriety as a U.S. representative (1858–63) from Ohio during the U.S. Civil War, when he was the leading Northern critic of the government's policy toward the Confederacy. An admirer of the South, Vallandigham vehemently attacked the war policies of President Abraham Lincoln. Essentially a conservative, he feared the changes buffeting Civil War America. He opposed industry, centralization of government, and emancipation, while favoring peace, state rights, and white supremacy. These principles led him to support a negotiated peace on terms favorable to the South, to denounce military conscription, and to become the leader of the COPPERHEADS, or Peace Democrats.

In 1862, Vallandigham lost a bid for reelection. The next year he was convicted of treasonable utterances and exiled to the Confederacy; he soon left the South for Canada. Running in absentia, he lost the 1863 Ohio gubernatorial election; he returned to the United States in 1864.

Vallayer-Coster, Anne [vah-lay-yay'-kohs-tair']   The French painter Anne Vallayer-Coster, b. Dec. 21, 1744, d. Feb. 27, 1818, was most highly acclaimed for her still lifes; in 1770 she was admitted to the Académie Royale du Peinture et de Sculpture. Her first recorded painting (1762) was a portrait; among her other paintings of people is *Woman Writing and Her Daughter* (1775; Bowes Museum, Barnard Castle, England). It was Vallayer-Coster's still lifes, however, that were most enthusiastically praised. Within this genre, her range of subject matter was vast, including musical instruments, military trophies, fruits and vegetables, flowers, lobsters, and dead game. She continued to exhibit in the Paris Salon until 1817.

Valle d'Aosta [vahl'-lay dah-oh'-stah]   Valle d'Aosta is a region in the Alps of northwestern Italy, bordering France and Switzerland. Its area is 3,262 km^2 (1,260 mi^2), and its population is 114,760 (1989 est.). The Italian slopes of Mont Blanc and the Matterhorn are there. The capital is Aosta (1983 est. pop., 37,355). Tourism, farming, the manufacture of textiles, iron, and steel, and hydroelectric-power generation are important. Conquered by Rome about 25 BC, the region was later held by the Goths, Lombards, and dukes of Burgundy. It belonged to the house of Savoy (later the rulers of Sardinia-Piedmont) from 1238.

Vallejo [vuh-lay'-oh]   Vallejo (1990 pop., 109,119) is a port city on San Pablo Bay in California about 40 km (25 mi) northeast of San Francisco. Its industries include flour milling, food processing, petroleum refining, smelting, and port activities. Gen. Mariano G. Vallejo founded the city in 1850 as the new state capital, but the legislature met there only briefly in 1852–53.

Vallejo, César   The Peruvian poet César Vallejo, b. Mar. 16, 1892, d. Apr. 15, 1938, focused on the theme of human suffering in the modernist poems of his first book, *Los heraldos negros* (The Black Heralds, 1918). In the more daring poems of *Trilce* (1922), with their unconventional grammar, dislocated syntax, and interior monologue, he related the impotence and isolation of people victimized by inexplicable forces. After moving to Paris in 1923, he devoted much of his energy to supporting Marxism and, later, the Republican cause in the Spanish Civil War. Vallejo's *Human Poems* (1939; Eng. trans., 1968), his last book of poetry, expresses in more direct language than that of *Trilce* his solidarity with all victims of injustice.

Valletta [vahl-let'-tah]   Valletta (1990 est. pop., 9,196) is the capital of Malta and a major Mediterranean port. The core of the city, founded in 1565, is located on a rocky promontory overlooking two deepwater harbors on the island's northwestern coast. British and NATO forces maintained bases there until 1979. Commercial shipping and tourism are the city's major activities.

Valley Forge   Valley Forge, 40 km (25 mi) west of Philadelphia, was the campground of 11,000 troops of George Washington's Continental Army from Dec. 19, 1777, to June 19, 1778. Because of the suffering endured there by the hungry, poorly clothed, and badly housed troops, 2,500 of whom died during the harsh winter, Valley Forge came to symbolize the heroism of the American revolutionaries. Despite adverse circumstances, Baron Friedrich von Steuben drilled the soldiers regularly and improved their discipline. Today the historic landmarks and monuments are preserved within Valley Forge National Historical Park (established 1976).

Valley of the Kings   The Valley of the Kings in western Thebes, Egypt, contains royal burial sites dating from the 18th dynasty (c.1570–1320 BC) and from the 19th dynasty (1320–1200 BC) of the New Kingdom. In the necropolis, the various chambers of the earlier tombs are built along a curving axis, whereas in the later examples chambers and corridors are arranged in parallel lines. More than 60 royal tombs are known, but many, such as that of Ramses II, are not yet accessible. Notable tombs include that of Ramses VI, containing a well-preserved painted relief of religious scenes. Directly beneath this tomb is that of Tutankhamen, which was discovered (1922) by Howard Carter. The tomb of Seti I, also known as Belzoni's Tomb after the Italian adventurer who first entered it in 1817, is noted for magnificent astronomical reliefs in its vaulted ceiling. At present the entire Valley of the Kings is being mapped.

Valley of Ten Thousand Smokes   The Valley of Ten Thousand Smokes is located in southern Alaska in the Aleutian Range, 40 km (25 mi) southwest of Anchorage. The valley, 150 km² (60 mi²) in area, is uninhabitable. Formerly rich in plant and animal life, it was devastated in 1912 when a new volcano, Novarupta, emerged, covering the valley floor with sand and lava up to 200 m (700 ft) deep. Volcanic Mount Katmai also erupted, creating a 5-km-wide (3-mi) crater and leaving a lake about 1,100 m (3,700 ft) below the rim. At the same time, fissures opened in the valley floor, emitting steam heated to up to 648° C (1200° F). In 1918 the U.S. government moved to protect the valley, creating the Katmai National Monument.

Vallonet Cave [vahl'-oh-nay]   The archaeological cave site of Le Vallonet, on the Mediterranean coast near Roquebrune-Cap-Martin, 5 km (3 mi) west of Menton, France, is the earliest known human habitation site in Europe and may have been used by some of the first hominids migrating into Europe from Northern Africa. It has been dated to the end of the Lower Pleistocene, between 1,300,000 and 700,000 years ago. The site, which consists of a small inner chamber preceded by a narrow passage, was inhabited during a cold period (the Günz glaciation). No evidence for the use of fire exists, nor were human remains found. A few Lower Paleolithic pebble tools and flakes of limestone, quartzite, and flint were discovered, associated with many fragments of elephants, horses, deer, cattle, wild boar, and even parts of stranded whales. Some of the bones and antlers appear to have been cut or chipped for use as tools.

Valois (dynasty) [vahl-wah']   The Valois dynasty produced the 13 kings who ruled France between 1328 and 1589. A branch of the Capetian family, the Valois were descended from Charles of Valois (1270–1325), the younger brother of Philip IV. Charles was succeeded as count of Valois by his son, who became King Philip VI in 1328. The Valois succession was challenged by the kings of England, descended from a daughter of Philip IV. This was a major factor contributing to the Hundred Years' War (1337–1453) and gave anti-Valois nobles an excuse to fight on the English side. For a time the English were also supported by the powerful dukes of Burgundy, a cadet line of the Valois. After Charles VII finally drove the English out of France in 1453, the Valois monarchs strengthened royal authority. On the death (1498) of Charles VIII the crown passed to the Orléans branch of the family in the person of Louis XII. He was succeeded

(1515) by his cousin of the Angoulême branch, FRANCIS I. The last rulers of the dynasty were beset by the Wars of Religion (see RELIGION, WARS OF). The Valois dynasty ended with the assassination (1589) of HENRY III and was followed by the Bourbon dynasty.

Valois, Dame Ninette de Through a combination of vision and single-mindedness, Ninette de Valois (Edris Stannus), b. June 6, 1898, in Baltiboys, Ireland, created Britain's national ballet. The company she founded in 1931 at Sadler's Wells Theatre in a working-class district of London is now the Royal Ballet. De Valois was a member of the Ballets Russes de Serge Diaghilev from 1923 to 1925. In 1926 she joined the London Old Vic Theatre to teach movement to its actors and to arrange dances for plays and operas at that theater. For some years she was a successful choreographer; *Job* (1931), *The Rake's Progress* (1935), and *Checkmate* (1937) are still performed in Great Britain. In 1963 she resigned as director of the Royal Ballet but has maintained a close connection with the company and its school.

Valparaíso [val-puh-ry'-zoh or vahl-pah-rah-ee'-soh] Valparaíso, the capital of Valparaíso province, is one of Chile's major cities, with a population of 288,300 (1989 est.). Located on a bay of the Pacific Ocean in the central part of the country, it is also Chile's most important seaport. Elevators and cable railroads connect the waterfront and port with the hillside residential section of Los Cerros. Valparaíso's mild climate attracts many tourists each year. The city is an important producer of textiles, foodstuffs, chemicals, and leather goods. Two universities and the Chilean naval academy are also located there, as is the new national congress building, constructed during 1989–90 (the executive branch of the government remains based in Santiago, the capital).

On his arrival in 1536, the Spanish conquistador Juan de Saavedra renamed the small Indian fishing village of Quintil and the surrounding bay Valparaíso (Valley of Paradise) for his birthplace in Spain. The city was sacked by English and Dutch pirates several times in the 16th century and was rocked by earthquakes in 1730, 1822, 1839, 1873, 1906–07, and 1971. Valparaíso's major growth began after Chilean independence (1818).

value-added tax A value-added tax (VAT) is one levied on goods and services at each stage of production and distribution. For example, instead of a buyer's paying a 10 percent retail sales tax on a record player, VAT would be collected in bits and pieces at each stage of production—first from the makers of the record player's components, then from the firm that assembled it, then from the wholesaler, and finally from the retailer. Each firm involved in the chain of production would add the rate of the tax, 10 percent in this example, to the value of the goods it sells, bill its customers for the total including the tax, take a credit for whatever VAT it has paid on its raw materials, and then owe the difference, on the value it has added to the product, as tax. The entire tax is ultimately passed on to the consumer as a proportionately higher price.

VAT was introduced in France in 1954 and has been adopted by the Common Market members, including Great Britain. It has been proposed as an alternative to either the United States federal corporate-income tax or the Social Security tax. VAT's opponents consider it a regressive tax that hits low- and moderate-income people, who spend a large part of their incomes on consumption, harder than the rich.

See also: INCOME TAX; TAXATION.

valve A valve is a mechanical device serving to control the flow of gases or liquids through a pipe or other flow system. Incorporated in a vast range of mechanical equipment, from water faucets to nuclear reactor systems, valves are movable parts that can either completely permit or block flow, or partially block flow. They are usually made of brass, bronze, steel, iron, or plastic, depending upon their function. They include gate, plug, globe, butterfly, check, safety, and spool valves.

A gate valve is basically a wedge-shaped disk that is lowered into a pipe to block flow. A plug valve, often found in the burettes that are used for chemical titrations, is a plug that has a hole that can either be lined up with the pipe, permitting flow, or turned perpendicular to the pipe's opening in order to block flow. A globe valve, used to lessen or increase flow, is a plug or disk that fits in a seat; water faucets most frequently have globe valves to regulate flow.

A butterfly valve is a circular disk, inside a pipe, that rotates on a hinge and allows alternating obstruction and passage of flow in rapid sequence. Gas is fed into an internal combustion engine by means of a butterfly valve in the carburetor. A check valve allows flow in only one direction; a simple example is the spherical plug of a snorkel, which permits a swimmer to breathe air but does not admit water to the tube.

Safety valves are designed to open when pressure within the flow system exceeds a maximum. The spool valve is a sliding valve with a complex system of inflow and outflow openings. Used in hydrostatic flow systems, the spool valve is powered to slide back and forth over the openings in such a manner that the flow of oil to various machine parts is regulated.

vampire In Slavic folklore a vampire is an evil spirit that takes possession of a corpse and, rising from its grave at night, sucks the blood of sleeping persons. The victims become vampires after death. Vampires are the ghosts of criminals, heretics, or suicides and can be put to rest only by having a wooden stake driven through their hearts.

See also: DRACULA.

vampire bat see BAT

Van, Lake

Van, Lake [vahn]   Lake Van, the largest lake in Turkey, covers an area of about 3,800 km^2 (1,470 mi^2) in the easternmost part of the country. It is extremely saline and has no outlet. The main economic activities of the area are extraction of sodium carbonate, fishing, and ferry service connecting cities onshore.

Van Allen radiation belts

Van Allen radiation belts   The Van Allen radiation belts consist of concentric doughnut-shaped regions of energetically charged particles that encircle the Earth within the MAGNETOSPHERE. The belt nearest to the Earth, located within 1 Earth radius from the Earth's surface, was discovered by James A. Van Allen and his associates on the basis of data received from Geiger counters carried by the first U.S. satellites (*Explorers 1* and *3*) in January and March 1958, and by S. N. Vernov on the basis of similar data received from *Sputnik 2*. In December 1958 a second belt, at a distance of about 2 to 3 Earth radii from the Earth's surface, was discovered by Van Allen's group. The first belt has been termed the *inner belt* and the second one the *classical outer belt*. In reality, no clear distinction separates the belts; the more energetically charged particles exist closer to the Earth, and belts of lower-energy particles extend outward to about 26,000 km (16,000 mi).

The Van Allen belts are doughnut-shaped zones of highly energetic charged particles within the Earth's magnetosphere, or magnetic-field region. The solar wind (yellow lines) distorts the magnetosphere, causing it to take the form of a teardrop with the tail pointing away from the Sun (A). Solar particles compress the Earth's magnetic field at the shock front (1) and flow around the field's boundary, or magnetopause (2). The most intense Van Allen belts include an inner zone of protons (3) and an outer zone of electrons (4).

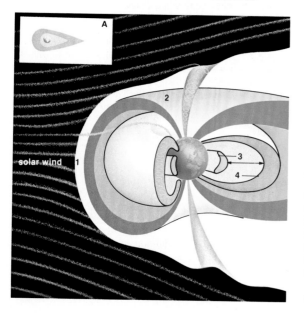

The energetically charged particles in these belts arise from various sources. Cosmic-ray particles (coming from interplanetary space), colliding with atmospheric atoms, produce neutrons that decay into energetic protons (10 million to 1 billion electron-volts) and electrons. The resulting charged particles immediately get trapped by the Earth's magnetic field. Some charged particles also penetrate from interplanetary space into the magnetosphere and diffuse slowly toward the Earth. The closer they approach the Earth, the more they are energized. Additionally, a large belt of protons, with energies of the order of 50,000 electron-volts, extends from about 3 to 9 Earth radii above the Earth's surface. This proton belt becomes greatly enhanced during a MAGNETIC STORM.

A large belt of electrons, with energies of the order of 10,000 to 50,000 electron-volts and with an extent similar to that of the ring current belt, also surrounds the Earth. This belt is fed during auroral activity (see AURORAS).

Van Buren, Martin

Van Buren, Martin [van buer'-en]   Martin Van Buren, eighth president of the United States (1837–41), governed during the Panic of 1837, America's worst economic crisis up to that time. He played a key role in organizing the Democratic party and was the first president to be born a U.S. citizen.

Early Career. Of Dutch descent, Van Buren was born on Dec. 5, 1782, in Kinderhook, N.Y.. He studied law and was admitted to the bar in 1803. Active in Democratic-Republican politics, he served as state senator (1812–20) and as attorney general of New York (1816–19).

Van Buren was elected to the U.S. Senate in 1821. During the administration of John Quincy Adams (1825–29), he led Senate opposition to the president and played a major role in organizing the political coalition that elected Andrew JACKSON president in 1828.

Jackson's Lieutenant. While in the Senate, Van Buren continued to dominate New York State politics and was elected governor in 1828; however, he resigned after only a few months to accept appointment as Jackson's secretary of state. Soon involved in a bitter power struggle with Vice-President John C. CALHOUN, Van Buren became a close companion and advisor to Jackson. Van Buren's position was strengthened by Jackson's disaffection with Calhoun. Jackson had discovered that Calhoun had privately called for his censure in 1819 for his actions during the invasion of Florida, and was displeased with Calhoun's extreme state-rights views. To enable Jackson to remove the pro-Calhoun element from his cabinet, Van Buren resigned. After calling for the resignation of all other cabinet members, Jackson appointed Van Buren minister to Great Britain. The Senate, with Calhoun casting the tie-breaking vote, refused to confirm the appointment. Enraged, Jackson supported Van Buren for the vice-presidency and then chose him as his successor. In 1836, Van Buren easily won the Democratic presidential nomination as Jackson's protégé and then the election.

Presidency. Van Buren sought to hold Southern Democrats in the party by adhering to a strict state-rights poli-

AT A GLANCE

MARTIN VAN BUREN
8th President of the United States (1837–41)

Nicknames: "The Little Magician"; "The Red Fox of Kinderhook"

Born: Dec. 5, 1782, Kinderhook, N.Y.

Education: Kinderhook Academy (graduated 1796)

Profession: Lawyer

Religious Affiliation: Dutch Reformed

Marriage: Feb. 21, 1807, to Hannah Hoes (1783–1819)

Children: Abraham Van Buren (1807–73); John Van Buren (1810–66); Martin Van Buren (1812–55); Smith Thompson Van Buren (1817–76)

Political Affiliation: Democrat

Writings: *Inquiry into the Origin and Course of Political Parties in the United States* (1867); *The Autobiography of Martin Van Buren* (1920), ed. by John C. Fitzpatrick

Died: July 24, 1862, Kinderhook, N.Y.

Buried: Kinderhook Cemetery, Kinderhook, N.Y.

Vice-President: Richard M. Johnson

cy on slavery. He favored guarantees that the federal government would not interfere with slavery in the states. Van Buren was opposed to the expansion of slavery, however, and his refusal to support the annexation of Texas offended many Southerners. Meanwhile, his administration aroused further sectional opposition by conducting a costly war against the Seminole Indians in Florida—a conflict that many Northerners saw as a prelude to the admission of Florida as a slave state.

Van Buren's greatest political difficulties resulted from the nation's first major depression, the Panic of 1837. Committed to the Jeffersonian principle of limited government, Van Buren refused to yield to pressure for federal intervention to relieve economic distress. He saw his responsibility as limited to preventing the loss of federal funds as a result of the collapse of banks, whose alleged abuses he, like Jackson, had long criticized. Van Buren called for the establishment of an INDEPENDENT TREASURY SYSTEM that would divorce government and banking by placing all public money in federally owned depositories. After much debate Congress established such a system in 1840.

Cautious and tactful in his foreign policy, Van Buren in 1838 sought to conciliate Great Britain in the CAROLINE AFFAIR, which arose over the sinking in American waters of a vessel supplying Canadian insurgents. In 1839 he intervened to prevent the so-called AROOSTOOK WAR, involving skirmishes over a boundary dispute between Maine and New Brunswick, from becoming a full-scale conflict.

Unsuccessful Presidential Bids. Despite his ability as chief executive, Van Buren gained a reputation as a devious political operator, and his failure to take decisive action to alleviate the hardships of the Panic of 1837 undermined his popularity. In 1840 he was defeated for reelection by the Whig candidate, William Henry Harrison.

Seeking the Democratic presidential nomination in 1844, Van Buren entered the nominating convention with the support of a majority of the delegates. His refusal, however, to support the annexation of Texas, which President John Tyler had made a burning national issue, cost him the support of the South. The convention chose annexationist James K. POLK of Tennessee, who subsequently won the presidential election.

In 1848, Van Buren was nominated for the presidency by the Barnburners (see HUNKERS AND BARNBURNERS), a faction of Northern Democrats opposed to the extension of slavery. Despite his endorsement by the FREE-SOIL PARTY, Van Buren ran a poor third. He died at Kinderhook on July 24, 1862.

Van de Graaff generator see ACCELERATOR, PARTICLE

---

van der Meer, Simon Simon van der Meer, b. The Hague, Netherlands, Nov. 24, 1925, was awarded, along with Carlo RUBBIA, the 1984 Nobel Prize for physics for their work leading to discoveries of the W and Z FUNDAMENTAL PARTICLES. After obtaining an engineering degree from the Technical University in Delft, van der Meer joined, in 1956, the staff of CERN in Geneva (see EUROPEAN ORGANIZATION FOR NUCLEAR RESEARCH). Van der Meer's major contribution to the discovery of the W and Z particles was his design of a process, known as stochastic cooling, which was used to obtain large numbers of antiprotons.

---

van der Waals equation The van der Waals equation, derived by the Dutch physicist Johannes van der Waals (1837–1923), is an equation of state for gases and liquids that provides a reasonably good representation of the pressure-volume-temperature (PVT) data in the range of pressures and temperatures where the ideal gas law ($PV=nRT$) is invalid. The equation states: $(P + n^2a/V^2)(V - nb) = nRT$, where P = pressure, V = volume, T = temperature, n = moles of gas, R is the universal gas constant, and a and b are constants characteristic of the gas. The constants a and b are evaluated for each gas by fitting the equation to experimental measurements of PVT data. They may also be obtained by measurement of the critical temperature and critical pressure of the gas (see CRITICAL CONSTANTS). The constant a is then a measure of the attractive forces between the molecules, called van der Waals forces. The constant b is the approximate volume of a mole of the molecules in the liquid state.

See also: GAS LAWS.

Van Devanter, Willis [van duh-van'-tur] Willis Van Devanter, b. Marion, Ind., Apr. 17, 1859, d. Feb. 8, 1941, served (1911–37) as associate justice on the U.S. Supreme Court. He practiced law before being elected (1890) chief justice of the Wyoming Supreme Court. Van Devanter then served (1903–10) on the U.S. Circuit Court; in 1911 President William H. Taft appointed him to the U.S. Supreme Court. Justice Van Devanter became one of the conservative majority on the Supreme Court that thwarted much of the New Deal legislation of President Franklin D. Roosevelt.

Van Diemen's Land see TASMANIA

Van Dine, S. S. [van dyn] S. S. Van Dine was the pseudonym of Willard Huntington Wright, b. Charlottesville, Va., 1888?, d. Apr. 11, 1939, an American scholar, editor, and art critic who turned to the writing of fiction after his health declined. He wrote a series of detective novels with an amateur sleuth as protagonist: Philo

Vance, a languid purveyor of esoteric knowledge and icy logic, was a huge success. Between 1926 and 1938, 12 novels appeared, 11 of which were turned into movies, and, in the 1940s, Vance was also featured in a radio series. Among the best of the Van Dine novels are *The Greene Murder Case* (1928), *The Bishop Murder Case* (1929), and *The Scarab Murder Case* (1930).

van Dongen, Kees see DONGEN, KEES VAN

Van Doren, Carl The writer, editor, and teacher Carl Clinton Van Doren, b. Hope, Ill., Sept. 10, 1885, d. July 18, 1950, was an early proponent of the serious study of American literature. Managing editor (1917–21) of the *Cambridge History of American Literature,* and literary editor of the *Nation* (1919–22) and *Century* (1922–25), he wrote such critical studies as *The American Novel* (1921; rev. ed., 1940) and *American Literature: An Introduction* (1933). He was also the author of a novel, *The Ninth Wave* (1926), and a Pulitzer Prize–winning biography (1938) of Benjamin Franklin.

Van Doren, Mark A versatile writer, Mark Albert Van Doren, b. Hope, Ill., June 13, 1894, d. Dec. 10, 1972, a brother of Carl Van Doren, won a Pulitzer Prize for his *Collected Poems* (1940) and was an esteemed critic and university teacher. His numerous studies of authors—including Dryden, Hawthorne, and Shakespeare—his play *The Last Days of Lincoln* (1959), and his poetry, which explores the relation between man and nature, are still admired. His later poetry includes the collections *Spring Birth* (1953) and *Morning Worship and Other Poems* (1960).

---

van Dyck, Sir Anthony [van dyk] The Flemish painter Sir Anthony (Anton) van Dyck, b. Mar. 22, 1599, d. Dec. 9, 1641, was noted primarily for his portraits and religious canvases. Between 1618 and 1620 he collaborated with Peter Paul Rubens, working with him as a younger colleague rather than as a student. He was later to attain a reputation second only to Rubens as the greatest painter in mid-17th-century Europe.

Van Dyck's name is inextricably associated with the history of English painting; he made his first trip to London in 1620, where he was granted a court pension. With royal permission he left England in 1621 for Italy, where he studied, traveled, and painted until 1627. The full-length portrait *Marchesa Elena Grimaldi* (c.1625; National Gallery of Art, Washington, D.C.) exemplifies van Dyck's use of dark but harmonious color and an air of regal dignity bordering on arrogance that made his work so popular in the court of Charles I.

Van Dyck returned to Antwerp in 1627 and in 1630 became court painter to Archduchess Isabella, regent of the Netherlands. He settled in London in 1632 and was knighted and appointed principal painter to Charles I in the same year. He painted many portraits of the royal

Charles I of England in Hunting Dress (c.1634), one of several royal portraits by Sir Anthony van Dyck, helped establish a grandiose new tradition in English portraiture. (Louvre, Paris.)

traits of Sir Peter Lely, Thomas Gainsborough, and Sir Joshua Reynolds.

van Eyck, Jan   see EYCK, JAN VAN

▬

Van Fleet, James Alward   James Alward Van Fleet, b. Coytesville, N.J., Mar. 19, 1892, d. Sept. 23, 1992, commanded (1951–53) the U.S. 8th Army during the KOREAN WAR. A graduate (1915) of West Point, Van Fleet led a machine-gun battalion in World War I. During World War II, he commanded the regiment that made (1944) the initial assault on Utah Beach, in Normandy. He was (1948–50) chief of the U.S. military mission to Greece, which helped fight Communist insurgents. Replacing Gen. Matthew B. Ridgway as 8th Army commander in Korea, Van Fleet was promoted (1951) to four-star general.

▬

van Gogh, Vincent   [van goh]   Although almost wholly unknown during his brief lifetime, the painter Vincent Willem van Gogh, b. Mar. 30, 1853, is today probably the most widely known and appreciated representative of POSTIMPRESSIONISM. His work became an important bridge between the 19th and 20th centuries; it was particularly influential in the evolution of both FAUVISM and German EXPRESSIONISM.

At the age of 16, van Gogh went to work for Goupil and Company, an art gallery with which one of his uncles had long been associated; he was dismissed in 1876. In 1880 he chose art as a vocation and became dependent on his brother Theo for money. Theo had also gone to work for Goupil. Vincent's thinking during his short but prolific career (approximately 750 paintings, 1,600 drawings, 9 lithographs, and 1 etching) is well documented in more than 700 letters that he wrote to Theo and others.

Van Gogh's early period includes all his work from 1879 through 1885. Between August 1879 and November 1885 he worked in Etten, The Hague—where he received some instruction from his cousin, Anton Mauve—and in Nuenen, among other places. In Nuenen he painted The Potato Eaters (1885; Rijksmuseum Vincent van Gogh, Amsterdam), his first important picture, which underscores his lifelong interest in peasant subjects.

During the winter of 1885–86 van Gogh studied at the academy in Antwerp, where he was forced to draw from plaster casts and to adopt academic principles that did not suit him. He moved to Paris, where he lived with Theo.

The Paris period (March 1886–February 1888) is extremely important because it enabled Vincent to see and to hear discussed the work of virtually every major artist there. Although van Gogh admired many members of the avant-garde, he also admired Eugène Delacroix, Jean François Millet, and the painters of the Barbizon and Hague schools, and such Japanese printmakers as Hiroshige, Hokusai, and Kesaï Yeisen. Numerous self-portraits, still lifes, and cityscapes date from this period, such as Self-Portrait with a Straw Hat (1887; Metropoli-

family as well as of court dignitaries and the nobility. His Charles I on Horseback (1638; National Gallery, London), one of several equestrian portraits he executed of the king, is a tour de force of dazzling brushwork and foreshortening, conveying the image of majesty and overwhelming power the king wished to project. Although much of van Dyck's work for the king had something of the flavor of image-building and propaganda about it, he was also capable of keen penetration and expression of character. His oval double portrait, The Artist with Sir Endymion Porter (c.1635, Prado, Madrid) reveals two worldly men, the painter and his patron, of sensitivity and intelligence.

Van Dyck also painted numerous religious and mythological subjects throughout his career. His debt to Italian Renaissance prototypes is, perhaps, clearer in these than in his portraits, as can be seen in Cupid and Psyche (c.1639; Royal Collections, Buckingham Palace, London).

Prior to van Dyck's arrival in England, English portraiture tended to be formal and almost primitive in style, but he brought to it the full power of a completely articulated baroque style, and his influence extended through the 18th century. It is clearly visible in the portan Museum of Art, New York City), *A Pair of Shoes* (1886; Rijksmuseum Vincent van Gogh), and *Restaurant de la Sirène at Asnières* (1887; Louvre, Paris). During these years van Gogh's style shifted from the darker manner characteristic of his Nuenen period to a postimpressionist style heavily influenced by divisionism (also called pointillism; see SEURAT, GEORGES).

Van Gogh left Paris and moved to Arles in February 1888. His mature work and many of his most famous paintings date from the ensuing year. For example, he painted numerous blossoming orchards in the spring of 1888 (Rijksmuseum Vincent van Gogh), *The Night Café on the Place Lamartine, Arles* (1888; Yale University Art Gallery, New Haven, Conn.), *Still Life with Sunflowers* (several versions), and *The Bedroom at Arles* (1888; Rijksmuseum Vincent van Gogh).

In October 1888, Paul GAUGUIN came to live and work with van Gogh. After only two months, however, following

the first of Vincent's attacks of dementia, in which he amputated his own earlobe, Gauguin left, having first summoned Theo from Paris. Thereafter, Vincent was hospitalized intermittently until the spring of 1890; he was voluntarily confined in the Asylum of Saint-Paul in Saint-Remy from May 1889 until May 1890. He continued to paint, however, and in June 1889 executed the *Starry Night* (Museum of Modern Art, New York City) and the extraordinary *Self-Portrait* (Louvre).

In the three months following his release from the hospital in May 1890, at the village of Auvers-sur-Oise outside Paris, Vincent produced many notable works including the *Portrait of Dr. Gachet* (private collection, New York City), *Field under Thunderclouds,* and the famous *Crows in the Wheatfields* (both Rijksmuseum Vincent van Gogh). Although Vincent had finally begun to receive critical praise, he shot himself on July 27, 1890, and died two days later.

(Right) The Church at Auvers, *painted by Vincent van Gogh in June 1890, a month before his suicide, is in his high-keyed late style, with thick impasto, violent colors, strong contrasts, and deliberate distortion to achieve powerful expressive effects. The looming church silhouette is echoed by the pyramidal ground below it. (Louvre, Paris.)*

(Below) Self-Portrait with a Gray Hat *(1877) was painted by Vincent van Gogh during his 2-year stay in Paris; the pointillist technique (dots of color) is clear evidence of his new interest in the work of the impressionist painters whom he met there. (Rijksmuseum Vincent van Gogh, Amsterdam.)*

Van Rensselaer (family) [van ren'-suh-leer] The venerable Van Rensselaers of New York were noted for their wealth and social prominence. The family traces its origins to **Kiliaen Van Rensselaer**, 1595–1644, an Amsterdam jeweler and stockholder of the Dutch colony of New Netherland, who in 1630 acquired a huge estate surrounding Fort Orange (Albany). Rensselaerswyck, the first, largest, and only successful patroonship (feudal estate; see PATROONS) in America became in 1685 an English manor, a kind of land grant that carried no civil authority and excluded the city of Albany. Kiliaen was an absentee proprietor, but his sons **Nicholas Van Rensselaer**, b. Amsterdam, September 1636, d. 1678, a Dutch Calvinist minister, and **Jeremias Van Rensselaer**, b. Amsterdam, c.1630, d. October 1674, established the family in America. **Stephen Van Rensselaer**, b. New York, Nov. 1, 1764, d. Jan. 26, 1839, the eighth and last of the patroons, was assemblyman, state senator, and lieutenant governor of New York as well as militia general in the War of 1812 and U.S. representative (1822–29). Stephen contributed a great deal to the economic and educational development of New York State; in 1824 he founded Rensselaer Polytechnic Institute in Troy, the nation's first engineering school. The ANTIRENT WAR, a tenant uprising that prompted legislation ending perpetual leases and thus patroonships, began at Rensselaerswyck (1839–40).

Van Vechten, Carl [van vek'-ten] In a style that was the literary equivalent of Art Deco, Carl Van Vechten, b. Cedar Rapids, Iowa, June 17, 1880, d. Dec. 21, 1964, chronicled the smart, decadent New York society of the 1920s. His novels include *Peter Whiffle* (1922), *The Blind Bow-Boy* (1923), *Firecrackers* (1925), and *Parties* (1930). His best-known work, *Nigger Heaven* (1926), portrayed New York's black culture during the HARLEM RENAISSANCE, and *Spider Boy* (1928) satirized Hollywood. When the Great Depression came, Van Vechten abandoned fiction for photography.

Van Vogt, A. E. The American writer Alfred Elton Van Vogt, b. Winnipeg, Manitoba, Apr. 26, 1912, broke into science fiction by contributing stories to the magazine *Astounding* in 1939. *Slan* (1946), which depicts the persecution of a superior mutant, is considered his best novel.

vanadium [vuh-nay'-dee-uhm] Vanadium is a bright white metallic chemical element of Group VB of the first series of transition metals in the PERIODIC TABLE. It has the symbol V, its atomic number is 23, and its atomic weight is 50.9414. The element was discovered in 1801 by Andrés M. del Rio, but at the time it was dismissed as impure chromium. The element was rediscovered in 1830 by Nils G. Sefström, who named it in honor of the Scandinavian goddess Vanadis.

Among the 65 or so minerals in which vanadium occurs, the more important sources of the metal include carnotite, patronite, roscoelite, and vanadinite. Other sources of vanadium are phosphate rock, certain iron ores, and some crude oils in the form of organic complexes. Extraction from petroleum ash is a possible future source of the element. High-purity vanadium is obtained by reduction of vanadium trichloride (VCl_3) with magnesium or with magnesium-sodium mixtures. Because the major use of the metal is as an alloying agent for steel, pure vanadium is seldom extracted, and the bulk of the metal is currently made by the reduction of vanadium pentoxide (V_2O_5) with calcium.

Natural vanadium consists of two isotopes, ^{50}V and ^{51}V, the former being radioactive. The pure metal is soft and ductile, with a melting point of 1,890° C, a boiling point of 3,380° C, and a density of 6.11 g/cm^3.

Vanadium is resistant to corrosion by alkali, sulfuric and hydrochloric acids, and salt water but oxidizes rapidly above about 660° C. Because the metal has good structural strength and a low fission neutron cross-section, it finds extensive application in the nuclear industry. The metal is also used in forming rust-resistant spring and high-speed tool steels; about 80 percent of the production of vanadium is used to make ferrovanadium or as a steel additive. Vanadium pentoxide is used in ceramics and as a catalyst. Vanadium and its compounds are toxic.

Vanbrugh, Sir John [van-bruh'] Sir John Vanbrugh, christened Jan. 24, 1664, d. Mar. 26, 1726, was an English playwright and architect whose most renowned works are Blenheim Palace in Oxfordshire and Castle Howard in Yorkshire. After writing several popular comedies, including *The Relapse* (1696), Vanbrugh turned more and more to architectural work. His design (1699) for Castle Howard, the palatial country home of his friend and associate the earl of Carlisle, successfully incorporated English baroque and French elements and was widely praised by contemporary observers.

His most renowned—and most controversial—design was that of Blenheim Palace (begun 1705), a gift to John Churchill, 1st duke of Marlborough, from the nation. At Blenheim, Vanbrugh was able to work out the first entirely English version of baroque architecture, presenting an interplay of conflicting masses and idiosyncratic classical detailing, with Gothic and even Elizabethan elements in the skyline. Throughout the early 1700s, while still working at Blenheim, he collaborated with Sir Christopher Wren and Nicholas Hawksmoor on several projects and executed numerous dramatic and original designs, including Vanbrugh Castle (c.1717) in Greenwich and the remodeling of Kimbolton Castle in Huntingdonshire (1707–10). He was also involved in planning gardens at Stowe in Buckinghamshire and Castle Howard, which established him as one of the founders of what was called the "picturesque" landscape. His work was always highly inventive but not imitable, and he had no followers.

Vance, Cyrus R. [vans] Cyrus Roberts Vance, b. Clarksburg, W.Va., Mar. 27, 1917, was U.S. secretary of state from 1977 to 1980. A graduate of Yale Law School, he began his career in government as a special counsel for the Senate Armed Services Committee in 1957. He served as secretary of the army (1962–64) and deputy secretary of defense (1964–67). He later undertook a number of important diplomatic missions for President Lyndon Johnson. During the Cyprus crisis of 1967 he was credited by some observers with having averted a war between Greece and Turkey, and during the Paris peace conference on Vietnam he was deputy chief of the U.S. delegation (1968–69). As secretary of state in the Carter administration, Vance was involved in the Strategic Arms Limitation Talks (SALT), the negotiations leading to the Israeli-Egyptian peace treaty of 1979, and the prolonged efforts to secure release of the U.S. hostages in Iran. He resigned in protest against the commando attempt to rescue the hostages in April 1980.

Vancouver [van-koo'-vur] Vancouver is a city in southwestern Canada opposite Vancouver Island in the province of British Columbia. Vancouver is Canada's third largest metropolis and one of the fastest growing. The city's population is 431,147, and that of the metropolitan area, 1,380,729 (1986). Occupying one of the world's most attractive city sites, Vancouver is surrounded by water and overlooked by mountains. The Strait of Georgia is to the west, Burrard Inlet is on the north, and the Fraser River delta is on the south. Just beyond Burrard Inlet the Coast Ranges rise abruptly to heights exceeding 1,500 m (5,000 ft). The climate of the area is perhaps the mildest in Canada.

Vancouver is a major port of Canada. As the principal western terminus of Canada's transcontinental highway and rail routes, it is the primary city of western Canada as well as one of the nation's largest industrial centers. Major industries include the production of lumber and paper products, shipbuilding, food and fish processing, petroleum refining, and metal product manufacturing.

Vancouver is also a major destination of tourists. In addition to the city's scenic location, visitors enjoy beautiful gardens and world-famous Stanley Park, a combination of natural forest and parklands near the city center. The University of British Columbia was founded in Vancouver in 1908.

Vancouver was founded as a sawmill settlement called Granville on Burrard Inlet in the 1870s. The city was incorporated in 1886 and renamed for British naval captain George Vancouver, who had explored the area a century earlier. The first trans-Canada railway, the Canadian Pacific, arrived in 1887. Other railways came soon after, and trans-Pacific ocean trade began to develop strongly in the late 19th century. Since World War II many immigrants from continental Europe and Asia and from other parts of Canada have settled in Vancouver. In 1986 it was the site of a world's fair.

Vancouver, George George Vancouver, b. June 22, 1757, d. May 10, 1798, an English explorer, surveyed the west coast of North America from the San Francisco Bay area to British Columbia. He entered the Royal Navy in 1771 and sailed (1772–75, 1776–80) under Capt. James Cook. In 1791, Vancouver set out to explore the Pacific Northwest, obtain from the Spanish the return of Nootka (on what was later named Vancouver Island, in his honor), and search for a Northwest Passage. Sailing around the Cape of Good Hope, he surveyed portions of the Australian and New Zealand coasts. Between 1792 and 1794, he sailed along the North American coast as far south as San Luis Obispo, Calif., and as far north as

Vancouver, the leading city of western Canada, is situated along the Pacific coast of British Columbia, separated from Vancouver Island by the Strait of Georgia. The area was explored in 1792 by the British captain George Vancouver and first settled during the 1870s.

Cook Inlet, Alaska. He was the first to circumnavigate Vancouver Island. Vancouver regained Nootka and reported that there was no Northwest Passage.

Vancouver Island   Part of British Columbia, Canada, Vancouver is the largest island on the Pacific coast of North America. Covering 31,284 km^2 (12,079 mi^2), it is 459 km (285 mi) long and averages 80 km (50 mi) in width. The population is 510,233 (1986). VICTORIA, the principal city, is the capital of British Columbia.

Mountainous and heavily forested, Vancouver Island has a rugged coastline with deep fjords and bays. The highest peak, Golden Hinde, rises 2,200 m (7,220 ft). Economic activities include lumbering, paper manufacturing, fishing, and coal and iron-ore mining. Tourism is also important.

Originally inhabited by Nootka and Makah Indians, Vancouver Island was visited by James Cook in 1778 and subsequently settled by the Hudson's Bay Company. It became a British colony in 1849 and part of British Columbia in 1866.

Vandals   [van'-duhlz]   Among the barbarian peoples who attacked the Roman Empire in the 5th century AD were the Vandals, a Teutonic tribe that governed a North African kingdom from 439 to 534.

By the 4th century the Vandals were living in the area of the Tisza River (in what is now eastern Hungary). As the Huns moved west later in that century, they pushed the Vandals before them. In December 406 the Vandals crossed the Rhine and invaded Gaul. They ravaged Roman territory there and in 409 invaded Spain. Following a series of defeats inflicted in 417 by the Visigoths, who were fighting on behalf of the Romans, the Vandals moved south to Andalusia.

In 429 the new Vandal ruler GAISERIC abandoned Spain and invaded North Africa, which finally fell under his complete control in 439. Gaiseric, who ruled until 477, gained control of the western Mediterranean and sacked Rome in 455. The common noun *vandal* reflects the latter act.

In North Africa the Vandals, who were Arian Christians, persecuted orthodox Christians (in a reversal of Roman practice). Gaiseric's descendants had difficulty defending their frontiers, and in 533 the Byzantine general BELISARIUS invaded North Africa. By 534 the Vandal kingdom was in ruins.

Vandenberg, Arthur H.   [van'-den-burg]   Arthur Hendrick Vandenberg, b. Grand Rapids, Mich., Mar. 22, 1884, d. Apr. 18, 1951, a leading Republican and U.S. senator from Michigan (1928–51), was a key figure in the establishment of a bipartisan foreign policy after World War II. Active in state and local politics, he was appointed to fill a vacant seat in the Senate (1928), to which he was elected soon after. Vandenberg was a leading opponent of President Franklin D. Roosevelt's internationalist

policies before and during World War II, but in the mid-1940s he reversed his views and strongly supported the containment policies of Harry S. Truman's administration. As ranking Republican and chairman of the Senate Foreign Relations Committee (1947–49), he was influential in developing bipartisan support for such efforts as aid to Greece and Turkey in 1947, the Marshall Plan in 1948, and the North Atlantic Treaty Organization in 1949.

Vandenberg Air Force Base   Vandenberg Air Force Base, located at Point Arguello, Calif., about 240 km (150 mi) north of Los Angeles, is the U.S. site for launching satellites southward over the Pacific Ocean into polar and near-polar orbits. The explosion of a Titan 34D booster at the base in 1986, however, badly damaged the pad used for major polar-orbit launches.

Primarily an Air Force facility for test-launching intercontinental ballistic missiles, Vandenberg handles civilian launches through the Western Test Range office of the Kennedy Space Center. Established in 1958, it is named for Gen. Hoyt S. Vandenberg, a former Air Force chief of staff. Plans called for occasional SPACE SHUTTLE launches from the base to begin in the mid-1980s, but structural flaws found in the launch facility—plus delays resulting from the *Challenger* disaster in 1986—postponed these plans until the early 1990s.

Vanderbilt   (family) [van'-dur-bilt]   The Vanderbilt family owes its prominence to its early association with rail and water transportation. **Cornelius Vanderbilt**, b. Staten Island, N.Y., May 27, 1794, d. Jan. 4, 1877, began a ferry service between New York City and Staten Island at the age of 16. In 1818 he entered the shipping company of Thomas Gibbons. As a result of the U.S. Supreme Court decision (GIBBONS V. OGDEN, 1824) nullifying the navigation monopoly that New York State had granted to Robert Fulton and Robert R. Livingston, Vanderbilt was able to gain control of much of the shipping business along the Hudson River. During the gold rush of 1849 he successfully opened a steamship route from New York to California. In the 1850s, Vanderbilt entered into transatlantic competition with the Cunard and other lines. The 1860s marked his entry into the railroad field. By 1875, after he had bought and consolidated many small holdings, his New York Central Railroad controlled the lucrative route between New York and Chicago. He founded Vanderbilt University in 1875.

At his death, Cornelius Vanderbilt's fortune was estimated at $100 million. Of his 13 children, **William Henry Vanderbilt**, b. New Brunswick, N.J., May 8, 1821, d. Dec. 8, 1885, is notable for having expanded the family railroad holdings.

Vanderbilt University   Established in 1873, Vanderbilt University is a private coeducational institution in Nashville, Tenn. Law, dentistry, nursing, medical, and engineering schools are part of the university. In 1979 the university absorbed George Peabody College for Teachers (1785).

Vanderlyn, John [van'-dur-lin]   John Vanderlyn, b. Kingston, N.Y., Sept. 15, 1775, d. Aug. 23, 1852, was an American painter of landscapes and historical subjects. In Paris and Rome, Vanderlyn thrived, perfecting a neoclassical style in the manner of Jacques Louis David and Jean Auguste Dominique Ingres that, in 1808, earned him a gold medal from Napoleon for his painting *Marius among the Ruins of Carthage* (1807; M. H. de Young Memorial Museum, San Francisco). After 1815, however, when Vanderlyn returned to the United States, his hopes for fame were never realized. He opened a rotunda in Manhattan to exhibit his panorama, *Palace and Gardens of Versailles* (1815; Metropolitan Museum of Art, New York City), but failed to prosper, and there was little demand for his paintings. Finally, in 1837, the government recognized him with a commission to paint *The Landing of Columbus* for the rotunda of the Capitol, but it was too late for the aging and disgruntled Vanderlyn. Although he spent the next 8 years in Paris working on the project, it could not measure up to the ambitious vision of his youth.

Vane, Sir Henry [vayn]   An English statesman, Sir Henry Vane the Younger, b. 1613, d. June 14, 1662, was a leading parliamentarian during the ENGLISH CIVIL WAR. A Puritan convert, he was colonial governor of Massachusetts (1636–37). Returning to England, Vane became a member of the Short and the Long parliaments and negotiated (1643) the alliance bringing the Scots into the English Civil War on Parliament's side.

Although against the king's execution, Vane served on the Commonwealth's Council of State (1649–53), handling naval and foreign affairs. An advocate of parliamentary supremacy, he opposed the dissolution of the Rump Parliament by Oliver Cromwell in 1653 and was imprisoned (1656) for attacking Cromwell's Protectorate. In 1659 he supported the army's overthrow of Richard Cromwell. After the restoration of the monarchy, Vane was executed for high treason.

Vänern, Lake [ven'-urn]   Lake Vänern, the largest lake in Sweden, covers an area of 5,585 km^2 (2,156 mi^2). Located in southwestern Sweden, Lake Vänern is a major link in the Göta Canal, linking the Kattegat to the Baltic Sea. Karlstad, Kristinehamn, Vänersborg, and Lidköping are major industrial centers along its shores.

Vanguard   The Vanguard program, begun in 1955, culminated in the successful launching of three scientific satellites. Initially a U.S. Navy project, the program was turned over to NASA in 1958. *Vanguard 1* was intended to be the first U.S. SATELLITE; troubles, however, with its launch vehicle, also named Vanguard, enabled the U.S.

Army to orbit its *Explorer 1* first. *Vanguard 1*, successfully launched on Mar. 17, 1958, from Cape Canaveral, Fla., weighed 1.5 kg (3.3 lb) and transmitted data until May 1964. Instrumentation consisted only of two radio transmitters for tracking the satellite. *Vanguard 2*, launched on Feb. 17, 1959, weighed 10 kg (22 lb) and was instrumented with photocells and two optical telescopes to study Earth's cloud cover. *Vanguard 3* weighed 29 kg (64 lb). It was orbited on Sept. 18, 1959, and transmitted data through December 12 of that year. Its scientific instrumentation, provided by NASA's Goddard Space Flight Center, consisted of experiments to study Earth's magnetic field, the micrometeoroid flux in near-Earth space, and solar X rays.

---

vanilla   *Vanilla* is the name given both to a genus of tropical orchids and to the flavor extract obtained from the fruit pods of several of its species. The best and most important commercial extract is obtained from *V. planifolia*, which, like other members of the genus, is a climbing vine with aerial roots and fragrant, greenish yellow flowers. The Aztecs introduced Spanish explorers to vanilla in the early 16th century, and soon afterward it became popular in Europe.

In its native habitat vanilla is pollinated by bees and possibly hummingbirds; this yields a fruit set of only about 1 percent. When cultivated outside Central America, where its natural pollinators do not exist, vanilla normally does not set any fruit. Today vanilla beans are produced by hand pollination with a wooden needle. The harvested, unripe, golden green beans are cured by alternating night-sweating with daily sun-drying, which produces the characteristic flavor and aroma. The curing process continues for 10 to 20 days, after which the beans are bundled for drying and development of the full aroma. This curing and drying requires about 4 to 5 months. The resulting bean is wrinkled and chocolate colored.

The flavor and odor of the extract come partially from a white crystalline aldehyde, vanillin, which develops

The vanilla V. planifolia, a member of the orchid family, is an epiphyte and obtains its food and water from air while anchored to another plant. This tropical American plant is cultivated for its seedpod (right), which is used to flavor food and beverages.

during the curing process. Vanilla beans, vanilla extracts and tinctures (alcoholic extracts), and vanilla resinoids (hydrocarbon solvent extracts) are the foremost food flavors for ice cream, puddings, cakes, chocolates, baked goods, syrups, candies, liqueurs, tobacco, and soft drinks. Vanilla tincture is also used in perfumes. Vanillin is now produced artificially from eugenol (derived from clove-stem oil) or from acid hydrolysis of lignin (wood).

Vanity Fair see THACKERAY, WILLIAM MAKEPEACE

van't Hoff, Jacobus Henricus [vahn tawf] The Dutch chemist Jacobus Henricus van't Hoff, b. Aug. 30, 1852, d. Mar. 1, 1911, received (1901) the first Nobel Prize for chemistry for the development of laws of chemical dynamics and of osmotic pressure in dilute solutions. Van't Hoff's pioneering work, especially in the discipline of PHYSICAL CHEMISTRY, had a significant influence on the chemical, physical, biological, and geological sciences. Independently and at the same time as Joseph Achille Le Bel, van't Hoff postulated (1874) that the carbon atom in organic compounds had a three-dimensional tetrahedral structure (see ORGANIC CHEMISTRY; STEREOCHEMISTRY) and that the possibility of asymmetry in certain compounds explained their OPTICAL ACTIVITY. He showed the analogy between gases and dissolved substances, and he developed laws that govern the relationships among temperature, molecular concentration, and the osmotic pressure of dilute solutions. During his later years he investigated the origin and formation of oceanic salt deposits, which became greatly important to the German potash industry.

Vanuatu [vah-noo-ah'-too] Vanuatu (formerly New Hebrides), a group of about 12 islands and about 60 islets extending for approximately 800 km (500 mi) in the southwestern Pacific, is located about 1,600 km (1,000 mi) northeast of Australia. More than half the residents live on the islands of Efate (the site of Vila, the capital), Espiritu Santo (the largest island), Malekula, and Tanna. Most of the residents are Melanesian and speak Bislama, a pidgin.

Because the islands are mountainous in the interior, most inhabitants live on the coastal plains and practice subsistence agriculture. Commercial plantations produce copra, cocoa, and coffee for export, and fishing and meat production are also export oriented. Vanuatu has no direct taxation and is becoming a banking center. Tourism is also important to the economy, which was damaged by a severe hurricane in 1987.

In 1606 a short-lived Spanish settlement was established on Espiritu Santo. Capt. James Cook charted the islands and named them the New Hebrides in 1774. Soon British and French traders, planters, and missionaries arrived. Conflicts between Europeans and indigenous peoples, as well as between competing European interests, resulted (1887) in an agreement that led to joint British and French administration of the islands. In 1980, the year in which the islands were scheduled for independence, a rebellion on Espiritu Santo was put down by British and French troops. Independence was granted one week later, on July 30, 1980, and a parliamentary form of government was established. In 1986, Vanuatu became the first South Pacific nation to establish diplomatic relations with the USSR and Libya.

AT A GLANCE

REPUBLIC OF VANUATU

Land: Area: 14,763 km^2 (5,700 mi^2). Capital and largest city: Vila (1989 est. pop., 19,400).

People: Population (1990 est.): 165,006. Density: 11.2 persons per km^2 (28.9 per mi^2). Distribution (1989): 18% urban, 82% rural. Official languages: French, English, Bislama. Major religions: Presbyterianism, Roman Catholicism, Anglicanism.

Government: Type: republic. Legislature: Parliament. Political subdivisions: 11 island councils.

Economy: GNP (1989): $131 million; $860 per capita. Labor distribution (1985): agriculture—80%; government, trade, and services—20%. Foreign trade (1988 est.): imports—$58 million; exports—$16 million. Currency: 1 vatu = 100 centimes.

Education and Health: Literacy (1989 est.): 10–20% of adult population. Universities (1990): none. Hospital beds (1989): 361. Physicians (1989): 18. Life expectancy (1990): women—72; men—67. Infant mortality (1990): 36 per 1,000 live births.

Vanzetti, Bartolomeo see SACCO AND VANZETTI CASE

vapor pressure The vapor pressure of a liquid is the pressure exerted by its vapor, or gaseous state, when it is in equilibrium with the liquid state. The vapor pressure varies directly with the temperature.

When a liquid is introduced into an evacuated vessel, evaporation occurs until the pressure of the vapor reaches a definite maximum value and the two phases are in equilibrium. If the vapor is then compressed so that its pressure is momentarily greater than its equilibrium vapor pressure, some of it will condense to the liquid state to reestablish the equilibrium. A liquid boils (evaporates rapidly) when its vapor pressure equals the prevailing atmospheric pressure. The normal boiling point of any liquid is the temperature at which its vapor pressure equals one atmosphere (760 mm Hg).

Varanasi [vuh-rahn'-uh-see] Varanasi (or Benares) is a sacred city for Hindus in Uttar Pradesh state, northern India, situated on the north bank of the Ganges River. Its population is 704,772 (1981). Jewelry, brasswork, lacquered toys, and gold-embroidered saris are important handicraft products. The city's tourist industry caters to the many pilgrims who visit the holy city each year. Varanasi contains more than 1,500 temples and mosques. Almost all of the city's 5 km (3 mi) of river banks have been converted into ghats (brick steps), where worshipers bathe in the sacred Ganges. Benares Hindu University (1916) is one of India's most prominent seats of learning.

Originally known as Kasi, Varanasi is mentioned in late Vedic literature (c.8th century BC) and in the Hindu epics *Ramayana* and *Mahabharata*. The city encompasses SARNATH, where Buddha preached his first sermon in about 530 BC. From the 4th to the 6th century AD, Varanasi was a great cultural center, but Muslim occupation from 1193 resulted in the city's decline and the destruction of its ancient temples.

Varangians see RURIK; VIKINGS

Vardon, Harry [vahr'-duhn] The Briton Harry Vardon, b. May 9, 1870, d. Mar. 20, 1937, was the first of the great modern golfers. He won the British Open a record 6 times (1896, 1898–99, 1903, 1911, 1914) and entered the U.S. Open 3 times, winning once (1900) and twice finishing second. Although he did not invent the overlapping grip, Vardon popularized it, and today it is called the Vardon grip. During a 12-year period he represented England 18 times in international competitions. An award, the Vardon Trophy, is given annually to the professional golfer with the lowest average number of strokes per round on the Professional Golfers' Association (PGA) tour.

Varèse, Edgar [vah-rez'] The French composer Edgar Varèse, b. Dec. 22, 1883, d. Nov. 6, 1965, was one of the greatest musical innovators of the 20th century. From 1904 he studied composition in Paris with Vincent d'Indy and Albert Roussel. Befriended by Claude Debussy and Romain Rolland, as well as by Ferruccio Busoni in Berlin and Richard Strauss in Vienna, he had the prospect of pursuing a successful career in Europe, but World War I intervened. Discharged from the army because of ill health, he went to New York in 1915 and played a leading role in the avant-garde movement of the 1920s and '30s. He was one of the founders of the International Composers' Guild (1921–27) and the Pan-American Association of Composers (1928–34).

In his compositions, such as *Hyperprism* (1923), *Intégrales* (1925), *Arcana* (1925–27), and *Ionisation* (1930–33, for 13 percussion instruments), he rejected all traditional forms and melodic-harmonic procedures in favor of self-contained sound structures emphasizing percussion. His *Poème électronique* (1957–58) was done entirely with taped sound, using 425 loudspeakers to project the sound throughout a moving spatial pattern.

Vargas, Getúlio Dornelles [vahr'-gahs] Getúlio Dornelles Vargas, b. Apr. 19, 1883, d. Aug. 24, 1954, Brazilian president (1930–45, 1951–54), promoted the modernization of Brazil. He served his home state of Rio Grande do Sul as national congressman (1922–26) and governor (1928–30). From 1926 to 1927 he was finance minister in the national cabinet. Unsuccessful in his bid for the presidency in 1930, Vargas led a revolt that overthrew the government. During the next 15 years, he effected massive transformations in the public and private sectors. He was authoritarian, but his social-welfare programs gained him the working- and middle-class backing.

Vargas supported the Allies during World War II, but his popularity declined as democratic sentiment grew. In 1945 he was ousted by the army. Although he was reelected president in 1950, his second tenure was beset with scandals and economic difficulties. Faced with growing opposition, Vargas resigned and then committed suicide.

Vargas Llosa, Mario [vahr'-gahs yoh'-sah] The novels of the major Peruvian writer Mario Vargas Llosa, b. Mar. 28, 1936, contain a mercilessly penetrating view of Peruvian society. Vargas's first collection of short stories, *Los jefes* (The Chiefs, 1958), won the Leopoldo Alas prize, but such novels as *The Time of the Hero* (1962; Eng. trans., 1966), *Conversation in the Cathedral* (1969; Eng. trans., 1975), *Captain Pantoja and the Special Service* (1973; Eng. trans., 1978), *The War of the End of the World* (1981; Eng. trans., 1984), set in Brazil, and *The Storyteller* (1987; Eng. trans., 1989) brought international recognition. In 1990 he ran unsuccessfully for president of Peru.

variable A variable is a symbol that can be replaced by any element of some designated set of numbers (or other quantities) called the domain of the variable. Any member of the set is a value of the variable. If the set has only one member, the variable becomes a constant. If a mathematical sentence contains two variables related in such a way that when a replacement is made for the first variable the value of the second variable is determined, the first variable is called the independent variable and the second the dependent variable.

variable star Variable stars are stars that vary in brightness, color, or magnetic field strength. A variable star may be either an eclipsing or a physical variable. An eclipsing variable is a binary star in which each of the orbiting components passes in front of the other, as seen from the Earth, giving periodic variations in the total brightness with the same period as the orbital period of the binary. Physical variables are single stars whose variations are caused by intrinsic pulsations or eruptions within the star itself. Eruptive physical variables are believed to be due to a sudden eruption inside the star; the more common pulsating variables are believed to represent intrinsic pulsations of the whole star. This article concerns only physical, or intrinsic, variables; see BINARY STARS for a discussion of eclipsing variables.

Eruptive Variables. The light variations in eruptive variables may be large, as in NOVAE, or small, as in flare stars and T Tauri stars. Flare stars, also called UV Ceti stars, are cool, faint stars that brighten for only a few minutes. This phenomenon may be related to the solar flares found on the Sun. Only a few dozen such stars are known. T Tauri variables have no regular periods and are believed to be very young stars still in the contraction phase. There are also recurrent novae, R Corona Borealis stars, and other less-common types of eruptive variables.

Pulsating Variables. Pulsating variables may be divided into several broad groups. Cepheids have periods between about 1 day and 50 days. Long-period variables have periods of several hundred days. RR Lyrae stars have periods between a few hours and 1 day. W Virginis stars have periods of more than 1 day and are broadly similar to Cepheids, but with a smaller absolute magnitude. Several rarer kinds of stars are known, including RV Tauri stars and β Cephei stars. There are also many irregular variable stars known, plus others described as semiregular.

Of the 13,800 known pulsating variable stars, about 700 are classical Cepheids, 4,600 are long-period variables, 4,400 are RR Lyrae stars, and 3,900 are semiregular or irregular variables. Cepheids, RR Lyrae stars, and W Virginis stars have pulsation cycles that repeat with regularity. Long-period variables have cycles that essentially repeat, but with some differences from one cycle to the next: for example, one maximum may not be of the same brightness as the preceding maximum. In all these stars the whole star is successively expanding and contracting, accompanied by changes in surface temperature and total luminosity.

Several general relations apply to pulsating stars. The period-luminosity relation asserts that there is a relationship between the period of the variation of the brightness of a variable star and its absolute brightness. From the

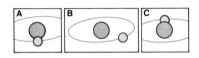

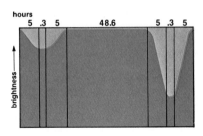

Algol, a double star system in the Perseus constellation, varies from maximum to minimum brightness every 69 hours. (A) When the bright star passes in front of the dim star, a slight drop in brightness is observed. (B) Maximum brightness results when neither star is eclipsed. (C) Minimum brightness occurs when the dim star covers the bright one.

observed period one can immediately deduce the absolute brightness of the star, and thus its distance. The period-density relation states that the product of the period of a variable star and the square root of the mean density of the star is approximately constant. The value of the constant depends on the type of star. In general, stars with long periods have small densities and hence are likely to be large supergiant stars.

Other Types of Variables. Among less-common types of variable stars are the δ Scuti stars, which seem to be related to the classical Cepheids but are fainter, have spectral types A to F, have much smaller amplitudes of variation, and exhibit a curious double periodicity. Also showing a double periodicity are β Canis Majoris stars of spectral type B. A number of magnetic variable stars are known, in some of which the magnetic-field variations are periodic, and in others irregular. The prototype periodic magnetic variable is α Canum Venaticorum. Its magnetic field varies from −1,400 to +1,600 gauss with a period of 5.5 days.

PULSARS, when first discovered, were so named because it was thought that they were a new kind of pulsating star. Later work indicated that pulsars are rotating neutron stars, so that their name is a misnomer.

variations *Variations* is a general term applied to a compositional style, known and practiced in music of both the Western and non-Western worlds, whereby a melody or harmonic-rhythmic complex is subjected to varied treatment—usually in a series of organized repetitions.

The principle of varying a theme (whether invented by the composer, or folk song, or plainsong) has been known and developed under different names at least since medieval times. The theme and variations as now understood began its long and still-active existence with the 16th-century lutenists, vihuelists, and composers for keyboard instruments. Byrd, Bach, Handel, Mozart, Haydn, Beethoven, Schubert, Schumann, Brahms, Schoenberg, Britten, and Copland are among the composers who have made significant contributions to the genre. The idea of variations has been fundamental to the development of JAZZ.

varicose vein   Varicose veins are abnormally dilated and tortuous veins. Although virtually any vein in the body can become varicose—HEMORRHOIDS, for example, are varicosities around the anus—most occur in the legs. In healthy veins, valves permit blood to flow toward the heart but not away from it. In varicose veins these valves do not work, perhaps because of patchy thinning of the vein walls. As a result the veins become inflated from the back pressure of blood.

Varicose veins occur more often in women than in men, especially during pregnancy, and some evidence exists that a predisposition to varicosity may be inherited. The condition is more likely to occur in people who stand for long periods of time or who do heavy lifting. Usually varicose veins cause no greater problems than an unsightly appearance, but sometimes they lead to a heavy feeling in the legs, especially by the end of the day. They may also cause skin discoloration, itching, or inflammation (see PHLEBITIS). Wearing support stockings can provide considerable relief from the condition. Occasionally, treatment may include surgery.

Varley, Frederick [vahr'-lee]   Frederick Horseman Varley, b. Sheffield, England, Jan. 2, 1881, d. Sept. 8, 1969, was one of Canada's most distinguished portrait painters. Although he was among the landscapists known as the GROUP OF SEVEN, Varley devoted himself primarily to portraiture for many years. His expressive portraits have often been favorably compared with those of the Englishman Augustus John. In 1926, Varley moved to Vancouver; there he began to paint richly colored landscapes whose calm spirituality reflects his interest in Eastern philosophy.

Varna [vahr'-nah]   Varna is a key port on the Black Sea in northeastern Bulgaria, with a population of 306,300 (1989 est.). The city is a major industrial center and naval base; industries include shipbuilding, flour milling, food processing, and the manufacture of electrical equipment and textiles. Health spas and sandy beaches make Varna a summer resort. It has a theater, an opera house, museums, a symphony orchestra, and art galleries. Nearby is the 6th-century Aladzha Monastery.

Founded in the 6th century BC by the Greeks and named Odessus, the city subsequently came under Thracian, Macedonian, and Roman rule. Known as Varna since AD 681, it was held by the Turks from 1444 to 1878, when it became part of independent Bulgaria. Between 1949 and 1956 the city was called Stalin.

varnish   A varnish is a solution of a hard RESIN, characteristically of natural origin; a drying oil, such as linseed or tung; metallic compounds that act as driers; and solvent. Varnishes are intended to provide an essentially continuous, transparent film to protect or enhance the appearance of wood or other materials without altering the underlying texture or color. PIGMENTS used in varnishes are intended solely to regulate level of gloss; they have no hiding or masking abilities at the levels employed. This absence of opacifying pigment distinguishes a varnish from either a stain or PAINT, although varnishes are frequently employed as paint binders.

The name *varnish* is believed to be derived from *vernix*, the Latin word for "amber." A natural resin, amber was an ingredient used in varnishes as long ago as 250 BC. Even though varnishes based on natural products continue to be used, numerous synthetically based polymer solutions have been developed that often offer superior qualities, particularly with regard to lightness of color, adhesion, exterior durability, and flexibility. Alkyd resin solutions are the most widely used synthetic varnishes. Varnish is principally used on furniture and floors and over paint coatings; it also has various marine applications and is used as a sealing compound.

Varro   Marcus Terentius Varro, 116–c.27 BC, was the first universal scholar of the Roman civilization. In the first civil war he fought on the losing side, but Octavius forgave him and appointed him head of his planned public library. After being proscribed by Mark Antony in 43, he escaped, was pardoned by Octavius, and then devoted himself fully to writing.

From his reputed output of more than 600 volumes, the titles of only about 50 works are known. Of these, his treatise *De Re Rustica* (On Agriculture), is preserved intact; approximately one-fourth remains from his important study *De Lingua Latina* (The Latin Language), and many fragments have survived from his *Menippean Satires*.

Vasa (dynasty) [vah'-zuh]   The Vasa dynasty, which ruled Sweden (1523–1654) and Poland (1587–1668), rose to power as a great Swedish noble family in the days of Swedish autonomy under Danish kings. In 1521, Gustav Vasa led a successful rising against the Danes and subsequently ruled (1523–60) as King GUSTAV I. Three of his sons also ruled as Swedish kings. One of these sons, **John III**, 1537–92 (r. 1568–92), married the sister of the Polish king; their son, who represented the union of the Vasas with the Polish JAGELLO dynasty, was elected (1587) king of Poland as SIGISMUND III; he also served as king of Sweden. Sigismund was succeeded in Poland by two of his sons, **Władysław IV**, 1595–1648 (r. 1632–48), and JOHN II. John, who was childless, abdicated in 1668, marking the end of the Vasa dynasty on the Polish throne.

In Sweden, Vasa monarchs GUSTAV II ADOLF and his daughter CHRISTINA reigned during an age of greatness as Sweden gained superiority over Denmark and established an empire that dominated the western and northern Baltic. Christina, the last Vasa ruler of Sweden, abdicated (1654) in favor of a cousin, Charles X.

Vasarely, Victor [vah-zah-ray-lee']   The Hungarian artist Victor Vasarely, b. Apr. 9, 1908, is perhaps the

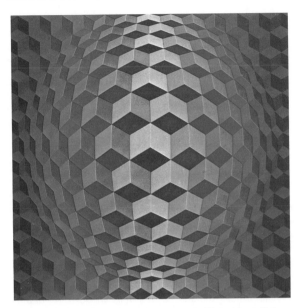

Cheyt-G *(1970), by the Hungarian-born artist Victor Vasarely, is an example of what is known as geometric, optical, or op art, in which the artist's intention is to bring about a striking, even dizzying, effect. (Artist's collection.)*

best-known exponent of post–World War II geometric painting. He worked as a graphic designer until 1944; this experience may have helped to shape the complex black-and-white patterns of his earliest paintings. Soon after, he added intense contrasts of color. Typically, the artist arranges a large number of small, nearly identical geometric shapes in patterns that generate vivid illusions of depth and, in some cases, motion. A citizen of France since 1959, Vasarely had some 150 solo exhibitions in the half-century span 1930–80 and has won many international prizes.

Vasari, Giorgio [vah-zah'-ree]   Giorgio Vasari, b. July 30, 1511, d. June 27, 1574, was an Italian writer, painter, and architect who is best known for his *Lives of the Most Eminent Painters, Sculptors, and Architects* (1550; rev. ed., 1568), which provides a thorough history of Italian Renaissance art through biographies of its principal practitioners. Modeled on the ancient Greek and Roman biographies of famous men, the *Lives* was the first book in Western history to concentrate exclusively on art and artists. Its underlying thesis—that art is an intellectual discipline practiced by individualistic geniuses, rather than a craft pursued by anonymous workers—ushered in the modern, as opposed to the medieval, view of artistic endeavor. Although it remains a primary source of information about Italian Renaissance and Mannerist artists, Vasari's work contains many lacunae and errors, particularly in the biographical data supplied, and its treatment of pre-15th-century artists is unreliable.

As a painter and architect Vasari displayed many of the tendencies associated with MANNERISM. His series of paintings (1570–72) in the Palazzo Vecchio of Florence celebrate the achievements of the Medici in highly stylized allegories replete with Manneristic exaggerations. Of his major architectural achievements, the Uffizi in Florence (1560–80), originally a governmental office building and now an art gallery and archive, is an important example of the Mannerist tendency to incorporate preexisting buildings in a new overall design. Vasari designed (1573), although he did not oversee the construction of, the Loggia in Arezzo. He also modernized and remodeled two important 13th-century churches in Florence, Santa Maria Novella (1565–72) and Santa Croce (1566–84).

Vasco da Gama   see GAMA, VASCO DA

vascular plant   see TRACHEOPHYTE

vasectomy   Vasectomy is the surgical sterilization of the male through the severing of the two sperm-carrying ducts, the vasa deferentia. This procedure prevents the sperm cells formed in the testes from reaching the storage structures called the ampullae. At the time of ejaculation, sperm cells in the ampullae are mixed with secretions of nearby glands to form the semen. Severing the vasa deferentia thus renders the semen sterile, that is, unable to fertilize an ovum.

Because the vasa deferentia lie almost entirely within the scrotum and thus outside the abdominal cavity, a vasectomy is a relatively simple procedure usually done under local anesthesia in a physician's office. Each vas deferens is exposed through a small incision, on the side of the upper part of the scrotum, and is severed; the severed ends of the vas deferens are then cauterized to seal them, and the incision is sutured. Sterility does not occur until residual sperm in the upper reproductive tract have left the body. Vasectomy has no effect on the production of the male hormone, testosterone.

Fertility may be restored by surgically rejoining the severed ends of the vasa deferentia; some clinicians have reported successful restoration in the majority of patients. Failures to reverse the procedure are due to such factors as infections and blood clots. By the mid-1980s vasectomy, along with tubal ligation in women, was the preferred method of birth control among U.S. couples who desired no further children.

Vasily III, Grand Duke of Moscow [vuh-see'-lee] Vasily III, b. 1479, d. Dec. 2, 1533, grand duke of Moscow (1505–33), succeeded his father, Ivan III. He annexed to Moscow the remaining independent Russian principalities (1510–23) and captured Smolensk from Lithuania (1514). He was succeeded by IVAN IV (the Terrible), his son.

vasopressin   see HORMONE, ANIMAL; PITUITARY GLAND

Vassar College   Established in 1861, Vassar College is a private liberal arts institution in Poughkeepsie, N.Y. One of the SEVEN SISTERS COLLEGES, it became coeducational in 1969. Vassar is basically an undergraduate college but also offers master's degrees in some modern languages, biology, chemistry, and drama.

Västerås [ves'-tuh-rohs]   Västerås (1988 est. pop., 117,563), a city in east central Sweden on the northern shores of Lake Mälaren, lies about 105 km (65 mi) northwest of Stockholm. It is Sweden's leading inland port and a major center for the manufacture of electrical appliances, machinery, turbines, and glass. An important trading and cultural center since the Middle Ages, the city has a 12th-century castle and a 13th-century cathedral. The early Swedish parliament frequently convened in the city, and the Reformation in Sweden was launched there in 1527.

Vatican City   Vatican City, the world's smallest state, occupies 0.44 km^2 (0.17 mi^2) on the west bank of the Tiber River, lying within the Italian capital city of Rome and almost completely surrounded by walls. Its population of 774 (1990 est.) consists primarily of employees of the Holy See, the central government of the Roman Catholic church. The Vatican also enjoys extraterritorial juris-

diction over Castel Gandolfo, the papal summer residence near Rome, and 13 churches and other buildings in Rome, including the Basilica of Saint John Lateran (Rome's cathedral). Both the temporal and spiritual authority of the Vatican is vested in the pope; in practice the city's civil administration is managed by the Papal Commission for Vatican City. The Vatican has its own newspaper (*L'Osservatore Romano*), railway station, postal service, police force, telephone system, radio, and bank.

Vatican City is also an important tourist center for Roman Catholics and those interested in art history (see VATICAN MUSEUMS AND GALLERIES). Visitors may enter Vatican City on the southeast through Giovanni Lorenzo Bernini's colonnade at Saint Peter's Square. SAINT PETER'S BASILICA is the largest and principal church of the Roman Catholic world. The Vatican Palace, constituting the Vatican proper, includes Michelangelo's frescoes on the ceilings of the SISTINE CHAPEL, Pintoricchio's frescoes in the Borgia Apartment, and Raphael's frescoes in the Raphael Rooms. The Vatican Library houses an extensive collection of manuscripts. Occupying a considerable portion of the city's land are the Vatican Gardens.

The Vatican's name derives from an isolated ridge of volcanic origin to the west of ancient Rome's low-lying hills. Saint Peter's Basilica was founded in the 4th century, and the area became increasingly associated with the papacy, especially during the Renaissance. Between 1860 and 1870 the PAPAL STATES were incorporated into the new Kingdom of Italy. The ensuing dispute between Italy and successive popes over church autonomy was settled by the Lateran Treaty (1929), which recognized the full and independent sovereignty of the Holy See in Vatican City. Although not a permanent member, the Vatican has an observer at the United Nations.

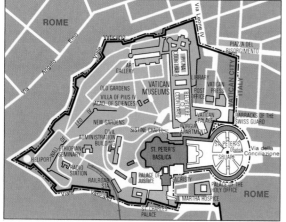

Vatican Council, First   The First Vatican Council, the 20th ecumenical council of the Roman Catholic church, is best known for its decree affirming the doctrine of papal INFALLIBILITY. It was opened by Pope PIUS IX in Saint Peter's Basilica on Dec. 8, 1869. Nearly 800 church leaders representing every continent attended, although the European members held a clear majority. Apparently the pope's primary purpose in convening the council was to obtain confirmation of the position he had taken in his *Syllabus of Errors* (1864), condemning a wide range of modern positions associated with the ideas of rationalism, liberalism, and materialism.

From the beginning, however, the question of infallibility dominated discussion. A vigorous minority opposed this doctrine on both theological and historical grounds and as being inopportune. Nonetheless, on July 18, 1870, the council solemnly accepted the proposition that when a pope speaks *ex cathedra* on faith or morals he does so with the supreme apostolic authority, which no Catholic may question or reject. Shortly after the vote on infallibility, the Franco-Prussian War and the successful invasion of the Roman state by the Italian army abruptly ended the council. The First Vatican Council marked the climax and triumph of the movement of ULTRAMONTANISM.

Vatican Council, Second The Second Vatican Council, the 21st ecumenical council of the Roman Catholic church, was announced by Pope JOHN XXIII on Jan. 25, 1959. On Oct. 11, 1962, after four years of preparation, the council formally opened. Four sessions convened; the last three (1963–65) were presided over by Pope PAUL VI, who succeeded John as pontiff in June 1963. The council ended on Dec. 8, 1965.

Unlike previous ecumenical councils, the Second Vatican Council was not held to combat contemporary heresies or to deal with awkward disciplinary questions but simply, in the words of Pope John's opening message, to renew "ourselves and the flocks committed to us, so that there may radiate before all men the lovable features of Jesus Christ, who shines in our hearts that God's splendor may be revealed."

The participants with full voting rights were all the bishops of the Roman Catholic church, of both the Western and Eastern rites, superiors-general of exempt religious orders, and prelates with their own special spheres of jurisdiction. Non-Catholic Christian churches and alliances and Catholic lay organizations were invited to send observers. These observers, however, had neither voice nor vote in the council deliberations.

The council produced 16 documents—all of which had to be approved by the pope before they became official. The most important of these for the subsequent life of the Roman Catholic church have been the Dogmatic Constitution on the Church, which gave renewed importance to the role of the bishops; the Constitution on the Sacred Liturgy, which authorized vernacularization of the liturgy and greater lay participation; the Pastoral Constitution on the Church in the Modern World, which acknowledged the need for the church to adapt itself to the contemporary world; the Decree on Ecumenism; and the Declaration on Religious Freedom. Together these documents present a church that is primarily a worshiping and serving community open to various points of view and religious traditions.

Vatican museums and galleries Set within the bastioned walls of VATICAN CITY are the Vatican Palaces, a large group of interconnecting buildings dating from the 14th to the 20th century, and SAINT PETER'S BASILICA. The palaces contain more than 1,400 rooms, most of which now house the museums, galleries, and libraries of the Vatican. Aside from the designated museums, a number of chapels and papal apartments are considered part of the museum collections and include the Stanze (rooms) of Julius II, frescoed by RAPHAEL and his school between 1508 and 1520; the Borgia Apartment of Alexander VI, with frescoes completed by Pintoricchio and his school in 1495; the Scala Regia (Royal Stairs), built during the 1660s for Urban VIII by Giovanni Lorenzo BERNINI; and the SISTINE CHAPEL, built by order of Sixtus IV in 1453, which contains, in addition to the monumental frescoes by MICHELANGELO, frescoes of scenes from the life of Moses by Sandro Botticelli, Perugino, and Luca Signorel-

li, among others. The collections of the seven major museums of the Vatican are among the largest, most important, and most valuable in the world.

In 1973, Paul VI inaugurated the Collection of Modern Religious Art, a group of 540 contemporary paintings, sculptures, and stained glass on permanent exhibition in the refurbished Borgia Apartment and its adjacent rooms. Selections from the Vatican Library's 60,000 manuscripts, 7,000 incunabula, and 950,000 printed books may be seen in the grandiose Sistine Hall and in adjoining exhibition rooms.

Vättern, Lake [vet'-urn] Lake Vättern, located in southern Sweden and that nation's second largest lake, averages about 130 km (80 mi) long and 30 km (20 mi) wide and has an area of about 1,900 km^2 (735 mi^2). The Göta Canal, connecting the Kattegat with the Baltic Sea, crosses the northern part of the lake. Jönkoping is at its southern end.

Vauban, Sébastien Le Prestre de [voh-bahn'] The French military engineer Sébastien Le Prestre de Vauban, b. May 1, 1633, d. Mar. 30, 1707, was the renowned director of French siege warfare during Louis XIV's wars. Vauban became a royal engineer in 1655, won the king's favor by his spectacularly successful siege (1667) of Lille, and formed and headed the separate army engineering corps after 1672. His innovative line of eastern border fortresses during the Dutch War (1672–78) provided unprecedented protection against foreign invasion; he eventually built or improved about 300 fortresses and captured about 50 others. Vauban also designed roads, bridges, canals, dikes, and aqueducts. A prolific and thoughtful writer on military engineering and many other subjects of public concern, he lost favor at court after publishing (1707) a proposal for a universal tax without exemption for nobility or clergy.

vaudeville see MUSIC HALL, VAUDEVILLE, AND BURLESQUE

Vaughan, Sarah Ranked as one of the foremost jazz song stylists, Sarah Lois Vaughan, b. Newark, N.J., Mar. 27, 1924, d. Apr. 30, 1990, began her career in the choir of her local Baptist church. In 1942 she won a contest at Harlem's Apollo Theater and, shortly afterward, a job as vocalist with the Earl Hines band. For most of her career, however, she worked as a soloist, achieving lasting fame for her jazz recordings with Dizzy GILLESPIE and Charlie PARKER in the early 1950s, for her complex bebop phrasing, and her impeccable scat singing. Although in much of her later recorded work she sang popular songs with bland orchestral backup, her voice remained a consistently virtuoso instrument.

Vaughan Williams, Ralph [vawn wil'-yuhmz] Ralph Vaughan Williams, b. Oct. 12, 1872, d. Aug. 26, 1958, was an English composer, also active at various times as organist, conductor, lecturer, teacher, editor, and writer. His influence on the development of 20th-century music in England was immense. He infused his works with the tradition of the Tudor-era composers and English folk music, creating a contemporary idiom rooted in the cultural soil of his country. He was music editor of the *English Hymnal*, edited two volumes of Purcell's welcome odes, conducted the London Bach Choir, and collected folk songs throughout England.

Four of Vaughan Williams's nine symphonies are descriptive: *A Sea Symphony* (no. 1, 1910), the *London* (no. 2, 1914), the *Pastoral* (no. 3, 1930), and the *Sinfonia antarctica* (no. 7, 1953). Other important works include *Fantasia on a Theme of Thomas Tallis* (1910) for string quartet and double string orchestra, and *The Lark Ascending* (1910) for violin and small orchestra. He also composed concertos for various instruments. Among his works for the stage are the two-act ballad opera *Hugh the Drover* (1924) and *Riders to the Sea* (1937), a one-act opera based on the play by J. M. Synge. Choral works form an important part of Vaughan Williams's achievement, and the most outstanding are the Mass in G Minor (1923); the oratorio *Sancta Civitas* (1926) for two soloists, three choruses, and orchestra; a *Magnificat* (1932); the *Serenade to Music* (1938) for 16 solo voices and orchestra; and *Hodie* (1954), a Christmas cantata. Vaughan Williams also produced solo songs, carols, and part-songs.

Ralph Vaughan Williams, a leading English composer of the 20th century, drew on English folk tradition and medieval and Tudor music to create a uniquely English compositional style.

vault see ARCH AND VAULT

Vaux, Calvert [vawks] The English architect Calvert Vaux, b. London, Dec. 20, 1824, d. Nov. 19, 1895, came to the United States in 1850 to work with the landscape architect Andrew Jackson DOWNING. Together they designed several picturesque villas in the Hudson River Valley. After Downing's death in 1852, Vaux completed a series of distinguished High Victorian designs, including his bridges and pavilions for Central Park (1857; with Frederick Law OLMSTED), and his Jefferson Market Courthouse (1876; with Frederick Withers), both in New York City. His most extraordinary conceptions were his compositions of infinitely extendable bays for the Metropolitan Museum of Art (1874–80) and the American Museum of Natural History (finished 1877; both with Jacob Wrey Mould), both in New York City, and the vast, arcaded iron and glass building he proposed for the Philadelphia Centennial Exposition of 1876.

Vazov, Ivan [vah'-zawf] Ivan Vazov, b. June 27, 1850, d. Sept. 22, 1921, is the most famous figure in modern Bulgarian literature. His poems—especially *Izbavlenie* (Deliverance, 1878), *Epopeya na zabravenite* (Epic of the Forgotten, 1881–84), and *Slivnitsa* (Fusion, 1886)—recount the historical hardships and patriotic aspirations of his people. His internationally famous novel *Under the Yoke* (1894; Eng. trans., 1894) describes Bulgarian village life in the years before Bulgaria's liberation (1878) from Turkish rule. Vazov's involvement in nationalist politics twice forced him into exile.

VCR see VIDEO RECORDING

VD see VENEREAL DISEASE

veal Veal, the flesh of slaughtered calves less than 1 year old, is considered a by-product of the dairy industry. Male calves are uneconomic for dairy farmers to raise, because they reduce the volume of milk available for sale. Some calves are killed within a week of birth. Their flesh, which is soft and watery, is called bob veal. Some calves are fed milk replacers containing vitamins, minerals, and fat for 8 to 10 weeks before being slaughtered. This diet promotes rapid growth and prevents the flesh from becoming the red color of beef. These calves are anemic and weak, compared to normal calves, and must be raised in scrupulously clean quarters with controlled temperature and humidity. (True milk-fed veal is a European specialty and is rarely found in the United States.) Veal is usually dense and fine grained with a light pink color.

Veblen, Thorstein B. Thorstein Bunde Veblen, b. Valders, Wis., July 30, 1857, d. Aug. 3, 1929, is best known for his book *The Theory of the Leisure Class* (1899), a classic of social theory that introduced the concept of CONSPICUOUS CONSUMPTION. He taught at the University of Chicago, Stanford University, and the University of Wisconsin.

Veblen argued that a fundamental conflict exists between the making of goods and the making of money. In *The Theory of Business Enterprise* (1904), he argued that the entrepreneur is a reactionary predator whose perspective is diametrically opposed to that of the engineer or industrialist. Veblen's businessperson makes profits not by providing an outlet for the forces of industrialization and social evolution but by distorting them: by engaging in monetary manipulations, by restricting output to keep prices artificially high, and by interfering with the engineers who actually produce goods and services. The founder of the so-called institutionalist school, Veblen believed that economics must be studied as an aspect of a changing culture.

vector analysis A vector, in mathematics, is a quantity stating both a magnitude and a direction. Force, velocity (speed in a particular direction), acceleration, angular momentum, and torque, for example, are quantities that are vectors. By contrast, a quantity with a magnitude but not a direction—mass and volume, for example—is called a scalar. Because physical quantities such as velocity and force are vectors, vector analysis—the mathematical manipulation of vectors—plays an important role in physics and engineering.

Whereas scalars follow the ordinary arithmetical laws of addition, subtraction, and so on, vectors must be dealt with by geometrical techniques because they involve direction as well. The most simple example of this is the addition of two vectors, such as two forces acting on a body in two different directions. Vectors are commonly represented by directed line segments—whose direction and length represent the direction and magnitude of the quantity—and are written in boldface. Thus, in the example, two forces **A** and **B**, of different magnitudes, act on a body in different directions. The resultant force **A + B** is found by constructing a parallelogram and drawing a directed line segment as the diagonal of the parallelogram. The length and direction of the diagonal are the magnitude and direction of the resultant vector of force acting on the body.

Subtraction of vectors can be performed in the same manner simply by reversing the direction of the representative line segment to be subtracted and constructing the appropriate parallelogram. More-complex problems involving vectors, however, require the use of advanced mathematical operations.

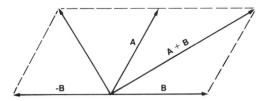

Vedanta [ve-dahn'-tuh] Vedanta, a term meaning "the final portions of the VEDAS," refers to those philosophical systems of HINDUISM which take their inspiration from the UPANISHADS.

The principal texts of Vedanta are the early Upanishads, particularly the *Brihadaranyaka* and *Chandogya*; the *Brahmasutras* (or *Vedantasutras*) of Baudarayana (dated between 100 BC and AD 100); and the BHAGAVAD GITA. Several distinct schools of interpretation emerged, the most notable of which are the Advaita (nondualist), Vishishtadvaita (qualified nondualist), and Dvaita (dualist) schools.

The earliest known exposition of Advaita Vedanta is in Gaudapada's *Karikas* on the Mandukya Upanishad (AD 600), but the school's most famous personage—and the most influential of classical Indian philosophers—was Shankara (early 8th century). A prolific writer, Shankara taught that there is only one reality, called either Brahman or Atman (the self); that all distinctions, all plurality is due to ignorance, or maya; and that liberation consists in eliminating ignorance and attaining that pure consciousness which is Brahman, or the True Self. This theory, although not the only Vedanta doctrine, is so popular among intellectuals in India that it is frequently and uncritically identified with Vedanta or with Indian philosophy as a whole.

Ramanuja (1056–1137) developed the more theistically oriented Vishishtadvaita Vedanta, in which Brahman is a personal God, immanent in all souls and the world, but without obliterating the differences among them. He roundly criticizes Shankara's theories of maya and pure consciousness.

Madhva (1238–1317) founded Dvaita, or dualist, Vedanta, in which differences between God, world, and souls are fully recognized. Other important systems include the Dvaitadvaita of Nimbarka (13th century) and the Shuddhadvaita of Vallabha (1481–1533).

Vedas [vay'-duhz] The Vedas (Sanskrit: "knowledge"), the most sacred books of HINDUISM and the oldest literature of India, represent the religious thought and activity of the Indo-European–speaking peoples who entered South Asia in the 2d millennium BC, although they probably also reflect the influence of the indigenous people of the area. The Vedic texts presumably date from between 1500 and 500 BC. This literature was preserved for centuries by an oral tradition in which particular families were entrusted with portions of the text for preservation. As a result, some parts of the texts are known by the names of the families they were assigned to.

In its narrowest sense, the term *Veda* applies to four collections of hymns (samhita): Rig Veda, Sama Veda, Yajur Veda, and Atharva Veda. These hymns and verses, addressed to various deities, were chanted during sacrificial rituals. In a wider sense, Veda refers to both these hymns and the materials that accreted around them: Brahmanas—prose texts that explain and illustrate the significance of the ritual; Aranyakas, or forest-treatises—esoteric texts providing symbolic or magical interpretations of ritual formulas; and the commentaries called UPANISHADS—the beginnings of Hindu philosophy.

Vedic rituals essentially involved offerings to and with fire under precisely prescribed conditions by which the sacrificer hoped to communicate with the deities and thus obtain desired results. Many of the deities addressed by the sacrifice were identified or associated with natural objects of forces such as fire, water, and wind. Among the most important were Indra (thunder, war, and perhaps creator), Varuna (guardian of the cosmic order and moral law), Agni (fire, light), and Soma (a liquid used in the sacrifice). The form and functions of one god, however, were not strictly distinguished from those of others, and as the Vedic period progressed, thought developed from polytheism to monotheism and thence, in the Upanishads, to monism.

The relation of Vedism to the Hinduism of later centuries is complex and not well understood. The originals of the major Hindu gods—SHIVA and VISHNU—can be found among the minor deities of the Vedas. The sacrifice has, however, all but disappeared from India in its Vedic form, replaced by different rites; and the analogy, central to the Vedic ritual, between actions on Earth and events in the heavens is replaced in Hinduism by the goal of liberation from actions on Earth, from life itself.

Vedder, Elihu [ved'-ur]   The American painter and illustrator Elihu Vedder, b. New York City, Feb. 26, 1836, d. Jan. 30, 1923, reveled in bizarre imagery. An expatriate, he lived in Rome from 1867 until his death. In *Questioner of the Sphinx* (1863; Museum of Fine Arts, Boston), the gigantic monument is being questioned by a wizened Arab. In *Memory* (c.1870; Los Angeles County Museum of Art), a disembodied head floats over a landscape. Vedder produced many book illustrations, the best known being the series (1884) of more than 50 in black and white for the *Rubaiyat of Omar Khayyam*.

Vega, Lope de [vay'-gah]   Lope Félix de Vega Carpio, b. Nov. 25, 1562, d. Aug. 27, 1635, was, with his follower Calderón de la Barca, one of the two most important playwrights of the Spanish Golden Age. Traditionally considered the founder of the *comedia*, Lope was also its most influential early practitioner.

The plays of the *comedia* always have three acts, are in verse, and employ a variety of metrical forms. Typically, they are filled with movement and intrigue and with vivid and dramatically convincing, though stereotypical, characters. The plays often include music and dance, and they mix scenes of the utmost gravity with those of comedy and farce. Most of these traits are singled out in Lope's *The New Art of Writing Plays* (1609; Eng. trans., 1914).

Called the Monster of Nature by his contemporaries because of his prodigious facility, Lope wrote about 800 plays, of which about 400–500 survive. He also wrote a bewildering variety of other works: hundreds of exquisite lyric poems, many long narrative poems on epic and mythological themes, numerous short stories and prose romances, and several didactic treatises in both verse and prose. Of all these nondramatic works, the single most important is *La Dorotea* (Dorothy, 1632), a long piece of fiction in dialogue form, based closely on Lope's own life.

Lope's enormous dramatic output is traditionally divided into various categories: *entremeses*—short comic interludes; *autos sacramentales*—allegorical works illustrating church doctrine; plays based on the Bible or on the lives of saints; plays dealing with historical episodes—for example, *Fuenteovejuna* (c.1611–18; Eng. trans., 1936) and *The Knight from Olmedo* (c.1615–26; Eng. trans., 1961); plays based on fictional sources—*Justice without Revenge* (1631; Eng. trans., 1961); cloak-and-dagger comedies—*The Dog in the Manger*

(c.1613–15; Eng. trans., 1961). His plays all have lively characterization, supple versification, natural and flowing dialogue, great dramatic momentum, and flashes of lyrical beauty. There is also the repeated celebration of certain cardinal virtues: love, honor, allegiance to the Catholic faith, loyalty to king and state.

Aptly, Lope's life was one of high personal drama. He was born in humble circumstances and rose to a position of great prominence and prestige. Along the way, he married twice; became embroiled in numerous love affairs, one of which led to a duel and subsequent banishment from Castile; served with the Spanish Armada; took orders in the church; and held the office of apostolic prothonotary.

---

vegetable   In horticulture, a vegetable is a herbaceous plant that is edible in whole or part. Parts usually eaten (and representative vegetables) include roots (beet); stems (asparagus); tubers (potato); leaf bases (onion); leaf petioles (celery); entire leaves (cabbage); flower parts (broccoli); immature fruit (cucumber); and mature fruit (tomato). Of great importance in the human diet, vegetables are rich in vitamins and minerals and supply fiber and bulk. Some are excellent protein sources when combined with other foods, such as beans with rice. They are usually low in calories.

Vegetables are cultured as annuals, with the exception of artichokes, asparagus, cardoon, chives, horseradish, and rhubarb, which are grown as perennials. Propagation is mostly by seed, but artichokes and rhubarb, for example, are propagated by divisions, and Irish potatoes by tubers or tuber sections.

Growth Requirements. Vegetables are variable in climatic requirements. Temperature and, to a lesser extent, length of day are the climatic components most influential in determining yields. Cool-season crops grow best from 12° to 20° C (54° to 68° F) and include green peas, lettuce, cabbage, onions, and spinach. Warm-season crops grow best from 18° to 28° C (64° to 82° F) and include beans, eggplant, okra, peppers, sweet corn, and tomatoes.

The precise climatic requirements of many crops have resulted in much centralization of production in those areas with suitable climate. An excellent example is the Salinas Valley of California, which, because of ocean cooling, provides ideal conditions for the culture of such cool-season crops as lettuce, celery, and broccoli during the summer months.

Rainfall during the growing season was formerly required for successful vegetable production. Today almost all commercially grown vegetables are raised under irrigated conditions or with supplemental irrigation. In some areas rainfall during the growing season is considered a detriment because it interferes with operations and promotes plant diseases.

Vegetables are grown on mineral or organic soils. Sandy loam and loam soils are the preferred types of mineral soils because of the desirable growth conditions and the ease of cultivation they provide. Heavier loams and clay soils are generally avoided. Organic soils, sometimes called peats or

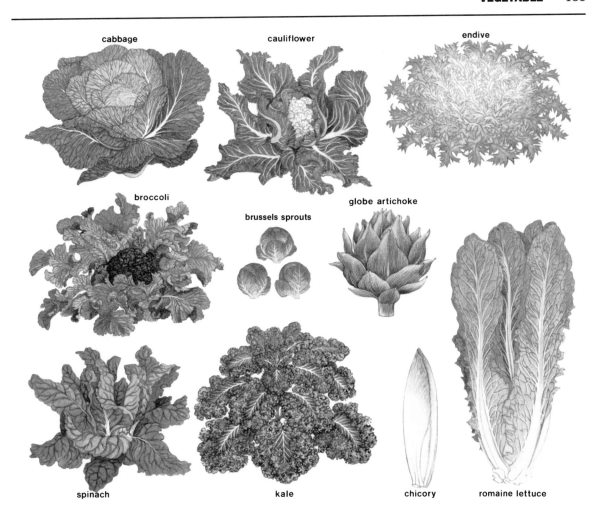

cabbage

cauliflower

endive

broccoli

brussels sprouts

globe artichoke

spinach

kale

chicory

romaine lettuce

(Above) *Greens commonly grown in temperate zones include varieties of cabbage—such as brussels sprouts, cauliflower, broccoli, and kale—and spinach, which is valued for its high iron and vitamin content. Lettuce varieties, such as romaine, as well as the herbs chicory and endive (whose popular names are sometimes reversed), are used as salad greens. Immature flower buds of the globe artichoke, when cooked, are considered a delicacy. (Below) The vegetable marrow (a variant of the zucchini eaten chiefly in Britain), pumpkin, and winter squash are among the gourd varieties of New World origin. The cucumber is an Asian gourd. Corn is a favorite food in America but has been used mostly for fodder in Europe.*

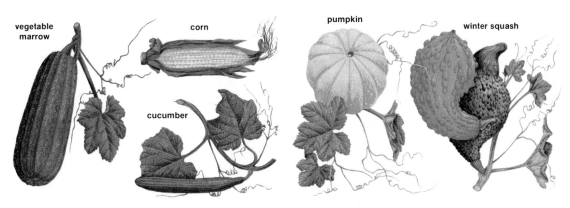

vegetable marrow

corn

pumpkin

winter squash

cucumber

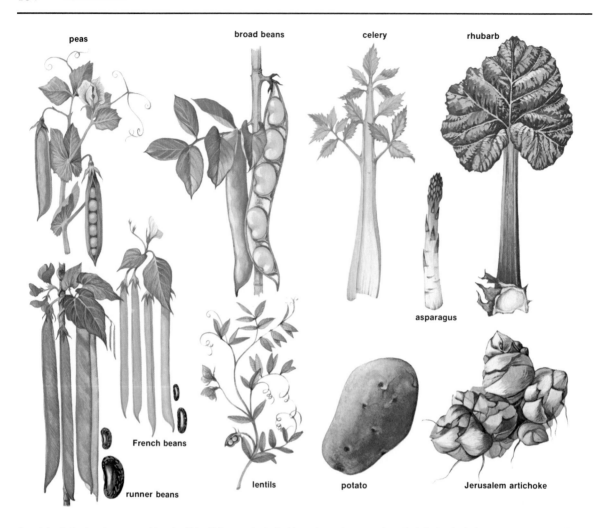

peas

broad beans

celery

rhubarb

asparagus

French beans

lentils

potato

Jerusalem artichoke

runner beans

A variety of plant parts are considered edible. Pulses—plants that have leguminous pods as their fruit—include garden peas, broad beans, runner beans, French beans, and lentils. Plants whose stems are eaten as vegetables include celery, asparagus, and rhubarb. Among tubers—enlarged underground stems of plants—are the potato and Jerusalem artichoke, the latter related to the sunflower.

The bell pepper, eggplant, and tomato are all members of the nightshade family. In earlier centuries the tomato, introduced into Europe from tropical America, was considered poisonous, but today it is one of the most valuable temperate-zone vegetable crops.

bell pepper

eggplant

tomato

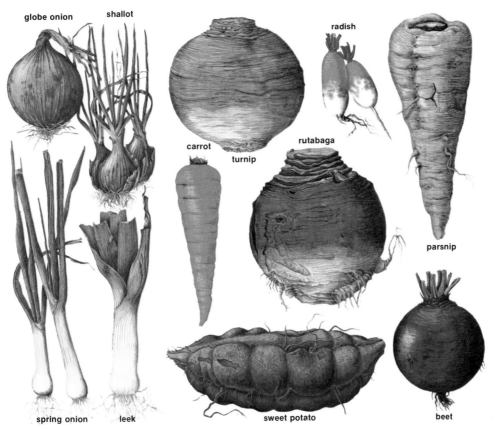

globe onion   shallot   radish   carrot   turnip   rutabaga   parsnip   spring onion   leek   sweet potato   beet

Onions are bulb vegetables used to season salads, soups, and cooked dishes. Common varieties include the globe onion, the shallot, the spring onion, and the leek. Such root vegetables as carrots, turnips, rutabagas, parsnips, and beets are harvested in autumn and winter; radishes are roots harvested in spring. The sweet potato, a tropical root vegetable, is related to the morning glory.

mucks, are important vegetable-growing soils in parts of Florida, New York, Michigan, Wisconsin, and California. Because of their productive capacity, muck soils are often reserved for growing the crops of highest value.

Liberal use of fertilizers ensures the continuous and rapid growth that is necessary for high quality and yields.

Vegetable Production. The production of vegetables is highly intensive as compared with the production of such field crops as corn, wheat, and sugar beets. The potential crop value is great and justifies the comparatively high expenditure on labor, water, fertilizer, farm chemicals, mechanization, and other resources. Production for canning, freezing, or dehydration is usually distinct from fresh production. Greenhouse growing of vegetables is important in some areas, and significant quantities of tomatoes, cucumbers, and lettuce are grown in forcing structures. Mushroom production is a specialized part of the vegetable industry. Commercial production is supplemented by the produce from home gardens. About half of the families in the United States grow some of their own vegetables.

Vegetable production requires considerable hand labor because of the intensive nature of cropping, the variable maturities of plants in a field, and the perishable nature of the harvest. Horticulturists, geneticists, and engineers have developed more-uniform plants and have designed intricate mechanical equipment for planting, cultivating, and harvesting vegetables. Perhaps the most notable example of this achievement has been the development of new tomato cultivars for processing, together with efficient field harvesters and a systematic approach to production. Virtually all processing tomatoes (those which will be canned or otherwise processed by the food industry) are now harvested mechanically.

Most vegetables are perishable and maintain peak quality for only a short period. A few, such as potatoes and onions, will remain in excellent condition for many months with good storage.

vegetable oils   Vegetable oils are oils obtained from certain field and tree crops. The field crops include soybeans, sunflowers, peanuts, rapeseed, safflower, sesame, cotton, corn, and flax. The most important tree crops are coconuts, palm, palm kernel, olives, castor, and tung.

The seven major vegetable oils—soybean, peanut, sunflower, coconut, palm, rapeseed, and cottonseed—are used primarily in food products. In the United States, salad and cooking oils, shortening, and margarine comprise a major share of the food-fat market; soybean oil is the primary vegetable oil used for these products.

Demand in the food-fat market has shifted from solid fats to liquid oils and from animal fats to vegetable oils, stimulating technological developments in the processing of vegetable oils to yield stable products. Soybean oil requires special processing because of its unstable linolenic-acid component. Palm oil, which is a highly saturated oil, is used mainly for shortening; however, technological improvements in the fractionation of palm oil yield a liquid oil similar to peanut or olive, which is finding use as a cooking oil. Edible oils also have important nonfood uses, but such industrial oils as tung, linseed, and castor have no food uses because of their toxic properties. Industrial vegetable oils are used in paints and varnishes, other drying-oil products, fatty acids, feeds, resins, and plastics.

Specialty vegetable oils include those obtained from nuts, particularly walnuts; from such herb seed crops as SESAME; and from plants whose commercial possibilities are being explored for the first time, such as the North American desert plant, JOJOBA.

The type of fat consumed in various food oils has become a major issue, spurred by concerns about high CHOLESTEROL levels leading to heart disease. Saturated fats, those containing large numbers of hydrogen atoms in their chemical composition, are suspected of raising cholesterol levels. "Tropical" vegetable oils—palm kernel, palm, and coconut, particularly—are high in saturated fats; soybean, corn, olive, cottonseed, and most other vegetable oils contain larger amounts of polyunsaturated oils, which are considered physiologically less threatening.

vegetarianism   Vegetarianism encompasses various religious, philosophical, and ethical beliefs, all of which involve a refusal to eat animal flesh, including red meat, poultry, and fish. The vegetarian diet consists mainly of cereal grains, legumes, nuts, seeds, vegetables, and fruits; soybeans, tofu (bean curd), and miso (fermented soybean paste) are popular sources of protein in many modern diets.

Vegetarians are classified according to which animal products are part of their diets. Vegans eat no dairy products or eggs. Lacto-vegetarians consume milk and cheese but not eggs. Ovo-vegetarians accept eggs but not dairy products. Lacto-ovo-vegetarians eat both dairy products and eggs. Some people abstain from eating meat for religious reasons, for example, Jains and most Buddhists and Hindus, for whom the killing and eating of animals violates the ethical precept of *ahimsa*, or nonviolence. Other, nonreligious people have embraced vegetarianism for similar ethical reasons. Still others believe that the vegetarian diet is healthier than a diet of meat. Some people have become vegetarians for ecological reasons because much less space and food outlay are needed to raise vegetables than livestock. They further argue that in a world of high population and scarce resources, vegetarianism is a practical method of averting world famine.

People who eat a well-balanced vegetarian diet generally have lower blood pressure, less cholesterol in the blood, and less excess fat than those who eat meat. Some doctors claim that vegetarians are less susceptible to heart disease

and some forms of cancer than are nonvegetarians. Vegetarians must take care, however, to eat the proper combinations of complementary foods in order to avoid protein and vitamin deficiencies. Grain-and-legume combinations are particularly important; rice and beans together, for example, provide complete protein equivalents to what is obtained by eating meat (see NUTRITION, HUMAN).

vegetation   see BIOME; PLANT; PLANT DISTRIBUTION

Veii [vay'-ee]   Veii, at the village of Isola Farnese, about 20 km (12 mi) northeast of Rome, is perhaps the most famous city of the ancient ETRUSCANS. It is known from Roman history, which describes Rome's wars with Veii, its close neighbor and rival. The historical account includes the slaughter of the noble family of the Fabii at the battle of the Cremera River (477 BC); the Roman general Camillus's capture of Veii and his *evocatio* (transfer) of the statue and cult of its patron goddess, Juno Regina, to Rome; and Rome's 10-year siege (modeled on the Trojan War) and subsequent annexation of Veii (396 BC). Numerous surviving *cuniculi* (drainage channels) show the Etruscans' skill in hydraulic engineering and may explain Roman tradition concerning Camillus's use of an underground passage to capture the city. Veii has also yielded some of the earliest Etruscan painted tombs, notably the Tomb of the Ducks (*c.*675–650 BC) and the Campana Tomb (*c.*600 BC).

Veil, Simone [vay, see-muhn']   The French lawyer and governmental official Simone Veil, b. Simone Jacob on July 13, 1927, was president (1979–81) of the first directly elected European Parliament and in 1982 became chairman of that organization's legal affairs committee. Veil was incarcerated in the Auschwitz concentration camp from 1944 to 1945. After graduating from the Institut d'Études Politiques Paris she worked (1957–65) in the Ministry of Justice. She served (1970–74) as secretary-general of the Higher Council of Magistrates before becoming (1974–79) minister of health, family, and social security.

vein   A vein is a vessel that carries blood from the tissues toward or into the heart. A vein is not subjected to the high blood pressures found in ARTERIES; its walls do have three layers, but they are thinner and contain fewer muscle cells and elastic fibers. Many veins contain valves that prevent the backflow of blood, especially in the legs.

The venous system begins with small veins, called venules, that collect blood from the capillaries; these converge into successively larger veins and culminate in two major veins of the body, which conduct blood directly to the heart. One major vein, the superior vena cava, carries blood from the tissues of the head, neck, arms, and chest; the other, the inferior vena cava, returns blood to the heart from all parts of the body below chest level. The latter is the largest vein in the body. The portal vein conducts blood from the intestines toward the heart, but unlike in other veins, the blood it carries enters the capillary system of the liver before passing into the inferior vena cava for return to the heart.

Disorders of veins include THROMBOSIS, involving a blood clot in a vein, and VARICOSE VEINS.

vein deposit   A vein is any tabular to sheetlike, quartz-rich body filling a fracture in rocks. The fractures may have been faults, joints, or other planar features. Miners and prospectors call any tabular body a vein if it is compositionally different from the surrounding rocks. A lode deposit consists of closely spaced, subparallel veins; a stockwork is a three-dimensional network of veinlets. Alteration minerals usually occur in rocks adjacent to mineralized veins, which generally originated in fractures across lower-grade mineralization. Veins continue to be important sources of gold, silver, uranium, and gems; the increased use of mining machinery, which ordinarily requires mining widths of 2 to 3 m (7 to 10 ft), has, however, rendered many veins uneconomic.

Vela   Vela was a series of 12 satellites developed for the U.S. Defense Advanced Projects Agency to detect nuclear detonations up to 160,000,000 km (100,000,000 mi) into deep space and, in the advanced models (*Vela 7* to *Vela 12*), in the Earth's atmosphere. The satellites have also provided data on solar flares and other solar radiation potentially hazardous to humans in space. The satellites were launched (1963–70) in pairs from a single vehicle and placed 180° apart, by thrust from a solid-propellant motor inside the satellite, in circular orbits of about 111,000 km (69,000 mi) altitude.

Velasco, Luis de [vay-lahs'-koh]   Luis de Velasco, d. July 31, 1564, Spanish colonial administrator and second viceroy of New Spain (1550–64), became known for his honesty, wisdom, and eagerness to protect the natives of Mexico. He freed many Indian slaves and strengthened government supervision of Indians held in peonage. The University of Mexico was founded (1553) during his administration.

Velasco unsuccessfully urged the crown to halt the importation of black slaves into New Spain. He expanded Spanish settlement northward, sent a colonizing expedition to Florida (1559), and equipped Miguel López de Legazpi's voyage to the Philippines (1564). His son, also called **Luis de Velasco**, b. 1534, d. Sept. 7, 1617, energetically continued his father's work by promoting the Indian economy as viceroy of New Spain (1590–95, 1607–11) and Peru (1595–1604).

Velasco Ibarra, José María   José María Velasco Ibarra, b. Mar. 19, 1893, d. Mar. 30, 1979, served as president of Ecuador five times. In 1934 he was elected president as leader of the conservatives but was deposed the next year. He regained the presidency in 1944 but

was deposed in 1947 by conservatives who feared his assumption of dictatorial powers. He again became president in 1952, serving until 1956, and was elected for the fourth time in 1960, but the austerity measures he imposed led to his ouster in 1961. In 1968, elected for the fifth time, Velasco Ibarra moved to establish a military dictatorship. He was deposed in 1972 when the army disapproved of his plan to return Ecuador to democratic rule.

Velázquez, Diego [vay-lahth'-kayth]   Diego de Silva Velázquez was a 17th-century Spanish painter whose genius for composition and brilliant brushwork place him in the first rank of Western artists. He was baptized in Seville on June 6, 1599, and died on Aug. 6, 1660. Although his surviving works comprise only about 100 paintings and perhaps a few drawings, he has remained one of the most influential artists of all time.

His first mature productions, which were executed in a naturalistic style related to that of CARAVAGGIO, usually depicted closely studied, small groups of ordinary people strongly modeled in chiaroscuro (light and shadow). Even at this early stage of his career, Velázquez imbued his figure groups with a dignity and profound humanity that are characteristic of his art. Outstanding among the *bodegones*, or tavern scenes, in which he specialized in this

Las Meninas (The Maids of Honor, 1656) is a puzzling masterpiece by the Spanish baroque master Diego Velázquez. One interpretation is that he is painting a portrait of the king and queen, whose reflections appear in the mirror on the rear wall. Watching them are their daughter, the Infanta Margarita, her ladies in waiting, the court dwarf, and, at rear, a courtier. (Prado, Madrid.)

period is *The Water Seller of Seville* (c.1619; Wellington Museum, London), whose solidly modeled figures are painted in a harmonious blend of greenish ocher and brown earth tones.

Shortly after moving (1623) to Madrid under the patronage of the Count-Duke of Olivares, he was named court painter to King Philip IV, whom Velázquez served for the rest of his life. He created vivid portraits and other paintings for his royal employer, including *Philip IV in Brown and Silver* (c. 1631; National Gallery, London) and a series of equestrian portraits. Contact with a wide variety of Italian works led him to experiment with increasingly fluid and loosely brushed paint, lighter colors, and multifigure compositions in interior settings, as in *The Forge of Vulcan* (1630; Prado, Madrid). Velázquez's masterpiece of the 1630s, *The Surrender of Breda* (1634–35; Prado), a sensitive group portrait, is set in a landscape representing the scene of a Spanish victory over the rebellious Dutch that had taken place a decade earlier; it exemplifies the virtue of magnanimity on the part of the victors.

From 1649 to 1651, Velázquez toured the cities of Italy in order to select paintings and sculptures to decorate the newly remodeled Alcázar in Madrid, then the royal residence. His famous portraits *Juan de Pareja* (1649–50; Metropolitan Museum of Art, New York City) and *Pope Innocent X* (1650; Galleria Doria Pamphili, Rome) were painted while he was in Rome and were greeted with great enthusiasm when they were displayed there.

Velázquez's achievements and aspirations are summed up in the celebrated painting known as *Las Meninas*, or *The Maids of Honor* (1656, Prado), in which he included a self-portrait as an ingenious claim to status for the painter and his art.

Velázquez de Cuéllar, Diego [vay-lahth'-kayth day kway'-yahr]   Diego Velázquez de Cuéllar, b. c.1465, d. June 12, 1524, a Spanish soldier, was the first governor of Cuba. He sailed to the New World with Christopher Columbus on the second voyage, to Hispaniola, in 1493. He returned to Spain and in 1511 received a commission to conquer Cuba. By 1514 the Spaniards controlled the whole island. Velázquez thereafter enjoyed considerable power as governor, founding Santiago (1514) and Havana (1515), and planning the conquest of Mexico. Two expeditions reached the coast in 1517 and in 1518. Velázquez put his brother-in-law, Hernán CORTÉS, in command of an expedition to the mainland in 1519, but, fearing Cortés as a rival, he sent Pánfilo de NARVÁEZ to countermand Cortés's orders. Cortés repulsed Velázquez's envoy, however, and proceeded to conquer the Aztec empire of Mexico. Velázquez was replaced as governor in 1521 but was reinstated in 1523.

Velikovsky, Immanuel [vay-lee-kahf'-skee]   The controversial American physician and historian Immanuel Velikovsky, b. Vitebsk, Russia, June 10 (N.S.), 1895, d. Nov. 17, 1979, argued that the configuration of the solar system

was changed in historical times and that this change caused cataclysmic upheavals on Earth. Macmillan, the original publisher of Velikovsky's *Worlds in Collision* (1950), transferred its rights to Doubleday after only two months of publication when Macmillan's sizable textbook business was endangered by a threatened boycott from many scientists who disapproved of Velikovsky's methodology.

In *Worlds in Collision*, Velikovsky claimed that a comet ejected from the planet Jupiter had, over a period of decades in the 15th century BC, temporarily stopped the Earth's rotation. He claimed further that in the 8th century BC the same comet shifted the orbit of Mars after a near collision with that planet before settling into its present orbit as the planet Venus.

Although Velikovsky's theory led him to make certain claims, such as a relatively hot temperature for Venus, that were subsequently verified, many scientists have questioned the plausibility of the celestial events described by Velikovsky and the mechanisms that he proposed to account for them. Velikovsky's other works include *Ages in Chaos* (1952), *Earth in Upheaval* (1955), *Oedipus and Akhnaton* (1960), *Peoples of the Sea* (1977), and *Ramses II and His Time* (1978).

vellum   SEE PARCHMENT

velocity   Velocity is the distance an object travels in a specified direction during a unit of time (see MOTION, PLANAR). Velocity thus differs from SPEED, for which the direction is unspecified. Because velocity is a vector quantity, it has two components: a magnitude, or speed of motion, and a direction of motion. The velocity of an object may vary from one moment to the next if either the speed or the direction of motion changes, or if both change at the same time. Either variation is an ACCELERATION. For example, an object revolving in a circle (see MOTION, CIRCULAR) undergoes acceleration; it may have constant angular (rotative) speed, but its direction of motion constantly changes.

velvet   Velvet is a fabric with a rich, soft texture produced by extra yarns in the warp that form a short pile. Originally made of silk, velvet may now be made of cotton or synthetic yarns. There are two methods of velvet manufacture. In one, the extra warp yarns are lifted over wires, and as the wires are withdrawn their knife-sharp ends cut the yarn. In the second method, two cloths are woven face-to-face, with the extra warp yarns interchanged between them, and are then cut apart to produce two pile fabrics.

Velvet has been used since the Middle Ages. Flattened or pressed velvet is called panne. Velvet with a high pile is called plush. Corduroy is a velvet whose pile has been cut in a striped pattern. Velveteen has pile made from extra fillings rather than from extra warp yarn.

Venda   The diverse groups that became known as the Venda, a BANTU-speaking people, moved southward into northeastern South Africa in the early 1700s and came under control of the Transvaal in 1898. The Venda are mostly farmers. Their religion centers on the worship of ancestral spirits, and the chiefs of the various tribal groups remain important. About two-thirds of all Venda live in the Venda homeland (1985 est. pop., 424,000), which was declared independent by the South African government in 1979. The homeland's area is 6,500 km² (2,510 mi²); Thonoyandou is the capital.

Vendôme, Louis Joseph, Duc de [vahn-dohm']
Louis Joseph, duc de Vendôme, b. July 1, 1654, d. June 15, 1712, a French general under Louis XIV, fought for Philip V, French Bourbon heir to the Spanish throne, in the War of the Spanish Succession (1701–14). He commanded the French forces defending Philip's Italian territories and defeated (1705) Prince Eugene of Savoy at Cassano. In Flanders, Vendôme was defeated (1708) by the duke of Marlborough at Oudenaarde. In Spain in 1710 he recaptured Madrid and defeated the Austrians at Villaviciosa.

---

veneer Veneer is a thin sheet of wood made from sliced or peeled logs. Veneer may be sliced longitudinally, by shaving thin layers of wood from a stationary log with a heavy knife. Peeled veneer results when a knife blade is pressed against a log so that a thin sheet of wood is peeled away as the log is turned. The veneer unwinds like cloth from a bolt. Peeled veneers, usually between 4.75 and 0.8 mm (0.19 and 0.03 in) thick and usually of softwood, are used to make packing crates and bushel baskets or are glued together to make plywood.

Sliced veneers have attractive grain patterns and can be as thin as 0.38 mm (0.015 in). Decorative plywood, made from sliced hardwood veneers, is used for paneling, doors, cabinets, and furniture. The inside layers may be made from peeled softwood, sliced hardwood, or particle board. Fine-grained veneers from decorative woods are often used as the surface layer on wood furniture.

Venera Venera, the Soviet program for the exploration of the planet Venus, has employed various types of spacecraft to measure the composition and dynamics of the Venusian atmosphere and to analyze and radar-map the planet's surface. During the most recent passage of Halley's comet around the Sun, in 1985–86, two Soviet craft sent to observe the comet also released balloon probes into the Venusian atmosphere while on their way.

The relative movements of Earth and Venus around the Sun provide a periodic "launch window" opportunity during which probes can be launched (a few weeks every 18 months). Beginning in February 1961 the USSR repeatedly launched two or three probes during each launch window. After ten failures, the eleventh probe, *Venera 4*, was launched on June 12, 1967, and successfully relayed data from the Venusian atmosphere. The first probe to transmit data from the surface was the 15th attempt, *Venera 7*, launched Aug. 17, 1970. Three more probes resulted in one more successful landing, on July 22, 1972.

The next Venus launch window was passed up in preparation for the launching of newer, heavier probes with the powerful Proton rocket in June 1975. *Venera 9* and *Venera 10* each dropped a probe into the Venusian atmosphere while maneuvering the main spacecraft into orbit around Venus. The probe relayed surface data and television pictures for 30 minutes each before losing contact with Earth. The Soviets launched two flyby-lander spacecraft, *Venera 11* and *Venera 12*, in 1978. The data transmission from the landing modules continued for 95 and 110 minutes after they landed in December of that year.

In 1981 the Soviets launched the flyby-landers *Venera 13* and *Venera 14*. They made successful landings in March 1982. The landers transmitted the first color pictures of the surface of Venus, tested the electrical conductivity of the rocks, drilled through the Venusian surface, and scooped up soil samples for analyses. In 1983, *Venera 15* and *Venera 16* were launched, entering orbit around Venus in October for extensive radar mapping.

In June 1985 four Soviet probes—two landers that analyzed soil, and two novel atmosphere balloons that briefly transmitted data from altitudes of 50–55 km (31–34 mi)—were dropped into the Venusian atmosphere by the Halley's-comet explorers, *Vega 1* and *Vega 2.*

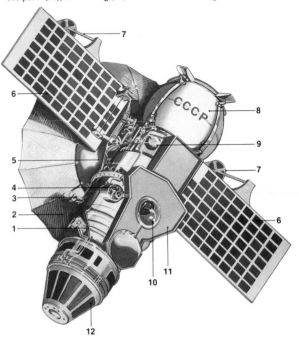

On Dec. 15, 1970, the Soviet Venera 7 *became the first artificial object to make a successful soft landing on Venus. Numbers indicate: pneumatic system (1) for operation of the nozzles of the orientation devices; high-gain umbrella antenna (2); cosmic-ray counter (3); sensor (4) for orienting spacecraft to the Sun; radiator cooler (5) for lowering vehicle temperature in Venus's atmosphere; solar panels (6); low-gain antennae (7); descent capsule (8); storage bottle (9) for compressed nitrogen; star-orientation sensor (10); protective panel (11); and housing (12) for course-correction engine.*

venereal disease   Gonorrhea, syphilis, and other venereal diseases are highly specific infections almost always acquired during sexual contact. Bacteria, protozoans, or fungi that cause venereal disease generally can attack only certain portions of the body, including the genital tract; they do not survive for long periods outside the human host, and so transmission by such objects as clothing or toilet seats is extremely rare. Venereal diseases range in effect from mild, annoying symptoms to life-threatening illnesses that spread from the reproductive tract to the entire body. The two most serious diseases are SYPHILIS and GONORRHEA; CHLAMYDIA, the most common venereal disease in the United States today, can also have serious effects. Other infections include chancroid, simple warts, cold sores, and vaginitis. None of these is acquired solely through sexual contact; the sexual partners of patients found to have a venereal disease, however, are likely infected. Therefore, people who have had sexual contact with infected patients should undergo examination and possibly therapy.

Common Syndromes

Asymptomatic Carriage. People with a sexually transmitted disease may have no symptoms or symptoms that are so mild that they do not prompt the patient to seek medical attention. Almost half of the women with gonorrhea have no significant symptoms, and up to 3 percent of men acquiring gonococcal infection of the penis will feel perfectly well. Gonococcal infections in the throat or rectum are usually asymptomatic. As many as 25 percent of women and almost all men with trichomoniasis feel perfectly well, and the organisms associated with nonspecific urethritis are frequently carried asymptomatically in women.

Penile Discharge and Urethritis. Most men who acquire gonorrhea in the penis will within 1 week develop a pus-like penile discharge and a burning sensation during urination. A more common cause of these symptoms is nonspecific urethritis, which can result from infection with a number of different organisms, especially *Chlamydia trachomatis.* Chlamydia infection usually results in a milder mucous discharge than that of gonorrhea; the discharge may be accompanied by very mild feelings of discomfort on urination. Symptoms often appear 1 to 3 weeks after acquiring the infection. Untreated chlamydia may spread to the sperm-carrying canals and could cause sterility. (In developing countries, chlamydia may also lead to TRACHOMA.) Women may experience burning during urination and have a mild vaginal discharge. If chlamydia is left untreated, however, inflammation of the fallopian tubes may occur, causing sterility, miscarriages, ectopic pregnancies, or possibly conjunctivitis in the newborn infant.

Vaginal Discharge. Many women note a vaginal discharge, which is a normal response to the action of female sex hormones. This normal discharge is usually free of odor and is not accompanied by vaginal irritation or soreness. Discharges associated with genital irritation or odor, however, may be symptoms of venereal disease. The most common venereal infection causing vaginal discharge is trichomoniasis. *Trichomonas vaginalis* is a pro-

tozoan that can infect the vagina and cause a thick, foul-smelling discharge to form. Infected women may have significant vaginal soreness and a burning sensation during urination. Men usually carry the parasite with no symptoms whatsoever. The bacterium *Corynebacterium vaginale* produces a milder form of vaginal irritation, which may be associated with a mild discharge and a distinctive fishlike odor. Once again, men often carry the organism without any symptoms at all. Vaginal discharge or irritation also can result from infection with the yeast *Candida albicans.* Oral contraceptives, antibiotics, and certain illnesses such as diabetes predispose to the development of vaginal CANDIDIASIS, and men having sexual contact with infected women may develop a superficial, itchy infection of the penis. The adult vagina is resistant to gonococcal infection, but the gonococcus can infect the mouth of the uterus and result in a cervical discharge that exits through the vagina.

Genital Skin Lesions

Blisters. Herpes simplex (type 2), a virus closely related to the one causing cold sores or fever blisters, produces genital infections that appear 3 to 7 days after contact (see HERPES). The initial lesions are groups of tiny blisters that quickly rupture, leaving painful shallow sores, which may last for several weeks before healing with crusting. Although the lesions heal completely, the virus remains in the nerves of the genital tract, and the lesions may recur at irregular intervals. While the lesions are present, the disease is highly contagious, but between recurrences the risk of transmission to the sexual partner is quite low. Women may have herpetic involvement of the uterine cervix, which can occur in the absence of painful skin lesions and therefore go unnoticed.

Ulcers. Herpes-simplex infections also are the most common cause of genital ulcers, affecting about ten times as many people as syphilis. Syphilis is another major cause of ulcers; one of the symptoms of syphilis is usually a single, relatively painless ulcer in the genital area. The sore, called a chancre, generally appears about 3 weeks after exposure at the site at which the infecting agent, *Treponema pallidum,* enters the body. Chancres have been found on the lips, mouth, and breasts and occasionally elsewhere. Even though the chancre always heals without treatment, the organisms are still present and may produce other manifestations of disease later in life. Somewhat larger, painful genital ulcers are symptomatic of a bacterial infection known as chancroid, common in Southeast Asia but rare in the United States.

Other Skin Lesions. Venereal warts, caused by the papilloma virus, appear on the external genitalia as rough-surfaced bumps. They are usually multiple and do not itch. Warts may appear up to 3 months following sexual contact. Small bumps or papules around the genitals or thighs may be molluscum contagiosum, a viral disease spread by contact; this infection is also acquired nonvenereally by young children. Itchy crusted lesions, or SCABIES, result when the mite *Sarcoptes scabiei* burrows into the skin. This disease is spread by skin-to-skin contact. Itching in the pubic-hair region may result from infestation with *Phthirus pubis*, the crab louse, which is spread by close contact.

Other Infections

Swelling of the lymph nodes in the groin may accompany many sexually transmitted infections and may be tender (herpes, chancroid) or painless (syphilis). Such swelling, called adenopathy, may be the only manifestation of a relatively rare sexually transmitted disease called lymphogranuloma venereum. Some forms of infectious hepatitis can be acquired by sexual contact, and gastrointestinal infections such as shigellosis and amebiasis have also been sexually transmitted.

Management of Sexually Transmitted Diseases

Prevention. Any sexually active person runs the risk of acquiring a sexually transmitted disease, and the risk increases with the number of sexual partners and with the likelihood of infection among those sexual partners. A person having sex with a single individual but whose partner has multiple contacts is at high risk for acquiring a sexually transmitted infection. Because venereal diseases may be present without any symptoms, asking partners about symptoms does not ensure good health. Mutual fidelity between sexual partners will keep the pair free of sexually transmitted infections; no other method provides complete protection against sexually transmitted diseases. The condom is partially effective if it is worn during all genital contact, but some of the genital area is still left uncovered. Washing the genitals or urinating immediately after intercourse also offers incomplete protection.

Treatment. Effective, rapid treatment is available for almost all of the sexually transmitted infections. Herpes-simplex infection has been a notable exception, but the drug acyclovir is proving useful in suppressing recurrent attacks.

See also: AIDS.

Veneto [vay-nay-toh]   Veneto is an administrative region of northeastern Italy, with an area of 18,364 km² (7,090 mi²) and a population of 4,380,597 (1989 est.). It borders Austria on the north and the Adriatic Sea on the east. The capital is VENICE. Other major cities are PADUA, VERONA, and VICENZA. The DOLOMITES form Veneto's northern rim. Southern Veneto consists of the fertile plain of the ADIGE and Piave rivers. The PO RIVER marks the southern boundary. The main economic activity is agriculture, and the chief crops are wheat, corn, sugar beets, hemp, and fruits. The textile, chemical, paper, food-processing, and shipbuilding industries are important.

Since the 15th century, Venice has dominated most of the region. After 1797, Veneto was held by Austria, and in 1866 it became part of unified Italy.

Venezuela [ven-ez-way'-luh or vay-nays-way'-lah]   Venezuela is located in northern South America, with the Caribbean Sea to the north. The republic borders Colombia on the west and southwest, Brazil on the south, and Guyana on the east. *Venezuela* means "Little Venice," a name

that early European explorers gave to the region of Lake Maracaibo, where Indian villages were built on pilings over the water. Venezuela's capital city is CARACAS. The country has abundant natural resources, but its development has been hindered by political and social problems.

Land and Resources

Venezuela is divided into three major regions: mountains, plains, and tropical forests. The Venezuelan ANDES stretch from the Colombian border northeastward for 322 km (200 mi) and contain Pico Bolívar, the nation's highest elevation, at 5,002 m (16,411 ft). The Cordillera del Norte runs east-west for 965 km (600 mi) in two parallel branches. South of the mountain regions are the llanos (plains), an extensive area of sparsely populated savannas and scrub forests, cut by the northern tributaries of the Orinoco River. Tropical forests characterize the highlands to the south of the Orinoco. ANGEL FALLS, cascading from Auyán-Tepui, is the world's highest cataract.

Soils. Venezuela's soils are low in fertility. Latosols cover most of the country, but mountain soils predominate in the highlands.

Climate. The Venezuelan climate is mostly tropical. Average annual temperatures range from 20° C (69° F) in the Andes to 28° C (82° F) in the Maracaibo Basin. Rainfall is abundant from May through December, averaging 533 mm (21 in) around Lake Maracaibo, 813 mm (32 in) in Caracas, 1,016 mm (40 in) in the llanos, and even larger amounts in the Andes.

Drainage. Lake MARACAIBO is the main feature of a depression north of the Andes. More than 130 rivers drain into this largest lake in South America. The ORINOCO RIVER, South America's second longest, drains 80% of the country. The extreme south is drained by the AMAZON RIVER.

Vegetation and Animal Life. Venezuela has a wide variety of animal life, including monkeys, jaguars, pumas, peccaries, manatees, sloths, anteaters, and armadillos. Tropical birds, such as parrots and macaws, are abundant.

Resources. Venezuela is a resource-rich nation. It is one of the world's largest petroleum producers, with proven reserves of about 58.5 billion barrels. The country also has reserves of iron ore, bauxite, coal, diamonds, gold, and silver.

People

Most people speak Spanish as their primary language and profess Roman Catholicism. About 67% of the people are mestizo, 21% white, 10% black, and 2% Indian. Major cities are Caracas, the petroleum center of MARACAIBO, VALENCIA, Barquisimeto, and Maracay. Life expectancy is rising, but malnutrition is still common, and access to quality health care remains a problem.

Education. Public education is highly centralized and is free. A six-year primary education is compulsory, and more than 80% of children in the relevant age group actually attend primary schools. Fewer than 40% receive secondary schooling, however. The National Training Institute (INCE) has trained several hundred thousand students, including adults and school dropouts, in various technical subjects.

AT A GLANCE

REPUBLIC OF VENEZUELA

Land: Area: 912,050 km² (352,144 mi²). Capital and largest city: Caracas (1990 est. pop., 1,290,087).

People: Population (1990 est.): 19,735,000. Density: 22 persons per km² (56 per mi²). Distribution (1990): 84% urban, 16% rural. Official language: Spanish. Major religion: Roman Catholicism.

Government: Type: republic. Legislature: National Congress. Political subdivisions: 20 states, 2 federal territories, 1 federal district, 1 federal dependency.

Economy: GNP (1989): $47.2 billion; $2,450 per capita. Labor distribution (1988): agriculture, forestry, and fishing—13.4%; manufacturing—17.5%; mining—1%; utilities—1%; construction—9.4%; trade, restaurants, and hotels—18.4%; transport, storage, and communications—6.3%; business and social services—32.5%; other—0.3%. Foreign trade (1988): imports—$11.5 billion; exports—$10.2 billion. Currency: 1 bolívar = 100 céntimos.

Education and Health: Literacy (1990): 86% of adult population. Institutions of higher education (1985–86): 82. Hospital beds (1987): 47,535. Physicians (1987): 28,400. Life expectancy (1990): women—77; men—71. Infant mortality (1990): 27 per 1,000 live births.

The Arts. Venezuelan literature owes much to novelists Rómulo GALLEGOS, Arturo Uslar Pietri, Guillermo Meneses, Ramón Díaz Sánchez, and Salvador Garmendía. Acclaimed poets include Andres Eloy Blanco, Juan Liscano, Antonio Arraiz, and Vicente Gerbasi. In the performing arts, Isaac Chocrón and Román Chalbaud are mainstays of the theater, whereas maestro Vicente Emilio Sojo revived interest in symphonic music.

Contemporary movements in the plastic arts are well represented: the kinetic school by Jesús Soto, Carlos Cruz-Diez, and Alejandro Otero; and the new figuration by Alirio Rodríguez.

Economic Activity

Once predominantly agricultural, the Venezuelan economy underwent a transformation during the 1970s based on petroleum wealth. The government's control of crucial natural resources resulted in tremendous profits from their exploitation and marketing. As a result of heavy spending and heavy borrowing, however, the Venezuelan economy encountered difficulties in the 1980s as oil prices fell. Inflation rose, and the repayment of foreign debt became an important issue. Venezuela, still the richest country in South America in terms of average income, instituted an economic austerity program in 1989.

Manufacturing. Industrial diversification, to reduce the country's dependence on oil revenues, is a government priority. The major development plan includes a steel complex, a tractor factory, aluminum plants, and bauxite, gold, and timber production.

Agriculture, Fishing, and Forestry. Agricultural development is another government priority. Only about 5% of arable land is utilized, the bulk of that for pasture. The main crops grown are sugarcane, bananas, rice, maize, sorghum, and cassava. The fishing sector has grown, but the timber wealth in the highlands has not been commercially developed.

Transportation and Trade. The main highway system, considered among the best in Latin America, is being upgraded, and an inadequate national railroad network has been targeted for improvement. Internal air transport is well developed.

Petroleum, by far the most important export, was the reason for a favorable trade balance until oil prices fell in the 1980s. Aluminum is the second most valuable export. Venezuela must import food and manufactured goods.

Government

The constitution of 1961 established a federal republic. The National Congress, made up of the Senate and the Chamber of Deputies, is the legislative branch. Governors of the 20 states are appointed by the president. General elections are held every 5 years; voting is univer-

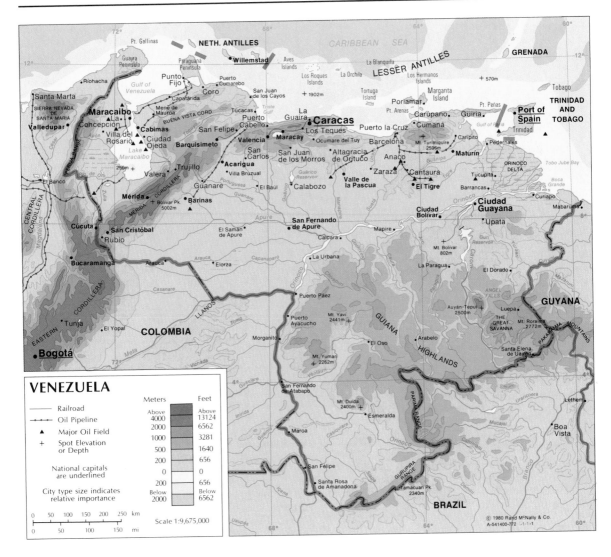

VENEZUELA

	Meters	Feet
——— Railroad		
·—·—· Oil Pipeline	Above 4000	Above 13124
▲ Major Oil Field	2000	6562
+ Spot Elevation or Depth	1000	3281
	500	1640
	200	656
National capitals are underlined	0	0
	200	656
City type size indicates relative importance	Below 2000	Below 6562

0 50 100 150 200 250 km
0   50   100   150 mi

Scale 1:9,675,000

© 1980 Rand McNally & Co.
A-541400-772 -1-1-1

sal and compulsory for those 18 years of age or older. The presidential incumbent is ineligible for two consecutive terms.

History

Long inhabited by ARAWAK and CARIB Indians, Venezuela was visited by Columbus in 1498. Settlements were established by the Spanish in 1523. In 1535, the Weiser brothers (German bankers who were granted rights to Venezuela by Holy Roman Emperor Charles V), financed an expedition to Venezuela and Colombia, but in 1556, the Weisers' contract was terminated, and Spain regained the region.

Venezuelan Creoles were active in the movement for independence from Spain. In 1806, Francisco de MIRANDA landed in Venezuela with a revolutionary force but was easily repulsed by loyalist troops. Venezuela's revolutionary congress declared its independence from Spain on July 5, 1811.

In 1830, Venezuela withdrew from Simón BOLÍVAR's Gran Colombia federation and became a sovereign state. The major political leaders in the following decades were José Antonio PAÉZ and Antonio GUZMÁN BLANCO. In 1899 the dictator Cipriano CASTRO seized control; nine years later he was replaced by Juan Vicente GÓMEZ, who ruled Venezuela until 1935. Gómez's successors were faced with the demands of an increasingly urban society and the democratic aspirations of the so-called Generation of 1928. A democratic interlude (1945–48) was followed by a decade of military rule.

Since 1958, Venezuela has had democratic rule. Figures of the Generation of 1928, such as Rómulo BETAN-

Angel Falls, the world's highest waterfall, descends 979 m (3,212 ft) from a massive plateau in Venezuela's remote Guiana Highlands. The cataract is the most dramatic feature of a vast national park in Venezuela's southeast interior.

COURT and Raúl Leoni of the Acción Democratica (AD) party, and younger men, such as Rafael Caldera of the Christian Democratic party (COPEI) and Luis Herrera Campíns (COPEI), have worked for democracy during their presidential administrations. Jaime Lusinchi (AD), president (1984–89) during a time of economic ills, was succeeded by Carlos Andrés Pérez (AD). Pérez, who was also president from 1974 to 1979, introduced austerity measures that provoked violent rioting in 1989.

Venezuela Boundary Dispute

In 1895, U.S. Secretary of State Richard OLNEY invoked the MONROE DOCTRINE against Great Britain in Britain's dispute with Venezuela over the boundary between Venezuela and British Guiana. Contention over the boundary began in 1814, when the British took their part of Guiana from the Dutch, but it became serious only in the 1880s, after gold was discovered there. Upon appeal by Venezuela, Secretary Olney, in July 1895, sent a belligerent note to Lord Salisbury, the British prime minister and foreign secretary, warning against British pressure on Venezuela. After Salisbury denied the Monroe Doctrine's applicability, President Grover Cleveland asked Congress to establish a boundary commission, its findings to be implemented by the United States. In 1896, Salisbury backed down and accepted arbitration. In 1899, an arbitral tribunal largely upheld Britain's pre-1880s claim; thereafter, diplomatic relations between Great Britain and Venezuela were renewed. After British Guiana gained independence as Guyana in 1966, Venezuela pressed its claim to more than half of the country.

Venice

Venice [ven'-is]   Venice (Italian: Venezia), the capital of Venezia province and of the Veneto region in northeastern Italy, lies on the Gulf of Venice at the north end of the Adriatic Sea. The political boundaries of the city were expanded in 1927 to include a mainland area around the Lagoon of Venice as well as the 118 small islands within the lagoon that comprise historic Venice. The city has a population of 327,700 (1987 est.).

The Historic City. The Grand Canal is historic Venice's main traffic artery. Although a causeway connects the mainland to the historic city, travel about the city is by motorboats, water-buses, curved-prow gondolas, or on foot. The smaller canals are crossed by footbridges, including the famous 16th-century Bridge of Sighs linking the ducal palace and the state prison. The largest of Venice's many squares is the Piazza San Marco, bordered on three sides by the Palazzo dei Procuratori (15th–16th centuries), and on the fourth by SAINT MARK'S BASILICA (9th century, rebuilt 11th–14th centuries). Between the church and the canal is the 99-m-high (325-ft) Campanile (a 1912 replica of the 12th-century original), and the Doge's Palace. Nearby is the Libreria Vecchia, begun in 1536 by Jacopo SANSOVINO. Across the Grand Canal is the Church of San Giorgio Maggiore, designed by Andrea PALLADIO. Among the city's many other notable churches is Santi Giovanni e Paolo (completed 1430), with a ceiling by Paolo VERONESE. The Church of Santa Maria dei Frari is the burial place of Titian. The Scuola Grande di San Rocco was originally decorated by TINTORETTO. Along the canal are the 15th-century Venetian-Gothic palace, Ca' d'Oro; the 17th-century Palazzo Rezzonico; and the Palazzo Vendramin-Calergi (1509). The Accademia di Belle Arti (Venice Academy) contains masterpieces from the Venetian school of art, including those by Giorgione; Jacopo, Gentile, and Giovanni Bellini; Gentile da Fabriano; Vittore Carpaccio; Canaletto; and Andrea Mantegna. In recent years many of Venice's treasures have been repaired and restored. Grand opera is still presented at the Teatro la Fenice, where works by Verdi, Rossini, Wagner, and Stravinsky were first performed.

Economy. Although tourism remains most important, modern Venice encompasses a newer, industrialized sector on the mainland, including Mestre and Marghera, the latter Venice's commercial port. Shipyards, petroleum refineries, and chemical and metallurgical industries contribute to the economy. Burano lace and Venetian glass are world renowned. Lido Beach, on one of the seaward islands, is a famous resort.

History. Mainlanders fleeing barbarians after the fall of Rome founded several settlements on the islands of the lagoon. In 697 authority was consolidated in Venice's

The Palazzo Ducale, or Doge's Palace, served as the residence of Venice's elected rulers and contained its governmental offices during the Middle Ages, when the city was capital of a powerful maritime empire.

first DOGE. Venice soon gained control of the Adriatic Sea, established outposts in the Levant, and became a staging area for the Crusades. The Venetian doge was instrumental in diverting the Fourth Crusade to conquer Constantinople in 1204. Thereafter, Venice was not only the unchallenged broker of most east-west commerce but also an interlocutor between the two cultures. In 1275 the Venetian Marco Polo reached Peking, opening a trade route between Europe and the Far East.

Venice continued to grow in power. In 1380 it defeated Genoa, its only European rival for mastery of the seas; at the Battle of Lepanto (1571), Venetian ships played an important role in the destruction of the Turkish fleet. The Portuguese discovery of an all-water route to the Far East around Africa and later the growing importance of the Western Hemisphere, led to Venice's decline. By the Treaty of Campo Formio (1797), the republic was dissolved, and the city came under the rule of the Austrians. Venice fought against foreign domination throughout the Risorgimento and, in 1866, became part of the united Kingdom of Italy.

Industrialization in the 20th century has brought about economic prosperity and rapid population growth in greater Venice. At the same time, however, the city's delicate ecosystem is threatened. Efforts to save the historic city from physical collapse have come from private funds and international organizations.

Venizélos, Eleuthérios [ven-ee-zel'-aws, el-ef-thair'-ee-aws] Eleuthérios Venizélos, b. Aug. 23, 1864, d. Mar. 18, 1936, several times prime minister of Greece, was one of the leading Greek politicians of his era. A native of Crete, he participated in the 1897 revolt against Turkish rule. In 1905, Venizélos proclaimed the union of Crete with Greece, a goal not realized until 1913.

Venizélos went to Greece in 1909 to advise the Military League shortly after its coup d'etat. He was the Liberal party's leader and became prime minister in 1910. During the BALKAN WARS (1912–13), Venizélos helped defeat the Turks. Favoring Britain and France in World War I he resigned in 1915 because of conflicts with the pro-German king CONSTANTINE I. Venizélos formed a rival government in Salonika in 1916. He returned to Athens as prime minister in 1917, after Franco-British pressure forced Constantine to abdicate.

After the war, Venizélos acquired substantial territory for Greece, particularly at Turkey's expense, but lost the elections in 1920. He served briefly as prime minister in 1924 and won the 1928 elections; in 1932 the worldwide depression led to his defeat. Implicated in the unsuccessful antimonarchist revolt of 1935, he fled Greece and died in exile in Paris.

Venn diagram Venn diagrams are pictures that display simple relationships among sets. Generally a large set U, which represents the entire universe under consideration, is fixed and represented as a rectangular region. Subsets of U are drawn as circles inside the rectangle, and the overlapping of two such regions indicates the intersection of the corresponding sets. In this way simple propositions in set theory may be understood pictorially. The method is also used to clarify the logic used in the study of SYLLOGISMS. A Venn diagram, however, should never be considered to constitute proof of a statement in set theory. Proofs can only be performed rigorously by working logically from the axioms. Also, Venn diagrams are not much help when a person deals with four or more subsets of U.

venom Venom is a poison secreted by certain snakes, insects, and other animals primarily for killing or paralyzing prey, and as digestive juices. The toxic components of snake venoms vary according to the species of snake and include neurotoxins and various enzymes, or hemotoxins. Neurotoxins interfere with nerve conduction and cause paralysis, including paralysis of the respiratory muscles. Hemotoxins hasten absorption of the venom, attack and destroy cells, or cause hemorrhage by interfering with blood coagulation.

Arachnid (scorpion and spider) venoms contain neurotoxins that in some species can cause death from respiratory paralysis. Although most spiders are venomous, in the United States only the brown spider and the black widow spider have venom potent enough to cause occasional deaths. The venoms of stinging insects such as bees, wasps, and hornets generally produce local irritation and swelling by the action of histamine and other substances.

See also: POISONOUS PLANTS AND ANIMALS.

ventriloquism [ven-tril'-uh-kwizm] Ventriloquism, from the Latin *venter*, meaning "belly," and *loquor*, meaning "to speak," is the ancient art of throwing the voice so that it seems to come from a source other than the speaker. The sounds are made with the lips motionless and the tongue drawn back so that only the tip of it moves. Entertainers heighten the illusion by using puppets who seem to talk.

Venturi, Robert [ven-tur'-ee] The American architect Robert Venturi, b. Philadelphia, June 25, 1925, is one of the most provocative and influential theorists of the post-1960 reaction against the functionalist aesthetic of modern architecture usually called the INTERNATIONAL STYLE. As stated most fully in his *Complexity and Contradiction in American Architecture* (1966), Venturi's aesthetic is grounded in a rejection of the "prim dreams of pure order" espoused by modernist architects in favor of an architecture of eclecticism, ambiguity, and humor. Even more controversial was his proclamation of the vitality and intrinsic worth of American roadside-strip architecture in *Learning from Las Vegas* (1972). Together, these two works have become the gospel of POSTMODERN ARCHITECTURE.

Venus (astronomy) Venus, the second planet (see PLANETS AND PLANETARY SYSTEMS) from the sun, is often called the Earth's sister planet because it so closely approximates the Earth in diameter, mass, and density, and probably also in composition and internal structure. Venus, however, is shrouded in thick clouds that completely hide the surface of the planet. Because these bright clouds act like a mirror and reflect 75% of the sunlight, many believed that surface temperatures would be nearly the same on both planets. Descriptions written in the

1950s pictured global seas of frothy liquids, out of which rose mist-shrouded islands, or extensive rain forests through which dinosaurs roamed. The atmosphere and surface of Venus are now known to be very different from that of the Earth, making it by no means a sister planet in terms of conditions for life.

Missions to Venus

The first successful flyby of Venus was made by the U.S. MARINER 2 craft on Dec. 14, 1962. This was followed by the *Mariner 5* flyby on Oct. 19, 1967, and the *Mariner 10* flyby on Feb. 5, 1974. The U.S. PIONEER *Venus 1* craft orbited Venus on Dec. 4, 1978, and this was accompanied by *Pioneer Venus 2*, which sent three probes through the Venusian atmosphere to the surface on Dec. 9, 1978. The Magellan spacecraft went into Venus orbit in August 1990 and mapped the entire planet at high resolution with its radar mapper.

The Soviet Union has had an even more ambitious Venus program, with 15 successful missions, including 10 landings. Between June 1967 and June 1983, 13 craft of the Soviet VENERA program flew by, orbited, or landed on Venus. In 1984 two Soviet craft, *Vega 1* and *Vega 2*— on their way to an encounter with Halley's Comet—deployed a pair of Venera-type landers and a pair of atmospheric balloons on Venus.

Orbit and Rotation

Venus orbits at an average distance of 108.2 million km (67 million mi) from the Sun and completes one revolution in 224.7 days. Surprisingly, Venus rotates backward compared to the Earth, and much more slowly—completing one rotation in 243 days. Tracking of weak features in the atmosphere reveals that the upper atmosphere also circulates backward once every 4 days.

The retrograde rotation of 243 days and the direct revolution about the Sun of 225 days combine to make the Venusian day—the time from one noon to the next— equal to 117 Earth days. The combined rotation and revolution also produce the unfortunate situation that every time Venus is closest to the Earth the same side of Venus is turned toward it. This unusual situation, including the slow backward rotation, may be caused by the gravitational force between the Earth and Venus.

The slow rotation may also be responsible for the apparent absence of a magnetic field on Venus. Like the Earth, Venus should have a large iron core, part of which, like the Earth's outer core, is expected to be molten. The slow spinning of Venus, however, apparently does not generate the kind of fluid motion within the core necessary to produce a magnetic field.

Atmosphere

Earth-based telescopic studies of the reflected spectrum of Venus were able to show that its atmosphere is different from that of the Earth. Carbon dioxide, first detected in 1932, is now known to make up 98% of the Venusian atmosphere. By contrast, CO_2 makes up only 0.03% of the Earth's atmosphere, although a far greater amount, about equal to the total quantity in the Venusian atmo-

(Below) *Venus, the second planet from the Sun, is surrounded by an atmosphere of carbon dioxide. Infrared radiation from the planet's surface is absorbed and radiated back by this atmosphere, producing surface temperatures as high as 480° C (900° F).*

(Above) *Radar mapping of Venus by* Pioneer Venus 1 *revealed a surface that is mainly a rolling plain with isolated highlands. Shown here is the largest such region. About half the size of Africa, it is tentatively named Aphrodite.*

sphere, is found in the rocks and oceans of the Earth. Nitrogen, the most abundant gas in the Earth's atmosphere, is less than 2% of the total on Venus. Present at a few parts per million are helium, neon, and argon.

Within the clouds, liquid and solid sulfur particles and droplets of sulfuric acid are the major constituents. The Pioneer Venus probes revealed that below the clouds the atmosphere is composed of 0.1% to 0.4% water vapor and 60 parts per million of free oxygen—an indication that Venus at one time had abundant water but has since then lost it by various processes.

Not only is the Venusian atmosphere made principally of compounds rare in the Earth's atmosphere, but the total surface pressure is much higher than at sea level on Earth. Spacecraft observations have given a value of 88 atmospheres (1,300 lb/in^2), or 88 times atmospheric pressure at sea level on Earth. The enormous amounts of CO_2 in the atmosphere cause this high pressure.

Because of the phenomenon known as the greenhouse effect, the thick CO_2 atmosphere on Venus is primarily responsible for the planet's extremely high temperature. (The recently detected water vapor provides a second strong solar heat trap.) Sunlight filtering through the clouds strikes the surface, which heats up as it absorbs the visible light. When it becomes hot enough the surface radiates away the absorbed heat as infrared radiation. Infrared waves are longer than visible light waves and are readily absorbed by carbon dioxide in the lower atmosphere. Thus the heat is kept near ground level. When the CO_2 atoms radiate away the infrared, a large fraction goes back into the surface, causing the temperature to rise further. The same process operates on Earth: water vapor in the lower atmosphere traps some of the outgoing radiation and raises the Earth's temperature about 30 C degrees; otherwise the average temperature of the Earth would be about −20°C (−4°F). The huge reservoir of CO_2 gas in the atmosphere of Venus has increased the surface temperature there to about 480° C (900° F), about 280 C

degrees more than what it would be if there were no greenhouse effect. Venus is actually hotter than MERCURY.

Although the clouds of Venus prevent much sunlight from ever reaching the surface, rocks near the Venera spacecraft cast sharp shadows, indicating the lower atmosphere is clear. From about 31 to 48 km (19 to 30 mi) above the surface a haze made up of tiny particles of sulfuric acid exists. Above this haze is the densest of Venus's cloud layers; about 3 km (2 mi) thick, it consists mostly of large sulfur particles. A brief clear space is above this cloud layer; above this, between 52 and 58 km (32 and 35 mi), there is a second layer of clouds that contains a large number of liquid and solid sulfur particles as well as sulfuric acid droplets. A third layer of clouds, consisting of sulfuric acid droplets, is present between the altitudes of 65 and 70 km (40 and 43 mi). Another haze layer, possibly due to the presence of water vapor or ice crystals, extends about 10 km (6 mi) above the tops of the clouds.

Winds at the surface are relatively gentle—about 13 km/h (8 mph), based on Soviet lander data. Faster winds exist higher up, as would be expected from the 4-day rotation of the upper atmosphere as compared to the 243-day surface rotation. Spacecraft have recorded 175-km/h (110-mph) winds at 45 km (28 mi) above the surface. Strong vertical winds were discovered in 1985 by the Vega craft. *Venera 11* and *Venera 12* also detected what appears to be lightning activity.

Surface

Venera 8, which landed on Venus in July 1972, found a granitic composition of radioactive elements uranium, thorium, and potassium, suggesting a crust like the continents of Earth. *Venera 9* and *Venera 10*, which landed in separate locations in October 1975, found basalt, which is the same material that erupts from Hawaiian-type volcanoes and forms the floors of the ocean basins on Earth.

Following radar observations from Earth and early

spacecraft, the Magellan spacecraft mapped the surface terrain at a resolution of 120 m (390 ft). The surface is largely rolling plain interrupted by areas of highlands, impact craters, spectacular mountains, and regions of ridges and canyons that are evidence of extensive tectonic activity. Volcanic flows cover about 80% of Venus; what may be the largest volcano in the solar system appears as a conelike rise more than 700 km (435 mi) across. A troughlike depression running across 1,400 km (870 mi) of surface is similar to the great rift valleys of Mars and may indicate rupturing of the crust. "Pancake" features, a series of domelike hills about 25 km (16 mi) across and 750 m (2,500 ft) high, may be due to viscous lava flows. Perhaps most surprising of all, Magellan showed no evidence of the plate-tectonics (continental-drift) mechanism that is so important in shaping Earth's geologic formations.

There is no liquid water on the Venusian surface, and this "missing water" has long been a puzzle to scientists who generally believe that Earth and Venus started out as very similar twin planets. Data from the U.S. Pioneer Venus probes, however, indicates that Venus may once, billions of years ago, have been covered by an ocean of water. Scientists speculate that the planet lost its water, the hydrogen dissipating into the atmosphere, the oxygen into the interior, possibly because of the runaway greenhouse effect that kept heat trapped close to the surface.

Venus (mythology)   An obscure deity of ancient Rome, by the 3d century BC Venus had become identified with the Greek goddess APHRODITE. Julius Caesar enshrined her as Venus Genetrix, the ancestor of his own family. In this aspect she was analogous to Mars, the paternal ancestor of the Romans. In Vergil's *Aeneid*, she is the mother of Aeneas and aids him in his adventures.

Venus of Willendorf [vil'-en-dohrf] The carved limestone statuette known as the Venus of Willendorf was discovered at Willendorf, Austria, in 1908. Dating from the

The Venus of Willendorf is a Paleolithic statuette representing one of the earliest forms of statuary art. The exaggerated form of the limestone Venus figurine may have served to emphasize her power of fertility as the goddess of birth and mother of all living things. (Naturhistorisches Museum, Vienna.)

Aurignacian period (*c*.30,000–*c*.25,000 BC) of the Old Stone Age, the 10.2-cm (4-in) female figure, which still bears traces of red pigment, has exaggerated breasts and hips and precisely arranged braids encircling the faceless head. The heavy stress on the female anatomical features and the absence of facial expression emphasize the sexuality of the figure, which may have served as a symbol of fecundity. The Venus, now in the Naturhistorisches Museum, Vienna, is considered a masterpiece of PREHISTORIC ART.

Venus's - flytrap   see CARNIVOROUS PLANTS

Veracruz (city) [vay-rah-kroos']   Veracruz, a major port on the Gulf of Mexico and the largest city of the Mexican state of Veracruz, has a population of 340,500 (1983 est.). Veracruz is Mexico's most important general cargo port, handling petroleum, fruits, molasses, and rum. The city is also a market center for a rich agricultural region and a tourist mecca. Many buildings dating from the colonial period have been preserved. The heart of Veracruz is the Plaza de la Constitución, the oldest Spanish plaza in North America.

Veracruz was established on Apr. 17, 1519, by Hernán Cortés to serve as his base for the conquest of Mexico. U.S. troops landed in the city during the Mexican War in 1847 and again in 1914 during the Mexican Revolution. Both the 1857 and 1917 Mexican constitutions were proclaimed in Veracruz.

Veracruz (state)   Veracruz is a long, narrow state in east central Mexico, along the Gulf of Mexico, with an area of 71,699 km^2 (27,683 mi^2) and a population of 6,215,-142 (1990). JALAPA is the capital, and the city of Veracruz is the largest urban center. Veracruz is primarily agricultural (coffee, sugarcane, bananas, and tobacco). Stock raising is concentrated on the lowlands; tropical forests yield dyewood, hardwoods, chicle, and rubber; and petroleum is produced. The Huastec and Totomac Indians live in Veracruz. Hernán Cortés landed there in 1519; Veracruz became a state in 1824.

verb   see PARTS OF SPEECH

verbena [vur-bee'-nuh]   *Verbena* is the generic name for about 200 species of herbs and subshrubs in the vervain family, Verbenaceae. Native to the warmer regions of North and South America, these plants, often called vervains, are popular garden ornamentals. Verbena leaves are lance-shaped and toothed, and the flowers are borne in broad clusters. The garden verbena, *V. hybrida*, is one of the most common garden annuals.

Verde, Cape (country)   see CAPE VERDE

Verde, Cape (promontory) [vurd]   Cape Verde is a narrow promontory in Senegal extending 32 km (20 mi) into the Atlantic Ocean to form Africa's westernmost extremity at 170°32' west longitude. Its name refers to its distinctive green vegetation. Cape Almadies is at its westernmost tip. Dakar is on the southern shore.

Verdi, Giuseppe [vair'-dee] Giuseppe Verdi, the foremost composer of Italian romantic opera, was born in the village of Le Roncole near Parma on Oct. 10, 1813, the son of an innkeeper. His first formal musical studies were with the organist Ferdinando Provesi in the nearby town of Busseto, where he lived in the home of the merchant Antonio Barezzi, who supported him financially and whose daughter Margherita was to become his first wife. He studied in Milan (1832–35), then returned to the post of organist in Busseto. After 3 years his desire to write for the theater brought him back to Milan, where his first opera, *Oberto*, was performed in 1839.

A series of personal tragedies—the death of his wife and both his children in the space of 22 months (1838–40)—interrupted Verdi's career, but in 1842 he was induced by his Milan producer to write *Nabucco*, the opera that brought him his first great success. For a decade thereafter he was sought by all the great opera houses of Italy, and he produced 18 operas in 15 years, culminating in 3 of his best-known works—*Rigoletto* (1851), *Il Trovatore* (The Troubadour, 1853), and *La Traviata* (The Fallen Woman, 1853).

By the early 1850s, Verdi was fulfilling commissions for theaters outside Italy—*Les Vêpres siciliennes* (Sicilian Vespers, 1855), *Don Carlos* (1867), and a revision (1865) of his earlier *Macbeth* (1847) for Paris; *La Forza del destino* (The Force of Destiny, 1862) for Saint Petersburg; and *Aïda* (1871) for a new opera house in Cairo. During this period he was elected to a term in the first Italian parliament after the unification of the country (1861). His election was not merely a tribute to his great popularity; Verdi had introduced patriotic elements into his operas as early as *Nabucco*, and his name had become an acronym for "Vittorio Emanuele, Re D'Italia" ("Vittorio Emanuele, king of Italy"—the rallying cry of the political movement for the unification of Italy).

After *Aïda*, Verdi went into semiretirement with his second wife, the singer Giuseppina Strepponi. The only other major work of the 1870s was his Requiem Mass (1874), in memory of the novelist Alessandro Manzoni. Through the cajoling of his publisher Giulio Ricordi and the librettist Arrigo Boito, who had assisted (1881) with the revisions of *Simon Boccanegra* (1857), Verdi was induced to take up first *Otello* (1887) and then *Falstaff* (1893). These two Shakespearean operas, one tragic and the other comic, were the crowning achievements of his old age. Verdi died in Milan on Jan. 27, 1901.

Verdi's early operas are constructed on a few conventional patterns, the most common comprising a pair of arias—a lyrical cantabile followed by an energetic cabaletta—for one of the principal singers. He favored compact librettos, typically with a tenor and soprano as protagonists opposed by a baritone who might be a romantic rival (as in *Il Trovatore*) or a father (as in *La Traviata*).

Giuseppe Verdi, one of the greatest Italian composers of the 19th century, created operas of dramatic intensity, soaring melody, and subtle characterization. La Traviata (1853), Aïda (1871), and Otello (1887) are three of his most highly acclaimed dramatic operas.

These baritone roles have a special prominence in Verdi's operas.

The operas that Verdi wrote for foreign theaters incorporate the spectacle and ballet associated with French grand opera of the same period. Accompaniments are richer, musical transitions more interesting, and structures less predictable (in particular, the crowd-pleasing cabalettas grow less frequent). As a result of this experimentation, perhaps, the operas of this period do not always make satisfactory wholes. No such problems exist in *Aïda, Otello*, and *Falstaff*, however. In these the dramatic compression of the early works is achieved anew. As he matured, Verdi made his structures more flexible and his accompaniments more expressive, without sacrificing the power of his melodies. The musical achievement of the last operas and the quality of Verdi's dramatic insight in general have long been recognized.

Verdun [vair-duhn'] Verdun is a city on the Meuse River in northeastern France, in the department of Meuse. Its population is 21,516 (1982). The city manufactures metal products and furniture. Verdun has an 11th-century cathedral and a 17th-century town hall now housing a war museum.

Verdun's importance as a commercial center and military stronghold predated the Roman Empire. The Treaty of Verdun, signed there in 843, divided the Carolingian empire. Under French control since 1552, Verdun was a strategic fortress during the Franco-Prussian War (1870–71). It was the site of one of the longest and bloodiest battles of World War I, the Battle of Verdun (Feb. 21–Nov. 26, 1916). The city was captured by the Germans in World War II (1940) and liberated by the Americans in 1944. Verdun has been largely rebuilt.

Verdun, Battle of see WORLD WAR I

Verdun, Treaty of The Treaty of Verdun (Aug. 10, 843) divided Charlemagne's Frankish Empire among the three sons of LOUIS I (Louis the Pious). The divisions coincided roughly with later national boundaries in Europe: CHARLES II (Charles the Bald) received lands corresponding to most of modern France; LOUIS THE GERMAN gained the lands east of the Rhine River (Germany); and LOTHAIR I, the eldest, took the imperial title and the Lombard kingdom (Italy) and lands to the north.

Verga, Giovanni [vair'-gah]   The finest Italian novelist of the late 19th century, Giovanni Verga, b. Sept. 2, 1840, d. Jan. 27, 1922, wrote realistic novels that caused him to be compared with Flaubert and Zola. His mature works depict—in a simple, naturalistic style that became associated with the term *verismo*—the life of impoverished Sicilian peasants. For example, his masterpiece, *The House by the Medlar Tree* (1881; Eng. trans., 1890), describes the futile efforts of a fishing family to better their lives. Italy's veristic theater was initiated by Verga's play *Rustic Chivalry* (1884; Eng. trans., 1955), on which Pietro Mascagni later based his opera *Cavalleria Rusticana* (1889).

Vergil [vur'-jil]   The great Roman poet Vergil (also spelled Virgil) was born Publius Vergilius Maro on Oct. 15, 70 BC in Andes, a village near Mantua in northern Italy. Vergil spent his childhood on his father's farm and was educated at Cremona, Milan, and then Rome, where he studied rhetoric. When civil war broke out in 49 BC, he retired to Naples, where he studied philosophy with the Epicurean Siro.

Beginning in 45 BC, encouraged by the statesman Pollio, Vergil spent eight or ten years composing the *Eclogues*, which were adapted to the stage as mimes, and thus made him a popular, if elusive, figure. After the publication of the *Eclogues*, Vergil joined the literary circle of Gaius Maecenas, which would later include the poets Horace and Propertius. Over a period of seven years he wrote the *Georgics*, a didactic poem on farming. The last years of Vergil's life were devoted to writing his epic poem, the AENEID. He died in Brundisium on Sept. 21, 19 BC, after catching a fever on a trip to Greece and Asia, during which he had intended to complete the *Aeneid*. Before setting out on the voyage, Vergil had asked that the *Aeneid* be destroyed if anything should happen to him before the poem was complete, but the emperor Augustus overturned the request and had it published.

The *Eclogues*, written from 45 to 37 (or 35) BC, were praised for the quiet beauty and charm with which they captured the pastoral landscape. Vergil arranged these ten poems to fit the design of the book as a whole. Poems of Theocritus provide a model for some of the Eclogues, which depict an idyllic Arcadia, with Roman political concerns and real people in pastoral guise intruding on the peaceful setting. The fourth Eclogue prophesies a new golden age that will begin with the birth of an unnamed child.

The *Georgics*, written from 36 to 29 BC, is a poem in four books purporting to teach farming. The influence of

Hesiod, Aratus, Callimachus, Varro, and Lucretius, as well as other poets in lesser degree, is evident in the poem. Vergil weaves together his diverse materials into a stunning creation that has been compared by many to a musical composition. Masterfully balancing the somber and the joyous, he evokes a love of the land that has seldom, if ever, been matched. Italy emerges as the "Saturnian land," fertile and varied in its produce, the beautiful land over which Saturnus ruled during the golden age. The horror of disease, embodied in the ravages of a plague, is relieved by the picture of the light and joyous bees, whose cultivation is said to have resulted in the tragedy of Orpheus and Eurydice. The poem ends with Aristaeus appeasing the offended deities and in the process discovering the art of beekeeping.

The *Aeneid* ("the story of Aeneas"), written from 26 to 19 BC, became the national epic. Vergil succeeded in unifying around the figure of Aeneas the theme of Homer's *Odyssey* (the search for a new home) in the first six books and that of the *Iliad* (the war and final reconciliation of the Trojans and the Latins) in the last six, with multiple correspondences between the two halves.

Vergil's greatness was recognized in his own lifetime, and in subsequent ages he was viewed as the supreme poet, orator, philosopher, prophet, and theologian. Copies of the *Aeneid* were placed in temples for consultation. In 4th-century Rome the pagan opposition to the church used Vergil as its Bible, and Fulgentius turned the *Aeneid* into an allegory of the stages of human life. Dante made Vergil his guide in the *Divine Comedy*. More recent scholarship has emphasized Vergil's art of cumulative imagery, his use of language, and the music of his hexameters: "the stateliest measure ever moulded by the lips of man" (Tennyson).

verismo [vair-ees'-moh]   Verismo (Italian for "realism"; sometimes Anglicized as *verism*), an artistic movement originating in the late 19th century, aimed at a realistic representation of contemporary life among ordinary people. The term is used for Italian opera of the period, which often featured violent plots and sordid surroundings resulting in melodrama that exploited individual moments of crisis at the expense of structural development and unity. The "pretty" tunes and virtuoso arias of operatic tradition were abandoned in favor of terser, less symmetrical melodies. Well-known examples of verismo operas include Mascagni's *Cavalleria Rusticana* (1890), Leoncavallo's *Pagliacci* (1892), and Charpentier's *Louise* (1900). Some of Puccini's operas also show the influence of verismo.

Verlaine, Paul [vair-len']   Paul Marie Verlaine, b. Metz, France, Mar. 30, 1844, d. Jan. 8, 1896, was one of France's finest symbolist poets, although he did not accept the designation himself. As a poet he was first associated with the PARNASSIANS, then with DECADENCE. In youth he was already troubled by the alcoholism and instability that were to torment his life. His marriage

(1870) to the teenage Mathilde Mauté ended in separation after he began a homosexual relationship with the poet Arthur RIMBAUD.

A bohemian figure, Verlaine was one of the most gifted writers of his age and, after his return to Catholicism in 1874, he wrote some of the century's most remarkable religious poetry, such as the sonnet sequence in *Sagesse* beginning "Mon Dieu m'a dit: Mon fils, il faut m'aimer" ("God said to me: My son, you must love me."). His limpid lyricism makes him one of the major French poets of the modern period.

In his first volume of verse, *Poèmes saturniens* (Saturnine Poems, 1866), Verlaine's musical gift is already apparent. In *Fêtes galantes* (1869) he is inspired in part by French painting of the 18th century. His later volumes, *La Bonne Chanson* (The Good Song, 1870), *Romances sans paroles* (Songs without Words, 1874), and *Sagesse* (Wisdom, 1881), contain many of his most exquisite and best-known poems. *Jadis et naguère* (Once upon a Time and Not Long Ago, 1885) contains his "Art poétique," which emphasizes the music of poetry, stresses nuance, and calls for the union of the vague with the precise. Verlaine's later collections of poems are of poorer quality. Among his prose writings are *Les Poètes maudits* (The Accursed Poets, 1884), *Mémoires d'un veuf* (Memoirs of a Widower, 1886), *Mes hôpitaux* (My Hospitals, 1891), *Mes prisons* (My Prisons, 1893), and *Confessions* (1895; Eng. trans., 1950). He died in a public infirmary and was buried in the Batignolles Cemetery in Paris.

See also: SYMBOLISM (literature).

In Jan Vermeer's Young Woman Standing at a Virginal *(c.1671) the artist has transformed a genre scene into a timeless, balanced composition through the meticulous placement of objects and a subtle distribution of color. (National Gallery, London.)*

Vermeer, Jan [vur-mayr']   Jan or Johannes Vermeer van Delft, b. October 1632, d. December 1675, a Dutch genre painter who lived and worked in Delft, created some of the most exquisite paintings in Western art. His works are rare. Of the 35 or 36 paintings attributed to him, most portray figures in interiors. All his works are admired for the sensitivity with which he rendered effects of light and color and for the poetic quality of his images.

Vermeer's earliest signed and dated painting, *The Procuress* (1656; Gemäldegalerie Alte Meister, Dresden), is thematically related to a Dirck van Baburen painting that Vermeer owned and that appears in the background of two of his own paintings. During the late 1650s he began to place a new emphasis on depicting figures within carefully composed interior spaces. Other Dutch painters painted similar scenes, but they were less concerned with the articulation of the space than with the description of the figures and their actions. In early paintings such as *The Milkmaid* (c.1658; Rijksmuseum, Amsterdam), Vermeer struck a delicate balance between the compositional and figural elements, and he achieved highly sensuous surface effects by applying paint thickly and modeling his forms with firm strokes. Later he turned to thinner combinations of glazes to obtain the subtler and more transparent surfaces displayed in paintings such as *Woman with a Water Jug* (c.1664–65; Metropolitan Museum of Art, New York City).

A keen sensitivity to the effects of light and color and an interest in defining precise spatial relationships probably encouraged Vermeer to experiment with the camera obscura, an optical device that could project the image of objects placed before it. Although he may have sought to depict the camera's effects in his *View of Delft* (c.1660; Mauritshuis, The Hague), it is unlikely that Vermeer would have traced such an image, as some have charged. Moralizing references occur in several of Vermeer's works, although they tend to be obscured by the paintings' vibrant realism and their general lack of narrative elements. In his *Love Letter* (c.1670; Rijksmuseum, Amsterdam), a late painting in which the spatial environment becomes more complex and the figures appear more doll-like than in his earlier works, he includes on the back wall a painting of a boat at sea. Because this image was based on a contemporary emblem warning of the perils of love, it was clearly intended to add significance to the figures in the room.

Vermigli, Pietro Martire [vair-meel'-yee]   The Italian reformer and theologian Pietro Vermigli (Peter Martyr), b. May 8, 1500, d. Nov. 12, 1562, helped in the preparation of the English Book of Common Prayer. An abbot in the Augustinian order, he became active in the Reformation. He moved to England in 1547 by invitation of Archbishop Thomas Cranmer and became professor of divinity at Oxford. In 1549 he took part in a famous disputation on the nature of the Eucharist. Imprisoned after the accession (1553) of the Catholic queen Mary, Vermigli was allowed to escape. He became (1556) a professor of Hebrew at Zurich.

Vermont   Vermont is the northwesternmost of the New England states. Its name is derived from the French phrase *monts verts*, "green mountains," just as its capital, MONTPELIER, is named for the French city of Montpellier. Samuel de Champlain in 1609 was the first European to explore the region, and Lake Champlain in the northwestern part of the state bears his name. To the east the Connecticut River follows Vermont's 322-km (200-mi) border with New Hampshire. Vermont is bordered by Massachusetts on the south, New York on the west, and the Canadian province of Quebec on the north.

The only New England state without a seacoast, Vermont traditionally has been the region's most important agricultural state. Since World War II, however, Vermont's economy has become increasingly diversified, with recreation and manufacturing assuming greater importance.

Vermont was admitted to the Union as the 14th state on Mar. 4, 1791, after having existed as an independent republic for 14 years.

Land and Resources

Vermont has 80 peaks exceeding 900 m (3,000 ft). The highest point, Mount Mansfield (1,339 m/4,393 ft), lies about 30 km (19 mi) almost due east of Burlington. Occupying much of northwestern Vermont, the Champlain Valley lies quite flat close to Lake Champlain. Toward the mountains to the east, relief gradually increases, and dairy farming gives way to other land uses.

The narrow Valley of Vermont, located south of the Champlain Valley, was a major settlement route into Vermont. Marble is quarried in the north.

The Taconic Mountains extend along the border with New York west of the Valley of Vermont. The highest summit is Mount Equinox near Manchester (1,163 m/3,816 ft). Slate is quarried along the western side. To the east of the valleys and extending the entire length of the state, forming its backbone, are the GREEN MOUNTAINS.

The Vermont Piedmont occupies most of the eastern portion of the state and includes the valleys of the White, West, and Black rivers, all of which drain into the Connecticut. With elevations less than 600 m (2,000 ft), the piedmont was an important area of early hill farming.

The Northeastern Highlands region, often referred to as the Northeast Kingdom, is a small, wild, and isolated mountainous area north of St. Johnsbury. The highest summit is Gore Mountain (approximately 1,000 m/3,330 ft), and nearly all of the region lies above 600 m (2,000 ft).

Soils. Although Vermont soils generally are acid podzol

AT A GLANCE

VERMONT

Land: Area: 24,903 km² (9,615 mi²); rank: 45th. Capital: Montpelier (1990 pop., 8,247). Largest city: Burlington (1990 pop., 39,127). Counties: 14. Elevations: highest—1,339 m (4,393 ft), at Mount Mansfield; lowest—29 m (95 ft), at Lake Champlain.

People: Population (1990): 564,964; rank: 48th; density: 23.5 persons per km² (60.8 per mi²). Distribution (1990): 32.2% urban, 67.8% rural. Average annual change (1980–90): +1%.

Government (1993): Governor: Howard Dean, Democrat. U.S. Congress: Senate—1 Democrat, 1 Republican; House—1 Independent. Electoral college votes: 3. State legislature: 30 senators, 150 representatives.

Economy: State personal income (1989): $9.3 billion; rank: 48th. Median family income (1989): $34,780; rank: 21st. Agriculture: income (1989)—$426 million. Lumber production (1991): 186 million board feet. Mining (nonfuel): value (1988)—$77 million. Manufacturing: value added (1987)—$2.5 billion. Services: value (1987)—$2.2 billion.

Miscellany: Statehood: Mar. 4, 1791; the 14th state. Nickname: Green Mountain State; tree: sugar maple; motto: Freedom and Unity; song: "Hail, Vermont!"

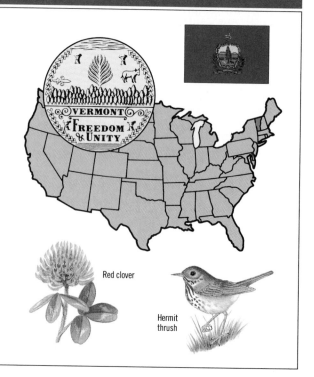

Red clover

Hermit thrush

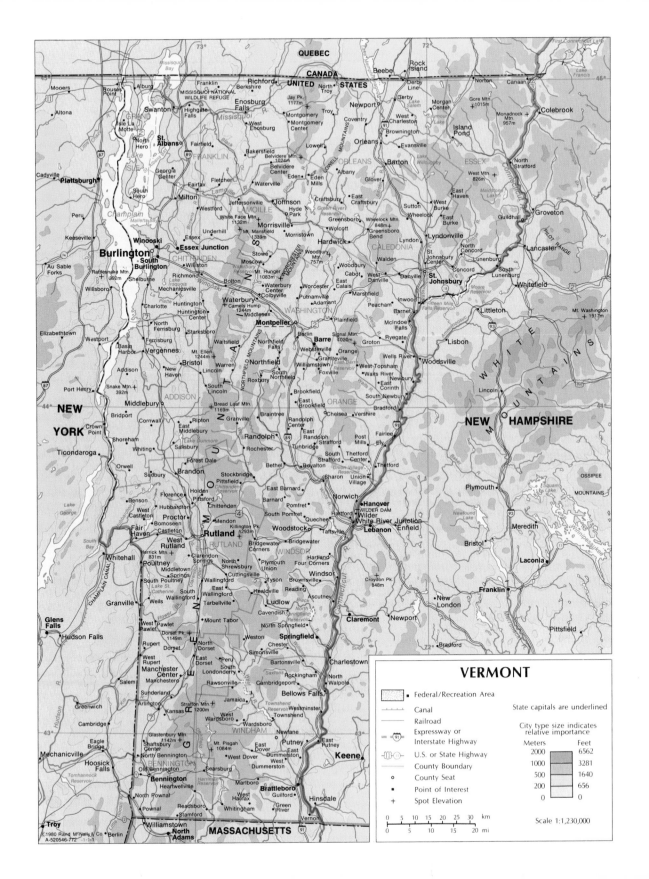

VERMONT

Federal/Recreation Area

Canal

Railroad

Expressway or
Interstate Highway

U.S. or State Highway

County Boundary

County Seat

Point of Interest

Spot Elevation

State capitals are underlined

City type size indicates
relative importance

Meters	Feet
2000	6562
1000	3281
500	1640
200	656
0	0

Scale 1:1,230,000

©1980 Rand McNally & Co.
A-520546-772   1-1-1

A sugar maple near Middlesex, a town along the Winooski River, is tapped for its sap, which is collected in buckets, transferred to a horse-drawn tank (background), *and boiled down into syrup.*

and podzolic, local relief differences result in wide variations. Nowhere are soils particularly fertile.

Rivers and Lakes. Much of the water from southwestern Vermont flows into the Hudson River; runoff in western Vermont drains into Lake Champlain (see CHAMPLAIN, LAKE), and thence into the St. Lawrence; and eastern Vermont lies within the CONNECTICUT RIVER drainage basin. The longest river in Vermont, Otter Creek in the Champlain Valley, extends only about 160 km (100 mi). After Lake Champlain (total area, 1,270 km²/490 mi²)—which is shared by New York State and Canada and is one of the largest freshwater lakes in the United States—Vermont's largest lake is Lake Memphremagog, partly in Canada.

Climate. Because of its inland location, Vermont receives little climatic impact from the Atlantic Ocean. Precipitation patterns mostly reflect elevation. The Champlain Valley receives an average of 813 mm (32 in) annually, whereas Somerset, at an elevation of 634 m (2,080 ft) in the Green Mountains of southern Vermont, receives more than 1,321 mm (52 in), and mountain summits even more, with snowfall totals of 3,810 mm (150 in) not uncommon. The average January temperature for the state is −8° C (18° F), whereas the July temperature averages 19° C (67° F).

Vegetation and Animal Life. Most of Vermont supports a natural vegetation of northern hardwoods, primarily birch, beech, and maple. Evergreens, especially balsam fir and spruce, predominate at higher elevations. White cedar is found in the Champlain Valley, as are stands of oak and hickory. About 70% of Vermont is forested.

White-tailed deer, weasels, shrews, red foxes, Canadian lynx, bobcats, beavers, porcupines, and snowshoe rabbits abound. Fishers, a species of marten, are becoming common once again, as are coyotes. Moose occasionally enter the state. About 300 black bears are shot annually. Spruce grouse and partridge furnish good hunting in autumn, and wild turkeys have been established in the southwestern part of the state.

Environment. Because of its proximity to large urban areas of the Northeast, Vermont has been experiencing considerable pressure on its natural resources. In response the legislature in 1970 passed one of the nation's most comprehensive environmental protection laws.

People

Vermont is the most rural state in the country, and most of the state's population live in places with fewer than 2,500 inhabitants or in isolated rural dwellings.

Only since 1960 has Vermont's population been growing in any significant way. In the 110 years between 1850 and 1960 the population went from 314,120 to 389,881, an increase of 24%. Since 1960 the rate of increase has been substantially greater. This recent growth (10.5% from 1980 to 1990, for example) has been the result of net in-migration in addition to natural increase. Vermont therefore is fast becoming an extension of the Atlantic coast urban region.

The most significant ethnic minority are French Americans. Welsh are uniquely concentrated in the slate districts in southwestern Vermont, and Italians are concentrated in the Barre granite area.

About 1% of the state's population are classed as black, Hispanic, Asian, or American Indian.

BURLINGTON remains Vermont's largest city, followed by RUTLAND, Essex Town and Essex Junction, BENNINGTON, Colchester, South Burlington, Brattleboro, Springfield, BARRE, and Montpelier.

Education. MIDDLEBURY COLLEGE and BENNINGTON COLLEGE are Vermont's best known private institutions of higher education. The University of Vermont, in Burlington, was founded in 1791. Primary and secondary education is carried out by Vermont's public and private or parochial schools.

Culture. The Shelburne Museum possesses one of the largest collections of Americana in the country and also boasts the sidewheel steamer *Ticonderoga*. The Athenaeum in St. Johnsbury is famous for its collection of 19th-century paintings. The American Precision Museum at Windsor exhibits the development of machine tools; and St. Johnsbury has the Fairbanks Museum and Planetarium. The Vermont Museum, in Montpelier, features an outstanding library and collections of Vermontiana.

The state has three symphony orchestras—the Vermont Symphony, the Vermont Philharmonic, and the University of Vermont Symphony.

Historical Sites and Recreational Areas. The Bennington Battle Monument dominates the town's skyline, and at East Hubbardton are the Hubbardton Battlefield and Museum. Windsor has the Old Constitution House, where Vermont's first constitution was written in 1777. The Revolutionary War fortifications on Mount Independence in Orwell, across from Fort Ticonderoga, N.Y., have been recently excavated.

The Green Mountain National Forest manages the thousands of hectares traversed by the APPALACHIAN TRAIL and the Long Trail. The Lye Brook and Bristol Cliffs wilderness areas also afford primitive solitude. Thousands of tourists visit the state's ski resorts.

Communications. Vermont has numerous AM and FM radio stations and several television broadcasting facilities. There are also cable television systems in operation in the state. Of the state's daily newspapers, the *Burlington Free Press* and the *Rutland Herald* have the largest circulations.

Economic Activity

Since World War II manufacturing and tourism have replaced agriculture as the state's economic mainstays.

Agriculture. Agriculture provides only a small percentage of Vermont's gross state product. Nevertheless, Vermont is an important agricultural state in New England, particularly in the area of dairy farming. Other valuable livestock products include beef cattle and calves, chickens, hogs, and turkeys.

Other agricultural products are derived from a few small truck farms. Principal products include maple syrup, Christmas trees, and potatoes. Apple orchards are important along the Lake Champlain shoreline and also near Brattleboro and Bennington.

Manufacturing and Energy. Among Vermont's leading industry groups are electrical and electronic equipment, food and food products, nonelectrical machinery, fabricated metal products, paper and paper products, printing and publishing, and lumber and wood products. Because the state lacks fossil-fuel resources, electrical bills in Vermont are higher than in many other states. The bulk of Vermont's electrical power is generated by nuclear energy. The second greatest source of energy is hydroelectricity, with the remainder coming from coal and petroleum.

Forestry and Fishing. About one-quarter of the state's manufacturing enterprises depend on the lumber industry. Furniture plants and small paper mills, small and medium-sized sawmills, and woodenware manufacturing plants are scattered across the state. Maple is the most valuable hardwood tree; softwoods of value include spruce and pine.

Workers prepare to hoist a slab of granite at the Wells-Lamson quarry near Barre. Situated in Washington County in central Vermont, Barre is the center of an area with the largest granite quarries in the United States.

Vermont has almost no commercial fishing, but many out-of-state visitors fish the state's lakes and mountain streams.

Mining. Mining in Vermont is limited to nonmetallic products, especially granite, marble, asbestos, slate, talc, and clay. The largest granite quarries in the United States are near Barre.

Transportation. Most freight transportation within the state is by truck. The Central Vermont, the state's leading rail carrier, however, is an important through-freight link between eastern Canada and the Atlantic seaboard. Lake Champlain provides barge transportation through canals to both the south and north.

Government and Politics

The state legislature consists of a senate, with 30 members, and a house of representatives, with 150 members. All state legislators are elected to 2-year terms, as is the governor.

Vermont has counties, cities, organized towns, unorganized towns, incorporated villages, and certain other areas called gores and grants. Local government is centered in towns; each town has its annual TOWN MEETING the first Tuesday in March, at which time the governing selectmen and other town officials are elected.

In national politics Vermont almost always votes Republican.

History

When Samuel de CHAMPLAIN traversed the lake that bears his name in 1609, Vermont was hunting territory for various ALGONQUIN and Iroquois tribes (see IROQUOIS LEAGUE), and Algonquin groups such as the ABNAKI and MAHICAN were probably already permanent inhabitants of western parts of the state.

Pierre de St. Paul, sieur de la Motte, built a blockhouse on Isle la Motte in 1666, and Captain Jacobus de Warm from Albany constructed a trading post on Chimney Point in 1690. A French fort was built on the same site in

Dairy cattle graze on a farm near Strafford, in the east central portion of the state. The majority of Vermont's farms are devoted to dairying and related operations.

1730, and the ruins of its chimneys that stood for years gave the place its unusual name.

Claims of Massachusetts, New Hampshire, and New York. Under the charter of the Massachusetts Bay Colony, Massachusetts had been granted the southern half of Vermont and southwestern New Hampshire, and to protect its settlements the colony erected a series of forts along the Connecticut River. Fort Dummer, the first permanent white settlement in what was to become Vermont, was built in 1724 near the present town of Brattleboro.

In 1741, however, George II ruled invalid Massachusetts's claims in Vermont and New Hampshire and fixed the northern boundary of Massachusetts at its present location. Gov. Benning Wentworth of New Hampshire saw this as an opportunity to grant lands west of the Connecticut River as far as a line about 30 km (20 mi) east of the Hudson River, the western boundary of both Massachusetts and Connecticut. In 1749 he granted the town of Bennington in southwestern Vermont, and subsequently, by 1764, he had granted a total of about 135 towns, making Vermont known as the "New Hampshire Grants."

But Wentworth's real-estate activities upset Gov. George Clinton of New York, who claimed that New York extended eastward to the Connecticut River. In 1764, King George III and his council declared "the western banks of the river Connecticut to be the boundary line between the said two provinces of New Hampshire and New York." New York thereupon declared all of Wentworth's grants null and void and began to make new grants to new grantees of lands already held and settled under New Hampshire title.

Independence and Statehood. Settlers were fearful of losing their lands, and violent outbreaks against New York authority were common, especially in western Vermont, where the GREEN MOUNTAIN BOYS organized by Ethan ALLEN in 1770–71 harassed holders of Vermont land with New York titles. As the only organized military group in Vermont, the Boys later were able to support the cause of the colonies against the British, notably by helping Benedict Arnold capture the British fortress at Ticonderoga in 1775.

With the Declaration of Independence on July 4, 1776, Vermont settlers pondered their future. At a convention at Windsor on July 2–8, 1777, 70 delegates unanimously adopted a constitution, and Vermont became the independent Republic of New Connecticut, alias Vermont, but the name *New Connecticut* was rarely used. After 14 years as an independent republic, Vermont was admitted to the Union as the 14th state on Mar. 4, 1791.

The 19th Century. During the War of 1812, America's first battleship, the *Saratoga*, built at Vergennes, was sent into action under Commodore Thomas MACDONOUGH on Lake Champlain. The Battle of Plattsburgh in September 1814 gave Americans control of the lake.

The opening (1823) of the Champlain Canal connecting Lake Champlain to the Hudson River made it possible for Vermont farmers to ship goods to New York City, stimulating agriculture and wool production, until the 1860s when dairy farming began to dominate. By the early 20th century, manufacturing replaced agriculture as the dominant economic activity.

A New Look. Today retirees, second-home owners, and new resident commuters from Connecticut, New York, and Massachusetts are settling in the state. The population is growing fast through migration, tourism is booming, and the stability and quiet so characteristic of more than 175 years of statehood is rapidly disappearing from the Green Mountain State.

---

vermouth   Vermouth is an alcoholic beverage with a white-wine base that is flavored with seeds, herbs, barks, flowers, and spices, according to each manufacturer's secret recipe. The drink is used primarily as an aperitif, or as an ingredient in martinis and manhattans. Sweet vermouth, also called Italian vermouth, is either *russo* (red) or *bianco* (white), whereas dry, or French, vermouth is white—pale amber, actually.

Vermouth is made by adding sugar syrup or *mistelle* (unfermented grape juice stabilized with brandy) to ordinary white wine. The herbs and flavorings that give the drink its characteristic flavor are macerated and steeped in alcohol, which is combined with the wine. Herbs used include cinnamon, rhubarb, nutmeg, cloves, quinine, and anise; as many as 50 herbs and flavorings may be included in the recipe. The flavored alcohol is added to the wine, and this fortified wine is then blended, clarified, pasteurized, refrigerated, filtered, stored for a few months, and bottled. The name is thought to derive from *wermut*, the German name for "wormwood," because blossoms of the wormwood plant, *Artemisia absinthium*, have been the BITTERS traditionally used in vermouth.

Verne, Jules [vurn]   The French novelist Jules Verne, b. Feb. 8, 1828, d. Mar. 24, 1905, almost single-handedly invented science fiction. He was educated in law but soon devoted himself to writing for the stage. The publi-

Jules Verne, a French science-fiction writer, anticipated many aspects of 20th-century technology in his popular novels. The concept of a powered submarine was popularized by his Twenty Thousand Leagues Under the Sea *(1870), and several peculiarities of space travel, notably weightlessness, are first mentioned in* From the Earth to the Moon *(1865).*

cation of *Five Weeks in a Balloon* (1863; Eng. trans., 1869) revealed his talent for stories of imaginary journeys. Verne had the ability to popularize science and created fantasies depicting journeys to the center of the earth, to the moon by rocket ship, and through the ocean by submarine; some of these tales have proved remarkably prophetic.

His creations have inspired filmmakers: TWENTY THOUSAND LEAGUES UNDER THE SEA (1870; Eng. trans., 1873), the story of the diabolical Captain Nemo and his submarine, and *Around the World in Eighty Days* (1873; Eng. trans., 1873) became successful movies in 1954 and 1956, respectively. The second of these works concerns Phileas Fogg, who, with his servant Passepartout, wagers that he can make what seemed in 1873 an impossibly fast journey. Mixing humor, adventure, and scientific discovery, it is probably Verne's best-loved work.

The Holy Family with Saint Barbara *(c.1562–70) displays the rich colors and air of opulence typical of Paolo Veronese's work. He was one of the most prolific and popular Venetian artists of the 16th century. (Uffizi, Florence.)*

Vernon, Edward   Edward Vernon, b. Nov. 12, 1684, d. Oct. 30, 1757, a British admiral, was known for his Caribbean exploits against the Spanish during the War of Jenkins's Ear (1739–41). Because he wore a coat of grogram (a coarse silk or silk-mix fabric), his men referred to him as "Old Grog." This nickname ("grog") was given to the rum-and-water mixture that he issued to them to control drunkenness. George Washington's family estate, Mount Vernon, was named for him.

Verona [vay-roh'-nah]   Verona, a city in northeastern Italy, is situated on the Adige River about 100 km (60 mi) west of Venice and has a population of 261,947 (1983 est.). Located at a major highway junction and served by railroads, Verona is an agricultural market town. The city's industries manufacture paper, textiles, leather goods, pharmaceuticals, chemicals, and metal products. Verona is especially known for its Soave, Bardolino, and Valpolicella wines. Historic sites include a Roman amphitheater and ruins of two gateways (1st century AD), the Church of Santo Zeno Maggiore (rebuilt 12th–13th centuries), the cathedral (12th–15th centuries), the Castel Vecchio (1354), and the Loggia del Consiglio (15th century).

Verona became a Roman colony (89 BC) and prospered because of its key location. Ruled in the early Middle Ages by Ostrogoths, Lombards, and Franks, Verona became a free commune in the 12th century. Prosperous and powerful under the SCALA family (1260–1387), Verona then fell into decline. It was ruled by Milan (1387–1405), Venice (1405–1797), and Austria (1797–1866), until it joined a united Italy.

Veronese, Paolo [vay-roh-nay'-zay]   Together with Titian and Tintoretto, Paolo Caliari, c.1528–1588, called Il Veronese for his birthplace of Verona, dominated Venetian painting of the 16th century. Veronese created a sensation in Venice with the brilliant color and illusionistic impact of the ceiling panels he painted (1553) for the

Room of the Council of Ten and other chambers in the Doge's Palace. In 1555 he undertook the decoration of the Church of San Sebastiano in Venice, which occupied him and his workshop intermittently for a decade. The San Sebastiano paintings exemplify Veronese's religious works and show his ability to integrate painting and architecture, whether real or fictive, in a single decorative ensemble. This talent is best seen in his masterpiece, the interior of the Villa Barbaro (now Villa Volpi) at Maser, which had been designed by Andrea Palladio. The trompe l'oeil (illusionist) architecture, landscapes, and human figures with which Veronese covered the villa's interiors recall the similar decorations of ancient country houses. Typical of this colorful blend of classical quotation and inspired illusionism is the ceiling fresco called *Abundance, Fortitude, and Envy* (c.1561), an ingenious masterpiece of *di sotto in su* ("from below looking up") perspective.

The theatrical quality of much of Veronese's art is exemplified in the series of supper scenes he painted for various monastic refectories in Venice and outlying areas. The most famous of these is his *Feast in the House of the Levi* (1573; Accademia, Venice), in which dozens of life-size figures populate a loggia that stretches in three open bays across the painting's 13-m (42-ft) width. Behind the figures an elaborate perspective opens like a stage set onto a clear blue sky. Although Christ and other familiar New Testament characters occupy the center, the rest of the composition is crowded with exotic characters not mentioned in the biblical text. The inclusion of these unorthodox details caused Veronese to be called before the Inquisition to defend his painting against charges that it lacked the requisite seriousness and piety for a depiction of the Last Supper. Given three months to modify the composition, the painter chose to adopt the present title, which indicates a less elevated theme. The very fact that

Veronese's painting caused a stir indicates the power of his greatest work and the great reputation he had achieved. His works exerted a profound influence on baroque artists such as Pietro da Cortona and on such rococo artists as Giovanni Battista Tiepolo.

Verrazano, Giovanni da [vair-raht-sah'-noh]

An Italian navigator and explorer in France's service, Giovanni da Verrazano, c.1485–c.1528, sailed up the east coast of North America in 1524 and discovered New York and Narragansett bays. Commissioned by King Francis I that year to search for a western sea route to China, he explored from around Cape Fear, N.C., to at least the Maine coast and mistook either Delaware or Chesapeake Bay for the opening to the Pacific Ocean. In 1528, Verrazano crossed the Atlantic again, heading for Central America. He never returned. According to one report, Verrazano was killed by Indians. The bridge connecting Staten Island, N.Y., and Long Island, N.Y., is named for him.

Verrazano-Narrows Bridge   see BRIDGE (engineering)

Verrocchio, Andrea del [vair-rohk'-kee-oh]

Andrea di Michele di Francesco di Cioni, called Andrea del Verrocchio, b. 1435, d. Oct. 7, 1488, was one of the most accomplished Florentine sculptors of the Early Renaissance and the head of an important workshop that numbered among its assistants Leonardo da Vinci, Lorenzo di Credi, and probably Perugino. Verrocchio apparently succeeded Donatello as the principal sculptor of the Medici family. His first major work for them was the tomb of Piero and Giovanni de'Medici (completed 1472; San Lorenzo, Florence); during the 1460s and '70s he fulfilled commissions from Lorenzo de'Medici for a bronze *David* (Bargello, Florence), the bronze *Putto with a Dolphin* (Palazzo Vecchio, Florence), and the *Resurrection* (Palazzo Vecchio) in terra-cotta relief. The Medici tomb is a virtuoso work of bronze and marble, but the other three pieces all invite comparison with Donatello in both the choice and interpretation of subject matter. The studied characterization of the warriors' varied reactions in the *Resurrection*, for example, seems a deliberate commentary on Donatello's own dramatic reliefs. These early efforts also prefigure Verrocchio's later concern with precise detail, technical virtuosity, and dramatic effects.

Verrocchio's major public work in Florence is the *Doubting of Thomas* (c.1465–83), a life-size group cast in bronze and placed in a niche at Or San Michele. While he was still working on this group Verrocchio was summoned (c.1483) to Venice to create an equestrian monument to the condottiere (mercenary captain) Bartolommeo Colleoni; a work of great dramatic power, it was completed (1495) after Verrocchio's death by the Venetian sculptor Alessandro Leopardi.

Although Verrocchio's workshop also produced a great number of paintings, only one, the Pistoia altarpiece (1478–85; Duomo, Pistoia), is clearly documented. The

Baptism of Christ (c.1470; Uffizi, Florence) bears clear evidence of Verrocchio's hand and also that of the young Leonardo.

Versailles [vair-sy']

Versailles, a city in north central France, is situated about 18 km (11 mi) southwest of Paris. The population is 91,494 (1982). Metal products, brandy, and footwear are manufactured locally. The city is an episcopal see as well as a local administrative and military center, and it has a national agricultural research station. Proximity to Paris makes Versailles a dormitory suburb. The economy, however, is chiefly based on tourists drawn by Louis XIV's world-renowned palace at Versailles, its grounds, and associated buildings.

Many historic events have taken place in Versailles. The declaration ending hostilities between the United States and Great Britain was signed there in 1783. The city served as headquarters of the German armies attacking Paris during the Franco-Prussian War (1870–71), and William I was crowned (1871) emperor of Germany in the palace. Versailles was the seat of the Allied War Council during World War I, and the Treaty of Versailles ending the war was signed in the Hall of Mirrors on June 28, 1919. The city was Allied General Headquarters (1944–45) in World War II.

Versailles, Palace of

The Palace of Versailles, for more than 100 years (1682–1790) the official residence of the kings of France, was the most elegant and sumptuous palace in Europe. Originally a royal hunting lodge, the Versailles complex was rebuilt and greatly expanded (from 1669) by King Louis XIV, who commissioned Louis LE VAU to create a great palace that would provide a suitable setting for the ceremonies of the royal court. Le Vau's splendid monument to the French classical style of the mid-17th century is complemented by the extraordinary formal GARDENS laid out by André Le Nôtre. The classicist Charles LE BRUN supervised the decoration of the palace's interior, which retains its sumptuous and grandiose appearance despite the melting down (1689) of the original silver furniture to pay for Louis XIV's wars. Typical of the lavishness of the interior decoration is the dazzling and hugely expensive Hall of Mirrors (begun 1678).

Le Vau's original design was expanded by Jules HARDOUIN-MANSART, who, with Robert de COTTE, designed the impressive Royal Chapel (1689–1710). The last major addition (1757–70) to the palace was Ange Jacques Gabriel's (see GABRIEL family) opera house, which is famous for its illusionistic mirrors. After the French Revolution, during which the palace was stripped of most of its furnishings, Versailles gave way to the Tuileries in Paris as the royal residence.

See also: BAROQUE ART AND ARCHITECTURE; FURNITURE; ROCOCO STYLE.

Versailles, Treaty of   see PARIS PEACE CONFERENCE

verse, free   see VERSIFICATION

versification   Versification is the art or practice of making verse. It is based on the principles of prosody, prosody being the theory of which versification is the practice. Discussion of either term leads to a consideration of those regular recurrences—rhyme, meter, stanza form—that distinguish verse from prose, and of those auxiliary recurrences and sound devices—alliteration, assonance, onomatopoeia (see FIGURES OF SPEECH)—found in both prose and verse but more frequently in verse.

Accent or Stress. In English the basis of verse is accent or stress. In all words of more than a syllable, one syllable is pronounced with more emphasis than the others; in all sentences, some words receive more emphasis than others. This emphasis—a combination of pitch, loudness, duration, and timbre—is accent or stress. Although many degrees of stress occur in any utterance, most prosodists are content to recognize not more than four levels, which for purposes of scansion, or metrical analysis, may be reduced to two—stressed and unstressed.

Meter. English prosody commonly recognizes four principal meters—iambic, trochaic, anapestic, dactylic—and eight line lengths—monometer, dimeter, trimeter, tetrameter, pentameter, hexameter, heptameter, octameter. The meters are named after the four principal kinds of feet: the iamb, consisting of an unstressed followed by a stressed syllable (x /); the trochee (/ x); the anapest (x x /); and the dactyl (/ x x).

Metrical patterning is seldom completely regular, but it must be sufficiently constant so that beneath the actual rhythm an identifiable paradigm can be heard. If a poem is said to be written in iambic pentameter, all of its lines will consist of five feet, and a majority of the feet will be iambs. Yet variation is important, for perfect regularity soon becomes monotonous, and in good verse, deviations from regularity help convey meaning.

Of the numerous ways of giving variation to verse, the most obvious is the use of substitute feet—for instance, a trochee for an iamb, or a spondee (//) for any of the other types. Extra unaccented syllables may also be added at the ends or beginnings of lines, and the weights of stressed or unstressed feet may vary considerably. A pronounced difference of effect exists between verse that is heavily end-stopped and verse that is run-on or enjambed in which the sense of one line flows without interruption into the next. Considerable variation may also be obtained by the use and positioning of the internal pause, or caesura. Such pauses, commanded by the grammatical or rhetorical shape of the sentence, may or may not be indicated by punctuation, but they affect the rhythm without affecting the meter.

Blank Verse. The essential difference between verse and prose is meter; other, optional differences are rhyme and stanza form. Indeed, so much of the greatest English poetry has been written in unrhymed iambic pentameter that it has been given a special name, BLANK VERSE. This is the meter Shakespeare used in his tragedies, Milton in his two epics, and Wordsworth, Keats, Tennyson, and Robert Frost in some of their finest poems.

Rhyme and Stanza Form. Rhyme is a feature of versification that by its recurrence at the ends of lines, regularly or irregularly arranged, further differentiates verse from prose; it can be used effectively to give musicality to the verse, to organize the lines, and to emphasize the words on which the rhymes fall. Like meter, rhyme can be both a formal and an expressive feature of verse. In addition, it can be used in conjunction with meter to organize a poem into a third pattern of recurrence—the stanza.

A stanza is a group of lines of fixed number, meter, and rhyme pattern, repeated throughout a poem. Many traditional stanza forms have special names. For example, ballad meter consists of four alternating iambic tetrameter and trimeter lines with a rhyme scheme of *a b c b*, whereas a Spenserian stanza consists of eight lines of iambic pentameter plus a ninth line of iambic hexameter, the whole having a rhyme scheme of *a b a b b c b c c*. Elegiac stanzas, rhyme royal, and ottava rima involve only iambic pentameter, with four, seven, and eight lines, respectively, and rhyme schemes of *a b a b, a b a b b c c,* and *a b a b a b c c.* In addition, meter and rhyme may prescribe the pattern for a whole poem, such as the LIMERICK or English SONNET.

Free Verse. Free verse, the principal vehicle of contemporary poetry, is, by these standards, not verse at all: that is, it is nonmetrical. Its only distinction from rhythmical prose is its arrangement on the page in lines of unequal length, determined by the writer on aesthetic grounds of cadence, breath, sound, or meaning. In prose the lines are of an equal length determined by the printer; thus, free verse has one rhythmical feature that prose lacks, the extra brief pause that usually accompanies a line end. The difference, however, is slight. Yeats divided a passage from Pater's prose into cadenced lines of unequal length and included it in his *Oxford Book of Modern Verse* (1936). It is a poem, but it is not verse in the sense of having identifiable meter.

Poetry. POETRY may be composed in either prose or verse. "Thirty days hath September,/April, June, and November" is verse but not poetry; Melville's *Moby-Dick* is prose but is highly poetic. That *Moby-Dick*, however poetic, is not a poem may be argued; but the issue is complicated by the prose poems of writers as diverse as Amy Lowell, Karl Shapiro, and Russell Edson. Verse and prose are mediums of meaning, and either may be the medium of poetry.

GLOSSARY

Accent   Special emphasis given to a syllable in pronunciation as a result of pitch, loudness, duration, and timbre. Usually used synonymously with stress.

Accentual meter   A meter in which only the number of accents is counted.

Accentual-syllabic meter   A meter in which there is a correspondence between the number of accents and the number of syllables, either two syllables for every accent (as in iambic and trochaic) or three syllables for every accent (as in anapestic and dactylic).

Alexandrine   A line of iambic hexameter.

Alliteration   The repetition of consonant sounds.

Anapest A three-syllable poetic foot accented on the last syllable.

Assonance The repetition of the same vowel sound.

Blank verse Unrhymed iambic pentameter.

Caesura An internal pause in a line, usually but not necessarily marked off by punctuation, which does not affect the meter.

Couplet A pair of lines, usually rhymed and usually having the same meter.

Dactyl A three-syllable poetic foot accented on the first syllable.

Dimeter A line of two feet.

End-stopped line A line followed by a long pause, usually marked off by punctuation.

Enjambment The flowing of the sense from one line into the next without interruption; the use of run-on lines.

Foot A metrical unit containing one stressed syllable and usually one or two unstressed syllables.

Free verse Rhythmical but nonmetrical lines used as a medium for poetry.

Heptameter A line of seven feet.

Heroic couplet A rhyming iambic-pentameter couplet.

Hexameter A line of six feet.

Iamb A two-syllable poetic foot accented on the second syllable.

Meter An ordered pattern of accents; rhythm that can be measured.

Monosyllabic foot A poetic foot containing one syllable only.

Octameter A line of eight feet.

Onomatopoeia The use of words whose sounds imitate their meaning, as *hiss, bang, buzz.*

Pentameter A line of five feet.

Pyrrhic A substitute poetic foot consisting of two unstressed syllables, always followed by a spondee.

Scansion The analysis of meter, usually with the aid of some graphic system of notation.

Spondee A two-syllable substitute poetic foot in which both syllables are accented, but the accent is conceived of as being divided between the two syllables.

Stanza A repeated unit of lines with a prescribed meter and rhyme scheme.

Syllabic meter A form of meter in which syllables only are counted; typical of Japanese verse, as in the haiku, and occasionally used by English and American poets.

Tetrameter A line of four feet.

Trimeter A line of three feet.

Trochee A two-syllable poetic foot accented on the first syllable.

vertebrae see SPINE

vertebrate see CHORDATE

Vertical Takeoff and Landing Aircraft see VTOL

vertigo Vertigo is a hallucination of spinning, either of oneself or of one's environment, that may be experienced as a sensation of imminent loss of consciousness, as a loss of balance without abnormal sensation, or as a vague lightheadedness. It is a subjective symptom or complaint rather than a disease, and it can occur in several physical disorders, including dysfunction of the vestibular organs of the ear (organs of balance), the brain, eyes, gastrointestinal tract, or other organs. It can also occur in the absence of organic disease, as in hyperventilation brought on by anxiety; as a result of alcohol or drug use; or as a result of motion sickness or fear of heights.

Vertov, Dziga [vair'-tuhf] Soviet filmmaker Dziga Vertov, pseudonym of Denis Kaufman, b. Jan. 2 (N.S.), 1896, d. Feb. 12, 1954, revolutionized the production of newsreel and documentary films. Beginning his career in 1918 as a newsreel editor for the Moscow Film Committee, Vertov displayed his new techniques to advantage in a newsreel series he produced (1922–25) and in informational films about Soviet achievements made for the Kino-Glaz group. His full-length documentary features include *The Man with the Movie Camera* (1929) and, following the introduction of sound, *Enthusiasm* (1931), *Three Songs about Lenin* (1934), and *Lullaby* (1937).

Verwoerd, Hendrik F. [fur-vohrt'] Hendrik Frensch Verwoerd, b. Sept. 8, 1901, d. Sept. 6, 1966, prime minister of South Africa (1958–66), was a leading figure in the establishment of APARTHEID in his country. As an infant he emigrated from Holland to South Africa with his parents. He later taught (1927–37) at Stellenbosch University. Verwoerd opposed South Africa's entry into World War II. As minister of native affairs (1950–58), he directed much apartheid legislation through parliament.

In 1958, Verwoerd was elected leader of the National party and prime minister. He played a major part in setting up Bantu "homelands" and separate black universities, but he relinquished the National party's previous policy of repatriating the Indians. His administration suppressed its critics but also carried out major slum-clearance plans and encouraged industrial development in the "homelands." Verwoerd was responsible for turning South Africa into a republic (1961). He was assassinated.

Very Large Array see NATIONAL RADIO ASTRONOMY OBSERVATORY

Vesalius, Andreas [vuh-say'-lee-uhs] Andreas Vesalius, b. Dec. 31, 1514, d. Oct. 15, 1564, was the Flemish anatomist and physician whose pioneering dissections of human cadavers and careful descriptions of human anatomy helped establish modern observational science. He is often called the father of anatomy. His major work, *De humani corporis fabrica* (On the Structure of the Human Body), an illustrated text of human anatomy, was published in 1543.

Vesey, Denmark [vee'-zee] The leader of an American slave revolt in Charleston, S.C., Denmark Vesey, b.

Africa, 1767, d. July 2, 1822, had been owned by a slave-ship captain before he purchased his freedom (1800) with $600 won in a street lottery. As a freedman in Charleston, he worked at carpentry, became a leader of his church, and read antislavery literature. In 1822 he devised an intricate conspiracy for an uprising in Charleston and vicinity. Informers divulged the plot, however, and 35 blacks, including Vesey, were executed.

Vespasian, Roman Emperor [ves-payz'-ee-uhn]

Vespasian, b. Nov. 17, AD 9, d. June 4, 79, Roman emperor (r. 69–79) and founder of the Flavian dynasty (69–96), pacified and strengthened the empire and pursued enlightened domestic policies. In 67 he was given the command against the Jewish rebels. During this campaign the eastern armies proclaimed him emperor (July 69). Having engineered the defeat of Vitellius, the last of the three imperial claimants following the death of NERO in 68, he was confirmed (December 69) by the Senate as emperor.

After satisfactorily ending the Jewish war and a Rhineland revolt, Vespasian turned to domestic reform. He eliminated Nero's treasury deficit through economy and increased taxation, at the same time beginning construction of the COLOSSEUM and other monuments in Rome. His foreign policies included the Romanization of provincials through grants of citizenship to selected towns, and annexations of territory in Anatolia and Germany. He also strengthened Roman rule in Wales and sent troops into Scotland.

To prevent a recurrence of civil war, Vespasian designated his son TITUS as his successor and appointed him prefect of the often volatile PRAETORIAN GUARD.

vespers   see DIVINE OFFICE

Vespucci, Amerigo [ves-poot'-chee]

Amerigo Vespucci, b. Florence, 1454, d. Feb. 22, 1512, an Italian explorer and navigator whose name was given to the New World, was the first to describe the Western Hemisphere as a previously unknown continent rather than as a part of Asia. Of his four possible voyages to the New World between 1497 and 1504, only the second and third are certain. He claimed a 1497 voyage, under Spanish auspices, that reached the Central American mainland. His 1499 voyage, undertaken for Spain, discovered Brazil and sailed northwest to Venezuela and then to Hispaniola. In 1501 he sailed to Brazil on Portugal's behalf and then continued south at least to the Río de la Plata. This voyage convinced him that he was exploring a new continent. Another expedition may have taken place in 1503–04, again to Brazil.

In 1507 the German cartographer Martin Waldseemüller published an account of Vespucci's voyages, along with a map and a treatise, *Cosmographiae introductio* (Introduction to Cosmography); Waldseemüller was the first to use the name *America* for the region Vespucci had explored.

Vesta [ves'-tuh]

In Roman mythology Vesta was the goddess of the hearth and symbol of the home. She watched particularly over households and family activities, and families made offerings to her at mealtime. Vesta was portrayed as a robed and veiled figure holding a scepter in one hand and the PALLADIUM in the other. She was identified with the Greek goddess HESTIA.

Vesta was worshiped both in individual homes and at a public shrine, where an eternal flame was tended by six vestal virgins. If one of these maidens lost her virginity during her 30-year term of duty, she was buried alive. If she permitted the fire to go out, she was flogged. The cult of the vestal virgins lasted into the early Christian period.

vestal virgins   see VESTA

vestments

Vestments are ceremonial garments worn by religious functionaries while performing sacred rites. In many religious traditions priests wear clothing that distinguishes them from the nonreligious; vestments, however, are associated with specific rituals and were traditionally given symbolic meanings. Among Christians, for example, the stole, a scarf adopted as the distinctive sign of the ordained minister, was customarily viewed as a yoke, symbolizing that the wearer was a servant of God. The eucharistic vestments worn by Roman Catholics, Episcopalians, and Lutherans include the alb, a white floor-length tunic (symbolizing purity) tied at the waist with a rope cincture, over which is worn the chasuble, a full cloak put on over the head. The amice, often made in the form of a collar or hood (symbolizing the helmet of salvation), is wrapped around the neck under the alb. The maniple, a length of material worn over the left arm, was originally a napkin and symbolizes the role of the minister as servant of the people of God. All of these garments are of early Christian origin (the stole, alb, and chasuble were derived from 4th-century Roman dress) and had become the liturgical norm by the 10th century. Later, other originally nonliturgical garments entered liturgical use. The black, full-length cassock, traditionally the outdoor dress of clergymen, was often retained under the liturgical vestments. Today the cassock is often worn with a white surplice, a full garment initially designed to cover the fur vests needed in cold churches. The Geneva, or pulpit, gown today worn for church services by many Protestant clergy was, with the cassock, the everyday dress of ministers in the 16th century.

Vestris (family) [ves'-tris]

The Vestris family, one of several important theatrical dynasties of the pre-romantic period, originated in Florence. **Teresa** (1726–1808), **Gaetano** (1728–1808), and **Angiolo** (1730–1809), children of **Tommaso Vestris**, were all dancers, of whom Gaetano, known as the God of the Dance, was the most celebrated and influential. Gaetano made his debut at the Paris Opéra in 1748, was appointed principal dancer in 1751, co-choreographer with Jean Dauberval in 1761, and chief choreographer in 1770. His chief pupil was **Auguste** (1760–1842), his illegitimate son by the dancer Marie Allard. Auguste was, like his father, ugly, conceited, and a technical prodigy. When Vestris and his son appeared together in London in 1781, Parliament suspended its sessions.

Auguste became a great teacher whose pupils included Charles Didelot, Jules Perrot, August Bournonville, and Marie Taglioni. Auguste's son **Armand** (1786–1825) worked mostly in London (1809–16) as a dancer and choreographer. He was married briefly to Lucia Elisabetta Bartolozzi, the famous Madame Vestris.

Vestris, Madame   Madame Vestris was the stage name of the English actress and theater manager Lucia Elisabetta Bartolozzi, b. London, Jan. 3, 1797, d. Aug. 8, 1856. She transformed London's Olympic Theatre into a showcase for the realistic presentation of drama by introducing, among other innovations, the three-walled "box" set with a ceiling, the first literal on-stage representation of a room. With her second husband, Charles James Mathews, she managed (1839–42) Covent Garden.

Vesuvius [vuh-soo'-vee-uhs]   Mount Vesuvius (Italian: Vesuvio), the only active volcano on the mainland of Europe, is located about 15 km (9 mi) southeast of Naples on the Bay of Naples in southern Italy. The volcano's crater, approximately 600 m (2,000 ft) in diameter and 300 m (1,000 ft) deep, lies within the remains of Monte Somma, a much larger ancient volcano. The height of the volcano, which varies with each eruption, was 1,280 m (4,199 ft) in 1970. Below the lava fields the fertile soil on the mountainsides supports agriculture.

Before AD 79, when a tremendous eruption buried the cities of HERCULANEUM, POMPEII, and Stabiae at its base, Vesuvius was thought to be extinct. From that time to 1631, when another major eruption occurred, about 10 smaller eruptions were recorded. Since 1631, Vesuvius has been continuously active, erupting 20 times; the most devastating eruptions occurred in 1794, 1872, and 1906. Its activity is now carefully monitored.

vetch   Vetch (or tare) is the common name for about 150 mostly north-temperate and South American species of climbing or straggling, weak-stemmed, viny herbs in the genus *Vicia* of the pea family, Leguminosae. They have compound leaves, and the terminal leaflets are transformed into tendrils. Some are cultivated as forage crops (hay, pasture, and silage); others are used as cover crops and as green manure.

Veterans Affairs, U.S. Department of   The U.S. Department of Veterans Affairs became the 14th cabinet department on Mar. 15, 1989—Congress having approved the transformation of the existing Veterans Administration (VA) to cabinet status in October 1988. The

VA, an independent government agency, had been created in 1930, supplanting several agencies that aided veterans. The department provides a wide range of services for veterans and their dependents, including hospital, nursing-home, and domiciliary care for eligible veterans, plus outpatient medical and dental care. It administers veteran pension plans and other compensation payments. Also, it directs the handling of educational programs, veterans' insurance policies, veterans' burial programs, and housing loans.

Veterans Day   see ARMISTICE DAY

Veterans of Foreign Wars   The Veterans of Foreign Wars (VFW) is a nationwide organization of U.S. veterans headquartered in Kansas City, Mo. The VFW was created in 1914. Membership is open to men who have served overseas in any branch of the military. A Ladies Auxiliary is open to female relatives of veterans and to women who have served overseas in the armed forces. Among the goals of the VFW are encouragement of patriotism and the provision of aid for disabled or needy veterans and their dependents. The VFW also sponsors community-service and youth-activity programs and maintains the VFW National Home for the children of deceased or disabled members in Eaton Rapids, Mich.

veterinary medicine   Veterinary medicine is that part of biology which deals with the health and disease of animals (see DISEASES, ANIMAL). Traditionally, it has involved principally the cure and treatment of disease; however, the emphasis is changing. Although cures and treatment are important, promotion of health is assuming its rightful place in veterinary medicine.

Veterinary medicine is concerned with a variety of animal species other than humans in a multitude of environmental circumstances. Humans are, however, the primary beneficiary of veterinary efforts. The practice of veterinary medicine may be applied by the veterinarian at a minimum of five levels: health promotion; specific prevention or protection; early diagnosis and prompt treatment; disability limitation; and rehabilitation or salvage.

History. Veterinary practice is probably as old as the domestication of animals. There are written records from 2000 BC in ancient Egypt and Babylonia. Aristotle and others wrote extensively describing veterinary practices in the Greek city-states. In the pre-Christian era no sharp distinction was made between the practice of human and of animal medcine. With the development of Judeo-Christian philosophies, however, the uniqueness of humans was emphasized. This caused a sharp line to be drawn between the physician and the veterinarian.

It was not until the 18th century AD that the veterinary profession developed in an ordered manner, after the founding of a college in Lyon, France. It had taken the Renaissance and Reformation to advance the science and art of all medical practice. Much of the present status and prestige of the veterinary profession has been realized only in the relatively brief period since World War II.

Education. As a consequence of changing needs and demand for veterinary service, the veterinary colleges in the United States have improved curricula and expanded facilities. A minimum of 6 years' academic preparation is now required before the student can become a doctor of veterinary medicine. The curriculum in the last 4 years includes the basic sciences, anatomy, physiology, pharmacology, pathobiology, microbiology, and the applied areas. These areas of study encompass basic principles and concepts as well as practical applications in diagnosis, therapy, preventive medicine, surgery, radiology, and many other areas of specialization.

Profession. In the late 1980s the American Veterinary Medical Association had a membership of about 43,000 veterinarians, a figure that represented 80% to 85% of all practicing U.S. veterinarians. Approximately 75% of these engage in private practice, and the remaining 25% are employed in governmental agencies, educational and research institutions, such industries as drug production, and a variety of miscellaneous enterprises.

About one-half of the veterinarians engaged in private practice confine their activities exclusively to pet or companion animals. The balance have what might be termed a "mixed" practice. Part of their time is spent on companion animals and part on food-producing or economic animals. Less than 10% of these veterinarians confine their activities to food or economic animals. Veterinarians in private practice spend most of their time with acute procedures (medical visits or calls and nonelective surgery) and preventive medical activities (routine medical visits or calls and examinations). A sizable portion of their time is spent in elective surgery.

Veterinarians outside of private practice are a much more diverse group. Their efforts range from primary animal health care through human health programs, with emphasis on environmental health, and zoonotic-disease programs. (Zoonotic diseases are those communicable from animals to humans.) Many are involved in teaching and research, and others in zoological work and wildlife programs. Several fields that may offer great opportunities for future veterinarians include SPACE MEDICINE, wildlife management, mariculture (cultivation of marine organisms), and marine biology.

veto A veto (Latin, "I forbid") is the right of one governmental branch (usually the executive) to refuse to assent to an act—or to negate an act—of another branch of government (usually the legislative). The veto can be absolute or limited. A limited veto is one that can be overridden in some way. An example of an absolute veto is the right of any one of the five permanent members of the United Nations Security Council to block action on nonprocedural matters.

Leaders of most modern governments have both formal and informal veto powers. The president of the United States has limited veto power granted by the U.S. Constitution (Article I, Section 7). A presidential veto can be overridden by a two-thirds majority in each house of Congress. The president can also use the so-called pocket veto: ordinarily if the president fails to act on legislation within 10 days of receiving it, it automatically becomes law; if Congress, however, adjourns before the 10 days have elapsed, the measure is automatically killed. The legislative veto (a device by which Congress grants the executive broad authority to act in a given area but reserves the right to veto any particular action taken under that authority) was declared unconstitutional by the U.S. Supreme Court in *Immigration and Naturalization Service* v. *Chadha* (1983).

viaduct [vy'-uh-duhkt] A viaduct is a bridge that usually rests on arches with high supporting towers and that is used to carry a road or railway over a valley or the streets of a city. The Romans built long, low viaducts at Salamanca, Córdoba, and Merida in Spain, as well as many high, multitiered stone arch structures such as the Pont du Gard near Nîmes, France.

From 1830 to 1860 more than 25,000 railroad bridges and viaducts were built in Great Britain alone. Isambard K. Brunel (see BRUNEL family) built a great number of timber viaducts for the Cornwall and Devon railways, with standard spans of 15 m (50 ft) and 20 m (65 ft). Although he used Baltic pine timber of the finest quality, none of his viaducts survived more than 60 years. In the last few decades reinforced concrete and steel have been used in viaduct construction.

Vianney, Saint Jean Baptiste Marie [vee-ahnay'] The patron saint of parish priests, Jean Baptiste Marie Vianney, b. May 8, 1786, d. Aug. 4, 1859, was the renowned priest and confessor of the French parish of Ars. He is known as the Curé of Ars. He achieved international fame as a spiritual counselor, with as many as 20,000 persons visiting him each year. He was canonized in 1925. Feast day: Aug. 4 (formerly Aug. 9).

vibraphone The vibraphone is a MARIMBA with metal bars, and resonators that have a controlled vibrato caused by a motor-driven mechanism that opens and closes them, thus altering the tone color and volume. For stopping the sound, the instrument is equipped with a damper pedal. Interesting effects may be achieved through its possibilities for sustained tones and by manipulation of the damper pedal. The vibraphone is one of the few instruments developed in the United States. Alban Berg, Olivier Messiaen, and Ralph Vaughan Williams have written for it, but it has been most popular in dance bands. The jazz musician Lionel Hampton brought it to wide public attention.

viburnum [vy-bur'-nuhm] *Viburnum*, or arrowwood, is an important genus of about 225 species of ornamental shrubs and small trees in the honeysuckle family, Caprifoliaceae. Native to America, Europe, and Asia, these plants produce simple deciduous or evergreen leaves, small white or pink flowers in flat-topped clusters, and small drupes.

Viburnums make attractive ornamentals, and many species are hardy in temperate North America. These plants enjoy sunlight, although they also do well in shade. The hobblebush, *V. alnifolium*, is a popular deciduous shrub that turns purple-red in autumn. Many species bear fragrant flowers. Some species are grown for their hydrangealike flower heads, including the Japanese snowball, *V. plicatum*.

vice-president of the United States   The vice-presidency of the United States is one of the two positions in the government of the United States that is filled in an election open to all eligible voters in every state and the District of Columbia. The vice-president is the second highest ranking officer in the executive branch of the federal government, beneath only the president. Both serve concurrent 4-year terms. The constitutional duties of the vice-president are relatively unimportant, however, and traditionally vice-presidents have had little influence on public affairs. The Founding Fathers who wrote the U.S. Constitution in 1787 provided that all of the "executive power" would rest in the hands of the president. Almost as an afterthought, they created the office of vice-president in order to provide for a successor should the president die or resign.

The significance of the office relates almost entirely to the fact that the vice-president succeeds to the presidency if the president dies, resigns, or is removed from office through the impeachment process. Altogether, eight presidents have died in office, and one has resigned. With the adoption in 1967 of the 25th Amendment to the U.S. Constitution, it is also possible for the vice-president to assume the duties of the presidency if the president becomes disabled.

President of the Senate. The vice-president is assigned only one responsibility by the Constitution, and that is in the legislative branch, not the executive branch. The vice-president is designated as the presiding officer of the Senate of the United States and has the additional responsibility of casting a tie-breaking vote whenever the votes of the senators are evenly divided on any roll call.

The vice-president's role as president of the Senate has not proved to be significant. The rules of parliamentary procedure adopted by the Senate provide little opportunity for the presiding officer to affect the course of the deliberations or to exercise political influence. Behind the scenes, however, some vice-presidents, particularly those who have previously served in the Senate, have been effective in winning votes for bills favored by the administration and in explaining administration policies to the members of the Senate and House of Representatives. In practice, the vice-president does not preside over the Senate with any frequency, except for ceremonial occasions.

The responsibility for casting tie-breaking votes is not a great one. First, if a vote on a measure has ended in a tie, it is regarded as defeated, and a negative vote by the

Lyndon Baines Johnson, who served as vice-president under President John F. Kennedy, takes the presidential oath shortly after Kennedy's assassination on Nov. 22, 1963.

vice-president would be superfluous. Thus, only if the vice-president favors a particular measure and casts an affirmative vote can the tie-breaking vote prove decisive. Second, the growth in the size of the Senate has reduced the statistical likelihood that tie votes will occur.

Nomination and Election. The U.S. Constitution as ratified in 1789 established a system for electing presidents and vice-presidents that remained in effect for only 15 years. In each presidential election the electors chosen by the states cast their ballots for president and vice-president. Each elector was permitted to vote for two candidates but was not permitted to indicate which choice he preferred for president and which for vice-president. The authors of the Constitution reasoned that an elector might well cast one vote for a resident of his own state and give the other vote to a political leader with a national reputation, and that when all of the votes were counted such a national figure would emerge with the most votes—and, hence, the presidency. It was further reasoned that the person who received the second greatest number of votes—hence, the vice-presidency—would also be some person of national reputation and the next best qualified person to serve as president.

The formation of political parties during the 1790s undermined the logic of this system, however. Each political party began to put up two-man teams, and the electors chosen by that party would vote for both men. In 1800 the candidates of the majority party, Thomas Jefferson and Aaron Burr, each received the same number (73) of electoral votes. Because of the tie, the responsibility for choosing the president fell to the House of Representatives. Everyone knew that Jefferson was the intended choice for president and Burr for vice-president, but the ambitious Burr allowed his name to remain in the running for the presidency, and he was supported by members of the House who opposed Jefferson. As a result, although Jefferson was ultimately chosen by the House, it was apparent that the electoral system had to be abandoned. The 12th Amendment to the Constitution, adopted in 1804, provided that the electors vote separately for the offices of president and vice-president.

The 12th Amendment created a new problem. American political parties traditionally have been composed of several factions. Parties quickly discovered a means of achieving a semblance of unity during each election campaign. After the contest for the presidential nomination was settled, the party leaders usually sought to console the losing faction by giving one of its members the nomination for vice-president, a process known as balancing the ticket.

This development, however, meant that if a president died in office it was highly possible that he would be succeeded by someone who had substantially different views on major issues. This situation arose on several occasions. As a result, the ideologically balanced ticket concept gradually fell into disfavor. Since World War II most party leaders have sought to nominate tickets composed of candidates who generally see eye-to-eye on key issues. Balance is achieved by other means, usually by nominating a candidate who comes from a different part of the country or who represents a different ethnic background.

In modern practice the presidential nominee consults with his advisors and with party leaders at the convention and then announces his choice for his vice-president, that is, running mate. The presidential nominee's choice is invariably nominated.

All major-party nominees for president and vice-president had been white males until 1984, when the Democrats nominated Geraldine Ferraro for the vice-presidency. African Americans have recently also received serious consideration for the post.

The Succession Problem. The Constitution originally provided that "In Case of the Removal of the President from Office, or of his Death, Resignation, or Inability to discharge the Powers and Duties of the said Office, the Same shall devolve on the Vice President...." Years later, a controversy arose over whether "the Same" referred to "Powers and Duties" or to "Office." In 1841, when President William Henry Harrison died in office, Vice-President John Tyler took the presidential oath and subsequently asserted that he was in fact holding the office of president. In all subsequent instances in which a president had died, his successor has been accepted by the public as the president both in power and in fact. The 25th Amendment to the Constitution, however, provides that if a president is disabled, the vice-president may exercise the powers and duties of the office, but only as acting president. The president, upon his recovery, may resume his duties. The 25th Amendment also provided that if the office of vice-president becomes vacant, the president must nominate someone to fill the vacancy. On approval of both houses of the Congress, the nominee is sworn in as vice-president.

The Constitution gives the Congress the responsibility for providing for the order of succession to the presidency should the offices of both president and vice-president be vacant at the same time. The succession statute was most recently rewritten in 1947, when Congress established the succession in this order: the Speaker of the House of Representatives, the president pro tempore of the Senate, and the heads of the departments in the executive branch of the federal government, in the order in which the departments were created, beginning with the secretary of state. The succession has never passed below the vice-president.

Political History of the Office. The most memorable event in the early history of the vice-presidency (after the

VICE-PRESIDENTS OF THE UNITED STATES

Vice-President	Term	President
1. John Adams	1789–97	Washington
2. Thomas Jefferson	1797–1801	John Adams
3. Aaron Burr	1801–05	Jefferson
4. George Clinton	1805–09	Jefferson
George Clinton*	1809–12	Madison
5. Elbridge Gerry*	1813–14	Madison
6. Daniel D. Tompkins	1817–25	Monroe
7. John C. Calhoun	1825–29	John Quincy Adams
John C. Calhoun†	1829–32	Jackson
8. Martin Van Buren	1833–37	Jackson
9. Richard M. Johnson	1837–41	Van Buren
10. John Tyler‡	1841	William Henry Harrison
11. George M. Dallas	1845–49	Polk
12. Millard Fillmore‡	1849–50	Taylor
13. William R. D. King*	1853	Pierce
14. John C. Breckinridge	1857–61	Buchanan
15. Hannibal Hamlin	1861–65	Lincoln
16. Andrew Johnson‡	1865	Lincoln
17. Schuyler Colfax	1869–73	Grant
18. Henry Wilson*	1873–75	Grant
19. William A. Wheeler	1877–81	Hayes
20. Chester A. Arthur‡	1881	Garfield
21. Thomas A. Hendricks*	1885	Cleveland
22. Levi P. Morton	1889–93	Benjamin Harrison
23. Adlai E. Stevenson	1893–97	Cleveland
24. Garret A. Hobart*	1897–99	McKinley
25. Theodore Roosevelt‡	1901	McKinley
26. Charles W. Fairbanks	1905–09	Theodore Roosevelt
27. James S. Sherman*	1909–12	Taft
28. Thomas R. Marshall	1913–21	Wilson
29. Calvin Coolidge‡	1921–23	Harding
30. Charles G. Dawes	1925–29	Coolidge
31. Charles Curtis	1929–33	Hoover
32. John N. Garner	1933–41	Franklin D. Roosevelt
33. Henry A. Wallace	1941–45	Franklin D. Roosevelt
34. Harry S. Truman‡	1945	Franklin D. Roosevelt
35. Alben W. Barkley	1949–53	Truman
36. Richard M. Nixon	1953–61	Eisenhower
37. Lyndon B. Johnson‡	1961–63	Kennedy
38. Hubert H. Humphrey	1965–69	Lyndon B. Johnson
39. Spiro T. Agnew†	1969–73	Nixon
40. Gerald R. Ford§	1973–74	Nixon
41. Nelson A. Rockefeller	1974–77	Ford
42. Walter F. Mondale	1977–81	Carter
43. George H. W. Bush	1981–89	Reagan
44. J. Danforth Quayle	1989–93	Bush
45. Albert Gore, Jr.	1993–	Clinton

*Died in office.
†Resigned.
‡Succeeded to presidency on death of president.
§Succeeded to presidency on resignation of president.

Jefferson-Burr controversy) was the competition between John C. Calhoun and Martin Van Buren to succeed President Andrew Jackson. Calhoun, who was vice-president during Jackson's first term, quarreled with the president over the issue of state rights and other matters and resigned as vice-president in frustration. Jackson chose Calhoun's adversary, Van Buren, to be the vice-president for his second term and was instrumental in securing Van Buren's election to the presidency in 1836.

From 1836 to 1988 no incumbent vice-president had been elected directly to the presidency; George Bush managed this feat in 1988. Many earlier vice-presidents were relatively unknown even in their own time.

Those vice-presidents who were elevated to the highest office through the death of the president provided some memorable moments in American history. President Zachary Taylor died during the debate over the Compromise of 1850, which he opposed. He was succeeded by Millard Fillmore, who supported the compromise, which, when adopted, helped avert the outbreak of civil war for a decade. Chester Alan Arthur, a product of the notorious spoils system, converted to the cause of civil-service reform and helped achieve its adoption after an advocate of reform, President James Garfield, was assassinated (by a disappointed office seeker). Warren Harding died in 1923 immediately before the discovery of serious scandals in his administration. He was succeeded by Calvin Coolidge, whose probity helped restore public confidence.

The modern history of the vice-presidency dates from World War II, when Franklin D. Roosevelt gave Vice-President Henry A. Wallace major responsibilities involving acquisition of natural resources required for the war effort. Thereafter, the concept of the working vice-president gradually evolved. Vice-presidents have received assignments that required them to deal with such problems as race relations, the space program, and unemployment. The vice-president is also a member of the National Security Council. Richard Nixon was the first vice-president to travel abroad extensively on diplomatic missions, and his successors have done the same.

Vicente, Gil [vee-sayn'-tuh]   Often called the father of the Portuguese theater, Gil Vicente, c.1470–1536, established the fundamentals of Portuguese drama. Writing in both Portuguese and Spanish, he produced short religious plays, called *autos*, and farces for the courts of Manuel I and John III. His trilogy of *autos*, *The Ships of Hell, Purgatory,* and *Glory* (1517–19; Eng. trans., 1929), has been called a Portuguese *Divine Comedy*. In his farces, which reflect popular poetry in their exquisite lyrics, Vicente used satire to ridicule the immoralities of his age. *Inês Pereira* (1523) is a typical example.

Vicenza [vee-chayn'-sah]   Vicenza is the capital of Vicenza province in the Veneto region of northeastern Italy, less than 60 km (40 mi) west of Venice at the confluence of the Bacchiglione and Retrone rivers. The population is 110,449 (1987 est.). Vicenza is an agricultural, commercial, and industrial center producing iron and steel, farm and textile machinery, furniture, glass, and chemicals. Notable buildings include a 13th-century Gothic cathedral and the 16th-century Renaissance Teatro Olimpico, Villa Rotunda, Basilica Palladiana, and Loggia del Capitanio, all designed by Andrea Palladio.

An ancient Ligurian town and then a Roman settlement, Vicenza became the seat of a Lombard duchy in the 6th century. It was later ruled by Verona and Milan before falling to Venice in 1404. Vicenza was governed by Austria from 1797 to 1866, when it joined the new Kingdom of Italy.

viceroy   Viceroy is the title formerly given by Spain and Great Britain to the governors-general of certain important dominions. Spain first used the title (Spanish, *Virrey*) in the 16th century to describe the governors of Peru and New Spain (Mexico). Traditionally, the British lord-lieutenant of Ireland was given the rank of viceroy, and after 1858 the governor-general of India was a viceroy.

Vichy [vee-shee']   Vichy, a town on the Allier River in the Allier department of central France, is about 320 km (200 mi) south of Paris and has a population of 30,527 (1982). It has many thermal springs that produce the famous Vichy water exported worldwide.

The Vichy springs, known to the Romans, began to attract visitors in the 17th century and were made highly fashionable by the visits of Napoleon III in the 19th century. During World War II, Vichy was the capital of unoccupied France from July 1940 until the German occupation of all of France in November 1942.

Vichy Government   The Vichy Government (1940–44), a right-wing authoritarian regime, succeeded the Third Republic in unoccupied French territory after Germany defeated France (June 1940) early in World War II.

Meeting in the resort town of Vichy, the French National Assembly, dazed by defeat and maneuvered by Vice-Premier Pierre LAVAL, voted 569 to 80 on July 10 to grant Premier Henri Philippe PÉTAIN full emergency and constitution-making power. The new government was composed of right-wing elements hostile to the Third Republic but did not include outright Fascists. Under German pressure, anti-Semitic measures were gradually enacted and reluctantly enforced.

Toward the Nazis, Vichy pursued an uneven wait-and-see and collaborationist policy. Premier Pétain remained relatively aloof from direct collaboration. Vice-Premier Laval, however, tended more to expediency, dealing with and yielding to Nazi demands and seeking a comfortable place for France in Hitler's "new order."

Opposition to Vichy was negligible at first, but by 1943–44, resistance forces and the rival Free French government under Charles de Gaulle isolated the regime, which had lost almost all autonomy after German troops entered unoccupied France in November 1942. Vichy ended ignominiously as a rump government in Germany after France's liberation in June 1944.

Vickers, Jon [vik'-urz] The operatic tenor Jon Vickers, b. Prince Albert, Saskatchewan, Oct. 29, 1926, made his debut (1956) as Aeneas in Berlioz's *Les Troyens* with London's Royal Opera. He moved into heldentenor roles as Siegmund in *Die Walküre*, at the 1958 Bayreuth Festival; his Metropolitan Opera debut was in 1960. An outstanding singing actor, Vickers is proficient in a variety of styles; apart from Wagner, he is especially celebrated as Florestan in Beethoven's *Fidelio* and as Benjamin Britten's Peter Grimes.

Vicksburg [viks'-burg] Vicksburg (1990 pop., 20,902) is a city in western Mississippi situated on high loess bluffs overlooking the Mississippi River at the mouth of the Yazoo River. It is the seat of Warren County and an important shipping, trade, and processing center. Vicksburg, settled in 1790, was the site of a pivotal Civil War battle. The city surrendered to Union forces in 1863, after a 66-day siege, giving the Union control of the Mississippi.

Vicksburg Campaign In the crucial Vicksburg Campaign (April–July 1863) of the U.S. Civil War, Union forces under Gen. Ulysses S. GRANT captured Vicksburg, Miss., the Confederacy's stronghold on the Mississippi River. The victory gave the Union control of the river and split the Confederacy in two. Vicksburg's capture, combined with the Union success at Gettysburg (July 1863), shifted the impetus of victory toward the North.

Foiled in several attempts to reduce Vicksburg during the previous fall and winter, Grant launched (April 1863) a combined army-navy operation. Ground forces marched south down the west bank of the Mississippi, while gunboats moved past the Vicksburg batteries to transport the troops back to the east bank at Bruinsburg, south of Gen. John C. Pemberton's heavy Vicksburg defenses. This daring move shifted the campaign to interior Mississippi as Grant, with about 33,000 men, moved inland toward Jackson. By that action, Grant drew Pemberton out of Vicksburg while separating him from Gen. Joseph E. JOHNSTON's approximately 20,000 Confederates in Jackson, whom the Union forces drove north (May 14). Grant then defeated Pemberton and pushed him back into Vicksburg. A siege of Vicksburg (May 18–July 4) ended when Pemberton, low on food and ammunition, surrendered the city and garrison.

Vico, Giambattista [vee'-koh, jahng-bah-tee'-stah] The Italian philosopher of history Giovanni Battista, or Giambattista, Vico, b. June 23, 1668, d. Jan. 23, 1744, was the most important forerunner of the historical view known as historicism: the idea that history is the key to any science of humanity. In his *Scienza nuova* (New

Science, 1725, 1730, 1744) and other writings, Vico stressed that history is the expression of human will and deeds and can therefore provide more certain knowledge about humanity than the natural sciences can. He saw each epoch as a whole in which all aspects of culture— art, religion, philosophy, politics, and economics—are interrelated, and he regarded myth, poetry, and art as important means of understanding the spirit of a culture. Vico outlined a conception of historical development in which great cultures go through cycles of growth and decline.

Victor Amadeus II, Duke of Savoy Victor Amadeus II, b. May 14, 1666, d. Oct. 31, 1732, duke of SAVOY, became the first king of Sardinia-Piedmont (1720–30). Son of Charles Emmanuel II, whom he succeeded as duke in 1675, he grew up under a regency headed by his mother. He ousted her in 1683, establishing an absolutist but reform-minded government. In 1690, Victor Amadeus joined the League of Augsburg against France. When his Spanish ally refused to let him have Milan, he made (1696) a separate peace with France, gaining Pinerolo. In the War of the Spanish Succession he began on France's side but in 1703 switched to the Habsburgs. At the Peace of Utrecht (1713) Victor Amadeus was elevated to the title of king and given Sicily. In 1720 he exchanged this island for Sardinia, which he turned into Italy's strongest state. He abdicated ten years later in favor of his son, Charles Emmanuel III.

Victor Emmanuel I, Italian King of Sardinia Victor Emmanuel I, b. July 24, 1759, d. Jan. 10, 1824, king of Sardinia-Piedmont (1802–21), resisted the liberal reforms resulting from the Napoleonic conquests. He succeeded his brother Charles Emmanuel IV (r. 1796–1802), who abdicated. Victor Emmanuel resided (1802–14) in Sardinia during the French control of Italy, which deprived the House of SAVOY of the rest of its possessions. He regained Piedmont, Nice, and Savoy in 1814. At the Congress of Vienna in 1815, he obtained Genoa. Utterly reactionary, he refused to grant a constitution. Faced with an uprising, he abdicated in 1821 in favor of his brother Charles Felix.

Victor Emmanuel II, King of Italy Victor Emmanuel II, b. Mar. 14, 1820, d. Jan. 9, 1878, a member of the SAVOY dynasty, was king of Sardinia-Piedmont (1849–61) and Italy (1861–78). Ascending the throne of Sardinia after the abdication of his father, Charles Albert, Victor Emmanuel preserved the new constitution that resulted from the 1848–49 revolt against Austria (see REVOLUTIONS OF 1848). In 1852 he appointed as premier the conte di CAVOUR, whose maneuverings were to make Victor Emmanuel the first king of a united Italy by 1861.

In 1860 the king secretly encouraged Giuseppe GARIBALDI to conquer Sicily and Naples. Victor Emmanuel then sent his army into papal territory, where it defeated the papal army at Castelfidardo and joined Garibaldi's

Victor Emmanuel II, originally king of Sardinia-Piedmont, became the first king of the nation of Italy after its unification by Cavour and Garibaldi. After expelling French troops from Rome, the king made the city his capital, ruling as a constitutional monarch.

force. The king took a more active part in government after Cavour died in 1861. With Prussian help, he annexed Venetia in 1866 and Rome in 1870, thereby completing the Italian RISORGIMENTO. Victor Emmanuel was succeeded as king of Italy by Humbert I, his son.

Victor Emmanuel III, King of Italy Victor Emmanuel III, b. Nov. 11, 1869, d. Dec. 28, 1947, king of Italy (1900–46), helped Benito MUSSOLINI come to power. Victor Emmanuel succeeded to the throne on the assassination of his father, Humbert I. He revealed his dislike for liberal government in 1922 when he invited the Fascist leader, Mussolini, to become premier and acquiesced to his dictatorship. After the Allies invaded Sicily in 1943, however, he conspired to arrest Mussolini and set up (July 25) a royal dictatorship with Marshal Pietro Badoglio. The undignified flight of both the king and Badoglio from Rome after the armistice (September 1943) with the Allies incurred much public hostility, and Victor Emmanuel was forced to relinquish all power to his son, Prince Humbert, on June 5, 1944. On June 2, 1946, Italy voted for a republic, forcing both kings into exile.

Victoria (Australia) Victoria is a state in southeastern Australia; its area is 227,629 km² (87,888 mi²). Although it occupies slightly less than 3% of the country's total area, it has a population of 4,260,300 (1988 est.), second only to that of New South Wales. More than 70% live in the metropolitan area of MELBOURNE, the capital city.

Victoria is divided into four physical regions. From north to south these are the plains of the Murray Basin, the Central Highlands—with a maximum elevation of 1,986 m (6,516 ft) at Mount Bogong—the Southern Plains, and the Southern Uplands. Forest covers most highland areas. The plains are largely grass. Numerous streams flow from the central highlands south into Bass Strait or north into the MURRAY RIVER, Victoria's northern boundary.

The majority of the people are of British stock, but many eastern or southern Europeans have immigrated to Victoria since 1947. Melbourne, the second largest city in Australia, is Victoria's only major metropolis. Other important cities include Ballarat and Geelong.

Victoria has a diversified economy, benefiting from abundant coal. Petroleum and natural gas are becoming increasingly important. Industries manufacture automobiles, metal products, machinery, textiles, and paper products. Agriculture is also of major importance, with leading commodities being wheat, wool, and dairy products. Melbourne is a focus of transportation routes—sea, land, and air—and almost equals Sydney as an import-export center. The state parliament consists of two elected houses: the Legislative Council (upper) and the Legislative Assembly (lower).

Explorers penetrated what is now Victoria during the 1820s, but it was not until the 1830s that permanent settlement began. In 1851, Victoria, originally part of New South Wales, became a separate colony. Gold discoveries during the 1850s attracted thousands of immigrants from Europe and China. In 1901, Victoria became a state in the Commonwealth of Australia.

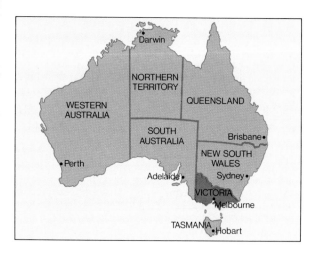

Victoria (British Columbia) Victoria is the capital city of British Columbia, Canada. Situated off the mainland on the southeast tip of Vancouver Island along the Juan de Fuca Strait, it is the island's principal city and has a population of 66,303 (1986). A major port and the base of a salmon-fishing fleet, Victoria also has shipbuilding and industries that process fish, lumber, and paper. It is connected to mainland Canada by air and ferry services. Victoria University (1902) is located in the city.

Victoria's first settlement, Fort Camosun, was established in 1843 by Sir James Douglas of the Hudson's Bay Company. Later renamed Fort Victoria in honor of Britain's queen, the city developed during the 1850s as the capital of Vancouver Island, by then a crown colony. After 1858, Victoria was a port for the gold-mining enterprises in the Cariboo Mountains. It became the capital of British Columbia in 1868, retaining this position when British Columbia joined (1871) the Canadian Confederation.

Victoria, Lake

Lake Victoria (or Victoria Nyanza), the largest lake in Africa and the second largest freshwater lake in the world (after Lake Superior), lies mostly within Uganda and Tanzania and borders on Kenya. Stretching over an area of 69,481 km^2 (26,828 mi^2), Lake Victoria's coastline is more than 3,220 km (2,000 mi) long. The lake is about 400 km (250 mi) long and approximately 240 km (150 mi) wide and is situated at an altitude of 1,134 m (3,720 ft). Lake Victoria's tributaries include the Kagera and the Mara, and it is a source of the NILE RIVER. Its only outlet is near Jinja, where a dam was built (1954) at Owen Falls to generate hydroelectric power. Ukerewe and the Sese Archipelago are the most important islands. The first European to explore the lake, John Hanning Speke (1858), named it for the British monarch, Queen Victoria.

Victoria, Queen of England, Scotland, and Ireland

Victoria, b. May 24, 1819, d. Jan. 22, 1901, queen of Great Britain and Ireland (r. 1837–1901), the longest-reigning monarch in English history, established the monarchy as a respected and popular institution while it was losing its place as an integral part of the British governing system.

Born in London, Victoria was the only child of Edward, duke of Kent and son of George III, and Princess Victoria, daughter of the duke of Saxe-Coburg. Taking the throne on the death of her uncle, William IV, Victoria became strongly attached to the Whig prime minister Lord MELBOURNE; after he resigned in 1839, Sir Robert PEEL, his would-be successor, suggested that she dismiss the Whig ladies of her court. Victoria, however, refused. In part because of this "bedchamber crisis," Melbourne resumed office for two more years.

Victoria and her court were greatly transformed by her marriage to her first cousin, Prince ALBERT of Saxe-Coburg, in 1840. Although her name now designates a supposedly prudish age, it was Albert who made a point of straitlaced behavior, and it was he who introduced a strict decorum in court. Victoria and Albert had nine children.

Albert taught Victoria the need for hard work if she was to make her views felt in the cabinet, and during the prince's lifetime Victoria did, by insistently interjecting her opinions, force the ministers to take them into account. She was partly responsible, for example, for the departure of Lord PALMERSTON as foreign secretary in 1851. Her political importance was based, however, on the temporarily factionalized state of Commons between 1846 and 1868, when royal intervention was needed to help glue together majority coalitions.

Always prone to self-pity, Victoria fully indulged her grief at Albert's death in 1861. She remained in mourning until her own death, and her popularity declined as a result. Victoria, however, regained the people's admiration

Queen Victoria, the longest reigning monarch in British history, populated most of the thrones of Europe with her descendants. Among her grandchildren were Emperor William II of Germany and Alexandra, consort of Nicholas II of Russia.

when she resumed her determined efforts to steer public affairs. She won particular esteem for defending the popular imperialist policies of the Conservative ministries of Benjamin DISRAELI, who flattered her relentlessly and made her empress of India in 1876. On the other hand, she intensely disliked William E. GLADSTONE, the Liberal prime minister. The celebrations of Victoria's golden and diamond jubilees in 1887 and 1897 demonstrated her great popularity.

In Victoria's later career, her attempts to influence government decisions ceased to carry significant weight. The Reform Act of 1867, by doubling the electorate, strengthened party organization and eliminated the need for a mediator—the monarch—among factions in Commons. Victoria was succeeded by her son, Edward VII.

Victoria, Tomás Luis de

[veek-tohr'-ee-ah] Tomás Luis de Victoria, b. c.1548, d. Aug. 27, 1611, was a great Spanish composer of Catholic church music who may have studied with Bartolomé Escobedo and Palestrina, but whose style is uniquely Hispanic. In Rome, where he first studied and later directed the music of the Jesuit Collegium Germanicum, Victoria gained experience as an organist and choirmaster, having competent choirs for the performance of his works. He entered the priesthood in 1575 but continued to compose and direct music in Rome until 1587, when he returned to Spain. This return coincided with his appointment as chaplain to dowager empress Maria, who lived in retirement at the Royal Convent of Barefoot Clarist Nuns in Madrid. Victoria served also as director of the choir of boys and priests attached to the convent, and in the last seven years of his life he was organist there. He wrote no secular music, but his religious works cover practically all the liturgical forms of his era—masses, motets, hymns, responsories, music for Holy Week, and a deeply moving *Officium defunctorum* for the funeral of the empress in 1603.

Victoria Cross

see MEDALS AND DECORATIONS

Victoria Falls Victoria Falls lies on the border of Zambia and Zimbabwe in south central Africa, on the middle course of the ZAMBEZI RIVER, where it is more than 1,676 m (5,500 ft) wide. The falls' African name is Mosi-oa-tunya—"the smoke that thunders." Islands divide the falls into Devil's Cataract, Main Falls, Rainbow Falls, and Eastern Cataract. The water drops into a 122-m-deep (420-ft) chasm and hits the wall of the chasm about 25–75 m (80–240 ft) above its floor. The highest of the falls is nearly 110 m (350 ft). Great clouds of water vapor from the falls keep the surrounding vegetation green and lush all year. A hydroelectric plant is powered by the falls. A 200-m (650-ft) railroad bridge crosses the chasm. Victoria Falls National Park surrounds the area. David Livingstone sighted the falls on Nov. 17, 1855, and named them for Queen Victoria.

Victoria Falls is one of the most impressive of Africa's many natural wonders. Victoria Falls National Park, established in 1952, is administered by the government of Zimbabwe and is among that country's leading tourist attractions.

Victoria Island Victoria Island, covering an area of 212,200 km² (81,930 mi²) in the Northwest Territories, is the third largest of Canada's Arctic islands. The main settlement is Cambridge Bay (1986 pop., 1,002). The island was discovered by Thomas Simpson in 1838 and explored by John Rae in 1851.

Victorian literature The first decades (1830s to 1860s) of Queen Victoria's reign produced a vigorous and varied body of literature that attempted to come to terms with the current transformations of English society, but writers in the latter decades (1870s to 1900) withdrew into AESTHETICISM, a preoccupation with sensation as an end in itself. Confronted by the shift from an agricultural to an industrial urban society and troubled by the erosion of traditional religious beliefs, the early Victorian writers held to a belief that literature should provide both an understanding of and fresh values for a new society. Novelists of the period explored the difficulty of forming a personal identity in a world in which traditional social structures appeared to be dissolving. With compassionate realism, George ELIOT described the slow dissolution of a

rural community. The many powerful novels of Charles DICKENS, William Makepeace THACKERAY, and Anthony TROLLOPE focused on the isolation of the individual within the city. Charlotte BRONTË dramatized the particular problems of creating a female identity. Among the writers of nonfiction, Thomas CARLYLE argued for the re-creation in industrial England of the lost sense of community among social classes. In contrast, John Stuart MILL spoke for the fullest development of the individual through freedom from social restraint. The foremost art critic of the time, John RUSKIN, showed the interdependence of great art and a society's moral health.

The major early Victorian poets, too, took the role of secular prophets. Alfred, Lord TENNYSON, in his major work, *In Memoriam* (1850), translated personal grief into an affirmation of religious faith. Matthew ARNOLD revealed how the spirit of his own age weakened emotional vitality. Although concerned with presenting his personal form of religious faith, Robert BROWNING used his dramatic monologues primarily to show the uniqueness of the individual personality.

By the 1870s, opposing what they now perceived as a repressive public morality, writers increasingly rejected any obligation to produce didactic art. Walter PATER argued that moments of intense sensation are the highest good and that the function of art must be to create such moments. In poetry, Dante Gabriel ROSSETTI and Algernon Charles SWINBURNE expressed their private erotic concerns in terms shocking to the general public. Such preoccupation with sensation led to the literary DECADENCE of the 1890s, epitomized by Oscar WILDE's play *Salomé* (1893), with illustrations by Aubrey BEARDSLEY. Along with a revitalization of prose fantasy (see William MORRIS; Robert Louis STEVENSON), the later Victorian period also saw a more searching realism, notably in the novels of Thomas HARDY.

Victorian style Victorian style is a catchall term often used to describe the eclectic and revivalist trends in British architecture and design during the reign of Queen Victoria (1837–1901). At one time dismissed as a superficial and inauthentic series of revivals of historical styles, the Victorian style has received more sympathetic and serious scholarly attention in recent years, in part because of a widespread reaction against the functionalist bias of modern architecture.

In searching for a style appropriate to the new structures required by urban-industrial civilization, Victorian architects revived historical styles and reapplied them to serve modern needs. These revivals included classical, Italianate, Gothic, Elizabethan, and French Empire styles. Most significant and widespread was the GOTHIC REVIVAL, which has as its great monument the Houses of Parliament (designed 1835; see WESTMINSTER PALACE) in London. Among the finest examples of eclectic architecture are the Royal Courts of Justice (1874–82; London) by George Edmund Street and Saint Pancras Station (1867–74; London) by Sir George Gilbert SCOTT. The leading theorists of the period, such as William MORRIS

The Royal Courts of Justice in the Strand, London, is a notable example of Victorian architecture. The Gothic exterior, designed by George Edmund Street (1824–81), reflects 19th-century Britain's fascination with the medieval past.

and John RUSKIN, anticipated modern design in stressing the idea of truth to the nature of the materials used.

Victorio [vik-tohr'-ee-oh]   Victorio, b. *c.*1825, d. Oct. 15, 1880, was a chief and military leader of the Warm Springs APACHE. During the 1870s he alternated between sporadic raiding and the bleak confinement of reservation life. Finally, in 1879, Victorio broke out from the San Carlos reservation in Arizona and led his people to their beloved Black Mountains. For 15 months he kept Mexican and U.S. troops off balance by striking swiftly at different points. His strategically located encampments permitted the enemy to use only limited numbers of attackers, comparable to his own 35 to 50 warriors. In October 1880, at Tres Castillos, on the Plains of Chihuahua, Victorio was surprised by the Mexicans. Unable to escape, he fought until his ammunition gave out and then killed himself.

vicuña [vi-koon'-yuh]   The vicuña, *Lama vicugna*, the smallest member of the camel family, Camelidae, is usu-

The vicuña lives in a band of 1 male and 5–15 females. The male guards his harem against predators by calling an alarm that warns away the females and by placing himself between the harem and the source of danger.

ally found in herds grazing on high-altitude semiarid plains of Peru, Ecuador, and Bolivia. Vicuñas stand about 85 cm (34 in) at the shoulder, are about 1.2 m (4 ft) long, and weigh about 57 kg (125 lb). Overhunted for their wool, they are now rare and protected.

Vidal, Gore [vi-dahl']   The American writer Gore Vidal, b. West Point, N.Y., Oct. 3, 1925, achieved success with his first novel, *Williwaw* (1946), inspired by his wartime service in the Aleutians. *The City and the Pillar* (1948), an account of homosexual life in the United States, and *The Judgment of Paris* (1952), a modernization of the ancient myth, won the respect of critics. *Myra Breckinridge* (1968), an outrageous spoof of Hollywood featuring a transsexual hero/heroine, brought him a much larger reading public. Vidal demonstrated his flair for dialogue and political understanding in two successful plays: *Visit to a Small Planet* (1957) and *The Best Man* (1960; film, 1964). His penchant for re-creating history in novel form led to *Julian* (1964), a fictional biography of the Roman emperor; *Burr* (1973); *Creation* (1981), about the 5th century BC; *Lincoln* (1984); *Empire* (1987); and *Hollywood* (1990). *Duluth* (1983) is a contemporary satire. Vidal's acerbic literary and political essays have been published in the collections *Homage to Daniel Shays* (1973), *Matters of Fact and Fiction* (1977), and *The Second American Revolution* (1982), and *At Home* (1988).

Videla, Jorge Rafael [vee-day-lah]   Jorge Rafael Videla, b. Aug. 20, 1925, was president of Argentina from March 1976 to March 1981. A professional soldier, Videla was commissioned into the army in 1944. He became commander in chief in 1975 and the following year led the coup that overthrew President Isabel Perón. In 1978 he resigned from active service and the ruling junta to assume a 3-year term as president. Most of the excesses of the so-called "dirty war" against terrorism occurred during Videla's early years as president.

After Argentina returned to civilian rule in 1983, Videla and eight other top military leaders were charged with human rights abuses and tried before a civilian court. On Dec. 9, 1985, Videla was sentenced to life imprisonment.

video   The term *video* originally was used in television as a form of shorthand to denote the portion of the electrical signal representing the picture, as opposed to that representing the sound, called *audio*. It was not until the 1970s, with the growth of the new visual electronic media, that it moved into the popular vocabulary, and today it is used to refer broadly to virtually all systems involving the electronic creation or re-creation of images. Television, which gave birth to video, is now one of its branches.

Video has become a dominant force in the lives of Americans. They watch television an average of more than 7 hours a day. As of the late 1980s, nearly 60 million households, or about two-thirds the total, owned videocassette recorders. As of 1990, nearly 54 million households (although not necessarily the same households) were connected to CABLE TV, and approximately half of those were equipped to receive special "premium," or pay-TV, channels. About 2 million families have backyard "dishes" to receive programs directly from COMMUNICATION SATELLITES. Americans make their own videos from cameras and camcorders, or store up TV programs for later viewing, buying some 350 million blank videocassettes per year. And they buy or rent movies or other programs on tape almost 1 billion times a year. Additional millions of Americans use office or home computers with VIDEO DISPLAY TERMINALS.

History

The concept of TELEVISION, the transmission of images over distances, had challenged scientists even before the invention of the movies or radio. The Nipkow scanning disc, invented in 1883, was a metal disc perforated by holes arranged in a spiral. When it revolved, the disc could scan a picture placed behind it. By rapidly changing the picture, the illusion of movement could be achieved and sent, via electric wires, from a transmitter to a receiver.

The present system of electronic television was proposed in detail by a Scotsman, A. A. Campbell-Swinton, in 1908. The many other early television schemes, however, envisioned transmission through wires, not over the air. Guglielmo Marconi's invention of the wireless radio (1895) spurred efforts toward over-the-air transmission of pictures, and in the late 1920s, radio, the motion picture, and television were combined. Charles Francis JENKINS, the inventor of the modern theatrical motion picture projector, in 1928 began regular broadcasts of crude "radiomovies" in Washington, D.C., using motion-picture film as a source. John Logie Baird in 1926 developed a similar mechanical TV system in Britain, which became the basis for the British Broadcasting Corporation's (BBC) first regular television broadcasts.

John Logie Baird's mechanical TV scanner (1926) used perforated, rotating discs to produce a 30-line image, repeated 10 times per second and transmitted electrically to a tiny receiver screen.

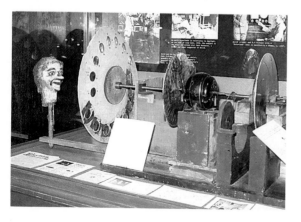

Electronic Television. Electronic television, which eliminated mechanical scanning discs at both the transmitting and receiving ends and substituted CATHODE RAY TUBES as receivers and transmitters, was developed simultaneously and independently in the early 1920s in the United States by Vladimir K. ZWORYKIN and Philo T. Farnsworth, both of whom built on the tube developed in 1897 by Karl Ferdinand Braun in Germany. The first regular broadcasts of electronic television for the public began in London in 1936 (see VIDEO TECHNOLOGY). In the United States an industry-wide engineering committee adopted standards for a 525-line system, but it was not until after World War II that regular broadcasting actually began. The U.S. system was known as NTSC, for the National Television System Committee, which developed it. After World War II, television developed rapidly throughout the world.

Color Television. In 1950 the FCC approved a color-television system that was incompatible with the millions of black-and-white sets then in use. This 441-line system never came into widespread use, and a second NTS Committee was convened to develop a compatible color system. The 525-line NTSC color system, compatible with its black-and-white system, gained FCC approval in 1953, but it was ten years before the public responded and bought color sets in any significant numbers. In Europe, two different 625-line color systems were introduced. These U.S. and European color TV standards are the basis for most video today.

Video Recording. Television's first decade was the "era of live TV," when most original programming was televised at precisely the time that it was produced, because no satisfactory method of VIDEO RECORDING except photographic film was available. Many live television shows actually were televised twice for different time zones. It was possible to make a record of a show, a film shot from the screen of a studio monitor, called a kinescope recording, but these recordings were expensive and of poor quality. It seemed logical that if signals representing audio could be stored on tape, their video counterparts could also be recorded.

The breakthrough came in 1956 from Ampex, the company that had introduced audio tape recording to the United States. The system was called "quad" because of its use of four recording heads; it remained the standard studio broadcast video recording system for nearly 20 years.

Electronic Newsgathering. One of the many early "home" recorders was the Sony-developed U-Matic (1971). It used a tape 0.75 inches (1.9 cm) wide, mounted in a two-reel cassette. A revolving head drum placed a track diagonally on the tape (the "helical scan" principle, used in most modern videocassette recorders). The U-Matic proved too expensive for consumers, but it was embraced by television stations and networks because its portability and good picture quality made possible electronic newsgathering, or ENG.

Just as the U-Matic revolutionized television news, videotape began to transform other aspects of TELEVISION PRODUCTION. (See also RADIO AND TELEVISION BROADCASTING.)

Video Today

Most of the major home video media originated as adjuncts to television broadcasting. These include videotape recording, cable television, and satellite reception, all of which have become, in one way or another, competitors of, or alternatives to, broadcast television. (See TELEVISION TRANSMISSION.)

The Home VCR. The most spectacular success story in the history of consumer electronics is the videocassette recorder, or VCR. The VCR itself was preceded by several other video devices designed to play recorded material, but not to record. The first was the EVR, or Electronic Video Recording system, a film-based video player unveiled by CBS in 1968. Next came the LaserVision optical VIDEODISC system, developed by Philips of Holland and MCA Laboratories of the United States and introduced to the market in 1978; it later became the basis for the successful digital audio COMPACT DISC (CD) system. RCA introduced (1981) the low-cost Capacitance Electronic Disc (CED) system, which used grooves and a stylus—similar to an acoustic phonograph record—to reproduce video.

In 1975, Sony marketed Betamax, a VCR based on its U-Matic system but using tape 0.5 inches (1.27 cm) wide in a smaller cassette. It was a quick success, both in Japan and the United States. The giant Matsushita Electric Industrial Corporation soon adopted another system called VHS (for Video Home System), which had been developed by its subsidiary, the Japan Victor Company (JVC).

The Betamax Case. VCRs initially were widely advertised as "time-shift" devices that allowed owners to record broadcasts when they were shown, but watch them at their own convenience. Two major motion picture studios, MCA and Disney, filed suit in 1976 against Sony, charging that the main purpose of the VCR was the violation of copyrights. Sony and its codefendants argued that viewers had the right to record programs from the public airwaves in the privacy of their own homes. In 1984, Sony (and by implication the VCR industry) won a complete victory in the U.S. Supreme Court, whose decision gave viewers the legal right to record programs broadcast by television stations.

Cassette Sale and Rental. With the rapid growth of the VCR population, sales and rental of recorded videocassettes—particularly motion pictures—became a huge business, giving rise to the new phenomenon of video stores, now omnipresent.

The Home Video Terminal. With the growing popularity of video devices—not only VCRs but home computers and sophisticated video games—the television set or receiver has evolved into a home video terminal. With many new signal sources in addition to off-air broadcasts, monitor-receivers are replacing receive-only sets. Such monitors have special video inputs that can accept video signals from a variety of devices.

Increasingly, receiver circuits are employing digital technology. Some monitor-receivers now use digital circuits for all signal processing, and thus they are, in effect,

This family possesses every electronic device needed for watching and recording TV; for hearing and taping music; for creating their own video images; and for making use of such systems as teletext.

computers that receive and display video pictures. The digital circuits are compatible with such other digital devices and systems as computers and TELETEXT and VIDEOTEX information retrieval services.

The Digital Future. In 1986 the first digital videotape recorders were introduced for broadcast use. These have made possible a degree of excellence never before obtained in professional video recording, particularly when editing requires the copying of one tape on another.

The Video Industries. Many of the basic principles and designs for video devices and products originated in the United States and Europe—for example, the videotape recorder, video cameras, and video display terminals. Their execution and production, however, have increasingly moved to the Far East, particularly Japan.

The first successful home video recorder was developed in Japan, and virtually all VCRs since then have been designed and manufactured there. Even industrial video equipment, such as that made for television stations, increasingly is coming from Japanese firms. Although RCA traditionally had been the dominant force in broadcast equipment, it left the field in 1985 after Sony took over the lead in that area. The picture tube has long been a U.S. product, but this area, too, is increasingly being dominated by imports from Korea and Japan.

The Impact of Video

In the decade of the 1950s television threw the motion picture industry into a deep depression as people stayed home to watch the free entertainment that TV provided. The movies fought back with 3D, color, Cinerama, and CinemaScope, and for a time, they managed to hold their own. But with the coming of the VCR and the videodisc player, both of which made movies easily and cheaply available for home viewing, the industry was pushed into another crisis. In response, motion picture producers are using videocassettes to sell their products. Within a matter of months—sometimes weeks—after a film's theatrical premiere, it may show up on videocassette. Shortly

The most dramatic proof of the power of television to attract and influence worldwide audiences of millions was provided by the Live Aid concert, held simultaneously in London and Philadelphia on July 13, 1985, to raise money for African famine relief. Such notable stars as Paul McCartney, David Bowie, Madonna, Joan Baez, and Tina Turner were on camera for a total of 14 hours. Truly international in scope, the broadcast also featured film from other concerts given in countries around the world, and the first televised live performance of a Russian rock group. The event was simulcast to 152 countries via the largest intercontinental satellite hook-up ever attempted. There were, it is estimated, some 1.5 billion people in the TV audience, and pledged donations totaled $70 million.

after its cassette debut, it may appear on one of the new "pay-per-view" cable services. Next in sequence is a regular premium or pay channel, such as Home Box Office or Showtime. The next outlet would be network television, followed by syndication to TV stations.

Thus, movies are now made with the small-screen audience as well as theatergoers in mind. Video techniques are now used in the production and editing of movies, many producers shooting movies simultaneously with video and film cameras for the greater flexibility in editing permitted by electronic recording. In some cases, features are made on videotape and then transferred to film.

The new video media have also had a strong effect on the original video medium, broadcast television. The competition of cable and the VCR for the time and attention of audiences, and the wide variety of choice now available, have reduced the audiences of the broadcast television networks and thus their advertising revenues.

Video is revolutionizing education and training, as schools and colleges learn to use this visual tool. Interactive videodiscs, in which the learner actively participates, are being used increasingly for training, notably in the U.S. armed forces. Some 8,500 private firms and organizations are estimated to have spent $2.3 billion to produce video programs for employees, shareholders, and others in 1985.

For the future, it seems inevitable that video will increase its presence and influence. Some significant factors should be the improvement in pictures through the adoption of high-definition standards; the increasing integration of the computer with the visual media, for more interactive forms of entertainment, education, and training; and the availability to vastly increased numbers of persons of the means of video production—especially, the camcorder and related devices.

GLOSSARY OF VIDEO TERMS

Note: terms followed by an asterisk (*) have separate entries in this encyclopedia.

analog   Information that is reproduced using a continuously varying electronic signal. In video terms, its opposite is digital.

aspect ratio   The proportions of a TV or film picture, generally given as the ratio of width to height. The standard TV picture has an aspect ratio of 4 × 3, or 4:3. High-definition video systems may have aspect ratios of 5 × 3 or greater.

bandwidth   The range of frequencies required for transmitting different types of electronic signals. Color TV needs a broad band—about 4.6 MHz; the telephone requires only a narrow band, less than 4 kHz.

Beta   The first successful home videocassette system, using ½-inch (1.27-cm) tape.

cable TV*   Method of nonbroadcast distribution of video programs directly to homes, generally employing coaxial or fiber-optic cable.

camcorder   One-piece combination video camera and recorder.

carrier wave   An electronic signal that is capable of carrying information when the signal is modulated.

CATV   Community antenna television; the predecessor of cable TV. The initials now often refer to cable TV.

CCD   (charge-coupled device*) A semiconductor chip used as a highly efficient light sensor in video cameras.

CCTV   Closed-circuit television.

CRT   (cathode-ray tube*) The screen usually used on a TV set or on a computer terminal.

database*   Computerized store of information that can be reached only via a computer.

DBS   Direct Broadcast Satellite; a system that sends TV broadcasts directly from a communications satellite to home antennas, or dishes.

digital television   TV transmission in the form of binary data, making possible more precise processing of the picture.

dish   The parabolic antenna used for transmitting and receiving signals from communication satellites.

earth station   The ground station that receives (downlink) and sends (uplink) signals to and from communication satellites.

edit, electronic   The removal, or the joining together, of sections of film or videotape material. In film editing, the material is actually cut out, or pasted together mechanically. In electronic editing of videotapes, videotape recorders make the required changes electronically.

8-mm Video   Videocassette format using tape 8 mm (about ⅓ in) wide, used primarily for camcorders.

ENG   Electronic newsgathering; the use of video cameras and tape recorders in place of film systems for news coverage by TV stations.

FAX   (facsimile* transmission) A system that transmits pictures or print electronically.

field   A set of scanning lines that, when interlaced with another set, makes up the "frame," or complete TV picture.

footprint   The particular patch of the Earth's surface reached by the signal from a communications satellite.

frame   A complete TV picture, comprising two fields. The U.S. transmission standard calls for 30 frames transmitted per second.

frequency*   The number of cycles per second of an electromagnetic transmission. 1 hertz (Hz) = 1 cycle per second; 1 kilohertz (kHz) = 1,000; 1 megahertz (MHz) = 1,000,000; 1 gigahertz (GHz) = 1 billion.

front projection   A type of projection TV system in which the picture is projected onto a reflective screen, which is viewed from the same side as the source of the projected picture.

geostationary orbit   The orbit of a communications satellite that allows it to move at the precise speed at which the Earth is rotating, thus remaining at the same spot in the sky relative to the Earth. The orbit is 35,900 km (22,300 mi) above the Earth and directly over the equator.

HDTV   High-definition TV; a technology aimed at producing a video picture containing as much detail as a 35-mm motion picture, with wide-screen aspect ratio and stereophonic sound.

head   In video and audio, an electromagnetic device that both lays down the magnetic track on recording tape and reads an existing track.

helical scan   The basis for most modern videotape recording, in which the signal is recorded as a diagonal track by recording heads on a rapidly revolving drum. The same heads, revolving at the same speed, are used for playback.

Intelsat*   International Telecommunications Satellite Organization; 112-member consortium of countries formed (1964) to launch and operate communications satellites.

kinescope   A TV picture tube. Also, a photographic film made from a TV transmission as it appears on the tube. Once used for recording TV programs, it has been replaced by videotape recording.

LaserVision, LaserDisc   Trade names for the optical videodisc* system in which picture and sound are recorded, and read out by laser.

LCD   (liquid crystal display) A thin, flat glass "sandwich" enclosing a layer of voltage-sensitive liquid. Widely used for calculator and watch displays and, more recently, for portable computer readouts and "pocket television" screens.

LPTV   Low-power TV; TV station with limited broadcasting range, often built in rural areas in order to pick up and amplify distant signals. Also used for broadcast programming to specific audiences.

lux   Unit of light illuminance. Used as a measure of low-light recording capacity in video cameras.

MATV   Master antenna television; a distribution system in which a single antenna is used to feed broadcast TV signals to the occupants of a building or development. SMATV provides the same service but uses a dish antenna to pick up satellite transmissions.

MDS   Multipoint distribution service; a method of distributing video programs from a central high point (usually a tall building) by microwave to subscribers equipped with special antennas. Sometimes called "wireless cable."

modem*   A device used for accessing computer data over telephone lines.

monitor   A video display used in TV studios and designed to receive direct input of video signals from studio cameras, videotapes, and other signal-producing equipment.

monitor-receiver   A television receiver that has video inputs enabling it also to serve as a monitor.

MTS   Multichannel TV sound; provides additional sound channels along with a single picture on a TV channel. The U.S. transmission system can include stereophonic sound as well as additional sound channels.

narrowcasting   Transmission to a specific, small audience (such as Japanese-speaking people, for example), often via low-power, UHF stations.

NTSC   National Television System Committee; a U.S. industry body that developed the black-and-white and color transmission standards used in most Western Hemisphere countries, in Japan, and in some other Far Eastern countries. The NTSC system uses a picture composed of 525 horizontal lines, with 30 frames (complete pictures) transmitted per second.

pay cable   Scrambled TV pictures of premium programs, transmitted by cable, designed for viewing only by those paying a monthly fee for home decoders.

pay-per-view, PPV   A form of pay TV where a specific fee is paid for watching each program selected.

pixel   Picture element; the smallest area of a video picture capable of being delineated by an electrical signal. The number of pixels in a complete picture determines the amount of detail or resolution in the picture. In the United States the TV picture generally holds a maximum of 150,000 pixels.

projection television   A television or video display system in which the picture is projected onto a screen, generally from three separate cathode-ray tubes, one for each primary color.

rear projection   A projection TV system wherein the picture is projected onto a translucent screen, which is viewed from the opposite side.

resolution   Standard measurement of the amount of detail that can be seen in a TV-screen image, expressed in the number of horizontal lines on a test pattern.

RF   Radio frequency; the electromagnetic wave "carrier" that conveys the modulated video signal from a TV station to a home receiver.

scrambling   A method of altering a cable or satellite transmission signal so that it can be seen only by those who own special decoders.

STV   Subscription TV; broadcast TV, transmitted in scrambled form, for which a decoder is needed.

teletext*   System of transmission of alphanumeric and other graphic information by TV stations along with their standard programs, for reception only by specially equipped TV receivers.

transponder   Device on a communications satellite that receives electromagnetic signals and transmits them back to Earth.

TVRO   TV receive-only Earth station; such as a home dish antenna.

UHF   Ultra high frequencies; used by TV channels 14 to 82.

VCR   Videocassette recorder; in which the tape is enclosed in a cassette and the loading within the machine is automatic.

VDT   Video display terminal*; generally used with a computer.

vertical blanking interval (VBI)   The 21 lines between TV frames, transmitted, like the frames, at a rate of 30 times per second. These lines are used for auxiliary information, including teletext, closed captions, and test signals.

VHF   Very high frequencies; used by TV channels 2 to 13.

VHS   A videocassette format, using ½-inch (1.27-cm) tape. VHS-C is a smaller VHS cassette. Super-VHS (S-VHS) incorporates advanced digital circuitry.

videodisc*   A disc resembling a phonograph record that stores both picture and sound for playback.

videotex*   Interactive (two-way) system for accessing written and graphic information on video screens and computer display terminals, which are linked to central computers via telephone lines.

VTR   Videotape recorder, using cassettes or open reels.

---

video, music   A music video is a brief performance on videotape that accompanies the recording of a single popular song. It is generally meant to embellish the song and to conceptualize it visually, and it usually features the vocalists and musicians of the recording. Music videos are available on videocassettes and are shown in nightclubs and theaters, but by far, their major outlet is television.

Although televised music is as old as television itself, music video became a pervasive artistic and social phenomenon only in the early 1980s. In Europe in the late 1970s, record companies began in a serious way to utilize video in order to promote their clients. Well-produced music videos were shown in nightclubs and on TV. The sales effect of these pieces eventually persuaded U.S. record companies to attempt this type of promotion, and in June 1981 the USA Network—a cable TV company—introduced "Night Flight," a weekend program featuring music videos. Two months later, Warner Amex Satellite Entertainment Company launched Music Television, or MTV, the first 24-hour music video channel.

---

video art   Video artists combine many different ways of using video equipment in order both to create and to record a variety of artistic expression. In its simplest manifestations, video art provides videotaped documents of musical, dance, and dramatic performances, of performance art, of on-the-street happenings, or even of self-portraits in motion of the artist at work. In this kind of usage, the video camera performs the same function as a motion picture camera, except that the resulting videotape can be shown on a television receiver immediately after it is shot—allowing performers, for example, to see their work in progress. Videotape editing and the addition of special effects can be done in the artist's studio, using relatively inexpensive and easily available video devices.

As this new medium was developing in the art world, the same small, lightweight video equipment was being used by documentary makers, social activists, and com-

The video for the 1984 song "You Might Think," a hit of the pop-rock group The Cars, won a raft of awards. In surrealistic fantasy, the song's hero appears wherever his girlfriend happens to look—as here, on her alarm clock.

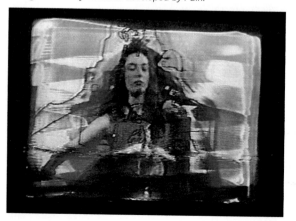
Nam June Paik's Global Groove (1973) featured his longtime partner, cellist Charlotte Moorman. Originally a live TV performance with videotape inserts, it created many of its effects through a video synthesizer developed by Paik.

The videotape Hatsu-Yume *(First Dream) was made in Japan by video artist Bill Viola in 1981. This still was photographed from the videotape by Kira Perov, who specializes in transforming the work of video artists into the quite different mode of still photography. "The passage from one medium to the other," she says, "from the original electronic video signal to the chemical emulsion of film, gives us new information. The image is no longer luminous. It does not emit light, but is printed only with the aid of light. Yet even without its electronic brilliance, the force of the image remains."*

munity groups. Some equipment was made available through cable TV public-access centers, as well as centers that were supported by government funds and private foundations. The technical advance that allowed both video artists and documentary makers to expand the potential in video art was the marketing (1971) of Sony's U-Matic tape recorder, which used ¾-inch (1.9-cm) tape inside a cassette. One-half-inch (1.27-cm) tapes became available in 1975, reducing the cost of a basic production package to about one-third that of ¾-inch tape. Video techniques were soon taught in many public school systems, community centers, and art departments in colleges and universities. Today, many video artists have grown up with television and know its techniques and much about its technology, which may be the same as broadcast television, or their own invention.

See also: COMPUTER GRAPHICS.

video camera   A video camera is capable of recording pictures (see VIDEO RECORDING) and sound on magnetic VIDEOTAPE, which can then be shown on a television screen, via a videocassette recorder (VCR). Small, hand-held amateur video cameras that record only in black and white have been available since the mid-1970s. Color cameras appeared in the late 1970s. Both types require the use of a portable VCR, usually connected to the camera by a cable. The large, professional studio camera, which differs considerably from the amateur camera in construction and technology, is described in VIDEO TECHNOLOGY.

The newest amateur camera technology is the camcorder, introduced in the early 1980s, which is a camera and a VCR combined into one lightweight, compact device.

The imaging technology in amateur video cameras is quite different from that of studio cameras. In a video camera, light collected by the lens is focused on the face-plate of an imaging device. In some cameras this may be a camera tube that contains a color stripe filter that produces the required electrical color signals. (Professional cameras, by contrast, require three separate tubes for the three primary colors.) The most recent video cameras have replaced the tube with a solid-state image sensor, usually a CHARGE-COUPLED DEVICE (CCD), that changes light energy into the electrical pulses that are recorded on videotape. The clarity and resolution of the videotaped pictures depend on the number of picture elements (pixels) that the CCD can create.

Camcorders are available with three separate types of recorder: Beta, VHS, and the relatively new 8-mm, which uses 8-mm (⅓-in) videotape instead of the more common ½-in (1.27-cm) tape found in most videocassettes. A variation of the VHS tape format, the VHS-C, is a miniature VHS cassette.

Automated features found on many video cameras and camcorders resemble those on photographic cameras; these include automatic aperture control, which eliminates the need to vary lens openings to compensate for different lighting conditions; automatic focusing; and manual or powered zoom-lens operation, to permit shooting a variety of scenes from wide-angle to close-up telephoto without changing lenses. Automatic or easily adjusted white-balance settings assure color accuracy with indoor and outdoor lighting.

Many cameras and camcorders also feature built-in electronic viewfinders—actually miniature black-and-white TV monitors that show exactly what the recorded picture will look like, and can be used for instant playback of scenes that have just been recorded. Microphones fitted to the camera pick up sound signals and record them on the appropriate section of the videotape, along with the video signals picked up by the camera itself.

A video camera capable of taking still pictures reached

The camcorder combines the video camera and videocassette recorder (VCR) in one compact, lightweight unit. Camcorders are available in Beta, VHS, VHS-C, and 8-mm tape formats as well as in the high-end S-VHS and S-VHS-C configurations. The Sony Betamovie, shown here, was the first camcorder on the market. Although the Betamovie uses standard Beta cassettes, its head drum is only 44.7 mm (1.76 in) in diameter. (The standard Beta VCR's head drum is 74.5 mm/2.93 in.) The drum rotates at 3,600 rpm, twice the speed of a standard VCR; with each revolution, its two heads each records information. The tape is almost completely wrapped around the drum—at a circumference of 300° instead of the usual 180°. It therefore uses less time to record a video field. To compensate, the recorded image is kept sharp by a high-speed scanning system. These design innovations produce a picture that is higher in quality than that of the standard Beta VCR, but they also prevent use of the Betamovie on the Beta VCR. Other camcorders differ in design both from the Betamovie and from each other. The VHS format, for example, uses four recording heads, records at the same speed as a standard VCR, and offers the possibility of instant playback. Many camcorders, however, use the smaller VHS-C format, which requires the use of an adapter to play the tapes in a home machine.

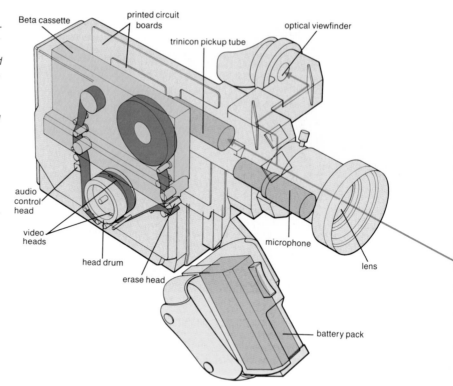

the market in 1986. Resembling a single-lens reflex film camera, this device records 50 still pictures on a floppy disk enclosed in a cartridge. The electronic imaging sensor is a CCD that can produce 380,000 pixels, giving its pictures slightly more definition than a high-quality TV image. With its auxiliary equipment, including a printer and a digital telephone transmitter, this camera has proved useful for professionals who need to transmit still pictures quickly.

video display terminal   A video display terminal (VDT) is the visual display screen of a computer. Most VDTs receive their images from a CATHODE-RAY TUBE, the same type as that used in conventional television receivers, although a few employ LIQUID CRYSTAL display technology. Originally, most VDTs displayed their information in green lettering on a dark background. This combination proved difficult to read, and many newer screens use color and offer much stronger resolution.

There are millions of VDTs now in use in factories and offices, and as computerization grows more commonplace the screen will become the standard workstation for a vast number of workers. Questions have been raised about the effects of these screens upon the health of workers. It has been suggested that they may induce high levels of stress, headaches, and eyestrain, and that in the case of pregnant women, they may increase the risk of miscarriage or birth defects. Although to date no deleteri-

ous connection has been established, the National Institute for Occupational Safety and Health (NIOSH) plans an extended study of the potential health effects of VDTs.

See also: INPUT-OUTPUT DEVICES.

video game   A video game is a contest between a player and a computer-designed program on a machine equipped with a video screen and a joystick or buttons that control the game's action. The machine may be designed to play one game, as are those in video-game arcades. On game consoles or home computers one can play any number of games, using different videotape game cartridges.

The first video games were created on mainframe computers by engineers and computer programmers in the late 1950s and early 1960s. In 1972, Nolan Bushnell produced the enormously popular Pong game, a machine in which two players attempted to hit a computerized ball into the opposition's net—all in black and white on a video screen. Space Race, Gotcha, Tank, the voracious disembodied mouth, Pacman, and—most popular of all—Space Invaders quickly followed. In Space Invaders, a movable cursor fires at an ever-oncoming line of shapes representing spaceships. Bushnell marketed Atari, a game console that plays through a TV set, beginning in 1979. Its formidable competitor, the Japanese Nintendo, had captured 85% of the U.S. video-game market by 1988.

In "Atomic Castle," a laser disc–operated video game, the choices made by the player will change the course of the game itself. The computer-controlled laser disc combines high-resolution graphics, animation, and live actors to achieve a remarkable visual realism.

There are those who feel that in order to play, one must accept the values implicit in these interactive games, which—like the often-condemned Dungeons and Dragons—may involve extremely violent or aberrant events and characters. Other types of games—especially those which use simulation (flying a plane, driving a car, escaping from a maze)—are simply highly imaginative tests of intelligence and skill. Defenders of the games claim that they help prepare children for later computer use and give them the opportunity to learn how to reach and carry out decisions quickly. (See also GAMES.)

video recording Several technologies for recording and playing back television pictures and sound are possible today, the most popular being the use of magnetic tape. The recording of electrical TV signals may also be accomplished with VIDEODISCS, using one of the three following methods. (1) The Capacitance Electronic Disc (CED) records in narrow grooves on discs resembling ordinary phonograph records, and plays back through a TV receiver using a mechanical stylus analogous to a phonograph stylus. (2) The Video High Density (VHD) technique uses a grooveless disc over which a stylus slides, sensing electric signal variations that are converted into television signals. (3) The optical, or laser, disc records TV signals in the form of tiny pits, which form a digital code. The code is both recorded and read back by a laser.

By far the most common means of storing television pictures, however, is through the use of a videocassette recorder (VCR), which is connected to the TV receiver and which employs magnetic tape as the signal-storage medium. Magnetic VIDEOTAPE is a plastic-based tape that has been coated with tiny magnetizable particles. During recording, tape heads—either one or two pairs, mounted on a rapidly rotating head drum inside the recorder—generate a magnetic field, which is transferred to the tape in the form of magnetized patterns. During playback, these magnetic patterns are electronically processed by the heads into a standard broadcast television signal that can be viewed or heard on a conventional TV set.

All home video recording systems employ tape that moves relatively slowly from one cassette reel to the other. The high density of information storage necessary for video signal recording is achieved by having the tape heads spin over the tape at 1,800 rpm, or 30 times a second. Each rotation traces a diagonal path across the tape in a technique known as helical scan recording. Each angled, magnetized video pattern corresponds to a single "field" of a video transmission, and two fields represent a complete frame, or picture (see VIDEO TECHNOLOGY). Thirty frames per second is the TV standard used in the United States; hence the head-drum rotational speed of 30 revolutions per second, or 1,800 rpm.

The sound track accompanying the video signals may be recorded either as a separate, horizontal track at the top or bottom of the tape; or, in so-called HiFi videocassette recordings, as an integral part of the video signal. In the latter case, audio quality is much improved and can be recorded stereophonically, on two separate sound tracks for left and right stereo channels. The newest 8-mm video recording systems make provision for several types of accompanying audio recording tracks, including a stereophonic system that uses a form of digital audio recording.

The first videotape recorder was demonstrated in 1951. It used 1-inch-wide (2.54-cm) tape traveling past stationary magnetizing tape heads at 100 inches per second, producing a very poor picture. By 1956, however, a tape recorder developed by the Ampex Corporation was used for the first time by a TV network. Its quality was so much superior to that of the kinescope—quick-developing film shot from the picture on a TV screen—that it became standard in TV studios, ending the era of the use of photographic film on television.

Sony's first videotape recorder, developed in the late 1960s, employed open-reel, ½-inch-wide (1.27-cm) tape. In 1971, Sony introduced U-Matic, a ¾-inch (1.9-cm) tape format that is still very much in use for professional applications, such as newsgathering by TV reporters in the field. Betamax, another Sony invention, was a ½-inch tape enclosed in a cassette that could be used in a relatively simple home recording machine, the videocassette recorder, or VCR. Barely a year later, Japan Victor Company (JVC) produced its first VHS-format (Video Home System) recorder, which, though similar in concept to the Beta machine, was incompatible with it.

The basic differences between Beta and VHS relate to the size of the tape cassettes and the method of loading, or wrapping the tape about the tape-recording head drum when a cassette is inserted in a VCR. Duration of recording differs as well. The maximum recording time for a Beta cassette (at the slowest Beta III speed) is 5 hours, whereas maximum recording time for a VHS cassette at its slowest speed, using extended-length tape on a thinner plastic base—which allows more tape to be wrapped around the cassette reel—is 8 hours.

The basic parts of a videocassette recorder include: control buttons (1); digital display panel (2); channel selectors (3); timer controls (4); power-supply units (5); power-supply transformer (6); power input (7); receiver and antenna attachments (8); tuner unit (9); main electronics (10); VHS videotape cassette (11); supply reel (12); take-up reel (13); motor for cassette loading (14); take-up tape disc (15); capstan shaft (16); audio control heads (17); inertia rollers (18); capstan motor (19); drum housing the video heads (20); erase head (21); tape tension arm (22); supply reel disc (23); rewind idler (24); and diagonal recording tracks (25). The top track records sound; the center contains the video signals; and the bottom track controls synchronization of sound and audio.

Portable videocassette recorders, which operate on battery power, have been available since the late 1970s. When combined with a color VIDEO CAMERA, such VCRs permit the making of home movies that can be played back through any compatible VCR and viewed on a TV screen. Recently, the functions of the video camera have been combined with those of a VCR in the form of lightweight camera-recorder combinations called camcorders.

Video recorders have had a profound effect on the way people seek entertainment. One can buy video recordings of the latest popular films, educational materials, self-help cassettes, and so forth or rent such cassettes at a nominal cost. A landmark U.S. Supreme Court decision has ruled that it is legal to record and play back programs broadcast by TV stations, so long as this is done for personal, noncommercial use. So-called time-shifting—setting VCR controls to record a program automatically, for viewing at a time later than the original broadcast—is a primary use of VCRs. Most machines can be programmed to record two or more events that will be broadcast up to four weeks later.

video technology   Modern video technology now encompasses imaging and display techniques that make it possible to convert optical images into electrical signals and vice versa. These video signals can be used to create an accurate optical reproduction of the original color image on a TELEVISION screen.

The imaging process depends on a number of photosensitive devices that convert light into electrical signals. These include vacuum-type camera tubes that are scanned by an electron beam, flying spot scanners that read photographic film and translate it into video images, and CHARGE-COUPLED DEVICES (CCDs), which are solid-state light sensors in chip form. The televised image can be re-created by a direct-view or projection CATHODE-RAY TUBE, by a LIQUID CRYSTAL display, by large-screen luminescent panels created by gas-plasma devices, or by light-valve projectors, which employ a fixed light source and special optical systems to project video images.

Video technology also includes complex analog and digital signal processing at the source, to mix images or create special effects. A similar, although much simpler, video-signal processing can take place in the monitor or home receiver, to display multiple images on the screen or to extract data from the video signal that provides useful information, including TELETEXT and VIDEOTEX.

Television depends on two fundamentals of physics, the conversion of light (photons) into commensurate electrical impulses (scanning and transmission), and the electroluminescence principle that generates light output in a chemical substance in proportion to an electrical input (display).

Between the original live image and the final reproduced image there lies a vast array of signal-processing techniques that permit the video signal to be manipulated and distributed to the end viewer.

Until the early 1970s, television signals were almost all analog, that is, the video signal representing a given optical scene was a continuously variable voltage, whose value at any point reflected the luminance (brightness) and chrominence (color hue and saturation) of the picture element being transmitted. As digital techniques developed, much of the analog video-processing circuitry was replaced by high-speed sampling methods that convert the continuously changing values of the video signal into binary digital bits, each representing a discrete signal level. (See DIGITAL TECHNOLOGY.)

The Picture Element

Television depends on the methodical sequential scanning of a color image, in order to relay it over a single channel from the source to its final destinations. To do so the original image must be broken down into picture elements called pixels. A pixel is the smallest area of a TV image that can be reproduced by an electrical signal.

For the television system to transmit properly, an exploring spot scans progressively across each picture element from the top left to the bottom right corner of the image. In scanning, the image is broken down into a series of horizontal lines (in the United States, 525 lines is the standard). In a process called interlaced scanning, the scanner "reads" every even line on one scan, producing one "field." The second scan reads the odd-numbered lines left empty during the first scan, producing the second field. The scanning process is repeated continuously, producing 30 frames, or complete scenes, per second. The continuous video signal generated by this action is interspersed by synchronizing pulses, and is relayed via a communications system to the home receiver. There, a reproducing spot, scanning the picture tube in synchronism with the scanning element in the studio, will re-create the image.

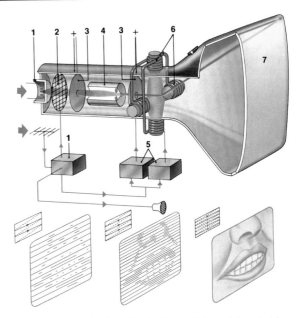

A black-and-white television set receives transmitted signals (arrow) *at its antenna. A tuner* (1) *selects the desired channel and separates the audio signal, which is processed the same as in FM radios. The visual signal is applied to a grid* (2) *in the picture tube to vary the intensity of the electron beam. This beam is accelerated by two positively charged anodes* (3) *and magnetically focused* (4). *Synchronization circuits* (5) *control horizontal and vertical magnetic deflectors* (6) *that sweep the beam across the phosphor-coated screen* (7). *The amount of detail is determined by the number of lines.*

In existing TV-broadcasting systems, the picture elements are defined by the system parameters, such as line structure and channel bandwidth. High Definition TV (HDTV), the most advanced TV transmission system, uses line structures ranging above 1,000 and bandwidths up to 30 MHz, thus allowing for sharper resolution, both horizontally and vertically. Japan is already broadcasting in HDTV, and Europe is developing its own system. It is hoped that if the United States can agree on HDTV standards U.S. transmission systems will also convert to HDTV.

The Camera Tube

The invention of the iconoscope by Vladimir ZWORYKIN and of the Image Dissector by Philo T. Farnsworth in the early 1920s led to electronic television as it is known today. Subsequent improvements in imaging-tube technology produced the orthicon and vidicon—which first transmitted images in black and white—and, as color television developed, the Plumbicon and Saticon were added. More recently, new imaging devices have been invented that use solid-state charge-coupled devices (CCDs) or metal oxide semiconductors (MOS) as image sensors.

Photoemission. The conversion of light into a series of electrical signals is accomplished by a variety of photo-sensitive devices that function as camera elements on which the scene to be televised is optically focused. The energy in the photons of light coming through the camera lens and falling on the photosensitive surface is converted into free electrons in a process called photoemission.

The most common photosensitive devices used in TV cameras are vacuum-tube types, such as vidicons, Plumbicons, and Saticons. Here, a thin layer of a complex metal alloy is placed on a substrate and located at the front end of a glass vacuum tube. An electron gun scans the rear of the substrate with an electron beam. Electrons freed from the photosensitive layer modulate the current flow from the electron gun in proportion to the light falling on the front surface of the light-sensitive metal-alloy layer. The readout of this variable current is the video signal, representing the actual brightness at each point in the scene.

Photoconduction. Another type of camera tube uses the process of photoconduction. Here the light falling on a layer of semiconducting material changes the conductivity of the material in proportion to the light intensity at a given point. A CCD is a photoconductor, a light sensor whose electrical conductivity is changed by the absorption of photons. In the CCD camera, three small solid-state chips (about $\frac{1}{3} \times \frac{1}{2}$ in/0.84 × 1.27 cm) replace the camera tubes and act as imagers for the red, green, and blue components of the color image. There are several varieties of semiconductor, solid-state imagers.

Whether the image sensor is the front "window" of a camera vacuum tube, or the exposed surface of a CCD chip, the method of producing a color television image is the same. The original image is picked up by the camera

Color-television cameras use dichroic mirrors (1) to split a colored image into red, green, and blue components that are fed into separate camera tubes (2). One encoding unit (3) combines the output signals into a luminance signal (4), intended for black-and-white sets. Other encoders (5, 6) convert the signals into a chrominance signal (7) containing information for color sets. The luminance signal is then amplified (8) and combined with the color signal for transmission (9).

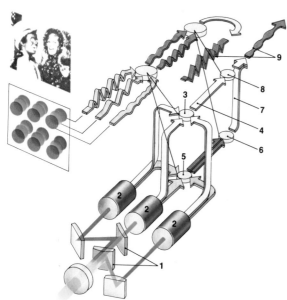

lens and relayed through an optical system that includes red and blue dichroic mirrors. These mirrors essentially split light into its primary colors: the red mirror reflects red, but allows blue and green to pass through; the blue mirror reflects blue, but allows the passage of red and green. In this way the reflected light from the scene is divided into its primary color elements, and each separate color is directed to its appropriate imaging device. The red, blue, and green video signals generated by the image sensors are then matrixed—that is, they are cross-mixed—and signals conveying luminance (brightness) and chrominance (color hue and saturation) are added.

When modulated on a radio frequency (RF) carrier on an assigned channel frequency, the signal can be picked up by a home receiver and decoded to display the original color scene on the picture tube.

The Picture Tube

On the display side, the vast majority of color-television sets use a direct-view picture tube, ranging in size from 2 to 40 in (5 to 92 cm) measured diagonally. These tubes have one of two basic fluorescent-screen structures, known as the dot phosphor shadow mask and the strip phosphor Trinitron (a trademark of the Sony Corp.).

In both cases, chemical compounds (phosphors) that convert electron-beam energy into radiant light, forming the additive primary colors (red, green, blue), are deposited on the inner face of the glass picture tube in precision arrays of dots or stripes with alternate colors. A power supply and scanning circuits provide the voltages that energize the picture tube. Processing circuitry decodes the video signal into the red, green, and blue components that drive the picture tube's electron guns. The video signal controls the intensity and position of the electron stream from the guns. As the beams scan the light-emitting phosphors in the tube, the color image is reconstructed on the face of the tube. The lag effect in the tube and the retentivity of the human retina both contribute to the illusion of a continuous image on the screen, even with rapid motion in the picture. The audio signal is detected, amplified, and fed to the speaker.

Flat-Screen TV. The ultimate television set will hang on the living room wall like a picture, and be only a few inches thick. The most promising technology in this field is the liquid crystal display (LCD), which has produced pocket-size portable TV sets with up to 4-in (10.2-cm) diagonal screens. While screen diagonals up to 12 in (30.5 cm) have been demonstrated as prototypes, none have the brightness, resolution, or contrast range of a direct-view picture tube.

At the other end of the scale, very large flat screens have been built for installation at large athletic parks, where they serve as giant scoreboards or huge television screens. The largest such screen by far was built by Sony at the Tsukuba Expo 85 in Japan. Using individual triads of red, green, and blue "trini-lites" (color phosphors arrayed together inside a cell), the screen stood 14 stories high and could easily be seen by 50,000 viewers.

Projection Television. Larger television images can be achieved through the use of a variety of projection sys-

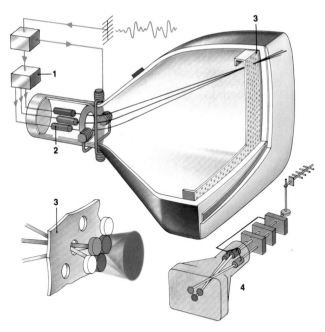

A color-television-set receiver has a decoding circuit (1) that separates the incoming signal into the red, green, and blue signals originally picked up by the camera tubes. Three electron guns (2), one for each color signal, emit beams that scan a television screen coated with phosphor dots arranged in triads. The dots fluoresce with a red, green, or blue glow when struck by an electron beam. Between the electron gun and screen is the shadow mask (3). The holes in the mask are arranged so that the electron beam from the blue gun, for instance, can bombard only the blue phosphor dots (4).

tems that are designed for home or professional environments. Home projection TV systems are usually the enclosed cabinet variety, with screens ranging from 40 to 50 in (92 to 127 cm) diagonally. The image comes from three high-brightness cathode ray tubes, each providing a primary color. These are projected through a folded mirror system, on the rear of the translucent screen.

Larger screens normally employ front projection, using either CRTs or light-valve techniques, and can produce television images on theater-size screens.

Digital and Analog in Video Technology

Both the sensing of a video image and its subsequent display are basically analog, created as they are by a continuously varying electric signal. However, the processing of video signals in their transition from the camera to the receiver screen can often be improved by converting them into digital form. The major advantage of handling a video signal in digital form is that it can be manipulated with special effects or used for image overlays or multiple-image mixing without any degradation in image quality. The digital signal is almost impervious to degradation.

Within the home receiver, conversion to digital will improve the visual display by adding features not normally possible with analog circuits. CCD memories within the receiver will permit a "picture in picture" display, allow-

ing the viewer to watch one channel on the full screen, with the video from another channel or from a VCR displayed in a small box in the corner of the screen.

Digital video techniques will continue to take over more of the TV image chain. As digital components become more plentiful and more cost effective, both TV studio equipment and consumer electronic devices will become more digitized.

Television Resolution

The quality of a television image is usually rated in lines of resolution and may range from 200 to 400 depending on the sophistication of the receiver circuitry. Even the best TV monitor or receiver, however, cannot display a better picture than the TV camera can produce on a given scanning system.

To improve television images beyond their fundamental limits and to create a high-definition television (HDTV) image will require a change of the basic scanning methods now in use. Several proposals have been made in the United States, Japan, and Europe for high-definition television systems using horizontal-line rates of 1,125 to 1,250, and expanding the picture to a 5:3 aspect ratio to give it a wide-screen look, thus emulating the cinema screen. These HDTV systems will produce television images with 4 to 6 times the visual information content of a normal TV picture, increase the contrast ratio, and remove the visible line structure common to standard TV images.

Television Transmission

The television channel that carries pictures and sound into the home receiver is part of a very rigid system of FREQUENCY ALLOCATIONS made by the International Telecommunications Union (ITU) to various regions around the world because space in the electromagnetic spectrum is so scarce and valuable. In the United States the Federal Communications Commission (FCC) handles frequency allocation.

A high definition TV (HDTV) image is projected on a screen measuring 10 ft (3.05 m) diagonally. The quality of the image rivals that of film. In the future, feature films might be made in HDTV and distributed via satellite simultaneously to thousands of electronic cinemas.

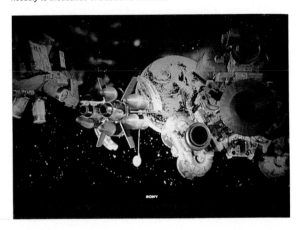

In North America the standard television channel is 6.0 MHz wide. Video signals are transmitted in a single sideband mode (sideband signals are present immediately above and below the carrier frequency), with the picture carrier at 1.25 MHz above the lower frequency boundary, and the sound carrier at 0.25 MHz below the upper boundary. This provides the video signal a 4.2 MHz channel, in which the color subcarrier is placed at 3.58 MHz above the picture carrier. (See also TELEVISION TRANSMISSION.)

Television signals must be transmitted in accordance with FCC regulations, with regard to the signal format, radiated power, modulation depth, and a variety of other parameters that adhere to the rules of good practice. These standards assure that the viewer will receive a stable, high-quality image and clear sound.

Video Recording Technologies

A permanent record of a television image or program can be made on film, on magnetic tape or discs, on optical discs, or in a solid-state memory called a frame buffer (see VIDEO RECORDING). Before the development of the first practical videotape recorder by Ampex Corporation in 1956, all television programs were recorded on film by kinescope recorders. Since then, videotape has become the preferred medium for almost every variety of programming applications.

Electronic cinematography has become the all-encompassing term for the use of television cameras to create program material, which is recorded, edited, and distributed on reels of videotape. In motion pictures there are three basic formats—35-mm professional, 16-mm industrial/educational, and Super 8-mm home movies. In the videotape world, things are not that simple. Professional videotape comes in 2-inch, 1-inch, ¾-inch, ½-inch, ¼ inch, and 8-mm widths, with enough different recording methods to create at least 15 noninterchangeable formats. In home video there are two half-inch formats, VHS and Beta, and the new 8-mm video format, none of which can play each other's tape cassettes.

Videotape Recording. VIDEOTAPE consists of a strip of plastic backing coated with a permanent layer of tiny metal particles imbedded in a durable resin. The videotape is capable of recording and then playing back the original video signal and the accompanying sound.

In broadcast television, videotape recorders can now reproduce television programs that are virtually indistinguishable from a live show, although such machines are relatively complex and expensive. Because videotaping a TV show permits correcting any mistakes made, and allows cost-effective scheduling of TV studio facilities, most major programs are taped, then replayed at the appropriate time slot in each time zone. (See also TELEVISION PRODUCTION.)

Camcorders. Television crews who go out in mobile vehicles to cover the news usually carry electronic cameras that incorporate a video recorder either as a separate portable unit or as a built-in cassette recorder on the camera. These self-contained battery-operated camcorders, weighing about 7 kg (15 lb), permit very flexible coverage in tight places and make possible pictorial results of very high visual impact. The imaging and videotape recording techniques developed for broadcasting have also resulted in the production of consumer-oriented devices, such as compact and affordable videocassette recorders.

Videocassette Recorders. Originally, home VCRs came in two incompatible formats, the Beta system developed by Sony and the VHS made by several manufacturers. Although both systems produced comparable images, the VHS configuration has now taken over the bulk of the market and is currently the leading format in sales, availability of prerecorded movies, and variety of accessories.

Optical Recorders. Video or audio signals can also be stored on optical discs by using lasers to record and play back the spiral tracks. The larger size VIDEODISC (30.5 cm/ 12 inches in diameter) can hold over one hour of normal television programming, one hour of a movie, or 15 minutes of high-definition TV, all with stereo sound. The COMPACT DISC can also be used for storing computer data, in which capacity it is called a CD-ROM (Read-Only Memory).

The advantage of the optical, or laser-read, disc over videotape is that it is virtually indestructible, since non-contact optical readout gives it an unlimited life. It also has a very high information-packing density and provides rapid random access to the information on the disc. The disadvantage, at least at present, is that the user cannot record a program but must buy a prerecorded disc.

Graphics Technology

Video Art. The development of COMPUTER GRAPHICS systems permit graphic artists to create images directly in the television medium, greatly influencing daily programming. This section emphasizes the technological aspects. For the artistic aspects, see VIDEO ART.

Electronic "paint systems" use a palette on which the artist renders the image with a stylus or light pen while watching a color television monitor to see the actual image being produced. The color monitor will also show the artist a wide selection of colors, a variety of print fonts, and various shapes such as circles, squares, and triangles (see PAINTBOX).

External images can also be entered through a video camera and digitized, so that they may be altered in size, position, or coloration. The more-advanced computer-graphics systems will also permit animation of the images to form a moving sequence.

TV station identification, logos, commercial spots, and news inserts are usually created on computer-graphics systems. The graphics can also be combined with live images.

Computer-graphics systems have steadily come down in size and price. These smaller systems are capable of three-dimensional rendering of television images and can be programmed to create animated segments for assembly on a videotape recorder.

Computerized Animation. The commercials and cartoons that are being produced today for television broadcasting are often made on computer-graphics systems with extended capabilities. While the individual images may be created by a system similar to the computer-

The digital TV set—the newest major consumer advance in video technology—replaces some 400 analog components with a digital chip and adds a computer memory to store image information. Among its advantages is the capacity to display several channels at once.

graphics system just described, the animation is dependent on larger computers with more memory and more capabilities. The key to generating the animation is to create a start "key frame" and an end "key frame." By telling the computer the rate at which the beginning and end images should progress, the computer will do all of the calculations, and produce the intermediate images to go smoothly from start to finish. Short animated sequences of this nature (up to 30 sec) can be stored on digital discs, from which they are transferred to tape and sequenced with past and future segments.

Video Special Effects. To heighten visual impact during a television show, images can be manipulated in a way that will make them appear more interesting. Because video signals can be digitized and put into a frame buffer (a color-information storage device) in pixel form, it is also possible to read out these pixels in a nonlinear form. The original image may have been rectangular, but with the proper software it can be read out as a trapezoid, circle, or some other shape. Similarly, the image may be zoomed, tumbled, overlaid with other images, or made to disappear into the horizon. These effects can be done in real time by a "joystick" and a series of function keys that select the type of effect desired. In many cases these digital video effects are recorded, and the tape is used for opening a new show. It is also possible to use these effects during live programming to enhance the appearance of the home viewers' image.

videocassette recorder   see VIDEO; VIDEO RECORDING

—

videodisc   Videodiscs resemble phonograph recordings in appearance and size but are able to store video as well as audio programming. Several types of videodiscs have been developed. The Philips Company of the Neth-

erlands developed the laser-optical type of videodisc in which video and audio signals are encoded in the form of microscopic pits beneath the surface of a reflective disc measuring approximately 30.5 cm (12 in) in diameter. A laser beam tracks and reads the video and audio data inscribed in this manner and translates the data into electrical signals that may then be seen and heard on a TV set or video monitor screen. (See also COMPACT DISC; VIDEO TECHNOLOGY.)

—

videotape   Videotape is thin, plastic tape—usually a polyester—covered with a surface layer of metallic particles and used for storing video and audio signals. For many years videotape was used almost exclusively by the television industry for recording programs for rebroadcast. Videotape is now available to the consumer for many uses, including recording off the television at home by means of a videocassette recorder and live-action recording with a VIDEO CAMERA.

Videotape recording employs the same analog, magnetic technology of audio tapes, whereby information converted into electromagnetic form causes metallic particles embedded in tape to orient themselves in correspondence with particular frequencies and dynamics (see SOUND RECORDING AND REPRODUCTION). The metal particles used most often to coat tape are ferric oxide (doped with cobalt) and chromium dioxide.

The methodology of video recording differs from that of audio recording. In recording video signals, the tape is moved slowly past recording heads that, instead of remaining stationary, sit along the edge of a wheel that rotates in a plane perpendicular to, or on a bias with, the passing tape. This perpendicular or helical scanning places more information on the tape—which is necessary for reproducing complex video images. This technique also allows for video stop-action: when the tape is stopped, the playback heads can continue to scan a single piece of tape, thereby reproducing a single picture frame. Ordinarily, the top and bottom edges of videotapes contain conventional audio tracks. Some types of tape, however, incorporate the audio signal into the diagonal video tracks, producing a much higher-fidelity sound. Audio on 8-mm tape, recorded in the same tracks as the video, can be used for audio recording alone, with a capacity of about 12 hours.

Videotape used by the television industry has a standard 2-in (5.08-cm) or 1-in (2.54-cm) width and is mounted on large reels. The more well-known consumer videotapes have a 0.5-in (1.27-cm) width and are contained within plastic cassettes for easy use in VIDEO RECORDING. The even thinner, 8-mm (0.31-in) tape is marketed for use in hand-held video camera/recorders, or camcorders. This latest tape technology requires a higher-density coating of pure metal particles (rather than oxides) in order to maintain picture quality.

—

videotex   Videotex is an interactive electronic technology that delivers information and transactional services such as banking and shopping through a computer/telephone communications system. Users can retrieve information or conduct transactions (such as paying bills, buying airline tickets, or relaying electronic messages) using a special terminal device hooked up to a TV set, or to a personal computer, and connected—generally via telephone lines—to a host computer. Customers pay a per-use charge or a monthly subscription fee to use the service. TELETEXT, a semi-interactive, information-supplying service, is available for television viewers who own special decoders. In contrast to videotex, it offers much smaller and more-restricted information categories.

Information and service providers (such as news organizations, banks, brokerage houses, merchandisers, and travel packagers) supply information for videotex systems and often manage their transactions (for example, ticket or stock purchases) through "gateways" that permit computerized information to be accessed from their own computers.

Videotex growth has been much slower than was originally predicted, despite the efforts of many organizations to develop and market videotex services. In North America, major newspaper publishers, banks, and computer and telephone companies have developed and tested videotex systems. Some projects have involved cable TV or alternative transmission technologies. Several have used special personal-computer software. From 1981 to 1986 about 60 videotex or hybrid videotex systems were created in the United States, most on a local or regional basis—although some offered nationwide services, such as electronic mail and coast-to-coast shopping. The most ambitious U.S. videotex ventures—few of which have succeeded—included Viewtron in Miami, Gateway in Los Angeles, and Keyfax in Chicago. All were developed by companies affiliated with major newspaper publishers.

On the other hand, videotex DATABASE systems—among them, CompuServe, The Source, and Dow Jones News/Retrieval—have attracted sizable national audiences, primarily individuals interested in services that provide such information as stock-market statistics, news reports, and business analysis.

In Europe and Japan, government-run telecommunications agencies have developed their own videotex systems. Often these systems are related to other communications services, such as computerized electronic phone directories. In France, since 1983 the Minitel project has given away about two million inexpensive terminals to telephone subscribers who use their videotex machines to obtain free directory information or, for a fee, real-estate listings, news stories, weather forecasts, restaurant guides, and TV schedules. Britain's Prestel, West Germany's Bildschirmtext, and Japan's Captain system—all government owned—have been moderately successful.

Vidor, King [vee'-dohr]   King Vidor, b. Galveston, Tex., Feb. 8, 1896, d. Nov. 1, 1982, was one of the pioneer directors of the U.S. film industry. He worked as a scriptwriter and newsreel cameraman in Hollywood before becoming an independent producer in 1918. *The Big Parade* (1925), one of the earliest films to depict World War I, was the director's first great success. Vidor's achievements as an innovative filmmaker reached their peak with *The Crowd* (1928), the all-black *Hallelujah* (1929), and *Our Daily Bread* (1934), works that display a growing interest in the editing techniques of the Soviet cinema. Also from this period were such charming light comedies as *The Patsy* (1928) and *Show People* (1928). Vidor became more stylistically conservative in such films as *The Citadel* (1938) and *Northwest Passage* (1940). Toward the end of his career he revealed a flair for melodrama in *Duel in the Sun* (1946), *The Fountainhead* (1949), and *Ruby Gentry* (1952). *War and Peace* (1956) was his last film epic.

Vieira, António [vy-ah'-ee-ruh]   The Portuguese Jesuit António Vieira, b. Feb. 6, 1608, d. July 18, 1697, was one of the most famous preachers and orators of his day, and his writings are considered models of Portuguese prose. During his long and varied life, he was court preacher and diplomat for King John IV of Portugal in the 1640s, a missionary in Brazil in the 1650s, a prisoner of the Inquisition from 1665 to 1667, and an advocate (in Rome) on behalf of the Portuguese Jews in the early 1670s.

Vienna   Vienna (German: Wien), in northeastern Austria, is located on the Danube River at an elevation of 202 m (664 ft). The capital of Austria and an autonomous province, it has a population of 1,482,825 (1988)—nearly one-quarter that of the entire country. Long the seat of the HABSBURG dynasty (Holy Roman emperors and, later, emperors of Austria), Vienna retains its imperial style.

Contemporary City. The heart of old Vienna is the Innere Stadt (Inner City), an area surrounded by a horseshoe-shaped wall that confined the city as late as the 1850s. In 1857, Emperor Francis Joseph decided to raze the wall and replace it with a 57-m-wide (187-ft) Ringstrasse (Ring Street). To line this beautifully landscaped boulevard, the Viennese erected a collection of buildings of varied styles, including the University of Vienna, the City Hall, and the State Opera House (Stadtsoper). Within the Innere Stadt is Saint Stephen's, a Gothic cathedral first built about 1135 and rebuilt during the 14th and 15th centuries. The oldest part of the Hofburg, the imperial palace of the Habsburgs, dates from the 13th century; the chapel (15th century) is now the home of the Vienna Boys Choir. As the strength of the empire grew, the Habsburgs moved to summer homes beyond the protection of the city walls. Schönbrunn Palace, in the southwest part of the city, dates from the late 17th century; the Belvedere, by Johann Lukas von HILDEBRANDT, from the early 18th century.

Vienna concentrated on developing its bureaucracy and service industries while the rest of Europe passed through the Industrial Revolution. It has a metallurgical industry, however, and produces precision instruments and electrical appliances; it also has a reputation for hand-finished goods and for pastries and confections. The city is

This view of Vienna's skyline shows two of the city's historic churches. On the left is the green dome of the Peterskirche, a baroque structure of the early 18th century; on the right, Saint Stephen's Cathedral, with its tall Gothic spire.

the headquarters of many international agencies.

Vienna is an autonomous province of Austria as well as the capital city. In addition to providing the usual municipal services, the city operates many small businesses.

Vienna has one of Europe's richest musical heritages. Franz Josef Haydn began his career in the boys' choir of Saint Stephen's. Beethoven, Mozart, the Strauss family, Schubert, Brahms, Bruckner, Mahler, Schoenberg, and Richard Strauss all lived and worked in Vienna. The VIENNA PHILHARMONIC ORCHESTRA is highly respected. The city's many museums include the Historical Museum of the City of Vienna, the Museum of Fine Arts, and the Albertina, in the Hofburg.

History. Originally a Celtic settlement called Vindobona, the site became a frontier encampment under the Romans. Repeatedly overrun in the great tribal migrations, the site had been resettled and fortified as Wena by the 11th century. It was chartered in 1137 and became the capital of the dukes of Austria. In 1278 the first of the Habsburgs took up residence there. The city was held (1485–90) by Matthias Corvinus of Hungary and unsuccessfully besieged by the Turks in 1529 and again in 1683. The Napoleonic Wars, during which Vienna was twice occupied (1805, 1809) by the French, ended with the Congress of Vienna (1814–15). During the late 19th and early 20th centuries, Vienna flourished as a cultural, philosophical, and scientific center. Following World War I, the Austrian Empire was dismembered, leaving Vienna the capital of a small republic. In 1938, Adolf Hitler annexed Austria to Germany. Badly damaged during World War II, Vienna underwent a quadripartite Allied occupation until 1955, when it was reestablished as the capital of an independent and permanently neutral Austria.

Vienna, Congress of The Congress of Vienna (September 1814–June 1815), convened by the states of Europe after the collapse of Napoleon I's empire, attempted to reestablish a balance of power and restore pre-Napoleonic dynasties where possible. The meeting was hosted by Austrian emperor Francis I (formerly Holy Roman Emperor Francis II) and attended by Emperor ALEXANDER I of Russia, King FREDERICK WILLIAM III of Prussia, and many lesser rulers. Viscount CASTLEREAGH for Great Britain, Prince Karl August von HARDENBERG for Prussia, Count Karl Robert NESSELRODE for Russia, and Prince Klemens von METTERNICH for Austria, representatives of the victorious powers, were the principal negotiators.

Charles Maurice de TALLEYRAND-PÉRIGORD of France was eventually brought into the group to break a deadlock over the demands of Russia for all of Poland and of Prussia for all of Saxony. Ultimately Prussia was given two-fifths of Saxony, and Russia received most of the grand duchy of Warsaw. In addition, Belgium was given to the Netherlands, Prussia received the Rhineland and Westphalia, Nice and Savoy went to Sardinia, and Lombardy and Venetia were given to Austria. A loose GERMAN CONFEDERATION was established primarily for defensive purposes, and Switzerland was neutralized under international guarantee. Denmark ceded Norway to Sweden in exchange for Lauenburg. Legitimate dynasties were restored in Spain, Portugal, and Italy. The settlement created a durable balance of power, but in ignoring nationalist yearnings it left unsolved problems that led to the REVOLUTIONS OF 1848 and later trouble.

See also: PARIS, TREATIES OF; QUADRUPLE ALLIANCE.

Vienna Philharmonic Orchestra No fewer than four dates, from 1833 to 1860, may be given for the founding of the Vienna Philharmonic (Wiener Philharmoniker); perhaps the most significant is 1842, when the orchestra of the Royal Court Opera performed in the Redoutensaal under Otto Nicolai. The Philharmonic, which is also the orchestra of the Vienna State Opera, makes its home in the acoustically superb Musikvereinsaal. Subscriptions to its concerts have remained within families for generations and are virtually unobtainable. Among its chief conductors since Nicolai have been Hans Richter, Gustav Mahler, Felix Weingartner, Wilhelm Furtwängler, Clemens Krauss, Bruno Walter, Herbert von Karajan, and, since 1971, Claudio Abbado.

Vientiane [vee-uhn-tee-en'] Vientiane is the capital and largest city of Laos, on the Mekong River in the northern part of the country, near the border of Thailand. The population is 377,409 (1981 est.). Vientiane is the major port and commercial center in Laos, serving the surrounding agricultural area.

Vientiane became the capital in 1563, when the government was moved from Luang Prabang under pressure of a threat from Burma. The city was sacked by the Thais in 1828. The French established their administrative capital for Laos in Vientiane in 1899. After independence in 1953, Vientiane remained the administrative capital while Luang Prabang served as the royal capital. With the Communist takeover in 1975, however, the kingdom was abolished and Vientiane became the sole capital.

Viet Cong [vee-et' kawng]   In the VIETNAM WAR the insurgent guerrilla movement that fought the South Vietnamese government and its ally, the United States, was known to its enemies as the Viet Cong ("Vietnamese Communists"). The name, coined by South Vietnamese leader Ngo Dinh Diem, was inaccurate because the Communists were only one of several groups that began isolated acts of rebellion in 1957. In 1960 these groups united into the National Liberation Front of South Vietnam (NLFSV), modeled on the earlier Viet Minh, and full-scale insurrection began. Most of the insurgents were South Vietnamese, but the movement depended increasingly on North Vietnamese aid and troops. In 1969 the NLFSV formed a Provisional Revolutionary Government, which participated in the peace negotiations in Paris. The NLFSV and the PRG were dissolved soon after the war's end (1975), but several members of the latter were included in the government of the unified Vietnam.

Viet Minh [min]   The Viet Minh was the shortened name for the League for the Independence of Vietnam, the chief political-military organization that battled the French for independence (1946–54). It was founded in 1941 in China by the Communist-nationalist HO CHI MINH. A coalition of nationalist groups under Communist control, it was the only significant organized resistance in Vietnam during the World War II Japanese occupation. In 1946 the Viet Minh assumed the leadership of the anti-French nationalist struggle. After the French defeat at the Battle of Dien Bien Phu in 1954, a Communist government was established in North Vietnam, and the Viet Minh was dissolved.

Viète, François [vee-et']   François Viète, b. 1540, d. Dec. 13, 1603, the greatest French mathematician of his time, was the founder of modern algebra and of modern algebraic notation. Viète founded the theory of equations and discovered general solutions to cubic and quartic equations. He was the first to use algebraic rather than geometric constructions in proofs. Viète also did important work in trigonometry and left an unpublished manuscript on mathematical astronomy.

Vietnam [vee-et'-nahm']   Vietnam, a nation located along the eastern coast of mainland Southeast Asia, has

had a turbulent history. Emerging as a distinct civilization during the 1st millennium BC, Vietnam was conquered by China during the early Han dynasty and subjected to 1,000 years of foreign rule. In AD 939, Vietnam restored its independence but in the 19th century was conquered once again and absorbed, along with neighboring Cambodia and Laos, into French INDOCHINA. After World War II, Communist-led VIET MINH guerrillas battled for several years to free the country from foreign subjugation. In 1954, at the GENEVA CONFERENCE, the country was divided into Communist-led North Vietnam and non-Communist South Vietnam. For the next 20 years, both North and South Vietnam were involved in the VIETNAM WAR. That conflict came to an end when Communist forces from the north occupied Saigon (now HO CHI MINH CITY) in April 1975.

Land and Resources

Vietnam extends about 1,600 km (1,000 mi) from the Chinese border to Point Ca Mau (Baibung) on the Gulf of Thailand. At its widest, it reaches a width of about 560 km (350 mi). In the narrow center, it is less than 50 km (30 mi) wide.

Much of Vietnam is rugged and densely forested. The Truong Son (Annamese Cordillera) extends more than 1,287 km (800 mi) from the YUAN RIVER delta east of HANOI to the Central Highlands south of Laos. For much of that distance, this mountain chain forms the border between Vietnam and Laos and Cambodia. The highest point in the country, Fan Si Pan, rises to 3,143 m (10,312 ft) near the Chinese border.

The large deltas of the Yuan River in the north and the MEKONG RIVER in the south are highly suitable for settled agriculture. In the Yuan delta, temperatures range from 5° C (41° F) in winter to more than 38° C (100° F) in summer. The Mekong delta is almost uniformly hot, varying from 26° to 30° C (79° to 85° F). The monsoon season extends from early May to late October, and typhoons often cause flooding in northern coastal areas.

Most of Vietnam's hardwoods and wild animals are found in the mountains. In the north are deposits of iron ore, tin, copper, apatite (phosphate rock), and chromite. Coal, mined along the coast near the Chinese border, is an important export and the main source of energy. There are modest oil reserves in the South China Sea.

People

Vietnam is one of the most homogeneous societies in Southeast Asia. Although more than 60 different ethnic groups live in the country, ethnic Vietnamese constitute nearly 90% of the total population. They speak Vietnamese (see SOUTHEAST ASIAN LANGUAGES).

The so-called overseas Chinese, descended from ethnic Chinese who arrived during the 17th and 18th centuries, settled for the most part in large cities. Thousands of ethnic Chinese fled abroad in 1978 in the wake of a government decision to nationalize commerce and industry in the south; about 2 million reportedly remain in the country.

Tribal peoples, including the MONTAGNARDS and the

AT A GLANCE

SOCIALIST REPUBLIC OF VIETNAM

Land: Area: 329,556 km^2 (127,242mi^2). Capital: Hanoi (1989 est. pop., 1,088,862). Largest city: Ho Chi Minh City (1989 est. pop., 3,169,135).

People: Population (1990 est.): 66,170,889 Density: 200.8 persons per km^2 (520 per mi^2). Distribution (1989): 20% urban, 80% rural. Official language: Vietnamese. Major religions: Buddhism, Caodaism, Hoa Hao, Roman Catholicism.

Government: Type: Communist state. Legislature: National Assembly. Political subdivisions: 37 provinces, 3 municipalities.

Economy: GNP (1989 est.): $14.2 billion; $215 per capita. Labor force (1989): agriculture and fishing—72%; manufacturing—11%; commerce and services—11%. Foreign trade (1988): imports—$2.55 billion; exports—$1.07 billion. Currency: 1 dong = 100 xu.

Education and Health: Literacy rate (1988 est.): 90% of adult population. Universities (1981): 3. Hospital beds (1989): 233,000. Physicians (1989): 21,300. Life expectancy (1990): women—66; men—62. Infant mortality (1990): 50 per 1,000 live births.

Meo, number about 3 million and live primarily in the Central Highlands and in the mountains of the north. Other smaller groups are the Khmer and the Cham, remnants of ancient states absorbed by the Vietnamese during their southward expansion.

Although the majority of ethnic Vietnamese traditionally considered themselves Buddhist or Confucianist, there are about 3 million Roman Catholics, most of whom live in the south. Members of two religious sects, the Cao Dai (an amalgam of Eastern and Western traditions) and the Hoa Hao (a radical form of Buddhism), number about 1 million each. Like the ethnic minorities, these religious groups have resisted assimilation into the majority culture.

The vast majority of the population live in overcrowded cities or in the densely populated delta areas and along the central coast. Large southern cities include Ho Chi Minh City, DA NANG, and HUE. Hanoi, the capital, and HAIPHONG, a port on the Gulf of Tonkin (see TONKIN, GULF OF), are the chief cities in the north.

Rapid population growth has strained limited health services, educational facilities, and food supplies. The government has instituted a family-planning program and attempted to relieve the problem of overcrowding by resettling several million people into "new economic areas" in the sparsely populated mountains and upland plateaus.

Education is under state control and is free at all levels. The leading institution of higher learning is Hanoi University. Although health facilities remain limited, there has been significant progress in health care since the reunification of the country in 1976.

For centuries, Vietnamese arts were heavily influenced by Chinese and Indian forms (see SOUTHEAST ASIAN ART AND ARCHITECTURE). More recently, Vietnamese painting borrowed from French styles and techniques. Traditional handicrafts are still practiced, and poetry remains the favorite literary genre. Vietnam's greatest poet was Nguyen Du (1765–1820).

Economic Activity

According to the evidence of contemporary archaeology, the Vietnamese were one of the first peoples of Asia to master the art of irrigation. Ever since, they have lived off the land, and their primary economic activity has been the cultivation of wet rice. The French increased rice production, developed coal mining, introduced cash crops, and built a modern rail and road network, but they were determined to maintain their colonies as a market for French manufactured goods and a source of cheap raw materials. After the French departed, economic development in both North and South Vietnam was hindered by the Vietnam War, and the country remained basically preindustrial.

The ultimate goal of the Communist regime that took power in 1975 was to transform all of Vietnam into an advanced industrial society based on socialist forms of ownership. Industry had been nationalized and agriculture collectivized in the north by the late 1950s, but Communist leaders delayed a similar socialist transformation in the south to avoid alienating the local population and to encourage economic recovery from the long years

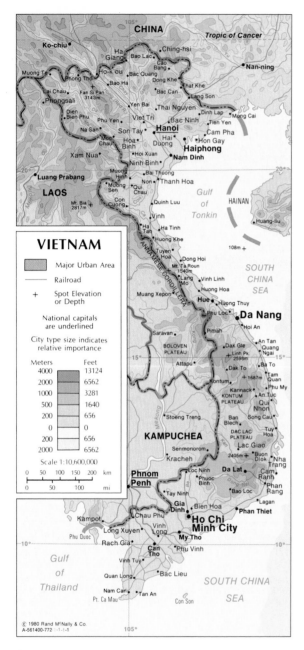

VIETNAM

- Major Urban Area
- ——— Railroad
- + Spot Elevation
  or Depth

National capitals
are underlined

City type size indicates
relative importance

Meters	Feet
4000	13124
2000	6562
1000	3281
500	1640
200	656
0	0
200	656
2000	6562

Scale 1:10,600,000

0   50   100 150 200 km
0   50   100   mi

© 1980 Rand McNally & Co.
A-561400-772 -1-1-1

ultimate objective of eliminating the private sector on a gradual basis was reaffirmed.

At present, Vietnam continues to make halting economic progress. Despite recurrent poor weather and rapid population growth, the country is now near agricultural self-sufficiency. Increasing pressure on arable lands has led to the recent planting of some hilly areas with cash crops such as coffee, tea, and rubber. Fishing, livestock raising, and forestry are also being encouraged. The industrial sector is showing signs of improvement, particularly in light industry and handicrafts, but consumer goods are in short supply, and growth rates remain low.

Government

Vietnam is a Communist republic. A new constitution in 1980 replaced the North Vietnamese constitution of 1959, which was extended throughout the country after the formal reunification of Vietnam on July 2, 1976. On paper, Vietnam has a parliamentary form of government, with supreme power vested in the unicameral National Assembly elected every five years by universal suffrage. The Assembly elects the Council of State, the collective presidency. Governmental functions are carried out by a Council of Ministers responsible to the National Assembly. In practice, real power resides in the hands of the Vietnamese Communist party.

History

By the middle of the 1st millennium BC, a small state based on irrigated agriculture and calling itself Van Lang had emerged in the Yuan delta. In 101 BC, Van Lang was overrun by forces from the north and gradually absorbed into the expanding Chinese empire. In the 10th century rebel groups drove out the Chinese and restored national independence. The new state, which styled itself Dai Viet (Greater Viet), accepted a tributary status with China. It resisted periodic efforts to restore Chinese rule, however, and began to expand its territory, conquering the state of CHAMPA to the south and eventually seizing the Mekong delta from the declining KHMER EMPIRE.

The difficulties of administering a long and narrow empire and cultural differences between the traditionalist and densely populated north and the sparsely settled "frontier" region in the Mekong delta led to civil war in the 17th century. Two major aristocratic families, the Trinh and the Nguyen, squabbled for domination over the decrepit Vietnamese monarchy. This internal strife was exacerbated by European adventurers who frequently intervened in local politics.

During the last quarter of the 18th century, a peasant rebellion led by the so-called Tay Son brothers in the south spread to the north, where the leading brother, Nguyen Hue, united the country and declared himself emperor. After his death in 1792, this dynasty rapidly declined and was overthrown by a scion of the princely house of Nguyen, who in 1802 founded a new Nguyen dynasty with its capital at Hue.

When the Nguyen dynasty failed to grant privileges to France in exchange for French aid, Napoleon III ordered an attack on Vietnam in 1857. Several provinces in the

of war. In 1979, after a disastrous 1978 attempt to nationalize industry and commerce and introduce rural collectives, the regime permitted the revival of private commerce and postponed the process of collectivization in the south. Economic production gradually recovered as emphasis shifted from heavy industry to consumer goods and farmers were allowed to sell surplus crops on the free market. In 1985 the regime decided that profit incentives would be temporarily retained to spur production, but the

An agricultural worker tends rice plants in a paddy along the Mekong River in southern Vietnam. Alluvial soils in the Mekong delta on the South China Sea have made it one of the most productive rice-growing regions in Southeast Asia.

south were ceded to France and transformed into a new colony of Cochin China. Twenty years later the French completed their conquest of Vietnam, dividing the northern and central parts of the country into protectorates with the historic names Tonkin and Annam. Between 1887 and 1893, all three regions were joined with the protectorates of Laos and Cambodia into the French-dominated Union of Indochina.

Deprived of a political and economic role by the colonial administration, Vietnamese patriots turned to protest or revolt. By the late 1930s the Communist party had become the leading force in the nationalist movement.

During World War II, Japan occupied Vietnam, but the French Vichy Government continued to administer the country until March 1945, when the Japanese established an autonomous state of Vietnam under Annamese emperor Bao Dai. When Japan surrendered in August the Viet Minh, an anti-Japanese and anti-French front founded by Ho Chi Minh in 1941, revolted and seized power. In early September, Viet Minh leaders declared the formation of the independent Democratic Republic of Vietnam (DRV). French forces returned by 1946, but negotiations to create a Vietnamese "free state" within the French Union collapsed. In December the First Indochinese War broke out between the Vietnamese and the French. In 1954 the Vietnamese defeated the French at Dien Bien Phu. Shortly after, the major powers met at Geneva and called for the de facto division of Vietnam at 17° north latitude into two separate states, the Communist-dominated DRV in the north and a non-Communist state in the south, with provision for eventual reunification.

The division of Vietnam lasted only two decades. In South Vietnam, the weak Bao Dai, reinstalled by the French in 1949, was replaced by Ngo Dinh Diem. Despite support from the United States, Diem was unable to suppress a continuing guerrilla insurgency. In November 1963, Diem was overthrown in a military coup, and North Vietnam intensified its efforts to seek reunification under Communist rule. In 1965, with the South Vietnamese regime on the verge of collapse, the United States decided to send combat troops to South Vietnam to defeat the insurgency. In January 1973, over the objections of South Vietnam's Nguyen Van Thieu (who served as president from 1967 to 1975), a peace agreement was signed in Paris calling for a cease-fire and the total withdrawal of U.S. troops. Vague provisions for a political settlement were ignored, however, and in the spring of 1975 the Communists launched a major offensive. North Vietnamese troops occupied Saigon in late April. In 1976, North and South Vietnam were formally united as the Socialist Republic of Vietnam, with Pham Van Dong as prime minister.

Relations between North Vietnam and China reached the breaking point at war's end because of territorial disagreements and a growing rivalry over Cambodia and Laos. In November 1978, Vietnam signed a treaty of friendship and cooperation with the USSR. Less than two months later Vietnamese forces invaded Cambodia, overthrew the pro-Chinese Khmer Rouge regime, and installed a new government sympathetic to Hanoi. Both China and the Association of Southeast Asian Nations (ASEAN) demanded a withdrawal of Vietnamese forces. Although a Cambodian peace accord was not signed until 1991, almost all Vietnamese forces were withdrawn in 1989. A new Vietnamese constitution adopted in April 1992 formalized the free-market reforms implemented since the 1980s. The former collective presidency was replaced by a single president elected from within the National Assembly, which was given greater powers. The Council of Ministers was replaced by a cabinet headed by a prime minister, whose powers were also enhanced. Vietnam remained a one-party state, but the Communist party was no longer to be involved in the day-to-day running of the government.

Bicycles are the chief mode of transportation in Hanoi, the capital of Vietnam. Hanoi's broad streets and architecture are reminders of an earlier time, when the city was the capital of French Indochina.

Vietnam Veterans Memorial A V-shaped wall bearing the names of Americans killed in the Vietnam War, the Vietnam Veterans Memorial, designed by architect Maya Yang Lin, was dedicated on Nov. 13, 1982; a bronze sculpture of three soldiers designed by Frederick Hart was added to it in 1984. The memorial was sponsored by the Vietnam Veterans Memorial Fund, which raised the money to build it from private donors and persuaded Congress to provide a site for it near the Washington Monument as a belated tribute to those who had fought in the Southeast Asian conflict.

A tribute to the Americans who fought in the Vietnam War, the Vietnam Veterans Memorial in Washington, D.C., was dedicated on Nov. 13, 1982, almost a decade after the United States withdrew from the war. The memorial consists of two black granite walls built into the earth and meeting at an angle. Inscribed are the names of more than 58,000 Americans killed or missing in Vietnam.

Vietnam War In the Vietnam War—which lasted from the mid-1950s until 1975—the United States and the southern-based Republic of Vietnam (RVN) opposed the southern-based revolutionary movement known as the VIET CONG (VC) and its sponsor, the Communist Democratic Republic of Vietnam (the DRV, or North Vietnam). The war was the second of two major conflicts that spread throughout Indochina, with Vietnam its focal point (see

VIETNAM). The First Indochina War was a struggle between Vietnamese nationalists and the French colonial regime aided by the United States. In the second war the United States replaced France as the major contender against northern-based Communists and southern insurgents. Communist victory in 1975 had profound ramifications for the United States; it was not only a setback to the containment of communism in Asia but a shock to American self-confidence.

The Origins of the War

French Indochina, which included Vietnam, Cambodia, and Laos, was occupied by Japanese forces during World War II. Vietnamese Communist leader HO CHI MINH and his VIET MINH movement organized resistance against the Japanese and in 1945 declared Vietnam an independent republic. Fearing Ho's Communism, the United States supported the restoration of French rule. When fighting erupted between France and the Viet Minh in 1947, the Americans aided the French and backed the French-sponsored government of Emperor Bao Dai.

The Partition of Vietnam. In 1954 the French, hoping to win a decisive victory, lured the Viet Minh into a set-piece battle at DIEN BIEN PHU, but were in turn besieged there. During the siege the exhausted government placed Indochina on the agenda of an international conference at Geneva (see GENEVA CONFERENCES). Defeat at Dien Bien Phu made France decide to withdraw from Indochina.

The conference terms were a mixed victory for the Viet Minh. Ho Chi Minh's Communist allies, the USSR and China, pressured him into accepting temporary division of Vietnam along the 17th parallel, pending elections to be held in two years. Laos, Cambodia, and Vietnam were granted independence, and no foreign troops were to be stationed there. In an exchange of population, thousands of northern Vietnamese Roman Catholics moved south, while Communists moved north. Neither the United States nor the South, now led by the U.S.-backed NGO DINH DIEM in Saigon, signed the accords.

Even before the conference's conclusion, Washington, whose policy was to oppose the spread of communism, began planning a regional security pact. The result was the Southeast Asia Treaty Organization (SEATO), which provided for future U.S. intervention in the event of danger to South Vietnam; the Indochinese states did not join.

The Two Republics. Providing economic and military aid, the United States supported Diem's refusal to hold the pledged elections, apparently assuming the popular nationalist Ho would win. After a shaky start, Diem began working to destroy the remaining Communist infrastructure in the South. His military force, the Army of the Republic of Vietnam (ARVN), was advised by some 700 Americans, who replaced the French in 1956. Increasingly dictatorial, the Catholic Diem incurred growing opposition from the Buddhist majority.

In the North, the DRV developed as a Communist state with ties to China and the USSR.

Early Stages of the Fighting

Armed resistance to Diem was organized by former Viet

Vietnamese leader Ho Chi Minh (center) discusses strategy with aides prior to the attack on the French garrison at Dien Bien Phu (March–May 1954).

Minh who became known as Viet Cong (Vietnamese Communists). The Viet Cong organized in 1960 as the National Liberation Front of South Vietnam (NLF). Communist-led and directed by Hanoi, it included all groups opposed to the Diem regime and its U.S. ally.

The NLF adopted the "people's war" strategy favored by Chinese Communist leader Mao Zedong: guerrillas using the civilian population as cover engaged in protracted warfare, avoiding conflict except in advantageous circumstances. Men and supplies infiltrated through Laos and Cambodia along a network of trails named for Ho Chi Minh. The Viet Cong used assassinations, terrorist activity, and military action against government-controlled villages. Diem moved peasants into "strategic hamlets" to separate them from the guerrillas. Peasant resentment at this policy aided Viet Cong recruitment.

U.S. intervention was based on belief in the "domino theory"—which held that if one Southeast Asian country were allowed to fall under Communist control, others would follow like a row of dominoes—and by an increasing concern for the credibility of U.S. opposition to communism after the Castro government came to power in Cuba (1959). Responding to Diem's request for help, U.S. president John F. Kennedy gradually increased the number of U.S. advisors to more than 16,000.

In Laos the PATHET LAO guerrilla movement grew following a U.S.-sponsored right-wing coup against the neutralist regime. Kennedy accepted (1962) a Laotian settlement that brought temporary neutralization. In South Vietnam the introduction of helicopters and more advisors briefly boosted morale in Saigon, but ARVN lost the battle of Ap Bac in January 1963 despite advice and superior technology.

The Fall of Diem. The South Vietnamese situation became critical by mid-1963. Buddhist monks protesting religious persecution dramatized their case by immolating themselves in the Saigon streets. Diem refused to placate the Buddhists, however. Fearing the war would be lost,

the United States supported a military coup that overthrew Diem on Nov. 1, 1963.

In the next two years Hanoi increased its strength in the South to 35–40 main-force battalions of the People's Liberation Army (PLAF), in addition to some 35,000 guerrillas and 80,000 irregulars. Whereas individual members of the DRV's People's Army of Vietnam (PAVN) had infiltrated south for some time, the first complete tactical unit arrived in December, moving along the newly completed Ho Chi Minh Trail. Most forces fighting in the South continued, however, to be locally recruited. Increasing Soviet as well as Chinese aid fueled the resistance.

The Tonkin Gulf Resolution. In Washington, Kennedy's successor, Lyndon B. Johnson, authorized the CIA, using mercenaries and U.S. Army Special Forces, to conduct covert diversionary raids on the northern coast, while the U.S. Navy, in a related operation, ran electronic intelligence missions in the Gulf of Tonkin. Johnson appointed General William WESTMORELAND to head the Military Assistance Command, Vietnam (MACV), increased the number of advisors to 23,000, and expanded economic assistance.

An incident in the Gulf of Tonkin served to justify escalation of the U.S. effort. On Aug. 2, 1964, an American destroyer in international waters involved in electronic espionage was attacked by North Vietnamese torpedo boats. Unharmed, it was joined by a second destroyer and on August 4 the ships claimed that both had been attacked. Evidence of the second attack was weak at best (and was later found to be erroneous), but Johnson ordered retaliatory air strikes and went before Congress to urge support for the TONKIN GULF RESOLUTION, a virtual blank check to the executive to conduct retaliatory military operations. There were only two dissenting votes.

After a Viet Cong attack (February 1965) on U.S. Army barracks in Pleiku, the United States commenced a restricted but massive bombing campaign against North Vietnam. Protection of air bases then provided the rationale for introduction of 50,000 U.S. ground combat forces, which were soon increased.

The Buddhist monk Quang Duc committed suicide by fire (June 1963) to protest against the regime of South Vietnam's Ngo Dinh Diem.

U.S. Escalation of the War

The decision to escalate slowly, to bomb selected military targets while avoiding excessive civilian casualties, and to fight a war of attrition in order to avoid possible confrontations with the USSR and China seriously misjudged the nature of the enemy and the strategy of people's war. Because the DRV fought a total war with a totally mobilized society, it could sustain high losses yet continue infiltrating as many as 7,000 men a month virtually indefinitely. Political cadres won support from, or at least neutralized, the Southern peasantry. Weak in air power, the Viet Cong fought from tunnels and retreated to sanctuaries in Cambodia when threatened.

U.S. attrition strategy depended on inflicting increasing pain through massive firepower against the North and Viet Cong–held areas until the revolutionaries found the cost too high. Territory gained was "cleared" but not held. In addition to bombing, the Americans and their allies—who ultimately included 70,000 South Koreans, Thais, Australians, and New Zealanders as well as 1,500,000 South Vietnamese—relied on the latest military technology, including napalm, white phosphorus, and defoliants, in an effort to hold down casualties. Agent Orange and other chemicals cleared vast areas of jungle, depriving the Viet Cong of cover as well as rice. Worldwide outcry over the use of chemical warfare and concern about its effect on the health of civilians and U.S. personnel led to discontinuance of defoliation in 1971.

In addition to conflict on the ground, water, and in the air, there was the struggle for what President Kennedy had termed the "hearts and minds" of the people. The Americans attempted to "search out and destroy" the enemy, leaving rural pacification to the poorly motivated ARVN. "Strategic hamlets" gave way to "revolutionary development," but the military junta headed by NGUYEN VAN THIEU, who took power in 1967, was unable to devise a successful pacification strategy.

As the war escalated, Johnson relied increasingly on selective service for manpower; nevertheless, the heaviest burdens of combat were placed on America's poor and minority groups.

The Antiwar Movement. Opposition to the war grew with increased U.S. involvement. Leftist college students and faculty, members of traditional pacifist religious groups, long-time peace activists, and citizens of all ages opposed the conflict. College campuses became focal points for rallies and teach-ins—lengthy series of speeches attacking the war. Marches on Washington began in 1965 and continued sporadically, peaking in 1968 and again in 1971. The antiwar movement probably played a role in convincing Lyndon Johnson not to run for reelection in 1968, and an even larger role in the subsequent victory of Richard Nixon over the Democrat Hubert Humphrey. Certainly its presence was an indication of the increasingly divisive effects of the war on U.S. society.

The Tet Offensive. By late 1967 the war was stalemated. Johnson urged Westmoreland to help convince a public growing more restive that the United States was winning. Although he promised "light at the end of the tun-

U.S. troops huddle around a tank in Hue during the Tet offensive of early 1968. Although the NLFSV and North Vietnamese failed to achieve their military goals, the offensive disproved U.S. government claims that the war was virtually over.

nel," increasing casualties as well as growing disbelief in public pronouncements—the "credibility gap"—fostered increasing skepticism. U.S. strategy was clearly not producing victory, and Johnson began a limited reassessment.

Meanwhile, Hanoi initiated a new offensive. As a first step, a massive attack was launched against the base at Khe Sanh. Attacks on cities began on Tet, the lunar holiday, Jan. 30, 1968. Hitting most provincial and district capitals and major cities, the Viet Cong also carried out a bold attack on the U.S. embassy in Saigon. The attack failed, but the attempt shocked U.S. public opinion. The Tet Offensive continued for three weeks. Although they failed in their military objectives, the revolutionaries won a spectacular propaganda victory. The Tet Offensive, as it was publicized in the U.S. media, seemed to confirm fears that the war was unwinnable. The public opposed the war in direct proportion to U.S. casualties, and these had topped a thousand dead a month.

The Significance of Tet. The Tet Offensive was a major turning point in the war. Although the Communists lost 40,000 troops, they had proved their ability to strike even in supposedly secure cities. Viet Cong, who had surfaced in anticipation of a general uprising that did not come, were decimated in the fighting or destroyed later by police, and from this point the insurgency was increasingly fought by the PAVN. Johnson sent 20,000 more troops in the next three months, bringing U.S. troop strength to a peak of 549,000. At the same time, the South was urged to do more in its own defense.

Tet crystallized public dissatisfaction with the war. It became increasingly clear that the public as a whole disapproved of the lack of progress. Further evidence of this came in March, when the antiwar senator Eugene McCarthy, running against the president, won 42 percent of the vote in New Hampshire's primary election.

On March 31, Johnson restricted bombing above the 20th parallel, paving the way for negotiations, and withdrew from a reelection bid. With Johnson's withdrawal and the assassination of Robert F. Kennedy, the Democratic nomination went to Vice-President Humphrey, who supported the war; the Republicans nominated Richard Nixon.

Negotiations began in May but quickly stalled over Hanoi's demands for a total bombing halt and NLF representation at the bargaining table. In November Johnson agreed to these terms. This aided Humphrey's campaign, but Nixon was victorious.

The Tet Offensive demonstrated that the RVN was able to act in its own defense, yet the generally weak ARVN performance led to increasing demands for its reform. Johnson determined that primary responsibility for combat in the South henceforth should be borne by ARVN. This policy—known as Vietnamization—meant pressuring the Thieu regime into a huge military buildup. At the same time, increasing suppression of dissent in that country brought protest from Buddhists and students.

The Nixon Administration and Vietnam

During the election campaign Nixon made vague promises to end the war. He was determined, however, to maintain credibility, preserve Thieu, and defeat the Communists. He and his foreign policy advisor Henry Kissinger conceptualized a strategy of détente, which involved harmonizing relations with the Soviets while encouraging Moscow to abandon Hanoi. They hoped that this linkage of diplomacy could produce "peace with honor" in Vietnam and allow a face-saving U.S. departure. The Soviets, however, recognized the Provisional Revolutionary Government (PRG) formed by the NLF in June 1969. No progress was made in the peace talks, either.

Meanwhile, the Vietnamization process continued, but ARVN remained poorly motivated and relatively ineffectual in combat. Its assumption of the brunt of the fighting, however, reduced U.S. casualties and enabled the United States to begin troop withdrawals.

At home, by the spring of 1970, public opinion was two to one against the war. When the public learned of the massacre of more than 300 civilians in the hamlet of MY LAI by U.S. troops, it reinforced beliefs that the war was a brutal, dehumanizing, and pointless affair from which the United States should withdraw.

Incursions into Cambodia and Laos. Nixon disliked confining the conflict to Vietnam instead of striking at Communist sanctuaries and supply points in neighboring neutral countries. Cambodia soon provided him the opportunity. In April 1970 a coup toppled the neutralist regime of Prince NORODOM SIHANOUK. He was replaced by the pro–U.S. LON NOL, who announced plans to interdict movement of Communist troops. When Hanoi then increased its pressure on Cambodia, U.S. forces were sent across the border. They were withdrawn again by June 30, but bombing raids continued until the end of the war.

The Cambodian incursion triggered protests in the United States. At Kent State and Jackson State universities, six students were killed in confrontations with police and National Guardsmen. One hundred thousand marched on Washington. Congress also protested, symbolically terminating the Tonkin Gulf Resolution.

Infiltration persisted despite the Cambodian incursion. Seeking to cut the Ho Chi Minh Trail, ARVN forces invaded Laos in February 1971. The operation escaped disaster only through U.S. air support.

Effects of the War on U.S. Troops. Withdrawals dropped U.S. troop strength in Vietnam to 175,000 by the end of 1971, exacerbating effects on troop morale even as it dampened protest at home. Drug and alcohol abuse became widespread among U.S. servicemen, and morale plummeted. Racial conflict grew as black soldiers, stimulated by the civil rights and black-power movements, increasingly resented fighting a "white man's war." Veterans of Vietnam formed their own antiwar organization.

The Easter Offensive. In March 1972, Hanoi launched a major conventional invasion of the South. The VC/PAVN forces encountered initial success, routing ARVN troops and overrunning Quang Tri province. President Nixon retaliated with an intensified bombing campaign, providing air support to areas under attack in the South and striking fuel depots in the Hanoi-Haiphong area. He also ordered the mining of Haiphong harbor, a naval blockade of the North, and massive sustained bombing attacks. Ultimately, U.S. bombing enabled ARVN to halt the offensive.

Negotiating and Fighting, 1971–72. Negotiations throughout 1971 made only limited progress. Meanwhile, playing on the Sino-Soviet split, the United States moved to normalize trade with China; Nixon and Kissinger both visited Peking, after which Nixon traveled to Moscow in May 1972. Both China and the USSR nonetheless increased aid to Hanoi.

Only after the Easter Offensive did negotiations become a top priority. In three weeks of intensive negotiations in late September and October, Kissinger and North Vietnamese representative Le Duc Tho shaped an agreement withdrawing U.S. troops, returning POWs, and providing for a political settlement through establishment of a tripartite council of reconciliation. Thieu, however, rejected it because it permitted Viet Cong forces to remain in place in the South, and Nixon supported him.

The Christmas Bombing and the Paris Peace Accords. Nixon, reelected by a huge majority in November 1972,

U.S. F-4C Phantoms release their bombs over North Vietnam. The bombing of North Vietnam, begun in 1965, was cut back or halted periodically to encourage peace negotiations and then resumed, culminating in the massive strikes of Christmas 1972.

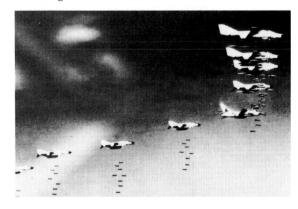

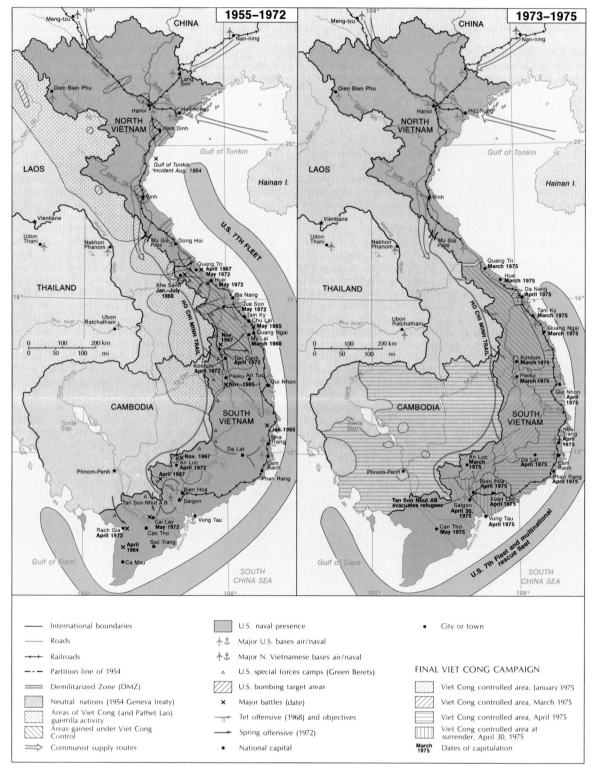

Between 1955 and 1965 the United States sent increasing military aid to prop up the South Vietnamese government against spreading insurrection. Then it began to deploy U.S. ground forces and aerial power on a massive scale against the insurrectionaries (Viet Cong) and their North Vietnamese allies. After 8 years of destructive but inconclusive fighting the United States withdrew its forces in 1973. Within 2 years the Viet Cong and North Vietnamese had won total control of South Vietnam and reunified the country.

then ordered massive bombing north of the 20th parallel. For 12 days beginning December 18, B-52s rained bombs on Hanoi and Haiphong. Women and children were evacuated and the cities defended with Russian-made surface-to-air missiles (SAMs). Fifteen B-52s were downed, 44 pilots captured, some 1,600 civilians killed, and Bach Mai hospital destroyed.

After the bombing, both sides were ready to resume negotiations: Hanoi had been seriously damaged and its stock of SAMs exhausted, while in Washington an angry Congress discussed limitations on the war. Six days of intense negotiations produced an agreement only slightly different from the October terms. Thieu refused to sign the agreement but did not actively oppose it.

The Paris Accords, signed Jan. 31, 1973, brought U.S. withdrawal and the return of the POWs but little else. Only a few civilian advisors and military personnel would remain. The Thieu government was left intact, but PAVN troops retained positions in the South. Political issues were left to negotiations between the two Vietnamese governments. A temporary four-party Joint Military Commission was to prevent a resumption of hostilities, and a four-power (Canada, Poland, Hungary, and Indonesia) International Commission of Control and Supervision was to supervise the cease-fire. The accords left unresolved the major issue of the war—the question of who would govern the South.

The Resolution of the Conflict

The RVN and the DRV used the time before implementation of the peace to seize more land, and Washington sent massive amounts of aid to Thieu. Both sides quickly violated the accords. The last POWs were returned in March. The United States continued to bomb Cambodia.

In the spring of 1973 Nixon's position was weakened by the involvement of his administration in the Watergate scandal. Taking advantage of this, Congress approved an amendment requiring the cessation of military operations in and over Indochina by August 15. In November 1973, Congress passed the War Powers Act, requiring the president to inform Congress within 48 hours of deployment of U.S. military forces abroad, withdrawing them within 60 days in the absence of explicit congressional endorsement. This virtually guaranteed the end of U.S. involvement in Indochina.

Renewed fighting led Thieu to declare the start of a third Indochina War in January. Although ARVN instituted new action, the North and the PRG won increasing victories. By the fall of 1974 the initiative had passed to the revolution. Thieu remained convinced that Nixon would not abandon him, but the Watergate crisis forced the latter to resign in August 1974.

In January 1975, Hanoi commenced a two-year campaign it believed necessary to defeat the South. Unexpected victory in the Central Highlands caused a speedup in the timetable. The ARVN retreat from the Highlands turned into a rout that became a disaster: troops fled south toward Saigon, anxious to protect their families. The loss of six central Vietnamese provinces led to the fall of the cities of Hué and Danang. Capitalizing on these

South Vietnamese president Nguyen Van Thieu and Richard Nixon address journalists following a joint strategy planning session at the U.S. base on Midway Island.

victories, Hanoi embarked on a campaign to "liberate" Saigon. The fall of the last resisting outpost, Xuan Loc, forced Thieu to recognize the gravity of the situation; he resigned and fled the country. Duong Van Minh became president, only to surrender unconditionally to the North on April 30.

While the world watched the dramatic evacuation of the Americans and some of their supporters from the roof of the U.S. embassy in Saigon, the other countries of Indochina fell less dramatically. Cambodia's KHMER ROUGE took Phnom Penh on April 17 and immediately evacuated the city, beginning a reign of terror that lasted for three years. The Pathet Lao had already gained participation in a coalition government in February 1973, and it took control of Laos peacefully after South Vietnam fell.

The Aftermath of the War

The attempt to find "lessons" in the defeat engaged the United States for the next decade. The domino theory was proved invalid, as no further nations in Southeast Asia adopted communism. Isolationist in the wake of war, the United States eschewed further interventions, and even limited covert operations, until Ronald Reagan became president in 1981. Inflation caused by the war costs racked the U.S. economy for the next eight years, and the social wounds of the divisive war were slow to heal. Frustrated and angry in defeat, America at first rejected its veterans as symbols of defeat in a war generally agreed to have been a mistake.

The war's statistics were grim: 2 to 3 million Indochinese killed, 58,000 Americans dead, the expenditure of three times the amount of U.S. bombs dropped on both theaters during World War II, overwhelming devastation in Indochina. The war cost the United States over $150 billion. The Viet Cong had proved willing to take one of the highest casualty rates in proportion to population in history. That the United States never lost a major battle proved irrelevant; concentrating on military objectives, it vastly

Refugees, many of them members of the South Vietnamese government, wait to board a helicopter on the roof of the U.S. embassy in Saigon on Apr. 29, 1975. The city was occupied by PRG and North Vietnamese troops the next day.

underestimated the political struggle, the nature of the enemy, and the consequences of supporting weak and unpopular regimes in the South.

By 1982 the wounds had begun to heal. The dedication of the VIETNAM VETERANS MEMORIAL in Washington, D.C., brought the veterans belated recognition for their sacrifices. The nation, recovering from its own posttraumatic shock, began embarking on new interventions against Communism. The legacy of the war embodied in the slogan "No More Vietnams" still had power, however, as opposition to these interventions demonstrated.

Vietnam was formally reunified in 1976, and Northerners quickly established dominance over the remnants of the PRG-NLF. The Vietnamese proved more able soldiers than managers. The move to socialize the economy hurt many, but it especially harmed the large Chinese entrepreneurial minority in the South, whose position was further weakened when China attacked Vietnam in 1978. More than 1.4 million Vietnamese, including large numbers of ethnic Chinese, fled the country by sea; as many as 50,000 of these "boat people" may have perished in flight. Nearly a million settled abroad, including some 725,000 in the United States.

Cambodia, renamed Kampuchea, was ruled by the despotic POL POT regime after the war. It murdered or starved some 1.5 million of its 7.5 million people and harassed its neighbor, leading the Vietnamese to invade in late 1978. Vietnam installed the Heng Samrin regime and retained an army of occupation. As a result of this violation of the UN charter, the United Nations ceased development aid and many Western countries followed suit, ceasing or sharply curtailing assistance. This led Vietnam to rely even more heavily on its ally the USSR, which had leased the port facilities at Cam Ranh Bay. The occupation of Kampuchea and the fate of some 2,500 Americans missing in action (MIAs) posed barriers to recognition by the United States. U.S. relations with Vietnam remained poor in the wake of the war and Hanoi's demands for reparations. By 1986, Vietnam had indicated plans to resolve two obstacles, cooperating in a resolution of the MIA issue and promising withdrawal from Kampuchea by 1990 in an effort to win U.S. recognition. Most Vietnamese forces were withdrawn by the end of 1989, and in 1990 the United States agreed to begin negotiations with Vietnam to explore the possibility of restoring normal diplomatic relations.

Vietnamese language   see SOUTHEAST ASIAN LANGUAGES

Vieuxtemps, Henri [vee-u-tahm']   The Belgian-born Henri Vieuxtemps, b. Feb. 17, 1820, d. June 6, 1881, one of the foremost violinists of 19th-century France, was called the king of the violin. He made his first concert tour at the age of 8 and from the age of 17 toured almost constantly, including triumphant visits to the United States (1844–45, 1857, and 1870). He also composed for the instrument, writing seven concertos and numerous concert pieces for violin and piano.

Viganò, Salvatore [vee-gah-noh']   Salvatore Viganò, b. Mar. 25, 1769, d. Aug. 10, 1821, was one of the greatest choreographers of the preromantic ballet. Viganò danced in Rome, Madrid, Paris, London, Brussels, Venice, and Vienna and choreographed his first ballet, Raoul, Signor de Créquis, in 1791. He wrote the music for many of his own ballets, but that for The Creatures of Prometheus (Vienna, 1801) was by Ludwig van Beethoven. Viganò was ballet master of La Scala, Milan (1813–21), where he choreographed numerous great dramatic ballets.

Vigée-Lebrun, Louise Élisabeth [vee-zhay'-luh-bruhn']   Louise Élisabeth Vigée-Lebrun, b. Apr. 16, 1755, d. Mar. 30, 1842, achieved an international reputation as a portraitist during her lifetime. She served as painter to Queen Marie Antoinette until the French Revolution forced her into an exile that lasted 12 years. Having escaped with her daughter to Italy, she continued to receive commissions as she traveled and was warmly welcomed in Europe's major capitals. In 1783 she was admitted to the Académie Royale.

Her style of portraiture catches her sitters looking alert; they are generally placed within their typical surroundings. For example, Marie Antoinette and Her Children (1787; Versailles Palace) is set in a room of the palace, and the painter in Hubert Robert (1788; Louvre, Paris) is seen at work, holding his palette and brushes.

According to her own memoirs, Vigée-Lebrun painted about 900 works, of which more than 200 were landscapes and the remainder mainly portraits.

Vigeland, Gustav [vee'-guh-lahn]   In their intense emotionalism, the works of the Norwegian sculptor

Gustav Vigeland, b. Apr. 11, 1869, d. Mar. 12, 1943, are akin to those of the painter Edvard Munch, his countryman and contemporary. Both men belonged to the fin de siècle intelligentsia of Paris and Berlin, and both absorbed its nihilistic despair. Vigeland's early style was strongly influenced by Auguste Rodin; his more expressionist mode emerged only later. He spent more than four decades on his major work, the huge outdoor sculpture complex in Frogner Park, Oslo, which contains more than 200 figures. Some of his later work at Frogner Park became routine; more subtle are his early sculptured portraits of famous Norwegians.

vigilantes   Until effective government reached the American frontier, volunteer vigilance committees were formed to maintain law and order. The most famous vigilante groups were in the mining and cattle towns of the Far West, communities that attracted many lawless individuals but often could not afford either a law officer or a jail. Some committees conducted judicial proceedings; others summarily banished, whipped, or hanged those they believed guilty.

The best known of these movements were those operating in San Francisco from 1849 to 1851 and a later committee of that city, which, in 1856, claimed 8,000 members. The San Francisco vigilantes generally conducted fair public trials and held hangings attended by thousands. In the early 1860s another famous movement, in Montana, eradicated the gang of the sheriff-turned-outlaw Henry Plummer. Most vigilante groups disbanded voluntarily once adequate law enforcement was established.

Vignola, Giacomo Barozzi da [veen-yoh'-lah] Giacomo Barozzi, called Giacomo da Vignola, b. Oct. 1, 1507, d. July 7, 1573, was an Italian architect of the Late Renaissance. He is best known for his *Regola delli cinque ordini d'architettura* (Rule of the Five Orders of Architecture, 1562), an architectural treatise that provided future generations of architects with models for the use of the classical orders and served as the basis of Vignola's influential design of the Church of Il Gesù in Rome.

Upon being appointed (1550) papal architect to Pope Julius III, he settled in Rome, where his first major commission was the design of the Villa Giulia (1551–55). Together with his redesign (begun 1559) of the Villa Farnese at Caprarola, the Villa Giulia reflects Vignola's ability to formulate inventive and graceful designs using classical elements.

Even more original in conception are the churches of Sant' Andrea in Via Flaminia (1550–54) and Sant'Anna dei Palafrenieri (begun 1565), whose oval-based plans represent a radical break with the Renaissance classical tradition and anticipate one of the most widely used forms in baroque architecture. Vignola departed from the oval format in building (from 1568) Il Gesù, the mother church of the Jesuit order. By eliminating side aisles he created an uncluttered and airy interior that influenced church architects for the next 200 years.

Vigny, Alfred de [veen-yee'] Alfred Victor, comte de Vigny, b. Mar. 27, 1797, d. Sept. 17, 1863, was the most stoical and pessimistic of the French romantic writers. In his verse, *Poèmes antiques et modernes* (Poems Ancient and Modern, 1826), in his collection of stories, *Stello* (1832), and in his play *Chatterton* (1835; Eng. trans., 1908) he deals with the condition of the poet, prophet, and genius in a noncomprehending society. His prose works, the novels *Cinq-Mars* (1826) and *Servitudes et grandeurs militaires* (1835; trans. as *The Military Condition,* 1964), present his belief in the brotherhood of humanity and the nobility of a military career. His adaptations and translations of Shakespeare, *Shylock* (1828) and *Othello* (1829), were presented with modest success at the Théâtre Français.

Vigo [vee'-goh] Vigo (1987 est. pop., 173,800) is a port on the Vigo Estuary, an inlet of the Atlantic Ocean in northwestern Spain, about 20 km (13 mi) north of the Portuguese border. Vigo is a naval base and a major fishing port, where lumber, paper, flour, soap, brandy, machinery, and tools are produced. Known to the Romans as Vicus Spacorum, Vigo became an important naval port in the 16th century.

Vigo, Jean Jean Vigo, b. Apr. 26, 1905, d. Oct. 5, 1934, the son of a celebrated anarchist, proved himself one of the great French filmmakers. *À Propos de Nice* (About Nice, 1930) is a short, personal film essay mixing sharp observation and adroit camera technique. His two major films, *Zéro de conduite* (Zero for Conduct, 1933) and *L'Atalante* (Atalanta, 1934), were both commercial disasters, and at the time of his death at the age of 29, Vigo remained almost unknown. His tiny output, however, now ranks among the great achievements of French cinema. His work draws uniquely sensitive pictures of private worlds (those of a group of schoolboys and a newly married couple, respectively), combining a respect for reality with virtually surrealist imagery.

Viking   The Viking space project produced, during the summer of 1976, the first two successful landings on the surface of MARS. *Viking 1,* consisting of a landing craft attached to a separate vehicle that would orbit the planet, was launched on Aug. 20, 1975, and entered orbit on June 19, 1976. On July 20 the lander touched down on the slope of a dry basin in a region known as Chryse Planitia. *Viking 2,* with an identical pair of coupled spacecraft, was launched on Sept. 9, 1975, reached Martian orbit on Aug. 7, 1976, and released its lander for a Sept. 3, 1976, arrival at a rock-strewn plain in a more northerly site called Utopia Planitia. This article describes only the spacecraft; its results may be found in the entry MARS (planet).

The Orbiters

The Viking orbiters were equipped for photography (in col-

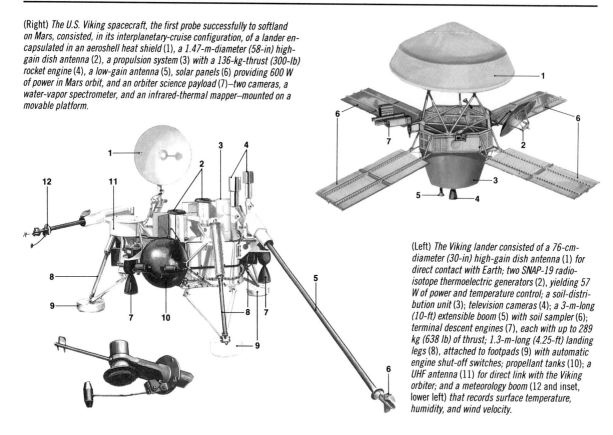

(Right) *The U.S. Viking spacecraft, the first probe successfully to softland on Mars, consisted, in its interplanetary-cruise configuration, of a lander encapsulated in an aeroshell heat shield (1), a 1.47-m-diameter (58-in) high-gain dish antenna (2), a propulsion system (3) with a 136-kg-thrust (300-lb) rocket engine (4), a low-gain antenna (5), solar panels (6) providing 600 W of power in Mars orbit, and an orbiter science payload (7)—two cameras, a water-vapor spectrometer, and an infrared-thermal mapper–mounted on a movable platform.*

(Left) *The Viking lander consisted of a 76-cm-diameter (30-in) high-gain dish antenna (1) for direct contact with Earth; two SNAP-19 radio-isotope thermoelectric generators (2), yielding 57 W of power and temperature control; a soil-distribution unit (3); television cameras (4); a 3-m-long (10-ft) extensible boom (5) with soil sampler (6); terminal descent engines (7), each with up to 289 kg (638 lb) of thrust; 1.3-m-long (4.25-ft) landing legs (8), attached to footpads (9) with automatic engine shut-off switches; propellant tanks (10); a UHF antenna (11) for direct link with the Viking orbiter; and a meteorology boom (12 and inset, lower left) that records surface temperature, humidity, and wind velocity.*

or, stereo, and through filters), atmospheric water-vapor detection, and surface-temperature measurement. Each orbiter carried two slow-scan cameras using television-type vidicon tubes.

The foremost task of the orbiter cameras was to aid in the selection of safe landing sites. The cameras then moved on to the task of photographing and mapping the rest of the planet, sometimes from altitudes as low as 298 km (185 mi). The orbiters also made extremely close passes by the Martian moons, PHOBOS and DEIMOS, enabling detailed photography of their surfaces and calculations of their masses based on their effects on the orbiters' trajectories.

The water-vapor detector aboard each orbiter consisted of an infrared spectrometer to measure solar infrared radiation that passed through the atmosphere after reflection from the surface of the planet. The infrared thermal mapper responsible for temperature measurements was a 28-channel radiometer capable of monitoring temperatures at the surface and in the upper atmosphere.

The Landers

The Viking landers were essentially three-legged platforms, with numerous instruments atop and within the platform structure, and were powered by nuclear sources called radioisotope thermoelectric generators (see SNAP).

The first measurements made by both landers came from a set of instruments—retarding potential analyzer, upper-atmosphere mass spectrometer, and pressure and temperature sensors—designed to make profile measurements of the atmosphere during the descent to the surface.

Among their surface instruments, the landers carried the first experiments ever sent from Earth with the specific intent of seeking life on another planet. Each lander carried a three-experiment biology instrument, miniaturized into less than 0.03 m^3 (1 ft^3) and using soil samples provided by each lander's extendable sampler arm.

The landers carried cameras, which were used not only for conventional photographs but also to measure light refraction in the atmosphere and to monitor the changing dust concentrations. The landers also carried seismometers, and meteorological instruments provided surface weather reports.

Vikings   The Vikings were venturesome seafarers and raiders from Scandinavia who spread through Europe and the North Atlantic in the period of vigorous Scandinavian expansion (AD 800–1100) known as the Viking Age. They appeared as traders, conquerors, and settlers in Finland, Russia, Byzantium, France, England, the Netherlands, Iceland, and Greenland.

The Vikings carried with them a civilization that was in some ways more highly developed than those of the lands they visited. Scandinavia was rich in iron, which seems to have stimulated Viking cultural development. Iron tools cleared the forests and plowed the lands, leading to a great increase in population. Trading cities such as Birka and Hedeby appeared and became the centers of strong local kingdoms. The Viking ship, with its flexible hull and its keel and sail, was far superior to the overgrown rowboats still used by other peoples. The rich grave goods of burial sites (see OSEBERG SHIP BURIAL), testify to the technical expertise of the Vikings in working with textiles, stone, gold and silver, and especially iron and wood. The graves also contain Arab silver, Byzantine silks, Frankish weapons, Rhenish glass, and other products of an extensive trade. Viking civilization flourished with its SKALDIC LITERATURE and eddic poetry, its runic inscriptions (see RUNES), its towns and markets, and, most of all, its ability to organize people under law to achieve a common task.

Expansion was apparently propelled by the search for new trading opportunities and new areas in which to settle. By the end of the 8th century, Swedish Vikings were in the lands around the Gulf of Finland, Danish Vikings were establishing themselves along the Dutch coast, and Norwegian Vikings had colonized the Orkney and Shetland islands.

During the 9th century they expanded beyond these three bases. Swedes called Rus or Varangians established fortified cities at Novgorod and then at Kiev, creating the first Russian state (see RURIK dynasty). Norwegian Vikings established kingdoms in Ireland, where they founded Dublin about 840, and in northwestern England. They settled Iceland and colonized Greenland in the 10th century and founded the short-lived North American colony called VINLAND in the early 11th century. Great armies of Danes and Norwegians conquered the area called the DANELAW in England. They attacked cities in France, Germany, the Low Countries, and Spain and, in 911, seized control of Normandy in France, where their descendants became known as the NORMANS.

The Vikings generally came under the cultural influence of the conquered peoples. Originally pagan worshipers of Thor and Odin, many became Christians, and during the 10th century they brought Christianity back to Scandinavia.

The process of conquest slackened during the 10th century as civil wars raged in Scandinavia. Out of these wars emerged powerful new kingdoms, and soon armies of a renewed Viking age were sailing forth. In 1013, SWEYN of Denmark conquered all of England. His son, CANUTE, built an empire that included England, Denmark, and Norway. After 1050, however, the emergence of stronger political systems and stronger armies in Europe, the development of new types of ships, and the redirection of military endeavor by the Crusades brought the Viking Age to an end.

(Below) *The Oseberg ship (AD c.800) is an example of a Viking long ship. Famed as shipbuilders and seafarers, the Vikings designed the ships, usually made of oak planks, with a high prow and stern, square sail, and rows of oars.*

(Above) *This naturalistic elk-antler carving, portraying a Viking warrior (11th century), ornamented the top of a stick found at Sigtuna, Sweden. Viking artisans excelled in stone- and wood-carving and metalworking.*

Villa, Pancho [vee'-yah]   Francisco "Pancho" Villa, originally named Doroteo Arango, b. June 5, 1878, d. July 20, 1923, Mexican bandit and revolutionary, became a folk hero as both a Robin Hood and an advocate of social reform. After killing a man in defense of his sister around 1894 he fled to the mountains. He then backed Francisco I. MADERO's revolution (1910–11) against dictator Porfirio Díaz and contributed to Díaz's fall.

While fighting for Madero's besieged government, Villa was condemned to death by Gen. Victoriano HUERTA, his commanding officer, in 1912, but Madero had Villa imprisoned instead. Villa soon escaped, and in 1913 he and his followers joined Venustiano CARRANZA in a revolt against Huerta.

After Huerta's ouster in 1914, Villa broke with the more conservative Carranza and occupied Mexico City with Emiliano ZAPATA. Defeated at Celaya and León in 1915 by Carranza's general, Álvaro OBREGÓN, Villa withdrew to Chihuahua, where he led guerrilla raids, including several into New Mexico in retaliation for U.S. president Woodrow Wilson's recognition of Carranza in October 1915.

After Carranza was killed (1920) in the rebellion of Agua Prieta, which toppled his regime, Villa was given an amnesty and a hacienda in return for laying down his arms. He lived in retirement until assassinated at Parral, Chihuahua, by followers of Obregón.

Pancho Villa, a Mexican military commander who played a key role in the Revolution of 1910, later led guerrilla forces against the Carranza government. In 1916 he raided the New Mexico town of Columbus, killing 17 Americans and provoking a U.S. punitive expedition into Mexico. Villa's exploits made him a folk hero throughout Mexico.

Villa-Lobos, Heitor [vee-lah-loh'-bohsh, ay'-tohr] Heitor Villa-Lobos, b. Rio de Janeiro, Mar. 5, 1887, d. Nov. 17, 1959, was a world-famous Brazilian composer. In his youth he traveled widely through Brazil, absorbing folklore and popular music. His formal musical training was scanty, and he was largely self-taught in composition. Befriended by the pianist Arthur Rubinstein, who played his music in the United States and Europe, Villa-Lobos was able to spend the years from 1923 to 1930 in Europe, living primarily in Paris. Audiences found his exotic compositions, such as *Rudepoema* (1923–26, for piano or orchestra) and the *Noneto* (1923), with its echoes of the Brazilian jungle, both exciting and fascinating.

After his return to Brazil he was active in music education and as organizer and director of people's choruses, while continuing his international career as composer and conductor. Extremely prolific, he composed in every category, from operas and symphonies to chamber music and songs, with many pieces for piano and several for guitar. Among his best-known works are the 9 *Bachianas Brasileiras* (1930–45) and the 14 *Chôros* (1920–28), written for a wide range of performance media, from solo guitar to full orchestra, band, and chorus. All are strongly imbued with Brazilian color. A favorite is the *Bachiana Brasileira no. 5* (1938) for soprano and 8 cellos.

Villahermosa [vil-ah-ayr-moh'-sah] Villahermosa (1980 pop., 250,903), the capital of Tabasco state, lies on the Gulf coastal lowlands of southeast Mexico near Campeche Bay. Petroleum is the major product, and the city is an agricultural marketing center. Villahermosa was founded by the Spanish in 1596.

Villanova University [vil-uh-noh'-vuh] Established in 1842 and administered by the Augustinian Fathers, Villanova University is a coeducational institution in Villanova, Pa. It has colleges of arts and sciences, nursing, and commerce and finance and a school of law.

Villanovans [vil-uh-noh'-vuhnz] The Villanovans, believed by some scholars to have been the predecessors of the ETRUSCANS, were the first people in central Italy to use iron. According to one school of thought they evolved out of the local Pianello culture; another school suggests that they were of foreign origin. They emerged during the 9th century BC and flourished between the Po and Tiber rivers. From there the rich culture of the Villanovans spread to the area around Bologna, where they established an important center near the present-day village of Villanova (for which they are named). The Villanovans worked the copper and iron mines of Tuscany and made fine metalwork that from the mid-8th century BC onward was influenced by Greek art.

Mystery surrounds the eclipse of the Villanovans. In the south they were replaced by the Etruscans during the 8th century BC, but in the north they continued until the 6th century BC, producing in the Po valley an art derived from the Greek Geometric.

Rome is built on the site of an 8th-century Villanovan settlement. This is compatible with the date of 753 BC that was in Roman tradition ascribed to the foundation of the Eternal City by Romulus.

Villanueva, Carlos Raúl [vee-ah-nway'-vah] Venezuela's major 20th-century architect, Carlos Raúl Villanueva, b. May 30, 1900, d. Aug. 16, 1975, established the National School of Architecture, where he taught for 16 years, and founded the Venezuelan Society of Architects, serving as its first president. He was also counselor to the Banco Obrero (a housing authority) and director of the National Commission on Urbanism. During the 1940s and '50s, Villanueva headed the design team that replaced the slums of Caracas with modern housing developments.

Villanueva's most important work, the monumental structures at the Central University of Caracas (1952), epitomizes his distinctive style, which attempts to integrate art and architecture on a grand scale. This project, incorporating the work of many contemporary artists and sculptors, is probably the world's best demonstration of how architecture, painting, sculpture, and stained glass can be integrated into a new, balanced synthesis.

Villars, Claude Louis Hector, Duc de [vee-yar']
Claude Louis Hector, duc de Villars, b. May 8, 1653, d. June 17, 1734, diplomat and soldier for Louis XIV of France, fought brilliantly during the War of the SPANISH SUCCESSION (1701–14); he was honored with the rare title of marshal general of France (1733). Villars won battles at Friedlingen (1702) and Höchstädt (1703) and pacified the rebellious French CAMISARDS. Although he lost the Battle of Malplaquet (1709) to the Anglo-imperial forces under the duke of Marlborough and Eugene of Savoy, his opponents suffered staggering casualties. Victory at Denain (1712) hastened the Peace of Utrecht (1713–14).

Villella, Edward [vil-el'-uh] The dynamic American dancer Edward Villella, b. Bayside, N.Y., Oct. 1, 1936, has done a great deal toward making dance an acceptable career for men. Upon graduation (1956) from New York State Maritime College, where he had been a boxing champion, Villella returned to his study of ballet. He joined New York City Ballet in 1957 and was immediately given leading roles. Among his most popular roles were those in *Prodigal Son* (1960), *Harlequinade* (1965), and *Rubies* (1967). Jerome Robbins created the leading role for him in his experimental ballet *Watermill* (1972). In 1976 Villella won an Emmy for his children's ballet for television, *Harlequin.* He contributed to Dance Perspectives Number 40, *The Male Image.* Villella has served on the National Council of the Arts and was chair (1978–79) of New York City's Commission on Cultural Affairs.

Villiers de L'Isle-Adam, Philippe [vee-lee-ay' duh leel-ah-dam'] Philippe Auguste Villiers de L'Isle-Adam, a French poet, novelist, dramatist and short-story writer, b. Feb. 28, 1838, d. Aug. 19, 1889, was a descendant of an impoverished noble family and lived in great poverty. He is best known for an esoteric symbolic play, *Axël* (1890), which was called by René Lalou "the last expression of European Romanticism, the Faust of the expiring nineteenth century." He also left two collections of short stories, *Cruel Tales* (1883; Eng. trans., 1963) and *Nouveaux contes cruels* (More Cruel Tales, 1888), and a novel, *L'Éve future* (The Eve of the Future, 1886).

Villon, François [vee-yohn'] François Villon, b. Paris, 1431, as François de Montcorbier or François des Loges, d. 1463?, was one of the finest French lyric poets. Of poor parents, he was brought up by a priest, Guillaume de Villon, whose name he took. He did graduate study in Paris until 1452 but three years later was banished from the city for fatally stabbing a priest in a brawl. *Le Petit Testament* (The Small Testament), known also as *Le Lais* (The Legacy), may have been composed at this time, and Villon's other long poem, *Le Grand Testament* (The Large Testament), known also simply as *Le Testament*, soon followed.

The Testaments are mock or imaginary wills in which bequests are made alternately with compassion and with irony. For example, to the Holy Trinity, Villon leaves his soul; to the earth, his body; to a Parisian, Denis, some stolen wine; to a madman, his glasses; to a lover, all the women he wants. At least two of Villon's shorter poems—"Ballad of Hanged Men" and "I Am François, They Have Caught Me"—were composed in 1462 while the author was awaiting execution for robbery. His sentence, however, was commuted to banishment, and Villon subsequently disappeared without a trace.

Villon, Jacques The French artist Jacques Villon, b. Gaston Duchamp, July 31, 1875, d. June 9, 1963, was the brother of the Dada artist Marcel Duchamp and the sculptor Raymond Duchamp-Villon. Villon adopted his favorite poet's surname in 1895, when he went to Paris to pursue an artistic career. He produced numerous posters and satirical newspaper drawings and became a printmaker of the first rank. His interest turned to cubist painting in 1911, and in 1912 he helped organize the avant-garde Section d'Or (Golden Section) exhibition in Paris.

During the 1920s and '30s, Villon alternated between formal abstraction and an extremely simplified realism bordering on cubism. In his later work, such as *Portrait of Marcel Duchamp* (1951; Henie-Onstad Museum, Oslo), Villon produced an elegant synthesis of both styles.

Vilna see VILNIUS

Vilnius [vil'-nee-uhs] Vilnius (Russian: Vilna), the capital of Lithuania, is located on the Neris River. With a population of 582,000 (1989), the city is an important cultural and industrial center, accounting for about one-fourth the manufacturing output of Lithuania. The principal products are precision instruments and electrical equipment. Vilnius has the ruins of a 14th-century castle. Its university was founded in 1579.

Settled during the 10th century, Vilnius became the capital of the Grand Duchy of Lithuania in 1323 and, despite destruction by the Teutonic Knights in 1377, developed into a major trading center. It declined after Lithuania was formally united with Poland in 1569. Vilnius passed to Russia in 1795. After World War I the city was disputed between the new governments of Lithuania and Poland; the Poles won control of it in 1920. The USSR took Vilnius from Poland in 1939 and ceded it to Lithuania, only to annex all of Lithuania the following year. From 1940 until 1990, when Lithuania declared its independence, the city was the capital of the Lithuanian SSR. Vilnius was an important Jewish center of Eastern Europe until the extermination of the Jews by the Germans during World War II.

Viña del Mar

[veen'-yah del mar] Viña del Mar (1989 est. pop., 302,800) is a seaside and gambling resort on the coast of central Chile, 8 km (5 mi) north of Valparaíso. Known for its superb gardens, a casino, a racetrack, and other recreational facilities, it also serves as an industrial and marketing center and is the site of Cerro Castillo, the summer retreat of Chilean presidents.

Vincennes

[vin-senz'] Vincennes (1990 pop., 19,-859), the oldest city in Indiana, lies on the Wabash River in the southwestern part of the state. It is the seat of Knox County and an industrial and commercial center. Glass, steel, shoes, and paper products are manufactured. Landmarks include the old cathedral of Saint Francis Xavier (1825) and the Indiana Territorial Capitol (1800). Vincennes was founded in 1702 by French fur traders and ceded to the British in 1763. During the American Revolution it was captured by Americans under George Rogers Clark in 1779.

Vincennes, François Marie Bissot, Sieur de

[van-sen'] François Marie Bissot, sieur de Vincennes, b. Montreal, June 17, 1700, d. Mar. 25, 1736, a French-Canadian soldier and explorer, promoted French interests in the Wabash country in present-day Indiana. Son of the explorer Jean Baptiste Bissot, sieur de Vincennes, he erected a fort c.1722 near present-day Lafayette, Ind., and in 1731 or 1732 built another at present-day Vincennes, Ind. Vincennes was defeated in a skirmish with the hostile Chickasaw Indians, who burned him at the stake near present-day Fulton, Miss.

Vincent, John Heyl

The Methodist clergyman John Heyl Vincent, b. Tuscaloosa, Ala., Feb. 23, 1832, d. May 9, 1920, was a leader in the Sunday school movement. As general secretary of the Methodist Episcopal Sunday School Union and Tract Society, he began publication of a large series of Sunday school materials. The culmination of his career came with the founding of the Chautauqua Sunday School Teachers Assembly in 1874. Out of this interdenominational project, which consisted of 8 weeks annually of summer school, developed the CHAUTAUQUA movement. Vincent was elected bishop in 1888.

Vincent de Paul, Saint

[van-sahn' duh pohl] The French priest Vincent de Paul, b. Apr. 24, 1581, d. Sept. 27, 1660, was the founder of numerous charitable organizations. Of peasant family, he founded the Congregation of the Mission (the Vincentians or Lazarists; 1625) to preach to the rural poor and, with Saint Louise de Marillac, founded the Daughters of Charity (1633), composed of peasant women who, in ministering to the poor, were the first sisters to work outside of the convent buildings in active service. Vincent also organized several seminaries to train young men for the priesthood and inaugurated the now-standard practice of a period of spiritual preparation for men about to be ordained to the priesthood. Canonized in 1737, he is the patron of all charitable works inspired by his example, including the famous lay organization of the St. Vincent de Paul Society. Feast day: Sept. 27 (formerly July 19).

Vincent Ferrer, Saint

[vin'-sent fer'-er] Spanish Dominican preacher Vincent Ferrer, b. c.1350, d. Apr. 5, 1419, worked to end the Great SCHISM. He was a protégé and friend of Pedro de Luna, whose confessor he became when de Luna was elected (1394) "antipope" at Avignon as BENEDICT XIII. After trying unsuccessfully to persuade Benedict to resign, Vincent began to denounce him publicly about 1412 and drew support away from the Avignon papacy, thus paving the way for the end of the Schism at the Council of Constance (1417). Vincent Ferrer was canonized in 1455. Feast day: Apr. 5.

Vindication of the Rights of Women, A

Mary WOLLSTONECRAFT's *A Vindication of the Rights of Women*, written in 1792, is a milestone in the history of modern feminism. Part of the spreading debate over human rights inspired by the French Revolution and a direct response to Jean Jacques Rousseau's *Émile* (1762), it was an appeal to French leaders of the period to include women in their proposed educational reforms. Its author argued that the rights of man applied equally to both sexes and that the cause of woman's oppression lay in a faulty education that had kept her inferior. Controversial in its time, Wollstonecraft's *Vindication* represents the first major demand for the redress of feminine grievances.

vinegar

Vinegar (from the French *vinaigre,* "sour wine") is an acidic liquid obtained from the fermentation of alcohol and used either as a condiment or a preservative. Vinegar usually has an acid content of between 4 and 8 percent; in flavor it may be sharp, rich, or mellow. Vinegar is made by combining sugary materials (or materials produced by hydrolysis of starches) with vinegar or acetic-acid bacteria and air. The sugars or starches are converted to alcohol by yeasts of the genus *Saccharomyces,* and the bacteria make enzymes that cause oxidation of the alcohol.

Several varieties of vinegar are manufactured. Wine vinegars, produced in grape-growing regions, are used for salad dressings and relishes and may be either reddish or white, depending on the wine used in the fermentation process. Tarragon vinegar has the distinctive flavor of the herb. Malt vinegar, popular in Great Britain, is known for its earthy quality. White vinegar, also called distilled vinegar, is made from industrial alcohol; it is often used as a preservative or in mayonnaise because of its less distinctive flavor and clear, untinted appearance. Rice vinegar, which has a piquant quality, is often used in Oriental countries for marinades and salad dressings.

Vinland [vin'-luhnd]   Vinland was a VIKING, or Norse, settlement on North America's east coast in the early 11th century. The land it occupied was probably first sighted c.986, when Bjarni Herjolfsson was blown off course. Later, c.1000, LEIF ERIKSSON led an expedition that touched Helluland (probably Baffin Island) and Markland (probably Labrador) and remained a year at Vinland. His brother Thorvald went to Vinland c.1004. THORFINN KARLSEFNI (c.1010) and two brothers, Helgi and Finnbogi (c.1013), also led expeditions. Vinland was abandoned c.1015, apparently because of the hostility of the native Skraelings.

Various spots have been suggested for Vinland's location, from the Virginia Capes to Newfoundland. The L'ANSE AUX MEADOWS site (northern Newfoundland) has many Norse artifacts, but the Vinland settlement's exact location remains in doubt. Yale University's Vinland map, a world map supposedly made about 1440, includes Vinland and Greenland, but by 1974 its New World portions had been proved a modern forgery.

Vinson, Frederick M.   Frederick Moore Vinson, b. Louisa, Ky., Jan. 22, 1890, d. Sept. 8, 1953, was 13th chief justice (1946–53) of the United States. Vinson was educated at the University of Kentucky and served (1922–38) as a Democrat in the U.S. House of Representatives. In 1938, President Franklin D. Roosevelt named him to the U.S. Court of Appeals. He resigned in 1943 to head the Office of War Mobilization, and, in 1945, President Harry S. Truman appointed him secretary of the treasury. In 1946, Truman named him chief justice. On the Supreme Court, Vinson was both criticized for failing to protect individual rights and praised for his record in cases involving religious freedom and the rights of blacks.

Vinson Massif   The Vinson Massif, Antarctica's highest peak, rises to 5,140 m (16,864 ft) in the Sentinel Range of the Ellsworth Mountains near the Ronne Ice Shelf. Sighted by Lincoln Ellsworth in 1935 during an aerial survey, it was first climbed in 1966.

vinyl   Vinyl plastic is usually the common thermoplastic polyvinyl chloride (see PLASTICS). Vinyl chloride is a gas produced by reacting ethylene or acetylene with hydrochloric acid. The reaction replaces one hydrogen atom in

ethylene with a chlorine atom, making the material nonburning. Before it was banned as a carcinogen in 1974, the gas had been used as a propellant in aerosols. Polymerization of vinyl chloride produces polyvinyl chloride (PVC), which is not considered dangerous. PVC is a rigid plastic but is soft and flexible if compounded with plasticizing materials.

More polyvinyl chloride is used than any other plastic except polyethylene. Uses include house siding, window frames, electrical insulation, eaves troughs, hoses, pipe, floor tile, phonograph records, household goods, and water-resistant sheeting, such as raincoats and shower curtains. Other vinyl plastics include polyvinyl fluoride, polyvinyl alcohol, polystyrene (polyvinyl benzene), and polyvinyl acetate.

viol   see MUSICAL INSTRUMENTS

viola [vee-oh'-luh]   The viola is the alto of the violin family, and it has the responsibility of playing the tenor part in the string quartet. Larger and heavier than the violin, it is tuned a fifth lower and has a darker, somewhat nasal tone. Preclassical viola parts were sometimes uninteresting, but in the music of Mozart they assumed an importance that has remained. Viola concertos are few, but the instrument plays an important role in chamber music and solo sonatas.

violet   Violets are about 500 species of temperate-zone flowers, genus *Viola*, in the violet family, Violaceae. They are low-growing herbs or subshrubs, and species bloom either annually or perennially. Violets may be stemmed—flowers and leaves growing on the same stem—or stemless—flowers and leaves growing on separate stalks. The shape of the leaves varies widely. Many species of violets produce two kinds of flowers: showy purple, blue, pink, yellow, white, or multicolored flowers are produced in the springtime, allowing cross-pollination by insects; self-pollinating, inconspicuous green flowers

The perennial sweet violet has broad, heart-shaped leaves and stemless flowers—growing on separate stems from the leaves. The flowers bloom in early spring, and colors range from violet, lilac, and pink to white. Although varieties of this species are cultivated, it also grows wild in moist, slightly sunny areas of Eurasia and Africa.

without petals are produced during the summer.

Although most species are wildflowers, several have been cultivated; these include the PANSY, classified as *V. tricolor* or *V. × wittrockiana* (a hybrid); Johnny-jump-up, *V. tricolor*; and sweet, or florist's, violet, *V. odorata*. Leaves of sweet violets can be added to salads, and the flowers can be candied or used to make violet jelly. Large numbers of the parma violet, *V. odorata* var. *semperflorens*, are grown in France and Italy to produce essential oils used in perfume; more than 2 million flowers are needed to yield about 0.5 kg (1 lb) of the oils. In the eastern United States and Canada, common wildflower species include the woolly blue violet, *V. papilionacea*, and the bird's-foot violet, *V. pedata*. The AFRICAN VIOLET, genus *Saintpaulia*, is not related to the true violet.

violin   The violin, the most commonly used member of the modern string family, is the highest-sounding instrument of that group. Its four strings are stretched over a high, arched bridge that permits the playing of one or two strings at a time, as well as the nearly simultaneous sounding of three or four as chords. The overall length of the violin averages about 60 cm (23.5 in), whereas the sounding length of the strings, from bridge to the nut at

The violin, which was perfected during the early 1700s by the Italian instrument maker Antonio Stradivari, has remained virtually unchanged to the present day. Profiles of the 18th-century instrument (A) and the modern violin (B) show minor adjustments that reflect the demands of changing music and technique. The bridge (1) was raised and arched slightly during the late 18th century, increasing string tension and providing the brighter tone that was desired. In order to facilitate playing, the wedge (2) was eliminated, and the neck (3) was set at an angle to the body to support the lengthened fingerboard (4). Playing positions have also changed, from the 18th-century posture with the left hand supporting the instrument to a position with the violin held between the shoulder and chin, freeing the left hand.

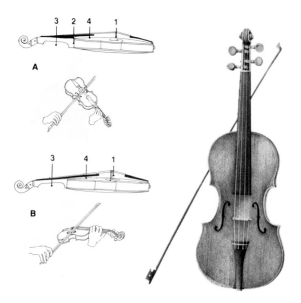

the end of the fingerboard, is about 32 cm (12.75 in). The instrument is held on the left side of the body, while the right hand holds the bow. The wider end of the instrument is placed between the player's left shoulder and chin, while the left hand encircles its neck, the fingers stopping the strings to produce the various pitches. Sound is produced by drawing the bow across the strings to make them vibrate, or by plucking the strings (pizzicato). The range of the violin extends from G, the lowest open string, upward nearly four octaves.

Introduced into Europe at a time when the viol was the commonest stringed instrument, this descendant of the medieval fiddle was considered more suitable for dance music and rustic merrymaking than for the church or nobleman's chamber. By the beginning of the 17th century, Giovanni Gabrieli and Claudio Monteverdi were using the violin in their instrumental ensembles, and general acceptance of the instrument followed shortly thereafter.

The earliest important center of violin making was Brescia, where Gaspara da Saló (1540–1609) and Giovanni Paolo Maggini (1581–1630) worked. Cremona became the center of manufacture when the instruments of the Amati family, and later those of the Stradivari, Guarneri, and Ruggieri shops, attracted the attention of the public (see AMATI family; GUARNERI family; STRADIVARI family). The Italian master builders of the 17th and early 18th centuries are esteemed above all others, but makers from other areas achieved high recognition, among them the Tyrolese brothers, Jakob and Markus Stainer, the Klotz family in Bavaria, and some English and French builders. The demand for instruments brought mass production to Mittenwald, Bavaria, where the Klotzes had worked, but also a decline in quality. There the custom originated of putting labels bearing the names of famous makers, mostly Italian, into instruments, not to deceive buyers, but to identify the style of instrument that was imitated. Owners of instruments with facsimile labels sometimes mistakenly believe that they have an undiscovered masterpiece, an all-but-impossible dream.

Excellent violin makers exist in the United States, but the old instruments possess a special aura that is prized by performers. Because the value of old instruments increases with time, the best of them are owned and treasured by professionals or housed in special collections.

Viollet-le-Duc, Eugène Emmanuel   The French architect Eugène Emmanuel Viollet-le-Duc, b. Jan. 27, 1814, d. Sept. 17, 1879, was known for his restorations of French medieval buildings. Among the important structures on which he worked were the Abbey Church of Vézelay (1840), the Sainte-Chapelle and Notre Dame in Paris (1845; in collaboration with Jacques Lassus), the walled city of Carcassone (1853), and the Château de Pierrefonds (1863–70).

Viollet-le-Duc educated himself during the 1830s through the firsthand study of buildings in France and abroad. In his theoretical writings he championed the Gothic style because he felt that its form was determined by structural necessity and its decoration both revealed and was derived from construction and materials. Thus he proposed the use of 19th-century techniques and materials, especially cast iron (see CAST-IRON ARCHITECTURE), according to the same rationalist principles employed by the Gothic masons.

violoncello   see CELLO

viper   Vipers are venomous snakes in which the venom apparatus has reached its greatest development. The fang-bearing bone (maxillary) on each side of the upper jaw not only is much shorter than in most other snakes but also can be rotated. The fangs, which are hollow like hypodermic needles, are normally carried folded and rest horizontally along the roof of the mouth. When preparing to bite, a viper erects these fangs to a perpendicular position by rotating each maxillary on the front end of the supporting prefrontal bone.

The viper family, Viperidae, is usually divided into two subfamilies: the Viperinae, or true vipers, and the Crotalinae, containing the PIT VIPERS. The true vipers are distributed extensively in the Old World. The African Gaboon viper, *Bitis gabonica,* reaching 1.8 m (6 ft) in length, is the largest of the true vipers; the African puff adder, *B. arietans,* another large viper, is responsible for more human and livestock deaths in Africa than any other snake; the Asiatic Russell's viper, *Vipera russelli,* exceeding 1.5 m (5 ft) in length, may carry more venom than any other viper; and the saw-scaled viper, *Echis carinatus,* a 60-cm (2-ft) snake of North Africa and Asia, has the most potent venom of any viper.

Pit vipers, such as the rattlesnakes, differ from the true vipers primarily by possessing heat-sensitive pits used to detect warm-bodied prey. Pit vipers occur in North, Central, and South America and also range from Eastern Europe across Asia to Japan and the Indonesian archipelago.

Most vipers are heavy bodied and terrestrial; however, some are adapted to life in the trees and are bright green with prehensile tails (*Bothrops, Trimeresurus,* and *Atheris*). Some vipers possess interesting appendages, the functions of which are unknown. The many-horned adder, *Bitis cornuta,* and the eyelash viper, *Bothrops schlegeli,* have spinelike scales over their eyes. A hornlike projection of the snout is found in the Patagonian viper, *Bothrops ammodytoides,* and the European sand viper, *V. ammodytes.*

The brilliantly colored rhinoceros viper has two or three horns above each nostril. It inhabits central African forests.

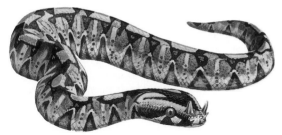

New World pit vipers bear living young, except for the bushmaster, *Lachesis muta,* which lays eggs. Most Old World pit vipers bear live young, although several species lay eggs. The majority of true vipers give birth to live young, but, as in the pit vipers, a few lay eggs. In the tropics vipers may breed every year, but species inhabiting colder regions and at least one species from the highland tropics are unable to acquire sufficient food reserves to produce young annually.

viperfish   Viperfish are elongated, deep-sea predators with large, expansive mouths containing several long, sharp, fanglike teeth. Making up the genus *Chauliodus,* family Chauliodontidae, viperfish are found in most oceans, usually in deep midwaters where they may make daily vertical migrations. They reach about 20 cm (8 in) in length and have adipose dorsal and ventral fins, a very elongated first dorsal spine, and many luminescent (light-producing) organs used to lure prey.

Viren, Lasse   [vir-eern', lahs'-suh]   Lasse Artturi Viren, b. July 22, 1949, is a Finnish long-distance runner whose feats in the 1972 and 1976 Olympic Games rank among the greatest in track-and-field history. Viren won both the 5,000- and 10,000-m (5,465- and 10,930-yd) runs in the 1972 Games, saving his most remarkable effort for the longer run, in which he not only broke the world record with a time of 27 min 38.4 sec, but did so after falling down halfway through the race. In the 1976 Olympics he became the first man ever to repeat the 5,000- and 10,000-m double victory; in those Games he ran the 5,000-m race in the Olympic-record time of 13 min 24.76 sec.

vireo   [vir'-ee-oh]   Vireos are small, mostly arboreal birds found from Canada through South America. More than 40 species, including the greenlets of South America, make up the family Vireonidae. Many are migratory, wintering in the tropics and breeding in cooler areas. Vireos are usually various shades of olive or gray above and white to gray below. Some have wing bars, eye rings, or head markings; both sexes are alike. They feed mostly on insects but may also eat berries. The female alone usually makes the lined cup nest, but the male helps in incubating the eggs and in caring for the young. The red-eyed vireo, *Vireo olivaceus,* a green-backed bird with a red eye, a white line over the eye, and a black-bordered blue gray cap, is common over its nesting range of southern Canada and the United States east of the Rocky Mountains.

Virgil   see VERGIL

virgin birth   The accounts of the birth of JESUS CHRIST in the Gospels according to Matthew and Luke, specifically the two Annunciation stories (Matt. 1:18–25; Luke 1:26–38), tell of a virginal conception by MARY through the power of the Holy Spirit. Belief that Jesus was thus conceived without a human father was more or less universal in the Christian church by the 2d century and is accepted by the Roman Catholic, Orthodox, and most Protestant churches. The origin of the tradition, however, is a controversial subject among modern scholars. Some believe it to be historical, based on information perhaps from Mary or her husband Joseph; for others it is a theological interpretation, affirming the divinity of Jesus Christ.

Virgin Islands

The Virgin Islands, a group of 7 main islands and more than 90 islets and cays, lie east of Puerto Rico in the Caribbean. Their total land area is 497 km² (192 mi²). Saint Thomas, Saint Croix, Saint John, and about 50 islets belong to the United States and have a population of 99,200 (1990 pop.). Anegada, Jost Van Dyke, Tortola, Virgin Gorda, and about 32 islets are possessions of the United Kingdom; their population is 11,585 (1985 pop.). CHARLOTTE AMALIE on Saint Thomas is the capital of the U.S. Virgin Islands. Road Town on Tortola is the capital of the British Virgin Islands.

Most Virgin Islanders are the descendants of slaves who worked colonial plantations. More recent immigrants to the islands have come from Puerto Rico, the United States, Venezuela, and the Lesser Antilles. Education and health standards are among the highest in the Caribbean.

Charlotte Amalie, the capital and largest city of the U.S. Virgin Islands, is situated on the Caribbean coast of the island of Saint Thomas.

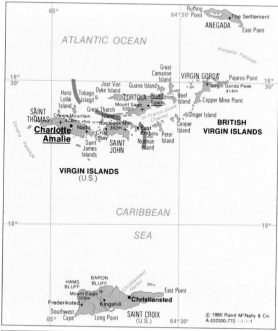

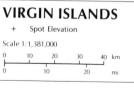

VIRGIN ISLANDS

+ Spot Elevation

Scale 1:1,381,000

0   10   20   30   40 km

0   10   20   mi

Saint Croix and Saint Thomas have divisions of the College of the Virgin Islands. Virgin Islands National Park is located on Saint John. Tourism dominates the economy. Fruits, vegetables, and coconuts are grown, and Saint Croix has petroleum refineries and bauxite-processing plants. Saint Thomas, with its large, protected harbor, has always been a commercial center.

Christopher Columbus landed at Saint Croix in 1493. The British took over the islands they now hold in 1666, and in the same year the Danes occupied Saint Thomas. In 1684 the Danes also occupied Saint John, and they acquired Saint Croix from the French in 1733. In 1917, because of the islands' strategic position on the approach to the Panama Canal, the United States purchased Saint Thomas, Saint Croix, and Saint John from Denmark. A major hurricane, *Hugo*, struck the islands in 1989, causing extensive damage on Saint Thomas and on Saint Croix, where there also was civil unrest.

virginal

The virginal is a keyboard instrument with strings that are plucked by a mechanism like that of a HARPSICHORD. However, there are differences between the instruments. The virginal is much smaller and has only one keyboard and a single set of strings. The strings themselves run more-or-less parallel to the front edge of the instrument. The harpsichord's strings, on the other hand, are placed at right angles to the front edge. The virginal can produce only a single timbre, whereas the harpsichord, with its several sets of strings and its "stops," can achieve a variety of tonal shades and textures. Because the longest strings of the virginal, the bass strings, are at the front, the instrument's shape can be varied.

The smaller, simpler virginal seems to have been much more common in late medieval and Renaissance Europe (the earliest mention of the instrument occurs in Germany in 1404) than the larger and more expensive harpsichord. Its name probably derives from the people who played it, most of whom were young women.

AT A GLANCE

VIRGINIA

Land: Area: 110,771 km^2 (42,769 mi^2); rank: 35th. Capital: Richmond (1990 pop., 203,056). Largest city: Virginia Beach (1990 pop., 393,069). Counties: 95. Elevations: highest—1,746 m (5,729 ft), at Mount Rogers; lowest—sea level, at the Atlantic coast.

People: Population (1990): 6,216,568; rank: 12th; density: 60.3 persons per km^2 (156.3 per mi^2). Distribution (1990): 69.4% urban, 30.6% rural. Average annual change (1980–90): +1.6%.

Government (1993): Governor: L. Douglas Wilder, Democrat. U.S. Congress: Senate—1 Democrat, 1 Republican; House—7 Democrats, 4 Republicans. Electoral college votes: 13. State legislature: 40 senators, 100 representatives.

Economy: State personal income (1989): $115.4 billion; rank: 11th. Median family income (1989): $38,213; rank: 13th. Agriculture: income (1989)— $2.06 billion. Fishing: value (1989)— $100 million. Lumber production (1991): 1.1 billion board feet. Mining (nonfuel): value (1988)—$495 million. Manufacturing: value added (1987)—$26.9 billion. Services: value (1987)—$28.5 billion.

Miscellany: Statehood: June 25, 1788; the 10th state. Nickname: Old Dominion; tree: dogwood; motto: *Sic Semper Tyrannis* ("Thus Always to Tyrants"); song: "Carry Me Back to Old Virginia."

Cardinal

Flowering dogwood

Virginia   Virginia, often regarded as the gateway to the South, occupies the middle position on the Atlantic seaboard of the United States. Named for Elizabeth I, England's "Virgin Queen," the state is also known as the Old Dominion—in recognition of the decision of Charles II to make the colony a fourth dominion of his realm, after England, Scotland, and Ireland—and as the Mother of Presidents, because it is the birthplace of eight U.S. presidents (George Washington, Thomas Jefferson, James Madison, James Monroe, William Henry Harrison, John Tyler, Zachary Taylor, and Woodrow Wilson).

Officially called the Commonwealth of Virginia, the state forms a rough triangle, with North Carolina and Tennessee to the south; Maryland, Chesapeake Bay, and the Atlantic Ocean to the northeast and east; and West Virginia and Kentucky to the northwest and west. Founded in 1607, Jamestown, near the southeastern corner of the state, represents the first permanent English settlement in North America. Virginia played a pivotal role in the American Revolution and the Civil War.

Land and Resources

Virginia has five distinctive topographical regions. Moving in from the Atlantic coast, the Tidewater, or coastal plain, is succeeded by the Piedmont or PIEDMONT PLATEAU, the BLUE RIDGE MOUNTAINS, the ridge and valley region, and the CUMBERLAND PLATEAU. The last three are part of the APPALACHIAN MOUNTAIN system.

Tidewater Virginia, including the Eastern Shore—the southern tip of the DELMARVA PENINSULA separated from the remainder of the state by CHESAPEAKE BAY—is generally low-lying and sandy, rising to about 90 m (300 ft) as it meets the Piedmont. Broad estuaries divide the western Tidewater into a series of peninsulas reaching into the bay.

The rolling hills of Piedmont Virginia extend southwest from Alexandria in the north. The towns of Fredericksburg, Richmond, and Emporia lie on the FALL LINE. The Blue Ridge rises from about 300 m (1,000 ft) at its base at the western edge of the Piedmont, reaching elevations of 350 m (1,200 ft) in the north to more than 1,700 m (5,500 ft) in the south. Virginia's highest point, Mount Rodgers, is found in the wider southern portion of the mountains.

The ridge and valley section of the state begins with the limestone-floored Great Valley and continues to the West Virginia border with a series of elongated hills and valleys trending northeast-southwest. In the extreme southwestern portion of Virginia lies a small part of the Cumberland Plateau of Kentucky.

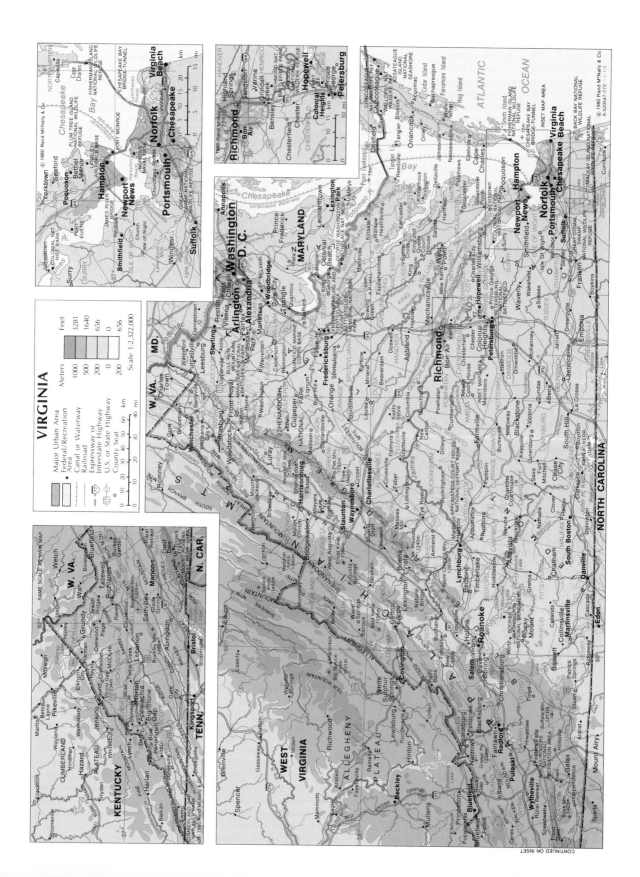

VIRGINIA

Scale 1:2,322,000

	Feet	Meters
	3281	1000
	1640	500
	656	200
	0	0
	656	200

Major Urban Area
Federal/Recreation Area
Railroad
Canal or Waterway
Expressway or Interstate Highway
U.S. or State Highway
County Seat

© 1980 Rand McNally & Co.
A-520547-772-1-1-1-1

CONTINUED ON INSET

The Blue Ridge Mountains, a segment of the Appalachian Mountain system, extends through Virginia from southwest to northeast. The highest point in the state, Mount Rogers (1,746 m/5,729 ft), is situated in the Blue Ridge Mountains near the North Carolina border.

Soils. Sandy loams dominate the Tidewater, but the Great Valley boasts dark, fertile limestone derivatives. In the mountains the thin soils are generally limestone based.

Rivers and Lakes. A series of rivers flowing east from the Blue Ridge drains most of Virginia. The POTOMAC follows Virginia's boundary with Maryland. To the south are the RAPPAHANNOCK, the York, and the JAMES RIVER, which enters Chesapeake Bay about 50 km (30 mi) north of the North Carolina line. Flowing north to join the Potomac, the SHENANDOAH RIVER drains the northern Great Valley; the western part of the state lies within the drainage basins of the Ohio and Tennessee rivers. The Roanoke drains the southwest toward North Carolina.

Virginia's only significant natural body of water, Lake Drummond (50 km^2/19 mi^2), lies at the center of the DISMAL SWAMP in the southeastern corner of the state. Several larger artificial lakes or reservoirs have been created along the course of the Roanoke River.

Climate. Virginia has a temperate climate; although summers are hot, winters are mild, and precipitation occurs throughout the year. July temperatures average 21° C (70° F) in the southwestern mountains but 27° C (80° F) in the southern Tidewater. In January the statewide average temperature drops to 4° C (39° F). Annual precipitation ranges from 760 mm (30 in) in the northwest to 1,400 mm (55 in) in the southeast.

Vegetation and Animal Life. Forests cover two-thirds of Virginia. Trees in the Tidewater are principally pines; in the western mountains, mostly hardwoods; and in the Piedmont, a mixture. Cypress trees grow in the Dismal Swamp, and azalea, rhododendron, and mountain laurel thrive in the western mountains.

Black bears inhabit the mountains and the Dismal Swamp, and deer can be found throughout the state. Smaller animals include foxes, rabbits, raccoons, squirrels, and opossums, and game birds such as turkeys, quail, grouse, doves, and woodcocks are found as well as such songbirds as robins, sparrows, and cardinals. Migrating ducks and geese fly across Virginia.

Resources. In the southwest, Virginia has large deposits of bituminous coal and small quantities of petroleum and natural gas. Other commercial minerals include sand and gravel, limestone, zinc, clays, lead, and soapstone (for talc). Groundwater resources are adequate in all sections of the state, often supplemented in the Tidewater by artesian wells.

People

More than half of Virginia's inhabitants live in the crescent-shaped urban corridor that stretches from ARLINGTON and ALEXANDRIA in the north, through FREDERICKSBURG, the state capital RICHMOND, and PETERSBURG, to NEWPORT NEWS, HAMPTON, PORTSMOUTH, and NORFOLK. The cities of CHARLOTTESVILLE, LYNCHBURG, and ROANOKE lie to the west. The rapid influx of people to northern Virginia gave the state a growth rate from 1980 to 1990 of 16.3%, compared to 10.2% for the nation as a whole.

The percentage of blacks, 18.8% (1990), in Virginia's population is declining. This relative drop is attributable to an in-migration of whites rather than an out-migration of blacks. Other minorities include 159,053 Asian and Pacific Islanders, 160,288 Hispanics, and 15,282 native Americans (1990). The Baptist, Methodist, Episcopal, and Presbyterian religious denominations together have the largest numbers of adherents.

Education. The first free school in the United States—the Syms Free School in Hampton—was founded in 1634 and the College of William and Mary, in Williamsburg, dates from 1693. The state constitution first provided for public schools in 1869. Thomas Jefferson founded the University of Virginia in 1819 (see VIRGINIA, UNIVERSITY OF). Today Virginia has 39 public institutions of

Thomas Jefferson designed Monticello, his classical revival residence, and directed its construction between 1770 and 1809. Located in Albemarle County in central Virginia, the mansion and its estate are maintained as a historical landmark.

higher education and 30 private institutions of higher education—including WASHINGTON AND LEE UNIVERSITY, Randolph-Macon College, and the University of Richmond.

Culture. The Virginia Museum of Fine Arts, located in Richmond, presents drama and music as well as art exhibits. Also in Richmond are the private Valentine Museum and the Museum of the Confederacy—the latter occupying Jefferson Davis's home, the so-called White House of the Confederacy. Norfolk boasts the Chrysler Museum; Newport News has the Mariners Museum.

The Barter Theatre in Abingdon has won national recognition, as has the federally funded Wolf Trap Farm Park for the Performing Arts. Many local public libraries and bookmobiles can draw on the resources of the Virginia State Library in Richmond.

Historical Sites and Recreational Areas. Virginia is famous for its historic homes—particularly George Washington's at MOUNT VERNON and Thomas Jefferson's at MONTICELLO; for the carefully restored colonial settlements of JAMESTOWN, WILLIAMSBURG, and Yorktown; and for its many Civil War battlefields, including those at Chancellorsville, Fredericksburg, Spotsylvania, Manassas, Petersburg, and the Wilderness. Appomattox Court House is the site of Gen. Robert E. Lee's surrender to Ulysses S. Grant on Apr. 9, 1865.

Among the sites administered by the National Park Service are Shenandoah National Park and Assateague Island National Seashore. National forests are also found within the state. Millions visit the state's beaches in summer and its mountain ski resorts in winter.

Communications. The *Virginia Gazette,* founded in 1736 by William Parks, was the colony's first newspaper; the *Alexandria Gazette* was begun in 1784. Among Virginia's leading newspapers today are the *Richmond Times-Dispatch* and *News Leader* and the *Norfolk Virginian-Pilot.* The state also has numerous radio and television broadcasting facilities as well as many cable television systems.

Economic Activity

This single most important source of income in Virginia is its government sector. Virginia has extensive military installations, and many Virginia residents work for the federal government in Washington, D.C. Manufacturing, services, and trade are also important sectors of the state's economy. Coal and timber are valuable resource industries. The millions of tourists who visit the state also contribute economically.

Agriculture. Important crops grown in Virginia are tobacco, hay, corn, soybeans, and apples. Tobacco accounts for more farm income than any other crop, but more than half of the state's farm income comes from cattle and poultry raising and dairy farming. Virginia is an important apple-growing state and a leading producer of turkeys.

Forestry and Fishing. Nearly two-thirds of Virginia's land area is forested. Much of the lumber harvested each year goes into making furniture. Virginia ranks among the leading U.S. fishing states. Major species caught include oysters, clams, crabs, menhaden, and alewives. Sport fishing is also popular in Virginia.

Mining. Coal and stone are the most important minerals mined in Virginia. The state's coalfields are found mainly in the Appalachian Mountains area. Limestone is found in Virginia's western valleys. Other stones produced are granite, marble, basalt, sandstone, slate, and talc. Virginia is also the nation's leading producer of kyanite.

Manufacturing. Virginia's major industrial products include tobacco products, chemicals, foods, electrical equipment, nonelectrical machinery, transportation equipment, rubber and plastic products, printing and publishing, textiles, and furniture. Important manufacturing centers in the state are Richmond, Hopewell, Norfolk, Newport News, Lynchburg, Roanoke, and Martinsville.

Transportation. Virginia's highways include long sections of interstate highways 81 and 95, two of the nation's most heavily traveled north-south arteries. Among the state's scenic roadways are the Blue Ridge Parkway, Colonial National Historical Parkway, and George Washington Memorial Parkway.

A number of freight rail lines operate in the state, and Amtrak provides passenger service to several cities. HAMPTON ROADS is one of the nation's leading ports. Major airports in the state are Dulles International Airport and Washington National Airport.

Energy. Major sources of electric power in Virginia are coal-fired and nuclear power plants. Other energy sources are hydroelectricity, oil-fired power plants, and gas.

Government and Politics

Virginia's original constitution, adopted in 1776, was superseded by updated documents in 1830, 1851, 1870, 1902, and 1971. The governor serves a 4-year term and cannot hold office twice in succession. The governor administers the state through an appointed cabinet.

The state general assembly—which can trace its roots to the colonial House of Burgesses, founded in 1619 and the oldest representative legislature in the country—consists of a senate, with 40 members serving 4-year terms, and a house of delegates, with 100 members serving 2-year terms. Virginia's judicial system ascends to a supreme court of appeals composed of 7 judges appointed by the legislature for 12-year terms. Virginia has 95 counties and 41 independent cities.

In U.S. presidential elections Virginia voted for the Democratic candidate from 1932 through 1948. Since 1952, with the exception of 1964, Virginia's electoral votes have been cast for the Republican candidate.

History

First settled as early as 10,000 years ago, Virginia was inhabited by Indian tribes belonging to three different language families at the beginning of the 17th century. Along the coast lived the POWHATAN, of the Algonquian family; the Piedmont was occupied by tribes of the Siouan family; and the Iroquoian family was represented principally by the SUSQUEHANNA at the northern end of Chesapeake Bay, by the CHEROKEE in the southwest, and by the Nottoway in the southeast.

First European Settlements. The European history of Virginia began in 1570 with a short-lived Spanish mission probably located on the York River. In 1584, Sir Walter RALEIGH obtained a grant from Queen Elizabeth to colonize all of North America not already possessed or occupied by other Christian people. The first expedition to the vast new territory, named Virginia in honor of the queen, arrived at Roanoke Island (see ROANOKE COLONY) in 1585. More settlers came 2 years later, but by 1590 all the colonists had died or disappeared.

After a few other false starts, on Dec. 20, 1606, the LONDON COMPANY sent out three ships—*Susan Constant, Discovery,* and *Goodspeed*—carrying 143 adventurers. The ships landed on Apr. 26, 1607, and the settlement of Jamestown, named in honor of the king, was established May 14, 1607.

Early Trials. The colony, the first permanent English settlement in the New World, suffered from poor leadership, famine, disease, disputes with the Indians, and failure to find a marketable product. Capt. John SMITH returned to England in 1609, and conditions grew so severe during the following winter that the colonists decided to abandon their settlement. As they set sail in June 1610, Lord DE LA WARR arrived with reinforcements and supplies.

In 1614, John ROLFE, who introduced tobacco into Virginia, married POCAHONTAS, daughter of the chief Powhatan, a union that led to a period of peace with the Indians. Under the leadership of Sir Thomas Dale and Sir George YEARDLEY, De La Warr's successors as governor, the colony began to prosper. The House of Burgesses was founded in 1619. That same year saw the importation of the first slaves to labor in the tobacco fields. In 1622 a new chief, Opechancanough, Powhatan's successor, organized a sudden attack that left 347 settlers—more than one-third of the whites—dead.

Growth of the Colony. The English crown took control of the colony in 1624, and by 1635 the population was 5,000. The capital was shifted to Williamsburg from Jamestown in 1699. Depressed tobacco prices, Indian

uprisings, and the refusal of Gov. Sir William BERKELEY to call new elections to the House of Burgesses led in 1676 to BACON'S REBELLION.

During the early 1700s, English settlers, encouraged by Gov. Alexander SPOTSWOOD, migrated from the coastal towns westward across the Piedmont, where they met Scots-Irish and German immigrants moving southward from Pennsylvania through the Great Valley. The westward movement helped focus attention on the conflicting land claims of Virginia and France, and Gov. Robert DINWIDDIE dispatched George WASHINGTON to expel the French from Fort Duquesne, now Pittsburgh. Washington's mission failed, as did the disastrous expedition of Gen. Edward BRADDOCK in 1755, but the FRENCH AND INDIAN WAR (1754–63) eventually resolved the matter in favor of the British.

The American Revolution. After the Boston Tea Party, Virginia's governor, Lord DUNMORE, dissolved the House of Burgesses to prevent its use as an antigovernment forum, but the members reassembled in Raleigh Tavern to call for a convention of all the colonies.

The First Continental Congress, as the convention was called, met in Philadelphia on Sept. 5, 1774, with Peyton Randolph (see RANDOLPH family) of Virginia presiding. A later state meeting that convened in Richmond to approve the actions of the congress received a motion from Patrick HENRY to call up the militia. The governor seized the available arms and retreated to a British warship. At the Second Continental Congress, Richard Henry Lee (see LEE family) of Virginia moved "to declare the United Colonies free and independent states," and Thomas JEFFERSON wrote the Declaration of Independence, adopted on July 4, 1776. The congress appointed Washington commander in chief of the Continental Army. Virginia became an independent commonwealth in June 1776, and adopted a constitution, including a bill of rights, drafted by George MASON.

Virginia's chief military contribution to the American Revolution was to be the provision of men and supplies to the army, although a small force under George Rogers CLARK secured the Northwest Territory in 1778–79. In 1781, Benedict Arnold laid waste to Richmond, but in May of that year Gen. Charles CORNWALLIS entered the state from the south for an unsuccessful campaign against the marquis de Lafayette, which ended with the British surrender at Yorktown on Oct. 19, 1781 (see YORKTOWN CAMPAIGN).

Early Years of the Republic. After the revolution Virginia dominated the early years of the republic, with Washington, Jefferson, Madison, and Monroe as presidents and John MARSHALL shaping the U.S. Supreme Court. Madison was also instrumental in replacing the loose Articles of Confederation with the present Constitution of the United States. Later Madison drafted (1798) the Virginia Resolution supporting state rights, while Jefferson produced the similar Kentucky Resolution (see KENTUCKY AND VIRGINIA RESOLUTIONS).

During the early 1800s, abolitionist sentiment was strong in the state, particularly in the west, and after the revolt in 1831 led by Nat TURNER, the Virginia House of Delegates almost voted to abolish slavery.

The Civil War. Conflict between the North and the South over slavery and tariffs grew during the first half of the 19th century, climaxed by John Brown's raid at Harpers Ferry in 1859 and by the election of Abraham Lincoln to the presidency in 1860. Virginia did not, however, join the Confederacy until Apr. 25, 1861, after Lincoln's call for troops. The capital of the Confederacy was moved to Richmond; thus Virginia soon became the major battleground of the war.

The fighting started at Bull Run, or Manassas, on July 21, 1861 (see BULL RUN, BATTLES OF). The following year Gen. George B. McCLELLAN attempted to come up the peninsula to Richmond but was repulsed by Gen. Robert E. LEE (see PENINSULAR CAMPAIGN). Also in 1862, Lee turned back Gen. John POPE at the second Battle of Bull Run (August 29–30) but was himself blocked by McClellan at Antietam.

Lee defeated the Union forces at the Battle of FREDERICKSBURG in December 1862 and again at the Battle of CHANCELLORSVILLE the following May. Other battles took place at Petersburg (see PETERSBURG CAMPAIGN) and in the Shenandoah valley. By the time Lee surrendered to Grant at Appomattox, the state was devastated.

Reconstruction and Its Aftermath. West Virginia had separated itself from Virginia in 1863, and the remainder of the state was readmitted to the Union in 1870. The radical Republicans who ran Virginia during RECONSTRUCTION were promptly expelled from power by more conservative elements. Except for a brief period in 1881, conservatives of varying stripes have been in the ascendancy ever since, with the Democrats holding the governorship from 1885 to 1969, and then recapturing the office in 1981. Harry F. BYRD became governor in 1926, and although he moved on to the U.S. Senate in 1933, he continued to dominate state politics until the early 1960s.

Recent Trends. The 1950s brought Virginia into conflict with the federal government over integration. Segregation eventually yielded, however, to a new political order. A milestone occurred in 1989, when Virginia elected L. Douglas WILDER governor—becoming the first state in the union to elect a black to the top state office.

The federal government continues to drive the state's economic growth, whether the income derives from military installations or from Virginians working for the government, many of them in adjacent Washington, D.C.

▬

Virginia, University of

Located in Charlottesville, Va., the University of Virginia was founded in 1819 by Thomas Jefferson, who designed the Rotunda, the lawn, and the surrounding pavilions and buildings. A college of arts and sciences and schools of education, law, medicine, nursing, commerce, business administration, engineering, and architecture are part of the university, which became fully coeducational by the 1970s. The library is a depository for documents of the United Nations, the United States, the state of Virginia, and other special collections. Clinch Valley College (1954), at Wise, is a 4-year college of the university.

▬

Virginia cowslip Virginia cowslip, or bluebells, is the common name for *Mertensia virginica*, a perennial herb of the family Boraginaceae. It grows up to 60 cm (24 in), bearing handsome blue to purple, trumpet-shaped flowers in nodding clusters. Virginia cowslip occurs naturally in rich woods and bottomlands from New York west to Ontario, Kansas, and Minnesota and south to Arkansas, South Carolina, and Alabama.

▬

Virginia creeper Virginia creeper is the common name for the woody vine *Parthenocissus quinquefolia* of the family Vitaceae. Native to eastern North America, this vine climbs by means of tendrils and is sometimes used, like ivy, to cover external walls. Its leaves usually have five leaflets and turn red in autumn.

Virginia Resolutions see KENTUCKY AND VIRGINIA RESOLUTIONS

▬

Virgo [vur'-goh] Virgo, the second largest constellation and one of the earliest to be distinguished, lies on the zodiac east of Leo and, in mid-latitudes of the Northern Hemisphere, is visible above the southern horizon on spring evenings. Most of its stars are faint, except for brilliant blue white Spica, the 15th brightest star in the sky. The autumnal EQUINOX, or the position of the Sun on the first day of autumn, is located in Virgo. The constellation is noted for containing a large cluster of galaxies (see EXTRAGALACTIC SYSTEMS).

▬

viroid Viroids are extremely small infectious particles that are thus far known to cause diseases only in higher plants, including the potato, tomato, and chrysanthemum. They consist solely of RNA and are about $\frac{1}{1000}$ the size of the smallest known virus. Viroids can cause stunting of overall plant growth, distortions of leaf shape, discoloration of leaves, or even death of the entire plant.

Viroids can be transmitted between plant generations through both pollen and ovules. They can also be transmitted from an infected to a noninfected plant by farm implements. Their mode of reproduction in host cells, however, has not yet been determined, nor has any protein been found in host cells that could be associated with a particular viroid. It is thought that viroids represent segments of normal cellular RNA that somehow have become transmissible, disrupting the host's metabolism.

virology see VIRUS

virtual image see LENS; MIRROR

virtual reality see CYBERSPACE

▬

virus Viruses are extremely small parasites that are able to reproduce only within the cells of their hosts, upon which they depend for many of their fundamental life processes. They are the causal agents of many INFEC-TIOUS DISEASES. Many hundreds of different types of viruses exist, each of which normally grows in a restricted range of hosts; different viruses, however, have a very wide variety of hosts, including bacteria, plants, and animals. Recently, scientists have found that viruses are more than 1,000 times more plentiful in water than originally suspected, possibly making them the most numerous life-forms on Earth.

Any given type of virus exists in several forms or stages. The free virus particle, or virion, consists of a molecule of nucleic acid—either DNA or RNA, depending on the specific virus—surrounded by protein and, in some viruses, also lipid and carbohydrate. The virion is inert, because it lacks many of the components that are necessary for independent life and reproduction; it does, however, provide for the transfer of the nucleic acid from host cell to host cell. Replication can occur only when the nucleic acid enters a host cell. Within the cell, the nucleic acid functions as genetic material and directs the synthesis of proteins. This results in the production of new virions, which then are released from the cell and can initiate new cycles of infection.

History

Viruses were discovered at the end of the 19th century. In 1892, Dimitri Ivanovsky, a Russian botanist, discovered that the sap from tobacco plants affected by mosaic disease could be passed through filters so fine as to exclude all known bacteria and still retain the ability to produce the disease in new plants. In 1898, Friedrich Loeffler and Paul Frosch reported similar results for the infectious agent of foot-and-mouth disease of cattle. They also showed that an animal inoculated with a tiny amount of filtered material could itself subsequently give rise to a very potent inoculum. This indicated that the infectious agent was able to reproduce itself within the infected animal. During the next three decades many viruses were discovered. Unlike other microorganisms, none of the viruses could be propagated in the absence of host cells, which led researchers to conclude that viruses are intracellular parasites.

Beginning in the 1930s, a number of new techniques were developed for virology, or the study of viruses. The discovery that many animal viruses can be grown in mice and in chicken embryos allowed the course of viral infection to be studied under controlled laboratory conditions. Very high-speed centrifuges were developed that made possible the preparation of highly purified virions. Chemical analysis showed that viruses consist primarily of nucleic acid and protein, and the development of the electron microscope during the 1940s permitted scientists to study the size and shape of these virions in great detail.

Because of the ease with which BACTERIA can be grown and manipulated in the laboratory, many of the features of intracellular viral development were first discovered by studying bacteriophages, which are viruses that grow in bacteria. During the late 1950s techniques for growing animal cells in tissue culture were developed, making

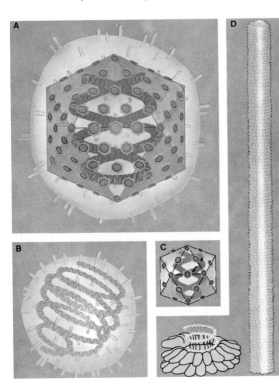

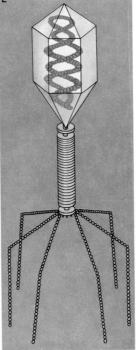

/\/\/\ · RNA
▮ DNA
▬ protein
/\/\/\ RNA + protein

A complete virus particle, or virion, consists of one molecule of nucleic acid—either DNA or RNA—and a protein coat called a capsid. The DNA of herpes virus particle (A) is enclosed by an icosahedral (20-sided) shell of 162 protein units, or capsomers, and by an outer spiked lipoprotein envelope; viruses of this type cause chicken pox and shingles in humans. A myxovirus (B), such as the influenza virus, has a protein and RNA core within a spiked lipoprotein envelope. The polyoma virus (C), which is associated with tumor induction, contains DNA in an icosahedral shell but lacks an outer envelope. Tobacco mosaic virus (D) consists of a helical strand of RNA with about 2,200 protein molecules coiled around it. The bacteriophage T2 (E) has a head—composed of DNA and a bipyramidal hexagonal (6-sided) protein shell—and a protein tail—made up of a tube core, a retractable sheath, and 6 tail fibers.

possible the detailed study of the intracellular growth of animal viruses.

Characteristics

The virions of different viruses vary greatly in size, shape, and complexity, but those of any given virus are uniform. The simplest types are rods and regular 20-sided polygons (icosahedrons); the tobacco mosaic virus, for example, consists of a single molecule of RNA surrounded by about 2,200 molecules of a single type of protein arranged in helical fashion to produce a rod 3,000 angstroms (1/100,000 in) long.

Many virions having a simple rod or polygonal shape are composed of several types of proteins, and some of these virions are surrounded by a less regularly shaped envelope, which often includes components of the host-cell membrane. At the other extreme of complexity, bacteriophage T4 has a virion composed of at least 25 different types of protein that make up a hollow head in which a DNA molecule is enclosed, and a tubular tail by which the virion attaches to its host cell and injects its DNA into it.

Reproduction. Virus reproduction begins when the virion comes into contact with a suitable host cell. The DNA or RNA enters the host cell and begins to function as genetic information by directing the synthesis of specific types of proteins that have enzymatic and structural roles. The infectious cycle usually consists of two different stages. In the first, the proteins are produced that are required for the reproduction of the viral DNA or RNA in conjunction with components of the host cell. In the second stage, proteins that make up the virion are produced; these combine with the DNA or RNA to form mature virions, which are then released from the cell. In some cases this release involves the complete disruption and death of the cell, a process known as lysis. In other cases individual virions are released through the cell membrane without killing the cell.

Transduction. Some viruses produce a small proportion of virions that contain host DNA in addition to or instead of viral DNA. These virions are able to transfer host genes from one cell to another. In bacteriophages, during the process called transduction, these genes can be incorporated into the recipient cell's chromosome, thus effecting genetic recombination.

Integration. Many viruses also interact with the host cell in such a way that the viral DNA, instead of replicating independently within the host cell, is integrated into the host-cell DNA. It is then replicated and passed on to daughter cells, as are the host cell's genes. Single or multiple copies of part or all of the viral DNA infecting animals may be incorporated into the host-cell DNA. When the viral DNA is integrated, virions are not produced and the host cell is not killed. When a complete copy of viral DNA is present, the cell may return at some time to a lytic mode of virus replication with subsequent production of new virions.

RNA as Genetic Material. The RNA-containing viruses

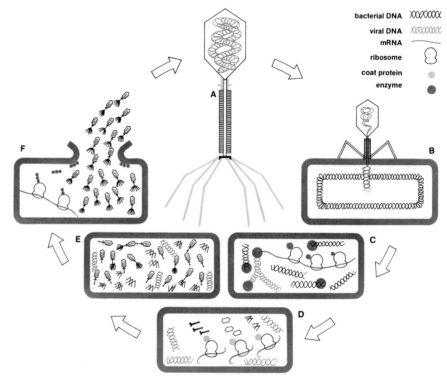

A virus contains the information needed to reproduce itself coded in its nucleic acid. Because it lacks its own protein-producing machinery, however, the virus must use the machinery of a host cell in order to multiply. A bacteriophage virion (A) attaches to a bacterial cell (B) and injects its DNA into the bacterium. Using bacterial ribosomes and enzymes, the viral DNA directs the synthesis (C) of messenger RNA (mRNA), enzymes that break up bacterial DNA, and enzymes that allow replication of viral DNA. Proteins are synthesized, using mRNA, from the DNA code; these proteins form heads, tails, and tail fibers (D), and the virus parts assemble into complete virions (E). An enzyme breaks up the bacterial cell (F) and liberates the new virions, which can infect other bacterial cells.

bacterial DNA
viral DNA
mRNA
ribosome
coat protein
enzyme

are unique among living systems because they use RNA as their primary genetic material. Some RNA-containing viruses produce enzymes that are capable of making new copies of RNA directly from the original molecule, thus circumventing DNA entirely. Retroviruses produce the enzyme called RNA-directed DNA polymerase, or reverse transcriptase, which can make a DNA molecule from the RNA molecule. This DNA formed from RNA then serves as the principal genetic molecule within the infected cell (see RETROVIRUS).

Importance of Viruses

Diseases. Although many viruses are apparently harmless to their hosts, certain viruses are responsible for important diseases of humans, other animals, and plants. Such diseases as CHICKEN POX, the common cold (see COLD, COMMON), ENCEPHALITIS, GERMAN MEASLES, HEPATITIS, genital and oral HERPES, INFLUENZA, MEASLES, viral MENINGITIS, MUMPS, POLIOMYELITIS, RABIES, SHINGLES, SMALLPOX, and YELLOW FEVER are all caused by viruses, and are due either directly or indirectly to the damaging effects of viral growth on the host cells. Of these diseases, only smallpox has been eliminated worldwide. Some of them, such as yellow fever, are caused by a class of viruses capable of growth and propagation in bloodsucking insects, where they cause no apparent harm. Such insects then act as vectors for transmitting the virus between animal hosts; in these hosts, however—including humans—the viruses cause diseases.

Viruses have been shown to cause certain types of cancer in animals. Two retroviruses have been associated with human leukemias, which are essentially cancers of T-cells (see IMMUNITY); another retrovirus has definitely been implicated with acquired immune deficiency syndrome (see AIDS). In addition, some of the PAPILLOMA viruses—the causes of various human tumors and WARTS—have been tentatively associated with diseases linked with the later development of cancer.

Vaccines. The smallpox vaccine, developed by Edward JENNER in 1796, was the first successful immunization against any infectious agent; vaccines were later found to be successful against other viral diseases, such as polio, hepatitis, influenza, and rabies. A vaccine consists of either killed virus or live virus that has been rendered incapable of causing disease. A vaccine causes the body to form antibodies, which provide protection against subsequent infections. The protection is only against the specific immunizing virus and viruses closely related to it. As an example, a new strain of the Rift Valley fever virus—borne by several species of mosquitoes and arachnids—swept eastern Africa in the late 1970s, causing epidemics that were combated by using a vaccine developed against the original strain during the 1960s. Through the use of GENETIC ENGINEERING techniques, researchers are creating various hybrid vaccines that are effective against more than one virus at a time (see VACCINATION; VACCINIA).

Interferon. Vertebrate animals also respond to viral infection by producing INTERFERON, a host-cell product that is formed and released by virus-infected cells. Interferon is taken up by uninfected cells, in which it inhibits the further growth of viruses. Once it is produced in response to one type of virus, it provides protection against a wide range of viruses.

virus, slow   Slow viruses are disease agents not yet identified but assumed to exist, because the diseases resemble viral diseases in their epidemiology. Slow-virus diseases are degenerative nerve disorders that take years to develop. They include the human diseases called kuru and Creutzfeldt-Jakob disease (see NERVOUS SYSTEM, DISEASES OF THE), a fatal sheep and goat disease called scrapie (see DISEASES, ANIMAL), and possibly a recently identified cattle disease called bovine spongiform encephalopathy, among others.

Theories on the nature of slow viruses include the PRION theory that they are nothing but infectious proteins; this idea is not generally accepted. The virino theory proposes that the agents do have nucleic acids, as do known viruses, but lack proteins. A third theory suggests that the agents are viruses that simply are very adept at hiding in body systems. Several known viruses can also act slowly, such as the AIDS virus and hepatitis viruses.

visa   see PASSPORT

viscacha   see CHINCHILLA

Visconti   (family) [vees-kohn'-tee]   The Visconti dynasty ruled the city of Milan and much of the surrounding region of Lombardy from 1277 to 1447. The name *Visconti* was formed from the family's title of viscount. The archbishop **Ottone Visconti**, b. 1207, d. Aug. 8, 1295, took possession of Milan in 1277, founding the dynasty's rule.

Archbishop **Giovanni Visconti**, b. 1290, d. Oct. 5, 1354, established unchallenged Visconti rule by expelling the rival Della Torre family. After his death, Lombardy was divided among his nephews: **Bernabò Visconti**, b. 1323, d. Dec. 19, 1385, a cruel and bizarre ruler, was given Milan; **Galeazzo II Visconti**, b. c.1320, d. Aug. 4, 1378, made his capital at Pavia. **Gian Galeazzo Visconti**, b. Oct. 16, 1351, d. Sept. 3, 1402, succeeded his father, Galeazzo II. Fearful of his uncle Bernabò's design to rule all Lombardy, Gian Galeazzo invaded Milan and probably poisoned Bernabò. He was made duke of Milan in 1395. He also conquered Verona and Vicenza, and during the 1390s he occupied Siena, Perugia, and Bologna. After he died of the plague his kingdom dissolved.

The family recouped its fortunes under **Filippo Maria Visconti**, b. Sept. 3, 1392, d. Aug. 13, 1447, who sought to maintain Visconti control over Lombardy. When he died without a male heir, the short-lived Ambrosian Republic (1447–50) was established in Milan. Lombardy soon passed, however, to Francesco Sforza (see SFORZA family), husband of the illegitimate **Bianca Maria Visconti**, b. 1423, d. Oct. 23, 1468.

Visconti, Luchino An aristocrat by birth and a Marxist by inclination, Italian filmmaker Luchino Visconti, b. Nov. 2, 1906, d. Mar. 17, 1976, is known for both his contributions to NEOREALISM and his frank aestheticism. His first film, *Ossessione* (1942), is one of the masterpieces of neorealist cinema. In the film self-destructive sexual passions are played out against a landscape of extraordinary beauty. Visconti used documentary techniques in his next film, *La Terra trema* (The Earth Trembles, 1948), to describe the lives of peasants in a Sicilian fishing village. A favorite theme was the tension between family solidarity and the destructive power of family relationships, best expressed in *Rocco and His Brothers* (1960) and *The Damned* (1969). Visconti's first film in color, *Senso* (1953), brilliantly portraying political and sexual conflicts during the Austro-Italian war of 1866, displayed the attention to detail and love for period reconstructions that would become his hallmarks in *The Leopard* (1963), *The Stranger* (1967), *Death in Venice* (1971), and *The Innocent* (1978).

viscosity [vis-kahs'-i-tee] Viscosity is a property of fluids (liquids or gases) that is a measure of a fluid's resistance to flow. When a fluid starts to flow under the action of a force, a shearing stress arises everywhere in the fluid that tends to oppose the motion. As one layer of the fluid moves past an adjacent layer, the fluid's molecules interact so as to transmit momentum from the faster layer to the slower layer tending to resist the relative motion. The simplest relation is in fluids for which the stress equals the coefficient of viscosity times the rate of shear. Such fluids are called Newtonian fluids, because their properties were first described by Isaac Newton. The viscosity of butter, a fluid that is non-Newtonian, decreases under a shearing stress, permitting the butter to be spread. Quicksand is a non-Newtonian fluid in which the viscosity increases when a shearing stress is applied.

viscount see TITLES OF NOBILITY AND HONOR

Vishnu [vish'-noo] One of the two premier gods of HINDUISM, Vishnu is frequently viewed as the preserver and protector of the world. The most popular contemporary forms or incarnations (avatars) of Vishnu are Rama, hero of the epic RAMAYANA, and KRISHNA, hero of the BHAGAVAD GITA. A kindly deity, Vishnu is represented riding on the bird Garuda or reclining on the snake Shesha and is sometimes worshiped symbolically by a small stone called a salagrama. His female consort is Lakshmi, goddess of well-being. The cult of Vishnu is called Vaishnavism. Particularly important sects are the Srivaisnavas of southern India, associated with the philosophy of Ramanuja (see VEDANTA); the Krishna cult of Brndaban, founded by Vallabha; and the Bengal movement, associated with the name of Caitanya (see HARE KRISHNA).

Visigoths see GOTHS

vision see EYE

visionary architecture The term *visionary architecture* is applied to a late-18th-century body of radically original architectural designs produced chiefly in France and principally by the architects Claude Nicholas LEDOUX and Étienne Louis BOULLÉE. In his works (1774–79) at the saltworks of Chaux at Arc et Senans, in his *Propylées* (customs houses) erected (1784–89) around Paris, and especially in his fantastic projects for the expansion of Chaux in his two-volume *Architecture considérée sous le rapport de l'art, des moeurs et de la législation* (The Relation of Architecture to Art, Customs, and Law, 1804 and 1847), Ledoux attempted to demonstrate a new and immediately comprehensible architectural language in which a cooper's house, for example, could be made in the shape of a barrel. As part of the contemporaneous search for natural, self-evident institutions and art, Ledoux's work eventually (1850s) came to be called *architecture parlante*, or "speaking architecture."

Architecture parlante involved a radical simplification of architectural forms that Boullée developed as an end in itself in his projects of the 1780s and '90s. In his *Essai sur l'art* (n.d.; pub. 1953 as *Boullée's Treatise on Architecture*), he conceived elaborate compositions of colonnades, domes, and unadorned masonry so arranged as to become huge architectural landscapes. A whole generation of architects produced similar designs: Jean Jacques Lequeu and Jean Nicholas Louis Durand in France, George Dance and Sir John Soane in England, Giuseppe Valadier in Italy, and Friedrich Gilly in Germany. Their designs presaged many of the concerns of modern architecture.

VISTA see ACTION

Vistula River [vis'-chu-luh] The Vistula River is a 1,069-km-long (664-mi) river flowing across central Poland. The country's longest river, it has a drainage basin of 198,500 km^2 (76,600 mi^2). Rising in the Carpathian Mountains in southernmost Poland, it flows generally northeast past Kraków, turns northwest toward Warsaw, and then north to the Baltic Sea at Gdańsk. Paralleled by railroads and canals along much of its route, it is navigable down to its tributary the San in southeastern Poland. Other tributaries include the Bug, Pilica, and Dunajec. The Vistula has long been a route for trade and expansion. Since World War II, dams and reservoirs have been built to improve navigation.

vital statistics see DEMOGRAPHY

vitamins and minerals Vitamins are carbon-containing substances that are required for normal METABOLISM but are not synthesized in the body. They are obtained, therefore, from such outside sources as food and water or are administered orally or intravenously. Exceptions to this definition include vitamin D, which is synthesized in the body to a limited extent, and vitamin B_{12}, which is synthesized by bacterial flora in the intestinal tract. Minerals also must be obtained from outside sources.

Vitamins and minerals function as "cofactors" in the metabolism of products in the body. Most aspects of bodily metabolism proceed with the aid of specific enzymes, but if additional catalysts were not present—for example, the cofactor vitamins and minerals—the reactions would proceed so slowly that they would be ineffective.

Daily Requirements

RDA. In the United States a Food and Nutrition Board was established to determine vitamin and mineral requirements. Since 1940 the board has periodically prepared a brochure listing the "Recommended Dietary Allowances" (RDA) of vitamins and other nutrients, based on existing knowledge. The RDA figures are estimations of the needs of most human beings; particular requirements will be less or more, depending on numerous individual factors such as genetics, environmental influences, and presence or absence of disease.

Supplements. Dietary supplements of vitamins are often recommended by physicians when any of the following conditions are present: diets obviously deficient in vitamins; conditions or diseases causing poor intestinal absorption; and increased needs that occur in relatively healthy individuals during periods of growth, hard physical work, pregnancy, lactation, and menstruation. Some disorders, including hyperthyroidism, infectious diseases, and tissue-wasting diseases, also cause increased tissue requirements.

Toxicity. Most of the water-soluble vitamins ingested in excessive amounts are rapidly excreted in the urine and thus rarely cause toxicity. The fat-soluble vitamins, on the other hand, are stored in body fat and are capable of causing severe toxicity when taken in excessive amounts.

Fat-Soluble Vitamins

Vitamin A. Vitamin A exists in a variety of forms, including retinol. Carotene, a pigment in some plants (see CAROTENOID), can be converted in the human body to vitamin A. Vitamin A is also highly concentrated in fish-liver oils. The normal diet contains adequate amounts of vitamin A.

Vitamin A is important to membrane integrity, especially of epithelial cells and mucous membranes; bone growth; reproduction; and embryonic development. A deficiency results in NIGHT BLINDNESS, in which the ability to see in dim light is impaired. Hypervitaminosis A results from excessive intake. Symptoms consist of irritability, vomiting, appetite loss, headache, dry skin, and scaling of skin. Intracranial pressure is increased, and bone changes occur.

Vitamin D. The active forms of vitamin D arise in the body from ingested precursors by exposure of the skin to ultraviolet light. Vitamin D interacts with PARATHYROID hormone and calcitonin (see HORMONE, ANIMAL) to control calcium levels.

A deficiency of vitamin D results in failure to absorb calcium and phosphorus, causing faulty formation of bone. In children the syndrome is known as RICKETS. Adult rickets, or osteomalacia, is characterized by generalized bone calcification and, eventually, gross bone deformities. Symptoms of hypervitaminosis D consist of weakness, fatigue, lassitude, headache, nausea, vomiting, and diarrhea. Urinary symptoms occur when calcium deposits build up in the kidneys.

Vitamin E. Vitamin E, or alpha tocopherol, is present in seed oils, especially wheat-germ oil. Few vitamins have been advocated for more diseases than has vitamin E, including such diverse disorders as coronary artery disease, muscular dystrophy, and schizophrenia. No persuasive evidence, however, demonstrates that vitamin E has any therapeutic value in these or other diseases. Fortunately, it is relatively nontoxic, and few adverse effects from excessive intake have been reported.

Vitamin K. Vitamin K is essential for synthesis by the liver of several factors necessary for the clotting of blood. A wide variety of vegetables, egg yolk, liver, and fish oils contain this vitamin. Deficiency of vitamin K rarely occurs, and its human requirements have not been specified.

Water-Soluble Vitamins

With the exception of vitamin C, water-soluble vitamins belong mainly to what are termed the *B complex* of vitamins. Yeast and liver are sources of most of these vitamins.

Thiamine. Thiamine (B_1) functions as a coenzyme and is important in carbohydrate intermediary metabolism. Thiamine deficiency, known as beriberi, causes peripheral neuritis marked by paralysis of the limbs and, finally, heart failure. Today thiamine deficiency most often occurs in nutritionally deficient alcoholics.

Riboflavin. In the body riboflavin (B_2) is conjugated by phosphate to yield compounds that serve as coenzymes for a wide variety of respiratory proteins. Riboflavin deficiency is characterized by growth failure in children, nerve degradation, sore throat, seborrheic dermatitis, and anemia.

Niacin. Niacin (B_3) compounds serve as coenzymes in conjunction with protein in tissue respiration and as dehydrogenases. Pellagra, caused by niacin deficiency, is characterized by a cutaneous eruption. The tongue becomes red and swollen, with excessive salivary secretion; diarrhea, nausea, and vomiting occur. Later, central-nervous-system symptoms appear, with headache, dizziness, insomnia, depression, and even overt psychosis.

Pyridoxine. Pyridoxine (B_6) exists in three forms, all of which may be converted in the body to pyridoxal-5-phosphate (PLP), the active coenzyme form. PLP functions in human metabolism in the conversion processes of amino acids.

Deficiency symptoms consist of facial skin lesions, irritability, convulsive seizures, and neuritis resulting in degeneration of peripheral nerves. Excessive dosages of vitamin B_6 over a period of time can also severely damage nerves.

Pantothenic Acid. Although pantothenic acid is widely distributed in nature, its role in human nutrition has not been clearly delineated. Biochemically, it is converted to coenzyme A, which serves a vital role for a variety of reactions involving transfer of 2-carbon fragments (acetyl groups). It is also essential for the production of metabolic products crucial to all living organisms.

Folic Acid. Folic acid, or pteroylglutamic acid, is converted in the body to a coenzyme that is important in the metabolism of many compounds. Nucleic-acid synthesis cannot take place without the presence of folic acid.

Deficiency in humans results in various ANEMIAS and can be produced by antivitamins such as methotrexate, which is used in cancer chemotherapy. Folic acid is present in many common foods, for example, vegetables and liver, but can be destroyed by excessive cooking. Deficiency is relatively rare unless caused by an antivitamin, tropical sprue, or pregnancy.

Cyanocobalamin (B_{12}). Vitamin B_{12} is involved in many of the synthetic steps required in the manufacture of nucleoproteins and proteins. Almost all organisms need this vitamin, but only in very small amounts. Vitamin B_{12} is present mainly in the liver, the kidneys, and the heart. In nature the source is believed to be solely synthesized by microorganisms.

The ability to absorb this vitamin depends on the production by the stomach of an intrinsic factor, a glycoprotein. B_{12} deficiency often involves defective production of an intrinsic factor. The symptoms of deficiency are identical to those of pernicious anemia: ineffective manufacture of red blood cells; faulty myelin synthesis, leading to a par-alyzing neuritis; and a failure to maintain the epithelium of the intestinal tract. Marked anemia and generalized debility, which eventually develop, are fatal unless treated.

Ascorbic Acid (Vitamin C). In the body ascorbic acid is involved in oxidation-reduction reactions. Unlike B-complex vitamins, it does not act as a cofactor. Citrus fruits are a major source of ascorbic acid. A deficiency of this vitamin results in SCURVY. The pathology affects mainly bone and blood vessels; teeth loosen and the gums become spongy and bleed easily. Hemorrhages in other tissues also occur easily with the slightest trauma. A sufficient daily intake of fresh orange juice provides enough vitamin C for most purposes. Controversy surrounds the practice of taking very large daily doses of vitamin C to prevent the common cold; medical research has not supported this notion. Intake of very large amounts for long periods of time can be harmful, even though vitamin C has a relatively low toxicity.

Biotin, Choline, Inositol, and PABA. Biotin is a coenzyme for several reactions involving carbon dioxide fixation. It is synthesized by intestinal bacteria and is widespread in food products. A natural deficiency in humans is unknown.

Choline is a component of lecithin and acetylcholine; the latter is an important neurotransmitter. Unlike most vitamins, choline can be synthesized in the body, if methionine intake is sufficient. It is present in large amounts in egg yolk, milk, and seafood. Human deficiency rarely occurs.

RECOMMENDED DIETARY ALLOWANCES (RDA)[*]

	Age (years)	FAT-SOLUBLE VITAMINS				WATER-SOLUBLE VITAMINS						
		Vitamin A RE†	Vitamin D (IU)	Vitamin E mg	Vitamin K (IU)	Vitamin B₁ (thiamine) mg	Vitamin B₂ (riboflavin) mg	Vitamin B₃ (niacin) mg	Vitamin B₆ mg	Vitamin B₁₂ μg	Folic Acid μg	Vitamin C (ascorbic acid) mg
Infants	birth–½	375	300	3	5	0.3	0.4	5	0.3	0.3	25	30
	½–1	375	400	4	10	0.4	0.5	6	0.6	0.5	35	35
Children	1–3	400	400	6	15	0.7	0.8	9	1.0	0.7	50	40
	4–6	500	400	7	20	0.9	1.1	12	1.1	1.0	75	45
	7–10	700	400	7	30	1.0	1.2	13	1.4	1.4	100	45
Males	11–14	1000	400	10	45	1.3	1.5	17	1.7	2.0	150	50
	15–18	1000	400	10	65	1.5	1.8	20	2.0	2.0	200	60
	19–24	1000	400	10	70	1.5	1.7	19	2.0	2.0	200	60
	25–50	1000	200	10	80	1.5	1.7	19	2.0	2.0	200	60
	51+	1000	200	10	80	1.2	1.4	15	2.0	2.0	200	60
Females	11–14	800	400	8	45	1.1	1.3	15	1.4	2.0	150	50
	15–18	800	400	8	55	1.1	1.3	15	1.5	2.0	180	60
	19–24	800	400	8	60	1.1	1.3	15	1.6	2.0	180	60
	25–50	800	200	8	65	1.1	1.3	15	1.6	2.0	180	60
	51+	800	200	8	65	1.0	1.2	13	1.6	2.0	180	60
Pregnant Women		800	400	10	65	1.5	1.6	17	2.2	2.2	400	70
Lactating Women	1st 6 mo.	1300	400	12	65	1.6	1.8	20	2.1	2.6	280	95
	2d 6 mo.	1200	400	11	65	1.6	1.7	20	2.1	2.6	260	90

[*]These vitamins and minerals are the amounts that should be present in a variety of common foods, which will also contain other nutrients, the requirements of which are less well defined. The amounts given allow for variation between individuals and ordinary environmental stresses.
†Retinal equivalents.

Inositol is a component of certain phospholipids. No coenzyme function has been established, but inositol promotes the growth of yeast.

Para-aminobenzoic acid (PABA) is not a human requirement, but it is needed by most microorganisms. Sulfonamides, a group of chemotherapeutic agents, act as antagonists to PABA. In order to survive, most microorganisms need to incorporate PABA into the molecule of folic acid. Sulfonamides prevent this, thus inhibiting the growth of bacteria.

Minerals

Unlike sodium and potassium, which are staple elements of the diet and are present in ample amounts in all food of vegetable and animal origin, certain minerals are additional dietary requirements. Although most are present in the average diet, these minerals may not always be ingested in quantities sufficient to satisfy metabolic needs, especially during growth, stress, trauma, and blood loss, and in some diseases.

Calcium. The body's calcium needs are generally met by dairy products, especially milk. Most calcium is stored in bone, with a constant exchange occurring among blood, tissue, and bone. The blood levels of calcium and its intestinal absorption, deposition, or mobilization from bone are all controlled by a complex interplay of vitamin D, parathyroid hormone, and calcitonin. Excessive dietary fiber can hinder calcium absorption (see NUTRITION, HUMAN).

RECOMMENDED DIETARY ALLOWANCES (RDA)

MINERALS

Calcium mg	Phosphorus mg	Iodine µg	Iron mg	Magnesium mg	Zinc mg
400	300	40	6	40	5
600	500	50	10	60	5
800	800	70	10	80	10
800	800	90	10	120	10
800	800	120	10	170	10
1200	1200	150	12	270	15
1200	1200	150	12	400	15
1200	1200	150	10	350	15
800	800	150	10	350	15
800	800	150	10	350	15
1200	1200	150	15	280	12
1200	1200	150	15	300	12
1200	1200	150	15	280	12
800	800	150	15	280	12
800	800	150	10	280	12
1200	1200	175	30	320	15
1200	1200	200	15	355	19
1200	1200	200	15	340	16

SOURCE: Table is modified from the National Academy of Sciences, Food and Nutrition Board, *Recommended Dietary Allowances*, 10th ed. (Washington, D.C.: National Academy Press, 1989).

Calcium promotes bone rigidity and is important in maintaining the integrity of intracellular cement and cellular membranes. It also regulates nerve excitability and muscle contraction and may be protective against high blood pressure. During periods of growth, pregnancy, and lactation, calcium intake should be increased. Diseases of calcium metabolism include vitamin D deficiency, hypervitaminosis D, hypo- and hyperparathyroidism, and some forms of renal disease.

Phosphorus. Phosphorus, ingested as phosphates, plays an important role in the hemostasis of calcium and in reactions involving carbohydrates, lipids, and proteins. The body's chemical energy is stored in phosphate compounds.

Iodine. Iodine is needed for the synthesis of thyroxine and the function of the thyroid gland. Seafood has a high iodine content. To prevent goiter, a small amount of iodine is often added to table salt (iodized salt). Elemental iodine is highly poisonous; its only use in medicine is as an antiseptic.

Iron. Iron is a vital component of hemoglobin and also of certain respiratory enzymes. Foods high in iron content include meat (liver and heart), egg yolk, wheat germ, and most green vegetables. Increased iron needs occur during the growth period and pregnancy, and with excessive menses and other instances of blood loss. Iron deficiency results in anemia.

Magnesium. Magnesium is essential for the activities of muscles and nerves, protein synthesis, and many other reactions. Magnesium deficiency may occur in alcoholism, diabetes mellitus, pancreatitis, and renal diseases. Prolonged deficiency can cause changes in heart and skeletal muscle. Excessive retention of magnesium can occur in renal disease and results in muscle weakness and hypertension.

Zinc. Zinc serves as a cofactor of dehydrogenases and carbonic anhydrase; its lack can cause skin rashes, taste disturbances, and mental lethargy. Zinc loss occurs during such stress situations as surgical operations, and its replacement aids in wound healing. Dietary programs often promote zinc loss, and the use of concentrated zinc supplements can lead to calcium deficiency. Overingestion of zinc or inhalation of its vapors can cause depression, vomiting, and headache.

Fluorine and Trace Minerals. Fluorine as fluoride is a requirement to bind calcium in bones. Microamounts of such elements as boron, chromium, chlorine, copper, manganese, molybdenum, selenium, silicon, sulfur, and vanadium are considered necessary to health. Normal diets would appear to provide adequate amounts of the trace minerals.

Vitoria [vee-toh'-ree-ah] Vitoria (1987 est. pop., 200,742) is the capital of Álava, one of the Basque provinces of northeastern Spain, and of the País Vasco autonomous region. The city underwent rapid industrialization from the late 1950s on and includes paper, furniture, leather goods, bicycles, and agricultural equipment among its manufactures. In 1813 the duke of Wellington won a major Peninsular War victory over the French there. A

14th-century cathedral is the principal landmark. Vitoria was founded by Visigoths during the 6th century and became part of Navarre in 1181.

Vitoria, Francisco de

Spanish Dominican theologian Francisco de Vitoria, b. *c.*1483, d. Aug. 12, 1546, was a leading humanist scholar and international jurist. He studied in Paris and, upon returning to Spain, was elected (1526) professor at Salamanca, where he remained until his death. He advised the Spanish king Charles (Holy Roman Emperor Charles V) on policy. Each year Vitoria began classes with a public lecture on important world problems; the notes from many of these lectures were later published, and they form the basis for his reputation in international law. In discussing Spanish colonization and Christianization of the New World, Vitoria was a staunch defender of the rights of the Indians. He also argued that war was justified only as a last resort in defense against aggression or to right a substantial wrong.

Vitruvius

[vi-troo'-vee-uhs]   The Roman architect and writer Marcus Vitruvius Pollio, active between 46 and 30 BC, wrote the sole surviving treatise on ancient architectural theory and practice; it is one of the most important treatises in the history of architecture. Called *De architectura*, it served Renaissance architects such as Leon Battista Alberti as their chief source of inspiration and remained influential up to the 20th century. The work consists of ten volumes: (1) the architect's training and aims, (2) materials, and the origin of architecture, (3) proportions, (4) the Greek orders and temples, (5) other civic structures, (6) domestic architecture, (7) stucco work and painting, (8) water and aqueducts, (9) astronomy, and (10) civil and military machines. Through his prefaces, Vitruvius reveals that his expertise brought him to the attention of Julius Caesar; later he worked for the emperor Augustus.

Vittorini, Elio

[vit-toh-ree'-nee]   A leader of the Italian neorealist movement, Elio Vittorini, b. July 23, 1908, d. Feb. 14, 1966, examined the political and moral aspects of fascism in his novels *In Sicily* (1941; Eng. trans., 1949), for which he was jailed (1943); *The Twilight of the Elephant* (1947; Eng. trans., 1951); and *The Red Carnation* (1948; Eng. trans., 1952). The critical essays in *Diario in pubblico* (Public Diary, 1957) constitute an important documentary record of his times.

Vivaldi, Antonio

[vee-vahl'-dee]   The Italian composer and violinist Antonio Vivaldi, b. Venice, Mar. 4, 1678, d. July (buried July 28), 1741, was a major figure in BAROQUE music and exercised a considerable influence on the development of the CONCERTO. He entered the priesthood, and because of his red hair he was known as "The Red Priest." From 1704 to 1740 he was teacher, conductor, and composer for the Ospidale della Pietà, a Venetian conservatory and orphanage for girls, whose musi-

The Italian baroque composer Antonio Vivaldi wrote numerous operas, oratorios, and secular cantatas but is remembered most for his 447 concertos that helped standardize the three-movement concerto form and that influenced the work of J. S. Bach.

cal performances were famous. He also traveled widely, producing operas in various European cities. His reputation diminished in later years, and he died destitute in Vienna.

Vivaldi's music was forgotten for a century after his death but began to arouse interest with the discovery of its influence on J. S. Bach, who arranged a number of Vivaldi's concertos for keyboard. Large quantities of his works have been found since the 1920s, and they are now widely published, performed, and recorded.

Vivaldi's output was enormous, encompassing most of the vocal and instrumental forms of his time. He claimed to have written 94 operas, of which 19 are preserved; these are rarely revived. He also wrote secular cantatas and church music for chorus, soloists, and orchestra in the form of oratorios, motets, and masses, the most popular today being the splendid *Gloria Mass*. His instrumental music, however, is the most admired. His greatest contribution is in his nearly 450 concertos. These are in various scorings—for orchestra alone (also called *sinfonias*), orchestra with one solo instrument, and orchestra with two or more solo instruments. More than half feature the violin, but other instruments are also represented— cello, viola d'amore, mandolin, and woodwinds and brasses. Most are in three movements with spirited outer movements framing a slow lyrical one. Some are descriptive, such as the popular four depicting the four seasons.

Vivar, Roderigo Díaz

see EL CID

Vivekananda

[vee-vuh-kuh-nuhn'-duh]   The Hindu thinker Vivekananda, b. Jan. 12, 1863, d. Jan. 4, 1902, founded the Ramakrishna order. Originally named Narendranath Datta, he became a follower of RAMAKRISHNA in 1881 and later his chief disciple. After Ramakrishna died (1886), Vivekananda traveled as a monk throughout India and went in 1893 to the World's Parliament of Religions in Chicago, where he represented Hinduism. His message of the truth of all religions made a remarkable impression. He returned to India and founded the Ramakrishna Mission at Belur, near Calcutta, in 1897. He made a second trip to the United States in 1899. Unlike Ramakrishna,

Vivekananda was an erudite thinker; he wrote and lectured extensively. The philosophy he propounded was Advaita VEDANTA, which he reinterpreted in a more rationalistic and activist vein.

viviparity [vi-vi-pair'-i-tee] Viviparity is the giving of birth to live offspring. This contrasts with oviparity, in which young are hatched from eggs deposited and incubated outside the body. Eggs of viviparous animals lack a hard or tough protective covering and contain little yolk; protection and nourishment for the embryo are supplied by the mother's body.

vivisection [vi-vi-sek'-shuhn] The term *vivisection*, most specifically referring to surgery on a living animal during scientific research, has come to mean all experimentation using live animals.

The practice of using live animals for scientific experiments has been opposed by numerous humane societies, frequently called antivivisectionists. In the 1870s a strong antivivisection movement emerged in Great Britain, culminating in the Cruelty to Animals Act of 1876. As a result of controversy concerning vivisection, the Animal Welfare Act (1970) was enforced by the United States Department of Agriculture, and the Laboratory Animal Act (1966) was enforced by the Food and Drug Administration. Voluntary controls for the benefit of laboratory animals are accreditation by the American Association for the Accreditation of Laboratory Animal Care and adherence to guidelines set by the National Institutes of Health.

Little doubt exists in the minds of most scientists and humane-society members that vivisection benefits humanity, nor does any question arise concerning the scientist's responsibility to society in the conduct of scientific experimentation. Scientists, however, are obliged to ask themselves whether or not animals are essential to the collection of data in a given experiment that will probably benefit humanity.

See also: ANIMAL RIGHTS; SOCIETY FOR THE PREVENTION OF CRUELTY TO ANIMALS.

Vizcaíno, Sebastián [veeth'-kah-ee-ee'-noh] Sebastián Vizcaíno, c.1550–c.1628, Spanish navigator and explorer, made the first systematic examination of the California coast (1602–03), sailing from Acapulco north to Cape Mendocino and discovering Monterey Bay. Later (1611–14), Vizcaíno sailed from Mexico to Japan and back.

vizsla [vizh'-luh] The vizsla is a medium-sized, robust, but rather lightly built hunting dog. Sometimes known as the Hungarian pointer, it stands 52–60 cm (21–24 in) at the shoulder, has pendant ears carried flat to the side, and a docked, or shortened, tail. Usual weight is 18–27 kg (40–60 lb). Its coat is smooth, short haired, and solidly colored in a distinctive rusty gold. Graceful and fast, the vizsla is a multipurpose hunting dog used on upland birds, rabbits, and waterfowl. The breed has been known in Hungary since the 14th century. It was recognized by the American Kennel Club in 1960.

Vlad the Impaler, Prince of Walachia [vlahd, wah-lay'-kee-uh] Vlad the Impaler, c.1431–c.1476, prince of Walachia (1456–62, c.1476), fought bitterly against the Turks and, because of his sadistic cruelty toward subjects and Turkish prisoners alike, became the source of the DRACULA legend. Deposed in 1462, he was later reinstated but soon was caught and beheaded by the Turks. His father was known as Vlad Dracul (Vlad the Devil)—hence the son's name Dracula (or son of the Devil).

Vladimir [vluh-dee'-meer] Vladimir is the capital of Vladimir oblast in the Russian republic of the USSR. It is situated on the Klyazma River, about 210 km (130 mi) east of Moscow. The city has a population of 350,000 (1989). One of the oldest of Russia's cities, Vladimir was founded in 1108 and was the center of the early Russian realm until absorbed by the newly dominant Moscow in the 14th century. The Golden Gate, a triumphal arch (1164), and the Assumption Cathedral (1158–61) are preserved. Industrial development has been moderate and includes the manufacturing of plastics, tractors, and electric machinery.

Vladimir I, Grand Duke of Kiev Vladimir I, b. c.956, d. July 15, 1015, grand duke of Kiev (c.978–1015), converted from paganism to Eastern Orthodox Christianity, thereby transforming the religious history of Russia. A descendant of the Varangian rulers of Kiev and a son of SVYATOSLAV I, who sent him (970) to govern Novgorod, Vladimir became grand duke after killing his brother Yaropolk; he thus united Kiev and Novgorod. Vladimir was initially anti-Christian, but about 988 he converted and subsequently married Princess Anna, sister of Byzantine Emperor Basil II. Requiring his subjects to undergo baptism, Vladimir also advanced Christianity by building churches, promoting religious charity, and establishing canon law. He was canonized by the Russian Orthodox church. Feast day: July 15.

Vladivostok [vlah-dee-vuh-stawk'] Vladivostok is the capital of the Maritime krai (territory) in the Russian republic of the USSR, in far eastern Siberia. It is a major domestic seaport on the Pacific coast and has a population of 648,000 (1989). An industrial center, Vladivostok is also the terminus of the TRANS-SIBERIAN RAILROAD and has a naval base. The city is closed to foreign shipping, which is diverted to the nearby foreign-trade port of Nakhodka. Vladivostok has shipyards and manufacturing plants and serves as a base for Soviet fishing and sealing fleets in the Pacific. The city lies in a picturesque amphitheater around a narrow, deep bay known as the Golden Horn.

Vladivostok was founded in 1860, when the region

passed from China to Russia; the presence of Russian power in the region was reflected in the city's name, which means "ruler of the east." After the Bolshevik revolution in 1917, Vladivostok served as a base for Japanese and U.S. interventionist forces from 1918 to 1922.

Vlaminck, Maurice de [vlah-mank']

The French painter Maurice de Vlaminck, b. Apr. 4, 1876, d. Oct. 11, 1958, was one of the original Fauves ("wild beasts"; see FAUVISM). The group of boldly colored and seemingly chaotic compositions that Vlaminck and his colleagues exhibited at the Salon d'Automne in 1905 ushered modern painting into the 20th century. Vlaminck's finest works employ jarring combinations of red, white, and blue with remarkable effectiveness. His *Tugboat at Chatou* (1906; private collection, New York City) exemplifies this effect.

Vlaminck, who had almost no art training, openly despised the tradition of French masters and boasted that he had never been inside the Louvre. Fascinated by the rhythms and tempo of urban life, he was filled with enthusiasm by the 1901 van Gogh retrospective in Paris and adopted the Dutch painter's energetic brushstrokes and brilliant palette. His most characteristic works stem from the following years. By 1908 he had begun to subdue his colors, and his compositions became more orderly.

Vlorë [vlohr'-uh]

Vlorë (Italian: Valona) is a major city and seaport in southwestern Albania, with a population of 71,700 (1989 est.). The city commands the Strait of Otranto at the entrance to the Adriatic Sea and was occupied as an Italian naval base from 1914 to 1920 and again during World War II. The principal economic activities are fishing and canning, the export of refined petroleum, and the manufacture of cement. Vlorë was founded *c.*750–680 BC as the Greek colony of Aulon and changed hands many times until conquered by the Ottoman Turks in 1464. Albanian independence from Turkish rule was proclaimed there in 1912.

Vo Nguyen Giap [voh nuh-win' dee-ahp']

As the Vietnamese military and political leader who organized the victory of the Viet Minh over the French at DIEN BIEN PHU in 1954, Vo Nguyen Giap, b. 1912, also set the strategy for the ensuing successful struggle against the South Vietnamese government and the United States. A member of the Vietnamese Communist movement, Giap fled to China in 1939, where, with Ho Chi Minh, he began organizing the Vietnamese revolutionary forces that marched into Hanoi in August 1945. He became a leading exponent of the theory and practice of guerrilla warfare. In 1946 he was made commander in chief of the People's Army of Vietnam. He became a deputy premier and defense minister of the Democratic Republic of Vietnam and a member of the politburo of the Lao Dong (Communist) party. Giap stepped down as minister of defense in 1980, and in 1982 he was dropped from the ruling politburo.

vocabulary   see ENGLISH LANGUAGE

vocal cords   see LARYNX

vocational education

Vocational education prepares students for industrial and commercial occupations that do not require a university degree. It includes training in such fields as manufacturing, building, business and health services, and agriculture. Vocational education programs are found in public and private secondary schools, community and junior colleges, industry, labor unions, penal institutions, adult education courses, and the military. Although vocational education students concentrate their efforts on learning a job-related skill, many schools require a program of academic study in order to ensure that students are competent in reading, writing, and arithmetic. In the United States in the early 1980s there were more than 10 million students in secondary vocational programs and 1.7 million men and women in postsecondary programs.

History of Vocational Education. Before the 19th century, vocational training was typically provided by a child's father or mother or through an APPRENTICESHIP. The Industrial Revolution of the early 19th century created a need for skilled workers that was greater than apprenticeship training could fulfill. As a result, the first vocational training programs in the United States were offered during the 1820s. The Gardiner Lyceum (Gardiner, Maine; 1821), the Franklin Institute (Philadelphia; 1824), and the Rensselaer Institute (Troy, N.Y.; 1824) were among the earliest vocational technical schools in the United States. In 1862 the Morrill Act provided for the establishment of LAND-GRANT COLLEGES.

Several European countries began teaching basic craft skills in schools during the second half of the 19th century. In 1876, at the Centennial Exhibition in Philadelphia, the Russian government displayed the projects of students from the Moscow Imperial Technical School. This demonstration, along with reports on other European manual-training programs, impressed John Runkle, president of the Massachusetts Institute of Technology, who used these ideas for shop courses at his school, and Calvin M. Woodward, who founded the St. Louis Manual Training School in 1880.

Vocational Education in Public Schools. At the turn of the century, the few vocational education programs offered by public schools were primarily in agriculture. During the early 1900s, efforts were made to obtain public support for formal vocational training in the secondary public schools, and distinctions were made between training for specific tasks and general education in practical skills. INDUSTRIAL ARTS PROGRAMS, formerly called manual-skill training courses, are designed for general education in the basic industrial processes, and strong competence in applied science and mathematics is required for TECHNICAL EDUCATION courses. Vocational education is concerned with the teaching of specific occupational skills. In an industrial arts program a student learns how to make objects out of wood, but a carpentry student in a vocational education program learns building-construction techniques.

The Smith-Hughes Act. The growing acceptance of the idea of providing job-related instructional programs in public schools gave rise to the Smith-Hughes Act of 1917, which specified certain occupational-preparation programs as eligible for federal support. This remained the basis of vocational education policy until the Vocational Education Act of 1963, which permitted federal money to be used for all vocational education programs in public secondary schools. As a result, vocational education programs and physical facilities grew rapidly during the 1960s. Later amendments (1968, 1972, 1976, 1984) to the 1963 act broadened the coverage of federal aid to include postsecondary and adult vocational programs, programs for handicapped and disadvantaged students, sanctions against sexual and racial discrimination, special programs in private institutions, and such support services as counseling and job placement. Since 1964, vocational training for young adults has also been provided by the JOB CORPS.

Contemporary Vocational Education. Many contemporary vocational programs offer opportunities for students to gain work experience in their chosen occupation. These cooperative work-experience programs allow a student to attend school for part of the day or year and also hold a part-time job. Such programs differ from general work-experience programs, which provide job opportunities, sometimes for pay, but not in a specified occupational area. These also differ from Work Experience Career Exploration Programs (WECEP), which are an aspect of CAREER EDUCATION.

vocational guidance   see CAREER EDUCATION

▬

vocoder   A vocoder (from voice coder) is an electronic apparatus that analyzes speech, transforms it into signals that can be transmitted over limited-frequency-bandwidth communications systems, and then re-creates the speech from the signals. The telephone vocoder has a speech analyzer at the transmitting end that can isolate and control such speech components as stress, pitch, inflection, duration, and levels of sound energy. The analyzed speech is fed into multiplexing equipment that combines it with other messages and transmits it. At the receiving end, demultiplexing equipment separates and routes the messages and feeds each to a speech synthesizer.

▬

vodka   The traditional liquor of Russia and Poland, vodka is a colorless, almost tasteless liquid made by distilling a mash of grain, sugar beets, potatoes, or other starchy food materials. The name is the Russian diminutive of *voda* ("water"). Vodka differs from WHISKEY principally in its lack of flavor (except that of alcohol itself) and color, a result of its distillation at so high a proof that flavoring substances are eliminated. Alcohol content is reduced by adding water, and most vodkas are sold at proofs ranging from 80 to 90 (40 to 45 percent alcohol

by volume). Some Russian and Polish vodkas are flavored by steeping aromatic grasses, berries, fruit peels, or seeds in the liquid. During the past 30 years vodka has gained in popularity in the United States and other Western countries, where it is used chiefly in mixed drinks (see ALCOHOL CONSUMPTION). Most U.S. vodkas are made from grain spirits purified by filtration through charcoal.

▬

Voice of America   The Voice of America (VOA), established in 1942 as part of the Office of War Information, is (since 1953) the international radio network of the U.S. INFORMATION AGENCY (formerly the U.S. International Communications Agency). It is charged with promoting a favorable understanding of the United States abroad—principally in Communist countries—a task it fulfills with a wide range of programs, including news and music. The USSR and other Soviet-bloc countries attempted to jam the VOA broadcasts directed to them between 1948 and 1963 and again between 1968 and 1973. The VOA has its headquarters in Washington, D.C.

voice recognition   see COMPUTER

▬

Voinovich, Vladimir [voyn'-oh-vich]   The Russian writer Vladimir Nikolaevich Voinovich, b. Sept. 26, 1932, is known in the USSR for his short stories. His fame in the West, however, rests on his novel *The Life and Extraordinary Adventures of Private Ivan Chonkin* (1975; Eng. trans., 1977), which draws on Soviet army life. The protagonist, Ivan Chonkin, a seemingly simple-minded Russian soldier, outwits the Soviet bureaucracy, both in the army and in civilian life. Later works include the autobiographical *The Ivankiad* (1976; Eng. trans., 1977), *Pretender to the Throne: The Further Adventures of Private Ivan Chonkin* (1979; Eng. trans., 1981), the satirical essays collected in *The Anti-Soviet Soviet Union* (1985; Eng. trans., 1986), and the novel *Moscow 2,042* (1987; Eng. trans., 1987). Voinovich left the USSR in 1980.

volcanic rock   see IGNEOUS ROCK

▬

volcano   A volcano is a vent in the Earth from which molten rock and gas erupt. The molten rock that erupts from the volcano (lava) often forms a hill or mountain around the vent. Derived from deep-lying molten material (see MAGMA) that tends to rise and infiltrate the Earth's crust, the lava may flow out as a viscous liquid, or it may explode from the vent as solid or liquid particles.

Types of Volcanoes. Lavas derived from the most fluid magmas erupt quietly and flow from the vent to form gently sloping shield volcanoes, a name derived from their resemblance to the shields of early Germanic warriors. Lava flows from shield volcanoes are usually only 1 to 10 m (3.3 to 33 ft) thick, but they may extend for great distances away from the vent. The volcanoes of Hawaii and Iceland are typical shield volcanoes.

Lavas formed from magmas with high gas contents and

©Gary Rosenquist/Earth Images

The explosive eruption of Mount St. Helens northeast of Vancouver, Wash., on May 18, 1980, was the most violent volcanic event yet to have occurred within the continental United States. The photographic sequence shows the top of the mountain as it disappeared in a cloud of ash and smoke, reducing St. Helens by some 400 m (1,300 ft) in height and strewing large regions with the fallout.

high viscosities are generally more explosive than those flowing from shield volcanoes. These gas-rich lavas are normally blown high into the air during an eruption. Lumps of

A cross section of a composite volcano reveals a steep-sided cone of ash and lava layers deposited around a cylindrically shaped conduit, or vent (1), leading from the surface to the magma source far below (2). Dikes, or sheets of lava that normally solidify along rising fissures beneath the Earth's surface (3), may sometimes serve as feeders through which lava may pass from a deep reservoir to a side vent, producing a parasitic cone (4). Magma may also solidify below the surface as thick bulges, or laccoliths (5), between sedimentary layers.

the lava fall as volcanic bombs, which accumulate with ash around the vent and form steep-sided but relatively small cinder cones. Volcanic bombs range in size from 3 cm (1.2 in) in diameter to house-sized blocks. Cinder cones most commonly consist of volcanic fragments anywhere from ash to small-pebble size, less than 3 cm in diameter.

Most of the tallest volcanoes are composite volcanoes. These form from a cycle of quiet eruptions of fluid lava followed by explosive eruptions of viscous lava. The fluid lava creates an erosion-resistant shell over the explosive debris, forming strong, steep-sided volcanic cones.

Types of Eruptions. A volcano may exhibit different styles of eruption at different times, and eruptions may change from one type to another as the eruption progresses. The least violent type of eruption is termed Hawaiian and is characterized by extensive fluid lava flows from central vents or fissures and occasionally accompanied by lava fountains. Strombolian eruptions are characterized by moderately fluid lava flows, usually accompanied by a violent lava-fountaining that produces an abundance of volcanic bombs and cinders. Vulcanian eruptions are characterized by viscous lavas that form short, thick flows around vents; very viscous or solid fragments of lava are violently ejected from these vents. Peléan eruptions are similar to Vulcanian eruptions but have even more viscous lava; domes form over the vents, and ash flows commonly accompany the dome formation. The most violent eruptions, such as that of Washington's Mount St. Helens in 1980, are termed Plinian after Pliny the Elder, who died in the Vesuvius eruption of AD 79. They include the violent eruption of large volumes of ash, followed by collapse of the central part of the volcano.

Eruption Prediction. Research continues to seek methods to accurately predict volcanic eruptions. Swarms of small earthquakes as the magma rises through the volcano, increases in sulfur-dioxide emissions, and physical swelling of mountain slopes all indicate that an eruption may be imminent. These factors were used to predict the 1991 eruptions of Mount Pinatubo in the Philippines and Mount Unzen in Japan.

Volcanic Origins. Most of the world's volcanoes are found along the margins of the huge plates into which the Earth's crust is divided (see PLATE TECTONICS). The largest volume of volcanic material emerges between these plates at centers of seafloor spreading such as the Mid-Atlantic Ridge. These MID-OCEANIC RIDGES are formed of lava that erupts quietly onto the ocean floor.

Where one crustal plate is subducted beneath another, chains of volcanoes such as the Andes form. Plate collisions also produce island arcs such as the volcanic Antilles, Aleutians, and Japanese Islands. Volcanoes formed over subduction zones may be among the most violent. Volcanoes also form over "hot spots" within a plate. The Hawaiian Islands and the Yellowstone volcanic field formed in this way.

▬

Volcker, Paul The American economist Paul Volcker, b. Cape May, N.J., Sept. 5, 1927, served as chairman of the Federal Reserve Board from 1979 to 1987, succeeding G. William Miller. Volcker was educated at Princeton, Harvard, and the London School of Economics. After working in several financial positions, he became a vice-president of Chase Manhattan Bank (1965–68). From 1969 to 1974 he served as undersecretary for monetary affairs in the Treasury Department and from 1975 to 1979 as president of the New York Federal Reserve Bank. Volcker's major achievement was curbing double-digit inflation through tight money policies.

▬

vole [vohl]   Voles are small, mouselike rodents found in North and Central America and northern Eurasia. About 47 species are classified in several genera, including the field voles (*Microtus*) and the red-backed voles (*Clethrionomys*), of the family Cricetidae. Voles are about 10 to 25 cm (4 to 10 in) long, including a short tail, and weigh up to 0.14 kg (5 oz). The long coat is grayish brown to black. Voles live in a wide variety of habitats, from moist meadows and semiswampy areas to woodland clearings and deserts. They often make runways under low vegetation or, where ground cover is scant, dig short burrows and build nests of shredded plant material. Some also live in rock crevices. Voles eat almost their own weight in vegetable matter each day.

▬

Volga River The Volga, the longest river in both European Russia and Europe as a whole, rises at an altitude of 228 m (748 ft) in the Valdai Hills, 320 km (200 mi) northwest of Moscow, and enters the Caspian Sea to the south after a course of about 3,690 km (2,290 mi). The Volga and its 200 tributaries drain an area of 1,360,000 km^2 (525,000 mi^2), about twice the size of Texas. The river is almost entirely navigable, although obstructed by ice for 3 or 4 months in the winter. The Volga and its 70

or more navigable tributaries carried about two-thirds of all Soviet river freight. Timber, petroleum, coal, salt, farm equipment, construction materials, fish, and fertilizers constitute the bulk of shipments. The river serves the cities of Tver, Rybinsk, Yaroslavl, Samara, Nizhni Novgorod, Kazan, Saratov, Volgograd, and Astrakhan. The construction of dams and reservoirs in the 20th century has turned the river into a series of artificial lakes between Rybinsk and Volgograd, facilitating navigation and supplying hydroelectric power.

The Upper Volga flows through the northern forests from its source to Nizhni Novgorod and links a number of lakes. The Middle Volga flows eastward from Nizhni Novgorod, where it is joined by the Oka, to just below Kazan, where it receives its largest tributary, the Kama. The Lower Volga flows southwestward to Volgograd and then southeastward to the Caspian Sea near Astrakhan. The Volga delta encompasses more than 19,000 km^2 (7,330 mi^2). Canals connect the Volga to the Baltic, Black, and White seas, the Sea of Azov, the Don River, and Moscow. The river is fed mainly by melting snow and summer rains.

Known to the ancient Greeks and mentioned by the geographer Ptolemy (2d century AD), the Volga became an important trade route linking Scandinavia, Persia, and central Asia in the 8th and 9th centuries. In the following centuries the Volga basin was settled by Slavs. By the end of the 16th century, Russian control extended to the entire Volga basin, with the fall of the Tatar khanates of Kazan and Astrakhan. The river's economic importance has been greatly enhanced since the 19th century with the coming of railroads, canals, dams, reservoirs, and industry.

▬

Volgograd [vohl-guh-graht']   Volgograd, the capital of Volgograd oblast in the Russian Federation, is located in southern European Russia, on the right bank of the Volga River at a rail junction. The population is 999,000 (1989). Principal industries include tractor manufacturing, steel and aluminum production, and petroleum refining. Woodworking plants process timber floated down the Volga. Other industries, including petrochemicals, synthetic fibers, and rubber, are found in the left-bank suburb of Volzhski (1989 pop., 269,000). Much of the electric power consumed by the industries is generated by the largest hydroelectric station in European Russia, completed in 1957.

Volgograd was founded in 1589 as a fortress guarding the Volga trade route after the Russians had seized the valley from the Tatars. It was originally called Tsaritsyn. Industrial and transport growth dates from the late 19th century. The city was called Stalingrad (1925–61), and it was at the Battle of Stalingrad (1942–43) that the Red Army stopped the advancing Germans in World War II.

▬

Volkswagen Designed by Ferdinand Porsche in the 1930s as the German "peoples' car"—a small automobile that would be inexpensive enough for the average family—the Volkswagen was not put into large-scale production until after World War II. The decision was then made to concentrate on a single model, the Volkswagen 1200 "Beetle," and to avoid annual model changes. The Beetle recalled Henry Ford's Model T in being simple in design, plain in style, and economical to operate. It was unique in that its four-cylinder air-cooled engine was mounted over the rear axle. The car became a phenomenal success, and, by 1978 when other Volkswagen models had achieved popularity, and the series was discontinued, 19,200,000 Beetles had been produced, making it the best-selling model in history. Volkswagen became (1978) the first important foreign manufacturer to build autos in the United States, and the firm opened factories in Latin America as well. Nevertheless, the VW Rabbit, the auto that was intended to take over the Beetle's market role, never achieved the popularity of its predecessor. By the early 1980s, Volkswagen sales in its overseas markets had plummeted.

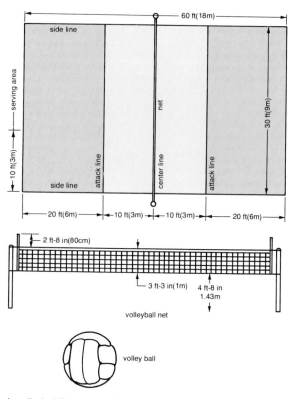

In volleyball 2 teams, each consisting of 6 players, use mainly their hands to hit a ball back and forth over a net. The game is played on an 18 x 9-m court (above, top) bisected by a net 2.43 m (2.24 m for women) high.

volleyball   Volleyball is a recreational and competitive team game that is played both in and out of doors by 2 teams of 6 players each. The object of the game is to try to score points in the course of hitting a ball with the hands across a net and within the boundaries of the court so that the opposing team cannot return the ball. In its official form volleyball is played on a rectangular court 18 m (59 ft 0.75 in) long and 9 m (29 ft 6.375 in) wide; a net placed 2.43 m (7 ft 11.625 in) high for men and 2.24 m (7 ft 4.125 in) high for women is suspended across the middle of the court. The ball weighs about 280 g (8.75–9.8 oz) and is made of supple leather or rubber.

To play, each team places 3 players—left, right, and center forwards—in the front line and 3 in the rear. The right rear player is stationed out of bounds in the service area and delivers the serve with a one-handed strike. The server hits the ball over the net, and the defensive team attempts to return service before the ball hits the surface of the court, using no more than 3 hits. The ball may not be caught in the hands, and no player may hit the ball twice in succession. If a serve goes out of bounds or fails to clear the net, play stops and the opposing team gains the serve. At each change of service the players rotate one position clockwise. This procedure allows each player a chance to serve during the course of the game. Only when serving may a team score points—1 point for each successful offensive rally—and the first team to score 15 points wins the game, except when the score is tied at 14. In this case a team must gain a 2-point advantage to win.

Volleyball was invented in 1895 by YMCA physical fitness director William G. Morgan, in Holyoke, Mass. Morgan hoped that his game of "mintonette" would be a substitute for basketball, a sport too strenuous for many of the older men he instructed. After World War II volleyball skills and distinct offensive and defensive patterns came into wide use.

Power volleyball, a style of play introduced by the Japanese, demanded that players dive and roll on the floor to recover shots and jump high to "spike" returns. Both the men's and women's teams of Japan, the Soviet Union, (East) Germany, and China have dominated international competitions using this style, but teams from other nations are fast catching up. Volleyball became an Olympic sport in 1964.

Volpone [vohl-poh'-nee]   *Volpone; or The Fox* (1606), Ben JONSON's best-known play, is a vigorous satirical comedy set in Venice that exposes human corruption and greed. The childless Volpone pretends to be dying in order to solicit rich gifts from his three would-be heirs: Corbaccio ("The Crow"), Corvino ("The Raven"), and Voltore ("The Vulture"). He is aided by his parasitic servant, Mosca ("The Fly"), whose elaborately arranged schemes make the drama seem like a series of plays within a play. By the end Volpone's schemes are confounded, all deceivers are unmasked, and virtue is rewarded.

Volstead, Andrew J. [vahl'-sted]   Andrew Joseph Volstead, b. Goodhue County, Minn., Oct. 31, 1860, d. Jan. 20, 1947, Republican U.S. representative (1903–23) from Minnesota, won fame when he wrote the Volstead Act

(1919), which outlawed the production, sale, and transportation of beverages containing more than one-half of one percent alcohol. The act, meant to enforce the 18th Amendment, was passed over President Woodrow Wilson's veto. Volstead also participated in efforts to check the power of big business, big cities, and labor unions. In 1922 he coauthored the Cooperative Marketing Act, which exempted farmer cooperatives from antitrust statutes.

◼

volt The volt, the unit of electromotive force (emf), is defined as the difference in electric potential that will cause a current of one ampere to flow through a resistance of one ohm. The volt is named for the Italian physicist Count Alessandro Volta of Como (1745–1827). Certain standards laboratories, such as the U.S. National Institute of Standards and Technology (NIST), keep standard voltaic cells whose emf is very precisely maintained. These cells are used to calibrate other emf sources and instruments, usually by measuring the potential drop across a standard resistor and comparing it to the standard's potential drop. In the laboratory the potential drop, or voltage, is measured with a resistometer-galvanometer combination known as an electrodynamic VOLTMETER, and the current it draws must be so small as not to alter the voltage measurably. To measure extremely high voltages, electrostatic voltmeters are used, in which the meter reading is proportional to the charge collected on a known capacitor and, by inference, to the voltage.

◼

Volta, Alessandro, Count [vohl'-tah] The Italian physicist Alessandro Giuseppe Antonio Anastasio Volta, b. Feb. 18, 1745, d. Mar. 5, 1827, was the inventor of the voltaic pile, the first electric battery. In 1775 he invented the electrophorus, a device that, once electrically charged by having been rubbed, could transfer charge to other objects. Between 1776 and 1778, Volta discovered and isolated methane gas. When Luigi Galvani's experiments with "animal electricity" were published (1791), Volta began experiments that led him to theorize that animal tissue was not necessary for conduction of electricity. Proof of this theory was the battery, which Volta invented in 1800. Volta taught at Como Gymnasium (1775–78) and at Pavia University (1778–1815). Napoleon made him a count in 1801. The unit of electric potential, the volt, is named in his honor.

◼

Volta River The Volta River, formed at the confluence of the Black and White Volta rivers in northern Ghana, West Africa, flows southward about 465 km (290 mi) to the Gulf of Guinea at Ada. The Akosombo Dam, completed at Ajena in 1965 to form Lake Volta, now regulates the river's flow, provides electricity for Ghana, and contributes to industrial growth.

◼

voltage regulator A voltage regulator is an electromechanical component or electronic circuit that delivers a constant output voltage; to a specified extent, the output is independent of variations in either the input voltage or the current demand of the load. Automobiles utilize a regulator (either electromechanical or solid-state) to govern the charging rate of the battery by the vehicle's generator or alternator, protecting the battery from overcharging. Many automobiles use a second voltage regulator to reduce the battery voltage to a level suitable for powering gauges. Electronic circuits utilize voltage regulators to deliver the various operating voltages required by the circuit.

◼

Voltaire [vohl-tair'] Voltaire, b. François Marie Arouet, in Paris, Nov. 21, 1694, d. May 30, 1778, was the most influential figure of the French ENLIGHTENMENT. Considered by his contemporaries as the greatest poet and dramatist of the century, he is now better known for his essays and tales. His precocious wit, his upbringing among a group of *libertins,* or freethinkers, and his predilection for aristocratic circles were to mark his life, as his classical education by the Jesuits was to form his taste.

For writing some satirical verses, he spent a year imprisoned in the Bastille (1717–18), after which he adopted the name Voltaire. Subsequently he quarreled with a nobleman, was returned briefly to the Bastille in April 1726, then went into exile in England for 3 years. Still unwelcome in Paris, he lived at Cirey in Lorraine from 1734 to 1744 with Madame du Châtelet, then at Versailles, Sceaux, and Lunéville. After Madame du Châtelet's death in childbirth in 1749, Voltaire was the honored guest of Frederick the Great at Potsdam, but increasing acrimony led to their abrupt separation in 1753. After 2 years of wandering, Voltaire settled at Les Délices, a château on the edge of Lake Geneva. Then, for safety, he moved (1759) to Ferney, just inside the French border, which remained his home until his triumphal return to Paris in February 1778.

Works. Voltaire catapulted to fame in 1718 with *Oedipe* (Oedipus), but his best tragedies were *Zaïre* (1732; Eng. trans., 1736), *Alzire* (1736; Eng. trans., 1736), *Mahomet* (1741; Eng. trans., 1744), and *Mérope* (1743;

Voltaire, one of the greatest literary and philosophical figures of the 18th century, embodied in his works the ideals of the French Enlightenment. Best known in his own day for his classical tragedies, Voltaire manifested a massive intellect in histories, essays, reformist tracts, poetry, and satirical tales.

Eng. trans., 1744). Voltaire's epic, *The Henriade* (1728; Eng. trans., 1732), was uninspired, but his light satiric verse—especially his long burlesque poem, *The Maid of Orleans* (1755; Eng. trans., 1758)—was unsurpassed. His historical works—*History of Charles XII* (1731; Eng. trans., 1732), *Age of Louis XIV* (1751; Eng. trans., 1752), *Essay on Manners* (1753–56; Eng. trans., 1759)—are landmarks of historiography.

Most of all, however, Voltaire was, and remains, famous as a *philosophe,* a fighter for reform. His ideas were expressed in poems, tracts, pamphlets, and tales. These last, particularly *Zadig* (1747; Eng. trans., 1749), CANDIDE, and *L'Ingénu* (1766; Eng. trans., 1786), are still universally read and admired. His philosophical works include the *Traité de métaphysique* (Treatise on Metaphysics, 1734), *Le Désastre de Lisbonne* (The Disaster of Lisbon, 1756), and the influential *Philosophical Dictionary* (1764; Eng. trans., 1765).

Ideas. Voltaire was the leader and chief organizer and propagandist of the reformist group called PHILOSOPHES. He strove for collaboration with the more radical of the encyclopedists—DIDEROT and d'HOLBACH—but in 1770 the two groups could not agree on the issue of atheism or on tactics. Voltaire preferred enlightened despotism for France; he fought not to dismantle the hierarchical ancien régime but to reform it. *Écrasez l'infâme,* "crush the infamous," was the famous slogan he raised against church, Christianity, and intolerance. Other of his targets were the horrendous systems of criminal justice and taxation and censorship of the press. Paradoxically, some consider Voltaire a fount of modern anti-Semitism. He constantly vilified the Jews, especially the ancient Hebrews, as superstitious fanatics, guilty of producing the Bible, Jesus Christ, and Christianity.

Voltaire long struggled with the idea of God. He felt that God was necessary to explain the universe and life, to justify morality, and to act as a police officer for the despised common people. His increasing preoccupation with evil, with humanity's estrangement from a universe foreign to human needs and aspirations, made his God into a removed, inactive deity, who had set up certain natural laws and the best possible original arrangement on earth, but then left human beings to shift for themselves.

Along with Hume and Gibbon, Voltaire was one of the originators of modern historiography. Although his use of history for nonhistorical purposes—propaganda, debunking, philosophical explanations—has been justly criticized, he demanded authentic documentation and broke with tradition in his conception of history as the history of civilization—social, economic, and cultural, as well as political.

voltmeter   The voltmeter is a device that converts electrical energy to physical energy in order to measure the electrical potential in volts. Most voltmeters are classical GALVANOMETERS that have been modified to measure the potential rather than the current. If a suitable resistor is placed in the circuit in parallel with the meter, the voltage can be determined as a product of the resistance value times the current; the meter can thus be calibrated directly in volts. In order to measure the voltage of alternating current, a rectifier must be provided, which is a device that converts alternating current into direct current.

Voltmeters are essential to electricians, scientists, and industrial workers. One basic meter movement is often used to measure volts, amperes, and resistance in ohms by providing suitable resistors and switches, and a small standard electrical source. Such a combination is called a multimeter or a Volt-Milliammeter (VOM).

volume   Volume is the measure of the capacity or space occupied or enclosed by a three-dimensional figure (a solid). The volume of a cube with edge e is e^3. If the measure of the edge is in meters (m), for example, the volume is in cubic meters (m^3).

The volume V of a rectangular parallelepiped (or simply, a box) with edges a, b, c, is $a \times b \times c$. For a right circular cylinder of radius r and height h, $V = \pi r^2 h$; for a sphere of radius r, $V = (4/3)\pi r^3$; for a pyramid of height h and area of base B, $V = (1/3) Bh$; for a cone of height h and radius of base r, $V = (1/3)\pi r^2 h$. In general, for any prismatoid (a polyhedron with all its vertices in two parallel planes) with height h, areas of bases B_1 and B_2, and plane section halfway between the bases of area M, $V = (h/6) (B_1 + 4M + B_2)$.

Volunteers in Service to America   see ACTION

Volunteers of America   Branching off from the original SALVATION ARMY based in England, the Volunteers of America became the first religious–social-welfare organization devoted to aiding the needy in the United States. It was founded in 1896 in New York City's Bowery section by Ballington Booth (a son of the Salvation Army's founder, William Booth) and his wife, Maud.

The Volunteers of America offers both spiritual and material help through individual counseling, group religious activities, and its social-service organizations. Assistance is provided to the homeless and the hungry, to prisoners in prerelease centers and halfway houses, to alcohol and drug abusers in residential homes and outpatient clinics, and to the mentally and physically handicapped in group homes. For the young and elderly, the organization operates day-care centers and nursing and retirement homes, and provides job-search assistance and home-feeding programs. The Volunteers of America is governed by a national board of directors, elected by its commissioned ministers.

Volvox [vahl'-vahks]   *Volvox* is a genus of freshwater green ALGAE. Hundreds to thousands of the single-celled algae, linked together by strands, form ball-shaped colonies. Each cell contains two flagella, a chloroplast, an eyespot, and a nucleus. Volvox colonies foreshadow multicellular differentiation. Some specialized cells reproduce asexually, releasing daughter cells to form new colonies. Volvox colonies also reproduce sexually, with tiny sperm fertilizing eggs to form a zygote that germinates into a cell that later divides to form a new colony.

von Braun, Wernher [vuhn brown]

The German-born engineer Wernher von Braun, b. Mar. 23, 1912, d. June 23, 1977, was a driving force in the development of manned space flight and directed the development of the rockets that put humans on the Moon. Von Braun received his bachelor's degree at the Berlin Institute of Technology in 1932 and his doctorate in physics at the University of Berlin in 1934. Prior to graduating, however, his work on rocketry had won him a research grant from the German Ordnance Department. His rocket research group was reorganized (1937) at Peenemünde on the Baltic coast. Von Braun and a select team of engineers and technicians there developed the A-4 ballistic missile, later designated V-2 (second vengeance weapon; see V-2) and used against Great Britain in World War II.

After the fall of the Third Reich, von Braun and more than 100 top engineers surrendered to the U.S. Army. After interrogation they were offered (1945) contracts to continue their research in the United States. This research was done first at Fort Bliss, Tex., near the White Sands Missile Range, N.Mex., and then at Redstone Arsenal at Huntsville, Ala. Under von Braun the army produced the REDSTONE battlefield rocket and the Jupiter intermediate range ballistic missile (see JUPITER, rocket).

The National Aeronautics and Space Administration on July 1, 1960, acquired von Braun's army team to form the nucleus of the Marshall Space Flight Center, also located in Huntsville. At Marshall he continued development of larger rockets started by the army: the Saturn I, then the largest U.S. rocket; the Saturn IB, used to launch the Apollo spacecraft on Earth-orbit missions; and the Saturn V rocket, which put humans on the Moon (see SATURN, rocket).

Wernher von Braun looks at a model of a Saturn rocket in this 1960 photograph. As director of the Marshall Space Flight Center in Huntsville, Ala., von Braun supervised the development of the Saturn V rocket used to launch Apollo spacecraft for lunar landing missions.

In 1970, von Braun became NASA deputy associate administrator for planning. Two years later he left NASA to become vice-president for engineering and development at Fairchild Industries in Germantown, Md.

Von Däniken, Erich [fuhn dahn'-i-ken]

The Swiss writer Erich Von Däniken, b. Apr. 14, 1935, has attracted immense interest from the public with his highly controversial theory that extraterrestrial visitors communicated their knowledge to primitive human beings in ancient times, enabling the latter to evolve into civilized humanity. Von Däniken travels and lectures widely, and his books—*Chariots of the Gods?* (1968; Eng. trans., 1970), *Gods from Outer Space* (1971), *The Gold of the Gods* (1973), *Miracles of the Gods* (1975), *In Search of Ancient Gods* (1976), *Signs of the Gods* (1980), *Pathways to the Gods* (1982), and *The Gods and Their Grand Design* (1984)—have sold millions of copies worldwide. Scientists discount the evidence presented in his books and dismiss his claims.

von Neumann, John [vuhn noy'-mahn]

John von Neumann, b. Dec. 28, 1903, d. Feb. 8, 1957, was a Hungarian-American mathematician who made important contributions to the foundations of mathematics, logic, quantum physics, meteorology, computer science, and game theory. At the age of 20, von Neumann proposed a new definition of ordinal numbers that was universally adopted. While still in his twenties, he made many contributions in both pure and applied mathematics that established him as a mathematician of unusual depth. His *Mathematical Foundations of Quantum Mechanics* (1932) built a solid framework for the new scientific discipline. During this time he also proved the minimax theorem of GAME THEORY. He gradually expanded his work in game theory, and with coauthor Oskar Morgenstern he wrote *Theory of Games and Economic Behavior* (1944).

In 1930, von Neumann journeyed to the United States, becoming a visiting lecturer at Princeton University; he was appointed professor there in 1931. He became one of the original six mathematics professors in 1933 at the new Institute for Advanced Study in Princeton, a position he kept for the remainder of his life. He became a U.S. citizen in 1937.

During the 1940s and '50s, von Neumann was one of the pioneers of computer science. He made significant contributions to the development of logical design, advanced the theory of cellular automata (see AUTOMATA, THEORY OF), and advocated the adoption of the bit as a measurement of computer memory.

During and after World War II, von Neumann served as a consultant to the armed forces, where his valuable contributions included a proposal of the implosion method for making a nuclear explosion and his espousal of the development of the hydrogen bomb. In 1955 he was appointed to the Atomic Energy Commission, and in 1956 he received its Enrico Fermi Award.

von Stroheim, Erich   see STROHEIM, ERICH VON

Von Sydow, Max [vuhn see'-dohf]   A tall, ascetic-looking Swedish actor, Max Von Sydow, b. Apr. 10, 1929, gave memorable performances in such Ingmar Bergman films as *The Seventh Seal* (1956), *Through a Glass Darkly* (1961), and *Hour of the Wolf* (1967). Although his best work has been done as a member of Bergman's company, he gained wider American recognition in the role of Christ in *The Greatest Story Ever Told* (1965) and in such films as *Hawaii* (1966), *Three Days of the Condor* (1975), and *Hannah and Her Sisters* (1986). His performance in the award-winning Danish film *Pelle the Conqueror* (1988) was acclaimed.

Vondel, Joost van den [vohn'-dul]   Joost van den Vondel, b. Nov. 17, 1587, d. Feb. 5, 1679, is generally regarded as the most important poet and dramatist of 17th-century Dutch literature. His early work was rooted in the tradition of the Rederijkers, but later writings belong to the mainstream of European literature.

The tragedy *Palamedes* (1625), attacking the stadtholder Maurits for the judicial murder of Johan van OLDENBARNEVELT, brought Vondel into conflict with the authorities. Two subsequent plays—*Gijsbreght van Aemstel* (Gijsbreght from Amsterdam, 1637), written for the inauguration of the new Amsterdam theater, and the pastoral *Leeuwendalers* (The Lion's Share, 1647)—likewise have blameless heroes. But in *Lucifer* (1654; Eng. trans., 1898)—which Milton may have drawn upon for the portrayal of Satan in *Paradise Lost*—the central personality is defeated by his own character flaws. Vondel elaborated biblical themes in his last plays, *Jeptha* (1659), *Adam in Exile* (1664; Eng. trans., 1952), and *Noah* (1667).

Vondel also translated many classical and Renaissance works from Greek, Latin, Italian, and French and composed a biblical epic, *Joannes de Boetgezant* (John the Baptist, 1662), in six cantos.

Vonnegut, Kurt, Jr. [vahn'-uh-guht]   Kurt Vonnegut, Jr., b. Indianapolis, Ind., Nov. 11, 1922, combines science fiction, social satire, and black comedy in his novels, which won a wide following during the 1960s. Vonnegut's themes spring from his contemplation of 20th-century horrors: dehumanization in a technological society in *Player Piano* (1952) and *Cat's Cradle* (1963), and the random destructiveness of modern war in *Slaughterhouse-Five* (1969; film, 1972). His play *Happy Birthday, Wanda June* was first produced in 1970; more recent works include *Breakfast of Champions* (1973), *Jailbird* (1979), *Galápagos* (1985), and *Bluebeard* (1987). Although his work has been criticized as simplistic, it has equally often been praised for its comic creativity.

voodoo   Voodoo is a religious system with followers predominantly in Haiti, the West Indies. Developed by slaves brought to Haiti by the French between the 17th and 19th centuries, it combines features of African and native West Indian religion, along with some of the Roman Catholic liturgy and sacraments. The voodoo deities, called loa, are closely related to African gods and may be spirits of natural phenomena—such as fire, water, or wind—or of the dead, including eminent ancestors. A feature of the cult is that at special ceremonies the loa have the power to make their presence known. They temporarily displace the astral body of a living person and occupy his or her physical body. The individual thus possessed is said to be mounted by the loa and behaves and acts as the loa directs, usually in a manner characteristic of the loa itself. Priests called *houngans* preside over these ceremonies.

Two main groups constitute the loa: the rada, often mild and helping, and the petro, dangerous and often deadly. Graveyards, coffins, shrouds, bones, and skulls figure prominently in the symbolism of the petro cult. The bocor, or priest, is especially dreaded for his supposed ability to create the ZOMBIE, a newly dead body that he reanimates by causing it to be possessed by an elemental spirit.

Voronezh [vuh-rawn'-ish]   Voronezh is the capital of Voronezh oblast in the Russian republic of the USSR. It is situated on the small Voronezh River, about 510 km (320 mi) south of Moscow. The city has a population of 887,000 (1989). During the Soviet period Voronezh has developed as a diversified manufacturing center, producing a wide range of machinery as well as synthetic rubber. Voronezh was founded in 1586 as a fortress on the southern approaches to Moscow and served as an early shipbuilding center under Peter I.

Voroshilov, Kliment Yefremovich [vuh-ruh-shee'-luhf]   Kliment Yefremovich Voroshilov, b. Feb. 4 (N.S.), 1881, d. Dec. 2, 1969, a Soviet military officer and political leader who joined the Social Democratic party in 1903, fought both in the civil war (1918–20) that followed the RUSSIAN REVOLUTIONS OF 1917 and in World War II. Allied with Joseph Stalin, Voroshilov became commissar for military and naval affairs (1925–34), commissar for defense (1934–40), and a member of the Communist party's politburo (1926–60). Early in World War II he suffered repeated defeats on the northern front and spent the remainder of the war in minor posts. After Stalin's death, Voroshilov served as chairman of the presidium (1953–60), a ceremonial position. He lost his major posts in 1960 but was restored to central committee membership shortly before his death.

Vorster, B. Johannes [for'-stur]   Prime minister of the Republic of South Africa from 1966 to 1978 and president from 1978 to 1979, Balthazar Johannes Vorster, b. Jamestown, South Africa, Dec. 13, 1915, d. Sept. 10, 1983, graduated (1938) in law at the University of Stellenbosch. He was interned during World War II because of his pro-Nazi sentiments and his leadership of a fascist organization. After World War II he joined the Nationalist party, entered (1953) the House of Assembly, and was appointed (1961) minister of justice in Hendrik Verwoerd's government. Vorster succeeded (1966) the latter when the Nationalist leader was assassinated. On Sept. 20, 1978, Vorster resigned as prime minister, for reasons of health, and was succeeded by Pieter W. Botha. After serving as president of South Africa, a ceremonial post, for 9 months, Vorster resigned in 1979 after being implicated in a financial scandal.

Vorticella [vor-ti-sel'-uh]   Vorticella is a genus of bell-shaped ciliated protozoans common in water-treatment systems and also found in fresh water and in the soil. Vorticella are usually attached to other surfaces by means of a long, springlike stalk with contractile, musclelike fibers. They may, however, develop cilia and become free-swimming. Winding rows of cilia on the anterior broad end sweep bacterial food into the mouth. Vorticella exhibit a type of sexual reproduction in which different-sized organisms conjugate (exchange nuclear material).

vorticism [vor'-ti-sizm]   Vorticism began as an abstract-geometric style of painting and sculpture among a few artists in London about 1912. It was publicized as a movement when the painter and writer Wyndham LEWIS published *Blast: Review of the Great English Vortex* (1914–15). *Blast*'s manifestos ridiculed many old, traditional values while praising modern technology and the dynamism of industrialized, urban society. Unlike the futurists (see FUTURISM), who embraced the speed, noise, and violence of modern life and attempted to convey them visually, the vorticists admired the hard, polished surfaces, sharp edges, and bare, precise shapes of the machine age; they strove to incorporate these attributes into their visual and literary works. The movement disintegrated after 1915, but some traces of its principles appear in the later work of Lewis and in the poetic theory and practice of Ezra POUND.

Vosges [vohzh]   The Vosges, a mountain range in eastern France, extend about 200 km (120 mi) through Alsace-Lorraine near the French-German border and the Rhine River. The massif has a core of ancient crystalline rock covered by Permian and Triassic sedimentary deposits. The summits of the High Vosges are gently rounded and rise above 1,220 m (4,000 ft); the Low Vosges in the north do not exceed 600 m (2,000 ft). The highest peak is Ballon de Guebwiller (1,424 m/4,672 ft).

Mostly forested, the slopes of the Vosges support beech forests to elevations of about 790 m (2,600 ft) and firs and pines above. Small glacial lakes are found throughout the range. The Moselle, Meurthe, Saar, and Ill rivers rise in the Vosges. Vineyards are cultivated on the steep Alsatian slopes; elsewhere, pulp and paper, textile, and other industries exploit the abundant water power.

Voskhod [vuhs-hohd']   The Soviet spacecraft Voskhod, based on modifications to the Vostok design, made two manned space missions—the first (1964) was the world's first multiperson spaceflight, and the second (1965) saw the first walk in open space by a space-suited cosmonaut. *Voskhod* in Russian means much the same thing as *vostok*, essentially a "moving upward"; the word is poorly translated as "sunrise."

In order to conduct impressive spaceflights prior to the beginning of the American GEMINI PROGRAM, Soviet chief space designer Sergei Korolev was ordered by Premier Nikita Khrushchev to modify the existing Vostok design to carry two additional crew members. These modifications were accomplished, despite the objections of Korolev, by removing the Vostok ejection seat and inserting three crew members into the spacecraft sideways and without spacesuits. The removal of the ejection seat eliminated any possibility of crew survival in the event of a booster malfunction early in the flight.

The Voskhod strongly resembled the Vostok spacecraft but was heavier—*Voskhod 1* weighed 5,320 kg (11,730 lb) and *Voskhod 2* weighed 5,685 kg (12,530 lb), compared to Vostok's 4,700 kg (10,400 lb). Voskhod had the same basic spherical command module as Vostok; an expanded service module, however, contained batteries, oxygen, and a rocket engine. An extra retro-rocket engine was mounted atop the command module in event of failure of the primary engine. The additional weight of the Voskhod required the use of a larger upper-stage rocket, although the lower stages were identical to those used to launch earlier Vostok and Sputnik flights.

VOSKHOD PROGRAM FLIGHTS

Name	Launch Date	Results
Cosmos 47	Oct. 6, 1964	Reentered or decayed Oct. 7, 1964; unmanned test
Voskhod 1	Oct. 12, 1964	Cosmonauts Konstantin Feoktistov, Vladimir Komarov, and Boris Yegorov recovered after 16 orbits (24 hr 17 min)
Cosmos 57	Feb. 22, 1965	Decayed Feb. 22, 1965; probably exploded; unmanned test
Voskhod 2	Mar. 18, 1965	Cosmonauts Pavel Belyayev and Aleksei Leonov recovered after 17 orbits (26 hr 2 min); Leonov accomplished first extravehicular activity (24 min)
Cosmos 110	Feb. 22, 1966	Dogs Vetorok and Ugolyok recovered after 330 orbits (22 days)

Vostok [vuhs-tawk']   Vostok, the first Soviet manned spacecraft, participated in six manned spaceflights between 1961 and 1963; these flights included the orbiting in space of the first man and the first woman and the first simultaneous flight of two manned spacecraft. Modified versions of the spacecraft were used in the Voskhod program and are still used as camera-carrying automatic photoreconnaissance satellites. The Russian word *vostok* is translated as "east" but actually connotes "upward," making it a particularly appropriate name for manned spaceflight.

Numbers for the Vostok vehicle and the final rocket stage indicate attitude-control thrusters (1); interstage attachments (2); final-stage rocket (3); access hatch (4); vernier nozzles (5); oxygen and nitrogen bottles (6); ejection seat (7); equipment-inspection hatch (8); portholes (9); tensioning bands holding reentry capsule (10); spherical reentry capsule with ablative heatshield (11); electronics package (12); whip aerials (13); control command aerials (14); multiplex connector (15); ejection-seat hatch (16, unseen); ejection seat rails (17); ejection-seat rocket motors (18); electric harness (19); paper-clip command aerial (20); rocket-stage extension (21), shrouding retrorocket of equipment module; external conduit (22); and VHF aerial (23).

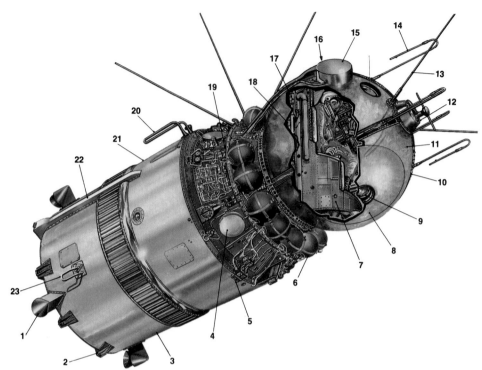

VOSTOK PROGRAM FLIGHTS

Name	Launch Date	Results
Sputnik 4	May 15, 1960	Unmanned prototype decayed Sept. 5, 1962; recovery on May 19, 1960, failed as cabin went into higher orbit; cabin decayed on Oct. 15, 1965
Sputnik 5	Aug. 19, 1960	Reentered Aug. 20, 1960; cabin with dogs Belka and Strelka recovered after 18 orbits
Sputnik 6	Dec. 1, 1960	Decayed Dec. 2, 1960; recovery attempt failed, resulting in loss of cabin with dogs Pshchelka and Mushka
Sputnik 9	Mar. 9, 1961	Cabin with dog Chernushka recovered after one orbit
Sputnik 10	Mar. 25, 1961	Cabin with dog Zvezdochka recovered after one orbit
Vostok 1	Apr. 12, 1961	First manned spaceflight; cosmonaut Yuri Gagarin recovered after one orbit (1 hr 48 min)
Vostok 2	Aug. 6, 1961	Cosmonaut Gherman Titov recovered after 17 orbits (25 hr 18 min)
Vostok 3	Aug. 11, 1962	Cosmonaut Andrian Nikolayev recovered after 64 orbits (94 hr 25 min)
Vostok 4	Aug. 12, 1962	Cosmonaut Pavel Popovich recovered after 48 orbits (70 hr 59 min); *Vostok 3* and *Vostok 4* formed the first group spaceflight and came within 6.5 km (4.0 mi) of each other during first orbit of *Vostok 4*
Vostok 5	June 14, 1963	Cosmonaut Valery Bykovsky recovered after 81 orbits (119 hr 6 min)
Vostok 6	June 16, 1963	Cosmonaut Valentina Tereshkova (first woman in space) recovered after 48 orbits (70 hr 50 min); *Vostok 5* and *Vostok 6* came within 5.0 km (3.1 mi) of each other during first orbit of *Vostok 6*

The Vostok weighed about 4,700 kg (10,400 lb) and was launched by an improved version of the same booster that had placed the first Sputnik satellites in orbit. For the Vostok program, an upper rocket stage was added.

The Vostok consisted of a spherical command module measuring 2.3 m (7.5 ft) in diameter and weighing about 2.4 tons, and a 2.3-ton service module containing batteries, oxygen, and a rocket engine. The pilot remained strapped to an ejection seat that could be thrown free if a booster exploded and that catapulted the pilot from the descending capsule at the end of the mission. All the Vostok cosmonauts bailed out of their ships at an altitude of 6,100 m (20,000 ft) and descended by individual parachute, although the account of the first landing was changed for propaganda reasons to insist that the pilot rode the capsule all the way to the ground.

voter registration   Voter registration is required in every state in the United States and in some foreign countries to maintain a list of all those qualified to vote and to preclude voting frauds. Massachusetts enacted the first registration laws in 1800, and the other New England states followed; New York instituted registration in the middle of the century, and most of the country had some statute enacted by 1900. In recent years a national system of registration by mail has been proposed.

Although guaranteed the right to vote under the 15th Amendment to the U.S. Constitution, southern blacks were long prevented from doing so by various methods ranging from the POLL TAX to violence. The best-known organized attempts to rectify this situation were made in Mississippi in 1962 and 1964. Ensuing federal legislation banned the poll tax and permitted federal examiners to register voters.

voting   see ELECTION

Voting Rights Act The Voting Rights Act was passed by the U.S. Congress in 1965. In 1957 and 1960 Congress had passed laws to protect the rights of black voters, and the 24th Amendment (1964) banned the use of POLL TAXES in federal elections. Nevertheless, in the presidential elections of 1964, blacks continued to have difficulty registering to vote in many areas. Voter registration drives met with bitter, and sometimes violent, opposition. In March 1965, Martin Luther King, Jr., led a march from Selma to Montgomery, Ala., to dramatize the voting issue (see CIVIL RIGHTS). Immediately after the march, President Lyndon B. Johnson sent a voting rights bill to Congress, and it was quickly passed.

The Voting Rights Act authorized the U.S. attorney general to send federal examiners to register black voters under certain circumstances. It also suspended all literacy tests in states in which less than 50% of the voting-age population had been registered or had voted in the 1964 election. The law had an immediate impact. By the end of 1965 a quarter of a million new black voters had been registered, one third by federal examiners. The Voting Rights Act was readopted and strengthened in 1970, 1975, and 1982.

Vouet, Simon [voo'-ay] The painter Simon Vouet, baptized Jan. 9, 1590, d. June 30, 1649, introduced the classical-baroque style to France, where it was to become dominant in the 17th century. Vouet, trained by his father, Laurent, went to England to work as a portraitist at the age of 14. After traveling to Constantinople and Venice he arrived in Rome in 1613. Vouet was influenced briefly by Caravaggio and, in the 1620s, by Annibale Carracci and Guido Reni. In 1627 he was called to Paris by Louis XIII, who named him painter to the king. Vouet's large studio supplied paintings—allegories, religious scenes, and portraits—for the king, the queen, and wealthy private patrons. *Time Vanquished by Hope, Love, and Beauty* (1627; Prado, Madrid) exemplifies his classical yet decorative style and his lush, sensual use of color.

Voyager The identical U.S. interplanetary probes *Voyager 1* and *2* were designed to explore the outer, giant planets of the solar system and their satellites. *Voyager 1*, launched from Kennedy Space Center on Sept. 5, 1977, made its closest approach to the cloud tops of JUPITER (272,000 km/170,000 mi) on Mar. 5, 1979, and to those of SATURN (126,000 km/78,000 mi) on Nov. 12, 1980. *Voyager 2*, launched on Aug. 20, 1977, on a slower and longer trajectory, made its closest approach to Jupiter (640,000 km/400,000 mi) on July 9, 1979, and to Saturn (101,000 km/63,000 mi) on Aug. 25, 1981. *Voyager 1* then headed on a trajectory taking it above the plane of the solar system toward interstellar space. *Voyager 2* sped toward an encounter with the planet URANUS, making its closest approach (80,000 km/50,000 mi) on Jan. 24, 1986. The probe then headed toward NEPTUNE,

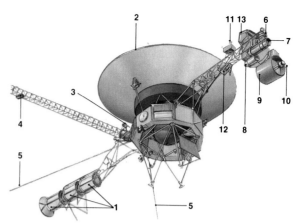

The unmanned Voyager spacecraft, developed specifically to explore the outer planets, is powered by plutonium radioisotope thermoelectric generators (1) and uses a large high-gain antenna (2) to return information to Earth. The space probe carries high- (3) and low-field (4) magnetometers, two long antennas (5) to detect planetary and plasma radio waves, wide- (6) and narrow-angle (7) television cameras, a photopolarimeter (8), infrared (9) and ultraviolet (10) spectrometers, and various instruments for detecting high-energy cosmic rays (11), low-energy charged particles (12), and plasma (13).

making its closest approach to that planet (5,000 km/3,100 mi) on Aug. 25, 1989. It, too, then headed toward interstellar space, but on a trajectory that took it below the plane of the solar system.

The Spacecraft. The central part of each 815-kg (1,797-lb) Voyager is a 10-sided aluminum framework ring. Above the ring is a high-gain antenna dish. The scientific equipment on each probe comprises a radio transmitter and 10 experiment packages. Voyager's optical scanners include a pair of television cameras, an infrared radiometer and interferometer-spectrometer, an ultraviolet spectrometer, and a photopolarimeter. The 4 particle and field detectors measure interplanetary plasmas, low-energy charged particles, cosmic rays, and magnetic fields. Each probe also carries 4 magnetometers. The remaining instrument package is a pair of 10-m-long (33-ft-long) antennas for studying planetary and plasma radio emissions.

Results. Both Voyager probes have carried out their functions with great success during their planetary encounters, the results of which are described in the separate entries on the planets and their major satellites. *Voyager 2*, in particular, which was designed to operate at peak performance only through its Saturn encounter, required extensive reprogramming in order to maintain adequate data transmission as its distance from the Earth continued to increase. One change in performance was a process called data compression, which reduced by more than 50% the number of bits of data required to transmit an image. Because the probe had to pass through the tilted plane of Uranus's satellite system at great speed, it also had to be reprogrammed for a technique called image motion compensation—that is, rotation of the craft while the camera shutter remained open. NASA also employed two or more of its Deep Space Network antennas to reinforce the very faint signals from *Voyager 2*—roughly equivalent to the wattage of a refrigerator lightbulb.

Messages to Extraterrestrial Civilizations. Because of the remote possibility that either probe might be recovered by some extraterrestrial civilization, scientists attached to both probes an identical gold-coated record. Encoded there are 117 pictures of Earth and of human beings, greetings in 54 different languages, and a 90-minute selection of the world's music.

voyeurism [voy-ur'-izm]   Voyeurism is the obtaining of sexual gratification from viewing others in a state of undress or engaged in sexual acts. Most voyeurs are male—hence the term *Peeping Tom* (see GODIVA, LADY)—and are prepared to spend considerable time in the hope of catching someone else unawares. Voyeurism probably originates as a psychological defense technique against possible negative judgment of one's own sexuality. Taking pleasure in viewing naked bodies or intercourse or in viewing one's sexual partner is not considered voyeurism. It becomes voyeurism only when it is a compulsive need and routinely supplants other available sexual activity.

Voysey, Charles Francis Annesley [voy'-zee]   The English architect Charles Francis Annesley Voysey, b. May 28, 1857, d. Feb. 12, 1941, was noted for his domestic architecture and his designs of furniture, chintzes, and wallpapers. Between 1888 and 1900 he built a number of houses in a simple, primitive style reminiscent of Gothic forms, which he felt to be especially English. His works include Perrycroft (1893–94; Cornwall); Greyfriars (1896; the Hog's Back, Surrey); Norney (1897; Shackleford, Surrey); and the Orchard (1900–01; Chorley, Hertfordshire). Voysey's influence in both England and the United States was considerable.

Voznesensky, Andrei [vuhz-nuh-sayn'-skee]   The Russian poet Andrei Andreyevich Voznesensky, b. May 12, 1933, became famous during the 1960s both in the USSR and abroad for such collections of poems as *Parabola* (1960; Eng. trans., 1967) and *Antiworlds* (1964; Eng. trans., 1967). Influenced by the works of Boris Pasternak and Vladimir Mayakovsky, Voznesensky's poetry is characterized by innovations in form and a predilection for philosophical questions. Some of his more recent poems are contained in *Story under Full Sail* (1974; Eng. trans., 1974) and *Nostalgia for the Present* (1978; Eng. trans., 1978).

Vries, Adriaen de [vrees]   The Dutch Mannerist sculptor Adriaen de Vries, 1545–1626, studied with Giovanni da Bologna in Florence and was one of the best assimilators of his master's bronze technique. Later, he helped to spread Italian Mannerism in Germany and Prague. His sensuous, delicate handling of the bronze

medium reveals a further debt to Benvenuto Cellini. De Vries's *Mercury and Psyche* group (*c.*1593; Louvre, Paris) and its companion piece, *Psyche* (*c.*1593; Nationalmuseum, Stockholm), are perfect examples of his elaborate but exquisite sense of composition.

Vries, Hugo De   The Dutch botanist and geneticist Hugo De Vries, b. Feb. 16, 1848, d. May 21, 1935, the foremost botanist of his time, proposed theories on heredity and variation in plants and rediscovered Mendel's laws and the phenomenon of mutation. In 1877 he was appointed the first lecturer in plant physiology at the newly established University of Amsterdam. Vries published (1889) one of the most important books in the history of genetics, *Intracellular Pangenesis,* which proposed the theory that "pangenes" carried hereditary traits in plants. In 1903, De Vries published his study of the phenomenon of variation and plant mutation, *The Mutation Theory,* the book that brought him fame. De Vries retired in 1918, actively contributing to scientific research until his death.

Vrubel, Mikhail Aleksandrovich [vroo'-buhl]   The symbolist, proto-expressionist art of Mikhail Aleksandrovich Vrubel, b. Mar. 17 (N.S.), 1856, d. Apr. 14 (N.S.), 1910, exerted a tremendous influence on avant-garde painters in Russia during the late 19th and early 20th centuries. Vrubel, who entered the Academy of Fine Arts in Saint Petersburg in 1880, also acquired experience through the restoration of medieval art treasures during his visits to Italy. By 1890 he had turned to a highly personal style that dwelt on distant eras and places and reflected his disturbed mental state, which became progressively worse until his death in an insane asylum.

VTOL   Vertical Takeoff and Landing (VTOL) AIRCRAFT are a general class of aircraft capable of takeoff and landing with no ground roll. VTOL aircraft hold promise for military applications, in which the ability to land and take off from unprepared fields or small ships presents a distinct operational advantage. Although a wide variety of methods to achieve vertical takeoff exist and numerous prototype aircraft have demonstrated the ability to take off and land vertically, the HELICOPTER is the only VTOL aircraft commonly used in military and commercial applications.

Jet-propelled aircraft have achieved vertical takeoff and landing by rotating the propulsion engines of the aircraft to the vertical, maintaining the fuselage level; by rotating the nozzles of the propulsion engines to deflect the jet engine exhaust downward; by using separate lifting engines; and by rotating the entire aircraft to the vertical. In propeller-driven VTOL aircraft the complete wing-propeller assembly or the propellers alone are rotated to the vertical for takeoff and landing. In order to achieve high-speed flight as well as good efficiency at high speeds, a relatively small propulsion device is required, with its axis aligned with the flight direction. A VTOL aircraft capable of high horizontal flight speeds, therefore, requires a jet engine; it will tend, however, to be inefficient in hovering and vertical flight.

Vuillard, Édouard [vwee-yahr'] The French postimpressionist artist Édouard Vuillard, b. Nov. 11, 1868, d. June 21, 1940, is best known as one of the principal figures of the NABIS, a group of young admirers of Paul Gauguin who banded together (c.1888–1900) in a close-knit group devoted to a radically antinaturalistic and mystical theory of painting. Around 1890, the rhythmic patterns and contrasting areas of flat color characteristic of Japanese works inspired Vuillard to explore the potential of two-dimensional compositions in which masses of color are manipulated to achieve delicate surface effects.

Less interested than the other Nabis in formulating a new theory of art based on the mystical association of images and feelings, Vuillard concentrated on small-scale decorative works featuring low-keyed, closely toned colors and blurred contours flushed with subtle light. In his best Nabis works, such as *Under the Trees* (1894; Cleveland Museum of Art, Ohio), he exhibits a delicate, brooding sensibility alive to the nuances of light and color. His remarkable series of domestic interiors (1895–1900) are notable for their intimacy and warmth. After 1900 Vuillard's works became more expansive and impressionistic, and the remainder of his career was devoted largely to portraits.

Vulcan [vuhl'-kuhn] In Roman mythology Vulcan was a god of fire, especially the destructive fire of volcanoes, and was invoked to prevent fires. Ugly and lame, he married VENUS, but she was constantly unfaithful. Vulcan was later identified with the Greek god HEPHAESTUS and was portrayed as a smith and artificer.

vulcanization see RUBBER

Vulgate see BIBLE

vulture Vultures are large birds of prey that live mainly as scavengers on carrion. They are divided into two groups: the New World vultures, family Cathartidae, and the Old World vultures, subfamily Aegypiinae, family Accipitridae. Both groups are placed in the order Falconiformes, together with hawks and eagles, and Old World vultures are in fact related to hawks. New World vultures, however, are of more ancient evolutionary origin and have been linked genetically to the storks. The combined classification resulted from superficial similarities produced by convergent evolution; thus the head and neck of all vultures are usually bare except for a thin covering of down, and both groups have weak feet adapted more for walking than clutching. Bills of New World vultures, however, are relatively weak; those of the Old World vultures are generally much stronger.

New World vulture species include the turkey vulture,

The turkey vulture grows to 81 cm (32 in) with a wingspan of up to 1.8 m (6 ft). The most widely distributed New World vulture, it ranges from southern Canada to southern South America.

Cathartes aura, and the black vulture, *Coragyps atratus*, both widespread in the Americas; the king vulture, *Sarcoramphus papa*, of tropical forest regions; and two South American *Cathartes* species. (In the United States, vultures are also called buzzards.) Turkey vultures have a keen sense of smell, whereas black vultures depend more on eyesight for finding carrion. The two CONDOR species include the California condor, *Gymnogyps californianus*, and the Andean condor, *Vultur gryphus*, which are among the world's largest flying birds.

Old World vultures inhabit the warmer parts of Europe, all of Africa, and the drier parts of Asia. They are most common in mountainous or open country and are seldom found in forests or in areas with high rainfall. All are carrion eaters except for the palm-nut vulture, *Gyphohierax angolensis*, which feeds principally on the fruit of the oil palm.

Vyshinsky, Andrei Yanuarievich [vish-een'-skee] Andrei Yanuarievich Vyshinsky, b. Dec. 10 (N.S.), 1883, d. Nov. 22, 1954, was a major participant of the Stalinist terror. Chief Soviet prosecutor from 1935 to 1939, he conducted the notorious GREAT PURGE trials in Moscow and developed the theory that confession alone was the determinant of criminal guilt. He was his country's chief delegate to the United Nations (1946–54) and its foreign minister (1949–53).

Vytautas, Grand Duke of Lithuania [vee-tow'-tahs] Vytautas, b. 1350, d. Oct. 27, 1430, grand duke of Lithuania, expanded Lithuanian territory to its maximum breadth and helped drive the TEUTONIC KNIGHTS from the country. Initially allied with the Knights, he won recognition from Polish king Władysław II (or V; see JAGELLO dynasty) in 1392 as Lithuania's grand duke, nominally subordinate to Władysław. Later, seeing the Knights as a threat to his power, Vytautas allied himself with Władysław to halt the westward expansion of the Knights at the Battle of Tannenberg in 1410.

Ww

GERMAN-GOTHIC	CLASSICAL LATIN	EARLY LATIN	ETRUSCAN	CLASSICAL GREEK	EARLY GREEK	EARLY ARAMAIC	EARLY HEBREW PHOENICIAN

W *W/w* is the twenty-third letter of the English alphabet. The letter is a doubling of the preceding letter, *V/v*, from which it was derived. *V/v* was used in Latin for both vocalic *u* and consonantal *w*, but in late Latin the sound of *w* became *v*, and the sounds *u, v*, and *w* were generally not distinguished in writing.

The modern letter *W/w* was introduced in the 11th century by the Norman scribes, who rejected the Anglo-Saxon runic letter *wyn* and replaced it with a double writing of the letter *U/V* then used in their version of the Latin alphabet. They called the letter *double vé* ("double V"), but because the letters *U* and *V* were the same at that time, the modern English name of the letter is "double U."

W/w is a voiced bilabial fricative and is made by expelling the voiced breath through the rounded lips with some raising of the back of the tongue. It is also called a semiconsonant and serves as a glide into the following vowel. The sound of *w* occurs only before vowels; otherwise, written *W/w* either is silent (*write, known, glow*) or spells *u* (*cow, brown*). The combination *wh* is pronounced either as *hw* (*where*) or with the *w* silent (*whole*). In some instances *W/w* before a vowel is silent, as in *two* or *sword*.

Wabash River [wah'-bash]   From its source in Grand Lake in western Ohio, the 765-km-long (475-mi) Wabash River flows generally westward across north central Indiana to Lafayette and then southward to Terre Haute before following part of the border between Illinois and Indiana and becoming a tributary of the OHIO RIVER southwest of Evansville. The Wabash drains about 85,900 km^2 (33,150 mi^2) of fertile farmland.

WAC [wak]   The Women's Army Corps (WAC), which was made a component of the U.S. Army in 1943, began as the Women's Army Auxiliary Corps (WAAC), created by the Congress in 1942. It had the same structure of ranks as other army units, and its members performed a wide variety of noncombat roles. Its peak strength during World War II was approximately 100,000 women, about 17,000 of whom served overseas. During the Korean War it increased from 7,000 to 12,000 members. In 1978 the WAC was dissolved and women were fully integrated into regular army units.

Waco [way'-koh]   Waco (1990 pop., 103,590), a city in east central Texas on the Brazos River, about 135 km (85 mi) south of Dallas, is the seat of McLennan County. It is a commercial and shipping center for a cotton-growing and cattle-raising area and began large-scale industrialization in the 1940s. Tires, glass, and aircraft parts are manufactured. Baylor University (1845) is located there. Waco was founded in 1849 on the site of a Waco Indian village and grew rapidly after the railroads' arrival (1881).

Wade, Benjamin Franklin   Benjamin Franklin Wade, b. near Springfield, Mass., Oct. 27, 1800, d. Mar. 2, 1878, was an influential Republican senator during the U.S. Civil War and RECONSTRUCTION eras. After practicing law in northern Ohio, he was elected to the U.S. Senate, serving continuously—first as a Whig and later as a Republican—from 1851 to 1869. He vigorously opposed the expansion of slavery into the territories.

In 1864 he sponsored the so-called Wade-Davis Reconstruction Bill, which proposed a more stringent Reconstruction policy than the one favored by President Abraham Lincoln. After Lincoln's pocket veto of the bill, Wade joined Henry Winter DAVIS in denouncing the president in the Wade-Davis Manifesto (Aug. 5, 1864). The Senate named Wade president pro tempore in 1867, putting him next in line for the presidency; he would have assumed the office had the impeachment of President Andrew Johnson been successful.

WAF [waf]   Women in the Air Force (WAF) serve in the U.S. Air Force in noncombat jobs. The WAF was established in 1948, when Congress authorized the permanent use of women volunteers. Women hold jobs similar to those held by men in supply, personnel, communications, and other support occupations and since 1977 have been allowed to fly military aircraft. The WAF directorate was rescinded in 1976. As of 1991 roughly 76,000 women served in the United States Air Force.

Wagner, Honus [wag'-nur]   John Peter "Honus" Wagner, b. Mansfield (now Carnegie), Pa., Feb. 24, 1874, d. Dec. 6, 1955, was an American professional baseball player whom historians of the game regard as the greatest shortstop ever. He played 3 seasons (1897–99) with the Louisville team of the National League (NL), and then joined the Pittsburgh Pirates in 1900. During the next 18 years he set numerous offensive records while displaying excellence and versatility at several infield positions. Wagner—who threw and batted right-handed, stood 1 m 80 cm (5 ft 11 in) tall, and weighed 90.6 kg (200 lb)—was deceptively fast. Nicknamed "the Flying Dutchman," he led the league in stolen bases 5 times and stole 722 in his career. He holds NL records for years leading in hitting (8) and for most triples (252) in a career. Wagner retired with 3,418 hits and a career batting average of .327. When the Baseball Hall of Fame was established in 1936, he was one of the first 5 inductees.

Wagner, Otto [vahg'-nur] Otto Wagner, b. July 13, 1841, d. Apr. 11, 1918, was an Austrian architect and teacher who believed that structural beauty could be attained only through practicality and rationalism. His earliest notable achievements were numerous stations and other structures for the Vienna Stadtbahn (1894–1901), in which exposed ironwork and metal floral decoration show Wagner's restrained handling of Art Nouveau motifs. Continuing in this manner, Wagner created the Majolika Haus (1898), an apartment complex with a flat, rectangular facade covered with colorful faïence plaques. Wagner's most audacious conception was the Postal Savings Bank (1903–06) in Vienna, a graceful building with a facade of thin marble slabs secured by exposed aluminum bolts. The same geometric rationalism is evident in his domed Steinhof Asylum church (1903–07).

His teaching at the Vienna Akademie, his textbook, *Moderne Arkitektur* (1895), and his serenely pragmatic later buildings make him one of the fathers of MODERN ARCHITECTURE.

Wagner, Richard The greatest composer of German opera, Richard Wagner, b. Leipzig, May 22, 1813, was the youngest of nine children of Friedrich and Johanna Wagner. His father, a police registrar, died 6 months after Richard was born, and his mother was remarried the following year to Ludwig Geyer, an actor and portrait painter, who moved the family to Dresden. Geyer died in 1821, and in 1827 the family returned to Leipzig.

Life. Wagner's first theatrical work was a spoken tragedy, *Leubald and Adelaide* (1828), which was heavily influenced by Shakespeare and Goethe. He began to teach himself the rudiments of muscial composition, and although his formal training was brief—about 6 months in 1831–32 with the Leipzig cantor C. T. Weinlig—during the 1830s, Wagner held a series of conducting posts with small theatrical companies. He wrote two operas, *Die Feen* (The Fairies, 1834) and *Das Liebesverbot* (Forbidden Love; after Shakespeare's *Measure for Measure*); the latter was performed without much success in 1836 in Magdeburg. His third opera, *Rienzi*, was conceived on a larger scale, in the futile hope of having it performed in Paris.

The success of *Rienzi* at Dresden in 1842, coupled with that of *Der fliegende Holländer* (The Flying Dutch-

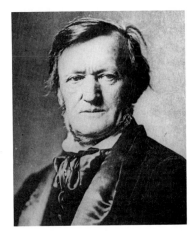

Richard Wagner is considered one of the greatest of the late-19th-century operatic composers. Tannhäuser (1845), Lohengrin (1848), and the tetralogy Der Ring des Nibelungen (1853–74) are among his most admired operas.

man) the following year, led to Wagner's appointment to an official conducting post there, where he completed *Tannhäuser* (1845) and *Lohengrin* (1848). This period of success ended in 1849, however, when his participation in revolutionary political activities forced him to flee to Switzerland.

During his exile from Germany, which lasted until 1860, Wagner devoted himself to speculation about the nature of opera. This took the form of several treatises, the most important of which (*The Artwork of the Future* and *Opera and Drama*) laid the foundation for his most ambitious work, *Der Ring des Nibelungen* (*The Ring of the Nibelung*), a cycle of four operas—*Das Rheingold* (*The Rhinegold*), *Die Walküre* (*The Valkyrie*), *Siegfried*, and *Götterdämmerung* (Twilight of the Gods)—that he began to compose in 1853 and did not finish until 1874. Work on the project was interrupted for 12 years while Wagner composed (1857–59) *Tristan und Isolde* and *Die Meistersinger* (1862–67).

Wagner and Bayreuth. The last great turning point in Wagner's fortunes occurred in 1864 when he was called to Munich by the eccentric young king of Bavaria, Ludwig II, an ardent admirer of his works and theories. Ludwig's patronage continued for the last 20 years of Wagner's life, making possible the performance of all his mature works and eventually the construction in BAYREUTH of a theater of Wagner's own design. It was opened in 1876 with the first complete production of the *Ring*. Bayreuth soon became the center for the promotion of Wagner's works and ideology. His last opera, *Parsifal,* was performed in 1882, with the ceremony normally accorded only to a religious event. Following Wagner's death on Feb. 13, 1883, control of the Bayreuth festival passed to his second wife, Cosima (a daughter of Franz Liszt), and later to their children and grandchildren, a succession that has continued to the present.

Works and Influence. In his early operas, Wagner moved easily from the German romantic style of Weber and Marschner (in *Die Feen*) to the Italian style of Rossini and Bellini (in *Das Liebesverbot*) to the grand-opera style of Spontini and Meyerbeer (in *Rienzi*). In the three works of the 1840s, however—*The Flying Dutchman, Tannhäuser,* and *Lohengrin*—he began to draw on legendary sources and reduce the contrast between aria and recitative, anticipating the new music-drama that he was to propose in the treatises written about 1850. He advocated a new synthesis of music, verse, and staging—what he called a *Gesamtkunstwerk* (unified work of art). The open-ended melody of the vocal line was to be supported by a symphonic accompaniment, continuously fluctuating with the sense of the text and unified by a web of motifs associated more or less directly with characters, things, ideas, or events. Wagner called these motifs *Grundthemen*, but they have become better known as *leitmotifs* ("leading motifs"). This theoretical music-drama was exemplified in its purest form in *Der Ring des Nibelungen*. Later works departed from it; for example, *Die Meistersinger* uses conventional rhymed verse in a historical, not a mythological, setting.

In turning to myth and legend for his dramatic materials, Wagner was seeking themes of lasting symbolic value. Particularly Wagnerian was the theme of fall and redemption, which recurs in all of the mature works except the comic *Die Meistersinger*. Although Wagner varied his treatment in each opera, the means of redemption is typically some combination of increased awareness on the part of the flawed male protagonist and the love and instinctive vision of his female counterpart. An equally important theme is the futility of opposing social (or artistic) change.

The extreme position formulated by Wagner made him the center of controversy. His influence on later generations of composers was above all through *Tristan und Isolde* and *Parsifal*. Extreme chromaticism, irregular resolution of dissonance, and continuously shifting key centers make *Tristan* a pivotal work in a progression leading ultimately to the atonality of Arnold Schoenberg and his followers. Although the impressionists, led by Debussy, favored other expressive goals and found other ways of weakening tonality, they, too, were influenced by Wagner's treatment of orchestral color (especially in *Parsifal*), his rich chords, and his subtle relation of motif to large-scale structure.

Wagner, Robert F., Sr. [wag'-nur] Robert Ferdinand Wagner, Sr., b. Germany, June 8, 1877, d. May 4, 1953, played an instrumental role in establishing the legislative foundations of a welfare state. He came to the United States with his parents in 1886. After attending the City College of New York and earning a law degree, he became affiliated with Tammany Hall and was elected state assemblyman (1904), state senator (1909), and justice of the state supreme court (1918). In 1927, Wagner won election to the U.S. Senate, where he served until his resignation in 1949. Regarded as a spokesperson for workers, immigrants, and the poor, Wagner supported unemployment insurance, social security, low-cost public housing, and a national health insurance plan. He sponsored the NATIONAL LABOR RELATIONS ACT of 1935, commonly known as the Wagner Act, which, by guaranteeing the right to organize and bargain collectively, spurred the growth of the trade union movement.

His son, Robert Ferdinand Wagner, Jr., b. New York City, Apr. 20, 1910, d. Feb. 12, 1991, served as mayor of New York City from 1954 to 1965.

Wagner Act   see NATIONAL LABOR RELATIONS ACT

wagon   A wagon is an animal-drawn, four-wheeled vehicle designed for the transport of bulk material. The somewhat archaic term for "wagon," *wain*, is still used in "wainwright" (a maker of wagons). The wagon is distinguished from the cart in that the latter usually has two wheels and is less sophisticated in design. Both vehicles are essentially boxes on wheels and are used primarily for transporting goods, unlike the COACH AND CARRIAGE, which are used mainly to carry passengers.

Origins. The earliest appearance of the wagon is dated back to the middle of the 4th millennium BC, but the precise location is a matter of some controversy. A Sumerian pictoglyph from the Protoliterate period (*c.*3200–3000 BC) in southern Mesopotamia seems to depict a modified sledge mounted on wheels (see SLED). Although many archaeologists believe Mesopotamia to be the area where wagons and carts first developed, others have argued that the absence of suitable wood in this area suggests that the steppe of Central Asia, where very early wagons have also been found, is a more likely birthplace. Significant evidence of carts and wagons used in the early 3d millennium BC has been found in various archaeological deposits. The evidence consists of clay models, representational paintings, and actual vehicles.

Technological Development. The earliest wagons and carts shared a similar design based on an "A-frame." Solid disk WHEELS that were either directly attached to the bed or fixed to an axle were used. The wheel and axle were designed to rotate as a single piece until sometime near the start of the 2d millennium BC, when the axle was made stationary and the wheels rotated around it. The spoked wheel, introduced *c.*2000 BC, permitted a significantly lighter and more maneuverable conveyance. By this time horses had been domesticated and were often substituted for the much slower oxen or onagers.

The royal tombs of the Shang dynasty in China reveal the use of wagons and CHARIOTS by 1500 BC. The very early appearance of bridles has also been confirmed by these tombs. Many improvements in design were made by the Chinese, including innovations in the wheel (dish or concave shaped), the bit, and the HARNESS.

A major technological development was the invention of the pivoted front axle. This advancement permitted far more flexibility in turning the wagon and enormously facilitated control over steering. This feature can be traced to Roman times, as can the elimination of the single-pole yoke. The single pole required a pair of draft animals, and its replacement by two parallel shafts permitted the use of a single draft animal. The earliest suspended carriages were used by the Romans. The suspension eliminates many of the bumps and jolts produced in passing over rough terrain.

Wagons in medieval Europe were relatively crude vehicles built on wheels and axles that turned in a single piece. Their major task was the hauling of heavy loads—generally farm produce—over relatively rough terrain. By the start of the 18th century, wagons were capable of hauling loads in excess of 6,800 kg (15,000 lb).

Covered Wagons. The covered cart and wagon date back to the Central Asian steppe during the 3d millennium BC, when protective covers typically were made of wickerwork. The use of metal hoops covered by leather or cloth can be traced back to Europe during the Middle Ages.

Well known in American folklore, the CONESTOGA, a type of covered wagon, was invented in the 18th century for the transportation of heavy loads over long distances.

Importance. For much of historical times (the last 5,000 years), only wheeled vehicles and river transport were capable of bringing large quantities of supplies to dense population centers, where craftsmen, merchants, and artisans depended on the farm produce obtained from the countryside. Thus, the existence of large towns and cities might have been impossible in a number of areas without wheeled vehicles.

Wahhabism [wah-hah'-bizm]   The term *Wahhabism* is an outsiders' designation for the religious movement within ISLAM founded by Muhammad ibn Abd al-Wahhab (1703–92). Members describe themselves as *muwahhidun* ("unitarians"), those who uphold firmly the doctrine that God is one, the only one (*wahid*). This self-designation points to the movement's major characteristic, its opposition to any custom and belief threatening and jeopardizing the glorification of the one God. It condemns as illegal and un-Islamic the practice of using the name of any prophet, saint, or angel in a prayer, of calling upon any such beings for intercession and making vows to them, and of visitations to tombs of saints.

Abd al-Wahhab, who had spent some years in Medina and various places in Iraq and Iran, won the support of Ibn Saud, ruler of the Najd (now in Saudi Arabia), in 1744, after being expelled from his native city, Uyayna, because of controversial teachings in his *Kitab al-tawhid* (Book of Unity). Between about 1763 and 1811 the Wahhabi Saudis established control of most of Arabia. Although pushed back by the Egyptian ruler MUHAMMAD ALI, they recovered part of their first empire between 1821 and 1833. In 1932, IBN SAUD succeeded in establishing the Kingdom of SAUDI ARABIA.

Wainwright, Jonathan M.   Jonathan Mayhew Wainwright, b. Walla Walla, Wash., Aug. 23, 1883, d. Sept. 2, 1953, was an American general who aided Gen. Douglas MACARTHUR in the defense of the Philippines early in World War II. After MacArthur was ordered to Australia in March 1942, Wainwright took command of the besieged defense forces until they were overwhelmed by the Japanese onslaught. Wainwright was taken prisoner (May 6, 1942) after the fall of Bataan and Corregidor. He remained a war prisoner until August 1945, one month before the Japanese surrender. Upon his return to the United States, he was made a full general and awarded the Medal of Honor.

Waite, Morrison Remick   Morrison Remick Waite, b. Lyme, Conn., Nov. 27, 1816, d. Mar. 23, 1888, was the seventh chief justice of the United States (1874–77). He wrote (1877) the notable opinion in *Munn* v. *Illinois*, holding that property which is devoted to public use must be subject to government regulation by the states. His highly restrictive view of the 14th Amendment became the accepted Supreme Court view until the 1930s.

Waiting for Godot [goh-doh']   *Waiting for Godot,* a "tragicomedy in two acts," was written in French by the Irish-born playwright Samuel BECKETT as *En attendant Godot* (1952) and was translated (1954) into English by Beckett. Two tramps, Vladimir and Estragon, await the mysterious Godot, who never arrives. The dialogue vaguely alludes to profound philosophic questions while appearing to burlesque them. Beckett stresses the absurdity of the human condition with a drama in which nothing happens, enacted by two pitiful but garrulous men, in a landscape containing only a dead tree.

Wajda, Andrzej [vy'-dah]   The distinguished Polish filmmaker Andrzej Wajda, b. Mar. 6, 1927, rose to fame with a trilogy—*A Generation* (1954), *Kanal* (1956), and *Ashes and Diamonds* (1958)—that vividly reflected the experience of an entire generation in postwar Poland. The most powerful of his wide-ranging later films are historical-political. *Man of Marble* (1977) and *Man of Iron* (1981) use historical contexts to inveigh against such contemporary oppressions as the secret police, the Communist party, and factory bosses. *Danton* (1983) views the French Revolution through the personalities of its leaders. *A Love in Germany* (1984) and *Korczac* (1991) continue his exploration of ordinary life within a political context.

wake   A wake is a widespread FUNERAL CUSTOM in which relatives and friends watch beside the body of the deceased, especially through the night, until burial. A custom prevalent in both the Western and non-Western worlds, the wake may range from a solemn affair to a boisterous feast and party. Most commonly the wake lasts from one to three nights, with watchers relieving each other.

In Christianity the wake originated from the belief that the departing soul is in need of consolation as it passes to another level of existence. Relatives and friends would offer prayers to the departed and also console the grieving kin. Customarily, the bereaved family served food and drink to those who participated. In all societies where it is practiced, the wake serves the social function of permitting family groups, or even whole tribes, as among the gypsies, to renew ties and give one another consolation.

Wake Island   Three small coral islets—Wilkes, Peale, and Wake—form the U.S. territory of Wake Island in the central Pacific, about 3,700 km (2,300 mi) west of Hawaii. Covering 8 km^2 (3 mi^2), the islets form a horseshoe around a shallow lagoon 7 km (4.5 mi) long and 3 km (2 mi) wide. The population is 195 (1990).

The uninhabited atoll was discovered by the Spanish in 1568 and later named for the British sea captain William Wake, who landed there in 1796. The United States seized the island in 1898 and began to build a naval base in 1941. Japan held the atoll from December 1941 until 1945. Since 1972, Wake has been administered by the U.S. Air Force.

Wakefield   Wakefield is a city in West Yorkshire in northern England, about 16 km (10 mi) south of Leeds, with a population of 60,800 (1981 est.). A market center for the surrounding agricultural region, Wakefield has been known for its textiles since the Middle Ages. Chemicals and machine tools are produced, and coal is mined. The 15th-century Church of All Saints and the Queen Elizabeth Grammar School (1591) are located there. The city also has a technical college.

Originally settled by Saxons and Danes, Wakefield grew up around a manor owned by King Edward the Confessor. During the Wars of the Roses (see ROSES, WARS OF THE), Wakefield was the scene of the battle (1460) in which Richard, duke of York, was killed by the Lancastrians.

Wakefield, Edward Gibbon   The British colonial reformer Edward Gibbon Wakefield, b. Mar. 20, 1796, d. May 16, 1862, one of the founders of New Zealand, was a major influence in British colonial policy. He wrote three works on colonization: *A Letter from Sydney* (1829), *England and America* (2 vols., 1833), and *A View of the Art of Colonization* (1849).

Wakefield argued that Britain should sell land in its colonies at a "sufficient price." He also urged a greater degree of self-government in the colonies and an end to the transportation of convicts to the colonies. His ideas were applied to New South Wales (in Australia) by the Colonial Office in 1832 and to South Australia in 1836 by the South Australian Association. Wakefield accompanied Lord DURHAM to Canada in 1838 and was influential in the writing of the so-called *Durham Report*, which advocated the legislative union of Upper and Lower Canada (Ontario and Quebec). In 1839, Wakefield founded the New Zealand Land Company, which initiated the settlement of that colony. He left (1852) England for New Zealand, where he served as advisor to the governor until his retirement in 1854.

Walachia   [wah-lay'-kee-uh]   Walachia (or Wallachia) is a historic principality of southeastern Europe, located in what is now southern Romania. It is bounded on the south by the DANUBE RIVER, on the north and west by the Transylvanian Alps, and on the east by the Dobruja region. The two principal provinces of Walachia today are Oltenia in the east and Muntenia in the west.

Part of the Roman province of Dacia, Walachia was subsequently occupied by the Lombards, Avars, Bulgarians, Cumans, and Mongols in succession. In 1290 a principality was established in the area by the Vlachs. Initially dominated by Hungary, it achieved independence in 1330. The fertile area attracted the Ottoman Turks, who made it (1417) a vassal state. Princes such as VLAD THE IMPALER and MICHAEL THE BRAVE briefly reasserted Walachian independence, but beginning in 1716 the Turks appointed outside rulers (Phanariots) to Walachia. In 1774, Walachia came under Russian protection while remaining part of the Ottoman Empire. That protection was ended in 1856, and, in 1859, Walachia joined with Moldavia to form the principality soon known as Romania.

Walburga, Saint   [wawl-bur'-guh]   Saint Walburga, b. c.710, d. Feb. 25, 779, often called Saint Walburga of Heidenheim, was an English missionary and abbess in Germany. The legend of Walpurgis (Walburga's) Night, when witches are said to congregate with the devil, originated from the coincidence of one of her feast days, May 1, with the date of a festival commemorating Waldborg, a pagan fertility goddess. Her other feast day is Feb. 25.

Walcott, Derek   [wawl'-kuht]   Derek Alton Walcott, b. St. Lucia, West Indies, Jan. 23, 1930, is considered by many the finest modern poet and playwright of the English-speaking Caribbean. He has written about 20 plays, produced in the West Indies, Europe, and the United States. His *Dream on Monkey Mountain* (1970) won an Obie award. Walcott has published more than a dozen volumes of poetry. His verse is technically brilliant and shows a keen sensibility. *Collected Poems 1948–1985* was published in 1985, and the epic poem *Omeros* in 1990.

Wald, Lillian D.   Lillian D. Wald, b. Cincinnati, Ohio, Mar. 10, 1867, d. Sept. 1, 1940, is known for her contributions to school nursing and child welfare. She founded (1893) the famous Henry Street Settlement for social services on New York City's Lower East Side, which she later expanded into a training center for nurses. Wald initiated (1902) municipal school nursing in New York and planned the development of the district nursing service of the American Red Cross. In 1912 her efforts on behalf of child welfare resulted in the establishment of the federal Children's Bureau.

Waldeck-Rousseau, René   [vahl-dek'-roo-soh']   Pierre Marie René Ernest Waldeck-Rousseau, b. Dec. 2, 1846, d. Aug. 10, 1904, headed two moderate French cabinets during the Third Republic. As minister of the interior (1881–85), he initiated the law legalizing trade unions (1884). In 1899 he formed a moderate repub lican government in response to demonstrations over the retrial of Alfred Dreyfus (see DREYFUS AFFAIR); later he helped secure Dreyfus's pardon. In 1901, Waldeck-Rousseau's cabinet enacted the Associations Law, aimed at regulating the activities of religious associations. When, in 1902, extremists fastened upon the law to implement their anticlericalism, Waldeck-Rousseau resigned in protest.

Walden [wawl'-den]

Walden [wawl'-den]   One of the seminal works of the New England transcendentalist movement, *Walden* (1854), by Henry David THOREAU, is a classic of 19th-century American literature. Influenced by Emerson's famous essay "Nature" (1836), Thoreau spent two years (1845–47) in a cabin he had built in the woods at Walden Pond near Concord, Mass., transforming his experience into a criticism of the "lives of quiet desperation" he believed to be the fate of most of humanity. There he learned that "a man is rich in proportion to the number of things which he can afford to let alone." In its criticism of the "busyness" of American life, *Walden* continues to exert a profound influence on the spiritual and political values of many readers.

Waldenses [wawl-den'-seez]   The Waldenses (Italian: Valdesi; French: Vaudois), an Italian Protestant communion of 20,000 members, traces its origins to the "poor men of Lyon," founded in the late 12th century by Peter Waldo, or Valdes (d. *c*.1218). Waldo, a wealthy Lyon merchant, disbursed his goods to the poor and became a traveling preacher about 1173, advocating voluntary poverty for the sake of Christ. He attracted a large following in southern France and sought papal recognition for his fellowship. Instead he was excommunicated for heresy in 1184.

Waldo's followers subsequently developed as a religious society with its own ministers. They promoted religious discipline and moral rigor, were critical of unworthy clergy and the abuses of the church, and rejected the taking of human life under any circumstances. In 1208 a crusade was authorized against the Waldenses and other groups (notably the Albigenses) in southern France. After the burning of 80 of their number at Strasbourg in 1211, the majority of Waldenses withdrew into Alpine valleys in northern Italy. They led a marginal existence until they joined (1532) with the Protestant reformers, at last becoming a separate church. The following three centuries were marked by intermittent persecution of them, growing out of the religious wars that raged between Protestants and Catholics. In 1848 they obtained full civil rights.

Waldheim, Kurt [vahlt'-hym]   The Austrian diplomat and politician Kurt Waldheim, b. Dec. 21, 1918, secretary-general of the United Nations from 1971 to 1981, was president of Austria from 1986 to 1992. After serving in the German army during World War II (when Austria was part of Hitler's Reich), Waldheim entered the Austrian diplomatic service. Austria's permanent UN rep-

resentative (1964–68) and foreign minister (1968–70), he ran unsuccessfully for the Austrian presidency in 1971. As secretary-general of the UN, he sometimes antagonized the United States and Israel by his deference to the USSR and the Third World countries. Waldheim won his second bid to become president of Austria despite revelations that he had concealed the extent of his involvement with Nazi Germany and had been accused of war crimes in occupied Yugoslavia. Although he was exonerated (1988) of direct involvement, he almost certainly knew of the commission of the crimes, and Austria suffered diplomatic isolation during his tenure.

Wales   Wales (Welsh: Cymru) is a principality lying in the west of Great Britain; it is one of four entities of the United Kingdom. Wales has an area of 20,761 km²

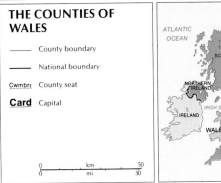

THE COUNTIES OF WALES

—— County boundary

—— National boundary

Cwmbra County seat

Card Capital

Cartographic Production by Lothar Roth & Associates

(Right) *During his conquest of Wales, King Edward I of England built (1285) Harlech Castle atop a cliff guarding the approach to Tremadog Bay, along the northwestern coast of Wales. Battles for this strategic castle occurred during the Wars of the Roses (1468) and the English Civil War (1647).* (Below) *Mount Snowdon, one of the highest peaks in the British Isles, rises to a height of 1,085 m (3,560 ft) in north-western Wales.*

(8,016 mi^2) and a population of 2,857,000 (1988 est.). Its capital is CARDIFF. Wales is bounded on the north by the Irish Sea, on the west by Saint George's Channel, on the south by the Bristol Channel and the River Severn, and on the east by England. Since 1974, Wales has consisted of eight counties: CLWYD; Dyfed; Gwent; Gwynedd; Powys; and Mid, South, and West GLAMORGAN. The Celtic people of Wales have their own language and heritage (see CELTIC LANGUAGES; WELSH LITERATURE). Only 20% of the population speak Welsh; virtually all speak English.

Land, People, and Economy. The Cambrian Mountains dominate Wales, with the highest point, Snowdon (1,085 m/3,560 ft), in the northwest. The Snowdonia massif is linked to the Brecon Beacons in the south by hills and plateaus. The most extensive lowlands are to the northwest on the island of Anglesey, to the southwest toward the sea, and near the English border. The vegetation of Wales is chiefly grassland and planted forests. Wales is drained by the Dee, Conwy (formerly the Conway), Clwyd, Dovey, Upper Severn, Taff, Neath, and Tawe rivers.

Dairying and sheep raising are the only major economic activities in the center and north. In the north, once-important coal mining and associated industries are giving way to a growing tourist trade. Most of the population live in the south, where heavy industry has developed. Coal mining and the manufacture of iron, steel, and tinplate are important. Paper and petrochemicals are also manufactured. The largest industrial centers—SWANSEA, Cardiff, and Newport—are in the south. The economy of south Wales was boosted by an influx of Japanese and U.S. investment in the late 1980s.

History. The Romans occupied Wales and exploited its mineral wealth (AD *c.*100–400). The region was divided into tribal kingdoms (*c.*450–600), which were gradually Christianized. The Welsh resisted the Anglo-Saxons but succumbed gradually to the Normans and their successors, who invaded South Wales (1093–1165). North Wales was conquered (1277–84) and fortified by EDWARD I. His eldest son was made Prince of Wales (1301), a title that has since been held by the monarch's eldest son. By the Acts of Union of 1536 and 1543, Wales was incorporated administratively into England (see GREAT BRITAIN, HISTORY OF). South Wales became heavily industrialized during the 18th and 19th centuries. Welsh nationalism revived in the 19th century, leading to the foundation of three university colleges, now part of the University of Wales.

Wałesa, Lech [vah-wen'-sah]   Lech Wałesa, b. Sept. 29, 1943, who first won fame as the leader of the SOLIDARITY labor movement, was elected president of Poland in 1990. An electrician at the Gdańsk shipyards, Wałesa organized a strike of shipyard workers in 1980 in defiance of Poland's Communist regime. He became chairman of Solidarity when it was established the following October, and was jailed for several months after the union was banned (December 1981) by the government because of its demands for democratic reforms. Awarded the Nobel Peace Prize in 1983, Wałesa again came to the forefront of Polish politics when Solidarity resumed open activity in 1988. He played a leading role in the formation (August 1989) of a Solidarity government, and won the presidency with nearly 75% of the popular vote in December 1990.

Walker, Alice   The poet, novelist, and short-story writer Alice Walker, b. Eatonton, Ga., Feb. 9, 1944, is known for her graphic depiction of the lives of southern blacks. Born into a sharecropper family, she took part in the civil rights movement of the 1960s while in college. Her experiences in the movement formed the basis for two novels, *The Third Life of Grange Copeland* (1970) and *Meridian* (1976), as well as for *In Love and Trouble* (1973), her poignant collection of stories about black women. Walker has published several volumes of poetry, including *Revolutionary Petunias* (1973), *Good Night Willie Lee* (1984), and *Her Blue Body, Everything We Know: Earthling Poems 1965–1990 Complete* (1991). Her novel *The Color Purple* (1982; film, 1985) won the Pulitzer Prize and the American Book Award in 1983; *The Temple of My Familiar* appeared in 1989.

Walker, David   David Walker, b. Wilmington, N.C., Sept. 28, 1785, d. June 28, 1830, was a black abolitionist, Boston correspondent for the antislavery newspaper *Freedom's Journal,* and author of *Appeal to the Coloured Citizens of the World* (1829), a pamphlet calling on slaves to rebel. Walker sought to have the *Appeal* smuggled into the South, leading to threats against his life; many believed that his death was due to poisoning.

Walker, Jimmy   James John Walker, b. New York City, June 19, 1881, d. Nov. 18, 1946, was mayor of New York City (1926–32). A Tammany Hall Democrat, he served in the state legislature for 12 years (1914–26). Walker was immensely popular as mayor, but was forced to resign from office (Sept. 1, 1932) following revelations of considerable corruption in his administration.

Walker, Margaret   Margaret Walker, b. Birmingham, Ala., July 7, 1915, had her first volume of poems, *For My People* (1942), included in the Yale Series of Younger Poets. The title poem is a powerful free-verse call to arms for African Americans, and the whole volume constitutes a technically accomplished and deeply felt tribute to the patience of her people. Walker's novel *Jubilee* (1965), based on the life of her great-grandmother, who was born a slave, won the author a Houghton Mifflin literary fellowship. *October Journey* (1973) contains her later poetry.

Walker, Mary Edwards   The American physician and feminist Mary Edwards Walker, b. Oswego, N.Y., Nov. 26, 1832, d. Feb. 21, 1919, played an active role in the women's suffrage movement. A graduate (1855) of Syracuse Medical College, she served as a nurse in the Union army during the Civil War. In 1864 she became the first woman commissioned as an assistant surgeon. After the war Walker worked briefly as one of the first women journalists in the United States.

Walker, Mickey   Edward Patrick "Mickey" Walker, b. Elizabeth, N.J., July 13, 1901, d. Apr. 28, 1981, was an American professional boxer who held the world welterweight (1922–26) and middleweight (1926–31) titles. His aggressiveness earned him the nickname "the Toy Bulldog." Although experts consider Walker one of the greatest champions in boxing history, many regret his unsuccessful fights against such larger, heavier boxers as Tommy Loughran, Maxie Rosenbloom, and Jack Sharkey. Walker, who became a member of the Boxing Hall of Fame in 1955, won 93 bouts in 111 career decisions.

Walker, Robert J.   Robert John Walker, b. Northumberland, Pa., July 19, 1801, d. Nov. 11, 1869, was a prominent American politician of the pre–Civil War period. He entered politics in Mississippi as a Democrat and won a place in the U.S. Senate (1836–45). An ardent expansionist, he became a leader in the drive to annex Texas. As secretary of the treasury (1845–49), Walker reestablished the INDEPENDENT TREASURY SYSTEM and helped pass the Walker Tariff (1846).

In 1857, Walker became territorial governor of Kansas. A supporter of POPULAR SOVEREIGNTY, he tried to have the proslavery LECOMPTON CONSTITUTION submitted to a vote but resigned (December 1857) when President James Buchanan refused to support him. Walker served as a Union financial agent in Europe during the Civil War and thereafter played a minor role in the purchase of Alaska (1867).

Walker, William   A lawyer-journalist turned soldier of fortune, William Walker, b. Nashville, Tenn., May 1, 1824, d. Sept. 12, 1860, tried in the mid-1800s to establish himself as a political force in Mexico and Central America. He was what was known as a FILIBUSTER. Heading an armed band, he made an abortive attempt to seize Baja California and Sonora in 1853. Two years later he led another expedition to Nicaragua, where he managed to set himself up as president (1856). A segment of American public opinion favored recognizing Walker's regime and possibly admitting Nicaragua as a slave state. After a conflict with some of his American business backers, however, Walker was expelled (1857). In August 1860 he landed in Honduras, where he was captured, court-martialed, and shot by local authorities.

walking fish   Walking fish is the name given to several species of fish that, equipped with accessory breathing apparatus, can live out of water for considerable periods of time and can travel short distances over land. The climbing perch, *Anabas testudineus,* of India and southeastern Asia uses spiny fin rays to move about. Mudskippers, of the genus *Periophthalmus,* found in the Old World tropics, use fleshy pectoral fins to skip about wet mud and sand. Other walking fish include certain catfish of the genus *Clarias.*

Wall Street   Wall Street is a short, narrow street in lower Manhattan that extends from Broadway to the East River; symbolically, the term *Wall Street* stands for the U.S. financial world because so many of the nation's stock-brokerage companies, banks, and commodity exchanges are located either on the street or in the immediate neighborhood. The name is taken from an old wall built in 1653 by Peter Stuyvesant across lower Manhattan Island, at what was then the northernmost boundary of the city, to protect the Dutch colonists. Wall Street landmarks include Trinity Church (1846), the New York Stock Exchange Building, the House of Morgan, and the old U.S. Sub-Treasury Building, on the site of which George Washington was inaugurated (1789) as first president of the United States. It was following the Civil War that the Wall Street district rapidly developed as the nation's financial center.

Wall Street Journal, The   *The Wall Street Journal*, an economics-oriented daily newspaper published by Dow Jones & Company, is known for its clearly written summaries of national and international news as well as its comprehensive analyses of business and financial trends. Its circulation of about 1,928,000, the largest of any daily in the United States, is in four editions, each of which contains some regional news. The *Journal*, employing many staff members who have won Pulitzer Prizes, is regularly included on lists of the ten best newspapers in the nation.

Walla Walla [wahl'-uh wahl'-uh]   Walla Walla (1990 pop., 26,478), the seat of Walla Walla County, lies in southeastern Washington near the Oregon border. The name means "little river" in the Cayuse Indian language. Economic activities include lumber milling, fruit and vegetable canning, and grain milling. Fort Walla Walla, a fur-trading post, was established near the site in 1818, and Marcus Whitman founded (1836) the Waiilatpu mission nearby. The present settlement, originally called Steptoeville, grew up around the military fort Walla Walla, established in 1856.

wallaby [wahl'-uh-bee]   Wallabies are small- to medium-sized members of the KANGAROO family, Macropodidae. They differ from the other small members of the family, the rat kangaroos, in a number of characteristics, including their long, oval-shaped ears, rudimentary or absent canine teeth, and relatively smaller upper front teeth (central incisors). Wallabies are found in grassy, brushy, or rocky terrain in Australia and New Guinea, and in the Bismarck Archipelago, an island group northeast of New Guinea. Hare wallabies, genus *Lagorchestes*, grow to about 50 cm (20 in) long, plus a 45-cm (18-in) tail, and weigh up to about 2.7 kg (6 lb). The nail-tailed wallabies, *Onychogalea*, are larger and have a horny tip at the end of

the tail. The brush wallabies, *Wallabia*, are among the fastest in the kangaroo family. They grow to about 1 m (40 in) long, plus a 75-cm (30-in) tail, and weigh more than 23 kg (50 lb).

The brush-tailed rock wallaby is an adept rock climber that can leap horizontally as much as 4 m (13 ft). A marsupial, the young climbs into the mother's pouch shortly after birth, where it feeds and grows for several months.

Wallace, Alfred Russel   The English naturalist and philosopher Alfred Russel Wallace, b. Jan. 8, 1823, d. Nov. 7, 1913, developed a theory of EVOLUTION by natural selection independently of Charles Darwin. After expeditions to the Amazon and the Malay Archipelago, Wallace wrote "On the Law Which Has Regulated the Introduction of New Species" (1855), in which he theorized that "species ... come into existence coincident both in space and time with preexisting closely allied species." Speculating on the possibility that Malthus's economic theory of "survival of the fittest" might be applicable to biological evolution, he shared his ideas with Charles Darwin—who had meanwhile developed the same ideas independently—in March 1858. The two naturalists presented their ideas jointly in July 1858.

Wallace, DeWitt   William Roy DeWitt Wallace, b. Saint Paul, Minn., Nov. 12, 1889, d. Mar. 30, 1981, an editor, publisher, and philanthropist, launched the *Reader's Digest* with his wife, Lila Acheson (1889–1984), in 1922. After their publishing business flourished, the Wallaces donated millions of dollars to numerous institutions, including New York's Metropolitan Museum.

Wallace, George   George Corley Wallace, b. Clio, Ala., Aug. 25, 1919, is a Democratic party politician and four-time governor of Alabama. Between 1946 and 1958, Wallace was, successively, assistant state's attor-

George Wallace, governor of Alabama for four terms (1963–67, 1971–79, 1983–87) and a third-party candidate for the presidency in 1968, first won regional support in the South as a leader of the anti-civil-rights movement and champion of state rights.

for publicly criticizing the administration's hard-line policy toward the USSR. In 1948, Wallace ran as the presidential candidate of the PROGRESSIVE PARTY, advocating extensive social reform and friendship with the USSR. He left the party in 1950 because it refused to support the Korean War and two years later sharply criticized the USSR. He devoted the rest of his life to agriculture.

Henry A. Wallace, the editor of a farming journal, was selected in 1933 by President Franklin Roosevelt as U.S. secretary of agriculture, a post his father had once held. Wallace won the vice-presidency as Roosevelt's running mate in 1940. He ran as Progressive party candidate for the presidency in 1948.

ney, a member of the state legislature, and a judge of the Third Judicial Circuit of Alabama. In 1962 he was elected governor after campaigning on a platform of defiant segregation. The following year he attempted to prevent African-American students from enrolling at the University of Alabama but yielded eventually to the authority of the National Guard. Wallace was ineligible to succeed himself as governor, and his wife, Lurleen, was elected to the post in 1966. In 1968 he won 46 electoral votes as the populist presidential candidate of the newly formed AMERICAN INDEPENDENT PARTY. In 1970 and 1974 he was reelected as governor. On May 15, 1972, while campaigning for the Democratic party's presidential nomination in Laurel, Md., he was shot in an assassination attempt that left him partially paralyzed. In 1982 he brought together a populist coalition of blacks and whites to win a fourth term as governor. He retired in 1987.

Wallace, Henry A.   Henry Agard Wallace, b. Adair County, Iowa, Oct. 7, 1888, d. Nov. 18, 1965, journalist, plant geneticist, agricultural leader, cabinet member, vice-president of the United States, and unsuccessful presidential candidate, was among the most controversial politicians of his time. As a farm journalist Wallace ran the family paper *Wallace's Farmer*, formerly run by his father, Henry Cantwell Wallace, who was secretary of agriculture from 1921 to 1924. As a plant geneticist Wallace developed the first commercial high-yield hybrid corn and founded (1926) a company to market the seed.

Appointed secretary of agriculture by Franklin D. Roosevelt in 1933, Wallace presided over New Deal programs that supported commodity prices and provided other assistance for farmers. As vice-president (1941–45) he became a leading advocate of liberal causes but alienated many powerful Democrats. In 1944, Harry S. Truman became Roosevelt's running mate, and in January 1945, Roosevelt appointed Wallace secretary of commerce. In September 1946, Truman, then president, fired Wallace

Wallace, Lew   Although Lewis Wallace, b. Brookville, Ind., Apr. 10, 1827, d. Feb. 15, 1905, had a distinguished career as a soldier (rising to the rank of major general during the Civil War) and diplomat (serving as minister to Turkey, 1881–85), he is best known as the author of *Ben Hur: A Tale of the Christ* (1880), a popular novel dealing with figures in the Roman world affected by the coming of Christ. The novel was even more popular in its two filmed versions (1925 and 1959). Wallace wrote other historical novels and also had a reputation as a biblical scholar.

Wallace, Sir William   The Scottish national hero Sir William Wallace, b. *c.*1272, d. Aug. 23, 1305, led the resistance against the attempt of EDWARD I of England to impose his rule on Scotland. In 1297, Wallace led a group of men who killed the English sheriff of Lanark, and he also defeated John de Warenne, earl of Surrey, the English governor of Scotland. Wallace then drove the English out of Scotland and invaded southern England. He became guardian of the realm in the name of the imprisoned John de BALIOL. Many Scottish nobles did not support Wallace, however, and in 1298, Edward defeated him at Falkirk. Wallace went to France in an unsuccessful bid for assistance. After his return he was arrested and executed for treason.

Wallenberg, Raoul   As a Swedish special diplomatic envoy to Hungary in 1944, Raoul Wallenberg, b. Aug.

4, 1912, rescued tens of thousands of Jews from the Nazis, chiefly by issuing them with Swedish passports. Wallenberg disappeared in 1945 on a trip to the Soviet zone, and later rumors claimed that he was still alive in a Soviet prison. In 1990 a former KGB official stated that Wallenberg had been executed before 1947.

Wallenda (family) [wuh-len'-duh]   The Wallenda family of show people and circus performers has roots going back to 18th-century Bohemia. The family is renowned above all for wire-walking at great heights. In 1928 a small troupe of Wallendas, led by the family's most eminent member, Karl Wallenda, b. Jan. 21, 1905, d. Mar. 22, 1978, came to the United States to appear with the Ringling Bros. and Barnum & Bailey Circus. A specialty of the troupe was a seven-man walking pyramid, until the pyramid collapsed during a show in Detroit in 1962, when two of the performers were killed and a third paralyzed. Later generations of the family remain active as circus performers. Karl himself—whose more spectacular feats included crossing the Houston Astrodome (1973) and the Tallulah Falls in Georgia—fell to his death from a high wire between two hotels in San Juan, Puerto Rico, at the age of 73.

Wallenstein, Albrecht Wenzel von [vahl'-en-shtyn]   Albrecht Eusebius Wenzel von Wallenstein, b. Sept. 24, 1583, d. Feb. 25, 1634, an Austrian general, fought for the Habsburgs as a mercenary during the THIRTY YEARS' WAR (1618–48). Descended from the minor Czech nobility, Wallenstein, a convert to Catholicism, remained loyal to Holy Roman Emperor FERDINAND II during the Bohemian rebellion (1618–23). In 1625, Wallenstein raised an army at his own expense for the emperor and was appointed imperial generalissimo.

A skillful military leader, Wallenstein defeated Ernst, Graf von MANSFELD (1626) and CHRISTIAN IV of Denmark (1627). He was rewarded (1629) with the imperial duchy of Mecklenburg, but his enemies, fearing the emperor's new power based on Wallenstein's 70,000-man army, persuaded Ferdinand to dismiss him in 1630.

The successful campaigns of GUSTAV II ADOLF, king of Sweden, forced Ferdinand in 1631 to recall Wallenstein. Wallenstein acted promptly and fought Gustav to a standstill, but the Swedes ultimately defeated Wallenstein's forces at Lützen in November 1632. Wallenstein began negotiating for peace, apparently hoping for terms that would make him a major European leader. Ferdinand feared that Wallenstein was plotting against him and ordered the general's capture—dead or alive. Wallenstein was assassinated at the fortress of Eger in Bohemia.

Waller, Edmund   Edmund Waller, b. Mar. 3, 1606, d. Oct. 21, 1687, was admired during the 17th and 18th centuries as a pioneer of harmonious versification. Today his reputation rests on the simplicity, elegance, and restraint of such lyrics as "Go, Lovely Rose" (1645). One of the CAVALIER POETS, he was banished for the so-called

Waller's plot (1643) to turn London over to Charles I. Pardoned by Cromwell in 1651, Waller composed the "Panegyric to My Lord Protector" (1655). Five years later he wrote the equally laudatory verses "To the King upon His Majesty's Happy Return," celebrating the accession of Charles II.

Waller, Fats   Thomas "Fats" Waller, b. New York City, May 21, 1904, d. Dec. 15, 1943, was a celebrated jazz pianist, organist, and composer. Early in the 1920s, Waller became the protégé of the famous pianist James P. Johnson and later accompanied such important vocalists as Florence Hills and Bessie Smith. His hundreds of recordings, including some early piano rolls, encompass ragtime, boogie-woogie, dixieland, and swing, although in his hands these styles are deftly recomposed into a unique Waller sound that influenced most of the jazz pianists of the following generation. His appearances on radio and in several motion pictures (notably *Stormy Weather*, 1943) brought Waller's talents to a wide audience. A major jazz creator, he wrote complete scores for such all-black shows as *Keep Shufflin'* (1928) and *Hot Chocolates* (1929) as well as many single pieces, especially the now-classic "Honeysuckle Rose," "Ain't Misbehavin'," and "Black and Blue."

---

walleye   A prized freshwater game fish of North America, the walleye, *Stizostedion vitreum*, is the largest member of the perch family but resembles the true pike and especially the sauger. Originally found in the cool, larger lakes of the eastern United States and Canada, walleyes have now been introduced into the western United States. Exceptionally flavorful, they weigh up to 11.5 kg (25 lb) and may be 90 cm (3 ft) long. Walleyes feed on smaller fish. Their bodies are spotted but have no distinctive stripes. These prolific fish spawn in the shallows of lakes and streams in early spring, each of the females producing from 25,000 to 700,000 eggs.

The walleye, a type of perch, is a spiny-rayed freshwater fish, found in the lakes and streams of North America.

Wallis and Futuna Islands [wahl'-is, foo-too'-nah]   A self-governing French overseas territory, the Wallis and Futuna Islands are two groups of islands in the southwestern Pacific Ocean. The Wallis group, consisting of the main island of Uvea (Wallis) and more than 20 surrounding islets, lies about 300 km (190 mi) west of

Western Samoa. The Futuna group (Îles de Horn) consists of the two islands of Alofi and Futuna, which lie approximately 225 km (140 mi) southwest of the Wallis group. The islands have a total land area of 321 km² (124 mi²) and a population of 14,910 (1990 est.). Mata Utu, the capital and principal city, is on Uvea. The Polynesian inhabitants depend on fishing; the growing of taro, fruit, and vegetables; and the production of copra.

Wallis was named for Samuel Wallis, an English navigator who visited the islands in 1767. French missionaries arrived in 1837, and a French protectorate was formed in 1887. The islands became an overseas territory following a referendum in 1959.

Walloons [wahl-oonz']

Walloons are an ethnic group in southern Belgium who speak a French dialect called Walloon. Their major city is LIÈGE, the center of a Walloon literary revival during the 19th century. Historically, the Walloons have clashed with the Flemish people of northern Belgium, who have had a different economy and whose language is a Germanic dialect. Hostility flared after 1831 when the Belgian kingdom was established; it was renewed at the end of World War II and again in the early 1960s. Belgium's recognition in 1970 of the cultural autonomy of the Walloons somewhat ameliorated the discord.

walnut

Walnut is the common name for about 20 species of deciduous trees of the genus *Juglans* in the walnut family, Juglandaceae. About six species are native to the United States; others occur in South America, the West Indies, southern Europe, and Asia. The leaves of walnuts are spaced alternately along the branches, and each is divided into an odd number—usually from 7 to 23—of small leaflets. Walnuts are monoecious: the male flowers are in long, unbranched, drooping catkins; the female flowers are borne singly or in short spikes. The fruit is a drupelike nut, with an outer leathery husk and an inner hard and furrowed stone, or nut. Walnuts provide fine wood for furniture and veneers, produce edible nuts, and serve as ornamental shade plantings.

The so-called English walnut, *J. regia*, actually is native to southeastern Europe and western Asia and does not thrive in England. It grows to more than 21 m (70 ft). It requires a long, warm growing season to properly mature the nut. The black walnut, *J. nigra*, is greatly valued for its fruit and fine-grained wood, the common dark-hued "walnut" of the furniture industry. Black walnut grows from Vermont and Maine west to southern Michigan and south to Texas and Georgia. The tree, the tallest of the walnuts, may reach 45 m (150 ft) in height. The butternut, *J. cinerea*, also a valuable lumber tree, has wood much lighter in color than that of the black walnut. This tree is found from New Brunswick, Canada, west to Minnesota and south to Arkansas.

Walpole, Horace, 4th Earl of Orford

The writer Horace Walpole, b. London, Sept. 24, 1717, d. Mar. 2, 1797, is best known for *The Castle of Otranto* (1764), the first Gothic novel in English, and for his exquisitely urbane letters, more than 3,000 of which survive. The youngest son of Sir Robert Walpole, Horace matriculated at Eton and Cambridge and made a two-year tour of the Continent with the poet Thomas Gray before being elected to Parliament in 1741. In 1747, Walpole purchased a small country home near Twickenham. Naming it Strawberry Hill, he transformed the house into a fantastic castle and furnished it with an eclectic art collection. It served as a major impetus for the GOTHIC REVIVAL in architecture.

Walpole, Sir Robert

Sir Robert Walpole, b. Aug. 26, 1676, d. Mar. 18, 1745, was the longest-serving (1721–42) of all British prime ministers. He began his career as a promising and uncompromising young Whig, holding office in several ministries. In 1717 he resigned in protest over the dismissal of his brother-in-law, Lord TOWNSHEND, as secretary of state. The ministerial scandals

Two widely cultivated walnut trees are the black walnut (left) and the English walnut (right). The fruit has a green, leathery rind and a woody, deeply grooved hull, which is easily cracked open. Both trees are valued for nuts as well as for timber.

Sir Robert Walpole brought a period of stable government to Britain during his long tenure as prime minister by skillful manipulation of the House of Commons. A dedicated servant of the Hanoverian dynasty, he tried to ensure its ascendancy by pursuing a policy of peace and national prosperity.

associated with the SOUTH SEA BUBBLE of 1720 led (1721) to his return to power with Townshend, and the two men worked together closely until 1730. Thereafter Walpole was virtually sole minister, and his skill as a courtier earned him the support of GEORGE I before 1727 and GEORGE II thereafter. Despite his Whig background, Walpole supported the Church of England, peace abroad, and retrenchment at home; he thus mollified the Tories and secured his success in Parliament.

Walpole's interest in financial reform led him to adopt (1733) an excise scheme that he was forced to withdraw. Subsequently, his position was weakened by his reluctance to begin—and inability to direct—a commercial war with Spain (the War of Jenkins' Ear), which led to his resignation in 1742. Created 1st earl of Orford, he continued to advise the king until his death. Despite his reputation for corruption and concealment, Walpole was unquestionably a shrewd politician who effectively created the premiership in its modern form of responsibility to Parliament.

Walpurgis Night   see WALBURGA, SAINT

—

walrus   A large marine mammal inhabiting open water at the edge of the Arctic ice pack, the walrus, *Odobenus rosmarus*, is closely related to the seal but forms its own family, the Odobenidae. Walruses lack external ears and have long tusks, a thick, wrinkled, nearly hairless skin ex-

cept for long bristles on the cheek pads, and reversible hind flippers that facilitate locomotion over ice. They grow to enormous size: males may be 3.7 m (12 ft) long and weigh up to about 1,400 kg (3,000 lb); females are only slightly smaller.

Walruses use their tusks to climb up onto the ice, to stir up clams and other bottom shellfishes, and in fighting. Most walruses live in herds, and in the late winter and spring they drift along on large floating ice fields. Their bellows can be heard up to 0.8 km (0.5 mi) away.

Female walruses have one calf every other year, in April or early May; the calf may stay with the mother for 2 years. Some walruses live for up to 40 years. Long a source of food, ivory, blubber-oil fuel, and hides to Eskimos, walrus populations have been greatly reduced by hunting.

—

Walsh, Raoul   The American film director Raoul Walsh, b. New York City, Mar. 11, 1887, d. Dec. 31, 1980, maintained his reputation as one of the foremost makers of action dramas from his first film, made in 1914, to his last, which appeared in 1964. His first film as a director, *The Life of General Villa* (1914), was composed of newsreel footage and staged scenes and starred Pancho Villa himself. From the 1920s, Walsh made many adventure films, commanding a wide range of styles, shown in *The Thief of Bagdad* (1924), *Me and My Gal* (1932), *Klondike Annie* (1936), starring Mae West, and *The Horn Blows at Midnight* (1945), with Jack Benny. During his later career he excelled in war films, Westerns, and gangster films, including the celebrated *White Heat* (1949), starring James Cagney.

—

Walsh, Thomas J.   The American legislator Thomas James Walsh, b. Two Rivers, Wis., June 12, 1859, d. Mar. 2, 1933, was one of the great liberal voices in the U.S. Senate early in the 20th century. Walsh practiced law (1884–90) in the Dakota Territory but moved to Montana in 1890. A Democrat, he entered the Senate in 1913 and remained there the rest of his life. He advocated women's suffrage, abolition of child labor, and arms limitation; he also favored U.S. membership in the League of Nations. Walsh headed the investigative committee that exposed (1921–22) the great Teapot Dome scandal.

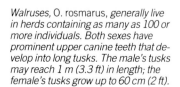

Walruses, O. rosmarus, generally live in herds containing as many as 100 or more individuals. Both sexes have prominent upper canine teeth that develop into long tusks. The male's tusks may reach 1 m (3.3 ft) in length; the female's tusks grow up to 60 cm (2 ft).

Walsingham, Sir Francis   Sir Francis Walsingham, b. *c.*1530, d. Apr. 6, 1590, was principal secretary to Queen ELIZABETH I of England from 1573 to 1590. As a zealous Protestant he went into exile on the Continent when Catholicism was restored by Mary I. Returning on Elizabeth's accession, he rapidly secured a prominent position among her advisors and sat in Parliament (1558–67). He served as ambassador in Paris (1570–73) and was then named principal secretary, succeeding William Cecil (later 1st Baron Burghley). Walsingham specialized in foreign policy, firmly advocating English involvement in Protestant causes. His other specialty was intelligence gathering; his information helped convict Mary, Queen of Scots, of treason, and his network of spies in the European capitals gave him advance knowledge of the impending attack of the Spanish Armada.

Walter, Bruno [vahl'-tur]   The German-born conductor Bruno Walter (originally B. W. Schlesinger), b. Sept. 15, 1876, d. Feb. 17, 1962, had his first instruction in music from his mother and made his debut as pianist at the age of 10. At 18 years of age he was engaged as assistant conductor at the Hamburg Opera, there beginning his friendship, which deepened later in Vienna, with Gustav Mahler. Walter conducted the posthumous premieres of Mahler's *Das Lied von der Erde* (1911) and his Symphony no. 9 (1912) and championed his works during their decades of relative neglect. A founder of the Salzburg Festival, Walter held a series of important musical posts in Munich, Berlin, Leipzig, and Vienna. Removed from his post by the Nazis, he settled (1938) in the United States, appearing at the Metropolitan Opera, serving as advisor to the New York Philharmonic (1947–49), and recording extensively.

Walter, Thomas U.   Thomas Ustick Walter, b. Philadelphia, Sept. 4, 1804, d. Dec. 30, 1887, is best known as architect of the dome (1855–65) and the Senate and House wings of the CAPITOL OF THE UNITED STATES. A student of architect William Strickland, Walter was most at ease with the GREEK REVIVAL style, as seen in Girard College (1833–47) and the Biddle house, Andalusia (1834), both in Philadelphia; however, his Moyamensing Prison in Philadelphia (1832–36; demolished) was partly Gothic Revival, partly Egyptian revival.

Walters, Barbara   The broadcaster Barbara Walters, b. Boston, Sept. 25, 1931, joined NBC's "Today Show" in 1961 as a writer and occasional on-the-air feature reporter. Within 4 years she became host Hugh Downs's assistant and in 1971 was given her own show, "Not for Women Only." Walters switched networks in 1976 to become co-anchor of "The ABC Evening News," at an unprecedented salary of $1 million a year. Since 1978 she has concentrated on special interviews.

Walther von der Vogelweide [vahl'-tur fuhn dair foh'-gel-vy'-de]   Walther von der Vogelweide, *c.*1170–*c.*1230, was the most important minnesinger, or German lyric poet, of the Middle Ages. Born in southern Germany, perhaps in the Tyrol mountains, to noble but impoverished parents, he spent most of his life wandering in Bavaria and Austria, supporting himself with his poems and songs. His *Under the Linden* is probably the most famous love poem in the German language. Walther's *Sprüche*, or maxims, survive, as do many of the melodies for his lyrics.

Walton, Bill   William Theodore Walton, b. La Mesa, Calif., Nov. 5, 1952, a 6-ft 11-in (2-m 11-cm) American basketball player, first drew national attention when he led San Diego's Helix High School to a 33-0 record while averaging 29 points and 22 rebounds per game his senior year. He then played center for the University of California at Los Angeles (UCLA). During his 3 varsity seasons (1972–74), Walton was College Player of the Year an unequaled 3 times and led UCLA to 2 undefeated seasons and National Collegiate Athletic Association titles (1972–73). As a professional, Walton was beset by injuries; he took the Portland Trail Blazers to the National Basketball Association championship in 1977, however, and was the NBA's Most Valuable Player in 1978. Walton joined the San Diego Clippers in 1979, but persistent leg injuries severely limited his playing time until the 1985–86 season, when he became a Boston Celtic. Walton contributed vitally to the Celtics' winning that year's NBA championship.

Walton, Ernest Thomas Sinton   see COCKCROFT, SIR JOHN DOUGLAS

Walton, Izaak   The English writer Izaak Walton, b. Stafford, Aug. 9, 1593, d. Dec. 15, 1683, is best known for his treatise on fishing, *The Compleat Angler* (1653), which in a conversational style combines anecdote, dialogue, quotation, and verse to present an eloquent testimony to the pleasures of a pastoral life. Walton also published important biographies of the poets Donne (1640), Wotton (1651), and Herbert (1670), and of the theologians Hooker (1665) and Sanderson (1678).

Walton, Sir William   The English composer Sir William Walton, b. Mar. 29, 1902, d. Mar. 8, 1983, came to public attention with *Façade* (1922), an entertainment for speaker and chamber ensemble, with poems by Edith Sitwell. Two overtures for full orchestra were inspired by visual art: *Portsmouth Point* (1925) for a print by Rowlandson, and *Scapino* (1941) for an etching by J. Callot. All four of his concerted works—*Sinfonia Concertante* (1928), Viola Concerto (1929), Violin Concerto (1939), and Cello Concerto (1957)—have remained in the repertory, as have his two symphonies, no. 1 (1934–35) and no. 2 (1960). Other important orchestral works include the *Johannesburg Festival Overture* (1956), the *Partita* (1958), and *Variations on a Theme by Hindemith* (1963). His film scores are numerous, the best known being those for *Henry V* (1944) and *Hamlet* (1948). Of the choral works, *Belshazzar's Feast* (1931) is the most vived and popular. His two operas are *Troilus and Cressida* (1954) and *The Bear* (1967). Outstanding among his chamber music is the Sonata for Violin and Piano (1949).

Sir William Walton, a contemporary English composer, achieved fame in 1922 with Façade, *a humorous musical setting for poems by Edith Sitwell. Such works as the dramatic oratorio* Belshazzar's Feast *(1931) and his Violin Concerto (1939) are noted for exacting craftsmanship and superb orchestration.*

waltz The waltz is a turning, gliding dance in ¾ time that dominated, social dancing from 1750 to 1900. Its most shocking innovation was the closed hold, in which each couple danced face to face with arms wrapped "immodestly" around one another, now the accepted ballroom position. A direct outgrowth of the German and Austrian *Ländler* and *Deutsche*, the waltz appeared in France after the Revolution (displacing the minuet) and in England in 1812. Its universal adoption marked the first occasion in centuries that mass taste prevailed in dance without the official sanction of either courts or dancing masters. The waltz required little skill; six evenly accented steps completed a full turn in two bars of music; the turns were repeated endlessly as the couples swiftly circled the dance floor. The Viennese waltz stressed the first step in the sequence and doubled the prevalent tempo.

Walvis Bay The territory of Walvis Bay, a South African enclave with the only deepwater harbor on the coast of Namibia, covers an area of 1,124 km² (434 mi²) and has a population of 16,607 (1985; city proper pop., 9,687). The port handles up to 90% of Namibia's exports; fishing is also important.

Walvis Bay was annexed by the United Kingdom in 1878, incorporated into the Cape of Good Hope in 1884, and administered as part of Namibia from 1922 to 1977, when it was returned to the direct control of the Cape Province. Despite Namibian claims to the enclave, South Africa refused to give it up when Namibia became independent in 1990.

Wampanoag [wahm-puh-noh'-ag] The Wampanoag, a North American Indian tribe of Eastern Algonquian linguistic stock, traditionally inhabited the territory around Narragansett Bay in present-day Rhode Island and Massachusetts. A horticultural people, during the early 17th century they occupied approximately 30 villages in the region. Their leader MASSASOIT welcomed the English during this period and remained at peace with them until his death (1661). By that time the Wampanoag had suffered grave privations, including epidemics that took most of the population.

When Massasoit's son Metacomet succeeded his father, he organized a major intertribal coalition and a war, lasting from 1675 to 1676, the purpose of which was to kill or drive away the English settlers (see KING PHILIP'S WAR). Metacomet and most of the chiefs were killed, and the Wampanoag were nearly exterminated. Except for a few villages that had remained at peace, the surviving Wampanoag took refuge among other tribes. One village, on Martha's Vineyard, persisted and has retained its identity to the present day.

wampum Wampum was a medium of value commonly used by aboriginal Woodland Indians who inhabited the Northeast region of the United States. It was originally composed of strings or belts of tubular beads made from the purple and white sections of hard clamshells. Adding to the value and prestige of wampum was the delicacy of the work needed in the production of the beads, despite a fairly limited drilling technology.

Strings of wampum served as sources of prestige, as badges of authorization or identification for intertribal ambassadors, and as mechanisms for recording and binding treaties. Cultural historians once believed that wampum was also used aboriginally as a special-purpose money in exchanges carried out among various tribes; it has since been shown that this use of wampum was inspired by European traders who needed a more readily available currency for trading with natives. With the introduction of metal drills and the mass production of wampum beads and belts in Europe, the value of wampum diminished, and it became used more for jewelry and decorating clothing.

These belts, crafted from shell beads, or wampum, held symbolic and ceremonial value for the Eastern Woodlands Indians. The value of an object made from wampum was determined by the intricacy of the workmanship, the color of the beads, and the size of the object.

Wananikwe [wah-nah-nik'-way]   Wananikwe, an Indian prophetess thought to be of Santee Sioux origins, founded (c.1876) an influential religious movement known as the Dream Dance, or Drum, Religion. Wananikwe is said to have had a visionary experience in which spirits taught her the tenets of a new religion that would protect Indians from white settlers. Although she disappeared soon after 1878, her religion was carried throughout the Great Lakes region by male Chippewa and Potawatomi disciples.

wandering Jew (botany)   Wandering Jew is the common name for *Tradescantia fluminensis* and *T. albiflora* of the spiderwort family, Commelinaceae. These perennial herbs are grown extensively as houseplants because they require little light and are easily rooted. Their green leaves may be striped or banded with white, yellow, or purple. Two other spiderworts are sometimes also called wandering Jew: *Zebrina pendula*, with red flowers and leaves of silver to purple green above and purple below; and *Commelina nudiflora*, with blue flowers.

wandering Jew (literature)   In European folk legend, the wandering Jew is a figure doomed to live until the Second Coming as punishment for having derided Jesus on his way to Calvary. The image of an aged, restless ascetic atoning through piety for his single rash act arose as early as the 13th century in both England and Italy. With its evocative overtones of the biblical story of Cain, the legend pervaded medieval Europe and has survived in literature and folklore to modern times. Wagner employed a related folk motif in *The Flying Dutchman*.

Wang Hsi-chih   see WANG XIZHI

Wang Mang, Emperor of China [wahng mahng] Separating the Earlier and Later HAN dynasties of China is the brief reign of Wang Mang, 33 BC–AD 23, a reformer who usurped the throne in AD 9, claiming divine election, and founded the Xin (New) dynasty. His reforms, intended to remedy the economic crisis into which the Han dynasty had fallen, were based on his revival of Zhou-dynasty classics concerning the ideal Confucian state and included such radical measures as nationalization of the land, currency debasement, abolition of slavery, and state loans to peasants at moderate interest rates. Opposition from wealthy landowners and provincial officials still loyal to the Han forced Wang Mang to rescind the reforms; his dynasty collapsed when he was murdered.

Wang Meng [wahng meng]   Wang Meng, b. c.1308, d. Oct. 14, 1385, was a leading Chinese landscape painter and one of the so-called Four Great Masters of the Yuan dynasty (1279–1368). Unlike the other three Yuan Masters, who were hermit painters, Wang led a politically active life that ultimately resulted in his death in prison. His paintings reflect a distinctively individual approach to the problems of space, form, and tactile quality in compositions of extraordinary density. The masterful landscape *Dwelling in the Jingbian Mountains* (1366; Shanghai Museum) embodies Wang's artistic goals and is a unique achievement in Yüan art.

Wang Wei [wahng way]   Wang Wei, 699–759, was a Chinese poet, painter, and scholar of the Tang dynasty. During the An Lushan rebellion he was captured and forced to serve the short-lived rebel regime. After order was restored he was condemned to die for treason but cleared his name with a poem, written during his captivity, that demonstrated his loyalty to the throne. Along with a significant body of lyrical poetry, Wang Wei executed delicately rendered landscape paintings that, like his poetry, reflect a love of nature and an inner tranquility derived from Buddhism and meditation. He is traditionally credited with founding the Southern school of Chinese landscape painting.

Wang Xizhi (Wang Hsi-chih) [wahng shee-ji]   Wang Xizhi, c.303–c.379, was a Chinese calligrapher whose work exerted a profound influence on later Chinese CALLIGRAPHY. He came from an eminent family and served in the government until 355. Well versed in all types of calligraphic scripts, he was best known for his running script, or *xingshu*, and his cursive script, or *caoshu*. Wang's *Preface to the Orchard Pavilion Gathering* (353) is widely acknowledged to be the best work produced in the running script, and his *On the Seventeenth* the best in the cursive script.

Wangs, Four   see CHINESE ART AND ARCHITECTURE

Wankel engine [wang'-kul]   The Wankel engine is an advanced type of internal-combustion engine developed in 1956 by Felix Wankel, a German mathematician. Currently, few automobile manufacturers use the Wankel rotary engine in the production of cars.

The Wankel engine differs greatly from conventional engines. It retains the familiar intake, compression, power, and exhaust cycle but uses, instead of a piston, cylinder, and mechanical valves, a triangular rotor that revolves around the eccentric. The three apexes, or tips, of this rotor remain in constant, snug contact with the combustion-chamber walls. The only other moving part is the crankshaft. The Wankel engine has 40 percent fewer parts and roughly one-third the bulk and weight of a comparable reciprocating engine.

In addition to the simplicity of design, there is little or no vibration in the Wankel. There are no problems with heat dissipation, hot spots, or detonation, all of which are considerations in the conventional reciprocating engine.

Wankel engines, most of which are liquid-cooled, are capable of running at unusually high speeds for long periods of time. The motor exhibits a high power-to-weight ratio and an exceptionally good torque curve at all engine speeds.

The Wankel engine is unique in that the power impulse is spread over approximately 270 degrees of crankshaft rotation, as compared to 180 degrees for the conventional reciprocating two-stroke engine.

The only major problem encountered so far with this engine has been with the apex seals. Experience has indicated that these seals have not been as efficient as they were expected to be and, as a result, the emission gases contain relatively high quantities of nitrogen oxides. Wankel-powered vehicles currently sold in the United States do, however, meet all U.S. emissions standards.

The North American wapiti is a large deer, second to the moose in size. Formerly hunted for its canine teeth—once used as a fraternal emblem—it is now few in number.

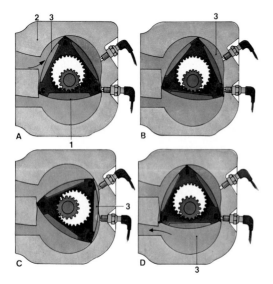

The Wankel engine (A) is an internal-combustion rotary engine. Its curved triangular rotor (1) orbits around a crankshaft inside a curved casing (2). As the rotor turns, its apexes slide along the casing, creating a series of combustion chambers of constantly alternating size. Gaseous fuel enters a chamber (3) through an intake port. (B) Rotary movement decreases the size of the chamber, compressing the fuel, which is ignited (C) by a spark plug. (D) Continuing movement of the rotor permits releases of exhaust gases through an exit port.

wapiti [wahp'-i-tee]   The wapiti, or American elk, *Cervus elaphus canadensis* of the family Cervidae, the largest living deer next to the moose, is now found only in remote areas of the Rocky Mountains and Canada, principally in national parks. Victims of declining open space and overhunting, wapiti require large tracts of semiopen woodland in which to forage for grasses, twigs, leaves, and other plant material. They must migrate between the mountains in winter and increasingly cultivated valleys in spring. Males grow to 2.4 m (7.8 ft) in length, 1.5 m (5 ft) in height at the shoulder, and as much as 450 kg (990 lb) in weight. Their antlers, with 12 powerful tines, may weigh from 20 to 25 kg (45 to 55 lb) and be 1.65 m (5.5

ft) wide. The neck and shoulders are covered with a shaggy mane; the coat is brownish gray with a whitish yellow rump patch. Calves stand soon after birth, and start grazing at 4 weeks.

war crimes   War crimes are violations by civilian or military personnel of the INTERNATIONAL LAW of war. Included are crimes against the peace, crimes against humanity, violations of the rules of conduct of hostilities, mistreatment of civilians and prisoners of war, and belligerent occupation of enemy territory.

Crimes against the peace (aggression) and crimes against humanity (including GENOCIDE) are comparatively recent additions to the code of war crimes. Although both have antecedents in international law, they were not authoritatively considered war crimes until the NUREMBERG TRIALS. Many of the norms about conduct of hostilities are derived from a body of customary principles formed over several centuries. These customary law principles continue in force, but much of the contemporary law on war crimes is found in the Hague Conventions of 1907 and the GENEVA CONVENTIONS of 1949. This body of law grows constantly, however, because new technologies and new problems in successive wars stimulate efforts to revise and update existing treaties.

War and Peace   *War and Peace* (1865–69), Count Leo TOLSTOI's major work, is considered by many the world's greatest novel. A magnificent panorama of Russian life, the book traces the fates of a host of characters during the Napoleonic Wars. Prince Andrei Volkonski searches for truth and significance but fails to find either because he is too much in control of his life; Countess Natasha Rostova is the embodiment of impulsiveness and spontaneity; and Count Pierre Bezukhov finds truth because he is open to life's irrational and unpredictable rhythms. Personal events are more important than public ones, and generals or kings delude themselves when they believe they determine the outcome of battles or the courses taken by nations. The insignificant, in fact, are often more in touch with history than are the mighty, because they move with its currents without attempting to direct it.

War of the Worlds, The

War of the Worlds, The   *The War of the Worlds* (1898), by H. G. WELLS, is a scientific fantasy and one of the precursors of SCIENCE FICTION. The novel concerns an invasion of earth by Martians who terrorize England with their superior technology and thirst for human blood. The panic-stricken population is saved from destruction only by the inability of the Martians to resist bacteria. In spite of its shortcomings, which include inadequate characterization and a plodding journalistic style, the novel was instantly popular and continues to be read. Orson Welles's 1938 radio-broadcast adaptation was thought by many listeners to be news reports of an actual invasion.

War of 1812

War of 1812   The War of 1812 was fought between the United States and Great Britain from June 1812 to the spring of 1815, although the peace treaty ending the war was signed in Europe in December 1814.

Background. From the end of the American Revolution in 1783, the United States had been irritated by the failure of the British to withdraw from American territory along the Great Lakes; their backing of the Indians on America's frontiers; and their unwillingness to sign commercial agreements favorable to the United States. American resentment grew during the French Revolutionary Wars (1792–1802) and the Napoleonic Wars (1803–15),

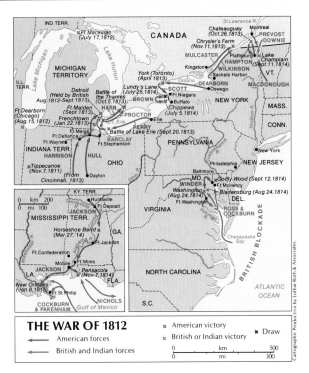

THE WAR OF 1812

← American forces
← British and Indian forces

✗ American victory
✗ British or Indian victory
✗ Draw

0 ___ km ___ 500
0 ___ mi ___ 300

The *Constitution* (right), *one of the first ships commissioned in the U.S. Navy, demolished the* Guerrière, *a British warship, on Aug. 19, 1812. Despite occasional U.S. naval victories, British sea power was never seriously threatened during the War of 1812.*

in which Britain and France were the main combatants. During the 1790s, French and British maritime policies produced several crises with the United States, but after 1803 the difficulties became much more serious. The British Orders in Council of 1807 tried to channel all neutral trade to continental Europe through Great Britain, and France's Berlin and Milan decrees of 1806 and 1807 declared Britain in a state of blockade and condemned neutral shipping that obeyed British regulations. The United States believed its rights on the seas as a neutral were being violated by both nations, but British maritime policies were resented more because Britain dominated the seas. Also, the British claimed the right to take from American merchant ships any British sailors who were serving on them. Frequently, they also took Americans. This practice of impressment became a major grievance.

In 1807, after the British ship *Leopard* fired on the American frigate CHESAPEAKE, President Thomas Jefferson urged and Congress passed an EMBARGO ACT banning all American ships from foreign trade. The embargo failed to change British and French policies but devastated New England shipping.

In November 1811 a group in Congress known as the War Hawks demanded war against Great Britain. These men were all Democratic-Republicans and mostly from the West and South. Among their leaders were John C. Calhoun of South Carolina, Henry Clay of Kentucky, and Felix Grundy of Tennessee. The FEDERALIST PARTY, representing New England shippers who foresaw the ruination of their trade, opposed war. Napoleon's announcement in

The British army that occupied Washington, D.C., after defeating the American militia in the Battle of Bladensburg, burned the Capitol and White House. (Military Collection, Brown University, Providence, R.I.)

1810 of the revocation of his decrees was followed by British refusals to repeal their orders, and pressures for war increased. On June 18, 1812, President James MADISON signed a declaration of war that Congress—with substantial opposition—had passed at his request. Unknown to Americans, Britain had finally, two days earlier, announced that it would revoke its orders.

Campaigns of 1812–13. The initial U.S. plan called for a three-pronged offensive: from Lake Champlain to Montreal; across the Niagara frontier; and into Upper Canada from Detroit. The attacks were uncoordinated, however, and all failed. In the West, Gen. William Hull surrendered Detroit to the British in August 1812; on the Niagara front, American troops lost the Battle of Queenston Heights in October; and along Lake Champlain the American forces withdrew in late November without seriously engaging the enemy.

American frigates won a series of single-ship engagements with British frigates. The captains and crew of the frigates CONSTITUTION and *United States* became renowned throughout America. Meanwhile, the British gradually tightened a blockade around America's coasts, ruining American trade, threatening American finances, and exposing the entire coastline to British attack.

American attempts to invade Canada in 1813 were again mostly unsuccessful. There was a standoff at Niagara, and an elaborate attempt to attack Montreal failed at the end of the year. The only success was in the West. The Americans won control of the Detroit frontier region when Oliver Hazard PERRY's ships destroyed the British fleet on Lake Erie (Sept. 10, 1813). This victory forced the British to retreat eastward from the Detroit region, and on Oct. 5, 1813, they were overtaken and defeated at the battle of the Thames (Moraviantown) by an American army under the command of Gen. William Henry HARRISON. In this battle the great Shawnee chief TECUMSEH, who had harassed the northwestern frontier since 1811, was killed while fighting on the British side.

Campaigns of 1814. In 1814 the United States faced

complete defeat, because the British, having defeated Napoleon, began to transfer large numbers of ships and experienced troops to America. The situation was particularly serious for the United States because the country was insolvent by the fall of 1814, and in New England opponents of the war were discussing separation from the Union. The HARTFORD CONVENTION that met in Connecticut in December 1814 and January 1815 stopped short of such an extreme step but suggested a number of constitutional amendments to restrict federal power.

The British appeared near success in the late summer of 1814. After winning the Battle of Bladensburg (August 24), they marched into Washington, D.C., and burned most of the public buildings. President Madison had to flee into the countryside. The British then turned to attack Baltimore but met stiffer resistance and were forced to retire after the American defense of FORT MCHENRY, which inspired Francis Scott Key to write the words of the "Star-Spangled Banner."

In the north about 10,000 British veteran troops advanced into the United States from Montreal. Only a weak American force stood between them and New York City, but on Sept. 11, 1814, American Capt. Thomas MACDONOUGH won the naval battle of Lake Champlain (Plattsburg Bay), destroying the British fleet. Fearing the possibility of a severed line of communications, the British army retreated into Canada.

Peace Treaty and the Battle of New Orleans. When news of the failure of the attack along Lake Champlain reached British peace negotiators at Ghent, in the Low Countries, they decided to forego territorial demands on the United States. The United States, although originally hoping that Britain would recognize American neutral rights, was happy to end the war without major losses. The Treaty of Ghent, signed by both powers on Dec. 24, 1814, supported, in essence, the conditions in existence at the war's onset. The U.S. Senate ratified the treaty unanimously on Feb. 17, 1815.

Andrew Jackson was the victorious American commander at the Battle of New Orleans. Due to slow communications, British commander Sir Edward Pakenham was unaware that the Treaty of Ghent, which formally ended the war, had been signed 15 days before he led the attack on New Orleans (Jan. 8, 1815).

Because it was impossible to communicate quickly across the Atlantic, the British attack on New Orleans went ahead as planned, even though the war had officially ended. In January 1815, Gen. Andrew JACKSON won a decisive victory at New Orleans over the attacking British forces: the British suffered more than 2,000 casualties; the Americans, fewer than 100. The accidental linking of the peace treaty with Jackson's victory at New Orleans convinced many Americans that the war had ended in triumph.

War on Poverty   The War on Poverty, declared in the State of the Union address on Jan. 8, 1964, was President Lyndon B. JOHNSON's attempt to break the cycle of poverty affecting nearly 35 million Americans. Economic expansion had reduced unemployment to 5.3 percent, but projections showed that 25 percent of young African Americans were destined for a life of irregular employment. Johnson, having enacted the modest antipoverty program of his predecessor, John F. Kennedy, wanted his own, and directed Sargent SHRIVER to steer the development and passage of an omnibus bill.

Rejecting an alternative of direct subsidies, the Economic Opportunity Act of 1964, signed into law by Johnson on Aug. 20, 1964, attempted to prepare the poor for successful competition in an expanding economy. It combined new and existing programs of services by professionals—Volunteers in Service to America, (VISTA), Neighborhood Youth Corps, JOB CORPS, College Work Study, and HEAD START—with the novel Community Action Programs (CAP), designed to involve recipients with "maximum feasible participation." Shriver's Office of Economic Opportunity (OEO) was given authority to run its own programs and supervise related agencies. Never adequate, however, funding for OEO was further reduced as spending for the Vietnam War increased.

War Powers Act   The U.S. Congress passed the War Powers Resolution, or Act, in 1973 in order to balance congressional and presidential powers. A key provision of the controversial law places a 60-day limit on any presidential commitment of U.S. forces abroad without specific authorization by Congress. The legislation was a reaction to actions taken by presidents Lyndon B. Johnson and Richard M. Nixon during the VIETNAM WAR.

warbler   The name *warbler* is used for birds of two subfamilies of the flycatcher family, Muscicapidae; for birds of the New World wood warbler family, Parulidae; and for several species of birds in the thrush family, Turdidae.

The Old World warblers are more than 300 species of birds constituting the subfamily Sylviinae of the flycatchers. They are generally grayish, greenish, or brownish, but some African species are highly colorful. Only three members of this subfamily occur regularly in the New World: the ruby-crowned kinglet, *Regulus calendula*; the golden-crowned kinglet, *R. satrapa*; and the Arctic warbler, *Phylloscopus borealis*.

Members of the flycatcher subfamily Melurinae are commonly known as Australian or wren warblers. These birds are found in Australia and as far east as Polynesia; they have cocked, wrenlike tails but brilliant colors.

The New World wood warblers usually have an unwarblerlike song and probably were named for their Old World counterparts because of their similar body shape, quick movements, and insectivorous habits. In addition to their songs, a prime difference between the New World wood warblers and the Old World warblers is that the former have nine primary feathers (flight feathers) whereas the latter have ten.

The morning warblers are three species of African birds, genus *Cichladusa* in the thrush family, Turdidae.

Ward, Artemus   Artemus Ward was the pseudonym taken by humorist Charles Farrar Browne, b. Waterford, Maine, Apr. 26, 1834, d. Mar. 6, 1867, as well as the name of the shrewd Yankee character he created for a popular series (1858–60) in the *Cleveland Plain Dealer*. He is the narrator of *Artemus Ward: His Book* (1862), *Artemus Ward: His Travels* (1865), and *Artemus Ward in London* (1867). His humor relied mainly on puns, misspellings, and—in lectures—a deadpan style of delivery that greatly influenced Mark Twain.

Ward, Montgomery   Aaron Montgomery Ward, b. Chatham, N.J., Feb. 17, 1844, d. Dec. 7, 1913, founded the U.S. mail-order house and retail department-store chain that bear his name. Ward worked during the 1860s as a traveling salesman in farm areas where he saw the advantages in selling low-priced goods by mail to rural customers. He founded a firm in 1872 and issued a one-page catalog of about 150 items. He began to offer (1875) his merchandise with a money-back guarantee to dissatisfied buyers. By 1888 the firm's sales exceeded $1 million annually, and by the time of Ward's death, $40 million.

Warham, William   [wohr'-uhm]   William Warham, b. c.1456, d. Aug. 22, 1532, was the last archbishop of Canterbury before the English church broke with Rome. After serving in several ambassadorial positions, he was appointed bishop of London (1502), archbishop of Canterbury and lord chancellor (1504), and chancellor of Oxford (1506). In 1515 he surrendered the lord chancellorship to Thomas WOLSEY, who thereafter eclipsed Warham. In 1531, Warham acknowledged Henry VIII as supreme head of the church with the proviso "so far as the law of Christ will allow." He subsequently protested all acts prejudicial to the authority of the pope.

Warhol, Andy   [wohr'-hohl]   The artist and filmmaker Andy Warhol, b. Pennsylvania, Aug. 6, 1928?, d. Feb. 22, 1987, was a founder and major figure of the POP ART movement. In 1960 he produced the first of his paintings

A single image of Andy Warhol's silk screen Elizabeth Taylor (1964) exemplifies the series of mechanical reproductions of celebrities he created during the early 1960s. Warhol was one of the most prominent exponents of the pop-art movement.

depicting enlarged comic-strip images—such as Popeye and Superman—initially for use in a window display. Warhol pioneered the development of the process whereby an enlarged photographic image is transferred to a silk screen that is then placed on a canvas and inked from the back. It was this technique that enabled him to produce the series of mass-media images—repetitive, yet with slight variations—that he began in 1962. These, incorporating such items as Campbell's Soup cans, Coca-Cola bottles, and the faces of celebrities, can be taken as comments on the American culture. Later in the 1960s, Warhol made a series of experimental films dealing with such ideas as time, boredom, and repetition; they include *Sleep* (1963) and *The Chelsea Girls* (1966). A celebrity himself, he founded *Interview* magazine.

warlords   Military governors, or warlords (*dujun*), effectively controlled large areas of China with their own armies during the period of anarchy following the death (1916) of YUAN SHIKAI, successor to SUN YAT-SEN as president, until the inauguration of a national government by CHIANG KAI-SHEK in 1928. There were hundreds of warlords—from those who commanded one district to those whose authority extended over two or three provinces—and their constant warring terrorized and impoverished the people. The Beijing government of Gen. Duan Qirui retained its claim of legitimacy, but the real control of the city and the bureaucracy was held by the more powerful warlords in the north, such as ZHANG ZUOLIN, Feng Yuxiang, Feng Gozhang, Wu Peifu, and Yan Xishan, either singly or in frequently shifting alliances.

In the south the nationalist KUOMINTANG movement of Chiang Kai-shek launched (1926) its NORTHERN EXPEDITION to eliminate the warlords and reunite China. Countless smaller warlord armies were absorbed along the way, and the major warlords in the north either fled in defeat or accepted a place in the new government.

Warm Springs   Warm Springs (1990 pop., 407) is a health resort in western Georgia, about 100 km (60 mi) southwest of Atlanta. The springs remain at a constant temperature of 31° C (88° F). Established as a resort during the 1830s, Warm Springs became famous when polio victim Franklin D. Roosevelt began to visit the town in 1924. Roosevelt's residence in Warm Springs came to be known as the "Little White House" during his presidency (1933–45), and after he died there it became a national shrine. The Warm Springs Foundation, founded by Roosevelt for the care of polio patients, is located there.

Warmerdam, Cornelius [wohr'-mur-dam]   Cornelius Anthony Warmerdam, b. Long Beach, Calif., June 22, 1915, was a pole vaulter during the era of the bamboo pole. No vaulter in history so completely outclassed the competition or maintained such domination of the event. Warmerdam was the first to surpass the height of 15 ft (4.57 m), on Apr. 13, 1940. On May 23, 1942, he set a world outdoor record by clearing 15 ft 7.75 in (4.76 m), and on Mar. 20, 1943, he achieved an indoor best of 15 ft 8.5 in (4.78 m). His outdoor record stood for 17 years, until pole vaulter Don Bragg cleared 15 ft 9.5 in (4.81 m) using an aluminum pole.

Warner, Pop   Glenn Scobey "Pop" Warner, b. Springville, N.Y., Apr. 5, 1871, d. Sept. 7, 1954, was an American college football coach who played football at Cornell University. In his first job he coached the University of Georgia to an undefeated season in 1896. He then coached Cornell the next 2 seasons before coaching (1899–1903) the Carlisle (Pa.) Indian School team. He returned to Cornell for 4 years but later rejoined Carlisle (1907–14). Warner earned national fame at Carlisle, especially with the legendary 1911–12 team that featured Jim Thorpe. Warner also coached Pittsburgh (1915–23), Stanford (1924–32), and Temple (1933–38). He retired with 313 coaching victories, one fewer than Amos Alonzo Stagg. The POP WARNER FOOTBALL leagues for young people are named for him.

Warner, Seth   Seth Warner, b. Roxbury, Conn., May 6, 1743, d. Dec. 26, 1784, a leader of Vermont's GREEN MOUNTAIN BOYS, captured (May 11, 1775) Crown Point at the beginning of the American Revolution and defeated (Oct. 31, 1775) a British force at Longueuil during the retreat from Canada. In 1777 he helped win the Battle of Bennington in the Saratoga campaign.

warrant   A warrant is a writ issued by a magistrate, justice of the peace, or other person in authority directing an officer of the law to execute certain functions proper to his or her office. Most warrants issued are warrants for arrest or SEARCH WARRANTS, but they can be issued to carry out or to prohibit many different kinds of actions, including seizure of goods and tax collection. According to the 4th Amendment of the U.S. Constitution, warrants must be supported by oath, must specifically describe the person or goods to be seized or the place to be searched, and can only be issued for "probable cause." Warrants are unnecessary if an officer of the law has probable cause to act immediately.

Warrau [wah-row']   The Warrau (or Warao) are a South American Indian people who occupy the vast delta lands of the Orinoco River in eastern Venezuela. Their language is distantly related to the Chibchan linguistic stock; their name means "boat people." Their population is concentrated among about 250 villages in Venezuela. The Warrau avoided absorption by European settlers and today are among the few Indian groups of the region to have survived.

Although they practice some horticulture, the Warrau rely on fishing from dugout canoes. Their settlements are composed of pole and thatch-roofed houses; households consist of several related families; the population of an average village is only about 50 people. Descent is traced through both parents, with authority vested in the male household elder. No paramount chiefs exist among the Warrau, and even the shamanism that constitutes their religion has no political implications. Unlike other tropical-forest peoples, the Warrau's SHAMANS, rather than just curing illnesses, fulfill a priestly role and propitiate supreme spirits.

Warren   Warren (1990 pop., 144,864) is an industrial city and northern suburb of Detroit. Automobile parts, tools, and dies are the major products. General Motors Technical Center is located there. Warren was first settled in 1837.

Warren, Earl   During his 16 years (1953–69) as the 14th chief justice of the United States, Earl Warren, b. Los Angeles, Mar. 19, 1891, d. July 9, 1974, made the U.S. Supreme Court a staunch defender of civil rights. Warren graduated from the University of California at Berkeley and served in World War I. After serving (1939–43) as California attorney general, Warren was elected governor of California (1942–53). In 1948 he was the Republican candidate for vice-president on the ticket headed by Thomas E. Dewey.

In 1953 he was appointed chief justice. One of his first decisions—an opinion he wrote for a unanimous Court—was the historic *Brown* v. *Board of Education of Topeka, Kansas,* which legally ended segregation in public schools. It set the stage for a long list of liberal decisions that marked the Warren Court, among them *Gideon* v. *Wainwright, Miranda* v. *Arizona,* and *Escobedo* v. *Illinois.* In 1963, President Lyndon B. Johnson appointed Warren head of the commission (see WARREN COMMISSION) to investigate the assassination of President John F. Kennedy. When he retired as chief justice in 1969, he was succeeded by Warren E. Burger.

Warren, Joseph   A Massachusetts physician and American Revolutionary patriot, Joseph Warren, b. Roxbury, Mass., June 10, 1741, d. June 17, 1775, drafted (1774) the Suffolk Resolves in protest against the British Intolerable Acts. On Apr. 18, 1775, he sent Paul Revere and William Dawes on their famous ride to Lexington. He was killed at the Battle of Bunker Hill.

Warren, Leonard   Leonard Warren, b. New York City, Apr. 21, 1911, d. Mar. 4, 1960, was probably the most acclaimed American baritone of his time. He studied at the Greenwich House Music School and at Columbia University and was singing in the Radio City Music Hall Glee Club when he entered the Metropolitan Opera's 1937 radio auditions, winning $5,000 for 6 months' study in Italy. On his return, he enjoyed a rapid rise to fame, beginning with his Metropolitan Opera debut in *Simon Boccanegra* on Jan. 13, 1939. He remained with the Met until his death, toured extensively in Europe and the Americas, and made many radio broadcasts and recordings. He died onstage at the height of his career, during a performance of Verdi's *La Forza del destino.*

Warren, Robert Penn   The writer and critic Robert Penn Warren, b. Guthrie, Ky., Apr. 24, 1905, d. Sept. 15, 1989, is perhaps best known for his Pulitzer Prize–winning novel, *All the King's Men* (1946; film, 1949), about a charismatic Southern politician whose career resembles that of Huey "Kingfisher" Long. While a student at Vanderbilt, Warren joined the group of poets known as the Fugitives and contributed an essay to their 1930 agrarian manifesto, *I'll Take My Stand.* After study (1928–30) at Oxford as a Rhodes scholar, he began a distinguished career as teacher and critic at several universities, notably Louisiana State (1934–42), where he edited the *Southern Review,* and Yale (1950–56, 1961–73). With Cleanth Brooks he wrote *Understanding Poetry* (1938) and *Understanding Fiction* (1943), two influential examples of NEW CRITICISM. Warren wrote ten other novels, including *A Place to Come To* (1977). He won two Pulitzer Prizes for poetry: for *Promises* (1957) and *Now and Then* (1979). More than half the entries in *New and Selected Poems, 1923–1985* (1985) were written after 1975. Warren was appointed the first U.S. poet laureate after that title was added (1985) to the position of consultant in poetry to the Library of Congress.

Warren Commission   The establishment of the Warren Commission, charged with investigating the Nov. 22, 1963, assassination of U.S. president John F. KENNEDY, was one of the first acts of Kennedy's successor, President Lyndon B. Johnson. Chief Justice of the United States Earl Warren chaired the commission. The other members were U.S. senators Richard B. Russell of Georgia and John Sherman Cooper of Kentucky; representatives Hale Boggs of Louisiana and Gerald R. Ford of Michigan; Allen Dulles, former head of the Central Intelligence Agency; and John J. McCloy, former president of the World Bank.

In September 1964 the *Report of the President's*

Commission on the Assassination of President John F. Kennedy was submitted. It concluded that Kennedy had been killed by 24-year-old Lee Harvey OSWALD. It found no evidence that either Oswald or Jack Ruby, the Dallas nightclub operator who killed Oswald as he was being transferred to Dallas County jail on November 24, was involved in a wider conspiracy.

The rejection of conspiracy as a factor behind the assassination reassured many Americans. Subsequently, however, critics contended that the commission acted hastily and that it ignored evidence linking others to the assassination. Oswald, they emphasized, had lived in the USSR and had worked for the pro-Castro Fair Play for Cuba Committee. Some critics argued that more than one person had fired at Kennedy.

Wars of the Roses   see ROSES, WARS OF THE

Warsaw

Warsaw Warsaw (Polish: Warszawa), the capital and principal city of Poland, is situated on the Vistula River. The city covers 445 km² (172 mi²), and its population is 1,651,000 (1989 est.).

Contemporary City. The old part of the city (Stare Miasto), on the west bank of the Vistula, was built around the market square (Rynek) and was enclosed by walls erected in 1380. Beginning in the 15th century the new town was added, and in the subsequent centuries suburbs developed. Most of Warsaw was reduced to ruins during World War II, but most of the Stare Miasto was restored; the rest of the city was rebuilt in modern architectural style.

In addition to serving as the political and administrative headquarters of Poland and the seat of the archbishop-primate of Poland, Warsaw is also the country's main financial and commercial center and railroad junction and an important port. Automobiles and locomotives, electrical equipment, chemical and pharmaceutical products, precision instruments, clothing, and processed foods are manufactured there. Warsaw has about 20 museums, including the National Museum. The 40-story Palace of Culture and Science has a convention center, exhibition halls, and theaters. The city's symphony orchestra is outstanding. Best known among Warsaw's theaters are the National Theater and the Polish Theater. The city is the seat of several institutions of higher learning, of which the largest is the University of Warsaw (1818).

History. Archaeological remains indicate that there was a settlement on the site of present-day Warsaw as early as the 10th century. In the 12th century, it was the residence of the dukes of Mazovia. With the extinction of their dynasty, the city was annexed by Poland and became (1596) the residence of the Polish kings.

In the 17th century Warsaw was occupied twice by the Swedes and twice by the Russians. A successful uprising against the Russians, led by Tadeusz KOŚCIUSZKO, was staged in 1794, but the Russians reconquered the city a few months later. In the third partition of Poland (see PO-LAND, PARTITIONS OF) in 1795, Warsaw was assigned to Prussia. Seized by Napoleon's armies in 1806, Warsaw subsequently became the capital of the duchy of Warsaw.

Warsaw, the capital of Poland, reemerged as the country's largest, most populous city after World War II: the Nazi occupation (1939–45) had left it depopulated and virtually destroyed.

In 1813 the city was retaken by the Russians and incorporated into imperial Russia.

With the restoration of independent Poland in 1918, Warsaw again became the country's capital. In September 1939 the city was seized by Hitler's armies and annexed by Nazi Germany. At that time the city's population was about 30% Jewish. In 1940 the Germans established a Jewish ghetto in the center of Warsaw. A massive rebellion that erupted in the ghetto in 1943 was brutally suppressed, and about 56,000 Jews were massacred. By the end of the war the remaining Jews had been exterminated. When the Soviet armies reached the eastern bank of the Vistula, the Polish underground in Warsaw staged, on Aug. 1, 1944, the so-called WARSAW UPRISING against the Germans. In reprisal the Germans razed much of the city. From 1945 to 1989, Warsaw was the capital of the Polish People's Republic, and thereafter of the Republic of Poland.

Warsaw Treaty Organization

Warsaw Treaty Organization   The Warsaw Treaty Organization (WTO), a military alliance between the USSR and its Eastern European satellites, was established on May 14, 1955, in Warsaw, as an Eastern counterpart to the NORTH ATLANTIC TREATY ORGANIZATION (NATO), one week after a rearmed West Germany entered that Western defense organization. The original Warsaw Pact nations were the USSR, Albania, Bulgaria, Czechoslovakia, the German Democratic Republic (East Germany), Hungary, Poland, and Romania. The WTO had a unified high command with headquarters in Moscow. Key posts in satellite forces were held by Soviet-trained or Soviet-born officers. In 1956, Hungary withdrew from the WTO but was pulled back into the alliance when Soviet troops crushed the

Hungarian revolt. In 1968, Czechoslovakia also attempted to withdraw but was forced back by an invasion by Warsaw Pact forces led by the Soviet Union. Albania resigned in 1968 because of its alliance with China. The whole status of the WTO became questionable with the fading of the cold war and the Communist regimes of Eastern Europe in 1989–90. German reunification in October 1990 ended East Germany's membership in the WTO, and in July 1991 the organization was disbanded entirely.

Warsaw uprisings   During World War II, Warsaw, the capital of Poland, was twice the scene of popular revolts against German occupiers.

In 1940 the German conquerors of Poland had confined more than 400,000 Jews in the crowded Warsaw Ghetto. About 300,000 were subsequently sent to concentration camps; but when the Germans attempted to deport the rest in January 1943, they met with resistance from the Jewish Combat Organization (ZOB). On April 19 about 2,000 German troops attacked the ghetto and were again resisted by the 60,000 remaining Jews. Setting the ghetto on fire, the Germans then flooded and smoke-bombed the sewers when the Jews attempted to use them as escape routes. On May 16, Nazi general Juergen Stroop reported that "the former Jewish quarter of Warsaw is no longer in existence."

Another rebellion, which is generally known as the Warsaw Uprising, was launched on Aug. 1, 1944, by the Polish anti-German resistance movement as Soviet troops approached the city. Although Soviet authorities promised to support the uprising, the aim of the anti-Communist resistance was to liberate the city from the Germans before the Soviets could do so. The uprising was backed by the Polish government in exile in London. In their suppression of the uprising, the Germans killed tens of thousands of Poles; meanwhile, the Soviet army remained inactive at the city gates until October 2, when the rebellion collapsed. The Germans exacted terrible revenge. Virtually the entire remaining population of Warsaw was deported to forced labor or concentration camps, and its buildings were systematically razed. The Soviets met little effective resistance when they set up (Jan. 1, 1945) a Soviet-dominated government in Poland.

wart   A wart is a small growth on the skin, usually measuring 2 to 10 mm (0.08 to 0.4 in) across. Warts are caused by PAPILLOMA viruses and affect many people at some time in their lives. They occur chiefly on exposed areas of the body such as the hands, fingers, face, scalp, and soles of the feet. Venereal warts occur on the rectum and vagina. When warts occur in a place subject to pressure—such as plantar warts on the soles of the feet—they may become callused and painful. Warts often disappear spontaneously—only to return in the same spot later. Physicians use a variety of local treatments to remove warts, including caustic chemicals, freezing with dry ice, burning with an electric needle, and surgical excision.

warthog   Warthogs are wild African hogs of the genus *Phacochoerus* in the pig family, Suidae. They are named for the pairs of warty growths, prominent in adult males, that are observed behind and below the eye, between the eye and the corner of the mouth, and at the side of the lower jaw. Warthogs have large, flat heads and curved tusks; they weigh up to 100 kg (220 lb) but are only 1 m (40 in) long. Dwellers of grasslands and open forests, they have acute senses of smell and hearing and eat grass, roots, bark, berries, and sometimes carrion. They often shelter in aardvark burrows and travel in small groups.

The warthog uses its curved tusks to dig for food and to defend itself when attacked. The male's upper tusks reach up to 63 cm (25 in) in length; the female's are smaller.

Warwick   [wawr'-wik]   Warwick is located on the western shore of Narragansett Bay in Rhode Island, 16 km (10 mi) southeast of Providence. The city has a population of 85,427 (1990). It is primarily a residential suburb of Providence, but it also has small manufacturing enterprises and is a summer resort and the site of the Theodore Francis Green airport, which serves the Providence metropolitan area. The city was settled in 1643 by Samuel Gorton, one of the founders of Rhode Island, and was later named for Robert Rich, earl of Warwick. During the 19th century the city was a textile-manufacturing center.

Warwick, Richard Neville, Earl of   Richard Neville, earl of Warwick, b. Nov. 22, 1428, d. Apr. 14, 1471, became known as the Kingmaker because of his great wealth and power. The son of Richard Neville, earl of Salisbury, he acquired Warwick lands by marriage and was made earl in 1450. As an ally of Richard, duke of York, he fought (1455) at Saint Albans (see ROSES, WARS OF THE) and invaded England from Calais in 1459 and again in 1460. His father's death made him outstandingly wealthy. After losing (1461) to the Lancastrians at the second Battle of Saint Albans, he supported EDWARD IV's successful bid for the throne. For the next three years

(1461–64) he virtually ruled England, but his position was undermined by his pro-French policies and by Edward's refusal to marry Bona of Savoy, the sister-in-law of Louis XI of France. In 1469, Warwick formed an alliance with Edward's brother George, duke of Clarence. The next year they fled to France, returning to effect a brief restoration of HENRY VI, who had been deposed in 1461. Edward reclaimed the throne in 1471; his troops met Warwick in battle at Barnet, Hertfordshire, where they slew him.

Warwickshire [wahr'-ik-shur] Warwickshire is a county in the MIDLANDS region of England. It has an area of 1,980 km^2 (765 mi^2) and a population of 477,000 (1991). Warwick is the county town. The Avon, the Cherwell, and the Trent rivers drain the county; dairying and wheat and orchard-fruit cultivation are economically important. Motor vehicles, metal goods, and textiles are manufactured. Tourists are drawn particularly to STRATFORD-ON-AVON, the home of William Shakespeare. Historic Kenilworth Castle (12th century; now in ruins), Baddesley Clinton Hall and Maxstoke Castle (both dating from the 14th century), and Rugby School are located in the county.

Wasatch Range [waw'-sach] Extending almost 400 km (250 mi) in a north-south alignment, the Wasatch Range of the middle ROCKY MOUNTAINS divides Utah in half. Rising sharply from basins on both sides, the conifer-forested upland rises to a high point of 3,660 m (12,008 ft) in Mount Timpanogos. The range was a barrier to early pioneer trails. Rich in minerals, the Wasatch is also an important source of irrigation water.

Washakie [wahsh'-uh-kee] Washakie, c.1804–1900, a chief of the Eastern SHOSHONI Indians of Wyoming, was noted for his exploits in fighting such tribal enemies as the Blackfoot and the Crow and also for his friendship with the white pioneers. When wagon trains were passing through Shoshoni country in the 1850s, Washakie and his people aided the overland travelers in fording streams and recovering strayed cattle. He was also frequently a scout for the U.S. Army during its campaigns against the Sioux, Cheyenne, and other tribes. He was later converted to the Protestant Episcopal church.

Washington Washington, named in honor of the nation's first president and popularly known as the Evergreen State because of its extensive forests, is located in the extreme northwestern corner of the continental United States. The Canadian province of British Columbia lies to the north, and the states of Idaho and Oregon form Washington's eastern and southern borders. Puget Sound and the Pacific Ocean lie to the west.

Encompassing 184,674 km^2 (71,303 mi^2), Washington ranks 18th among the states in land area and, with 4,866,692 inhabitants (1990), 18th in population. The population is increasing at a greater rate than the national average.

Thousands of years of occupancy by American Indians were interrupted during the late 18th century by the arrival of European and American explorers and traders. The ensuing fur trade gave way to permanent white settlement during the 1840s. Washington, with its capital at OLYMPIA, became a territory in 1853 and in 1889 became the 42d state. Long noted for its abundant natural resources of water, timber, and fish, today Washington is a leader in the aerospace industry, international trade, and tourism.

Land and Resources

Washington is characterized by greatly varying relief and scenery. Although the rough outline of Washington's coast totals only 253 km (157 mi), the actual coastline is 4,870 km (3,026 mi) because of the many inlets and small islands in PUGET SOUND. The Strait of JUAN DE FUCA and the adjoining Puget Sound and Strait of Georgia separate the Olympic Mountains (highest peak, Mount Olympus, at 2,428 m/7,965 ft) on the Olympic Peninsula from British Columbia's Vancouver Island. To the east and southeast of the sound is a coastal plain, the Puget Sound lowland. To the east the lowland gives way to the CASCADE RANGE (highest peak, Mount Rainier, at 4,392 m/14,410 ft), with its dormant volcanoes. Another volcano in the Cascades, Mt. St. Helens—dormant since 1857—erupted in 1980, causing extensive damage. To the far east lie the lower slopes of the ROCKY MOUNTAINS. In the north are the Okanogan Highlands. Enclosed by the mountains (except in the southeast) lies the roughly triangular-shaped Columbia Basin. The Columbia Basin and the Puget Sound lowland constitute Washington's only extensive level areas.

Soils and Drainage. Soils range from acidic, waterlogged peats to subhumid alkaline deposits. The most fertile are loess soils of the Palouse River valley and alluvial soils of the Puget Sound lowland.

The COLUMBIA RIVER and its tributaries, including the SNAKE, Okanogan, and Yakima, drain all of eastern Washington. The system's volume of flow is second only to that of the Mississippi. Short rivers, including the Skagit, Snohomish, and Chehalis, drain the western portion of the state. Fjordlike Lake Chelan on the eastern side of the Cascade Range is the largest and deepest of Washington's hundreds of natural lakes; Lake Roosevelt, formed behind GRAND COULEE DAM, is the largest artificial body of water in the state.

Climate. Under the influence of prevailing westerly winds and the rain-shadow effect of the Cascades, Washington is divided into two major climatic regions: a moist, temperate zone to the west with approximately 500 to 3,800 mm (20 to 150 in) of precipitation and an annual temperature fluctuation of 8 to 11 C degrees (14 to 20 F degrees), and a drier, some what continental eastern region with 200 to 635 mm (8 to 25 in) of precipitation and a temperature range of 25° to 28° C (45° to 50° F). Summer is the dry season throughout almost the entire state, and cyclonic storms from the west constitute the most frequent and regular meteorological disturbances.

AT A GLANCE

WASHINGTON

Land: Area: 184,674 km^2 (71,303 mi^2); rank: 18th. Capital: Olympia (1990 pop., 33,840). Largest city: Seattle (1990 pop., 516,259). Counties: 39. Elevations: highest—4,392 m (14,410 ft), at Mount Rainier; lowest—sea level, at the Pacific coast.

People: Population (1990): 4,866,692; rank: 18th; density: 28.2 persons per km^2 (73.1 per mi^2). Distribution (1990): 76.4% urban, 23.6% rural. Average annual change (1980–90): +1.8%.

Government (1993): Governor: Mike Lowry, Democrat. U.S. Congress: Senate—1 Democrat, 1 Republican; House—8 Democrats, 1 Republican. Electoral college votes: 11. State legislature: 49 senators, 98 representatives.

Economy: State personal income (1989): $84 billion; rank: 17th. Median family income (1989): $36,795; rank: 15th. Agriculture: income (1989)—$3.6 billion. Fishing: value (1989) $135 million. Lumber production (1991): 3.3 billion board feet. Mining (nonfuel): value (1988)—$459 million. Manufacturing: value added (1987)—$19 billion. Services: value (1987)—$19 billion.

Miscellany: Statehood: Nov. 11, 1889; the 42d state. Nickname: Evergreen State; tree: Western Hemlock; motto: *Alki* ("By and By"); song: "Washington, My Home."

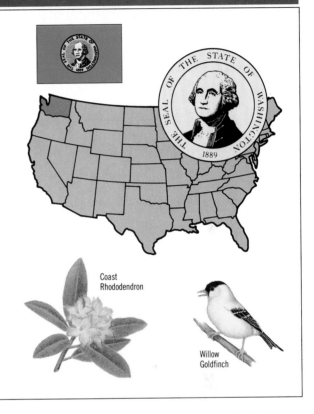

Coast Rhododendron

Willow Goldfinch

Vegetation and Animal Life. The humid western portion of Washington is dominated by forests of Douglas fir and hemlock, mixed with western red cedar, Sitka spruce, and other conifers, as well as various deciduous trees including alder, birch, and maple. At higher elevations subalpine fir and other hardy species take over, while to the east beyond the crest of the Cascades ponderosa pine becomes common. Sagebrush and bunch grass prevail throughout much of the Columbia Basin, but ponderosa pine, Douglas fir, and other western species reappear in the east and in the Okanogan Highlands.

Animal life abounds in Washington. Larger mammals include black bears, Roosevelt elks, deer, and cougars; smaller mammals include bobcats, marten, skunks, foxes, and coyotes. Major flyways bring many species of wildfowl through the state. Rivers and lakes are stocked with trout and sturgeon, and coastal waters abound with salmon, dogfish, Dungeness crab, and other shellfish.

Resources. The most valuable of Washington's varied and widely distributed natural resources are its Pacific salmon and shellfish; its Douglas fir and other softwoods found in the Olympics, Cascades, Blue Mountains (in the southeastern corner of the state), and Okanogan Highlands; its water resources in the Columbia Basin and

many western rivers; and its loess soils of the Palouse River valley. Principal mineral resources include clay, sand, gravel, and stone.

People

Washington's population is unevenly distributed. Density is greatest in the area around Seattle and Tacoma and lowest in the sparsely inhabited northwest corner of the state. The great majority of Washingtonians live in a narrow 17-km-wide (10-mi) corridor running north-south from the Canadian border at Blaine to the Columbia River at Vancouver (an outlier of the Portland, Oreg., metropolitan area). Eastern Washington claims the state's second largest city, SPOKANE, an important manufacturing, grain, and financial center. Smaller urban centers along the Columbia and its tributaries include YAKIMA, WALLA WALLA, and the tri-cities of Pasco-Richland-Kennewick. The Olympic Peninsula is thinly populated except in the vicinities of Aberdeen-Hoquiam and Port Angeles.

Between 1980 and 1990, Washington's yearly population increase was 1.8% as against an annual growth rate of 1.0% for the population of the United States as a whole. Whites make up the great majority of the population, while blacks and Hispanics constitute small minori-

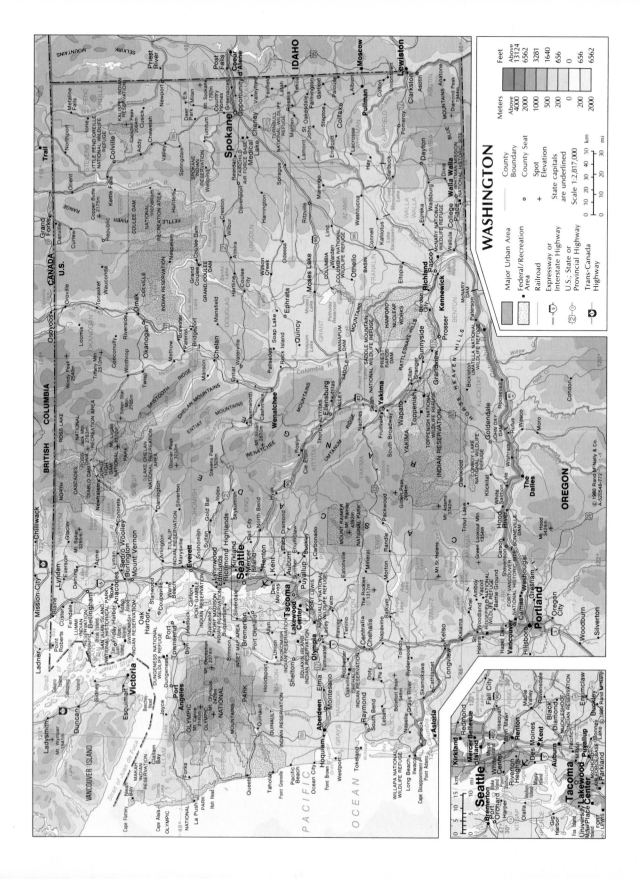

WASHINGTON

Feet
Above 13124
6562
3281
1640
656
0
656
6562

Meters
Above 4000
2000
1000
500
200
0
200
2000

Major Urban Area
Federal / Recreation Area
Railroad
Expressway or Interstate Highway
U.S.; State or Provincial Highway
Trans-Canada Highway

County Boundary
County Seat
Spot Elevation
State capitals are underlined

Scale 1:2,817,000

0 10 20 30 40 50 km
0   10   20   30 mi

© 1980 Rand McNally & Co.
A-520546-772 -1

ty groups within the state. Washington has an American Indian population as well, many of whom live on the state's Indian reservations. The Roman Catholic church is the largest religious group; other large groups are the Mormons, Methodists, and Lutherans.

Education. Since early territorial days Washington has had statewide primary and secondary education. Five state universities, including the University of Washington (1861) at Seattle and Washington State University (1890) at Pullman, are part of the public system of higher education. Private colleges and universities include the University of Puget Sound (1888) in Tacoma, Whitman College (1859) in Walla Walla, and Gonzaga University (1887) in Spokane.

Culture and Historic Sites. The state has symphony orchestras in Seattle, Spokane, Bellevue, and other communities; the Cornish School of Music is at Seattle. The State Capitol Museum is in Olympia. The Museum of History and Industry and the Pacific Science Center are both located in Seattle; the Museum of Native American Cultures is in Spokane.

The Whitman Mission National Historic Site near Walla Walla commemorates the Indian mission established in 1836 by Marcus Whitman.

Communications. Washington has numerous commercial radio and television broadcasting facilities, as well as public television broadcasts from Seattle, Spokane, and Tacoma. Major newspapers having wide regional coverage include the *Seattle Post-Intelligencer* and *Times*, the *Tacoma News-Tribune*, and the *Spokane Spokesman-Review* and *Chronicle*.

Economic Activity

Historically, Washington has depended heavily on abundant primary resources for its economic well-being, but in recent decades manufacturing and services, especially tourism and finance, have provided increasingly larger proportions of the state's income. Manufacturing makes up the single most important economic activity in the state.

Agriculture. Washington's leading agricultural commodities are wheat, dairy products, cattle, and apples, of which Washington is the nation's leading producer. Pears, hops, grapes, plums, and cherries are also leading products in various parts of the state; berries, poultry, and dairy farming are significant west of the Cascades.

Forestry and Fishing. The forest industries are highly developed in western Washington and parts of the northeast and southeast of the state. The leading timber trees are western hemlock and Douglas fir. Commercial fishing for salmon, halibut and shellfish is concentrated along the Pacific Coast and around Puget Sound. Sport fishing is also popular; major species caught include salmon and trout.

Mining. Coal is one of the state's valuable minerals and is its only major fossil-fuel resource. Smelting facilities located in Tacoma and Ferndale depend on ores from outside the state; nonetheless, Washington leads the nation in aluminum smelting. Nonmetalliferous minerals include sand, gravel, clay, and stone. Other minerals found in the state are gold, silver, copper, and uranium.

Manufacturing and Energy. Washington's leading manufacturing products are transportation equipment, particularly aircraft and space equipment; food products; and lumber and wood products. Boeing, a leading producer of commercial aircraft, is the state's largest employer, with plants in Seattle, Everett, Auburn, Kent, and Renton. The primary-metals industry is also important in the state, as is the manufacture of nonelectrical machinery, printing and publishing, and paper products. Industrial centers are heavily concentrated in the Puget Sound lowland. Smaller industrial regions have also grown up along the lower Columbia and in the tri-cities area and Spokane. In addition, Washington is a shipbuilding center, with shipyards in Bremerton, Seattle, and Tacoma.

Hydroelectric installations, primarily along the Columbia River or its tributaries, provide most of the electrical power in the state. The Hanford nuclear reactors, begun in 1943, were the first in the nation.

Tourism. With much of its total area available for recreational purposes, Washington has become a major tourist

Mount Rainier, rising 4,392 m (14,410 ft), is the highest peak in the state of Washington. A dormant volcano that last erupted more than 2,000 years ago, the peak is the center of Mount Rainier National Park, founded in 1899. Mount Rainier's slopes support one of the largest glacial systems in the United States.

Bucking, the process in which tree trunks are cut into logs, is facilitated by modern tree-harvesting equipment. The forest industries have been a major economic activity in Washington since the late 19th century.

state in recent decades. Three national parks (Olympic, Mount Rainier, North Cascades), several national forests (including Mount Baker-Snoqualmie, Gifford Pinchot, and Olympic), and various wilderness and national recreational areas, together with many state and county parks, provide opportunities for year-round recreation. Private resort areas include ski resorts, marinas, beach resorts, dude ranches, hunting lodges, and fishing camps.

Transportation and Trade. Major interstate highways in Washington include I-90, connecting Spokane and Seattle, and I-5, traveling in a north-south direction from Vancouver, British Columbia, through Washington to Portland, Oreg. State-owned ferry systems operate on Puget Sound and the Strait of Juan de Fuca. The Seattle-Tacoma International airport is the state's busiest. The port of Seattle shares the traffic of Puget Sound with harbors at Tacoma, Everett, and Bellingham; there are also Columbia River ports at Longview, Kalama, and Vancouver.

Government and Politics

The state constitution, approved in 1889 and since amended, provides for a bicameral legislature, a governor who serves a 4-year term and may run for reelection, and the power of legislation by public referenda. The house of representatives consists of 98 members, serving 2-year terms, and the 49 members of the senate serve 4-year terms. Since 1972 each equally populated legislative district elects 1 senator and 2 representatives. The judicial branch is headed by a supreme court of 9 justices, elected for 6-year terms. Despite numerous attempts to institute one, Washington does not have a state income tax.

Washington voters have generally chosen Republican candidates in presidential elections; they did not vote for a Democrat until 1932, when the state first helped elect Franklin D. Roosevelt. Democrats, however, often have managed to win other election contests. Henry M. JACKSON, a Democrat, held his Senate seat from 1953 until his death in 1983.

History

American Indians have inhabited Washington for more than 10,000 years. The settled Coast Salish bands of western Washington included the CHINOOK, NISQUALLY, and PUYALLUP. The plateau Indians of the interior included the NEZ PERCÉ, OKANOGAN, SPOKAN, and YAKIMA.

Exploration and Confrontation. Early contacts between Indians and Europeans were abrupt and often brutal, and the consequences for the Indians were serious. Smallpox, cholera, and measles severely reduced the tribes' population, and subsequent white settlement led to loss of Indian lands and the establishment of reservations.

Coastal exploration by the Spanish began during the 16th century. The first landing was made in 1775, by Bruno Heceta and Juan Francisco de la Bodega y Quadra, near Point Grenville, to forestall Russian expansion southward from Alaska. The English captain James Cook sailed along the coast in 1778, and the American captain Robert GRAY discovered the Columbia River in 1792. The same year, Capt. George VANCOUVER completed the first mapping of the entire coastline. Overland exploration, initiated by the LEWIS AND CLARK EXPEDITION in 1805–06, was completed within a decade by David THOMPSON and various fur traders.

The Fur Trade and White Settlement. The fur trade constituted Washington's first major industry. Two companies, John Jacob Astor's (see ASTOR family) Pacific Fur Company—a subsidiary of his AMERICAN FUR COMPANY—and the Montreal-based NORTH WEST COMPANY, competed for the furs. Economic success came only with the HUDSON'S BAY COMPANY's takeover in 1821. Under the direction of Dr. John McLOUGHLIN, Fort Vancouver became the headquarters of operations that ranged from California to Alaska.

An influx of American missionaries, led by Marcus WHITMAN and Jason Lee, into the Oregon country during the 1830s was followed in the next decade by the first rush—5,000 strong—of American settlers, and the competing British and U.S. claims quickly came to a climax. British preference for the Columbia River and America's political slogan of "Fifty-four forty or fight!" (referring to the latitude 54°40') gave way to compromise, however, when, in 1846, the 49th parallel was chosen as the boundary between Canada and the United States (see OREGON QUESTION).

Through the 1850s, Oregon's Willamette River valley drew most of the Northwest's new settlers. In eastern Washington, the Whitman massacre at Waiilatpu in 1847 was followed by protracted Indian wars that lasted throughout the next decade and delayed occupation of the Columbia Basin. Meanwhile, settlements were established around Puget Sound—Olympia in 1846, Seattle and Port Townsend in 1851, and Whatcom (later Bellingham) in 1852.

Economic Growth and Statehood. A proposal for a Columbia Territory was passed by Congress in March 1853, with the name *Washington* being substituted by amendment. Isaac I. Stevens became the first territorial governor, and during the next few years treaties were signed between the United States and the Indian tribes, notably the Treaty of Point Eliot (1856). By the early 1860s most accessible land was owned and occupied. During the next three decades lumbering operations proliferated along Puget Sound. Coal and gold were discovered and mined, salmon canning begun, the Palouse River valley occupied and the so-called inland wheat empire established, irrigation of parts of the Columbia Basin attempted, and railroad lines built, notably the Northern Pacific and the Great Northern. By 1880 the population exceeded 75,000, and by 1890 it had reached 357,000. Seattle, Spokane, and Tacoma had emerged as major urban centers. In 1889, Washington became the 42d state.

20th Century. The 1893 depression was a major setback to growth, but by 1900 the state once again was making rapid progress, politically and socially as well as economically. The Depression years of the 1930s saw the inauguration of the Columbia Basin Project and the Bonneville Power Administration, to build dams and provide hydroelectric power. During the 1940s, Boeing emerged as a major international company, and manufacturing other than processing of local resources, finance, and tourism began to assume major roles in the state's economy. World War II and the wars in Korea and Vietnam provided further economic incentives. An economic downturn during the early 1970s, with massive layoffs by Boeing, has been succeeded by a new era of steady economic growth.

Washington, Booker T.

Booker Taliaferro Washington, b. Franklin County, Va., Apr. 5, 1856, d. Nov. 14, 1915, was a leading African-American educator. As a child he worked for 9 months of the year in the coal mines and attended school for 3. In this manner he worked his way through Hampton Institute, graduating in 1875. In 1881 he was appointed the first president of Tuskegee Institute (now TUSKEGEE UNIVERSITY), an Ala-

Booker T. Washington, an American educator and lecturer, was appointed (1881) head of Tuskegee Institute and oversaw its development as one of the first significant educational centers for blacks in the United States.

bama trade school for blacks. Tuskegee opened with one teacher, about 50 pupils, and funds of $2,000 a year from the state of Alabama. By its 25th anniversary under Washington's leadership, the school had more than 1,500 students training in 37 industries.

Believing that blacks would advance only if they were educated, Washington advocated training black people for trades so as to build up their economic strength. This strategy was opposed particularly by W. E. B. DU BOIS, who favored a more direct fight for racial equality. From 1895, Washington rapidly gained the attention of white leaders and became influential in channeling contributions to black causes and in getting blacks appointed to federal jobs. He advised Presidents Theodore Roosevelt and William Howard Taft on racial matters. Washington's autobiography, *Up From Slavery*, appeared in 1901.

Washington, D.C.

Washington, the capital of the United States, is located in and coterminous (as of 1878) with the DISTRICT OF COLUMBIA, a federally owned enclave surrounded on three sides by Maryland and across the Potomac River from Arlington and Fairfax counties, Va. The city is the center of a metropolitan area that is the eighth most populous in the country. The population of the city proper is 609,909 (1990), and that of the metropolitan area, 3,923,574. Washington is divided along a north-south axis by Rock Creek. Additions to the city's total land area—at present 179 km² (69 mi²)—have been made by adding landfill along the shores of the Potomac.

Contemporary City

As the seat of the U.S. government, Washington plays a unique role both in national and international life. As the only major planned city in the country, it is also one of the eastern seaboard's most impressive. The central northwestern portion of the city, surrounding the Mall, is the focus of governmental activity and is defined by the structures housing the various units of government: the CAPITOL, atop Capitol Hill; the WHITE HOUSE, at 1600 Pennsylvania Avenue; the Supreme Court; the LIBRARY OF CONGRESS; the State Department; the Justice Department; the Federal Bureau of Investigation; and many more. Interspersed among these buildings are the Washington Monument (163 m/535 ft; 1884); the Lincoln (1922) and Jefferson (1943) memorials on either side of the Tidal Basin, around which a profusion of Japanese cherry trees flowers each spring; and the imposing neo-Gothic facade of the SMITHSONIAN INSTITUTION. The PENTAGON complex lies across the Potomac in Virginia adjacent to ARLINGTON NATIONAL CEMETERY.

Economy. The economy of the city is predicated on its governmental role. More than a third of the work force is federally employed, with large numbers also employed in retailing, construction, and printing. Little manufacturing takes place. The embassies of more than 100 nations as well as several major international organizations, such as the World Bank, the International Monetary Fund, and the Organization of American States, are located there. Also headquartered in Washington are hundreds of na-

Some of the land-marks of Washington, D.C., the capital of the United States, include the Washington Monument (left), *the Capitol* (center), *and the Jefferson Memorial* (right foreground), *which overlooks the Tidal Basin and is adjacent to East Potomac Park.*

tional associations, nonprofit organizations, and research institutes, including the National Academy of Sciences, the Carnegie Institution, and the Brookings Institution. Tourism is Washington's second largest industry, catering to an estimated 17,500,000 annual visitors.

Washington has excellent national and international air linkage from Washington National and Dulles International airports as well as rail service to New York and Boston, Chicago, and points south. The city is a focal point on the Interstate Highway System, although direct access is only by way of a beltway girdling the city. A subway system (the Metro) began operating in downtown Washington in 1976.

Education and Culture. The city's major institutions of higher learning include Georgetown University (1789), The George Washington University (1821), Howard University (1867), Catholic University of America (1887), and American University (1893). Some of the world's outstanding art collections are located in the NATIONAL GALLERY OF ART, the National Portrait Gallery, the Hirshhorn Museum and Sculpture Garden, the Corcoran Gallery of Art, the Byzantine and pre-Columbian collections at DUMBARTON OAKS, the Freer Gallery of Art, and the Phillips Collection. Constituent parts of the Smithsonian Institution include museums devoted to arts and industries, natural history, air and space, and history and technology. The Library of Congress possesses the world's largest collection of books, manuscripts, and documents; the FOLGER SHAKESPEARE LIBRARY contains the largest collection of Shakespeareana. The National Archives houses the nation's historic documents and treasures. Among historic points of interest that can be visited are Ford's Theatre and the Frederick Douglass Home, now the Museum of African Art. A recent addition to the face of the city is the KENNEDY CENTER FOR THE PERFORMING ARTS. The Robert F. Kennedy Stadium is the home of the Washington Redskins. Recreational facilities include the National Arboretum; the National Zoo, located in Rock Creek Park (710 ha/1,754 acres), the city's largest in an extensive park system; and a boat basin on the Potomac.

History

George Washington personally selected the site of the nation's permanent capital in 1791, and the government was officially transferred there in 1800. Located close to the geographic center of the original 13 colonies, the area allotted measured 259 km² (100 mi²) and encompassed the existing port towns of Alexandria and Georgetown. The land west of the Potomac was returned to Virginia in 1846. Pierre Charles L'ENFANT's design (1791) for the city, developed after 1801, was limited to the area south of the present Florida Avenue. It consisted of a physical framework for the siting of major government buildings and a grid street pattern overlaid by broad radial avenues, with a series of squares and circles reserved for monuments.

The barely completed capital of the infant republic was captured and burned (1814) by the British during the War of 1812, but it was soon reconstructed. By 1860 its population was 61,100. Washington's first great period of development took place following the Civil War. The city's growth accelerated during the 1930s and particularly after World War II. The district's black population, which averaged a quarter to a third of the city's total between 1870 and 1950, now represents approximately two-thirds of the population, a trend reflecting the flight of the middle classes away from the urban center. The result is a capital city whose residential pattern is sharply divided along class and color lines. In addition to blacks, there are growing numbers of Hispanics (5.4%) and Asians (1.2%).

Today, between the historic core Washington and its mid-20th-century suburbs, lie a somewhat dilapidated 19th-century city east of Rock Creek, occupied mostly by blacks, and an early-20th-century city west of Rock Creek (which envelops the exclusive 18th-century and early-Federal Georgetown section), occupied largely by affluent whites. Black frustrations following the assassination of Martin Luther King, Jr., led to major riots in Washington in 1968. Today, as is the case with many other U.S. cities, Washington is contending with a major drug problem.

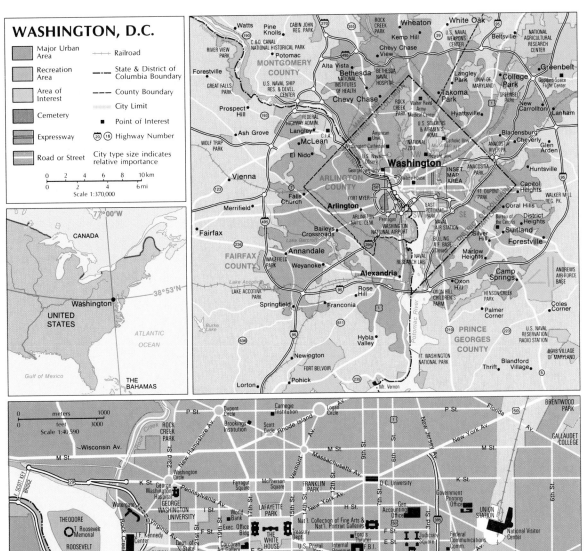
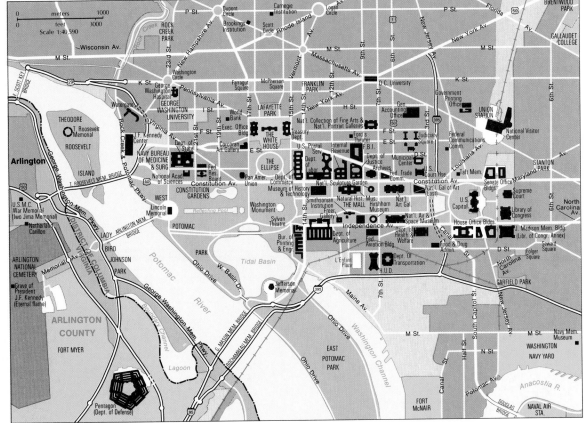

GEORGE WASHINGTON
1st President of the United States (1789–97)

Nickname: "Father of His Country"

Born: Feb. 22, 1732, Pope's Creek, Va.

Profession: Soldier, Planter

Religious Affiliation: Episcopalian

Marriage: Jan. 6, 1759, to Martha Dandridge Custis (1731–1802)

Children: None

Political Affiliation: Federalist

Writings: *Writings* (39 vols., 1931–44), ed. by John C. Fitzpatrick

Died: Dec. 14, 1799, Mount Vernon, Va.

Buried: Mount Vernon, Va. (family vault)

Vice-President: John Adams

Washington, George   George Washington was commander in chief of the Continental army during the AMERICAN REVOLUTION and first president of the United States (1789–97).

Early Life and Career. Born in Westmoreland County, Va., on Feb. 22, 1732, George Washington spent his early years on the family estate on Pope's Creek along the Potomac River. His early education included the study of such subjects as mathematics, surveying, the classics, and "rules of civility." His father died in 1743, and soon thereafter George went to live with his half brother Lawrence at MOUNT VERNON, Lawrence's plantation on the Potomac. Lawrence, who became something of a substitute father for his brother, had married into the Fairfax family, prominent and influential Virginians who helped launch George's career. In 1748 he secured an appointment to survey Lord Fairfax's lands in the Shenandoah Valley and

was later appointed surveyor for Culpeper County. When Lawrence died in 1752, George inherited the Mount Vernon estate.

By 1753 the growing rivalry between the British and French over control of the Ohio Valley, soon to erupt into the FRENCH AND INDIAN WAR (1754–63), created new opportunities for the ambitious young Washington. He first gained public notice when, as adjutant of one of Virginia's four military districts, he was dispatched (October 1753) by Gov. Robert DINWIDDIE on a fruitless mission to warn the French commander at Fort Le Boeuf against further encroachment on territory claimed by Britain. Washington's diary account of the dangers and difficulties of his journey, published at Williamsburg on his return, may have helped win him his ensuing promotion to lieutenant colonel at only 22 years of age.

French and Indian War. In April 1754, on his way to establish a post at the Forks of the Ohio (the current site of

Pittsburgh), Washington learned that the French had already erected a fort there. Warned that the French were advancing, he quickly threw up fortifications at Great Meadows, Pa., aptly naming the entrenchment Fort Necessity, and marched to intercept advancing French troops. After a skirmish Washington pulled his small force back into Fort Necessity, where he was overwhelmed (July 3) by the French. Surrounded by enemy troops, with his food supply almost exhausted and his dampened ammunition useless, Washington capitulated. Under the terms of the surrender signed that day, he was permitted to march his troops back to Williamsburg.

Discouraged by his defeat and angered by discrimination between British and colonial officers in rank and pay, he resigned his commission near the end of 1754. The next year, however, he volunteered to join British general Edward BRADDOCK's expedition against the French. When Braddock was ambushed by the French and their Indian allies on the Monongahela River, Washington, although seriously ill, tried to rally the Virginia troops. Whatever public criticism attended the debacle, Washington's own military reputation was enhanced, and in 1755, at the age of 23, he was promoted to colonel and appointed commander in chief of the Virginia militia, with responsibility for defending the frontier. In 1758 he took an active part in Gen. John FORBES's successful campaign against Fort Duquesne.

Virginia Politician. Assured that the Virginia frontier was safe from French attack, Washington left the army in 1758 and returned to Mount Vernon, directing his attention toward restoring his neglected estate. He erected new buildings, refurnished the house, and experimented with new crops. With the support of an ever-growing circle of influential friends, he entered politics, serving (1759–74) in Virginia's House of Burgesses. In January 1759 he married Martha Dandridge Custis, a wealthy and attractive young widow with two small children.

After 1769, Washington became a leader in Virginia's opposition to Great Britain's colonial policies. As a delegate (1774–75) to the First and Second Continental Congress, Washington did not participate actively in the deliberations, but his presence was a stabilizing influence. In June 1775 he was Congress's unanimous choice as commander in chief of the Continental forces.

American Revolution. Washington took command of the troops surrounding British-occupied Boston on July 3, devoting the next few months to training the undisciplined 14,000-man army and trying to secure urgently needed powder and other supplies. Early in March 1776, using cannon brought down from Ticonderoga by Henry KNOX, Washington occupied Dorchester Heights, effectively commanding the city and forcing the British to evacuate on March 17. He then moved to defend New York City against the combined land and sea forces of Sir William HOWE. In New York he committed a military blunder by occupying an untenable position in Brooklyn (see LONG ISLAND, BATTLE OF), although he saved his army by skillfully retreating from Manhattan into Westchester County and through New Jersey into Pennsylvania. In the last months of 1776, Washington was desperately short of men and supplies. He had lost New York City to the British; enlistment was almost up for a number of the troops, and others were deserting in droves; civilian morale was falling rapidly; and Congress, faced with the possibility of a British attack on Philadelphia, had withdrawn from the city.

Colonial morale was briefly revived by the capture of Trenton, N.J. (see TRENTON, BATTLE OF), a brilliantly conceived attack in which Washington crossed the Delaware River on Christmas night 1776 and surprised the predominantly Hessian garrison. Advancing to Princeton, N.J., he routed the British there on Jan. 3, 1777, but in September and October 1777 he suffered serious reverses in Pennsylvania—at BRANDYWINE and Germantown. The major success of that year—the defeat (October 1777) of the British at Saratoga, N.Y.—had belonged not to Washington but to Benedict ARNOLD and Horatio GATES. The contrast between Washington's record and Gates's brilliant victory was one factor that led to the so-called CONWAY CABAL—an intrigue by some members of Congress and army officers to replace Washington with a more successful commander, probably Gates. Washington acted quickly, and the plan collapsed due to lack of public support and Washington's overall superiority to his rivals.

After holding his bedraggled and dispirited army together during the difficult winter at VALLEY FORGE, Washington learned that France had recognized American independence. With the aid of the Prussian Baron von STEUBEN and the French marquis de LAFAYETTE, he concentrated on turning the army into a viable fighting force, and by spring he was ready to take the field again. In June 1778 he attacked the British near Monmouth Courthouse, N.J., on their withdrawal from Philadelphia to New York (see MONMOUTH, BATTLE OF). Although American general Charles LEE's lack of enterprise ruined Washington's plan to strike a major blow at Sir Henry CLINTON's army at Monmouth, the commander in chief's quick action on the field prevented an American defeat.

In 1780 the main theater of the war shifted to the south. Although the campaigns in Virginia and the Carolinas were conducted by other generals, including Nathanael GREENE and Daniel MORGAN, Washington was still responsible for the overall direction of the war. After the arrival of the French army in 1780 he concentrated on coordinating allied efforts and in 1781 launched, in cooperation with the comte de ROCHAMBEAU and the comte d'Estaing, the brilliantly planned and executed YORKTOWN CAMPAIGN against Charles CORNWALLIS, securing (Oct. 19, 1781) the American victory.

After the war Washington returned to Mount Vernon, which had declined in his absence. Although he became president of the Society of the Cincinnati, an organization of former Revolutionary War officers, he avoided involvement in Virginia politics, preferring to concentrate on restoring Mount Vernon. His diary notes a steady stream of visitors, native and foreign; Mount Vernon, like its owner, had already become a national institution.

In May 1787, Washington headed the Virginia delegation to the CONSTITUTIONAL CONVENTION in Philadelphia and was unanimously elected presiding officer. His presence lent prestige to the proceedings, and although he made few direct contributions, he generally supported the advocates of a strong central government. After the new Constitution was submitted to the states for ratification and became legally operative, he was unanimously elected president (1789).

The Presidency. Taking office (Apr. 30, 1789) in New York City, Washington acted carefully and deliberately, aware of the need to build an executive structure that could accommodate future presidents. Hoping to prevent sectionalism from dividing the new nation, he toured the New England states (1789) and the South (1791). An able administrator, he nevertheless failed to heal the widening breach between factions led by Secretary of State Thomas JEFFERSON and Secretary of the Treasury Alexander HAMILTON. Because he supported many of Hamilton's controversial fiscal policies—the assumption of state debts, the Bank of the United States, and the excise tax—Washington became the target of attacks by Jeffersonian Democratic-Republicans.

Washington was reelected president in 1792, and the following year the most divisive crisis arising out of the personal and political conflicts within his cabinet occurred—over the issue of American neutrality during the war between England and France. Washington, whose policy of neutrality angered the pro-French Jeffersonians, was horrified by the excesses of the French Revolution and enraged by the tactics of Edmond GENÊT, the French minister in the United States, which amounted to foreign interference in American politics. Further, with an eye toward developing closer commercial ties with the British, the president agreed with the Hamiltonians on the need for peace with Great Britain. His acceptance of the 1794 JAY'S TREATY, which settled outstanding differences between the United States and Britain but which Democratic-Republicans viewed as an abject surrender to British demands, revived vituperation against the president, as did his vigorous upholding of the excise law during the WHISKEY REBELLION in western Pennsylvania.

Retirement and Assessment. By March 1797, when Washington left office, the country's financial system was well established; the Indian threat east of the Mississippi had been largely eliminated; and Jay's Treaty and Pinckney's Treaty (1795) with Spain had enlarged U.S. territory and removed serious diplomatic difficulties. In spite of the animosities and conflicting opinions between Democratic-Republicans and members of the Hamiltonian Federalist party, the two groups were at least united in acceptance of the new federal government. Washington refused to run for a third term and, after a masterly Farewell Address in which he warned the United States against permanent alliances abroad, he went home to Mount Vernon. He was succeeded by his vice-president, Federalist John Adams.

Washington spent his last years in happy retirement at Mount Vernon. In mid-December, he contracted what was probably quinsy or acute laryngitis; he declined rapidly and died at his estate on Dec. 14, 1799.

Washington, Martha   Martha Dandridge Custis Washington, b. New Kent County, Va., June 2, 1731, d. May 22, 1802, the wife of George Washington, had previously been married (1749) to Daniel Parke Custis, a wealthy Virginia planter who died in 1757. She and Custis had four children: John Parke Custis (d. 1781), Martha Custis (d. 1773), and two others who died in infancy. Her marriage (1759–99) to Washington was childless. A gracious, sensible woman, Martha Washington acted as hostess for her husband but took no part in public affairs.

Martha Washington, the heiress of a Virginia landowning family, was a 27-year-old widow when she married George Washington in 1759. Washington adopted her two children and, later, two of her grandchildren.

Washington, Mount   Mount Washington, the highest peak in the northeastern United States, rises to 1,917 m (6,288 ft) in the Presidential Range of the WHITE MOUNTAINS in northern New Hampshire. The mountain is a popular outdoor sports area. Numerous hiking trails, a cog railway (1869), and a highway lead to the top. Known for its severe climate, the mountain is the site of a weather station that has recorded many of the strongest winds in the United States.

Washington, Walter   Walter Edward Washington, b. Dawson, Ga., Apr. 15, 1915, served (1975–78) as the first elected mayor of Washington, D.C. A Democrat, Washington had considerable government experience, particularly in the field of housing. Graduating from Howard University, he became executive director of the Capital Housing Authority (1961–66) in Washington, D.C., and was chairman of the New York City Housing Authority (1966–67).

Washington Conference   The Washington Conference (1921–22) was the first of several attempts at naval disarmament made after World War I. It was also an effort to stabilize East Asia and to provide for an independent Republic of China. The key political settlement of the conference was the Four Power Treaty (Dec. 13, 1921), in which the United States, Britain, Japan, and France pledged to consult one another if any of their island possessions in the Pacific were threatened. The same powers and Italy signed the Five Power Naval Armaments Treaty (February 1922), heralded as the most successful disarmament pact in history. It provided for a 10-year hiatus in building warships of more than 10,000 tons and established a ratio among the signatories regarding the number of these ships they could have. The London Naval Conference of 1930 (see LONDON, TREATIES AND CONFERENCES OF) extended the Washington agreement to cruisers and destroyers, but the Japanese abrogated the treaties in 1934.

Washington and Lee University

Washington and Lee University Established in 1749, Washington and Lee University is a private 4-year liberal arts school—originally for men but coeducational as of 1985—in Lexington, Va. Robert E. Lee was president of the school from 1865 to 1870. The college has a law school.

Washington Post, The

Washington Post, The Founded in 1877 and, since 1963, under the guidance of owner Katharine GRAHAM, *The Washington Post* is generally regarded as among the most authoritative and influential U.S. newspapers. The *Post*'s staff includes political cartoonist Herbert Block (Herblock) and editor Benjamin Bradlee. Reporters Carl Bernstein and Bob Woodward (see BERNSTEIN, CARL, AND WOODWARD, BOB) led the investigation into the WATERGATE scandal. Daily circulation is about 720,000. The Washington Post Company also owns *Newsweek* magazine, Newsweek Books, and several television stations.

Washo

Washo [wah'-shoh] The Washo are a North American Indian tribe of the Hokan linguistic stock who traditionally have lived in the Sierra Nevadas of California and western Nevada. They probably numbered between 1,000 and 3,000 before the mid-19th century. Families lived in conical, brush or tule-rush structures, sometimes covered with earth, in small villages seldom composed of more than 50 to 60 people. Leadership was informal and based on dreams, through which special powers were conferred to an individual by beings who appeared as animals, birds, or ghosts. SHAMANS cured the tribe's illnesses.

After about 1860, California gold seekers, settlers, and silver miners in Nevada gradually disrupted the Washo economy and way of life. The U.S. government made no treaty with the Washo but furnished an agent and allotted pine-nut gathering areas to individual families in accordance with the Dawes Act of 1887. Lacking a reservation, the Washo formed scattered settlements around ranches and then around towns. Today, probably fewer than 600 Washo live in colonies in California and Nevada.

wasp

wasp The term *wasp* generally refers to stinging members of the suborder Apocrita, order Hymenoptera, ex-

cluding bees and ants. Some nonstinging members of the suborder Symphyta (for example, the wood wasps) are also termed *wasps*. The term is derived from Anglo-Saxon words that apparently originated from the root *wefan* ("to weave"), in reference to the "woven" nests made by social paper wasps.

Of the Apocrita two superfamilies, Sphecoidea (sphecoid wasps) and Vespoidea (vespoid wasps), comprise the so-called true wasps. The sphecoid wasps are usually solitary. The sphecids (family Sphecidae) constitute a large group of graceful and colorful wasps that range from about 0.5 to 5 cm (0.25 to 2 in) in length. The vespoid wasps, either solitary or social, are usually combinations of black, red, or yellow. They include the hornets, the yellow jackets, the spider wasps, the tiphiids, and the scoliids.

In predaceous wasps the female ovipositor is modified as a sting and does not function as an egg-laying tool. The sting is used for defense and for subduing other insects, which are gathered as food for their young. These wasps usually build a nest of mud or plant material or excavate a nest in soil, crevices, or plant stems, where the prey is hidden and the egg is laid. Most such wasps are solitary and thus are not commonly noticed. The social wasps, however, live in colonies of up to several thousand members and are often conspicuous. In nonstingers, or wasps that live a "parasitic" form of life, the females use their ovipositor to inject an egg into or onto a host insect or spider. There is no nest construction, and the host is eventually killed by wasp larvae that feed on it.

Habits. All wasps undergo a complete metamorphosis, that is, there are egg, larval, pupal, and adult stages. Wasp larvae are rarely seen, because they are almost always hidden in a protected nest or host insect. Each species of predaceous, solitary wasp will generally collect only one type of prey, but some may take unrelated insects or, rarely, even act as scavengers, taking dead or dying insects.

There is great diversity in habits among solitary wasps. The mud-dauber (genus *Sceliphron*) nests in protected places, building mud cells that it provisions with several small spiders. The spider wasps (family Pompilidae), which dig their nest in the ground, prey on spiders, using one for each nest. The cicada killer (genus *Sphecius*) digs a hole in the ground, then buries a cicada in the nest with an egg.

Social Wasps. In the social wasps, also referred to as paper wasps, hornets, or yellow jackets, one to several females begin a colony by making small paper cells of masticated plant material mixed with saliva. One egg is laid per cell, and when it hatches the larva is fed chewed bits of other insects, especially caterpillars. Colonies of hornets and yellow jackets (genus *Vespula*) are founded by a single queen, but colonies of other paper wasps (such as the genus *Polistes*) may have several founder females. Eventually, however, only one female, the queen, lays eggs. When the larvae transform to adults, they join the queen in building and provisioning the colony.

Two basic types of paper nest are made in North America. One type has only a single layer of cells and is built above ground. The other type has multiple layers and is sur-

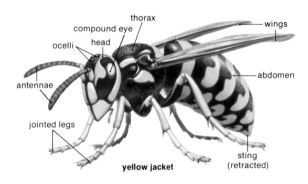

yellow jacket

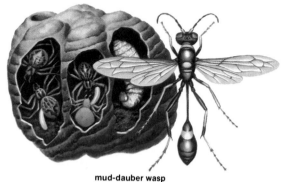

mud-dauber wasp

The yellow jacket is a paper wasp with a striking black-and-yellow pattern on its abdomen. Its external anatomy is typical of most wasps; the female has a sting—a modified ovipositor—in the tip of the abdomen. The mud dauber is a solitary wasp that builds its nest from mud; each cell within the nest is stocked with paralyzed spiders to feed the developing larvae.

rounded by a paper "envelope." It is often built in trees or in protected places such as abandoned animal burrows.

Importance. Solitary wasps are nonaggressive; even the largest generally sting humans only when handled. The social wasps, however, are aggressive and easily provoked, and they sting in numbers when disturbed. Despite this hazard most wasps aid humans greatly by destroying many insect pests.

Wassermann, August von [vahs'-ur-mahn] The German immunologist August Paul von Wassermann, b. Feb. 21, 1866, d. Mar. 16, 1925, developed (1906) the Wassermann reaction test, a blood test to detect antibodies in people infected with the syphilis bacteria, *Treponema pallidum*. The Wassermann test has been largely replaced by more specific and rapid tests. Wassermann earlier worked on developing an inoculation against cholera and an antitoxin against diphtheria. He later devised diagnostic tests for tuberculosis.

Wassermann, Jakob The German novelist Jakob Wassermann, b. Mar. 10, 1873, d. Jan. 1, 1934, first

achieved recognition with *The Dark Pilgrimage* (1897; Eng. trans., 1933), a novel that concerns the plight of persecuted Jews seeking salvation in a new community. His most famous work, *Caspar Hauser* (1908; Eng. trans., 1928), was based on the true incident of a youth who suddenly appeared on the streets of Nuremberg in 1828 and could neither walk nor speak. In his ambitious Kerkhoven trilogy—*The Maurizius Case* (1928; Eng. trans., 1929), *Doctor Kerkhoven* (1931; Eng. trans., 1932), and *Joseph Kerkhoven's Third Existence* (1934; Eng. trans., 1934)—Wassermann postulated a system of ethics and religion that would save humanity from decadence.

waste disposal systems The problem of waste management and disposal becomes increasingly pressing as human population, industrial activity, and material consumption expand. The collection and disposal of municipal wastes poses the most visible solid-waste management problem; agricultural and mining wastes, however, dwarf urban wastes in magnitude, and industrial wastes present a severe danger to the environment.

Agricultural and Mining Wastes. Agricultural and mining wastes are generally disposed of on the land from which they came. When not adequately contained, however, these wastes have caused the contamination of runoff and receiving waters. Agricultural wastes, particularly animal wastes, contain valuable nutrients that traditionally were returned to the soil. Recently, however, agricultural wastes have come to be seen as a disposal problem rather than as a usable commodity.

As the cost of chemical fertilizers increases, the residuals from organic-waste treatment, or the untreated wastes themselves, may once again become a significant source of soil nutrients.

Industrial Wastes. Hazardous industrial wastes, although often in liquid form, are generally treated the same as solid wastes because they must be kept from receiving waters. Radioactive or chemically toxic wastes must be adequately contained in special disposal areas.

Municipal Wastes. The residential and commercial wastes of municipalities cause litter, open dumps, leaching of water pollutants, ocean contamination, air pollution from burning wastes, and wasted resources. Before the 1960s most of the urban refuse produced in the United States was burned in open dumps or in inadequate incinerators. Today, most municipal waste is buried in sanitary LANDFILLS. Many landfills, however, are nearly filled, and are closing.

Urban refuse contains large quantities of potentially usable paper fiber, glass, metals, organic material for compost, and energy (see RECYCLING OF MATERIALS). A traditional urban waste-disposal method is incineration, which reduces the volume of the waste by about 90%. Drawbacks to incineration include air pollution and the disposal of the residue, or "fly ash," that remains after the incineration process (see POLLUTANTS, CHEMICAL).

Energy Recovery. Energy is perhaps the easiest resource to extract from solid waste. About 70% to 80% of residential and commercial solid waste is combustible, and it has about one-third the heating value of an equal weight of coal.

Energy can be recovered in several ways. First, the raw wastes can be incinerated with the heat used to produce steam for heating buildings; noncombustible materials can be recovered from the ashes. Second, the refuse can be shredded into small pieces, then air-classified by blowing the wastes up into a column, separating out the light material (termed RDF, for refuse-derived fuel), which is suitable as fuel; the heavy material remaining at the bottom of the column contains reclaimable metals and glass. Third, the separated combustibles can be incinerated in clean combustion units, such as fluidized beds, to produce high-pressure gases that can run gas turbines and generate electricity. Finally, the lighter organic wastes may be decomposed chemically by PYROLYSIS to produce oil or gas fuels.

With the cost of energy increasing in the 1970s, the use of the energy content of solid wastes began to receive more attention. Several cities have constructed or are planning facilities to extract energy from waste. About 70 energy-recovery plants are already in operation or are undergoing testing in the United States.

Efforts to increase the extraction of energy and materials from urban refuse will continue as the costs of energy, disposal, and raw materials rise. Although the movement toward recycling and energy production from wastes may be helpful, it is not expected to reduce waste-disposal loads so long as a high-consumption, throwaway society continues to generate increasing quantities of discarded material.

See also: POLLUTION, ENVIRONMENTAL.

Waste Land, The

Waste Land, The T. S. ELIOT's most famous poem, *The Waste Land* (1922) helped establish and is considered prototypical of the so-called modern sensibility in literature and the arts. Replete with obscure literary, historical, and mythical allusions, as well as intricate patterns of symbolism, the five-part poem represents the modern world as vacuous and lacking in spiritual vitality. Eliot uses an array of cultural references and an interplay of reflection and description in order to demonstrate the possibility of existence becoming a ceremonious order testifying to physical and spiritual well-being. *The Waste Land*, originally almost twice its published 434-line length, was edited by Ezra Pound.

watch see CLOCKS AND WATCHES

Watch Tower Bible and Tract Society see JEHOVAH'S WITNESSES

water Water is the most common substance on Earth, covering more than 70 percent of the planet's surface. All living things consist mostly of water; for example, the human body is about two-thirds water. Earth, air, fire, and water were considered by the ancient philosophers to be the four chemical elements, a concept that persisted through the Middle Ages. It was not until 1781 that Henry Cavendish showed that water was obtained by the combustion of hydrogen. Shortly afterward the discovery was made that water could be electrolytically decomposed into two volumes of hydrogen and one volume of oxygen, but the chemical formula of water was a matter of controversy until 1860, when Stanislao Cannizzaro established it as H_2O.

Water is a clear, colorless liquid that appears blue when its depth is at least 6 m (20 ft). The color results not only from physical causes but also from suspended impurities. In terms of its chemical composition, water has an unusually high boiling point (100° C/212° F) and freezing point (0° C/32° F). These discrepancies result from the strong attraction that each water molecule has for others (see HYDROGEN BOND), so that the energy required to melt the solid and boil the liquid is greater than might be predicted. Water also shows unusual volume changes with temperature. As warm water cools, it contracts until it reaches its maximum density at 4° C (39° F); further cooling effects an expansion of the liquid phase, and another expansion occurs when the liquid freezes to ice. Both of these peculiarities occur because of the formation of highly ordered arrangements of hydrogen bonding of the water molecules.

Pure water is a poor conductor of electricity, but the impurities found in natural water transform it into a relatively good conductor. The ability of water to act as a universal solvent as well as its high dielectric constant (about 80) are a result of the polar nature of the water molecule.

water, desalination of see DESALINATION

water beetle Water beetles spend both their larval and adult life stages in fresh water. Also known as diving beetles, about 4,000 species make up the family Dytiscidae. Air-breathing, water beetles come to the surface at intervals, fly between bodies of water, and approach light at night. The adults and larvae, known as water tigers, are voracious, feeding on small animal matter. The term *water beetle* is also applied to water scavenger beetles and whirligig beetles.

water boatman The water boatman is a small aquatic insect—any of about 200 species making up the family Corixidae—often abundant in freshwater ponds and lakes. Less than 1 cm (0.4 in) long, it is dark, oval, and somewhat flattened, with long, oarlike hind legs used for swimming. Air bubbles carried on the body surface or under the wings provide water boatmen with oxygen when they are underwater, clinging to bottom debris for prolonged periods. They eat algae and microorganisms.

water buffalo   see ANIMAL HUSBANDRY; BUFFALO

water bug   Water bug is a name commonly given several different insects that spend all or part of their lives in water. These include the water strider, water boatman, water beetle, and backswimmer. The true giant water bugs, found in most tropical and temperate regions, make up the family Belostomatidae. Large, flat, usually brownish insects, they have strong beaks, front legs adapted for prey capture, and back legs adapted for swimming. Strong fliers, they often approach light at night and hence are frequently called electric light bugs; they can inflict a painful wound if handled.

water chestnut   The water chestnut may be one of two quite different kinds of plants. The trapa nut, *Trapa natans*, a Eurasian plant naturalized in the eastern United States and also kept in ponds and aquariums, has floating leaves and edible seeds 2.5 to 5 cm (1 to 2 in) in diameter. The Chinese water chestnut, *Eleocharis dulcis*, is an Old World sedge grown in flooded fields under tropical conditions. Its tubers, which reach 4 cm (1.5 in) in diameter, are used in Chinese dishes. It is also grown in the southern United States.

water clock   see CLEPSYDRA

water hyacinth   Water hyacinth is the common name for the aquatic herb *Eichhornia crassipes* of the family Pontederiaceae. Native to tropical America, it has become naturalized to the ponds, quiet streams, and ditches of the southeastern United States. The plants have ovate leaves with large, inflated petioles that aid in flotation, and long, trailing, feathery roots. The large, showy violet flowers have conspicuous markings.

Water hyacinth has become a troublesome weed, clogging otherwise navigable watercourses and irrigation ditches in the United States and Australia. It is a good absorber of pollutants, however, and may be useful in water-treatment systems and sewage-disposal plants.

water lily   Water lily is the common name for more than 40 species of aquatic plants of the water lily family, Nymphaeaceae. Some species are known as LOTUSES. Found throughout temperate and tropical regions, water lilies are characterized by large, nearly circular, leathery floating leaves and by white, yellow, pink, red, scarlet, blue, or purple flowers that float or are supported by stems above the water surface.

Water lilies are generally divided into two groups: tropicals, which are usually annuals and are further classified as day or night bloomers; and hardy varieties, which grow as perennials. The night-blooming tropicals are normally fragrant; the scent attracts insects for pollination.

Following the return of the rains, primitive peoples witnessed the rise of the undefiled water lily from the bottom

The common North American water lily produces small, lotuslike flowers that are attached to underwater stems. Its floating leaves are known as lily pads.

of dried-up watercourses and considered the living blooms symbols of immortality and resurrection.

water moccasin   The water moccasin, or cottonmouth, *Agkistrodon piscivorus*, is a venomous snake. Because it has heat-sensory pits located behind the nostrils, it is classified in the pit viper family, Crotalidae. Related to the copperhead, water moccasins inhabit freshwater swamps, shallow lakes, and slow-moving streams in the southeastern United States. They may leave the water to hibernate on ledges, and occasionally they enter salt water. The water moccasin ranges from 76 to 114 cm (30 to 45 in) in length, with a few reaching 1.8 m (6 ft). The young have light and dark bands of brown and a yellow tail, and the adults are dark olive, brown, or black. Their diet consists of frogs, fish, and other small animals. Water moccasins mate in spring and bear 5 to 12 young in late summer.

The water moccasin's threatening posture, with the head lifted and the mouth wide open, reveals the mouth's white lining—hence the name *cottonmouth*. The bite is rarely fatal but causes severe pain and local tissue damage.

The water moccasin, or cottonmouth, is a venomous snake found in the southeastern United States.

water mold The water mold, genus *Saprolegnia*, is an aquatic MOLD belonging to the phylum Oomycetes of the kingdom Fungi. Water mold appears most commonly as a gray fuzz on dead animals in water. The mold causes diseases in fish and fish eggs and may do significant damage in fish hatcheries.

water pollution see POLLUTION, ENVIRONMENTAL

water polo The sport of water polo is a team game that demands swimming skills, body balance and control, and passing and throwing abilities. It is one of the world's most demanding sports. The object is to score as many goals as possible by throwing the waterproofed ball into the opponent's goal. In the Olympic Games and other formal competitions, water polo is played in a pool with a playing area 30 m (98.4 ft) long and 20 m (65.6 ft) wide. The minimum depth must be 2 m (6.56 ft) in order to prevent the players from standing on the pool bottom. A team consists of a goalie—the only player allowed to hold the ball with two hands—three defenders, and three forwards. Each player must wear a colored and numbered cap. Fouls are called by the referee for taking the ball underwater, holding a player who does not have the ball, holding onto the side of the pool or pushing off from it

According to internationally observed regulations, a water polo team consists of 11 players, 7 of whom are permitted in the water at any one time. The players of opposing teams are distinguished by their caps (1). Play begins when the single referee (2) throws the ball into the pool at the half-distance line (3) and players swim out from their respective goal lines (4) to retrieve the ball. While on offense, no player may pass the 2-m line (5) without possesion of the ball. Penalty shots are awarded in the case of major fouls. Such shots are attempted from a line 4 m (6) from the goal.

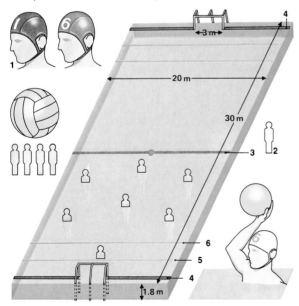

with the feet, and touching the ball with both hands at the same time. For serious infractions a team is awarded a free throw or a penalty shot at the opponent's goal. Teamwork is very important. The ball is advanced or passed with one hand, or dribbled by pushing the ball forward between the arms with the chest or forehead on the water. Defenders may "tackle" the player with the ball to impede his or her motion.

Water polo originated in Great Britain in the early 1870s when both swimming and polo were enjoying great popularity. The game was originally called water football because of the characteristics it shared with soccer. The early game was unsafe and rough; in the modern game excessively rough play is penalized. Water polo was first played in the United States in 1888 and introduced into the Olympics in 1900. Hungary, Yugoslavia, and the Soviet Union have traditionally dominated international and Olympic competition, but in recent years U.S. teams have been stronger than previously.

water quality The suitability of water for aquatic life and for human use depends on its quality. All natural waters contain dissolved inorganic and organic substances. The total dissolved-solids burden of rivers is generally between 20 and 2,000 parts per million and may be higher in groundwater. In natural (unpolluted) surface waters, the major dissolved solids are calcium, magnesium, sodium, potassium, sulfate, chloride, carbonate, bicarbonate, and silica. In the United States the average concentration of dissolved matter ranges from about 50 parts per million in the humid western mountains and the Appalachians up to 1,000 parts per million in the arid nonmountainous regions of the West.

Many pollutants may also be found in solution, either as large increases of substances normally present, such as nitrates, phosphates, and certain metals, or as synthetic substances, such as pesticides (see POLLUTION, ENVIRONMENTAL). The pH of water—a measure of acidity or alkalinity—is an important quality factor. The acidity of rainwater has been greatly increased (from a normal pH of 5.6 to between pH 4 and 5) in some regions by atmospheric pollutants (see ACID RAIN). Another measure of water quality is dissolved oxygen. Animals that live in water depend on dissolved oxygen for life. A marked decrease of dissolved oxygen because of bacterial decay of organic wastes has been a major impact of water pollution (see EUTROPHICATION).

Suspended sediment affects water quality by reducing light penetration, smothering fish eggs and other bottom life, filling lakes and reservoirs, and making water undesirable for many uses. Fecal-coliform bacteria in water are an important index of water quality. Derived from the intestines of mammals (including humans), they indicate the possibility that disease organisms are present. Water temperature, a final qualitative factor, influences the metabolic rate of aquatic organisms and the rates of chemical reactions. Significant increases of temperature caused by industrial discharges of heated water may be detrimental to aquatic life, a condition termed *thermal pollution*.

water resources The Earth's water resources comprise the total volume of fresh water available for human use and management. Less than 3% of the Earth's total volume of water is fresh, and almost four-fifths of this is essentially unavailable because it is in the form of glacial ice. Of the remaining quantity of liquid fresh water, most is underground, with an average of only 5% present as surface water—lakes and streams—at any time.

Water resources are more meaningfully measured in terms of flow rates, rather than volumes, however. The average precipitation rate is the rate at which water is delivered to the land, but a significant portion of this (two-thirds on a worldwide basis) returns directly to the atmosphere by evapotranspiration (see HYDROLOGIC CYCLE). The difference between precipitation rate and evapotranspiration rate is called the runoff rate or water yield. This runoff eventually enters the surface-water system of rivers, streams, and lakes, either directly or as groundwater seepage.

Runoff

The world average runoff rate represents about 39,000 km^3 per year (28.1×10^{12} gal/day). This flow is the amount theoretically available for direct human use and management, and represents a maximum estimate of world water resources.

The groundwater component of runoff is not a separate water resource from surface water. GROUNDWATER is recharged by percolation of rain and snowmelt and flows into lakes and streams as an integral part of the interconnected system by which runoff drains ultimately to the ocean. The actual amount of water available to supply human needs is substantially less than the total average runoff, streamflow being highly variable over time, so runoff from groundwater represents the more realistic estimate of the manageable water resource available on a continental basis.

Variability of streamflow is the critical factor in developing a practical estimate of the water resources of a region. This variability is determined by the climate, particularly the seasonal and year-to-year variations in PRECIPITATION, evapotranspiration, and snowmelt; the degree to which groundwater seepage contributes to streamflow; and the degree to which lakes, swamps, and reservoirs store streamflow and compensate for its variability.

Uses and Needs

Consideration of WATER QUALITY as well as of flow variability is also important in evaluating water resources, because water cannot be applied to a given use unless its quality is suitable for that use.

Use of water can be classified in two major ways: instream use versus withdrawal, and consumptive use versus nonconsumptive. Instream uses include navigation, generation of hydroelectric power, maintenance of water quality, provision for fish and wildlife habitat, and fulfillment of aesthetic goals. Withdrawal uses involve removal of water from streams or groundwater. Water that is either evaporated, transpired, incorporated into products, or discharged into a saltwater body, where it is not available for reuse, is said to be consumed.

The demand for the water resource in any stretch of river is the sum of the amount required for instream purposes (such as maintenance of water quality), plus the amount required for withdrawal. That which is withdrawn but not consumed is available for reuse downstream, usually after treatment.

Total worldwide water withdrawal is approximately 2,400 km^3/yr (1.7×10^{12} gal/day) and is allocated as follows: 2% to rural domestic uses, 8% to urban domestic uses, 8% to industrial uses, and the remaining 82% to agricultural IRRIGATION. Projections for the middle of the 21st century are an almost tenfold growth in world water withdrawals, to about 20,000 km^3/yr (14.5×10^{12} gal/day), well beyond the amount that the world's rivers can supply. Water may therefore become a scarce resource, limiting population growth during the next century.

In the United States, total withdrawals of fresh water amount to about 480 km^3/yr (0.35×10^{12} gal/day), of which 74% is from surface water and 26% from groundwater. This water is allocated as follows: 58% to industry, 34% to irrigation, 7% to urban water supplies, and 1% to rural water supplies. Of the water withdrawn, only 23% is used consumptively. Irrigation is by far the heaviest consumer of water, accounting for 83%, whereas urban supplies account for 7%, industry for 6%, and rural supplies for 4%.

The United States, the Soviet Union, India, and China are by far the world's largest users of water. Together the four nations withdraw approximately 45% of the total amount worldwide. As compared to the United States, the Soviet Union uses about 51% of its withdrawn water for irrigation, roughly 45% for industry and electricity production, and about 4% for domestic purposes. India uses almost 96% of its withdrawn water for irrigation, only about 3% for industry and electricity production, and 1% for domestic purposes. China uses about 93% of its withdrawn water for irrigation, approximately 5% for industry and electricity production, and 2% for domestic purposes.

Of these four leading nations, the United States is the only one that already has more land under irrigation than it requires. In fact, some areas have already stopped crop irrigation because of depletion of groundwater supplies. All four nations face increasing problems of pollution of their water resources, and China, India, and the Soviet Union also face special problems of distribution of those resources.

water softener A water softener is a device or a substance that removes, or renders inactive and isolates, ions such as calcium, magnesium, iron, or manganese in hard water. Water containing dissolved calcium and magnesium salts, or ferrous iron, in amounts greater than 120 mg/l is considered hard. Hard water forms scale—a deposit of carbonate salts—on the inner surfaces of boilers, cooking utensils, and pipes that carry hot water or steam. Iron oxidizes, reddening the water. Mineral salts precipitate the fatty acids from soap in the form of a scum or a gelatinous curd.

Because of the problems created by hard water, both for industry and for domestic water users, various types of water softeners have been developed. Water passed through a polystyrene ion-exchange filter gives up calcium and magnesium ions for sodium ions from ZEOLITES in the filter. The addition of lime to hard water precipitates mineral salts. Borax and sodium carbonate are also precipitating softeners. Trisodium phosphate, once a major ingredient of detergent washing powders, is an efficient water softener but is no longer used because of the pollution problems it creates.

water spaniel   see AMERICAN WATER SPANIEL

water strider   Water striders are aquatic insects (family Gerridae) often found in large numbers on quiet pond waters. They use their long, slender, hair-covered middle and hind legs to steer and propel themselves on the water surface, making little dimples on the surface film. Shorter, grasping forelimbs are used to capture small insect prey. With the exception of one marine genus—*Halobates*—all water striders are found in fresh water, and a few are specialized for swift-moving waters.

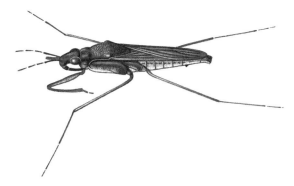

The water strider, or pond skater, of Europe lives on ponds and similar quiet waters. Fine, dry leg bristles keep it afloat. It detects its prey, mostly insects, by sight and vibrations sensed through its legs.

water supply   A water supply provides water for use in homes and industries, for irrigation, for extinguishing fires, for street cleaning, for carrying wastes to treatment facilities, and for many other purposes. The three most important factors in any water supply are its quality, the quantities available, and the location of the water supply relative to the points of use.

A typical water-supply system consists of six functional elements: a source of supply; storage facilities; transmission facilities for transporting water from the points of storage to a treatment plant; treatment facilities for altering water quality; transmission facilities for transporting water to intermediate points, such as standpipes or water towers; and distribution facilities for bringing water to individual users.

Sources

Rainwater falls on a watershed (catchment area) and either flows above ground to streams and rivers or soaks into the ground to reappear in springs or to be drawn from wells (see HYDROLOGIC CYCLE).

The amount of rainwater that will enter a water-supply system depends on the amount of precipitation and the volume of the runoff. About two-thirds of the annual average precipitation in the United States is lost to the atmosphere by evaporation and transpiration. The remaining water becomes runoff into rivers and lakes or, through infiltration, replenishes groundwater (see WATER RESOURCES).

Surface Water. Surface water is obtained from lakes, streams, rivers, or ponds. Storage reservoirs—artificial lakes created by constructing DAMS across stream valleys—can hold back higher-than-average flows and release them when greater flows are needed. Water supplies may be taken directly from reservoirs or from locations downstream of the dams.

Groundwater. GROUNDWATER supplies come from natural springs, from wells (see WATER WELL), and from infiltration galleries, basins, or cribs. Most small, and many large, North American water systems use groundwater as their source of supply.

Water Reuse. Only a small portion of the water that is supplied to dwellings, commercial and industrial establishments, and public facilities is consumed by evaporation and processing. The remaining wastewater (usually after treatment) is discharged to the soil and either infiltrates to groundwater or is discharged to surface watercourses.

Transmission and Distribution Systems

Water from a river, lake, or reservoir flows through an intake structure into the transmission system. The intake pipe from a groundwater source is connected to a pump and transmission conduit that conveys the water to a distribution system.

Transmission. A good example of a large city's water-supply and transmission system is that of New York City. This complicated system draws water from as far as the east branch of the Delaware River and conveys the water in gravity tunnels over a course that exceeds 160 km (100 mi). The New York City system was begun in 1830 with the building of the Croton Reservoir, an impoundment of the Croton River. The reservoir was completed in 1842 and captured the flow from a watershed draining 975 km² (375 mi²). The system has grown along with the population.

Distribution. In cities the distribution system generally follows the street patterns, but it is also affected by topography; types of residential, commercial, and industrial developments; and location of treatment facilities and storage works. Street mains usually have a minimum diameter of 15–20 cm (6–8 in) to provide adequate flows for buildings and for fighting fires. The pipes connected to buildings may range down to as small as 2.5 cm (1 in) for small residences.

Water Treatment

All natural waters contain inorganic and organic substances. The types and amounts of these substances depend upon exposure to physical, chemical, and biological actions in the hydrologic cycle (for example, addition of sediment from erosion) and contamination by pollutants caused by human activities. The treatment of water supplies depends on the quality of the source of the surface water or groundwater and the standards established for a specific water use.

Many water supplies can be used with little or no treatment for cooling and for many types of agriculture. Substantial treatment may, however, be needed for some types of industrial processes and for domestic uses. All public water supplies must meet the standards established by the 1974 Safe Drinking Water Act, which relate to physical and chemical characteristics and to pesticide contaminants. These standards are updated periodically by the Environmental Protection Agency.

Water-treatment plants are generally designed to remove the following principal contaminants: pathogenic bacteria; trace organic compounds; substances producing color, taste, and odor; suspended materials; and minerals causing hardness. To meet drinking-water standards, water is treated by any number of combinations of processes that can be broken down into two distinct categories, physical and chemical.

Physical Treatment. The most common methods of physical treatment are screening, aeration, flocculation, sedimentation, and filtration. Screening usually requires the use of coarse screening or bars 2.5 to 5 cm (1 to 2 in) apart to remove large floating and suspended debris from the water. Microscreens are drumlike fine-mesh screens (23- to 65-micron aperture sizes) designed to remove fine suspended material. Aeration is a gas-transfer operation used to remove carbon dioxide and hydrogen sulfide, and to oxidize dissolved iron and manganese and volatile oils.

Flocculation is a gentle agitation of flocculant precipitates that result from the addition of coagulant chemicals. The purpose of this gentle agitation is to conglomerate particulates into large clumps that will settle. Sedimentation removes particles from the water by allowing them to settle in a tank. Filtration removes finely suspended material from the water by the use of a layer of sand—or sand with crushed coal—supported by a gravel bed.

Chemical Treatment. The more common methods of chemical treatment include coagulation, disinfection, water softening, adsorption, and oxidation. Coagulation involves the addition to water of a chemical, such as alum, that induces the formation of precipitates of fine and colloidal suspended material. This material forms flocs that will settle in a sedimentation basin.

Disinfection is the destruction of pathogenic organisms in a water supply. Chlorine is the most commonly used disinfectant, and chlorination is usually the last step in a water-treatment system. The extent of chlorine use is being reduced because of evidence of the formation of cancer-causing compounds in chlorination.

Water softening (see WATER SOFTENER) is the removal from water of minerals that cause hardness, such as calcium and magnesium.

Adsorption is a process for the removal of organic chemicals—some of which cannot be removed by conventional water-treatment processes—by activated carbon. Adsorption is the clinging of materials to the surface of the carbon granules. Activated carbon presents a tremendous amount of surface area in relation to the net volume of granules used.

Oxidation, a type of chemical reaction, is used to convert undesirable substances to less-harmful forms.

DESALINATION (desalting), the conversion of saline water to fresh water, is a technique that is increasingly used where freshwater supplies are insufficient. Methods of desalination include distillation, freezing, demineralization by ion exchange, electrodialysis, or reverse osmosis.

Wastewater Collection and Disposal

Wastewater Collection. Seventy to ninety percent of the water distributed in a community by a public water-supply system is discharged after use to wastewater collection and disposal systems. In small communities, dispos-

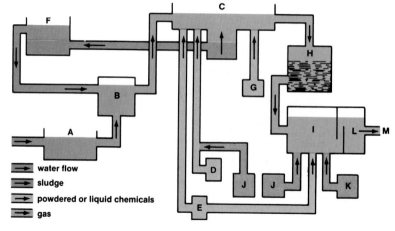

A modern water-treatment plant uses a combination of physical and chemical methods to make polluted water safe for consumption. Raw water from a river source is screened at the intake (A). Pumps (B) draw the water into an upward-flow sedimentation tank (C), to which is added aluminum sulfate (D), as a flocculant, and lime slurry (E), as a softener and acidity regulator. Sludge formed in the tank is pumped to a sludge lagoon (F), where its liquid is recycled. As the water leaves the tank, activated carbon (G) is added to adsorb impurities that produce unpleasant tastes, odors, and colors. The water passes through a filter in a rapid-gravity sand tank (H), then continues to a contact tank (I) where it is treated with additional lime, sterilized with chlorine gas (J), and dechlorinated with sulfur dioxide (K). Pumps (L) convey the purified water to the main water-supply system (M).

→ water flow
→ sludge
→ powdered or liquid chemicals
→ gas

al is often by individual building facilities, such as septic tanks and tile fields that extend into the soil. In larger cities, and in small communities where soil conditions are not appropriate for individual systems, extensive piping systems, following the street alignments, accept wastewater discharges and lead to wastewater treatment plants. The pipes in the wastewater-collection systems are usually placed on down slopes to sustain gravity flow.

Wastewater Disposal. Wastewater can be treated by a number of systems. The conventional method, however, is a combination physical-chemical-biological system that removes specified amounts of organic matter, nitrogen, phosphorus, and other material. A typical plant would include primary settling tanks for the removal of readily settleable solids. This is usually followed by a biological treatment unit, such as a trickling filter or an activated sludge-aeration tank, in which microorganisms digest the organic matter in the waste and develop cell mass while reducing concentrations of organic wastes. The waste stream then enters a sedimentation basin in which the cell mass and other suspended materials are settled out. The water that leaves this basin is then chlorinated and discharged to a receiving stream or other water body. (See SEWERAGE; WASTE DISPOSAL SYSTEMS.)

Critical Water-Supply Issues

Problems of inadequate water and sanitation facilities exist throughout the world and have been particularly acute in the poorer countries. The World Health Organization estimated that at the end of 1975, 25% of the people in developing countries had no access to potable water by house connections or standpipes. In rural areas, almost 80% did not have reasonable access to safe water. Considering both rural and urban populations, only 35% were adequately served. Although many new systems have been constructed in recent years, the growth of population has imposed even greater needs, and there has probably been little overall improvement.

In the economically advanced countries, close to 100% of the urban population and most of the rural population is served by safe and dependable supplies. Most water-supply systems in the United States have dependable supplies, control waterborne disease, and provide water with acceptable color, odor, and taste; critical problems of water supply do exist, however, in various locations in the United States.

Competing offstream uses of water for energy, agriculture, and municipal and industrial needs, coupled with associated environmental and instream flow requirements (for hydroelectric power, for example), have caused severe basinwide and local problems. Diminished water pressure, declining spring and stream flow, land subsidence, and saltwater intrusion have resulted from excessive withdrawals of ground water.

Pollution in watercourses used for water supplies is a problem in many areas, caused by direct and indirect discharges of municipal and industrial wastes and by surface runoff from rainfall on urbanized, agricultural, and mining areas. Groundwater pollution is recognized increasingly as a serious problem, due to contamination from animal feedlots, community landfills, toxic and hazardous materials, septic tanks and cesspools, and municipal and industrial discharges. Once contaminated, groundwater recovery is typically slow, and the cost of treating water from such sources is high.

At least 4,000 cases of waterborne illness, primarily of bacterial or viral origin, are still reported each year, but the actual total, including more-difficult-to-identify chemical poisonings, is larger. Medical science has begun to address the issues of chemical carcinogens that involve latency periods of 20 or more years before disease symptoms can be identified, as well as problems of acute chemical toxicity.

Development of Public Water-Supply Systems

Water-supply and disposal systems began with the growth of ancient cities. The earliest record of central water-supply and wastewater disposal dates back to the city of Nippur in Sumer, 5,000 years ago. Water there was drawn from wells and cisterns, and an extensive drainage system conveyed the wastes from palaces and residential areas of the city.

Water-treatment knowledge dates from 2000 BC, when Sanskrit writings indicate that methods for purification of foul water consisted of boiling in copper vessels, exposing to sunlight, filtering through charcoal, and cooling in earthern vessels.

The most notable ancient water-supply and waste-disposal systems were those of Rome. In AD 97, Sextus Julius Frontinus, then water commissioner of Rome, reported the existence of nine aqueducts of lengths varying from 16 to more than 80 km (10 to 50 mi), with cross sections of $\frac{1}{2}$ to $4\frac{1}{2}$ m^2 (7 to 50 ft^2). Such a system had an estimated aggregate capacity of 84 million gallons per day.

The strides in water supply and waste disposal in ancient times were notable; quality control and public-health practices, however, are of recent origin. The Industrial Revolution created industrial centers to which people flocked for employment. Because of inadequate city water-supply and waste-disposal systems, disease began to increase significantly. Water was drawn from polluted rivers and shallow wells contaminated by untreated, disease-bearing sewage.

The large cities had been provided with extensive storm-drainage systems, and the discharge of human wastes into them had been forbidden until the crowding in the cities, which caused sanitation problems of monumental proportions, forced their use. The use of the storm drains offered a cheap and ready way to ease the problems caused by overcrowding; the simple conveyance of sewage from the city to nearby rivers, lakes, and tidal estuaries, however, only transferred the problem to these bodies of water, and they in turn became heavily contaminated with pathogenic organisms. Because these contaminated water bodies supplied many cities with water, many types of disease persisted.

Cholera appeared in London in 1848 and claimed thousands of lives. The spread of the disease was linked to the contaminated water supply, and the control of the disease was hindered by the lack of sewers. Finally, in

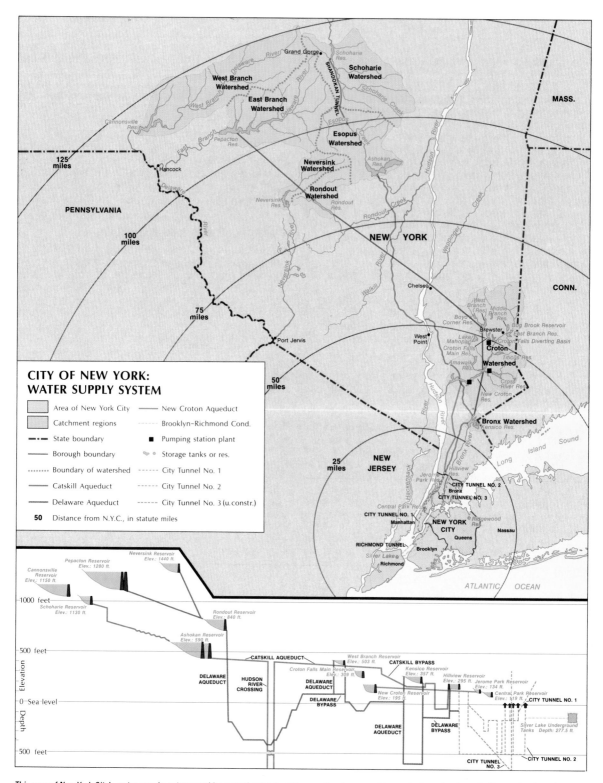

CITY OF NEW YORK: WATER SUPPLY SYSTEM

Area of New York City
Catchment regions
State boundary
Borough boundary
Boundary of watershed
Catskill Aqueduct
Delaware Aqueduct

New Croton Aqueduct
Brooklyn-Richmond Cond.
Pumping station plant
Storage tanks or res.
City Tunnel No. 1
City Tunnel No. 2
City Tunnel No. 3 (u. constr.)

50 Distance from N.Y.C., in statute miles

This map of New York City's water-supply system provides a good example of the complex storage and transmission network needed to supply adequate water to a densely populated urban center. Lengthy aqueducts had to be constructed in order for the city to tap distant watersheds in upstate New York. Not shown on the map are the system's treatment facilities or the distribution network within the city that supplies water to individual users. In the future the city may also draw some water from the Hudson River.

1855, an act of Parliament provided the basis for the Metropolitan Commission of Sewers to provide an adequate system.

In the United States the growth of population from 2.5 million at the time of the American Revolution to more than 200 million and the conversion from an essentially rural economy to about 25% urban population after the Civil War and to some 75% urban population today, has required the extensive development of public water-supply systems. In the second half of the 19th century and the early part of the 20th century, concern with the quality of these supplies became dominant as the result of serious outbreaks of waterborne disease. More than 50,000 people died from typhoid fever due to contaminated water in a five-year period from 1900 to 1904.

Whereas filtration was employed in Europe as early as 1829, it was not used in the United States until 1871. Even by 1900, only 10 filtration plants were in operation. The reliability of water treatment increased greatly when disinfection began to be employed, first in 1908 with chlorine compounds and then from 1911 when chlorine gas was introduced. By the 1930s waterborne diseases were largely eliminated from U.S. cities.

The historical problems of waterborne diseases would have been much worse if it were not for the development of uncontaminated water supplies requiring little or no treatment. Thus, groundwater supplies have been used when they were adequate, particularly for small cities. Many of the larger cities have developed large surface-water supplies from remote catchment areas protected from contamination. The Boston metropolitan area, since 1930, has been served by a system dependent on tributaries of the Connecticut River.

Other large 20th-century interbasin river-transfer developments for municipal and industrial water supply and for other purposes have included the Colorado River aqueduct serving the Los Angeles metropolitan district, the transmountain aqueducts carrying water across the Continental Divide to Denver, the aqueduct system to transfer

A blimp warns New Yorkers to conserve water during the summer drought of 1965. Another drought, caused by minimal snowfall the preceding winter and subnormal rainfall in catchment areas, brought the reservoirs supplying New York City to less than half their capacity in the summer of 1985.

Delaware River water to New York City, the Central Valley Project in Southern California using excess waters moved from the northern part of the state, and numerous water supplies from federal multipurpose reservoirs. Such long-distance transfers have not only sustained large urban population growths but have also made possible the irrigation of vast areas of farmland in rainfall-deficient regions, particularly in the southwestern United States.

water table The water table, also called the GROUNDWATER table, is the level in the ground below which the Earth is saturated with water. Because of the difficulty of determining the saturation level of material in the deep subsurface, the water table is usually defined as the elevation of water surfaces in shallow, nonpumping wells (which penetrate only short distances into the saturated zone). In many places the first saturated rocks encountered underground are so impermeable that water cannot flow into shallow wells. Therefore a water table is considered to be present only where the uppermost saturated rocks are sufficiently permeable to yield well water. In areas where the uppermost saturated rocks are too impermeable, deeper underlying beds that do yield water are classified as being under confined conditions rather than water-table conditions.

By measuring the elevations of water levels in wells and plotting the data, water-table maps can be constructed. These maps reveal that the water table in most humid and subhumid regions generally follows the contours of the surface; in arid regions, however, this is generally not the case.

Water-table maps yield valuable information about subsurface water supplies. If the elevation of the land

A network of aqueducts brought pure water to ancient Rome from distant rivers, springs, and lakes at the rate of over 300 million l (80 million gal) daily.

surface is known, water-table maps indicate the general depth to which it is necessary to drill for water. This information, in turn, allows cost estimates to be made for drilling wells and pumping groundwater.

---

water thrush   Neither aquatic nor thrushes, water thrushes are North American passerine birds belonging to the wood-warbler family Parulidae. They do live in the vicinity of streams, however, and the Louisiana water thrush, *Seiurus motacilla*, of the eastern United States, tends to sing to the background of rushing water. Unlike most warblers, which are arboreal, water thrushes habitually walk on the ground. Generally 12 cm (5 in) long, they are olive-colored above and have a light stripe over the eye, and a spotted breast.

---

water wave   Water waves are a major mechanism for transporting energy from one point to another on the sea surface (see OCEAN-ATMOSPHERE INTERACTION). They are produced when the air-sea interface is distorted by a disturbing force such as the wind. A restoring force such as gravity, surface tension, or the Coriolis force then acts to return the surface to equilibrium. The disturbance propagates on the surface of the water as a wave.

Wave Periods. Wind generates waves that have a wide range of frequencies, or periods. It is responsible for pure capillary waves (ripples), which have periods less than 0.1 sec, and for most gravity waves, which have periods from 0.1 sec to approximately 30 sec. Wind-driven gravity waves contain, on the average, more energy than waves of any other period. Seas (waves being actively generated by the wind during a storm) have periods of 4 to 10 sec, and swells (waves that have radiated from the wind storm) have periods of 10 to 30 sec. Wind storms are also responsible for waves with periods longer than 30 sec; these storms excite seiches (standing waves that do not move forward but instead move up and down), whose typical periods range from 5 to 10 min, and storm surges

(large waves having periods from 1 to 100 hr).

Disturbing Forces. Wind is the most important disturbing force for most ocean waves. Other important forces are seismic activity—earthquakes, volcanic eruptions, and landslides—which can produce TSUNAMIS with periods from 10 min to 1 hr 15 min, and the influence of the Sun and Moon, which produce tides that can have periods from 12 to 24 hr. Forced waves such as the astronomical tides exhibit at all times the periods of the forces generating them. All other waves are free; their periods depend on the medium in which they are propagating and have no fixed relation to the generating force. Wind-generated waves represent a delicate balance of forced and free waves.

Restoring Forces. Gravity is the dominant restoring force for waves with periods from 1 sec to 1 hr. Waves with periods less than 1 sec, such as ripples, are influenced by surface tension. The Coriolis force, an effect of the Earth's rotation, has an influence on waves with periods of more than 1 hr (see CORIOLIS EFFECT).

Shoaling Waves. Waves propagating into shallow water toward a beach undergo a shoaling transformation: the crests steepen, troughs flatten, and wavelength and phase speed decrease. In addition, orbital velocities of the water particles increase. Eventually the orbital velocities (maximum at the wave crest) exceed the phase speed of the wave, and the wave breaks. On entering shallow water, waves are also refracted toward regions of lesser depth, which can cause selective erosion of shoal regions and coastal promontories.

During calm weather, beaches are subject to long-period swell. In shallow water a net transport of water and often sand and sediment occurs in the direction of propagation, and beaches are often replenished by sand that was previously eroded during these periods. During stormy weather, commonly associated with winter, beaches are subject to short-period waves, which can produce erosion.

Wave Refraction. On entering shallow water, incoming waveforms are increasingly influenced by the offshore submarine topography and are refracted such that the

All waves can be described in terms of a crest, or highest point (5); a trough, or lowest point (11); a midpoint, or still-water level (8); a height, or crest-to-trough vertical distance (6); and a wavelength, or horizontal distance between successive crests or troughs (12). Each water particle in deep water moves in a circular orbit. Because of friction, the particle orbits and energies decrease with water depth and become negligible at the wave base (7). As a wave approaches a beach (1), the water-particle orbits become flattened ellipses. If the shore slope is steep, the wave peaks rapidly (4), and a plunging breaker results (3). The water moves up the shore as a translation wave (2). If the waves pass over a gently sloping sandbar (10), they will move slowly toward the shore as spilling breakers (9).

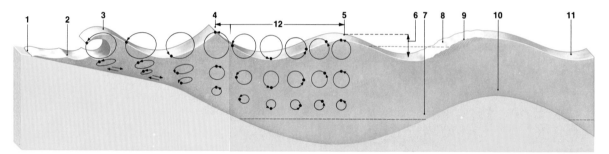

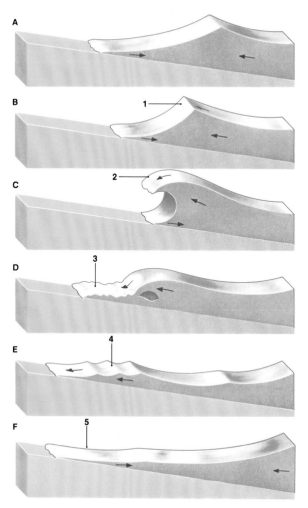

(A) *As a wave passes into water shallower than half its wavelength, frictional interaction with the bottom slows the waves near the shore.* (B) *Waves farther out then overtake those closer in and increase the wave height to a peak (1).* (C) *If the shore slope is steep, the crest peaks rapidly and curls over the friction-retarded lower wave portion. Because no underlying water supports the curled crest, the crest eventually breaks, or collapses, and crashes down as a plunging breaker (2).* (D) *After breaking, the water rushes up the beach as a swash (3).* (E) *It continues its forward movement as a translation wave (4).* (F) *The water then returns down the slope as a backwash (5).*

wave crests tend to parallel the depth contours. Waves traveling directly toward straight coastlines with parallel depth contours and a sloping beach are slowed and experience a reduction in wavelength. Waves traveling obliquely toward a beach with parallel depth contours are refracted so that the crests more nearly parallel the beach. Along an irregular coastline, waves are refracted toward promontories and away from indentions in the coast, a phenomenon that aids in selective erosion and tends to straighten the irregularities.

water well A water well is a hole or shaft excavated or drilled into the Earth's crust to a depth below a free water level, or into a water-bearing stratum or an AQUIFER. The type of well to be constructed is determined by the nature of the soil and the depth to a suitable water-bearing stratum.

Dug wells consist of a vertical hole 1 to 3 m (3 to 10 ft) in diameter that is excavated in the soil until the water-bearing stratum is encountered. The well is then lined with concrete, brick, rough stone, or vitrified tile. The portion of the lining extending from about 0.3 m (1 ft) above the ground surface to at least 3 m (10 ft) below the surface is made watertight to exclude any surface drainage. Normally a dug well is used where the water-bearing stratum is close to the surface.

Driven wells are used when GROUNDWATER is within 8 m (25 ft) of the surface and where there are no boulders or intervening rock formations present. The simplest type of driven well consists of a perforated brass strainer that is cone-shaped at one end and attached at the other to the end of an iron pipe. The pipe is driven through the upper soil layers and into the water-bearing stratum.

Bored wells, constructed where the soil is cohesive enough to prevent serious caving, are usually bored with hand augers or by machinery. The auger retains the soil as the well is bored and must therefore be periodically raised to remove the soil. A well casing and screen are placed in the bored hole and cemented in place after the water-bearing stratum is reached.

When the top soil strata are too hard or do not contain groundwater, wells must either be drilled in rock, where

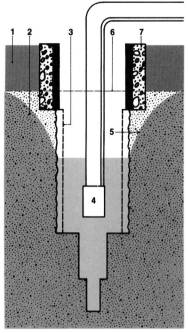

The borehole of a well passes through the soil layer of the Earth's crust (1) and penetrates an aquifer, a water-bearing stratum (2). The lower end of the hole is lined with screens (3). Groundwater from the aquifer seeps through the screens and is piped upward by an electric pump (4). Solid particles that slip through the screens fall to the bottom of the well. The action of the pump creates a "cone of depression" (5) in which the water level inside the borehole drops below the level of the water table (6). The upper part of the well is lined with cement (7) to prevent polluted surface water from entering.

water may be obtained from crevices, or through the soil to deeper water-bearing strata. Drilled wells are usually 10 to 30 cm (4 to 12 in) in diameter and are drilled by percussion or rotary DRILLING. A tube well is a deep rotary-drilled well in which the sections of casing are welded together and driven down the shaft as it is being drilled.

Shallow wells are usually pumped by horizontal centrifugal PUMPS equipped with sand catches on the main suction pipe. Deep-well pumps vary and include air-lift pumps, reciprocating pumps, jet pumps, and vertical centrifugal pumps. Small-bore wells are pumped by air lifts or reciprocating deep-well pumps; large-bore wells are pumped by deep-well turbine pumps.

Waterbury

Waterbury is a city in western Connecticut about 32 km (20 mi) northwest of New Haven. It is located at the confluence of the Naugatuck and Mad rivers and has a population of 108,961 (1990). A center of the brass industry since the mid-18th century, Waterbury is a regional financial and commercial center. Rubber goods, electronic components, clocks, watches, machine tools, shell casings, and textiles are manufactured there. The city has notable buildings of red brick and white marble designed by Cass Gilbert in the early 20th century, including the Municipal Building, the Chase Building, and the Waterbury National Bank.

The site of present-day Waterbury was known to local Indian tribes as "the place where no trees will grow" because of repeated flooding. A nearby settlement dating from 1674 was abandoned and the present site chosen in 1677. The city was most recently damaged by floods in 1955.

watercolor

Watercolor is a painting technique in which pigments suspended in a gum-arabic solution are applied to a surface with brush and water. In general, watercolor provides a brilliant transparency and freshness

The luminosity achieved through transparent watercolor wash is exhibited in Albrecht Dürer's The Great Piece of Turf *(1503). (Albertina, Vienna.) Dürer's handling of this medium was not equaled until the latter half of the 18th century.*

The immediacy of Winslow Homer's watercolors is seen in Woodcutter and the Fallen Tree *(1891). Homer vitalized American watercolor painting. (Museum of Fine Arts, Boston.)*

and allows very free brushwork.

The watercolor medium contains gum arabic, which acts as a binder; glycerin, to keep the paint moist; a plasticizer, such as hydromel or sugar water; a wetting agent, to achieve a uniform flow of paint on surfaces; and a preservative, such as phenol. Watercolors are usually applied with hair brushes to special, handmade watercolor paper characterized by a rich but subtle absorbency and texture. The white of the paper plays a major role in the luminosity of the watercolor painting.

Water as a medium for paint and gum arabic as a binder have been known since ancient times. Water paints were used on illuminated manuscripts in the Middle Ages, and in the early 16th century the German artist Albrecht DÜRER developed the wash technique (overlapping layers of highly diluted pigments) to a refined level. Watercolor in the modern sense (since the late 18th century) designates a technique in which wash is the vehicle for color and the white of the paper is reserved for the highlights. Because the effects of watercolor lend themselves to landscape, British landscape artists such as J. M. W. TURNER exploited the virtues of the medium to its fullest advantage. By the late 1700s watercolor paints were being made commercially in the form of hard, dry cakes. The more familiar pantype watercolor, which has glycerine added to it, was introduced in 1835. Collapsible watercolor tubes appeared about 1900.

During the late 19th and early 20th centuries major American artists such as Winslow HOMER and John MARIN explored new possibilities with watercolor. Pablo PICASSO and Joan MIRÓ were influenced by the aesthetic of watercolor to dilute oil paint with solvent to a washy thinness. Following their example, several modern American painters have used watercolor techniques with oil- and acrylic-based paint, allowing the paint to flow freely over the painting surface.

watercress Watercress, *Nasturtium officinale,* is a floating or creeping water plant of the mustard family, Cruciferae. A perennial, it grows best in fresh water, particularly in cool streams and ponds, and in wet soil. Its round, edible leaves are pungent to the taste and commonly used as salad greens or as a garnish. Cutting the leaves encourages further leaf growth, although once the plant's small white flowers appear, the leaves become too harshly flavored to eat. Watercress is native to Europe and was transplanted to several parts of the world. It grows widely in North America, where it is cultivated as a commercial crop.

waterfall A waterfall is an often spectacular vertical or nearly vertical section in the longitudinal profile of a river channel. The sharp alteration in stream gradient greatly increases flow velocity, causing abrasion in underlying rock formations. The falls' eddying spray and the pot lakes developed in the plunge pool effectively scour the rocks underlying the ledge of the falls. This erosional activity undercuts the falls and causes them to migrate upstream, leaving a gorge in front of the falls.

As the stream channel evolves and equilibrates, the falls are transformed into rapids. The rapids may persist for long periods of time, until they are smoothed and no discernible break exists in the stream profile.

Falls may occur simply as a result of differential erosion, where a resistant formation is underlain by a more easily eroded rock. Continual undermining of the less resistant rock will form and maintain a waterfall, as at NIAGARA FALLS.

Small waterfalls are often found where streams flow over hanging valleys into a main valley. Such falls commonly occur in glacially eroded alpine mountains, where the main valleys are scoured more deeply than the tributary valleys. In such instances, the tributary stream must drop vertically to its confluence with the main stem of the river, as at YOSEMITE FALLS in California.

Recent tectonic activity can also cause waterfalls to

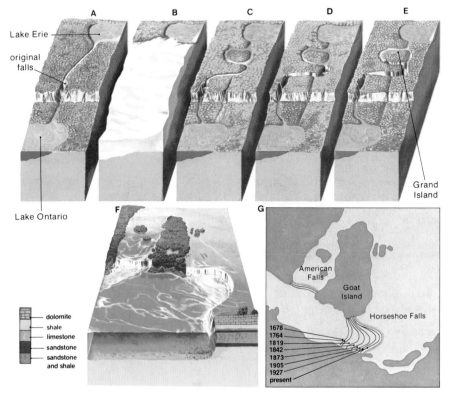

Lake Erie

original falls

Lake Ontario

A B C D E

Grand Island

dolomite
shale
limestone
sandstone
sandstone and shale

F G

American Falls

Goat Island

Horseshoe Falls

1678
1764
1819
1842
1873
1905
1927
present

Niagara Falls lies along the course of the Niagara River, which flows north from Lake Erie to Lake Ontario. (A) Experts believe that the original falls began south of the present-day falls, forming Saint David's Gorge about 14,000 years ago. (B) The gorge became glaciated about 13,000 years ago. Once the ice retreated (C), about 11,000 years ago, the river ran along a new course beside Saint David's Gorge. The power of the water gradually eroded the riverbed to the present-day position of the falls (D). In the future (E) the falls will divide at Grand Island and ultimately will reach Lake Erie. (F) The top layer of rock beneath the river is highly resistant Lockport dolomite; deeper layers of shale, limestone, and sandstone, however, are easily eroded from underneath the dolomite, which then breaks off in large pieces. (G) The retreat of the falls from 1678 to 1927 is illustrated. Each minute 432 million l (114 million gal) of water can flow over Horseshoe Falls and 23 million l (6 million gal) over American Falls.

form. Discontinuities in river gradient occur where crustal blocks have been displaced by recent faulting. Kabalega Falls on the White Nile River and VICTORIA FALLS on the Zambezi River were established in this manner.

—

Waterford   Waterford (Irish: Port Láirge) is the seat of Waterford County in MUNSTER province and the main port and largest city in southeastern Ireland (1986 pop., 39,529). Waterford County has an area of 1,839 km^2 (710 mi^2) and a population of 236,008 (1986). Located on the River Suir, Waterford has food-processing and brewing industries. Waterford crystal became famous for its fine luster and the brilliance of its cutting. The Waterford glassworks founded by George and William Penrose in 1783 closed in 1851, but the Waterford glass industry was revived in 1939.

Norse invaders (Vikings) founded Waterford in the early 10th century. Besieged by Oliver Cromwell in 1649, the city fell to the parliamentary general Henry Ireton in 1650.

—

waterfowl   Waterfowl is a common term for birds of the family Anatidae, order Anseriformes—swans, geese, and ducks. More than 140 species are found throughout the world, but geese are most abundant in the Northern Hemisphere. Many are prized as food and game. As swimming or semiaquatic birds, waterfowl are adapted to life on the surface of water. They generally have broad, rather flat bodies lightened by air sacs; short legs; and webbed feet. The neck is long, for reaching down below the water surface for food, and the bill is usually short, straight, and flattish, with grooves along the sides for straining food from water. The plumage, underlaid with down, is very dense and kept oiled to repel water.

Waterfowl are gregarious birds that form large flocks, particularly when migrating. They move in tight bands, often in V or chevron formation, from wintering grounds to breeding sites. To achieve flight, some species, especially geese and swans, run on the water, pounding the surface with their feet and the tips of their wings. All waterfowl lay unspotted eggs, often 10 to 20 in a clutch. The young are down-covered and able to swim almost immediately after hatching. Adults molt after breeding, losing not only their nuptial plumage but also their wing quills; they are unable to fly for several weeks.

Swans are elegant-looking, long-necked birds that feed on vegetation on the bottoms of ponds, rivers, and bays. Geese are smaller than swans and somewhat less aquatic; most feed on land, usually in grassy meadows or grain fields. Ducks are generally smaller than geese. Some are surface feeders, or dabblers, feeding on vegetation, insects, and other small invertebrates in shallow marshes and lakes. Other ducks are divers, feeding on deep-water and bottom-dwelling organisms.

Three species of large South American birds known as screamers are also sometimes considered waterfowl. The term *waterfowl* is also sometimes applied to other birds that spend all or part of their lives on or near water: pelicans, gannets, boobies, frigate birds, cormorants, grebes, loons, and related species; such seabirds as albatrosses, petrels, fulmars, and shearwaters; such shorebirds as gulls, plovers, skimmers, sandpipers, terns, and snipes; such marsh birds as cranes, rails, and coots; and such stilt-legged birds as herons, bitterns, ibises, spoonbills, and flamingos.

—

Watergate   Watergate refers to the political scandal and constitutional crisis that began when five burglars broke into (June 17, 1972) Democratic National Committee headquarters at the Watergate office building in Washington, D.C. It ended with the resignation (Aug. 9, 1974) of President Richard M. NIXON.

In January 1973 the burglars and two coplotters—G. Gordon Liddy and E. Howard Hunt—were convicted of charges of burglary, conspiracy, and wiretapping and were sentenced to prison terms by District Court Judge John J. Sirica. He was convinced that pertinent details had not been unveiled during the trial and proffered leniency in exchange for further information. As it became increasingly evident that the Watergate burglars were tied closely to the Central Intelligence Agency and the Committee to Re-elect the President (CRP), some of Nixon's aides began talking to federal prosecutors.

The defection of aides such as Jeb Stuart Magruder, assistant to CRP director John N. MITCHELL, quickly implicated others in Nixon's inner circle. The Senate established (February 1973) an investigative committee headed by Sen. Sam ERVIN, Jr., to look into the growing scandal. Amid increasing disclosures of White House involvement in the Watergate break-in and its aftermath, Nixon announced the resignations of John Ehrlichman and H. R. Haldeman, two of his closest advisors, and the dismissal of his counsel John W. Dean III.

Growing suspicion of presidential involvement in the

John Dean III, former White House counsel, is sworn in before the Senate Select Committee on Presidential Campaign Activities, convened in May 1973 to investigate charges stemming from the break-in and electronic surveillance of Democratic headquarters.

scandal resulted in an intensification of the investigation. Leaders in this inquiry included Judge Sirica, reporters for the *Washington Post*, the Ervin committee, and Archibald Cox, who was sworn in as special prosecutor in May 1973. Dean told the Ervin committee in June that Nixon had known of the cover-up. A month later, former White House staff member Alexander Butterfield revealed that Nixon had secretly tape-recorded conversations in his offices. Both Cox and the Ervin committee began efforts to obtain selected tapes. Nixon, citing EXECUTIVE PRIVILEGE, refused to relinquish them and tried to have Cox fired. On Oct. 20, 1973, Attorney General Elliot L. Richardson, refusing to dismiss Cox, resigned in protest. His deputy, William Ruckelshaus, also refused and was fired. Nixon's solicitor general, Robert H. Bork, who was next in command, then fired Cox. The "Saturday night massacre," as the events of that evening became known, heightened suspicions that Nixon had much to hide.

Leon Jaworski, who replaced Cox as special prosecutor on November 1, continued to press for the tapes. On Mar. 1, 1974, a federal grand jury indicted seven men, including Haldeman, Ehrlichman, Mitchell, and White House special counsel Charles Colson, for conspiracy to obstruct justice. At the same time, the House Judiciary Committee began investigating the Watergate affair and related matters.

The president released (April 30) edited transcripts containing suspicious gaps. Not satisfied, Judge Sirica subpoenaed additional tapes. When Nixon refused, the case moved to the Supreme Court, which ruled (July 24) against him by an 8–0 vote. The Court conceded that a president could withhold national security material but insisted that Watergate was a criminal matter.

On July 27–30, the House Judiciary Committee, whose public hearings had disclosed evidence of illegal White House activities, recommended that Nixon be impeached on three charges: obstruction of justice, abuse of presidential powers, and trying to impede the impeachment process by defying committee subpoenas.

A beleaguered President Nixon released three tapes to the public on Aug. 5, 1974. One revealed that he had taken steps to thwart the FBI's inquiry into the Watergate burglary. The tape made it clear that Nixon had been involved actively in the cover-up from its beginnings. These disclosures destroyed the president's remaining congressional support. With House impeachment inevitable and Senate conviction probable, Richard Nixon resigned (Aug. 9, 1974), the first U.S. chief executive to do so.

Waterloo, Battle of The Battle of Waterloo, fought 19 km (12 mi) from Brussels on June 18, 1815, marked the end of the NAPOLEONIC WARS (1803–15). It pitted the 72,000-man force of NAPOLEON I against the duke of WELLINGTON's 68,000-man Anglo-German-Dutch army and the 90,000-man Prussian army of Gebhard BLÜCHER. The climax of a three-day campaign, the battle began at 11 AM; it had been delayed by rain, giving the Prussians time to march to Wellington's aid. French marshal Michel NEY delivered the main attack at La Haye Sainte at about 1 PM. The tide of the battle turned when Blücher's army, having eluded the pursuing French columns of Emmanuel Grouchy, attacked Napoleon's right flank. Although Ney pierced Wellington's line by 6:30 PM, the Prussian troops eventually overwhelmed the French right, leading to the deployment of the French Imperial Guard in a des-

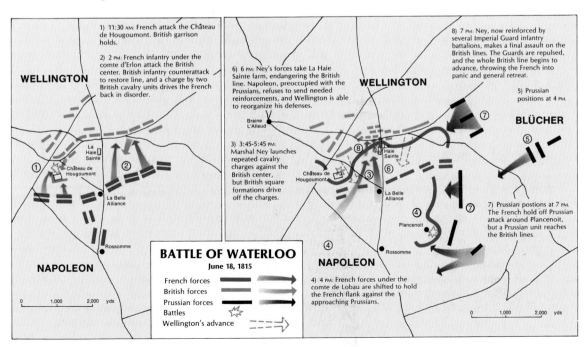

1) 11:30 AM: French attack the Château de Hougoumont. British garrison holds.

2) 2 PM: French infantry under the comte d'Erlon attack the British center. British infantry counterattack to restore line, and a charge by two British cavalry units drives the French back in disorder.

WELLINGTON

La Haie Sainte
Château de Hougoumont
La Belle Alliance
Rossomme

NAPOLEON

BATTLE OF WATERLOO
June 18, 1815

French forces
British forces
Prussian forces
Battles
Wellington's advance

0   1,000   2,000   yds

6) 6 PM: Ney's forces take La Haie Sainte farm, endangering the British line. Napoleon, preoccupied with the Prussians, refuses to send needed reinforcements, and Wellington is able to reorganize his defenses.

Braine L'Alleud

3) 3:45–5:45 PM: Marshal Ney launches repeated cavalry charges against the British center, but British square formations drive off the charges.

8) 7 PM: Ney, now reinforced by several Imperial Guard infantry battalions, makes a final assault on the British lines. The Guards are repulsed, and the whole British line begins to advance, throwing the French into panic and general retreat.

5) Prussian positions at 4 PM.

WELLINGTON

La Haie Sainte
Château de Hougoumont
La Belle Alliance
Plancenoit
Rossomme

NAPOLEON

BLÜCHER

7) Prussian postions at 7 PM. The French hold off Prussian attack around Plancenoit, but a Prussian unit reaches the British lines.

4) 4 PM: French forces under the comte de Lobau are shifted to hold the French flank against the approaching Prussians.

0   1,000   2,000   yds

perate last-ditch attempt to salvage the battle. By 7:30 PM, Wellington was able to take the offensive and drive the French from the field. Napoleon's casualties were 31,000; Wellington suffered 11,900; and Blücher had more than 7,000.

watermark   Watermarking is a technique used to create a pattern or mark in a sheet of PAPER that is visible when the sheet is held to a light. The marking is made by wires woven into the surface of a mold, in the production of handmade papers, or into a revolving cylinder for machine-made papers. The thickness of the wire creates a corresponding displacement of fiber in the wet sheet during its formation, so that when dried the pattern is easily visible. The watermark has a long history as a maker's trademark and as a guarantee of quality; the first recorded trade watermark appeared during the 13th century. In paper to be used for currency the watermark has a security function, serving as a guarantee of authenticity.

watermelon   Watermelon is an annual trailing vine, *Citrullus vulgaris,* of the cucumber family, Cucurbitaceae, native to Africa and now grown in warm regions throughout the world for its large, sweet-fleshed fruits. The fruit was introduced into North America during the 16th century. In the United States the leading producers today are Florida and Texas. Watermelon vines are tender to frost and require a long growing season. The number of fruits per vine varies from 2 to 15, and the weight of each watermelon ranges from 1.4 kg (3 lb) to 22.5 kg (50 lb). Depending on the variety, the flesh color may be red, pink, yellow, or white.

Waters, Ethel   The actress and singer Ethel Waters, b. Chester, Pa., Oct. 31, 1900, d. Sept. 1, 1977, starred in such Broadway musicals as *Africana* (1927), *Blackbirds* (1930), and *As Thousands Cheer* (1933) and popularized the hit songs "Stormy Weather" and "Dinah." In 1950 she won the New York Drama Critics' Circle Award for her performance in *Member of the Wedding.*

Waters, Muddy   The blues singer and guitarist Muddy Waters, b. McKinley Morganfield in Rolling Fork, Miss., Apr. 4, 1915, d. Apr. 30, 1983, was a seminal figure in the creation of the music style known as RHYTHM AND BLUES. Waters began his career with an acoustic guitar—his country blues were recorded in 1941 for the Archives of American Folksong of the Library of Congress—but he switched to electric guitar in 1943. In the 1950s, Waters established an innovative approach to the blues by using a band consisting of amplified guitar, harmonica, piano, and drums. Waters inspired countless musicians, including Bob Dylan, Elvis Presley, and Mick Jagger. Although he had been a star performer at international blues, folk, and jazz festivals, Waters never gained the kind of commercial success accorded to imitators.

waterskiing   Waterskiing is an internationally popular recreational and competitive sport in which participants plane across the water's surface on one or two specially designed skis while being towed by a powerboat. The precise origins of the sport are obscure. Shortly after the development of the motorboat in the early 1900s came the introduction of the flat-board aquaplane, a device that water enthusiasts stood on while being towed by a boat. In 1925, Fred Waller of Huntington, N.Y., received a patent for water skis. In 1935, on Long Island Sound, the first waterskiing contest was held. Four years later the first national championships were contested.

Competitions are held for men and women in slalom, jumping, and trick ski events. The winner is decided by the best all-around performance in three events. For the jump to count in ski jumping, the skier must successfully pass over the ramp, land, and ski to the end of the course. Points are awarded for distance and for style in approach and in landing. In the slalom event, the skier must negotiate a course set with marker buoys. As the boat passes through the center of the course the skier must pass across the outside of the buoys. Points are awarded for each buoy successfully negotiated. In trick skiing, competitors execute difficult maneuvers such as turns and jumps. Each individual trick is awarded 20 to 450 points by a panel of judges. Some extremely talented skiers are able to ski without the aid of skis, planing on the soles of the feet.

A waterskier is shown slalom skiing, in which both feet are positioned on one ski. The nearly prone position of the skier (as well as the huge spray created) indicates the difficulty of turning sharply at a high rate of speed.

waterspout   Waterspouts are funnel clouds extending from the bases of cumulonimbus clouds to the sea surface. A product of high surface temperatures and humidities, they are common in all equatorial oceans and inland seas. Waterspouts and TORNADOES result from similar formative processes. Rapid updrafts within the cumulonimbus cause an inflow of moist low-level air. Conservation of angular momentum causes the air to spiral faster and faster toward the updraft region, where the reduction in pressure cools the air to temperatures below dew point and condensation droplets form.

Unlike tornadoes, which are usually associated with foul weather and are very destructive, waterspouts may occur in fine weather and rarely cause damage.

waterwheel

The waterwheel, which dates back two millennia, was the first device designed to harness a power source other than animals. In a typical waterwheel, flowing water is directed from a natural stream or reservoir to cups or buckets attached to the perimeter of a wheel or to the ends of wide spokes. The waterwheel's rotating axle may turn a generator, machinery, or a mill, either directly or by means of gears or belts.

In a horizontal waterwheel the flowing water strikes only one side, causing the wheel to rotate. Vertical waterwheels may be grouped generally as undershot, where the water is directed toward the bottom of the waterwheel; overshot, where the water meets the waterwheel at or near its top; and breast, where water meets the waterwheel about midway between the top and bottom. Over the years improvements in the design of waterwheels have led to the development of hydraulic turbines, which are enclosed wheels with scientifically designed blades and which use the energy in the flowing water more efficiently.

See also: HYDROELECTRIC POWER; TIDAL ENERGY.

This engraving (1749) depicts one of the large undershot waterwheels at London Bridge that were used between 1582 and 1822 to supply the city of London with water. Waterwheels provided power for many industrial purposes before the development of the steam engine.

Watie, Stand

Stand Watie, b. Dec. 12, 1806, d. Sept. 9, 1871, was a CHEROKEE Indian chief who signed the Treaty of New Echota of 1835, ordering the Cherokee to give up their land east of the Mississippi and move westward to INDIAN TERRITORY. Cherokee factions opposed to the treaty sentenced him to death, but he lived on to serve as brigadier general, leading a Confederate Cherokee regiment. Watie was the last Confederate officer to surrender to the Union.

Watlings Island   see SAN SALVADOR ISLAND

Watson (family)

Thomas John Watson, b. Campbell, N.Y., Feb. 17, 1874, d. June 19, 1956, was a U.S. businessman who promoted (1924–49), as its president, the International Business Machines Corporation (IBM) to a position of world prominence. In 1914, Watson was made president of the Computing-Tabulating-Recording Company, a firm that changed its name to IBM in 1924. He greatly expanded IBM's product line to include all kinds of business machines and after World War II developed electronic computers. By the time of his death the firm sold its products in 82 countries and had assets in excess of $630 million. In his private life Watson was a philanthropist and art patron and collector. His son, **Thomas John Watson, Jr.**, b. Dayton, Ohio, Jan. 8, 1914, became president of IBM in 1952 and chairman of the board in 1961. He graduated from Brown University in 1937 and began to work for IBM in sales before serving in the Army Air Force during World War II. From 1979 to 1981 he served as U.S. ambassador to the USSR.

Watson, Elkanah

Elkanah Watson, b. Plymouth, Mass., Jan. 22, 1758, d. Dec. 5, 1842, was an American agriculturist, merchant, and canal builder. Watson spent his early years as a merchant in New England and was sent (1779) to France to carry funds and dispatches to Benjamin Franklin, American agent in Paris. Watson was impressed by the inland waterways of Holland, and in 1789 he organized the Bank of Albany, N.Y., and began to promote canal building. He secured (1798) a charter that permitted his company to dig a canal around Niagara Falls. After retiring from his canal enterprises, Watson began experimenting with scientific agricultural practices at his farm in the Berkshires.

Watson, James D.

The biologist James Dewey Watson, b. Chicago, Apr. 6, 1928, helped determine the molecular structure of deoxyribonucleic acid (DNA), the hereditary material of most cells. For this work he shared the 1962 Nobel Prize for physiology or medicine with two British scientists, Francis CRICK and Maurice Wilkins. After earning a Ph.D. in zoology from Indiana University in 1950 and doing postgraduate work in Copenhagen, Watson joined the Cavendish Laboratories at the University of Cambridge. In collaboration with Crick and using X-ray diffraction pictures of DNA from Wilkins, Rosalind Franklin, and others, he worked to determine the exact chemical structure of the DNA molecule. In 1953, Watson and Crick succeeded in constructing a molecular model of DNA; they showed it to have a double-helix arrangement

James D. Watson, an American biochemist, is famous for his role in determining the three-dimensional double-helix molecular structure of DNA, or deoxyribonucleic acid. This chemical, which is found in living cells, is involved in the transmission of hereditary properties.

likened to a spiral staircase. This model, known as the Watson-Crick model, had a profound impact on biology, opening new avenues of research in genetics and biochemistry.

Subsequently, while working and teaching at the California Institute of Technology and Harvard University, Watson helped break the genetic code by determining how proteins are synthesized in the cell. In 1968 he became director of Cold Spring Harbor Laboratory of Quantitative Biology in New York, where he conducts cancer research. In 1988 he was appointed head of the Office for Human Genome Research (see GENOME) at the National Institutes of Health.

Watson, John B.   The psychologist John Broadus Watson, b. Greenville, S.C., Jan. 9, 1878, d. Sept. 25, 1958, was the principal spokesperson for rigorous BEHAVIORISM during the formative years of American psychology. Strongly influenced by mechanistic materialism in biology and neurology at the University of Chicago, where he received (1903) his doctorate, Watson shunned the prevailing methods and concerns of the then dominant school of introspectionism. He studied animal behavior and described it in terms of two categories: stimulus and response. Later he borrowed the terminology of conditioning from the Russian reflexologists Vladimir Bekhterev and Ivan Pavlov.

Watson first experimented solely with animals but later (1918) extended his research and explanatory principles to behavior in children and to BEHAVIOR MODIFICATION. Throughout his career Watson stressed the preponderant role of the milieu in determining behavior and character.

Watson, Thomas E.   Thomas Edward Watson, b. Columbia County, Ga., Sept. 5, 1856, d. Sept. 26, 1922, was one of the leaders of the POPULIST PARTY of the 1890s. A Georgia lawyer, Watson served (1891–93) in the U.S. House of Representatives as a Farmers' Alliance Democrat. He became active in the Populist party and was its vice-presidential nominee in 1896. In 1904 he was the party's presidential candidate but polled only 117,183 votes. After 1908, Watson became a champion of the Ku Klux Klan, engaging in vitriolic tirades against Catholics, Jews, blacks, and socialists. He was elected to the Senate in 1920 as a Democrat but died less than two years into his term.

Watson, Tom   Thomas Sturges Watson, b. Kansas City, Mo., Sept. 4, 1949, was the premier professional golfer in the United States during the late 1970s and early 1980s. Watson won the Missouri Amateur title three times. He graduated from Stanford University in 1971 and turned professional in 1973. In addition to many other tournament victories, Watson has won eight major championships: the British Open five times (1975, 1977, 1980, 1982–83), the Masters twice (1977, 1981), and the U.S. Open (1982). He has also won the World Series of Golf twice (1975, 1980). The leading money winner on the Professional Golfers Association (PGA) tour five times (1977–80, 1984), Watson was voted the PGA Player of the Year six times (1977–80, 1982, 1984). In 1980 he became the first golfer to earn $500,000 in prize money in a single year. For the years 1977–79 he also won the Vardon Trophy, awarded annually to the player with the best average score per round. Watson was inducted into the PGA/World Golf Hall of Fame in 1988.

Watson-Watt, Sir Robert Alexander   Sir Robert Alexander Watson-Watt, b. Apr. 13, 1892, d. Dec. 3, 1973, was a Scottish physicist whose work on radiolocation instruments became the basis for Great Britain's RADAR system during the early years of World War II. From 1915 to 1936, Watson-Watt worked at the British government's Meteorological Office and Department of Scientific and Industrial Research. In 1919 he patented his first radar device, designed for use in atmospheric studies. Successive instruments improved the instrument's accuracy and sensitivity, and his 1935 patent was central to the radar system that proved effective against German air raids. Watson-Watt was knighted in 1942.

watt   The watt is the unit of power ordinarily employed in mechanics and electricity. One watt equals 1 joule per second, or 10^7 ergs, and 746 watts equal 1 horsepower (hp). The power in watts developed in an electrical circuit is equal to the potential (volts) times the current (amperes). In heat measurement, which customarily uses calories and Btu's as energy units, 1 watt equals 0.239 calories per second or 3.4192 Btu/h. Multiplying a unit of power by a time unit, such as is done to obtain kilowatt hours (kW h), gives units of energy.

Watt, James James Watt, b. Jan. 19, 1736, d. Aug. 25, 1819, was a Scottish engineer and inventor who played an important part in the development of the STEAM ENGINE as a practical power source. In 1757 he was appointed instrument maker at the University of Glasgow; there he met the physicist Joseph Black, who was studying the thermodynamic (heat) properties of steam. Watt studied the Newcomen steam engine then in use and made a number of important improvements. In 1769 he patented a separate condenser (a chamber for condensing the steam) for the engine. He formed (1774–1800) a partnership with·the manufacturer Matthew BOULTON. The Boulton and Watt steam engines soon replaced the Newcomen engines that were being used to pump water out of mines. Other improvements developed by Watt included the twin-action piston·engine (in which steam is supplied to both sides of the piston), obtaining power from the expansion of the steam inside the cylinder, a mechanism for transforming the reciprocating motion of the piston into rotary motion, and the centrifugal governor (a device that made use of the principle of FEEDBACK to keep the steam engine at a constant speed). Although Watt did not invent the steam engine, his improved engine was really the first practical device for efficiently converting heat into useful work and was a key stimulus to the Industrial Revolution.

Antoine Watteau's La Gamme d'Amour *(c.1718), an elegant* fête galante—*a courtly scene of aristocratic dalliance in an idyllic park—catches a moment when the two lovers pause in thier duet to exchange glances. (National Gallery, London.)*

The Scottish inventor James Watt's development of an improved steam engine was a landmark in the early part of the Industrial Revolution. Patented in 1769, the engine's design included a separate condensing chamber and insulated engine parts. (National Portrait Gallery, London.)

Watteau, Antoine [wah-toh'] Jean Antoine Watteau, b. Valenciennes, Oct. 10, 1684, d. July 18, 1721, was the finest French painter and draftsman of the early 18th century. His art celebrates the grace and charm of the life enjoyed by elegant society in his time.

In 1712, Watteau showed a work (now lost) to the Académie Royale; it so impressed the judges that he was immediately named a provisional member of the Académie. He was elected (1717) a full member when he submitted his *Pilgrimage to Cythera* (Louvre, Paris), a po-

etic evocation of a theme that permeates all of Watteau's art: that love is the central experience of human existence. As a painter of fêtes galantes—depictions of the pastoral pleasures of high-born lovers—Watteau won vast admiration, and his pictures were avidly collected in France and in England.

Watteau pursued a lifelong interest in theater scenes and theatrical costuming and began to depict personages from the theater—especially those from the popular Italian comic theater, the *commedia dell'arte*—as representatives of universal character types. His *Mezzetin* (*c.*1718; Metropolitan Museum of Art, New York City), for example, typifies the unrequited lover, and his great *Gilles* (1720–21; Louvre) the awkward, lonely outsider. As a result of his association with Claude Audran, a leading designer of decorative ornament, Watteau gained an appreciation of the joyous colorism and brushwork of Peter Paul Rubens. These elements coalesced in such mature masterpieces as *Love in the French Theater* (*c.*1718; Staatliche Museen, Berlin) and *The Shepherds* (*c.*1717; Schloss Charlottenburg, Berlin).

Watteau's contemporaries praised his realism as much as his grace. A mastery of realistic detail is especially evident in his magnificent drawings, many executed in three colors of chalk—black, white, and red—as well as in one of his last works, the *Gersaint Signboard* (1721; Schloss Charlottenburg). Originally intended to be an outdoor shop sign, this depiction of the interior of his friend Gersaint's Parisian gallery served its intended function for only 15 days; then it was removed to be treasured as one of the greatest paintings of the time.

Watts, Isaac   Nonconformist minister Isaac Watts, b. July 17, 1674, d. Nov. 25, 1748, has been called the father of English hymnody. As assistant minister (1699) and then pastor (1702) of an Independent congregation at Mark Lane, London, he composed some of his best-remembered hymns, including "Our God, Our Help in Ages Past."

Watutsi   see TUTSI

Waugh, Evelyn [waw]   The major English comic novelist Evelyn Arthur St. John Waugh, b. London, Oct. 28, 1903, d. Apr. 10, 1966, wrote some of the most brilliant and bitingly satirical novels of his day. His formal innovations, notably the assimilation of several inconsequential plots into an ordered whole, and his love for the bizarre and for black humor have influenced a generation of younger writers.

A high degree of sophistication and a caustic wit displayed in polished, deceptively simple prose are the marks of such works as *Decline and Fall* (1928), *Vile Bodies* (1930), *Black Mischief* (1932), *A Handful of Dust* (1934), and *Put Out More Flags* (1942). In his later, more serious novels—such as *Brideshead Revisited* (1945) and the wartime trilogy *Men at Arms* (1952), *Officers and Gentlemen* (1955), and *Unconditional Surrender* (1961)—Waugh's conservative Catholicism, arch-Tory views, and deep-seated pessimism increasingly influence his themes. The Hollywood way of death is the subject of *The Loved One* (1948). *The Ordeal of Gilbert Pinfold* (1957) is a semiautobiographical account of a novelist who suffers from hallucinations. *A Little Learning* (1964) covers the author's youth and education, and Waugh's posthumous *Diaries* (1976) disclose the real identities of many of the people ridiculed in his novels. A collection of Waugh's letters was published in 1980.

Waukegan [waw-kee'-guhn]   Waukegan (1990 pop., 69,392), an Illinois port city on Lake Michigan, 64 km (40 mi) north of Chicago, is the seat of Lake County. It is the most industrialized of Chicago's northern lakeshore communities, manufacturing pharmaceuticals, wood and metal products, and outboard motors. The Great Lakes Naval Training Center is also there.

A French stockade and trading post later known as Little Fort was built on the site about 1675. After the French withdrew about 1760, Little Fort became a Potawatomi Indian village. In 1836 the Indians were forced out by a treaty favoring white settlers. Already a busy port by 1846, Little Fort became the village of Waukegan in 1849, deriving its name from the Potawatomi word for "fort" or "house."

wave, water   see WATER WAVE

wave mechanics   see QUANTUM MECHANICS

waveguide   A waveguide is a device that confines and guides electromagnetic waves within fixed boundaries. A familiar audio-frequency analogy to the electromagnetic waveguide is an organ pipe, through which sound waves are carried. A waveguide usually takes the form of a hollow metal tube used to conduct MICROWAVES. Waves transmitted as power or a signal by a waveguide are used as critical elements of sophisticated communications systems, radar equipment, microwave ovens, and mass spectrometers.

Wavell, Archibald Percival Wavell, 1st Earl [way'-vul]   Archibald Percival Wavell, 1st Earl Wavell, b. May 5, 1883, d. May 24, 1950, was a British soldier and administrator. An officer in the Black Watch regiment, he served in the South African War, on the Indian frontier, and in Belgium, Turkey, and Palestine during World War I. In 1937–38, at the time of Arab-Jewish disturbances, he had charge of British troops in Palestine. Wavell's two major World War II commands, in the Middle East (1939–41) and Southeast Asia (1941–42), were plagued by bad luck and strategy disputes with his superiors in London. Initial success against the Italians in North Africa in 1940 was followed by disaster there and in Greece in 1941. Following the loss of Singapore and Burma to the Japanese in 1942, Wavell was transferred to the Indian command and later promoted to viceroy (1943–47). His efforts to prepare the Indians for self-government and to mediate between Hindus and Muslims were largely frustrated.

Waves   Women in the Naval Service are known as Waves, an acronym derived from Women Accepted for Volunteer Emergency Service in World War II. About 86,000 women served in the Waves at its peak strength during the war. In 1948, Congress established Women in the Naval Service on a permanent basis. Waves serve alongside men in the medical and supply corps and in other noncombat fields such as personnel, administration, and communications, and since 1972 have served on ships at sea. In 1991 about 60,000 women were serving in the U.S. Navy.

waves and wave motion   Waves are the result of a disturbance of some sort—the motion of an object, a change in an electrical current, or an alteration of an electromagnetic field. The disturbance is transported from one point to another by a wave, but the medium through which it travels does not undergo a net displacement.

Types of Waves

Most waves may be classified as either longitudinal or transverse, according to the motion of the particles of the medium that transports the wave. There are other types of waves, such as rotational waves and Alfvèn waves (see

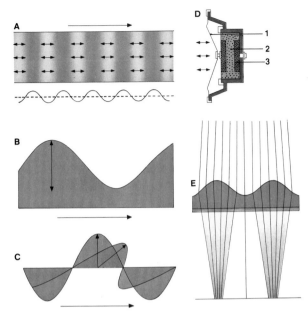

The form a wave takes depends on the nature of the oscillating source and the medium through which the wave travels. Sound moves as a longitudinal wave (A), in which particles of the medium—such as air or water—oscillate back and forth in the wave's direction of travel. This can be depicted as a sine wave (below), with zones of greatest compression as maxima. A water wave (B) is a transverse wave, in which water particles move at right angles to the wave's direction of travel. An electromagnetic wave (C) can be depicted as a transverse wave in which electric and magnetic forces act at right angles. To measure a wave, the wave is usually converted to some other form of energy. For example, a microphone (D) can be used to intercept a sound wave. The vibration of the diaphragm (1) compresses carbon granules (2) and alters the resistance between blocks (3), producing electrical pulses that correspond in amplitude to the sound wave. A water wave (E) can focus light on a screen to measure amplitudes.

MAGNETOHYDRODYNAMICS), but these are difficult to describe and are of less general importance.

Longitudinal Waves. In longitudinal waves vibrations occur in the direction of wave motion. Acoustic (sound) waves are longitudinal waves. When air is the medium, the air molecules oscillate back and forth in a direction parallel to the direction the waves travel. Acoustic waves are a particular member of the general class of elastic waves and require a medium having both inertia and elasticity. The effect on the medium is a series of compressions and rarefactions, regions where the particles are alternately more crowded and then more spread out than they would be in the absence of the wave. After the passage of the wave the particles resume their equilibrium positions and motion; the wave has caused no net displacement.

Transverse Waves. In transverse waves oscillations occur perpendicular to the direction of the wave. The effect is easily demonstrated by tying one end of a rope to a post and giving the other end a sharp flip up and down. A section of the rope appears to travel toward the post; this is a

single wave pulse. A quick series of flips sends a succession of pulses toward the post. Obviously, the rope itself does not move forward and any particle in it undergoes only up-and-down motion; thus the disturbance caused at one end is conveyed to the other by a transverse wave. All electromagnetic waves are transverse waves; they do not require a medium and can travel in a vacuum.

Wave Characteristics

Waves are typically described in terms of their frequency, μ, or wavelength, λ. These are not independent but are related to a third quantity, the velocity, v, by λ m = v. The frequency is measured in cycles per second (cps), or hertz (Hz). Frequency is usually used to specify a given wave because it remains constant under all conditions except when there is relative motion between the observer and the source (see DOPPLER EFFECT). On the other hand the velocity, and therefore the wavelength, depends on the medium. Whenever a wave is specified by its wavelength, as is done with light, the wavelength given is the length that the wave has in a vacuum when it travels at the fixed value c, the speed of light.

The amplitude of a wave is its maximum displacement from equilibrium and is proportional to the amplitude of its source. The intensity of the wave, and therefore the energy it contains, is proportional to the square of the amplitude.

Under suitable conditions all waves are subject to the phenomena of REFLECTION, REFRACTION, DIFFRACTION, and INTERFERENCE. The successful interpretation of light diffraction in terms of wave theory by Augustin FRESNEL was sufficient to end (temporarily, at least) the question of whether light is a wave or a stream of particles. Although modern quantum mechanics stipulates wavelike properties to objects, and vice versa, it is still considered that diffraction, interference, and so forth are evidence of the wave nature of a beam.

Wave Motion

The simplest form of a wave is one represented by a sine or cosine function, indicating that the particles move with simple harmonic motion (see MOTION, HARMONIC).

Superposition of Waves. Not all motions are simple harmonic motion, and a wave may be the result of several superimposed vibrations. When these are of the same frequency, the phenomenon of interference occurs. The waveform is still sinusoidal and has the same frequency, but the resultant intensity may be either greater than or less than either of the contributing waves, according to the phase difference. Waves that are "in phase" peak at about the same time and add to each other; waves that are "out of phase" subtract and can cancel each other out entirely.

Two sound waves that differ slightly in frequency can combine to produce beats. The separate waves are alternately in phase and out of phase, causing the loudness of the tone to wax and wane. Waves of the same type (say, a group of electrical waves) but having different frequencies can be superimposed to produce a new waveform. This, in fact, is the principle of AM (amplitude modulation) radio, in which an electrical wave containing the acoustic information (20–20,000 Hz) is mixed with an electrical wave with suitable transmission properties (about 1 MHz) for broadcasting. The radio receiver then separates the audio-frequency signal from the radio-frequency carrier wave.

Although the sound wave produced by a tuning fork has a pure frequency, a note from most instruments, as well as one produced by the human voice, is complex, a mixture of frequencies consisting of the fundamental (the lowest frequency of the mixture) and overtones, or HARMONICS, which have frequencies that are simple multiples of the fundamental. Any complex waveform, even the sawtooth and pulsed waves common in electronics, can be produced or represented by the addition of simple harmonic waves. The branch of mathematics that treats this resolution of periodic functions is called FOURIER ANALYSIS.

Standing Waves. When two waves having the same wavelength and amplitude travel in opposite directions, the result is a standing wave. There is a waveform, but it does not advance. At regular intervals along the waveform there are points called nodes where no oscillations take place. Standing waves are generally produced by reflection—the meeting of the returning wave and the incoming wave generates the effect. Standing waves may be produced in any substance—liquid, solid, or gas—or in a vacuum. Nearly all sounds created by musical instruments are the result of the formation of standing waves.

See also: SOLITON.

---

wax Waxes comprise a broad group of opaque, water-repellant, essentially solid materials having varied chemical composition and many diverse applications. Some are natural in origin; others are totally synthesized by the chemical industry. Unlike fats, which often have a similar physical appearance, natural waxes are not glyceryl esters (see FATS AND OILS) but are more complex blends of esters, acids, alcohols, and hydrocarbons.

Waxes are usually solids at room temperature but soften or become liquids at elevated temperatures. They are relatively inert as used and are soluble in petroleum solvents or are readily emulsifiable in water. Many of the uses of waxes depend upon their ability to be molded or to form a thin film on otherwise permeable substrates, such as the material for milk and juice containers.

Natural Waxes

The waxes found in nature are directly derived from mineral, vegetable, and animal sources.

Mineral waxes, which are all obtained from fossil sources, include montan, which is extracted from coal or lignite; ozocerite, from shale; and paraffin, from petroleum. Paraffin, used for candles and protective coatings, is by far the most widely used of all waxes.

Vegetable waxes exist in nature as coatings on leaves, stems, and trunks of plants and trees. They generally retain moisture in plants which are indigenous to tropical or arid areas. Carnauba wax is beaten from branches cut from the carnauba palm, which is cultivated in Brazil. Valued for its hardness and high melting point, carnauba is the key ingredient in fine auto waxes. Candelilla wax is obtained from the stem and leaves of a small perennial rush found in southern Texas and Mexico. The wax, separated from the plant by immersion in hot water, approaches the quality of carnauba wax. Sugarcane wax is a by-product of sugar processing and is inferior in quality to carnauba wax.

Foremost among the waxes obtained from the animal kingdom are beeswax and spermaceti. Beeswax is the widest-known and probably the longest-used wax. It is believed to have been used in early Egypt both as a cosmetic base and for lighting. Spermaceti is a wax extracted from the head cavity and blubber of sperm whales along with sperm oil. It has excellent lubricating properties under high shear conditions, a feature difficult to duplicate with synthetic lubricants.

Synthetic Waxes

A number of waxy acids and polymers have wide application in both pure and blended form, including stearic and cetyl alcohol, chlorinated paraffins, ethylene oxide polymers, polyethylene, and numerous synthetic glycerides. Many of the polymeric grades are used to increase the melting points of the softer, natural waxes such as paraffin, while others are used as diluents for high-performance natural grades typified by carnauba wax.

wax museum see TUSSAUD, MADAME

---

waxbill Waxbills are small, attractive, often brightly colored finches found in tropical areas from Africa to Australia. Together with the grass finches and mannikins, the group includes 28 species that are classified in the family Estrildidae. They are seed eaters with conical bills and are found mainly in grasslands, in forest clearings, or near human habitations. They often gather in large flocks, sometimes reaching pest proportions. The sexes are similar. In some species courtship is complicated, with the males carrying grass, singing, and dancing. Bulky, often domed nests are attached to twigs or placed on the ground and typically have side entrances. Both parents incubate the eggs and care for the young.

---

waxwing Distributed over much of the Northern Hemisphere, waxwings are members of the bird family Bombycillidae that are distinguished by their rich, neatly preened plumage. Named for the waxlike red spots usually found on their wings, they are chiefly arboreal birds and take insects on the wing, flycatcher-style. A little larger than the house sparrow, they are generally a blend of fawn and chestnut to dark gray, with yellow-tipped tails and black chins. The Bohemian waxwing, *Bombycilla garrula*, is known for its sudden mass wintertime invasions of specific areas of Europe.

Wayne, Anthony The American general Anthony Wayne, b. near Paoli, Pa., Jan. 1, 1745, d. Dec. 15, 1796, won major recognition in the American Revolution and in Indian warfare. Known as Mad Anthony, Wayne served in Canada in 1776 and at Brandywine and Germantown in 1777; he encamped at Valley Forge during the winter of 1777–78. At the end of 1778 he was given command of a corps of light infantry. His most successful action was a surprise attack on the British at Stony Point on the Hudson River in July 1779.

After the Revolution a series of American defeats by the Indians in the Old Northwest caused Wayne to be given (1792) command of the Northwest army. On Aug. 10, 1794, he won a decisive victory at the Battle of Fallen Timbers on the Maumee River. Under provisions of the ensuing Treaty of Greenville (1795), Wayne obtained a large cession from the Indians. After the British had agreed in JAY'S TREATY to vacate their posts in the Old Northwest, Wayne led the American force that took possession of the forts in 1796.

Wayne, John The American film actor John Wayne, stage name of Marion Michael Morrison, b. Winterset, Iowa, May 26, 1907, d. June 11, 1979, epitomized the archetypal hero of the American Western frontier. He appeared in more than 150 films, many of them directed by his lifelong friend John FORD, whose *Stagecoach* (1939) made Wayne a star. He gave some of his best performances in Ford's *She Wore a Yellow Ribbon* (1949) and *The Searchers* (1956) and in Howard Hawks's *Red River* (1948) and *Rio Bravo* (1959); he won an Academy Award for his role as the crusty, aging westerner in *True Grit* (1969). His notable non-Western films include *The Long Voyage Home* (1940), *They Were Expendable* (1952), and *The Quiet Man* (1952), all directed by Ford. Wayne both directed and acted in *The Alamo* (1960) and *The Green Berets* (1968).

John Wayne, long one of Hollywood's leading box-office attractions, appears in the role of J. B. Books, the title character from his last film, The Shootist *(1976). Ironically, the film deals with a gunfighter dying of cancer, the disease to which Wayne succumbed in 1979.*

WCTU The National Woman's Christian Temperance Union (WCTU) of the United States, founded in 1874 in Cleveland, Ohio, is an organization of women who seek to improve public morals, especially through abstinence from alcoholic beverages and narcotics. Frances WILLARD, an early president (1879–98) of the WCTU, organized (1883) the world WCTU, which now has branches in more than 70 countries.

weak interactions   see FUNDAMENTAL INTERACTIONS

weakfish Also known as sea trout, the weakfishes constitute the genus *Cynoscion* of the drum family, Sciaenidae. They are named for their soft flesh and easily torn mouths. Found near shore from Cape Cod to Mexico, weakfishes are important commercial and game fishes. They average about 2.25 kg (5 lb) in weight. They produce strumming sounds by vibrations of their swim bladders.

Wealth of Nations, An Inquiry into the Nature and Causes of the   see SMITH, ADAM

weapons   see ARTILLERY; BOW AND ARROW; CHEMICAL AND BIOLOGICAL WARFARE; FIREARMS; NUCLEAR STRATEGY; ROCKETS AND MISSILES; SWORD AND KNIFE; and related articles

weasel The weasel family, Mustelidae, comprises 67 species of long, slender-bodied, short-legged, vigorous mammals. Found on all continents except Antarctica and Australia in nearly all habitats, weasels are the world's most widespread carnivores. The family includes the true weasels, such as the ERMINE, FERRET, MARTEN, MINK, POLECAT, WOLVERINE, and fisher, and also the BADGER, OTTER, SKUNK, and honey badger.

True weasels vary in size from the small least weasel, *Mustela nivalis rixosa* (30–70 g/1.1–2.5 oz), a predator of voles and mice, to the large, powerful wolverine *Gulo gulo* (7–32 kg/15–71 lb), which can kill animals much larger than itself. Many male weasels can be up to twice the size of females of the same species. Some weasels consume only one type of prey; the black-footed ferret, *M. nigripes,*

The long-tailed weasel, found from Canada to South America, is one of the largest weasels. Its body averages 25–30 cm (10–12 in) in length, and it has a tail 10–20 cm (4–8 in) long.

for example, feeds almost exclusively on prairie dogs and is threatened with extinction because of prairie-dog–eradication programs throughout its rangeland habitat. Most weasels, however, eat a variety of small mammals and birds. Weasels play an important role in controlling the numbers of some of their prey, particularly voles and mice. They have become serious pests when they are introduced into new areas; following the introduction of ermines and ferrets into New Zealand from Europe, severe predation of native birds occurred.

Both wild and domesticated weasels are highly valued in the fur trade. Pelts of SABLE, ermine, mink, and wolverine are especially prized. Some valuable weasels have been overharvested in the past, and the trapping of most species is now closely regulated in most areas.

—

weather   *Weather* refers to the state of the atmosphere and includes the temperature, precipitation, humidity, cloudiness, visibility, pressure, and winds (see PRECIPITATION, weather; WIND). Weather, as opposed to climate, includes the short-term variations of the atmosphere, ranging from minutes to months. CLIMATE is typically considered the weather that characterizes a particular region over time.

The weather must be measured and records kept to gain an understanding of the forces at work and to yield the information on the averages and extremes (see METEOROLOGICAL INSTRUMENTATION; METEOROLOGY; WEATHER FORECASTING). By studying weather records, atmospheric scientists may be able to predict the weather ahead on scales of weeks to months with greater accuracy and modify more successfully the weather to increase precipitation or ameliorate severe storms (see WEATHER MODIFICATION).

Causes of Weather. The five factors that determine the weather of any land area of the Earth are: the amount of solar energy received because of latitude; the area's elevation or proximity to mountains; nearness to large bodies of water and relative temperatures of the land and water; the number of such storm systems as CYCLONES, HURRICANES, and THUNDERSTORMS resulting from air-mass differences; and the distribution of air pressure over the land and nearest oceans, which produces varying wind and air-mass patterns.

How these five factors interact over the North American continent is an excellent example of how the weather of the United States is produced. Because the landmass of North America encompasses a greater range of latitude than longitude (10° to 80° north latitude), a great amount of differential heating occurs, which in turn creates airmass differences. The indentation of the Gulf of Mexico on southern states affects the character of air masses and placement of pressure centers and storm systems over the eastern half of the continent. Warm, moist air from the south often meets cold, dry air from the north over the central United States. These contrasting air masses include: continental Arctic and polar, from cold land sources; maritime polar, from cold ocean regions; and the warmer and moist Gulf or Atlantic oceanic sources. Air from the Pacific Ocean affects the weather in the western mountains of the United States, which in turn affects the cold-and-warm-air interaction in the eastern United States.

The air movements resulting from these five weather-producing factors of North America provide an exceptional variety of weather among regions and include DROUGHTS, floods, and every known form of severe storm, including TORNADOES, HAIL, and ice storms. These extremes alternate with calm periods of either clouds or sunshine. Thunderstorms in the United States yield about half of the total precipitation in most of the nation—80% in drier mountain climates, 65% in the Great Plains, 50% in the Midwest, and 40% in the East.

The weather in most places is sensitive to a few key factors. For example, severe drought in the sub-Saharan region of Africa is thought to occur when onshore winds from the Atlantic Ocean change direction by at least 60 degrees in a relatively small area. A seasonal shift of this type is presumably related to slight differences in ocean temperatures, which in turn may have resulted from changes in cloudiness related to a slight shift in hemispheric pressure patterns.

Cycles. In most locales the weather changes as a result of the diurnal cycle—between night and day—and the annual cycle—which encompasses daily, monthly, and seasonal variations. These two cycles, the diurnal and annual, are related to the Earth's motion around the Sun and reveal the Sun as the major factor influencing the weather. At a given time the weather differs greatly with distance; during heavy rains, for example, the differences in the amount of rainfall between regions of close proximity are often great.

The diurnal cycle exists everywhere but varies by climate type; within a climatic zone it varies by season. Honolulu, with an equitable oceanic weather regime dominated by the trade winds, has a night-to-day range of 6 C degrees (11 F degrees) in July, whereas St. Louis, Mo., with a continental climate, has an average diurnal range of 12.8 C degrees (23 F degrees) in July. In January, however, the St. Louis diurnal range is 9 C degrees (16 F degrees).

Averages. All weather information for a particular area is derived by a local weather station, and the daily high and low temperature values for a month are averaged to yield the "mean," or "normal," monthly temperature. The highest average values of precipitation occur in locales having strong maritime or orographic influences; these values occur in either warm or cold climates. The extremely low precipitation averages occur either in interior zones far from moist air or at locales where cold oceanic currents stabilize the air.

In a similar fashion, the daily wind and humidity values are averaged to yield their monthly means, and the daily rainfall and snowfall values are totaled, along with the number of days with rain, thunderstorms, freezing temperatures, and clear or cloudy skies. Certain monthly extremes are also identified on a monthly basis, including the highest and the lowest temperature, the heaviest 1-day precipitation (rain or snow), and the greatest wind speed. These monthly summaries are often combined and become the basis for describing the weather of a region. Atmospheric scientists also study weather-producing conditions, such as fronts and high- and low-pressure areas, to describe how the weather of the region is produced.

Extremes. Weather variations that are excessive during a given time span are often called extremes. Records of weather are examined to define extremes; absolute extremes are the highest and lowest values of a weather element observed over the entire period of record.

Among record temperature extremes, the highest temperature ever recorded is 57.8° C (136° F), in the Libyan desert; the lowest is –89.2° C (–128.6° F), in Antarctica. The world's highest 1-year precipitation for a given area was 26,461 mm (1,042 in), at Cherrapunji, India; the lowest was 0.8 mm (0.03 in), in the Chilean desert.

Great temperature extremes have been recorded at a number of points within the United States. For example, the record highest and lowest temperatures at Fairbanks, Alaska, are 37.2° C and –54.5° C (99° F and –66° F), respectively, a difference of 91.7 C degrees (165 F degrees). Those at Boise, Idaho, are 45.6° C and –42.8° C (114° F and –45° F), a range of 88.4 C degrees (159 F degrees). The greatest temperature change during a 24-hour period in the United States occurred in Billings, Mont., when the temperature fell 56.1 C degrees (101 F degrees), from 7.8° C to –48.3° C (46° F to –55° F).

weather forecasting

The task of predicting the weather that will be observed at a future time is called weather forecasting.

The Forecasting Process. Making a weather forecast involves three steps: observation and analysis, extrapolation to find the future state of the atmosphere, and prediction of particular variables. The standard extrapolation technique is to assume that weather features will continue to move as they have been moving. In some cases the third step simply consists of noting the results of extrapolation, but actual prediction usually involves efforts beyond this.

Weather forecasting stations use computers to process large amounts of data from the National Weather Service. The resulting forecast represents a best possible estimate, making use of regional weather data as well.

The National Severe Storms Laboratory at Norman, Okla., studies the nature of severe local storms and hazardous weather phenomena of all kinds.

The tools that meteorologists can use for forecasting depend on the intended range of the forecast, that is, how far into the future it is supposed to extend. Short-range forecasts, sometimes called "nowcasts," extend up to 12 hours ahead. Daily-range forecasts are valid for 1 to 2 days ahead; this is the range where numerical forecasting techniques have made their greatest contribution. In the 1980s, however, the techniques also became useful in the development of medium-range forecasts, which extend from 3 to 7 days ahead. Extended-range forecasts, which extend more than a week ahead, depend on a combination of numerical and statistical forecast guidance. Finally, short-term climate forecasts, such as the 1-month and 3-month average forecasts issued by the Climate Analysis Center of the NATIONAL WEATHER SERVICE (NWS), depend mostly on statistical guidance.

Observation and Analysis. Meteorological observations taken around the world include reports from surface stations, radiosondes (balloon-borne radio transmitters), ships at sea, aircraft, radar, and weather satellites (see METEOROLOGICAL INSTRUMENTATION). The data are transmitted on the Global Telecommunications System (GTS) of the WORLD METEOROLOGICAL ORGANIZATION (WMO) to regional and global centers, where they are collated, redistributed back across the GTS, and, with the help of interactive computer systems, used in various numerical forecast models.

Extrapolation. Whenever possible, meteorologists rely on numerical models to extrapolate the state of the atmosphere into the future. The reason is that these models are based on the actual equations that describe the behavior of the atmosphere. Different models, however, have widely varying levels of approximation to the equations. The more exact the approximation, the more expensive it is to use the model, because more computer time is required to do the work.

Forecast-model activity in the United States is concentrated in the NWS's National Meteorological Center (NMC) in Suitland, Md. A large Class 6 computer there is

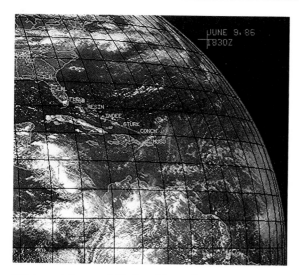

This image is from a satellite-based forecasting system developed by the University of Wisconsin. Several organizations use the system, including the commercial delivery service Federal Express, one of whose plane routes appears in the photograph.

kept busy running four different models twice a day from data observed at 0000 and 1200 Universal Coodinated Time (UTC; 7 AM and 7 PM Eastern Standard Time, respectively). Two of the models focus on North America and surrounding waters. The other two models uniformly cover the entire globe. One model for each domain is relatively simple, intended for a quick computation as an early update even when computer problems arise. The other model for each domain is more complete, providing a better answer at greater expense.

Additional models are run on the computer as needed—as, for example, during hurricanes. After each model is run, selected results are further processed and transmitted to the NWS offices, other governmental agencies, universities, private meteorologists, and the general public, and to the GTS for international distribution.

A separate numerical modeling operation is carried out at the European Center for Medium-Range Weather Forecasting (ECMWF) in Bracknell, England. The consortium of European nations that organized the ECMWF chose to construct a global model with more spatial detail and costlier approximations than any other model in existence. Forecast computations are performed only once a day (from 0000 UTC data), and the results are sent to the member states of the consortium. Selected results are broadcast on the GTS.

Some countries, including Australia, Canada, China, Great Britain, and the Soviet Union, carry out a numerical forecast effort on either the regional or global domain. Many other countries choose to use the numerical forecast products available on the GTS and to allocate their own resources to the predictive step of forecasting.

Prediction. When a forecaster sets out to predict a specific variable—for example, the minimum temperature on a given night at the city where he or she is located—a great deal of observed and model-generated data is available. None of the data, however, provide a definitive prediction. The forecaster must also apply a knowledge of average climatic conditions, local microclimate variations, and typical model behavior in the current situation. The NWS has undertaken extensive efforts to express this kind of additional information in the form of so-called statistical regression equations. These equations have coefficients that vary with geographical location and season. As a result, the NMC forecast material also includes objective, statistically based predictions of temperature, wind, precipitation, and other variables at 286 stations around the United States. Such statistical products are relatively rare elsewhere, because a large amount of data—including model-generated data—is required.

Most forecasters in the United States have available all of the information described above. Their job is to evaluate the situation, compare different sources, and arrive at the best possible estimate for the variables of interest, such as air temperature and the likelihood of precipitation. Polar-front theory can be used to help the forecaster synthesize the results of complicated numerical models, just as it helps synthesize patterns in real data. The variety of forecasts observed in the media on any given day represents differing estimates based on the same information. For example, statistical products are very useful but cannot be accepted blindly, so the forecaster must decide which guidance—if any—to accept.

Severe-Weather Events. Great attention is paid to weather forecasts during times of severe events such as BLIZZARDS, HURRICANES, and TORNADOES. Accordingly, the NWS commits significant resources to the forecast of such events. Blizzards or strong extratropical cycles are handled through the usual forecast-information channels, with the local NWS office issuing special advisories as appropriate.

The National Hurricane Center in Coral Gables, Fla., has prime responsibility for tracking and forecasting hurricanes—and their antecedent conditions—in the Atlantic, Caribbean, and eastern Pacific. Despite the variety of satellite-borne sensors available, "hurricane hunter" aircraft still fly around and through such storms to gather data. As with conventionally obtained information, these extra data both define the current state of a storm and provide the starting point for numerical forecasts. The forecast problem is complicated by the fact that populations have grown so quickly along the Gulf and Atlantic coasts that certain regions need more than 24 hours of warning for evacuation before a hurricane makes landfall. Despite research, however, conditions can exist under which it is recognized that a correct 24-hour forecast is unlikely.

The Severe Storm Forecast Center (SSFC) in Kansas City, Mo., has primary responsibility for severe events

Synoptic weather maps, such as that on the opposite page, are published daily by the United States Weather Bureau, showing weather conditions existing over a wide area at a given time. The maps are drawn from atmospheric data collected by observers at selected locations and are used for weather forecasting.

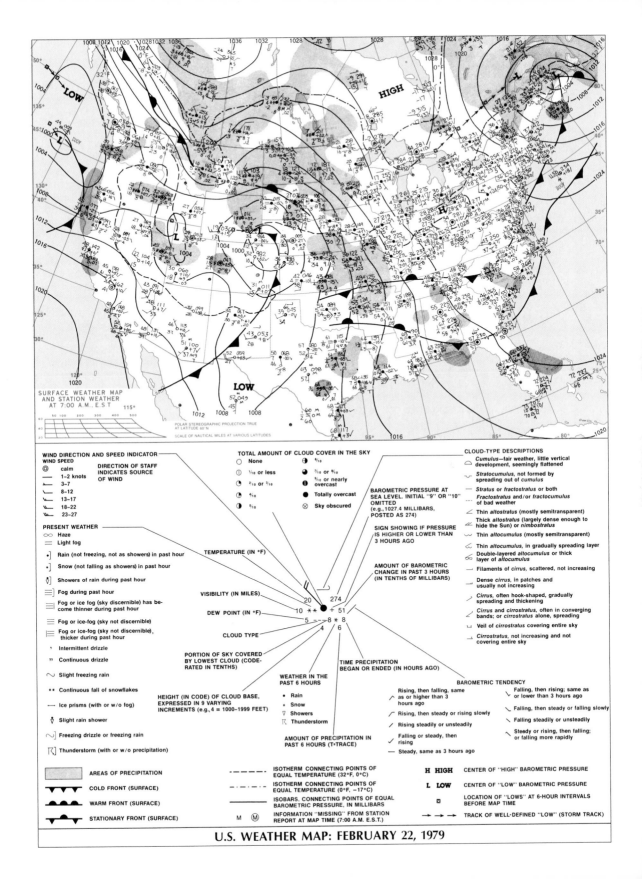

SURFACE WEATHER MAP
AND STATION WEATHER
AT 7:00 A.M., E.S.T.

POLAR STEREOGRAPHIC PROJECTION TRUE
AT LATITUDE 60°N
SCALE OF NAUTICAL MILES AT VARIOUS LATITUDES

50 100 200 300 400 500

WIND DIRECTION AND SPEED INDICATOR
WIND SPEED

◎	calm

DIRECTION OF STAFF
INDICATES SOURCE
OF WIND

⌐	1–2 knots
⌐—	3–7
⌐——	8–12
⌐———	13–17
⌐————	18–22
⌐—————	23–27

PRESENT WEATHER

∞ Haze
≡ Light fog

•¦ Rain (not freezing, not as showers) in past hour
*¦ Snow (not falling as showers) in past hour
⩒ Showers of rain during past hour
≡ Fog during past hour
≡ Fog or ice fog (sky discernible) has be-
come thinner during past hour
≡ Fog or ice-fog (sky not discernible)
≡ Fog or ice-fog (sky not discernible),
thicker during past hour
, Intermittent drizzle
,, Continuous drizzle
∿ Slight freezing rain
** Continuous fall of snowflakes
— Ice prisms (with or w/o fog)
⩒ Slight rain shower
∿ Freezing drizzle or freezing rain
⍔ Thunderstorm (with or w/o precipitation)

HEIGHT (IN CODE) OF CLOUD BASE,
EXPRESSED IN 9 VARYING
INCREMENTS (e.g., 4 = 1000–1999 FEET)

TOTAL AMOUNT OF CLOUD COVER IN THE SKY

○	None	◑	⁶/₁₀
◔	¹/₁₀ or less	◕	⁷/₁₀ or ⁸/₁₀
◔	²/₁₀ or ³/₁₀	◕	⁹/₁₀ or nearly overcast
◑	⁴/₁₀	●	Totally overcast
◑	⁵/₁₀	⊗	Sky obscured

BAROMETRIC PRESSURE AT
SEA LEVEL. INITIAL "9" OR "10"
OMITTED
(e.g., 1027.4 MILLIBARS,
POSTED AS 274)

SIGN SHOWING IF PRESSURE
IS HIGHER OR LOWER THAN
3 HOURS AGO

AMOUNT OF BAROMETRIC
CHANGE IN PAST 3 HOURS
(IN TENTHS OF MILLIBARS)

TEMPERATURE (IN °F)

VISIBILITY (IN MILES)

DEW POINT (IN °F)

CLOUD TYPE

```
      ‖
  20    274
10 **  + 51
 5     8 * 8
   4     6
```

PORTION OF SKY COVERED
BY LOWEST CLOUD (CODE-
RATED IN TENTHS)

WEATHER IN THE
PAST 6 HOURS

• Rain
* Snow
▽ Showers
⍁ Thunderstorm

TIME PRECIPITATION
BEGAN OR ENDED (IN HOURS AGO)

AMOUNT OF PRECIPITATION IN
PAST 6 HOURS (T=TRACE)

CLOUD-TYPE DESCRIPTIONS

◠ *Cumulus*—fair weather, little vertical
development, seemingly flattened
⌒ *Stratocumulus*, not formed by
spreading out of *cumulus*
— *Stratus* or *fractostratus* or both
⎵ *Fractostratus* and/or *fractocumulus*
of bad weather
∠ Thin *altostratus* (mostly semitransparent)
⩘ Thick *altostratus* (largely dense enough to
hide the Sun) or *nimbostratus*
∾ Thin *altocumulus* (mostly semitransparent)
⌇ Thin *altocumulus*, in gradually spreading layer
�double-layered *altocumulus* or thick
layer of *altocumulus*
⌇ Filaments of *cirrus*, scattered, not increasing
⌇ Dense *cirrus*, in patches and
usually not increasing
⌇ *Cirrus*, often hook-shaped, gradually
spreading and thickening
⌇ *Cirrus* and *cirrostratus*, often in converging
bands; or *cirrostratus* alone, spreading
⌣ Veil of *cirrostratus* covering entire sky
⌇ *Cirrostratus*, not increasing and not
covering entire sky

BAROMETRIC TENDENCY

∧ Rising, then falling, same
as or higher than 3
hours ago
⌃ Rising, then steady or rising slowly
⌿ Rising steadily or unsteadily
⌿ Falling or steady, then
rising
— Steady, same as 3 hours ago
⌀ Falling, then rising; same as
or lower than 3 hours ago
⌁ Falling, then steady or falling slowly
⌁ Falling steadily or unsteadily
⌁ Steady or rising, then falling;
or falling more rapidly

▨	AREAS OF PRECIPITATION	
▼▼	COLD FRONT (SURFACE)	
◖◗	WARM FRONT (SURFACE)	
▼◗	STATIONARY FRONT (SURFACE)	

– – – – ISOTHERM CONNECTING POINTS OF
EQUAL TEMPERATURE (32°F, 0°C)
– · – · – ISOTHERM CONNECTING POINTS OF
EQUAL TEMPERATURE (0°F, –17°C)
———— ISOBARS, CONNECTING POINTS OF EQUAL
BAROMETRIC PRESSURE, IN MILLIBARS
M Ⓜ INFORMATION "MISSING" FROM STATION
REPORT AT MAP TIME (7:00 A.M. E.S.T.)

H HIGH CENTER OF "HIGH" BAROMETRIC PRESSURE
L LOW CENTER OF "LOW" BAROMETRIC PRESSURE
⊠ LOCATION OF "LOWS" AT 6-HOUR INTERVALS
BEFORE MAP TIME
→ ⇢ TRACK OF WELL-DEFINED "LOW" (STORM TRACK)

U.S. WEATHER MAP: FEBRUARY 22, 1979

connected with thunderstorms, including tornadoes, downbursts, hail, and lightning. A so-called "convective outlook" is issued a day ahead, delimiting the general region of expected activity. Detailed forecasting then takes place in the range of 1 to 3 hours. Once a severe event is reported, the SSFC works with local NWS and government authorities to obtain additional observations and to warn localities expected to be affected.

Forecasting Research. A number of new observing systems are being developed for forecasting purposes. These include the Next-Generation Radar (NEXRAD) digital weather radar, which employs the DOPPLER EFFECT to detect motions toward or away from the radar installation. The Doppler effect is also employed in so-called "wind profilers" that continuously report horizontal wind speeds at various heights above the ground. New generations of satellite-borne sensors are intended to increase the weather information obtainable from space by some 100 to 1,000 times the current volume. In addition, automated systems are being developed for taking observations at surface stations and on board buoys, ships, and aircraft. The communications, processing, and display systems intended to govern this torrent of further data are still being elaborated. The Program for Regional Observation and Forecast Systems (PROFS), a project of the NATIONAL OCEANIC AND ATMOSPHERIC ADMINISTRATION (NOAA) in Boulder, Colo., is developing interactive computer systems for extracting needed information from a vast array of data sources.

New numerical models continue to be developed as supercomputers become more powerful (see COMPUTER MODELING). It is not simply a matter of doing more and more computations, however. Some approximations in such models depend on other parts of the solution being sufficiently simple to make the resulting approximation satisfactory. For example, the treatment of incoming SOLAR RADIATION is relatively unimportant for models that are no longer useful after 2 days. Some scheme for solar radiation must be included, however, for models that are still useful for up to 7 or 8 days.

As numerical models improve, meteorologists are reconsidering the concept of predictability. How far ahead can time- or area-averaged quantities be usefully predicted? Is it possible to identify occasions when the atmosphere is more predictable than at other times? Meteorologists recognize that in the predictive step of forecasting, current statistical models should in time be replaced with expert systems, an outgrowth of research into ARTIFICIAL INTELLIGENCE. This idea, however, has only begun to be developed. The greatest potential for improvement in forecasting appears to lie in the short and medium ranges, whereas experimental work will characterize the extended range. Improvements in daily forecasting are likely to increase at a relatively slow pace.

---

weather modification Weather modification includes both planned efforts and accidental actions that alter natural atmospheric phenomena. The use of chemicals to make rain (cloud seeding) and to dissipate fog is the most common form of planned weather modification.

Inadvertent changes such as ACID RAIN and smog are created by the chemical waste products of industrial complexes, cities, and certain agricultural practices.

Cloud Seeding. The major effort in weather modification has been the chemical seeding of clouds. The physical basis for cloud seeding is the induction of an internal change in the cloud either prematurely or with greater efficiency than occurs in nature. Most cloud-seeding projects presume that at least a portion of the cloud to be treated contains supercooled water (unfrozen water drops existing at temperatures below freezing), that more ice particles can be produced, and that treatment with chemical agents or refrigerants will change a portion of the cloud into ice.

After seeding, the resultant mixture of water and ice is unstable; water vapor is rapidly deposited on the ice crystals, while simultaneously water evaporates from the supercooled water droplets in the cold upper part of the cloud. The ice crystals become sufficiently large to fall relative to the remaining droplets, and the crystals collect water vapor and droplets as they descend through the cloud. These particles of ice or water can grow large and heavy enough to fall from the cloud as precipitation.

The chemical agents used in cloud seeding primarily have been dry ice or silver iodide. Dry ice produces enormous numbers of ice crystals—an effect first observed in 1946—but it must be broadcast from high altitudes. Silver iodide is introduced into clouds in the form of smoke either by smoke generators or by pyrotechnic (burning) devices. Urea, an organic compound commonly used as fertilizer, has also been used in cloud seeding.

Hail and Lightning Suppression. Projects to suppress hail use large amounts of silver iodide to transform nearly all the supercooled water into ice crystals; the results of these programs are uncertain. Lightning suppression to reduce the violence of thunderstorms or the threat of fire in dry areas has been attempted by seeding thunderstorms with metallic chaff to produce a current that is supposed to neutralize the electrical field. Silver iodide is also introduced, to produce ice-crystal dipoles. The results are inconclusive.

Cloud Dissipation. The alteration of precipitation from layer clouds—those normally appearing with large-scale cyclonic storm systems common during cold weather—has not been established. Seeding certain layer clouds such as stratus with freezing nuclei, however, can dissipate them; this technique has been successfully used to dispel clouds over airports.

Snow Induction. Experiments and operational projects involving silver iodide seeding of mountain-produced (orographic) clouds during winter in Colorado and California have indicated that increases in snowfall ranging from 10 percent to 30 percent can be induced under certain conditions. Snow induction would benefit ski resorts and also provide a source of water.

Fog Suppression. The two basic types of fog, cold and warm, each require a different approach for suppression. The dissipation of cold fogs, which are fogs made up of liquid droplets at temperatures below freezing, has become a routine weather-modification technology that is performed at a number of U.S. airports. Aircraft flying over the fog broadcast crushed dry ice or silver iodide. Warm fogs—those with droplets at temperatures above freezing—have defied attempts at modification. Numerous schemes have been tried, including heating the air to evaporate the fog (attempted during World War II) and drying the fog with chemical agents.

Hurricane Experiments. A hurricane contains huge quantities of supercooled water, and silver iodide seeding conceivably could produce some changes in storm behavior. Aircraft seeding tests have suggested some minor, short-lived changes in the wall cloud of the hurricanes, resulting in diminished wind speeds for a few hours. Results regarding hurricane-modification technology, however, are inconclusive.

Technologies do not exist for modifying rainfall and severe storms over major population and agricultural areas of the world in a way that would be economically useful. Research in this area must be concerned not only with technical problems but with social and environmental issues. Public controversies have occurred and will continue to occur unless planned weather modification is both effective and properly managed for the general welfare.

weather satellite see SATELLITE, ARTIFICIAL

Weatherford, William William Weatherford, also known as Red Eagle, b. c.1780, d. Mar. 9, 1824, was a CREEK Indian chief noted for his role in the Creek War, 1812–14. On Aug. 30, 1813, having forewarned the commander, Weatherford led 1,000 Creek Indians of the Red Stick faction in an assault on Fort Mims, Ala. Nearly 500 soldiers and settlers were killed. Weatherford then led his forces north along the Tallapoosa. At Horseshoe Bend, on Mar. 27, 1814, they were defeated by Andrew Jackson and his Indian allies. The battle cost the Creek 600 warriors and about half of their lands in Alabama. Weatherford, pardoned by Jackson, lived out the remainder of his years farming in peace.

weathering Weathering has been defined in several ways; in simplest terms it is the rock breakdown, decomposition, and rotting that take place at or near the surface of the Earth. Weathering involves both physical and chemical reactions, so it depends on such factors as climate, topography, vegetation, time, and the composition and texture of the parent rock.

Temperature and rainfall are significant climatic factors; rock decay is most rapid in warm, humid climates. Both the direction of water movement through the rocks and the leaching of soluble components depend on the amount of rainfall and its seasonal distribution. In a continuously wet climate water moves downward; in a dry climate the prevailing water movement may be upward, and the decay components may not be removed from the weathering zone.

Topography controls the vertical movement of groundwater, the rate of erosion, and the rate of removal of weathering products (see EROSION AND SEDIMENTATION). In low, flat areas there is little movement of water through the soils and rocks and therefore relatively little leaching.

Vegetation is important because the products of organic decay, particularly in cool, humid climates where abundant organic acids can be produced, greatly affect the alteration process. The type of vegetation—that is, trees, grasses, and other plants—has a significant effect on the decomposition of the parent minerals and the resultant decomposition products.

Time plays a role in the development of weathering products because weathering processes are relatively slow. In the initial stages of weathering certain reactions may take place that are very different from subsequent reactions after the more soluble components are removed.

A variety of chemical reactions take place in weathering, including hydrolysis, ion exchange, oxidation, carbonation, and solution. Water is a factor in hydrolysis, ion exchange, and solution. Oxidation involves the combination of elemental oxygen with the atoms or ions in the rock or mineral. Carbonation is the combination of carbonate or bicarbonate with rock elements such as calcium, magnesium, and iron.

Some of the end products of the weathering process are of economic significance. Among the most important and widespread of these are the clay called kaolin and an aluminim ore called bauxite (see ORE DEPOSITS).

Double Arch and other features in Arches National Monument, Utah, were formed by the erosion of an ancient sandstone bed. Depending on the materials in sedimentary layers, varied weathering effects can contribute to the striking appearance of such formations.

weaver Weavers are birds of small to medium size, many of which are known for weaving complex nests. More than 150 species, including the well-known house SPARROW, *Passer domesticus* (also called English sparrow), are found throughout the world; weavers are especially prevalent in the Old World, particularly Africa. These species make up the family Ploceidae, closely related to the WEAVER FINCH family, Estrildidae.

Weavers usually have bodies 7.5 to 25 cm (3 to 10 in) long but are variable in total length because some, such as the African whydah, *Coliuspasser progne*, have long tails, sometimes 63 cm (25 in) in length. Most have short, conical bills that are good for cracking seeds, their chief food.

In general, weavers build globular nests with side or bottom entrances often extended into tubes or spouts. The nest fabric, usually strong and pliant, is woven by the use of intricate stitching techniques. The nest of the social weaver, *Philetairus socius*, is particularly elaborate, with vertical tunnels leading to canopied retort-shaped chambers. Many species are colonial; the extreme is reached by the red-billed dioch, *Quelea quelea*, an African bird that breeds in large colonies with up to 10 million nests. These weavers migrate in locustlike flocks, causing great damage to crops.

Weaver, James B. The American politician James Baird Weaver, b. Dayton, Ohio, June 12, 1833, d. Feb. 6, 1912, was the presidential candidate of the GREENBACK PARTY in 1880 and of the POPULIST PARTY in 1892. An Iowa lawyer and Union officer, Weaver served (1879–81) in the U.S. House of Representatives as a Greenbacker. On the Greenback ticket he polled 308,578 votes for president. Weaver served again (1885–89) in the House of Representatives, winning two terms as candidate of both the Greenback-Labor and Democratic parties. A Populist party founder, he garnered more than a million popular votes and 22 electoral votes as its presidential nominee.

Weaver, Robert C. Robert Clifton Weaver, b. Washington, D.C., Dec. 29, 1907, was the first African American to hold a cabinet post in the U.S. government. An economist, he began his government service during the New Deal, serving the Roosevelt administration in various capacities. After World War II he taught economics, and in 1949–55 he directed the opportunity fellowship program of the John Hay Whitney Foundation. In 1961, President John F. Kennedy appointed Weaver to administer the Housing and Home Finance Agency; in 1966, when the Housing and Urban Development department was created, he became its first secretary. Weaver retained this post until 1968.

weaver finch Weaver finches are small, often brightly colored, seed-eating birds with conical bills. Found in the Old World tropics, the more than 100 species—many popular as cage birds and including WAXBILLS, mannikins, and grass finches—make up the family Estrildidae, closely related to the weavers of the family Ploceidae. Many species construct complicated nests with side entrances. The young have bright spots, sometimes reflective, on the tongue, palate, and gape that presumably help the parents feed them in the darkness of the covered nest.

weaving Weaving is the process of interlacing two sets of yarns to produce a fabric. First one set of yarns, the longitudinal warp, is laid in place on a LOOM. Then the second set, called the weft or filling, is interlaced at right angles to the warp. The weft yarn is usually wound around a shuttle, which passes through the warp, unwinding the yarn as it moves.

History. It is generally believed that weaving techniques were first used in BASKETRY, where plant fibers, such as thin vines and reeds, were readily available as basket-making materials. After the invention of the loom and the spindle, advances in weaving techniques took place rapidly. Fine linen cloth was being manufactured in Europe perhaps as early as 7,000 years ago. Devices that raise alternate warp threads simultaneously (heddles) were used in Egypt in the 4th millennium BC and in Bronze Age Europe and Asia. Foot-operated heddles are believed to have originated in ancient China.

These early looms were capable of producing complex weaves. The Inca of Peru, for example, produced woven wool and cotton fabrics in brilliant colors and sophisticated patterns. Although weaving machinery is now for the most part powered and almost entirely automatic, the basic weaves remain those that were developed in the early age of the hand loom.

Basic Weaves. All woven fabrics, however complex, are made using variations of the three basic weaves.

The plain weave is the most common, the strongest, and the least complicated. In plain-woven fabrics, the weft is carried over all odd-numbered warps and under all even-numbered warps. For the next pick, or pass of the shuttle, the weft passes over the even-numbered warps, and under the odd.

The twill weave is formed when the weft passes over warps 1 and 2 and under warps 3 and 4, and in the next pick, passes over warps 2 and 3 and under warps 4 and 5. Twill fabrics have diagonal lines running either right or left on the fabric face.

In the satin weave, the weft "floats" or skips over as many as 12 warps before being woven in. The next pick repeats the float, but on a different set of warps.

In addition to the weave, which determines the structure of the fabric, several other factors influence the fabric's appearance. Within a given area of cloth, the ratio of warps to wefts may be equal, producing a square-count fabric where warp and weft have equal prominence; the number of warps may be larger (warp-face); or the number of wefts may be larger (weft-face). Held so that the weave's most prominent features are highlighted, a plain-weave cloth in warp-face will emphasize horizontal lines,

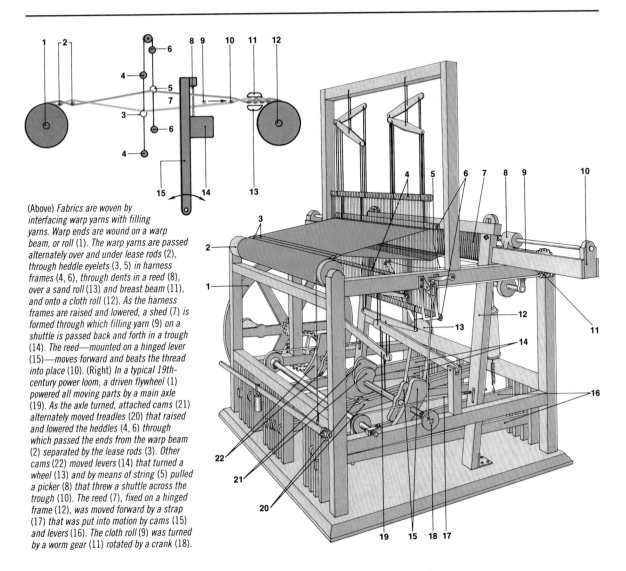

(Above) *Fabrics are woven by interfacing warp yarns with filling yarns. Warp ends are wound on a warp beam, or roll (1). The warp yarns are passed alternately over and under lease rods (2), through heddle eyelets (3, 5) in harness frames (4, 6), through dents in a reed (8), over a sand roll (13) and breast beam (11), and onto a cloth roll (12). As the harness frames are raised and lowered, a shed (7) is formed through which filling yarn (9) on a shuttle is passed back and forth in a trough (14). The reed—mounted on a hinged lever (15)—moves forward and beats the thread into place (10). (Right) In a typical 19th-century power loom, a driven flywheel (1) powered all moving parts by a main axle (19). As the axle turned, attached cams (21) alternately moved treadles (20) that raised and lowered the heddles (4, 6) through which passed the ends from the warp beam (2) separated by the lease rods (3). Other cams (22) moved levers (14) that turned a wheel (13) and by means of string (5) pulled a picker (8) that threw a shuttle across the trough (10). The reed (7), fixed on a hinged frame (12), was moved forward by a strap (17) that was put into motion by cams (15) and levers (16). The cloth roll (9) was turned by a worm gear (11) rotated by a crank (18).*

whereas a weft-face weave will show longitudinal lines.

The light-reflective quality of woven cloth is exploited in patterns of great complexity—for instance, a plain-weave fabric may have its design woven in a satin weave that alone catches and is outlined by light. Pattern may also be determined by the use of different-colored yarns, and by the relationship of color to warp and weft. For example, a stripe may run longitudinally in warp-face material, or from side to side in a weft-face fabric.

Along with the many different effects produced by warp or weft emphasis, and the almost infinite number of variations of the basic weaves and their combinations, several other techniques are used to produce special fabrics. In double-face weaving, which is used for heavy woolens such as blankets, two sets of warp yarns are interwoven with one set of weft (or two of weft and one of warp), creating a two-faced fabric that may often have a different weave on either surface. Double cloth uses two sets of both warp and weft, with the warp sets regularly pulled through the opposite weft to intermesh the two surfaces. Pile fabrics, such as terry-cloth toweling, are also woven with two sets of warp or weft. One set forms the "ground," while the other forms the raised loops that characterize terry cloth. Velvet is a warp-pile fabric; the warp is a double set, and it is cut to form the pile.

Lappet weave is one of several weaves that use extra warp threads as floats on the fabric's surface. The extra warp, woven in on a regular pattern, is cut (as in dotted swiss) or laid on the surface, as in the many fabrics with a raised pattern that seems almost embroidered. Brocade weaves also produce a raised-pattern effect, by using extra weft threads as floats.

Light, sheer fabrics woven of silk, cotton, or rayon may be made in a gauze weave, where some of the warp threads are interlaced with each other by the weft, producing an open, lacelike texture.

In some hand-woven carpets, the weft is not passed through on a shuttle, but instead is tied to pairs of warp threads, with the weft ends left free to form the pile. In the Middle East, rugs are still woven in which the warp threads are picked up individually by hand, and a flat piece of wood is used to hold them open while the weft is inserted and tied.

web-fed press Web-fed presses are PRINTING machines that receive paper from a continuous roll (web) rather than as separate sheets. They are used for printing newspapers, magazines, books, catalogs, stationery, and various packaging materials. The presses are often known by the printing process being used—web-offset, rotary letterpress, rotogravure—and can be of single-unit or multiunit construction.

In web-fed printing, a roll of paper is suspended in a reel stand and fed into the press. The web is pulled through one or more printing units, maintaining constant tension and pressure on the web so that such faults as misregister (improper alignment of color images), breaks in the web, or wrinkling do not occur. Each unit of a web-fed press is able to print a certain number of pages, depending on the width of the web and the circumference of the printing cylinder versus the width and height of the page. After passing through the printing units, the full web is cut into smaller webs called ribbons. These ribbons are collected in the press-folder system and cut and folded into a section called a signature. Some presses can paste ribbons together before folding into signatures. One method toward maximum output on modern web presses is achieved by a "flying paster"; a new roll of paper is joined (pasted) to the end of another roll while the press is running at high speed.

web spinner Web spinners, or embiids, are slender, fragile insects, from 4 to 7 mm (0.15 to 0.28 in) long, that live in large groups in silk-lined galleries in the soil or under bark, stones, or debris. The silk is spun from glands in the front legs as the insects run forward and backward. Most males are winged, but females are wingless. Most of the species, which make up the order Embioptera, are found in the tropics.

Webb, Sidney and Beatrice Sidney James Webb, b. July 13, 1859, d. Oct. 13, 1947, and Beatrice Potter Webb, b. Jan. 22, 1858, d. Apr. 30, 1943, were two English social and economic reformers and theorists, who for half a century influenced the socialist thought of their time. They were both active in social work and with labor unions when they met and married in 1892. Sidney was one of the early members (1884) of the FABIAN SOCIETY, and Beatrice, before she knew Sidney, had published (1891) *The Co-operative Movement in Great Britain*. Sid-

ney was elected (1902) as a Progressive party member of the new London County Council. Among numerous activities to advance social justice and education, the Webbs were the power behind the Educational Acts of 1902 and 1903; they were principal founders of the London School of Economics (1895); and in 1913 they founded *The New Statesman*, which is still one of Britain's leading political journals. Sidney was an executive member of the Labour party from 1915 to 1925; he entered the House of Commons in 1922; and he was president of the Board of Trade in the first Labour government (1924). He resigned his seat in 1928 but the following year agreed to serve in the second Labour government as colonial secretary; he was raised to the peerage as Baron Passfield (Beatrice objected strongly and refused to be called Lady Passfield).

Weber, Carl Maria von [vay'-bur] The German composer Carl Maria von Weber, b. Nov. 18, 1786, d. June 5, 1826, is best known for his romantic operas. First cousin of Mozart by marriage, he shared something of the same precocious talent, writing an opera, *Das Waldmädchen* (The Forest Maiden), which was produced at Freiburg in 1800, and *Peter Schmoll*, performed at Augsburg in 1803. His first appointment as a conductor came in 1804 at the Stadttheater in Breslau. He resigned this post in 1806 when he became director of music to Duke Eugen of Württemberg at Carlsruhe, and he later served as music master to the duke's brother, Ludwig, at Stuttgart. His opera *Silvana* was well received at Frankfurt in 1810, the title role being sung by his future wife, Caroline Brandt. *Abu Hassan* followed in 1811 (Munich) and proved that he possessed great talent as a writer of Singspiel.

Weber toured widely and with great success as a pianist and earned respect as a conductor in Prague and Dresden. His Dresden appointment, by the King of Saxony, crowned his artistic development and gave him the leisure to pursue new operatic ventures, notably *Der Freischütz* (The Freeshooter), whose libretto (by Friedrich Kind) was based on a book of ghost stories. The resulting musical and dramatic mixture of mystery, love, and suspense, all heightened by Weber's skillful and imaginative use of the orchestra, captivated the public at the first performance (1821) in Berlin and established romantic opera in Germany. Although *Euryanthe* (1823) was less successful, due to a poor libretto, his last opera, *Oberon*, first performed at Covent Garden in 1826, met with an enthusiastic reception. In addition to his operas, he wrote much incidental music, three masses, various occasional cantatas, two symphonies, several concertos and concertinos (piano, horn, clarinet, bassoon), works for piano solo and duet, and numerous songs and part-songs.

Weber, Dick [web'-ur] Richard Anthony Weber, b. Indianapolis, Ind., Dec. 23, 1929, began bowling at an early age, and when he was 25 years old he was asked to join (1955) the Budweiser team. In his first year he helped the team win the national title. The following year he and Ray Bluth won the first of 4 national doubles titles. During 1961 and 1962, Weber gained 7 Professional Bowlers Association (PBA) victories. In 1965 he became the first bowler to roll three 300 games in one tournament. Weber was named Bowler of the Year by the Bowling Writers Association 3 times (1961, 1963, 1965) and an All-American 15 times, and he is a member of the PBA and American Bowling Congress (ABC) Halls of Fame.

Weber, Max (painter)   The painter Max Weber, b. Russia, Apr. 18 (N.S.), 1881, d. Oct. 4, 1961, emigrated to Brooklyn, N.Y., in 1891 and later became one of the first Americans to participate in the Parisian art movements of the early 1900s. Because he knew most of the advanced Parisian painters personally, he was then the best-informed painter of the American avant-garde. This knowledge is evident in his work, which reflects these European influences and, later, also those of cubism and futurism. Working in the futurist style, Weber also produced some of the first abstract sculpture in the United States, such as *Spiral Rhythm* (1915; Hirshhorn Museum and Sculpture Garden, Washington, D.C.). After 1917, Weber's work became less abstract and more decorative in its use of line and color. During the 1930s his concern for social issues predominated in his choice of subjects, but after World War II his interests centered on genre scenes, musical themes, and religion.

Weber, Max (sociologist) [vay'-bur]   Max Weber, b. Apr. 21, 1864, d. June 14, 1920, was a German social scientist and one of the founders of modern SOCIOLOGY. After studying in several German universities, working briefly as a legal assistant, and completing his doctoral

Max Weber, a German social scientist and theorist, greatly influenced 20th-century sociology through his techniques of analysis and his contributions to such fields as the sociology of religion and political sociology. His work The Protestant Ethic and the Spirit of Capitalism *(1904–05) is still widely debated.*

dissertation, Weber was appointed professor at the University of Freiburg (1894) and then professor at the University of Heidelberg (1896). Although nearly incapacitated by a nervous breakdown in his mid-thirties, Weber nevertheless managed to produce a prodigious body of work.

Weber is known for his work in three areas. His studies in the sociology of religion, including his analysis of the influence of Lutheranism and Calvinism on the development of capitalism, were initiated by his influential book *The Protestant Ethic and the Spirit of Capitalism* (1904–05; Eng. trans., 1930). His political sociology has been the foundation for many modern analyses of politics, social stratification, and bureaucracy, although Weber's works in political sociology were not available in English until the translation of *Economy and Society* (1922) in 1968. His *Methodology of the Social Sciences* (1922; Eng. trans., 1949) remains influential in the development of systems of inquiry into the nature of social science.

Fundamental to Weber's thought were his concept of BUREAUCRACY and his theory of rationalization. He maintained that the bureaucratization of the political and economic spheres of society was the most significant development in the modernization of Western civilization.

Weber, Wilhelm Eduard   The German physicist Wilhelm Eduard Weber, b. Oct. 24, 1804, d. June 23, 1891, is famed for his work on electricity and magnetism. The unit of magnetic flux, the weber, is named in his honor. From 1831 to 1836, Weber was a professor of physics at the University of Göttingen, where he collaborated closely with Carl Friedrich GAUSS, one of the world's most brilliant mathematicians. Together they established a network of magnetic observatories; to correlate local measurements, they created the first practical long-range galvanic telegraph. While professor of physics at the University of Leipzig, Weber published (1846) his law of electrical force. To test it Rudolph Kohlrausch measured the ratio between the electrodynamic and electrostatic units of charge, a measurement that played a key role in James Clerk MAXWELL's formulation of the electromagnetic theory.

Webern, Anton von [vay'-burn]   Although he is now considered one of the founders of 20th-century SERIAL MUSIC, Anton Webern, b. Vienna, Dec. 3, 1883, worked in relative obscurity until his death at Mittersill in the Austrian Alps on Sept. 15, 1945, mistakenly shot by an American soldier. After his high school graduation in 1902, he went to Bayreuth to hear the festival performances of Wagner's music-dramas. Inspired by this experience, he threw himself into music studies at the University of Vienna. In 1904 he began four years of study with Arnold Schoenberg, to whom he remained devoted for the rest of his life. Both Webern and his fellow pupil Alban Berg closely followed Schoenberg's evolution from tonality through atonality to the twelve-tone system.

Webern is noted for the extreme brevity and delicacy

of many of his compositions. Some are less than a minute long, and the music is rarely loud. He developed the concept of *Klangfarbenmelodie* (tone-color melody): the division of a melody among a succession of different instruments, each playing just one or two notes. Schoenberg wrote of Webern's brief pieces, "Every glance is a poem, every sigh a novel."

As might be expected, most of Webern's music is for small instrumental and vocal ensembles. Such pieces include the Six Bagatelles for String Quartet (1913), the Concerto for Nine Solo Instruments (1934), and two chamber cantatas to texts by Hildegard Jone (1939 and 1941–43).

Webster, Daniel Daniel Webster, b. Salisbury, N.H., Jan. 18, 1782, d. Oct. 24, 1852, statesman, lawyer, and orator, was his era's foremost advocate of American nationalism. A farmer's son, he graduated from Dartmouth College in 1801. After a legal apprenticeship, Webster opened a legal practice in Portsmouth, N.H., in 1807.

Rising quickly as a Federalist party leader, Webster was elected (1812) to the U.S. House of Representatives. After two more terms in the House, Webster left Congress in 1816 and moved to Boston. Over the next six years he won major constitutional cases before the Supreme Court (most notably, DARTMOUTH COLLEGE V. WOODWARD, GIBBONS V. OGDEN, and MCCULLOCH V. MARYLAND), establishing himself as the nation's leading lawyer and an outstanding orator. Webster was returned (1823) to Congress and was elected (1827) senator from Massachusetts.

With the Federalist party dead, Webster joined the National Republican party, allying himself with westerner Henry CLAY and endorsing federal aid for roads in the West. Webster also backed the high-tariff bill of 1828. Angry Southern leaders condemned the tariff, and South Carolina's John C. CALHOUN argued that his state had the right to nullify the law. Replying to South Carolina's Robert HAYNE in a Senate debate in 1830, Webster triumphantly defended the Union. His words "Liberty *and* Union, now and forever, one and inseparable!" won wide acclaim.

Webster and President Andrew Jackson joined forces in 1833 to suppress South Carolina's attempt to nullify the tariff. But Webster and other opponents of Jackson—now known as Whigs (see WHIG PARTY, United States)—battled him on other issues, including his attack on the National Bank. Webster ran for the presidency in 1836 as one of three Whig party candidates but carried only Massachusetts.

In 1841, President William Henry Harrison named Webster secretary of state. The death of Harrison (April 1841) brought John Tyler to the presidency, and in September 1841 all the Whigs but Webster resigned from the cabinet. Webster remained to settle a dispute with Great Britain involving the Maine-Canada boundary and successfully concluded the WEBSTER-ASHBURTON TREATY (1842). Whig pressure finally induced Webster to leave the cabinet in May 1843.

The annexation of Texas in 1845 and the resulting war with Mexico, both opposed by Webster, forced the country to face the issue of the expansion of slavery. Webster opposed such expansion but feared even more a dissolution of the Union over the dispute. In a powerful speech before the Senate on Mar. 7, 1850, he supported the COMPROMISE OF 1850, denouncing Southern threats of secession but urging Northern support for a stronger law for the recovery of fugitive slaves. Webster was named secretary of state in July 1850 by President Millard Fillmore and supervised the strict enforcement of the Fugitive Slave Act. Webster's stand alienated antislavery forces and divided the Whig party, but it helped to preserve the Union.

Webster, John John Webster, b. London, *c.*1580, d. *c.*1634, is celebrated for his two great tragedies, *The White Devil* (1612) and *The Duchess of Malfi* (1613). Although fascinated by the reputation of Italian Renaissance courts for intrigue, debauchery, and violence he portrays in the duchess a memorably pure and suffering woman. Vittoria Corombona, the white devil, is so subtly depicted that her greatness of spirit almost conceals her evil nature. Webster also wrote the tragicomedy *The Devil's Law Case* (1619–20) and collaborated with Thomas DEKKER on the comedies *Northward Ho* (1603–04), *Westward Ho* (1605), and *The Famous History of Sir Thomas Wyatt* (1607).

Webster, Noah Noah Webster, b. West Hartford, Conn., Oct. 16, 1758, d. May 28, 1843, was an American lexicographer and author. He wrote textbooks and compiled the first dictionary that distinguished American usage from British. His spelling book, known as the "blue-backed speller," was instrumental in standardizing American spelling. It sold millions of copies. His series of dictionaries culminated in the two-volume *American Dictionary of the English Language* (1828), which re-

Daniel Webster, a prominent lawyer and gifted orator, became one of the most influential members of the U.S. Congress, where he championed the interests of the northeastern states.

Noah Webster, the American lexicographer famous for An American Dictionary of the English Language (1828), championed the development of a distinct national culture, independent of England's influence. Webster also wrote medical and scientific texts, composed political tracts, and served in the Massachusetts state legislature.

flected his extensive research. He also advocated uniform copyright laws and was a founder of Amherst College.

Webster, William H.

U.S. public official William Hedgcock Webster, b. St. Louis, Mo., Mar. 6, 1924, was a federal judge when he became director of the Federal Bureau of Investigation in 1978. He was credited with restoring the FBI's reputation, which had been tarnished by improper activities. In 1987, Webster succeeded William J. Casey as director of the Central Intelligence Agency, then implicated in the IRAN-CONTRA AFFAIR. Webster resigned that post in 1991.

Webster-Ashburton Treaty

The Webster-Ashburton Treaty (Aug. 9, 1842), negotiated by U.S. Secretary of State Daniel WEBSTER and special British envoy Lord Ashburton, settled a long-standing dispute over the boundary between Maine and New Brunswick, Canada, while also resolving other issues. Under the terms of the agreement, which was hastened by the AROOSTOOK WAR between residents of Maine and New Brunswick, the United States received about 7,000 of the 12,000 disputed square miles, the rest going to Great Britain. The treaty also defined the U.S.-Canadian boundary between Lake Superior and the Lake of the Woods.

Weddell Sea

[wed'-ul] The almost continuously ice-covered Weddell Sea of the Atlantic Ocean covers an area of about 8 million km^2 (3 million mi^2) within the Antarctic Circle. It lies southeast of South America, east of Palmer Land, and west of Coats Land. Charted by the British navigator James Weddell in 1823, the sea is the site of scientific bases.

Wedekind, Frank

[vay'-de-kint] The German playwright Frank Wedekind, b. July 24, 1864, d. Mar. 9, 1918, is today recognized as the great forerunner of EXPRESSIONISM on the German stage. Going far beyond his naturalistic contemporaries in what he chose to present—and to argue—and mixing the tragic with the farcical, Wedekind was the creator of a grotesque style in drama which, in his later, lesser-known plays, became almost purely expressionistic. His first tragedy, *The Awakening of Spring* (1891; Eng. trans., 1909), about adolescent sex, was immediately banned; *Earth Spirit* (1895; Eng. trans., 1914) and *Pandora's Box* (1903; Eng. trans., 1918) provided the German theater with the ultimate love goddess, Lulu, an embodiment of insatiable sexuality and of primal energy. Later, more autobiographical plays—*The Marquis of Keith* (1901; Eng. trans., 1952), *Such is Life* (1901; Eng. trans., 1912), and *Hidalla* (1904)—deal with misunderstood genius. Wedekind acted in his own works, and his bizarre style of performance became the model for the concept of acting that Bertolt Brecht introduced into EPIC THEATER. After his death, Wedekind became a cult figure for all those who attacked traditional morality.

Wedgwood, Josiah

Josiah Wedgwood, b. July 12, 1730, d. Jan. 3, 1795, was the most important figure in British ceramic history. He set up his own pottery works in Burslem in 1759. At first he worked to improve the cream-colored earthenware body (called creamware) that, in varying quality, had been in use by Staffordshire potters for about 10 to 15 years. After 1765, Wedgwood was permitted to name his creamware "Queen's ware," after furnishing tableware to Queen Charlotte, the consort of George III.

In 1766, Wedgwood built a new factory specifically to make ornamental wares in the neoclassic revival style. The factory was named Etruria, after the region of central Italy where classical vases had been recently discovered.

This blue jasper-ware vase (c.1785), designed by the renowned English potter Josiah Wedgwood, exemplifies one of the most popular types of ceramic ware created at the Wedgwood manufactory in Etruria, Staffordshire. Born into a family of established potters, Wedgwood improved the quality of earthernware and introduced neoclassical styles into ceramics during the 18th century. (Victoria and Albert Museum, London.)

Thomas Bentley, his partner and London agent, was largely responsible for the quality and sophistication of these wares. The first were made in the "Black Basalt" body, but after further research, in 1776, Wedgwood perfected his well-known "Jasper ware" in various colors. His most famous productions in this technique were his copies of the Portland Vase (AD 3d century; British Museum, London), a Roman glass amphora with white relief decoration on a dark blue ground. Wedgwood's creamware, however, ensured the prosperity of his business and was always his main product. Its refinement and practicality made it the most desirable utilitarian pottery of the late 18th century. The Wedgwood firm continues to produce pottery and china today.

Wedgwood was also inventor of the pyrometer, which measures high temperatures, and he was the first industrialist to install (1782) a steam engine in his factory.

Wedgwood, Thomas   The son of Josiah Wedgwood, Thomas Wedgwood, 1771–1805, first conceived the idea of photography by applying 18th-century discoveries of the light sensitivity of silver nitrate to the production of images of designs and objects. Placing objects in the sun on surfaces coated with the chemical, he attempted to capture their images using a CAMERA OBSCURA. With Sir Humphry DAVY, Wedgwood published (1802) his results, but he died before finding a way to fix his silhouette images or to make a photograph.

Weed, Thurlow   Thurlow Weed, b. Greene County, N.Y., Nov. 15, 1797, d. Nov. 22, 1882, was William H. SEWARD's political manager and editor of the *Albany* (N.Y.) *Evening Journal* from 1830 to 1863. Long years of political management gave him an unsavory reputation for receiving government favors and dominating Seward, but Seward frequently took more advanced positions than Weed in reform causes. In 1856, Weed—thinking defeat probable—held Seward back from vigorous contention for the Republican presidential nomination. Seward lost the nomination to Abraham Lincoln in 1860, but Weed's influence with the administration remained substantial.

Although he was known as dictator of New York's Whigs, Weed never had complete control of the state's patronage during the Civil War. By 1863 he felt that abolitionist fanatics controlled Lincoln and hoped for a War Democrat to replace him. The "peace plank" in the 1864 Democratic platform, however, kept Weed in Republican ranks, and he retained influence with Lincoln's administration to the end.

week   see CALENDAR

weever   Weevers, or weeverfishes, are marine fishes with hollow, venom-containing spines on each gill cover and on a small dorsal fin. They typically lie buried in sand or mud and often inflict very painful wounds on people who unwittingly step on them or touch them. Several spe-

cies, making up the family Trachinidae, are found in coastal waters of Europe and the Mediterranean region. They attain lengths of about 35 cm (14 in) and are most active at night.

weevil [wee'-vul]   A weevil is a specialized beetle with an elongated head and a protruding, often curved snout that bears the mouthparts and antennae. Most weevils are less than 7 mm (0.28 in) long, but some are as much as 7.5 cm (3 in) long. Most are plainly or concealingly colored, but a few are bright. Adults are commonly found on flowers and fruit, often escaping potential predators by pretending to be dead. Females lay eggs in plant parts, some developing without fertilization through parthenogenesis. The legless, often blind larvae frequently burrow into seeds, buds, fruits, or underground roots.

Many weevils are among the worst insect pests. The larvae of the cotton boll weevil, *Anthonomus grandis*, feed on developing COTTON bolls, ruining crops. The granary weevil, *Calendra granaria*, and rice weevil, *C. oryzae*, damage wheat and rice in storage; the alfalfa weevil, *Hypera postica*, reduces the yield of hay; and pine weevils, *Pissodes*, damage branch tips on pine trees. Other weevils destroy fruit and nut crops, turfgrass, corn, ornamental shrubs, and other plants.

More than 40,000 species of weevils constitute the family Curculionidae of the beetle order Coleoptera. Almost 2,000 species of long, slender, primitive weevils, found mostly in the tropics, make up the family Brentidae.

The boll weevil has been a cotton pest in the southern United States since 1800. Because of the heavy financial losses it caused white plantation owners, black musicians before the Civil War used it in song lyrics as a symbol of rebellion.

Wegener, Alfred Lothar [veg'-e-nur]   The German meteorologist and geophysicist Alfred Lothar Wegener, b. Nov. 1, 1880, d. November 1930, stated the earliest seriously argued and factually supported hypothesis that the continents slowly drifted apart from a single landmass. He first presented (1912) his hypothesis of CONTINENTAL DRIFT in a lecture. The published version *The Origin of the Continents and Oceans* (1915; Eng. trans., 1924) received a generally hostile reception, and only in recent decades, with acceptance of PLATE TECTONICS, has Wegener become widely acknowledged as a revolutionary thinker.

In order to conduct meteorological and geological research, Wegener participated (1906–08, 1912–13, 1929–30) in three expeditions to Greenland. On his second expedition he jointly undertook the longest crossing of the ice cap ever accomplished. He died while leading a third Greenland expedition.

Weicker, Lowell P.   Lowell Palmer Weicker, Jr., b. Paris, May 16, 1931, was elected governor of Connecticut in 1990, the state's first independent governor since the 1850s. A graduate of Yale University and the University of Virginia law school, Weicker, a former Republican, was a U.S. senator from Connecticut from 1971 to 1989. He served as a member of the Senate investigative panel that looked into the WATERGATE scandal of 1972–74. Earlier in his political career he was a state legislator (1963–69), 1st Selectman, Greenwich, Conn. (1964–68), and a one-term member of the U.S. House of Representatives (1969–71).

Weidman, Charles [wyd'-muhn]   Charles Weidman, b. Lincoln, Neb., July 22, 1901, d. July 15, 1975, was a pioneering figure in American modern dance. A member of the Denishawn company from 1921 to 1928, he and Doris HUMPHREY left to establish their own school and company. In 1945 he founded a school by himself and 3 years later, a small dance group, the Charles Weidman Dance Company. Toward the end of his life he collaborated with the sculptor Mikhail Santaro on theater pieces. As a choreographer, Weidman's best works were humorous and satirical, such as *And Daddy Was a Fireman* (1943) and *Fables for Our Time* (1947). In the 1930s he choreographed several important Broadway shows, including *As Thousands Cheer* (1933) and *I'd Rather Be Right* (1937). Among his pupils was choreographer Bob Fosse.

Weierstrass, Karl Theodor [vy'-ur-shtrahs]   Karl Theodor Wilhelm Weierstrass, b. Oct. 31, 1815, d. Feb. 19, 1897, was (next to Gauss and Riemann) one of the most important German mathematicians of his century. After he had held several minor teaching positions, his work became recognized, and in 1856 he became a member of the faculty of the University of Berlin. His successful lectures in mathematics attracted students from all over the world. The topics of his lectures included the introduction to the theory of analytic functions, the theory of elliptic functions, and the application of these theories to problems in geometry and mechanics. He dealt with the theory and applications of Abelian functions. In his work outside the lecture room he reestablished the theory of analytic functions on a firmer basis than it had been prior to his work. The standards of rigor that he set affected generations of mathematicians.

weight (mathematics)   A weight is a numerical coefficient that is used to give more preference to some numbers than to others when treating statistical data. For example, when an instructor gives 3 quizzes and a final exam and counts the final exam double, the student's grade will be a weighted mean (see AVERAGE).

weight (physics)   Weight is a property of an object that exists by virtue of its MASS and the force of gravity. It is therefore distinct from mass, which is unaffected by the strength of the gravitational field. Weight is properly expressed in the same units (see UNITS, PHYSICAL) as force—the pound in the English system and the newton in the METRIC SYSTEM. Because of the customary determination of mass by its weight in the Earth's gravitational field, the weight of an object is frequently expressed in terms of the mass units kilograms and grams.

weight lifting   Weight lifting (and power lifting) is a sport that requires lifting a bar loaded with metal weights. It is both a competitive amateur sport and a form of exercise. The principle behind weight lifting is that a muscle will become stronger, harder, and larger if it works against increasingly heavier loads. Dumbbells, short metal bars with weights on either end, are used for exercising each hand; in competition athletes use both hands to lift a 2.2 m (7 ft 2 in) barbell with weights on the ends.

The three lifts in power-lifting competition are the squat (in which the bar is lifted from supports to the back of the shoulders, after which the lifter squats and straightens up), the bench press (in which the lifter lies on his or her back, lifts the barbell from the chest and extends the arms fully, locking the elbows), and the dead lift (in which the lifter raises the barbell from the floor to the thighs in one motion). Powerful weight lifters can lift 2½ times their body weight in a dead lift and 2 times their body weight in a bench press.

The three lifts in Olympic competition were, until 1972, the press (in which the lifter raises the barbell from the floor to the level of the shoulders and then above the head), the snatch (in which the barbell is lifted over the head in one uninterrupted movement), and the clean and jerk (in which the lifter pulls the barbell to the chest, then jerks it overhead in a separate motion). Accomplished weight lifters can snatch and press well above their own body weight, and jerk up to 2 times their weight and more. In both forms of competition the combined weight of the three lifts is the contestant's score. In 1972 the press was eliminated from Olympic and international competition.

Before the 20th century, weight lifting was primarily a stage and circus feat, although there were competitive events in Egypt, Japan, Turkey, and Europe. Weight lifting is now organized and governed by the International Weightlifting Federation, and the sport in its current form has been on the agenda of the Olympic Games since 1920.

weight loss   see DIET, HUMAN; OBESITY

weightlessness   The state of weightlessness—a condition in which an object experiences no gravitational pull—is created not by leaving the region of gravitational influence of Earth or of other celestial bodies but by balancing the force of gravity with the speed of a vehicle. Such a state is created, for example, when a space vehicle orbits the Earth. Near the Earth's surface, a weightless state can be produced for only brief periods (30 to 40 sec) by flying parabolic maneuvers in an aircraft. A weightless state produces effects on a body's cardiovascular and nervous systems as well as on its blood, muscles, skeleton, body fluids, and electrolytes (see SPACE MEDICINE).

weights and measures Weights and measures are standard units used to express specific quantities such as weight, capacity, or length. They are defined in terms of units and standards (see UNITS, PHYSICAL). A unit is the name of a given quantity such as a yard or pound; and a standard, until recently, has been the physical embodiment of a unit, something concrete that can be seen or touched. Now, however, the speed of light in a vacuum is used to define the meter, and only the kilogram standard remains a physical artifact. The science of weights and measures, called metrology, facilitates commercial, industrial, and scientific interaction.

Prehistoric Times. Systems of weights and measures evolved gradually and were subject to many influences. Thus, it is difficult to trace a clear or logical course. Counting was probably the earliest form of measure. Among prehistoric communities quantities of the principal product of each tribe often were used as a unit of barter. For example, a farmer might trade 20 handfuls of grain to a shepherd for a sheep. This simple barter system endured for thousands of years.

The development and application of linear measure probably took place between 10,000 and 8000 BC, before the development of measures of weight or capacity. The units of measure in these early systems were based on natural objects. People realized that some simple proportions exist among certain dimensions of the human body, so that it was logical to use parts of the body for standards of linear measure. For example, the Egyptians defined the cubit as the distance between the elbow and the tip of the middle finger.

Early humans also learned that there was a uniformity of weight among similar seeds and grains, and so these became used as standards of weight. The carat, used by modern jewelers as a unit for weighing precious stones, was derived from the carob seed. The grain, which is still used as a unit of weight, was originally the weight of a grain of wheat or barley. Other arbitrary measures of capacity were used: for example, cupped hands, hollow gourds, pots, and baskets.

All these methods of measurement depended on units that varied greatly. As primitive societies became more sophisticated, the need arose for a standardized system of weights and measures.

Egypt. Probably the earliest known unit of linear measure is the cubit. Used by the Egyptians, Sumerians, Babylonians, and Hebrews as a prime unit, its origin is uncertain. Because the distance between the elbow and

the tip of the middle finger varied from person to person (from about 17.6 to 20 in), so did the cubits used among various civilizations. The Egyptians had two cubits, a short one of 0.45 m (17.7 in) and a royal cubit of 0.524 m (20.6 in). The Egyptian royal cubit was divided into units of seven palms, the palm being the width of four fingers. In turn, each palm could be subdivided into four digits, the breadth of the middle finger.

Egyptian weight standards were based on a unit of grain. For example, in the decimal kedet system, 140–150 grains made up a kedet; ten kedets were a deben; and ten debens equaled a sep.

Greece and Rome. The Greeks probably adopted some of their standards from the systems developed by the Egyptians and Babylonians. The Greeks, however, also introduced a new unit, the foot, which they usually divided into 16 fingers. When political, military, and commercial power in the Mediterranean passed from the Greeks to the Romans, the latter adopted and modified the Greek system of measurement.

One of the most important contributions of Rome to the modern system of measurement was the division of the foot into 12 units called inches. Five feet equaled one pace (a pace being one double step), and 1,000 paces equaled a Roman mile. The 5,000 feet of the Roman mile is closely related to the modern mile of 5,280 feet.

The Romans used two different systems of weights. The smallest unit was the *uncia*, abbreviated to *oz*, from which the term *ounce* is derived. One system had 16 unciae, or ounces, to one *pondus*, or pound. A second system used a pound called the *libra* (abbreviated *lb*), which equaled 12 *unciae*.

Roman systems of weights and measures were among the many customs adopted by the peoples conquered by the Romans throughout Europe and western Asia. With the decline of imperial power in the 3d century AD, however, arbitrary local systems emerged. This led to widespread confusion.

Middle Ages. In the Middle Ages, little uniformity existed among systems. Not only did each country have its own standard but frequently there were differences within the country. In medieval France, for example, weight units varied not only between provinces but also between cities. France did not achieve uniformity in weights and measures until the metric system was established in the early 19th century.

As in France, England lacked standardized systems of weights and measures. In about 1300, London merchants, influenced by the French, adopted a weight system called *avoirdupois* (from the old French term, *aveir-de-peis*), meaning "goods of weight." This system, used to weigh bulkier goods, was based on a pound of 7,000 grains or 16 ounces. It is still used in many English-speaking countries.

During the 15th century the troy system, probably named for the ounce of Troyes, France, was used by jewelers to weigh gold, silver, and precious metals. The troy ounce is made up of 480 grains, with 12 ounces to the pound. Although the actual standards vary, both the troy

WEIGHTS AND MEASURES

Unit	Abbreviation	Equivalents	Unit	Abbreviation	Equivalents
Weight			**Volume**		
gram	g	1 g = 0.001 kg = 0.032150737 oz (troy or apothecary) = 0.035273962 oz (avoirdupois)	milliliter liter	ml l	1 ml = 1 cm^3 1 l = 1,000 cm^3 = 1,000 ml = 0.001 m^3 = 1.056688 qt (U.S.) = 0.2641721 gal (U.S.)
kilogram	kg	1 kg = 1,000 g = 2.204623 lb			
metric ton	metric ton	1 metric ton = 1,000 kg = 2,204.6226 lb (av) = 2,679.2289 lb (t or ap)	cubic meter	m^3	1 m^3 = 1,000,000 cm^3 = 1,000 l = 1 kl = 35.31467 ft^3 = 264.1721 gal
pounds (avoirdupois)	lb or lb av	1 lb av = 116.666 drams (t or ap) = 256 drams (av) = 7,000 grains = 453.59237 grams = 14,583333 oz (t or ap) = 16 oz (av) = 1.215277 lb (t or ap)	**Volume, Liquid**		
			hectoliter	hl	1 hl = 100 l = 0.1 m^3
			pint	pt	1 pt (U.S.) = 28.875 in^3 = 473.1765 cm^3 (ml) = 0.4731765 l 1 pt (U.K.) = 34.678 in^3 = 0.568261 l (Can. and Austral.) = 0.568262 l (U.K.)
pounds (troy or apothecary)	1 lb t or lb ap	1 lb t or lb ap = 5,760 grains = 373.24172 grams = 96 drams (t or ap) = 210.65143 drams (av) = 12 oz (t or ap) = 13.165714 oz (av) = 0.8228571 lb (av)	quart	qt	1 qt (U.S.) = 75 in^3 = 946.353 cm^3 (ml) = 0.946353 l 1 qt (U.K.) = 69.355 in^3 = 1.136522 l (Can. and Austral.) = 1.136523 l (U.K.)
Length			gallon	gal	1 gal (U.S.) = 231 in^3 = 3.785412 l = 3,785.412 cm^3 (ml) 1 gal (U.K.) = 277.42 in^3 = 4.546090 l (Can. and Austral.) = 4.546092 l (U.K.)
meter	m	1 m = 100 cm = 1,000 mm = 39.370079 in = 3.280840 ft			
kilometer	km	1 km = 1,000 m = 0.6214 mi	**Volume, Dry Measure**		
inch	in	1 in = 0.08333 ft = 0.027777 yd = 2.54 cm	pecks (U.S.)	pk	1 pk (U.S.) = 537.605 in^3 = 8,809.7675 cm^3 (ml) = 16 pt (U.S. dry) = 8 qt (U.S. dry) = 0.25 bushels (U.S. dry) = 7.999999567 qt (U.K. dry)
mile (statute)	mi	1 mi = 63,360 in = 5,280 ft = 1,760 yd = 1.609344 km			
nautical mile (international)	naut mi	1 naut mi = 1.852 km = 1.51 mi	pecks (British imperial)	pk	1 pk (U.K.) = 554.8385 in^3 = 9,092.175 cm^3 (ml) = 16 pt (U.K. dry) = 8 qt (U.K. dry) = 0.25 bushels (U.K. dry) = 8.256449 qt (U.S. dry)
Area					
square meter	m^2	1 m^2 = 10,000 cm^2 = 10.76391 ft^2 = 1.195990 yd^2			
square kilometer	km^2	1 km^2 = 1,000,000 m^2 = 0.3861 mi^2			
are	a	1 a = 100 m^2 = 119.60 yd^2			
hectare	ha	1 ha = 10,000 m^2 = 2.471054 acres			
acre	acre	1 acre = 43,560 ft^2 = 4,840 yd^2 = 4,046.8564 m^2			

and avoirdupois pounds are similar to the Roman pounds.

The system that had been developed by medieval apothecaries and used until very recently was similar to the troy system, with 5,760 grains or 12 ounces to the pound. Now, however, most pharmacists and physicians use the metric system.

Metric System. The creation of the METRIC SYSTEM was one of the most significant contributions of the French Revolution. It was initially adopted in 1793 and, though discarded in 1812, was reinstituted in 1840 as the only legal and permissible standard system of weights and measures for France.

The metric system is a decimal system based on multiples of ten. Its basic unit, the meter (from the Greek *metron*, which means "measure"), was first defined as 1 ten-millionth of the length of the meridian from Dunkerque to Barcelona. In 1983 the meter was redefined as the length of the path traveled by light in a vacuum in 1/299,792,458 of a second. This standard is laboratory reproducible.

Today the acceptance of the metric system is almost worldwide. When Great Britain joined the Common Market in 1972 it became imperative for the country to adopt metric weights and measures. The United States is the only major power that lags behind the rest of the world in accepting the metric system, but it is in the (slow) process of converting to this system.

International System of Units. Just as primitive humans had to create more sophisticated systems of measure as life became more complex, advances in modern science and technology have created a need for new units of measure. In 1960 the Eleventh General Conference of Weights and Measures in Paris named a new and comprehensive system of weights and measures: the International System of Units, or *Systeme International* (abbreviated SI). This system is based on six units: the meter to measure length, the kilogram for mass, the second for time, the AMPERE for electric current, the kelvin for thermodynamic temperature (see KELVIN SCALE), and the candela for light intensity. Not only does this system give unity to worldwide interchange, it also is adaptable to scientific advancement.

See also: MEASUREMENT.

Weil, Simone [vyl]   Simone Weil, b. Feb. 3, 1909, d. Aug. 24, 1943, was a French social philosopher, religious thinker, mystic, and political activist. In 1936 she was involved in the French worker strikes. She identified with all human suffering and often undertook physically demanding work, despite her poor health: she spent a year working in an auto factory and living with working women to learn the effect of industry on workers. Politically, she was a radical leftist. She worked for the Loyalists during the Spanish Civil War by joining and training with an anarchist unit; being a pacifist, however, she refused to use her rifle. Jewish by birth, Weil wanted to know the suffering of those who were victims of Nazism. Refusing to eat

more than the ration allowed in German-occupied France, she died of hunger.

Weill, Kurt [vyl]   The German-American composer Kurt Weill, b. Dessau, Germany, Mar. 2, 1900, d. Apr. 3, 1950, is best remembered for his collaborations with the playwright Bertolt Brecht on two satiric operas, The THREEPENNY OPERA and *The Rise and Fall of the City of Mahagonny* (1930; first production in English, 1979). After coming to the United States in 1935, Weill turned out a string of successful Broadway musicals, including *Knickerbocker Holiday* (1938) and *Lost in the Stars* (1949) with Maxwell Anderson and *One Touch of Venus* (1943) with Ogden Nash. He also wrote instrumental works, including two symphonies. Weill's wife, the singer Lotte LENYA, performed in many of his shows.

Weimar [vy'-mahr]   Weimar (1980 pop., 63,326) is a city in east central Germany on the Ilm River. It is a rail center where agricultural machinery, textiles, chemicals, pharmaceuticals, and processed foods are manufactured. The Goethe-Schiller Archives (1896) are located in Weimar, as are the Weimar State Theater, the Goethe National Museum, and the Liszt Museum. Near the city is the BUCHENWALD National Memorial honoring those who died in the concentration camp located there (1937–45).

Weimar was founded in 1254. The city became important as the capital of the Saxe-Weimar duchy in 1547 and of a grand duchy (Saxe-Weimar-Eisenach) in 1815. It became a great intellectual center in the late 18th century. The writers Johann Wolfgang von Goethe and Johann Christoph Friedrich von Schiller and the philosopher Friedrich Wilhelm Nietzsche lived and died in Weimar. Franz Liszt was musical director there during the mid-19th century. The German National Assembly met in the city in 1919 and adopted a new constitution for the democratic republic popularly called the Weimar Republic. The republic, which gave Germany its first national experience of democracy, was overthrown by the National Socialists in 1933.

Weimar Republic   see GERMANY, HISTORY OF; WEIMAR

Weimaraner [vy'-mah-rahn-ur]   The Weimaraner is a large, gray German sporting dog. Males stand 63.5 to 68.5 cm (25 to 27 in) high at the shoulders, females 58.5 to 63.5 cm (23 to 25 in). The breed is smooth-coated, sleek, and solid-colored in gray tones ranging from mouse to silver. The eyes are gray green or amber. Originally called the Weimar pointer, the dog is pointerlike in general outline and similar to the German short-haired pointer, only larger. The ears are carried flat to the side of the head. The tail is docked and about 15 cm (6 in) long in mature dogs. The breed was developed around Weimar, Germany, at the beginning of the 19th century. The dogs were first cultivated by nobility, later by sports enthusi-

The Weimaraner was originally a breed sponsored by 19th-century German nobility in Weimar. It is considered an all-around gun dog and is used to hunt a variety of game.

asts. The first specimen was brought to the United States in 1929, and the breed was officially recognized by the American Kennel Club in 1943.

Weinberg, Steven   Physicist Steven Weinberg, b. New York City, May 3, 1933, shared the 1979 Nobel Prize for physics with Abdus Salam and Sheldon GLASHOW for their efforts to formulate an approach to a UNIFIED FIELD THEORY that would unite the four FUNDAMENTAL INTERACTIONS of matter as aspects of a single phenomenon. In 1967 he and the Pakistani physicist Salam jointly presented a system of equations unifying the electromagnetic force and the weak force. Later experiments confirmed certain particle behaviors that had been predicted by their work. Weinberg has also written on science for a general audience. His works include *The First Three Minutes* (1977), on cosmology, and *The Discovery of Subatomic Particles* (1982).

Weinberger, Caspar Willard   As President Ronald Reagan's secretary of defense (1981–87), Caspar Willard Weinberger, b. San Francisco, Aug. 18, 1917, presided over the largest peacetime military buildup in U.S. history, with expenditures of $2 trillion. Weinberger had earlier headed (1972–73) the Office of Management and Budget under President Richard Nixon, where his reputation as one of Washington's most effective economizers earned him the nickname "Cap the Knife." During the Nixon administration he also served (1973–75) as secretary of health, education, and welfare. Returning to private business in 1975, Weinberger worked as an executive of the Bechtel Group until Reagan nominated him, as one of Reagan's longtime trusted advisors, as defense secretary.

Weingartner, Felix [vyn'-gahrt-nur]   Felix Weingartner, b. June 2, 1863, d. May 7, 1942, was one of the greatest Austrian conductors. Completely self-confident in his artistic judgment, he was not averse to making drastic cuts in major works, justifying his decisions in long letters to the press. As a youth he attended Leipzig Conservatory on a scholarship and studied piano with Liszt. From 1884 he conducted widely in Germany and Austria, occupying positions with the Berlin Opera (1891–98), the Vienna State Opera (1908–10), and the Vienna Volksoper (1919–24).

Weiss, Peter [vys]   A German playwright and novelist who helped develop the concept of documentary drama, Peter Weiss, b. Nov. 8, 1916, d. May 5, 1982, is most famous for his play *Marat/Sade*, which uses the French insane asylum of Charenton in 1808 as a metaphorical image of contemporary society. His first three plays—*The Tower* (1948; Eng. trans., 1966), *Die Versicherung* (Insurance, 1952), and *Night with Guests* (1963; Eng. trans., 1968)—show the influence of Kafka and the THEATER OF THE ABSURD. With *Marat/Sade* (1963; Eng. trans., 1965; film, 1966), Weiss's political perspective changed, and in his next plays, all experiments in documentary theater—*The Investigation* (1965; Eng. trans., 1966), *Song of the Lusitanian Bogey* (1965; Eng. trans., 1970), and *Vietnam Discourse* (1968; Eng. trans., 1970)—he employed the alienation techniques developed by Bertolt BRECHT to raise the audience's social consciousness to explore different kinds of political and racial oppression. Weiss also published a series of autobiographical novels and stories, notably *Leavetaking* (1961; Eng. trans., 1962) and *Vanishing Point* (1962; Eng. trans., 1966).

Weissmuller, Johnny [wys'-muhl-ur]   John Weissmuller, b. Freidorf, Hungary (now Romania), June 2, 1904, d. Jan. 20, 1984, was an American who became the first swimmer to win 5 gold medals in Olympic Games competition. He completely dominated swimming during the 1920s and won 51 U.S. national championships and set 67 world records during his career. In the 1924 Olympics Weissmuller won gold medals in the 100-m freestyle, the 400-m freestyle, and the 4 × 200-m freestyle relay; in the 1928 Olympics he took gold medals in the 100-m freestyle and the 4 × 200-m freestyle relay. From 1932 to 1948 he acted in films, playing the part of Tarzan.

Weizmann, Chaim [vyts'-mahn, hy'-im]   Zionist leader Chaim Weizmann, b. Nov. 27 (N.S.), 1874, d. Nov. 9, 1952, was president of the World Zionist Organization (1920–30, 1935–46), first president of Israel (1949–52), and an internationally renowned scientist. A native of Russia, he studied chemistry at the University of Freiburg in Switzerland and received his doctorate there in 1900. Weizmann joined the University of Manchester faculty in 1904 and became a leader of the British Zionist movement. He was influential in the formulation of the BALFOUR DECLARATION (1917), committing the British government to work toward the establishment of a Jewish homeland in Palestine. He headed the Zionist Commission to Palestine in 1918 and played the key role in establishing the Jewish Agency for Palestine in 1929.

As president of the World Zionist Organization, Weizmann stressed the need for extensive Jewish settlement work in Palestine, backed by the world Jewish community, in implementing the Balfour Declaration. Although he advocated a Jewish state, his policy of compromise with Britain after World War II was opposed by David BEN-GURION, and Weizmann was not reelected to head the World Zionist Organization in 1946. He was president of Israel's Provisional Council of State (1948–49) and in February 1949 was inaugurated as the first president of Israel. Weizmann was a founder of the Hebrew University in Jerusalem (1918) and was instrumental in establishing the Sieff Research Institute at Rehovot (1934).

Weld, Theodore Dwight   The American abolitionist Theodore Dwight Weld, b. Hampton, Conn., Nov. 23, 1803, d. Feb. 3, 1895, was perhaps the most effective organizer of the United States antislavery movement. By 1830, Weld had established himself as a persuasive lecturer who brought many prominent people into the ABOLITIONIST movement. The agents trained by Weld were extraordinarily successful in spreading abolitionism through Indiana, Ohio, and upstate New York.

Weld helped to establish the then abolitionist Oberlin College after being expelled (1834) from Lane Seminary in Cincinnati for organizing an antislavery debate. In 1838 he married the abolitionist-feminist Angelina Grimké (see GRIMKÉ, SARAH MOORE AND ANGELINA EMILY). She helped him write the famous tract *American Slavery As It Is* (1839), which inspired Harriet Beecher Stowe's novel *Uncle Tom's Cabin*. Weld later retired from active abolitionism to teach.

welding and soldering   Welding and soldering are methods of joining metals by the application of heat, sometimes combined with pressure, with or without the use of a filler metal. The welding process joins metals by melting them, fusing the melted areas, and then solidifying the joined area to form a metallurgical bond. In soldering, a molten solder (a liquid-metal filler) is used to join two metals; the solder's melting temperature must be below those of the metals to be joined. Technically, all soldering done with a solder that melts at temperatures above 450° C (840° F) is called brazing. The decision whether to weld or to solder metals depends on such factors as the comparative ease of joining, the joint strength needed, the corrosion resistance, and the time and costs involved.

Welding technology is used in building structural components, in aircraft manufacture, in pressure vessels, in food and chemical containers, in the automotive industry,

In the metal-arc method of welding, heat generated by an electric arc melts a coated metal electrode, forming filler material that can be used to join two iron or steel pipes.

and in nuclear reactors. Soldering is used to repair jewelry, toys, and electrical connections for household appliances. Virtually every manufacturing endeavor utilizes some form of a welded, brazed, or soldered joint.

Several welding processes are available for use. Shielded metal-arc welding uses an electric arc between an electrode and the work to be joined; the electrode is a coated metal rod that decomposes to protect the weld area from contamination and melts to form filler metal. Gas-shielded arc welding produces a welded joint under a protective gas, which may or may not be inert. Submerged-arc welding uses a flux to promote fusion as the heating arc produces the weld. Other, more specialized types of welding include cold welding, which uses pressure alone to join metals, with no heat being applied during the operation; explosion welding, which uses a controlled explosion to press two metals together under enormous pressure; diffusion welding, which produces a joint by applying pressure to the pieces at elevated temperatures; laser-beam welding, which makes use of the intense heat of laser light to melt and join metals; and ultrasonic welding, which creates a bond through the application of high-frequency vibratory energy while the parts to be joined are held together under pressure.

If the welding engineer decides that melting the metals to join them is not suitable, they may be brazed or soldered at a lower temperature. To obtain a soldered joint, the parts are heated to a suitable temperature and a filler metal is distributed between the closely fitted surfaces of the joint. This filler metal, or solder, solidifies to unite the parts into a single assembly.

Weldon, Fay   An English novelist and playwright known for the dark comedy she finds in the war between the sexes, Fay Weldon, b. Sept. 22, 1933, has written a number of stage, radio, and television plays, including a segment (1972) of *Upstairs, Downstairs*. Her novels *Down Among the Women* (1971) and *Female Friends* (1974) established her reputation for sardonic analysis of the often obsessive or demented ways in which men and women cope with the impossible demands of traditional sex roles. Other Weldon novels include *The Shrapnel Academy* (1987) and *The Cloning of Joanna May* (1989).

Welensky, Sir Roy [wuh-len'-skee] A moderate white Rhodesian statesman, Sir Roy Welensky, b. Jan. 20, 1907, d. Dec. 5, 1991, was prime minister of the Federation of Rhodesia and Nyasaland (1956–63). A leader in trade unions and politics in Northern Rhodesia (now Zambia), he helped (1953) form the federation that united Northern Rhodesia, Southern Rhodesia (now Zimbabwe), and Nyasaland (now Malawi). As deputy minister (1953–56) and prime minister, Welensky favored a policy of interracial "partnership." He was unable to prevent the federation's breakup in 1963. In 1965, refusing to back white supremacist Ian Smith's unilateral declaration of Southern Rhodesian independence from Britain, Welensky retired from politics.

Welf (family) [welf] The Welfs, or Guelphs, a German family, contested with the HOHENSTAUFENS for the throne of the Holy Roman Empire during the 12th century. The family traced its descent from the 9th-century Swabian count Welf. In 1070, Welf IV was named duke of Bavaria. After the death of Holy Roman Emperor Henry V (1125), the Welf-Hohenstaufen struggle began. The German princes chose as Henry's successor LOTHAIR II (r. 1125–37), whose personal heir was Henry the Proud, Welf duke of Bavaria. Henry the Proud inherited the duchy of Saxony from Lothair, but in 1138 the princes elected the Hohenstaufen CONRAD III (r. 1138–52) king. Conrad then deprived Henry of his duchies, precipitating a civil war.

The Hohenstaufen emperor FREDERICK I (r. 1152–90) restored Bavaria to HENRY THE LION, son of Henry the Proud (he had already recovered Saxony). After new disputes, however, Frederick confiscated (1180) all Welf holdings except those in Saxony, which were later (1235) designated the duchy of Brunswick (Braunschweig).

The most important of the later Welf branches were those of Brunswick-Lüneburg and Brunswick-Wolfenbüttel. In 1692 the duke of Brunswick-Lüneburg became an elector, and his territories became known as the electorate of Hanover. In 1714, Elector George succeeded to the English throne as GEORGE I (see also HANOVER dynasty).

See also: GUELPHS AND GHIBELLINES.

welfare see SOCIAL AND WELFARE SERVICES

welfare state The term *welfare state* has been used since World War II to refer to the acceptance by democratic governments of the responsibility for the economic and social well-being of all their people. Programs of the welfare state, known collectively as SOCIAL SECURITY, have aimed primarily at alleviating hardships caused by unemployment, disability, and old age, and at securing for all, regardless of income, adequate medical care and other essential services.

Governments have long attempted to enlarge economic and social opportunities and to promote justice, education, and health for their citizens, but early programs tended to be limited and selective. In the 1880s, Germany introduced insurance to cover sickness and old age for wage earners. Great Britain's National Insurance Act of 1911 provided UNEMPLOYMENT INSURANCE. In 1935 the United States, with the Social Security Act, adopted a program that subsidized pensions for the elderly, WORKERS' COMPENSATION for wage earners, and pensions for their surviving spouses with dependent children. The act also led to the creation of unemployment insurance programs administered by various states. (The Social Security Amendments of 1965 added MEDICAID and MEDICARE, health insurance plans for low-income citizens and the elderly, respectively.) By the end of the 1930s, Sweden had established health and unemployment insurance for wage earners, housing subsidies, old age pensions, and paid vacation and maternity leave plans.

The extraordinary development of the welfare state after 1945 may be attributed largely to the experience of two great wars and an intervening and persistent commercial depression. As early as 1936 the British economist John Maynard KEYNES argued that a free-market economy could not maintain full employment (see EMPLOYMENT AND UNEMPLOYMENT) without compensatory taxation and public expenditures, but it took the outbreak of World War II in 1939 to end the depression by means of massive increases in public spending and government assumption of the control of much economic activity. Characteristic of postwar developments was the expansion of social insurance programs, of which the British National Health Service is a prime example. Since 1948 it has provided medical care to all residents, financed out of general tax revenues, although some services were curtailed by the government of Margaret THATCHER during the 1980s.

The Netherlands, West Germany, France, and the Scandinavian countries also experienced an impressive postwar expansion of social services. In Scandinavia today, for example, children's allowances are paid regardless of the parents' income; national health schemes are modeled on Britain's service; and comprehensive unemployment insurance plans include retraining and relocation assistance.

In all countries, however, there remain those who have exhausted their insurance benefits, or who are not eligible for them, or who have special problems. In most countries these benefits are usually available only after demonstration of need through a means test. Such direct support of the poor, the elderly, and the malnourished is at the heart of the SOCIAL AND WELFARE SERVICES offered by the modern industrial state.

Public funds also support training and placement programs intended to improve the employability of the young, the hard-core unemployed, and the handicapped. DAY-CARE CENTERS for young children allow their mothers to attend training programs and then find paid employment. Day care, by exposing disadvantaged children to a stimulating environment early in life, also gives them a better foundation for success in their schoolwork. Publicly financed housing has supplied shelter for those who cannot afford rents high enough to attract private investors.

Virtually all citizens are substantially dependent on government intervention in social welfare at some point in their lives. The availability of jobs, for instance, is significantly affected by the level of taxes, public expenditures of all sorts, credit policies, and subsidies. Governments have recently granted loans, or guarantees for private credit, to those establishing new enterprises (notably U.S.–minority-group members) or promising to hire the long-term unemployed. This growing dependence, together with the high cost to taxpayers of such programs, the massive administrative expansion entailed, and a growing feeling that governments cannot effectively operate such a range of programs, is the cause of much recent criticism of public welfare policies in the United States. In view of its widespread political support, however, the welfare state seems unlikely to disappear anytime soon.

Welk, Lawrence   The orchestra leader Lawrence Welk, b. Strasburg, N.Dak., Mar. 11, 1903, d. May 17, 1992, maintained his longtime popularity with a musical style that seemed to satisfy a widespread interest in nostalgia. Welk earned his first accordion by hiring himself out as a farm laborer and began his career playing at rural celebrations. He formed his first dance band in 1925, performing at dance halls and occasionally on the radio. Radio, then television, gradually brought his music to a national audience. From 1955 to 1982, Welk had his own television show; reruns continue to be popular.

Welland Ship Canal   [wel'-uhnd]   The 45-km-long (28-mi) Welland Ship Canal, part of the ST. LAWRENCE SEAWAY, connects Port Colborne on Lake Erie with Port Weller on Lake Ontario. The canal bypasses Niagara Falls. It has a minimum depth of 9 m (30 ft) and eight locks to compensate for the 100-m (328-ft) difference in elevation between the two lakes. Opened in 1932 and modernized in 1972, the present canal replaces one opened in 1829.

Welles, Gideon   The American journalist and political leader Gideon Welles, b. Glastonbury, Conn., July 1, 1802, d. Feb. 11, 1878, was secretary of the navy (1861–69) under Presidents Abraham Lincoln and Andrew Johnson. From 1826 to 1836, he edited the *Hartford Times*. As a Democrat he served (1827–35) in the Connecticut legislature. He left the Democrats, however, over the slavery issue, helped to organize the Republican party, and in 1854 founded the *Hartford Evening Press*, one of the country's first Republican newspapers. At the outset of the Civil War, Lincoln appointed him secretary

of the navy. Quickly, Welles built an adequate navy from virtually nothing. Under his direction, Union ships closed ports on both Confederate coasts, and he established a fleet of gunboats and ironclads on the Mississippi. After the war, Welles supported President Johnson's Reconstruction policy.

Welles, Orson   Although the American actor-director George Orson Welles, b. Kenosha, Wis., May 6, 1915, d. Oct. 10, 1985, worked on the stage and in films for nearly 50 years, his fame rests principally on two projects he completed before he was 30 years of age. The first, his 1938 radio adaptation for the Mercury Theatre of H.G. Wells's *The War of the Worlds,* created a panic among listeners who believed it was a report of an actual Martian invasion. The second was his first and greatest film, the extraordinary *Citizen Kane* (1941). A character study loosely modeled on the life of publisher William Randolph HEARST, it embroiled Welles in legal battles, won Academy Awards for him and cowriter Herman Mankiewicz, and established his reputation as Hollywood's boy wonder. Although *Kane* drew vast critical praise, it was initially unsuccessful at the box office and the Hollywood studios withdrew their endorsement of Welles's directorial autonomy, an artistic and financial hindrance that would plague him his entire career.

Welles began as an actor with Dublin's Gate Theatre in 1931, but he soon turned to writing and directing, producing a notable all-black version of *Macbeth* in 1936 before founding the Mercury Theatre with John Houseman in 1937. After the double triumph of *War of the Worlds* and *Citizen Kane*, he directed *The Magnificent Ambersons* (1942), *The Lady from Shanghai* (1948), and a new *Macbeth* (1948) before moving to Europe, where many of his subsequent films, beginning with *Mr. Arkadin* (1955), were made. *Touch of Evil* (1958) is a shadowy American FILM NOIR. *The Trial* (1962) is a bleak adaptation of Kafka. *Chimes at Midnight* (1966), a study of Fal-

The American actor and director Orson Welles appears in the title role of Citizen Kane *(1941), an Academy Award-winning film that he also coauthored and directed.*

staff, and the unfinished *Don Quixote* (1957–66) reflect Welles's fascination with extravagant, outsize characters, many of whom he himself played to perfection.

Welles starred in many of his own films, but his screen credits also include distinguished performances in *Jane Eyre* (1944), *The Third Man* (1949), *Moby Dick* (1956), *A Man for All Seasons* (1966), and *Catch-22* (1970).

Welles, Sumner   Sumner Welles, b. New York City, Oct. 14, 1892, d. Sept. 25, 1961, American diplomat, was an expert on Latin America who served as President Franklin D. Roosevelt's assistant secretary and undersecretary of state. He was assistant chief (1920–21) and chief (1921–22) of the State Department's Latin American Affairs Division. As assistant secretary (1933–37) and undersecretary of state (1937–43), he helped formulate Roosevelt's hemispheric GOOD NEIGHBOR POLICY. During the first part of World War II he organized Latin American support for the Allies.

Wellesley, Richard Colley Wellesley, Marquess [welz'-lee]   The British statesman Richard Colley Wellesley (originally Wesley), b. June 20, 1760, d. Sept. 26, 1842, has been overshadowed in history by his younger brother, Arthur, the duke of WELLINGTON. One of the lieutenants of William PITT (the Younger), Richard Wellesley was governor general in India (1797–1805) after serving in the Irish and British parliaments. He envisioned British paramountcy over the Indian subcontinent and annexed new territories. He came into conflict with the East India Company, however, by thinking in terms not of the company's trade but of Anglo-Indian commerce and Asiatic power. While foreign secretary (1809–12) he sustained the military efforts of his brothers in the Iberian campaign. Later, as lord lieutenant of Ireland (1821–28; 1833–34), Wellesley attempted to ease Catholic-Protestant tensions there.

Wellesley College   Established in 1870, Wellesley College is a private 4-year liberal arts school for women in Wellesley, Mass. One of the SEVEN SISTERS COLLEGES, Wellesley has a cross-registration program of study with the Massachusetts Institute of Technology, in nearby Cambridge, Mass.

Wellington   Wellington, the capital city and principal port of New Zealand, is situated on the southern coast of North Island at Port Nicholson inlet of Cook Strait. The city's population is 135,400 (1989 est.). Wellington is the center of government, finance, and commerce for New Zealand; its harbor, which is almost landlocked, is among the world's finest. The city proper has a shortage of building space (much of Wellington is built on landfill) and contains commercial areas, docks, and government buildings, including the Houses of Parliament.

Most industry, which includes the production of auto-

mobiles, chemicals, textiles, and machinery, is located in the Hutt Valley, east of the city. Residential areas are in the steep hills surrounding the harbor, along the bay on the western side of the harbor, and in nearby suburbs. The city exports meat, wool, and dairy products. Cultural attractions in Wellington include the New Zealand Symphony Orchestra; the National Art Gallery (1936); the National Museum; the Botanical Gardens; and the Zoological Gardens. Victoria University of Wellington (1897) is there.

Wellington was settled by the first group of British immigrants to New Zealand, who landed at Port Nicholson in 1840. The city became the capital of New Zealand in 1865.

Wellington, Arthur Wellesley, 1st Duke of   The British soldier and statesman Arthur Wellesley, duke of Wellington, b. May 1?, 1769, d. Sept. 14, 1852, defeated Napoleon I at the Battle of Waterloo and later served in several Tory ministries, including one he headed (1828–30) as prime minister.

The son of an impoverished family of the Irish gentry, Wellesley (originally Wesley), received military training in France. He won his first military triumphs in India (1796–1805) under the governor-generalship of his older brother, Richard, Marquess WELLESLEY.

In 1808, Arthur Wellesley was ordered to the Iberian peninsula against Napoleon; he was virtually the only effective general of the allied forces in the NAPOLEONIC WARS. Although he was made Viscount Wellington after winning at Talavera (1809), he was much criticized at home because his victories were not followed up or were followed by strategic retreats. By constructing and holding the lines of Torres Vedras (1810) near Lisbon, however, he maintained a British lodgment on the Continent, and after his victories at Salamanca (1812) and Vitoria (1813) he advanced (1814) into France from the south, helping to force Napoleon's abdication (1814).

Having been made a duke, Wellington replaced the foreign secretary, Viscount CASTLEREAGH, as negotiator at the Congress of Vienna in February 1815. After Napoleon's return to power, Wellington defeated him at Water-

The duke of Wellington, a British soldier and statesman, appears in a portrait by Francisco Goya (1812). Wellington, whose military career reached its climax with the defeat (1815) of Napolean at Waterloo, became an important figure in British politics as a leader of the most conservative elements within the Tory party.

loo on June 18, 1815 (see WATERLOO, BATTLE OF). Afterward, the Great Duke—as he was subsequently known—was drawn into British politics. When George CANNING became prime minister (1827), Wellington, who opposed his European policy and his favorable stand on CATHOLIC EMANCIPATION, led half the cabinet in resigning.

As prime minister (from early 1828), however, Wellington seemed a realist when, for example, he modified the Tory stance and worked for reforms that removed electoral disabilities for dissenters and Catholics. But he proved politically naive after the 1830 elections, when he declared the British electoral system (with its rotten boroughs) flawless; he subsequently had to yield power to Whigs and Canningites.

In 1832, Wellington tried unsuccessfully to form a government to pass a pettier Reform Bill than the one that became law that June. Asked to form a ministry in 1834, he insisted that Robert PEEL be prime minister. Under Peel, he served as foreign secretary (1834–35) and minister without portfolio (1841–46), working at times against his own strong prejudices, as when he helped abolish the CORN LAWS.

As commander in chief of the army (1827–28, 1842–52), Wellington calmly prevented violence in 1848 when the Chartists (see CHARTISM) threatened an uprising. In his later years he also served as chancellor of the University of Oxford (1834–52) and as an advisor to Queen Victoria.

■

Wells, Fargo and Company   Wells, Fargo and Company, founded in 1852 by Henry Wells, William G. FARGO, and others to establish express service to California, provided essential communication, transportation, and banking functions on the trans-Mississippi frontier. In the 1850s the company began providing banking services for gold miners and soon expanded into general banking. With the purchase of the Overland Stage Company and Pioneer Stage Company, it acquired a near monopoly of western express service and became heavily involved in passenger transportation. Adjusting to the railroad era, the company established its own transcontinental rail system by 1888. The beginning of government parcel-post delivery in 1912 was a fatal blow to the company's express service. In 1918, Wells, Fargo and Company and other express carriers were merged into the American Railway Express Company.

■

Wells, H. G.   The English writer Herbert George Wells, b. Bromley, Kent, Sept. 21, 1866, d. Aug. 13, 1946, was one of the world's most prominent literary personalities in the era between 1895 and 1920. With Jules Verne, he was the inventor of SCIENCE FICTION; in the tradition of Dickens, he also was a master of the comic novel.

His father was a shopkeeper, his mother a lady's maid. Wells left school at the age of 14 but 4 years later won a scholarship to the Normal School of Science in South Kensington, where he studied under Thomas Henry Huxley. Another grant took him to London University, from which he graduated with a degree in biology in 1890. By

The English novelist and social theorist H. G. Wells correctly predicted the advent of space exploration, atomic power, and other technological developments. Although originally a firm believer in the ability of science to create a more perfect world, Wells later felt that the human race was likely to destroy itself.

the time he was 30, he had already embarked on his famous series of scientific romances, notably *The Time Machine* (1895), *The Invisible Man* (1897), and The WAR OF THE WORLDS (1898).

These were followed by several first-rate comic novels, three of which—*Love and Mr. Lewisham* (1900), *Kipps: The Story of a Simple Soul* (1905), and *The History of Mr. Polly* (1910)—have become minor classics. The novels *Ann Veronica* (1909), dealing with women's emancipation, *Tono-Bungay* (1909), incorporating Wells's views on science and progress, and *Mr. Britling Sees It Through* (1916), on World War I, also were popular. Wells outlined his socialist and internationalist solutions to civilization's ills in *Anticipations* (1901), *A Modern Utopia* (1905), *New Worlds for Old* (1908), and *The Shape of Things to Come* (1933). His *Outline of History* (1920; rev. ed. 1931) is perhaps the best one-volume history of humankind ever compiled by a single author.

Welsh corgi   see CARDIGAN WELSH CORGI; PEMBROKE WELSH CORGI

Welsh language   see CELTIC LANGUAGES

■

Welsh literature   Welsh literature begins with the 6th-century bardic poetry attributed to Aneurin and Taliesin, which praises patrons and elegizes fallen warriors. The former existence of genealogical traditions, mythic tales, and epic accounts of such heroic figures as King Arthur and the poet-wizard Merlin (Myrddin; see ARTHUR AND ARTHURIAN LEGEND) may be inferred from surviving prose tales of the 11th century and later, particularly the *Four Branches of the Mabinogi*, for mythological lore; native Arthurian tales and such others as *Peredur* and *Owein* showing Norman French influence; and native historical accounts, such as *The Dream of Maxen Wledig*.

The poetry of 12th-century Wales includes works by court bards and by poets who were themselves princes, like Owain Cyfeiliog (c.1140–97). From the later 14th century, the much-imitated poetry of DAFYDD AP GWILYM, directed to a new, nonaristocratic audience, presents considerable metrical innovation and an emphasis on themes of romantic love.

Religious movements—first the Reformation and later the Methodist revival—had a profound effect on Welsh literary tradition. These movements suppressed many old themes and genres, including much popular, folkloristic literature, but also offered new ones, such as the hymns of William Williams (Pantycelyn) (1717–91). The 19th century produced the lyric poets John Hughes (Ceiriog) and John Jones (Talhaiarn), and the novelist Daniel OWEN. The vigorous prose and poetic traditions of Welsh literature continue in the work of such contemporary writers as Kate Roberts and Saunders Lewis.

Welsh pony   see HORSE

Welsh springer spaniel   The Welsh springer spaniel is a medium-sized, red and white dog with the coat, feathering, and pendant ears characteristic of spaniels. It weighs 16 to 20 kg (35 to 44 lb). The Welsh springer spaniel makes a good household dog and noisy guard. It is at its best, however, as a gun dog in the country. The breed's lineage is unclear, but it is doubtless related to the English springer spaniel and has been known in Wales for at least two centuries. It is among the rarest purebred breeds in the United States; only a handful are registered each year.

Welsh terrier   The Welsh terrier is a small, rough-coated dog with small drop ears and an erect, docked tail. The coat is black and tan, the black forming a saddle over the back. The Welsh terrier stands about 38 cm (15 in) at the shoulder and weighs about 9 kg (20 lb). It is hardy and game but quiet and less excitable than the fox terrier. Developed in Wales to hunt foxes, badgers, and otters, the breed was first imported into the United States in the late 19th century.

The Welsh terrier is a medium-sized, rough-coated terrier. A sporting dog developed in North Wales during the 19th century, its coat is wiry and usually black and tan in color. The Welsh terrier is now primarily a show dog and a pet.

Welty, Eudora [wel'-tee]   The distinguished southern writer Eudora Welty, b. Jackson, Miss., Apr. 13, 1909, is best known for such novels as *Delta Wedding* (1946), *Losing Battles* (1970), and the Pulitzer Prize–winning *The Optimist's Daughter* (1972). She has also produced seven volumes of short stories, among them *The Golden Apples* (1949), *The Bride of the Innisfallen* (1955), and *A Sweet Devouring* (1969). Both novels and stories are usually set in Mississippi, but whereas the former tend to focus on family complexities, the latter typically examine the lives of isolated individuals. In 1980 she published her collected stories and received the Presidential Medal of Freedom.

Photo Jill Krementz © 1972

Eudora Welty, one of the most respected 20th-century American writers, draws on the rich traditions and social complexities of the American South in her novels and short stories. The recipient of many literary honors, including six O. Henry awards and a Pulitzer Prize, Welty is widely acclaimed for her ability to capture the nuances of rural Mississippi life.

Wenatchee [wen-ach'-ee]   The Wenatchee are North American Indians who formerly occupied the drainage of the Wenatchee River in present-day Washington. Bands speaking related dialects of the Interior SALISH language bordered the Wenatchee on the north. Typical Plateau people, they relied heavily on the salmon runs in their river system. Each band had its winter village site where semisubterranean earth lodges were built, torn down in spring to dry out pit and timbers, and then rebuilt in fall. In summer they lived in aboveground mat lodges.

Social structure was based on small village bands of kinship-based affiliation. Religion revolved around simple First Salmon rites, guardian spirit quests and dances, and shamanistic curing. In addition to the introduction of horses, Plains influence gave rise to bands composed of a group of villages united under a common war chief. In 1780 the Wenatchee's estimated population was 1,200. Measles, smallpox, and other diseases drastically reduced their numbers during the early 19th century. In 1910 fewer than 75 Wenatchee were reported living on the Colville Agency in Washington.

Wenceslas, Saint [wenz'-suhs-las]   A duke of Bohemia and Christian martyr, Wenceslas, b. c.907, d. Sept. 28, 929, is the patron saint of Czechoslovakia. About 924 he overthrew the regency of his mother, who was persecuting the Christians. His continuation of the Christianization of Bohemia and his submission to the German king HENRY I aroused strong opposition from a group of the nobility and led to Wenceslas's murder by his brother Boleslav I, who succeeded him. Feast day: Sept. 28.

Wenceslas I, King of Bohemia   Wenceslas I, b. 1205, d. Sept. 22, 1253, king of Bohemia (1230–53), succeeded his father, Ottokar I, founder of the Bohemian kingdom. He added Austria to the possessions of the Přemysl dynasty by compelling the Austrians to recognize his son OTTOKAR II as duke. The influx of German colonists into Bohemia continued under Wenceslas and brought prosperity, although Moravia was attacked by the Mongols in the 1240s and the Bohemian nobles rebelled from 1248 to 1250.

Wenceslas II, King of Bohemia   Wenceslas II, b. 1271, d. June 21, 1305, son and successor of OTTOKAR II as king of Bohemia (1278-1305), encroached on Polish territory and eventually became king of Poland (1300–05). After a regency to 1283, Wenceslas overcame dissidents headed by Záviš, his mother's lover and, later, husband, whom he executed in 1290. During his reign Bohemia's silver mines were developed.

Wenceslas, King of Germany and Bohemia   Wenceslas, b. Feb. 26, 1361, d. Aug. 16, 1419, successor to his father, Holy Roman Emperor CHARLES IV, as German king (1378–1400; he was never crowned emperor) and king of Bohemia (1378–1419), tried vainly to halt the disintegration of the empire. At the same time, his kingdom of Bohemia was torn by the problem of the HUSSITES.

The empire faced serious problems, such as the independence of the towns and the depredations of the petty nobility, but Wenceslas was distracted by controversies provoked by his brothers SIGISMUND (later Holy Roman emperor) and John of Görlitz and his cousin Jobst of Moravia, as well as by the papal schism, which began in 1378. After 1394 he virtually ignored Germany. In Bohemia, Wenceslas quarreled with the clergy and ordered the torture and killing of (1393) Saint JOHN NEPOMUCENE, the vicar general in Prague. In 1394, Jobst led a revolt of Bohemian magnates that resulted in Wenceslas's brief imprisonment.

In 1400 the German princes deposed Wenceslas and elected Rupert of the Palatinate in his place. Wenceslas was deposed in Bohemia by Sigismund in 1402 but regained power. He won popular favor by initially backing anti-German religious ferment centering around John HUSS; his decree of Kutná Hora (1409), giving the Czechs greater control over the University of Prague, resulted in the election of Huss as rector. Wenceslas later regretted his encouragement of the Hussites after Huss was executed (1415) and the Hussite wars began.

Wentworth, William Charles   Australia's first great patriot, William Charles Wentworth, b. Oct. 26, 1790, d. Mar. 20, 1872, sought self-government for New South Wales. Following an education in England, he returned to New South Wales and in 1813 participated in the first crossing of the Blue Mountains, which opened up the western plains. In 1824, he began editing a newspaper, *The Australian*, that allied itself with the emancipists (freed convicts) against the wealthy free settlers. Having become a wealthy settler himself, Wentworth held more conservative views when he entered the Legislative Council in 1843, but he helped secure squatters' rights, a primary education system (1848), the first British colonial university, in Sydney (1850), and a constitution for New South Wales (1855).

werewolf [wair'-wulf]   In European folklore a werewolf is a man who at night transforms himself or is transformed into a wolf (a process called lycanthropy) and roams in search of human victims to devour. The werewolf must return to human form at daybreak by shedding his wolf's skin and hiding it. If it is found and destroyed, the werewolf dies. A werewolf who is wounded immediately reverts to his human form and can be detected by the corresponding wound on his body. Similar creatures exist in folklore all over the world.

Werfel, Franz [vair'-ful]   A versatile and prolific Austrian writer, Franz Werfel, b. Sept. 10, 1890, d. Hollywood, Calif., Aug. 26, 1945, is remembered especially for his best-selling novel *The Song of Bernadette* (1941; Eng. trans., 1942; film, 1942), based on the life of Saint Bernadette of Lourdes. After producing several popular plays—including the Faustian trilogy *Mirror Man* (1920; Eng. trans., 1920) and the realistic *Goat Song* (1921; Eng. trans., 1926)—he began to develop religious themes, especially evident in *The Eternal Road* (1935; Eng. trans., 1936), a biblical verse pageant, and *The Forty Days of Musa Dagh* (1933; Eng. trans., 1934), a novel about the Armenians' persecution at the hands of the Turks in 1915. Werfel fled Austria in 1938; the comic play *Jacobowsky and the Colonel* (1944; Eng. trans., 1944) reflects his sense of exile.

Wergeland, Henrik Arnold   [vair'-guh-lahnd] Considered Norway's national poet, Henrik Arnold Wergeland, b. June 17, 1808, d. July 12, 1845, published his monumental cosmological poem *Skabelsen, Mennesket og Messias* (Creation, Mankind, and Messiah) in 1830; it was followed by the lyrical works *Jan van Huysums Blomsterstykke* (Jan van Huysum's Flowerpiece, 1840) and

Den engelske Lods (The English Pilot, 1844). A champion of his country's independence from Denmark, he wrote a history of the Norwegian constitution (1841–43) and engaged in polemics with his contemporary J. S. C. Welhaven.

Werner, Abraham Gottlob [vair'-nur] The German mineralogist and geologist Abraham Gottlob Werner, b. Sept. 25, 1749, d. June 30, 1817, was the first to develop and teach a geological theory or system that was universally and historically applicable to the Earth and based on observation of geologic phenomena in nature. Werner taught at the mining academy at Freiberg from 1775 until his death. In his first book (1774), a field guide for the identification of minerals, Werner classified minerals by their external characteristics. Later he also investigated the chemical composition of minerals.

Werner's geological system was built upon stratigraphic succession—the concept that the Earth's crust contains rocks in a successive order that reveals the Earth's history. According to his theory, an ocean once covered the entire surface of the Earth. Rocks settled from the universal ocean by sedimentation, and thus water had the principal role in forming the Earth's crust. Werner's claim that all basalt is an aqueous precipitate conflicted with the ideas of the geologist James HUTTON, who argued that the original rocks of the crust were formed by heat.

Wertheimer, Max [vairt'-hy-mur] Max Wertheimer, b. Prague, Czechoslovakia, Apr. 15, 1880, d. New Rochelle, N.Y., Oct. 12, 1943, was a psychologist and philosopher who founded the influential school of GESTALT PSYCHOLOGY. He was educated at the Universities of Prague, Berlin, and Würzburg, and in 1910, at the Psychological Institute in Frankfurt, he began experimental studies of apparent motion (published in 1912) that inaugurated the Gestalt school. Together with Wolfgang KÖHLER and Kurt KOFFKA, who served as subjects in these experiments, Wertheimer elaborated the Gestalt theory. He left Germany because of the rise of the Nazis and taught at the New School for Social Research in New York from 1933 until his death. In 1923 he published an influential paper on the principles of organization in perception, and his Gestalt analysis of human thought, *Productive Thinking*, was published posthumously (1945).

Wertmuller, Lina [wairt'-muhl-ur] A highly original and controversial Italian filmmaker, Lina Wertmuller, b. c.1926, specializes in melodramatic tragicomedies characterized by an idiosyncratic blend of wit, irony, socialist dialectics, and sheer grotesquerie. She has taken on such themes as economic exploitation and the inability of the striving worker to rise above it in *The Seduction of Mimi* (1972), an anarchist's abortive attempt to assassinate Mussolini in *Love and Anarchy* (1973), the subordination of natural love to class interests in *Swept Away* (1975), and the insanities to which chauvinism—male or national—can lead in *Seven Beauties* (1976).

Weser River [vay'-zur] A 437-km-long (271-mi) waterway in Germany, the Weser River is formed by the Fulda and Werra rivers at Münden in central Germany and flows northward into the North Sea at Bremerhaven. It enters the North German Plain at Minden and is linked by canals with other major German rivers.

Wesley (family) [wes'-lee] The Wesley family was made famous by the two brothers, John and Charles, who worked together in the rise of METHODISM in the British Isles during the 18th century. They were among the ten children surviving infancy born to **Samuel Wesley** (1662–1735), Anglican rector of Epworth, Lincolnshire, and **Susanna Annesley Wesley**.

John Wesley, b. June 28, 1703, d. Mar. 2, 1791, was the principal founder of the Methodist movement. The rescue of little "Jackie" from the burning rectory ("a brand plucked from the burning") has become legendary. John was elected (1726) fellow of Lincoln College at Oxford University. He was ordained in 1728.

After a brief absence (1727–29) to help his father at Epworth, John returned to Oxford to discover that his brother Charles had founded a Holy Club composed of young men interested in spiritual growth. John quickly became a leading participant of this group, which was dubbed the Methodists.

John Wesley, founder of the Methodist church, was a zealous reformer, championing such causes as abolition of slavery, civil rights, and prison reform. (National Portrait Gallery, London.)

In 1735 both Wesleys accompanied James OGLE-
THORPE to the new colony of Georgia, where John's attempts
to apply his then high-church views aroused hostility. Discouraged, he returned (1737) to England; he was rescued
from this discouragement by the influence of the Moravian preacher Peter BOEHLER. At a small religious meeting
in Aldersgate Street, London, on May 24, 1738, John
Wesley had an experience in which his "heart was
strangely warmed."

After this spiritual conversion, which centered on the
realization of salvation by faith in Christ alone, he devoted
his life to evangelism. Beginning in 1739 he established
Methodist societies throughout the country.

Late in life Wesley married Mary Vazeille, a widow. He
continued throughout his life a regimen of personal
discipline and ordered living. He died at 88, still preaching, still traveling, and still a clergyman of the Church
of England. In 1784, however, he had given the Methodist societies a legal constitution, and in the same year
he ordained Thomas COKE for ministry in the United
States; this action signaled an independent course for
Methodism.

Charles Wesley, b. Dec. 18, 1707, d. Mar. 29, 1788,
was perhaps England's greatest hymn writer. Educated at
Oxford, he was ordained in 1735 and went to Georgia as
Oglethorpe's secretary. He returned a year earlier than
John. After a religious experience similar to John's, he
continued for many years in close association with the
Methodist movement. After 1756, however, he left the
itinerant ministry and settled first in Bristol and later in
London. He wrote more than 5,000 hymns, among them
"Hark, the Herald Angels Sing" and "Love Divine, All
Loves Excelling."

Charles's son, **Samuel Wesley** (1766–1837), and
grandson, **Samuel Sebastian Wesley** (1810–76), were
both distinguished composers of sacred music.

Wesleyan University [wes'-lee-uhn]   Established in
1831, Wesleyan University is a private coeducational liberal arts school in Middletown, Conn. Doctorates are giv-
en in sciences and music.

Wessex   The most durable of the Anglo-Saxon kingdoms, Wessex formed the nucleus about which the future
English nation coalesced. Located in southwestern England, the kingdom grew from settlements established
perhaps as early as the late 5th century. Saxon kings accepted Christianity in the early 7th century, and Wessex
shortly thereafter was unified. The native Britons, who
were Celts, and their Germanic conquerors became equal
before the law under the legal code issued by King Ine (r.
688–726). After the Danish Vikings invaded England, the
West Saxon king ALFRED successfully resisted a Danish
attempt to invade Wessex and established (886) West
Saxon leadership over all the Anglo-Saxon rulers who had
not succumbed to Danish rule. Alfred's son EDWARD THE
ELDER and grandson ATHELSTAN expanded gradually into
the DANELAW (areas controlled by the Danes) and complet-

ing the reconquest in 927. The crown of Wessex then became the crown of England. EDGAR the Peaceful (r. 959–
75) enjoyed the most extensive rule of any Wessex king.
In 1016, King ÆTHELRED II lost England to the Danes.
After the Danish line ended, EDWARD THE CONFESSOR, the
last king in the Wessex line, ruled (1042–66).

Wessex culture   The term *Wessex culture* is used to
describe a group of rich, Bronze Age burials (1800–1400
BC) found in southern England. The most famous is that
of Bush Barrow, Wiltshire, which yielded two bronze dag-
ger blades, a bronze axehead, a mace or scepter with zig-
zag bone mountings, and a series of gold mountings.
These burials are now generally held to represent the
presence in southern England of settlers from Britanny,
where similar graves have been found. The term *Wessex
culture* is somewhat misleading; there is little or no evidence that the inhabitants of Wessex developed a culture
significantly different from those of their contemporaries
elsewhere in Britain. The earliest Wessex graves contained fine ornamental goldwork that reflects the influence of the BEAKER CULTURE.

During the era when the Wessex culture flourished,
STONEHENGE was completed. Wessex chiefs also may have
been responsible for establishing a vigorous trade with
Ireland, the European continent, and the Mediterranean—including Mycenae. Amber appears to have been
one of the commodities traded by the Wessex chiefs, and
amber cups have been found in Wessex graves. The reason for the collapse of the Wessex culture is not known,
but it appears to coincide with a major cultural break in
Britain that has been attributed to deteriorating climatic
conditions.

West, Benjamin   Benjamin West, b. Springfield,
Pa., Oct. 10, 1738, d. Nov. 3, 1820, was the first American artist to achieve an international reputation. In 1760
he left for Europe, and in Rome, where he remained until
1763, he was welcomed and praised as a prodigy from
the wilderness. West was one of the earliest artists to
work in the classical style that dominated European
painting for the next half century. His *Agrippina with the
Ashes of Germanicus* (1768; Yale University Art Gallery,
New Haven, Conn.) caused King George III of England to
commission *The Departure of Regulus* (Kensington Palace, London) soon after. West and the king became close
friends, and the artist received many commissions from
him, most notably *The Progress of Revealed Religion*, an
uncompleted 36-part series, now destroyed, that was intended for the Royal Chapel.

West hoped to combine those aspects of the old masters which he most admired into a perfect, eclectic style.
Many art students were attracted to his London studio,
especially students from America. In 1768 he helped organize the Royal Academy and 4 years later was named
Historical Painter to the King. In 1792 he succeeded Sir
Joshua Reynolds as president of the Royal Academy. His
later large religious works, such as *Christ Healing the Sick*

Benjamin West's Penn's Treaty with the Indians *(1772), one of the first historical paintings of an American subject, illustrates the balanced composition and dignified heroism of West's neoclassical style. An influential American among London artists, West was the first to portray historical figures in contemporary rather than classical attire. (Pennsylvania Academy of the Fine Arts, Philadelphia.)*

(1811; Pennsylvania Hospital, Philadelphia) find few admirers today. In London he did portraits, but his fame now largely rests on his earlier scenes of contemporary history. In *Penn's Treaty with the Indians* (1772; Pennsylvania Academy of the Fine Arts, Philadelphia) he combined the rustic and the exotic in a grouping of almost classical nobility. In the same year, *The Death of Wolfe* (National Gallery of Canada, Ottawa) showed the British general expiring on the battlefield of Quebec, surrounded by grieving Indians and loyal officers. Although consciously grand and derivative, they are still impressive and perhaps the most influential of all his works. *Death on a Pale Horse* (1802; Philadelphia Museum of Art) is an example of the romantic style he adopted late in life.

West, Jerry   Jerry Alan West, b. Cheylan, W.Va., May 28, 1938, is considered one of the greatest basketball players ever. At the University of West Virginia the 6-ft 3-in (1-m 90-cm) guard was an All-American for 2 years and became the first draft choice of the Los Angeles Lakers in 1960. In his 14 years with the Lakers, his scoring, ball-handling, and defensive talents earned him a place on 13 consecutive all-star teams. In the 1969–70 season he led the National Basketball Association (NBA) in scoring with a 31.2 average and in 1971–72 led the league in assists with 747. West retired after the 1973–74 season ranking third in regular-season career scoring, with 25,192 points, and first in points per game in playoff competition. He was elected to the Basketball Hall of Fame in 1979.

West, Jessamyn   The American novelist Jessamyn West, b. North Vernon, Ind., July 18, 1902, d. Feb. 23, 1984, is best known for *The Friendly Persuasion* (1945; film, 1956), a group of sketches about Quaker settlers in Indiana who remain good and gentle in a disorderly world. Some of West's best work explores women's crises, such as adolescence in *Cress Delahanty* (1953) and death in *A Matter of Time* (1966). *The Massacre at Fall Creek* (1975) examines the effect on a frontier community of the first trial of a white man for the murder of an Indian. West's memoirs are *The Woman Said Yes* (1976), *The Life I Really Lived* (1979), and *Double Discovery* (1981).

West, Mae   Mae West, b. Brooklyn, N.Y., Aug. 17, 1892, d. Nov. 22, 1980, a legend in American entertainment for more than 50 years, began her career in burlesque and subsequently became famous on Broadway for her quick wit, double entendres, and exaggerated sexiness, which she displayed in her own plays *Sex* (1926), *Drag* (1927), and *Diamond Lil* (1928). In 1926 she was jailed for ten days for obscenity. She also wrote the screenplays of her films *She Done Him Wrong* (1933), *I'm No Angel* (1933), *Going to Town* (1934), and *My Little Chickadee* (1940), with W. C. Fields. She made a comeback in *Myra Breckinridge* (1969) and, at the age of 84—her inimitable style still intact—starred in *Sextette* (1977). Her memoir *Goodness Had Nothing to Do with It* appeared in 1959.

West, Nathanael A satiric novelist whose disillusioned vision of the United States early won him a small but enthusiastic following, Nathanael West, b. Nathan Weinstein in New York City, Oct. 17, 1903, d. Dec. 22, 1940, is most highly regarded for *Miss Lonelyhearts* (1933; film, 1959). The novel is an arresting satire involving a columnist for the lovelorn who becomes enmeshed in the pathetic lives of several of his correspondents. All West's works, influenced by French surrealism, have a bizarre and dislocated quality that anticipates such contemporary fictional trends as black humor and absurdist irony. His first novel, *The Dream Life of Balso Snell* (1931), was begun while the author was still attending Brown University. *A Cool Million* (1934) takes politics as the subject of its satire, and *The Day of the Locust* (1939; film, 1975) presents a violent view of the Hollywood that West had come to know through his work as a scriptwriter.

West, Rebecca Rebecca West is the pseudonym of the English writer Dame Cicily Isabel Fairfield Andrews, b. Kerry, Ireland, Dec. 25, 1892, d. Mar. 15, 1983. A prolific writer and an outspoken feminist ("Rebecca West" is the strong-willed heroine in Ibsen's play *Rosmersholm*), West was briefly an actress and for most of her life a journalist, as well as a novelist, critic, and political essayist. Among her many books the most celebrated are *Black Lamb and Grey Falcon* (1941), a work that combines West's account of her journeys in Yugoslavia with an analysis of Balkan civilization, politics, and history; *The Meaning of Treason* (1947), a study of two contemporary British traitors; and *A Train of Powder* (1955), her coverage of the German war-crimes trials at Nuremberg.

West Africa The term *West Africa* usually refers to the southern half of the western bulge of the African continent, bounded on the north by the Sahara Desert and on the south and west by the Atlantic Ocean. Although the term is a vague one, the independent nations of Benin, Cameroon, Gambia, Ghana, Guinea, Guinea-Bissau, Ivory Coast, Liberia, Nigeria, Senegal, Sierra Leone, and Togo are generally considered West African. Sometimes the countries of the transitional Sahel zone—including Mali, Mauritania, and Niger—are also included. The region was exploited and colonized by Arabs and by the Portuguese, British, and French.

West Bank The West Bank refers to disputed lands located west of the Jordan River between Israel and Jordan. The West Bank has an area of about 5,900 km^2 (2,270 mi^2) and includes numerous sites of religious and historic significance to Jews, Christians, and Muslims. The population (1990 est., including East Jerusalem) of 1,238,122 includes more than 1,000,000 Palestinian Arabs, many of whom were displaced when Israel was created in 1948 and live in United Nations–administered refugee camps. The Jewish population (about 18%) has increased rapidly since 1979, when the Israeli government permitted Israelis to purchase private land. Hebron and Nablus are the largest cities.

The region was part of biblical Samaria and Judea. From 1920 to 1948 the West Bank was included in the British Mandate for Palestine. In 1947, the United Nations voted to partition Palestine into Jewish and Arab states, with the West Bank part of Arab territory. Jordanian forces occupied the West Bank during the first of the Arab-Israeli Wars; the area was formally annexed by Jordan in 1950, an act not recognized by the United Nations, the United States, or the Arab League. After the June 1967 Six-Day War, the West Bank came under Israeli military administration. UN Security Council Resolution 242 of Nov. 22, 1967, called for the withdrawal of Israeli troops and a peaceful settlement, but no peace agreement was reached. A 1974 Arab summit meeting at Rabat adopted a resolution declaring the Palestine Liberation Organization (PLO) the sole representative of the Palestinian Arabs.

The Camp David Accords of September 1978 and the Egyptian-Israeli peace treaty of March 1979 proposed a five-year period of self-rule for West Bank Palestinians. Many Palestinian and Arab leaders oppose limited autonomy and seek an unconditionally independent Palestinian state, a prospect that Israel vigorously opposes for security reasons. Egyptian-Israeli talks on the issue and a peace plan proposed by the United States in 1982, which called for the creation of an autonomous Palestinian confederation linking the West Bank and Gaza Strip to Jordan, made little progress. Meanwhile, Israelis continued to settle on the West Bank, about 65% of which was declared off-limits to Arab residence. In December 1987, West Bank and Gaza Strip Palestinians launched an uprising to end Israeli occupation. As the uprising continued, it contributed to Jordan's severing all legal and administrative links to the West Bank in favor of the PLO in July 1988 and to the PLO's declaration of an independent Palestinian state in November. Plans for holding elections in the occupied territories made little progress; a further setback to a negotiated settlement was PLO support for Iraq in the 1991 Gulf war.

West Bengal   see Bengal

West Florida Controversy In the years between the Louisiana Purchase of 1803 and the Adams-Onís Treaty of 1819, Spain and the United States disputed possession of West Florida, a strip of land below 31° north latitude between the Mississippi and Perdido rivers. When Napoléon Bonaparte acquired the Louisiana Territory from Spain, its boundaries were not specified. The United States purchased Louisiana from France under the same vague terms but chose to include West Florida. Spain disagreed.

In 1810, when American settlers in Baton Rouge rebelled against Spanish authority, declared their independence, and asked for U.S. annexation, the U.S. government occupied West Florida east to the Pearl River. The area became part of the state of Louisiana in April 1812. In May 1812, Congress incorporated the section of West Florida between the Pearl and Perdido rivers into the Mississippi Territory. Mobile remained in Spanish hands until April 1813, when it was captured by Gen. James Wilkinson. In 1819, John Quincy ADAMS negotiated the Adams-Onís Treaty, by which Spain yielded both West and East Florida to the United States.

West Germany   see GERMANY

—

West Highland white terrier   The West Highland white terrier is a small, sturdy, short-legged dog with a foxy face and erect, undocked tail. Often known as a Westie, it makes an excellent companion dog and is lively without the aggressiveness typical of a terrier. Westies stand about 28 cm (11 in) high at the shoulder and have a compact, substantial, squarish body. The white outer coat is straight and hard and should be free of all curl and not silky. Known in Scotland in the 19th century, the breed was brought to the United States in the early 1900s.

—

West Indies   The West Indies are a chain of about 1,000 islands in the CARIBBEAN SEA, extending in an arc from the southern tip of Florida to the northeastern corner of South America. They consist of three groups: Bahama Islands, Greater Antilles, and Lesser Antilles (see ANTILLES, GREATER AND LESSER). Ranging in size from Cuba (110,922 km²/42,827 mi²) to Saba (13 km²/5 mi²), the islands of the West Indies have a total land area of about 236,000 km² (91,000 mi²). The largest islands, part of the Greater Antilles group, are Cuba, Hispaniola (divided between the Dominican Republic and Haiti), Jamaica, and Puerto Rico. Most of the Lesser Antilles islands, which include the WINDWARD ISLANDS and the LEEWARD ISLANDS, Barbados, and Trinidad and Tobago, are formed by peaks of volcanic mountains. The highest point of the West Indies is in the Dominican Republic, where Pico Duarte (Duarte Peak) reaches 3,175 m (10,417 ft). The climate is tropical.

The original inhabitants of the West Indies were ARAWAK and CARIB Indians, but the present population consists primarily of descendants of Spanish, French, British, Dutch, Portuguese, Swedish, and Danish settlers; African slaves mostly from West Africa; and Asian Indians, who arrived from India during the 19th century as indentured workers.

The West Indies produce a wide variety of tropical fruits, spices, sugar, coffee, and cacao. Petroleum is extracted from Trinidad and its surrounding waters, and bauxite is mined in Jamaica, Haiti, and the Dominican Republic. Manganese, nickel, and copper are found on some of the other islands, including Cuba. Industries include sugar, rum, tobacco, and fruit processing, textile

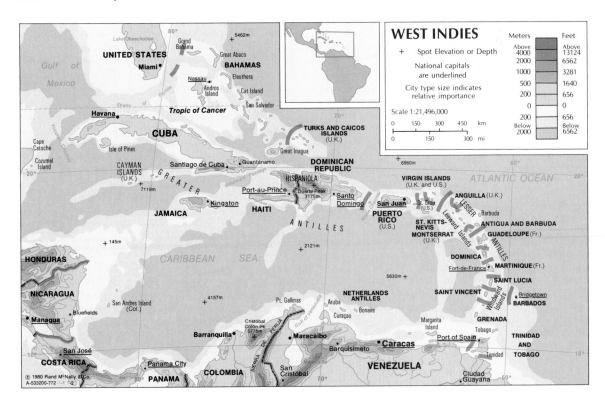

manufacture, and mineral refining. Tourism is a major source of income.

Sighted by Christopher Columbus and other Spanish explorers during the late 15th and early 16th centuries, the islands in the Caribbean were called the West Indies because they originally were thought to be part of Asia. In subsequent centuries, the West Indies were colonized by European powers, but most of the larger and many of the smaller islands by now have become independent. The remaining islands are possessions of the United Kingdom, the United States, France, and the Netherlands.

West Indies Associated States   Between 1965 and 1967 the former British colonies among the Leeward Islands of the Lesser Antilles in the Caribbean Sea—ANTIGUA AND BARBUDA, DOMINICA, GRENADA, SAINT KITTS–NEVIS and ANGUILLA, SAINT LUCIA, and Saint Vincent (see SAINT VINCENT AND THE GRENADINES)—were accorded the status of associated states by Britain. Under this arrangement Great Britain was responsible for the foreign affairs and defense of the associated states. The local governments—each headed by an assembly and a chief minister—were autonomous and subject only to fiscal audit of their financial affairs by Britain. Additionally, the status of association was completely voluntary and terminable at any time by either party.

The associated states were formerly part of the West Indies Federation, which existed from 1959 until 1962. Antigua, Dominica, Grenada, Saint Lucia, and Saint Vincent held the status of associated states until each achieved independence during the 1970s and early 1980s. Anguilla was initially part of the same associated state as Saint Kitts–Nevis and retained this formal status even after gaining administrative independence in 1971. It became a fully separate British dependency in 1981. Like the other former associated states, except Anguilla, Saint Kitts–Nevis achieved full independence, terminating its status of association, in 1983.

West Irian   see IRIAN JAYA

West Pakistan   see PAKISTAN

West Palm Beach   West Palm Beach (1990 pop., 67,643), the seat of Palm Beach County, is a winter resort and industrial city in southeastern Florida. Aircraft parts, computers, and transistors are manufactured there. Founded in 1880, it developed as a commercial center for nearby Palm Beach after 1893.

West Point   see UNITED STATES MILITARY ACADEMY

West Virginia   West Virginia, the only landlocked South Atlantic state, is bordered by Pennsylvania on the north, Maryland and Virginia on the east, and Kentucky and Ohio on the west. Very irregular in shape, with two panhandles—a northern one jutting up between Pennsyl-

vania and Ohio and an eastern one squeezed by Maryland and Virginia—West Virginia has about five-sixths of its 1,880-km (1,170-mi) border marked by rivers or mountain ridges. Lying wholly within the APPALACHIAN MOUNTAINS, and thus well deserving of its nickname, the "Mountain State," West Virginia claims the highest mean elevation (approximately 450 m/1,480 ft) of any state east of the Mississippi and the most rugged terrain.

During the 1970s, revived interest in West Virginia's primary resource, coal, drew many new residents to the state and increased the population by 11.8% to 1,950,279 (1980); however, the population has since dropped (1990, 1,801,625).

Land and Resources

West Virginia lies within three physiographic provinces. At Harpers Ferry a scenic and strategic pass of the Potomac provides a gateway through the BLUE RIDGE MOUNTAINS. To the west the Ridge and Valley region occupies most of the eastern panhandle. A prominent east-facing escarpment, the Allegheny Front of the ALLEGHENY MOUNTAINS, marks the beginning of the Appalachian Plateau, which covers three-fifths of the state. The highest elevations in West Virginia—Spruce Knob (1,482 m/4,861 ft), Bald Knob (1,476 m/4,842 ft), and Big Spruce Knob (1,418 m/4,652 ft)—are found along the eastern edge of the plateau.

Soils.   West Virginia's steep slopes generally offer shallow, clayey, acidic soils, favoring the growth of forests. Occasional river floodplains provide blacker, more fertile soils, and limestone bedrock helps neutralize acidity.

Rivers and Lakes.   The state's northwestern boundary follows the right bank of the OHIO RIVER for 412 km (256 mi), and the POTOMAC marks West Virginia's northern border with Maryland. Fish and Middle Island creeks and the Little Kanawha, Kanawha, and Guyandotte rivers flow across the Appalachian Plateau northwestward into the Ohio. The north-running West Fork and Tygart rivers join in Marion County to form the MONONGAHELA, which flows north into Pennsylvania.

West Virginia has about 70 smaller public fishing lakes and ponds but no large natural body of water. Artificial reservoirs on the New, Gauley, and Tygart rivers afford flood protection, low-flow augmentation, and recreation.

Climate.   With a mid-latitude continental climate, featuring cyclonic storms in winter and thunderstorms in summer, West Virginia receives about 100 mm (4 in) of rain each month. Greater amounts occur at higher elevations, but downwind or eastward of mountains precipitation drops to as low as 810 mm (32 in) a year in parts of Pendleton County. Temperatures range from January's average of 1° C (34° F) to July's 22° C (72° F).

The many steep, narrow valleys make flash flooding West Virginia's most feared weather-related phenomenon.

Vegetation and Animal Life.   Deciduous hardwoods of valleys, notably cherry and Appalachian oak, give way at higher elevations to scattered patches of conifers. Wildlife includes deer, bears, squirrels, rabbits, foxes, skunks, opossums, and raccoons. Mountain streams teem with trout, carp, and perch.

WEST VIRGINIA

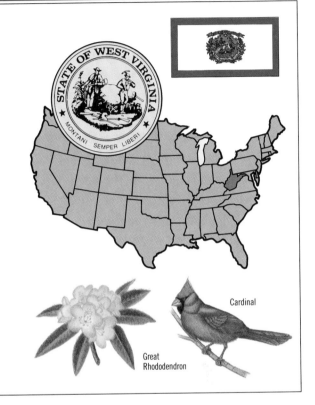

Land: Area: 62,759 km^2 (24,231 mi^2); rank: 41st. Capital and largest city: Charleston (1990 pop., 57,287). Counties: 55. Elevations: highest—1,483 m (4,861 ft), at Spruce Knob; lowest—73 m (240 ft), at the Potomac River.

People: Population (1990): 1,801,625; rank: 34th; density: 28.7 persons per km^2 (74.3 per mi^2). Distribution (1990): 36.1% urban, 63.9% rural. Average annual change (1980–90): −0.8%.

Government (1993): Governor: Gaston Caperton, Democrat. U.S. Congress: Senate—2 Democrats; House—3 Democrats. Electoral college votes: 5. State legislature: 34 senators, 100 representatives.

Economy: State personal income (1989): $22.9 billion; rank: 35th. Median family income (1989): $25,602; rank: 48th. Agriculture: income (1989)—$314 million. Lumber production (1991): 399 million board feet. Mining (nonfuel): value (1988)—$127 million. Manufacturing: value added (1987)—$5.4 billion. Services: value (1987)—$4.9 billion.

Miscellany: Statehood: June 20, 1863; the 35th state. Nickname: Mountain State; tree: sugar maple; motto: *Montani Semper Liberi* ("Mountaineers Are Always Free"); songs: "The West Virginia Hills"; "This Is My West Virginia;" "West Virginia, My Home Sweet Home."

Cardinal

Great Rhododendron

Resources. Commercial timberland covers about 80% of West Virginia's land area. The brines of the Kanawha River valley provided the initial incentive to bore holes into the earth to remove salt and other valuable resources. The technology developed for salt mining was utilized in drilling the world's first petroleum well at Titusville, Pa., in 1859. A year later a successful well at Burning Springs in Wirt County began West Virginia's petroleum boom. Since the 1890s, however, coal has constituted the state's most valuable mineral resource. It has been estimated that 55% of West Virginia is underlain with minable coal.

People

Most West Virginians live along the Kanawha, Ohio, and Monongahela rivers. CHARLESTON (the capital), Huntington, Wheeling, Morgantown, Parkersburg, Fairmont, and Weirton are the only cities with more than 20,000 inhabitants. About one out of 9 residents live in the state's most populous county, Kanawha (1990 pop., 207,619), centered on Charleston, but West Virginia's population is still predominantly rural.

West Virginia has about 56,000 blacks, 8,500 Hispanics, and 7,500 Asians. Major European ethnic groups include the English, Scots-Irish, and Germans. Those of English descent generally tend to belong to Baptist and Episcopalian congregations. Scots-Irish are usually Presbyterian, and the Germans of the eastern panhandle belong to Amish, Mennonite, or Church of the Brethren congregations. Later Roman Catholic immigrants from Ireland and eastern and southern Europe are concentrated in the industrial centers and in the coalfield areas.

Education. West Virginia's institutions of higher learning include 10 state-supported institutions as well as private institutions—such as Alderson-Broaddus, Bethany, Davis and Elkins, Salem, and West Virginia Wesleyan, all founded by 1904, and Wheeling College, established in 1954.

Culture. In 1976, Charleston opened a new center for both performing arts and display of arts and crafts. Huntington and Parkersburg also have art galleries. Several cities have symphony orchestras.

Historical Sites. HARPERS FERRY was the scene of John BROWN's famous raid (1859) that foreshadowed the violence of the Civil War. At the other end of the state, downstream from Parkersburg, Harman Blennerhasset built a mansion (c.1800) on an island in the Ohio that still retains his name. There, Aaron Burr, with Blennerhasset's unwitting assistance, set about to establish an empire in the southwest.

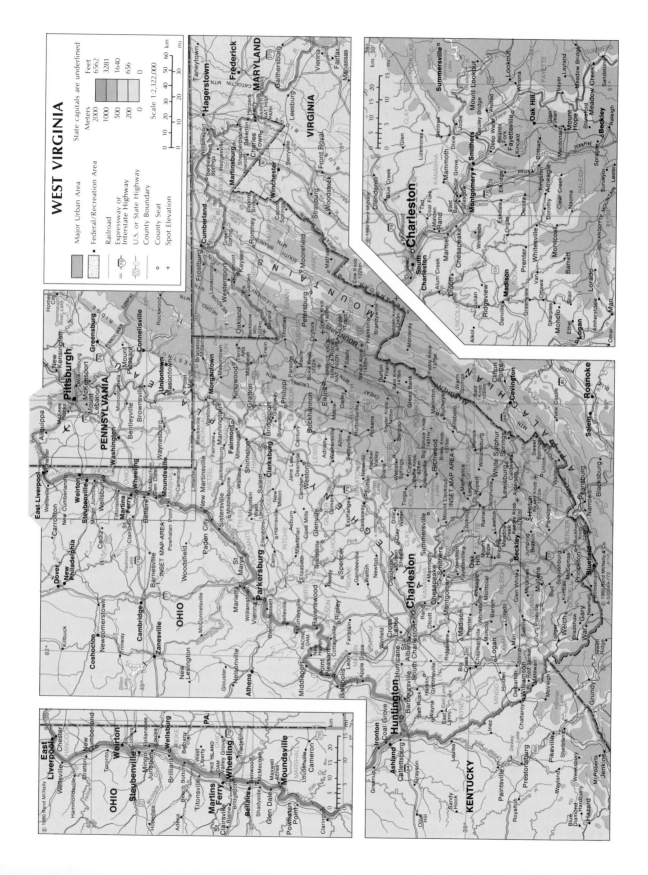

WEST VIRGINIA

State capitals are underlined

Meters	Feet
2000	6562
1000	3281
500	1640
200	656
0	0

Scale 1:2,322,000

Major Urban Area

Federal/Recreation Area

Railroad

Expressway or Interstate Highway

U.S. or State Highway

County Boundary

County Seat

Spot Elevation

Communications. West Virginia has numerous television and radio stations. The state's major newspapers include the *Charleston Gazette* and *Daily Mail*, the *Huntington Herald-Dispatch*, the *Parkersburg News*, and the *Wheeling Intelligencer* (founded in 1852) and *News-Register*.

Economic Activity

West Virginia's economy is dominated by coal mining, concentrated in the Monongahela valley and south of the Kanawha valley, and by a chemicals industry located along the Kanawha and Ohio rivers and based on the state's natural resources of salt, coal, petroleum and natural gas.

Agriculture. Since World War II, West Virginia's agricultural production has shifted from dairying and general farming to livestock breeding. The eastern panhandle specializes in apples and peaches, and Hardy County along the Virginia border raises about 10 million chickens annually.

Forestry and Fishing. West Virginia has more hardwood sawtimber than any other state in the union. Approximately three-quarters of the state's area is woodland.

Hunting and fishing are major recreation industries. Squirrels, rabbits, deer, grouse, and wild turkeys constitute the most popular game.

Mining. Coal, natural gas, and petroleum are West Virginia's most important mineral products. The state is the country's third most important producer of coal, after Kentucky and Wyoming. When the industry slumps, as it did seriously in the mid-1980s, the entire state suffers.

James Wilson discovered the nation's first natural-gas well in 1815 at Charleston, while digging for water. The state also produces significant amounts of petroleum, as well as limestone, clay, gravel, sand, and salt.

Manufacturing. West Virginia's leading industries produce primary and fabricated metals, glass, chemicals, wood products, textiles and apparel, and machinery.

Tourism. West Virginia's 35 state parks receive millions of visitors each year. The Monongahela and other national forests encompass approximately 7,500 km^2 (2,900 mi^2). In Wheeling the municipal Olgebay Park draws guests from Ohio and Pennsylvania as well as from West Virginia.

Transportation. Three interstate highways meet at Charleston: I-64, I-77, and I-79.

The Ohio, Monongahela, and part of the Kanawha have 3-m (9-ft) navigation channels. Every year millions of tons of coal are barged on the rivers of West Virginia. Additional millions of tons (but generally a smaller percentage) are trucked, and the remaining tonnage—usually the biggest share—is carried by railroads. A network of pipelines transports petroleum and gas. The state's busiest airport is at Charleston.

Energy. West Virginia is an energy-exporting state, sending out electricity, as well as coal, gas, and petroleum. Electric-power production totaled 99.3 billion kW h in 1988. The state's generating plants, capable of 15.2 million kW, include two major hydroelectric installations on the Cheat and Gauley rivers.

West Virginia's rolling landscape, although unsuitable for extensive cultivation, provides good pasturage. Poultry and livestock, account for most of the state's agricultural production.

Government and Politics

West Virginia's present constitution, adopted in 1872, calls for a governor, who may serve any number of 4-year terms but no more than 2 in succession, and for a bicameral legislature comprising a senate, whose 34 members are elected to 4-year terms, and a house of delegates, whose 100 members serve 2-year terms.

West Virginia's secession from Virginia in 1863 ended much of the east/west sectionalism of the mother commonwealth, but in both states north/south political divisions continued unabated. The Civil War saw lower- and upper-class West Virginians of southern heritage fighting for the Confederacy; the middle classes of cities and towns and the Scots-Irish farmers tended to side with the North. The Union sympathizers, under the auspices of the Republican party, pushed for statehood and chose as capital the northern-panhandle city of Wheeling. When, following the war, the southern adherents regained political control, they made Charleston the capital (1870). Wheeling was the capital again from 1875 to 1885, at the end of which time Charleston recovered the honor. Even though Republicans returned to power during the 1890s with a program of industrial growth, Charleston remained the capital. The Depression of the 1930s gave back to the Democrats an ascendency that, with a few exceptions, they have maintained ever since.

History

The earliest inhabitants of what is now West Virginia used campsites subsequently buried in the alluvial deposits of the Ohio and Kanawha rivers. They left behind small piles of shells near their villages. The Mound Builders of the Adena culture, who occupied the region 2,000–3,000 years ago, fashioned hundreds of burial mounds, one of the largest of which, Grave Creek Mound, is at Moundsville, in the northern panhandle.

Continuous mining equipment, used in most underground mining operations, greatly facilitates coal extraction. Coal is West Virginia's most valuable mineral resource, and the state is one of the leading U.S. producers of bituminous coal.

European Settlement. By 1669, when the German-born explorer John Lederer crested the Blue Ridge, the Mound Builders had long since disappeared and the CHEROKEE, DELAWARE, SHAWNEE, and SUSQUEHANNA roamed the area looking for game. West Virginia remained unsettled until the power of the Indians was broken about 1726, when Morgan Morgan, a Welsh immigrant, journeyed south through the Ridge and Valley region from Pennsylvania and erected a cabin at Bunker Hill, south of Martinsburg. Soon (*c.*1727), a band of German pioneers established New Mecklenburg (now Shepherdstown) on the right bank of the Potomac, south of Hagerstown, Md. More pioneers—Scottish, Irish, and German—arrived from Pennsylvania, settling first in the eastern panhandle, in the Greenbrier valley, and then along the Ohio at such sites as Wheeling (1769), Point Pleasant (1774), and Parkersburg (1785). Charleston, upstream on the Kanawha River, was founded in 1788.

The American Revolution. The wave of new settlers arriving on the Appalachian Plateau felt threatened by the French, lodged at FORT DUQUESNE (site of present-day Pittsburgh, Pa.). But after the British had won the last of the FRENCH AND INDIAN WARS in 1763, King George III, fearing further trouble from the Indians, forbade any settlement west of the Allegheny Mountains. Ignoring the king's proclamation, no fewer then 30,000 pioneers occupied the land between the Alleghenies and the Ohio by 1775. Indian power was ended by the retreat of the Shawnee from Point Pleasant in 1774. In 1782, the year after the British surrender at Yorktown supposedly ended the Revolution, British troops and Indians raided Fort Henry at Wheeling.

The Civil War and Separation. As early as 1776, the settlers of western Virginia had petitioned the second Continental Congress in Philadelphia for a separate government. It became increasingly clear during the early 1800s that, whereas eastern Virginia shared the social and economic interests of the South, the western part of the state—because of both geography and ethnic heritage—had more in common with the North (especially western Pennsylvania) and the West.

On Apr. 12, 1861, Confederate troops fired on Fort Sumter; 5 days later, at a state convention in Richmond, Virginians had to decide whether to join the CIVIL WAR on the side of the Confederacy or the Union. A majority voted for an ordinance of secession, but delegates from the northwestern part of the state returned home and set up their own convention at Wheeling on June 11.

Declaring the government at Richmond void, the Wheeling convention established a "restored" government of Virginia and appointed Francis H. PIERPONT governor. In a public referendum on Oct. 24, 1861, voters overwhelmingly supported creation of a new state, Kanawha.

The next month a second convention met at Wheeling, changed the name of the state to West Virginia, and began to draft a constitution. Voters approved the new constitution in April 1862, and a year later President Abraham Lincoln proclaimed West Virginia a state, to be admitted to the Union 60 days later, on June 20, 1863.

Industrialization and Labor Strife. John Peter Salley had discovered coal near Racine as early as 1742, and in 1794 at King's Creek in the northern panhandle Peter Tarr constructed the first iron furnace west of the Alleghenies. Industrialization on a large scale, however, did not begin until after the Civil War. Organizers from the United Mine Workers of America (UMW) came to West Virginia in 1890. On Dec. 6, 1907, the worst mining disaster in U.S. history left 361 dead at Monongah.

Frequent strikes and lockouts, particularly in 1912–13 and 1920-21, led to violent battles between miners on the one hand and company guards, local police, state militia, and federal troops on the other. Turmoil continued into the 1940s, when the UMW took the miners out on strike at the height of World War II. During the 1970s, wildcat strikes plagued the coalfields as union men defied their leadership. Recently, renewed interest in coal for electric power generation and for coal gasification has aroused national attention, and West Virginia's economic future again appears promising if labor-management cooperation can be realized.

westerlies Between latitudes 30° and 60° in the Northern and Southern hemispheres lie belts of winds called the prevailing westerlies. Separated by the tropical easterlies, they blow from the west and ring the poles over the most densely populated areas of the Earth. The westerlies extend more than 20 km (12.5 mi) above the Earth's surface. The strongest winds, with speeds of more than 300 km/h (185 mph), occur at about 12 km (7.5 mi); these are the JET STREAMS, which extend from the tropics to the poles.

In the Southern Hemisphere, where there are few landmasses to disturb their development, the westerlies are stronger and more extensive than in the Northern Hemisphere; they are widest and strongest in the winter months. Northern westerlies also are widest and strongest in winter, but they show seasonal variation, which accounts for the dry summers and wet winters along the westerlies' southern edge.

The westerly belts are the sites of many short-lived, fast-moving cyclonic disturbances as cold, polar easterlies interact with warm, mid-latitude westerlies. Because of these traveling low- and high-pressure disturbances, the westerlies have more storms than any of the other wind belts.

Western Australia Western Australia, Australia's largest state, occupies the western third of the continent and has an area of 2,527,632 km² (975,920 mi²), nearly four times that of Texas. It has a population of 1,594,700 (1989 est.). The capital, PERTH, is located on the southwest coast, where most of the people live.

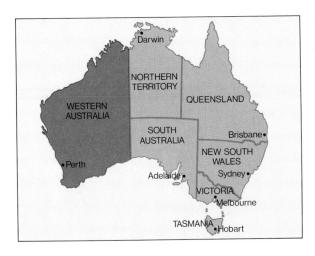

The Western Plateau, which covers most of the state, is a shield of ancient rock with an elevation generally between 230 and 460 m (750 and 1,500 ft). Three climatic regions can be found in Western Australia: the southwest, which has warm to hot, dry summers and mild, rainy winters; the hot, monsoonal northern fringe; and the vast interior, which is hot and arid.

Western Australians are English speaking and predominantly Australian-born. The population is highly urbanized (about 85%), but the state's population density is low, about 0.66 per km² (1.7 per mi²). Major towns other than Perth include Bunbury, Geraldton, Albany, and Freemantle on the southwest coast, and Kalgoorlie, Coolgardie, and Port Hedland.

Western Australia has long exported wool, wheat, and beef. Since the 1960s the focus has shifted to the extraction and processing of minerals, and improved transportation and communications facilities have reduced the state's isolation. Leading ores include iron, gold, nickel, and bauxite. Petroleum and gas have also been developed.

Permanent settlement of Western Australia began in 1829. Chronic labor shortages prompted the colonists to seek convict labor, and prisoners were sent there during the mid-19th century. A series of gold rushes during the 1880s spurred development. Western Australia became a state in 1890.

Western Europe The term *Western Europe* is usually applied to a geographical area that encompasses Scandinavia, the Netherlands, Belgium, Luxembourg, France, Portugal, Spain, and Italy. Natural boundaries include the Atlantic Ocean on the west, the Arctic Sea on the north, and the Mediterranean Sea on the south. To the east lie the countries of Central Europe. Politically, the term *Western Europe* often refers to the non-Communist countries of Europe.

Western Sahara Western Sahara, formerly Spanish Sahara, is a 266,000-km² (103,000-mi²) area in northwestern Africa on the Atlantic coast. Although much of Western Sahara is covered with infertile desert soils, the area is rich in minerals. Estimates of the traditionally nomadic population vary widely.

Spain established a colony there with El Aaiún (now Aiún) as its capital in 1884. After large deposits of high-grade phosphate were discovered in 1963, Morocco and Mauritania pressured Spain to relinquish its hold on the area; Algeria, and later Libya, backed an indigenous proindependence group known as the Polisario Front. In 1975 the World Court ruled that Western Sahara should be granted self-determination. Morocco's King HASSAN II ordered a mass march of 350,000 civilians (the Green March) into the territory. Spain withdrew in 1976, ceding the northern two-thirds to Morocco and the remainder to Mauritania. In 1979, Mauritania signed a treaty with the Polisario renouncing its claims; Morocco then annexed the entire area.

By the early 1980s Morocco, which had divided the area into four provinces, accepted in principle the idea of a referendum but rejected demands by the Organization of African Unity for direct negotiations with the Polisario. To thwart guerrilla attacks, Morocco built a fortified wall that eventually enclosed most of Western Sahara, including the bulk of the population, the mineral resources, and the rich coastal fisheries. Drought drove many formerly nomadic Sahrawis into towns behind the wall, where Moroccan investment and settlement sparked an economic boom. In 1988, Morocco and the Polisario agreed to accept a United Nations peace plan calling for a referendum on the future of the area.

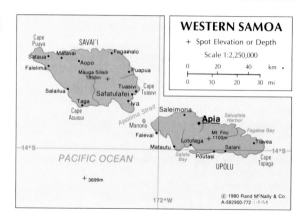

Western Samoa [suh-moh'-uh]   Western Samoa, which with nearby American Samoa is part of the Polynesian SAMOA Archipelago in the Pacific Ocean, is located about 2,800 km (1,700 mi) northeast of New Zealand.

Land, People, and Economy. Western Samoa comprises two large islands, Upolu (1,100 km²/425 mi²)—where APIA, the capital and principal urban center, is located—and Savai'i (1,820 km²/700 mi²), as well as several smaller islets. The islands are of volcanic origin and surrounded by coral reefs. Mauga Silisili, the nation's highest point, rises to 1,858 m (6,096 ft) on Savai'i. About 65% of the country's fertile land is forested. Yearly temperatures average 27° C (80° F), and precipitation ranges from 2,500 to 7,000 mm (100 to 275 in).

Present-day Samoans are descended from Polynesians who arrived more than 2,000 years ago. Most of the inhabitants live in small coastal villages, where they engage in subsistence fishing and agriculture, growing root crops and fruits. The principal cash crops are copra, cacao, and bananas. Most manufacturing is limited to light industries primarily for local use. Tourism is important to the economy.

Although education is not yet free or compulsory, most children receive a primary education. The former Alafau Agricultural College (1966) is now part of the University of the South Pacific, which has its main campus on Fiji.

Government and History. The 1960 constitution provides for the election of the head of state to a 5-year term by the legislative assembly after the death of the remaining paramount chief. The head of state appoints the prime minister, with assembly approval. *Matai*, or local chiefs, elected most assembly members until 1991.

AT A GLANCE

INDEPENDENT STATE OF WESTERN SAMOA

Land: Area: 2,842 km² (1,097mi²). Capital and largest city: Apia (1983 est. pop., 35,000).

People: Population (1990 est.): 186,031. Density: 65 persons per km² (170 per mi²). Distribution (1989 est.): 21% urban, 79% rural. Official languages: Samoan, English. Major religions: Congregationalism, Roman Catholicism, Methodism.

Government: Type: constitutional monarchy. Legislature: Legislative Assembly (Fono). Political subdivisions: 11 districts.

Economy: GNP (1989 est.): $114 million; $720 per capita. Labor distribution (1983): agriculture—59%; other—41%. Foreign trade (1988): imports—$51.8 million; exports—$9.9 million. Currency: 1 tala = 100 sene.

Education and Health: Literacy (1990): virtually 100% of adult population. Universities (1990): none. Hospital beds (1987): 642. Physicians (1988): 44. Life expectancy (1990): women—69; men—64. Infant mortality (1990): 48 per 1,000 live births.

The first European to visit (c.1771) Western Samoa was the Dutch navigator Jacob Roggeveen. During the 1830s the London Missionary Society became active there, and subsequently U.S., British, and German commercial interests competed for economic dominance of the islands. By a treaty of 1899, Western Samoa became a German colony. Following World War I, New Zealand assumed control under a League of Nations mandate. Independence was achieved on Jan. 1, 1962. Because only one-tenth of the population was eligible to vote under the *matai* system, universal suffrage was instituted in 1991, although only *matai* could stand for election.

Westerns

A highly conventional romance form native to American culture, Westerns pervade television, movies, and paperback novels. Set in the last third of the 19th century and located west of the Mississippi, where law and order are threatened by anarchy, Westerns present violent clashes between idealized heroes and villains. Important icons of the genre are the gun, horse, saloon, and open prairie. The stories resolve an essential tension between the need to express individual impulses and the need for social groupings.

Well-known Western novelists include Max BRAND, Zane GREY, Louis L'AMOUR, and Owen WISTER. Influential Western films include *The Great Train Robbery* (1903), *The Covered Wagon* (1923), *Stagecoach* (1939), and *Shane* (1953); among the many actors who have starred in Westerns are Tom MIX, Gary COOPER, John WAYNE, and Clint EASTWOOD. John FORD was the Western's most enduring and highly regarded film director.

See also: FILM, HISTORY OF.

Westinghouse, George

George Westinghouse, b. Central Bridge, N.Y., Oct. 6, 1846, d. Mar. 12, 1914, was an American inventor and industrialist who during his lifetime obtained approximately 400 patents, including that on the air BRAKE. In 1865 he patented a device for replacing derailed freight cars on tracks; 3 years later he developed the railroad frog, which permits the wheel on one rail of a track to cross another rail of an intersecting track. In 1869 he founded the Westinghouse Air Brake Company. By the early 1880s, Westinghouse had developed interlocking switches and a complete railroad signal system (see SIGNALING) and established (1882) the Union Switch and Signal Company. In 1886 he founded the Westinghouse Electric Company, which established the use of alternating current for electrical generating and transmitting apparatuses and electrical appliances in the United States.

Westlake, Donald E.

A versatile American crime novelist, Donald Edwin Westlake, b. New York City, July 12, 1933, has written three distinct types of novels. Under the pseudonym Richard Stark, he published a chilling series of hard-boiled novels whose protagonist is a professional thief. The films *The Split* (1968) and *Point Blank*

(1967) were based on *The Seventh* (1966) and *The Hunter* (1963), respectively. As Tucker Coe, Westlake published mystery novels, including *Murder among Children* (1968), that focus on the psychology of their hero, a guilt-ridden ex–police officer. Under his own name, Westlake writes hilarious farces such as *The Hot Rock* (1970; film, 1972) and *Bank Shot* (1972; film, 1974), about inept criminals or unlucky innocents. *A Likely Story* (1984) satirizes the publishing industry.

Westminster Abbey

London's Collegiate Church of Saint Peter in Westminster, popularly called Westminster Abbey, is one of Britain's principal historic monuments. It was originally attached to a Benedictine abbey dissolved in 1560. After the demolition of a Norman church built (c.1050) on the site by Edward the Confessor, work on the present structure was begun in 1245, but the nave was not completed until the early 16th century. The two prominent western towers were added in the 18th century. The architect of the first building campaign was Henry of Reims. In general terms the design closely follows the French Gothic plan first established (c.1194) at Chartres Cathedral; the key elements of this plan are the four-part rib vaults, the three-story elevation, the round piers with attached colonnettes, and the tall, narrow proportions of the main spaces. Among the subsidiary elements of the abbey complex, the octagonal Chapter House (1250–1253?) is one of the most beautiful examples of a particularly English type of building. The axial radiating chapel from the church (1503) is a superb example of English Late Gothic architecture.

Famous as the place where the British sovereigns are crowned, the abbey contains the 13th-century coronation chair of Edward I, the Shrine of Edward the Confessor, the Tomb of the Unknown Warrior, and the Poets' Corner, with memorials to many of Britain's greatest writers.

Westminster Abbey, begun under the 13th-century architect Henry of Reims, reflects French Gothic influence throughout its design. The abbey has been the site of all English coronations since its construction.

Westminster Palace   Westminster Palace, the correct name for the building commonly called the Houses of Parliament, occupies the site of the London residence of the kings of England from the 11th to the 16th centuries. The only surviving medieval element on the site is the Great Hall, built (1097–99) by William II and rebuilt (1291) by Edward II; measuring approximately 75 m (246 ft) in length, it is the largest open-timber hall in Europe. Henry VIII removed the royal offices to Whitehall, reserving Westminster for the use of Parliament and other public bodies. The entire Westminster complex with the exception of the Great Hall was destroyed in an 1834 fire and replaced (1840–60) by the present building, which was designed by Sir Charles Barry and decorated by A. W. N. Pugin. The most striking parts of Barry's neo-Gothic design are the River Front, which extends about 290 m (950 ft) along the Thames River, and the Clock Tower, the 97-m-tall (318-ft) home of Big Ben.

Westmoreland   see CUMBRIA

Westmoreland, William C.   The American general William Childs Westmoreland, b. Spartanburg County, S.C., Mar. 26, 1914, commanded (1964–68) U.S. forces in South Vietnam in the VIETNAM WAR. A 1936 graduate of the United States Military Academy (West Point), he participated in the World War II Normandy invasion. He served in the Korean War and from 1960 to 1963 was superintendent of West Point. During his command in Vietnam, U.S. involvement grew from a few thousand advisors and technicians to more than 500,000 American troops. From 1968 to 1972, Westmoreland was army chief of staff. In a $120 million libel suit against CBS Westmoreland claimed that the network had defamed him in a 1982 television documentary about Vietnam. After a prolonged trial (1984–85), he finally dropped the suit before it was sent to the jury.

Weston, Edward   With his crisp, probing, often sensual images of natural forms, Edward Weston, b. Highland Park, Ill., Mar. 24, 1866, d. Jan. 1, 1958, helped change the direction of modern photography. He first won a reputation for his soft-focused pictorial work. In the early 1920s, however, influenced by the leading exponents of straight photography, Alfred Stieglitz and Paul Strand, Weston turned to working with a sharply focused lens during trips to the east coast and Mexico. Together with the photographers Ansel Adams, Imogen Cunningham, John Paul Edwards, Sonya Noskowiak, and Henry Swift, Weston founded (1932) Group f/64, a short-lived but influential association based on Weston's theories of the previsualization and nonmanipulation of the final print.

Weston's use of an 8x10-inch view camera permitted him to see the image of the object he was photographing on the ground glass and thus to determine the final printed image. He then contact-printed the negative on glossy paper the same size as the negative, reproducing as many of the light-reflecting surfaces as possible. Best known for his close-range photographs of female nudes, rocks, shells, and vegetables, Weston also photographed landscapes in the South and West and experimented with abstractions.

Westphalia   [west-fay'-lee-uh]   Westphalia (German: Westfalen), a historic region in Germany, is now part of the states of North Rhine–Westphalia, Lower Saxony, and Hesse. The region's boundaries have varied widely through the centuries but in general are marked by the Rhine River to the west, the Weser River to the east, the Netherlands to the northwest, the former Prussian province of Hanover to the north and east, and Hesse-Nassau to the south and southeast. The terrain consists of northern lowlands, the RUHR VALLEY to the west, and hilly country south of the Ruhr River. The major rivers are the RHINE, WESER, Ems, Lippe, and Ruhr. Westphalia is heavily populated and industrialized, especially in the Ruhr Valley and urban concentrations, but agriculture is still important. Major cities include DORTMUND, DUISBURG, DÜSSELDORF, and ESSEN.

The Westphalians, a western Saxon people, moved into the region during the early Middle Ages. Westphalia was granted (1180) as a duchy to the archbishop of Cologne. The archbishops were nominal overlords of the region until 1803. The Peace of Westphalia (1648), which ended the Thirty Years' War, was signed at MÜNSTER. Under Napoleon I, Westphalia was divided between the grand duchy of Berg and the short-lived (1807–13) kingdom of Westphalia under Jérôme Bonaparte. In 1816 most of Westphalia became a Prussian province, retaining a political identity until after World War II.

Westphalia, Peace of   The Peace of Westphalia comprises the series of treaties that ended the THIRTY YEARS' WAR in Germany in 1648. These treaties created a compromise settlement between Protestants and Roman Catholics, destroyed the Holy Roman Empire as a significant entity by recognizing the virtual sovereignty of the German states, established France as the major European power, and made Sweden the dominant Baltic nation.

After the Preliminary Treaty of July 1642, peace congresses opened at Münster and Osnabrück in Westphalia, northwest Germany, in 1643. In January 1648, Spain and the United Provinces of the Netherlands made peace, Spain formally recognizing Dutch independence (see DUTCH REVOLT). On Oct. 24, 1648, the other treaties were signed. Holy Roman Emperor FERDINAND III accepted French claims to Upper Alsace. Sweden obtained the bishoprics of Bremen and Verden and divided Pomerania with Brandenburg, whose prince-elector also obtained Magdeburg. Bavaria kept the Upper Palatinate and the Palatinate electorate. The emperor recognized Swiss independence. The German princes obtained the formal right to make alliances and choose their religion for themselves and their subjects, leaving the emperor with few powers.

Wexford Wexford, a county in LEINSTER province, southeastern Ireland, has an area of 2,351 km² (908 mi²) and a population of 99,081 (1981). Enniscorthy, New Ross, and the county seat of Wexford are the major towns. Wexford consists of lowlands bordered by the Blackstairs Mountains in the west and by Saint George's Channel on the east and south. Cattle raising and the cultivation of cereals, wheat, and turnips are important. The first part of Ireland to be invaded by Anglo-Normans in 1169, Wexford was subjugated by Oliver Cromwell in 1649.

Weyden, Rogier van der [vy'-duhn] Rogier van der Weyden, b. c.1399, d. June 16, 1464, was one of the principal founders of the Netherlandish tradition of painting. His reputation was such that his influence dominated northern European painting for at least 50 years after his death.

Although van der Weyden was probably apprenticed in Tournai, Belgium, to Robert Campin, the most innovative Flemish artist of the early 15th century, his debt to Jan van Eyck is also visible. In van der Weyden's early painting *Saint Luke Drawing a Portrait of the Virgin* (c.1435; one version, Museum of Fine Arts, Boston), the naturalistic description and lack of such supernatural elements as halos is characteristic of Campin, but the composition as a whole is borrowed from van Eyck. The dramatically physical presence of the Virgin appearing to Saint Luke, the patron saint of artists, epitomizes van der Weyden's emphasis on the concrete, which is reinforced by a realistic domestic interior and the careful rendering of a Flemish town in the background. He also imposes a personal elegance on the composition, which is most evident in the complementary poses of Luke and the Virgin. Similar characteristics can be seen in van der Weyden's masterwork, the *Descent from the Cross* (before 1443; Prado, Madrid), in which the powerful physicality of the figures and the detailed textural description are offset by a carefully balanced and interlaced composition. The naturalism and emotional theatricality are countered by the shallow space in which the action takes place and by the gilded background.

Throughout his career van der Weyden attempted to balance in his art the convincing visual description characteristic of Netherlandish painting and a medieval heritage of isolated devotional images. His production consisted of large altarpiece images, small icons of the Virgin and Child or Christ, and portraits. Van der Weyden's elegantly simple compositions, his beautiful yet formulaic figures, and his earnest piety provided a readily imitable formula for several generations of copyists and imitators in the Netherlands and Germany.

Weygand, Maxime [vay-gahn'] After completing a long army career, French general Maxime Weygand, b. Jan. 21, 1867, d. Jan. 28, 1965, returned to the military during World War II and rose to become supreme French commander (May–June 1940). He could not, however, prevent France's fall (June 22, 1940) to the Germans. Thereafter he served the Vichy government. The Germans imprisoned him (1942–45) because he was suspected of aiding the resistance. In 1948, Weygand was acquitted of charges of collaboration with the Germans.

whale Whales are the larger members of the order Cetacea. This order of aquatic mammals is divided into three suborders: the Mysticeti, the baleen whales; the Odontoceti, the toothed whales; and the Archaeoceti, an extinct group known only through fossils. The Odontoceti also include the smaller DOLPHINS and PORPOISES.

The large baleen whales comprise three families and about a dozen species. All these species lack teeth except as vestiges in the embryos. Instead, they possess a row of fringed plates of baleen (whalebone), which is a keratinaceous (horny) material developed from the gums. The plates act as a filter, or sieve, straining small marine organisms from the water. The baleen whales are primarily plankton feeders and derive most of their nourishment from marine organisms that may be only a few millimeters (several hundredths of an inch) in length. Their principal food in the polar regions, especially in the Antarctic, consists of small, shrimplike crustaceans collectively known as "krill." Commonly known baleen whales include the right whale, genus *Balaena*; the gray whale, *Eschrichtius gibbosus*; the blue whale, *Balaenoptera musculus*; the fin whale, *B. physalus*; and the humpback whale, *Megaptera novaeanglia*. The largest species, and the largest animal that has ever lived, is the blue whale. Specimens up to 30 m (100 ft) in length have been recorded, with weights estimated at more than 130 metric tons (143 U.S. tons).

The toothed whales are all predators, feeding actively on fish and squid. They possess sharp teeth, usually in both jaws, used to catch their prey. The odontocetes that are commonly called whales comprise 5 families and about 30 species, including such forms as pilot whales, *Globicephala*; beaked whales, *Mesoplodon*; the beluga or white whale, *Delphinapterus leucas*; the killer whale, *Orcinus orca*; the pygmy sperm whale, *Kogia*; and the species best known through Herman Melville's novel *Moby-Dick*, the sperm whale, *Physeter catodon*. Sperm whales have been recorded up to 19 m (62 ft) in length.

General Characteristics. The general form of whales is torpedo-shaped, and their bodies are smooth and streamlined. The front limbs are modified into a pair of flippers and are used primarily as stabilizers or steering mechanisms. The hind limbs are represented only by a few bony vestiges. A dorsal fin is usually present, and the tail fin consists of a pair of horizontal flukes. The primary thrust in locomotion is derived from up-and-down movements of the tail and flukes.

Some baleen whales—including the blue, fin, and humpback—have longitudinal furrows on their undersides and are known as rorquals. The skin of whales is smooth and hairless, except for the stiff bristles, or vibrissae, in the head region of some whales, such as the fin whale and other rorquals, and the vestiges of hair and hair

narwhal

sperm whale

pilot whale

killer whale

beluga

gray whale

blue whale

right whale

humpback whale

finback whale

(Opposite page) *Whales are large aquatic mammals with torpedo-shaped bodies, horizontal tail fins, front limbs modified into flippers, and no external hind limbs. Like other mammals they are warm blooded, bear live young, and breathe air (by surfacing at regular intervals). Whales are divided into two groups: the Odontoceti, or toothed whales, and the Mysticeti, or baleen whales. The toothed whales are predators with sharp teeth and wide throats. They include the narwhal, a small whale with a maximum length of about 5.5 m (18 ft) excluding the male's spiral tusk, which may reach an additional 2.7 m (9 ft). The beluga, or white whale, is slightly smaller and lacks the tusk but has a similar body shape. The pilot whale is found in schools with several hundred members. The black-and-white killer whale cooperatively hunts in packs that number from 3 to 50. Largest of the toothed whales, the sperm whale, reaches a maximum size of about 20 m (65 ft) and maximum weight of about 50 metric tons. The baleen whales are generally large whales that feed primarily on plankton. They lack teeth but instead have plates of baleen, or whalebone, on the upper jaw, which filter small organisms from the water. The gray whale reaches a maximum size of 15 m (50 ft). The right whale is slightly larger and has a bonnet, or horny protuberance, on its head. Largest of all whales—and the largest animal known—is the blue whale, which may reach 30 m (100 ft) with an estimated weight in excess of 130 metric tons. The finback whale has a gray-to-black body with a white underside and may grow to 24 m (80 ft). The similarly colored humpback whale may reach 15 m (50 ft). Like the blue whale, they are rorquals—baleen whales with many longitudinal furrows running from the chest to the throat.*

follicles in the embryos of the sperm whale and certain other species. The humpback whale commonly possesses many large, rough-surfaced growths on parts of its head. The function of these is unknown. Underneath the whale's skin is a thick layer of dense fatty tissue, the blubber, the primary function of which appears to be as an aid in maintaining the body temperature of these warm-blooded mammals at 34°–37° C (93°–99° F). Because they are air-breathing mammals, all whales must rise to the surface to breathe. Some species, such as the sperm whale, are capable of diving to depths of more than 1,000 m (3,300 ft) and remaining underwater for 50 minutes or more. A single breath of a whale consists of a rapid explusion of air. The exhalation is followed immediately by a slower inhalation. The spout of a whale is often erroneously thought to be water. Because the exhaled air is normally warmer than the outside atmosphere, a rapid condensation of water occurs, giving the spout the appearance of a jet of steam. It emerges from the top of the head, from the blowhole. In reality, the blowhole is the nostril, single in odontocetes and double in mysticetes.

Reproduction. Little is known about the reproductive behavior of whales, and much of it is derived from studies on small cetaceans, such as porpoises, in captivity. The gestation period for cetaceans in general is about 10 to 12 months, including even the gigantic blue whale. Some estimates give as long as a 16-month gestation period for the sperm and killer whales. Whales usually bear a single calf per pregnancy. The young are nursed from about 5 to 7 months in the blue and fin whales and up to about a year in most odontocetes. Life spans for cetacean species are estimated from about 30 years in the smaller odontocetes to perhaps 90 or even 100 years for the large baleen whales.

Distribution. Whales can be found in all oceans and seas of the world and at any latitude. Gray whales follow migration paths along the Pacific coasts of Asia and North America, some of them undertaking the longest round-trip migration of any mammal, up to 22,000 km (14,500 mi). The blue whale, the sperm whale, and possibly other species have a circumpolar distribution, and there appear to be distinct noninterbreeding populations in the Northern and Southern hemispheres.

Behavior. Although little is known directly about the social behavior of whales, it is clear that most are gregarious, traveling in schools, also called pods or gams. Occasion-

ally, whales thrust themselves completely out of the water, leaping into the air, and falling back with a huge splash. This "breaching" is thought to be associated with some aspects of reproduction or courtship, but may be only incidental to some other behavior as yet undetermined.

Virtually all species of cetaceans are known to produce sounds, and these sounds may serve as an important means of interaction and communication. All odontocetes thus far investigated produce short, pulse-type sounds that function in echolocation. In addition, most species are also known to emit high-pitched squeals and whistles that appear to be used as part of social behavior. Although there is no evidence that these sounds represent anything comparable to a true language, there is little doubt that they are used to denote specific emotional states, for example, fright, hunger, or sexual readiness. For the mysticetes, there is much less evidence available on the function of sounds because none have yet survived in captivity for study.

whaling Whales have been hunted and used for meat and oil since earliest times. Subsistence whaling has always been practiced by the Eskimos of the Arctic. The harvesting of whales in commercial quantities dates back at least to the 11th century.

Whale oil, rendered from the blubber, was used originally for lamp fuel and later as a principal ingredient of soaps, margarine, paint oils, and lubricants. Spermacetic oil, a waxy material extracted from the head of the sperm whale, was highly prized for making candles, fine lubricants, cosmetic oils, and shoe polish. Whalebone, or baleen, the long bony plates that act as a sieve in the mouths of baleen whales, are extremely strong and flexible, and were used as stays in women's corsets. Ambergris, an odorous substance accumulated in the intestines of the sperm whale (and sometimes found washed up on beaches), acts a a stabilizer in the manufacture of perfumes and other fragrances and is still used, although it is largely replaced by synthetics now. Whale meat has always been a staple in the diet of certain Eskimos and is widely eaten in Japan.

Growth of Commercial Whaling. The first significant era of commercial whaling occurred during the 12th and 13th centuries, when captures of the Atlantic right whale by Basque whalers operating along the shores of the Bay

A 19th-century woodcut of a whaling expedition in the South Seas shows sailors in wooden boats attempting to harpoon a sperm whale at close range. The term Nantucket sleighride *was coined to describe the situation to which a boatload of sailors anchored by a towline to a harpooned whale were subjected as the wounded animal tried to escape.*

of Biscay reached industrial proportions. Subsequent declines in the whale population, coupled with increased demand, resulted in voyages of ever-increasing length.

During the 17th century, Dutch, English, French, and German whalers pursued the Arctic right whale, or bowhead whale, along the ice edge of the Arctic and North Atlantic oceans from Spitzbergen to the Davis Strait. The initial colonization of North America during the early 17th century resulted in modest harvests of Atlantic right whales along the New England coast. The discovery (early 18th century) of the sperm whale farther offshore catapulted the U.S. whaling industry into prominence. When the tryworks, the brick ovens used for rendering whale blubber, were moved from land to the decks of the whaling ships, there was no longer any need to return to shore with a load of blubber. Whaling voyages often lasted years—as long as it took to fill the oil casks in the hold.

Right whales were discovered off the Pacific coast of South America and by 1840 had been hunted almost to extinction. Whalers then sought right whales and bowhead whales in the Bering Sea and along the coast of Asia; they hunted gray whale along the southern California coast. By killing juvenile whales and nursing calves, and concentrating their attacks on a single species at a time, whalers eventually depleted the stocks of all hunted whales, with the exception of the gray whale.

The rise of the petroleum industry effectively ended the era of the great sailing fleets of whalers, as petroleum products replaced whale oil for lighting. The U.S. fleet, once numbering more than 700 vessels, shrank to insignificance, as did the much smaller fleets of the European nations.

Modern Whaling. In the 1860s, a Norwegian, Svend Foyn, invented a cannon-fired harpoon with an explosive head. His harpoon gun was improved upon until, by the 1870s, it had reached its present form: a cylindrical steel device shot from a cannon-type gun and trailing a heavy rope. The force of the shot carried the harpoon great distances and penetrated deep into the whale's body. A

charge on the tip exploded, and movable barbs opened out to fasten the weapon snugly inside the whale. Most whales sink when they die (the sperm whale is the sole exception), so dead whales were pumped full of air to keep them afloat.

The harpoon gun was the first major technological advance in the art of whaling. With the advent of engine-powered ships, other changes became inevitable. By the mid-1920s the factory ship, with its attendant fleet of "catcher" boats, was in wide use. A huge vessel carrying everything needed for extended whaling voyages, it contained modern tryworks, laboratories, refrigerators, and the machinery for reducing the entire whale to usable products.

The small catcher boats, guided by the reports of a whale spotter in an airplane—later, by helicopters or SO-NAR—sighted and harpooned the whale, inflated its body, and marked its position with a buoy before continuing the hunt. Factory-ship fleets would accompany a group of whales, killing large numbers every day until not a single whale remained. Ships hunted the blue, sei, and fin whales—creatures that swam too fast for sailing ships to follow. By the 1960s the smaller minke whale was also taken.

The sale of whale oil had once again become profitable in the early 20th century, because HYDROGENATION made the oil usable in soaps, shortenings, and margarines. Factory-ship pressure cookers extracted every ounce of oil from whale meat and bone; what was left of the whale was ground into bone meal or animal feed. An entire whale could be completely disassembled and rendered into its component products in less than one hour. In the 1930s almost every industrialized seagoing nation launched factory fleets. As a result, Antarctic blue whales were decimated. The Pacific-humpback and sperm-whale populations dwindled to insignificance. More than 30,000 whales were killed annually until World War II temporarily ended the slaughter.

In the immediate postwar era the need for fats and oils to supplement meager European diets drove more whaling fleets out to sea. Yet the vastly diminished whale numbers soon made whaling a far less profitable enterprise. The United States and the European nations—with the exception of Norway and Iceland—gradually ended their whaling industries. By the 1960s, only the Soviet Union and Japan maintained large factory-ship fleets.

Whale Conservation. The International Whaling Commission (IWC) was formed in 1946 to regulate whaling worldwide. The commission at first prohibited the killing of right and gray whales, limited the taking of other whale species, and established closed areas and seasons. Whaling nations, however, were not bound by IWC rulings, and large numbers of whales continued to be taken for some years afterward.

U.S. concern for the declining whale populations resulted in a ban on importation of all whale products in 1970 and in passage of the Marine Mammal Protection Act of 1972, which prohibited all commercial exploitation of whales in U.S. waters. Worldwide a variety of wildlife and conservation organizations spoke out against the practice of commercial whaling, and sentiment grew to end whaling altogether.

In 1982 the IWC, whose membership had increased from 14 members to 38, voted to ban all commercial whaling at the end of the 1984–85 season. The effects of the ban were to be reviewed to determine whether commercial quotas should be resumed, but Japan and Norway, the major whaling nations, filed objections and have continued to take small numbers of minke and sei whales, for "scientific research." The legally permissible hunting of whales by Eskimos and other aboriginal peoples may also be contributing to the critical depletion of some species.

Wharton, Edith Edith Wharton, b. New York City, Jan. 24, 1862, as Edith Newbold Jones, d. Aug. 11, 1937, is unique among American novelists for her ironic, insider's portrayal of the clashes accompanying the displacement of New York City's pre–Civil War high society by the parvenu society of the postwar years.

Wharton belonged to old New York families by both birth and marriage. She began to write fiction and publish poems at an early age, and her professional writing career was launched by a how-to book, *The Decoration of Houses* (1897, with Ogden Codman, Jr.). Her marriage in 1885 to Edward Wharton, 12 years her senior, ended in divorce in 1913. She never remarried and divided most of the rest of her life between Paris and the French Riviera.

Meanwhile, Wharton had enjoyed her first great literary success with *The House of Mirth* (1905), the pathetic tale of Lily Bart, a New York debutante whose ill-advised speculations in courtship and gambling cause her to descend through ever-lower circles of society until she dies, perhaps a suicide. By contrast, the sardonic *The Custom of the Country* (1913) follows an unscrupulous midwestern social climber through several marriages to the pinnacle of society. *The Age of Innocence* (1920), which won the Pulitzer Prize, looks backward nostalgically at the power of a rigidly decorous older society to destroy a blossoming but indiscreet romance. Quite different is the popular short novel ETHAN FROME, a grim tale of frustrated infatuation in a decaying New England village.

Edith Wharton is considered one of the most distinguished writers of the first quarter of the 20th century. Her themes focus on the parochial mores and inevitable decline of the established upper-class society of New York City during the late 19th and early 20th centuries.

During World War I, Wharton was a vehement partisan of France and celebrated its cause in *The Marne* (1918) and *A Son at the Front* (1923). She then returned to the New York of her childhood as a setting for *The Old Maid* (1924); *Hudson River Bracketed* (1929) and its sequel, *The Gods Arrive* (1932); and *The Buccaneers* (1938), an unfinished novel containing some of her best writing. Wharton's autobiography, *A Backward Glance,* was published in 1934.

wheat A highly important cereal crop of the genus *Triticum* of the grass family, Gramineae, wheat was probably first cultivated in the Euphrates Valley nearly 9,000 years ago. Since that time wheat has been a significant food source for people and animals. The most important species include common wheat, *T. vulgare*, used in BREAD; durum wheat, *T. durum*, used in pasta products; club wheat, *T. compactum*, used in cakes and pastries; and Polish wheat, *T. polonicum.*

Most of the approximately 30 species of wheat have hollow stems. The leaves are long and narrow. The head is characterized by flowers numbering 20 to 100 and occurring in spikelets. Fertilization of the flowers produces grain. A deep crease extends the length of a kernel, and many short hairs occur on the kernel's small end. The entire kernel is surrounded by the pericarp, or outer bran, which is difficult to remove and represents 15% of the kernel. The rest of the kernel is composed of endosperm (83%) and germ (1.5%). The object of FLOUR milling is to separate these constituents.

Cultivation. The wheat plant adapts to a wide range of environmental conditions, from those in the Arctic Circle to those in the tropics. It is best cultivated in temperate areas with 250 to 750 mm (10 to 30 in) of yearly rainfall. Wheat cultivation spread throughout the world with the advent of trade. It was unknown in the Western Hemisphere until the Spanish brought it to the Americas in 1519. For thousands of years the sickle remained the common method for cutting wheat, and threshing was done by beating to separate the kernels from the hulls. When the reaper was invented in about 1830, mechanical operations were used for cutting and threshing. Today self-propelled combines are common.

Depending on variety, planting time, and environment, commercial wheats are classified as hard or soft, spring or winter, white or red, or durum wheat. After the wheat seed is planted, it starts to absorb moisture and swell, and soon the pericarp, located at the germ end, ruptures. The primary bud emerges, then lateral rootlets. The plant pushes up through the soil, soon forming foliage. Leaves grow from the base area near the stem; therefore, grazing or cutting does not prevent renewed growth. Winter wheat can thus be pastured without harming the plant.

As the plant grows, short stems form branches, called tillers, close to the ground; these become straw. The head begins to develop and emerges from the leaf sheath, flowering takes place, and fertilization occurs. Some flowers are sterile.

Environmental hazards to the wheat plant are drought,

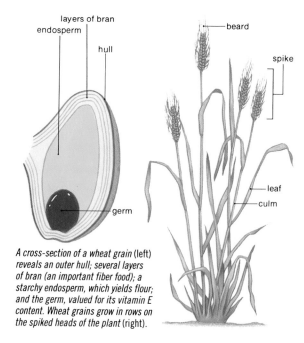

A cross-section of a wheat grain (left) *reveals an outer hull; several layers of bran (an important fiber food); a starchy endosperm, which yields flour; and the germ, valued for its vitamin E content. Wheat grains grow in rows on the spiked heads of the plant* (right).

freezing temperatures, and wind erosion. Wheat is subject to numerous diseases (mosaics, smuts, and rusts, for example) and insects (such as grasshoppers and locusts, Hessian flies, green bugs, army worms, and weevils). Plant breeding research has eliminated or drastically reduced damage caused by many of the diseases and insects that afflict wheat.

Breeding. Wheat-breeding programs in many worldwide research centers have sought higher yields, improved baking quality, and enhanced nutrition. The first big stride in yield potential occurred with the introduction of semidwarf varieties responsive to fertilizer applications and insensitive to length of day. Semidwarf wheat, because of its shorter straw, leaves less material on the field during harvesting.

Improving the chemical and physical properties of the wheat kernel depends on the plant breeder's skill and knowledge in manipulating the genes controlling these characteristics. The hard-wheat breeding programs have two objectives: to increase protein content and to enhance protein quality. Until recently, improved yields have decreased protein content; however, newer varieties are high yielding and maintain high protein content as well. The nutritive value of wheat protein does not differ much among varieties as measured by amino-acid analysis. Lysine is a limiting amino acid; consequently, efforts have been directed to producing varieties with a higher lysine content.

Wheat and other cereal grains do not contain appreciable amounts of vitamin A, D, or C but do contribute minerals and the vitamins thiamine, riboflavin, and niacin.

Breeding programs can be expected eventually to improve the total nutritive value of wheat.

Production. When environmental conditions permit, seeding occurs in the fall so that the roots can develop and use the warmth, moisture, and sunlight in the spring. Moisture in semiarid regions is conserved by allowing the land to remain idle for one entire growing season, a practice called fallowing. The physical and chemical properties of wheat proteins differ from those of other plants because the proteins form gluten, which retains gas during fermentation. Gluten development and gas-retention properties are altered by variety, soil, and growing conditions. Wheats thus differ in quality from season to season and place to place.

The leading wheat-producing countries in order of output are the USSR, the United States, China, India, Canada, and Australia. The United States, however, has a higher yield per hectare than the USSR, whose geography is not ideally suited for wheat cultivation.

Marketing. After harvest, wheat is transported from areas of production to areas of utilization and then to regions of consumption. Wheat is moved to the local elevator as the first collection point, then shipped to terminal elevators, which in turn supply the processors or ship to export locations. Flour mills usually are located near centers of population because wheat can be shipped at a lower cost than can the commodities manufactured from wheat. Different kinds of flour are required by the baking industries; consequently, wheat of different qualities must be segregated for delivery to mills for manufacturing special products.

Uses. Wheat ground into flour and made into baked products is the form in which most wheat is consumed;

Wheat is among the world's oldest and most important cultivated grains. Under the Grains Standard Act of 1916, the United States, a major producer of wheat, classified five varieties of wheat. Of these, soft red winter, common white, and durum are used in making pastry dough, macaroni, and other pasta, and hard red winter wheat and spring wheat are used to make bread flour.

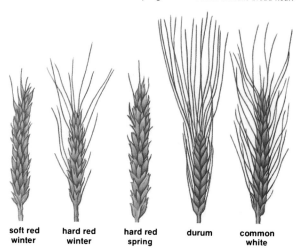

soft red winter   **hard red winter**   **hard red spring**   **durum**   **common white**

however, pasta products are popular and represent an expanding market. Durum wheat is especially suitable for pasta. Puffed, flaked, and rolled wheat is used in breakfast foods. A wheat food-product called bulgur is prepared by cooking, dehydrating, and peeling wheat. It resembles rice in appearance but not in eating qualities. Processed wheat germ is used in various specialty foods and to produce vitamin E.

Wheat for animal feed or pet foods is restricted because it is usually higher priced than other cereal grains of comparable nutritive value. Much wheat, however, is fed to animals in regions throughout the world where no distinction is made between food and feed grains. The by-products of the flour-milling operations are bran, shorts, germ, and low-grade flour usually marketed as feed. Monosodium glutamate, a common condiment, is derived from gluten.

Gluten is used mainly in the bread-baking industry. Dried gluten contains 75% to 85% protein, 5% to 10% lipids, and some starch. Gluten is also hydrolized for use as meat extenders, meat substitutes, pet foods, and food flavors. When gluten is separated from wheat, the marketing of starch becomes necessary. Wheat starch can be used for essentially all usual food and industrial purposes.

wheaten terrier see SOFT-COATED WHEATEN TERRIER

———
Wheatley, Phillis The first recognized African-American poet, Phillis Wheatley, 1753–84, was brought to America as a slave and took the name of her master, the merchant John Wheatley. She published her first poem at the age of 13. *Poems on Various Subjects, Religious and Moral* (1773) received praise in America and England.

Wheatstone bridge see BRIDGE CIRCUIT

———
wheel A wheel is a circular frame of wood, metal, or other hard substance, either in the form of a solid disk or a ring or rim with spokes radiating from a central part (nave). A wheel is designed so that it can be attached at its center to an axle with or around which it rotates.

The invention of the wheel is considered to be one of the great milestones in the history of humanity. Many have thought the wheel essential to the formulation of both ancient and modern civilizations. Although modern archaeologists have moderated this earlier view, it is generally agreed that the wheel is vital to most societies.

Although the precise date and place of its discovery are unknown, the wheel is believed to have been invented in ancient Mesopotamia, sometime during the 4th millennium BC. (This invention may have been preceded by the invention of the POTTER'S WHEEL.) The area between the Tigris and Euphrates rivers in modern Iraq, where the ancient civilization of Sumeria arose, provides the earliest unequivocal evidence of the wheel's existence. In exca-vating the courtyard of the Eanna Temple in the ancient city of URUK, archaeologists found a clay tablet containing a pictograph of a wheeled cart that dates from the period 3200–3100 BC. Some experts argue that the wheel's actual invention may have come as much as 1,000 years earlier, but archaeological excavations have not uncovered evidence from an earlier period.

The sturdy, solid construction of the early wheel is thought to have served admirably on what were probably rough roads (see ROADS AND HIGHWAYS), and the simplicity of design allowed for its swift repair. Both two- and four-wheeled vehicles were used to transport goods.

The wheel's military potential was perceived relatively early. A depiction at Ur shows war chariots running down enemy troops (see CHARIOT). Royal funerary processions made use of the earliest hearses. Whether for transportation or war, all conveyances were drawn by domesticated animals that included oxen, onagers, and the Asiatic ass.

Although no conclusive evidence exists, many experts believe that the wheel was invented only once and then diffused to the rest of the world. According to this hypothesis, the initial spread was to areas adjacent to southern Mesopotamia, so that by 2600 BC the wheel was actively used in Assyria. By the end of the 3d millennium BC, it may already have reached the Ukraine. Its consistent use in organized warfare, however, created a demand for a lighter-weight wheel structure that would permit greater speed.

Early in the 2d millennium BC the spoked wheel was created. Its birthplace is believed to be in northern Syria or possibly Anatolia, and its invention is attributed to the Hittites or the Mitanni. By the 18th century BC, horse-drawn war chariots with spoked wheels were being made by the Hyksos, who used them to invade Egypt in 1680 BC.

Indian tradition indicates that metal-using barbarians arrived in India in the 14th century BC with horse-drawn chariots used for both war and sport. The peoples of the Indus civilization adapted these vehicles to transport foodstuffs from distant rural areas to the large cities, using both two-wheeled carts and larger, four-wheeled WAG-ONS (see COACH AND CARRIAGE). All vehicles were drawn by the humped ox. Similar conveyances with the same basic wheel design were found in Indian villages as late as the 1930s.

Sculptures of chariots found in ancient Chinese tombs reveal that the spoked wheel had arrived in China by the 13th century BC, effectively completing the diffusion of the wheel to the major centers of civilization of the Old World. The wheel was not used anywhere in the New World (although it was used on children's toys) until introduced by Europeans in the 16th century AD.

No major design changes in the spoked wheel were made until the advent of railroads during the 19th century and automobiles during the 20th century. Special solid-metal wheels were created for railroad cars; later, tubed, and then tubeless, rubber TIRES were developed for automobiles, permitting very high speeds by greatly reducing surface friction.

Archaeologists have come to believe that the wheel is

nave lathe

mortising cradle

(Left) The craft of the wheelwright has been passed down with few changes since the Middle Ages. In the first stage of the wheelmaking process, the nave of the wheel is shaped from well-seasoned elm on a hand-driven lathe. Using a chisel, the wheelwright cuts grooves into which iron bands will be fitted to provide strength. The nave is then placed on a mortising cradle, where holes are made to receive the spokes.

(Below) The spokes, cut from sturdy heart-of-oak, are driven into the mortises with a hammer. Next, the rim of the wheel is constructed in sections known as fellies. Each section, made of ash wood, is shaped with an adze. Using an instrument called a spoke dog, the wheelwright hammers the fellies onto the spokes. The fellies are then joined together with dowels.

spoke

mortise

adze

felly

spoke dog

dowel

metal strake

square-head nail

hot metal band

tyring tongs

tyring clamp

straking

tyring platform

tyring

(Left) An ironworker adds a metal rim by one of two methods, straking or tyring. In straking, several metal bars are fastened to the wheel with square-head nails. These nails protrude from the finished wheel, giving extra traction but causing damage to roadways. In tyring, a metal bar is heated, bent into a ring, and dropped over the wheel by ironworkers using tongs. Water is then thrown on the red-hot band. The resulting contraction causes it to tighten onto the wheel with a spectacular cracking noise. During this procedure the wheel rests on a tyring platform, held in place by a clamp. The metal rim is secured with nails, and the wheel is sanded and painted.

not an absolute necessity for the growth of civilization. The Sphinx and Pyramids of Egypt were constructed well before the wheel was introduced. Moreover, the great civilizations of the New World evolved without benefit of the wheel. It is now thought that unless a suitable system of roads is established and large draft animals are available, wheeled vehicles will prove of little value.

Wheeler, Joseph   Joseph Wheeler, b. Augusta, Ga., Sept. 10, 1836, d. Jan. 25, 1906, was a U.S. Army officer and politician. During the Civil War he commanded (April 1862) a Confederate infantry regiment at Shiloh and then became (October 1862) chief of cavalry in the Army of Mississippi, earning the nickname "Fightin' Joe."

After the war Wheeler served as a U.S. representative from Alabama (1881–82, 1883, 1885–1900). He led a cavalry unit in Cuba during the Spanish-American War and commanded a brigade in suppressing the Philippine insurrection (1899–1900).

Wheeler, William Almon   William Almon Wheeler, b. Malone, N.Y., June 30, 1819, d. June 4, 1887, served a term as U.S. vice-president (1877–81) under President Rutherford B. Hayes. A lawyer and a Whig New York State assemblyman (1850–51), he became a Republican in 1855. In 1858–59 he was president pro tempore of the state senate. Wheeler presided over the New York constitutional convention of 1867–68 and was a U.S. representative (1861–63, 1869–77). He was trusted for his integrity and in 1875 formulated the "Wheeler compromise" to resolve a disputed election in Louisiana.

Wheeling   Wheeling, a city in northern West Virginia, is the seat of Ohio County. Its population is 34,882 (1990). Situated on the Ohio River, Wheeling is an industrial community and a distribution center for the coal and natural gas produced in the area. Major products of the city's varied industries are enamelware, glass, iron and steel, pottery, textiles, and tobacco products. Wheeling Island in the Ohio River, part of the city, is connected to the mainland by bridges. Oglebay Institute Mansion Museum (1830) contains exhibits of 19th-century furniture and a glass collection.

Wheeling was settled in 1769 by Col. Ebenezer Zane and his brothers. The city was the site of a battle (1782) during the American Revolution. During the 19th century, Wheeling thrived as a junction of the Cumberland Road and as a city on the Baltimore and Ohio Railroad. The city was twice the capital of West Virginia (1863–70, 1875–85).

Wheelock, Eleazar   The Congregationalist minister Eleazar Wheelock, b. Windham, Conn., Apr. 22, 1711, d. Apr. 24, 1779, founded DARTMOUTH COLLEGE. In 1754 he began a school for Indians in Lebanon, Conn., with the object of sending his students back to their people as Christian missionaries. Wheelock later moved to Hanover, N.H., where he established (1770) Dartmouth for both whites and Indians. It became an important source of preachers for the northeast frontier.

Wheelwright, John   The colonial American clergyman John Wheelwright, b. England, c.1592, d. Nov. 15, 1679, supported his sister-in-law, Anne HUTCHINSON, in the controversy over antinomianism in Massachusetts. Banished (1638) from the colony, he formed a dissident church in Exeter, N.H., and later in Wells, Maine. In 1644 he was reconciled with the Massachusetts authorities after formally acknowledging that he had been in error.

whelk [welk]   Whelk is the common name for a group of generally large marine snails with pointed shells, classified in the genera *Buccinum* and *Busycon* of the class Gastropoda, phylum Mollusca. Whelks generally have a head with scraping radula, eyes, and tentacles; a large foot; and visceral organs, turned counterclockwise, encased in a heavy spiral shell. The entire animal can withdraw into the shell completely, closing a horny trapdoor disk called an operculum, thus protecting itself from mechanical injury, chemical irritants, or excessive dryness. Whelks are generally found on sandy bottoms, moving through the sand in search of food—clams, mussels, or other marine invertebrates.

Whig party (England)   The Whig party of England had its origins in the 17th century as a party of opposition to the king; during the first half of the 18th century, however, Whigs administered nearly every government, and they continued to hold office periodically until the mid-19th century, when they coalesced with other groups in the LIBERAL PARTY. The Whig party's origins are traceable to 1679, when the House of Commons attempted to exclude the Roman Catholic duke of York (the future JAMES II) from the throne. King CHARLES II prorogued the exclusionist Parliament of that year at intervals, and during the following year exclusionists petitioned the king to meet Parliament immediately. These petitioners were nicknamed *Whigs* for the whiggamores, who were Scottish Presbyterian rebels.

Responsible for overthrowing King James in the GLORIOUS REVOLUTION of 1688, the Whigs used as their justification the teachings of philosopher John LOCKE. Gradually, they came to advocate responsible constitutional government, but they held no radical views. Their opponents, the Tories, eventually accepted many of the Whigs' tenets of constitutionalism but disappeared as a potent political force after 1714 (see TORY PARTY).

The Whig party began to advocate electoral and parliamentary reform during the era of the French Revolution. It opposed the revived Tory party, which represented more conservative interests. After the death of Lord Palmerston in 1865 and the passing of the second Reform Act in 1867, Whigs, radicals, and Peelites (or left-wing Tories) formed the Liberal party, and the name *Whig* vanished as a political term.

Whig party (United States)   The Whig party (1834–56) of the United States was formed to oppose Andrew Jackson and the Democratic party. The Whig coalition's antecedent was the National Republican party organized to support President John Quincy ADAMS (1825–29). Led by Henry CLAY of Kentucky and Daniel WEBSTER of Massachusetts, National Republicans advocated an active federal role in the nation's economic development. Known as the American System, their program called for federally sponsored roads and canals, a high tariff to protect American manufacturers, and a powerful national bank.

The leaders and the program proved no match against Jackson. He defeated Adams in 1828, rejected federal aid for roads in 1830, vetoed the recharter of a National Bank in 1832, and later that year decisively won reelection against Clay. The repeated defeats led to the formation in 1834 of a new opposition party, initially united on little but hostility to Jackson's bold use of executive power. Joining the economic nationalists in the party were several state-rights Southerners, including for a time John C. CALHOUN of South Carolina.

The wide diversity of views within the Whig party made it difficult to unify around a common program or leader. In the 1836 presidential contest the Whigs backed three regional candidates, Gen. William Henry HARRISON, Hugh Lawson WHITE, and Webster, all of whom lost to Jackson's successor, Martin Van Buren. In 1840 the Whigs backed a single candidate, Harrison, who, like Jackson, was a military hero.

After winning the presidency Harrison was prepared to let Clay seek congressional passage of an energetic Whig program that included a new tariff and national bank. But Harrison died in April 1841, and his successor, former state-rights Democrat John TYLER of Virginia, vetoed the Whig program and was expelled from the party. The Whigs nominated Clay for president in 1844. The Democrats made the "reannexation of Texas" the campaign's major issue, thereby reviving the dangerous controversy over the extension of slavery. The Whigs, more sharply divided than the Democrats over this matter, suffered a narrow defeat.

Ultimately the slavery issue destroyed the Whigs. In 1848 they won the presidency with another military hero, Gen. Zachary TAYLOR. Whig Senate leaders Clay and Webster, however, fearing disunion over slavery, played key roles in securing the COMPROMISE OF 1850, which included a stronger Fugitive Slave Law that offended many Northern Whigs. In 1852 many Southern Whigs defected in reaction to the party's nomination of Gen. Winfield SCOTT for president and the deaths of Unionists Clay and Webster. Furious sectional controversy over the KANSAS-NEBRASKA ACT dealt the party its final blow.

whip The political party officer in the U.S. Congress charged with "whipping" the members into line, enforcing attendance, and voting discipline is called the whip. Each party has its own whip in each house. The office was formally initiated in the House of Representatives in 1899 and in the Senate in 1913. The office and its name originated in the British Parliament, where failure to follow the whip on important votes is tantamount to withdrawing from the parliamentary party.

whiplash Now used for any general injury to the spinal cord and spine resulting from sudden extension of the neck, the term *whiplash* was first coined for the snapping back and then forward of a passenger's head in an automobile accident. Whiplash symptoms may include headaches, and pain and tenderness in the supporting muscles and structures of the head and neck; sometimes they may not appear until several hours after the abrupt injury. Mild forms of whiplash are treated with moist heat and immobilization of the neck with a cervical collar during waking hours.

whippet [wip'-it] The whippet is a lean, swift dog—similar to a small greyhound—that is popular for hunting rabbits and for racing. Males are 48 to 54 cm (18 to 21 in) high at the shoulder; females are shorter. Elegant and slender in outline, whippets have rose ears, smooth coats, and long, thin tails carried low. The breed was developed in England during the 19th century to course rabbits in an enclosure; later, whippets were raced.

The whippet was developed in England more than 100 years ago, most likely by crossing small English greyhounds with terriers and, later, Italian greyhounds. With its streamlined body and long legs, the whippet is considered the fastest domestic animal of its weight, running as fast as 55 km/h (34 mph).

Whipple, Abraham Abraham Whipple, b. Providence, R.I., Sept. 26, 1733, d. May 27, 1819, was an American naval officer in the Revolutionary War. He commanded a privateer during the French and Indian War (1754–63) and participated in the destruction of the British revenue cutter *Gaspee* in 1772. Commissioned a captain in the Continental Navy in 1775, he served in Commodore Esek Hopkins's expedition to the Bahamas in 1776. In 1779 his squadron captured eight British merchant ships with cargoes valued at more than $1 million. He was taken prisoner at the capture of Charleston, S.C., in 1779.

whip-poor-will [wip'-ur-wil] The whip-poor-will, *Caprimulgus vociferus*, is an infrequently seen but often heard nocturnal bird widespread in wooded areas of the eastern United States and southern Canada. In winter it migrates to Mexico and the Gulf of Mexico region. A closely related species, the Ridgway's whip-poor-will, *C. ridgwayi*, is found in New Mexico. Whip-poor-wills belong to the goatsucker-nightjar family, Caprimulgidae.

Whip-poor-wills are about 25 cm (10 in) long. Like other caprimulgids, they have an enormous gape with which they scoop up insects on the wing. They have prominent mouth bristles, large eyes that shine in the dark, and tiny, weak feet almost useless for perching. The plumage is mottled gray and brown, providing excellent camouflage among leaves on the ground or on a low tree limb. The birds are best known for their loud, persistent calls; they may utter several hundred *whip-poor-will* sounds in rapid succession.

Whip-poor-wills lay two white or creamy white eggs blotched with brown. The eggs are laid on the bare forest floor with no semblance of a nest. Both the eggs and the incubating bird are well camouflaged.

whirlpool   A whirlpool is a circular eddy or vortex that may be found in the sea or any inland watercourse. It is formed by the meeting of two currents or as the result of flow.disruption caused by structural anomalies within a drainage channel. The term *maelstrom* is used to describe large oceanic whirlpools.

whiskey   Whiskey (or whisky), from the Scottish Gaelic *uisge beatha*, "water of life," is one of the distilled alcoholic beverages. Other distilled alcoholic beverages include brandies, rums, and vodkas. Percentages of alcohol commonly range from 40% to 50%, expressed as proof. In the United States a spirit with 50% alcohol by volume is termed *100 proof*.

Production. Whiskey, like the other distilled spirits, is generally distilled from a fermented, or alcohol-containing, mash of grains, which may include barley, rye, oats, wheat, or corn. Because distillation requires an alcohol-containing liquid, it is necessary to ferment the grain. Part of the process of whiskey production includes converting the starch in the grain to sugar so that fermentation and ultimately distillation can take place. The grain is ground, then cooked until it becomes gelatinous, releasing the starch from its coating. Barley malt is added

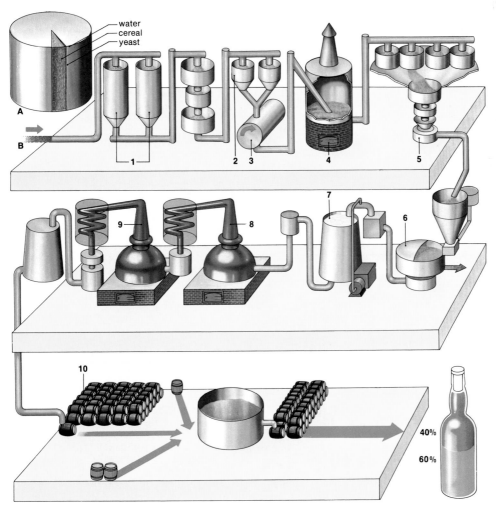

Whiskey is made from water, cereal, and yeast, combined and processed in correct proportions (A). Manufacture of whiskey (B) begins with the harvesting of barley, which is saturated with water (1), steeped (2), and allowed to germinate inside a rotating drum (3). Here enzymes in the barley convert its starch to the sugar maltose. The malted barley is heated in a peat furnace (4), ground (5), and mashed with water, creating a liquid called wort, from which waste material is discarded (6). Sugar in the cooled wort is changed to alcohol (fermented) by the addition of yeast (7). The mixture is distilled twice (8, 9), then diluted. Aging and flavoring take place in oak casks (10). The whiskey is blended with water at a ratio of 40 to 60, and bottled.

because it is rich in amylase, an enzyme that enables starch to be converted to sugar. The mash is then ready for fermentation, and yeast is added. It ferments for 72 hours, creating an alcoholic liquid known as beer. The beer undergoes selective distillation to become whiskey. The product of distillation is colorless and of varied flavor. Fuller-flavored whiskeys mellow with wood maturation. This aging will vary with the spirit, the material and size of the cask, and the storage conditions.

Types. Straight whiskeys are flavorful. They are made from at least 51% of a particular grain and are aged in new, charred white-oak barrels for at least 2 years.

The predominant ingredient in light whiskey is corn; the higher the amount of corn, the lighter the flavor. Bourbon, the most popular whiskey made in the United States, must have at least 51% corn in the mash; it may have as much as 79%. Other grains present are rye and barley malt, which also contribute flavor. Light whiskey is stored in seasoned, charred oak casks, which impart little color or flavor.

Blended whiskey, erroneously known as rye whiskey, is a combination of straight (at least 20%) and light whiskey. The final product may have as many as 40 to 50 different components. Tennessee whiskey is usually made from corn, but any grain may be used. A bourbon-type whiskey, it is very full because it is treated with maplewood charcoal to remove the lighter flavors. Canadian whiskey is always a blend. It is ordinarily at least 6 years old when sold. Delicate and light bodied, it is often confused with American blended whiskey and thus called rye. All Scotch whiskeys are imported, and nearly all are blends. They are normally distilled from barley malt cured with peat, giving the spirit a smoky flavor.

___

Whiskey Rebellion   The first serious test of the U.S. government's ability to enforce federal laws, the Whiskey Rebellion was an uprising against the federal excise tax on corn liquor in 1794 in western Pennsylvania. There, whiskey was distilled to use up surplus corn. The farmers refused to pay the federal tax, first levied in 1791, regarding it as a tyrannical levy akin to the pre-Revolutionary Stamp Act. In 1794 tax collectors faced violent resistance. On the advice of Alexander Hamilton, who was seeking an opportunity to demonstrate federal power, President George Washington called out the militia, causing the rebellion's immediate collapse. All those tried as participants were later acquitted or pardoned.

___

Whiskey Ring   One of the major scandals of President Ulysses S. GRANT's second term (1873–77), the Whiskey Ring involved a conspiracy among whiskey distillers, revenue collectors, and high federal officials to avoid taxation through fraudulent reports on whiskey production. Although the ring was begun before Grant's administration, it flourished after 1870. Its leaders included John A. McDonald, a collector of internal revenue, and Grant's personal secretary, Orville E. Babcock. Relentless investigation by Secretary of the Treasury Benjamin H.

BRISTOW secured 230 indictments (no convictions), exposed McDonald and Babcock, and broke up the ring in May 1875. The president apparently was not involved and told investigators: "Let no guilty man escape if it can be avoided"; Grant helped Babcock, however, to secure an acquittal for his part in the ring.

___

whist   Whist, one of the first card games to use the trump-suit concept, is played by four people in partnerships. All 52 cards of a standard deck are dealt facedown except for the final card, which is turned up to establish the trump suit. The dealer adds that card to his or her hand when it is the dealer's turn to play. The person to the dealer's left begins play by leading a card, and the other players follow suit, if possible. The trick is won by the highest card of the suit led or by a trump card played from a hand with no cards in the suit led. If more than one player lacks cards in the suit led, the trick is won by the highest trump card played. Unless a trump is led, however, a player void in the suit has the option of trumping or of discarding any card from another suit. The winner of each trick leads next. Six tricks are called a book; each additional trick counts one point; and the first partnership to score seven points wins the game.

Whist developed during the 18th century from the French game of *triomphe,* or "triumph," which began during the 16th century and is the origin of the word *trump.*

___

Whistler, James Abbott McNeill   The cosmopolitan American painter and etcher James Abbott McNeill Whistler, b. Lowell, Mass., July 10, 1834, d. July 17, 1903, became part of a circle of young artists who were shaping new pictorial attitudes. In 1859 he moved to London, where, in response to various stimuli, he created a strikingly original style.

Portrait of Lady Seymour Haden at the Piano (1859; Cincinnati Art Museum, Ohio), with its noticeable impasto, reveals Whistler's early admiration for Gustave Courbet, but instead of emulating the realist's emphasis on the density of the subject matter, the technique emphasized precision of form. His elongated, Botticelli-like *The Little White Girl: Symphony in White No. 2* (1864; National Gallery of Art, Washington, D.C.) resembles the spiritual yet exotic women painted by the English Pre-Raphaelites but is free of their accumulated religious and literary references. Its subtitle demonstrates that Whistler intended a harmony of various tones of one color.

Whistler subtitled his later figural compositions *Arrangements,* another musical term, indicating that his purpose was as much artistic as representational. Objects in *Arrangement in Gray and Black, No. 1, Portrait of the Artist's Mother* (1872; Louvre, Paris) appear in such exquisite equilibrium that this pictorial rightness evokes his mother's New England character. Like the French impressionists, Whistler collected 18th-century Japanese colored wood-block prints, which suggested the odd perspectives the impressionists used to transpose everyday reality into art. The high-placed architectural fragment in

In Symphony in White No. III *(1867), James Abbott McNeill Whistler experimented with assymetrical composition and a monochromatic palette in gradations of white and green. (Barber Institute of Fine Arts, Birmingham, England.)*

Nocturne in Blue and Gold: Old Battersea Bridge (1872–73; Tate Gallery, London), however, is submerged in a non-Japanese atmosphere. Whistler, unlike the impressionists, preferred fugitive effects of light occurring after sunset; his forms, therefore, are blurred in haze rather than obscured by brilliant reflections. After 1872, Whistler subtitled his twilight scenes *Nocturnes* to accent the melancholy mood conveyed by their cool blue harmonies. Their elusiveness was further heightened by the thinness of the color washes. Whistler was a friend of the poet Mallarmé's, and his *Nocturnes* approach the evocative ambiguity of symbolist poetry. Like the symbolists, Whistler rarified a sentiment, projecting it by means of an artistic symbol, the color blue. He also achieved this evanescent quality in the series of Venetian views that place him among the greatest masters of etching.

White, Andrew Dickson   Andrew Dickson White, b. Homer, N.Y., Nov. 7, 1832, d. Nov. 4, 1918, was an American historian, diplomat, and the first president of CORNELL UNIVERSITY. As chair of the New York State Senate's committee on education, he was responsible for the founding of New York's land-grant university and for its charter, including provisions for religious freedom and the admission of women. As president (1867–85) of Cornell, White introduced the elective system, treated students as adults, and expanded the college curriculum to include subjects other than agriculture and the mechanical arts. White was minister to Germany (1879–81), to Russia (1892), and to The Hague Peace Conference (1899). He was the first president of the American Historical Association.

White, Byron R.   Byron Raymond White, b. Fort Collins, Colo., June 8, 1917, was appointed (1962) an associate justice of the U.S. Supreme Court by President John F. Kennedy. After graduating from the University of Colorado in 1938, "Whizzer White," as he was known, played professional football for one season, went in 1939 to England as a Rhodes scholar, and, with the outbreak of World War II, returned to the United States to enroll in Yale Law School. When the United States entered the war, he joined the navy. Returning to Yale after serving in the South Pacific, he received (1946) his law degree and began clerking for Chief Justice Frederick Vinson before subsequently joining a Denver law firm. White was named deputy attorney general in 1961 and a year later became the first Kennedy appointee to the Supreme Court. He often votes with the Court's conservative bloc.

White, E. B.   A distinguished American essayist, editor, and author of children's fiction, Elwyn Brooks White, b. Mount Vernon, N.Y., July 11, 1899, d. Oct. 1, 1985, was associated from 1927 with the *New Yorker*; some of his "Talk of the Town" columns, which helped establish the magazine's crisply urbane style, are collected in *The Wild Flag* (1946). Among his best-known books for adults are *Is Sex Necessary?* (1929), a group of humorous sketches done with James Thurber; *One Man's Meat* (1944), a selection of columns from his association (1938–43) with *Harper's*; *The Elements of Style* (1959), a standard manual for writers, revised from the work of William Strunk, Jr.; and his *Essays* (1977).

White's juvenile books, *Stuart Little* (1945), CHARLOTTE'S WEB (1952), and *The Trumpet of the Swan* (1970), have become classics, as has his affectionate guide, *Here Is New York* (1949). In 1978, White received a special Pulitzer Prize, "for the full body of his works over many decades."

White, Edward Douglass   Edward Douglass White, b. Lafourche, La., Nov. 3, 1845, d. May 19, 1921, was an associate justice of the U.S. Supreme Court (1894–1910) and ninth chief justice (1910–21). A former Confederate soldier and Louisiana jurist, White served (1890–94) in the U.S. Senate and was named to the Supreme Court by President Cleveland. When President Taft named him chief justice he became the first associate to be so promoted. Although generally a conservative, he upheld the antitrust laws and the 8-hour working-day legislation.

White, Edward H., II   The American astronaut Edward Higgins White II, b. Nov. 14, 1930, was the first American to walk in space. He graduated (1952) from the U.S. Military Academy, received (1959) an M.S. degree in aeronautical engineering from the University of Michigan, and served as an air force test pilot before being selected as an astronaut in 1962. On the third revolution of his only mission in space, the 4-day *Gemini 4* (June 3–7, 1965) flight, White maneuvered outside the Gemini with a hand-held oxygen gas gun while remaining linked with the craft. The space walk lasted 21 minutes instead of the scheduled 10. White was to have flown on the first manned Apollo mission, *Apollo-Saturn*

Ed White, during the third revolution of his Gemini 4 flight, became the first U.S. astronaut to undertake a space walk. He died in a fire that occurred during a ground test of the spacecraft slated to make the first manned Apollo spaceflight.

204. During a ground launch simulation on Jan. 27, 1967, however, a fire broke out in the command module, asphyxiating White, Roger Chaffee, and Commander Virgil I. Grissom.

White, Hugh Lawson

Hugh Lawson White, b. Iredell County, N.C., Oct. 30, 1773, d. Apr. 10, 1840, was a U.S. senator (1825–40) and an unsuccessful presidential candidate in 1836. He was a Tennessee judge and legislator and president of the state bank. As chairman of the Senate Committee on Indian Affairs, he played an important part in the forcible removal westward of many Indians. An early supporter of fellow Tennessean Andrew Jackson, White later broke with the president and ran against Jackson's handpicked successor, Martin Van Buren, as one of the Whig-backed presidential candidates in the 1836 election.

White, Minor

One of the most influential photographers of the 20th century, Minor White, b. Minneapolis, Minn., July 9, 1908, d. June 24, 1976, was best known for his extension of Alfred STIEGLITZ's concept of "equivalence." In pursuit of his interest in mystical or psychological "readings" of photographs, White developed (1945–47) a metaphorical and sequential approach to the medium in which he saw photographs as equivalents for emotions and experiences.

White, Patrick

The novelist and playwright Patrick Victor Martindale White, b. London, May 28, 1912, of Australian parents, d. Sept. 30, 1990, became (1973) the first Australian to win the Nobel Prize for literature. His education began in Australia; later he attended Cambridge University (1932), where he studied modern languages. During World War II, White served as an intelligence officer in the Middle East and Greece. When the war ended, he settled on a small farm at Castle Hill, New South Wales.

White's first publications were two collections of verse, *Thirteen Poems* (1929) and *The Ploughman and Other Poems* (1935). *Happy Valley* (1939), his fourth novel but the first to be published, was awarded the Australian Literature Society Gold Medal, as was *The Tree of Man* (1955). He was twice the winner of the Miles Franklin Literary Award for the best Australian novel of the year—for *Voss* (1957) and for *Riders in the Chariot* (1961). His other books include the novels *The Vivisector* (1970), *A Fringe of Leaves* (1976), *The Twyborn Affair* (1980), and *Memoirs of Many in One* (1986); a collection of stories, *The Cockatoos* (1974); *Four Plays* (1965); and the autobiography *Flaws in the Glass* (1982).

White, Peregrine

Peregrine White, b. Nov. 30, 1620, d. July 22, 1704, was the first child to be born of English parents in New England. The son of William and Susanna White, he was born on the *Mayflower* in Cape Cod Bay.

White, Stanford

Stanford White, b. New York City, Nov. 9, 1853, d. June 25, 1906, was an important American architect and one of the founders (1880), with Charles Folen McKim and William Rutherford Mead, of the influential architectural firm of McKIM, MEAD, AND WHITE. White received his education in architecture as an apprentice (1872–78) in the office of Henry Hobson RICHARDSON, whom he assisted (1872–77) in the construction of Trinity Church in Boston.

Either in collaboration with his partners or alone, White designed a wide variety of public, institutional, and religious buildings executed in a lavish Italian Renaissance style and many large mansions done in what has come to be known as the Shingle style. Among the firm's New York City buildings attributed mainly to White's design efforts are the Washington Arch (1889), the first Madison Square Garden (1890), the Vanderbilt residence (1905), the New York Herald Building (1894), and the Madison Square Presbyterian Church (1906). Of these, only the Washington Arch still stands.

White was shot and killed by Harry Thaw, the jealous husband of former chorus girl Evelyn Nesbit.

White, T. H.

The English writer Terence Hanbury White, b. Bombay, India, May 29, 1906, d. Jan. 17, 1964, is best known for his tetralogy, *The Once and Future King* (1958), published separately as *The Sword in the Stone* (1938), *The Witch in the Wood* (1939), *The Ill-Made Knight* (1940), and *The Candle in the Wind* (1958). Based loosely on Malory's *Morte Darthur* (c.1469), the stories inspired a Broadway musical, *Camelot* (1960); a film (1967) based on the musical; and a Disney cartoon fantasy (1963). Among White's other works are the autobiographical *England Have My Bones* (1936) and *America at Last* (1965) and the novels *Mistress Masham's Repose* (1946) and *The Master* (1957). *The Book of Merlyn*, a fifth book concluding *The Once and Future King*, was published posthumously in 1977.

White, Theodore   Theodore Harold White, b. Boston, May 6, 1915, d. May 15, 1986, was a writer and journalist famed for his "Making of the President" books about the U.S. presidential campaigns from 1960 through 1972. He won a Pulitzer Prize for *The Making of the President 1960*. This series was followed by *Breach of Faith: The Fall of Richard Nixon* (1975), *America in Search of Itself: The Making of the President 1956–80* (1982), and his memoir *In Search of History* (1978). White began his career as a correspondent in China for *Time* magazine (1939–45).

White, Walter   Walter Francis White, b. Atlanta, Ga., July 1, 1893, d. Mar. 21, 1955, an African-American leader, was assistant secretary (1918–30) and executive secretary (1931–55) of the NATIONAL ASSOCIATION FOR THE ADVANCEMENT OF COLORED PEOPLE (NAACP). White investigated numerous lynchings and race riots and dealt with racial issues in two nationally syndicated newspaper columns and six books. After World War II he became a U.S. government advisor on the United Nations.

White, William   William White, b. Philadelphia, Apr. 4, 1748, d. July 17, 1836, was one of the founders of the Protestant EPISCOPAL CHURCH in the United States. In a 1782 pamphlet, *The Case of the Episcopal Churches in the United States Considered*, White suggested a national church separated from the jurisdiction of the English crown but continuing the spiritual tradition of the Church of England. Consecrated (1787) a bishop in England, he returned to the United States to help organize the Protestant Episcopal Church (1789). He also revised the Book of Common Prayer.

White, William Allen   The writer, editor, and publisher William Allen White, b. Emporia, Kans., Feb. 10, 1868, d. Jan. 29, 1944, bought the *Emporia Gazette* for $3,000 in 1895 and turned it into the most respected small-town newspaper in the country. Many of his editorials were gathered in *The Editor and His People* (1924) and *Forty Years on Mainstreet* (1937). White also published a collection of short stories, *In Our Town* (1906), and a novel, *A Certain Rich Man* (1909). He is probably best remembered, however, for the eulogy "Mary White" (1921), written on the death of his 16-year-old daughter.

white-collar crime   White-collar crime refers to violations of the law committed by salaried or professional persons in conjunction with their work. The term was first used by the American criminologist Edwin Sutherland in 1939. Today crimes that are identified as white-collar include illegal lobbying, bribery, illegal campaign contributions, laundering of funds, consumer fraud, environmental pollution, price fixing, embezzlement, income-tax fraud, computer break-ins (see COMPUTER CRIME), and securities violations.

Despite the harm done by white-collar crime, law enforcement agencies have historically paid scant attention to this phenomenon. When a conviction does occur, it has resulted more often in a fine and an admonition than in a prison term. A shift became apparent in the late 1970s when the FBI's ABSCAM investigation (1978–80) resulted in the conviction of several U.S. legislators for bribery and related charges.

Insider trading, or the illegal manipulation of stocks and bonds for personal profit, by powerful Wall Street financiers was the white-collar crime most in the news from the mid-1880s to the early 1990s. The federal crackdown on securities violators netted such prominent offenders as stock speculator Ivan Boesky, sentenced in 1986 to 3 years in prison and a $100 million fine; the investment firm Drexel Burnham Lambert, which in 1989 was required to pay a $650 million penalty for securities violations prior to filing for bankruptcy; and junk-bond king Michael Milken, who, threatened by a 98-count indictment that the government brought against him in 1989, agreed in 1990 to plead guilty to 6 criminal counts of securities fraud and pay a $600 million fine. The most powerful and highly paid financier of the 1980s, whose junk-bond marketing fueled the corporate takeovers and leveraged buyouts of a decade, Milken was sentenced to 10 years in prison and 5,400 hours of community service upon completion of his term and was permanently barred from working in the securities business.

white dwarf   White dwarfs are STARS that are nearing the end of their lives, having exhausted the hydrogen and helium in their interiors by nuclear reactions. They are considered the next-to-final stage in STELLAR EVOLUTION for stars less than 1.4 times as massive as the Sun, the final stage being black dwarfs, or burned-out stars. The best-known white dwarf is the companion of SIRIUS, the brightest star in Earth's sky.

White dwarfs have radii about 0.01 times the Sun's radius, absolute visual magnitudes ranging from +10 to +16, and surface temperatures ranging from below 4,000 to 25,000 K. Their extremely dense matter is in a degenerate state; that is, atomic nuclei are stripped of their electrons. The term *white* is a misnomer for many of these stars, which are often reddish and show a wide range of spectral types.

White House   The White House, since 1800 the official residence of the president of the United States, is located at 1600 Pennsylvania Avenue in Washington, D.C. The winner of a 1792 competition for its design was the Irish-American architect James HOBAN, whose dignified neoclassical plan was a virtual copy of a project in James Gibbs's *Book of Architecture* (1728). As early as 1807, Benjamin LATROBE, the principal architect of the CAPITOL,

A colonnaded portico forms the main entrance to the White House, official residence of the president of the United States. The neoclassical mansion, designed by James Hoban and built on a site chosen by George Washington, was burned by British troops in 1814 and restored shortly thereafter.

sought to improve the building by preparing designs for pavilions at either end (added that year in collaboration with Thomas Jefferson), for interior alterations, and for porticos on both fronts. After the building was burned (1814) by the British, it was reconstructed (1815–17) by Hoban. Later Hoban added (1826) the semicircular South Portico that Latrobe had proposed and completed (1829) Latrobe's North Portico.

The White House was extensively remodeled (1902) by the firm of McKim, Mead, and White, which also added the East Gallery and the Executive Office Wing. Between 1948 and 1952 the building, deemed structurally unsound, was gutted and its interior structure replaced with steel framing, within which the original rooms were reconstructed. Since 1961 each First Lady has contributed to a continuing effort to refurbish the interior. The resultant enhancement has made the White House a veritable museum of decorative arts of the first quarter of the 19th century.

White Mountains   The White Mountains, the northernmost part of the Appalachian Mountains, contain the highest elevations in New England. They cover about 3,370 km² (1,300 mi²) in northern New Hampshire and western Maine. The highest portion is the Presidential Range, which has several peaks exceeding 1,520 m (5,000 ft) in elevation, including Mount Washington (see WASHINGTON, MOUNT). The best known among the area's tourist attractions is Franconia Notch, with the "Great Stone Face" of the Old Man of the Mountains.

white rot fungus   White rot FUNGI grow on dead wood by breaking down its constituents into nutrient materials. This ability is of great interest because LIGNIN, a major constituent of wood, is a complex polymer that resists degradation and is mainly a waste by-product in industries that process wood, as in paper manufacturing. An enzyme, called ligninase or lignase, enables the white rot fungus *Phanerochaete chrysosporium* to feed on wood. The enzyme is being studied for use in obtaining chemical products from lignin as well as in solving pollution problems that it causes. The enzyme can also degrade other pollutants, such as phenols.

White Russia   see BELORUSSIA

White Sands Missile Range   White Sands Missile Range is one of the oldest U.S. missile test ranges. Located at White Sands National Monument in New Mexico, it covers an area about 66 km (41 mi) wide and 201 km (125 mi) long. It was selected by the U.S. Army in early 1945 as a secure, flat, accessible site for missile tests. Shortly after Nazi Germany fell, the first captured V-2 rockets were fired at White Sands Proving Ground, as it was known until 1958. Administrative and support facilities are located nearby at Fort Bliss, Tex. White Sands Missile Range continues to be used for the testing of battlefield missiles, warheads, and civilian space motors.

White Sea   The White Sea (Russian: Beloye More) is a large inlet of the BARENTS SEA in the northwestern European USSR, bounded by Karelia on the west and the Kanin Peninsula on the east. It covers an area of about 90,650 km² (35,000 mi²) and reaches a maximum depth of 340 m (1,115 ft). Numerous rivers, including the Northern Dvina and Onega, drain into the sea, which is partially frozen from November to May. The shores are irregular and mostly swampy. The largest harbor is

Arkhangelsk on the western shore; another important Soviet port, Murmansk on the Barents Sea, is linked with the White Sea by the Kola River. The principal islands are the Morzhovets and the Solovetskiye group. The White Sea–Baltic Waterway connects the sea with Leningrad.

White Sulphur Springs   White Sulphur Springs (1990 pop., 2,779) is a resort city in southeastern West Virginia known for its mineral waters. Settled about 1750, it became a fashionable health spa in the early 1800s, and many U.S. presidents spent their summers there. The first U.S. golf club is believed to be the predecessor of the modern Greenbrier Club, located in the city.

Whitefield, George [wit'-feeld]   The English preacher George Whitefield, b. Dec. 16, 1714, d. Sept. 30, 1770, was a leader of the Evangelical Revival on both sides of the Atlantic, participating in the GREAT AWAKENING in the colonies and the Wesleyan movement in Great Britain. He was educated at Oxford and was a member of the WESLEY brothers' Holy Club. After ordination (1736) as an Anglican deacon he made the first of seven voyages to America in 1738. He subsequently took orders as a priest, but he was soon excluded from Anglican pulpits because of his evangelistic fervor. As a result he began preaching in religious societies and the open air, making a major contribution to the Evangelical Revival and the growth of METHODISM.

Theological differences led to conflict with John Wesley and a partial separation of the movements they represented. Whitefield identified himself more closely with the Countess of Huntingdon Connection, which was essentially Calvinist in theology (in contrast to the Arminianism of the Wesleys).

whitefish   Whitefishes are among the most important of freshwater food fishes. They are marketed both fresh and smoked, and their roe is sometimes used for caviar. Whitefishes are closely related to salmon and trout, family Salmonidae, but are usually classified in their own family, Coregonidae. Distributed throughout northern Europe, Asia, and North America, most species are found only in fresh water, but a few live in the sea and return to fresh water to spawn. Whitefishes are silvery white with darker backs and have a small adipose fin following the dorsal fin. Several species known as ciscoes are fished in the Great Lakes. The iconnu, *Stenodus leucichthys*, is a popular game fish of Arctic Asia and North America.

Whitehead, Alfred North   The English mathematician and philosopher Alfred North Whitehead, b. Ramsgate, Kent, Feb. 15, 1861, d. Dec. 30, 1947, exercised broad influence on 20th-century thought. Whitehead en-

tered (1880) Trinity College, Cambridge, and studied mathematics. Elected to a fellowship in 1884, he remained at Cambridge until 1910, when he moved to the University of London. In 1924 he accepted a chair in philosophy at Harvard University, where he taught until retirement in 1937.

In 1903, Whitehead and Bertrand RUSSELL, his most important student, began work on the *Principia Mathematica* (3 vols., 1910–13), an attempt to construct the foundations of mathematics on a rigorous logical basis. Next, he turned his attention to epistemology and the philosophy of science, in an attempt to explain the relation of formal mathematical theories in physics to their basis in experience. In *The Principle of Relativity* (1922), Whitehead presented a critique and an alternative to Einstein's general theory of relativity.

Science and the Modern World (1925), a series of lectures given in the United States, served as an introduction to his later metaphysics. There he began to develop his views about the unity of knowledge and experience. Whitehead constructed a theory of perception that relied on the transformation of received stimuli by the organism into experiences that can be further transformed into objects of knowledge. Whitehead's most important book, *Process and Reality* (1929; rev. ed. 1978), expanded upon this theory. In contemporary thought he is closely associated with the philosophy of process (see PROCESS PHILOSOPHY).

Whitehorse   Whitehorse (1986 pop., 15,199), the capital (since 1952) of the Yukon Territory, Canada, lies at the head of navigation on the Yukon River and is a major city on the Alaska Highway. It is linked by rail with Skagway, Alaska, and is an important distribution center. Whitehorse was founded in 1898 during the Klondike Gold Rush.

Whiteman, Paul   Paul Whiteman, b. Mar. 28, 1890, d. Dec. 29, 1967, was a classically trained musician who became famous as the leader of a jazz orchestra during the 1920s and '30s. Known as the King of Jazz, he brought that idiom into the homes of middle-class America and gave it a respectability that it had not previously enjoyed. Heavily orchestrated and arranged, his music allowed only minimal scope for solo improvisation. Despite this, Whiteman was able to attract some of the foremost white jazz players as soloists. One of his major achievements was the initial performance of George Gershwin's *Rhapsody in Blue*, in 1924. Although jazz styles later turned away from the symphonic format represented by Whiteman, he remained a celebrated popularizer of jazz.

Whitgift, John   John Whitgift, b. *c.*1530, d. Feb. 29, 1604, archbishop of Canterbury (1583–1604) during the last years of Elizabeth I's reign, firmly upheld the episcopal structure and ritual uniformity of the Church of England against Puritan opposition. His severity toward the

Puritans provoked the *Marprelate Tracts* (1588–89), a series of pseudonymous pamphlets satirizing the authoritarianism of the church.

Whitlam, Gough

Whitlam, Gough [wit'-luhm, gahf] Edward Gough Whitlam, b. July 11, 1916, was prime minister of Australia from December 1972 to November 1975.

Whitlam joined the Australian Labor party (ALP) in 1945, and in 1959 he became a member of its federal parliamentary executive. In 1967, Whitlam was elected party leader.

In the general election of December 1972, Whitlam led the ALP to its first victory in a generation, over the conservative coalition of the Liberal and National Country parties. As prime minister he aimed to build a foreign policy independent of the United States, and a domestic policy based on democratic-socialist ideals. He ended conscription, ordered Australian troops home from Vietnam, and backed legislation furthering the claims of the aborigines, other ethnic minorities, and women. He also recognized the governments of Communist China and North Vietnam.

Beginning in 1973, however, as a result of the world economic crisis brought about by the Arab oil boycott, inflation spiraled and unemployment reached its worst level since World War II. The Australian electorate came to resent the higher taxes necessitated by the ALPs social-welfare programs. Finally, in a severe budget crisis, Whitlam was dismissed by the governor-general, Sir John Kerr. In the election that followed, the ALP was routed. Whitlam remained as leader of the opposition, but after his second election loss in 1977 he retired from politics.

Whitman, Marcus

Whitman, Marcus Marcus Whitman, b. Rushville, N.Y., Sept. 4, 1802, d. Nov. 29, 1847, was a medical doctor and pioneer missionary to the American Northwest. After a preliminary tour of the West in 1835 to select mission sites, he returned to the Oregon country in 1836 with his wife, Narcissa, and three others. Sponsored by the American Board of Commissioners for Foreign Missions, they founded a mission among the Cayuse Indians west of present Walla Walla, Wash. It faltered, however, and Whitman returned (1843) east to persuade the board not to abandon it.

On his journey back Whitman helped guide the first of many large parties of settlers to Oregon. Unfortunately, these travelers brought with them diseases (such as measles) that caused many deaths among the Indians, who were, in any case, increasingly alienated by Whitman's demands that they give up their old ways. Finally, the Cayuse massacred the Whitmans and 12 others.

Whitman, Walt

Whitman, Walt The greatest of 19th-century American poets, Walt Whitman, b. West Hill, Long Island, N.Y., May 31, 1819, d. Mar. 26, 1892, abandoned his given name, Walter, when he published (1855) his first book of poetry, LEAVES OF GRASS, one of the seminal works of American literature.

Whitman was born on a small farm that the family left in 1824 when they moved to Brooklyn. At the age of 11 he began to learn printing, a trade with which he remained associated for many years as printer, journalist, and newspaper editor. In 1838–39 he edited a weekly newspaper, the *Long Islander*.

For the next ten years Whitman drifted from one job to another. He occasionally taught school, wrote short stories and poems for magazines, and edited such newspapers as the New York *Aurora* and *Evening Tatler* and the *Brooklyn Daily Eagle*. As a contributor (1848) to the New Orleans *Crescent*, he made a trip to the South. About 1850 he returned to his family in Brooklyn and, until the death of his failing father in 1855, assisted him in the building business.

Late in 1862, Whitman went to the battlefront in Virginia to find his brother George, who had been wounded, and then returned to Washington, where he worked in various government departments. He served as a volunteer nurse to soldiers, Northern and Southern, who were sick and dying in the unhygienic military hospitals in Washington.

Poetry. Paid for, and in part typeset, by Whitman himself, *Leaves of Grass* (1855), including the famous "Song of Myself," launched his career as a poet. The book did not win universal acclaim, however, because his irregular poetry as well as his candid anatomical references antagonized many early readers. In *Drum-Taps* (1865), Whitman printed poems based on his wartime experiences; *Sequel to Drum-Taps* (1865–66) contained what later became two of his most famous works, "When Lilacs Last in the Dooryard Bloom'd" and "O Captain! My Captain!" commemorating the death of Lincoln. A prose volume, *Democratic Vistas* (1871), followed a few years later.

Retirement. Whitman remained in Washington until 1873, when he suffered a paralytic stroke that left him

Walt Whitman was the first American poet to abandon most of the conventions of earlier poetry and create a distinctly national idiom to address those he celebrated as the "American masses." The first edition of Leaves of Grass *(1855), printed by Whitman himself, was found indecent by many of its early readers.*

permanently crippled. Moving to Camden, N.J., to be near his mother and his brother George, he remained there until his death. Although he never again held a job, he regained some of his former strength and supported himself by printing and selling his own books and writing for newspapers and magazines. *Leaves of Grass*, which was constantly expanded, slowly became known in the United States and abroad; and Whitman, now acknowledged as a major literary figure, welcomed writers and artists from all over the world to his modest house on Mickle Street. He collected his autobiographical reminiscences in *Specimen Days and Collect* (1882), which incorporated the earlier *Memoranda during the War* (1875).

Although frequently in great pain after 1885, Whitman continued to write poems and prose pieces. He completed the last revision of *Leaves of Grass* shortly before his death; he is buried in a tomb, which he designed himself, in Harleigh Cemetery, Camden.

Having set himself a difficult task—to create a poetry that would reflect the American melting pot of races and nationalities, the democratic aspirations of the people, and the physical vastness of the United States—Whitman replaced traditional English form and meter with a rhythmic unit based on the meaning and natural flow of the lines. The subject matter, like the rhythm, was intended to be as free as the people and included topics usually avoided by the era's poets—commonplace experiences, labor, sexuality. He remains the nation's great celebrator and affirmer of democracy, freedom, the self, and the joys of living.

Whitney, Eli Eli Whitney, b. Westboro, Mass., Dec. 8, 1765, d. Jan. 8, 1825, was the inventor of the COTTON GIN and a pioneer in the use of mass-production methods. He graduated from Yale College in 1792 and by April 1793 had designed and constructed a machine called a cotton gin that quickly and easily separated cottonseed from the short-staple cotton fiber. Whitney's cotton gin

Eli Whitney, whose invention (1793) of the cotton gin made short-staple cotton the principal cash crop of the southern United States, designed his machine in just a few days while visiting a Georgia plantation. His later use of interchangeable parts in firearms manufacture was among the earliest instances of mass production.

was capable of maintaining a daily output of 23 kg (50 lb) of cleaned cotton, and its effect was far-reaching, making southern cotton a profitable crop.

In 1798, Whitney obtained a government contract to make 10,000 muskets. He demonstrated that machine tools—manned by workers who did not need the highly specialized skills of gunsmiths—could produce standardized parts to exact specifications, and that any part could be used as a component of any musket. The firearms factory he built in New Haven, Conn., was thus one of the first to use mass-production methods.

Whitney, Mount Mount Whitney, the highest peak (4,418 m/14,494 ft) in the conterminous United States, is located in the SIERRA NEVADA range, in Sequoia National Park, California. The first white persons to see the peak were Josiah D. Whitney and his geological surveying party in 1864.

Whitsunday see PENTECOST

Whittaker, Charles Evans Charles Evans Whittaker, b. Troy, Kans., Feb. 22, 1901, d. Nov. 26, 1973, was an associate justice of the U.S. Supreme Court from 1957 to 1962. After serving on the U.S. District Court for Western Missouri (1954–56) and on the U.S. Court of Appeals for the 8th Circuit (1956–57), he was appointed to the Supreme Court by President Eisenhower. Whittaker was known as a middle-of-the-road conservative.

Whittier, John Greenleaf One of the best-loved American poets of the 19th century, John Greenleaf Whittier, b. Haverhill, Mass., Dec. 17, 1807, d. Sept. 9, 1892, won national fame with his nostalgic poem "Snow-Bound" (1866), celebrating the rural world of New England. A Quaker, Whittier began his career as a journalist for William Lloyd Garrison, committing himself to the abolitionist cause in the celebrated pamphlet *Justice and Expediency* (1833) and thereafter, throughout the Civil War, in numerous polemics and volumes of patriotic verse. He is best remembered for such popular poems as "Maud Muller" (1854), "The Barefoot Boy" (1855), and "Barbara Frietchie" (1863). The town of Whittier, Calif., was named for him in 1887.

Whitworth, Kathy Hall of Fame golfer Kathrynne Ann Whitworth, b. Monahans, Tex., Sept. 27, 1939, has won more professional tournaments (88) than anyone in history, man or woman. In her career (1959–), Whitworth has won the Ladies' Professional Golfers Association (LPGA) championship tournament three times (1967, 1971, 1975) and been voted LPGA Player of the Year seven times and Associated Press Woman Athlete of the Year twice (1965–66). She led the LPGA in prize money for eight seasons and has accumulated about $1.7 million in career earnings.

Who, The   A British rock group, The Who were popular in England from the mid-1960s, as much for their bizarre stage performance as for their music. By 1967 they had become a major rock band in the United States as well. Their "My Generation" (1965) is ranked among the earliest true rock-music songs; the rock opera *Tommy* (1969) and the work of guitarist and composer Peter Townshend (b. May 19, 1945) achieved considerable fame. The Who members include Townshend, bassist John Entwistle (b. Sept. 10, 1944), and singer Roger Daltrey (b. Mar. 1, 1944). The death of drummer Keith Moon, b. Aug. 23, 1946, d. Sept. 7, 1978, only temporarily slowed the group's resurgence in the late 1970s. The Who was still touring in the late 1980s.

wholesaling   Wholesaling is the buying of goods from the manufacturer (or producer) and their subsequent sale, not to consumers, but to retail stores and other businesses, which in turn sell them to the public. This "middleman" function has evolved largely because of the great differences—in size, in needs, in business orientation, and in geographic location—between national or regional manufacturers and local retailers. Although practices vary from industry to industry, the services performed by the wholesaler generally include some or all of the following: storage of large quantities of goods at locations convenient to the retailer; delivery of goods on the retailer's request; extension of credit or other financial assistance to the retailer; servicing of goods sold; sales promotion and publicity, maintenance of a sales force to call on and assist retailers, and market research; and billing, collections, and record keeping.

Wholesalers, who may also be called distributors or jobbers, are distinguished from brokers by the fact that they actually buy and hold title to the goods they distribute, whereas brokers do not. (When brokers are involved, legal ownership remains with the producer until the broker sells the product.) A hybrid variety, called a drop shipper, takes orders and arranges shipment of goods directly from the manufacturer's plant. Wholesalers range in size from multimillion-dollar regional organizations to small rack jobbers, who stock and service specific displays in different stores.

whooping cough   Whooping cough, or pertussis, is an acute infectious disease that is a leading cause of death in infants unprotected by immunization. The infective agent, the bacterium *Bordetella pertussis,* is transmitted by inhalation of material expelled by the coughing of infected patients. After an incubation period of about a week, symptoms at first resemble those of the common cold; after 7 to 10 days, coughing increases and becomes distinctive. A series of short coughs of increasing intensity is followed by a long indrawing of breath with the characteristic crowing sound or "whoop." The patient's face often becomes blue during the frightening spasms; clear sticky mucus is expelled, and vomiting commonly occurs.

Pneumonia is a dangerous complication. The younger the patient, the greater the risk of serious illness. Treatment includes careful nursing, sedatives, and plenty of fluids. Antibiotics are needed only for the treatment of complications, such as pneumonia. Prevention is by immunization with a vaccine containing killed pertussis bacteria.

whooping crane   The whooping crane, *Grus americana,* is one of the largest North American birds and one of the most seriously endangered. Standing nearly 1.5 m (5 ft) tall and with a 2.3-m (7.5-ft) wingspread, it is larger than the much more common North American sandhill crane, *G. canadensis.* Like other cranes, the whooping crane is a long-necked, long-legged bird of prairie and marsh. The long, powerful bill is used for killing snakes, frogs, and other small animals. Adults have completely white plumage, except for black primary feathers on the wings, black legs, and bare red areas on the head. They are known for their loud whooping cries, which can be heard as the birds migrate between winter and summer homes. After elaborate courtship rituals, cranes build a nest of vegetation on moist ground. Usually two eggs are laid, but only one chick survives to fly south for winter.

Whooping cranes formerly occupied widespread breeding areas in Canada and the northern United States, but their numbers have diminished greatly. The bird is now protected by law on its breeding grounds near Great Slave Lake in Canada, on its wintering grounds in the

The whooping crane (background) *is now being bred in captivity in an effort to save the species from extinction. Eggs laid by captive whooping cranes are hatched in the wild by sandhill cranes* (foreground), *which then raise the young.*

Aransas National Wildlife Refuge in Texas, and all along its migration route.

Whorf, Benjamin Lee [wohrf]

The linguist Benjamin Lee Whorf, b. Winthrop, Mass., Apr. 24, 1897, d. July 26, 1941, is best remembered for the Whorf-Sapir hypothesis (also called the Whorf or Whorfian hypothesis; see ANTHROPOLOGICAL LINGUISTICS), which states that each language shapes the view of reality of its speakers. This relativistic conception is diametrically opposed to that of universal grammar, which holds that languages have all their basic features in common.

After earning a B.S. in chemical engineering at MIT in 1918, Whorf joined the Hartford Fire Insurance Company, remaining with the firm for the rest of his life and becoming an authority on fire prevention. His interest in biblical Hebrew, Aztec, and Mayan led to study with Edward SAPIR at Yale in 1931. In addition to several theoretical papers on linguistics, Whorf published much basic research on American Indian languages, especially Aztec and Hopi.

Who's Afraid of Virginia Woolf?

Edward AL-BEE's most popular play, *Who's Afraid of Virginia Woolf?* (1962), presents a grim yet comic sex duel between the middle-aged Martha and her husband, George, a history professor at a small college. Martha invites a new instructor, who turns out to be an opportunist, and his barren wife for a drink. During the drunken night that follows, the four characters' inhibitions dissolve, and their increasingly sadistic arguments and behavior reveal the individual and shared secrets and despairs that have degraded their lives. The most striking aspect of the play is the sardonic humor that characterizes the verbal exchanges.

Wichita (Indian tribe) [wich'-i-tah]

The Wichita are a North American Indian tribe of Caddoan linguistic stock. They called themselves Kitikitish; the French called them Pani Pique ("Tattooed Pawnee") because they practiced tattooing. In 1541, Francisco Coronado contacted the Wichita in legendary Quivira, southeast of the great bend of the Arkansas River in south central Kansas. Lured by trade and driven by the APACHE and other hostile tribes, they relocated (early 18th century) in Oklahoma.

A semisedentary agricultural people, the Wichita were active traders during the 18th century, exchanging maize, melons, and French trade goods for COMANCHE horses, mules, and captives. After signing (1835) a peace treaty with the United States, the Wichita were assigned (1859) a reservation along the Washita River in INDIAN TERRITORY. During the Civil War, harassed by the slave-owning FIVE CIVILIZED TRIBES loyal to the Confederacy, the Wichita fled to Kansas but returned to Oklahoma in 1867. In 1901 their reservation was greatly reduced by the U.S. government, which opened much of their land to white settlement. From an estimated 3,200 in 1780, the Wichita

population had dwindled to a mere 385 in 1937. The Wichita tribe in Oklahoma numbered an estimated 869 members in 1989.

Wichita (Kansas)

Wichita is a city in south central Kansas and the seat of Sedgwick County. The largest city in the state, it has a population of 304,011 (1990), with 485,270 persons in the metropolitan area. Wichita is the principal commercial and industrial center of southern Kansas. Most of the nation's private and business aircraft are manufactured there; the production of tools and appliances, petroleum refining, meat processing, and flour milling are also important. The city's cultural and educational institutions include the Wichita Art Museum, Wichita State University (1892), and Friends University (1898).

The Wichita Indians had a village on the city's site, and in 1864, James R. Mead, aided by the scout Jesse Chisholm, established a trading post there. In 1868 the first settlers arrived, and the city became a stopover for the cattle drives along the CHISHOLM TRAIL. Wichita expanded farther when the Santa Fe Railway reached the city in 1872. The settlement grew rapidly as a cow town, with scouts, Indians, cowboys, ranchers, and gamblers crowding into it. During the late 1870s farms began obstructing the cattle trail, and Wichita became a trade and grain-milling center.

Wichita Falls

Wichita Falls (1990 pop., 96,259), a diversified industrial city in northern Texas about 200 km (125 mi) northeast of Dallas, is the seat of Wichita County. It is a center of the petroleum industry, and electronic equipment, pharmaceutical products, petroleum field equipment, and leather goods are manufactured there. Settled in 1876, Wichita Falls became a cattle- and grain-shipping center after the arrival of railroads in 1882.

Wickersham, George W. [wik'-ur-shuhm]

George Woodward Wickersham, b. Pittsburgh, Pa., Sept. 19, 1858, d. Jan. 25, 1936, served (1909–13) as attorney general under President William Howard Taft. He strongly enforced the Sherman Anti-Trust Act, particularly against the American Tobacco and Standard Oil companies. From 1924 to 1929 he worked with the League of Nations. In 1929, Herbert Hoover appointed Wickersham chairman of the so-called Wickersham Commission, investigating the effectiveness of American law enforcement. It concluded that the federal machinery of enforcement was inadequate and advocated, among other things, modification of the prohibition laws.

wickiup [wik'-ee-uhp]

The wickiup, a circular or oval structure of arched poles covered with brush and mat, was traditionally used as a temporary dwelling by various hunting and foraging Indians of North America living in semidesert areas of the Great Basin, Southwest, and California. The term is most commonly used to describe the traditional APACHE dwelling.

widgeon [wij'-uhn] A widgeon is a moderate-sized, freshwater duck, family Anatidae, with a white wing patch and greenish speculum. The American widgeon, *Anas americana*, found in North America, has a grayish head, white forehead and crown, and greenish markings behind the eye; it is often called the baldpate. The European widgeon, *A. penelope*, of Eurasia and northern Africa, has a reddish head and golden forehead. The Chiloë widgeon, *A. sibilatrix*, of southern South America, has a black neck and crown and a white face with green behind the eyes. Widgeons feed by grazing on land to a greater extent than do most other *Anas* species, but they also feed in water.

Widor, Charles Marie [vee-dohr'] The French composer Charles Marie Jean Albert Widor, b. Feb. 21, 1844, d. Mar. 12, 1937, was one of the great masters of the organ. A skillful improviser even as a child, Widor was named organist at Saint Sulpice in Paris in 1869 and held that post for more than six decades. He also taught at the Paris Conservatory, conducted an oratorio society, and wrote criticism under the name Auletes. With his pupil Albert Schweitzer he edited many of J. S. Bach's organ works. Widor's compositions include operas, three symphonies, concertos, chamber works, piano music, and songs, but he is best known for his works for the organ, especially the eight Symphonies, or suites, which are showpieces in the romantic style, a test of both the organist and organ.

Wieland, Christoph Martin [vee'-lahnt] A versatile representative of the German Enlightenment, the poet and novelist Christoph Martin Wieland, b. Sept. 5, 1733, d. Jan. 20, 1813, began his writing career as a sentimentalist but soon turned to rationalism. Witty, lucid, and light, Wieland is best known for *The History of Agathon* (1766-67; Eng. trans., 1773), a philosophical novel; *Der goldene Spiegel* (The Golden Mirror, 1772), a political novel that earned him the post of tutor at the Weimar court; *The Republic of Fools* (1774; Eng. trans., 1861), satirizing German provincialism; and two elegant verse epics, *Musarion* (1768) and *Oberon* (1780; Eng. trans., 1798). Wieland also translated 22 of Shakespeare's plays into German.

Wiener, Norbert [wee'-nur] The American mathematician Norbert Wiener, b. Columbia, Mo., Nov. 26, 1894, d. Mar. 18, 1964, established the science of CYBERNETICS, which deals with the common factors of control and communication in automatic machines, living organisms, and organizations. He also contributed to the theory of stochastic processes and to the theory of Brownian motion, the construction of a rigorous mathematical description of a physical process that is subject to random change.

Wiener helped build the mathematics department at the Massachusetts Institute of Technology (MIT) into an outstanding research facility. He taught there from 1919 until his retirement in 1960. His 3-volume *Collected Works* were published between 1975 and 1982.

Wiesbaden [vees'-bah-den] Wiesbaden, the capital of Hesse state in southwestern Germany, is located on the Rhine River to the south of the Taunus Mountains, 32 km (20 mi) west of Frankfurt am Main. The city's hot saline springs make Wiesbaden an important resort spa. The population is 268,900 (1984 est.). Metal goods, chemicals, plastics, and textiles are also produced. Wiesbaden is the site of the annual International Festival of Music, Ballet, and Drama. Important landmarks include the old town hall (1610), the Hessian State Theater (1894), and the Kaiser-Friedrich Baths (1913).

A popular spa (Aquae Mattiacorum) in Roman times, the city was fortified by the Romans in 12 BC, AD 83, and c.370. It became an imperial free city in 1241. It passed to the counts of Nassau in 1255 and was the capital of the duchy of Nassau from 1806 to 1866, when it passed to Prussia.

Wiesel, Elie [wee-zel'] Prolific author and educator Eliezer Wiesel, b. Sighet, Romania, Sept. 30, 1928, is known as the survivor of the Holocaust who most eloquently speaks for the dead. He continuously strives to reconcile the belief in a just God with the world's seemingly pervasive evil. Wiesel's novels, many based in his concentration-camp experiences, include *Night* (1960), *Dawn* (1961), *A Beggar in Jerusalem* (1970), *The Oath* (1973), *The Testament* (1981), and *The Fifth Son* (1984). His essays on Hasidic and biblical figures include the collections *Souls on Fire* (1972) and *Messengers of God* (1976). He has also written two plays, *Zalmen; or, The Madness of God* (1975) and *The Trial of God* (1979). Wiesel was awarded the Nobel Peace Prize in 1986.

wig The wig is a cosmetic head covering of artificial or human hair. The Egyptians adorned themselves with formalized multitiered or thickly plaited wigs in vivid colors, often interwoven with gold jewelry. In Greece wigs were used by both men and women.

Louis XIII wore a wig of long curls to conceal his baldness, and the style became widespread in England during the reign of Charles II. Elaborate wigs were gradually replaced by smaller, neater ones, and by the 1790s the fashion had begun to die out. Wigs are still worn by British barristers and judges.

Since World War II the toupee, which simulates real hair, has been worn to conceal baldness, and ornamental wigs have become a fashion accessory for women. Most wigs are machine-made from synthetic fibers. Some are made of real hair, mostly in Spain and Italy. Between 50,000 and 200,000 strands are needed to make a full wig.

Wiggin, Kate Douglas   The writer and educator Kate Douglas Wiggin, b. Philadelphia, Sept. 28, 1856, d. Aug. 24, 1923, wrote such best-selling children's books as *The Birds' Christmas Carol* (1887) and *Rebecca of Sunnybrook Farm* (1903; films, 1917, 1932, and 1938). In San Francisco she organized (1878) the first free kindergarten in the Far West.

Wigglesworth, Michael   A Puritan poet and cleric, Michael Wigglesworth, b. Yorkshire, England, Oct. 18, 1631, d. June 10, 1705, attended Harvard and from 1656 until his death served as pastor in Malden, Mass. His enormously popular *The Day of Doom* (1662) vividly depicts the terrors of the wicked on the Day of Judgment. Wigglesworth's other poems include *God's Controversy with New England* (written 1662; published 1871) and *Meat out of the Eater* (1669).

Wight, Isle of   see ISLE OF WIGHT

Wigman, Mary   Mary Wigman (Marie Wiegmann), b. Hannover, Germany, Nov. 13, 1886, d. Sept. 18, 1973, was, during the 1920s and '30s, the most highly regarded modern dancer and choreographer in central Europe and one of the principal reasons for the ascendancy there of MODERN DANCE. An assistant of Rudolf von LABAN, she opened a highly successful school in Dresden in 1920. The style of dancing Wigman evolved was, in her words, mostly "dark, heavy, and earthbound." It was an attempt, by means of personally conceived movement, to increase the emotional expressiveness, and therefore the relevance, of dance. Wigman's ideas and teaching methods were brought to the United States by her pupil Hanya HOLM, who opened a Mary Wigman School of Dance in New York in 1931.

Wigner, Eugene Paul   Eugene Paul Wigner, b. Budapest, Hungary, Nov. 17, 1902, is an American physicist known for his work on group theory and as one of the early developers of nuclear power. From 1942 to 1948 he worked on the MANHATTAN PROJECT; his research on nuclear chain reactions aided in the development of the atomic bomb. Wigner received the Enrico Fermi Award of the Atomic Energy Commission (1953) and the Atoms for Peace Award (1960) and shared the 1963 Nobel Prize for physics with Jo Jensen and Marie Goeppert-Mayer.

Wigtown   [wig'-tuhn]   Wigtown is a former county located in southwestern Scotland, between the Irish Sea and the North Channel, and including the Mull of Galloway, Scotland's most southerly point, in the west. The towns of Wigtown, Stranraer, and Whithorn are the principal urban centers. Sheep and cattle raising, dairying, and fishing form the basis of the economy. About AD 397, Wigtown became the site of Scotland's first Christian mission center, Saint Ninian's Candida Casa. The area was included later in the ancient territory of Galloway, ruled by Scottish-Norse kings, and became part of Scotland in 1455. In 1975, Wigtown was included in the new DUMFRIES AND GALLOWAY administrative region.

wigwam   [wig'-wahm]   The wigwam was a housing structure traditionally used by nomadic and seminomadic Indian tribes of the Upper Great Lakes of North America. It consisted of saplings inserted into the ground, bent over, and tied in the middle to form a domelike, sometimes elongated, roof. Bark and woven rush mats were tied over this framework.

Wilberforce, William   Philanthropist, reformer, and orator William Wilberforce, b. Aug. 24, 1759, d. July 29, 1833, led the fight in Britain for the abolition of the slave trade. In 1780 he became a member of Parliament, where he was a consistent supporter of his friend William Pitt the Younger. After converting (1785) to Evangelical Christianity, Wilberforce was persuaded to remain in Parliament rather than take holy orders. His *Practical View of the Prevailing Religious System of Professed Christians* (1797) was an attempt to win the ruling classes to "vital Christianity" and established him as the leader of the Evangelicals. Wilberforce's fame, however, was established by his campaign against the slave trade, which was abolished in 1807. He continued to fight against slavery itself and lived to see its complete abolition in 1833.

Wilbur, Richard   One of the most highly praised poets and translators of his generation, Richard Wilbur, b. New York City, Mar. 1, 1921, demonstrated his talent in his first volume of verse, *Beautiful Changes* (1947). *Things of This World* (1956) won him the Pulitzer Prize and National Book Award and helped ensure his dominant place among American poets who write in traditional modes.

Some critics felt that Wilbur was limited by care and fastidiousness in his constant production of disciplined verse. As if in response, *Advice to a Prophet* (1961) contained some bolder poems that addressed topics more contemporary than those the poet had usually handled. In *Walking to Sleep* (1969), however, he showed that his finer gifts are artistry and gracefulness. His best work may well be his verse translations of Molière's *The Misanthrope* (1955) and *Tartuffe* (1963), both of which enjoyed successful Broadway runs and delighted audiences with their balance and incisive wit.

wild children   see FERAL CHILDREN

wild rice   Wild rice, also known as water oats, is two or three species of aquatic grasses, genus *Zizania*, family Gramineae, that have broad blades and long, reedy stems. They grow in shallow water of still ponds and lakes. The wild rice of the northern United States and southern Canada, *Z. aquatica*, is also known as Indian rice because Indian tribes collected the grains and used them as a cereal food. Manchurian wild rice, *Z. caducifolia*, has smaller grains than its American counterpart and is also edible. Long available only as a wild crop, wild rice has now been successfully cultivated.

wildcat

Wildcat is the common name of several species of closely related small, Old World wildcats and occasionally of such North American cats as the lynx, bobcat, and feral domestic cats. The true wildcat, *Felis silvestris*, is found from Scotland through Europe, except Scandinavia, and in parts of Asia and Africa. It has the general form of a house cat but has a longer, squarer head, longer legs, and a full, short tail with a rounded tip. The male is 58 cm (23 in) long, on the average, plus a 31-cm (12-in) tail. It may stand 38 cm (15 in) high at the shoulder and weigh about 6 kg (13.2 lb). A lone night hunter, the wildcat kills large birds and small mammals and may take poultry and lambs from farms. After a gestation period of about 68 days, the wildcat gives birth to 3 to 6 kittens. The wildcat interbreeds with its cousin, the domestic house cat.

The wildcat, a heavily built, fierce cat of forest regions, somewhat resembles a domestic tabby but cannot be tamed.

Wilde, Oscar

[wyld]   Known above all for his aphoristic wit, the Irish writer Oscar Fingal O'Flahertie Wills Wilde, b. Dublin, Oct. 16, 1854, d. Nov. 30, 1900, was also the most scandalous personality of his time. He wrote one of the English stage's finest comedies, *The Importance of Being Earnest* (1895); the sparkling novel *The Picture of Dorian Gray* (1891); and several splendid literary essays, notably "The Critic as Artist" (1890).

Wilde's mother composed patriotic Irish verse under the name Speranza; his father, an eminent physician, published about 20 books, including several on Irish folklore. At Trinity College, Dublin (1871–74), Wilde won the Berkeley Gold Medal for Greek, and at Magdalen College, Oxford (1874–78), he was awarded (1878) the prestigious Newdigate Prize for his poem *Ravenna*.

Early Career. Deeply influenced by John Ruskin and Walter Pater at Oxford, Wilde became known during the early 1880s as a minor poet. He was already a major public figure, however, and is thought to be the target of Gilbert and Sullivan's satire on aesthetes in the light opera *Patience* (1881). By 1890, Wilde's literary personality had clearly emerged, especially in such essays as "The Truth of Masks," "The Decay of Lying," and "The Portrait of Mr. W. H." The next two years brought "The Critic as Artist" and "The Soul of Man under Socialism" (1891).

Philosophy. Wilde's poetry is reminiscent of Keats's, Dante Gabriel Rossetti's, and Swinburne's, and his philosophy was a dandyism taken from Baudelaire and the French critic Barbey d'Aurevilly, and from Carlyle's remarks in *Sartor Resartus* (1833–34) on the "dandiacal body." To such familiar propositions as "clothes are the man," "form is content," and "beauty is truth," Wilde added his own, such as "manners before morals," that, for the Victorians at least, were full of menace.

In the 1890s, Wilde became one of London's most prominent playwrights with such successes as *Lady Windermere's Fan* (1892), created for the actress Lillie Langtry; *A Woman of No Importance* (1893); and *The Importance of Being Earnest*. A fourth play, *Salomé* (1893), written in French but translated (1894) by Lord Alfred Douglas, was produced (1896) in Paris after it was banned from the English stage.

Prison. Wilde was at the height of his career when the marquess of Queensberry—provoked by Wilde's affair with his son, Lord Douglas—accused him of "posing as" a sodomite. Wilde sued Queensberry for libel and lost; then the government prosecuted Wilde for indecent acts and won. He was sentenced to two years (1895–97) at hard labor, during which time he composed *Ballad of*

Oscar Wilde, seen in a caricature (1884) by Carlo Pellegrini ("Ape"), was a poet, essayist, novelist, and dramatist and one of the most publicized figures of Victorian England. Cultivating the pose of an aesthete, Wilde became equally known for his scintillating conversation and his brilliant theatrical comedies, most notably Lady Windermere's Fan *(1892) and* The Importance of Being Earnest *(1895). (National Portrait Gallery, London.)*

Reading Gaol (1898) and the autobiographical essay *De Profundis* (1905).

A complete edition of Wilde's literary works and critical writings appeared in 1908 (repr. 1969); his letters were not collected and published until 1962, however.

wildebeest [wil'-duh-beest]   The wildebeest, or gnu, of the genus *Connochaetes* in the family Bovidae, is an antelope with down-curving horns from the grassy plains of central and southern Africa. Body length is up to 2 m (6.5 ft), shoulder height is about 1.4 m (4.5 ft), and weight is up to 270 kg (600 lb). The black wildebeest, *C. gnou*, is almost extinct. The blue wildebeest, *C. taurinus*, ranges widely in herds numbering in the thousands.

The wildebeest, or brindled gnu, is an African antelope with brown stripes on its sides. Both the male and female have manes, beards, and heavy, curved horns.

Wilder, Billy [wyl'-dur]   Whether comedies or melodramas, the films of American writer-director Billy Wilder, b. Vienna, June 22, 1906, have been distinguished by their cynicism and sophistication. Wilder established his talent for farce with the first Hollywood film he directed, *The Major and the Minor* (1942), and his mastery of film noir with the corrosive thriller *Double Indemnity* (1944). Subsequent films in the acidulous Wilder mode include the Academy Award–winning *The Lost Weekend* (1945), *Sunset Boulevard* (1950), and *Ace in the Hole* (1951). Wilder's later work included the poignant *Love in the Afternoon* (1957), the popular comedy *Some Like It Hot* (1959), the Academy Award–winning *The Apartment* (1960), and the farcical *Buddy, Buddy* (1981).

Wilder, Laura Ingalls   The American writer Laura Ingalls Wilder, b. Pepin, Wis., Feb. 7, 1867, d. Feb. 10, 1957, wrote the *Little House* series of autobiographical novels about growing up on the American frontier, which have become classics of children's literature. Her first

novel, *Little House in the Big Woods* (1932), began the nine-novel series that includes *Little House on the Prairie* (1935) and inspired a television series in 1974.

Wilder, L. Douglas   Lawrence Douglas Wilder, b. Richmond, Va., Jan. 17, 1931, was elected governor of Virginia in 1989, the first African-American governor ever to be elected in the United States. The grandson of slaves, Wilder left his home state to study law at Howard University in Washington, D.C., because Virginia barred blacks from its law schools at the time (1956). Despite such experiences, Wilder was not a civil-rights activist. He entered politics in 1969, winning election as a state senator. He served as lieutenant governor from 1986 to 1990. In the gubernatorial election, his pro-choice stance on the abortion issue was a major factor in his narrow victory.

Wilder, Thornton   Thornton Niven Wilder, b. Madison, Wis., Apr. 17, 1897, d. Dec. 7, 1975, was an American playwright and novelist whose works reveal a conviction that life is meaningful only when lived with full awareness of the value of the present moment. The novel *The Cabala* (1926) describes contemporary Roman society as glimpsed by young Americans. *The Bridge of San Luis Rey* (1927; Pulitzer Prize) is a narrative of obsessive love set in colonial Peru, and *The Woman of Andros* (1930) is set in ancient Greece. Wilder's collection of fanciful playlets, *The Angel That Troubled the Waters* (1928), similarly reflects a fondness for distant times and places.

The Long Christmas Dinner and Other Plays in One Act (1931) includes six plays, the best of which are set in the United States and couched in colloquial idioms. Wilder's fourth novel, *Heaven's My Destination* (1935), relates the comic misadventures of a young textbook salesman obsessed with religion. Next came three full-length plays. In the classic, Pulitzer Prize–winning *Our Town* (1938), written to be performed without scenery, Wilder depicted a typical New Hampshire village as representing the center of creation. *The Merchant of Yonkers* (1938), later revised and retitled *The Matchmaker* (1954), is a robust farce set in the 1880s. *The Skin of Our Teeth* (1942), another Pulitzer Prize winner, traces the course of humankind from prehistory to the present.

Wilder's last major works were three novels: *The Ides of March* (1948), an existentialist treatment of the last days of Julius Caesar; *The Eighth Day* (1967), an exploration of the metaphysical implications of a murder and its aftermath; and *Theophilus North* (1973), an amusing study of a young man learning and teaching others how to cope with the temptations and disappointments of life.

Wilderness Campaign   In the Wilderness Campaign (May–June 1864), a series of U.S. Civil War clashes in Virginia, the Union forces used their superior manpower to wage a war of attrition. In May 1864, Gen. Ulysses S. GRANT, newly in command of the Union armies, directed an attack on Gen. Robert E. LEE's Army of Northern Virginia. Gen. George G. MEADE launched the assault with more than 100,000 men. Lee, with about 70,000 men, met the initial Union thrust in a tangled woodland called the Wilderness, about 80 km (50 mi) northwest of Richmond.

Heavy fighting on May 5 and 6 (in the Battle of the Wilderness) cost about 18,000 Union lives, but Grant ignored losses and ordered Meade southeast to Spotsylvania Court House. More than 14,000 Union soldiers were killed there from May 8 through May 18, but Grant kept pressing against Lee's right, moving southward to Cold Harbor just north of Richmond. Furious fighting there cost 13,000 Union lives from June 3 through June 12, and there were approximately 12,000 Union casualties in an 8-minute period on June 3. From the Wilderness to Cold Harbor the Union army suffered about 20,000 casualties. Grant kept on receiving reinforcements, but Lee finally could find no more. Grant then moved south and began the PETERSBURG CAMPAIGN. The Wilderness Campaign deprived Lee of room to maneuver and trapped him at last in the defense of Richmond.

Wilderness Road   The Wilderness Road, the major route for American pioneers traveling into Kentucky and the Ohio Valley, was cleared and marked by Daniel BOONE and 30 axmen in 1775. It extended from eastern Virginia through the Cumberland Gap to the Kentucky River near the present city of Lexington and later to Louisville. By 1800, 200,000 settlers had used the road.

---

wildlife refuge   The major purposes of a wildlife refuge are to provide protection for animals that have become significantly reduced in number and to improve the habitat sufficiently so that animals will breed and grow in number. Traditionally, a wildlife refuge has been a marked area of land or water on which hunting, trapping, trespassing, and fishing are forbidden or restricted. The contemporary definition is more inclusive; several national wildlife refuges now permit managed hunting, fishing, and trapping on selected areas.

State refuges existed long before federal refuges in the United States. The first state refuge was established in 1870 at Lake Merritt, Calif. Several decades later, such states as Pennsylvania (1905), Alabama (1907), Massachusetts (1908), and Louisiana (1911) established wildlife refuges primarily to benefit upland game, particularly white-tailed deer and turkeys.

The first federal refuge was established (1903) in Florida by executive order of President Theodore ROOSEVELT. This refuge, intended to protect brown pelicans, was located on Pelican Island in the Indian River. The Migratory Bird Conservation Act of 1929 provided the authority for purchasing land and establishing refuges for migratory birds. The Fish and Wildlife Act of 1956 gave further impetus to the federal refuge program by authoriz-

ing the U.S. Fish and Wildlife Service to acquire land for refuge purposes for all kinds of wildlife. The Endangered Species Preservation Act of 1966 provided protection for endangered wildlife and also gave official designation to the National Wildlife Refuge System, which now encompasses 13.8 million ha (34 million acres) within about 420 refuges.

Although disturbances from lumbering and oil drilling must not seriously hurt the functions of a refuge, these activities often are carried out on lands owned by the U.S. Fish and Wildlife Service. Under present policy a large number of federal refuges have portions open for activities such as hunting, fishing, boating, camping, and hiking.

Migratory-bird refuges account for three-fourths of all refuges established; concern for waterfowl has resulted in breeding, flyway, and wintering refuges. The Souris River National Wildlife Refuge in North Dakota is an example of a waterfowl breeding habitat. The Chautauqua National Wildlife Refuge in the Illinois River bottom is a flyway refuge where waterfowl can find food and protection while migrating to wintering grounds. The Delta National Wildlife Refuge in the Mississippi River delta is provided for wintering waterfowl.

Refuges also exist for endangered species such as the whooping crane, which finds protection at its winter home in the Aransas Refuge of Texas. Key deer in Florida benefit from the Key Deer Refuge there. Desert bighorn sheep find protection in the Desert Game Refuge of Nevada.

Privately owned wildlife refuges have been established by diverse groups. Protection by individual ranchers in the West saved remnant numbers of antelope, and a few timber companies in the Southeast saved populations of deer and wild turkey. Mrs. C. N. Edge of a private conservation committee leased and developed the Hawk Mountain Sanctuary in eastern Pennsylvania, which provides protection to migrating hawks. The National Audubon Society has established a number of refuges, many of which provide protection for rookeries of ibises, egrets, and herons.

National refuges exist in Africa, protecting such game as elephants and lions and also lesser-known, rare species of animals; such refuges also have been established in numerous other regions worldwide. Populations of the giant sea turtle, fur seal, and unique bird species of the Galápagos Islands have been protected under the Charles Darwin Foundation for the Galápagos Islands, established (1959) with the support of UNESCO and the International Union for the Conservation of Native and Natural Resources.

Wilfrid, Saint   An English bishop, abbot, and missionary, Saint Wilfrid, b. 634, d. Apr. 24, 709, helped bring about the adoption of Roman observances (replacing Celtic forms) by the Northumbrian church at the Synod of Whitby in 664. Having served as abbot of Ripon since 661, he became bishop of York in 669. Conflicts with the Northumbrian kings, however, twice forced him to flee. He agreed to resign the see of York and become bishop of Hexham. He spent his last years at Ripon. Feast day: Oct. 12.

Wilhelm   for German rulers of this name, see WILLIAM

Wilhelm, Hoyt   James Hoyt Wilhelm, b. Huntersville, N.C., July 26, 1923, was one of the finest knuckleball pitchers in major league baseball history. Starting with the N.Y. Giants (National League) in 1952, he played for 9 teams in both leagues and became the first pitcher to win the earned-run-average title in both leagues (1952, 1959). Used primarily as a relief pitcher, he registered a no-hitter as a starter for the Baltimore Orioles in 1958. When he retired in 1972, Wilhelm had won 143 games—124 of them in relief, a major league record. He set another record by pitching in 1,070 games during his career. Wilhelm was inducted into the Baseball Hall of Fame in 1985.

Wilhelmina, Queen of the Netherlands   [vil-hel-mee'-nah]   Queen Wilhelmina, b. Aug. 31, 1880, d. Nov. 28, 1962, reigned over the Netherlands for more than half a century. In 1890 she succeeded her father, William III, to the throne under the regency of her mother; she assumed personal rule in 1898. Although committed to observe the constitution, Wilhelmina considered herself a ruler by divine right and frequently intervened in political affairs. After the German invasion on May 10, 1940, Wilhelmina fled to England, leading a government in exile from London and becoming popular as a rallying point for Dutch freedom. In declining health, she abdicated in favor of her daughter Juliana on Sept. 4, 1948.

Wilkes, Charles   Charles Wilkes, b. Apr. 3, 1798, New York City, d. Feb. 8, 1877, was a U.S. naval officer and explorer. He commanded a government-sponsored scientific expedition (1838–42) that explored the region in Antarctica now bearing his name (Wilkes Land), the western coast of North America, and about 300 Pacific islands. As commander of the U.S.S. *San Jacinto* during the Civil War he intercepted (1861) the British mail vessel *Trent* and removed Confederate officials on board, touching off the TRENT AFFAIR. Later in the war he angered foreign governments in the West Indies over violations of neutrality and was court-martialed and suspended from duty in 1864.

Wilkes, John   A London politician and journalist, John Wilkes, b. Oct. 17, 1727, d. Dec. 26, 1797, was one of the founders of modern British radicalism. Elected to Parliament for Aylesbury in 1757, he used his political periodical *North Briton* to launch (1762) a series of scurrilous attacks on the political activities of King GEORGE III and his supporters. The attacks culminated in the devastating "No. 45" issue of April 1763 and led to his expulsion from the House of Commons and his prosecution by the government.

After four years of exile, Wilkes aroused still more controversy in 1768. Three times elected by Middlesex and three times expelled by a vengeful Commons, he claimed martyrdom in the cause of electoral rights, provoking a nationwide campaign on his behalf that initiated the movement for parliamentary reform. His cause was not assisted, however, by his unsavory reputation in personal and financial dealings. Wilkes returned to Parliament as member for Middlesex in 1774, serving until 1790. He never again attracted the support he had in the 1760s.

Wilkes-Barre   [wilks'-bar-ruh]   Wilkes-Barre, a city in northeastern Pennsylvania and the seat of Luzerne County, is located on the Susquehanna River in the Blue Ridge Mountains, about 26 km (16 mi) southwest of Scranton. The city has a population of 47,523 (1990). The industries of Wilkes-Barre produce textiles, tobacco products, wire and cable, and electronic and metal goods.

Settled in 1769 by a group of colonists from Connecticut, Wilkes-Barre was named for the English politicians John Wilkes and Isaac Barré, known for their support of the American colonists. It was the site of violent land-claim conflicts called the Pennamite Wars (1769–99) between the New Englanders and Pennsylvanians. The city was severely damaged by floods in 1972.

Wilkins, Sir Hubert   George Hubert Wilkins, b. Oct. 31, 1888, d. Dec. 1, 1958, was an Australian explorer and aviator who pioneered the use of the airplane and submarine for polar exploration. His earliest expeditions took him to the Arctic with Vilhjalmur Stefansson (1913–16) and the Antarctic with Sir Ernest Shackleton (1920–22). In April 1928, Wilkins and Carl Ben Eielson made the first transarctic airplane flight over unknown territory; Wilkins was knighted for this feat. Later in 1928, Wilkins and Eielson flew over the Antarctic, and in 1931, Wilkins led a submarine voyage under Arctic ice.

Wilkins, Roy   Roy Wilkins, b. St. Louis, Mo., Aug. 30, 1901, d. Sept. 8, 1981, led the NATIONAL ASSOCIATION FOR THE ADVANCEMENT OF COLORED PEOPLE (NAACP) from 1955 to 1977. A graduate (1923) of the University of Minnesota, he joined the staff of the NAACP in 1931. Ar-

Succeeding Walter White as executive secretary (later executive director) of the NAACP in 1955, Roy Wilkins led that organization into increasing militancy in the 1960s but rejected the extremism of the black-power advocates.

chitect of the legal challenge that led to the historic Supreme Court school-desegregation decision of 1954, Wilkins was at the forefront of the civil rights struggle of the following decades and remained a staunch advocate of constitutional means of achieving black equality.

Wilkinson, Bud

Charles Burnham "Bud" Wilkinson, b. Minneapolis, Minn., Apr. 23, 1916, was an American football coach. He played (1934–36) quarterback and guard for the University of Minnesota before gaining national recognition coaching (1947–63) at the University of Oklahoma, where his teams won 145, lost 29, and tied 4. From 1954 to 1956 his teams were undefeated, winning 47 consecutive games. During his tenure as coach Oklahoma won 14 conference and 3 national championships. After leaving Oklahoma Wilkinson worked as a sports broadcaster. He returned to football in 1978 as coach of the St. Louis Cardinals of the National Football League (NFL) but was discharged during the 1979 season.

Wilkinson, James

An American soldier and adventurer, James Wilkinson, b. Calvert County, Md., 1757, d. Dec. 28, 1825, was involved in conspiracies to separate the West from the Union. During the American Revolution, he won promotion to brigadier general (1777). Appointed (1778) secretary to the Board of War, Wilkinson was soon forced to resign because of his involvement in the CONWAY CABAL against Washington.

In 1784, Wilkinson moved to Kentucky, where he accepted (1787) a Spanish bribe and pledged to work for Western secession. While still in the pay of the Spanish, he accepted (1791) an army commission and became (1796) the highest-ranking officer. In 1805 he became governor of the Louisiana Territory and entered into an agreement with Aaron BURR perhaps aimed at creating an independent republic in the American West. He betrayed Burr, however, and was the chief prosecution witness in Burr's trial (1807). He was cleared by court-martial in 1811 and promoted to major general in 1813. His military career ended during the War of 1812, when his Montreal campaign failed (1813).

Wilkinson, Jemima

Calling herself the "Universal Publick Friend," American religious leader Jemima Wilkinson, b. Cumberland, R.I., Nov. 29, 1752, d. July 1, 1819, formed a society of Universal Friends and founded (1794) a community for her followers in Jerusalem Township, N.Y. After a vision in which she died and returned to Earth, she preached a combination of Quaker ideals, celibacy, millennialism, mystical interpretations of dreams, and the doctrine that she was God's divine messenger.

will (law)

In law, a will is a written document that directs how a person's property shall be distributed at death. Anyone who is legally an adult, of sound mind, and not under the undue influence of an interested party can make a valid will. It must be signed by the person who makes it, and in most U.S. states two or three other persons must also sign the will as witnesses. Within limits, persons may dispose of their property as they choose. State statutes, however, usually stipulate that a surviving spouse cannot be disinherited.

The person who makes a will is called a testator, if a man, and a testatrix, if a woman. In the will the maker appoints a person to take care of his or her estate after death. That person is called an executor (male) or an executrix (female). When the maker dies, the will is taken to the appropriate county office (called a PROBATE court, orphan's court, or surrogate's court) to establish that it is a valid will, properly executed. If the will does not specify an executor, the court will appoint an administrator, who will perform the same functions as an executor.

The assets of the deceased person must then be gathered together by the executor, who is responsible for paying debts and distributing what is left to the heirs in accordance with the directions contained in the will. The executor usually employs a lawyer to take care of the legal details and may be required to make a formal accounting to the court before carrying out the final distribution.

A person who dies without a valid will is said to die intestate. The person's property is then distributed in accordance with a state statute for intestate succession. If the decedent was single, the statute usually provides for the property to go to the next of kin, in the following order: parents or surviving parent, brothers and sisters, nephews and nieces, grandparents, uncles and aunts, and cousins. If the decedent has no relatives within the statutory limit, the estate goes to the state itself, by a process called escheat. If the intestate person was married, the surviving spouse usually receives at least one-third of the entire estate, but statutes differ and offspring always have rights. In making a will, it is prudent, but not essential, to have the assistance of a lawyer familiar with the laws of inheritance and taxation.

will (philosophy)

In philosophical discussion, will is usually paired with reason as one of two complementary activities of the mind. The will is considered the faculty of choice and decision, whereas the reason is that of deliberation and argument. Thus a rational act would be an exercise of the will performed after due deliberation.

The will has figured prominently in the thought of many philosophers, among them the 19th-century thinkers Arthur Schopenhauer and Friedrich Wilhelm Nietzsche. Historically, debate has centered on the issue of the will's freedom, a question of prime importance for the analysis of human action and moral responsibility.

Philosophers have often thought that persons are responsible only for those actions which they have the option either to do or not to do or to will or not to will. If all acts, including acts of will, are predetermined, then this option does not appear to exist.

In the philosophy of mind, the question is whether reasons in the mind are identical with or reducible to events in the brain and, if so, whether physical events determine choices, decisions, and acts. A wide variety of answers have been proposed, including ones derived from Freudian psychoanalysis and the various forms of behaviorism. Some philosophers in the analytic tradition have argued that DETERMINISM is a matter of causes and decisions a matter of reasons and that the two are mutually exclusive. The issue remains controversial.

Willamette River [wil-am'-it]   Formed in western Oregon by the confluence of the Coast and Middle Forks rivers, the 485-km-long (301-mi) Willamette River flows northward·from near Eugene to join the COLUMBIA RIVER near Portland. It is widely used for irrigation and hydroelectricity and is navigable by small vessels.

Willard, Emma Hart   Emma Hart Willard, b. Berlin, Conn., Feb. 23, 1787, d. Apr. 15, 1870, was a pioneer in the movement for higher education for women. She lobbied in New York State for female seminaries and opened her own schools, training hundreds of teachers. Her introduction of mathematics and history into the curriculum was a radical innovation. In 1895 the seminary she had founded in Troy, N.Y., in 1821 was renamed the Emma Willard School.

Willard, Frances   The American reformer Frances Elizabeth Caroline Willard, b. Churchville, N.Y., Sept. 28, 1839, d. Feb. 18, 1898, was the founder (1874) of the National Women's Christian Temperance Union (WCTU); in 1891 she was elected president of the World WCTU. An effective lecturer and organizer, she also sought to reform working conditions in industry and promoted women's suffrage.

---

willemite [wil'-uh-myt]   The SILICATE MINERAL willemite (Zn_2SiO_4) has been an important zinc ore for more than 125 years. Willemite occurs as white, greenish, yellow, gray, pink, green, and brown six-sided prismatic crystals (hexagonal system) and as disseminated grains and fibrous masses. Hardness is 5½, luster is vitreous to resinous, streak is colorless, and specific gravity is 3.9 to 4.2. Willemite has been mined from crystalline limestone in Sussex County, N.J. Its brilliant yellow green fluorescence was used in early television tubes.

Willemstad [vil'-uhm-staht]   Willemstad (1985 est. met. area pop., 125,000), the capital of the Netherlands Antilles, is the largest town on Curaçao. A petroleum-refining and tourist center, it was settled by the Dutch during the 1630s. Its historic buildings include the oldest (1732) synagogue in the Western Hemisphere.

William of Auvergne   William of Auvergne, also called William of Paris, b. c.1190, d. Mar. 30, 1249, was

a French theologian and philosopher. Although his thought was largely in the tradition of Saint Augustine, he was among the first medieval Western writers to make wide use of Aristotelian and Arabic philosophy. He adopted Aristotle's definition of the soul as the "form" of the body, but he argued against any doctrine inconsistent with Christianity. William's major work is *Magisterium divinale* (The Divine Teaching, c.1223), a collection of treatises.

William of Champeaux   French theologian William of Champeaux, b. c.1070, d. January 1122, helped to develop systematic SCHOLASTICISM. In the discussion of UNIVERSALS, he proposed an extreme realist position that claimed a real identity of natures in two existing individuals of the same species, a position he later modified under the attacks of Peter ABELARD. Entering the Abbey of Saint-Victor at Paris in 1108, William made it one of the foremost schools of his time. In 1113 he was consecrated bishop of Châlons-sur-Marne and began a reform of the clergy.

William the Lion, King of Scotland   William I (the Lion), b. 1143, d. Dec. 4, 1214, was king of the Scots (1165–1214). He inherited (1152) the earldom of Northumberland, but five years later HENRY II of England annexed it. William succeeded his elder brother, Malcolm IV, to the Scottish throne. Hoping to regain Northumberland, William invaded England in 1174 but was captured at Alnwick. He subsequently signed the Treaty of Falaise (1174) in which he acknowledged Henry as his feudal superior. William later (1189) recovered the overlordship of Scotland by the Quitclaim of Canterbury, paying RICHARD I, the new English king, 10,000 marks. In 1192, Pope Celestine II declared the Scottish church independent of any English archbishop.

William and Mary, College of   Chartered in 1693 by King William III and Queen Mary of England, the College of William and Mary, in Williamsburg, Va., is the second oldest college in the United States. PHI BETA KAPPA, the national honor society, was founded there in 1776. Sir Christopher WREN designed the main building, the oldest academic edifice still in use in the United States. The college, which grants bachelor's, master's, and doctoral degrees, has programs in arts and sciences, the oldest law school (1779) in the country, and schools of marine science, education, and business administration.

William of Occam   William of Occam, or Ockham, b. Ockham, England, c.1285, d. c.1349, ranks among the most important philosopher-theologians of the Middle Ages. In 1324 he was called to the papal court at Avignon to answer a charge of heresy in a trial that dragged on without a formal conclusion. In 1328, Occam and Michael Cesena, the Franciscan minister-general, fled

Avignon. Although under a ban of excommunication, they were welcomed by the pope's enemy, Holy Roman Emperor Louis IV, to whom Occam is reputed to have said: "Defend me with your sword and I will defend you with my pen." It is believed that he died in Munich, a victim of plague.

Occam has been called the greatest logician of the Middle Ages; using his logical faculty, he elaborated a theology that remained influential for centuries. Occam adopted a nominalist (see NOMINALISM) solution to the problem of UNIVERSALS. He maintained that all existing things are individuals and that universality exists only in concepts or names. It followed that (1) God, unhampered by any universal essences, was free to create every individual unconnected with every other and (2) subsequent causal connections among such individuals were not necessary. Occam accepted the Aristotelian dictum that science is demonstration based on certain, secure premises. He rejected the Thomistic view that theology is a proper science and therefore rejected rational demonstrations of God's existence, of divine attributes, and of the immortality of the soul. Against the philosophical explanations of others, he used a principle sometimes called Occam's razor: "A plurality (of reasons) should not be posited without necessity."

In law and ethics, Occam's nominalist views led him to voluntarism and emphasis on the divine command. He concluded that the ultimate source of value and obligation lay not in any "natures" of things but in the free will of God. He regarded the rightness or wrongness of human acts as a function of their being commanded or forbidden by divine authority.

A detail from the Bayeux tapestry (c.1080), which depicts the Norman conquest of England, shows William I with messengers. William's seizure of the English throne established Norman feudalism in the Anglo-Saxon state. (Musée de la Reine Mathilde, Bayeux, France.)

William I, King of England

William I, King of England (William the Conqueror) Duke of Normandy and one of the greatest English kings, William I, b. c.1028, d. Sept. 9, 1087, led the Norman conquest of England and provided stability and firm government in an age of great disorder. The illegitimate son of the Norman duke Robert I, he inherited Normandy in 1035 and consolidated his rule by 1042. After 1050 he began to take an interest in acquiring land in England—perhaps given some encouragement by the English king EDWARD THE CONFESSOR. Following Edward's death (Jan. 5, 1066), Vikings under King HAROLD III of Norway moved on England, and William soon followed. The new English king, HAROLD II, defeated the Vikings and confronted the Normans near Hastings in October 1066 (see HASTINGS, BATTLE OF). William's forces achieved a decisive victory, and on Christmas Day 1066, William was crowned king of England, founding the Anglo-Norman monarchy and realm.

A highly capable, intelligent, and determined man, William I established a strongly personal monarchy and brought England into the mainstream of continental development. Imposing royal authority directly on courts and other institutions, William ordered the inquests that resulted in the monumental DOMESDAY BOOK. He revolutionized the social, political, and military structures of England, replacing the English nobility with French nobles, thus introducing continental FEUDALISM, a structure in which nobles held land in return for service in the royal army.

As the Anglo-Saxon state was Normanized, so too was the English church: English bishops and abbots were replaced by clerics from the Continent, including LANFRANC of Bec, who became (1070) archbishop of Canterbury. The Conqueror had been a great reformer of the church in Normandy, and he continued this role in England. He established the archbishop of Canterbury as primate of the English church, held reforming councils (which he attended), and exercised not only his rights but also his responsibilities over the church. The bishops were among his closest advisors. William I kept a close but cool relationship with the papacy, supporting ecclesiastical reform while carefully maintaining his control over the English church. He was succeeded as duke of Normandy by his eldest son, Robert II, and as king of England by his sons, first William II, then Henry I.

William II, King of England

William II, King of England (William Rufus) William Rufus, b. c.1056, d. Aug. 2, 1100, king of England, continued, and indeed intensified, the policies of his father, William I (the Conqueror), bringing the English baronage close to the point of open rebellion by the time of his death in an alleged hunting accident—possibly an assassination. Ascending the English throne in 1087, William Rufus was a strong monarch with a lofty regard for kingship and its responsibilities. He increased the centralization of royal justice and administration and strengthened the Anglo-Norman realm. Regarded as the oppressor of the English church, William drove Saint ANSELM, archbishop of Canterbury, into exile (1097) over issues of church-state relations and reform. William II was succeeded by his younger brother, Henry I.

William III, King of England, Scotland, and Ireland

William III, b. Nov. 4, 1650, d. Mar. 8, 1702, prince of Orange and later king of England, Scotland, and Ireland, devoted most of his life to resisting the expansionist designs of the powerful French monarchy. He was the posthumous son of William II, prince of Orange; his mother, Princess Mary, was the sister of England's Charles II and James II.

Dutch republicans, who had been angered by William II's efforts to extend his authority, sought to exclude the ORANGE dynasty from political power after his death. In 1672, when French and British troops invaded the Netherlands, however, William III was summoned to direct the defense of the country. William formed alliances with Austria and Spain, made peace with England in 1674, and compelled the French to accept the treaty of Nijmegen in 1678. Meanwhile, in order to cement an English alliance, he had married (1677) his English cousin Mary, daughter of the future James II.

In 1688, William, a Protestant, was invited to invade England by the political enemies of his father-in-law, a Catholic convert. James fled England, and on Feb. 13, 1689, William and his wife were jointly offered the throne. They (she as MARY II) were crowned on Apr. 11, 1689, and thus was concluded the bloodless GLORIOUS REVOLUTION. In May, William induced the English Parliament to join the alliance against France. After crushing James's invasion of Ireland in 1690 he spent the next 7 years campaigning in the Spanish Netherlands (see GRAND ALLIANCE, WAR OF THE). In 1697 he concluded a favorable peace at Ryswick. William later negotiated two partition treaties (1698, 1700) with LOUIS XIV to prevent the French monarch from claiming the entire Spanish empire for his son or grandson when the childless king of Spain died. Louis, however, repudiated the treaty, and William's last diplomatic action was the negotiation of another Grand Alliance against the French. The ensuing War of the SPANISH SUCCESSION began shortly before William's death.

In England, William was never popular. During his reign he approved the Toleration Act (1689) for Nonconformists, and his Whig ministers established (1694) the funded national debt and the Bank of England. He was also compelled to accept a BILL OF RIGHTS (1689) and the Triennial Act (1694) requiring that a new Parliament should meet at least once every 3 years. The Act of SETTLEMENT (1701) further restricted royal prerogatives. William was succeeded on the British throne by Mary's sister, Queen Anne.

William IV, King of England, Scotland, and Ireland

William IV, b. Aug. 21, 1765, d. June 20, 1837, known from his earlier service in the Royal Navy as the Sailor King, ruled Great Britain and Ireland from 1830 to 1837. He was the third son of George III. After his niece Charlotte died (1817) and he became heir presumptive, he married Princess Adelaide of Saxe-Meiningen; their two children died in infancy, however. Succeeding his brother, GEORGE IV, William briefly welcomed the accession to power of the Whigs and Canningites with their parliamentary Reform Bill. Other Whig proposals soured him, however. To pass the REFORM ACT in the House of Lords, he reluctantly agreed (1832) to create new peers (an action that eventually proved unnecessary). His refusal late in 1834 to accept Lord John Russell as leader of the Commons was virtually a dismissal of Lord MELBOURNE's Whig government and gave a definite advantage to the Tory party. After the Whigs narrowly won the 1835 election, William welcomed the Tories' power of obstruction in the House of Lords. He was succeeded by Queen Victoria, his niece.

William I, Emperor of Germany

William I, b. Mar. 22, 1797, d. Mar. 9, 1888, king of Prussia and later the first German emperor, was a cautious ruler who presided over the rise of the Prussian HOHENZOLLERN dynasty. His military career earned him a reputation as a reactionary, and he commanded Prussian troops in suppressing a revolt in Baden in 1849. He succeeded his ill elder brother, FREDERICK WILLIAM IV, first as regent in 1858 and then as king of Prussia in 1861. Initially, William's devotion to the constitution of 1848 seemed to herald a New Era. His insistence, however, on reorganizing the army to increase efficiency and political reliability brought on a constitutional conflict (1862) with the Chamber of Deputies. Rejecting the compromise suggested by Otto von BISMARCK, whom he appointed as prime minister, William strengthened both his ascendancy over the army and his opposition to parliamentary control. He commanded the army with the advice of his other chief advisor, Helmuth K. B. von MOLTKE.

William was content to stay out of the limelight in favor of the able men he retained in office. Although favoring German unity, he resisted his proclamation as German emperor at Versailles on Jan. 18, 1871, considering it a diminution of Prussian power. William was innately conservative, desiring slow internal development to strengthen the monarchy and favoring strong ties with Russia. His conscientiousness and his modest, direct manner won him great popularity with the German people. He was succeeded briefly by his son, Frederick III.

William II, Emperor of Germany

King of Prussia and the third German emperor, William II, b. Jan. 27, 1859, d. June 4, 1941, led Germany into WORLD WAR I. William developed a strong antagonism toward England, the country of his strong-willed mother, Victoria, the daughter of the British queen Victoria. His father, the less dominant parent, did not achieve the throne—as FREDERICK III—until March 1888, when he was already dying.

William identified with the conservative policies of his grandfather, William I, although he lacked the older man's ability to judge character. Despite his intelligence and good intentions, William was poorly prepared when he succeeded his father on June 15, 1888. His youth, inexperience, and desire to rule on his own brought a decisive clash with Chancellor Otto von BISMARCK, who opposed further extension of social-welfare measures—temporarily desired by William to counteract August Bebel's Social Democrats.

With Bismarck's dismissal in 1890, William gradually extended his own authority. Volatile, unpredictable, and never applying himself methodically, he was unable to coordinate government policy. His chancellors—Georg Leo, Graf von CAPRIVI; Chlodwig, Fürst zu Hohenlohe-Schillingfürst; Bernhard, Fürst von BÜLOW; and Theobald von BETHMANN-HOLLWEG—made halfhearted suggestions that concessions should be made to effect the gradual transformation of a monarchy dominated by landowners and industrialists into a state more responsive to the majority of the people. Such suggestions were thwarted, however, by William's insistence on absolutism and his opposition to parliamentary control.

In his foreign policy William aimed to enhance German prestige, expressing a strident nationalism in warlike speeches that alarmed all Europe and backing colonial expansion and Admiral Alfred von TIRPITZ's construction of a large battle fleet. William abandoned Bismarck's ties with Russia in 1890 and alienated his cousin Russian emperor NICHOLAS II by his tactlessness. Britain—offended by William's encouragement of the Boers in his telegram (1896) to South African president Paul KRUGER—was disturbed by German imperialism and commercial competition and threatened by the German navy. William's attempts to frighten France into alliance, notably in the first of the Moroccan Crises (1905–06), only strengthened French ties with Britain and Russia. He also encouraged Austro-Hungarian expansion in the Balkans. In July 1914, William wavered between peace and war; it was his tragedy to bear heavy responsibility for the outbreak of World War I through his sword rattling, his backing of Austria, his fleet increases, and his approval of the war plan of Alfred, Graf von SCHLIEFFEN.

By removing himself to army headquarters during the war (1914–18), William lost contact with the German people and identified the monarchy with the war's outcome. He contributed to defeat by supporting far-reaching annexationist plans and unrestricted submarine warfare, which brought the intervention of the United States, and by opposing peace proposals and domestic reform. He lost authority to the party leaders in the Reichstag and to the dictatorship (1916–18) of Paul von HINDENBURG and Erich LUDENDORFF. With the armistice of November 1918, William fled to the Netherlands, where he abdicated on Nov. 28, 1918; he died in exile there.

___

William I, King of the Netherlands   William I, b. Aug. 24, 1772, d. Dec. 12, 1843, prince of Orange-Nassau and first king of the Netherlands, renounced the throne when he was forced to accept a constitutional monarchy. He was the son of stadholder William V (see ORANGE dynasty). Commander of the Dutch army during the French Revolutionary Wars, he went into exile after the downfall of the Dutch Republic in 1795.

William returned to the Netherlands as sovereign prince in 1813, and in 1815, with the assent of the Congress of Vienna, became king of a United Netherlands, including Belgium and the Grand Duchy of Luxembourg. He encouraged economic growth, but his policies in the provinces, offending both the Roman Catholic church and liberals, led to the Belgian Revolution of 1830. When revision of the constitution became necessary after the recognition of Belgian independence in 1839, he had to accept ministerial responsibility. He abdicated on Oct. 7, 1840, in favor of his son William II.

___

William II, King of the Netherlands   The reign of William II, b. Dec. 6, 1792, d. Mar. 17, 1849, was marked by the adoption of a new constitution, which gave the Netherlands the political institutions by which it is still governed. Exiled to England in 1795 with his father, who later became King William I, he commanded Dutch troops at Waterloo (1815). In 1831 he again commanded an army, defeating the separatist Belgians.

In October 1840 he succeeded to the throne on the abdication of his father. Hoping to keep his country free from the revolutionary ferment of 1848, William took the initiative in the enactment of a new constitution, written by the liberal statesman Johan Thorbecke, which firmly established the supremacy of the States-General.

___

William III, King of the Netherlands   King William III, b. Feb. 19, 1817, d. Nov. 23, 1890, opposed the advanced liberal constitution adopted in 1848, but after he ascended to the throne in 1849 parliamentary government was consolidated in the Netherlands. An anti-Catholic, William retained political influence through the cabinet, giving special attention to religious matters. His attempt in 1867 to sell France the Grand Duchy of Luxembourg met Prussian hostility and had to be abandoned. As a result, his political stature at home suffered irreparably. William's personal life was troubled, first by separation from his wife, Sophia of Württemberg, and then by plans to divorce her and marry his mistress, a French actress.

___

William I, Prince of Orange   (William the Silent) William I, b. Apr. 25, 1533, d. July 10, 1584, prince of Orange, led the revolt of the Low Countries against PHILIP II of Spain, founding in the process a separate Dutch nation in the northern Netherlands (see DUTCH REVOLT). Born in Germany, he inherited in 1544 the vast possessions of his cousin, René of Chalon, in the Low Countries and the principality of Orange. He thereafter lived in the Netherlands and became a favorite of Holy Roman Emperor Charles V. Although Philip II, Charles's successor in the Low Countries and Spain, named (1559) William stad-

William I (the Silent), prince of Orange, led the Dutch Revolt against the Spanish from 1568 until his assassination in 1584. The northern provinces of the Netherlands formed the Union of Utrecht in 1579 and in 1581 declared their independence of Spain, naming Willliam as their stadholder (governor).

holder (governor) of Holland, Zeeland, and Utrecht, William became the leader of the high nobility's resistance to Philip's efforts to introduce monarchical absolutism and to repress Protestantism. It was at this time that Cardinal Granvelle, William's principal opponent, called him "the Silent" because, although he spoke eloquently, he did not reveal his inner thoughts.

An armed revolt broke out in the Netherlands in 1566. Withdrawing to Germany when the duque de ALBA entered the Netherlands with a powerful Spanish army the next year, William unsuccessfully attempted counteroffensives from Germany in 1568 and 1572. After a rebel naval force, the Sea Beggars, captured the little Dutch port of Brielle on Apr. 1, 1572, however, a "free" States of Holland confirmed William as stadholder, and he went to Holland to continue the resistance. Between 1576 and 1579 he was able to hold together a broad union of all the Low Countries in resistance to Spain.

Raised first as a Lutheran and then (from 1544) as a Catholic, William had become (1573) a Calvinist but promoted toleration among creeds. His all-Netherlands policy collapsed in 1579 with the establishment of a separate union of the southern provinces, which favored reconciliation with Philip. Meanwhile the rebellion continued in the north.

In 1580, William was outlawed by Philip, and a price was put on his head; the States-General renounced allegiance to Philip in 1581. William was assassinated at Delft in 1584, but the rebellion continued under the leadership of his son, MAURICE OF NASSAU, and Johan van OLDENBARNEVELT, who consolidated the independence of the Dutch Republic.

William II, Prince of Orange

William II, b. May 27, 1626, d. Nov. 6, 1650, prince of Orange and stad-holder of six provinces of the Dutch Republic, sought to break the dominance of Holland over the other provinces by a coup d'etat in 1650. William, who had married the daughter of the English King Charles I in 1641, succeeded his father in 1647.

Failing to prevent a separate Dutch peace with Spain in 1648, William tried to crush the peace party in Holland in 1650. He took advantage of the other Dutch provinces' jealousy of Holland by arresting its leaders and by a siege of Amsterdam, which was unsuccessful. A compromise was reached, but before William could effect his foreign schemes, he died of smallpox. His posthumous son later became WILLIAM III of England, Scotland, and Ireland.

Williams, Edward Bennett

Edward Bennett Williams, b. Hartford, Conn., May 31, 1920, d. Aug. 13, 1988, was an American trial lawyer. He graduated from Holy Cross College in 1941 and, after serving in the army during World War II, took a law degree at Georgetown University. He then established a law practice and soon became famous for his willingness to accept the most difficult cases. In a single year (1954), Williams represented Sen. Joseph R. McCarthy in the Senate censure action case against him, as well as two Hollywood writers who had been accused of Communist activities.

Williams, Eleazer

Eleazer Williams, b. Caughnawaga, Canada, c.1789, d. Aug. 28, 1858, was a Protestant Episcopal missionary to the Iroquois Indians. The son of a Saint Regis Indian, he was raised by relatives in Longmeadow, Mass. Appointed lay reader and catechist, he worked among the Oneida Indians. In 1822 he helped lead the movement of the Oneida to a reservation in the Green Bay area of what is now Wisconsin. His work there failed after 1832. In 1839, Williams told a newspaper editor that he was the Lost Dauphin (Louis XVII) of France, and rumors about his identity followed him the rest of his life.

Williams, Emlyn

The Welsh playwright, director, and actor George Emlyn Williams, b. Mostyn, Flintshire, Nov. 26, 1905, d. Sept. 25, 1987, gained renown for such thrillers as *A Murder Has Been Arranged* (1930), *Night Must Fall* (1935), and *The Druid's Rest* (1944), as well as for his sensitive evocation of boyhood in a Welsh mining town in his drama *The Corn Is Green* (1938). Equally acclaimed were his one-man shows in which he impersonated, and read from the works of, Charles Dickens (1951) and Dylan Thomas (1955). He performed internationally with his Dickens show and also was in films.

Williams, Eric

Eric Eustance Williams, b. Sept. 25, 1911, d. Mar. 29, 1981, chief minister of Trinidad and Tobago from 1956 until his death, led his country to independence in 1962. After studying at Oxford, Williams taught (1939–53) social and political science at Howard University. In 1955 he returned to Trinidad and founded the country's first formal political party, the People's National Movement. After his election as chief minister, Williams attempted to build a political and economic federation of West Indian nations; when this failed, he turned to diversifying industry and agriculture, improving education, and attracting foreign investment.

Williams, Hank   The country singer Hank Williams, b. Georgiana, Ala., Sept. 17, 1923, d. Jan. 1, 1953, became the most popular country-music star in the United States during the last 6 years of his brief life. Williams could not read music (his formal education ended during his sophomore year at high school), but he learned to play on a $3.50 guitar with the help of a black Alabama street singer named Rufe Payne. As the leader of a small music group, the Drifting Cowboys, Williams was heard regularly on local radio from 1937, and he won national prominence in 1949, when he became a star of the GRAND OLE OPRY. Since that year his records and compositions have dominated the field of country music. His son is the singer Hank Williams, Jr. (b. Shreveport, La., May 26, 1949).

Williams, John   The American cleric John Williams, b. Roxbury, Mass., Dec. 10, 1664, d. June 12, 1729, was minister at Deerfield, Mass., during the Indian massacre of the townspeople in 1704. Taken prisoner with most of his immediate family, he was held captive until 1706. Williams, who then returned to his pastoral post, wrote *The Redeemed Captive Returning to Zion* (1707), a widely circulated account of his experiences.

Williams, John A.   John Alfred Williams, b. Jackson, Miss., Dec. 5, 1925, is an African-American writer whose novels—particularly *The Man Who Cried I Am* (1967), *Sons of Darkness, Sons of Light* (1969), and *!Click Song* (1982)—are bitter, violent portrayals of the black man's position in a racist America. On the other hand, *The Junior Bachelor Society*, 1976, is a comparatively gentle book, made into a 1981 television film, *Sophisticated Gents*. Williams's many works of nonfiction include *This Is My Country Too* (1965), based on his travels through the United States, and *The King God Didn't Save* (1970), a harsh analysis of the ideas and actions of Martin Luther King, Jr.

Williams, Roger   Roger Williams, b. London, *c.* 1603, d. March? 1683, was a radical Puritan thinker and founder of the colony of Rhode Island. The son of a London merchant tailor, the intellectually brilliant Williams graduated (1627) from Cambridge and was ordained in the Church of England. His developing Puritanism, how-

ever, alienated him from the church, and in the first year of the Puritan migration to New England, Williams left England with his family, arriving at Boston in 1631.

Welcomed warmly at first, Williams refused the ministry of the Boston congregation because it had not formally separated from the English church. He moved to Salem, to Plymouth, and back to Salem, his "strange opinions" arousing controversy everywhere. He insisted that the lands given to Massachusetts and Plymouth belonged to the Indians and denied that government could enforce religious laws. The rulers of Puritan Massachusetts, by contrast, believed that they were obligated to maintain a godly community and protect true religion. Williams was expelled (October 1635) from the colony by the Massachusetts General Court. He fled (January 1636) with a few Salem acquaintances to the Indians on Narragansett Bay. At the head of the bay he bought land and named the tiny settlement, the first in Rhode Island, Providence.

For the next 40 years Williams left a profound imprint on Rhode Island, making it a haven for heterodoxy. In England, in 1644, Williams secured a patent for the colony from Parliament; several years later a representative government was established with complete religious freedom. He was governor of the colony from 1654 to 1657. In 1663, King Charles II granted Rhode Island a royal charter confirming all of its liberal institutions.

Although Williams had helped to found the first Baptist congregation in America (1639), he left it in a few months to become a Seeker, opposed to all sects and creeds. Williams's work among the Indians enabled him to learn their language and to write *A Key into the Language of America* (1643). His defense of religious freedom, *The Bloudy Tenent of Persecution* (1644), was one of the great Puritan tracts.

Williams, Ted   The American professional baseball player Theodore Samuel Williams, b. San Diego, Calif., Aug. 30, 1918, was one of the greatest hitters in major

Ted Williams, an outfielder with the Boston Red Sox, is generally recognized as one of the greatest hitters in the history of baseball. He is the last player to bat for a seasonal average of more than .400– .406 in 1941.

league history. A lifetime .344 batter with 521 home runs in 19 years (1939–60) as a left-hand-hitting outfielder for the Boston Red Sox, Williams won 6 American League (AL) batting titles—his last at the age of 40, in 1958—4 home-run crowns, and 9 slugging-average championships (lifetime slugging average: .634—2d only to Babe Ruth). Nicknamed The Splendid Splinter, he won baseball's prestigious Triple Crown (most home runs, most runs batted in, and highest batting average) in both 1942 and 1947. Williams was the AL's Most Valuable Player in 1946 and 1949. His most notable season came, however, in 1941, when he won his first batting crown, with a .406 average. No hitter has since reached the .400 mark. Williams led the AL in bases on balls 8 times, and he accumulated 2,019 career walks to rank 2d, again behind Babe Ruth. Although Williams missed nearly 5 full seasons fulfilling his military obligation during World War II and the Korean conflict, he still compiled many impressive career statistics. Williams retired in 1960 but returned to baseball in 1969 as manager of the Washington Senators (later, the Texas Rangers). He retired from managing in 1972. In 1966, Williams was elected to the Baseball Hall of Fame.

Williams, Tennessee Thomas Lanier ("Tennessee") Williams, b. Columbus, Miss., Mar. 26, 1911, d. Feb. 25, 1983, was an outstanding American playwright and the author of film scripts, short stories, novels, and verse. He vividly conveyed the sexual tensions and suppressed violence of his tormented characters, winning Pulitzer Prizes for A STREETCAR NAMED DESIRE and CAT ON A HOT TIN ROOF.

Williams began his career auspiciously with a Group Theater award (1939) for four one-act plays later published (1948) under the collective title *American Blues*. After a disappointment in his first professional production, *Battle of Angels* (1940), Williams combined semiautobiographical material with innovative technique in *The Glass Menagerie* (1945; film, 1950), and secured

Tennessee Williams, one of the foremost American playwrights of the mid-20th century, is best known for works that explore the failures, frustrations, and tensions of human relationships. A Streetcar Named Desire *(1947) and* Cat on a Hot Tin Roof *(1955) each received the Pulitzer Prize and the New York Drama Critics' Circle Award.*

Photo Jill Krementz © 1973

both that year's New York Drama Critics' Circle Award and lasting fame in the American theater.

Themes of Sexual Frustration. The unsuccessful dramatization of a D. H. Lawrence story, *You Touched Me!* (1945), on which Williams collaborated with Donald Windham, was followed by the first of a series of plays dealing with sexual frustration, *A Streetcar Named Desire* (1947; film, 1951), the most effective of all Williams's works. A compelling portrait of personal disintegration, this drama, like *The Glass Menagerie* before it and most of Williams's subsequent plays, has a cast of naturalistic characters whose personalities are illuminated by imaginative staging. Williams studied the problems of solitary women in two more plays: *Summer and Smoke* (1948; revised as *The Eccentricities of a Nightingale*, 1965), a melodrama in which a Southern spinster attempts to ignore the sensual side of her nature, and *The Rose Tattoo* (1951; film, 1955), a lusty comedy in which a mature widow, after a long inner struggle, rediscovers love.

Pursuing the experimental aspect of his work, Williams, in *Camino Real* (1953), peopled a Latin American town with historical and literary characters, lost souls, and sadists. This play was eclipsed in public attention by *Cat on a Hot Tin Roof* (1955; film, 1958), which returns to Williams's theme of frustrated female passion, this time with the added dimension of male homosexuality. For his next three plays, *Orpheus Descending* (1957, a revised version of *Battle of Angels*; filmed as *The Fugitive Kind*, 1960), *Suddenly, Last Summer* (1958; film, 1960), and *Sweet Bird of Youth* (1959; film, 1961), Williams borrowed elements of the ancient myth of Orpheus and Eurydice to create violent modern plots involving murder, cannibalism, and emasculation. With *Period of Adjustment* (1959) he pursued a lighter, comic vein in a play about two couples, one just married, and their minor emotional difficulties. *The Night of the Iguana* (1961; film, 1964), which won both a Drama Critics' Circle Award and a Tony Award, is set in an out-of-the-way Mexican hotel and portrays the interactions of three oddly assorted characters—the widow who runs the hotel, a defrocked minister, and a spinsterish woman who travels with her ancient grandfather.

Later Works. Although Williams continued to offer new plays—such as *I Can't Imagine Tomorrow* (1970, for television), *Demolition Downtown* (1976), *This Is an Entertainment* (1976), and *Vieux Carré* (1979)—the quality declined after *The Night of the Iguana* and *The Milk Train Doesn't Stop Here Anymore* (1962). An exception was *Small Craft Warnings* (1972), set in a seacoast bar peopled by a typical Williams cast of wounded characters. Of his nondramatic works, the novel *The Roman Spring of Mrs. Stone* (1950; film, 1961) is the best known. *The Knightly Quest* (1967) and *Eight Mortal Ladies Possessed* (1974) are short-story collections. Verse collections include *In the Winter of Cities* (1956) and *Androgyne, Mon Amour* (1977). Although Williams's *Memoirs* (1975) reveal a great deal about his personal life, they are disappointing in their lack of comment on his dramaturgy.

Williams, William Carlos   One of the most innovative of modern American poets, William Carlos Williams, b. Rutherford, N.J., Sept. 17, 1883, d. Mar. 4, 1963, was also a pediatrician who practiced medicine in his birthplace for most of his long life. Williams published his first book, *Poems*, in 1909, only 3 years after graduating from the University of Pennsylvania Medical School. From that time until his death he published nearly 40 more volumes of poetry, fiction, plays (*Many Loves and Other Plays*, 1961), essays, biography, and autobiography.

The importance of Williams as a modern writer lies partly in his insistence that American art be based on American experience. His characters, his settings, his language—all are drawn from the most common American sources. His experiences as a physician continuously influenced his aesthetic theory and the poetry and fiction that grew from that theory. Williams was important also for his interest in new ways of expressing the timeless truths with which literature deals: to him, innovation was the index of a writer's merit.

From such early verse collections as *The Tempers* (1913) and *Al Que Quiere!* (1917) to the prose poem *Kora in Hell: Improvisations* (1920) and *Spring and All* (1923), Williams was intent on comparing the new imagist poetics (see IMAGISM) with paintings by Charles Sheeler, Paul Klee, Charles Demuth, the impressionists, and others. Williams's poems are filled with people and their speaking voices, but they are also close observations of nature—poems of the real and the concrete—exemplifying a method that Williams described as "objectivist." They illustrate his contention, in *Paterson*, that abstractions do not reach the reader, that there can be "no ideas but in things."

Williams produced at least 50 short stories and four novels, the best of which, *White Mule* (1937), portrayed the life of a poor immigrant American family. His major sustained work followed his wide experimentation in both short poetry and fiction. The five books of the epic poem *Paterson* (1946–58) created his permanent literary reputation as a writer who cared deeply about his country and its culture. Williams's last three books of poems, collected in 1962 as *Pictures from Brueghel*, won the Pulitzer Prize.

Williams, William Sherley   One of the mountain men who trapped and explored in the American West, William Sherley Williams, b. Rutherford County, N.C., June 3, 1787, d. Mar. 21, 1849, served as an interpreter and guide for various U.S. government surveying expeditions. He moved near St. Louis, Mo., in 1794, and at the age of 16 he went to live among the Osage Indians for 25 years. During this time Williams, known as Old Bill, served as government interpreter and scout. Beginning in 1824 he spent much of his time trapping in the southern Rockies. Later he was a guide on the 1845 and 1848 expeditions of John C. Frémont. Williams was ambushed and killed by Indians.

Williams College   Established in 1793, Williams College is a private coeducational school in Williamstown, Mass. Master's degrees are offered in several fields.

Williamsburg   Williamsburg is an independent city in southeastern Virginia located between the James River and the York River. It has a population of 11,530 (1990). The city contains a leading U.S. colonial restoration (1926). In a re-creation of the buildings and activities of Williamsburg's colonial period, the restoration contains 88 restored buildings and is a major tourist attraction and the city's main source of income. Williamsburg is also the seat of the College of William and Mary (1693), the second oldest college in the United States.

The settlement of Middle Plantation, founded in 1633 on Williamsburg's site, served as Virginia's temporary capital during the rebuilding of Jamestown in 1698. Renamed and made the permanent capital in 1699, Williamsburg was the colony's political and cultural center and was the scene of dramatic events in the American independence movement during the 1760s and '70s. After Richmond was made the capital of Virginia in 1779, Williamsburg declined.

The Capitol at Williamsburg was the seat of Virginia's colonial government throughout most of the 18th century. Much of this city, located in southeastern Virginia, was restored during the 1930s.

Williamsport   Williamsport, the seat of Lycoming County, Pa., has a population of 31,933 (1990). The city lies on the west branch of the Susquehanna River, about 110 km (70 mi) north of Harrisburg. A major lumbering center in the 1860s, Williamsport is now an industrial city. Plastic, metal, leather, and electronic products, paper and lumber, and textiles are produced there. Little League baseball was founded in Williamsport in 1939 and the Little League World Series is played annually nearby. The city is also the site of Lycoming College (1812). Williamsport was founded in 1795.

Willkie, Wendell L.

The American politician Wendell Lewis Willkie, b. Elwood, Ind., Feb. 18, 1892, d. Oct. 8, 1944, was the Republican presidential nominee in 1940. Willkie was a corporation lawyer until 1933, when he became president of Commonwealth and Southern Corporation, a private utilities company. He gained renown as an opponent of public power but remained a Democrat until 1939. In 1940 the eastern liberal wing of the Republican party, with the help of extensive grassroots support, engineered Willkie's nomination for president. He endorsed many New Deal social reforms and repudiated isolationism, but he lost to President Franklin D. Roosevelt by almost 5 million votes. During World War II, Willkie toured the world as Roosevelt's envoy and advocated a postwar international organization to promote peace, most notably in *One World* (1943).

willow

Willow is the common name for about 300 species of deciduous trees and shrubs of the genus *Salix* in the willow family, Salicaceae. Leaves are linear-lanceolate to elliptic, and the tiny flowers lack petals and sepals. The bark of this softwood is scaly or furrowed. About 100 species, most of which grow as shrubs, are native to North America.

Willows are shallow-rooting plants that favor moist soils typical of riverbanks and are used in these locations for erosion control. They provide nectar for bees in the spring. The flexible twigs of the basket willow, *S. viminalis*, are used in basketry, and the showy catkins of the pussy willow, *S. discolor*, are used in decorations. The black willow, *S. nigra*, is the only willow used for lumber, and it is used only when great strength is not required. Popular ornamentals in the United States include the weeping willow, *S. babylonica*, and the brittle willow, *S. fragilis*.

Wills, Garry

The American writer Garry Wills, b. Atlanta, Ga., May 22, 1934, is known for his scholarship in classical languages and literature as well as for his articles and books on contemporary events, especially the celebrated *Nixon Agonistes* (1970). A listing of some of his books indicates the wide range of Wills's interests and competence: *Roman Culture* (1966); *The Second Civil War* (1968), about the struggle for civil rights for African Americans; *Politics and Catholic Freedom* (1964) and *Bare Ruined Choirs* (1972), about religion; *Inventing America: Jefferson's Declaration of Independence* (1978) and *Explaining America: The Federalist* (1981); *Confessions of a Conservative* (1979); and *The Kennedy Imprisonment: A Meditation on Power* (1982).

Wills, Helen Newington

Helen Newington Wills, b. Centerville, Calif., Oct. 6, 1905, was an outstanding tennis champion known for her excellent ground strokes. She started playing tennis at the age of 13 and won her first women's singles title 4 years later. During her career she won the Wimbledon singles title 8 times (1927–30, 1932–33, 1935, and 1938), the U.S. championship 7 times (1923–25, 1927–29, and 1931), and the French 4 times. Wills also won the women's doubles title at Wimbledon on 3 occasions and the U.S. doubles 4 times.

Willson, Meredith

Meredith Willson, b. Mason City, Iowa, May 18, 1902, d. June 15, 1984, tapped a rich vein of Americana in his Broadway musicals. He wrote the books, lyrics, and music for *The Music Man* (1957) and *Here's Love* (1963), as well as the lyrics and music for *The Unsinkable Molly Brown* (1960).

(Left) *The Babylon weeping willow is frequently planted along riverbanks.* (Right) *The American pussy willow bears silky buds on long, slender branches.*

Wilmington (Delaware) Wilmington, the largest city in Delaware and the seat of New Castle County, has a population of 71,529 (1990). It is located in the northern part of the state, on the Delaware River at the junction of Brandywine Creek and the Christina River, and is important both as a trading center and as a port of entry. The nearby Delaware and Chesapeake Canal provides access for shipping into Chesapeake Bay. The city is important for chemical manufacturing, which is dominated by the du Pont Corporation. Other major products are textiles, rubber and leather products, explosives, floor coverings, and railroad cars. Historic buildings include Old Swedes Church (1698) and the Old Town Hall (1798). The WINTERTHUR MUSEUM contains early American furniture and decorative arts.

Wilmington was first settled in 1638 by Swedish immigrants, who were supplanted by the Dutch and then the British during the mid-17th century. The Battle of the Brandywine (1777) of the American Revolution was fought nearby. The du Pont powder mills were established in 1802.

Wilmington (North Carolina) Wilmington (1990 pop., 55,530) is the principal seaport of North Carolina and the seat of New Hanover County. It is situated on the west bank of the Cape Fear River, 48 km (30 mi) north of the Atlantic Ocean, and was for many years the largest city in the state. Wilmington's economy is based on shipping and rail transportation, tourism, and the manufacture of textiles and wood and metal products. Wilmington, founded in 1730, was occupied by the British under Charles Cornwallis in 1781. During the Civil War it was a leading Confederate port defying the Union blockade.

Wilmot Proviso David Wilmot (1814–68), a U.S. representative from Pennsylvania, introduced a fateful amendment to an appropriations bill in 1846 and thereby injected the slavery issue into the debates concerning the MEXICAN WAR. Anticipating Mexico's cession of territory, President James K. Polk had asked for $2 million to facilitate negotiations. The Wilmot Proviso stated that in any resultant treaty "neither slavery nor involuntary servitude shall ever exist in any part of said territory."

The bill as amended passed the House on Aug. 8, 1846, but lost in the Senate. Early in 1847 another bill, this time for $3 million, was similarly amended and passed by the House but not the Senate. The principle of the Wilmot Proviso reappeared in congressional debates thereafter and became a plank in the platforms of the Free-Soil and Republican parties.

Wilson, Angus The English writer Angus Frank Johnstone Wilson, b. Aug. 11, 1913, d. May 31, 1991, achieved success with the publication of his first novel, *Hemlock and After* (1952). The many books that followed include his masterpieces, the novels *Anglo-Saxon Atti-*

tudes (1956) and *Old Men at the Zoo* (1961); studies of Dickens (1970) and Kipling (1979); and selections from his critical essays, *Diversity and Depth in Fiction* (1984), and from his travel writings, *Reflections in a Writer's Eye* (1986).

Wilson, August African-American playwright August Wilson, b. Pittsburgh, Pa., 1945, made his theatrical breakthrough with the play *Ma Rainey's Black Bottom* (1984). *Fences* (1987; Pulitzer Prize), *Joe Turner's Come and Gone* (1988), and *The Piano Lesson* (1989) followed. All four examine the question of black identity as twisted and transformed through generations of African Americans. The plays constitute perhaps the most important body of black drama since the theater of Imamu BARAKA.

Wilson, Charles Thomson Rees The Scottish physicist Charles Thomson Rees Wilson, b. Feb. 14, 1869, d. Nov. 15, 1959, was awarded the 1927 Nobel Prize for physics for his invention and improvement (1895–99, 1910–11) of the CLOUD CHAMBER, an apparatus that revolutionized the study of particle physics. Wilson's cloud chamber became indispensable in nuclear research.

Wilson, Edmund Edmund Wilson, b. Red Bank, N.J., May 8, 1895, d. June 12, 1972, was the preeminent American critic of his time. He also wrote novels, plays, stories, and poems, as well as hundreds of book reviews.

Wilson attended Princeton University, where he was a close friend of F. Scott Fitzgerald. After World War I he became a journalist, first at *Vanity Fair* (1920–21) and later at the *New Republic* (1926–31) and the *New Yorker* (1944–48). In later years he spent much time at his family's house in Talcottville, N.Y., about which he wrote affectionately in *Upstate* (1971). By then he had published more than 30 books, of which the most important are *Axel's Castle* (1931), a pioneering study of the symbolist movement; *To the Finland Station* (1940), a series of extended and subtle portraits of the great figures from the socialist-communist tradition; and *Patriotic Gore* (1962), a study of various personalities and books connected with the U.S. Civil War.

Although Wilson's commitment to historical and biographical criticism was profound, he never doubted that the critic's first task was to evaluate, "to tell good from bad, the first-rate from the second-rate." This process can be viewed most clearly in his collections of literary journalism from the 1920s and '30s, *The Shores of Light* (1952), and from the 1940s, *Classics and Commercials* (1950).

Wilson, Harold James Harold Wilson, b. Huddersfield, Yorkshire, Mar. 11, 1916, was prime minister of the United Kingdom from 1964 to 1970 and from 1974 to 1976. He was knighted in 1976 and created a life peer, Baron Wilson of Rievaulx, in 1983.

Elected to Parliament as a Labour member in 1945, Wilson was made president of the Board of Trade in 1947. He resigned in 1951 over the introduction of charges in the free National Health Service. Hugh Gaitskell, leader of the Labour party from 1955, died in 1963, and Wilson succeeded him. On Oct. 15, 1964, when Labour won a narrow victory in the general election, Wilson became prime minister, the youngest in the century. With the hope of increasing his majority in the House of Commons, Wilson called for an election on Mar. 31, 1966; Labour was returned with a large majority. The Conservatives won the 1970 election, but Wilson returned to office in 1974. On his retirement in 1976, he was succeeded by James Callaghan.

Wilson's ability to hold the bitterly divided Labour party together was a major achievement of his leadership. One of the most divisive issues was Britain's membership in the European Economic Community (EEC), which was opposed by the party's left wing. Britain entered the EEC in 1973 (while the Conservatives were in power). When Labour came back into office in 1974, Wilson reopened negotiations with the EEC and submitted the issue of Britain's membership to the public in the form of a national referendum in 1975. The voters indicated a two-to-one preference for retaining Britain's membership, a margin that was regarded as a victory for Wilson. Wilson's efforts, however, to settle the Rhodesia problem and to restrain inflation were unsuccessful.

Wilson, Henry   Henry Wilson, originally Jeremiah Jones Colbath, b. Farmington, N.H., Feb. 16, 1812, d. Nov. 22, 1875, was a U.S. vice-president (1873–75) and antislavery leader. After serving as apprentice to a cobbler in Natick, Mass., he became a successful shoe manufacturer. Wilson entered politics as a Whig and served in the Massachusetts legislature from 1841 to 1852. Convinced that Southern slaveowners were plotting to expand their power over the entire United States, he helped organize (1848) the Free-Soil party, joined (1854) the Know-Nothing party, and finally became (1856) a member of the new Republican party. Nicknamed the "Natick cobbler," Wilson served (1855–73) in the U.S. Senate, eventually emerging as an influential Radical Republican and advocating full political rights for blacks once the Civil War was over. Vice-president during the second term of Ulysses S. Grant, Wilson died in office.

Wilson, James   James Wilson, b. Carskerdo, Scotland, Sept. 14, 1742, d. Aug. 21, 1798, was an American jurist and Revolutionary statesman. Immigrating to America in 1765, he eventually settled in Carlisle, Pa., where he became a prominent lawyer. In 1774 he was made head of the Carlisle Committee of Correspondence; he published several notable pamphlets denying the power of the British Parliament over the colonies. As a member

(1774; 1775–77) of the Continental Congress he signed the Declaration of Independence. In Congress again (1783; 1785–86) under the Articles of Confederation, he worked for the creation of a stronger central government.

In Pennsylvania politics, Wilson was an extreme conservative, opposing the state's democratic constitution of 1776. An influential member of the Constitutional Convention of 1787, he was responsible for the introduction of the electoral college. He served as associate justice of the U.S. Supreme Court (1789–98). His most notable opinion was *Chisholm* v. *Georgia* (1793), upholding federal over state authority.

Wilson, Robert   Robert Wilson, b. Waco, Tex., Oct. 4, 1944, is a director-designer-playwright whose productions combine dance, music, and art and are known for their surrealist imagery, anarchic texts, and immense duration. Among them are *The Life and Times of Joseph Stalin* (1973); *Einstein on the Beach* (1976), a collaboration with composer Philip Glass; *The Golden Windows* (1982); and *the CIVIL warS*, a 5-part operatic saga with musical collaborators including Glass (*Act V, The Rome Section*, 1986) and David Byrne (*The Knee Plays*, 1986).

Wilson, Robert W., and Penzias, Arno A.   The American radio astronomers Arno A. Penzias, b. Munich, Apr. 26, 1933, and Robert Woodrow Wilson, b. Houston, Tex., Jan. 10, 1936, shared the 1978 Nobel Prize for physics for their detection in 1965 of low-temperature radio emissions from the entire universe. They concluded that this BACKGROUND RADIATION constituted the heat remaining from the big bang about 18 billion years ago, from which the universe has been theorized to have evolved.

Wilson, Teddy   Jazz pianist Theodore Wilson, b. Austin, Tex., Nov. 24, 1912, d. July 31, 1986, is as important in musical history as his colleagues, the great pianists Earl Hines, Art Tatum, and Fats Waller. Classically trained, Wilson had a fluid, sophisticated style that marked a generation of jazz pianists. It was his association with Benny Goodman's trio and quartet (he was the first black to play publicly with a white group), and his work with the young Billie Holiday, that made his name known in the 1930s and has kept his recorded work popular up to the present day. From the late 1940s, Wilson taught, as well as touring with his own trio.

Wilson, W. B.   William Bauchop Wilson, b. Blantyre, Scotland, Apr. 2, 1862, d. May 25, 1934, an American coal miner, union leader, and legislator, served (1913–21) as the nation's first secretary of labor. Taken to Pennsylvania as a child, he was working in the coal mines by the age of nine. He served (1900–08) as secretary-treasurer of the United Mine Workers. A Democratic representative (1907–13), Wilson chaired the House committee that wrote the legislation creating the Department of Labor.

Wilson, Woodrow   Woodrow Wilson, 28th president of the United States (1913–21), secured a legislative program of progressive domestic reform, guided his country during WORLD WAR I, and sought a peace settlement based on high moral principles, to be guaranteed by the LEAGUE OF NATIONS.

Early Life and Career. Thomas Woodrow Wilson was born in Staunton, Va., on Dec. 28, 1856. He attended (1873–74) Davidson College and in 1875 entered the College of New Jersey (later Princeton University), graduating in 1879. Wilson studied (1879–80) at the University of Virginia Law School, briefly practiced law in Atlanta, and in 1883 entered The Johns Hopkins University for graduate study in political science, receiving a Ph.D. in 1886.

Wilson taught at Bryn Mawr College (1885–88) and Wesleyan University in Connecticut (1888–90) before he was called (1890) to Princeton as professor of jurisprudence and political economy. A popular lecturer and a prolific writer, Wilson was the unanimous choice of the trustees to become Princeton's president in 1902. His reforms included reorganization of the departmental structure, revision of the curriculum, raising of academic standards, tightening of student discipline, and the still-famous preceptorial system of instruction.

In 1910, George Harvey, editor of *Harper's Weekly*, with help from New Jersey's Democratic party bosses, persuaded Wilson to run for governor. After scoring an easy victory, Wilson cast off his machine sponsors and launched a remarkable program of progressive legislation, including a direct-primary law, antitrust laws, a corrupt-practices act, a worker's compensation act, and measures establishing a public-utility commission and permitting cities to adopt the commission form of government.

Success in New Jersey made Wilson a contender for the Democratic presidential nomination in 1912; he won the nomination after 46 ballots. Offering a program of reform that he called the New Freedom, Wilson ran against a divided Republican party. In November, with only 42 percent of the popular vote, he won 435 electoral votes to 88 for Progressive candidate Theodore Roosevelt and 8 for the Republican candidate, President William Howard Taft.

Progressive as President. Employing personal persuasion as well as patronage and appealing to the American

AT A GLANCE

WOODROW WILSON
28th President of the United States (1913–21)

Nickname: "Schoolmaster in Politics"

Born: Dec. 28, 1856, Staunton, Va.

Education: College of New Jersey (now Princeton University; graduated 1879)

Profession: Teacher, Public Official

Religious Affiliation: Presbyterian

Marriages: June 24, 1885, to Ellen Louise Axson (1860–1914); Dec. 18, 1915, to Edith Bolling Galt (1872–1961)

Children: Margaret Woodrow Wilson (1886–1944); Jessie Woodrow Wilson (1887–1933); Eleanor Randolph Wilson (1889–1967)

Political Affiliation: Democrat

Writings: *Congressional Government* (1885); *George Washington* (1896); *A History of the American People* (5 vols., 1902); *Constitutional Government in the United States* (1908); *Papers of Woodrow Wilson* (1966–), ed. by Arthur S. Link, et al.

Died: Feb. 3, 1924, Washington, D.C.

Buried: National Cathedral, Washington, D.C.

Vice-President: Thomas R. Marshall

public with his stirring rhetoric, Wilson won passage of an impressive array of progressive measures. The Underwood Tariff Act (1913), the first reduction in duties since the Civil War, also established a modest income tax. The Federal Reserve Act (1913) provided for currency and banking reform. Antitrust legislation followed in 1914, when Congress passed the Federal Trade Commission Act and the Clayton Anti-Trust Act. In 1915, Wilson supported the La Follette Seamen's bill, designed to improve the working conditions of sailors. The following year he signed the Federal Farm Loan Act, providing low-interest credit to farmers; the Adamson Act, granting an 8-hour day to interstate railroad workers; and the Child Labor Act, which limited children's working hours.

In foreign policy, Wilson was faced with greater problems than any president since Abraham Lincoln. He attempted to end U.S. dollar diplomacy and promote the mediation of disputes. He rejected a loan to China on the grounds that it impaired Chinese sovereignty, and he helped thwart Japanese designs on the Chinese mainland. He approved Secretary of State William Jennings BRYAN's efforts to minimize the danger of war through a series of "conciliation treaties" and joined him in an unsuccessful attempt to negotiate a Pan-American pact guaranteeing the integrity of the Western Hemisphere.

In attempting to deal with revolutionary Mexico, Wilson first sought to promote self-government by refusing to recognize the military usurper Victoriano HUERTA and forcing him to allow free elections. When Huerta resisted, Wilson tried to force him out by ordering (April 1914) limited American intervention at Veracruz and by supporting constitutionalist Venustiano CARRANZA. Mediation by Argentina, Brazil, and Chile helped to prevent a general conflict and led to Huerta's resignation in July 1914. A year later, Wilson recognized Carranza's provisional government, and in 1916 he intervened again after Carranza's rival, guerrilla leader Pancho VILLA, had raided a town in New Mexico, killing several Americans. In 1915 and 1916 he reluctantly sent troops to Haiti and Santo Domingo to establish U.S. protectorates.

After the outbreak of the European war in August 1914, Wilson struggled to maintain U.S. neutrality in the face of the British blockade of Germany and the latter's introduction of submarine warfare. He warned Germany in February 1915 that it would be held to "strict accountability" for the loss of American lives in the sinking of neutral or passenger ships. After the LUSITANIA was sunk in May 1915 (with the loss of 128 Americans), he negotiated with such firmness that Secretary Bryan, fearing a declaration of war, resigned in protest. In September 1915, Wilson won pledges from Germany to provide for the safety of passengers caught in submarine attacks, and in May 1916 the Germans agreed to abandon unrestricted submarine warfare.

Running on his record of reform and with the slogan "He kept us out of the war," Wilson sought reelection in 1916 against Republican Charles Evans Hughes. The president won a narrow victory, receiving 277 out of 531 electoral votes.

Wartime Leader. When Germany renewed all-out sub-marine warfare in 1917, Wilson severed diplomatic relations. In April he asked Congress for a declaration of war, asserting that "the world must be made safe for democracy."

As war president, Wilson made a major contribution to the modern presidency as he led Americans in mobilizing the nation's resources. Establishing a series of war agencies, he extended federal control over industry, transportation, labor, food, fuel, and prices. In May 1917 he forced through Congress a Selective Service bill under which 2.8 million men were drafted by war's end. He sought and received legislative delegation of increased powers, thus leaving for his successors the precedents and tools to meet future crises.

Wilson the Peacemaker. In 1915 and 1916, Wilson sent his advisor and confidant, Col. Edward M. HOUSE, to Europe to work toward a negotiated peace and postwar cooperation. In the spring of 1916, Wilson joined the call for a postwar association of nations; on Jan. 22, 1917, he called for a peace without victory and reaffirmed his support for a league of nations. With the United States in the war, Wilson hoped to have a stronger influence on the peace settlement. On Jan. 8, 1918, he presented his FOURTEEN POINTS, a comprehensive statement of war aims.

After the war ended in November 1917, Wilson headed the U.S. delegation to the PARIS PEACE CONFERENCE. He erred seriously, however, by not developing bipartisan support for his peace plans; he did not appoint a prominent Republican to the delegation, and he called on voters to reelect a Democratic Congress in 1918 as a vote of confidence. Most contests were decided on local issues, and when Republicans captured both houses of Congress, his leadership seemed repudiated.

Wilson was hailed as a hero on his arrival in Europe, and he worked tirelessly for a peace along the lines of his Fourteen Points; only his shrewd bargaining prevented even harsher terms from being imposed on Germany. Wilson characterized the Versailles Treaty as the best obtainable compromise and put his hopes in the League of Nations, an integral part of the treaty, as the institution to maintain peace.

Senate Republicans refused to approve the peace treaty without significant modifications of the U.S. commitment to the League. Wilson accepted some compromise but then turned to the people. In a national speaking tour he eloquently defended the League and U.S. membership as essential to lasting world peace. Long months of exhausting labor had weakened the president, however, and he collapsed on Sept. 25, 1919, following a speech in Pueblo, Colo.

A week later Wilson suffered a stroke that left him partially incapacitated for the remainder of his life. The Senate rejected the treaty in November 1919 and March 1920. Wilson urged that the 1920 presidential election be a referendum on the League. Republican Warren G. Harding, who had established a reputation as an opponent of the League, won in a landslide. The following month Wilson won the Nobel Peace Prize for 1919. He died in Washington, D.C., on Feb. 3, 1924.

wilt   see DISEASES, PLANT

Wiltshire [wilt'-shir]   Wiltshire is a county in southern England with an area of 3,481 km² (1,344 mi²) and a population of 557,000 (1988 est.). Trowbridge is its administrative center; other major cities include SALISBURY, Marlborough, and Swindon. Two-thirds of the area is covered by the great chalk Salisbury Plain. The county's major rivers are the Avon and the Kennet. The economy is based mainly on agriculture. Industries include food processing, textile manufacturing, and the production of carpets, agricultural machinery, and rubber goods. AVEBURY and STONEHENGE, the prehistoric monuments, are famous attractions. Salisbury Cathedral and Wilton House, the latter designed by Inigo Jones, are also well known. Wiltshire has been inhabited since the Neolithic Period.

Winchell, Walter   A syndicated columnist who was published in 800 U.S. newspapers during his heyday, Walter Winchell, b. New York City, Apr. 7, 1897, d. Feb. 20, 1972, was the father of the modern gossip column; when he adapted (1932) the format for a Sunday night network radio broadcast, he reached up to 20 million listeners. Starting in vaudeville at the age of 13, Winchell began writing about show business for the *New York Evening Graphic* in 1924 and for the *New York Daily Mirror* in 1929. After his daily column, "On Broadway," became nationally syndicated, he expanded its coverage to include political figures. Winchell's brash mixture of coined words, gossip, and tips on the stock market remained popular until the 1950s. On radio, a breathless delivery and the staccato of a telegraph key between stories distinguished his style.

Winchester   Winchester, the county town of Hampshire, lies on the west bank of the Itchen River in southern England. The population is 30,642 (1981). An ancient Roman commercial center that still serves as an agricultural market, Winchester rivaled London as the seat of royal government, culture, and learning during the Middle Ages. The most notable landmark is the famous Norman cathedral, begun in 1079, which contains the tombs of many English kings and authors, including those of Jane Austen and Izaak Walton. Winchester College, the first independent school in England, was founded in 1382 by William of Wykeham. Alfred, king of Wessex, made Winchester his capital during the 9th century, and William the Conqueror was crowned there as well as in London.

Winckelmann, Johann [ving'-kul-mahn]   The German art historian and classical archaeologist Johann Joachim Winckelmann, b. Dec. 9, 1717, d. June 8, 1768, laid the foundations for the modern study of ancient art. Unlike many of his colleagues of later times, he worked primarily at scholarship rather than excavation. Having studied philosophy, languages, literature, and drawing, he produced his first study, on the influence of Greek art, which became an essential document in neoclassical art criticism. In 1755, Winckelmann obtained access to various little-known collections of classical sculpture in Rome; he also traveled extensively in southern Italy, and in 1763–64 published his most influential work, *Geschichte der Kunst des Altertums* (History of the Art of Antiquity). By personally observing ancient monuments Winckelmann showed that art can be studied as history—as a progression of the aesthetic ideals promoted by specific schools, cultures, or centuries.

---

wind   Wind is air in motion relative to the rotating surface of the Earth. Horizontally, winds typically reach speeds of 50 km/h (31.25 mph), although in JET STREAMS speeds in excess of 300 km/h (187.5 mph) have been recorded. Vertically, velocities are much smaller, measured in tenths of a kilometer per hour. In meteorology, the location from which the wind blows is used to indicate the wind's direction; for example, a northwesterly wind blows from the northwest.

Causes and Effects. As Isaac Newton's LAWS OF MOTION would lead one to expect, the movement of air is produced by force imbalances. In the atmosphere, large temperature variations are the cause of such imbalances. Equatorial and polar regions vary the greatest in temperature; this temperature variation, together with a resulting pressure gradient and the CORIOLIS EFFECT, forms the basic

At the equator, air heated by the Sun rises and cold air from polar regions moves in, creating a general circulation of air and causing permanent wind belts. The equatorial area, a region of frequent calms and light winds, is called the doldrums. Trade winds of the latitudes 0° to 30° blow fairly constantly, whereas the prevailing westerlies are variable in velocity. As the hot air moves toward the poles, it descends and cools, developing into high-velocity polar easterlies. In both hemispheres are belts of calms known as horse latitudes.

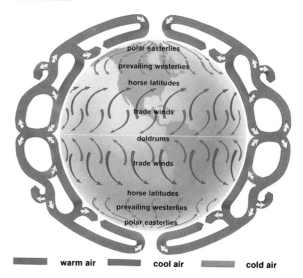

warm air   cool air   cold air

planetary wind fields. The wind flow that is produced is an attempt by the ATMOSPHERE to return to equilibrium. Because global heating gradients are continually maintained by the Sun, an equilibrium is never attained; instead, a steady state is reached in which relatively constant planetary winds carry heat from the equator toward the poles.

Three basic physical effects govern the distribution of wind: the basic driving forces that produce the motion in the atmosphere; the effect of dissipative processes, such as friction, which reduce the kinetic energy of the wind; and the Coriolis effect, caused by the rotation of the Earth. All scales of winds, ranging from planetary to regional, are governed by these processes.

The effects of friction create eddies in the turbulent boundary layer of the atmosphere. At altitudes of more than 1 km (0.62 mi), winds are generally smooth. The air, however, may be quite turbulent near jet streams. As energy is dissipated by friction at the lower boundary, the winds throughout the entire troposphere adjust to replenish the lost energy. In this manner, the entire atmosphere is affected by the dissipative processes at the lower boundary.

Coriolis Effect. The Earth's rotation modifies wind by means of the Coriolis effect, which can be described as the force produced by the Earth's rotation. This force is zero at the equator and reaches its maximum at the poles. Because the Coriolis effect vanishes at low latitudes, winds there tend to flow directly from high to low pressure; at higher latitudes, where the effect comes into play, winds flow almost parallel to the isobars.

In middle and high latitudes, the frictional forces that act in the opposite direction to the wind create a balance of forces (Coriolis force, pressure-gradient force, and friction), which causes a change in wind direction in the vertical vector as the wind speed decreases to zero at the ground. This effect is called the Ekman spiral.

Types of Winds. The three groups of winds are the planetary winds, which include the trade winds and middle-latitude westerlies; the secondary winds, sea breezes, monsoon winds, and cyclonic winds; and regional anabatic and katabatic winds.

In planetary winds, which are a major component of the general circulation, a rising motion occurs in the low latitudes, where low pressure is created by maximum solar heating. A compensating inflow occurs at low levels in each hemisphere, producing the northeast trade winds of the Northern Hemisphere and southeast trade winds of the Southern Hemisphere. The outflow of air from the tropics in the upper troposphere is diverted by the Coriolis force to produce strong westerlies.

The westerlies may become unstable and produce such mid-latitude disturbances as jet streams, cyclones, and anticyclones as well as associated secondary wind systems; they remain essentially westerly, however, if stable. The westerlies penetrate the atmosphere to the Earth's surface, where they are dissipated by friction.

Secondary winds develop to minimize local imbalances. Monsoons, for example, minimize the temperature gradient between warm landmasses and adjacent cooler oceans by producing an onshore flow of cooler air. Affected by the Coriolis force, the summer monsoon winds approach Asia from the southwest. In winter, air flows off extremely cold Asian landmasses toward the warmer oceans as the northeast monsoons.

Among the middle-latitude secondary winds are the winds associated with transient weather systems (see CYCLONE AND ANTICYCLONE). Besides possessing specific directions relative to the pressure centers, the winds associated with these systems are characterized by gales.

A more benign system is the sea breeze, which is usually confined to within 20 km (12.5 mi) of a coastline and to a vertical column of a few kilometers. If daytime heating is strong enough, as in the tropics, the moist onshore flow, which is forced to rise by surface heating, may form large convective clouds that yield brief, heavy showers. The cooling of the land at night reverses the sea-breeze circulation, resulting in a weak offshore surface flow.

Regional winds are usually the effects of such geographic features as mountain ranges. A moist wind upon a mountain is forced to rise and may produce significant climatological effects. Cooling adiabatically, the rising air may produce rainfall on the windward side of the mountain. As the air descends on the lee side, the adiabatic heating, plus the heat added to the system from condensation on the windward side, causes a very warm wind. Such winds may be very turbulent and can inflict severe damage. Ascending winds are termed anabatic, whereas descending winds are called katabatic (see CHINOOK). A potentially destructive katabatic wind called a microburst, an intense localized downdraft that spreads along the ground, causes the condition known as wind shear. Often associated with THUNDERSTORMS and rain showers, wind shears are characterized by sudden shifts in wind speed and direction.

Secondary Effects. Winds cause a number of secondary effects—for example, the wind energy that is dissipated at the lower boundary of the atmosphere over ocean regions produces ocean waves (see WATER WAVE) and drives large OCEAN CURRENTS (see also OCEAN-ATMOSPHERE INTERACTION). This energy is dissipated on coastlines or transmitted to the deep ocean by turbulent eddies. Wind energy can be harnessed either directly by windmills or indirectly through the extraction of energy from ocean waves (see WINDMILLS AND WIND POWER).

Wind patterns also produce a variety of erosional and depositional landforms (see EROSION AND SEDIMENTATION). The ability of wind to erode, carry, and deposit sediments is somewhat similar to that of water, but air is much less dense than water and can carry only smaller particles. Wind erosion, therefore, is significant only in arid or semiarid areas, where fine-grained sediment is not held firmly in place by moisture or vegetation.

wind chill Wind chill, the additional cooling effect produced by wind at low temperatures, results from rapid removal of heat from the body by convection and by evaporation from the skin. In physical terms it is defined as the dry convective cooling power of the atmosphere and may be expressed as the number of calories of heat lost per unit area at a given wind speed and temperature. The equivalent wind-chill temperature, a more common index, is the temperature of calm air that would cause the same cooling effect as the combination of air temperature and wind speed.

wind instruments   see MUSICAL INSTRUMENTS

wind tunnel
The wind tunnel, a device widely used for experimental research in aerodynamics and in the design and development of new AIRCRAFT and other objects, consists of a channel in which an airstream is produced. The use of the wind tunnel is based on the principle that the effect produced on an object moving through the air depends only on the velocity of the air relative to the object; consequently, no difference results in the effect if the object is stationary and the airstream is moving, or vice versa.

A wind tunnel includes a test section, where the model is mounted. The test section may be an open or closed channel, and the airstream through the test section is usually produced by a propeller or fan if the air speed through the test section is less than the speed of sound. If a supersonic airstream is required, large tanks of compressed gas usually are employed, producing the high-velocity stream by allowing the gas to expand through a suitably shaped nozzle into the test section. Instrumentation is provided in the test section to permit measurement of forces and pressures acting on the model and to measure other quantities of interest. Techniques are available to allow the visualization of the air flow as well.

Wind tunnels in use today have test sections with cross-section dimensions as large as 12 to 24 m (40 to 80 ft). Velocities up to 20 times the speed of sound are produced in supersonic wind tunnels.

Wind in the Willows, The
The major theme of the children's story *The Wind in the Willows* (1908), by Kenneth GRAHAME, is the struggle between the noisy, common way of life and the quiet and genteel. The Wild Wooders, including the stoats and the weasels, epitomize the former, while the River-Bankers, including Badger, Mole, Rat, and Toad, represent the latter. Toad, perhaps a projection of the author, is a lovable rebel who does not fit well into either camp. Structurally, the fantasy is a small epic in prose, partly paralleling the events in Homer's *Odyssey*.

Windhoek
[vint'-hook]   Windhoek (1988 est. pop., 114,500), the capital and largest town of Namibia, is centrally located in the Khomas Highlands and has rail and air links with South Africa. It ships lambskins and has meat-processing and engineering industries. Windhoek was founded by Germans in 1890 and became the capital of Southwest Africa (now Namibia) in 1892.

windmills and wind power
Windmills, or wind machines, are devices that generate power or perform work by using the force of the wind. They usually consist of two or more blades or sails mounted on a shaft, from which power is taken; the power is usually used to pump water or to turn a generator to produce electricity.

The first windmills were used for irrigation in Persia in about the 5th century AD; their use had spread throughout

This traditional flour mill is supported by a vertical center post around which the entire mill revolves. The center post usually is aobut 80 cm (31 in) square and about 6 m (19.8 ft) high and weighs up to 1.5 metric tons (3,300 lb). Four posts, or crosstrees, below the mill housing support the center post. The sail mechanism (detail) of the post mill is connected to the grinding stones by means of wheels and gears. The fantail at the rear turns two vertical iron shafts that connect to the two fantail wheels. When sidewinds turn the fantail, and thus the wheels, the mill is brought around so the sails face into the wind again.

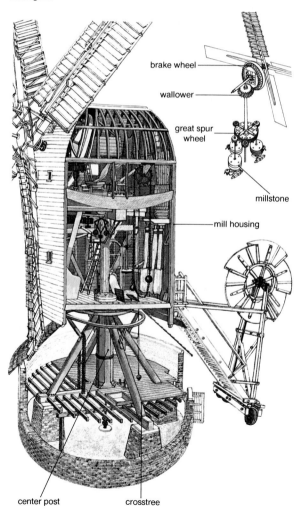

brake wheel

wallower

great spur wheel

millstone

mill housing

center post   crosstree

Europe by the 12th century. Early European windmills pumped water or turned the grindstones of corn mills. Windmills were used in Holland to drain the polders after the dikes were built; the largest of their time, they became and remain a symbol of the Netherlands. The Dutch mills, as well as smaller mills, were made of wooden frames over which canvas was stretched to form sails that turned in the wind.

During the late 19th century thousands of windmills were in use in Europe and in the rural United States, mostly for irrigation purposes. They were gradually displaced in Europe, however, by steam engines running on cheap coal, and in the United States, by the rural electrification program of the 1930s to 1950s. With the sharp rise in energy prices in the 1970s, interest revived in using machines to harness the "free" energy of the wind. The U.S. government rapidly increased funding for research and development of wind-power technology, and many other nations also invested in wind-energy programs. Commercially available small wind turbines were generally rated at 2 to 10 kW output; larger units planned by power utilities were designed to produce up to 4 MW. Proposed "wind farms" of more than 100 such machines could generate hundreds of megawatts of electric power. In addition, such relatively lightweight machines as the "sailwing" developed by Princeton University showed promise for use in irrigation projects and small-scale electric-power generation.

Types. Although an enormous number of devices to exploit wind energy have been proposed, most modern machines fall into one of two general classes: horizontal-axis machines and vertical-axis machines. Within these two categories they can be further classified as lift devices, which use the principle of the airplane wing to produce rotation, and drag devices, which are driven simply by the impulse of moving air striking their blades.

Examples of horizontal-axis machines are the familiar multibladed windmills of the prairies in the United States, used primarily for pumping water, and modern two- and three-bladed lift devices similar to huge airplane propellers. Such devices may have rotors more than 90 m (295 ft) in diameter and are usually equipped with a servomotor that keeps them facing the wind at all times. Their propeller-tip speeds can be 5 to 6 times the wind velocity, and they operate at high efficiency.

Vertical-axis machines include lift devices, such as the Darrieus rotor (or "eggbeater"), and drag devices, such as the S-shaped Savonius rotor. Both these types have the advantage that they need not be turned to face the wind, and therefore do not require the pitch and pivoting mechanisms used on propeller-type windmills.

Recently, energy designers have begun investigating the Magnus Effect rotor, a rotating cylinder or sphere immersed in moving air or water. Under these circumstances an area of low pressure is produced on the side of the object moving into the wind, whereas high pressure occurs on the opposite side. This pressure differential creates a force at right angles to the direction of the wind, a force that can be used to create energy.

Future Prospects. Electricity produced by wind power is somewhat more expensive than that produced by conventional means, but this situation will change as experimentation provides high-efficiency models. Much wind power of the future may be generated by highly efficient, small wind machines for individual homes and businesses. Present experimentation, however, has focused primarily on large-scale projects. Because of their huge size—the approximate height of a 25-story building—and the complexity of the devices needed to operate them, giant windmills have been plagued with structural and other problems. The smaller windmills built in huge arrays on wind-farms have proved more successful, although they present problems of noise pollution and disruption of radio and television reception. If these problems can be solved, or if Darreius and Magnus Effect rotors prove as efficient as their prototypes, wind power may eventually provide significant amounts of energy.

window   see HOUSE (in western architecture)

Windsor (dynasty) [win'-zur] Windsor has been the family name of the British royal house since 1917. During World War I, when Britain was at war with Germany, King George V announced (1917) that the family no longer would be known by the German name Wettin—which came from Prince Albert of Saxe-Coburg-Gotha, husband of Queen Victoria—but as Windsor, derived from Windsor Castle, a royal residence. At the same time, the family relinquished all its German titles. British monarchs bearing the name *Windsor* have been GEORGE V, EDWARD VIII (who abdicated in 1936 and was made duke of Windsor), GEORGE VI, and ELIZABETH II. In 1960, Queen Elizabeth issued a decree by which her descendants other than those titled *prince* or *princess* (meaning her own children and the children of her sons) were to be called Mountbatten-Windsor, Mountbatten being the family name of the queen's consort, Prince Philip. This meant that Windsor remained the name of the royal house.

Windsor (Ontario) Windsor, a city in southern Ontario, Canada, on the south bank of the Detroit River, opposite Detroit, has a population of 193,111 (1986). Located on water and rail routes, Windsor has become a center of automobile manufacturing. Other industries include iron and steel plants, breweries, and canneries for the surrounding agricultural region. The University of Windsor (1857) and Western Ontario Institute of Technology (1958) are located there. Landmarks include the Hiram Walker Historical Museum (1812) and the riverfront Dieppe Gardens. The first land grants for settlement were made in 1749. Known as The Ferry, Richmond, and South Detroit, Windsor received its present name in 1836.

Windsor Castle Windsor Castle, in Windsor, Berkshire, England, a small town on the Thames River west of London, has been the premier residence of the royal family of Great Britain since the reign (1066–87) of William I. The castle, set in a small park, occupies the site of a Roman fort and is surrounded by a series of defensive walls. The core of the complex, the Middle Ward, is Norman in layout, although its so-called Round Tower is a later (1272) addition by Henry III that was extended in 1344 by Edward III. To the west are the Lower Ward, the Horseshoe Cloister, the Chapel of Saint George, and the Deanery—all late-medieval structures. The Upper Ward, begun by Henry II (r. 1154–89) and completed by Charles II (r. 1660–85), contains the Throne Room, Saint George's Hall, and the great Reception Room. Continuous restoration of the castle, especially during the 19th century, has made it very difficult to distinguish accurately the old parts from the new.

Windward Islands   The Windward Islands make up the southern group of tropical islands situated in the Lesser Antilles of the West Indies between the Caribbean Sea and the Atlantic Ocean. They include from north to south the islands of DOMINICA, MARTINIQUE, SAINT LUCIA, SAINT VINCENT AND THE GRENADINES, and GRENADA. The LEEWARD ISLANDS lie to the north.

wine   Wine is an alcoholic beverage made from fermented grape juice. Growing grapes for wine is one of the world's most important farming activities, and the industry is a major feature of the economy of many wine-producing countries. Wines may be either red, white, or rosé and also dry, medium, or sweet. They fall into three basic categories: natural, or "table," wines, with an alcohol content of 8% to 14%, generally consumed with meals; sparkling wines, containing carbon dioxide, of which CHAMPAGNE is archetypal; and fortified wines, with an alcohol content of 15% to 24%, drunk either as an aperitif or with dessert, depending on their sweetness. The various types include PORT, SHERRY, and aromatic wines and bitters, such as VERMOUTH.

History

Old World. Cultivation of the vine began several thousand years before Christ and is mentioned many times in the Old Testament. The ancient Egyptians made wine; the early Greeks exported it on a considerable scale. During the Roman Empire vine cultivation was extended to such a degree that a surplus ensued, and in AD 92 the emperor Domitian decreed that half the vines outside Italy be uprooted. When replanting was later permitted, vineyards extended into northern France and Germany and even into southern England.

The Middle Ages, AD c.400–1200, saw little progress in viticulture. From about 1200, monasteries kept alive the art of wine making. Later the nobility also owned extensive vineyards. The French Revolution and the secularization of the German vineyards by Napoleon, however, removed many vineyards from ecclesiastical hands.

From the beginning of the 13th century, the wines of Bordeaux (an area under the English crown from 1152 to

Some of the most important wine-grape varieties are pictured here. (A) Portugieser makes a light, red Rhine wine. (B) Pinot Blanc, a white grape of the famous Pinot family, produces white burgundies in France, California, and northern Italy. (C) Traminer makes spicy white Rhine wines. (D) Riesling produces the most distinctive Alsace and Moselle wines. (E) Merlot makes a soft, fruity red wine. (F) The white Sylvaner grows in such northern wine regions as Austria and Switzerland. (G) Cabernet Sauvignon is California's finest red wine grape. (H) Müller Thürgau, a German grape, is the product of a cross between Riesling and Sylvaner. (I) Pinto Gris makes fine white wines in northern Italy, Germany, and Alsace. (J) Pinot Noir is the great red Burgundy grape. (K) Gutedel is grown in Germany as a table as well as a white wine grape. (L) Sauvignon Blanc produces such fine Bordeaux wines as Graves, Sauternes, and Pouilly Fumé.

1435) were commonly shipped to England, the Hanseatic ports, and the Low Countries. By the 14th century wines from Spain and Portugal were also widely exported.

For convenience in commerce, the Bordeaux merchants classified their finest red wines as early as 1725, but it was not until 1855 that such a classification, based on the market price for each wine, received official recognition.

During the middle and second half of the 19th century the European vineyards suffered from a series of disastrous diseases and pests, particularly mildew, *Oidium*, and the plant louse, *Phylloxera*. First discovered in 1863, *Phylloxera* destroyed the vines by attacking their roots. Not until about 1880 was the grafting of European vine species onto immune American rootstock accepted as the only viable solution.

Simultaneously, a movement began to ensure the authenticity of wine, culminating (1936) in France when the *appellation contrôlée* (quality control) law, now the model for similar legislation in other countries, came into effect.

New World. European colonists endeavored to produce wine wherever possible and were particularly successful in Australia, South Africa, South America, and California. Franciscan monks planted the first vineyards in California in 1769, but it was not until the mid-1830s that wine was produced on a commercial scale. The industry grew, until the devastation to the wine market caused by PROHIBITION. Following repeal of prohibition in 1933, the California wine industry revived gradually. Today methods of viticulture and enological practices in California are now among the most advanced in the world.

Major Wine Areas

France. French wines lead the world in quality. The area adjacent to the port of Bordeaux is the home of the widely planted "noble" vine, the Cabernet Sauvignon, which, with other related varieties, principally Cabernet Franc and Merlot, produces such famous red wines as the châteaux Lafite-Rothschild, Latour, Margaux, and Mouton-Rothschild in the Médoc district; Haut-Brion from the Graves; Cheval-Blanc and Ausone in Saint Émilion; and Pétrus in Pomerol. Equally renowned is Château d'Yquem, a white wine produced in Sauternes from Sauvignon Blanc and Sémillon grapes.

Burgundy is a smaller region but produces many famous wines from two related grape varieties: Pinot Noir for reds and Chardonnay for whites. The best reds come from the Côte d'Or, a narrow strip of hilly land that follows the course of the Saône River and extends roughly from Dijon for 60 km (37 mi) south to Chagny. The Côte d'Or is traditionally divided between the stronger, heartier red wines of the Côte de Nuits, such as Gevrey-Chambertin, Chambolle-Musigny, and Nuits-Saint-Georges, and the more delicate reds of the Côte de Beaune, such as Beaune, Pommard, and Volnay. Of equal standing are the dry white Burgundies: Chablis from the north; and Corton-Charlemagne, the Montrachets, and the Meursaults from the southern part of the Côte d'Or.

The Champagne region in northern France produces indisputably the best sparkling wine in the world. Other good sparkling wines are produced in the Loire, Burgundy, Savoie, and elsewhere. The Rhône valley produces excellent full-bodied reds such as Châteauneuf-du-Pape, Côte Rôtie, and Hermitage; rare and subtle whites such as Condrieu and Château Grillet; and the most renowned rosé, Tavel. Alsace, in the Rhine valley to the east, produces consistently good quality white wines named for the grape variety: Riesling, Gewürztraminer, Muscat, Sylvaner, and others. The Loire valley, in west central France, produces excellent, light, and refreshing white wines such as Sancerre and Muscadet; the well-known rosé d'Anjou; and the minor reds Chinon and Bourgueil. The Midi and Provence regions in the south of France produce a great deal of ordinary wine, as well as some aperitif and dessert wines and popular rosés.

Germany. Mainly light, fruity white wines are made in Germany. The finest of these are made of the Riesling grape from three districts on the banks of the Rhine: from the Rheingau, Rheinhesse, and Rheinpfalz; from the Nahe Valley; and from the Mosel/Saar/Ruwer valleys. The alcoholic content of German wine is low, about 9%, and the wines vary from dry to extremely sweet.

Spain. From southern Spain comes sherry, the most versatile and classic fortified wine. Sherry ranges from the dry manzanilla and fino through the medium-dry amontillado to the sweet oloroso and "cream" styles. Sherry is blended, may be sweetened, and is usually fortified with brandy.

In northeast Spain, on the banks of the Ebro River, is the Rioja, now acknowledged as the country's leading table-wine area, producing excellent, long-lived reds and dry whites.

Portugal. Portuguese wines vary from such popular light, slightly sparkling pink wines as Mateus and Lancers to the most renowned of all fortified dessert wines, port. The best reds come from the north central Dão region, which also produces some whites. In the far north of Portugal the light, acidic *vinho verde* ("green wine") is made.

Madeira is made on and called after the Portuguese-owned island in the Atlantic Ocean, off the coast of Morocco. Along with sherry and port, Madeira is one of the oldest and greatest classic dessert wines.

Italy. More wine is produced by Italy than by any other country. The best-known wines are from the north: Barolo, Asti Spumante, and vermouth from Piedmont; Chianti from Tuscany; Soave, Valpolicella, and Bardolino from Veneto; and the sparkling, sweetish red Lambrusco, from central Italy. Grape varieties are almost as numerous as the controlled appellations and include indigenous grapes, such as the Nebbiolo from Piedmont.

Other Areas. Wine is produced in many other countries, including most of those in southern and southeastern Europe and a few in northern Africa. South Africa, Australia, Argentina, and Chile also have significant wine industries.

United States. Nine-tenths of the U.S. vineyards are in California, where an ideal grape-growing climate and the support of wealthy and knowledgeable amateurs have encouraged growers and wine makers to strive for the highest standards. As a result California produces a large quantity of good commercial wines and some of very high quality.

Although wine is made in no fewer than 34 states, only California wines can be said occasionally to rival those of France. French wines are usually named by the region, town, or vineyard where they are produced, and, occasionally, by a generic name (Beaujolais). California wines, on the other hand, are often named for the principal grape variety used in making the wine. The finest California red wines are made from the Cabernet Sauvignon grape. Others include the Pinot Noir, Grenache (a rosé grape), Zinfandel, and Petite Sirah. Fine whites are led by the Chardonnay, by the Pinot Blanc, and by some late-harvested Rieslings. Wines from the Chenin Blanc and Sémillon grapes are not in the same class. The finest wines are made in the Napa and Sonoma valleys north of

San Francisco, in nearby Sonoma and Mendocino counties, and in an expanding grape-growing area to the south of San Francisco Bay as far as Monterey. Mass-produced table and dessert wines come mainly from the Central Valley.

Every size and class of producer is found in California: small, family-owned premium wineries whose production is limited but highly valued; medium-sized quality firms such as Martini and Robert Mondavi; corporation-backed growers, including Inglenook and Beaulieu vineyards; and

The diagram indicates some of the processes involved in wine making. White wine grapes are crushed (1), and the juice is filtered free of skins and stems (2) and pumped into a fermenting vat (3). Fermentaton may continue for up to 50 days for very dry white wines, which are then drawn off and bottled (4). For rosé wines, juice and pulp are fermented with skins and stalks (5), then filtered (6) and bottled (7). In making red wines, the crushed grapes, pulp, skins, and stalks are fermented together (5) as in rosé making, but the solids are then pressed out (8) and the filtered juice drawn into a second fermenting vat (9). Finings—substances that precipitate suspended particles—are added (10) and then removed by filtration (11). Some wine is pasteurized (12) before bottling. The purple shading on the map locates major grape-growing areas.

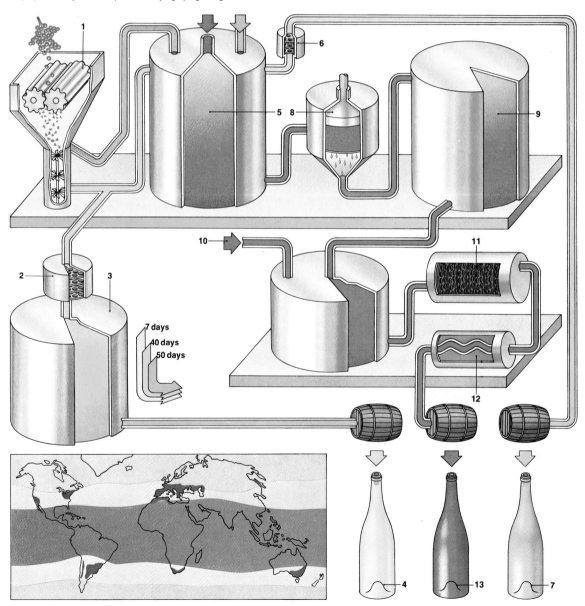

larger, commercial operations such as Almaden, Paul Masson, and—largest of all—Gallo. In addition to the wines already mentioned, many sparkling white wines are made in California, and there is also a large production of inexpensive fortified wines.

The second most important U.S. wine-producing area is New York State, particularly the Finger Lakes region, south of Lake Ontario. Large and small growers battle high heat in the growing season and extreme cold in the winter to produce a large quantity of wines of varying quality.

Wine Making

The quality and quantity of grapes depend on geographical, geological, and climatic conditions in the vineyards, and on the grape variety and methods of cultivation. Some of these factors may be governed by local laws.

Harvesting. The crop is harvested in the autumn when the grapes contain the optimum balance of sugar and acidity. For the sweet white wines of Bordeaux and Germany, picking is delayed until the grapes are affected by a beneficial mold, *Botrytis cinerea,* which concentrates the juice by dehydration.

Vinification. For red wine, the grapes are crushed immediately after picking and the stems generally removed. The yeasts present on the skins come into contact with the grape sugars, and fermentation begins naturally. Cultured yeasts, however, are sometimes added. During fermentation the sugars are converted by the yeasts to ethyl alcohol and carbon dioxide. The alcohol extracts color from the skins; the longer the vatting period, the deeper the color. Glycerol and some of the esters, aldehydes, and acids that contribute to the character, bouquet, and taste of the wine are by-products of fermentation. Traditional maturation of red wine, as practiced, for instance, in Bordeaux, then takes up to two years in 50-gallon oak casks, during which time the wine is racked—drawn off its lees, or sediment—three or four times into fresh casks to avoid bacterial spoilage. Further aging is usually advisable after bottling.

The juice of most grape varieties is colorless. Grapes for white wine are also pressed immediately after picking, and the must starts to ferment. Fermentation can proceed until it is completed, which will make a dry white wine; or it can be stopped to make a sweeter wine. Maturation of white Burgundy and some California Chardonnays still takes place in oak casks, but vintners tend now to use large tanks of such modern materials as stainless steel. Minimum contact with the air retains the freshness of the grapes.

To make rosé wines, the fermenting grape juice is left in contact with the skins just long enough for the alcohol to extract the required degree of color. Vinification then proceeds as for white wine.

The best and most expensive sparkling wines are made by the champagne method, in which cultured yeasts and sugar are added to the base wine, inducing a second fermentation in the bottle. The resulting carbon dioxide is retained in the wine. Other methods, such as carbonation, are also used.

The alcohol content of fortified wines is raised by adding grape spirits. With port and madeira, brandy added during fermentation kills off the yeasts, stopping fermentation, and leaves the desired degree of natural grape sugar in the wine. Sherry is made by adding spirit to the fully fermented wine. Its color, strength, and sweetness are then adjusted to the required style before bottling.

Storage and Use

Wine bottles should be laid on their side to prevent the corks from drying out and the air getting at the wine. There should be no great fluctuation in temperature: 13–16° C (55–60° F) for reds, 10–13° C (50–55° F) for whites being ideal. Humidity should be 70% to 80%, and the storage place should be free from drafts, light, and vibration.

Red wine should be served at room temperature, 18–22° C (65–72° F). White and rosé wines should be at refrigerator temperature, 6–10° C (43–50° F). Only wines that have thrown a sediment in the bottle, such as vintage port, red Bordeaux, and red Burgundy, need be decanted before drinking.

Winesburg, Ohio Sherwood ANDERSON's *Winesburg, Ohio* (1919), a collection of loosely connected short stories about the inhabitants of a small town in Ohio, established him as one of the best American fiction writers of his generation. George Willard, a young reporter, is the book's central character, to whom other inhabitants of the town tell their stories. Most characters speak of their humble but poignant memories and aspirations, revealing the complexity of private life beneath social appearance.

Wingate, Orde British army officer Orde Wingate, b. Feb. 26, 1903, d. Mar. 24, 1944, commanded a British-Indian guerrilla force, the "Chindits," in Burma in World War II. He served in the Sudan (1928–33) and in Palestine (1936–39). In World War II his forces captured (1941) Addis Ababa, Ethiopia. Sent to India, he organized the Chindits to enter Burma and, supplied by air, to harass the Japanese forces there from behind their lines during February–May 1943. Shortly after being promoted to acting major general in command of an airborne thrust into Burma in March 1944, he died in an air crash.

Winnebago [win-uh-bay'-goh] The Winnebago were the major Siouan-speaking tribe of North American Indians occupying present-day Wisconsin when the first French explorers arrived (1634). Their name is Algonquian for "people of the filthy water," referring to the algae-rich, dead-fish-clogged Fox River and Lake Winnebago, where the tribe lived. A horticultural people settled in permanent villages, they periodically hunted bison.

During the mid-17th century the Winnebago were nearly exterminated by disease and through warfare with the ILLINOIS tribes. As their population recovered, they became known as one of the most numerous, powerful, and warlike peoples of the Great Lakes region. They were active in the fur trade. During the 19th century Winnebago lands were ceded to the United States in a series of treaties. After prolonged migrations and much hardship, the U.S. government eventually (1865) assigned them a reservation in Nebraska. Large numbers returned (1875) to Wisconsin, however, and were given homestead lands. The Wisconsin and Nebraska Winnebago on or near federal reservations numbered an estimated 3,952 in 1989.

Winnebago, Lake   Lake Winnebago, Wisconsin's largest lake, is about 48 km (30 mi) long, as much as 16 km (10 mi) wide, and covers an area of 557 km^2 (215 mi^2). It is fed and drained toward the Great Lakes by the Fox River.

Winnie-the-Pooh   A. A. MILNE'S *Winnie-the-Pooh* (1926), illustrated by Ernest Howard SHEPARD, became an immediate best-seller throughout the world. The story was in part inspired by Milne's wife, Dorothy, who created nicknames and adventures for the stuffed toys belonging to her son, Christopher Robin. Milne's humorous and rhythmical prose enlivens the presentation of the greedy Pooh bear, timid Piglet, melancholy Eeyore, irrepressible Tigger, Kanga, baby Roo, and other friends of Christopher Robin.

Winnipeg   [win'-i-peg]   Winnipeg, a city in south central Canada, is the capital of the province of Manitoba. Located at the confluence of the Assiniboine River and the Red River of the North, the city lies 100 km (60 mi) north of the Minnesota border and has a population of 594,551 (1986). Excellent transportation facilities make modern Winnipeg a chief commercial, industrial, and distribution center for the prairie provinces. Industries include meat-packing, flour milling, brewing, and textile manufacturing. The University of Manitoba (1877) and its affiliates and the University of Winnipeg (1871) are located there. The city is known for the Royal Winnipeg Ballet and its symphony orchestra.

Established in 1738 as Fort Rouge by the French explorer Pierre Gaultier de Varennes, sieur de La Vérendrye, the site of Winnipeg was later settled (1812) by Scottish colonists as part of the Red River Settlement. The city was made provincial capital in 1870. With the arrival of the Canadian Pacific Railroad in 1885, Winnipeg became a major grain distribution center.

Winnipeg, Lake   Lake Winnipeg, the third largest lake entirely in Canada, is located in south central Manitoba about 72 km (45 mi) north of Winnipeg. It is 425 km (264 mi) long, up to 109 km (68 mi) wide, and covers an area of 24,389 km^2 (9,417 mi^2). The Saskatchewan, Red, and Winnipeg rivers feed into the lake; its outlet is the Nelson River, which drains northeastward into Hudson Bay. The first white to visit Lake Winnipeg was the fur trapper the sieur de La Vérendrye in the 1730s.

Winnipesaukee, Lake   [win-i-puh-saw'-kee]   Lake Winnipesaukee (named for an Indian word meaning "smile of the great spirit") in southern New Hampshire is about 40 km (25 mi) long and 20 km (12 mi) wide and covers 184 km^2 (71 mi^2). Its wooded shoreline and 274 islands make it a popular summer resort.

Winslow, Edward   Edward Winslow, b. Droitwich, England, Oct. 18, 1595, d. May 8, 1655, was a founder and leader of the PLYMOUTH COLONY and its most effective diplomat. A member of the PILGRIM community in Leiden, he helped arrange the passage of the group to America on the MAYFLOWER. In 1620 he negotiated a treaty with Indian chief MASSASOIT, and he subsequently went on several missions to secure supplies and establish fur-trading posts. He procured cattle on his first trip (1623–24) to England. During a later mission (1635), Archbishop William Laud imprisoned him for 17 weeks for his religious activities. Winslow was governor of the Plymouth Colony for three years (1633–34, 1636–37, 1644–45) and, except for those years, an assistant from 1624 to 1646. Winslow went to England in 1646 to defend the Massachusetts Bay Colony and never returned to New England.

Winslow, John Ancrum   John Ancrum Winslow, b. Wilmington, N.C., Nov. 19, 1811, d. Sept. 29, 1873, a Union naval officer, participated (1861–62) in operations on the upper Mississippi during the U.S. Civil War. Promoted to captain in 1862, he commanded (1863–64) the U.S.S. *Kearsarge* in pursuit of Confederate raiders in European waters. On June 19, 1864, the *Kearsarge* sank the notorious privateer *Alabama* (see ALABAMA, ship) off Cherbourg, France.

Winston-Salem   Winston-Salem, in the Piedmont of north central North Carolina, is the seat of Forsyth County and is the state's second largest city (1990 pop., 143,485). Although it has many diversified industries, the city's position as the state's foremost industrial center stems from its manufacture of tobacco products. Textiles, electronic equipment, clothing, and furniture are also produced. Winston-Salem is the home of Wake Forest University (1834), Winston-Salem State University (1892), and Salem Academy and College (1772). The southern headquarters of the Moravian Church in America is located in the city.

Winston-Salem was created when two communities were united in 1913. Salem, first settled in 1766 by members of the Moravian Church from Pennsylvania, grew as a religious, cultural, and trade center. Winston was established in 1849 as the county seat; in 1875, R. J. Reynolds founded a factory there that expanded to become the world's largest cigarette manufacturing plant.

Winter Palace   The Winter Palace (Russian: Zimniy Dvorets), principal residence of the Russian tsars from 1762 to 1917, was built in Saint Petersburg (now Leningrad) during a period of 50 years. Begun in 1711 at the order of Peter the Great, the original Dutch-style structure was replaced (1716) by a simple two-story building designed by the German architect Johan Mattarnovy. The Swiss-Italian architect Domenico Tressini later enlarged this second palace. Bartolommeo RASTRELLI gave the Winter Palace its final design (completed 1762), although work continued well into the 19th century. The immense scale, Italianate features, and brilliant color of Rastrelli's palace are typically Russian baroque. The present interiors date from a 19th-century restoration by the architect A. P. Briullov, undertaken as the result of a severe fire (1837). The Winter Palace complex houses the vast HERMITAGE MUSEUM, a storehouse of the artistic treasures accumulated by the tsars.

winterberry   Winterberry is the common name for several evergreen or deciduous shrubs or small trees in the genus *Ilex* of the holly family, Aquifoliaceae. These plants have conspicuous red, white, black, or yellow berries that persist through winter. Mountain winterberry, *I. ambigua* var. *montana*, is found in mountainous areas of the eastern United States and has lanceolate leaves with marginal teeth; the shrub produces red berries. The common winterberry, *I. verticillata*, is native to eastern North America and grows in swampy, acidic soils.

wintergreen   Wintergreen is the common name for 8 species of evergreen herbs of the genus *Chimaphila* and 12 species of *Pyrola,* both genera of the family Pyrolaceae, and most notably *Gaultheria procumbens* of the family Ericaceae. *Gaultheria* is the original source of oil of wintergreen.

Wintergreen G. procumbens yields spicy-tasting red berries, which are eaten by animals and birds during cold weather when other food is scarce. Oil of wintergreen is used as a flavoring in confectionary and pharmaceutical preparations.

Winter's Tale, The   SHAKESPEARE's tragicomedy *The Winter's Tale* (1610–11), one of the last plays he wrote, is among the poet's most mature works. The protagonist Leontes, king of Sicilia, unjustly accuses his admirable wife, Hermione, and good friend Polixenes, king of Bohemia, of adultery. Hermione is imprisoned, where she bears a daughter (Perdita), and is then reported dead to Leontes, who begins a long period of grief. With various subplots, the action moves between Sicilia and Bohemia, to be resolved with a reuniting of king and queen. Replete with echoes of many of Shakespeare's other plays, *The Winter's Tale* is at once Christian and pagan, romantic and realistic. It is thematically complex as well, examining innocence and play, jealousy and love, fancy and imagination. The principal plot source is Robert Greene's prose romance *Pandosto: The Triumph of Time* (1588).

Winterthur   [vin'-tur-toor]   Winterthur (1987 est. pop., 84,548) is an industrial and commercial center located in Zurich canton, northeastern Switzerland. Textiles, locomotives, and machinery are major products. The largest technological college in Switzerland is found there. Historic landmarks include the Church of Sankt Laurenz (1264) and the town hall, which dates from the 1780s.

Founded by the counts of Kyburg about 1180, Winterthur passed to the Habsburgs in 1264 and remained under their influence until 1467, when it was sold to Zurich.

Winthrop   (family)   The Winthrops of New England were among colonial America's foremost political leaders and scientists. **John Winthrop**, b. Jan. 12, 1588, d. Mar. 26, 1649, country squire and lawyer in Suffolk, England, was a founder of the MASSACHUSETTS BAY COMPANY. In 1630 he left for Massachusetts with the first major group of Puritan emigrants. Winthrop was often elected the colony's governor (1629–33, 1637–40, 1642–44, 1646–49) and had the greatest influence in shaping the settlement into a Bible Commonwealth. He was also deputy governor for ten years. His *Journal* (1630–49) is the major source of knowledge of the colony's early years. His eldest son, also called **John Winthrop**, b. England, Feb. 12, 1606, d. Apr. 5, 1676, founded Ipswich, Mass. (1633), and Saybrook (1635) and New London (1646), Conn. In 1662, while governor of Connecticut (1657, 1659–76), he obtained from Charles II a royal charter uniting the colonies of Connecticut and New Haven. Interested in chemistry and astronomy, he was the first American admitted to the Royal Society of London.

In 1693, John Jr.'s son, **Fitz-John Winthrop**, b. Ipswich, Mass., Mar. 14, 1638, d. Nov. 27, 1707, convinced William III to reaffirm Connecticut's charter, which had been questioned, and was subsequently the colony's governor (1698–1707).

John Winthrop, b. Boston, Dec. 19, 1714, d. May 3, 1779, a great-great-grandson of the first John Winthrop, was a leading American scientist of the 18th century. Hollis professor of mathematics and natural philosophy at Harvard (1738–79), he introduced (1751) the study of calculus there. Winthrop built the first experimental physics laboratory in America (1746), made significant astronomical observations, and was elected to the Royal Society of London (1766).

wire

wire Wire is a usually flexible metal rod or thread of uniform diameter. It has many uses, particularly in electrical wire and cable applications; in medical, farming, and industrial tools; and in hardware such as bolts, nails, nuts, screws, rivets, and needles. In construction, steel-wire cables are used to reinforce suspension bridges. Wire is also used in more delicate apparatuses, such as stringed instruments and watch springs.

Production. Wire is made by "drawing out" metals such as copper, iron, brass, aluminum, gold, silver, and platinum. In wire drawing, the metal is first heated and then run through a series of rollers that press it into thin rods. The rods are then coiled by machine, allowed to cool, cleaned with sulfuric acid or other chemicals, neutralized, and lubricated, followed by reheating to alleviate brittleness. They reach their final form by being drawn through a series of progressively smaller holes, known as dies, which reduce their diameters and increase their lengths. The finished wire is then wound around a rotating drum.

History. Wire was used as an ornament by the Egyptians as early as 3000 BC. Although the Romans used perforated pieces of iron as drawing dies, until the Middle Ages wire drawing was largely done by hand; the resulting threads had to be hammered and joined to each other to produce wire of a desired length. The first mechanical wire-drawing equipment was developed (c.1350) by Rudolf of Nuremberg.

Because of the Industrial Revolution, the demand for cable suspension bridges, the telegraph, the telephone, and the electric light, as well as the growing demand for fencing and barbed wire, spurred production of greater lengths and strengths of wiring. In this century, carbide drawing dies were developed that could withstand high speed and long wear and provide increased accuracy. With a die capable of standing up to the drawing of greater quantities of wire at the desired gauge through a single hole, machines that drew continuously came to the fore.

Advanced welding techniques now allow long, continuous coils of rod and wire to be drawn.

wirehaired pointing griffon

wirehaired pointing griffon The wirehaired pointing griffon, a dog resembling the German wirehaired pointer, is somewhat smaller (50 to 60 cm/19.5 to 23.5 in) and thicker-set. The coat is harsh and steel gray with chestnut splotches. The breed is Dutch in origin but French in development. Examples of the breed were shown in the United States in the 1880s but never became popular. These dogs have excellent scenting and retrieving characteristics and are slow, deliberate workers in the field.

wiretapping

wiretapping Wiretapping, also called bugging, traditionally refers to the secret tapping of a telephone or telegraph line in order to eavesdrop on another person. The term now has been expanded, however, to include other forms of electronic surveillance. Radio transmitters with integrated microcircuits have been made small enough to permit their insertion into bits of cardboard or behind wallpaper. More recently, the laser technique of focusing light beams on the tapped party has permitted monitoring ordinary voices from miles away.

Wiretapping is used in international espionage; in personal lawsuits (especially in divorce actions); to gain market information; and especially by law-enforcement officers. Innocent people, however, can be victimized, harmed, and embarrassed by wiretapping. In the United States the practice has been attacked as an invasion of privacy (see PRIVACY, INVASION OF). Wiretapping has been regarded as a kind of unreasonable search (unconstitutional under the 4th Amendment) and as a method that, in effect, compels one to testify against oneself (which is also constitutionally prohibited under the 5th Amendment).

In its first ruling on a wiretap case the U.S. Supreme Court held in *Olmstead* v. *United States* (1928) that police wiretapping was not a violation of the 4th Amendment's ban on unreasonable search and seizure. In his famous dissent, however, Associate Justice Oliver Wendell Holmes, Jr., called the practice a "dirty business" and said that the government had no business resorting to it. In the Communications Act of 1934 the Congress outlawed wiretapping, which made evidence garnered by bugging inadmissible in court. Subsequently, several states passed laws that permitted law-enforcement officials to gather evidence against potential criminals by wiretapping. In 1967, however, the Supreme Court ruled, in *Katz* v. *United States,* that wiretapping does violate 4th Amendment rights, in effect reversing the *Olmstead* ruling. The Crime Control Act of 1968 provides a carefully drawn system for judicially approved wiretapping. Since then the Court has ruled that court orders must be obtained even in cases involving national security.

Wisconsin

Wisconsin Wisconsin is located in the northern interior of the United States in the upper Midwest. It is bounded on the north by Lake Superior and the Upper Peninsula of Michigan, on the south by Illinois, on the west by Iowa and Minnesota, and on the east by Lake Michigan. Wisconsin extends about 475 km (295 mi) east to west at its widest point, and about 515 km (320 mi) north to south. The state took its name from its principal river, the Wisconsin, whose name had been derived from an Ojibwa Indian word thought to mean "gathering of the waters." Wisconsin's nickname, the Badger State, comes not from the wild animal of that name, but from the nickname given to lead miners of the 1830s who burrowed into hillsides looking for shallow deposits of ore.

Wisconsin ranks 16th (1990) in population among the 50 states, and ranks 13th in the value of its manufacturing. As urbanized as the state has become, Wisconsin remains the nation's leading dairy state—accounting for almost 17% (1988) of U.S. milk and about half of U.S. cheese production—and it is a leader in the production of green peas, string beans, and sweet corn.

AT A GLANCE

WISCONSIN

Land: Area: 169,653 km^2 (65,503 mi^2); rank: 23d. Capital: Madison (1990 pop., 191,262). Largest city: Milwaukee (1990 pop., 628,088). Counties: 72. Elevations: highest—595 m (1,951 ft), at Timms Hill; lowest—177 m (581 ft), at Lake Michigan.

People: Population (1990): 4,906,745; rank: 16th; density: 28.8 persons per km^2 (74.7 per mi^2). Distribution (1990): 65.7% urban, 34.3% rural. Average annual change (1980–90): +0.42%.

Government (1993): Governor: Tommy G. Thompson, Republican. U.S. Congress: Senate—2 Democrats; House—4 Democrats, 5 Republicans. Electoral college votes: 11. State legislature: 33 senators, 99 representatives.

Economy: State personal income (1989): $80.1 billion; rank: 18th. Median family income (1989): $35,082; rank: 19th. Agriculture: income (1989)—$5.3 billion. Lumber production (1991): 511 million board feet. Mining (nonfuel): value (1988)—$205 million. Manufacturing: value added (1987)—$31.7 billion. Services: value (1987)—$16 billion.

Miscellany: Statehood: May 29, 1848; the 30th state. Nickname: Badger State; tree: sugar maple; motto: Forward; song: "On, Wisconsin!"

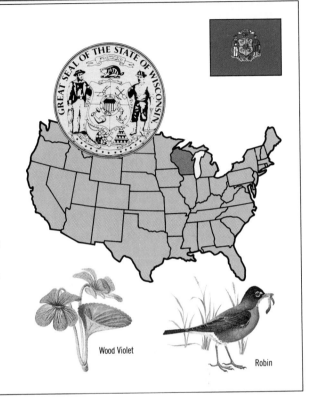

Wood Violet

Robin

Land and Resources

Wisconsin may be divided into five physiographic regions: the Lake Superior lowland; the northern highland; the central sandy plain; the western upland, extending across the southwestern portion of Wisconsin; and the eastern ridges and lowlands.

The Lake Superior lowland is a level to gently rolling red clay plain along Lake Superior in the northwestern corner of the state. The northern highland extends south from the Lake Superior lowland and covers the northern third of the state. It consists essentially of a gently rolling glaciated plain of low local relief, although Rib Mountain towers about 250 m (800 ft) above the city of Wausau in Marathon County, and the state's highest point, Timm's Hill, at 595 m (1,952 ft), is located in southeastern Price County. In the crescent-shaped central sandy plain, edging along the southern margin of the northern highland, local relief varies from the flattish beds of ancient glacial lakes to rolling glacial moraines and, in a few western sections, scattered mesas and buttes.

The western upland, in the southwest, contains some of Wisconsin's roughest landscape. Glaciation covered little of the region, so mature river systems have had millions of years to cut an intricate, hilly landscape. By contrast, the eastern ridges and lowlands region has low relief because of recent glaciation, but occasional moraines of up to 100 m (300 ft) mark places where glacial lobes stopped prior to withdrawal.

Soils. The Lake Superior lowland contains iron-rich soils of fair to good fertility. The northern highland and central sandy plain contain mostly gravelly or sandy soils interspersed with claylike mucklands. Because of the steep terrain, deep soil deposits in the western upland are limited to valley bottoms and broad ridge tops. The eastern ridges and lowlands have some of the state's most fertile soils; the land is of limestone origin.

Drainage. The MISSISSIPPI RIVER flows along most of Wisconsin's western border with Minnesota and Iowa. About 30% of Wisconsin lies within the GREAT LAKES drainage basin and about 70% is within the basin of the Mississippi River. The highland area of northern Wisconsin is the source for most of the state's seven major drainage systems. The principal ones are the Wisconsin River, which begins on the Michigan-Wisconsin border and empties into the Mississippi just below Prairie du Chien; the Chippewa-Flambeau, which drains the northwest interior and also empties into the Mississippi; and the Wolf-Fox river system, which empties into GREEN BAY and thence into Lake MICHIGAN.

About 8,500 interior lakes, most of them in the north and east, cover more than 4,000 km² (1,500 mi²). Lake WINNEBAGO, Wisconsin's largest lake, has an area of 557 km² (215 mi²); Green Lake, the state's deepest lake, reaches 72 m (236 ft).

Climate. Mild to warm summers and cold, snowy winters characterize Wisconsin's humid, continental climate. Average July temperatures range from 18° C (65° F) in the north to 24° C (75° F) in the south; January temperatures vary between –14° C (7° F) and –4° C (24° F). Lakes Michigan and Superior exert a moderating influence during both the summer and winter. Precipitation averages 760 mm (30 in) statewide.

Vegetation and Animal Life. By the early 1920s most of Wisconsin's vegetation had been removed by lumbering or deliberate burning to clear land for farming. Today, however, developing young forests—mostly in the north and consisting of aspen, oak, maple, and birch—cover 42% of the state.

The buffalo and the passenger pigeon did not survive the 19th-century pioneers; even the marten, fisher, and timber wolf disappeared for a time. Conservation agencies have had some success reintroducing the wild turkey, and prairie chickens would be gone had it not been for the formation of a society dedicated to their survival. The coyote has recently moved into the state. As a result of careful management, white-tailed deer are more numerous today than ever. Skunk, fox (red and gray), and various species of rabbit seem to go through population cycles independent of human influences.

Resources and Environment. Drought—especially in summer—is a serious problem in Wisconsin. In some areas even enough water for human consumption may be lacking for weeks or months.

Most of the state's important commercial minerals are nonmetallic—sand, gravel, and building stone. Iron and zinc-lead ores are mined, but the vast quantities of copper and zinc discovered in the north remain unexploited. Wisconsin's commercial forests—97% of the total forest—cover about 58,800 km² (22,700 mi²), but little is harvested. State regulation of natural resources began in 1867 when a forest commission was established.

People

Of the five eastern north central states—Illinois, Indiana, Michigan, Ohio, and Wisconsin—Wisconsin is the least populous, as well as the least densely populated. Yet Wisconsin has been growing faster than any of the other four states. Generally, southeastern Wisconsin has the highest density, and the wooded north has the lowest. The major cities are MILWAUKEE, MADISON (the capital), RACINE, GREEN BAY, KENOSHA, APPLETON, SHEBOYGAN, OSHKOSH, and LA CROSSE; all, except for La Crosse, are in the southeastern quadrant of the state. Until recently the migration trend within Wisconsin was from rural to urban areas and from older city centers to newer suburban areas. Recently, however, some reversal of this trend has occurred in the state.

African Americans constitute the largest minority in the state and make up nearly one-fourth of the population of the city of Milwaukee. Other minority groups in the state are Hispanics and American Indians. Of the white majority, of European origin, more than 20 groups are represented, the largest of which are those of German, Scandinavian, Slavic, English, and Irish descent. The largest religious groups in Wisconsin are Roman Catholics and Lutherans. Other principal denominations include Methodists, the United Church of Christ, Baptists, and Presbyterians.

Education. Wisconsin's 1848 constitution provided for free public education, and in 1911 the first system of vocational, technical, and adult education in the nation was enacted by the Wisconsin legislature. The University of Wisconsin system (see WISCONSIN, UNIVERSITY OF) includes all public institutions of higher education in the state. Wisconsin's private colleges and universities include Beloit College (1846), Lawrence University (1847), and Marquette University (1857).

Culture. Leading museums include the Milwaukee Public Museum and the State Historical Society at Madison. The Milwaukee Art Center possesses an outstanding collection of 20th-century art, and the Milwaukee Symphony has achieved national recognition. The Milwaukee Repertory Theater, Ballet Company, and Florentine Opera, as well as the Symphony, all perform from the city's Performing Arts Center. Specialized museums include the Circus World Museum in Baraboo and the National Railroad Museum in Green Bay.

Historical Sites. Built in 1926, Little Norway, near Mount Horeb, re-creates an early 19th-century Norwegian village. The Villa Louis (built 1843) at Prairie du Chien was the home of Hercules L. Dousman, a fur trader. The Roi-Porlier-Tank Cottage (erected 1776) in Green Bay is the oldest standing building in the state.

Communications. Leading newspapers in the state are the *Milwaukee Journal,* the *Milwaukee Sentinel,* the *Green Bay Press Gazette,* and the *Wisconsin State Journal* in Madison. The state is also served by numerous commercial and educational radio and television stations and by various television cable systems.

Economic Activity

Manufacturing is Wisconsin's single most important economic activity. In the early 1980s, however, an economic slump caused a permanent loss of some manufacturing jobs in the state. Economic growth areas since that time have been in service industries. Farming, particularly dairying, traditionally has been important to the state's economy and remains significant.

Agriculture, Forestry, and Fishing. About 80% of the agricultural receipts comes from livestock (cattle, hogs) and livestock products, especially milk and cheese. Leading field crops include corn, hay, oats, barley, soybeans, tobacco, and wheat. Wisconsin also is a large producer of vegetables and fruits, including potatoes, and sweet corn, beets, green peas, snap beans, cabbage, carrots, lima beans, cranberries, cherries, apples, and cucumbers.

In most years only small numbers of people are employed in logging camps or by logging contractors. Far more people, however, work in forest-based manufacturing in-

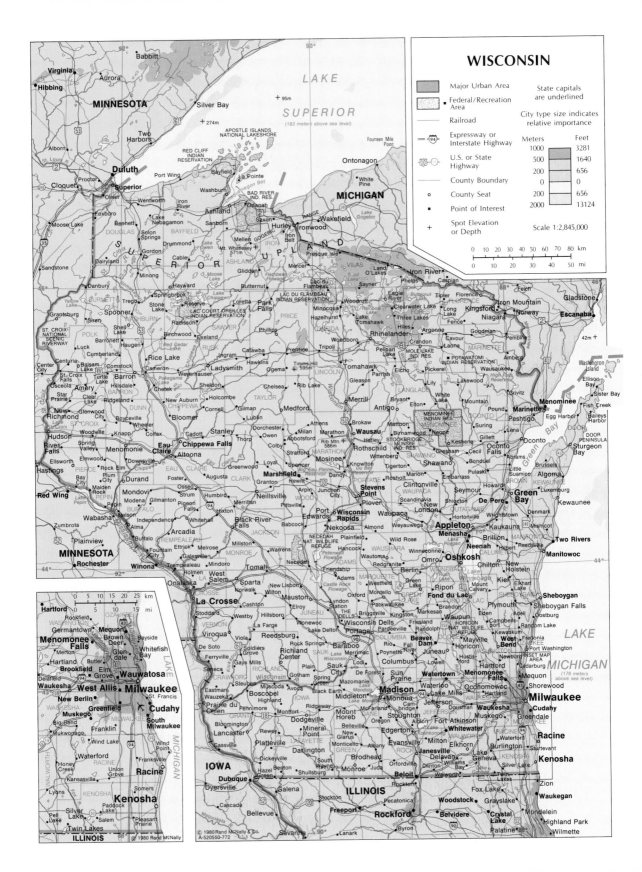

WISCONSIN

Major Urban Area

Federal/Recreation Area

Railroad

Expressway or Interstate Highway

U.S. or State Highway

County Boundary

County Seat

Point of Interest

Spot Elevation or Depth

State capitals are underlined

City type size indicates relative importance

Meters	Feet
1000	3281
500	1640
200	656
0	0
200	656
2000	13124

Scale 1:2,845,000

0 10 20 30 40 50 60 70 80 km
0 10 20 30 40 50 mi

© 1980 Rand McNally & Co.
A-520550-772

dustries, and the value of wood products made in Wisconsin far exceeds that of the state's lumber production.

Because of pollution, overfishing, and the depredations of the sea lamprey, the state's commercial fishing industry, located primarily along lakes Michigan and Superior, has been in decline since 1945. Sport fishing, however, thrives in the state.

Mining. Mineral production is of minor significance to Wisconsin's economy. The most important minerals are sand and gravel, stone, and iron ore.

Manufacturing and Energy. Wisconsin is an important industrial state. Among its leading products are nonelectrical machinery, food products, paper products, fabricated metal products, and transportation equipment. The main area of industrial activity is in the southeastern part of the state, particularly the Milwaukee metropolitan area. Major paper-production areas are in the Fox River and Wisconsin River valleys. Wisconsin is also a leading beer-producing state. Milwaukee has long been a major brewery center, and there is also beer production in La Crosse. Most of Wisconsin's coal, oil, and natural gas come from sources outside the state. The state's energy needs are supplied by steam-generating plants, hydroelectric power plants, and nuclear power.

Tourism. Wisconsin's travel and recreation industry is one of the state's major sources of income. The famous Wisconsin Dells draws many visitors to that scenic region of the state, and deer, rabbit, and squirrel attract numerous hunters each fall. The state's many lakes are used for boating, camping, fishing, and waterskiing. Chequamegon and Nicolet national forests cover extensive areas in northern Wisconsin. The Apostle Islands in Lake Michigan and the adjacent coastline are designated a national lakeshore; two separate areas of the Saint Croix River are national scenic river sites shared with Minnesota.

Transportation. Wisconsin's major interstate highways are I-90 and I-94, which cross the state in a northwest-southeasterly direction. Milwaukee's Mitchell Field is the busiest of the state's airports. Airlines also serve Green Bay, Madison, and other Wisconsin cities. Most of Wisconsin's cities and villages receive railway freight service, and Amtrak provides passenger service to some Wisconsin cities.

Wisconsin ports, including Milwaukee, Green Bay, and Superior, handle significant water-traffic tonnage on the Great Lakes. The Mississippi River remains an important route for barges navigating from Minnesota to the Gulf of Mexico. Wisconsin has barge ports at Alma, La Crosse, Prairie du Chien, and Cassville.

Government and Politics

Wisconsin has had the same constitution ever since becoming a state in 1848, although it has been amended. The governor serves a 4-year term and can be reelected indefinitely. The legislature comprises a senate, whose 33 members hold office for 4 years, and an assembly, whose 99 members serve 2-year terms. Wisconsin's judicial system ascends to a supreme court composed of 7 justices elected to 10-year terms.

The Republican party dominated Wisconsin politics during the second half of the 19th century. During the first two decades of the 20th century, however, Robert M. LA FOLLETTE and his Progressive movement held center stage. Since that time Republicans and Democrats have been in the ascendancy by turns. This holds true for presidential and congressional elections in Wisconsin as well as for local contests.

History

Skilled big-game hunters arrived in Wisconsin 13,000 to 14,000 years ago. About 6,000 years ago, the so-called Old Copper Indians lived in pole-frame structures covered with hides or bark. Early Woodland cultures (see MOUND BUILDERS) occupied portions of the state by about 600 BC. The Middle Woodland or Hopewell people arrived from the south about 100 BC. Overlapping in time with the Hopewell in southern Wisconsin, the Effigy Mound Builders left behind spectacular burial mounds, such as one near Madison that is in the form of a huge bird 2 m (6 ft) high with a wingspread of 190 m (624 ft).

The erosional action of the Wisconsin River has carved out the Wisconsin Dells, whose sandstone cliffs and rock formations reach about 46 m (150 ft) above the river.

Cheddar cheese is produced at the Lake to Lake Dairy Cooperative plant in Kiel. Cooperatives, which developed during the late 19th century, were a key factor in the growth of Wisconsin's dairy industry.

By AD 1000, ancestors of the WINNEBAGO settled near Oshkosh and Platteville. By the time the first Europeans arrived during the 17th century, they found FOX, HURON, ILLINOIS, KICKAPOO, MENOMINEE, MIAMI, OJIBWA, OTTAWA, POTAWATOMI, SAUK, and SIOUX, as well as the Winnebago.

European Period. The Frenchman Jean NICOLET, the first European to visit Wisconsin, arrived in the Green Bay area in 1634 to extend the fur trade. By 1665 the western Great Lakes basin was occupied by several hundred French fur traders, including Pierre Esprit RADISSON and Médard Groseilliers, who subsequently set up the field base for what would later become the HUDSON'S BAY COMPANY. The Jesuit priest Claude Jean ALLOUEZ established a mission at De Pere, just south of Green Bay, in 1671; also during the 1670s, Jacques MARQUETTE and Louis JOLLIET explored the upper Mississippi River region.

Beginning about 1735, French and Indian raiders, led by Charles Michel de LANGLADE, attacked the British along the Appalachian Mountains. Even before the last of the French and Indian Wars was over in 1763, however, the British had occupied former French outposts in Wisconsin. Twenty years later, following the American Revolution, possession of Wisconsin passed to the United States; it was not until shortly after the War of 1812, however, that the federal government garrisoned a post in the state.

Territory and State. To protect Wisconsin's growing number of American settlers, the federal government began, in 1817, to build Forts Howard (Green Bay), Crawford (Prairie du Chien), and Winnebago (Portage). From 1818 to 1836, Wisconsin was administered as part of the territory of Michigan. A lead rush to the southwestern corner of Wisconsin encouraged Congress to grant separate territorial status on July 4, 1836. Belmont, a small crossroads village in Lafayette County, was chosen as the seat of the first territorial legislature. Present-day Madison was later chosen as the permanent territorial capital.

Another influx of immigrants between 1840 and 1850, much of it into eastern Wisconsin, increased the population of the territory tenfold to 305,000. On May 29, 1848, Wisconsin became the 30th state.

Wisconsin saw its population burgeon during the 1850s to more than 700,000. During that decade nearly 300,000 immigrants entered the state, 45% of them from Germany.

The Civil War interrupted Wisconsin's economic growth. The frontier of settlement remained virtually unchanged from 1860 to 1870. The next decade, however, saw farming expand northward. After the mid-1870s some farmers turned to dairying, at first concentrating on butter but later on cheese, because it spoiled less easily. Next to agriculture, lumbering was the state's leading industry from 1890 to 1910.

Twentieth Century. A population that was 60% rural in 1900 was more than half urban by the time the Depression of the 1930s struck. World War II cut unemployment and increased wages but brought new problems in its wake. Greater industrialization has depleted natural resources and has created pollutants that threaten tourism and dairy farming.

The thousands of blacks that have come to Wisconsin since 1945 suffer disproportionately from poor housing, high unemployment, and other social ills. In the early 1960s the federal government, believing that Indians would benefit from an end to reservations, made the Menominee Indian reservation Wisconsin's 72d county. When this experiment turned out to be a failure, reservation status was restored by Congress in 1973.

Wisconsin, University of The University of Wisconsin was founded in Madison, Wis., in 1849 as a coeducational land-grant and sea-grant institution. It has colleges of letters and science, engineering, and agriculture and life sciences, which grant bachelor's, master's, and doctoral degrees, and schools of law, medicine, education, journalism, nursing, pharmacy, social work, and business.

The university also has campuses in Milwaukee, Green Bay, and Parkside, which were joined in 1971 by the nine state universities—Eau Claire, La Crosse, Oshkosh, Platteville, River Falls, Stevens Point, Superior, Whitewater, and Stout. In addition to the 13 senior colleges there are 14 community colleges.

Wisdom, John Arthur John Terrence Dibben Wisdom, b. 1904, is one of the leading philosophers of the analytic school that developed in England in the 1920s. Educated at Cambridge University, Wisdom was influenced by Bertrand Russell and G. E. Moore. As a fellow of Trinity College at Cambridge, Wisdom became associated with Ludwig Wittgenstein, who had a permanent and profound effect on his thinking.

With the paper "Philosophical Perplexity" (1936), Wisdom began to evolve a critique of philosophical method derived from Wittgenstein. This view of philosophy in terms of engaging in discourse rather than putting forward theories has been influential in many areas of contemporary philosophy. Wisdom, however, has had the greatest influence in the philosophy of religion, primarily through his article "Gods" (1945).

Wisdom, Book of   Wisdom, a defense of the Jewish way of life, is one of the books of the APOCRYPHA; in the Septuagint and Vulgate it is included in the Old Testament. The book is ascribed to King SOLOMON and stands in the same intellectual tradition as such earlier collections of proverbial wisdom as Proverbs and the Book of Sirach—hence its full title, the Wisdom of Solomon. The work was actually written in Greek about 75 BC or perhaps as late as AD 40. Its author was an Alexandrian Jew who was attempting to strengthen the religious commitment of the Hellenistic Jewish community and, if possible, to convert the Gentiles.

Wise, Isaac Mayer   A product of the German Jewish Enlightenment, Rabbi Isaac Mayer Wise, b. Steingrub, Bohemia, Mar. 29, 1819, d. Mar. 26, 1900, was the leading force in American Reform Judaism for a half-century. Immigrating to the United States in 1846, he served eight years in an Albany, N.Y., congregation before moving (1854) to Cincinnati, Ohio. There he helped organize the Union of American Hebrew Congregations (1873), Hebrew Union College (1875), and the Central Conference of American Rabbis (1889)—all of which he served as president until his death.

Wise held that Judaism is a rational religion that should not be bound by archaic Halakhic laws. He eliminated two-day holidays, skullcaps, and much Hebrew from Reform liturgy and introduced choirs, organs, Sunday service, and sermons.

Wise, John   American Congregational clergyman John Wise, b. Roxbury, Mass., August 1652, d. Apr. 8, 1725, has been called the first great American democrat. As minister of the Chebacco church in Ipswich, Mass., he led resistance to a provincial tax imposed (1687) by the administration of Sir Edmund Andros, urged moderation during the Salem Witch Trials (1692), and articulated democratic ideas about civil and ecclesiastical government. In *A Vindication of the Government of New-England Churches* (1717), Wise praised Congregationalism for basing itself on democratic principles in accord with natural law and right reason.

Wise, Stephen Samuel   Rabbi Stephen Samuel Wise, b. Budapest, Hungary, Mar. 17, 1874, d. Apr. 19, 1949, was one of the most influential Jewish leaders in the United States during World War II. After serving (1900–06) a congregation in Portland, Oreg., he went to New York City, where he established (1907) the Free Synagogue and became active as a reformer in city politics. Soon the foremost spokesperson for Reform Judaism, Wise quickly organized (1916) the American Jewish Congress in response to pogroms in eastern Poland. He

was the first to propose, in 1933, a total boycott of German goods in the United States in retaliation for Nazi oppression of Jews.

Wise Men, Three   see MAGI

Wiseman, Fred   A former lawyer and professor, Frederick Wiseman, b. Boston, Jan. 1, 1930, makes controversial documentary films about public, tax-supported institutions, through which he reveals the more general attitudes of U.S. society. His free-form, nonnarrative method involves filming hours of undirected footage and subsequently creating a structure through extensive editing. Wiseman made his first film, *Titicut Follies* (1967), at a Massachusetts institution for the criminally insane; his later films include *High School* (1968); *Law and Order* (1969), about the police; *Hospital* (1970); *Welfare* (1975); *Blind* and *Deaf* (both 1986); and *Missile* (1989)

Wister, Owen   The American writer Owen Wister, b. Philadelphia, July 14, 1860, d. July 21, 1938, was an easterner who, like his friend Theodore Roosevelt, came to love the American West. His famous novel *The Virginian* (1902) successfully combines local color, frontier humor, and adventure and contains the brave and reticent hero who became the model for the popular image of the cowboy. The novel inspired a successful stage play, three films (1914, 1929, 1946), and a television series (1962–69). Wister's collections of stories include *Lin McLean* (1898) and *The Jimmyjohn Boss* (1900).

wisteria [wis-tir'-ee-uh]   *Wisteria* is the generic and common name for 9 or 10 species of woody lianas in the pea family, Leguminosae. Native to temperate Asia and North America, they are grown extensively as ornamental vines. The twining stems support alternate leaves and small, attractive, pea-shaped flowers.

Wisteria in bloom adds an old-fashioned, delicate appearance to a garden, a fence, or a wall. Its mildly scented flowers hang in long clusters from branches.

wit The complexity of the term *wit*, derived from Old English *witan*, "to know," is suggested by C. S. Lewis's judgment that "if a man had time to study one word only, 'wit' would perhaps be the best word he could choose." Its general reference is to mental capacity. It is used in that sense in the derogatory term *half-wit*, as well as in the question "Have you lost your wits?" The plural form originated in theories of faculty psychology, in which the interior faculties (common sense, imagination, memory, reason, and fancy) were called wits. The modern sense of wit has been developed over centuries of English and American writing, ranging from John Donne's poetry to H. L. Mencken's mordant essays.

During the 17th century, *wit* became a critical term, equivalent to the current word *genius*, and was used to translate the Latin *ingenium* and the French *esprit* and *génie*. Wit was associated more with imagination (poetry) than with judgment (reason and facts). The qualities associated with the term were held in lower regard by the end of the century, largely as a result of the acceptance of the associative psychology of Thomas Hobbes (in *Leviathan*, 1651) and John Locke (*Essay Concerning Human Understanding*, vol. 1, 1690). To them, judgment (the scientific or historical faculty) discerned differences between things or facts that are similar. Wit (the poetic faculty), using memory or fancy, discovered similarities between things or ideas that are different. Indeed, by the early 19th century, wit often implied mere cleverness, particularly verbal, a meaning that had always existed parallel to the critical meanings.

In modern critical writing the kind of wit that is meant is usually qualified, for example, as *metaphysical, trenchant*, or *satirical*. The adjectives *romantic* or *Victorian* would not be used to characterize wit because neither contains the idea of the conscious manipulation of words and ideas in a clever way, often with satiric intent, and always with the purpose of causing delight. An epigram by Alexander Pope concerning the collar of the king's dog is witty: "I am his Highness' dog at Kew;/Pray tell me Sir, whose dog are you?" The wit here comes from the play on the word *dog*.

One of the finest and most illuminating examples of wit can be found in act 1 of Oscar Wilde's *The Importance of Being Earnest* (1895). If *witty* is substituted for its synonym *clever*, the following lines constitute an accurate definition of wit, with its emphasis on phrasing (style) and verbal play, its cynicism and its unexpectedness:

Algernon: All women become like their mothers. That is their tragedy. No man does. That's his.
Jack: Is that clever [witty]?
Algernon: It is perfectly phrased! and quite as true as any observation in civilized life should be.
See also: COMEDY; EPIGRAM.

witch doctor see SHAMAN

witch hazel Witch hazel is the common name for about 100 species of trees and shrubs in the family Hamamelidaceae but is most commonly applied to *Hamamelis virginiana*. This shrub or small tree is usually found in moist soils along streams from New Brunswick to Iowa and south to Arkansas and Florida, where it may grow up to 9 m (30 ft) tall.

Leaves are alternate with widely spaced marginal teeth and grow up to 15 cm (6 in) long and 8 cm (3 in) wide. Foliage is a dull green above and lighter below, with hair on the midrib and veins. Flowers are yellow with thin, elongated petals and produce a two-valved, woody capsule that splits and ejects the black seeds when mature.

An alcoholic extract made from the leaves and bark is used on bruises and inflammations and as a rubbing lotion.

witchcraft In the modern world, witchcraft is a form of nature religion that emphasizes the healing arts. The term is also applied to various kinds of MAGIC practiced in Asian, African, and Latin American communities.

In traditional European society, however, witchcraft was believed to be a kind of harmful sorcery associated with the worship of Satan, or the devil (in Christian belief, a spirit hostile to God).

Witches were blamed for causing lingering illnesses or death to humans and domestic animals, sending demons into people's bodies, and destroying crops with hailstorms. They reputedly met together at gatherings called Sabbats, where they parodied Christian rituals, did obscene homage to the devil, and held bizarre orgies. Because of their pact with Satan, they were supposed to have a special mark or scar on their bodies that never bled or hurt when pricked by sharp instruments.

Geographically, the center of witch-hunting lay in Germany, Austria, and Switzerland, but few areas were left untouched by it. In southwestern Germany alone, more than 3,000 witches were executed between 1560 and 1680. In England, where torture was prohibited, only about 20 percent of accused witches were executed (by hanging); in Scotland, where torture was used, nearly half of all those put on trial were burned at the stake, and almost three times as many witches (1,350) were killed as in England. In the Dutch republic, no witches were executed after 1600, and none were tried after 1610. In Spain and Italy accusations of witchcraft were handled by the INQUISITION, and although torture was legal, only a dozen witches were burned out of 5,000 put on trial. Ireland apparently escaped witch trials altogether. Many witch trials were provoked, not by hysterical authorities or fanatical clergy but by village quarrels among neighbors. About 80 percent of all accused witches were women. Traditional theology assumed that women were weaker than men and more likely to succumb to the devil.

All these aspects of witchcraft crossed over to the Americas with European colonists. In the Spanish and French territories cases of witchcraft were under the jurisdiction of church courts, and no one suffered death on this charge. In the English colonies about 40 people were executed for witchcraft between 1650 and 1710, half of them in the famous SALEM WITCH TRIALS of 1692.

Witch trials declined in most parts of Europe after 1680; in England the death penalty for witchcraft was abolished in 1736. In the late 17th and early 18th centuries one last wave of witch persecution afflicted Poland and other areas of eastern Europe, but that ended by about 1740. The last legal execution of a witch occurred in Switzerland in 1782.

Beginning in the 1920s, witchcraft was revived in Europe and America by groups that considered it a surviving link with pre-Christian religious practices. This phenomenon was partly inspired by such books as Margaret Murray's *The Witch Cult in Western Europe* (1921). Some forms of modern witchcraft follow the traditions of medieval herbalists and lay healers.

witchweed Witchweed is the common name for about 50 species of parasitic plants constituting the genus *Striga* in the figwort family, Scrophulariaceae. About 10 species of witchweeds, native to the Old World tropics, may be parasitic on agricultural crops. One species, *S. lutea*, a red-flowered, annual herb native to India, was accidentally introduced into the United States and is now a problem in North and South Carolina.

The minute seeds of witchweed may lie dormant for 15 to 20 years. When a seed does germinate, the roots of the seedling seek and interconnect with the roots of a host plant, from which they draw water and nutrients. Even after emerging from the soil and producing leaves that photosynthesize food, the witchweed continues to draw from its host.

Plants of the figwort genus *Alectra* that are also sometimes called witchweeds are parasites in tropical areas.

Witherspoon, John The Scottish-American clergyman, political leader, and educator John Witherspoon, b. Scotland, Feb. 5, 1723, d. Nov. 15, 1794, served as president of Princeton University and was the only minister to sign the Declaration of Independence. Educated at the University of Edinburgh, Witherspoon was ordained a Presbyterian minister in 1743. In 1768 he went to America as president of the College of New Jersey (later Princeton University), a position he held until his death. He also served as New Jersey's representative to the Continental Congress from 1776 to 1782 (with brief interludes).

Witkiewicz, Stanisław Ignacy [vit'-kee-uh-vich] The Polish playwright and novelist Stanisław Ignacy Witkiewicz, b. Feb. 24, 1885, d. Sept. 18, 1939, is recognized as a major figure in European avant-garde literature. His plays—*Water Hen* (1922; Eng. trans., 1968), *Madman and the Nun* (1925; Eng. trans., 1968), and *Crazy Locomotive* (1923; Eng. trans., 1968)—present images of a world gone mad and heading for destruction. His antiutopian novel, *Insatiability* (1930; Eng. trans., 1977), portrays a decadent Europe succumbing to Chi-

nese communism. Witkiewicz also wrote on aesthetics, philosophy, and drug experimentation. He committed suicide when the Nazis invaded Poland.

witness A witness, in a court of law, is one who gives EVIDENCE or information under oath or affirmation. In order to testify, a witness usually must have first-hand (rather than hearsay) evidence of what occurred in order to provide testimony that is relevant and accurate. A witness must be considered competent in order to testify—that is, among other things, able to understand and remember what was witnessed and aware of what it means to offer testimony under oath. The 6th Amendment to the U.S. Constitution gives the accused the right to confront hostile witnesses and to compel (see SUBPOENA) the attendance of favorable witnesses. The Supreme Court extended these rights to state trials in 1965 and 1967 through the DUE PROCESS clause of the 14th Amendment. A witness, however, can never be compelled to give evidence that may be self-incriminating. Those who are accused cannot be required to give evidence in court or testify against themselves in a criminal prosecution, because compelling individuals to act as a witness against themselves would also violate the SELF-INCRIMINATION clause of the 5th Amendment. According to the common-law doctrine of privileged communications, lawyers of accused persons cannot be required to testify against those persons in regard to what they may have learned in their official capacities. The same privilege also usually extends to doctors, members of the jury, and spouses.

Witt, Johan de [vit] Johan de Witt, b. Sept. 25, 1625, d. Aug. 20, 1672, was the political leader of the Dutch Republic from 1653 to 1672. An opponent of the house of Orange, he was elected (1653) grand pensionary of Holland three years after the death of William II. De Witt stubbornly upheld government without stadholders, despite strong popular feeling for the young prince of Orange, William III (later King WILLIAM III of England). In 1654 de Witt took the United Provinces out of the disastrous first ANGLO-DUTCH WAR (1652–54). He defeated the British decisively during the second Anglo-Dutch War (1665–67), but he faced a combined French-English assault in 1672. After the French invaded the country in June of that year, de Witt was wounded in an assassination attempt, and he resigned in August, a month after William had been named stadholder. De Witt and his brother Cornelis were murdered by a pro-Orange mob.

Witt, Katarina [vit] (East) German figure skater Katarina Witt, b. Dec. 3, 1965, dominated her sport in the 1980s to an extent rivaled only by Sonja Henie in the 1930s. From 1983 to 1988 the graceful and expressive Witt, with flirtatiousness of style, captured 6 consecutive European championships, 4 world titles (1984–85, 1987–88), and 2 Olympic gold medals (1984, 1988).

Witte, Sergei Yulivich, Count   The Russian states-man Count Sergei Yulivich Witte, b. June 29 (N.S.), 1849, d. Mar. 13 (N.S.), 1915, was a gifted administra-tor who as minister of finance (1892–1903) used the state's resources to modernize the Russian economy. By establishing a protective tariff, creating a favorable bal-ance of trade, placing Russia on the gold standard, and attracting foreign investment, he engendered substantial industrial growth. He fared less well in attempting to re-form the peasant economy. Although he was dismissed as finance minister in 1903, Witte remained active and ne-gotiated the Treaty of Portsmouth ending the Russo-Japa-nese War in 1905. During the 1905 revolution he con-vinced Emperor Nicholas II to issue the October Manifes-to, which promised constitutional government. Witte then became prime minister (1905–06), but he proved so un-popular that Nicholas was forced to dismiss him.

Wittelsbach (family) [vit'-uhls-bahk]   The Wittelsbach family of Germany founded the dynasty that ruled Bavar-ia from 1180 to 1918. In 1180, Holy Roman Emperor Frederick I granted Otto VI, count of Scheyern, the duchy of Bavaria. He became Duke Otto I, the dynasty's founder. His grandson, Otto II, through marriage added (1214) the Rhenish Palatinate to his holdings. Duke Lou-is III, as Holy Roman Emperor Louis IV (r. 1314–47), brought the Wittelsbachs to their peak of power, but he also divided (1329) the succession between an elder branch, which inherited the Rhenish Palatinate and the Upper Palatinate (an area of northern Bavaria), and a younger branch, which received Bavaria. The former was given an electoral title in 1356.

During the Reformation the Bavarian branch champi-oned Roman Catholicism, and the Palatinate branch es-poused Protestantism. In the course of the Thirty Years' War, the Palatinate's electoral vote and the Upper Palati-nate were transferred (1623) to Bavaria under Duke Max-imilian, but another electoral vote was created for the Rhenish Palatinate in 1648.

Elector Charles Albert of Bavaria became Holy Roman Emperor Charles VII (1742–45), the only non-Habsburg emperor after 1438. The death of his son, Maximilian III, ended (1777) the younger line of Wittelsbachs, and in 1799 all the Wittelsbach lands—both the Palatinate and Bavaria—were reunited under Maximilian Joseph. In 1806 he became king of Bavaria as Maximilian I. The dy-nasty ended with Louis III, who abdicated when the Ba-varian monarchy was abolished in 1918.

Wittenberg [vit'-en-bairk]   Wittenberg is a city in east central Germany with a population of 53,560 (1987 est.). A rail center with an inland harbor on the Elbe River, the city lies between Berlin and Leipzig. Manufactures include machinery, chemicals, rubber, leather and paper products, clothing, and foodstuffs. The burial places of Protestant theologian Martin Luther and reformer Philipp Melanch-thon are located in the city. Wittenberg University, founded in 1502, is now part of the University of Halle (1817).

Chartered in 1293, Wittenberg was the residence of the electors of Saxony from the 13th to the 15th century. The Protestant Reformation started in Wittenberg in 1517 when Luther posted his 95 theses questioning Catholic doctrine there. Wittenberg became part of Prussia in 1815.

Wittgenstein, Ludwig [vit'-gen-shtyn]   Ludwig Jo-sef Johann Wittgenstein, b. Vienna, Apr. 26, 1889, d. Apr. 29, 1951, was one of the most original and influen-tial philosophers of the 20th century. He became inter-ested in the foundations of mathematics and studied (1912) with Bertrand Russell at Cambridge. Having given away a large inheritance, Wittgenstein taught elementary school from 1920 to 1926 in rural Austria and subse-quently served as gardener in a monastery near Vienna. In 1929 he returned to Cambridge, and in 1939 he was ap-pointed to the chair in philosophy formerly held by G. E. Moore. Wittgenstein wrote continually, and lecture notes, as well as dictated manuscripts, circulated widely, al-though often against his wishes.

Early Philosophy. In the *Tractatus Logico-Philosophi-cus* (1921), Wittgenstein claimed that the problems of philosophy arise when "the logic of our language is mis-understood." He also claimed to have given "on all essen-tial points, the final solution of the problems." Wittgen-stein thought he had provided this solution by analyzing the relation of language to the world, showing the bound-aries of what can intelligibly be said or thought. Central to his analysis is a theory of meaning, usually referred to as the picture theory. The picture theory states that simple objects exist, out of which complex ones are constructed. The relations of these objects to one another are repre-sented, or pictured, in language, and only what can be so pictured can be stated intelligibly. The nature of the pic-turing relationship cannot be stated; because it is not a fact or an object, it can only be shown. Even though the relation cannot be articulated, it is possible to see it, and

Ludwig Wittgenstein, an Austrian philoso-pher who taught at Cambridge Universi-ty, profoundly affect-ed the course of 20th-century philos-ophy with his analy-ses of language and meaning. His work influenced logical positivism and other developments in contemporary thought.

it must hold if language is to represent the way the world is. For Wittgenstein, therefore, the traditional problems of philosophy are not solved, but rather dissolved, because they arise from a failure to understand the picturing relations; consequently, the problems ask for answers to questions that are nonsensical.

Later Philosophy. Although the *Tractatus* retained considerable influence in LOGICAL POSITIVISM, it was Wittgenstein himself, in his later philosophy, who eventually produced the most devastating critique of his early work. He still viewed philosophical problems as arising in some way from confusion about language, and he still saw his work as a means of dissolving these problems. In the *Tractatus*, however, Wittgenstein had thought of language primarily as giving and manipulating the names of given objects. In his later work he considered this inadequate, because naming can take place only in the context of a developed language, for which there already exist rules for picking out objects, properly using names, and properly carrying out operations. The criteria for these activities, in turn, are to be found not in logic but in the actual practice of a language-using group. Thus, while his early philosophy equates meaning with representing, or picturing, the later philosophy sees meaning in terms of doing, of participating in what he calls a "language game." Wittgenstein held that any general theory of meaning would be inadequate to dispel philosophical perplexity and that the way to escape the bewitchment of the mind by language is to examine in detail how the language in question is used in the particular language game in which it is found.

Witwatersrand [wit'-wawt-urz-rand]   Witwatersrand, also The Rand, is a ridge about 240 km (150 mi) long, located in the Transvaal in northeastern South Africa. It is Africa's largest industrialized region and possesses the world's largest goldfield. It centers on JOHANNESBURG and extends east and west to form a nearly continuously urbanized area that also includes the cities of Germiston, Benoni, Boksburg, Brakpan, Krugersdorp, Maraisburg, and Springs. The Rand traditionally produces about two-thirds of South Africa's and one-third of the world's total gold output. Gold was discovered in 1884. The region's mines are among the deepest in the world, between 1,220 and 3,500 m (4,000 and 11,500 ft) deep. Uranium is extracted, and silver and uranium oxide are recovered as a by-product from gold mining. Other industries include metallurgy and the manufacture of chemicals, machinery, and textiles.

Witz, Konrad [vits]   The German-Swiss painter Konrad Witz, b. *c*.1400–1410, joined the Guild of Painters in Basel (now Switzerland) in 1434 and continued to work there until his death *c*.1444–1446. He seems to have been responsible for replacing the so-called soft Gothic International Style with the new, more realistic style of 15th-century Flemish painters. His most important work was the *Saint Peter Altarpiece*, signed and dated 1444. One of the two surviving wing panels, the dramatic representation of *Christ Walking on the Water and the Miraculous Draught of Fishes* (Musée d'Art et d'Histoire, Geneva) is especially important because it is one of the first examples in Western art of an actual landscape setting—a view of Lake Geneva.

Wizard of Oz, The   A fantasy written by L. Frank BAUM, *The Wonderful Wizard of Oz* (1900) tells the story of Dorothy, a young farm girl from Kansas who is carried away by a tornado to a strange land called Oz. To return home she must travel to its capital, Emerald City, and ask the assistance of the Wizard of Oz. Along the way she meets three companions—a tin woodsman, a talking scarecrow, and a cowardly lion—with whom she has a series of adventures. Oz emerges as a more interesting place than home, despite the didactic point of the story that "there's no place like home." The novel was adapted into an extraordinarily popular film (1939) starring Judy Garland.

Wobblies   see INDUSTRIAL WORKERS OF THE WORLD

Wodehouse, Sir P. G. [wud'-hows]   The English humorist Pelham Grenville Wodehouse, b. Oct. 15, 1881, d. Feb. 14, 1975, created the delightfully incompetent Bertie Wooster and his butler, Jeeves, the heroes of one of his most popular series, in 1917. Other works center on the equally comic world of Blandings Castle, with its eccentric upper-class inhabitants forever locked into an unchanging world of the 1920s. In addition to 96 novels, Wodehouse wrote 18 plays, such as *Leave It to Psmith* (1930), and lyrics for 33 musicals, including *Oh, Boy!* (1917), *Show Boat* (1927), and *Anything Goes* (1934). In 1941, Wodehouse made several political radio broadcasts while a prisoner of the Germans. He became a U.S. citizen in 1955 but received a British knighthood in 1975. His autobiography, *Author! Author!*, appeared in 1962.

Woden   see ODIN

Wöhler, Friedrich [voh'-lur]   The German chemist Friedrich Wöhler, b. July 31, 1800, d. Sept. 23, 1882, discovered the salts known as cyanates in 1822 and within six years carried out the first synthesis of an organic compound, urea, by the rearrangement of ammonium cyanate. This achievement began the decline of the vitalistic theory that had dominated organic chemistry and that had required the existence of a "life force" for organic synthesis. Wöhler later studied minerals; prepared phosphorus, crystalline boron, and silicon; and discovered silicon hydride.

Wolcott (family) [wul'-kuht]   The Wolcott family of Connecticut was prominent in American colonial and early national politics. **Roger Wolcott**, b. Jan. 4, 1679, d.

May 17, 1767, sat in Connecticut's legislature almost continuously from 1714 to 1741; he was second in command of the force that took Louisbourg in 1745. Wolcott served as Connecticut's deputy governor (1741–50) and governor (1750–54). His son, **Oliver Wolcott**, b. Nov. 20, 1726, d. Dec. 1, 1797, a Connecticut delegate to the Continental Congress (1775–78, 1780–84), signed the Declaration of Independence. In August 1776 he was a militia commander in the defense of New York. Wolcott helped negotiate the Treaty of Fort Stanwix (1784) with the Iroquois. He was Connecticut's lieutenant governor (1787–96) and governor (1796–97). His son, **Oliver Wolcott**, b. Jan. 11, 1760, d. June 1, 1833, was comptroller of public accounts (1788–89) for Connecticut and auditor (1789–91) and comptroller (1791–95) of the new federal treasury. In 1795 he became secretary of the treasury. Loyal to Alexander Hamilton's faction of the Federalist party, Wolcott resigned his post in 1800 after participating in Hamilton's intrigue against President John Adams during that year's election. Later, he was Connecticut's governor (1817–27).

wolf Possibly no animal has been so misunderstood, feared, hated, and persecuted throughout history as the wolf. The gray wolf, also called the timber wolf, is the largest of about 41 wild species within the dog family, Canidae, of the order Carnivora. With the exception of the red wolf of southeastern Texas and southern Louisiana, all living wolves are considered a single species, *Canis lupus*. The red wolf, *C. rufus*, is similar to but smaller than the gray wolf and is intermediate in many characteristics between gray wolves and coyotes; indeed, it has been suggested that the red wolf originated as a fertile cross between gray wolves and coyotes.

Characteristics. The size of wolves varies with geographic locality. Adults range from about 127 to 164 cm (5 to 6.5 ft) from nose to tip of tail, from 65 to 90 cm (26 to 36 in) high at the shoulder, and from 18 to 80 kg (40 to 175 lb) in weight. The red wolf is at the lower end of this range, seldom exceeding 30 kg (66 lb) in weight. Coat colors vary from pure white, which is predominant in

The gray, or timber, wolf is the largest wild canine. Hunting alone or in a pack, it can pursue its prey—including moose and caribou—for hours at speeds of 32 km/h (20 mph) or more.

the far north, through mottled gray to brown or black. Grizzled gray is the most common color. The red wolf is usually a reddish tan.

Occurrence. Wolves can live in a variety of habitats, ranging from Arctic tundra to forest and prairie, if suitable prey is present. They are absent from deserts and the highest mountains. At one time the wolf occurred throughout most of the Northern Hemisphere north of 20° north latitude, or approximately from the Arctic to south central Mexico. Attempts to exterminate the animal have reduced this range considerably. In the Old World wolves still exist in the Soviet Union, China, northern India, Eastern Europe, and, in very small numbers, Western Europe. Most New World wolf populations are in Canada and Alaska. A small population exists in Mexico. Of the 48 contiguous states only Minnesota currently has a wolf population large enough to maintain itself.

Social Behavior. The basic social unit of wolf populations is the pack, which usually consists of a mature male and female plus offspring one or more years of age. Pack size can reach 36, but usually 2 to 8 individuals are present. Each pack ranges over its own area of land, or territory—which may vary from 130 to 13,000 km^2 (50 to 5,000 mi^2)—and will defend all or much of this area against intruders. Members form strong social bonds that promote internal cohesion. Order is maintained by a dominance hierarchy. The pack leader, usually a male, is referred to by behaviorists as the alpha male. The top-ranking (alpha) female normally is subordinate to the alpha male but dominant over all other pack members.

When two wolves meet, each shows its relationship to the other by indicating dominance or submission through facial expression and posture. Additional modes of wolf communication are howling and other vocalizations, and scent marking. One function of howling is to communicate position or assemble the pack; advertisement of territory to neighbors is probably another. Scent marking involves deposition of urine or feces on conspicuous objects along travel routes, usually by dominant wolves. This behavior appears to function in territory maintenance and in intrapack communication.

During the course of each year wolf packs alternate between a stationary phase from spring through summer and a nomadic phase in autumn and winter. Activities during the stationary phase involve caring for pups at a den or homesite. During summer most movements are toward or away from the pups, and adults often travel and hunt alone. By autumn pups are capable of traveling extensively with the adults.

Life Cycle. Generally only the highest ranking male and female in a pack will breed. The breeding season can vary from January in low latitudes to April in high latitudes. Pups are born about 63 days after breeding; an average litter is 6 pups. The mother wolf stays close to her young for the first 2 months while other pack members bring food. Pups are weaned at about the fifth week. The pups approach adult size by autumn or early winter. Sexual maturity usually is attained at 2 years.

The major prey of wolves are large hoofed mammals, including deer, moose, elk, caribou, bison, musk-oxen, and mountain sheep. Beaver is eaten when available. In summer a variety of smaller foods, such as small rodents and berries, supplement the diet. Animals killed are typically young, old, or otherwise weaker members of their populations because they are easiest to capture. Healthy wolves rarely, if ever, attack humans. Mortality factors affecting wolves include persecution by humans, killing by other wolves, diseases, parasites, starvation, and injuries by prey. Probably few wolves live more than 10 years in the wild.

Wolf, Hugo

Wolf, Hugo [vohlf]   The Austrian composer Hugo Wolf, b. Mar. 13, 1860, d. Feb. 22, 1903, is ranked with Franz SCHUBERT as a master of the German lied. Wolf studied (1875–77) at the Vienna Conservatory, and from 1883 to 1887 he was music critic of the fashionable weekly *Wiener Salonblatt*. Despite the encouragement and, often, the financial support of many of Vienna's musicians, Wolf's work received little notice until the late 1880s, when he embarked on several years of intense composition. Early in 1888 he wrote 43 songs set to poems by Eduard Mörike and composed 50 Goethe songs later that year. The *Spanisches Liederbuch* (1889–90) and the *Italienisches Liederbuch* (1890–91, 1896) were songs set to German translations of Spanish and Italian verse. The Vienna Opera rejected Wolf's one finished opera, *Der Corregidor* (1896). This rejection precipitated Wolf's mental breakdown; he eventually died from syphilis in a Viennese mental hospital.

Wolf-Ferrari, Ermanno

Wolf-Ferrari, Ermanno [vohlf-fay-rah'-ree]   At the turn of the 20th century, the graceful, melodious comic operas of Ermanno Wolf-Ferrari, b. Venice, Jan. 12, 1876, d. Jan. 21, 1948, were welcomed by German audiences as an antidote to lengthy and serious Wagnerian music-dramas. *I quattro Rusteghi* (*The Four Ruffians*, 1906) and *Il secreto di Susanna* (*The Secret of Susanna*, 1909) are still sometimes performed in Europe, and the overture and intermezzo from his tragic opera *I gioielli della Madonna* (*The Jewels of the Madonna,* 1911) have remained in the concert repertoire.

Wolfe, James

Wolfe, James   James Wolfe, b. Jan. 2, 1727, d. Sept. 13, 1759, English general, commanded the British force that captured Quebec from the French in 1759, paving the way for the British conquest of Canada. He entered the army in 1742 and fought in the siege of Louisbourg (1758) as a brigadier general. This battle won him the rank of major general and the command of an expedition against Quebec in 1759. After launching a series of unsuccessful attacks, Wolfe in September led his men up the cliffs to the Plains of Abraham, southwest of the city, to await an expected French attack. This, under Gen. Louis Joseph MONTCALM, came prematurely (September 13) and was easily broken by disciplined British firepower. Wolfe, however, was killed during the fighting and subsequently became a legendary hero on whom many unearned attributes were bestowed.

See also: FRENCH AND INDIAN WARS.

Wolfe, Thomas

Wolfe, Thomas   Thomas Clayton Wolfe, b. Asheville, N.C., Oct. 3, 1900, d. Sept. 15, 1938, was one of the great American novelists of the 20th century. In 1916 he left home for the University of North Carolina, where he became a charter member of the Carolina Playmakers and began his literary career writing one-act plays about mountain folk. He continued his playwriting at Harvard, in George Baker's workshop.

In 1924, Wolfe became an English instructor at New York University, where he taught intermittently until 1930. Unable to find a producer for *Welcome to Our City* or for *Mannerhouse* (posthumously published, 1948), his Civil War drama, he began work on *Look Homeward, Angel* (1929), a novel about a boy named Eugene Gant growing up in the South. Wolfe then conceived the idea of an epic novel that would capture the restlessness of the modern American and convey the vastness and variety of the continent. His plans expanded to include a series of novels spanning the history of the nation; but after four years, overwhelmed by the bulk and complexity of his scheme, Wolfe turned for aid to Maxwell PERKINS, his editor at Scribner's. Perkins helped him turn one portion of his material into *Of Time and the River* (1935), an account of Eugene Gant at Harvard and in New York and Europe. A year later, when Wolfe revealed in *The Story of a Novel* how Perkins had come to his aid, critics charged that he was unable to produce his novels without editorial help. After the publication of *From Death to Morning* (1935), a collection of stories, Wolfe put aside his plans for six novels about Gant in order to create a less autobiographical book about an innocent, gullible man discovering life's realities through trial and disillusionment.

When Wolfe died suddenly in 1938 after unsuccessful surgery, he left behind a fragmentary narrative of more than a million words. Out of this manuscript, his new edi-

Thomas Wolfe wrote two major autobiographical novels, Look Homeward, Angel *(1929) and* You Can't Go Home Again *(1940), which established him as a major figure in American literature.*

tor, Edward Aswell of Harper & Brothers, drew three books: *The Web and the Rock* (1939), the story of George Webber's boyhood in the South and of his stormy love affair with Esther Jack later in New York; *You Can't Go Home Again* (1940), the struggles of Webber as a young novelist who finds he cannot escape change and its responsibilities; and *The Hills Beyond* (1941), an incomplete cycle of tales about Webber's mountain kinfolk. Wolfe's *Complete Short Stories*, edited by Francis E. Skipp, appeared in 1987.

Wolfe, Tom   Spokesperson for the New Journalism, Thomas Kennerly Wolfe, Jr., b. Richmond, Va., Mar. 2, 1931, is known for his lively rhetoric and amusing observations of American social life. As a contributor to *Esquire*, he established a type of journalism that is characterized by the flagrant use of fictional devices to present intentionally colored facts. Wolfe analyzed its development in his introduction to *The New Journalism* (1973), an anthology that followed four controversial books, including *The Kandy-Kolored Tangerine-Flake Streamline Baby* (1965) and *The Electric Kool-Aid Acid Test* (1968). His other books include *The Painted Word* (1975), a commentary on art; *The Right Stuff* (1979), about the Mercury astronauts; *From Bauhaus to Our House* (1981), on modern architecture; and the novel *The Bonfire of the Vanities* (1987; film, 1990), about ambition and greed in a nightmarish New York City.

Wolff, Christian   Christian Wolff, b. Jan. 24, 1679, d. Apr. 9, 1754, was a leader of the German ENLIGHTENMENT. As a professor of mathematics and natural science at the University of Halle (1706–23), he was opposed by pietist (see PIETISM) theologians. Wolff became chancellor of the university in 1743.

Wolff was a rationalist (see RATIONALISM), both in his metaphysics of essences and in his epistemology, in which he rejected John Locke's view of the mind as a tabula rasa. Wolff held a mechanistic concept of the cosmos and considered the cosmological argument the best proof for the existence of God. In ethics he argued the position of enlightened DEISM, namely, that good could be discovered by reason and without revelation.

Wolff popularized Leibniz and the Enlightenment, established the tradition of German academic philosophy, and greatly influenced the early work of Immanuel Kant.

wolffish   see BLENNY

wolfhound   see BORZOI; IRISH WOLFHOUND

wolfram   see TUNGSTEN

Wolfram von Eschenbach   [vohlf'-rahm fuhn esh'-en-bahk]   The German poet Wolfram von Eschenbach, *c.*1170–*c.*1220, is remembered primarily for *Parzival* (1200), a long narrative poem recounting the knight PAR-

SIFAL's quest for the Holy Grail. Little is known of Wolfram's life, except that he was a poor aristocrat patronized by Landgrave Hermann I of Thuringia, for whom he wrote the unfinished epic *Willehalm*, about William of Toulouse, who battled the Moors in 783 but ended his life as a monk. Wolfram also left two fragments of a stanzaic romance, *Titurel*, and some fine lyric poems.

wolframite   [wulf'-ruhm-yt]   The principal ore of tungsten is the iron and manganese tungstate mineral wolframite [$(Fe,Mn)WO_4$]. It forms dark gray to brownish black tabular crystals (monoclinic system) and bladed, lamellar, or granular, cleavable masses. Hardness is 4 to 4½, luster is submetallic, streak is reddish brown to black, and specific gravity is 7.0 to 7.5. Wolframite is found in acidic igneous rocks, often associated with cassiterite, as well as in sulfide veins and placer deposits.

Wolgemut, Michael   [vohl'-ge-moot]   Michael Wolgemut (1434–1519) was a German painter and woodcut designer who worked principally in Nuremberg. His paintings reflect the influence of the Flemish realist school. Wolgemut's workshop in Nuremberg produced two of the most famous books of the 15th century, Stefan Fridolin's *Schatzbehalter* (Treasurechest, 1491) and Hartmann Schedel's *Nuremberg Chronicle* (1491–93). The latter, a history of the world, included 645 separate woodcuts, among which the most famous are the views of European towns. With these volumes Wolgemut achieved his goal of establishing the woodcut as a significant artistic creation in its own right. Apart from his paintings and woodcuts, Wolgemut is best known as the teacher of Albrecht Dürer.

Wollongong   [wul'-uhn-gawng]   Wollongong (1986 pop., 167,863) is a rapidly growing industrial city and seaport on the east coast of Australia about 64 km (40 mi) south of Sydney. Coal mining, copper smelting, and steel fabrication are major industries. The University of Wollongong (1975), a former technical college, is located there. Wollongong was founded in 1834 and was merged in 1947 with Bulli, Port Kembla, and other municipalities to form Greater Wollongong (1988 est. pop., 235,300).

Wollstonecraft, Mary   [wul'-stuhn-krahft]   The English writer Mary Wollstonecraft, b. Hoxton, Middlesex, Apr. 27, 1759, d. Sept. 10, 1797, was an early feminist. Her tract *A VINDICATION OF THE RIGHTS OF WOMEN* influenced many 19th-century suffragists.

After trying to support herself as a governess, Wollstonecraft went to work in 1787 for the London publisher James Johnson. She had already written *Thoughts on the Education of Daughters* (1787), as well as a story, "Mary" (1788), based on her friendship with Fanny Blood. She was soon to achieve renown as a controversialist, first with *A Vindication of the Rights of Man* in 1790, and then two years later with its more famous companion piece.

Thwarted in her love for the painter Henry Fuseli, Wollstonecraft left for Paris in 1792. There she lived with Gilbert Imlay, an American who deserted her soon after the birth of a daughter, Fanny, in 1794. Returning to England she married the writer and philosopher William GODWIN in 1797, but died a few months later, 11 days after giving birth to a second daughter, Mary Wollstonecraft SHELLEY, the future author of *Frankenstein* and wife of the poet Percy Bysshe Shelley.

Wolsey, Thomas [wool'-zee]   Thomas Wolsey, b. *c.*1475, d. Nov. 29, 1530, English statesman and prelate, virtually ruled England as chief advisor (*c.*1513–29) to HENRY VIII and papal legate (1518–29). His rise to power was the more spectacular because of his lowly birth as the son of a butcher. A brilliant child, Wolsey graduated from Oxford at the age of 15 and in 1509 became Henry VIII's almoner. He gained the king's particular favor by organizing a successful military invasion of France in 1513. He was named bishop of Lincoln (1514), then archbishop of York (1514), lord chancellor (1515), and a cardinal (1515). Through his appointment as papal legate in 1518, Wolsey became England's most powerful cleric, the pope's direct agent.

Wolsey was only partially successful in his attempts to maintain a balance of power between France and the Holy Roman Empire. He became unpopular for his own material greed, demonstrated by his construction of a splendid residence for himself at Hampton Court. By expanding the power of the court of Star Chamber over the nobility, Wolsey earned enmity from that class. Wolsey's diplomatic and personal ambitions left little time for his planned reforms of church, but he did suppress a number of monasteries to finance a new college at Oxford, which survives as Christ Church.

In 1529, Wolsey fell from power because he could not persuade Pope CLEMENT VII to grant Henry VIII a divorce from CATHERINE OF ARAGON. He was arrested and died on his way to answer charges of treason.

Wolstenholme Towne   The Wolstenholme Towne site, on the James River 16 km (10 mi) east of the site of JAMESTOWN, Va., offers evidence of the earliest town plan yet excavated in British colonial North America; it was similar to some settlements built in Ireland in the early 17th century. Founded in 1619, the town featured a 920-m^2 (10,000-ft^2) trapezoidal palisade or fort with widely spaced posts (3 m/9 ft apart) and planks between them. Among the artifacts found were two close helmets (armets). Restricting movement, hampering vision, and muffling sound, these heavy helmets were designed for European-style fighting rather than for Indian attacks. A massacre apparently occurred in 1622. When a ship came from England bearing reinforcements, only 20 of the more than 200 original settlers of Wolstenholme Towne remained. Occupation of the site apparently continued only through the 1650s.

wolverine [wul-vur-reen']   Although the wolverine, *Gulo gulo*, looks rather like a small bear, it is in the weasel family, Mustelidae. Males measure to 86 cm (34 in), plus a 25-cm (10-in) tail, and weigh up to 27 kg (60 lb). Males share territories with two or three females. Wolverines live in cold, northern forests worldwide and are solitary, nocturnal predators; they also eat carrion. Their glossy black fur sheds and was prized by Indians.

The wolverine Gulo luscus *is a member of the weasel family found in northern areas of Eurasia and North America.*

woman suffrage   SEE SUFFRAGE, WOMEN'S

Woman's Christian Temperance Union   see WCTU

wombat [wahm'-bat]   The wombat is a burrowing, herbivorous, marsupial mammal in the family Phascolomidae, including two living genera in Australia and Tasmania: *Vombatus,* coarse haired with a naked nose; and *Lasiorhinus,* with soft fur and a hairy muzzle. Wombats are grayish brown, thick-bodied animals ranging from 70 to 120 cm (27 to 47 in) and weighing up to 27 kg (60 lb). The ventral pouch opens posteriorly. Wombats' large and numerous burrows are a hazard to domestic range animals.

The island wombat is a heavyset marsupial that can be tamed and becomes a playful pet.

Women in the Air Force   see WAF

women in society   As individuals, women have participated in essentially all of the activities performed in human societies. As a group, however, women have been identified with particular roles ascribed to them by their societies. These roles have commonly been presented as naturally linked to women's physiology—childbearing and infant care. Even in societies where women have been given broader responsibilities and power, men have normally dominated political life. The emergence of classes, states, and major religions has universally strengthened male dominance, and the rise of capitalism has furthered this tendency.

Preliterate Cultures. In both hunting and foraging and early settled agricultural societies, women contribute directly and indispensably to subsistence, frequently controlling or collecting the essentials for survival. No known societies have entrusted any technological activities specifically to women. Although such female activities as food preparation and cooking approximate technology, men monopolize hunting, butchering, and the processing of hard materials. KINSHIP provides the basic social organization in preliterate societies; work is allocated according to gender and generation.

Some 19th-century scholars, notably Johann Jakob Bachofen, believed that the matriarchal family was the foundation of human society. More recent work has discredited this myth of MATRIARCHY. Many preliterate societies in the past, however, were matrilineal (descent was traced through the family of the mother) or matrilocal (newly married couples resided with and worked for the family of the mother). Among the Iroquois, women's influential roles were based on female control of the group's economic organization. As a rule, in societies in which hunting predominated, there was greater sexual segregation in work and child-rearing, greater emphasis on competition, and a masculine cast to creation myths and cosmology (see CREATION ACCOUNTS). In more settled societies, which relied marginally or not at all on hunting, there was greater sexual integration, less competitiveness, and a feminine cast to creation myths and cosmology.

Western Cultures. By *c.*3000 BC, in SUMER, the first of the Bronze Age patriarchal civilizations of Mesopotamia, recognizable class divisions and royal dynasties had appeared, consolidating women's exclusion from politics. According to their class position, women continued to exercise varied roles and to enjoy some legal protection for property. Symbolically, the early role of priestesses was transformed into the roles of concubines and prostitutes in the god's harem. The legal code of the Old Babylonian king Hammurabi (r. *c.*1792–1750 BC; see HAMMURABI, CODE OF) carried the patriarchal tendencies of Sumer to their logical severity by including draconian punishments for women who challenged male dominance.

By contrast, the Minoan society of Crete, which also took shape about 3000 BC, perpetuated women's preponderant influence in religion and social life and granted them equal political authority with men. Minoan women, belonging to a trading rather than a warrior society, drew strength both from their membership in corporate kinship groups and from their institutionalized ties with other women. (See AEGEAN CIVILIZATION.)

The classical myths of origin, recorded and shaped by

Among preliterate peoples, women perform culturally ascribed activities. Papago Indian women of Arizona were expert basketweavers.

HESIOD during the 8th century BC, set forth a complex anthropomorphic cosmology in which women, such as PANDORA and APHRODITE, figure prominently as disruptive forces, or, like ATHENA and ARTEMIS, as asexual virgins. Hesiod explicitly depicted the progress of civilization as the triumph of male power and principles of justice over the reproductive forces of women.

In keeping with its cultural hostility toward women, classical Greek civilization (5th–3d century BC) severely curtailed women's political participation. Athens firmly relegated women, with slaves and children, to the household, or *oikos*, which male citizens dominated and represented in the polity. The married woman nonetheless earned respect from her management of the *oikos*. The more authoritarian Spartans, who also displayed deep misogyny (hatred of women) and radically segregated women and men, allowed women defined public roles. The fear of and hostility toward women that permeated Greek culture was institutionalized in law and indirectly expressed in men's idealization and love of other men, particularly young boys.

Traditional Judaic society also restricted women's social role and encouraged sexual segregation. Judaism probably also reflected a historic revolt against a prehistoric female-centered cosmology. By historic times, Jewish monotheism was clearly founded upon the worship of a male creator and lawgiver.

The Roman state, with its principle of *patriapotestas* ("right of the father"), granted women even fewer rights than did the Greek states but probably permitted them greater personal freedom. Although a husband possessed the right of life and death over his wife, Roman culture never expressed deep hostility toward female sexuality, nor a sharp polarity between the sexes.

Christianity emerged in part as a reaction to the perceived laxity of late Hellenistic and Roman morals and the internal crisis of Jewish society. Although women figured prominently among early converts and proselytizers, the architects of Christian orthodoxy, notably Saint Paul, mistrusted sexuality in general and women in particular. Increasingly, Christianity stressed both Eve's responsibility for the fall of the human race from divine grace and Mary's virginity. Women were denied official religious roles until, eventually, a place was made for them in the religious orders.

The Germanic tribes that overran the Roman Empire seem to have regarded women largely as property to be exchanged by men. The Roman historian Tacitus, however, emphasized Germanic women's roles as seers and prophets, and subsequent Christian chroniclers praised women's efforts to convert their men. Laywomen remained strictly subordinate to husband and family, however.

By the 9th century, women's legal position had improved as a result of complex social change. Women's ability to inherit property strengthened their position within the family and influenced society at large. The Carolingian rulers reinforced the church's policy of the indissolubility of marriage, thus protecting women against repudiation for childlessness. Property and marital security enabled women to play more-active roles in the early Middle Ages. From the 11th century on, however, women's freedoms were steadily restricted, first by the church and later by lay society. The rise of monarchies strengthened male control of families and increased male opportunities in the public sphere. The cult of COURTLY LOVE, which simultaneously idealized women as objects of male devotion and drew them from religious devotion to romantic love of men, provided cultural compensation for declining female independence.

During the Renaissance the individualistic, secular culture that might have invited female as well as male participation self-consciously defined itself as the male mind triumphing over (female) nature. Renaissance thought still portrayed women as dangerous and disorderly. Urban institutions followed the Athenian pattern of associating men with politics and women with the household. The Reformation, which recognized the importance of women's participation in their own salvation, glorified marriage, and benefited from female support, nonetheless repudiated the implications of sexual equality. In the 15th and 16th centuries, female initiative continued to be channeled into religious vocation, social promotion through marriage, or family interests. Some upper-class women, such as Elizabeth I and other noblewomen, enjoyed unusual opportunities because of their family status. Peasant and lower-class women worked with and for their families in agriculture, crafts, and the home.

The Puritan Revolution of 17th-century England promoted a close identification of women with domestic life that gained broad acceptance throughout the 18th century. Although the American Revolution and French Revolution yielded mixed benefits for women, both restricted citizenship to men. The NAPOLEONIC CODE approximated the Roman *patriapotestas* in its subjugation of married women to their husbands. The individualism of Enlightenment thought, however, combined with the revolutionary defense of individual rights, sowed the seeds of modern FEMINISM. Mary WOLLSTONECRAFT's *A Vindication of the Rights of Women* (1792) was the opening shot in the coming campaign for equal rights.

Throughout the Western world the gradual development of liberal and democratic institutions encouraged the emergence of a model of womanhood for women of all classes and the doctrine of separate spheres. From the 17th century, the rise of capitalism, followed by industrialization, was accompanied by the disruption of peasant communities and the growth of a wage labor force in which working women participated, although for lower wages than men. The colonialism that preceded and accompanied this process wrenched West African women, like men, into enslavement on the plantations of the Americas. The progress of industrialization and the organization of labor discriminated against women who, increasingly, accepted the goal of a male wage that could support entire families.

During the 19th century, women became more concerned with social reform and improvement of their own position. Many argued that their interest in nursing, social work, temperance (see TEMPERANCE MOVEMENT), and even the vote (see SUFFRAGE, WOMEN'S) was in keeping with true womanhood. A decline in the birthrate and infant mortality left more and more women with years unencumbered by childbearing. Women fought for and won gradual improvement in the rights of married women to property, divorce, and child custody. By the 20th century they began to claim full citizenship and control over their own reproductive powers. By the time the new feminist wave broke in the 1960s, women had gained individual rights and opportunities undreamed of by women in other ages and other parts of the world. Male dominance in the household and the public sector still flourished, however. Women had gained many of the uncertainties and responsibilities of individualism without equal access to its benefits.

Eastern Cultures. The dominant cultures of the Islamic countries, India, China, and Japan rested on sharp social distinctions and on the labor of peasants or tribal masses.

The traditional Chinese custom of footbinding—the wrapping of young girls' feet with strips of linen to prevent further growth—was particularly favored by the upper classes as a sign of beauty and gentility. The custom, which resulted in grotesque deformation, was banned in 1912.

As Western countries became industrialized, more women joined the labor force, although at wages lower than men's. In this French hat factory, c.1900, all work was performed by women.

Normally, official ideologies and ruling elites saw the seclusion of women as essential to social and political order. Women's only alternative to domestic confinement was to join a religious order or to become a wandering mendicant like Mirabai, the 16th-century Rajput princess.

Generally, Islam (established in the 7th century AD) confirmed or strengthened female subordination among the peoples it conquered and, by including women's status in holy law, or SHARIA, made subsequent change difficult. Allowing polygyny (see POLYGAMY), it restricted the number of wives to four and insisted on equal treatment. Declaring a woman worth half a man with respect to inheritance and testimony, it encouraged female INFANTICIDE. Islam veiled women and isolated them from all men other than their own relatives. Yet Islamic women were entitled to full support for themselves and their children from their husbands.

In India, caste ENDOGAMY stressed marriage as the central purpose of a woman's life. Marriage policies and a deep mistrust of female sexuality, especially among the Brahmans, resulted in prepuberty marriage, SUTTEE, bans on remarriage by widows, and a neglect of female children, who were considered economic liabilities. Hinduism emphasized the dual nature of women as benevolent wives but dangerous mothers. The penetration (13th century) of Islam into northern India introduced the constraints of Sharia and, at least for aristocratic women, purdah, or seclusion from public observation.

Strict patrilineal values governed the position of women in the Chinese Empire. Confucianism, originating in the 6th century BC, emphasized the importance of the family to social order and of gender and generational hierarchy within families. In marriage the wife was totally subject to her husband and, especially, to his parents. Although there was no polygyny, the husband could take concubines. Upper-class women lived lives of leisure and extreme seclusion. The growth of cities (10th–16th century) was accompanied by an increase in female literacy

and by an impression of female immorality. Systematic confinement and oppression reached its height during the Qing dynasty (1644–1911) with FOOT-BINDING, prostitution and concubinage, and social pressure on widows to remain chaste or to commit suicide.

In Japan, beginning in the 8th century, the influence of Buddhism, Confucianism, and specific clans steadily restricted the image and political roles of women. By the Heian period (794–1185), women were secluded and used as pawns in marriage politics. The absence of patrilocality made them more valuable than sons for ambitious clans. Excluded from official learning, women writers developed special skills in vernacular literature and produced brilliant works of fiction, such as MURASAKI SHIKIBU's *The Tale of Genji* (11th century). The high point of women's rights to inherit and own property was reached in the Kamakura period (1185–1333). Under Tokugawa feudalism (1600–1867), women were viewed as inferior to men and were subject to male relatives; they also lost most of their property rights and all political roles. Men practiced polygyny, kept concubines, and could repudiate their wives at will. The Meiji Civil Code of 1898 perpetuated much of this subordination.

Women's Status Today. Since World War II the position of women around the globe has begun to change at an accelerating rate. Women have gained most in politically progressive or economically developed countries, but there is no single explanation for women's gains, and in no country do women enjoy full political, legal, economic, social, educational, and sexual equality with men.

In highly developed countries women normally account for 30%–40% of the labor force, but in less developed countries with a large subsistence sector they may constitute less than 10%, and even less than 5% in some orthodox Muslim countries. Most women remain concentrated in low-paying, low-status, "female" jobs, especially primary and secondary school teaching, service jobs, and some clerical and sales jobs. Throughout the world women continue to earn less than men for comparable

Supporters and opponents of the Equal Rights Amendment demonstrate in Illinois before the proposed amendment's ultimate defeat. The ERA fell 3 states short of the 38 needed for ratification before the deadline of June 30, 1982.

work and to be excluded from the best-paid and most-prestigious jobs. With rising male unemployment in recent times, women's participation in the labor force has even declined in Japan, Italy, Peru, and India. Perhaps as many as 50% of the world's farmers are women, largely bound to a declining and ever less profitable subsistence economy. Yet 38% of the world's women are unpartnered: single, widowed, or divorced; they support themselves and often others.

Women's near exclusion from the highest incomes and most dynamic economic sectors is closely related both to their formal political and legal rights and to the persistence of traditional religious, cultural, and family values. Much of the world is subject to the influence of three traditional legal systems: COMMON LAW, CIVIL LAW, and Sharia. Legislation that promotes sexual equality has not eradicated their influence. The legal position of women most closely approximates that of men in such countries as the USSR, China, and Cuba. American feminists have insisted that piecemeal reform, including suffrage and the Civil Rights Act of 1964, does not provide the same protection as would the comprehensive EQUAL RIGHTS AMENDMENT.

Although women generally have acquired the vote, they do not exercise political power in proportion to their numbers. A few, exceptionally, have attained the highest political offices: Indira GANDHI, Golda MEIR, and Margaret THATCHER. In Communist countries, although they are more heavily represented in governing political bodies, women have rarely attained membership in the ruling politburo of the Communist parties.

Women have also failed to gain equal access to higher (especially technical) education. Women's illiteracy has declined dramatically in the past few decades, but only during the 1970s and '80s have American women finally constituted 20% of those in professional training—medicine, business, law. In the Third World, preference is normally given to the education and training of men for the advanced economic and governmental sectors. Furthermore, in many countries, defenders of traditional family, religious, and cultural values vigorously oppose the liberation of women as one more manifestation of Western domination.

Overall, while the needs of women in different countries vary, and the rate of progress is inconsistent, increasing numbers of women around the world are recognizing their need to be full and equal members of society.

Women's Army Corps   see WAC

Wonder, Stevie   Rock-music star Stevie Wonder, b. Steveland Morris Hardaway in Saginaw, Mich., May 13, 1950, who was born blind, has been a recording artist since the age of 10, when he was signed by MOTOWN records. Among rock music's most highly paid, most esteemed performers, Wonder composes, arranges, produces, sings, and plays piano, clarinet, drums, organ, and harmonica on his recordings. *Music of My Mind*

(1972), *Innervisions* (1973), *Songs in the Key of Life* (1976), *Journey through the Secret Life of Plants* (1979), and *In Square Circle* (1985) reflect his ability to draw on diverse themes and a rich variety of musical ideas and techniques.

wood   Wood is the hard, fibrous substance found beneath the bark of trees and shrubs. It is composed of specially hardened cells whose two main functions are transporting water and dissolved minerals from the roots to the leaves and supporting the plant body. Most wood cells are dead. Only young cells, those laid down during the current growing season, are alive (primary xylem). Once the xylem cell hardens with lignins, it is referred to as secondary xylem. The ratio of dead to living wood cells increases as the girth of the tree increases.

Wood, a fibrous cellulosic material obtained from trees, is valued in construction because of its varied properties and availability. The products of different trees differ in color, density, grain pattern, texture, hardness, and strength. Wood is classified as hardwood or softwood, but these terms bear no relation to actual hardness. Hardwoods are produced by broad-leaved trees, such as ash, linden, beech, teak, oak, mahogany, walnut, and rosewood. Softwoods are obtained from conifers, or needle-leaved trees, including spruce, Douglas fir, pine, and red cedar. Most softwoods are used for building construction; hardwoods usually go into furniture.

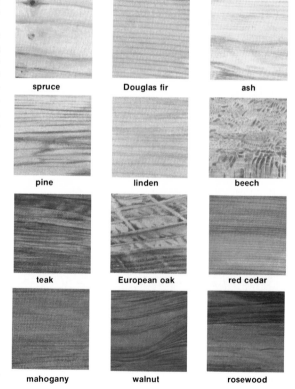

spruce   Douglas fir   ash

pine   linden   beech

teak   European oak   red cedar

mahogany   walnut   rosewood

Composition and Structure

The wall of the wood cell consists of two principal chemicals: cellulose and lignin. Cellulose constitutes 70% of the dry cell wall and is more important economically. Lignin fills the spaces within the cellulose network. Cellulose is a polymerized carbohydrate; many glucose molecules are linked together in long chains to form macromolecules. The cellulose becomes arranged in long, threadlike fibrils. Cellulose wound in this fashion is as strong as an equivalent thickness of steel. Lignins also add rigidity to the cell wall.

Structurally, the dense aggregations of wood cells in woody plants are secondary xylem elements interlaced with rays. As a young twig grows, special undifferentiated cells at the twig tips (the apical meristems) are able to divide and produce the specialized tissues known as wood, bark, pith, cambium, and so on. Most of these tissues are incapable of further division, except for the cambium and the cork cambium. The cork cambium gives rise to bark; the cambium gives rise to wood.

The cambium is a lateral meristem; like the apical meristem, it is capable of dividing every spring during the growing season. It divides in the horizontal plane, however, increasing the diameter of the tree, whereas the apical meristem divides in the vertical plane, increasing the tree's height. The apical and the lateral usually are active at the same time. The cambium actually assumes the form of an inverted cone in every twig, stem, trunk, and root. This cone produces phloem to the outside and xylem to the inside. Phloem translocates photosynthates from the leaves to other living cells, providing them with nourishment. Xylem cells conduct water with dissolved minerals from the roots to all portions of the tree.

Every spring the cambium manufactures new xylem and phloem. It is this new annual growth that produces growth rings in wood. In most instances, the age of a tree can be determined by counting the rings of a trunk's cross section. Another tissue type generated by the cambium is wood rays. Wood rays, consisting of parenchyma cells, conduct the water laterally from the xylem to the living cells.

Wood is further classified into sapwood and heartwood. Sapwood is the part of the wood that conducts water. It consists of the xylem vessels that lie closest to the cambium. Usually several years' worth of xylem vessels will make up the sapwood. Each year, as the cambium generates new xylem vessels, the older xylem vessels of the sapwood become clogged with metabolic wastes, such as tannins, dyes, and resins. As a result, the vessels lose their ability to conduct water and become heartwood.

Heartwood provides structural support for the tree. Heartwood generally makes better lumber than does sapwood. It is often drier, has a richer color than sapwood because of dye accumulation, and is more resistant to decay because of certain chemical deposits such as tannins.

Properties of Wood

Wood is a poor conductor of heat and therefore is useful as an insulator. It does not conduct electricity. Moreover, wood can be recycled many times. It is easy to fasten, shape, smooth, and reshape, and it is enduring. Wooden structures many hundreds of years old have remained in good condition with minimal care.

Different woods have different uses because the properties of wood differ from species to species. Density, the weight per unit volume, is compared to an equal volume of water to yield the specific gravity. Most woods have a specific gravity less than 1.0—they are lighter than water and therefore float—because of the numerous air spaces.

The hardness of wood, which varies greatly, refers to the resistance of wood to a saw or an ax across the grain. Hardness is dependent primarily on weight, degree of seasoning, and the structure of the wood elements.

Wood is termed as *hardwood* or *softwood.* Hardwoods generally comprise broad-leafed trees, such as elm and oak. Softwoods, or conifers, typically are trees with scale-like leaves, such as cedar, fir, and pine. Exceptions may be found in both groups, and these designations can be inaccurate.

The terms *porous* and *nonporous* are also used. Porous refers to vessels (large cells or pores) that conduct sap in hardwoods. When these vessels are absent (nonporous), as in softwoods, the structure of the wood is relatively homogeneous, and resin ducts are often present.

Durability is the ability of wood to resist decay, insect infestation, chemicals, fungi, and marine organisms. The most decay-resistant species are often used where decay could be a problem. Catalpa, cedar, chestnut, black locust, and Osage orange trees are resistant to decay; aspen, cottonwood, fir, and willow are prone to decay.

Wood grain, or the arrangement of the cells, is specific to each species and is a desirable property in decorative wood. When a log is cut, different grain patterns are visible, depending on whether the wood is cut perpendicular to the grain (crosscut) or parallel to the grain. Parallel cuts can be either along the radius of a log or tangential to the log. A highly prized form of wood grain is derived from burls—large bulbous growths peculiar to certain species, in which the grain swirls in an unusual pattern. Burls are obtained from California laurel, redwood, many fruitwoods, and maples.

Uses

Lumber. The need for LUMBER makes this industry the greatest consumer of wood in the United States. Nearly 40 billion board feet of lumber are produced annually, most of which are softwoods. More than three-fifths of this harvest is from the western states, and most of the remainder is from the southeastern pine forests. The Allegheny Mountain region yields many choice hardwoods, including cherry.

Waste materials from logs, including edgings, trimmings, shavings, and sawdust, are used extensively. For example, slabs and trimmings are used for pulp and particleboard, and bark as mulch. Pulpwood is used mostly for paper. One source of pulpwood is from timber species unsuitable for lumber. Chips and sawdust from the milling process are also used, as are selected eastern hardwoods.

Fuelwood. In North America only 10% of the timber harvest is used for fuel. Usage is increasing, however, because of rising costs of petroleum products. Europe uses 30% of its timber for fuel; Latin America, Africa, and Asia (exclusive of the USSR) use between 75% and 90%.

Veneers, Particleboard, and Plywood. These wood products are used in construction for facing large areas and in the manufacture of furniture. VENEERS and plywood are both thin, laminar pieces of wood glued together to form a strong product. Particleboard is composed of wood chips and shavings combined with a bonding agent to form panels. Veneer is a thin slice of a log cut in sheet form. Once cut, the more decorative veneers, especially from choice hardwoods such as cherry, walnut, and pecan, are used in furniture manufacture or for other applications where appearance is important. Other veneers are glued together in layers with the grain of one layer lying perpendicular to that of the next. This strong, durable product is called plywood.

Posts, Poles, and Pilings. Close to 500 million posts, poles, and pilings are required each year in the United States. Fence posts are usually made from cedar, cypress, Osage orange, or black locust because of their durability. Telephone poles account for more than 6 million new poles annually. Douglas fir, southern pine, and lodgepole pine are favored for telephone poles.

Rayon. RAYON, the first commercially produced synthetic fiber, is still used for textiles and tire cord. In rayon production, pulp is broken down chemically to free the cellulose, processed, hardened into fine filaments, and spun together to form rayon thread or yarn.

___

Wood, Fernando Fernando Wood, b. Philadelphia, Pa., June 14, 1812, d. Feb. 14, 1881, was a U.S. representative (1841–43, 1863–65, 1867–81) from New York and a Tammany Hall leader. Elected mayor of New York City in 1854 and 1856, he was expelled from Tammany for not sharing patronage with other bosses. Wood formed a rival organization, Mozart Hall, and won another term as mayor in 1859. During the Civil War he advocated peace by conciliation between North and South.

___

Wood, Grant During the 1930s the American regionalist painter Grant Wood, b. Anamosa, Iowa, Feb. 13, 1891, d. Feb. 12, 1942, won both popular and critical acclaim for his elegant, meticulously composed canvases. During his four visits to Europe in the late 1920s, Wood was strongly influenced by the work of such 16th-century Flemish painters as the van Eyck brothers. Their paintings helped to shape the stylized form of realism through which he expressed his strong midwestern American themes. Wood's witty approach to his subjects, within the

Grant Wood's American Gothic *(1930), a major American regionalist work, is a subtle and witty commentary on midwestern rural life. (Art Institute of Chicago.)*

concepts of the American regionalist school, forms the basis for his most famous works, such as *American Gothic* (1930; Art Institute of Chicago) and *Daughters of Revolution* (1932; Cincinnati Art Museum). Like his fellow American regionalists Thomas Hart Benton and John Steuart Curry, Wood rejected the innovations of modernism. He died on the eve of his 51st birthday and at the peak of his fame.

___

Wood, Leonard Leonard Wood, b. Winchester, N.H., Oct. 9, 1860, d. Aug. 7, 1927, American soldier and colonial administrator, served in Cuba and the Philippines. He received his M.D. from Harvard in 1884 and entered the Army Medical Corps in 1885. He ultimately rose to the rank of major general (1903) in the regular army and was later (1910–14) chief of staff.

Wood participated (1885–86) in the Apache wars, and during the Spanish-American War (1898) commanded the "Rough Riders," made famous by his friend Theodore ROOSEVELT, with whom he became politically allied. Wood was named military governor (1898–99) of Santiago, Cuba, then (1899–1902) of all Cuba. Extremely successful in these posts, he became highly popular on the island. From 1903 to 1906, Wood was governor of Moro province in the Philippines and harshly suppressed insurrectionist activity. Later he was (1921–27) governor-general of the islands, but his tight reign generated serious opposition among independence groups there. Wood dabbled in politics and in 1920 was a leading candidate for the Republican presidential nomination but lost to Warren G. Harding.

wood alcohol   See METHYL ALCOHOL

—

wood carving   Wood carving, or wood sculpture, is one of the oldest and most widespread forms of art. Because of the near universality of trees, the relative simplicity of the necessary technology, and the relative durability of the product, wood carving has been practiced in almost all cultures from the earliest times. Wood can be fashioned by chopping, riving or splitting, sawing, and gouging and cutting with implements made of stone, bone, or metal. Objects of wood are fashioned by a basically subtractive method, although multiple blocks or pieces can be fastened together to form large pieces. The carving can be in shallow relief or fully three-dimensional; it can be an end in itself, as a carved boat or architectural ornament, or it can be a step in a more complex process, as in block printing of textiles or MARQUETRY in furniture. Most work is done with a hand-held knife or with a chisel struck with a hammer. The art of the wood carver depends on knowledge of the characteristics of specific

The wooden reliefs decorating the choir stalls of the Cathedral of Amiens (1220–88), created during the early 16th century, are among the cathedral's most beautiful sculptures. These reliefs reflect medieval sculptural traditions in the choice of material and in the iconography.

The elaborately carved totem poles of the Kitwancool, a group of the Tsimshian people of British Columbia, exemplify the highly developed wood-carving traditions of the native Americans of the Northwest Pacific coast. Totem poles display symbolic, stylized representations of human and animal forms.

woods, skill in fashioning the material, and talent in design.

Of all the major traditions of wood carving, the closest in structure and suggestive form to the tree is the so-called totem pole of the American Northwest Coast Indians. Carved of red cedar logs, these cylindrical sculptures of stacked animal and human figures sometimes reached heights of 25 m (80 ft) or more. The frontally erect, bilaterally symmetrical figures are shaped in relief within the overall pillar form. In the earliest recorded (18th century) examples, the facial features, particularly the eyes, were outlined in color; by the late 19th century, paints obtained in trade were used to polychrome the entire surface of the totem pole (see INDIANS OF NORTH AMERICA, ART OF THE).

Relief sculpture was the primary form of wood carving for medieval European artists, who usually concentrated on the decoration of flat surfaces on altar screens, choir stalls, and doors. Three-dimensional wood carving from the medieval period exists in the form of single figures and groups for major altarpieces and for niches in large architectural screens. During the 16th century these figures assumed a grace of pose and realism of detail that represent a high point in the art of wood sculpture.

This wood sculpture of the Bodhisattva Kuan-yin, seated in the Maharajalila position, or "Repose of the Great King," is representative of the sophisticated wood sculpture of the Song dynasty (960–1279). (Museum van Aziatische Kunst, Amsterdam.)

During the Renaissance and baroque periods, stone was the preferred medium for sculpture. In 17th-century England, however, Grinling GIBBONS revived the use of wood reliefs, as interior ornamentation for both ecclesiastical and secular buildings. Realistic panels were cut from blocks of laminated limewood in remarkably high, deeply undercut relief designed to punctuate the wall surface in paneled rooms.

In the West the emphasis in wood sculpture has moved increasingly from the spiritual to the secular, culminating in such 20th-century works as Robert Laurent's *The Flame* (c.1917; Whitney Museum of American Art, New York City) that emphasize the grain, color, and texture of the wood. Three-dimensional Oriental carving tends to emphasize fluidity and grace of line in both overall form and detail. Typical is the Chinese figure, *Guanyin* (AD 1168; Yale University Art Gallery, New Haven, Conn.), seated in the position of ease; the figure's rounded curves emphasize the tone of serenity and calm. Executed—as is most large-scale wood sculpture—of joined blocks of wood, the figure was originally painted and, subsequently, gilded—features that contribute to the figure's aura of remoteness.

A more strongly stylized and expressive treatment of the human form characterizes African wood sculpture. In a Mende female cult figure (19th century; British Museum, London), for example, anatomical elements are simplified, reduced, or exaggerated to create a sense of directness and stability. The potency of sculpture to communicate and to perform a magical function—in this case to cure illness in women—are the fundamental aspects of almost all African wood carving (see AFRICAN ART).

wood louse   see ISOPOD

wood sorrel   Wood sorrel is the common name for small herbs with cloverlike leaves that fold up at night or in darkness. Also known as sour grass and lady's sorrel, approximately 850 species make up the genus *Oxalis* of the wood sorrel family, Oxalidaceae. Representatives are found on all continents but are most abundant in Central and South America and southern Africa. Wood-sorrel leaves are divided into three segments, with each segment heart-shaped and notched. When ripe seedpods are touched, they open explosively, scattering seeds widely. The sour taste of the plant is due to oxalic acid, which is poisonous, particularly in large quantities.

There are several yellow-flowered species. Yellow wood sorrel, *O. stricta*, is a common North American lawn and field weed; creeping sour grass, or lady's sorrel, *O. corniculata*, a common Old World perennial with a creeping stem and small flowers, has an agreeable taste.

Of the purple-flowered species, the violet wood sorrel, *O. violacea*, is common in open woods and on shaded slopes and banks of North America. In the high Andes of South America, one species, oca, *O. tuberosa*, has a tuber that is used as a potatolike, starchy food.

wood turtle   see POND TURTLE

wood warbler   Wood warblers comprise about 120 species and subspecies of birds of the New World family Parulidae. Small (11–18 cm/4–7 in), often brightly marked and variously colored, most wood warblers are arboreal, but some are terrestrial. Some catch insects on the wing, as do flycatchers, and others crawl about on trees, as do creepers.

Most North American wood warblers nest in the upper latitudes, winter in South and Central America, and migrate in abundant, invasionlike waves. Wood warblers have quick movements and abrupt, high-pitched songs.

woodbine   Woodbine is the common name for several woody vines and twining shrubs, including the approximately 15 species of *Parthenocissus* in the grape family, Vitcaceae. These high-climbing, deciduous vines include the VIRGINIA CREEPER, *P. quinquefolia*, and Boston IVY, *P. tricuspidata*. Other plants called woodbine are the HONEYSUCKLE species *Lonicera caprifolium* (Italian woodbine) and *L. periclymenum* (one variety of which is called Dutch woodbine).

woodchuck   see GROUNDHOG

woodcock   The five or six species of woodcock belong to the sandpiper family, Scolopacidae, and inhabit damp woods and bogs in many parts of the world. The American woodcock, *Philohela minor*, ranges over eastern North America; the somewhat larger (35 cm/14 in) European woodcock, *Scolopax rustica*, is found over much of temperate Europe and Asia. Other species inhabit New Guinea and adjacent islands.

Squat-bodied with long bills, woodcocks feed on earthworms and insect larvae and, with the exception of the Javanese woodcock, *S. saturata,* live and nest on the ground. Their wood-brown coloring allows them to blend in with their surroundings. Because their eyes are set so high and far back, woodcocks have overlapping fields of vision both in front and in back of their heads. Twice each spring, courting males slowly circle overhead, making various sounds. The females lure the males to the ground with a special call.

woodcreeper   Woodcreepers are birds of the family Dendrocolaptidae, order Passeriformes, suborder Furnarii. The 13 genera and 48 species occur from Mexico through Central and South America as far as northern Argentina, Bolivia, and Peru, as well as Trinidad and Tobago. Woodcreepers may be from 15 to 37 cm (5.75 to 14.5 in) long. They are basically olive or grayish brown, often with streaks, bars, or spots of black, gray, or white. The bill ranges from short and straight to long and decurved, the long tail feathers have rigid shafts, and the feet are strong. These features are associated with the woodcreepers' habit of climbing upward on tree trunks, using the tail as a brace in a manner like that of woodpeckers. Climbing up a tree in a spiral around the trunk, they probe for insects in the bark. A few species also feed on the ground.

woodcuts and wood engravings   The woodcut is the earliest graphic printing process (see GRAPHIC ARTS), dating from about the 9th century in China and the 15th century in Europe. It is a relief printing technique—that is, the design stands out from the body of the wood block, which is a flat, close-grained wood piece that has been sawed along the grain. All areas of the block except the design itself are cut away with a sharp knife and a gouge. The projecting surface is inked and a sheet of paper laid on it. The design is transferred to the paper by rubbing or pressing. The woodcuts of Albrecht DÜRER and Hans HOLBEIN the Younger show the height of the art form as it was practiced in Renaissance Europe. From the 17th through the 19th century, such Japanese artists as HARUNOBU, KIYONAGA, and UTAMARO perfected the art of the colored woodcut print, using a separate block for each color and treated rice paper for the print.

The woodcut was superseded as a fine printing process by the invention and development of intaglio metal techniques such as ENGRAVING and ETCHING on copper and zinc. By the 18th century the woodcut had degenerated to the crudest kind of popular print used to decorate cheap song sheets and other ephemeral printing.

A regeneration occurred with the invention of the wood-engraving technique. This seems to have first taken place in 18th-century England, and it was brought to perfection by the illustrator Thomas BEWICK. In this process a block of wood, usually boxwood, chosen for its density and hardness, was prepared from a cross-grain section, and a graver—akin to a metal-engraving tool—was used. This technique led to a different kind of print relying for its definition on the use of a white line instead of the isolated black line of the woodcut. Wood engraving is capable also of finer detail and stands up better to pressure and repeated use than do woodcuts. As the demand for illustration increased in the 19th century, wood engraving degenerated to a reproductive process. It was superseded by the photographic halftone process.

Edvard Munch's Clair de lune (1896) *displays the fine white lines produced by the wood-engraving technique. Colored prints are made by successive printings with separate blocks inked in different colors. (Graphische Sammlungen, Munich.)*

Wooden, John   John Robert Wooden, b. Martinsville, Ind., Oct. 14, 1910, one of the greatest college basketball coaches, compiled 667 victories (winning percentage: .806) in his career (1946–75). Wooden was a 3-time All-American player (1930–32) at Purdue before coaching in high school, then college. In 1948 he arrived at UCLA, and that school's 1964–75 domination of college basketball is unrivaled: 10 national titles in 12 years, including 7 straight (1967–73); a record 88 consecutive victories along the way; and 4 Coach of the Year awards. He was elected to the Basketball Hall of Fame as both a player (1959) and a coach (1972), the only person so honored.

Woodhull, Victoria   [wud'-huhl]   Victoria Claflin Woodhull, b. Homer, Ohio, Sept. 23, 1838, d. June 10, 1927, was an American publicist of causes and the first woman to become a presidential candidate. She established (1868) a brokerage firm on Wall Street, created her own political party, campaigned for the presidency (1872) after being nominated, and published a journal

Victoria Woodhull, an outspoken advocate of women's suffrage, free love, and a form of socialism termed pantarchy, *was the first American woman to run (1872) for the U.S. presidency. With her sister, Woodhull established (1868) a successful Wall Street brokerage firm and founded* Woodhull and Claflin's Weekly *(1870–76), a journal supporting various reform movements.*

Woodpeckers obtain food by drilling holes in the bark of trees with their strong, straight, chisellike beaks and extracting insects. Clockwise from the top are: the pileated woodpecker; *the* hairy woodpecker; *and the* red-bellied woodpecker.

(1870–76) devoted to controversial issues. Responding to attacks on her advocacy of free love, she precipitated (1872) a scandal by claiming that Rev. Henry Ward Beecher had committed adultery with a parishioner. Having lost her bid for the presidency and accused of destroying the moral fiber of American life, she left for England, where she married a wealthy banker and settled down to a quiet life.

Woodland culture   see MOUND BUILDERS

---

woodpecker   Woodpeckers are well-known birds, attracting attention with their habit of drilling and pounding trees with their bills to obtain insect food. About 180 species, including sapsuckers and flickers, make up the subfamily Picinae. Together with piculets and wrynecks, they constitute the family Picidae. Woodpeckers are found over most of the world except Madagascar, New Guinea, Australia, and New Zealand.

Woodpeckers range from about 8 cm (3¼ in) to nearly 60 cm (2 ft) in length. They have strong, straight, chisellike bills and extraordinarily extensible tongues that are often barbed and coated with a sticky salivalike substance to help in catching insects. The legs are short, and the sharply clawed toes are frequently arranged with the two middle toes forward and the first and fourth toes backward to help in climbing and clinging to trees. The tail feathers, stiff and often spine-tipped, are used as a brace, providing support on tree trunks. The species vary greatly in color, with both sexes usually similar but with the males having extra red or yellow markings on the head. Woodpeckers occasionally utter harsh cries but generally remain silent or make drumming noises with the bill. Woodpeckers excavate a hole in a tree and line the bottom of it with a few wood chips for the eggs. Both parents incubate the eggs and care for the young.

The largest woodpecker—now virtually extinct—is the ivory-billed woodpecker, *Campephilus principalis*, a crow-sized, black, white, and red bird of the southeastern United States and Cuba. The slightly smaller pileated woodpecker, *Dryocopus pileatus*, is common in North America.

---

woodruff [wud'-ruhf]   Woodruff is the common name for the small herbs of the *Asperula* and *Galium* genera in the madder family, Rubiaceae. Native to Eurasia and Australia, the plants now grow throughout the world's temperate zones, doing best in moist soil. Fresh woodruff has no odor; when dried, it has a vanillalike odor and flavor. *G. odoratum* is a fragrant perennial whose dried foliage is used to flavor German May wine and to scent linens and pillows. The plant carpets the beech forests of northern Germany, where it is known as *Waldmeister*, or master of the woods. It is used in some perfumes for the scent of new-mown hay. *A. orientalis*, a popular annual in U.S. gardens, bears sprays of dainty blue flowers.

Woods Hole scientific institutions   The hamlet of Woods Hole, at the southern heel of Cape Cod, Mass., is the site of two famous scientific establishments. The Woods Hole Marine Biological Laboratory (founded 1888) is a research facility for scholars interested in marine biology and ecology and the natural history of marine forms. The laboratory conducts research in ecology, neurobiology, and the genetics of marine organisms and offers courses at all university levels.

The Woods Hole Oceanographic Institution, one of the world's leading centers in OCEANOGRAPHY was founded in 1930. It supports a wide range of research and educational programs in all phases of the marine sciences and offers graduate degrees in a cooperative program with the Massachusetts Institute of Technology. The institution also participates in numerous large projects such as the JOIDES deep-sea drilling program (see JOIDES; OCEAN DRILLING PROGRAM) and operates interdepartmental research programs on the social and economic effects of human exploitation of marine resources.

The institution has a research laboratory and several research vessels and operates the *Alvin*, a deep-sea research submarine that has taken part in ocean-bottom surveys.

Woodson, Carter Godwin Carter Godwin Woodson, b. New Canton, Va., Dec. 19, 1875, d. Apr. 3, 1950, was a pioneer in the study of black history. The son of a former slave, he began high school at the age of 20 but went on to study at Berea College, the University of Chicago, the Sorbonne, and Harvard University (Ph.D., 1912). He founded (1915) the Association for the Study of Negro Life and History to train black historians and to collect, preserve, and publish documents on blacks. He also founded *The Journal of Negro History* (1916) and the *Negro History Bulletin* (1937). His writings include *The Education of the Negro Prior to 1861* (1915) and *The Negro in Our History* (1922).

Woodstock Festival A rock-music festival, the Woodstock Music and Art Fair, held Aug. 15–17, 1969, on a farm near Woodstock, N.Y., was the culminating event of the era of the COUNTERCULTURE in America. Attracted by the presence of the most famous ROCK MUSIC bands and performers of the time, a huge crowd of perhaps 500,000 fans camped in a meadow and for 3 days lived in a heady atmosphere of amplified music, drugs, and togetherness. Documented in the movie *Woodstock* (1970) and covered in detail by all the major news media, Woodstock became a symbol of solidarity for the generation of flower children, Vietnam War resisters, hippies, and other young people in their revolt against "The Establishment."

Woodville, Elizabeth Elizabeth Woodville, b. 1437, d. June 8, 1492, was the wife of King EDWARD IV of England. Married to Edward in 1464, she was unpopular at the Yorkist court because of the many favors bestowed on her family, previously Lancastrian supporters. When Edward died (1483), his brother Richard, duke of Gloucester, claimed that Elizabeth's two sons by Edward—EDWARD V and Richard of York—were illegitimate. He imprisoned them in the Tower of London (where they were murdered) and became king as RICHARD III. One of Elizabeth's daughters later married Henry VII.

Woodward, Bob see BERNSTEIN, CARL, AND WOODWARD, BOB

Woodward, C. Vann The American historian Comer Vann Woodward, b. Vanndale, Ark., Nov. 13, 1908, became Sterling professor of history at Yale in 1961 and is a leading authority on the American South. From his earliest work, *Tom Watson: Agrarian Rebel* (1938), through such books as *Origins of the New South, 1877–1913* (1951) and *The Strange Career of Jim Crow* (1955), his writings have cast a new light on Southern history. *Mary Chesnut's Civil War*, Woodward's edition of the wartime diaries of a Southern aristocrat, won a 1982 Pulitzer Prize.

Woodward, Joanne The actress Joanne Woodward, b. Thomasville, Ga., Feb. 27, 1931, has demonstrated her talent in a variety of stage, film, and television roles. Her best films include the Academy Award–winning *The Three Faces of Eve* (1957), *Rachel, Rachel* (1968), *Summer Wishes, Winter Dreams* (1973), and *The Glass Menagerie* (1987). She is married to actor Paul Newman.

woodwind instruments see MUSICAL INSTRUMENTS

woody plant see SHRUB; TREE

wool Wool is the fine, soft, wavy hair that forms all or part of the protective coat of domestic sheep. It has been harvested from ancient times to provide clothing and household coverings and holds an important place in today's textile trade because of its properties of insulation, absorbency, resilience, and ability to take dye well. The coats of other animals are also called wool for manufacturing purposes. Such "wool" includes that from angora goats, camels, and alpacas, among other animals. CASHMERE is a fine wool produced from the Kashmir goat.

About half the wool in world trade is grown in the Southern Hemisphere, particularly Australia, New Zealand, and Argentina. More than three-quarters of world use is in the Northern Hemisphere, notably France, the United Kingdom, Japan, the USSR, and China. Estimated annual world wool production in the late 1980s was almost 3 million metric tons (3.3 million U.S. tons), uncleaned. The main contributing countries were Australia, the USSR, New Zealand, China, Argentina, Uruguay, and South Africa.

Wool Fiber

Wool fiber is composed of keratin, a protein present in all horny cells (hair, horn, and hoof). Keratin consists of helical chains of AMINO ACIDS. Because the chains are coiled, they stretch when the wool is pulled, and then recoil back into shape.

The fiber grows from a follicle in the dermal layer of the sheep's skin. Follicles also produce grease, or wax, secreted by the sebaceous glands and suint secreted by the sweat glands. Wool grease can be commercially refined into lanolin, an important skin-care product.

Wool-fiber production is a continuous process, in con-

Sheep shearing for wool on this Patagonian ranch is done using hand shears. After the wool is shorn, it is separated according to type, grade, and yield.

trast to the intermittent hair growth and periodic shedding of the coat of most other hair-growing animals. Production of wool fiber depends on the sheep's rate of growth, which in turn is affected by such factors as breed and diet. The type of coat, or fleece, is dictated largely by heredity. For instance, most lambs born with a rough, uneven coat will subsequently have a rough fleece, which is generally composed of an inner coat of fine, short wool fibers and an outer coat of long, coarse hair fibers. This kind of fleece is usually unsuitable for processing into wearing apparel but is useful for carpet yarns. A smooth, curly birthcoat usually presages a more even fleece that will be acceptable for use in apparel.

Types of Wool

Among the 450 breeds of domestic SHEEP in the world, great differences exist in the amount and the kind of wool produced. Merino sheep, for instance, produce extremely fine (in fiber diameter) and soft wool used for apparel. "Down" breeds, such as Southdown, Hampshire, and Suffolk, produce short, spongy wool suitable for specialty lines of knitwear and fabrics. Such breeds as Romney, Corriedale, Border Leicester, English Leicester, and Lincoln produce long, medium to coarse wool, which is used for knitwear, tweeds, and blankets. The coarser wools and wool produced by such Asian breeds as Sikkim Bera and Tatarian are used for carpets.

Harvesting and Processing

Wool is harvested from sheep by mechanical shearing or hand shearing and is separated by skilled sorters according to four basic classifications. First, the wool is judged to be a certain type, which indicates its suitability for a particular form of processing. Second, the wool's quality,

meaning the thinness or coarseness in diameter of the fiber, is judged. Third, the grade is assessed—an estimate of excellence that is affected by fiber length, color, evenness, damage, and contamination. Yield—the percent of clean wool present after removal of grease and dirt—is the fourth classification.

After the wool is sorted it is cleaned in a process known as wool scouring. Many wools are then carded—a process using a tool with rows of bent wire teeth—to disentangle the fibers and remove debris. After cleaning, fibers are processed to fabric by one of three basic systems: worsted, woolen, and felting.

The worsted system requires long, sound wool, combed to remove short fibers. The longer fibers are arranged more or less parallel before spinning. The wool is then woven or knitted. Worsted yarn is smooth, and the resulting worsted cloth is particularly favored for fine suiting and hosiery fabrics.

The woolen system uses short wool, or that containing both long and short fibers. No combing is done; the woven cloth, known as a woolen fabric, has a rougher appearance than that of worsted and is most suitable for blankets, overcoats, and tweeds.

The felting system depends on the movement and entanglement of fibers as they are padded in warm, soapy solution. The chief products are hats and industrial felts.

See also: FIBER, NATURAL; TEXTILE INDUSTRY.

Woolf, Virginia A sensitive critic and an important innovator in modern British fiction, Virginia Woolf, b. Adeline Virginia Stephen, Jan. 25, 1882, d. Mar. 28, 1941, is known especially for her experimental novels *Mrs. Dalloway* and TO THE LIGHTHOUSE. The daughter of the wealthy scholar-editor Sir Leslie Stephen, and delicate in health, she was educated at home. With a precocious mastery of writing, she began to contribute to the *Times Literary Supplement* in her early twenties.

Her father's death in 1904 caused the first of several nervous breakdowns that darkened Woolf's adult life. With her sister Vanessa and brother Adrian, she moved to the Bloomsbury section of London and there gathered about her the brilliant avant-garde artists, writers, and philosophers who became known as the BLOOMSBURY GROUP. She married the journalist and political essayist Leonard Woolf in 1912. Dividing their time between London and a country home in Sussex, in 1917 they began the Hogarth Press, a publishing house that later brought to public notice E. M. Forster, Katherine Mansfield, and T. S. Eliot.

Novels. Published to slight critical attention, Woolf's first two novels, *The Voyage Out* (1915) and *Night and Day* (1919), were traditional in form, giving little hint of the experiments to come. These began with *Jacob's Room* (1922), an impressionistic novel in which Jacob's character is developed not through his conversation or actions but through fragmentary comments by the people around him. Three other brilliant, innovative novels quickly followed: *Mrs. Dalloway* (1925), in which Woolf uses the STREAM OF

Virginia Woolf, one of the most distinguished novelists and critics of the first half of the 20th century, made major contributions to the development of modern fiction. Among her innovations in narrative form are the interior-monologue and stream-of-consciousness techniques and the manipulation of time.

CONSCIOUSNESS and interior-monologue techniques to reveal a woman's life as she moves about London in the course of one day; *To the Lighthouse* (1927), which deals symbolically with time and art; and *Orlando: A Biography* (1928), a fantasy tracing the development of its English protagonist's self-consciousness through three centuries and one change of sex.

Critical Writings. In 1925, Woolf collected and published her critical essays as *The Common Reader.* In these essays, as in those of *The Second Common Reader* (1932), she showed an undogmatic sensitivity to a wide variety of literature, writing in a lucid and informal style that contrasts sharply with the self-conscious mannerisms of her novels. Both volumes are now recognized as being among the best in their genre, and two feminist works concerned with women's needs and rights—*A Room of One's Own* (1929) and *Three Guineas* (1938)—have recently found a wider audience.

Although she experimented further with the novel form in *The Waves* (1931) and *The Years* (1937), Woolf continually fought nervous exhaustion and abnormal sensitivity; only her husband's selfless attention prevented her psychological collapse. When England declared war against Germany, even the Woolfs' retreat in Sussex was touched by anxiety. On Mar. 28, 1941, sensing the beginning of another nervous breakdown and fearing the incursion of madness, Woolf drowned herself. *The Death of the Moth and Other Essays* (1942), much criticism, and several volumes of diaries and letters were published posthumously.

Woollcott, Alexander [wul'-kuht] An iconoclastic theater and literary critic and prominent member of the Algonquin Roundtable group, Alexander Humphreys Woollcott, b. Phalanx, N.J., Jan. 19, 1887, d. Jan. 23, 1943, was celebrated for his acid wit and chatty theater gossip. After graduation (1909) from Hamilton College, he wrote for several New York newspapers, and his essays were collected in *Shouts and Murmurs* (1922) and *En-*chanted Aisles (1924). Woollcott had his own radio show—"The Town Crier" (1929–42)—and he also appeared once on stage in George S. Kaufmann and Moss Hart's *The Man Who Came to Dinner* (1939) as Sheridan Whiteside, an exasperating, irascible character modeled on Woollcott himself.

Woolley, Sir Leonard A brilliant British field archaeologist, Sir Charles Leonard Woolley, b. Apr. 17, 1880, d. Feb. 22, 1960, spent most of his career excavating various sites in the Middle East, beginning in Nubia in 1907. Although he also worked at the ancient Egyptian site of Tell el-AMARNA, Woolley's major projects were elsewhere. In 1912 he assumed leadership of the CARCHEMISH excavations (1912–14, 1919), assisted by T. E. Lawrence. From southeastern Turkey and northern Syria, Woolley shifted (1922) to Mesopotamia. Renowned for his excavations at UR, he systematically exposed, over 13 years, a sequence covering millennia but known best for its Sumerian remains. He returned (1936) to Syria and, from then until 1949, devoted himself to excavations at ALALAKH and Al Mina, work that greatly elucidated local and interregional events, especially of the 2d and 1st millennia BC.

Woolman, John Quaker minister John Woolman, b. Rancocas, N.J., Oct. 19, 1720, d. Oct. 7, 1772, was a prominent antislavery leader of the 18th century. After working as a farmer, tailor, shopkeeper, and schoolmaster, he became (1741) a minister in the Society of Friends (Quakers). Beginning in 1743 he went on a series of missionary travels to Quakers in the South, the Middle Colonies, and New England. On his travels, in conversations with slaveholders, and by his writings, Woolman persuaded Quakers throughout America of the necessity of manumission (freeing) of slaves. The 1754 publication of Woolman's *Some Consideration on the Keeping of Negroes* marked the first public proclamation by a religious body of the evil of slavery. In 1755, when the Pennsylvania assembly levied a tax to pay for the war with the French and Indians, Woolman supported those who refused to pay the tax, arguing that compliance was inconsistent with pacifism.

Woolworth Building The Woolworth Building in New York City was erected in 1909–13 by the architect Cass GILBERT for Frank Winfield Woolworth, the self-made 5-and-10-cent-store magnate, who paid for it in cash ($13,500,000). It was intended to be a technological monument to American commercial success. In 1913 its 60 stories made it the world's tallest building (241 m/792 ft), which it remained until 1930 (see SKY-SCRAPER). It has its own power plant, which runs 28 electronically dispatched high-speed elevators, the first of their kind. The white terra-cotta cladding of its steel skeleton is Gothic in detail.

ILLUSTRATION CREDITS

The following list credits or acknowledges, by page, the source of illustrations used in this volume. When two or more illustrations appear on one page, they are credited individually left to right, top to bottom; their credits are separated by semicolons. When both the photographer or artist and an agency or other source are given for an illustration, they are usually separated by a slash. Those illustrations not cited below are credited on the page on which they appear, either in the caption or alongside the illustration itself.

3 Photographie Giraudon; Center for UFO Studies and N.I.C.A.P.
6–7 Rand McNally & Company
8 Leo deWys Inc./Joachim Messerschmidt
9 Tass from Sovfoto
10 Magnum Photos/Abbas; Sipa Press/Shone
11 Picture Group/Rosen
12 Tass from Sovfoto; Sygma/Gransanti
13 Tass from Sovfoto
14 Sipa Press/Jane Schneider
15 Picture Group/Koch/Contrasto; Wide World Photos
17 Rand McNally & Company
20 Rand McNally & Company
21 Robert Harding, Picture Library Ltd.; Sergio Dorantes
22 Photo Researchers/Gordon Johnson
23 Picturepoint, London; Picturepoint, London
25 Vandaag BV
26 Picturepoint, London; Photo Researchers/Susan McCartney
28 Black Star/Leo Choplin
32–33 Rand McNally & Company
34 Photo Researchers/Laurence Lowry; Photo Researchers/Esther Henderson
35 Photo Researchers/Jim Amos; Photo Researchers/Van Bucher
36 Photo Researchers/James Hanley
38 Photo Researchers/George Hollis; Photo Researchers/Esther Henderson; Photo Researchers/Dan Guravich
41 Picturepoint, London; Photo Researchers/Inez and George Hollis
42 Superstock/Shostal/Fire
44 Photo Researchers/Frank S. Miller; Photo Researchers/Tom Hollyman
45 Photo Researchers/Van Bucher; Black Star/Tom Sobolik
48 Metropolitan Museum of Art, New York, Gift of Junius S. Morgan, 1919; New York Public Library Astor, Lenox, and Tilden Foundations, The I. N. Phelps Stokes Collection of American Historical Prints
50 Abby Aldrich Rockefeller Folk Art Collection, Williamsburg, Va.
51 New York Public Library Astor, Lenox, and Tilden Foundations, Rare Book Division; The Bettmann Archive
52 New York Public Library Astor, Lenox, and Tilden Foundations, The I. N. Phelps Stokes Collection of American Historical Prints

53 The Bettmann Archive; Yale University Art Gallery
54 The Bettmann Archive; The Bettmann Archive
56 Denver Public Library Western History Department; Museum of Fine Arts, Boston, Gift of Joseph W., William B., and Edward H. R. Revere
60 The Bettmann Archive; Scala, Florence
61 Union Pacific Railroad Company
62 Museum of the City of New York
64 UPI/Bettmann Newsphotos; Missouri Historical Society, St. Louis; Henry Ford Museum Ford Archives
65 Life Magazine © Time, Inc./Margaret Bourke-White; Museum of the City of New York
66 Naval Photographic Center; Official U.S. Coast Guard Photo; Imperial War Museum, London
68 The Bettmann Archive; Stefan Lorant: The Glorious Burden (author's edition)
69 NASA; Magnum Photos/Bruce Davidson
70 Magnum Photos/Philip Jones-Griffith
71 UPI/Bettmann Newsphotos; Sygma/Franken
72 Sipa Press/Trippett; The White House/Pete Souza
73 U.S. Army Photo
74 U.S. Naval Academy
83 Photo Researchers/Georg Gerster
87 NASA; NASA; NASA
95 Rand McNally & Company
97 Photo Researchers/Carl Frank
100 Rand McNally & Company
101 Photo Researchers/R. G. Everts; Photo Researchers/Porterfield-Chickering
110 Brown Brothers
115 White House Historical Society
120 Photo Researchers/Joe Munroe
128 Lothar Roth and Associates
130 The Bettmann Archive
143 Rand McNally & Company
144 Photo Researchers/Gianni Tortoli
145 Photo Researchers/Porterfield-Chickering
147 NASA; NASA
149 The Bettmann Archive
153 Rand McNally & Company
154 Photo Researchers/Michael P. Manheim
155 Courtesy Vermont Department of Development; Courtesy Vermont Department of Development

156 Brown Brothers
164 UPI/Bettmann Newsphotos
168 The Bettmann Archive
169 The Bettmann Archive
170 Photo Researchers/Georg Gerster
171 Robert Harding Picture Library
172 Telegen/Donna Foster-Roizen
173 Picture Group/Horan
174 Sygma/Bytes
176 Courtesy Elektra Records; Collection of Visual Studio Workshop
177 © Kira Perov
179 Laser Games/Thom Kidrin
183 Telegen/Donna Foster-Roizen
185 Telegen/Donna Foster-Roizen
187 Leo deWys/Peer
190 Rand McNally & Company
191 Sem Presser; Sygma/Spengler
192 Picture Group/Shepard Sharbell
193 Black Star/Vietnam News Agency; Wide World Photos
194 UPI/Bettmann Newsphotos
195 U.S. Air Force
197 UPI/Bettmann Newsphotos
198 UPI/Bettmann Newsphotos
201 University Museum of National Antiquities, Oslo, Norway; Antikvarish Topografish, Stockholm
202 The Bettmann Archive
208 Rand McNally & Company; Photo Researchers/Fritz Henle
210 Rand McNally & Company
211 Peter Arnold/Horst Schafer
212 Photo Researchers/Jacques Jangoux
222 Culver Pictures
226 All pictures—Earth Images/Gary Rosenquist
229 Brown Brothers
231 UPI/Bettmann Newsphotos
239 The Bettmann Archive
243 Lothar Roth and Associates
244 Superstock/Shostal/Carle; Superstock/Shostal/Streichan
247 UPI/Bettmann Newsphotos; Brown Brothers
250 The Bettmann Archive
252 The Bettmann Archive; Michael Holford Library
255 The Bettmann Archive; Lothar Roth and Associates
256 Brown University Library/Ann S. K. Brown Military Collection; The Bettmann Archive
258 Snark International
260 Photo Researchers/Tomas D. W. Friedman
264 Rand McNally & Company
265 Stock Photos West/Keith Gunnar
266 Photo Researchers/Porterfield-Chickering
267 The Bettmann Archive
268 Photo Researchers/Van Bucher
270 White House Historical Society
272 The Bettmann Archive
283 The Bettmann Archive; Time Magazine/Ben Martin

286 Cooper Bridgeman Library
288 UPI/Bettmann Newsphotos
290 All-Sport/Vandystadt
291 Aldus Archives
292 UPI/Bettmann Newsphotos
293 National Portrait Gallery, London
297 Black Star/Sipa Press
299 Rainbow/Hank Morgan; Visions/J. Ross Baughman
300 Aviation Week & Space Technology, © 1987 McGraw-Hill Inc. All Rights Reserved
303 Photo Researchers/Barry Hennings
307 Ullstein Bilderdienst
308 The Bettmann Archive
309 Brown Brothers; Victoria and Albert Museum, London
316 Photo Researchers/Rafael Macia
318 The Hark Group Ltd./Slidemakers
319 The Bettmann Archive
320 The Bettmann Archive
323 National Portrait Gallery, London
327 Rand McNally & Company
330 Rand McNally & Company
331 Photo Researchers/Linda Bartlett
332 Courtesy West Virginia Department of Travel and Commerce/T. Evans
334 Rand McNally & Company
335 A. F. Kersting
340 The Bettmann Archive
341 Brown Brothers
350 NASA
352 Edward Teitelman
354 The Bettmann Archive
355 The Bettmann Archive
360 National Portrait Gallery, London
363 UPI/Bettmann Newsphotos
366 Magnum Photos/Lessing
369 Nassau/Mauritshuis
370 Wide World Photos
372 Hedrich-Blessing
376 White House Historical Society
382 Het Spectrum
391 Rand McNally & Company
392 Photo Researchers/Thomas B. Hollyman
393 Photo Researchers/Joe Munroe
397 Aldus Archives
400 Courtesy Charles Scribner's Sons
403 Historical Picture Service
404 Historical Picture Service
405 The Bettmann Archive; Wide World Photos
409 Superstock/Shostal
412 The Bettmann Archive
414 Bruce Coleman Inc./Jen and Des Bartlett
415 BBC–Hulton Picture Library